MAGILL'S QUOTATIONS
IN CONTEXT
Second Series

Magill's

QUOTATIONS

in Context

SECOND SERIES

Edited by
FRANK N. MAGILL

Associate Editor
TENCH FRANCIS TILGHMAN

1817

HARPER & ROW, PUBLISHERS

NEW YORK AND EVANSTON

FIRST EDITION

LIBRARY OF CONGRESS CATALOG CARD NUMBER: 65-21011

PREFACE

MAGILL'S QUOTATIONS IN CONTEXT, Second Series, is an extension of the original work published in 1965. It contains 1,500 additional quotations handled in the same manner as those in the earlier work except that in most cases the *Context* paragraph is longer and the number of lines quoted from the original source is greater. This change in format is the result of evaluations of comments and suggestions from users, many of whom expressed the desire to have a more extensive background commentary and see more of the original quoted material even if this arrangement meant fewer quotations overall.

In this series we have been concerned not only with familiar aphorisms; we have also included many literary expressions which may not be thought of by most readers as "familiar quotes" but which represent important and well-known sequences from much-esteemed literary works. Many readers will thus encounter expressions that remind them of works previously read, and indeed some may find here opening wedges leading eventually to pleasant discoveries and a broadening literary horizon.

For example, "God tempers the wind to the shorn lamb" (included in an earlier volume) is a lead-in to a delightful and touching sequence from Laurence Sterne's A SENTIMENTAL JOURNEY THROUGH FRANCE AND ITALY, wherein the simpleminded Maria credits the Almighty with showing special mercy to those of His creatures who are flawed through circumstance. Yorick (Sterne) learns that Maria has been wandering about the roads of France on her own. Searching, he comes upon her weeping quietly by the roadside near her home. She tells him of her travels, and he relates her story thus:

> "—She had since that, she told me, stray'd as far as Rome, and walk'd round St. Peter's once—and return'd back—that she found her way alone across the Apennines—had travell'd over all Lombardy without money,—and through the flinty roads of Savoy without shoes—how she had borne it, and how she had got supported, she could not tell—but God tempers the wind, said Maria, to the shorn lamb."

Here, then, is a reminder of Sterne's humane approach in his writings—a most attractive characteristic.

Deserving to be remembered, too, are such phrases as "Freedom and not servitude is the cure of anarchy," which can lead one to a full and rewarding study of Edmund Burke's determined efforts at conciliation between Great Britain and the American Colonies. Or, a wry comment such as "A well-written life is almost as rare as a well-spent one" is surely a challenge for one to examine Carlyle's FREDERICK II OF PRUSSIA.

"Simplify, simplify" may not seem striking as a "quote," yet it takes us to Thoreau and thence across the entire spectrum of his philosophy. Consider "The rest is silence." Not dramatic standing alone, yet as a lead-in to the death of Hamlet and indirectly to a review of his moody, turbulent life, the expression becomes noteworthy indeed.

Hence, this work is meant to be more than a book of quotations. There are fifteen hundred opportunities for the reader to travel a path which leads behind the quotation itself and on toward a rapport with the creative sensibility from which it sprang.

Entries in this book are alphabetical by quotation, without regard to author or chronology. There are, however, three complete indexes, enabling the user to find readily any quotation in the book. Two of these indexes appear ahead of the text: The Alphabetical List of Quotations, showing every entry in alphabetical order, and a Key Word Index. The purpose of the latter list is to assist those who may not remember a quotation verbatim but who recall a key word or an identifying phrase. This index, also, is alphabetical, and quotations that contain several key words may appear in this special index several times in different word arrangements. The first word of the true quotation is always given in italics so that the user of the Key Word Index may readily recognize the quotation sought once he has found it in the rearranged form of the line. An Author Index will be found at the end of the book.

It should be pointed out that quotations appearing at the top of an entry do not always agree verbatim with the actual quotation as it appears in the context. Instead, these top lines are treated as *titles* for the entries, a procedure that enabled the editors to take certain minor liberties with the material as it is quoted in the contextual excerpt itself—which is always verbatim. The purpose here was to eliminate archaic spellings or words that have long since disappeared from the quotation as we use it today. Modernization was not attempted in every case, however; who would dare, for example, to disturb "Up roos the sonne, and up roos Emelye"? Inasmuch as our title line need not scan, contractions which may be necessary in a line of poetry as it appears in the context were usually eliminated.

Our hard-working staff joins me in the hope that most of the literary expressions in this book will prove rewarding to readers of all tastes, and that the volume will afford much pleasure to those who use it.

FRANK N. MAGILL

ALPHABETICAL LIST OF QUOTATIONS

ALPHABETICAL LIST OF QUOTATIONS

They'll take suggestion as a cat laps milk, 1077
They're only truly great who are truly good, 1078
Things that love night love not such nights as these, 1079
Think of your forefathers and of your posterity!, 1079
Think only what concerns thee and thy being, 1081
Thinking is the greatest fatigue in the world, 1082
Third among the sons of light, 1083
This and that way swings the flux of mortal things, 1083
This is hell, nor am I out of it, 1084
This is war, 1085
This music crept by me upon the waters, 1086
This night thy soul shall be required of thee, 1086
This submerged tenth, 1088
This weak piping time of peace, 1089
This will never do!, 1090
This world is a comedy to those that think, a tragedy to those that feel, 1091
Those who have much to hope and nothing to lose, will always be dangerous, 1091
Thou art in a parlous state, 1092
Thou didst eat strange flesh, 1093
Thou god of our idolatry, the press, 1093
Thou hast conquered, O pale Galilean, 1094
Thou hast nor youth, nor age, 1095
Thou speakest wiser than thou art ware of, 1096
Though her body die, her fame survives, 1096
Though I be poor, I'm honest, 1097
Though it be a foul great lie: set upon it a good face, 1098
Though poor in gear, we're rich in love, 1099
Thought which saddens while it soothes!, 1100
Three things I never lends—my 'oss, my wife, and my name, 1101
Three-o'clock-in-the-morning courage, 1102
Thrice he routed all his foes; and thrice he slew the slain, 1103
Thy eternal summer shall not fade, 1104
Thy necessity is yet greater than mine, 1104
Thy soul was like a star, and dwelt apart, 1105
Time hath an art to make dust of all things, 1106
Time hath, my lord, a wallet at his back, 1107
Time, not Corydon, hath conquered thee, 1107
Time, the avenger, 1108
Time, thou devourer of all things, 1109
Time will run back, and fetch the age of gold, 1110
Tip me the black spot, 1111
'Tis an awkward thing to play with souls, 1111
'Tis beauty calls, and glory shows the way, 1112
'Tis Death is dead, not he, 1113
'Tis death that makes life live, 1114
'Tis not in mortals to command success, but we'll do more, Sempronius; we'll deserve it, 1115
'Tis not too late to-morrow to be brave, 1116
'Tis not what man does which exalts him, but what man would do!, 1117
'Tis pride that pulls the country down, 1117
'Tis safest in matrimony to begin with a little aversion, 1118
To be constant, in nature were inconstancy, 1119
To Carthage I came, 1120
To compare great things with small, 1121
To die in the last ditch, 1122

KEY WORD INDEX

(The *italicized* word indicates the beginning of a quotation)

Buckingham, *Off* with his head. So much for, 803
Bucket, A, *Drop* of a, 234
Bugle horn were worth a thousand men, *One* blast upon his, 819
Build, let us think we build forever, *When* we, 1251
Bull story, *Cock* and, 155
Bullied out of vice, *More* people are flattered into virtue than, 714
Burden, The, *Grasshopper* shall be a, 369
Bush, *Good* wine needs no, 363
Business, *Dispatch* is the soul of, 218
Business is nobody's business, *That* which is everybody's, 1046
Butter no parsnips, *Fine* words, 291
Butterfly, *Kill* not the moth nor, 563
Buttons, *I* had a soul above, 479
Byron; open thy Goethe, *Close* thy, 152

Caesar and his fortune, *You* carry, 1313
Caesar, *I* appeal unto, 470
Caesar might be great!, *What* millions died that, 1232
Caesar never knew, *Regions*, 908
Candle in the sun, *To* set a, 1132
Candle!, *Out*, out, brief, 842
Candle throws his beams, *How* far that little, 458
Candle to the sun, *It* is hardly necessary to light a, 547
Cakes and ale, *No* more, 757
Candid friend, *Save*, oh, save me, from the, 941
Canker lives in sweetest bud, *Loathsome*, 629
Cannon's mouth, *Seeking* the bubble reputation even in the, 947
Canoe, *Paddle* your own, 844
Carnivorous production, *Man* is a, 667
Carthage I came, *To*, 1120
Case, A, *Lady* in the, 575
Cast, *I* have set my life upon a, 484
Castle, A, *Man's* house is his, 680
Cat, A, *Harmless* necessary, 394
Cat in, to make all split, A, *Part* to tear a, 848
Cat laps milk, *They'll* take suggestion as a, 1077
Cat than choking her with cream, *More* ways of killing a, 715
Cause! for the Church! for the Laws!, *For* God! for the, 303
Celt, The, *Blind* hysterics of the, 99
Certain, because it is impossible, *It* is, 546
Chains, *You* can make better use of iron than forging it into, 1312
Change, The, *Ringing* grooves of, 922
Character, *Education* has for a chief object the formation of, 241
Charities of man to man, The, *Cold*, 156
Charity, *Give* him a little earth for, 334
Charity more than the dead, The, *Living* need, 629
Chaste, and unexpressive she, The, *Fair*, the, 273
Cheerful as any man could do in that condition, *Looking* as, 635
Cherubins, *Quiring* to the young-eyed, 900
Chess, *Life* is too short for, 613
Chevalier, *Charlie* is my darling, the young, 138
Child, I spake as a child, *When* I was a, 1246
Child of earth, A, *Happy*, 390
Child, An, *Old* man is twice a, 812

xl

Exalts him, but what man would do!, *'Tis* not what man does which, 1117
Excess are wrong, The, *Best* things carried to, 89
Exercise is to the body, *Reading* is to the mind what, 904
Expressive to be blue, too lovely to be grey, *Eyes* too, 267
Extinction of unhappy hates, *Endless,* 244
Eye, in a fine frenzy rolling, The, *Poet's,* 875
Eye of the beholder, *Beauty* is in the, 81
Eyes, The, *Cynosure* of neighboring, 183

Face is a letter of recommendation, A, *Good,* 359
Faces like a flint, *Set* your, 952
Factions are volcanoes burnt out, *Old* religious, 812
Facts, *What* I want is, 1229
Fair, *Divinely* tall, and most divinely, 221
Fair, whatever you do!, *Drink,* 233
Fairies!, *Farewell,* rewards and, 280
Fairy Lilian, *Airy,* 14
Faith in all, *Unfaith* in aught is want of, 1165
Faith is lost, when honor dies, the man is dead!, *When,* 1243
Faith, *O* thou of little, 794
Faith, *Punic,* 896
Faith; vain faith, and courage vain, *Courage* and, 174
Faith's absurd, A, *Scientific,* 943
Falchions in fair hands, *Fans* turn into, 279
False fire!, *What,* frighted with, 1225
False man, *Man:,* 663
Falsehood hath!, *What* a goodly outside, 1221
Falsehood to the heart, *Who* speaks the truth stabs, 1270
Fame survives, *Though* her body die, her, 1096
Fame while woman wakes to love, *Man* dreams of, 662
Families last not three oaks, *Old,* 811
Famous, *I* awoke one morning and found myself, 471
Fancy bred, *Tell* me where is, 1041
Fancy, *Chewing* the food of sweet and bitter, 140
Fancy-free, *Maiden* meditation, 658
Fancy's child, *Sweetest* Shakespeare, 1029
Far from home, The, *Night* is dark, and I am, 748
Fashion, *After* the high Roman, 11
Fashion, The, *Glass* of, 339
Father's business, *I* must be about my, 490
Fathom five, *Full,* 320
Fatigue in the world, *Thinking* is the greatest, 1082
Fault, and honesty is his, *Every* man has his, 256
Fault, *Clever* to a, 151
Faults is to be conscious of none, The, *Greatest* of, 381
Fault's with time, The, *Only,* 830
Fear thou not at all, *Hope* thou not much, and, 454
Feast!, *Liberty's* a glorious, 607
Feather for each wind that blows, *I* am a, 463
Feathers, An, *Upstart* crow, beautified with our, 1173
Feeling, a woman as old as she looks, A, *Man* is as old as he's, 671
Fell who fell, *Freely* they stood who stood, and, 313
Fester smell far worse than weeds, *Lilies* that, 620
Few words are the best men, *Men* of, 703

xlv

Horne, *Triton* blowing loud his wreathed, 1149
Horrors, hail!, *Congenial,* 166
Horse amble true, *Hard* is to teach and old, 391
Hottentot, *Consider* him as a respectable, 171
Hour, *You* come most carefully upon your, 1314
How a man dies, but how he lives, *It* matters not, 554
Hub of the solar system, *Boston* State House is the, 109
Human for being devout, *I* am not the less, 468
Humanities of old religion, The, *Fair,* 272
Humour, A, *Holiday,* 447
Hung upon his lips, *Persuasion,* 857
Husband, A, *Light* wife doth make a, 617
Husband than the best of men, *No* worse a, 762

Iago, the pity of it, *O,* 789
Idealistic nation in the world, *America* is the only, 37
Idols, *God* keeps a niche in heaven to hold our, 349
Ignorance, *O!* more than Gothic, 791
Ills from beauty spring, *What,* 1230
Ill-spent youth, *To* play billiards well was a sign of an, 1129
Image of death, *In* every parting there is an, 523
Impeachment, *I* own the soft, 493
Imperator, those about to die salute thee, *Hail,* 386
Impotently great, *Ignobly* vain, and, 514
Impunity a rose, *Any* nose may ravage with, 45
Impure what God declares pure, *Defaming* as, 204
Inconstancy, *To* be constant, in nature were, 1119
Increment, *Unearned,* 1164
Incurable disease, *Life* is an, 611
Indictment against a whole people, *I* do not know the method of drawing up an, 477
Indifference, *Nothing* is so fatal to religion as, 779
Indifferent to me, *Nothing* human is, 776
Industry, *Captains* of, 130
Infelicity, *Too* quick a sense of a constant, 1144
Infinite spaces terrifies me, The, *Eternal* silence of these, 250
Injured they also hate, *Whom* they have, 1275
Inn, *No* room in the, 759
Inn, The, *World,* I count it not an, 1301
Innocence but sin, *Ignorance* is not, 514
Innovate is not to reform, *To,* 1125
Institution, It's more than a game. *It's* an, 556
Instructor, Time, The, *Grand,* 365
Insult, An, *Injury* is much sooner forgotten than an, 533
Insult to injuries, *Adding,* 6
Intoxication, The, *Best* of life is but, 88
Invisible, The, *Choir,* 144
Iron enter into his soul, *I* saw the, 495
Iron pokers into true-love knots, *Wreathe,* 1307
Iron than forging it into chains, *You* can make better use of, 1312
Island, *No* man is an, 755
Ivory, *Gates* of, 325

Jangled out of tune, *Sweet* bells, 1024
Jargon of the schools, *All,* 20
Jargon of their Babylonian pulpits, The, *Confused,* 165

1

Jenny's case, *Vengeance* of, 1179
Jester, *How* ill white hairs become a fool and, 458
Jew eyes?, *Hath* not a, 395
Jilted than never be courted at all, *Better* be courted and, 90
Joan, *Some* men must love my lady, and some, 993
Job, The, *Patience* of, 850
Jolly, *Some* credit in being, 990
Joy be unconfined, *Let,* 597
Joys, like griefs, are silent, *Great,* 372
Judgment, thou art fled to brutish beasts, *O,* 790
Jurisprudence, The, *Gladsome* light of, 338
Just, *Whatever* is, is in its causes, 1240

Kalends, *They* will pay on the Greek, 1076
Key Shakespeare unlocked his heart, *With* this, 1289
Killing a cat than choking her with cream, *More* ways of, 715
Kin, and less than kind, A, *Little* more than, 624
King, A, *Cat* may look at a, 133
King, A, *Leper* once he lost and gained a, 593
Kingdom, The, *Keys* of the, 562
Kings, that privates have not too, *What* have, 1226
Knave, A, *Rascally* yea-forsooth, 903
Knaves; 'tis in their own defense, *Men* must be, 700
Knots, *Wreathe* iron pokers into true-love, 1307
Know, The, *Master* of those who, 688
Know thee who thou art, *I,* 489
Knowledge, The, *Bonded* warehouse of my, 104
Knowledge in the making, *Opinion* in good man is but, 834
Knowledge, *Science* is organized, 941
Knowledge to be my province, *I* have taken all, 484

Labor too, and tires as much, *Pleasure* is, 871
Laboring man, *Sleep* is sweet to the, 977
Ladder, *Jacob's,* 559
Ladies, A, *Lion* among, 621
Lady Disdain, *My* dear, 728
Lady fair, *Faint* heart ne'er wan a, 269
Lady of old years, *Some* lost, 991
Language of a tear, *With* the persuasive, 1288
Lark and go to bed with the lamb, *We* rise with the, 1209
Last ditch, *To* die in the, 1122
Last, Him midst, and without end, *Him* first, Him, 436
Law, *All's* love, yet all's, 33
Law, *Reason* is the life of the, 905
Law, The, *Safety* of the people shall be their highest, 935
Law, thou mine, *God* is thy, 348
Laws! *For* God! for the Cause! for the Church! for the, 303
Lay, The, *Unpremeditated,* 1169
Leak will sink a ship, and one sin will destroy a sinner, *One,* 823
Lean on one another, *Laws,* like houses, 585
Leap, *Look* before you, 632
Learned in a lady's eyes, *Love,* first, 642
Lecture, *She* looked a, 960
Led, *When* we think we lead, we are most, 1252

Strange, 'twas passing strange, *'Twas*, 1156
Strayed like lost sheep, *Erred* and, 249
Street to street, The, *Harlot's* cry from, 393
Study, and not study to live, *I* would live to, 505
Stumbled when I saw, *I*, 499
Stupidity, *There* is no sin except, 1057
Style, The, *Grand*, 368
Subject for conversation in a mixed company, *Religion* is by no means a proper, 908
Submerged tenth, *This*, 1088
Success pays the failure of years, A, *Minute's*, 709
Suckle fools, and chronicle small beer, *To*, 1133
Sudden glory, *Laughter* is nothing else but, 583
Suffer, and to die, The, *Lot* of man; to, 639
Suffering entereth, *Knowledge* by, 572
Summer, left blooming alone, The, *Last* rose of, 579
Summer rose, *My* life is like the, 731
Summer while 'twas May, *Squandered* a whole, 1004
Sun, *All* things that love the, 29
Sundry places, The, *Scripture* moveth us in, 944
Sure as death, *As*, 64
Swallow dares, *Daffodils*, that come before the, 184
Swap horses while crossing the river, *It* is not best to, 548
Sweeten this little hand, *All* perfumes of Arabia will not, 28
Sweetly solemn thought, *One*, 828
Sweets, A, *Wilderness* of, 1280
Symbols, and inhabit symbols, *We* are, 1200

Tails you lose, *Heads* I win, 419
Tale in everything, *You* would find a, 1320
Talent does what it can, *Genius* does what it must, and, 329
Talismans and spells, *Books* are not seldom, 107
Tangled web we weave when first we practice to deceive, *Oh!* what a, 808
Taskmaster's eye, *My* great, 729
Tax and to please is not given to men, *To*, 1134
Taxes must, at last, fall upon agriculture, *All*, 26
Teach, *Gladly* would he learn and gladly, 337
Tears, *Child* of misery, baptized in, 141
Tears, *Crocodile's*, 178
Tears for misfortune, *There* are, 1052
Tears, *Hence* these, 430
Tears, *Smiling* through, 980
Teeth, sans eyes, sans taste, sans everything, *Sans*, 939
Tell, *You* must not kiss and, 1316
Teller, The, *Nature*, of bad news infects the, 738
Teller, *Truth* never hurts the, 1155
Tempora! O mores! *O*, 793
Tenderest, the loving are the daring, The, *Bravest* are the, 112
Tenders, *Fan* spread and streamers out, and a shoal of fools for, 279
Tether time or tide, *Nae* man can, 734
Thebes never knew, *Riddles* of death, 918
Their like again?, *Where* wilt thou find, 1258
Theme, The, *Imperial*, 521
Thickens, and the crow makes wing, *Light*, 616
Thickens, The, *Plot*, 872

MAGILL'S QUOTATIONS
IN CONTEXT
Second Series

Absalom, my son, my son

Source: II SAMUEL 18:33
Author: Unknown
First transcribed: 1100-400 B.C.
Type of work: Religious history

Context: Absalom, the son of David, plots against his father, the king. When men from all over Israel flock to Absalom's side, David says to his people that for safety they must flee Jerusalem with him, and go into the wilderness. Absalom moves into the city upon David's departure, even taking over King David's concubines, as a sign that he has become the ruler. Ahithophel, one of Absalom's counselors, asks to be allowed to pursue the forces of David and destroy them, but Hushai, who is a secret agent of King David, advises differently. When Ahithophel sees that his counsel is not taken, he goes to his home and hangs himself. Following the advice of Hushai, Absalom takes a force to go out and crush David's loyal followers. But David and his people meet Absalom and his force in battle in the wood of Ephraim and defeat them. Absalom loses twenty thousand men in the battle. Absalom himself is caught in the branches of a great oak tree when his mule passes beneath; there he hangs, alive, till found by David's men. Joab, one of David's lieutenants, stabs Absalom with three darts, and his men then beat Absalom to death, despite King David's injunction to his followers not to harm Absalom. Ahimaaz and Cushi are sent as runners to tell David of the victory; Ahimaaz does not reveal Absalom's death, but Cushi does. King David, who loves Absalom dearly, despite the son's great treachery, is saddened beyond measure by Absalom's death, and the victory over the rebel and his men becomes a day of mourning. The king is distraught over his son's death:

And the king was much moved, and went up to the chamber over the gate, and wept: and as he went, thus he said, O my son **Absalom, my son, my son** Absalom! would God I had died for thee, O **Absalom, my son, my son!**

. . .

And the people gat them by stealth that day into the city, as people being ashamed steal away when they flee in battle.

But the king covered his face, and the king cried with a loud voice, O my son Absalom, O **Absalom, my son, my son!**

The absent are always in the wrong

Source: L'OBSTACLE IMPRÉVU (Act I, sc. vi)
Author: Philippe Néricault Destouches (1680-1754)
First published: 1717
Type of work: Dramatic comedy

1

Context: As Jean Baptiste Poquelin (1622–1673) took the pen name of Molière, to publish his plays, so Philippe Néricault became known as the popular playwright Destouches, being especially remembered for his comedy of interclass marriage, *Le Glorieux* (1732) in which the pride of a haughty nobleman takes a fall. *L'Obstacle imprévu ou L'Obstacle sans obstacle* (The Unforeseen Obstacle or the Obstacle without an Obstacle) achieved popularity when first performed in Paris in 1717. It was later condensed by L. Monrose into three acts. Following the usual classical formula, it observes the unities, taking place in the home of Lisimon, an elderly man. Valère is his foppish son. He is also guardian of Julie, his niece. She and Leandre are in love. Again, according to formula, each of them has a servant who is a friendly adviser, like the *gracioso* in Spanish comedies. Julie has her confidante Nérine. Leandre has Crispin, and Valère is served by Pasquin. The comedy opens with a discussion between Valère and Pasquin. The son is complaining about his inability to get along with his father, and the servant is trying to stop such talk. If Valère will cease behaving foolishly, there will be no trouble. To push home his point, Pasquin acts out that morning's discussion between father and son about the way the young man had spent the previous evening among a lot of over-dressed dandies, when he should have been thinking about Angelique, to whom his father had arranged a marriage. There is another love complication, one between Julie and Leandre. She has the idea that there is an obstacle to their marriage, and she intends to enter a convent. Nérine, down-to-earth like all classical comedy servants, suggests that if Julie cannot marry Leandre, she look for another sweetheart. Crispin comes to report in a mixed-up speech an overheard and puzzling conversation about confusion between two daughters of an Italian in Paris and some skullduggery between Julie's guardian and her uncle. In Scene vi, Lisimon shows that he intends to marry Julie himself. Her mother is dead. She has been left in his care by her supposed father, now in the Indies, who also gave him power to marry her off. Now he tries to persuade Nérine to work on her mistress to give her consent to marry him. The servant knows the situation and refuses to coöperate, saying that Julie could never love a bilious and choleric old man who wants her only for her inheritance, about which she is ignorant. Julie loves Leandre. All that prevents their marriage is that for the moment neither of them has money. He is trying to keep her from taking her vows until he can earn a living, which he says he will do or die. In Nérine's conversation with Lisimon, she tells him the situation. Here is a translation of the French original.

NÉRINE

They wanted to get married, but when he had to come to the point, Leandre learned that Julie hadn't a centime and that she was living on an allowance from her uncle, ever since her mother had left her in Paris without telling anybody where she was going.

LISIMON

Was the young man rich?

NÉRINE

His riches, present and future, amounted to a large sum of tenderness and beautiful sentiments.

. . .

LISIMON

They could hardly establish a home on that!

NÉRINE

He had a servant, too, named Crispin, who was a nice young man.

LISIMON

Did you like him?

NÉRINE

Must you ask? A maid always yearns for the servant of the man who comes courting her mistress. That's the way it always is, in plays.

LISIMON

Tell me, is your mistress still in love with that Leandre?

NÉRINE

Of course! She's no fickle girl. She's not like me. I was sort of in a hurry, and since **the absent are always in the wrong,** and Pasquin was on hand, why, I went ahead and married him.

Abstract liberty is not to be found

Source: SPEECH ON MOVING HIS RESOLUTIONS FOR RECONCILIATION WITH THE
      COLONIES
Author: Edmund Burke (1729-1797)
First published: 1775
Type of work: Political Speech

Context: Burke was the greatest and the most articulate defender of the American Colonies in the English Parliament. He foresaw the great loss England would suffer if the colonies were alienated and lost as a result of harsh suppression. He pleaded desperately with Parliament not to take the strong measures of taxation and military aggression, which, he admitted, were strictly legal measures, but he begged instead for an act of redress, for which the acts of redress toward Ireland and Wales were

3

valid historical precedents. He fully realized the intensity of the sense of freedom and liberty in the colonies and knew that revolution would result from repression:

> . . . This fierce spirit of liberty is stronger in the English colonies probably than in any other people of the earth; and this from a great variety of powerful causes; . . .
> First, the people of the colonies are descendants of Englishmen. England, Sir, is a nation, which still I hope respects, and formerly adored, her freedom. The colonists emigrated from you when this part of your character was most predominant; and they took this bias and direction the moment they parted from your hands. They are therefore not only devoted to liberty, but to liberty according to English ideas, and on English principles. **Abstract liberty,** like other mere abstractions, **is not to be found.** Liberty inheres in some sensible object; and every nation has formed to itself some favourite point, which by way of eminence becomes the criterion of their happiness. It happened, you know, Sir, that the great contests for freedom in this country were from the earliest times chiefly upon the question of taxing.

Accurst be he that first invented war

Source: TAMBURLAINE THE GREAT (Part I, Act II, sc. iv, l. 664)
Author: Christopher Marlowe (1564-1593)
First published: 1590
Type of work: Dramatic tragedy

Context: Mycetes, King of Persia, finds his kingdom menaced by the forces of Tamburlaine, a former Scythian shepherd. Anxious to rid his crown and his lands of this threat, Mycetes sends Theridamas at the head of a thousand richly armed cavalrymen to subdue Tamburlaine and his few hundred foot soldiers. But Theridamas, impressed by Tamburlaine at a parley, decides to join forces with him. Mycetes' brother, Cosroe, meanwhile, plots to become king, disdaining Mycetes as a weak monarch. He joins forces with Tamburlaine, expecting to use Tamburlaine to defeat Mycetes and thus win the crown of Persia. During the ensuing battle Mycetes leaves the field to hide his crown. He is found alone by Tamburlaine, who tells Mycetes he may keep the crown till Tamburlaine can pull it publicly from his head. Mycetes makes his comment about war just before meeting Tamburlaine:

MYCETES
Accurst be he that first invented war,
They knew not, ah, they knew not simple men,
How those were hit by pelting Cannon shot,
Stand staggering like a quivering Aspen leaf,

4

Fearing the force of *Boreas* boisterous blasts.
In what a lamentable case were I,
If Nature had not given me wisedomes lore?
For Kings are clouts that every man shoots at,
Our Crown the pin that thousands seek to cleave.
Therefore in pollicy I think it good
To hide it close: a goodly Strategem,
And far from any man that is a fool.
So shall I not be knowen, or if I be,
They cannot take my crown from me.
Here will I hide it in this simple hole.

An acre of Middlesex is better than a principality in Utopia

Source: LORD BACON
Author: Thomas Babington Macaulay (1800-1859)
First published: July, 1837
Type of work: Biographical essay and book review

Context: The essays of Lord Macaulay, based on wide reading and a memory that seemed never to forget a fact, made him a welcome magazine contributor. His reviews of biographical volumes usually turned out to be more biographies than reviews. He could provide interesting parallels and illustrations. The fact that his knowledge did not extend to art or science and was superficial was not important to his readers. Like them, he judged everything from the viewpoint of a liberal Whig. When asked to review Basil Montagu's sixteen-volume *The Works of Francis Bacon, Lord Chancellor of England* (London: 1825–34), Macaulay substituted for an opinion of the merits of this lengthy work, an essay on Lord Bacon, that was published in the *Edinburgh Review,* in July, 1837, declaring that while the aim of the philosophy of Plato was to exalt man into a god, something noble, Bacon's philosophic aim was the more obtainable one of supplying man's vulgar (i.e., ordinary) wants. Tennyson was to write in *Locksley Hall* (1842): "Better fifty years of Europe than a cycle of Cathay" (that is, a long while in China). Macaulay localizes the idea to England. Utopia refers to an imaginary and idealistic island described by Sir Thomas More (1478–1535) in a Latin romance of the same name, written in 1516.

. . .

An acre of Middlesex is better than a principality in Utopia.
The smallest actual good is better than the most magnificent promises of impossibilities. The wise man of the Stoics would, no doubt, be a grander object than a steam-engine. But there are steam-engines. And the wise man of the Stoics is yet to be born. A philosophy which should enable a man to feel perfectly happy while in agonies of pain, may be better than a philosophy which assu-

5

ages pain. But we know that there are remedies which will assuage pain; and we know that the ancient sages liked the tooth-ache just as little as their neighbors.

. . .

Adding fuel to the flame

Source: SAMSON AGONISTES (Line 1351)
Author: John Milton (1608-1674)
First published: 1671
Type of work: Dramatic tragedy

Context: The play opens with the last phase of the life of Samson, the Old Testament hero. The Philistines have blinded him and hold him prisoner in Gaza. The play, structured as a Greek tragedy, depicts the restoration of the fallen Samson to the grace of God. Samson has already been tested by God and failed the test. Having been punished and having repented his sin, he now undergoes trials of his will and integrity to prove that he is worthy to be tested a second time. The last of these trials comes when Harapha, a strong man of Gath, taunts Samson for his blindness and helplessness. Samson makes a humble admission of his sins and finds his punishment just. He still hopes for God's pardon. Samson challenges Harapha to single combat that they might find whose god is strongest, but the champion from Gath declines. Samson is then summoned to entertain the nobles at the feast of the god Dagon, but he refuses. As the officer leaves to report his refusal, the Chorus warns:

> Consider, Samson; matters now are strain'd
> Up to the highth, whether to hold or break;
> He's gone, and who knows how he may report
> Thy words by **adding fuel to the flame?**
> Expect another message more imperious,
> More Lordly thund'ring then thou well wilt hear.

Adding insult to injuries

Source: THE FOUNDLING (Act V, sc. ii)
Author: Edward Moore (1712-1757)
First published: 1748
Type of work: Dramatic comedy

Context: Edward Moore began his writing career as an author of fables, offering to the public *Fables for the Female Sex,* in 1744. They have been compared to the earlier fables by John Gay, better known for *The Beggar's Opera.* Like his predecessor, Moore also turned to the theater, and

6

in 1748 offered to the actor David Garrick, then manager of Theatre Royal in Drury Lane, his first attempts, *The Foundling.* Its reception was mixed. Some critics applied to it a couplet Garrick had meant as a general comment on comedies, written as Epilogue for the performance:

"From such dull stuff, what profit can you reap?
You cry:—' 'Tis very fine!' and fall asleep."

Henry Brooke in his preface to the printed edition damned it with faint praise. Some of the audience found revolting the character of Faddle, and said he had a mind too deformed for public exhibition. His friend, young Belmont, the play's hero, is only a step above him in baseness, and that because he does possess courage. But the great Mrs. Cibber put life into the insipid character of "The Foundling," and the play continued to be performed, and was even translated into French. Out of it all, the dramatist found a wife. A poetic spinster, falling in love with him, sent a letter in verse to her young cousin:

"Would you think it, my coz, for the fault I must own,
Your Jenny, at last, is quite covetous grown:
Though millions, if fortune should lavishly pour,
I still should be wretched, if I had not More."

The poem circulated. Moore got the message, and out of curiosity sought out Jenny. Liking what he saw, he gambled on his luck, married her, and wrote a greatly improved tragedy, *The Gamester.* In the plot of *The Foundling,* Sir Charles Raymond has a son, Colonel Raymond, in love with Rosetta Belmont. Her father, Sir Robert, has another child, young Belmont. Rosetta has a passion for William Faddle, unprincipled but full of fun. Rosetta has made friends with Fidelia, about whose parentage little is known, and so young Belmont thinks he can enjoy her without marrying her, with Faddle's help. He puts out the story that she is an heiress, but will not comment on her family. His sister backs his love affair in hopes the girl can redeem him from his wildness. The situation is cleared at the end. Fidelia is really Harriet, the lost daughter of Sir Charles. While he was in France, her nurse stole her, announcing that the girl was dead, and then putting out the story that she had discovered a foundling at her steps. Having brought her up, she sells her at the age of twelve to Villiard, who now claims to be her guardian. But the repentent nurse confesses, Sir Charles welcomes his missing daughter, and marries her to a reformed young Belmont. Colonel Raymond marries Rosetta for a general pairing-up. At the beginning of Act V, Fidelia and Belmont are trying to clarify their situation when the two parents and Villiard appear, the latter accusing young Belmont of stealing his ward.

7

VILLIARD

My doors were broken open at midnight by this gentleman, myself wounded, and Fidelia ravished from me. He ran off with her in his arms. Nor, till this morning, in a coach which brought her hither, have my eyes ever beheld her.

SIR ROBERT

A very fine business, truly, young man! [*To his son.*]

FIDELIA

He has abused you, sir. Mr. Belmont is noble—

BELMONT

No matter, Fidelia. Well, sir, you have been robbed, you say? [*To Villiard.*]

VILLIARD

And will have justice, sir.

BELMONT

Take it from this hand then. [*Drawing.*]

SIR CHARLES

Hold, sir. This is **adding insult to injuries.** Fidelia must be restored, sir.

SIR ROBERT

Ay, sir, Fidelia must be restored.

FIDELIA

But not to him. Hear but my story. . . .

Adventure brave and new

Source: RABBI BEN EZRA (Stanza 14)
Author: Robert Browning (1812-1889)
First published: 1864
Type of work: Dramatic monologue

Context: Rabbi Ben Ezra was a distinguished Jewish philosopher, physician, astronomer, and poet of the twelfth century. The ideas found in this poem are drawn largely from the Rabbi's own writings and correspond closely to Browning's own philosophy of life. The Rabbi's monologue opens on the optimistic, almost exultant, note as he declares: "Grow old along with me! / The best is yet to be, / The last of life, for which the first was made," He does not grieve for the past hopes and fears of youth. He

8

finds hope in the philosophic doubt which assails him. This doubt he sees as evidence of the spark of God within each man. Man is exalted by what he aspires to be rather than by what he actually becomes. The Rabbi declares that the Maker's plan is perfect, and that we should be thankful to be men. "For pleasant is this flesh; / Our soul, in its rose-mesh / Pulled ever to the earth, still yearns for rest." All that is past is ever with us. Our experiences and our desires are God's potter's wheel on which our souls are shaped. The Rabbi expectantly approaches old age and the life after death:

> Therefore I summon age
> To grant youth's heritage,
> Life's struggle having so far reached its term!
> Thence shall I pass, approved
> A man, for aye removed
> From the developed brute—a God, though in the germ.
> And I shall thereupon
> Take rest, ere I be gone
> Once more on my **adventure brave and new;**
> Fearless and unperplexed,
> When I wage battle next,
> What weapons to select, what armor to indue.

After life's fitful fever he sleeps well

Source: MACBETH (Act III, sc. ii, l. 23)
Author: William Shakespeare (1564-1616)
First published: 1623
Type of work: Dramatic tragedy

Context: Advised by three witches that he will be king, Macbeth gives way to his ambition, murders King Duncan, and usurps the throne. In his hasty grab for power, Macbeth has lost something more precious, peace, which, ironically, he has given to the slain king. The new king addresses Lady Macbeth.

MACBETH
· · ·
>   . . . Better be with the dead,
> Whom we, to gain our peace, have sent to peace,
> Than on the torture of the mind to lie
> In restless ecstasy. Duncan is in his grave.
> **After life's fitful fever he sleeps well,**
> Treason has done his worst; nor steel, nor poison,
> Malice domestic, foreign levy, nothing,
> Can touch him further.

9

LADY MACBETH
Come on.
Gentle my lord, sleek o'er your rugged looks,
Be bright and jovial among your guests to-night.

MACBETH
So shall I, love, and so I pray be you. . . .

After strange gods

Source: DEUTERONOMY 31:16
Author: Unknown
First transcribed: 1000-300 B.C.
Type of work: Homiletic religious law and history

Context: When the book of Deuteronomy begins, Moses has arrived with his people at the threshold of the promised land. Behind them lie forty years of wandering, to which they were condemned by the Lord for their lack of faith. Moses recites the history of these years for them: their deliverance from Egypt and from the pursuit by Pharaoh, their idolatry in the encampment at Sinai, their sojourn in the deserts. He reminds them of the miracles by which they were fed, and of the angel they have followed. The Amorites, whom they once refused to attack when commanded to do so, have been defeated. So has Og, king of Bashan: much territory east of the Jordan now belongs to the Israelites. Now they must cross to the west bank of the river and destroy all who dwell there. At this point Moses preaches to his followers, setting forth a long and detailed code of laws by which they must live. Some of these laws deal with sanitation and the prevention of disease, and more than one present-day writer has found them remarkably sound in the light of modern discoveries. Again and again Moses warns his people away from any form of heathenism, and it is clear that this is his chief concern. Forty years of wandering have eliminated the older generation, that would always be likely to return to Egyptian ways; the few survivors will not be allowed to cross the Jordan. But even the younger ones, raised up under the laws of Moses, cannot be depended upon. They are like children, difficult to manage and forever running after some novelty. More than twenty times during his discourse, Moses reminds them of the Lord's promise to punish them severely if they take up with other gods. He reminds them at the same time that they are God's chosen people and will flourish if they abide by his commandments. Moses is now one hundred and twenty years of age; he will not live to cross the river and is ready to hand over the command to Joshua. He warns his people again and again, once angrily:

And the LORD said unto Moses, Behold, thy days approach that thou must die: call Joshua, and present yourselves in the tabernacle of the congregation, that I may give him a charge. And Moses and Joshua went, and presented themselves in the tabernacle of the congregation.

And the LORD appeared in the tabernacle in a pillar of a cloud: and the pillar of the cloud stood over the door of the tabernacle.

And the LORD said unto Moses, Behold, thou shalt sleep with thy fathers; and this people will rise up, and go a whoring **after the gods of the strangers** of the land, whither they go to be among them, and will forsake me, and break my covenant which I have made with them.

Then my anger shall be kindled against them in that day, and I will forsake them, and I will hide my face from them, and they shall be devoured, and many evils and troubles shall befall them; so that they will say in that day, Are not these evils come upon us, because our God is not among us?

And I will surely hide my face in that day for all the evils which they shall have wrought, in that they are turned unto other gods.

Now therefore write ye this song for you, and teach it the children of Israel: put it in their mouths, that this song may be a witness for me against the children of Israel.

For when I shall have brought them into the land which I sware unto their fathers, that floweth with milk and honey; and they shall have eaten and filled themselves, and waxen fat; then will they turn unto other gods, and serve them, . . .

After the high Roman fashion

Source: ANTONY AND CLEOPATRA (Act IV, sc. xv, l. 87)
Author: William Shakespeare (1564-1616)
First published: 1623
Type of work: Dramatic tragedy

Context: Dissension and struggle for power mark the rule of the Roman Empire by the triumvirate, Antony, Octavius Caesar, and Lepidus. Antony loses influence to young Caesar when he becomes romantically entangled with Cleopatra, the betwitching queen of Egypt. When the forces of Caesar and Antony finally meet in battle, Antony is defeated. Accusing Cleopatra of double-crossing him and causing his downfall, Antony vows to kill the queen. Cleopatra dispatches word to Antony that she is dead, hoping to bring her lover to repentance. Antony, distraught, falls upon his sword and is taken to die in the arms of Cleopatra. Cleopatra faints with her dead lover in her arms, but quickly recovers and commands Charmian and her other attendants to put aside their sorrow and to prepare a noble funeral befitting the noble Roman who has died:

CLEOPATRA
. . . How do you do, women?

11

What, what, good cheer! Why how now Charmian!
My noble girls! Ah women, women, look
Our lamp is spent, it's out. Good sirs, take heart.
We'll bury him. And then, what's brave, what's noble,
Let's do it **after the high Roman fashion,**
And make death proud to take us. Come, away.
This case of that huge spirit now is cold.
Ah women, women! Come, we have no friend
But resolution, and the briefest end.
                    [*Exeunt, bearing off* ANTONY's *body.*]

After the scole of Stratford atte Bowe

Source: THE CANTERBURY TALES (Prologue, l. 125)
Author: Geoffrey Chaucer (1343?-1400)
First transcribed: c. 1387-1392
Type of work: Collection of tales

Context: The Canterbury pilgrims, a diverse group, having lodged by chance at the Tabard Inn in Southwark, decide to travel together to the shrine of Thomas à Becket at Canterbury and to tell tales to alleviate the tedium of the journey. In the Prologue, which establishes the framework for the pilgrimage and introduces the tale-tellers, Chaucer describes the physical appearance and gives the background of each of the pilgrims. Among them is a prioress whom the poet, although he respects her greatly, may be satirizing very gently. The school at Stratford at Bow, for example, could hardly compare its French with that of Paris.

Ther was also a Nonne, a PRIORESSE,
That of hir smylying was ful symple and coy;
Hire gretteste ooth was but by Seinte Loy;
And she was cleped madame Eglentyne.
Ful weel she song the service dyvyne,
Entuned in hir nose ful semely,
And Frenssh she spak ful faire and fetisly,
After the scole of Stratford atte Bowe,
For Frenssh of Parys was to hire unknowe.

The age of chivalry is gone

Source: REFLECTIONS ON THE REVOLUTION IN FRANCE
Author: Edmund Burke (1729-1797)
First published: 1790
Type of work: Political treatise

Context: Burke was a believer in law and order, and all that contributed to the preservation of law and order he admired. He was equally a lover of liberty, and he saw in the French Revolution a threat to law and order, and to liberty, throughout the European world, as well as in his beloved England. He saw the Revolution's leaders use abstract theories to produce chaos and bloodshed in the name of liberty, and the sight led him to continue his advocacy of slow change in government and equally slow change in the bounds of liberty.

He was particularly struck by the mistreatment of the French royal family during the Revolution, as he was impressed by what he termed "the serene patience" with which Marie Antoinette, the Queen of France, endured her mistreatment. In writing about her and her fate he says he would have expected ten thousand Frenchmen to have leaped to her defense with their swords if she had been even looked at insultingly, but, he remarks:

> . . . **the age of chivalry is gone.** That of sophisters, economists, and calculators, has succeeded; and the glory of Europe is extinguished for ever. Never, never more shall we behold that generous loyalty to rank and sex, that proud submission, that dignified obedience, that subordination of the heart, which kept alive, even in servitude itself, the spirit of an exalted freedom. The unbought grace of life, the cheap defence of nations, the nurse of manly sentiment and heroic enterprise, is gone! It is gone, that sensibility of principle, that chastity of honor, which felt a stain like a wound, which inspired courage whilst it mitigated ferocity, which ennobled whatever it touched, and under which vice itself lost half its evil, by losing all its grossness.

Ah Christ! if only I had known, known, known

Source: THE DEFENCE OF GUENEVERE (Line 41)
Author: William Morris (1834-1896)
First published: 1858
Type of work: Narrative poem

Context: William Morris, who was highly interested in everything medieval, wrote a number of poems utilizing materials from the Arthurian legends. This poem is based upon the famous story, puzzling and disturbing to the British in the age of Queen Victoria, of King Arthur's queen, Guenevere, who fell in love after her marriage with one of the greatest, some legends say the greatest, of the Knights of the Round Table, Sir

Lancelot. In this poem Queen Guenevere is called upon, after charges have been made, particularly by Sir Gauwaine, to defend her conduct, which for a queen involves treason, not merely adultery. Guenevere loves Lancelot and does not pretend otherwise, but she compares herself to a dying man who is presented with cloths of two colors by an angel and asked to choose which is the color of Hell and which of Heaven. With no

13

one, nor anything, to help, the dying man must choose between the red and the blue cloths held by the angel —making his choice for eternity. Choosing the blue, as the color of the heavens, the dying man unwittingly chooses Hell. Guenevere says to the court that the judges should try to envision themselves in the dying man's place, as she feels she has a similar decision:

> "After a shivering half-hour you said,
> 'God help! heaven's color, the blue;' and he said, 'Hell.'
> Perhaps then you would roll upon your bed,
>
> "And cry to all good men who loved you well,
> **'Ah Christ! if only I had known, known, known;'**
> Lancelot went away, then I could tell,
>
> "Like wisest man how all things would be, moan,
> And roll and hurt myself, and long to die,
> And yet fear much to die for what was sown."

Airy, fairy Lilian

Source: LILIAN (Stanza 1)
Author: Alfred, Lord Tennyson (1809-1892)
First published: 1830
Type of work: Lyric poem

Context: In this early poem by Tennyson, the speaker is fascinated by Lilian's "black-beaded eyes," "lightning laughters," and "gaiety without eclipse." She is light and frivolous and only teases him. Yet this very light and flitting quality "wearieth" her admirer as time passes and she fails to return his love. Her coyness and laughter soon irritate him to the point that in the final stanza he asserts that "If prayers will not hush thee,/ Airy Lilian,/ Like a rose-leaf I will crush thee."

> **Airy, fairy Lilian**
> Flitting, fairy Lilian,
> When I ask her if she loves me,
> Claps her tiny hands above me,
> Laughing all she can;
> She'll not tell me if she love me,
> Cruel little Lilian.

Airy tongues that syllable men's names

Source: COMUS (Line 207)
Author: John Milton (1608-1674)
First published: 1637
Type of work: Masque

Context: When *Comus* was presented at Ludlow Castle to celebrate the installation of the Earl of Bridgewater as the President of Wales, the earl's daughter and two sons had leading roles in the production. The three, making their way to Ludlow, are benighted in a forest inhabited by the vile enchanter Comus and his rabble rout of followers. The Lady, becoming separated from her brothers, who left her, too weary to proceed further into the tangled wood, to find fruits and berries to refresh her, hears the wild, tumultuous music that accompanies a dance by Comus's crew. She is filled with misgiving at the sound of the riotous and ill-managed merriment, as it is the kind of music that stirs up the loose, unlettered rustics when they celebrate the harvest season. She reflects that she would be loath to encounter the rudeness and insolence of a band of midnight drinkers, but her situation is such that she is compelled to seek any sort of aid that offers itself. She is afraid that her brothers have wandered so far away that they will not be able to find her again. She makes her way to where the revelry was, but finds no one. She says:

> This is the place, as well as I may guess,
> Whence even now the tumult of loud mirth
> Was rife and perfect in my listening ear,
> Yet nought but single darkness do I find.
> What might this be? A thousand fantasies
> Begin to throng into my memory
> Of calling shapes, and beckoning shadows dire,
> And **airy tongues, that syllable men's names**
> On sands and shores and desert wildernesses.
> These thoughts may startle well, but not astound
> The virtuous mind, that ever walks attended
> By a strong-siding champion conscience.—
> O welcome, pure-eyed faith, white-handed hope,
> Thou hovering angel, girt with golden wings,
> And thou unblemished form of chastity,
> I see ye visibly, and now believe
> That he, the supreme good, t'whom all things ill
> Are but as slavish officers of vengeance,
> Would send a glistering guardian, if need were,
> To keep my life and honor unassailed.

15

Alas! the fleeting years!

Source: ODES (Book II, Ode 14, l. 1)
Author: Horace (65-8 B.C.)
First transcribed: 23-13 B.C.
Type of work: Ode

Context: Inevitably death comes to every man, says the poet, in a short poem filled with allusions familiar to his contemporaries. Pluto, God of the Underworld and Death, unappeased by righteousness or by elaborate sacrifice, comes to both rich and poor, and all, though they may have escaped the wrath of Mars, God of War, or the fierce waves of the Adriatic Sea, must finally gaze upon Cocytus, the underworld river of lamentation and the dead of Rome, leaving behind those they hold dear—wives, children—and their possessions. In one translation, the passage reads:

> **Alas,** my Postumus, **our years**
> **Glide silently away.** No tears,
> No loving orisons repair
> The wrinkled cheek, the whitening hair
> That drop forgotten to the tomb.
> Pluto's inexorable doom
> Mocks at thy daily sacrifice.
> Around his dreary kingdom lies
> That fatal stream whose arms infold
> The giant race accurst of old:
> All, all alike must cross its wave,
> The king, the noble, and the slave.

All art constantly aspires towards the condition of music

Source: THE RENAISSANCE ("The School of Giorgione")
Author: Walter Pater (1839-1894)
First published: 1873
Type of work: Aesthetic criticism

Context: In *The Renaissance,* Pater is concerned with a discussion of the artists whose work best reflects the essential qualities of the era, an age which he describes not merely as a revival of classical antiquity but as a period of general excitement and enlightening of the human mind. He traces its beginnings far back into the Middle Ages, "with its motives already clearly pronounced, the care for physical beauty, the worship of the body, the breaking down of the limits which the religious system of the middle age imposed on the heart and on the imagination." But he finds in Italy the dominant Renaissance expression—in the concrete works of art and its prominent personalities. One of the essays, "The School of

16

Giorgione," describes the fervid artistic activity in Venice at the turn of the sixteenth century, with the experimentation in light, the harmonious and splendid color, the large and free design. Giorgione was an accomplished musician, and his canvases can aptly be termed symphonies in paint. It is this symphonic quality with which Pater is concerned in the opening paragraphs in which he discusses the separate, yet similar, aspects of art. There is rhythmic design in canvas painting, just as there is body and color in music; all art is but a translation "into different languages of one and the same fixed quantity of imaginative thought":

All art constantly aspires towards the condition of music. For while in all other kinds of art it is possible to distinguish the matter from the form, and the understanding can always make this distinction, yet it is the constant effort of art to obliterate it. That the mere matter of a poem, for instance, its subject, namely, its given incidents or situation—that the mere matter of a picture, the actual circumstances of an event, the actual topography of a landscape—should be nothing without the form, the spirit, of the handling, that this form, this mode of handling, should become an end in itself, should penetrate every part of the matter: this is what all art constantly strives after, and achieves in different degrees.

All by my own-alone self

Source: BROTHER WOLF FALLS A VICTIM
Author: Joel Chandler Harris (1848–1908)
First published: 1883 in *Nights with Uncle Remus*
Type of work: Short story

Context: Joel Chandler Harris, always referred to by his full name, made his reputation by a series of animal stories, supposedly told by an elderly Negro ex-slave, Uncle Remus. He published the first one in *The Atlanta Constitution* with which he was associated from 1876 to 1900. The stories attribute human traits to Brer (Brother) Rabbit and to other animals, and are told in the Negro dialect of middle Georgia. In Europe it was the Fox, not the Rabbit, who was the trickster hero of folk tales. But in Chapter 36 of Harris's second book, as the title declares, "Brother Wolf Falls a Victim" (to Brother Rabbit). In the conversation, the little boy who is listening asks whether Uncle Remus ever saw the Witch-Rabbit, Mammy-Bammy Big-Money. The elderly Negro replies that if he has ever run across her, she disappeared so fast he never caught a glimpse of her.

The result of this good-humored explanation was that the child didn't know whether Uncle Remus had ever seen the Witch-Rabbit or not, but his sympathies led him to suspect that the old man was

17

thoroughly familiar with all her movements.

"Uncle Remus," the little boy said after a while, "If there's another story about Mammy-Bammy Big-Money, I wish you would tell it to me **all by my own-alone self."**

All have not the gift of martyrdom

Source: THE HIND AND THE PANTHER (Part II, l. 59)
Author: John Dryden (1631-1700)
First published: 1687
Type of work: Religious allegory

Context: Having been converted in 1686 to Catholicism, Dryden championed his new Church in a long poem, *The Hind and the Panther.* In his allegory, animals represented England's various religious groups. The hares were the Quakers; the apes, the freethinkers; the boar, the Anabaptists; the fox, the Unitarians; the wolf, the Presbyterians. "The milk white Hind" was the Roman Catholic Church, in danger of being attacked by the Panther (The Church of England), but defended by the British Lion (King James II). In the second part, the Panther accompanies the Hind through the woods, and they talk together. The Panther congratulates her at having escaped the hunter's snares. The Hind retorts that the snares were laid for the Panther, who twisted out of them. Some people are born to be martyrs, she tells her companion, while others are unwilling to suffer for a just cause. Instead, from fear and selfishness, they do everything to escape. The use of the word "gift" shows the poet's admiration of those who suffer for righteousness' sake.

. . .

"Long time you fought, redoubled batt'ry bore,
But, after all, against yourself you swore:
Your former self; for ev'ry hour your form
Is chopp'd and chang'd, like winds before a storm.
Thus fear and int'rest will prevail with some;
For **all have not the gift of martyrdom."**
    The Panther grinned at this, and thus replied:
"That men may err was never yet denied.
But if that common principle be true,
The cannon, dame, is level'd full at you." . . .

All heiresses are beautiful

Source: KING ARTHUR OR THE BRITISH WORTHY (Act I, sc. i)
Author: John Dryden (1631-1700)
First published: 1691
Type of work: Dramatic opera

18

Context: Henry Purcell (1659–1695) provided the music for this play as he and other famous composers did for the many songs by Dryden, so popular in late seventeenth century drawing rooms. As the curtain rises on *King Arthur or The British Worthy,* Conon, Duke of Cornwall, Albanact, Captain of Arthur's Guards, and Aurelius, a friend of the king, discuss the coming battle that will determine whether Arthur or the invading Saxons will rule Britain. Oswald, King of Kent, the Saxon leader, had come earlier to Conon's court seeking to marry the duke's daughter, Emmeline. Because she was in love with Arthur, his suit was refused. Determined to marry her, he began the present war. The soldiers ponder Oswald's motives, since the princess is blind, but one of them remarks that her wealth is bound to make her attractive. The man who marries her will not get a "blind bargain." He knows well how advantageous it will be. Conon then describes Oswald, as he seemed to be at the court of Cornwall.

CONON

Revengeful, rugged, violently brave; and once resolved,
    is never to be moved.

ALBANACT

Yes, he's a valiant dog, pox on him!

CONON

This was the character he then maintained,
When in my court he sought my daughter's love,
My fair, blind Emmeline.

ALBANACT

I cannot blame him for courting the heiress of Cornwall;
All heiresses are beautiful; and, as blind as she is, he
Would have no blind bargain of her.

All is gas and gaiters

Source: NICHOLAS NICKLEBY (Chapter 49)
Author: Charles Dickens (1812-1870)
First published: 1838-1839
Type of work: Novel

Context: At a gathering in the Nickleby residence in London are Mrs. Nickleby and her daughter, Kate; Miss La Creevy, the artist; Mr. Linkinwater, who professes to admire Miss La Creevy; and Frank Cheeryble, who, with his brother Charles, employs Nicholas Nickleby. While the company is engaged in conversation, a muffled voice singing in melancholy tones issues from a neighboring room. The company, upon investigation, finds a pair of legs in coarse gray stockings dangling from the chimney, and when they are sharply pulled a gentleman in small clothes, that is, tight-fitting knee breeches, appears. Kate says that he is a madman who has escaped from the neighboring house, but Mrs. Nickleby insists that he is the victim of a plot to rob him of his wealth. His demanding bottled lightning, a thunder sandwich, a fricassee of boot-tops with goldfish sauce rather substantiates Kate's opinion of him. He greets Miss La Creevy as his lost love and says that all is gas and gaiters, by which expression he seems to mean that now everything is all right:

> "Aha!" cried the old gentleman, folding his hands, and squeezing them with great force against each other. "I see her now; I see her now! My love, my life, my bride, my peerless beauty. She is come at last—at last—and **all is gas and gaiters!"**
>
> Mrs. Nickleby looked rather disconcerted for a moment, but immediately recovering, nodded to Miss La Creevy and the other spectators several times, and frowned, and smiled gravely; giving them to understand that she saw where the mistake was, and would set it all to rights in a minute or two.
>
> "She is come!" said the old gentleman, laying his hand upon his heart. "Cormoran and Blunderbore! She is come! All the wealth I have is hers if she will take me for her slave. Where are grace, beauty, and blandishments, like those? In the Empress of Madagascar? No. In the Queen of Diamonds? No. In Mrs. Rowland, who every morning bathes in Kalydor for nothing? No. Melt all these down into one, with the three Graces, the nine Muses, and fourteen biscuit-bakers' daughters from Oxford-street, and make a woman half as lovely. Pho! I defy you."

All jargon of the schools

Source: ON EXODUS 3:14 (Stanza vi)
Author: Matthew Prior (1664-1721)
First published: 1707
Type of work: Philosophic poem

Context: English poet and diplomat, Matthew Prior is known chiefly for his epigrams, satires, and society verse. With his Tory party affiliation, he was thrown into close literary association with Alexander Pope and John Arbuthnot. In his public life, he took part in several important European treaty negotiations, including the Treaty of Ryswick and the Treaty of Utrecht. "On *Exodus* 3:14: I am That I am: An Ode," written in 1688, originated as an exercise at St. John's College, Cambridge. In many ways it anticipates in a limited fashion Pope's *An Essay on Man*. Prior berates "foolish man," who scarce knows himself, for his presumptuous curiosity—his "daring Pride and insolent Delight"—which would attempt to fathom the mysteries of God's universe. He avers that God's laws will never submit to "Reason's Batteries, or the Mines of Wit." The perspective of faith is man's only recourse; as Pope was to describe it: "Whatever is, is right." At one point Prior takes to task the petty knowledge of the schools and laboratories, always claiming the answers to some enigma of the universe or of human nature, yet ever replacing the "answers" of yesterday with the new hypotheses and theories of today:

> Man does with dangerous Curiosity
> These unfathom'd Wonders try:
> With fancy'd Rules and arbitrary Laws
> Matter and Motion he restrains;
> And study'd Lines and fictious Circles draws:
> Then with imagin'd Soveraignty
> Lord of his new Hypothesis he reigns.
> He reigns: How long? 'till some Usurper rise;
> And he too, mighty Thoughtful, mighty Wise,
> Studies new Lines, and other Circles feigns.
> From this last Toil again what Knowledge flows?
> Just as much, perhaps, as shows,
> That all his Predecessor's Rules
> Were empty Cant, **all Jargon of the Schools;**
> That he on t'other's Ruin rears his Throne;
> And shows his Friend's Mistake, and thence confirms
> his own.

All men would be cowards if they durst

Source: A SATYR AGAINST MANKIND (Line 158)
Author: John Wilmot (Second Earl of Rochester, 1647–1680)
First published: 1675
Type of work: Verse satire

Context: In this verse satire Rochester expresses a general and cold contempt for human life as he saw and lived it. He begins, as does Boileau in his eighth satire, with a picture of the contempt in which man is held by the beasts for his supposed reason, or "common sense." A clergyman interrupts for a brief dialogue, protesting Rochester's slander of "Blest glorious Man, to whom alone kind Heav'n / An everlasting Soul hath freely giv'n;" a gift which enables him to reason. The poet responds that it is "This super-nat'ral Gift, that makes a Mite / Think he's the Image of the Infinite." Reason, in Rochester's philosophy, is useful only when leagued with knavery and hypocrisy. Concerning man's martial accomplishments, the poet observes that animals kill out of necessity but man from wantonness and lust for power "for the which alone he dares be brave:"

> Look to the bottom of his vast Design,
> Wherein Man's Wisdom, Pow'r, and Glory join;

21

The Good he acts, the Ill he does endure,
'Tis all for Fear, to make himself secure.
Merely for safety, after Fame we thirst;
For **all Men would be Cowards if they durst:**
And Honesty's against all common sense—
Men must be Knaves; 'tis in their own defence,
Mankind's dishonest; if you think it fair,
Amongst known Cheats, to play upon the square,
You'll be undone—
Nor can weak Truth, your Reputation save;
The Knaves will all agree to call you Knave.
Wrong'd shall he live, insulted o'er, opprest,
Who dares be less a Villain than the rest.

All places are distant from Heaven alike

Source: ANATOMY OF MELANCHOLY (Partition II, sec. 3, memb. 4)
Author: Robert Burton (1577-1640)
First published: 1621-1651
Type of work: Essays

Context: As an early forerunner of Freud, the vicar Burton, who dabbled in every field of learning, spent much of his life writing a thick book that might be called "An Analysis of Morbid Psychology." But there was no body of applied science on which Burton could draw, so he took from every sort of source to produce a series of informal essays on ways of curing man's dissatisfaction with the universe. In the first two of his three Partitions, he considered first the causes and then the cures of melancholy. Section 3 of Partition II concerns remedies for discontent. No one should be unhappy at servitude, for everybody is subservient to some one: nobles to their king, lovers to their mistresses, and rich men to their gold. Imprisonment is not sufficient cause for discontent, since all life is a prison. Nor should one who is banished or forced to change his residence feel himself a slave at the orders of a master. His new place of residence is attractive to some one who considers the newcomer lucky to be there. A man can travel as quickly to Heaven from one place as from another.

. . . There is a base Nation in the north (saith Pliny), called Chauci, that live amongst rocks and sands by the seaside, feed on fish, drink water: and yet these base people account themselves slaves in respect, when they come to Rome . . . so it is. Fortune favors some to live at home to their further punishment: 't is want of judgment. **All places are distant from Heaven alike,** the Sun shines happily as warm in one city as in another, and to a wise man there is no difference of climes, . . .

22

All places shall be hell that are not heaven

Source: THE TRAGICAL HISTORY OF DOCTOR FAUSTUS (Scene V, l. 27)
Author: Christopher Marlowe (1564-1593)
First published: 1604
Type of work: Dramatic tragedy

Context: The death of the greatest of Elizabethan dramatists, next to Shakespeare, "Stab'd with a dagger" by a drinking companion, Ingram Frizer, at the age of twenty-nine, has been ascribed to a plot by the Puritans because of the playwright's atheistic and heretical religious principles. Yet how could any heretic write such a Puritanical sermon as the struggle of Dr. Faustus with his conscience, his final awful soliloquy, and the terrifying climax of this play, where amid thunder and lightning the devils carry him off to hell? The German scholar brings his punishment on himself. Reviewing the vast knowledge he possesses, Dr. John Faustus pronounces it futile. He decides to take up magic and with a spell conjures up Mephostopilis with whom he signs a pact: his soul in return for twenty-four years of service from Lucifer's chief minister. Receiving the signed document, the Minister of Hell speaks:

MEPHOSTOPHILIS
Now, Faustus, ask me what thou wilt.

FAUSTUS
First will I question with thee about hell.
Tell me, where is the place that men call hell?

MEPHOSTOPHILIS
Under the Heavens.

FAUSTUS
Aye, so are all things else, but whereabout?

MEPHOSTOPHILIS
Within the bowels of these elements,
Where we are tortured and remain forever.
Hell hath no limits, nor is circumscribed
In one self place, for where we are is hell,
And where hell is, there must we ever be:
And, to be short, when all the world dissolves
And every creature shall be purified,
All places shall be hell that are not heaven.

FAUSTUS
I think hell's a fable.

23

MEPHOSTOPHILIS
Ay, think so still, till experience change thy mind.

All poets are mad

Source: ANATOMY OF MELANCHOLY: DEMOCRITUS JUNIOR TO THE READER
Author: Robert Burton (1577-1640)
First published: 1621-1651
Type of work: Essays

Context: The seventeenth century was a time of intellectual ferment when scholars tried to master all they could of human knowledge. Burton called himself Democritus Junior, after the Greek philosopher of the fifth and fourth centuries B. C. who, besides studying the physical world and theorizing about atoms, held that the true end of life was happiness achieved through inner tranquility. Burton's book has no special theme or thesis, but into it he poured his immense sum of learning. A lengthy introduction, "Democritus Junior to the Reader," is a satirical catalog of the follies of mankind. Parts sound very modern: the injustice of a system where a lawyer gets more money in a day than a philosopher in a year, and where wise men are degraded and fools preferred. He gives his recipe for a New Utopia. Quoting Tully (Cicero), he writes: "I prefer silent Wisdom to talkative Folly," He gives his own opinions, sometimes footnoting them by references to ancient writers, many of whom are no longer mentioned in the most minute biographical volumes. Frascatorious (1483–1553) was an Italian physician and poet whose long poem about Syphilis gave that disease its name. Scaliger (1484–1558) wrote *Poetics* (published in 1561).

> . . . I esteem a man wise, not according to his words but to his deeds. Make the best of him, a good orator is a turn-coat, an evil man, his tongue is set to sale, he is a mere voice, as he said of a nightingale, gives a voice without thought, an hyperbolical liar, a flatterer, a parasite, and as Amnianus Marcellinus will, a corrupting cozener, one that doth more mischief by his fair speech, than he that bribes by money; for a man may with more facility avoid him that circumvents by money, than he that deceives by glozing terms; which made Socrates so much abhor and explode them. Frascatorius, a famous poet, freely grants all Poets to be mad; so doth Scaliger, and who doth not? Either mad or making verses (saith Horace); (saith Virgil) it pleases one to be mad, i.e., to make verses; So Servius interprets it, **all Poets are mad.** . . .

24

All service ranks the same with God

Source: PIPPA PASSES (Part IV, "Night")
Author: Robert Browning (1812-1889)
First published: 1841
Type of work: Dramatic poem

Context: Pippa Passes is the first of a series of little pamphlets which Browning called *Bells and Pomegranates.* It did not achieve immediate recognition; a previous poem, *Sordello,* had done him considerable harm because of its obscurity, and some time elapsed before *Pippa Passes* began to receive the attention it deserved. It eventually became one of Browning's most popular poems. This story of an innocent little girl and her love of life reflects one of his basic beliefs—that life and intensity are the same thing and that they are good. His religious conviction was that the right would always triumph in the end, and that the Divine love he found manifested through nature and intellect could have no other effect. To Browning, love is not a passion dedicated to human perfection; it is instead a Divine tolerance of imperfect humanity. Pippa is unaware that she is an instrument of Divine love and justice—she is just a child who loves life and sings because of it. All the same, when she passes by and people hear her song, their lives are affected dramatically. A very poor child, she works the year round at a silk mill in Asolo, Italy. On her one holiday, New Year's day, she goes about the town to see the homes of four people she admires and considers the happiest in the city. In the first house she passes, an adulterer and murderer hears her song, is conscience-stricken, and expiates his crime with poison; in the second, a sculptor enmeshed in the world's complexities receives new inspiration and resolves to go elsewhere rather than kill a man; in the third house, an unstable youth duped by others musters his courage and goes forth to destroy an evil at its source. Pippa passes the fourth house in time to prevent an evil man from selling a child into prostitution—and the child she saves is herself. Pippa returns home unaware that she has influenced anyone; she is content with her lot and not envious, but she has enjoyed imagining herself in the places of these high and happy people. Regretting that her holiday is over, she prepares to sleep:

Now, one thing I should like to really know:
How near I ever might approach all these
I only fancied being, this long day:
—Approach, I mean, so as to touch them, so
As to . . . in some way . . . move them—if you please,
Do good or evil to them some slight way.
For instance, if I wind
Silk tomorrow, my silk may bind
           [*Sitting on the bedside.*]
And border Ottima's cloak's hem.

Ah me, and my important part with them,
This morning's hymn half promised when I rose!
True in some sense or other, I suppose.
[*As she lies down.*]
God bless me! I can pray no more tonight.
No doubt, some way or other, hymns say right.
All service ranks the same with God—
With God, whose puppets, best and worst,
Are we; there is no last nor first.
[*She sleeps.*]

All silent, and all damned

Source: PETER BELL (Part I, Original Edition)
Author: William Wordsworth (1770-1850)
First published: 1819
Type of work: Narrative poem

Context: As the author explains in his preface to this long, unsuccessful poem, "the Imagination . . . does not require for its exercise the intervention of supernatural agency"; quite the contrary, the poet can stimulate his readers' imaginations by faithfully adhering to "the humblest departments of daily life." The story of the poem, an attempt to illustrate everyday occurrences, earned the laughing scorn of practically all of Wordsworth's major contemporaries: a potter named Peter Bell is a sinful man who not only has a dozen wives but also is so insensitive that he does not appreciate nature. One day he comes upon a starving ass that has remained where its master died, and from the patient loyalty of the animal (as well as from his own guilt) he learns the wickedness of his ways and repents. The quotation occurs near the end of the first part of the original poem: Peter Bell, discovering that the ass is dying, loses his temper and begins to beat the poor beast, but as he maltreats it, he is seized with irrational fear and thinks that he hears noises such as demons might make:

Is it a party in a parlour?
Cramm'd just as they on earth were cramm'd—
Some sipping punch, some sipping tea,
But, as you by their faces see,
All silent, and all damn'd!

All taxes must, at last, fall upon agriculture

Source: THE DECLINE AND FALL OF THE ROMAN EMPIRE (Chapter 8)
Author: Edward Gibbon (1737-1794)
First published: 1776-1788
Type of work: History

Context: In Chapter 8 of his narrative of Roman history, Edward Gibbon leaves the chronicle of the Roman Empire itself to inform his reader of the nature of Rome's enemies from without, the tribes which were to invade the outer provinces of the Empire at first and, later, overrun the Empire as a whole and sack the city of Rome itself. These invaders Gibbon calls "the nations who avenged the causes of Hannibal and Mithridates." He first tells of the Persians, including in his narrative a succinct, but clear, account of their religion, Zoroastrianism. He then relates how Artaxerxes wrested the control of the Near East from the Parthians and established his own vigorous administration throughout Persia by subduing each of the under-kings who had ruled under his predecessor. The quotation about taxes and agriculture is credited to Artaxerxes by Gibbon, who notes that it can be found in D'Herbelot's *Bibliothèque Orientale,* under the entry "Ardshir," another form of Artaxerxes' name. The quotation appears in a paragraph in which Gibbon praises the Persian ruler for his intelligent and effective rule:

> The reign of Artaxerxes . . . forms a memorable era in the history of the East, and even in that of Rome. His character seems to have been marked by those bold and commanding features that generally distinguished the princes who conquer, from those who inherit, an empire. Till the last period of the Persian monarchy his code of laws was respected as the ground-work of their civil and religious policy. Several of his sayings are preserved. One of them in particular discovers a deep insight into the constitution of government. "The authority of the prince," said Artaxerxes, "must be defended by a military force; that force can only be maintained by taxes; **all taxes must, at last, fall upon agriculture;** and agriculture can never flourish except under the protection of justice and moderation. . . .

All the live murmur of a summer's day

Source: THE SCHOLAR-GYPSY (Stanza 2)
Author: Matthew Arnold (1822-1888)
First published: 1853
Type of work: Philosophical poem

Context: Arnold's poem is derived from a passage in Joseph Glanvil's *Vanity of Dogmatizing* (1661) which tells of a scholar who, for lack of money, abandoned his studies at Oxford and joined a band of gypsies. The scholar was admitted to the confidence of the gypsies, who communicated to him the secrets of their knowledge and philosophy. After he had been with them for several years, two of his fellow students at Oxford chanced upon him, and to them he said that the gypsies have the power to bind the imagination of others with their own. He asserted that when he was perfect in the knowledge he would communicate it to the world.

Arnold's poem begins with the poet's telling the shepherd to go to the hills to release the sheep from the fold, but in the evening, when tired men and dogs have gone to rest, the shepherd is to renew his quest for knowledge. The poet sits in a corner of the field where the reaper stored his basket of food, his jug of drink, and his coat while he was working. The poet will sit and wait for country sounds to come to him—the bleating of sheep, the cries of the reapers, and all the live murmur of a summer's day.

> Here, where the reaper was at work of late—
> In this high field's dark corner, where he leaves
> His coat, his basket, and his earthen cruse,
> And in the sun all morning binds the sheaves,
> Then here, at noon, comes back his stores to use
> Here will I sit and wait,
> While to my ear from uplands far away
> The bleating of the folded flocks is borne,
> With distant cries of reapers in the corn—
> **All the live murmur of a summer's day.**

All the perfumes of Arabia will not sweeten this little hand

Source: MACBETH (Act V, sc. i, ll. 56-57)
Author: William Shakespeare (1564-1616)
First published: 1623
Type of work: Dramatic tragedy

Context: Lady Macbeth receives a letter from her husband telling her of the prophetic words of three witches that he will become king. When the chance comes to kill King Duncan as he sleeps, an overnight visitor in Macbeth's castle, Lady Macbeth urges Macbeth to murder his liege and cousin and to usurp the throne. The deed is done, Macbeth is crowned king, and yet the queen does not enjoy her new estate. Finally insane, Lady Macbeth is obsessed with the murder of Duncan and the idea that his blood would not wash off her hands after she had smeared it upon the grooms who slept by their king.

LADY MACBETH
Here's the smell of the blood still: **all the perfumes of Arabia will not sweeten this little hand.** Oh, oh, oh!

DOCTOR
What a sigh is there! The heart is sorely charged.

GENTLEWOMAN
I would not have such a heart in my bosom for the dignity of the whole body.

DOCTOR

Well, well, well.

GENTLEWOMAN

Pray God it be sir.

DOCTOR

This disease is beyond my practice. Yet I have known those which have walked in their sleep who have died holily in their beds.

All things that love the sun

Source: RESOLUTION AND INDEPENDENCE (Stanza 2)
Author: William Wordsworth (1770–1850)
First published: 1807
Type of work: Didactic poem

Context: Although the second half of this poem has been made famous by two parodies of it (Edward Lear: "Incidents in the Life of My Uncle Arly" and Lewis Carroll: "The White Knight's Ballad"), it remains an important work from the author's early period when his inspiration was still at its height. The poem, twenty stanzas in length, shows that the author, who had so often declared his faith in nature as a guide, a teacher, and a friend, was also aware that nature could at times be very unkind. The subject arose from an actual experience that Wordsworth encountered in the Lake District: that of meeting, during one of his walks, an old man, badly crippled by an accident and yet struggling to make some kind of a living. The old man's fortitude amidst these reverses of fortune compelled the poet's admiration but reminded him that all men—especially poets—are subject to these same reverses. The poem breaks into two parts: the first describes the beauty of the moors early in the morning after a heavy storm; the second recounts the poet's meeting with the old leech-gatherer and the conversation that ensued. It was this second section that inspired the parodies of Lear and Carroll, and it must be admitted that Wordsworth's questions and his inattention to the old man's replies are fit subjects for parody. But in the early part of the poem, Wordsworth expresses his usual view of his kinship with nature and his attribution of human qualities to all of her manifestations:

There was a roaring in the wind all night;
The rain came heavily and fell in floods;
But now the sun is rising calm and bright;
The birds are singing in the distant woods:
Over his own sweet voice the stock-dove broods;
The jay makes answer as the magpie chatters;
And all the air is filled with pleasant noise of waters.

29

All things that love the sun are out of doors;
The sky rejoices in the morning's birth;
The grass is bright with raindrops;—on the moors
The hare is running races in her mirth;
And with her feet she from the plashy earth
Raises a mist, that, glittering in the sun,
Runs with her all the way wherever she doth run.

All things work together for good

Source: ROMANS 8:28
Author: Paul
First transcribed: c.50-60
Type of work: Religious epistle

Context: Romans is a letter which Paul wrote to his fellow-Christians in Rome; it is a letter to strangers, because he had never been to Rome and had no part in founding the church there. For this reason his epistle is more a treatise on the principles and practice of Christianity than a letter. It is evident that he wishes to offer his readers encouragement and reassurance in their faith; at the same time, he is anxious to furnish as many arguments as possible which can be used by them in gaining converts to Christianity. His principal concern is for the Jews; most of his work has been done among these people, and it has been his habit as a missionary to go to the synagogue whenever he arrives in a community. There he begins his effort by arguing scripture and preaching. He has found the Jews very resistant to conversion. In the first eight chapters of this epistle he draws upon his long experience and enumerates all the objections to Christianity that members of the Jewish faith are likely to raise. For each of the objections he provides an answer. Paul begins the epistle with a statement of his qualifications; he then blesses his readers and states his gospel for them, reminding them that God offers salvation through it to all men regardless of their origin. He adds that all men are sinners and that to satisfy the outward requirements of faith is useless unless one's belief is genuine. To observe the law is good, but its observance without faith is vain: belief in man's redemption through Christ transcends the law. At this point Paul turns to a discussion of sin and its nature, adding the reassurance that ancient sins are wiped out by baptism. He then returns to his discussion of the law; no earthly law has power over us after death. The true Christian is dead to sin because his law is Christ. In Chapter 8 Paul goes back to an earlier point, that to be one with Christ is to be pure and free from condemnation. He elaborates his theme of the transcendency of spiritual things over material:

For we are saved by hope: but hope that is seen is not hope: for
what a man seeth, why doth he yet hope for?

30

But if we hope for that we see not, then do we with patience wait for it.

Likewise the Spirit also helpeth our infirmities: for we know not what we should pray for as we ought: but the Spirit itself maketh intercession for us with groanings which cannot be uttered.

And he that searcheth the hearts knoweth what is the mind of the Spirit, because he maketh intercession for the saints according to the will of God.

And we know that **all things work together for good** to them that love God, to them who are the called according to his purpose.

For whom he did foreknow, he also did predestinate to be conformed to the image of his Son, that he might be the firstborn among many brethren.

Moreover whom he did predestinate, them he also called: and whom he called, them he also justified: and whom he justified, them he also glorified.

What shall we then say to these things? If God be for us, who can be against us?

He that spared not his own Son, but delivered him up for us all, how shall he not with him also freely give us all things?

Who shall lay any thing to the charge of God's elect? It is God that justifieth.

All this and heaven too

Source: THE LIFE AND DEATH OF THE REV. PHILIP HENRY (Chapter V)
Author: Matthew Henry (1662-1714)
First published: 1696-1697?
Type of work: Biography

Context: Matthew Henry writes the life of his father, Philip Henry (1631 –1696), a non-conformist minister whose entire existence lay in preaching the gospel. After a pleasant and tranquil beginning to his career as a minister, he was, during much of the reign of King Charles II, barred from preaching in public and was subjected to various other harassments because his conscience forbade his conforming to the church regulations set up by parliament at the instigation of the king. Although he was deprived of his pulpit, he was, because he had married a woman of some wealth, never in want for the necessities of life. He contrived to lead a useful and pleasant life, although he was several times imprisoned for short terms for his lack of conformity. As, however, other ministers of the gospel were incarcerated at the same time as he was, he rather enjoyed the experience, as it gave him the opportunity to discuss religion with his peers, an opportunity he did not have while at liberty. He was always charitable and used to season his gifts to the poor with wholesome advice and gentle admonitions for erring conduct. He always took great pleasure in being able to contribute to the poor, believing that anything material he gave would be returned to him in gifts of the spirit:

. . . though he did not delight himself in the abundance of wealth; yet, which is far better, he delighted himself in the "abundance of peace." . . . All that he had and did, observably prospered, so that the country oftentimes . . . called his family, "a family which the Lord had blessed." And his comforts of this kind were (as he used to pray they might be) "oil to the wheels of his obedience," and in the use of these things he served the Lord his God with "joyfulness and gladness of heart"; yet still mindful of and "grieved for, the afflictions of Joseph." He would say sometimes, when he was in the midst of the comforts of this life, as that good man who exclaimed, **"All this and heaven too!** surely then we serve a good Master." Thus did the Lord bless him, and make him a blessing; and this abundant grace, through the thanksgiving of many, redounded to the glory of God.

An allegory on the banks of Nile

Source: THE RIVALS (Act III, sc. iii)
Author: Richard Brinsley Sheridan (1751-1816)
First published: 1775
Type of work: Dramatic comedy

Context: In this scene of Sheridan's play, Captain Absolute appears to Lydia Languish as "Ensign Beverley," which is a fictitious identity he has taken on to woo the fanciful, but beautiful, young heiress. He knows that with her romantic notions she wants to marry the penniless "ensign" for love, rather than the real Captain Absolute, who is heir to wealthy Sir Anthony Absolute. The situation is complicated further by the fact that Mrs. Malaprop, the girl's guardian, knows the suitor for Lydia is Captain Absolute, but she does not know that he is also the fictitious "ensign," whom she despises. During the interview between the young people Mrs. Malaprop enters unseen to eavesdrop. Hearing Lydia say that she will never marry Captain Absolute, Mrs. Malaprop comes forward to berate the headstrong girl. As usual when she speaks, Mrs. Malaprop uses wrong words, here saying "allegory" for "alligator":

MRS. MALAPROP
[*Aside.*] Ay, poor young man!—down on his knees entreating for pity!—I can contain no longer.—[*Coming forward.*] Why, hussy! hussy! I have overheard you.

CAPT. ABSOLUTE
[*Aside.*] Oh, confound her vigilance!

MRS. MALAPROP
Captain Absolute, I know not how to apologize for her shocking rudeness.

32

CAPT. ABSOLUTE

CAPT. ABSOLUTE

[*Aside.*] So all's safe, I find.—[*Aloud.*] I have hopes, madam, that time will bring the young lady—

MRS. MALAPROP

Oh, there's nothing to be hoped for from her! She's as head-strong as **an allegory on the banks of Nile.**

All's love, yet all's law

Source: SAUL (Line 242)
Author: Robert Browning (1812-1889)
First published: 1855
Type of work: Dramatic monologue

Context: David, the shepherd boy, has cured King Saul of his melancholic despair of pleasure in all things. It is now the next morning, and David recounts, step by step, the events of the previous evening in Saul's camp: his meeting with Abner, his entry into Saul's darkened tent, and his first glimpse of the king "erect as that tent prop, both arms stretched out wide / On the great cross-support in the center, that goes to each side." There is then a catalogue of all the good things of the earth for which Saul should thank heaven. On his harp, David tells of the God-given signs of order in all creatures and of men working together as a society. A moan breaks from Saul's lips, a sign that the melancholy is somewhat broken. David sings of the joys of living and of the king's great worth. Slowly, Saul regains his kingly habits and bearing. It is through David's deep love and desire to help that the boy suddenly attains a mystical glimpse of Truth. He breaks off singing to speak aloud:

I have gone the whole round of creation; I saw and I spoke;
I, a work of God's hand for that purpose, received in my brain
And pronounced on the rest of his handwork—returned him again
His creation's approval or censure; I spoke as I saw;
Reported as man may of God's work—**all's love, yet all's law.**

. . .

I but open my eyes—and perfection, no more and no less,
In the kind I imagined, full-fronts me, and God is seen God
In the star, in the stone, in the flesh, in the soul and the clod.

Am I no a bonny fighter?

Source: KIDNAPPED (Chapter 10)
Author: Robert Louis Stevenson (1850-1894)
First published: 1886
Type of work: Novel

Context: David Balfour, a Scots lad, is sent by a rascally uncle to enforced service in the American colonies. While aboard the ship bound to America, he becomes the cabin-boy for the "Covenant." Shortly afterward the ship runs down a small boat; one man is saved after the accident, a Jacobite adventurer named Alan Breck, a Highlander with a price on his head. Alan Breck demands that the "Covenant's" master set him ashore in Scotland; the captain agrees to put the new passenger on land, but plots to deliver the man to the authorities so he may receive the bounty for turning Breck in. David Balfour overhears the captain and the second officer plotting against the Highlander and warns the man of his peril. Breck and the lad take refuge in the ship's roundhouse, where they hold off the ship's crew, who endeavor to capture them by force. Breck with his sword, and David Balfour with pistols, drive off the crew, killing the second officer and three other men, as well as wounding the captain and several others. Having driven the survivors below decks, Breck returns to the roundhouse, now described by young Balfour:

> The roundhouse was like a shambles; three were dead inside, another lay in his death agony across the threshold; and there were Alan and I victorious and unhurt.
>
> He came to me with open arms. "Come to my arms!" he cried, and embraced and kissed me upon both cheeks. "David," said he, "I love you like a brother. And O, man," he cried in a kind of ecstasy, **"am I no a bonny fighter?"**
>
> Thereupon he turned to the four enemies, passed his sword clean through each of them, and tumbled them out of doors one after the other. As he did so, he kept humming and singing and whistling to himself, like a man trying to recall an air; only what *he* was trying to do was to make one. All the while the flush was on his face, and his eyes were as bright as a five-year-old child's with a new toy. . . .

Ambition can creep as well as soar

Source: LETTERS ON A REGICIDE PEACE (Letter III)
Author: Edmund Burke (1729-1797)
First published: 1796-1797
Type of work: Open letter

Context: As Burke's life approached its end so did the life of the French Revolution. In Paris horror succeeded horror, culminating in the execution of the king and queen; the Army moved in, and under the command of Napoleon, protected what was of permanent value in the increasing shambles of the disintegrating Revolution. To the astonishment of many, France, wracked by violent internal conflicts and collapsing credit, was able to break up the European coalition arrayed against her. In England a movement was afoot to make peace with the Revolutionary government, and peace talks were actually opened at one point. Burke, ever a firm and stanch enemy of the French Revolution, was equally firmly opposed to this peace movement. In a series of four open letters he argued his case for France as a menace to all of Europe. In this third letter Burke insisted that France had at one time contemplated an invasion of England and that the peace terms offered to England by the Directory were positively humiliating; he derided and cast suspicion on those who encouraged peace as an apology for England's military actions against France:

> There is one thing in this business which appears to be wholly unaccountable, . . . I cannot help asking, Why all this pains to clear the British nation of ambition, perfidy, and the insatiate thirst of war? At what period of time was it that our country has deserved that load of infamy of which nothing but preternatural humiliation in language and conduct can serve to clear us? If we have deserved this kind of evil fame from anything we have done in a state of prosperity, I am sure that it is not an abject conduct in adversity that can clear our reputation. Well is it known that **ambition can creep as well as soar.** The pride of no person in a flourishing condition is more justly to be dreaded than that of him who is mean and cringing under a doubtful and unprosperous fortune. . . .

Ambition's debt is paid

Source: JULIUS CAESAR (Act III, sc. i, l. 83)
Author: William Shakespeare (1564-1616)
First published: 1623
Type of work: Dramatic tragedy

Context: Following his stirring victories over Pompey, Julius Caesar has returned to Rome and is swept up in the plaudits of "the common herd." In the rush of this popular acclaim, there is rumor that Caesar is on the verge of allowing himself to be crowned emperor. Such a period of political instability is the season of discontent both for those who, fed by personal ambition, see their own opportunities for power thwarted and also for those who are apprehensive lest the law of the land is to be subordinated to the individual and the freedom of the Republic lost forever. These two kinds of individuals are, of course, philosophies apart, but rebellion makes strange bedfellows. Thus it is that the ambitious aristocrats Cassius, moved by envy in his hatred of Caesar and possessed of "an itching palm," and Casca, who holds in high disdain the "tag-rag" multitude which heaps accolades upon Caesar, are joined in rebellion against their Roman leader. As for Brutus, he is as idealistic as his compatriots are practical. His love of Caesar is great, but his love for Rome greater. In the desperate efforts which he is convinced are necessary to save the Republic, he becomes a part of that which, were it for personal gain, he would loathe. Following the mo-ment of Caesar's murder, he attempts to quiet the distracted populace:

CAESAR

Et tu Brute? Then fall Caesar.

CINNA

Liberty! Freedom! Tyranny is dead.
Run hence, proclaim, cry it about the streets.

CASSIUS

Some to the common pulpits, and cry out,
Liberty, freedom, and enfranchisement!

BRUTUS

People and senators, be not affrighted,
Fly not, stand still. **Ambition's debt is paid.**

.   .   .

METELLUS

Stand fast together, lest some friend of Caesar's
Should chance—

BRUTUS

Talk not of standing. Publius, good cheer,
There is no harm intended to your person,
Nor to no Roman else: so tell them Publius.

America is the country of young men

Source: SOCIETY AND SOLITUDE (Chapter 12, "Old Age")
Author: Ralph Waldo Emerson (1803-1882)
First published: 1870
Type of work: Moral essay

Context: Emerson begins this essay by relating how the appearance of former President Josiah Quincy of Harvard at the annual Phi Beta Kappa Society dinner there in 1861 as the oldest living Phi Beta Kappan and oldest living alumnus of Harvard, had caused him to return home to look again at Cicero's famous essay on old age, and to write down his own comments about it. Emerson notes that the trappings of old age are often an illusion, that a gray head of hair, or a bald head, can make a person seem older than he really is. The real value is in what a person has learned —so that some men are old, in a good sense, while still very young in years. He adds that the experience of age is important, pointing out, "Life and art are cumulative; and he who has accomplished something in any

36

department alone deserves to be heard on that subject." He notes that as one approaches old age another advantage is the sense of relief one can enjoy at having escaped so many dangers, even fates. There is also, Emerson says, yet another capital advantage to age, that as one gains years a success more or less signifies not as much to one's self and to those about one. A third benefit or felicity of age is that it has already found the expression that youth so badly wants. And, lastly, Emerson suggests that old age sets its house in order by completing secular affairs. The essayist then notes, as if in contrast:

America is the country of young men, and too full of work hitherto for leisure and tranquillity; yet we have robust centenarians, and examples of dignity and wisdom. I have lately found in an old notebook a record of a visit to ex-President John Adams, in 1825, soon after the election of his son to the Presidency. It is but a sketch, and nothing important passed in the conversation; but it reports a moment in the life of a heroic person, who, in extreme old age, appeared still erect and worthy of his fame.

America is the only idealistic nation in the world

Source: ADDRESS AT SIOUX FALLS (September 8, 1919)
Author: Woodrow Wilson (1856-1924)
First published: 1919
Type of work: Speech

Context: On January 8, 1918, long before World War I was over, Woodrow Wilson delivered an address in which he presented the "Fourteen Points" under which he hoped a lasting peace could be established. When the Germans proposed an armistice, the Allied Powers named Wilson their common spokesman; he accordingly went to Paris to aid in peace negotiations. The previous Congressional election had resulted in a Republican Congress hostile to Wilson's ideals of peace, and there was other opposition to the Fourteen Points, which would commit all men to open diplomacy, freedom of the seas, self-determination of peoples, free trade, free access to harbors, disarmament, and—most important to Wilson—a League of Nations that would settle disputes and guide the world. In spite of the veneration accorded Wilson abroad, it was soon apparent that his ideals represented more self-sacrifice than any nation cared to undertake. He fought for his Fourteen Points but was forced to make concessions. During a brief trip home, he warned his opposition that the League and the Treaty would be so closely interwoven that either both or none would be the choice. He did succeed in his principal goal at Paris; the League of Nations was made a part of the Treaty of Peace. The concessions he made had weakened his position, however, and when he at length presented a completed Treaty to the Senate on July 10, 1919, he met with vio-

37

lent opposition. He continued to fight for his work and his dreams; he made a speaking tour of the country in order to tell the American public, in person, what he was trying to achieve. The grueling schedule sometimes involved several lengthy addresses in one day, and the result was a collapse from which he never really recovered. The following extract, taken from an address given in the Coliseum at Sioux Falls, illustrates both his idealism and his concept of America:

. . . You cannot establish freedom, my fellow citizens, without force, and the only force you can substitute for an armed mankind is the concerted force of the combined action of mankind through the instrumentality of all the enlightened Governments of the world. . . . Your choice is between the League of Nations and Germanism. I have told you what I mean by Germanism—taking care of yourselves, being armed and ready, having a chip on your shoulder, thinking of nothing but your own rights and never thinking of the rights of anybody else, thinking that you were put into this world to see that American might was asserted and forgetting that American might ought never to be used against the weak, ought never to be used in an unjust cause, ought never to be used for aggression; ought to be used with the heart of humanity beating behind it.

Sometimes people call me an idealist. Well, that is the way I know I am an American. America, my fellow citizens—I do not say it in disparagement of any other great people—**America is the only idealistic Nation in the world.** When I speak practical judgements about business affairs, I can only guess whether I am speaking the voice of America or not, but when I speak the ideal purposes of history I know that I am speaking the voice of America, because I have saturated myself since I was a boy in the records of that spirit, and everywhere in them there is this authentic tone of the love of justice and the service of humanity. . . .

America! thou half-brother of the world!

Source: FESTUS (Scene VIII)
Author: Philip James Bailey (1816-1902)
First published: 1839
Type of work: Philosophical poetic dialogue

Context: Festus is a dialogue between Lucifer and Festus, a character who evidently derives from Christopher Marlowe's Faustus, in that he has a craving to find answers to all the philosophical questions that have vexed the mind of man from the beginning of time. In Scene VIII Lucifer provides two horses, Ruin and Darkness, upon which the pair of speakers ride over the world to perceive the characters of the various lands that they pass. In rapid succession they view France, Spain, Italy,

38

Greece, Switzerland, Germany, Poland, Russia, Hindustan, and Egypt. They then plunge into the depths of the sea to make their way to America, which is characterized as a compound of something good and something evil found in all of the countries on earth; this compounding of qualities makes America the half-brother of the world. Festus is much concerned that America is a slave-holding country; he prophesies that eventually the slaves will be freed, and then there will be no blot upon the stars of the flag of the country that is dedicated to freedom. In the quotation below the two travelers have just emerged on their horses from the depths of the sea:

LUCIFER

There! now we stand
On the world's-end-land!
Over the hills
Away we go!
Through fire, and snow.
And rivers, whereto
All others are rills.

FESTUS

Through the lands of silver,
The lands of gold;
Through lands untrodden,
And lands untold.

. . .

LUCIFER

By strait and bay
We must away;
Through swamp, and plain,
And hurricane;

FESTUS

And that dark cloud of slaves
Which yet may rise;—
Though nought shall blot the bannered stars
From Freedom's skies.
America! thou half-brother of the world!
With something good and bad of every land;
Greater than thee have lost their seat—
Greater scarce none can stand.
Thy flag now flouts the skies,
The highest under Heaven. . . .

An amiable weakness

Source: THE SCHOOL FOR SCANDAL (Act V, sc. i)
Author: Richard Brinsley Sheridan (1751-1816)
First published: 1777
Type of work: Dramatic comedy

Context: Sheridan's contemporaries called him "The modern Congreve," after the Restoration master of the comedy of manners, William Congreve (1670–1729). Others, thinking of Tom Jones called the characters Joseph and Charles, "the Blifil and Tom Jones of the comedy." Its screen scene has been termed "the best one-act play in the English language." Many pirated editions appeared, but no authorized version was published in England during Sheridan's lifetime. The expression "an amiable weakness" can be found in Tom Jones (1749) (X, viii): "The too inordinate fondness of a father . . . must be allowed the name of an amiable weakness," and in Gibbon, Decline and Fall of the Roman Empire (1776), where in Chapter XIV the author speaks of "the amiable weakness of human nature." In Sheridan's play, it occurs in the last act when Sir Oliver Surface, returning after fifteen years abroad, is trying to decide which of his two nephews is the more deserving to be his heir. He visits Joseph in the guise of Mr. Stanley, a poor relative, to ask for charity. He has already made a generous present of cash to each of his nephews. The comment of his nephew, Joseph Surface, shows Sir Oliver how little gratitude the young man has, for he lies about his uncle's gifts. He also boasts falsely about his own generosity toward his brother. "Congou tea" is an excellent quality of black tea; avadavats are oriental birds of the finch family; pagodas were Indian gold coins of the period.

JOSEPH

. . . Sir Oliver is a worthy man—a very worthy man; but avarice, Mr. Stanley, is the vice of age. I tell you, my good sir, in confidence, what he has done for me has been a mere nothing—though people, I know, have thought otherwise, and for my part I never chose to contradict the report.

SIR OLIVER

What! has he never transmitted you bullion—rupees—pagodas?

JOSEPH

O, dear sir, nothing of the kind!—No, no—a few presents now and then—china, shawls, congou tea, avadavats, and Indian crackers—little more, believe me.

SIR OLIVER [aside.]

Here's gratitude for twelve thousand pounds! Avadavats and Indian crackers!

Then, my dear sir, you have heard, I doubt not, of the extravagance of my brother: There are very few who would credit what I have done for that unfortunate man.

SIR OLIVER [*aside.*]

Not I, for one!

JOSEPH

The sums I have lent him!—Indeed I have been exceedingly to blame; it was **an amiable weakness,** however, I don't pretend to defend it,—and now I feel it doubly culpable since it has deprived me of the pleasure of serving you, Mr. Stanley, as my heart dictates.

SIR OLIVER [*aside.*]

Dissembler! . . .

Among new men, strange faces, other minds

Source: IDYLLS OF THE KING ("The Passing of Arthur," Line 406)
Author: Alfred, Lord Tennyson (1809-1892)
First published: 1869
Type of work: Narrative poem

Context: Sir Bedivere, the last surviving knight of the Round Table, relates the final scenes of the life of King Arthur. First comes the ghost of Gawain, warning of the hollowness of delight and of Arthur's impending death. Second, Modred's forces are pressed back to the western boundary of Lyonesse. Third, is the great battle, fought on winter solstice in a chill white mist in which friend and foe seem like shadows. Only Arthur, Bedivere, and Modred survive the battle. In the last act of his kingship, Arthur slays Modred and receives, himself, a mortal wound. Bedivere bears Arthur to a nearby chapel which has, symbolically, a broken chancel and a broken cross. Arthur, realizing that death is near, asks Bedivere to return his sword, Excalibur, to the water from whence it came. Bedivere, his sense of right and wrong clouded, twice lies to Arthur. The third time, however, he throws the sword into the water and sees it caught by a white hand, which brandishes it three times before taking it down into the mere. Arthur asks to be taken to the edge of the lake. Standing under the winter moon, amid the icy caves, frosty chasms, and bare, black cliffs, they see a dusky barge bearing three black-hooded queens. Arthur is taken aboard. As the barge prepares to cast off, Bedivere asks:

"Ah! My Lord Arthur, whither shall I go?
Where shall I hide my forehead and my eyes?

For now I see the true old times are dead,
When every morning brought a noble chance,
And every chance brought out a noble knight.
    .   .   .
But now the whole Round Table is dissolved
Which was an image of the mighty world;
And I, the last, go forth companionless,
And the days darken round me, and the years
Among new men, strange faces, other minds."
And slowly answered Arthur from the barge:
"The old order changeth, yielding place to new,
And God fulfills himself in many ways,
Lest one good custom should corrupt the world."
    .   .   .

And lo! Ben Adhem's name led all the rest

Source: ABOU BEN ADHEM AND THE ANGEL (Last time)
Author: Leigh Hunt (1784-1859)
First published: 1844
Type of work: Lyric poem

Context: As editor of *The Examiner,* Leigh Hunt recognized and encouraged the poetic ability of Shelley and Keats. For a slighting comment on the fat "Adonis of fifty," later George IV, Hunt was imprisoned for two years (1813–1815), during which time his cell was a meeting place for young radicals. He is chiefly remembered, however, for his light essays and his delightful autobiography (1850), though he also wrote and published many short poems, of which "Jennie Kissed Me" and "Abou Ben Adhem" are those best remembered today. They show his efforts, as leader of the "Cockney School of Poetry," toward a colloquial style. In his *Bibliothèque Orien-* *tale* (1781), D'Herbelot told the legend of Abou-Ishak Ben Adhem. Hunt gave it poetic form, perhaps for Mrs. S. C. Hall's album, though it was first published in her husband's *Books of Gems,* Vol. III. It underscores the idea that a man can show his love of God and receive His blessing by loving his fellow-men. Abou Ben (son of) Adhem awakens one night to see an angel writing in a book of gold. He asks what the vision is doing, and receives the answer: "Writing the names of those who love the Lord." Asked whether Abou's name is there, the angel replies, "No." "Well, at least write down my name as one who loves his fellow-men," Abou insists.

The Angel wrote, and vanished. The next night
It came again with a great wakening light,
And showed the names whom love of God had blessed,
And lo! Ben Adhem's name led all the rest.

Another race hath been, and other palms are won

Source: ODE. INTIMATIONS OF IMMORTALITY FROM RECOLLECTIONS OF
EARLY CHILDHOOD (Stanza 11)
Author: William Wordsworth (1770-1850)
First published: 1807
Type of work: Ode

Context: In the earlier stanzas of his celebrated ode, Wordsworth has written of his awareness of a loss of freshness and radiance in living and of his temporary grief over the loss. (See "The rainbow comes and goes.") But though he is now in middle age and will not know again "the hour/ Of splendour in the grass, of glory in the flower," he will not grieve but rather find strength in what remains: in "primal sympathy" and compassion for man, in faith, and in the development of a philosophical view. As he concludes his ode, he weighs his losses and his gains and finds himself richer than before. The earth still shows its beauties, and because of what has happened in the growth of his heart and mind, he may still win palms in the remaining race of life:

> I love the Brooks which down their channels fret,
> Even more than when I tripped lightly as they;
> The innocent brightness of a new-born Day
>   Is lovely yet;
> The Clouds that gather round the setting sun
> Do take a sober colouring from an eye
> That hath kept watch o'er man's mortality;
> **Another race hath been, and other palms are won.**
> Thanks to the human heart by which we live,
> Thanks to its tenderness, its joys, and fears,
> To me the meanest flower that blows can give
> Thoughts that do often lie too deep for tears.

Answer came there none

Source: THE BRIDAL OF TRIERMAIN (Canto III, x)
Author: Sir Walter Scott (1771-1832)
First published: 1813
Type of work: Narrative poem

Context: During the early nineteenth century Walter Scott, known for his ballads, narrative poems, and historical novels, captured the Romantic interest in the medieval past. The descendant of a family related to the old Scotch clan of Buccleuch, he cherished the ambition to become a landed aristocrat and attempted to recapture the flamboyancy and magnificence of the past through the construction of the mansion of Abbotsford on the banks of the Tweed. He was known to his readers as "The Wizard of the North" and, until the sudden advent of Byron on the literary scene with the publication of *Childe Harold,* was the most popular writer of his day. One of Scott's later poems, "The Bridal of Triermain," is the first of a long series of nineteenth century treatments of the "Matter of Arthur." Around the Arthurian characters he winds the legend of Sleeping Beauty, thus creating a tone of the marvelous and supernatural which is commonplace to the metrical romance. Lord Roland de Vaux, motivated by a strange and inexplicable sound of the harp, undertakes a perilous journey both to test his chivalry and to search for a bride for Triermain. At one point he must pass through a forbidding valley which, following sunset, takes on a ghastly hue and is filled with strange and shrieking sounds. Dauntless, Roland rushes from his cave-shelter to do battle with whatever adversary there may be, only to find the sounds and the sight a phantasy of the enchanted mind:

He paused perforce, and blew his horn,
And on the mountain-echoes borne
Was heard an answering sound,
A wild and lonely trumpet-note;
In middle air it seem'd to float
High o'er the battled mound;
And sounds were heard, as when a guard
Of some proud castle, holding ward,
Pace forth their nightly round.
The valiant Knight of Triermain
Rung forth his challenge-blast again,
But **answer came there none;**
And 'mid the mingled wind and rain,
Darkling he sought the vale in vain,
Until the dawning shone; . . .

Antony should conquer Antony

Source: ANTONY AND CLEOPATRA (Act IV, sc. xv, ll. 16-17)
Author: William Shakespeare (1564-1616)
First published: 1623
Type of work: Dramatic tragedy

Context: Battling against Octavius Caesar for the right to rule the Roman Empire, Mark Antony is twice defeated, once at the Battle of Actium and again later, near Alexandria. Antony's defeats are caused by his love for Cleopatra. Twice she deserts him in battle, leaving the scene with her forces, and twice he loses a victory because of her defection. Realizing that his love for Cleopatra has cost him victory, the empire, and even his honor, Antony vows revenge, despite his love. But when

Cleopatra learns of his anger she sends him the false news of her suicide. These tidings persuade Antony that Cleopatra truly loved him, and in remorse he falls upon his sword, fatally wounding himself. Before he dies, however, members of his guard carry him to the monument where Cleopatra has taken refuge. The dying Antony assures Cleopatra that he dies of his own will, personally unconquered by Octavius Caesar. That he should slay himself is proper, replies Cleopatra.

ANTONY

Peace!
Not Cæsar's valour hath o'erthrown Antony,
But Antony's hath triumph'd on itself.

CLEOPATRA
So it should be, that none but **Antony
Should conquer Antony,** but woe 'tis so!

ANTONY
I am dying, Egypt, dying; only
I here importune death a while, until
Of many thousand kisses the poor last
I lay upon thy lips.

Any nose may ravage with impunity a rose

Source: SORDELLO (Book VI)
Author: Robert Browning (1812-1889)
First published: 1840
Type of work: Narrative poem

Context: The story of Sordello, the forerunner of Dante, is a painful history of a man of imagination born in the midst of civil war and political confusion. As a young man, Sordello tries to change the history of poetry but miserably fails, yet as he grows older, he finds that failure may be success, and turning from his deeply subjective vision joins the political disputes. However, the clash of personal vision and public involvement turns his mind into a feverish mass of contradictions that prevent any peace or happiness. Only when he realizes that there is a life after death can he reconcile himself to his apparent failure; he realizes that earthly fame is pallid beside immortal joy, and he accepts the fact that his vision, however great, was unfulfilled but will inspire others. Having told his painful tale, Browning directly addresses the reader to remind him that a story is more than the immediate reaction it calls up in the reader's mind; in fact, the poem is written so that the revelations of the poet do not come immediately but only after the reader has thought much about the surface story

and has come to see that in the   profound psychological insight.
poem's obscurity lies the clarity of

> Wake up! The ghost's gone, and the story ends
> I'd fain hope, sweetly; seeing, peri or ghoul,
> That spirits are conjectured fair or foul,
> Evil or good, judicious authors think,
> According as they vanish in a stink
> Or in a perfume. Friends, be frank! ye snuff
> Civet, I warrant. Really? Like enough!
> Merely the savor's rareness; **any nose**
> **May ravage with impunity a rose;**
> Rifle a musk-pod and 't will ache like yours!
> I'd tell you that same pungency ensures
> An after-gust, but that were overbold.
> Who would has heard Sordello's story told.

Anybody can be good in the country

Source: THE PICTURE OF DORIAN GRAY (Chapter 19)
Author: Oscar Wilde (1856-1900)
First published: 1891
Type of work: Novel

Context: The relationship between young Dorian Gray and his older friend Lord Henry Wotton resembles that of Faust and his tempter Mephistopheles. Through the influence of Lord Henry, Dorian lives for some years a life that on the surface is filled with sensation and pleasure but that at the same time is destroying his soul. His pleasures bring pain, suffering, and even death to others. At his country home Dorian is hunting one day with a friend who accidentally shoots and kills a man. When Dorian discovers that the dead man is James Vane, who had been pursuing him because he had caused the suicide of Vane's sister eighteen years earlier, he is at first pleased and relieved to be safe from Vane's revenge. Afterward, however, he determines to give up his evil ways, and Lord Henry mocks him:

> . . . "My dear boy," said Lord Henry, smiling, **"anybody can be good in the country.** There are no temptations there. That is the reason why people who live out of town are so absolutely uncivilized. Civilization is not by any means an easy thing to attain to. There are only two ways by which man can reach it. One is by being cultured, the other by being corrupt. Country people have no opportunity of being either, so they stagnate."

The apparel oft proclaims the man

Source: HAMLET (Act I, sc. iii, l. 72)
Author: William Shakespeare (1564-1616)
First published: 1603
Type of work: Dramatic tragedy

Context: With much fatherly advice, Polonius, Lord Chamberlain in the court of Denmark and a tedious old man, sends his son Laertes, returned to Denmark for the coronation of the king, back to Paris, where he has been in school. The main body of the speech follows:

> POLONIUS
> . . . There—my blessing with thee.
> And these few precepts in thy memory
> Look thou character. Give thy thoughts no tongue,
> Nor any unproportioned thought his act.
> Be thou familiar, but by no means vulgar.
>   •   •   •
> Give every man thy ear, but few thy voice;
> Take each man's censure, but reserve thy judgement.
> Costly thy habit as thy purse can buy,
> But not expressed in fancy; rich, not gaudy,
> For **the apparel oft proclaims the man;**
> And they in France of the best rank and station,
> Or of the most select and generous, chief in that.
>   •   •   •
> This above all, to thine own self be true,
> And it must follow, as the night the day,
> Thou canst not then be false to any man.
> Farewell, my blessing season this in thee.

Applaud the hollow ghost which blamed the living man

Source: GROWING OLD (Stanza 7)
Author: Matthew Arnold (1822-1888)
First published: 1867
Type of work: Lyric poem

Context: With a definite note of melancholy and irony, this poem discusses the physical and emotional developments characteristic of the aging process. Growing old is characterized by loss of vitality and strength as well as of a vision for the future. Feeling and sensitivity fade into nothingness. "Ah, 'tis not what in youth we dream'd 'twould be!" The days stretch out into meaningless hours. But, as the final lines tell us, when an old person does die, the world finally remembers he has been a living man and commemorates him with a funeral. The irony lies in the fact that the world that gave the old person no praise, only blame, while he was living lavishes attention upon him after he has no need of it.

> It is—last stage of all—
> When we are frozen up within, and quite
> The phantom of ourselves,
> To hear the world **applaud the hollow ghost**
> **Which blamed the living man.**

Apples of gold for the king's daughter

Source: THE KING'S DAUGHTER (Line 4)
Author: Algernon Charles Swinburne (1837-1909)
First published: 1866
Type of work: Literary ballad

Context: In their search for inspiration that might give poetry a new foundation, the Romantic poets frequently turned to the Middle Ages where they discovered the almost forgotten traditional ballad. The ballad was adopted as a medium through which the nineteenth century poet could create a literature of mysteriously enchanting beauty such as Keats' "La Belle Dame sans Merci" or Coleridge's "Ancient Mariner." Swinburne, more than any other British poet, came to the ballad tradition with an ear for the rhythm and an eye for the form; as a result, he created literary ballads that are unique in English poetry, for they capture the primitivism of the traditional ballad as well as their form and brevity of expression. This poem, one of his most successful ballads, is a chant in which nine sisters give their gifts to the daughter of the king, their niece; the unlimited jealousy that the women still have because they were not chosen by the king's son slowly unfolds as the gifts become more and more curses.

> We were ten maidens in the green corn,
>   Small red leaves in the mill-water:
> Fairer maidens never were born,
>   **Apples of gold for the king's daughter.**

> We were ten maidens by a well-head,
>   Small white birds in the mill-water:
> Sweeter maidens never were wed,
>   Rings of red for the king's daughter.

48

The appropriate title of "agnostic"

Source: SCIENCE AND CHRISTIAN TRADITION (Chapter 7)
Author: Thomas Henry Huxley (1825-1895)
First published: 1889 (Chapter 7)
Type of work: Essay

Context: Huxley was an English biologist and teacher who became famous through his defense of Darwin's evolutionary theories. He lectured widely and wrote a number of works designed to popularize science. In addition he produced a number of writings in which he examines Scripture critically and with some effort at scientific detachment. He once engaged in a controversy with Gladstone, the British statesman, in which theories of evolution were compared with Biblical tradition. Huxley's opinions are elaborated in a group of essays written from 1887 to 1892; these were collected and published in one volume under the title, *Science and Christian Tradition.* Huxley considered himself an agnostic, and in his essay on agnosticism, which forms Chapter 7, he explains how he came to invent the term. Before doing so, however, he retraces the history of his thinking in regard to Christian Scripture, particularly the Gospels. This essay was written primarily in reply to Dr. Wace, Principal of King's College, who had stated flatly that an agnostic and an infidel are one and the same. Huxley's reply is to the effect that he does not know the truth but is searching for it in a scientific manner. He notes that the Gospels were written some time subsequent to the death of Jesus, and that variant texts all reveal additions and elaborations by their transcribers; that it is therefore difficult to determine precisely what Jesus actually said and did; and that early Christian rites and customs differed greatly from those of our own time. He can prove nothing either way; and if he must be faithful, then to which of the many Christian doctrines? Huxley then tells his readers how the term "agnostic" originated:

When I reached intellectual maturity and began to ask myself whether I was an atheist, a theist, or a pantheist; a materialist or an idealist; a Christian or a freethinker; I found that the more I learned and reflected, the less ready was the answer; until, at last, I came to the conclusion that I had neither art nor part with any of these denominations, except the last. The one thing in which most of these good people were agreed was the one thing in which I differed from them. They were quite sure they had attained a certain "gnosis,"—had, more or less successfully, solved the problem of existence; while I was quite sure I had not, and had a pretty strong conviction that the problem was insoluble. . . .

This was my situation when I had the good fortune to find a place among the members of that remarkable confraternity of antagonists, long since deceased, but of green and pious memory, the Metaphysical Society. Every variety of philosophical and theological opinion was represented there, and expressed itself with entire openness; most of my colleagues were -*ists* of one sort or another; and, however kind and friendly they might be, I, the man without a rag of a label to cover himself with, could not fail to have some . . . uneasy feelings . . . So I took thought, and invented what I conceived to be **the appropriate title of "agnostic."** It came into my head as suggestively antithetic to the "gnostic" of Church history, who professed to know so much about the very things of which I was ignorant. . . . To my great satisfaction, the term took, . . .

That is the history of the origin of the terms "agnostic" and "agnosticism. . . ."

Aristocracy of the Moneybag

Source: THE FRENCH REVOLUTION (Vol. II, Book IX, chapter 7)
Author: Thomas Carlyle (1795-1881)
First published: 1837
Type of work: History

Context: Carlyle was determined to be a historian. Frustrated in his purpose to enter the clergy according to the wishes of his parents, and by a revulsion against eighteenth century rationalism, he shifted to the study of law. However, he found it dull reading in the office of an Edinburgh lawyer. Frustration brought on illness and a breakdown which he cured with a new interest. He learned German and began delving into German philosophy and literature that gradually introduced him to the idea of an orderly universe and an immanent and friendly .God, postulated by Fichte and Goethe. He capitalized on his experiences in his spiritual autobiography, *Sartor Resartus,* appearing first in a magazine in 1835, as an attack on the materialization of his era. Carlyle's knowledge of German led to assignments as book reviewer for several magazines. Generally each book served as text for a biographical essay on its subject. The success of *Sartor Resartus* permitted him and his wife to move to London, where they found a house near the British Museum, and he began reading and note-taking for his most ambitious work, *The French Revolution: A History.* His tragedy with the first draft is literary history. Having completed his Volume I, he took his only copy to get the opinion of his friend, John Stuart Mill (1806 –1873) philosopher and economist, with special interest in France. A stupid maid, seeing a pile of scribbled papers in her employer's study, burned them. However, Carlyle started his task again and by 1837 had completed the two volumes. In his essays and lectures, Carlyle frequently expressed the opinion that great men were the causes of great movements and human progress. He saw the French Revolution as evidence of man's divinity exemplified by the deeds of its great leaders. And so his history is actually a series of portraits of those involved. But added to them, to give brilliancy to his story, are graphic recreations of great scenes of the Revolution, the assassination of Marat by Charlotte Corday, the execution of Marie Antoinette, the capture of the Bastille, so exciting that occasional distortions of history pass unnoticed. For the writing of *Sartor Resartus,* Carlyle devised a Teutonic sort of English; for his French Revolution, his style is more vivacious French-English, with exclamations, questions, comments to the reader, quotations in French, and an abundance of footnotes that show the extent of his preparatory reading. His thesis that the aristocracy of blood and documents was wiped out by an aristocracy of money appears early in his history. In Chapter 7 of Book VII, the author declares: ". . . (Demoiselle) Thèroigne had bags of money, which she distributed over Flandre:—furnished by whom? Alas, with money-bags, one seldom sits on insurrectionary cannon. Calumnious Royalism!" In the last book of his second volume, Carlyle reverts to this idea:

> . . . Confused wreck of a Republic of Poverties, which ended in Reign of Terror, is arranging itself into such composure as it can. Evangel of Jean-Jacques, and most other Evangels, become incredible, what is there for it but to return to the old Evangel of Mammon? *Contrat-Social is true or untrue.* Brotherhood is Brotherhood or Death, but money always will buy money's worth; in the wreck of human dubitations, this remains indubitable, that Pleasure is pleasant. Aristocracy of Feudal Parchment has passed away with a mighty rushing; and now, by a natural course, we arrive at **Aristocracy of the Moneybag.** . . . Apparently a still baser sort of Aristocracy? An infinitely baser; the basest yet known.

Aroint thee witch the rump-fed ronyon cries

Source: MACBETH (Act I, sc. iii, l. 6)
Author: William Shakespeare (1564-1616)
First published: 1623
Type of work: Dramatic tragedy

Context: Macbeth and Banquo, generals in the army of King Duncan of Scotland, pass along a heath near Forres as they return home from a battle in which they have successfully put down a rebellion against the king. Three witches await their approach to pronounce the words of prophecy that Macbeth, who is Thane of Glamis, will bear the titles of Thane of Cawdor and finally king, and that the heirs of Banquo will ascend the throne. As the witches wait, they discuss their day's adventures, the first witch filling her sisters with indignation as she tells them of the way a despicable, mangy (ronyon) sailor's wife, fat-bottomed from eating refuse (rump-fed) refused to share with her the chestnuts she is eating, yelling at her to be gone.

51

A sailor's wife had chestnuts in her lap,
And munched, and munched, and munched.
 Give me, quoth I.
Aroint thee witch the rump-fed ronyon cries.
Her husband's to Aleppo gone, master o'th' Tiger;
But in a sieve I'll thither sail,
And like a rat without a tail,
I'll do, I'll do, and I'll do.

Art never expresses anything but itself

Source: THE DECAY OF LYING
Author: Oscar Wilde (1856-1900)
First published: 1889
Type of work: Literary essay

Context: To support a wife, Oscar Wilde became editor of *The Woman's World,* a position that kept him in funds and allowed him to indulge in his favorite sport of talking. The loss of that job drove him to the writing of magazine articles, usually *résumés* of his monologues. One was "The Decay of Lying," later included in *Intentions* (1891). In it he pleaded for imagination and the *beau ideal* instead of the crude and raw life of the realists. While the essay established his reputation among critics, it seemed to the average Englishman more like a cynical defense of mendacity. Its form is a Plantonic dialogue between Vivian and Cyril, in a country house in Nottinghamshire. Vivian reads his unfinished essay, while Cyril interrupts and objects. Vivian sees Art not as holding a mirror up to Nature, but as revealing Nature's imperfections and lack of design. To him, Art does not imitate Life; Life imitates Art. His arguments almost convince Cyril.

CYRIL—You have proved it to my dissatisfaction. But even admitting this strange imitative instinct in Life and Nature, surely you would acknowledge that Art expresses the temper of its age, the spirit of its time, the moral and social conditions that surround it, and under whose influence it is produced.
VIVIAN—Certainly not! **Art never expresses anything but itself.** This is the principle of my new aesthetics; and it is this, more than that vital connection between form and substance, on which Mr. Pater dwells, that makes Music the type of all the arts. . . .

The art of pleasing consists in being pleased

Source: THE ROUND TABLE ("On Manner")
Author: William Hazlitt (1778-1830)
First published: 1817
Type of work: Essay

Context: Hazlitt was very much an individualist, and his free-ranging style is essentially his own. His lack of formal education and the narrow limits of his reading furnished ammunition to his enemies, of whom he had many; he admitted the truth of their charges but was not cowed by them. A lover of art in all its forms, he felt that his function as a critic was to sense what is good in art and to furnish reasons for the faith he had in it. Thus his critical opinions depended less on knowledge than on his "depth of taste," as his friend Keats evaluated it. This faculty seldom went astray; Hazlitt's judgements of his contemporaries usually anticipate those of posterity. As an essayist he commands a respectable place in English literature. *The Round Table,* similar to a number of other volumes by him, is a collection of essays on a variety of subjects. Hazlitt's usual method is to begin with a specific idea and then to follow it with a rapid series of examples and associations; this, together with his terseness and clarity, gives the writing a sense of excitement. He does not usually end with a definite conclusion. In the essay, "On Manner," Hazlitt begins by noting that Lord Chesterfield believed manner was more important than matter; and he adds that the practice of the world seems to bear this opinion out. He then defines his terms: "What any person says or does is one thing; the mode in which he says or does it is another. The last of these is what we understand by *manner.*" He then presents a rush of examples. Manner is involuntary or incidental, betraying our sincerity or lack of it; the way we confer a favor is often far more valuable than the favor itself; the difference between a good actor and bad one is the manner in which the part is played. He then discusses humor:

. . . The same story told by two different persons shall, from the difference of the manner, either set the table in a roar, or not relax a feature in the whole company. We sometimes complain (perhaps rather unfairly) that particular persons possess more vivacity than wit. But we ought to take into the account, that their very vivacity arises from their enjoying the joke; and their humouring a story by drollery of gesture or archness of look, shews only that they are acquainted with the different ways in which the sense of the ludicrous expresses itself. It is not the mere dry jest, but the relish which the person himself has of it, with which we sympathise. For in all that tends to pleasure and excitement, the capacity for enjoyment is the principal point. One of the most pleasant and least tiresome persons of our acquaintance is a humourist, who has three or four quaint witticisms and proverbial phrases, which he always repeats over and over; but he does this with just the same vivacity and freshness as ever, so that you feel the same amusement with less effort than if he had startled his hearers with a succession of original conceits. Another friend of ours, who never fails to give vent to one or two real *jeu-d'esprits* every time you meet him, from the pain with which he is delivered of them, and the uneasiness he seems to suffer all the rest of the time, makes a much more interesting than comfortable companion. If you see a person in pain for himself, it naturally puts you in pain for him. **The art of pleasing consists in being pleased.** To be amiable is to be satisfied with one's self and others. Good-humour is essential to pleasantry.

Art remains the one way possible of speaking truth

Source: THE RING AND THE BOOK (Book XII, "The Book and the Ring," Line 842)
Author: Robert Browning (1812-1889)
First published: 1868-1869
Type of work: Dramatic monologue

Context: It is fitting that Browning concludes his longest work with one of his favorite observations about art. Because men live in a world that they experience only through their senses and because the senses are not always reliable, no two men will agree about the world. The differences in opinion about the most trivial experiences are, therefore, essentially the same as the controversies between philosophers or theologians. Art, unlike the disputers, speaks obliquely, addressing all men so that, while there may remain disagreement, the underlying truth of the human condition is apparent. In *The Ring and the Book* Browning has illustrated this belief by telling the story of the Roman murder trial from different, often divergent, points of view, leaving to the reader the responsibility of sifting the evidence to reach a conclusion. Like the human condition, the truth of the murder case is hidden within the differing reports, and only the skillful mind has the ability of figuring out the truth.

So, British Public, who may like me yet,
(Marry and amen!) learn one lesson hence
Of many which whatever lives should teach:
This lesson, that our human speech is nought,
Our human testimony false, our fame
And human estimation words and wind.
Why take the artistic way to prove so much?
Because, it is the glory and good of Art,
That **Art remains the one way possible
Of speaking truth,** to mouths like mine at least.

Arts to rule as they desired

Source: THE SCHOLAR-GYPSY (Stanza 5)
Author: Matthew Arnold (1822-1888)
First published: 1853
Type of work: Philosophical poem

54

Context: As in many of his works, Arnold in this poem is trying to teach the people of his age. He wanted men to have a better view of life, to understand the futility of meanness of mind, to understand the glory of living an enlightened life. In this poem he begins by having the narrator imagining himself on a hill above Oxford, on a summer day, looking down from a corner of a field to the towers of the university. Beside the speaker of the poem is a book, identifiable as Joseph Glanvil's *Vanity of Dogmatiz-* *ing* (1661), in which is found the story of an Oxford student forced by his poverty to leave the university, whereupon he joins a band of gypsies. Arnold transforms the young man of Glanvil's tale into an ideal, a young man who rejects his own time and seeks higher goals. The fifth stanza of the poem relates how two of the scholar-gypsy's former fellow students met him in a country lane, how they asked him of his new life, and how he replied to them.

But once, years after, in the country-lanes,
  Two scholars, whom at college erst he knew,
    Met him, and of his way of life enquired;
  Whereat he answered, that the gypsy-crew,
    His mates, had **arts to rule as they desired**
      The workings of men's brains,
And they can bind them to what thoughts they will.
    "And I," he said, "the secret of their art,
      When fully learn'd, will to the world unpart;
But it needs heaven-sent moments for this skill."

As far as angel's ken

Source: PARADISE LOST (Book I, l. 59)
Author: John Milton (1608-1674)
First published: 1667
Type of work: Epic poem

Context: Milton asks his epic question, who seduced our original parents into disobeying God? The answer is, the infernal serpent, whose pride had cast him out of heaven; with him there fell a host of rebel angels. Satan, motivated by envy of God and by the desire to be revenged on Him for what he considered injustice, deceived Eve, the mother of all mankind. For his revolt, God hurled him and his cohorts out of heaven, down to bottomless perdition, there to dwell in adamant chains and penal fire. Milton here was probably drawing on the classical account of Zeus's hurling of the defeated Titans into the underworld, where they were perpetually imprisoned. Milton, however, quickly abandons the idea of the unbreakable chains—if he ever had it— as the devils are free to travel through the universe, especially up to the earth. But for nine days the devils lie stunned on a fiery lake. "Ken," usually "knowledge," is here "range of view."

Nine times the space that measures day and night
To mortal men, he with his horrid crew
Lay vanquished, rolling in the fiery gulf,
Confounded though immortal: but his doom
Reserved him to more wrath; for now the thought
Both of lost happiness and lasting pain
Torments him; round he throws his baleful eyes
That witnessed huge affliction and dismay,
Mixed with obdúrate pride and steadfast hate:
At once **as far as angel's ken** he views
The dismal situation waste and wild,
A dungeon horrible, on all sides round
As one great furnace flamed, yet from those flames
No light, but rather darkness visible
Served only to discover sights of woe,
Regions of sorrow, doleful shades, where peace
And rest can never dwell, hope never comes
That comes to all; . . .

As fresh as is the month of May

Source: THE CANTERBURY TALES (Prologue, l. 92)
Author: Geoffrey Chaucer (1343?-1400)
First transcribed: c. 1387-1392
Type of work: Collection of tales

Context: Little is known with certainty about the life of Geoffrey Chaucer. He was probably born in London, but when? In 1386, while a witness concerning a coat of arms, he testified that he was "forty years of age and more," which would make his birthyear nearer 1343 than the traditional date of 1340. He also said he had "born arms for twenty-seven years." Part of this service included his year in France with the English army, in 1359–1360, during the Hundred Years War. It was not a very important campaign, but in one of the skirmishes, at Réthal, near Rheims, he was captured. The amount of his ransom, £16, amounting to about $2,400 today, indicates Chaucer's importance, when common soldiers were freed for a pound or two. After a gap of six years, Chaucer's history can be picked up again, as a yeoman in the household of King Edward III. In 1368, he was an esquire; and in 1369, in the army of John of Gaunt, he took part in a raid on Picardy, along with 600 men at arms and 150 other members of the king's household. This part of his life may well have been in his mind when he included a squire among those on the Pilgrimage from London to Canterbury. The Squire, too, had been on a military expedition in Flanders, Artois, and Picardy. There are thirty in the group, twenty-eight Pilgrims, the host of the Tabard Inn at Southward, across the Thames River from London, and the author. To entertain themselves on the journey to the tomb of Thomas à Becket, each agrees to tell two stories, and two more on the return trip. Actually only twenty-two of the proposed 120 appear in Chaucer's volume, set down in iambic pentameter. The Prologue, introducing the members of the company, declares that in April when the showers wake up nature, birds sing, the crops begin growing, and people like to go on pilgrimages. By his selection of pilgrims, Chaucer gave a complete panorama of the English social classes of his day, from the clergy and knights to the humble plowman. The Knight, though the highest in rank of all the pilgrims, is modest and prudent. Chivalry was on the decline in the fourteenth century, but Chaucer makes his Knight an ideal character, untouched by satire. Though veteran of wars for king and religion all over the known world, he is dressed in sober garb and accompanied by only two retainers, a yeoman clad in green, and his son of about twenty, who had also fought in several campaigns. His duty as Squire is to attend his father and carry his lance. His dress is the height of fashion, and he has the courtly accomplishments. He can sing and play the flute. Though he loves the ladies so passionately that at night he sleeps no more than a nightingale does, he is as fresh as May, that month of beauty and flowers used by many poets in their similes. Tennyson in his *Idylls of the King,* commands: "Blow, Trumpet, for the world is white with May." Many poets have written of the "Merry month of May," and only an occasional cynic like Lowell declares: "May is a pious fraud of the almanac." Chaucer says about the Squire:

With hym ther was his sonne, a yong SQUIER,
A lovyere and a lusty bacheler
With lokkes crulle, as they were leyd in presse.
Of twenty yeer of age he was, I gesse.
Of his stature he was of evene lengthe,
And wonderly delyvere and of greet strengthe.
And he hadde been somtyme in chivachye
In Flaundres, in Artoys, and Pycardie,
And born hym weel, as of so litel space,
In hope to stonden in his lady grace.
Embrouded was he, as it were a meede,
Al full of fresshe floures, whyte and rede.
Syngynge he was or floytynge, al the day
He was **as fressh as is the monthe of May.**

As fresh as paint

Source: FRANK FAIRLEGH (Chapter 41)
Author: Francis Edward Smedley (1818-1864)
First published: 1850
Type of work: Novel

Context: Smedley was just one of the   many writers of the Victorian era who produced a vast number of exceedingly sentimental novels which were quickly bought up by a sentimental reading public and as quickly forgotten. Since, says the author of this novel, many volumes have appeared concerned with " 'Schoolboy Days' and 'College Life,' " but none concerned with "the mysteries of that paradise of public-school-fearing mammas—a 'Private Tutor's,' " this novel was produced to fill that void.

It chronicles the adventures in the life of a private pupil. In Chapter 41, Oaklands, a friend of the hero, laments that Fairlegh's sister seems very apathetic and lacking in interest in anything and asserts that he shall raise her spirits by having her ride horseback every day. Oaklands, who has been very ill, is overheard by Lawless, who has entered unperceived and misunderstands the context:

"Horseback, eh!" exclaimed Lawless, who had entered the cottage without our perceiving him. "Ay, that's a prescription better than all your doctor's stuff; clap her on a side-saddle, and a brisk canter for a couple of hours every day across country will set the old lady up again in no time, if it's your mother that's out of condition, Frank. Why, Oaklands, man, you are looking **as fresh as paint**; getting sound again, wind and limb, eh?"

As full of valor as of kindness

Source: KING HENRY THE FIFTH (Act IV, sc. iii, l. 15)
Author: William Shakespeare (1564-1616)
First published: 1600
Type of work: Historical drama

Context: The English army begins battle at Agincourt against the forces of France in a contest in which King Henry of England eventually gains the crown of France. Some of the English leaders, speaking briefly before going into battle, note that the French have three thousand troops, or five to each English soldier. The Duke of Bedford and the Earl of Exeter bid farewell to the Earl of Salisbury as he leaves for battle:

BEDFORD
Farewell good Salisbury, and good luck go with thee.

EXETER
Farewell kind lord; fight valiantly to-day.
And yet I do thee wrong, to mind thee of it,
For thou art framed of the firm truth of valor.
[*Exit* SALISBURY.]

BEDFORD
He is **as full of valour as of kindness;**
Princely in both.

As hardy as the Nemean lion's nerve

Source: HAMLET (Act I, sc. iv, 1. 83)
Author: William Shakespeare (1564-1616)
First published: 1603
Type of work: Dramatic tragedy

Context: In the frosty night before the castle at Elsinore, Hamlet encounters the ghost of his father. He is bursting with impatience to know what the purpose of the apparition is: "What may this mean. . . . What should we do?" But the ghost wishes to speak to Hamlet in private, and since others are present—the sentinels and Hamlet's friend, Horatio— the spirit beckons Hamlet away. However, no one knows, at this point, whether the spirit is the ghost of Hamlet's father or a demon in his father's shape; therefore, the prince's companions warn Hamlet against following. But Hamlet insists that he will follow. He hears his destiny calling, and every artery in his body feels as bold as the great lion whose slaying was the first of the Twelve Labors of Hercules, and he insists that he will create another ghost of anyone who hinders—"lets"—him:

HAMLET
It waves me still.
Go on; I'll follow thee.

MARCELLUS
You shall not go my lord.

HAMLET
Hold off your hands.

HORATIO
Be ruled, you shall not go.

HAMLET
My fate cries out,
And makes each petty artery in this body
As hardy as the Nemean lion's nerve.
Still am I called. Unhand me gentlemen—
By heaven I'll make a ghost of him that lets me.
I say, away!—Go on, I'll follow thee.
[*Exeunt* GHOST *and* HAMLET.]

As he who, seeking asses, found a kingdom

Source: PARADISE REGAINED (Book III, 1. 242)
Author: John Milton (1608-1674)
First published: 1671
Type of work: Epic poem

tempted by Satan, first with great luxury and second with wealth and earthly power that will provide fame. Christ resists both of these temptations and points out that both Job and Socrates achieved great glory by entirely peaceful means; military conquerors, He says, are mere destroyers. He says that he seeks not his own glory but the glory of Him that sent him. But Satan does not easily give up the chance to seduce Christ with the prospect of glory, which, he says, God the Father himself receives, but Christ rebuts this argument by pointing out that God's glory is a byproduct of His goodness, for which He desires only thanks. This argument strikes Satan dumb, as he had fallen from heaven through his desire for glory. Recovering his presence of mind, he urges that Christ assume the kingdom that he is to inherit. Christ says that that is no concern of Satan's, and His assuming of His kingdom will be Satan's destruction. Satan, however, says that perhaps Christ hesitates because of a lack of worldly experience; after all, He has hardly seen the towns that neighbor his own home. The wisest, he says, will be fearful to act if they lack experience: Saul, a simple country boy, hunted asses and found a kingdom. (I Samuel, 9) Satan says:

> The world thou hast not seen, much less her glory,
> Empires, and monarchs, and their radiant courts,
> Best school of best experience, quickest in sight
> In all things that to greatest actions lead.
> The wisest, unexperienced, will be ever
> Timorous and loth, with novice modesty,
> **(As he who seeking asses found a kingdom)**
> Irresolute, unhardly, unadventurous:
> But I will bring thee where thou soon shalt quit
> Those rudiments, and see before thine eyes
> The monarchies of earth, their pomp and state,
> Sufficient introduction to inform
> Thee, of thyself so apt, in regal arts,
> And regal mysteries; that thou mayst know
> How best their opposition to withstand.

As many men, so many minds

Source: PHORMIO (Act III, sc. iii)
Author: Terence (Publius Terentius Afer, c. 190-159 B.C.)
First transcribed: Second century, B.C.
Type of work: Dramatic comedy

Context: Demipho, an aged Athenian, goes abroad, leaving his grown son at home in Athens. During the father's absence, the son, named Antipho, marries Phanium without his father's consent, an act unheard of in classical times. Upon Demipho's return he is righteously angry about his son's marriage, and becomes even angrier when Antipho refuses to come to explain the matter to him. In his anger and his anxiety, Demipho turns to his three legal advisers—Hegio, Crito, and Cratinus—for their opinions on what to do in the matter, hoping they can give him advice about what action to take. When Hegio speaks in his turn, he makes the comment about the diversity of men's opinions. The comment has been translated variously, although always with the same meaning.

DEMIPHO
You see how matters stand? What shall I do? Tell me, Hegio.

HEGIO
I? I think Cratinus ought to give his opinion, if you have no objection.

DEMIPHO
Tell me, Cratinus.

. . .

CRATINUS
Well, I think you should do what is best; what this son of yours has done in your absence should be undone. In that way you will secure justice. . . .

DEMIPHO
Now you, Hegio.

HEGIO
I believe that Cratinus has spoken with good sense. But it's a fact that **"As many men, so many minds"**: each man after his own fashion. Now, it doesn't seem to me that what has been done by law can be undone; and it's wrong to try to change it.

As savage as a bear with a sore head

Source: THE KING'S OWN (Chapter 26)
Author: Frederick Marryat (1792-1848)
First published: 1830
Type of work: Novel

Context: Twenty-six volumes are included in the standard edition of works by Captain Marryat. Son of a member of Parliament, young Frederick several times ran away from school until finally at the age of fourteen, he was allowed to join the British navy. There he served against Napoleon and in the Burmese War, and reached the rank of Commander. However, his articles attacking the system of recruiting by press gangs lost him favor, and he resigned in 1829, to spend the rest of his life as a writer. *The King's Own* is his only tragic novel; and it has a more artful plot than his other books. Its hero is drawn from the novelist's second and favorite son, William, who died at the age of seven. Captain M——is a portrait of his first commander, Lord Cochrane, later admiral of Chile's navy during its struggle for independence. The book was completed on shipboard, during a six weeks' charting expedition in the Atlantic. The novelist's variety of interests may explain its many digressions. The book's most famous scene, the sea fight and shipwreck, is patterned on a naval battle between the French and English in 1797. Though the novel will never be as popular as Marryat's *Peter Simple* or *Mr. Midshipman Easy,* many critics consider it his best work. Chapter 26 contains one of the digressions, a story told by the coxswain Marshall, to Surgeon Macallan. On a previous ship, a pet cat had made dirt on the master's sextant case. Though usually even-tempered, the captain has ordered the crew to kill the cat. None of the sailors is willing, but finally, under the captain's eye and in order to keep the ship's deck clean, the cat is thrown overboard and shot while in the water.

> "Well, sir, I never seed a ship's company in such a farmant, or such a nitty kicked up 'tween decks, in my life . . . all agrees that no good would come to the ship a'ter that, and very melancholy they were, and couldn't forget it.
> "Well, sir, our sailing orders come down the next day, and the first cutter is sent on shore for the captain, and six men out of ten leave the boat, and I'm sure that it warn't for desartion, but all along of that cat being hove overboard and butchered in that way —for three on 'em were messmates of mine, . . . and if they had had a mind to quit the sarvice, I should have know'd it. The captain was **as savage as a bear with a sore head,** and did nothing but growl for three days afterwards, and it was well to keep clear on him, for he snapped right and left, like a mad dog."

As she would catch another Antony in her strong toil of grace

Source: ANTONY AND CLEOPATRA (Act V, sc. ii, ll. 350-351)
Author: William Shakespeare (1564-1616)
First published: 1623
Type of work: Dramatic tragedy

Context: The love of Antony, one of the reigning triumvirs of the Roman Empire, and Cleopatra, voluptuous Queen of Egypt, has run its course, with Antony, dead from his own sword and Cleopatra from a poisonous snake. Caesar, in Egypt to carry its mighty queen back to Rome as a display for his own grandeur, views the bodies of Cleopatra and her attendants, unmarred by the venom of the asp.

62

CAESAR
O noble weakness!
If they had swallowed poison, 'twould appear
By external swelling; but she looks like sleep,
As she would catch another Antony
In her strong toil of grace.

DOLABELLA
Here on her breast,
There is a vent of blood, and something blown.
The like is on her arm.

FIRST GUARD
This is an aspic's trail, and these fig-leaves
Have slime upon them, such as the aspic leaves
Upon the caves of Nile.

CAESAR
Most probable
That so she died; for her physician tells me
She hath pursued conclusions infinite
Of easy ways to die. . . .

As sober as a judge

Source: DON QUIXOTE IN ENGLAND (III, xiv)
Author: Henry Fielding (1707-1754)
First published: 1734
Type of work: Dramatic comedy

Context: Fielding began this comedy in 1728, then was dissuaded from completing it by his actor friends Booth and Cibber. However, when Drury Lane actors needed a play in a hurry, he resurrected it, completed it, and saw it performed at the New Theatre. Sancho Panza and Don Quixote enter an English inn where they find people as mad as they are. Each scene ends with a song by one of the actors. As in the Cervantes' novel, Don Quixote believes that since he is a knight-errant, the world owes him a living. The point of the play is expressed in one of its songs:

"The more we see of human kind,
The more deceits and tricks we find,
In every land as well as Spain."

Squire Badger is important in the coming elections; also being rich, he is sought as husband for Dorothea, the daughter of Sir Thomas Loveland, though she in turn loves Fairlove. Don Quixote also loves her. In this scene of Act III, Sir Thomas goes to Badger to arrange a marriage, but the squire reveals himself as such a bore that Dorothea's father agrees to let his daughter marry her true love, Fairlove. "Oons" and " 'sbud" are euphemisms for the oaths "God's Wounds," and "God's Blood!" A be-

wigged judge sitting in court certainly gives the impression of being sober.

Squire Badger

Oons! what's the matter with you all? Is the devil in the inn, that you won't let a man sleep? I was as fast on the table, as if I had been in a feather bed. 'Sbud, what's the matter? Where's my Lord Slang?

Sir Thomas Loveland

Dear squire, let me entreat you would go to bed; you are a little heated with wine.

Squire Badger

Oons, sir, do you say that I am drunk? I say, sir, that I am **as sober as a judge;** and if any man say that I am drunk, sir, he's a liar.

As sure as death

Source: EVERY MAN IN HIS HUMOUR (Act II, sc. i, l. 119)
Author: Ben Jonson (1573?-1637)
First published: 1598
Type of work: Dramatic comedy

Context: In the title *Every Man in his Humour,* the word humour means whim or quirk of behavior; consequently, the play is filled with characters who consistently pursue courses of action in accordance with their ruling follies. Some of the characters are Old Knowell, who has the confidence of action produced by the belief that he knows everything; Edward Knowell, his son, around whom most of the action centers; Brainworm, a mad, rascally servant who is a prime mover of the action; Master Stephen, a loutish country cousin of Edward Knowell who has the humour to be a city dandy; Master Matthew, a city gull, or fool, who wishes to be a gentleman poet; Captain Bobadill, a braggart soldier who is at heart a coward; Wellborn, a city sophisticate, companion of Edward Knowell; Kitely, a cowardly merchant; and Squire Downright, a forthright and plain-speaking, no-nonsense fellow. In Act I, scene i of the play, Kitely is complaining to Downright of the way in which his lodger, Wellborn, acts; he has turned Kitely's house into a tavern or a stews by introducing into it his ritous companions. They mock Kitely and say that he is jealous in his behavior because he has recently married a young and pretty wife and lodges her attractive sister in his house also—as sure as death they say it!

Whilst they, sir, to relieve him in the fable,
Make their loose comments upon every word,
Gesture, or look, I use; mock me all over,
From my flat cap unto my shining shoes;
And, out of their impetuous rioting phant'sies,
Beget some slander that shall dwell with me.
And what would that be, think you? marry, this:
They would give out, because my wife is fair,
Myself but lately married, and my sister
Here sojourning a virgin in my house,
That I am jealous!—nay, **as sure as death,**
That they would say: and how that I had quarelled
My brother purposely, thereby to find
An apt pretext to banish them my house.

At the feet of Gamaliel

Source: ACTS 22:3
Author: Unknown (traditionally Luke)
First transcribed: 60-150 (probably c. 80-90)
Type of work: Religious history and tradition

Context: The Acts of the Apostles is the only contemporary account of the early Christian Church and its beginnings which remains to us. Its author may or may not have been Luke the physician; in any case he evidently wrote both Luke and Acts, and it is probable that Luke supplied much of the material. Acts begins with the Resurrection and the commission Jesus laid upon His apostles, then tells the story of their missionary activities. It is an inspiring record of struggle and of moral courage, and of the growth of an institution. Chapters 15 through 28 cover the efforts of Paul. The story of his career as wandering evangelist is eloquent testimony of the difficulties these early missionaries had to face. His travels took him through Syria, Greece, and into Asia Minor. It was his custom to enter the synagogues in cities which had them, and there to argue scrip-ture with the Jews. He preached publicly, labored when necessary to sustain life, and persevered with great singlemindedness in the face of hardship and widespread hostility. To be an evangelist in the time of the apostles was to accept persecution and strife, and to thrive on it if possible. In Thessalonica, Paul was the center of a riot when ruffians were persuaded, or hired, to break up the activities of the Christians; the agitators followed him to Berea. Much later, in Ephesus, he was again the focal point of a riot started by silversmiths who feared his success at winning converts would stop the sale of figurines representing Diana, and thus wreck their business. After he leaves Ephesus Paul insists, in spite of warnings, on going to Jerusalem. Here he is recognized and accused in the temple by persons who have seen him in Asia Minor; he is dragged from the temple by a mob and the centurions arrive to conduct him to prison. He gains permission to tell the people how he became a Christian; they are not appeased by his words; only the fact that he is a Roman citizen saves him from a scourging.

> Men, brethren, and fathers, hear ye my defence which I make now unto you.
> (And when they heard that he spake in the Hebrew tongue to them, they kept the more silence: and he saith,)
> I am verily a man which am a Jew, born in Tarsus, a city in Cilicia, yet brought up in this city **at the feet of Gamaliel,** and taught according to the perfect manner of the law of the fathers, and was zealous toward God, as ye all are this day.
> And I persecuted this way unto the death, binding and delivering into prisons both men and women.
> As also the high priest doth bear me witness, and all the estate of the elders: from whom also I received letters unto the brethren, and went to Damascus, to bring them which were there bound unto Jerusalem, for to be punished.
> And it came to pass, that, as I made my journey, and was come nigh unto Damascus about noon, suddenly there shone from heaven a great light round about me.
> And I fell unto the ground, and heard a voice saying unto me, Saul, Saul, why persecutest thou me?
> And I answered, Who art thou, Lord? And he said unto me, I am Jesus of Nazareth, whom thou persecutest.
> And they that were with me saw indeed the light, and were afraid; but they heard not the voice of him that spake to me.

Avarice, the spur of industry

Source: ESSAYS (XII "Of Civil Liberty")
Author: David Hume (1711-1776)
First published: 1752
Type of work: Political essay

Context: The Scottish philosopher David Hume, described as having a face broad and fat with an expression of imbecility, with wide mouth and eyes vacant and spiritless, and who was further handicapped by a body "to communicate the idea of a turtle-eating alderman," stirred his era by essays whose determined skepticism was practically unanswerable on empirical grounds. Most of Hume's devastating essays were completed before he was forty, his *Essays Moral and Philosophical,* in 1741, and his *Philosophical Essays,* in 1748. He also wrote an exhaustive History of England (1754–1761) whose errors in fact, especially in flattering the Stuarts, were compensated for by its style; its readability kept it a standard text for years. Surprisingly, not until 1817 did an edition of his Essays appear in the United States, and then Dr. Thomas Ewell of Virginia edited

66

Hume's Essays in two volumes, dedicated to President Monroe. Dr. Ewell enters a defense of the supposed atheism of Hume. Perhaps the author's stand on miracles is objectionable, but the physician maintains that the essays should be read by every clergyman as training in thought and reflection that will increase the ability to preach convincingly. On many points, the apologist insists, Hume showed himself benevolent, with a universal love of mankind. Hume's "Essay of Civil Liberty" includes most of the qualities that made him admired and feared. He laments that the world is too young to have determined general truths in politics. Not only is the art of reasoning still imperfect, but sufficient facts are lacking. Machiavelli's reasoning produced many maxims about the Prince that can be completely refuted, especially in regard to absolute government. Trade, too, is just beginning to be esteemed as an affair of state. Only the modern maritime nations see the importance of an extensive commerce, which was neglected by the ancients. So, too, in comparing civil liberty and absolute government, Hume fears that what he writes may be refuted by further experience and rejected by posterity. However, he sees that Greece, the home of culture, lost that culture when it lost its liberty and when learning was transported to Rome, the only free nation at the time in the world. However, the idea that arts and sciences flourish only in a free government can be refuted by a look at France, which scarcely ever enjoyed any established liberty. Commerce, however, does fix its seat in free government.

> . . . there is something hurtful to commerce inherent in the very nature of absolute government, and inseparable from it, though the reason I should assign for this opinion is somewhat different from that which is commonly insisted on. Private property seems to me almost as secure in a civilized European monarchy as in a republic; nor is danger much apprehended in such a government, from the violence of the sovereign; more than we commonly dread harm from thunder or earthquakes, or any accident the most unusual and extraordinary. **Avarice, the spur of industry,** is so obstinate a passion, and works its way through so many real dangers and difficulties, that it is not likely to be scared by an imaginary danger. . . . Commerce, therefore, in my opinion, is apt to decay in absolute governments, not because it is there less secure, but because it is less honorable. . . .

The awkward squad

Source: WORKS OF BURNS; WITH HIS LIFE (Volume I, p. 344, 1834 ed.)
Author: Allan Cunningham (1784-1842)
First published: 1834
Type of work: Biography

Context: Allan Cunningham, Scottish poet and man of letters, was well acquainted with many of the writers of his native land, including the Ettrick Shepherd, James Hogg (1770–1835). Cunningham wrote three original novels and many songs, one of them "A Wet Sheet and a Flowing Sea" (1825). His imitations of old Scotch ballads, published in Cromek's *Remains of Nithsdale and Galloway Song* (1810), seemed so authentic that they attracted the attention of Sir Walter Scott and led to a lifelong friendship. Cunningham was also a biographer. He began with a six-volume *Lives of the Most Eminent British Poets, Sculptors, and Architects* (1829–1834), and a three-volume life of the Scottish genre and portrait painter, Sir David Wilkie (1785–1841), who began his work in a humble Scotch home and ended painting kings. However, the works for which Cunningham will be longest remembered are his accounts of his friendship with another humble Scotsman, Robert Burns (1759–1796). Burns was one of the most prolific and varied of lyric poets. He sent 160 songs to Johnson's Museum. For his friend Thomson, he wrote at least a hundred more, some of them recasting old and imperfect songs of his country. Not until the very end of Burns's life, when he realized he had little time to live, did he write to Johnson to beg that his poems—or copies of them—be returned to him to allow them to be put into perma-

nent shape for publishing, but by then it was too late, and he was too ill. So it was left to his young friend, Allan Cunningham, to collect the prose and verse scattered around the country at random. At least a third of these works had never been published. He edited them in an eight volume *Works of Robert Burns; With his Life* (London; James Cochrane, 1834), with a second edition the following year. The first volume, of 380 pages, is devoted to the life. In the final section, describing Burns' last days, Cunningham tells of the poet's trip to the seashore where Dr. John Maxwell, his physician, hoped salt water bathing would be beneficial. He returned home late in July, 1796, knowing that his end was near. In 1794, at the possibility of an invasion by France, Burns had enlisted in the Dumfriesshire Volunteers. Though he never saw military service, he knew he would receive a military funeral, and joked about it. In describing the funeral, Cunningham wrote: "When the first shovelfull of earth sounded on the coffin-lid, I looked up and saw tears on many cheeks where tears were not usual. The Volunteers justified the surmise of Burns by three ragged and straggling volleys: the earth was heaped up, and the vast multitude melted silently away." Earlier in the account, Cunningham wrote:

Though Burns now knew he was dying, his good humor was unruffled, and his wit never forsook him. When he looked up and saw Dr. Maxwell at his bed-side,—"Alas!" he said, "what has brought you here? I am but a poor crow, and not worth plucking." He pointed to his pistols and desired that Maxwell would accept them, saying they could not be in worthier keeping, and that he should never more have need of them. This relieved his proud heart from a sense of obligation. Soon afterward he saw Gibson,

68

one of his brother-volunteers, by the bedside with tears in his eyes. He smiled and said,—"John, don't let **the awkward squad** fire over me!"

An ax to grind

Source: WHO'LL TURN GRINDSTONE?
Author: Charles Miner (1780-1865)
First published: 1810
Type of work: Essay

Context: Charles Miner, editor of *The Gleaner and Luzerne Advertiser,* of Wilkes-Barre, Pennsylvania, wrote for his paper a number of short essays which were collected into book form in 1815 as *Essays from the Desk of Poor Robert the Scribe, Containing Lessons in Manners, Morals, and Domestic Economy.* The essay *Who'll Turn Grindstone?* tells of an incident in the author's early boyhood. One cold winter morning a smiling stranger with an ax over his shoulder accosted him and asked permission to grind his ax on the boy's grandfather's grindstone. The stranger had the lad get some hot water for the stone and then flattered him into turning the crank. Then, patting the lad on the head, he called him "my man" and "one of the finest lads I have ever seen." It was a new ax and took a great deal of grinding. Time to go to school came and went, and still the little boy toiled and tugged away until his hands were blistered:

> The school bell rung, and I could not get away;—my hands were blistered, and it was not half ground. At length, however, the axe was sharpened, and the man turned to me, with "Now you little rascal, you've played the truant—scud to school, or you'll buy it." Alas, thought I, it was hard enough to turn grindstone, this cold day; but now to be called "little rascal" was too much. It sunk deep in my mind, and often have I thought of it since.
> When I see a merchant, overpolite to his customers—begging them to taste a little brandy, and throwing half his goods on the counter—thinks I—That man has **an axe to grind.**

Babbled of green fields

Source: KING HENRY THE FIFTH (Act II, sc. iii, 1. 17)
Author: William Shakespeare (1564-1616)
First published: 1600
Type of work: Historical drama

Context: In a street in Eastcheap, London, in front of the Boar's Head Tavern, Pistol announces to his cronies the death of Sir John Falstaff, the roguish and lewd knight who has whiled away many hours at the

69

Boar's Head Tavern and has been a favorite drinking companion of Prince Hal before his coronation as King Henry V. Bardolph says he wishes he were with Falstaff whether he be in heaven or in hell, but the hostess says that Falstaff is in Arthur's bosom and proceeds to give the particulars of the death and last words of the merry knight:

HOSTESS

Nay sure, he's not in hell; he's in Arthur's bosom, if ever man went to Arthur's bosom. 'A made a finer end, and went away an it had been any christom child; 'a parted ev'n just between twelve and one, ev'n at the turning o' th' tide: for after I saw him fumble with the sheets, and play with flowers, and smile upon his finger's end, I knew there was but one way; for his nose was as sharp as a pen, and 'a **babbled of green fields**. . . .

Back and side go bare, go bare

Source: GAMMER GURTON'S NEEDLE (Act II, Song)
Author: William Stevenson (Sixteenth century)
First published: 1575
Type of work: Dramatic comedy

Context: Gammer Gurton's Needle, which dates from about 1553, is one of the first regular English comedies. In five acts, it follows the classic Latin pattern; but it is completely English in all other respects. The author, a "Mr. S.," has been identified with William Stevenson, M.A. of Christ's College, Cambridge, where the play was originally performed. The setting is an English village; the characters are likeable and morally upright, though their speech is earthy enough to have a certain shock value even today. The plot is complex. Gammer Gurton has lost her precious needle, an article of great value upon which many villagers depend. She was putting a patch on the breeches of Hodge, her servant (the entire seat had fallen out of them), when she saw Gib, her cat, in the milk pan. Throwing down her mending, she chased Gib out of the house. When she returned, the needle had vanished. Gammer, Tib her maid, and Hodge are equally upset when the play opens. Hodge is recounting the tragedy to Diccon, an eccentric who has been released from Bethlehem Hospital (Bedlam) and who now wanders harmlessly around the village. Diccon proceeds to the tavern where he hopes to beg some ale, while Hodge goes home to help in the search. The fire is out, and he sifts through the ashes; Gib has taken refuge at the back of the hearth, and Hodge sees her eyes glowing. She dashes up the stairs; Hodge, thinking the glowing eyes are sparks in her fur and fearing she will fire the thatched roof, charges up the stairway in pursuit. He is rewarded with two cracked shins. (The needle will not be found until the last act, when Hodge puts on his breeches and sits down on it). Diccon, meanwhile, arrives at the

tavern in time to hear a robust drinking song; it is rendered by Dame

Chat, tavern keeper and friend of
Gammer Gurton:

Back and side go bare, go bare,
Both foot and hand go cold;
But belly, God send thee good ale enough,
Whether it be new or old.

I cannot eat but little meat,
My stomach is not good;
But sure I think that I can drink
With him that wears a hood.
Though I go bare, take ye no care,
I am nothing a-cold;
I stuff my skin so full within
Of jolly good ale and old.
        Back and side go bare, go bare, . . .
            • • •
Now let them drink till they nod and wink,
Even as good fellows should do;
They shall not miss to have the bliss
Good ale doth bring men to;
And all pour souls that have scoured bowls,
Or have them lustly trolled,
God save the lives of them and their wives,
Whether they be young or old.
        Back and side go bare, go bare, . . .

Bad laws are the worst sort of tyranny

Source: SPEECH AT BRISTOL PREVIOUS TO THE ELECTION, 1780
Author: Edmund Burke (1729-1797)
First published: 1780
Type of work: Political speech

Context: Edmund Burke faced an
election at the time he made this
speech at the guildhall in Bristol,
which he had been representing in
Parliament for six years. The speech
is a bid for re-election and also a defense of his conduct as a member of
the House of Commons. He notes
that he is accused of neglecting his
constituents by not visiting Bristol, of
being wrong in his stand upon the
Irish trade acts, of being wrong in his

opinions and mode of proceeding on
Lord Beauchamp's debtors' bills, and
of voting wrongly on bills having to
do with religious freedom for Roman
Catholics. He defends himself against
these charges one by one. In answering the last-named accusation, he describes how laws against Roman
Catholics came into existence during
the seventeenth century, especially
how one law had been passed ironically in 1699. This particular law had

71

been intended to seem so harsh that it could not pass, but it did. And, says Burke, "The effects of the act have been as mischievous as its origin was ludicrous and shameful. From that time every person of that communion, lay and ecclesiastic, has been ob-liged to fly from the face of day." Burke shows specific examples of the cruel effects of this law, the repeal of which he had worked for. After challenging his hearers, "Let him stand forth that disapproves what we have done!" Burke comments on bad laws:

> Gentlemen, **bad laws are the worst sort of tyranny.** In such a country as this they are of all bad things the worst, worse by far than anywhere else; and they derive a particular malignity even from the wisdom and soundness of the rest of our institutions. For very obvious reasons you cannot trust the crown with a dispensing power over any of your laws. However, a government, be it as bad as it may, will, in the exercise of discretionary power, discriminate times and persons; and will not ordinarily pursue any man, when its own safety is not concerned. A mercenary informer knows no distinction. Under such a system, the obnoxious people are slaves, not only to the government, but they live at the mercy of every individual; they are at once the slaves of the whole community, and of every part of it; and the worst and most unmerciful men are those on whose goodness they most depend.

Bankrupt of life, yet prodigal of ease

Source: ABSALOM AND ACHITOPHEL (Part I, l. 168)
Author: John Dryden (1631-1700)
First published: 1681
Type of work: Satiric poem

Context: Absalom and Achitophel is generally regarded as the finest political satire in the English language. Though it appeared anonymously, everyone recognized Dryden's acid pen. He finally acknowledged his authorship in his *Discourse Concerning Satire* (1692), though no published version during his lifetime carried his name as author. The use of a Scriptural story for satirical purposes was not a new idea. Absalom, weak and misguided, but full of good intentions, represents the Duke of Monmouth. Achitophel, who by his counsel guided Absalom into rebellion, was the Earl of Shaftesbury, and in the poem there are excellent portraits of other contemporary politicians. There is some basis for the rumor that Dryden began the poem at the urging of King Charles II. Many editions followed, to weaken the already declining influence of Shaftesbury. Part II appeared in 1692. Shaftesbury was small in stature, but had an active brain. To describe his son, a man of little capacity, the poet rephrases Plato's definition of a man. Cataloguing the conspirators in the "Popish Plot," Dryden reminds readers of the belief that there is only a

72

thin division between genius and insanity. The intelligent Shaftesbury must have slipped over the edge, or he would never, in his declining years and having already achieved honor and wealth, have continued to punish his body that had so little life left, just to help a worthless son. Why not be wasteful of the leisure that he possessed in abundance?

> Of these the false Achitophel was first;
> A name to all succeeding ages curst:
> For close designs and crooked counsels fit;
> Sagacious, bold, and turbulent of wit;
>
>   • • •
>
> A fiery soul, which, working out its way
> Fretted the pigmy body to decay,
>
>   • • •
>
> Great wits are sure to madness near allied,
> And thin partitions do their bounds divide;
> Else why should he, with wealth and honor blest,
> Refuse his age the needful hours of rest?
> Punish a body which he could not please;
> **Bankrupt of life, yet prodigal of ease?**
> And all to leave what with his toil he won,
> To that unfeather'd two-legg'd thing, a son?

Bare ruined choirs, where late the sweet birds sang

Source: SONNET 73 (Line 4)
Author: William Shakespeare (1564-1616)
First published: 1609
Type of work: Sonnet

Context: A mood of melancholy is sustained in this sonnet, in which the poet, likening his estate to the end of the autumn, to the end of the day after the sunset, and to the final dying embers of the fire, reckons yet that his beloved must count him dearer because of the nearness of the time of separation. A forceful image is created in the likening of the bare branches of the trees to the arches of a ruined cathedral, both deserted by their choirs. The entire sonnet reads:

> That time of year thou mayst in me behold,
> When yellow leaves, or none, or few, do hang
> Upon those boughs which shake against the cold,
> **Bare ruin'd choirs, where late the sweet birds sang.**
> In me thou seest the twilight of such day,
> As after sunset fadeth in the west,
> Which by and by black night doth take away,
> Death's second self, that seals up all in rest,
> In me thou seest the glowing of such fire,

That on the ashes of his youth doth lie,
As the death-bed whereon it must expire,
Consum'd with that which it was nourish'd by.
This thou perceiv'st, which makes they love more strong,
To love that well which thou must leave ere long.

Battering the gates of heaven with storms of prayer

Source: SAINT SIMEON STYLITES (Line 7)
Author: Alfred, Lord Tennyson (1809-1892)
First published: 1842
Type of work: Dramatic monologue

Context: The darkness of the human mind that leads to guilt and the frenzied, practically insane, drive and the means men use to purge themselves of this guilt are here explored through the dying speech of a Christian saint who does not want to be sainted. Obsessed with his guilt yet unable to determine its source, Simeon follows the route of the medieval saints who so hated their bodies that they tortured themselves in the hopes of earning heaven. He has tied coarse ropes around his loins until the ulcers betrayed his penance; he has lived for three years with his leg chained to a mountain crag; but, for most of his life, he has lived on the tops of great columns where, exposed to all kinds of weather, he has suffered privation, starvation, and the pains of exposure. After such a lifetime, he believes that he is about to die; still obsessed with his guilt, he prays for the last time, begging for forgiveness and hoping that his pain will allow him to enter heaven.

Altho' I be the basest of mankind,
From scalp to sole one slough and crust of sin,
Unfit for earth, unfit for heaven, scarce meet
For troops of devils, mad with blasphemy,
I will not cease to grasp the hope I hold
Of Saintdom, and to clamor, mourn, and sob,
Battering the gates of heaven with storms of prayer,
Have mercy, Lord, and take away my sin! . . .

Be bold, be bold—but not too bold

Source: THE FAERIE QUEENE (Book III, Canto 11, stanza 54)
Author: Edmund Spenser (c. 1552-1599)
First published: 1590
Type of work: Allegorical poem

Context: The exemplification of love's aspects is the major theme of Book III. Britomart, the lady-knight of Active Chastity, is fervently seeking her love, Sir Artigall, the knight of Justice. While on this quest, she finds Scudamore, the Shield of Love, weeping on the ground because Busirane has held Amoret captive for seven months by means of black magic. Busirane, who represents the negation of Chastity and of the will of love, is Lust. Britomart accompanies Scudamore to Busirane's castle where the entrance is guarded by a sulphurous smoking flame. Britomart, alone, is able to penetrate the flame. Inside the castle, she passes through three rooms, each of which teaches her something of the transforming nature of love. In the first, she sees a tapes-try depicting the many disguises under which Jove made love, showing that even gods can debase themselves and become bestial in the search for love. Britomart passes through a door capped with Busirane's motto: *Be bold*. She finds herself in a room of pure gold hung with Cupid's "warlike spoils" which show the destructive effect of love on personal and political power. These two rooms have portrayed graphicly the boldness of love: desire, pursuit, victory. Over the centuries, Spenser's lines have undergone a change in the popular memory.

> And as she lookt about, she did behold
> How over that same dore was likewise writ,
> **Be bold, be bold,** and every where Be bold,
> That much she muz'd, yet could not construe it
> By any ridling skill, or commune wit.
> At last she spyde at that roomes upper end,
> Another yron dore, on which was writ,
> **Be not too bold;** whereto though she did bend
> Her earnest mind, yet wist not what it might intend.

Be it ever so humble, there's no place like home

Source: HOME, SWEET HOME (from the opera, *Clari, or, The Maid of Milan*)
Author: John Howard Payne (1791-1852)
First published: 1823
Type of work: Lyric

Context: Payne was an itinerant actor and dramatist; he left his home in Easthampton, Long Island, at the age of fifteen and spent several years in New York City, where he worked for a counting-house by day and edited a theatrical paper at night. After two years of college he made his first appearance on the stage (1809). He then went to London and spent a number of years there, writing several dramas and adapting others; all are forgotten now. He wrote a highly successful tragedy, *Brutus,* in which he had intended to play the leading role; however, Kean took the part and was made famous by it. In addition to producing several other popular works, Payne wrote a number of critical reviews. He returned to the United States in 1832 and in spite of a substantial income from his plays was in financial difficulties most of the time. He was United States Consul at Tunis, Algeria, from 1841 to 1845 and again in 1851 to 1852, dying there. While in London in 1823, Payne had written the lyric for an operatic aria; it is for this that he is still remembered. Henry R. Bishop, on a commission by the manager of Covent Garden Theatre, adapted a French play into an opera. Its title is *Clari, or, The Maid of Milan*. The song, "Home, Sweet Home," is presented several times in the course of the opera—in the overture, as an aria by Clari during the first act, as a song by peasants in the third act, and finally as a chorus. According to Bishop, the melody is partly founded on a Sicilian air. In the lyrics Payne, a homeless wanderer himself, expresses all the heartfelt longing for home that strikes us—either with pain or with nostalgia—at some time in the course of our lives. This yearning for a stability he could never have has touched the sentiments of millions over nearly a century and a half of time. The first and last stanzas are given below:

'Mid pleasures and palaces though we may roam,
Be it ever so humble, there's no place like home;
A charm from the sky seems to hallow us there,
Which, seek through the world, is ne'er met with elsewhere.
    Home, Home, sweet, sweet Home!
There's no place like Home! there's no place like Home!

. . .

To thee I'll return, overburdened with care;
The heart's dearest solace will smile on me there;
No more from that cottage again will I roam;
Be it ever so humble, there's no place like home.
    Home! Home! sweet, sweet, Home!
There's no place like Home! there's no place like Home!

Be neither saint nor sophist-led, but be a man!

Source: EMPEDOCLES ON ETNA (Act I, sc. ii, 1. 136)
Author: Matthew Arnold (1822-1888)
First published: 1852
Type of work: Poetic drama

Context: Empedocles, the poet and philosopher, is an exile on Mount Etna. Disillusioned, because he has questioned until the glory of life and the splendor of nature are dead; and hopeless, because he is torn between the blind faith of religion and the critical logic of philosophy, he can understand neither the young poet nor the physician. Callicles, the poet, advocates a romantic escape into idyllic beauty, but Empedocles cannot stop asking the questions that make such escape impossible. Pausanias, the physician, is interested only in the magic of healing people in a civilized society, but Empedocles cannot escape the lure of poetry that promises,

76

however feebly, the hope of beauty. In one of his moods, Empedocles breaks off his conversation with Pausanias to listen to Callicles, seizes his harp, and in a long monologue characterizes the dilemma that drives men from youthful hope to the adult despair. The quotation occurs in the part of the monologue where Empedocles describes how differences in opinions make the individual sink into his own subjectivity.

> And we feel, day and night,
> The burden of ourselves—
> Well, then, the wiser wight
> In his own bosom delves,
> And asks what ails him so, and gets what cure he can.
> The sophist sneers: Fool, take
> Thy pleasure, right or wrong.
> The pious wail: Forsake
> A world these sophists throng.
> **Be neither saint nor sophist-led, but be a man!**

Be wise today; 'tis madness to defer

Source: THE COMPLAINT: OR, NIGHT THOUGHTS ("Night the First," l. 390)
Author: Edward Young (1683-1765)
First published: 1742
Type of work: Philosophical poem

Context: The poet awakes from uneasy, dream-ridden sleep in the middle of the night and in the darkness and silence reflects upon man's place on earth and in the future life. Man is a wonderful creature, midway in the great chain of being between mere nothing and the deity—a worm and yet a god. His true place is in the infinite with God, but he spends his time here on earth busying himself with trivial concerns. Because man is a selfish creature, he pays attention to his own wants and desires here on earth, but by so doing he stores up woes in the future life. Man is really a petty creature, without vision; he tries to gain deceptive earthly joys, and ambition leads him towards what he foolishly believes are worthy goals. When he has almost reached them, death, whose hungry maw demands millions of human lives every day, consumes him. No one is ever ready for death; man never prepares for it: he should be wise and to-day be waiting for his long journey—it is madness to delay so important an activity. But procrastination is the thief of time.

> Not e'en Philander had bespoke his shroud:
> Nor had he cause; a warning was denied;
> How many fall as sudden, not as safe!
> As sudden, though for years admonished home.
> Of human ills the last extreme beware,

Beware, Lorenzo! a slow sudden death.
How dreadful that deliberate surprise!
Be wise to-day; 'tis madness to defer;
Next day the fatal precedent will plead;
Thus on, till wisdom is pushed out of life.
Procrastination is the thief of time;
Year after year it steals, till all are fled,
And to the mercies of a moment leaves
The vast concerns of an eternal scene.
If not so frequent, would not this be strange?
That 'tis so frequent, this is stranger still.

Be your oriflamme today the helmet of Navarre

Source: IVRY: A SONG OF THE HUGUENOTS (Line 30)
Author: Thomas Babington Macaulay (1800-1859)
First published: 1824
Type of work: Ballad

Context: The original Huguenot was "one who took an oath." It comes from the earlier French *eiguenot,* changed because of a fancied resemblance to the name Hugh, and was applied to the sixteenth and seventeenth century French Protestants. Though Henry IV (1553–1610) of France, was brought up as a Protestant, he wavered back and forth toward Catholicism. His claim to the French throne was recognized by Coligny, chief of the Huguenots, in 1569. When he was named to the throne, the Catholic League, to force him to abjure Protestantism, waged the War of the Three Henrys. The League was defeated at the Battle of Ivry, in northern France, where Henry IV issued his gallant order: "If you lose your standards, follow my white plume." Later, with the explanation, "Paris is worth a Mass," he permanently became a Roman Catholic. Navarre lies across the Pyrenees Mountains and was formerly an independent kingdom. Now the southern part forms Spain's Basque region, while the northern section is part of France. In one of his miscellaneous poems, Macaulay tells of the Battle of Ivry. The oriflamme was the ancient royal standard of France, with flame-shaped streamers.

The king is come to marshal us, in all his armor drest,
And he has bound a snow-white plume upon his gallant
    crest.
He looked upon his people, and a tear was in his eye;
He looked upon the traitors, and his glance was stern and
    high.
Right graciously he smiled on us, as rolled from wing to
    wing,
Down all our line, a deafening shout, "God save our Lord
    the King!"

"And if my standard-bearer fall, as fall full well he may,
For never saw I promise yet of such a bloody fray,
Press where ye see my white plume shine, amidst the ranks
   of war,
And **be your oriflamme to-day the helmet of Navarre.**"

A beauteous evening, calm and free

Source: IT IS A BEAUTEOUS EVENING, CALM AND FREE (Line 1)
Author: William Wordsworth (1770-1850)
First published: 1807
Type of work: Sonnet

Context: This beautiful sonnet was composed on the beach near Calais in the autumn of 1802. The girl walking with Wordsworth is Caroline, his natural daughter by Annette Vallon.The father is deeply moved by the beauty of the evening and the sound of the sea, but the child seems indifferent. Yet, says Wordsworth, you have a divinity in you and a worshipful spirit, even though you appear untouched. "Abraham's bosom" is the place where souls rest in heaven after death. Luke 16:22: "And it came to pass, that the beggar died, and was carried by the angels into Abraham's bosom." The sonnet follows:

It is **a beauteous evening, calm and free,**
The holy time is quiet as a Nun,
Breathless with adoration; the broad sun
Is sinking down in its tranquillity;
The gentleness of heaven broods o'er the Sea:
Listen! the mighty Being is awake,
And doth with his eternal motion make
A sound like thunder—everlastingly.
Dear Child! dear Girl! that walkest with me here,
If thou appear untouched by solemn thought,
Thy nature is not therefore less divine:
Thou liest in Abraham's bosom all the year;
And worshipp'st at the Temple's inner shrine,
God being with thee when we know it not.

The beautiful uncut hair of graves

Source: SONG OF MYSELF (Canto 6)
Author: Walt Whitman (1819-1892)
First published: 1855
Type of work: Lyric poem

Context: After experiences as printer,   journalist, and newspaper editor, during which he published a few poems and articles, Walt Whitman, under an abbreviated first name that he used for the rest of his life, published at his own expense a small volume, *Leaves of Grass,* containing twelve lyric poems, among them "Song of Myself." The book was largely ignored except by Ralph Waldo Emerson, who wrote him a congratulatory letter. In subsequent years through commercial publishers, Whitman issued ten editions, each radically different. At first Whitman was criticized for his daring subject matter and for his long, rhythmical, but unrhymed lines. Readers thought he well characterized himself when he wrote about his "barbaric yawp." Today, however, critics recognize the greatness of some poems, amid the false greatness and mediocrity of the rest. Some of the best of Whitman appeared in its longest poem, "Song of Myself," in 52 cantos. It shows the poet as a mystic, a pantheist, and a lover of humanity. In Canto 6, he combines two of his favorite themes: death and democracy.

A child said *What is the grass?* fetching it to me with
full hands;
How could I answer the child? I did not know what it
was any more than he . . .

Or I guess it is the handkerchief of the Lord,
A scented gift and remembrance designedly dropt,
Bearing the owner's name someway in the corner, that
we may see and remark, and say *Whose?* . . .

Or I guess it is a uniform hieroglyphic,
And it means, Sprouting alike in broad zones and narrow
zones,
Growing among black folk as among white,
Kanuck, Tuckahoe, Congressman, Cuff, I give them the
same, I receive them the same.

And now it seems to me **the beautiful uncut hair of graves.**

Beauty in distress

Source: TO FLORENCE (Stanza 7)
Author: George Gordon, Lord Byron (1788-1824)
First published: 1812
Type of work: Lyric poem

Context: On Byron's first trip to Europe, he and his companion, John Hobhouse, spent some time in Malta where they met Spencer Smith and his wife Constance. Hers was a fantastic story, quite apart from her adventures with the Marquis de Salvo. In 1806 she incurred the enmity of Napoleon and was imprisoned. She escaped down a rope ladder in male disguise.

Byron was immediately taken with her, perhaps because of her near-sightedness and habit of looking at men with bewildered vagueness, like a romantic lady in distress. But she was realist enough to defraud the poet of a costly yellow diamond. Byron wrote to his mother that he was in love with a German lady with fat arms, though his references to her in *Childe Harold's Pilgrimage* II, 30–35, do not make him appear very much infatuated with her. Her actual name was Constance, but in his narrative the poet gives her the more romantic name of Florence. Thomas Moore, who used Byron's Memoirs in writing the poet's biography, declared —and Byron's friend Hobhouse agreed—that Byron's references to her were cold. With the passing of time, however, Byron idealized her in a number of short poems, and made passionate references to their relationship. The poems include "Stanzas Composed during a Thunderstorm," "Stanzas written in Passing the Ambracian Gulf," and "To Florence," of which the first, seventh, eighth, and final stanzas are here given. He tells her he loves her and wants her to look on him as a friend, and he will think of her when he sees her birthplace, Stamboul.

> Oh Lady! when I left the shore,
>   The distant shore which gave me birth,
> I hardly thought to grieve once more,
>   To quit another spot on earth: . . .
>   .   .   .
> And who so cold as look on thee,
>   Thou lovely wand'rer, and be less?
> Nor be, what man should ever be,
>   The friend of **Beauty in distress?**
>
> Ah, who could think that form had past
>   Through Danger's most destructive path,
> Had braved the death-winged tempest's blast,
>   And 'scaped a tyrant's fiercer wrath? . . .
>   .   .   .
> And though I bid thee now farewell,
>   When I behold that wondrous scene,
> Since where thou are I may not dwell,
>   'T will soothe to be, where thou hast been.

Beauty is in the eye of the beholder

Source: MOLLY BAWN (Chapter XII)
Author: Margaret Wolfe Hungerford (c. 1855-1897)
First published: 1878
Type of work: Novel

Context: Molly Bawn is the nick-name Philip Massereene has given his pretty step-sister Eleanor. Philip, a poor but honest gentleman of Victorian England, owns a small homestead south of London where he lives with his wife, Letitia, and Molly. Molly has a fierce old grandfather who disowned her mother when she married beneath her and who has never seen his granddaughter, but as he becomes ill in his old age he sends for her. In the meantime, however, Molly has fallen in love with Teddy, a friend of her brother. The two cannot marry because Teddy, whose full name is Tedcastle, has an inadequate income. Molly, interrupting her courtship to visit her wealthy but ill-natured grandfather, meets her cousin Marcia, a scheming but beautiful girl. One evening soon after Molly's arrival, several neighbors come to visit, including Lady Stafford, who is met at the door by Marcia. Lady Stafford inquires concerning the arrival of the other guests:

"One moment, Marcia. Many people come yet? Tedcastle?"

"Yes, and Captain Mottie, with his devoted attendant, and the Darleys."

"Maudie? Is she as fascinating as ever? I do hope, Marcia, you have got her young man for her this time, as she was simply unbearable last year."

"I have not," laughing: "it is a dead secret, but the fact is, he *wouldn't come*."

"I like that young man. Though I consider he has sold us shamefully. Any one else?"

"My cousin, Eleanor Massereene."

"*The* cousin! I am so glad. Anything new is such a relief. And I have heard she is beautiful: is she?"

"Beauty is in the eye of the beholder," quotes Marcia, in a low tone, and with a motion of her hand towards the open door inside which sits Molly, that sends Lady Stafford up-stairs without further parley.

Beauty is the lover's gift

Source: THE WAY OF THE WORLD (Act II, sc. ii)
Author: William Congreve (1670-1729)
First published: 1700
Type of work: Dramatic comedy

Context: Mrs. Millamant, attended by her admirer Witwoud, joins Mrs. Fainall and Mirabell, whom she loves. Mrs. Millamant has been late in arriving for this rendezvous and gropes for an explanation for her tardiness. She finally says that she had been reading a batch of just-arrived letters. She loathes letters, which serve only one useful purpose—to pin up one's hair. It seems that those in prose are useless; she tried some once and her hair was in such a wretched condition that her maid, Mincing, had to work all morning in an effort to rectify matters. Letters in poetry, however, make the hair sit properly the next day. It then develops that

82

Mrs. Millamant loves to inflict pain, as when one parts with her cruelty she parts with her power; when one parts with her power she is old and ugly. Mirabell, however, says that if a woman destroys her lover she destroys herself. She is no longer beautiful when she has lost her lover, because her beauty dies in the instant of losing him. It is the lover who bestows beauty on the beloved; the old and ugly, who cannot bear to look in their mirrors, can be flattered, for the mirror reflects men's praises—what they say about their ladies—rather than accurate reflections of the faces.

MIRABELL

Ay, ay, suffer your cruelty to ruin the object of your power, to destroy your lover—and then how vain, how lost a thing you'll be! Nay, 'tis true: you are no longer handsome when you've lost your lover; your beauty dies upon the instant; for **beauty is the lover's gift;** 'tis he bestows your charms—your glass is all a cheat. The ugly and the old, whom the looking-glass mortifies, yet after commendation can be flattered by it, and discovers beauties in it; for that reflects our praises, rather than your face.

Beauty unadorned

Source: THE ROVER; OR, THE BANISH'D CAVALIERS, PART TWO (Act IV, sc. i)
Author: Aphra Behn (1640-1689)
First published: 1681
Type of work: Dramatic comedy

Context: The Rover, a Cavalier named Willmore, is an Englishman, a soldier of fortune since his banishment from England for supporting the crown during the civil wars. He comes to Madrid, where he falls in love with La Nuche, a Spanish courtesan, who also loves him. Their love affair is complicated in several ways. There is, of course, La Nuche's reputation as a courtesan. Also, Ariadne, a young lady of quality, bids for Willmore's love, as a rival to La Nuche, even though she is engaged to marry Beaumond, Willmore's friend. La Nuche, truly in love with Willmore, grumbles from time to time about being a courtesan and finding it difficult to prove to Willmore that she really loves him. One of the persons to whom she complains is Petronella Elenora, her bawd, who is herself a worn-out courtesan. Petronella tries, as she does in this passage, to persuade La Nuche that she ought not to worry about love in general or Willmore, a penniless man, in particular. She admonishes La Nuche that wealth is everything:

LA NUCHE
. . .
Oh give me Love: I will be poor and love.

She's lost—but hear me—

LA NUCHE

I won't, from Childhood thou hast trained me up in Cunning,
read Lectures to me of the use of Man, but kept me from the
knowledge of the Right; taught me to jilt, to flatter and deceive:
and hard it was to learn th' ungrateful Lessons. But oh how soon
plain Nature taught me Love, and shew'd me all the cheat of thy
false Tenents—No—give me Love with any other Curse.

PETRONELLA

But who will give you that when you are poor? when you are
wretchedly despis'd and poor?

LA NUCHE

Hah!

PETRONELLA

Do you not daily see fine Clothes, rich Furniture, Jewels and
Plate are more inviting than **Beauty unadorn'd?** be old, diseas'd,
deform'd, be any thing, so you be rich and splendidly attended,
you'll find your self lov'd and ador'd by all. . . .

Begin with the beginning

Source: DON JUAN (Canto I, stanza 7)
Author: George Gordon, Lord Byron (1788-1824)
First published: 1819 (Cantos I-II)
Type of work: Satirical poem

Context: In the literary world, the
Spanish Don Juan Tenorio is the
symbol of the great lover, the profli-
gate libertine, with feudal power but
without feudal obligation. One is not
sure how much Byron knew of the
Spanish play that introduced this
character to the literary world, the
Golden Age *El Burlador de Sevilla*
(The Mocker of Seville) by Tirso de
Molina (1584?–1648). *Don Juan
Tenorio* (1844) by the romantic
dramatist José Zorrilla (1817–1893)
did not appear until later. Certainly
Byron did not know how to pronounce the Spaniard's name, for instead of Don Hwahn (to rhyme with
"John"), he rhymed it with "ruin."
But then, he rhymed Cádiz with "ladies" and the three-syllable "capote"
with "boat." Nor did he follow the
story line of the Spanish original.
Started out like a bedroom farce, it
let him indulge his talent for insults
and ridicule. Its dedication insults
Wordsworth, Coleridge, and "Sir
Laureate" Robert Southey, who lives
to sing about kings "very ill." About
Coleridge, Byron remarks that the
poet explained metaphysics to the na-

tion, then adds: "I wish he would explain his explanation." Wisely, the publisher, Murray, who published Cantos I and II in July, 1819, and Cantos III, IV, and V in August, 1821, issued them without mentioning either his name or the name of the author. Of course the authorship was quickly guessed, and upon Byron fell a storm of obloquy for their voluptuousness and skepticism. Consequently Murray refused to publish any later cantos. They were printed in sets of three by John Hunt in 1823 and 1824. Byron was writing Canto XVII when he died of a fever in Greece. Byron announced that he intended to write an epic of modern life; however, the poem fails to follow the epic tradition, since the poet departs from the story with frequent digressions, as he does in *Childe Harold's Pilgrimage*. He refers to many people and things, as well as indulging in bitter tirades against England, society, wealth, and power. So the adventures of the Don are incidental to a satire that is, in the opinion of many critics, the greatest in English, as well as the poem above all others of his pen into which are gathered the most outstanding traits of his genius. It is written largely in ottava rima, an Italian meter: eight lines of ten syllables with the first six rhyming alternately, and a rhymed couplet at the end. As an example, see the stanza quoted here. In the opening lines of the first canto, Byron remarks: "I want a hero," and therefore he takes Don Juan, familiar as a figure in the pantomime, sent to the devil before his time. Then the author digresses to list some of the heroes of the present and past, all of whom he finds unfit for his poem. He also comments on the usual way of plunging somewhere into the middle of the action in an attempt to seize attention at once. But as he comments:

That is the usual method, but not mine—
　My way is to **begin with the beginning;**
The regularity of my design
　Forbids all wandering as the worst of sinning,
And therefore I shall open with a line
　(Although it cost me half an hour in spinning)
Narrating somewhat of Don Juan's father,
And also of his mother, if you'd rather.

Believing where we cannot prove

Source: IN MEMORIAM (Prologue, stanza 1)
Author: Alfred, Lord Tennyson (1809-1892)
First published: 1850
Type of work: Elegy

Context: When Arthur Henry Hallam, Tennyson's beloved friend, suddenly died in Vienna at the age of twenty-two years, Tennyson composed in his honor one of the great elegies in the English language. He begins his work with a prologue addressed to Love, the son of God. We

85

have not seen Love face to face; we accept its existence on faith alone, believing something that we cannot prove. In this passage Tennyson is echoing the conclusion of the gospel of *John* (20:24–29): the disciple Thomas said that he would not believe that Christ had risen from the dead until he had put his finger into the print of the nails in Christ's hands and thrust his hand into the wound in his side. Christ invites him to do what he demanded and then said, "Thomas, because thou hast seen me, thou hast believed; blessed are they that have not seen and yet have believed." Tennyson, following Christ, is saying in different form that belief grounded on proof is inferior in merit to the accepting of what cannot be proved, which is true faith.

> Strong Son of God, immortal Love,
>   Whom we, that have not seen thy face,
>   By faith, and faith alone, embrace,
> **Believing where we cannot prove;**
>
> Thine are these orbs of light and shade;
>   Thou madest Life in man and brute;
>   Thou madest Death; and lo, thy foot
> Is on the skull which thou has made.
>
> Thou wilt not leave us in the dust:
>   Thou madest man, he knows not why,
>   He thinks he was not made to die;
> And thou hast made him: thou art just.

Beneath the Good how far—but far above the Great

Source: PROGRESS OF POESY (Last line)
Author: Thomas Gray (1716-1771)
First published: 1757
Type of work: Pindaric ode

Context: Gray wrote poetry for his friends. He had little but scorn for the intellectual qualities and knowledge of the general public. Therefore, he declared, concerning the lines and references in his poem that traced the history of poetry from the Greek Pindar to the great English figures, that they were "vocal to the intelligent; for the many they need interpreters." However, many of its footnotes were in Greek that would be of little help to the general reader. Most of the names mentioned in the ode are familiar today. After the poet's tribute to Shakespeare (see, "Nature's darling") and to Milton (see, "He pass'd the flaming Bounds"), Gray lauds the greatness of Dryden. However, now that Dryden is dead, Gray asks who will inherit the lyre of the Theban Eagle (Pindar). Perhaps some one still a child will one day prove how far goodness can outshine greatness. (See, "They're only truly great").

> Yet oft before his infant eyes would run
> Such forms as glitter in the Muse's ray,
> With orient hues, unborrowed of the Sun;
> Yet shall he mount, and keep his distant way
> Beyond the limits of a vulgar fate;
> **Beneath the Good how far—but far above the Great.**

The best in this kind are but shadows

Source: A MIDSUMMER NIGHT'S DREAM (Act V, sc. i, l. 213)
Author: William Shakespeare (1564-1616)
First published: 1600
Type of work: Dramatic comedy

Context: As the wedding festivities of Theseus and Hippolyta draw to a close, Philostrate, Master of Revels, is commanded to bring a dramatic performance before the royal group. Various selections are rejected as inappropriate for the nuptial occasion: the eunuch reciting the battle with the centaurs, the riot of the tipsy Bacchanals, the thrice three muses mourning for the death of learning. Instead, Theseus prefers the Athenian handicraftsmen's production of *The Most Lamentable Comedy, and Most Cruel Death of Pyramus and Thisbe.* Philostrate is quick to caution the duke that the quality of performance leaves much to be desired, but Theseus replies that "never anything can be amiss,/ When simpleness and duty tender it." He informs his bride of the honesty and sincerity of such a group in comparison with the finely polished performances of deceit. Moreover, if the rustics confuse line, meter, and meaning in their delivery, it will be no worse than "great clerks" who have come to me with "premeditated welcome," but who "shiver and look pale," making "periods in the midst of sentences" and throttling "their practis'd accent in their fears." Following the duke's example, the courtiers attempt to receive the performance with graceful pleasure, but, when the character representing Wall informs the crowd his part is concluded and stalks off stage, the farce is more than Hippolyta can bear. Again Theseus reminds her that all players are but shadows of the mind which must be fitted to proper form by the imagination:

WALL
Thus have I, Wall, my part discharged so;
And, being done, thus Wall away doth go. [*Exit.*]

THESEUS
Now is the Moon to see between the two neighbours.

87

DEMETRIUS

No remedy my lord, when walls are so wilful, to hear without warning.

HIPPOLYTA

This is the silliest stuff that e'er I heard.

THESEUS

The best in this kind are but shadows; and the worst are no worse, if imagination amend them.

HIPPOLYTA

It must be your imagination then, and not theirs.

THESEUS

If we imagine no worse of them than they of themselves, they may pass for excellent men.

The best of life is but intoxication

Source: DON JUAN (Canto II, stanza 179)
Author: George Gordon, Lord Byron (1788-1824)
First published: 1819 (Cantos I and II)
Type of work: Satiric poem

Context: The young Don Juan, as punishment for an amorous scrape that has resulted in a divorce and a scandal which has all Spain talking, has been banished from his homeland and packed off to sea on his pious mother's assumption that the salt air will somehow bring about a change of heart and a return to innocence. Who knows but that her scheme might have worked had not a great storm come up, battering the ship to pieces, killing all of Juan's fellow voyagers, and depositing him, half-drowned, on an island coast. Two ladies, the beautiful Haidée, "The greatest heiress of the Eastern Isles," and her companion, find the unconscious and emaciated youth lying on the sand, carry him to a cave, and nurse him back to health and alas! to love. As the lovely Haidée accompanies the handsome Juan on his first venture from the cave since his rescue, the poet describes the "wild and breaker-beaten coast" along which the lovers stroll. He then digresses a bit and speaks up in favor of old wine!

And the small ripple spilt upon the beach
  Scarcely o'erpassed the cream of your champagne,
When o'er the brim the sparkling bumpers reach,
  That spring-dew of the spirit! the heart's rain!
Few things surpass old wine; and they may preach
  Who please,—the more because they preach in vain,—

Let us have wine and women, mirth and laughter,
Sermons and soda-water the day after.

Man, being reasonable, must get drunk;
 The best of life is but intoxication:
Glory, the grape, love, gold, in these are sunk
 The hopes of all men, and of every nation;
Without their sap, how branchless were the trunk
 Of life's strange tree, so fruitful on occasion!
But to return,—Get very drunk; and when
You wake with headache, you shall see what then.

The best things carried to excess are wrong

Source: THE ROSCIAD (Line 1039)
Author: Charles Churchill (1731-1764)
First published: 1761
Type of work: Satiric poem

Context: A dissipated clergyman, Churchill won both fame and notoriety as a satiric poet during the last four years of his life. He was associated with and defended John Wilkes, the unscrupulous editor of the *North-Briton.* Much of the harsh and vitriolic nature of Churchill's satire seems to have been formed by this association. In *The Rosciad,* his first important poem, Churchill attacked a number of theatrical personalities with such witty satire that it was at one time regarded as the most important satiric work between those of Pope and Byron. Near the end of the poem, after a long catalogue of contemporary stage personalities, all subjected to biting attack, came the famous actor David Garrick, followed by a train of critics. The first critic accuses Garrick of being too short to play a hero because "Your Hero always should be tall, you know":

 Another can't forgive the paltry arts,
By which he makes his way to shallow hearts;
Mere pieces of finesse, traps for applause.—
"Avaunt, unnat'ral start, affected pause."

 For me, by Nature form'd to judge with phlegm,
I can't acquit by whosesale, nor condemn.
The best things carried to excess are wrong:
The start may be too frequent, pause too long;
But, only us'd in proper time and place,
Severest judgment must allow them Grace.

Better be courted and jilted than never be courted at all

Source: THE JILTED NYMPH (Stanza 3)
Author: Thomas Campbell (1777-1844)
First published: 1842
Type of work: Humorous poem

Context: Thomas Campbell took more pride in having founded the University of London than in his poetry, even his heroic and patriotic poetry that stirred Great Britain between 1800 and 1840. That is well, because the university continued and grew, while Campbell's reputation as a poet diminished until he is now almost forgotten. One section of his collected poems is headed "Songs, chiefly Amatory," and contains thirty poems to almost as many ladies. He started with two "To Caroline" poems, written in 1795, just after he left the University of Glasgow. He was eighteen and Caroline, seventeen. He wrote "Ode to Content" in 1800, dedicated to Matilda Sinclair, whom he later married. Then came poems to Julia, to Florine who married one of his best friends, to Margaret, a lovely table maid, and to three celebrated Scottish beauties: Jemima, Rosa, and Eleanore. Many of the poems were trite, but Campbell could turn a phrase and incorporate humor, as he did when one young lady in 1840 begged him for something original for her album. His response was: "An original something, fair maid, you will win me/ To write—but how shall I begin?/ For I fear I have nothing original in me—/ Excepting Original Sin." How many times he loved, he was too much the gentleman to boast. How many times he lost, he was too proud to confess. But like Samuel Butler in *The Way of All Flesh* (Chapter 77), and Tennyson in *In Memoriam,* Campbell agreed " 'Tis better to have loved and lost/Than never to have loved at all." In his song, "The Jilted Nymph," he phrased it differently. It was written to be sung to the Scots tune of "Woo'd and married and a'." The first, part of the third, and the last stanzas are given here. In the lines omitted, the nymph tells of her sad experiences with various temporary suitors.

I'm jilted, forsaken, outwitted;
   Yet think not I'll whimper or brawl—
The lass is alone to be pitied
Who ne'er has been courted at all;
Never by great or small
Wooed or jilted at all;
   Oh, how unhappy's the lass
Who has never been courted at all!
     • • •

What though at my heart he has tilted,
   What though I have met with a fall?
Better be courted and jilted
   Than never be courted at all . . .
     • • •

90

But lately I've met with a suitor
   Whose heart I have gotten in thrall,
And I hope soon to tell you in future
   That I'm wooed and married and all.
Wooed and married and all,
What greater bliss can befall?
   And you all shall partake
   Of my bridal cake,
When I'm woo'd and married, and all.

The better day the worse deed

Source: AN EXPOSITION OF THE OLD TESTAMENT (Genesis 3:6)
Author: Matthew Henry (1662-1714)
First published: 1708-1710
Type of work: Biblical commentary

Context: Matthew Henry was an English noncomformist clergyman whose father, Philip Henry, was a clergyman before him and was persecuted for his beliefs. Matthew became minister of a Presbyterian church in Chester in 1687, remaining there until 1712. In the latter year he moved to Hackney, and two years later he died suddenly at Nantwich. He wrote a number of doctrinal works and a moving biography of his father, but he is best remembered for his commentaries on the Bible. These represent a truly monumental achievement and were published under the title *Expositions of the Old and New Testaments.* To many, this lengthy and exhaustive work still holds first place for general usefulness in its field. The lessons which Henry draws from his text are both sound and sensible, and he presents them in memorable fashion. Much use is made of metaphor, analogy, and illustration; the language is direct and simple, homely and warm without loss of dignity. His writing abounds with pithy observations and quotable expressions, and his reflective statements give evidence that his work was a labor of devotion. It is obvious to the reader that Henry had a warm understanding of the world and of man, that he was deeply pious, and that his knowledge of scripture was keen and searching. His commentaries are practical and devotional in nature; they are expositions and explanations of the material and do not undertake to criticize it. In his discussion of the third chapter of Genesis, he describes the transgression of Eve when she partook of the forbidden fruit, and the transgression of Adam when he joined her in surrendering to the wiles of the Serpent. Then he explains the enormity of Adam's guilt in no uncertain terms:

. . . In neglecting the tree of life which he was allowed to eat of, and eating of the tree of knowledge which was forbidden, he plainly shewed a contempt of the favours which God had be-

91

stowed on him, and a preference given to those God did not see fit for him. He would be both his own carver, and his own master; would *have* what he pleased, and *do* what he pleased; his sin was, in one word, *disobedience* . . . to a plain, easy, and express command, which, probably, he knew to be a command of trial. He sins against great knowledge, against many mercies, against light and love, the clearest light, and the dearest love, that ever sinner sinned against. He had no corrupt nature within him to betray him; but had a freedom of will, not enslaved, and was in his full strength, not weakened or impaired. He *turned aside quickly.* Some think he fell the very same day on which he was made: though I see not how to reconcile that with God's pronouncing all *very good,* in the close of that day: others suppose he fell on the sabbath day; **the better day the worse deed:** however, it is certain that he kept his integrity but a very little while; being in honour, he *continued not.* But the greatest aggravation of his sin, was, that he *involved all his posterity* in sin and ruin by it. God having told him that his race should replenish the earth, surely he could not but know that he stood as a public person, and that his disobedience would be fatal to all his seed; and if so, it was certainly the greatest treachery as well as the greatest cruelty that ever was.

Better one suffer than a nation grieve

Source: ABSALOM AND ACHITOPHEL (Part I, l. 416)
Author: John Dryden (1631-1700)
First published: 1681
Type of work: Satiric poem

Context: In his poetical rewriting of the Biblical story of the revolt of Absalom against King David (II Samuel, 13–18) Dryden, England's leading poet of his time, incorporated a thinly disguised allegory of the frustrated attempts of the Whigs to make the illegitimate James Stuart, Duke of Monmouth, the successor of Charles II. If Dryden thought to conceal his authorship by publishing it anonymously, he failed. The rhymed couplets, handled in a way none of his contemporaries could match, were as good as a signature. When another James, the Roman Catholic Duke of York, brother of Charles II, loomed as heir to the English throne, the Earl of Shaftesbury headed a plot to legitimatize Monmouth. When details were made public, in 1678, the attempt became known as "The Popish Plot." At the start of this satire, Shaftesbury, as Achitophel, is attempting, by saying that the right of succession sometimes brings harm to a nation, to persuade Absalom (Monmouth) to appeal to the people to dethrone King David and give him the throne. Rather than the "right of kings," he argues, there is such a thing as the "right of people" to decide how they shall be governed. The "right of succession," when it would bring harm to a country, should be abrogated. Perhaps the heir to the throne would suffer, but what is the unhappiness of one person in comparison to that of a whole nation?

> . . . the people have a right supreme
> To make their kings; for kings are made for them.
> All empire is no more than pow'r in trust,
> Which, when resum'd, can be no longer just.
> Succession, for the general good design'd,
> In its own wrong a nation cannot bind;
> If altering that the people can relieve,
> **Better one suffer than a nation grieve.**

Between craft and credulity, the voice of reason is stifled

Source: LETTER TO THE SHERIFFS OF BRISTOL
Author: Edmund Burke (1729-1797)
First published: 1777
Type of work: Political treatise

Context: Burke's letter was written to John Farr and John Harris, the sheriffs of Bristol, about the state of affairs between Great Britain and the American Colonies. Burke was elected to the House of Commons in 1774, as the representative of Bristol, whose citizens had broad commercial interests which made them sympathetic to Burke's liberal views on the war between Great Britain and the colonists. Burke was not a man to adhere blindly to abstract principles in the way of many of his fellow countrymen; he cared nothing for his country's right to coerce the Colonies or its so-called dignity. He asked always what was the humane action and what was in Great Britain's best interests in the long run. In his letter to the sheriff he writes to them about the most recent acts of Parliament with respect to the Colonies and what he calls the civil war then going on. He recounts how one of the acts brands men aboard American privateers and warships as buccaneers, to be tried and hanged as pirates when they are captured. Such action, along with the insistence upon trying Americans for treason only in Great Britain, Burke feels to be wholly unjustified. He also comments on the fact that New York, Long Island, and Staten Island should have been restored, but have not, to trade when they submitted voluntarily to British rule. Burke then comments:

> . . . But we see well enough to what the whole leads. The trade of America is to be dealt out in *private indulgences and graces;* that is, in jobs to recompense the incendiaries of war. They will be informed of the proper time in which to send out their merchandise. From a national, the American trade is to be turned into a personal monopoly; and one set of merchants are to be rewarded for the pretended zeal of which another set are the dupes; and

93

thus, **between craft and credulity, the voice of reason is stifled,** and all the misconduct, all the calamities of the war are covered and continued.

Beware of those who are homeless by choice

Source: THE DOCTOR (Chapter 34)
Author: Robert Southey (1774-1843)
First published: 1834-1847)
Type of work: Literary miscellany

Context: In his own time, Robert Southey was a literary innovator and leader; he explored new areas in writing, pioneered in a number of styles, and was the only "entire man of letters" in his day. He supported and helped to found the romantic movement, experimented with a number of departures from eighteenth century rigidity, and established paths for others to follow. These include the ballad, the reintroduction of blank verse, the epic, and the exotic oriental setting. He wrote voluminously in all fields; in addition to his poetry, he proved himself a competent historian, essayist, biographer, and critic. He was named poet laureate of England in 1813 and held the post for thirty years. A tireless scholar and a conscientious craftsman whose mind eventually failed from overwork, Southey now appears to have been far inferior in genius to his friends Coleridge, Wordsworth, and Scott; to present-day critics, his importance is almost purely historical and he is remembered for a handful of minor poems —and a nursery classic, "The Three Bears." It is generally agreed that his talents were not equal to his ambitions; and the epics, which he was certain would ensure his lasting reputation, are now considered failures. Nonetheless there is much of interest in his writings, and much of the unusual. *The Doctor* is an example of his prose; a lengthy and curious work which Southey wrote for amusement in his leisure time, it is a collection of nearly everything: fantasy, fiction, whimsy, opinion, criticism, lore of all sorts, anecdotes, and an overriding facetiousness. The last quality seems labored to a modern reader, whose attention is nonetheless held by the endless variety of the book. Many of his comments are sound and perceptive; for example, his distrust of the "world citizen" who acknowledges no ties, owes no allegiances, accepts no responsibilities, and cannot be involved in life:

Whatever strengthens our local attachments is favorable both to individual and national character. Our home,—our birth place, —our native land,—think for a while what the virtues are which arise out of the feelings connected with these words; and if thou hast any intellectual eyes thou wilt then perceive the connection between topography and patriotism.
Shew me a man who cares no more for one place than another,

94

and I will shew you in that same person one who loves nothing but himself. **Beware of those who are homeless by choice!** You have no hold on a human being whose affections are without a tap-root. The laws recognize this truth in the privileges which they confer upon freeholders; and public opinion acknowledges it also, in the confidence which it reposes upon those who have what is called a stake in the country. Vagabond and rogue are convertible terms; and with how much propriety any one may understand who knows what are the habits of the wandering classes, such as gypsies, tinkers, and potters.

Beware the fury of a patient man

Source: ABSALOM AND ACHITOPHEL (Part I, l. 1005)
Author: John Dryden (1631-1700)
First published: 1681
Type of work: Satiric poem

Context: According to warnings supplied to the British government by Titus Oates in August, 1678, conspirators were plotting the murder of King Charles, who would be replaced by James Duke of York, acting as an agent of the Jesuits. The French would then play a role to suppress the Protestants. Dryden satirized what was called "The Popish Plot," in the guise of retelling the Biblical story of Absalom's plot against his father, King David. Anthony Cooper, Earl of Shaftesbury, who at first sided with the king, later changed sides and became a strong supporter of the Exclusion Bill, whose purpose was to deprive the Duke of York of right of succession. He is cast in the poem as Achitophel. Absalom represents Monmouth, illegitimate son of Charles II. David is Charles II. Though the details of the plot reported by Oates were largely false, there was enough truth in them so that an investigation did reveal an actual conspiracy. King Charles II was forced to take action against Parliament (called "The Sanhedrin" in Dryden's allegory). James went into temporary exile; and in 1681, the year of the appearance of Dryden's poem, Shaftesbury was arrested for treason. In the lament of King David, close to the conclusion of the poem, one is reminded of Maxim Number 289 by Publilius Syrus of the first century, B.C.: "An overtaxed patience gives way to fury," as well as of the colloquial: "Even a worm will turn." Here David (Charles II) is sorry that the conspirators had mistaken his merciful treatment of them for fear. Now that his patience has been overtaxed, he will be forced to act cruelly and decisively.

· · ·

Must I at length the sword of justice draw?
O curst effect of necessary law!
How ill my fear they by my mercy scan,
Beware the fury of a patient man.

95

Law they require, let Law then show her face;
They could not be content to look on Grace,
Her hinder parts, but with a daring eye
To tempt the terror of her front and die.

. . .

Big-Endians and Little-Endians

Source: GULLIVER'S TRAVELS (*Voyage to Lilliput,* Chapter IV)
Author: Jonathan Swift (1667-1745)
First published: 1726
Type of work: Satirical fiction

Context: Lemuel Gulliver, ship-wrecked off the coast of Lilliput and captured by its tiny inhabitants, is exhibited before the Lilliputians, including their emperor. Instructed in the language, Gulliver is brought to the chief city, Mildendo, and into the court, where he discusses politics with a leading official. He is informed that a controversy over which end of an egg is to be broken has led to the formation of two political parties, the Big-Endians and the Little-Endians, with a result that Lilliput has been at war for thirty-six moons with the neighboring land of Blefescu. The author first recounts the historical episode, and scholars explain the meaning in a footnote:

> . . . It began upon the following occasion. It is allowed on all hands, that the primitive way of breaking eggs before we eat them, was upon the larger end: but his present Majesty's grandfather, while he was a boy, going to eat an egg, and breaking it according to the ancient practice, happened to cut one of his fingers. Whereupon the Emperor his father published an edict, commanding all his subjects, upon great penalties, to break the smaller end of their eggs.[3] . . .

---

[3] The **Big-Endians and Little-Endians** are no doubt the Roman Catholics and Protestants. But here, as elsewhere, the analogy must not be strained too far. The King who cut his finger is Henry VIII, the father of Edward VI.

The bird that flutters least is longest on the wing

Source: THE TASK (Book VI, ll. 930–931)
Author: William Cowper (1731-1800)
First published: 1785
Type of work: Meditative poem in blank verse

Context: This quotation is taken from that section, or book, of *The Task* entitled "The Winter Walk at Noon." The poet intersperses meditations on many topics with descriptions of the English countryside during a winter noon when snow blankets all the earth, except the places beneath the forest trees. Toward the end of this book, which is the last section of the poem, he meditates upon the end of creation and invokes the aid of God, Who will bring the end and the restoration of man. The poet, having been forced out of an active life by severe mental illness, seeks to vindicate the life, in spiritual terms, of the human being who has lived a life of retirement from the usual activities and pace of the world. He notes that the world scorns the pleasures of the retired person, as he overlooks the world's pleasures for what is beyond. The poet then explains why the spiritual man is not interested in the usual activities of this world.

> He seeks not hers, for he has proved them vain.
> He cannot skim the ground like summer birds
> Pursuing gilded flies, and such he deems
> Her honours, her emoluments, her joys;
> Therefore in contemplation is his bliss,
> Whose pow'r is such, that whom she lifts from earth
> She makes familiar with a heav'n unseen,
> And shows him glories yet to be reveal'd.
> Not slothful he, though seeming unemploy'd,
> And censured oft as useless. Stillest streams
> Oft water fairest meadows; and **the bird**
> **That flutters least is longest on the wing.**
> Ask him, indeed, what trophies he has raised,
> Or what achievements of immortal fame
> He purposes, and he shall answer—None.
> His warfare is within.

A bitter heart, that bides its time and bites

Source: CALIBAN UPON SETEBOS (Line 167)
Author: Robert Browning (1812-1889)
First published: 1864
Type of work: Dramatic monologue

Context: This poem, although subtitled "Natural Theology in the Island," is an attack upon such deterministic religious sects as Calvinism, which picture a God who saves or damns human beings, punishes or rewards them, wholly according to whim. The speaker of the poem is Caliban, the brutish monster-slave of Prospero in Shakespeare's *Tempest*. Caliban speculates upon his god, Setebos, who may be all-powerful or who may be under another god called the Quiet. Setebos is strong but devoid of any feelings of affection for the thing that he has created, man, although he may feel envy and spite. He is all alone in the cold, since to have made a mate would have been like making himself. Caliban says that Setebos is like what he himself would be if he could give life to creatures he might make of clay. He might make a bird that would break its leg; when the poor creature cried out in pain, Caliban might pluck off its remaining leg, or, on the other hand, he might give it two more legs. Whichever he did, he would feel pleasure at the display of his power. As a line of crabs marched past him, he might smash one now and then— or give one a special reward. And again the whimsical display of power would be pleasing. Setebos has made things that are better than he is, but they must submit to his power. Setebos, however, looks up to the Quiet and envies it; then he looks down and makes imitations of a world and creatures that he can never reach. It is as though he had captured a sea beast which he had penned, blinded and with the webs of its feet split, in a pool. The creature, powerless as it is, yet has bitterness in its mind and bites at its master.

And hath an ounce sleeker than youngling mole,
A four-legged serpent he makes cower and couch,
Now snarl, now hold its breath and mind his eye,
And saith she is Miranda and my wife:
'Keeps for his Ariel a tall pouch-bill crane
He bids go wade for fish and straight disgorge;
Also a sea-beast, lumpish, which he snared,
Blinded the eyes of, and brought somewhat tame,
And split its toe-webs, and now pens the drudge
In a hole o' the rock and calls him Caliban;
A bitter heart, that bides its time and bites,
'Plays thus at being Prosper in a way,
Taketh his mirth with make-believes: so He.

The bivouac of the dead

Source: THE BIVOUAC OF THE DEAD (Stanza 1)
Author: Theodore O'Hara (1820-1867)
First published: 1847
Type of work: Ode

Context: Theodore O'Hara was primarily a soldier, exemplifying in his career the colorful reputation of the Irish. He was a Kentuckian by birth and during his checkered lifetime held numerous responsible posts in civilian life. But the world of the military evidently had first call upon him. After receiving his college education he was for a time Professor of Greek; he then practiced law and was later employed by the U.S. Treasury Department. When the Mexican War broke out, he served throughout the campaign and was brevetted for gallantry. After the war he practiced law again in Washington, D.C., but apparently could not settle down to the humdrum routines of peacetime. Becoming interested in the struggles for independence of patriots in other nations, he abandoned his law practice and led a regiment at Cardenas in support of Lopez for the liberation of Cuba. He returned severely wounded from this adventure, and as soon as he had recovered he joined Walker's filibustering expedition. Following this adventure, he resumed a peacetime existence and was connected editorially with several newspapers until the outbreak of the Civil War. During this conflict he served in the Confederate Army, first as Commander of the fort at Mobile Bay and later as Chief of Staff for General Breckenridge. O'Hara's devotion to military life and his understanding of the soldier give his poem "The Bivouac of the Dead" a certain personal quality that lifts it above many sentimental tributes of its time to those killed in the nation's wars. These are men he knew, men who fought beside him and shared the rigors of the campaign. The poem is one which O'Hara read at the dedication of a monument to the soldiers of Kentucky who were killed in the Mexican War; it enjoyed considerable popularity, and lines from it appeared frequently on monuments and gates in the various national cemeteries during the last half of the nineteenth century. The first two stanzas are given below:

The muffled drum's sad roll has beat
   The soldier's last tattoo;
No more on life's parade shall meet
   That brave and fallen few.
On Fame's eternal camping-ground
   Their silent tents are spread,
And glory guards with solemn round
   The bivouac of the dead.

No rumor of the foe's advance
   Now swells upon the wind—
No troubled thought at midnight haunts
   Of loved ones left behind;
No vision of the morrow's strife
   The warrior's dream alarms;
No braying horn or screaming fife
   At dawn shall call to arms.

The blind hysterics of the Celt

Source: IN MEMORIAM (Part CIX, stanza 4)
Author: Alfred, Lord Tennyson (1809-1892)
First published: 1850
Type of work: Elegy

Context: This elegy was written as a monument to Arthur Henry Hallam, a young man of extraordinary promise and an intimate friend of Tennyson's, who died suddenly in Vienna at the age of twenty-two. The poem records the slow, spiritual progress of Tennyson from his initial depth of personal sorrow to the gradual healing of grief through a sense of spiritual contact with Hallam in a wider love of God and humanity. Through intuition rather than reason, Tennyson has achieved a certainty that the spirit exists divorced from the body, that the spirit survives death. In Part CIX, the poet dwells on the completeness of Hallam's character, analyzing the characteristics of this ideal man. Hallam was original, yet critical; logical and forceful in "impassion'd logic;" a lover of good, yet not ascetic; a passionate, yet pure lover. Hallam had:

> A love of freedom rarely felt,
>   Of freedom in her regal seat
>   Of England; not the schoolboy heat,
> **The blind hysterics of the Celt;**
>   • • •
> All these have been, and thee mine eyes
>   Have look'd on: if they look'd in vain,
>   My shame is greater who remain,
> Nor let thy wisdom make me wise.

Bliss was it in that dawn to be alive, but to be young was very Heaven!

Source: THE PRELUDE (Book XI, ll. 108-109)
Author: William Wordsworth (1770-1850)
First published: 1850
Type of work: Autobiographical poem

Context: When still a young man, Wordsworth, like many of the British liberals, believed that the French Revolution marked the inauguration of a new age of political equality and freedom from tyranny; the old ways that had enslaved men were being changed by Reason, and dreams were coming true because people were concentrating on the problem of how to make life on earth pleasant rather than on how to earn an eternal life of joy. After he had grown apart from nature and momentarily accepted the rationalistic doctrine that man could form a perfect society on earth, Wordsworth was blinded to the full implications of the Revolution. In fact, he believed so strongly in the power of Reason that the Reign of Terror and the execution of the royal family came as a disillusioning shock to him and threw him into such a quandary that for a while he could find nothing solid upon which to build his life. The quotation comes from his account of the dreams of his youth before the period of disillusionment began.

Bliss was it in that dawn to be alive,
But to be young was very Heaven! O times,
In which the meagre, stale, forbidding ways
Of custom, law, and statute, took at once
The attraction of a country in romance!
When Reason seemed the most to assert her rights,
When most intent on making of herself
A prime enchantress—to assist the work
Which then was going forward in her name!

Blond beast

Source: A GENEALOGY OF MORALS (First Essay, section 11, as translated by
    William A. Hausemann)
Author: Friedrich Wilhelm Nietzsche (1844-1900)
First published: 1887
Type of work: Philosophy

Context: The influence of Nietzsche upon certain areas of twentieth century thought has been considerable. Although students of his work have divided his development into three periods, his underlying ideas remained much the same and his changes lay in his consideration of them. His third, or ethical, period is usually considered most important; in it he seeks to define the ultimate good. To Nietzsche there are two standards of good and evil, one for the masters and one for the slaves. According to the first standard, whatever expresses the will of the individual or forms a part of him is good; all else is evil. Under the second standard, anything painful is bad and whatever makes life more endurable is good. Western standards are at present those of the slaves; Nietzsche blames this state of affairs on a plot by the Jews. Self-assertion is his moral ideal: the will to power lies at the root of all things, and power is the sole good which can be gained. In connection with this idea may be mentioned the concept most often associated with him—the doctrine of the superman. Nietzsche believed that man will evolve into a higher species. He also believed in External Recurrence, an old theory that history is a great cycle and repeats itself in every detail. To it he added the idea that life is good because of suffering, not in spite of it. He believed the ultimate good in art is a mixture of dream and intoxication evoking an underlying truth, a goal most nearly achieved in Wagnerian opera. A number of his ideas were incorporated into the ideology of Adolf Hitler and Nazi Germany. Nietzsche's writing style is somewhat incoherent; much of his life was spent in a struggle against the insanity which destroyed his mind in 1889. In the following selection Nietzsche, who has been discussing the cramped and cowardly outlook of the servile mentality, contrasts with it his ideal man—the lusty and amoral young savage:

101

. . . those very men, who by manners, reverence, usage, gratitude, and still more by mutual superintendence, by jealousy *inter pares* are rigorously held within bounds, and who, on the other hand, in their conduct among one another prove themselves so inventive in regardfulness, self-restraint, delicacy, faith, pride and friendship,—these same men are towards that which is without, which to them is foreign, a foreign land, not much better than so many disengaged beasts of prey. Here they enjoy liberty from all social restraint; the wilderness must compensate them for the tension produced by a long incarceration and impalement in the "peace" of society; they step *back* into the innocence of the conscience of the beast of prey, as exultant monsters, which, perhaps, walk away from an abominable sequence of murder, burning down, violation, torture, with such wantonness and equanimity, as if merely some student-trick had been accomplished; with the conviction, that now for a long time again the poets will have something to celebrate and sing of. At the ground of all these noble races, the beast of prey, the splendid, **blond beast,** lustfully roving in search of spoils and victory, cannot be mistaken. An outlet is necessary from time to time for this hidden ground; the animal must come out again, must go back into wilderness: Roman, Arabian, Germanic, Japanese nobility, Homeric heroes, Scandinavian vikings—in this need they all are *one*. It is the noble races, that left the concept "barbarian" on every trace, wherever they passed; even in their highest civilisation the consciousness of this fact is visible and even a certain pride in it. . . .

The blood of the martyrs is the seed of the Church

Source: APOLOGETICUS (50)
Author: Tertullian (c.155-c.220)
First transcribed: c.197
Type of work: Religious philosophy

Context: Educated in his native Carthage and in Rome in law and in rhetoric, Tertullian was well prepared for the position he holds as ablest of the early defenders of the Christian faith. Among his writings are *De Carne Christi,* a rebuttal to Marcion and other heretics, and a number of treatises on morality and the discipline of the Church. His *Apologeticus* points out the guilt of many non-Christians of the very acts of immorality for which Christians are falsely accused and for which they suffer martyrdom. Ironically *"the blood of the martyrs is the seed of the Church,"* contends Tertullian, for Christian believers multiply with each incidence of martyrdom:

. . . Nor does your cruelty, however exquisite, avail you; it is rather a temptation to us. The oftener we are mown down by you, the more in number we grow; **the blood of Christians is seed.** Many

102

of your writers exhort to the courageous bearing of pain and
death, as Cicero in the *Tusculans,* as Seneca in his *Chances,* as
Diogenes, Pyrrhus, Callinicus. And yet their words do not find so
many disciples as Christians do, teachers not by words, but by
their deeds. . . .

Blood will have blood

Source: MACBETH (Act III, sc. iv, l. 122)
Author: William Shakespeare (1564-1616)
First published: 1623
Type of work: Dramatic tragedy

Context: Macbeth orders Banquo and his son, Fleance, murdered the night of his feast. The murderers kill Banquo, but Fleance escapes. One of the murderers comes to tell Macbeth what has happened just as the celebration is beginning. Macbeth, knowing full well Banquo is dead, wishes for his presence and is confronted by his wounded and gory ghost sitting in the place of honor. Shocked almost into madness, Macbeth babbles of blood and murders. Lady Macbeth hastily excuses him on grounds of an old infirmity, but when the ghost returns a second time, Macbeth is completely unnerved. Lady Macbeth asks the guests to leave immediately. Macbeth is sure the ghost is a horrible omen of things to come.

LADY MACBETH
I pray you speak not; he grows worse and worse.
Question enrages him. At once, good night.
. . .

MACBETH
It will have blood, they say; **blood will have blood.**
Stones have been known to move, and trees to speak.
Augurs and understood relations have
By maggot-pies and choughs and rooks brought forth
The secret'st man of blood. What is the night?

Blow winds, and crack your cheeks

Source: KING LEAR (Act III, sc. ii, l. 1)
Author: William Shakespeare (1564-1616)
First published: 1608
Type of work: Dramatic tragedy

Context: King Lear, old and foolish, has attempted to rid himself of the responsibilities of kingship by dividing his realm among his three daughters on the condition that each daughter declare her love for him. When the youngest daughter, Cordelia, refuses to indulge in the effusive love of her sisters, she is disinherited. Lear, however, soon discovers the seeming love of Goneril and Regan, his oldest daughters, and when Regan puts Kent, the king's courtier, into stocks and Goneril refuses to take the part of the aged monarch, he calls his daughters "unnatural hags" and rushes into the stormy night. On the heath with his faithful fool, he cries out against the elements:

LEAR

Blow winds, and crack your cheeks. Rage, blow,
You cataracts, and hurricanoes, spout
Till you have drenched our steeples, drowned the cocks.
You sulphurous and thought-executing fires,
Vaunt-couriers of oak-cleaving thunderbolts,
Singe my white head. And thou all-shaking thunder,
Strike flat the thick rotundity o' th' world,
Crack nature's moulds, all germens spill at once,
That makes ingrateful man.

The bonded warehouse of my knowledge

Source: HANDLEY CROSS (Chapter 27, 1843 edition; Chapter 32, 1854 edition)
Author: Robert Smith Surtees (1803-1864)
First published: 1843
Type of work: Novel

Context: Robert Surtees, as editor of *The New Sporting Magazine,* established a place in literature for himself with a long series of humorous sketches which he contributed to its pages. The principal character which he developed as humorist and chronicler of the hunting field is that of John Jorrocks, a wholesale grocer in London whose greatest ambition is to become a Master of Foxhounds. These sketches were first collected in book form in *Jorrocks' Jaunts and Jollities* (1838); another collection entitled *Handley Cross* was published in 1843. A second edition of *Handley Cross,* greatly enlarged with additional characters and episodes, appeared in 1854. The sleepy little village of Handley Cross, located in the Vale of Sheepwash, has experienced a sudden burst of prosperity and become a flourishing community. Now approaching urban status, it desires more formality in its social institutions. The hunt is one of these. Jorrocks has become widely known by this time because of his frequent country excursions, during which he combines business with pleasure by taking orders for groceries while riding with the huntsmen. This is the reason the Committee of Management, seeking a likely candidate for Master of the Handley Cross Hunt, sends its invitation to Jorrocks. His dreams come true, Jorrocks arrives in a state of great agitation; he delivers an impassioned acceptance speech to the townspeople and nearly breaks down in the middle of it. He describes the ideal M.F.H., and assures his listeners he is prepared to meet those qualifications; furthermore, he intends to deliver a series of "lectors" on various matters pertaining to the hunt. It is soon evident that whenever Jorrocks allows himself to dwell upon the joys of the chase, his emotions get the best of him. In his first lecture, he instructs novices in the art of acquiring a horse; in the second, he takes up another important matter:

"Frinds and fellow-countrymen! Lend me your ears. That's to say, listen to wot I'm a goin' to say to you. This night I shall enlighten you on the all-important ceremony of takin' the field." (Loud applause.)

"TAKIN' THE FIELD!" repeated he, throwing out his arms, and casting his eyes up at the elegant looping of his canopy. "TAKIN' THE FIELD! glorious sound! wot words can convey anything 'alf so delightful?

"In my mind's eye I see the 'ounds in all their glossy pride a trottin' around Arterxerxes, who stamps and whinnies with delight at their company. There's old Pristess with her speckled sides, lookin' as wise as a Christian, and Trusty, and Tuneable, and Warrior, and Wagrant, and Workman, and Wengence, and all the glorious comrades o' the chase.

"But to the pint. Ingenious youth, having got his 'oss, and learned to tackle him, let me now, from **the bonded warehouse of my knowledge,** prepare him for the all-glorious ceremony of the 'unt.

"How warious are the motives," continued Mr. Jorrocks, looking thoughtfully, "that draw men to the kiver side. Some come to see, others to be seen; some for the ride out, others for the ride 'ome; some for happetites, some for 'ealth, some to get away from their wives, and a few to 'unt. Ah! give me the few. . . ."

The bone of manhood

Source: SPEECH ON MOVING HIS RESOLUTIONS FOR RECONCILIATION WITH THE COLONIES
Author: Edmund Burke (1729-1797)
First published: 1775
Type of work: Political speech

Context: As a member of Parliament, Burke defied George III, who was attempting to overthrow established political traditions and centralize governmental power, and he strongly urged that Parliament should not suppress the American Colonies, citing the acts of redress for both Ireland and Wales as precedent. Not only, he argued, would justice and right be served by a reconciliation between the colonies and the mother country, but such action would also be profitable for England as a result of the many imports, exports, and industries of the colonies, especially their whaling and fishing activities:

> . . . No sea but what is vexed by their fisheries. No climate that is not witness to their toils. Neither the perseverance of Holland, nor the activity of France, nor the dexterous and firm sagacity of English enterprise, ever carried this most perilous mode of hard industry to the extent to which it has been pushed by this recent people; a people who are still, as it were, but in the gristle, and not yet hardened into **the bone of manhood.** When I contemplate these things; when I know that the colonies in general owe little or nothing to any care of ours, and that they are not squeezed into this happy form by the constraints of watchful and suspicious government, but that, through a wise and salutary neglect, a generous nature has been suffered to take her own way to perfection; . . . when I see how profitable they have been to us, I feel all the pride of power sink, and all presumption in the wisdom of human contrivances melt and die away within me. My rigour relents. I pardon something to the spirit of liberty.

A book in breeches

Source: A MEMOIR OF THE REVEREND SYDNEY SMITH BY HIS DAUGHTER LADY HOLLAND (Chapter 11)
Author: Sydney Smith (1771-1845)
First published: 1855
Type of work: Biographical memoir

Context: A considerable part of Saba, Lady Holland's, biography of her father, the Reverend Sydney Smith, is devoted to quotations from his general conversation, in Combe Florey where he preached. Begun in 1843, the biography was not published until ten years after his death. Most of his quips and comments appear in unconnected paragraphs. One of the longest paragraphs reports his comment about Thomas Babington Macaulay (1800–1859). Many people have been called "a walking encyclopedia." Here is a more original description of a well-informed man, "like a book in breeches." Macaulay read widely and voraciously, and many have testified to his retentive memory.

> Some one speaking of Macaulay: "Yes, I take great credit to myself; I always prophesied his greatness from the first moment I saw him, then a very young and unknown man, on the Northern Circuit. There are no limits to his knowledge, on small subjects as well as on great; he is like **a book in breeches.** . . . Yes, I agree, he is certainly more agreeable since his return from India. His en-

emies might perhaps have said before (though I never did so) that he talked rather too much; but now he has occasional flashes of silence that make his conversation perfectly delightful. . . ."

Books are not seldom talismans and spells

Source: THE TASK (Book VI, l. 98)
Author: William Cowper (1731-1800)
First published: 1785
Type of work: Meditative poem in blank verse

Context: This quotation is from the sixth book, or section, of the poem, entitled "The Winter Walk at Noon." As in the other books of the poem, Cowper here mingles meditations on many subjects with descriptions of nature. In this book, as in the one preceding, the descriptions are of the English countryside in the wintertime. One also finds in this section the poet's thoughts on a wide variety of subjects: bells ringing in the distance, the origin of cruelty to animals, the difference between lawful and unlawful destruction of animals, man's extravagant praise of himself, and, among other topics, the effect the spring season has upon the shrubbery. The particular quotation is taken from the section containing Cowper's commentary on meditation, in which he opines that meditation is better for man than the study of books. Walking in the silent woods of winter, the poet says, "Meditation here may think down hours to moments." He says also that he believes the heart must give lessons to the head, that knowledge and wisdom often have little or nothing in common. He goes on to compare knowledge and wisdom:

> Knowledge dwells
> In heads replete with thoughts of other men;
> Wisdom in minds attentive to their own.
> Knowledge, a rude unprofitable mass,
> The mere materials with which wisdom builds,
> Till smooth'd and squared and fitted to its place,
> Does but encumber whom it seems t'enrich.
> Knowledge is proud that he has learn'd so much;
> Wisdom is humble that he knows no more.
> **Books are not seldom talismans and spells**
> By which the magic art of shrewder wits
> Holds an unthinking multitude enthrall'd.

Books are the legacies that a great genius leaves to mankind

Source: THE SPECTATOR (Number 166)
Author: Joseph Addison (1672-1719)
First published: September 10, 1711
Type of work: Essay

Context: The Spectator, a periodical issued by Joseph Addison and his friend and classmate Richard Steele, amused and enlightened the English public by telling, among other matters, of the conversation of a small club meeting at a coffee house. The members of the club included a country gentleman, Sir Roger de Coverley, the author, known as Mr. Spectator, and several other members representative of the general populace. In issue Number 166, Addison discusses the concept of Aristotle that the world is a transcript of the mind of the first being and that the ideas of men are transcripts of the world. Following this logic, says Addison, books are the legacies left by geniuses to mankind:

> There is no other method of fixing those thoughts which arise and disappear in the mind of man, and transmitting them to the last periods of time; no other method of giving a permanency to our ideas, and preserving the knowledge of any particular person, when his body is mixed with the common mass of matter, and his soul retired into the world of spirits. **Books are the legacies that a great genius leaves to mankind,** which are delivered down from generation to generation, as presents to the posterity of those who are yet unborn.

Books, clad in black and red

Source: THE CANTERBURY TALES (Prologue, l. 294)
Author: Geoffrey Chaucer (1343?-1400)
First transcribed: c. 1387-1392
Type of work: Collection of tales

Context: Chaucer, to bind together his collection of tales, establishes the framework of a group of pilgrims traveling from the Tabard Inn in Southwark to the shrine of Thomas à Becket at Canterbury and telling tales to make the trip less tiresome. In the Prologue, the pilgrims are introduced and described in sharp detail. Among the most memorable of the travelers is a poor clerk, or student, who would choose from the world's riches a mere collection of books.

> A CLERK ther was of Oxenford also,
> That unto logyk hadde longe ygo.
> As leene was his hors as is a rake,
> And he nas nat right fat, I undertake,
> But looked holwe, and therto sobrely.
> Ful thredbare was his overeste courtepy;
> For he hadde geten hym yet no benefice,
> Ne was so worldly for to have office.
> For hym was levere have at his beddes heed
> Twenty **bookes, clad in blak or reed,**

Of Aristotle and his philosophie,
Than robes riche, or fithele, or gay sautrie.

Boston State House is the hub of the solar system

Source: THE AUTOCRAT OF THE BREAKFAST-TABLE (Chapter 6)
Author: Oliver Wendell Holmes (1809-1894)
First published: 1858
Type of work: Essay

Context: Chapter Six of *The Autocrat of the Breakfast Table* opens with a discussion of famous sayings by men of Boston, starting with Benjamin Franklin's comment, "He that has once done you a kindness will be more ready to do you another than he whom you yourself have obliged." This is followed by a comment attributed to the Autocrat's friend, the Historian, "Give us the luxuries of life, and we will dispense with its necessaries." The Autocrat adds a third, "Good Americans, when they die, go to Paris." A stranger at the boarding-house table, a young "jaunty-looking" chap, says he has heard a fourth saying, about Boston and its views.

Under some prodding from the other guests, the young man gives the quotation above. It is followed by a discussion of the parochialism that one finds in every city. The people of Boston, suggests the Autocrat, are no different in their attitudes toward their native city from those of other towns, large or small. He goes on to comment, "Boston is just like the other places of its size;—only, perhaps, considering its excellent fish-market, paid fire-department, superior monthly publications, and correct habit of spelling the English language, it has some right to look down on the mob of cities."

A jaunty-looking person, who had come in with the young fellow they call John,—evidently a stranger,—said there was one more wise man's sayings that he had heard; it was about our place, but he didn't know who said it.—A civil curiosity was manifested by the company to hear the fourth wise saying. I heard him distinctly whispering to the young fellow who brought him to dinner, *Shall I tell it?* To which the answer was, *Go ahead!*—Well,—he said,—this was what I heard:—

"**Boston State-House is the hub of the solar system.** You couldn't pry that out of a Boston man, if you had the tire of all creation straightened out for a crowbar."

Bottled lightning

Source: NICHOLAS NICKLEBY (Chapter 49)
Author: Charles Dickens (1812-1870)
First published: 1838-1839
Type of work: Novel

Context: After the great success of *Pickwick Papers* and *Oliver Twist* had established his reputation, Dickens looked around for a new subject to which he could direct his humanitarian and reforming zeal. As a child, he had heard of the notorious "Yorkshire schools," the name given to a type of school, many of them located in that county, which, while masquerading as educational institutions, were in reality only places to which unwanted children could be sent to be kept out of the way. They were run by ignorant and often brutal men, and the ill-treatment to which the helpless boys were subjected had become a byword. Dickens traveled to Yorkshire under an assumed name and with the pretext of being a parent in search of such a school. He soon assembled his material and created the figure of Wackford Squeers, headmaster of Dotheboys Hall, one of his most loathsome scoundrels. To develop the complicated and melodramatic type of plot at which he excelled, Dickens interwove the story of Squeers and his school with that of the usurer Ralph Nickleby, uncle of the naïve hero of the novel. Around the main characters Dickens grouped a supporting cast of the humorous and eccentric minor figures that his inexhaustible imagination produced. One of these is Mrs. Nickleby, the verbose, rattle-brained, and totally impractical mother of the hero. In one of the comic side episodes of the story, Mrs. Nickleby and her daughter Kate are entertaining some callers, when their attention is attracted by strange noises from the next room. The group rushes to investigate and discovers that a man is climbing down the chimney; his feet and legs are already visible. When he is pulled out, he is revealed as "the gentleman in small-clothes" (that is, tightly-fitting knee breeches), a harmless lunatic living in the next house who fancies himself in love with Mrs. Nickleby. His first demand, after a rambling speech by that lady, in which she expresses her inability to accept his attentions, has given us a phrase still applied to liquor of unusual strength:

. . . He did not appear to take the smallest notice of what Mrs. Nickleby said, but when she ceased to speak he honoured her with a long stare, and inquired if she had quite finished.

"I have nothing more to say," replied that lady modestly. "I really cannot say anything more."

"Very good," said the old gentleman, raising his voice, "then bring in the **bottled lightning,** a clean tumbler, and a corkscrew."

Nobody executing this order, the old gentleman, after a short pause, raised his voice again and demanded a thunder sandwich. This article not being forthcoming either, he requested to be served with a fricassee of boot-tops and goldfish sauce, . . .

Bowels of compassion

Source: I JOHN 3:17
Author: Unknown (traditionally John the Apostle)
First transcribed: c.95-100
Type of work: Pastoral epistle

Context: The author of this epistle was a man of great authority in early Church matters, and it is probable that he was also the author of the fourth Gospel. It is not known with certainty that he was John the Apostle; but if not, he was apparently either an eyewitness to much of Jesus' ministry or knew those who were. The present epistle forms part of a battle of the early Church to preserve its identity. Gnosticism was a growing religious movement of the time which sought to combine all religions and to embrace all religious systems and philosophies under a universal method. There were some able thinkers connected with it, and it offered something of a synthesis, capable of endless adaptation, and having some philosophical basis. It offered a kind of pantheism in which the various gods were represented by spiritual essences, and all manner of ceremonies were connected with it. Being more a method or system than a result, it could include both puritanical fanatics and debased libertines. There were early Christians who wished for such a tolerant arrangement; but John and his contemporaries saw a very real danger in it. If Christianity should be absorbed into such a system, its entire meaning and identity would cease to be important and would soon be destroyed. Too, there were opponents of Christianity who were promoting the Gnostic adoption of Christianity, probably for that very reason. This was a time when sects were proliferating, and most of the Gnostic-Christian groups had already withdrawn from the parent Church. John's epistle represents an effort on his part to strengthen those who remain faithful to it; he sets forth Christian principles simply and clearly for them, that they may not be tempted to abandon the Church in favor of a debased substitute.

Whosoever is born of God doth not commit sin; for his seed remaineth in him: and he cannot sin, because he is born of God.

In this the children of God are manifest, and the children of the devil: whosoever doeth not righteousness is not of God, neither he that loveth not his brother.

For this is the message that ye heard from the beginning, that we should love one another.

Not as Cain, who was of that wicked one, and slew his brother. And wherefore slew he him? Because his own works were evil, and his brother's righteous.

Marvel not, my brethren, if the world hate you.

We know that we have passed from death unto life, because we love the brethren. He that loveth not his brother abideth in death.

Whosoever hateth his brother is a murderer: and ye know that no murderer hath eternal life abiding in him.

Hereby perceive we the love of God, because he laid down his life for us: and we ought to lay down our lives for the brethren.

But whoso hath this world's good, and seeth his brother have need, and shutteth up his **bowels of compassion** from him, how dwelleth the love of God in him?

My little children, let us not love in word, neither in tongue; but in deed and in truth.

111

The bravest are the tenderest, the loving are the daring

Source: A SONG OF THE CAMP (Stanza 11)
Author: Bayard Taylor (1825-1878)
First published: 1860
Type of work: Lyric poem

Context: A Song of the Camp relates an incident in the Crimean War. The English, Irish, and Scottish troops have temporarily ceased from bombarding the enemy forts when a guardsman, announcing that they are to storm the forts tomorrow, calls for a song. The songs the soldiers sing are of love, not of Britain's glory. All sing "Annie Laurie," but each soldier thinks of a different name as he sings. Voice after voice catches up the song, until it rises like an anthem, and many a soldier has the powder stains washed off his face by tears of honest emotion. The next day the battle resumes:

> Beyond the darkening ocean burned
>   The bloody sunset's embers,
> While the Crimean valleys learned
>   How English love remembers.

> And once again a fire of hell
>   Rained on the Russian quarters,
> With scream of shot, and burst of shell,
>   And bellowing of the mortars!

> And Irish Nora's eyes are dim
>   For a singer, dumb and gory;
> And English Mary mourns for him
>   Who sang of "Annie Laurie."

> Sleep, soldiers! still in honored rest
>   Your truth and valor wearing:
> **The bravest are the tenderest,—**
> **The loving are the daring.**

Brazil, where the nuts come from

Source: CHARLEY'S AUNT (Act I)
Author: Brandon Thomas (1849-1914)
First published: 1892
Type of work: Dramatic comedy

Context: Brandon Thomas, British dramatist, is best remembered today for his comedy "Charley's Aunt;" it was tremendously popular and its initial run lasted four years. It is still frequently revived, and over the past three-quarters of a century has moved millions to tears of laughter. Jack Chesney and Charles Wykeham, undergraduates at Oxford, are both in love—Jack with Kitty Verdun and Charles with Amy Spettigue. Neither has found himself able to declare the fact. Charley's aunt, Donna Lucia d'Alvadorez, is coming to pay him a visit. She is from Brazil, is wealthy and is a widow; but Charley has never seen her and knows nothing about her beyond these basic facts. Jack's father drops by to leave his son an allowance check, and while there informs Jack that their fortune is in difficulties; Jack tells him about the impending visit of Charley's aunt and suggests that his father try to win her hand. The boys invite Kitty and Amy to their lodgings for luncheon, since all will be chaperoned by the aunt— but a message arrives from that lady, saying she will be delayed. Jack and Charley are determined to have their luncheon anyway, but must not compromise the girls. A solution to this dilemma occurs in the form of a fellow undergraduate, Lord Fancourt Babberley, who is to impersonate an old lady in some amateur theatricals. The boys force him into his costume and pass him off as Charley's aunt. Kitty and Amy make a great fuss over him when they arrive, to his obvious delight. Presently Amy's uncle appears, bent on breaking up the party; Lord Fancourt scolds him and sends him on his way, unaware that both Spettigue and Jack's father will be competing for Charley's Aunt's vast fortune and her hand in marriage. As Spettigue leaves, Lord Fancourt shies a book at him and knocks off his hat. Spettigue exits, muttering to himself. As soon as he is gone, Jack and Charley and the two girls come back into the room.

KITTY [*to* LORD FANCOURT.]
It was sweet of you!

AMY
You darling!
[*One on each side of* LORD FANCOURT, *they kiss him.*]

CHARLEY
Look at him, Jack!

JACK [*to* CHARLEY.]
I'll punch his head if he does it again!
Here's my father!

JACK [*to* LORD FANCOURT.]
Donna Lucia!
[*Aside.*] Take care, here's my father.

LORD FANCOURT
Look here, am I any relation to him?

113

JACK

No; You're *Charley's* Aunt, from **Brazil.**

LORD FANCOURT

Brazil! Where's that?

JACK

You know—er—**where the nuts come from.**

The bread of life

Source: JOHN 6:35
Author: Unknown (traditionally John the Apostle)
First transcribed: By 130
Type of work: Gospel

Context: In Chapter 6 of his Gospel, John describes the miracle of the loaves and fishes, in which Jesus miraculously feeds an audience of five thousand persons with five barley loaves and two small fish. He gives these to his disciples to distribute among the crowd, and after everyone is fed all he can eat there are twelve baskets of food left over. According to Matthew, this incident occurs while Jesus is sorrowing for the brutal execution of John the Baptist; but the writer of this Gospel does not connect the two. Both Gospels record that Jesus afterward sends the disciples ahead by ship and asks the multitudes to return to their homes; and thus excusing Himself, He ascends into a mountain to pray. The implication in Matthew is that He wishes to be alone because of His grief concerning the Baptist; according to John, Jesus retires to the mountain to pray for another reason: the people wish to make Him king. An excellent case could be made that the two accounts do not conflict with each other, and that if the two were combined a fuller and probably more accurate rendering of the event would result. Such an assumption does much to emphasize those trials of the spirit that Jesus was continually beset with. It is the belief of some scholars that John's intention was to supplement the other Gospels with information and events which they do not include. His description of the miracle which followed that of the loaves and fishes is in substantial agreement with Matthew: after Jesus' disciples have embarked, they are caught in a storm, and Jesus walks to them across the water. He reassures them, the storm dies, and they reach port safely. John does not mention Peter's test of faith, when he tried to walk on the water and partially succeeded. John relates that the multitude, on the following day, goes in search of Jesus; and when they find Him He obliges them with a sermon.

Jesus answered them and said, Verily, verily, I say unto you, Ye seek me, not because ye saw the miracles, but because ye did eat of the loaves and were filled.

114

Labour not for the meat which perisheth, but for that meat which endureth unto everlasting life, which the Son of man shall give unto you: for him hath God the Father sealed.

Then said they unto him, What shall we do, that we might work the works of God?

Jesus answered and said unto them, This is the work of God, that ye believe on him whom he hath sent.

They said therefore unto him, What sign shewest thou then, that we may see, and believe thee? what dost thou work?

Our fathers did eat manna in the desert; as it is written, He gave them bread from heaven to eat.

Then Jesus said unto them, Verily, verily, I say unto you, Moses gave you not that bread from heaven; but my Father giveth you the true bread from heaven.

For the bread of God is he which cometh down from heaven, and giveth life unto the world.

Then said they unto him, Lord, evermore give us this bread.

And Jesus said unto them, I am **the bread of life:** he that cometh to me shall never hunger; and he that believeth on me shall never thirst.

Bred en bawn in a brier patch

Source: HOW MR. RABBIT WAS TOO SHARP FOR MR. FOX
Author: Joel Chandler Harris (1848-1908)
First published: 1880 in *Uncle Remus: His Songs and His Sayings*
Type of work: Short story

Context: The feud between Brer (Brother) Fox and Brer Rabbit is the origin of a number of tales, supposedly told by old Uncle Remus, on a plantation in middle Georgia. Their author, always known by his full name, Joel Chandler Harris, wrote them for *The Atlanta Constitution,* on which he advanced from reporter to editor between 1876 and 1900. In 1880 he gathered 34 of his animal fables into *Uncle Remus, His Songs and His Sayings.* The best known story of them begins in Chapter 2, "The Wonderful Tar-Baby Story," and continues in Chapter 4, "How Mr. Rabbit Was Too Sharp for Mr. Fox." To capture his annoying enemy, Brer Rabbit, Brer Fox mixes tar with "turkentine," and models a Tar-Baby. Along comes the Rabbit. Angry because the creature will not answer his greeting, the Rabbit punches its head, and his fist sticks in the sticky mess. In a second attempt to punch it, the Rabbit's other fist sticks tight. So do his feet, when he tries to kick the Tar-Baby. Now he cannot move. At this point, Uncle Remus interrupts the story. He looks at the little boy and sees that "Old Man Nod wuz ridin' on his eyelids." In Chapter 4, he finishes the tale. To all the cruel threats made by Brer Fox about what he is going to do with his victim, Brer Rabbit has only one reply: "I don't keer what you do wid me, Brer Fox, so you don't fling me in dat brier-patch." Deciding to punish the Rabbit in the way he feared most, Brer Fox:

> cotch 'im by de behinn legs en slung 'im right in de middle er de brier-patch . . . Brer Fox sorter hang 'roun' fer ter see w'at wuz gwine ter happen. Bimeby he hear somebody call 'im, en way up de hill he see Brer Rabbit settin' cross-legged on a chinkapin log koamin' de pitch out'n his ha'r wid a chip. Den Brer Fox know dat he been swop off mighty bad. Brer Rabbit wuz bleedzd fer ter fling back some er his sass, en he holler out:
> **"Bred en bawn in a brier-patch,** Brer Fox!" . . . en wid dat he skip out des ez lively ez a cricket in de embers.

Bright Apollo's lute, strung with his hair

Source: LOVE'S LABOUR'S LOST (Act IV, sc. iii, l. 343)
Author: William Shakespeare (1564-1616)
First published: 1598
Type of work: Dramatic comedy

Context: The Court of Navarre shall become "a little Academe" pledge King Ferdinand and his lords, Berowne, Longaville, and Dumaine, as they vow for three years to forsake women, to fast, and to study. The arrival of the Princess of France and three attractive attendants on a diplomatic mission upsets the academicians, who fall in love with the ladies, forsake their former vows, and pledge themselves to pursue love and happiness. Love, says Berowne, which enhances the senses, is "as sweet and musical" as the golden lyre of Apollo, a favorite god of the Greeks associated with light, truth, and beauty:

BEROWNE
· · ·
Love's feeling is more soft and sensible
Than are the tender horns of cockled snails.
Love's tongue proves dainty Bacchus gross in taste.
For valour, is not Love a Hercules,
Still climbing trees in the Hesperides?
Subtle as Sphinx, as sweet and musical
As **bright Apollo's lute, strung with his hair.**
And when Love speaks, the voice of all the gods
Make heaven drowsy with the harmony.
Never durst poet touch a pen to write
Until his ink were tempered with Love's sighs.
O then his lines would ravish savage ears
And plant in tyrants mild humility.
· · ·

116

The bright face of danger

Source: ACROSS THE PLAINS, WITH OTHER MEMORIES AND ESSAYS ("The Lantern-Bearers," Part IV)
Author: Robert Louis Stevenson (1850-1894)
First published: 1892
Type of work: Literary essay

Context: In his essay *The Lantern-Bearers,* Stevenson investigates the poetic impulse which he feels to be universal in man. Painting a vivid word picture of his youth in a sea-coast village, he describes a local custom among the boys: in autumn they bought tin bull's-eye lanterns of the type once worn by policemen. These had a shutter which cut off the dim light they produced and were called dark-lanterns. They were sometimes used also by burglars, but the boys were imitating neither. Each wearing his lantern concealed under his top-coat, the boys would sally forth and foregather in the early darkness to talk of the things they felt at their age to be serious. "But the talk, at any rate," says Stevenson, "was but a condiment; and these gatherings themselves only accidents in the career of the lantern-bearer. The essence of this bliss was to walk by yourself in the black night; the slide shut, the top-coat buttoned; not a ray escaping, whether to conduct your footsteps or to make your glory public . . . and to exult and sing over the knowledge."

It is said that a poet has died young in the breast of the most stolid. It may be contended, rather, that this (somewhat minor) bard in almost every case survives, and is the spice of life to his possessor. Justice is not done to the versatility and the unplumbed childishness of man's imagination. His life from without may seem but a rude mound of mud; there will be some golden chamber at the heart of it, in which he dwells delighted; and for as dark as his pathway seems to the observer, he will have some kind of a bull's-eye at his belt. . . .

The average man . . . is just like you and me, or he would not be average . . . this harping on life's dulness and meanness is a loud profession of incompetence; it is one of two things: the cry of the blind eye, *I cannot see,* or the complaint of the dumb tongue, *I cannot utter.* To draw a life without delights is to prove I have not realised it. . . .

For to miss the joy is to miss all. In the joy of the actors lies the sense of any action. That is the explanation, that the excuse. To one who has not the secret of the lanterns, the scene . . . is meaningless. And hence the haunting and truly spectral unreality of realistic books . . . in each, life falls dead like dough . . . ; each is true, each inconceivable; for no man lives in the external truth, among salts and acids, but in the warm, phantasmagoric chamber of his brain. . . .

In nobler books we are moved with something like the emotions of life. . . . These are notes that please the great heart of man.

117

Not only love, and the fields, and **the bright face of danger,** but sacrifice and death and unmerited suffering humbly supported, touch in us the vein of the poetic. We love to think of them, we long to try them, we are humbly hopeful that we may prove heroes also.

A bright particular star

Source: ALL'S WELL THAT ENDS WELL (Act I, sc. i, l. 97)
Author: William Shakespeare (1564-1616)
First published: 1623
Type of work: Dramatic comedy

Context: Helena, daughter of the late physician of great renown Gerard de Narbon, has been taken into the household of the Countess of Rousillon, where she is loved and treated as a daughter. As the play begins, Bertram, the Countess' son, is commanded to attend the king at his court and takes sorrowful leave of his mother and the strangely reticent Helena. Upon Bertram's departure, Helena in soliloquy pours out her secret love for him and thus explains her melancholy silence. Not of noble birth, she has held her love within her heart alone rather than embarrass the Countess, for whom she has great affection. Later in the act, the Countess will discover Helena's secret, encouraging her to take active pursuit by traveling to the king's court in order to be near Bertram and in order to attempt to cure the king of a fistula by a rare prescription which her father has left her. In this present soliloquy, however, she assumes her love to be futile and foolish; her love for a star in the heavens far above would be just as hopeless. As long as Bertram was physically present, she could observe him every hour, but now in his absence the pangs of undeclared love grow unbearable:

> . . . My imagination
> Carries no favour in't but Bertram's.
> I am undone, There is no living, none,
> If Bertram be away. 'Twere all one
> That I should love **a bright particular star,**
> And think to wed it, he is so above me.
> In his bright radiance and collateral light
> Must I be comforted, not in his sphere.
> The ambition in my love thus plagues itself;
> The hind that would be mated by the lion
> Must die for love. 'Twas pretty, though a plague,
> To see him every hour, to sit and draw
> His arched brows, his hawking eye, his curls,
> In our heart's table: heart too capable
> Of every line and trick of his sweet favour.
> But now he's gone, and my idolatrous fancy
> Must sanctify his reliques.

118

Britannia rules the waves

Source: ALFRED, A MASQUE (Finale: "Ode in Honour of Great Britain")
Author: James Thomson (1700-1748)
First published: 1740
Type of work: Song lyric

Context: James Thomson's reputation as a poet rests solidly on his long poem *The Seasons,* the first poetic work of such length (well over 5000 lines) devoted primarily to the description of nature and scenery. His best-known work, however, is a song. In 1740 Thomson, in collaboration with David Mallet, wrote the words for a patriotic masque entitled *Alfred.* The music for this production was composed by Dr. Thomas Augustine Arne (1710–1778), contemporary of Handel and one of England's finest native composers. The masque, an art form long popular in England, was a type of pageant combining spectacle, drama, and music; it was frequently allegorical or symbolic, and often very elaborately staged. The shorter masques were frequently inserted into plays as diversions or interludes. The more spectacular forms, however, were produced as separate works. *Alfred* is one of the latter. Replete with splendor, it culminated in a triumphant anthem for full orchestra and chorus which was instantly popular and has remained so to this day: the song now universally known as "Rule, Britannia." The anthem has, of course, undergone a certain amount of evolution over the years; the more difficult passages have been modified to accommodate untrained voices, and in its most frequently-quoted line the word *rule* was changed in use to *rules.* Thus, what was originally a sacred command soon became a statement of fact. In any case, "Rule, Britannia" has those vital ingredients which any great national anthem must have—a happy combination of spirited, soaring melody and words of rousing patriotic inspiration. Three of the six stanzas are given below as they first appeared.

When Britain first, at Heaven's command,
    Arose from out the azure main,
This was the charter of the land,
    And guardian angels sang this strain:
      Rule, Britannia, rule the waves!
    Britons never will be slaves!

The nations not so blest as thee,
    Must in their turns to tyrants fall,
Whilst thou shalt flourish great and free,
    The dread and envy of them all.
      Rule, Britannia, rule the waves!
    Britons never will be slaves!

. . .

The Muses, still with freedom found,
    Shall to thy happy coast repair;
Blest isle, with matchless beauty crowned,

119

And manly hearts to guard the fair!
Rule, Britannia, rule the waves!
Britons never will be slaves!

The brother of death exacteth a third part of our lives

Source: ON DREAMS
Author: Sir Thomas Browne (1605-1682)
First published: 1836
Type of work: Philosophy

Context: As physician, philosopher, and amateur theologian, Browne produced a number of literary works on a variety of subjects. This short essay concerning seventeenth century dream psychology survived, with a number of Browne's other works, in manuscript until the nineteenth century. Dreams, says Browne, are in part the result of the day's thoughts and actions; virtuous men have pleasant and peaceful sleep while vicious men are troubled and tormented by their dreams. What we dream is influenced not only by our character, however, but may also be determined by the foods we eat. The images appearing in dreams, he continues, are often symbolic and require subtle interpretation; this theory he illustrates by citation of classical examples. Some dreams contain useful intelligence, but others may delude and mislead us if we do not interpret them with care. Since we spend one-third of our lives asleep, we should give due attention to the dreams that come to us during that period:

> Half our days we pass in the shadow of the earth, and **the brother of death exacteth a third part of our lives.** A good part of our sleeps is pieced out with visions, and phantastical objects wherin we are confessedly deceived. The day supplyeth us with truths, the night with fictions and falsehoods, which uncomfortably divide the natural account of our beings. And therefore having passed the day in sober labours and rational enquiries of truth, we are fain to betake ourselves unto such a state of being, wherin the soberest heads have acted all the monstrosities of melancholy, and which unto open eyes are no better than folly and madness.

A brotherhood of venerable trees

Source: MEMORIALS OF A TOUR IN SCOTLAND, 1803: SONNET COMPOSED AT
————CASTLE (Line 6)
Author: William Wordsworth (1770-1850)
First published: 1807
Type of work: Sonnet

Context: This sonnet is addressed to William Douglas (1724–1810), fourth Duke of Queensbury, a celebrated rake of the time. Douglas had the ancient plantations of trees felled at Neidpath, or Nidpath, Castle, referred to in the poem, to provide a dowry for Maria Fagniani, whom he supposed to be his daughter. Another notable of the time also provided her with a dowry for the same reason; historians of the period believe that both of them might have been mistaken in their beliefs about their relationship to the lady; at least one certainly was. Wordsworth arrived at Nidpath in time to see the trees lying scattered on the ground; he wrote the sonnet that same night. The act of felling the trees met with considerable resistance in the neighborhood. The poet says that the traveler will gaze with pain at such an outrage, but nature, which has a multitude of sheltered places, nooks, bays, mountains, and the gentle River Tweed, hardly seems to notice such acts of vandalism.

Degenerate Douglas! oh, the unworthy Lord!
Whom mere despite of heart could so far please,
And love of havoc, (for with such disease
Fame taxes him,) that he could send forth word
To level with the dust a noble horde,
A brotherhood of venerable trees,
Leaving an ancient dome, and towers like these,
Beggared and outraged!—Many hearts deplored
The fate of those old Trees; and oft with pain
The traveler, at this day, will stop and gaze
On wrongs, which Nature scarcely seems to heed:
For sheltered places, bosoms, nooks, and bays,
And the pure mountains, and the gentle Tweed,
And the green silent pastures, yet remain.

Budge doctors of the Stoic fur

Source: COMUS (Line 707)
Author: John Milton (1608-1674)
First published: 1637
Type of work: Masque

Context: Milton wrote the masque *Comus* to celebrate the installation of the Earl of Bridgewater as President of Wales; parts were acted by the earl's daughter and two sons. The three endeavor to reach Ludlow Castle, where the masque was presented; they pass at night through a wild wood in which the wicked enchanter, son of Bacchus and Circe and a symbol of license and debauchery, holds sway. Comus meets the earl's daughter, known as the Lady, who has become separated from her brothers; he offers to show her the way through the wood, but instead of doing so, takes her to his palace, the scene of his immoral revels. He threatens to deprive the Lady of physical motion by waving his magic wand, but, as she says, he cannot touch the freedom of her mind, which is dedicated to virtue. She further says that in spite of all of Comus's promises of the good that will befall her if she succumbs to his blandishments, only good people can bestow good on others. To this Comus replies that people are foolish to listen to moralists who preach abstinence. Stoic moralists in doctor's gowns preach things contrary to nature. In the quotation, budge meant a fur used to trim doctoral gowns during the time that Milton was a student at Cambridge; he seems to have had unpleasant memories of his professors. The hair-splitting scholastic philosophers who preached a degraded Stoicism were especially the objects of Milton's scorn.

LADY

. . .

And wouldst thou seek again to trap me here
With lickerish baits fit to ensnare a brute?
Were it a draught for Juno when she banquets,
I would not taste thy treasonous offer; none
But such as are good men can give good things,
And that which is not good, is not delicious
To a well-governed and wise appetite.

COMUS

O foolishness of men! that lend their ears
To those **budge doctors of the Stoic fur,**
And fetch their precepts from the Cynic tub,
Praising the lean and sallow abstinence.
Wherefore did Nature pour her bounties forth
With such a full and unwithdrawing hand,
Covering the earth with odors, fruits, and flocks,
Thronging the seas with spawn innumerable,
But all to please and sate the curious taste?

. . .

Bulls of Bashan

Source: PSALMS 22:12
Author: Unknown
First transcribed: c.400-200 B.C.
Type of work: Religious poetry

Context: The poet, in a psalm prophetic of the passion of the sorrowful Christ, weeps because he is forsaken by God, unlike his forefathers who were delivered from exile. The plight of the poet is so overwhelming that he describes himself as being surrounded by roaring bulls of Bashan (a region of the northern kingdom of Israel between Gilead and Hermon, originally assigned to the tribe of Manasseh):

Many bulls have compassed me: strong **bulls of Bashan** have beset me round.

They have gaped upon me with their mouths, as a ravening and a roaring lion.

I am poured out like water, and all my bones are out of joint: my heart is like wax; it is melted in the midst of my bowels.

My strength is dried up like a potsherd; and my tongue cleaveth to my jaws; and thou hast brought me into the dust of death.

For dogs have compassed me: the assembly of the wicked have inclosed me: they pierced my hands and my feet.

I may tell all my bones: they look and stare upon me.

They part my garments among them, can cast lots upon my vesture.

Business first; pleasure afterwards

Source: THE ROSE AND THE RING, OR THE HISTORY OF PRINCE GIGLIO AND PRINCE BULBO (Chapter 1)
Author: William Makepeace Thackeray (1811-1863)
First published: 1854
Type of work: Christmas story

Context: In his "Prelude" to this story, Thackeray tells how at one Christmas in a foreign city he drew a set of Twelfth-Night characters for the English children and then composed *The Rose and the Ring* as a story to accompany the pictures and serve as a Christmas pantomime for the English children and their parents. Chapter I of the story, entitled "Shows How the Royal Family Sate Down to Breakfast," introduces King Valoroso XXIV of Paflagonia; his queen, humorously called by her husband Mrs. V; and their daughter, Princess Angelica. The king, left alone when his wife and daughter finish breakfast, falls to drinking many egg-cupfuls of brandy to raise up his courage for his conscience bothers him. He is really a villain, despite his kind treatment of his queen and daughter in matters of gifts and allowances for parties and dresses, for he has usurped the throne from Prince Giglio upon the death of the late king, Valoroso's older brother and Giglio's father. Following his consumption of several draughts of brandy, King Valoroso sits down at the table again, to complete his breakfast and read the newspapers. The queen, meanwhile, wonders whether she should go visit Prince Giglio, who is convalescing from an illness; she considers the matter to herself:

". . . Not now. **Business first; pleasure afterwards.** I will go and see dear Giglio this afternoon; and now I will drive to the jeweller's, to look for the necklace and bracelets." The Princess went up into her own room, and made Betsinda, her maid, bring out all her dresses; and as for Giglio, they forgot him as much as I forget what I had for dinner last Tuesday twelvemonth.

Business was his aversion; pleasure was his business

Source: THE CONTRAST (Chapter 1)
Author: Maria Edgeworth (1767-1849)
First published: 1804
Type of work: Didactic short story

Context: While seldom read today except by scholars or literary historians, Maria Edgeworth was once the leading best-seller of England and enjoyed such fame that she was praised by the writers of America and Europe. What these men found in her short stories was a remarkable ability to describe character within a short space. Although her stories are primarily didactic — or "moral," as she would have said it — she seldom fell back on the stereotyped characters that are often the backbone and the fault of the sermonizing story. Quite the contrary, as she shows in the description of Philip Folingsby, one of the minor characters in this story, she could pinpoint a man's personality with a few choice words that so strike the reader that the character is unforgettable.

. . . he was a man whose head was at this time entirely full of gigs, and tandems, and unicorns: **business was his aversion; pleasure was his business.** Money he considered only as the means of pleasure; and tenants only as machines, who make money. He was neither avaricious nor cruel; but thoughtless and extravagant.

The busy trifler

Source: EXPOSTULATIONS (Line 322)
Author: William Cowper (1731-1800)
First published: 1782
Type of work: Essay in verse

Context: William Cowper, frequently suffering from a sense of wrong-doing and several times confined in an insane asylum for religious mania, remonstrates in 734 lines with his country for her ungodly ways. "Why weeps the Muse for England?" he queries in his opening line. Everything looks attractive and successful in the land, yet things are wrong. He reminds his readers that, before its downfall, prophets wept for Israel even when it seemed favored by God. And he goes still farther into antiquity to Assyria, called upon to repent, then to Greece and Rome, whose glories faded. At the conclusion, he calls on his country to take stock of itself and not be over-proud or seek comfort in the feeling that other nations are just as guilty of wrong-doing. God, not man, is responsible for the present blessings of the world. Man is only a busy trifler, making much ado about nothing. The poet uses a similar phrase, "important trifler," in *Conversations* (line 250).

Know, then, that heavenly wisdom on this ball
Creates, gives birth to, guides, comsummates all;
That, while laborious and quick-thoughted man
Snuffs up the praise of what he seems to plan,
He first conceives, then perfects his design,
As a mere instrument in hands divine:
Blind to the workings of that secret power,
That balances the wings of every hour,
The busy trifler dreams himself alone,
Frames many a purpose, and God works his own.

Butchered to make a Roman holiday

Source: CHILDE HAROLD'S PILGRIMAGE (Canto IV, stanza 141)
Author: George Gordon, Lord Byron (1788-1824)
First published: 1818 (Canto IV)
Type of work: Narrative poem

Context: In Canto IV of Byron's long poem, Childe Harold (Byron) visits Venice, Florence, and Rome. His pilgrimage ends at Rome, the goal toward which all his journeying has tended. The title "Childe" is one which candidates for knighthood bore, in the days of chivalry, until their pilgrimage was done and knighthood was conferred upon them. The poem's title thus symbolizes Byron's wanderings over Europe, seeking an escape from himself and from the world that wearies him. His love and admiration for Rome, the eternal city, "lone mother of dead empires," is such that he declares it his country. Saddened by the ruins of its former glory and conscious of its past greatness, he calls the roll of famous men who made the city what it was. Some of them were tyrants; Byron considers the nature of tyranny and despairs of the achievement of true freedom by mortal men. Byron's passionate devotion to freedom is not merely rhetorical: at the age of thirty-six he will die of a fever contracted while fighting in the name of Greek liberty. Now he visits ancient tombs, wondering about the lives of those who were buried there. In the ruins he sees "the moral of all human tales" retraced: "First Freedom and then Glory— when that fails, / Wealth, vice, corruption,—barbarism at last." Byron ponders the sequence as Rome experienced it: the greatness which passed into softness, indulgence and orgy— until, too fat and corrupt to resist, the great empire fell before hordes of barbarians. Contemplating the vastness of the Colosseum, Byron envisages the bloody spectacles that were staged there for the excitement and entertainment of bored and sated crowds—part of that degeneracy which led to the nation's fall:

I see before me the Gladiator lie:
He leans upon his hand—his manly brow
Consents to death, but conquers agony,
And his dropp'd head sinks gradually low—

125

And through his side the last drops, ebbing slow
From the red gash, fall heavy, one by one,
Like the first of a thunder-shower; and now
The arena swims around him—he is gone,
Ere ceased the inhuman shout which hail'd the wretch who won.

He heard it, but he heeded not—his eyes
Were with his heart and that was far away;
He reck'd not of the life he lost nor prize,
But where his rude hut by the Danube lay,
There were his young barbarians all at play,
There was their Dacian mother—he, their sire,
Butcher'd to make a Roman holiday—
All this rush'd with his blood.—Shall he expire
And unavenged?—Arise! ye Goths, and glut your ire!

A button-hole lower

Source: LOVE'S LABOUR'S LOST (Act V, sc. ii, 1. 706)
Author: William Shakespeare (1564-1616)
First published: 1598
Type of work: Dramatic comedy

Context: Don Adriano de Armado, Costard, a clown, and several others are presenting a play for the Princess of France and her court with King Ferdinand of Navarre and his nobles. In this play Costard plays the part of Pompey. While Armado, who plays Hector, delivers his lines, Berowne—an attendant lord to the king—whispers to Costard some alarming information about Jaquenetta and Armado. And then, while Armado is still playing the part of Hector, Costard—with his newly gained knowledge—confronts him with the fact that Jaquenetta, a country "wench" is "two months on her way" with his child. Armado challenges Costard to a duel because of this public charge, and the two are led on by the onlookers who keep referring to them as Pompey and Hector. Then Moth, page to Armado, steps in to remind his master of his position and to head off a duel not worthy of his master's fighting. He reminds Armado that his position is not that of the play hero, Hector, being challenged by a lofty antagonist; rather, the challenge is from Costard the clown concerning a mere country wench. Thus, Moth's desire is to bring Armando "a button-hole lower," out of the play and back into reality.

MOTH

Master, let me take you **a button-hole lower.** Do you not see Pompey is uncasing for the combat? What mean you? You will lose your reputation.

126

By night an atheist half-believes in God

Source: THE COMPLAINT: OR, NIGHT THOUGHTS ("Night the Fifth," l. 176)
Author: Edward Young (1683-1765)
First published: 1742
Type of work: Philosophical poem

Context: The poet excoriates the use of "wit" in poetry, which too often is used to exalt sensuality and not virtue. The bulk of the poetry of sensuality far exceeds that of virtue, which should be the true subject of poetry. The poet goes on to say that night is the time for thought; during daylight, virtue, a frail and fair thing, suffers in the crowd. Few people bring back to their homes at evening the manners they possessed in the morning; their thoughts are blotted by the corruption of the world, their good resolutions are shaken, their thoughts tainted. The example of others is a bad thing; people see vain ambition and are stimulated to pursue their own ambitions. The riot, pride, and perfidy everywhere evident undermine otherwise good and virtuous people and set them upon wrong courses. A single glance can carry infection. Safety lies only in remaining remote from the crowd. At night, freed from the fevers and distractions of the day, we are close to the deity; we realize our faults and vice loses its allurements and looks as black as the night itself. At night even the atheist has doubts about his spiritual questionings and almost believes in God.

> This sacred shade, and solitude, what is it?
> 'Tis the felt presence of the deity.
> Few are the faults we flatter when alone,
> Vice sinks in her allurements, is ungilt,
> And looks, like other objects, black by night.
> **By night an atheist half-believes in God.**

By thunders of white silence overthrown

Source: HIRAM POWERS' GREEK SLAVE (Line 14)
Author: Elizabeth Barrett Browning (1806-1861)
First published: 1850
Type of work: Sonnet

Context: As a poet of the mid-nineteenth century, Mrs. Browning was influenced by the school of idealism, especially in terms of her understanding of the nature and role of art; according to this school, a work of art transcends reality and lifts the spectator into the realm of ideas wherein the anguish and pain of life are harmonized into cosmic order. Accepting this didactic and elevated view of art, Mrs. Browning was always interested in social reform and in the lamentable conditions of the lower classes; to her, poetry and the fine arts were instruments for the amelioration of so-

127

ciety. In the 1840's and 1850's there was much talk against the slave trade, especially in relationship to the United States since England had already outlawed slavery; as a social reformer, Mrs. Browning, horrified by attempts to rationalize the practice, turned to art as a means of lifting men's minds to a universal truth. By drawing her readers' attentions to the statue of the Greek Slave, she hopes to uplift their spirits to the point that art and universal truth will triumph and thus end slavery. Hiram Powers was an American sculptor working in Italy during the time of the Brownings' residence there. His "Greek Slave" (1843) was one of the most famous sculptures of this period.

> Pierce to the centre,
> Art's fiery finger! and break up ere long
> The serfdom of this world! appeal, fair stone,
> From God's pure heights of beauty against man's wrong!
> Catch up in thy divine face, not alone
> East griefs, but west, and strike and shame the strong,
> **By thunders of white silence overthrown.**

Call me early, mother, I'm to be Queen of the May

Source: THE MAY QUEEN (Stanzas 1 and 11)
Author: Alfred, Lord Tennyson (1809-1892)
First published: 1832
Type of work: Lyric poem

Context: "The May Queen" is filled with vain young Alice's joyous anticipation of her one-day reign as Queen of the May. Other girls are fair and black-eyed, but none, she exults, "so fair as little Alice in all the land they say." She will "sleep so sound all night" that her mother must wake her with a loud call, to "gather knots of flowers, and buds and garlands gay." She boasts of the sharp look she gave Robin, who must have thought her a ghost, "for I was all in white." She knows her reputation for cruelty, "but I care not what they say." Though Robin is not dying of love, as reported, his heart may be breaking, but "what is that to me?" Many a bolder lad will woo her "any summer day." Her mother, her little sister Effie, and shepherd lads from far away will come to see her crowned. Honeysuckle, cuckoo-flowers, and marsh-marigolds are all in bloom. Night-winds blow and seem to brighten the stars above, and Alice predicts, "There will not be a drop of rain the whole of the livelong day." All the valley will be "fresh and green and still," cowslip and crowfoot will cover the hillside, and the rivulet in the dale below will "merrily glance and play," for Alice is to be Queen of the May. Thus she ends as she began, exulting, and reminding her mother:

So you must wake and call me early, **call me early, mother
dear,**
To-morrow 'ill be the happiest time of all the glad New-year:
To-morrow 'ill be of all the year the maddest merriest day,
For I'm to be Queen o' the May, mother, **I'm to be Queen o'
the May.**

Calm's not life's crown

Source: YOUTH AND CALM (Line 23)
Author: Matthew Arnold (1822-1888)
First published: 1852
Type of work: Lyric poem

Context: Never a genuinely happy person, Arnold developed a view of life that fully accepted the harsh facts of existence and the torment of human anguish; however, he was not a man to luxuriate in misery, unwilling to make a compromise with his world. Slowly learning that the promises of youth are seldom fulfilled, he came to accept life on its own terms: man's responsibility was to seek calm, not joy. Such stoicism gradually led to a mature serenity, freed from the passions and romantic dreams of youth; this serenity enabled him to rise above his own suffering into a state of calm detachment wherein he achieved his fame as a man who had found the compromise with life that preserves sanity without despair. This quotation comes from a passage in which he makes one of the clearest statements of his view of life:

> Youth dreams a bliss on this side death.
> It dreams a rest, if not more deep,
> More grateful than this marble sleep;
> It hears a voice within it tell:
> **Calm's not life's crown,** though calm is well.
> 'Tis all perhaps which man acquires,
> But 'tis not what our youth desires.

Calumnies are answered best with silence

Source: VOLPONE (Act II, sc. ii, l. 20)
Author: Ben Jonson (1573?-1637)
First published: 1607
Type of work: Dramatic comedy

Context: Volpone, the Fox, a wealthy Venetian, pretends to be upon his death's bed in order to extort rich presents from a crew of legacy-hunters, each member of which believes that he is to be Volpone's heir. Volpone is aided in his masquerade by a servant as unprincipled as himself,

129

Mosca, the Fly. After a visit by Corvino, the Crow, Mosca describes the charms of Corvino's young, beautiful, and virtuous wife, Celia, whom Corvino keeps under lock and key, so great is his jealousy and his fear that she will find a lover. Volpone decides that he must see this paragon and has Mosca set up a bench upon which he can stand to sell his medicines, as he is announced to the public as Scoto of Mantua, a famous mountebank, or traveling seller of remedies for all kinds of diseases. A naïve and credulous English knight, Sir Politick Would-be, who believes that he sees deep meanings in events that strike others as unimportant commonplaces, takes it upon himself to tell a gentleman traveler, Peregrine, all about Scoto of Mantua. Mountebanks, according to Sir Politick, are the only knowing men in Europe, scholars, physicians, statesmen, and counsellors to states. Peregrine replies that he has heard they are mere lewd imposters, but Sir Politick, pitying his ignorance, tells him that one does well to disregard such attacks upon character and refuse to say a word, for calumnies are answered best with silence.

SIR POLITICK

Pity his ignorance.
They are the only knowing men of Europe!
Great general scholars, excellent physicians.
Most admired statesmen, professed favorites,
And cabinet counsellors to the greatest princes;
The only languaged men of all the world!

PEREGRINE

And, I have heard, they are most lewd imposters;
Made all of terms and shreds; no less beliers
Of great men's favors, than their own vile med'cines;
Which they will utter upon monstrous oaths;
Selling that drug for twopence, ere they part,
Which they have valued at twelve crowns before.

SIR POLITICK

Sir, **calumnies are answered best with silence.** . . .

Captains of Industry

Source: PAST AND PRESENT (Book IV, chapter 4, chapter title)
Author: Thomas Carlyle (1795-1881)
First published: 1843
Type of work: Book of essays on economics and society

Context: Carlyle was something of a romanticist about the past. Like others in the Victorian period, both in England and in the United States, he looked to the past to see only what was good; he therefore believed it to be superior to his own age and exaggerated its glories. But he also acquired the truth which the great historian always learns: by studying the past we can learn, if we will, how to avoid the mistakes of the generations of mankind who have preceded us. In this particular essay Carlyle looks at nineteenth century industrialists in Great Britain and finds them wanting, seeing them merely as men who are busy gathering up thousand-pound notes as American Indians were alleged to gather scalps, as trophies giving visible evidence of prowess over one's enemies and fellowmen. But Carlyle expresses hope that the pursuit of money, Mammonism, as he calls it, will not always be the end for which the leaders of industry strive. He hopes for the improvement, he says, to come from the industrialists themselves. Government, he says, can help, but government cannot do it all, if for no other reason than that the government merely reflects the people. The remedies, he says, must be found "by those who stand practically in the middle of it; by those who themselves work and preside over work"—in short, by the men he calls captains of industry. Carlyle issues a ringing challenge to these men:

. . . *Captains of Industry* are the true Fighters, henceforth recognizable as the only true ones: Fighters against Chaos, Necessity and the Devils and Jotuns; and lead on Mankind in that great, and alone true, and universal warfare; the stars in their courses fighting for them, and all Heaven and all Earth saying audibly, Well done! Let the **Captains of Industry** retire into their own hearts, and ask solemnly, If there is nothing but vulturous hunger for fine wines, valet reputation and gilt carriages, discoverable there? Of hearts made by the Almighty God I will not believe such a thing. . . .

Carthage must be destroyed

Source: PARALLEL LIVES ("Cato the Censor")
Author: Plutarch (c.45-c. 125)
First transcribed: c. 105-115
Type of work: Biography

Context: Marcus Portius (234–149 B.C.), called Cato the Censor and Cato the Elder to distinguish him from his grandson, the Stoic philosopher, was given the name of Cato, or Wise Man, because of the admiration of his fellow citizens. He was a soldier who when he was only seventeen fought against Hannibal. Rising in the political world, he was consul in 195 B.C., and in 187, censor, the official with rights to inquire into the lives and morals of Rome's citizens, and punish disorders and immorality. He spent his life trying to restore what he thought were the morals and simplicity of the old days. Sent on a diplomatic mission to Carthage, he returned convinced that that city-state was a danger to Rome and should be destroyed. Carthage, near modern Tunis, was supposedly built by Dido on the site of old Utica. By the fifth century B.C. it was gaining power in the Mediterranean and, under Hannibal, it became very strong. Rome challenged it in the third century in the Punic Wars, so-called because Rome called the Phoenicians "Poeni." The First Punic War ended with Carthage's loss of Sicily. In the Second Punic War, Fabio and Scipio Africanus defeated Hannibal at the Battle of Zama (202 B.C.). Still because of its commercial power, many Romans felt it should be razed and its streets sprinkled with salt. Chief advocate was Cato the Censor, who ended all his speeches in the Senate, regardless of their topic, with the words: "Ceterum, censeo, Carthaginem esse Delendam" (For the rest, I vote that Carthage should be destroyed). Plutarch repeats Cato's demands in slightly different words. Plutarch, the biographer, was born in Greece, but after study in Athens visited Rome, where he probably wrote most of his works. One was *Parallel Lives,* in which he linked twenty-three great Greeks with their Roman counterparts, then added other biographies, including that of Cato. Plutarch was a moralist. His interest in noteworthy men of the past was in what they could teach about morality. By their deeds, rather than by the social and historical period in which they were involved, he wanted them judged, and he was not above occasional distortion of history to prove his point. Ethics ranked high in his thoughts: "Generosity brings reward as arrogance earns punishment." Did he have Cato's hatred of Carthage in mind when he wrote that "no beast is more savage than a man possessed with power added to his rage?" Cato, by continually preaching the destruction of Carthage, brought on the Third Punic War (149–146 B.C.) that completely ended its existence at the hands of an army under the command of the son of the Scipio who had proclaimed his belief that it should be left standing. Speaking of Cato the Censor, said Plutarch:

It is said that at the conclusion of his speech he shook the lap of his gown, and purposely dropped some Libyan figs; and when he found that the Senators admired them for their size and beauty, he told them, that the country where they grew was but three days' sail from Rome. But what was a stronger instance of his enmity to Carthage, he never gave his opinion in the Senate upon any other point whatever, without adding DELENDA EST CARTHAGO, **Carthage must be destroyed.** Scipio made a point to mention the contrary, and concluded his speeches: "And my opinion is, that Carthage should be left standing."

Castles in Spain

Source: THE ROMAUNT OF THE ROSE (Fragment B, l. 2573)
Author: Geoffrey Chaucer (1343?-1400), translator of part of the *Roman de la Rose* by Guillaume de Lorris (died c. 1235)
First transcribed: 1360?-1372
Type of work: Allegorical romance

132

Context: The English translation of Guillaume de Lorris's and Jean de Meun's *Roman de la Rose* exists in three fragments, A, B, and C, and comprises but a fraction of the French poem. Some critical opinion holds that Fragment B was not translated by Chaucer. The poet says that the lover should set his thoughts on loving and place his heart in but one place and never remove it. He should give his heart freely and gladly, but never show it to the world. When his beloved is absent he will mourn; he will constantly try to catch a sight of her. When he fails to see her, he will be in great sadness; when he does see her, his spirits will be immeasureably quickened. When he comes into her presence, he will be dumb, and afterwards he will reproach himself for not having spoken. Finally, night will come and the lover will have to make his sad way to his lonesome bed, there to dream he has her at his side, a situation as imaginary as building a Castle in Spain.

Thanne shall thee come a remembraunce
Of hir shap and hir semblaunce,
Whereto non other may be pere.
And wite thou wel, withoute were,
That thee shal seme, somtyme that nyght,
That thou hast hir, that is so bright,
Naked bitwene thyne armes there,
All sothfastnesse as though it were.
Thou shalt make **castels** thanne **in Spayne,**
And dreme of joye, all but in vayne,
And thee deliten of right nought,
While thou so slombrest in that thought,
That it so swete and delitable,
The which, in soth, nys but a fable;
For it ne shall no while laste.

A cat may look at a king

Source: ALICE'S ADVENTURES IN WONDERLAND (Chapter 8)
Author: Lewis Carroll (Charles Lutwidge Dodgson, 1832-1898)
First published: 1865
Type of work: Imaginative tale for children

Context: The English proverb, "A cat may look at a king," was already old when John Heywood (1497–1580) included it in his collection of English colloquial sayings, *Proverbes.* This was the first volume of its kind and was published in 1546. The meaning of the proverb is that there is safety in insignificance: an inferior may do certain things in the presence of a superior without fear, simply because he is beneath the latter's notice. The most delightfully memorable use of this saying is undoubtedly that which occurs in Lewis Carroll's dream-tale, *Alice's Adventures in Wonderland.* After a series of strange experiences, Alice finds her-

133

self lost in a forest and uncertain which way she should go. The Cheshire Cat appears in a tree and counsels her in such a way that she is more confused than ever. He has the pleasant ability to appear and disappear at will; normally the process is gradual, and his fixed grin is the first and last part of him which is visible. As he vanishes, he informs Alice that he will see her later at the Queen's croquet-match. In time Alice does find herself part of this festive event, in which the mallets are flamingoes, the hoops are soldiers bent double, and the balls are hedgehogs. This arrangement does not make the game easy to play, and the Queen's ferocious disposition is upsetting. "The players all played at once, without waiting for turns, quarrelling all the while, and fighting for the hedgehogs; and in a very short time the Queen was in a furious passion, and went stamping about, and shouting, 'Off with his head!' or 'Off with her head!' about once in a minute." Alice wonders that there is anyone left alive. At this point the cat reappears, though it halts the process while only its head is visible.

"How do you like the Queen?" said the Cat in a low voice.

"Not at all," said Alice: "she's so extremely—" Just then she noticed that the Queen was close behind her, listening: so she went on "—likely to win, that it's hardly worth while finishing the game."

The Queen smiled and passed on.

"Who *are* you talking to?" said the King, coming up to Alice, and looking at the Cat's head with great curiosity.

"It's a friend of mine—a Cheshire Cat," said Alice: "allow me to introduce it."

"I don't like the look of it at all," said the King: "however, it may kiss my hand, if it likes."

"I'd rather not," the Cat remarked.

"Don't be impertinent," said the King, "and don't look at me like that!" He got behind Alice as he spoke.

"A cat may look at a king," said Alice. "I've read that in some book, but I don't remember where."

"Well, it must be removed," said the King very decidedly; and he called to the Queen, who was passing at the moment, "My dear! I wish you would have this cat removed!"

The Queen had only one way of settling all difficulties, great or small. "Off with his head!" she said without even looking round.

"I'll fetch the executioner myself," said the King eagerly, and he hurried off.

Caterpillars of the commonwealth

Source: KING RICHARD THE SECOND (Act II, sc. iii, 1. 166)
Author: William Shakespeare (1564-1616)
First published: 1597
Type of work: Historical drama

Context: Henry Bolingbroke, banished from England on charge of treason, hears that King Richard II has confiscated his inheritance upon the death of John of Gaunt, Duke of Lancaster, his father and uncle of the king. While the king is in Ireland to oversee his wars, and the affairs of state are left in the hands of another uncle, the Duke of York, Bolingbroke returns and finds that York will not stand in the way of his claim to his title and inheritance. When the Duke of York proposes that Bolingbroke spend the night at Bristol Castle, Bolingbroke quickly accepts, confessing that he has sworn to rid the castle of the low companions of the king:

BOLINGBROKE

An offer uncle, that we will accept,
But we must win your Grace to go with us
To Bristol Castle, which they say is held
By Bushy, Bagot, and their complices,
The **caterpillars of the commonwealth,**
Which I have sworn to weed and pluck away.

YORK

It may be I will go with you—but yet I'll pause,
For I am loth to break our country's laws.
Nor friends, nor foes, to me welcome you are.
Things past redress are now with me past care.
[*Exeunt.*]

Caverns measureless to man

Source: KUBLA KHAN (Line 4)
Author: Samuel Taylor Coleridge (1772-1834)
First published: 1816
Type of work: Narrative-lyric poem

Context: By his poetry, Wordsworth put magic into ordinary situations. His friend Coleridge tried to make exotic and supernatural situations sound real. They collaborated in *Lyrical Ballads* (1798–1800), a work that ushered in the English Romantic Movement. Coleridge needed to be pressured into writing. The sight of Wordsworth's activity did serve as a spur, and most of his poetry was produced while he lived near Wordsworth and his sister Dorothy in the lovely Lake Region of England. Coleridge's greatest work was "The Ancient Mariner" included in *Lyrical Ballads*. The story of another of his poems has often been told. One day in 1797, he had taken a dose of the opium to which he had become accustomed for his pain. Then while endulging in his other opiate, reading, he fell asleep. He had been reading *Purchas, His Pilgrimage* (1613), into which an English clergyman named Samuel Purchas (1577–1626) had gathered stories of peoples and religions of the world. He had finished a

135

chapter dealing with the Mongol Emperor Kublai Khan (1215?–1294), grandson of Jenghiz Khan, and the palace he had built at Cambaluc, now Peiping, which Marco Polo saw and described. Sleeping profoundly, Coleridge dreamed out a long poem, as John Masefield reported he had seen in a dream and set down later one of his masterpieces. However, Coleridge did not have the same good fortune. He opened his eyes and began feverishly to write down all he could remember. While working, he was interrupted by a caller from the town of Porlock, probably a creditor. By the time Coleridge could send him away, the rest of the poem had slipped from his mind. Only the fragment that he had put onto paper remained. Critics ever since have raged against the interruptor. Yet in its present state, the fifty-four lines of "Kubla Khan" make one of the most magical poems in the English language, full of exquisite music and haunting phrases. Byron used one of the lines: "And woman wailing for her Demon Lover," as the motto for his *Heaven and Earth* (1823). Perhaps it is even two poems, because after the pause at line 35, the poet is reminded of a vision he once had of an Abyssinian maid playing her dulcimer. He cries that if he could only re-create within himself her music, he could rebuild that ancient pleasure-dome and cave of ice to be so real that people would be frightened and believe him some spirit come from Paradise. Scholars have found the inspiring paragraph that supplied some of Coleridge's phrases. It occurs in the 1626 edition, Book IV, chapter xiii, p. 418: "In Xamdu did Cublai Can build a stately palace encompassing sixteene miles of plaine ground with a wall, wherein are fertile meadowes, pleasant Springs, delightful Streams, and all sorts of beasts of chase and game, and in the middest thereof a sumptuous house of pleasure." This is the way Coleridge transmuted the prose into poetic beauty:

> In Xanadu did Kubla Khan
> A stately pleasure-dome decree;
> Where Alph, the sacred river, ran
> Through **caverns measureless to man**
>   Down to a sunless sea.
> So twice five miles of fertile ground
> With walls and towers were girdled round:
> And here were gardens bright with sinuous rills,
> Where blossomed many an incense-bearing tree;
> And here were forests ancient as the hills,
> Enfolding sunny spots of greenery.

Chaos is come again

Source: OTHELLO (Act III, sc, iii, 1. 92)
Author: William Shakespeare (1564-1616)
First published: 1622
Type of work: Dramatic tragedy

cer pleads with Desdemona, wife of the valiant Moor, to speak for him. She consents, but, in the course of her persistent pleading, becomes mildly annoying to Othello, who loves her so much that he cannot really find fault with her. He compares life without her love to the disorder before the creation of the world.

DESDEMONA
. . . What, Michael Cassio,
That came a-wooing with you; and so many a time,
When I have spoke of you dispraisingly,
Hath ta'en your part; . . .

. . .

OTHELLO
I will deny thee nothing.
Whereon, I do beseech thee, grant me this,
To leave me but a little to myself.

DESDEMONA
Shall I deny you? No. Farewell my lord.

. . .

OTHELLO
Excellent wretch! Perdition catch my soul
But I do love thee; and when I love thee not,
Chaos is come again.

Chapter of accidents

Source: LETTERS TO HIS FRIENDS (To Solomon Dayrolles, No. LXXIX, February 16, 1753)
Author: Philip Dormer Stanhope, Lord Chesterfield (1694-1773)
First published: 1777
Type of work: Personal letters

Context: To his friend and protégé, Solomon Dayrolles (d. 1786), the Earl of Chesterfield writes that he has been silent for a long time (the last previous letter to Dayrolles was written two months before this one). He complains that he constantly grows deafer and consequently more isolated from people. He can now say, what is he to the world, or the world to him. He is discouraged about the prospect of regaining his hearing, as he has tried a thousand remedies, but all have been ineffective. But al-

137

though knowledge is severely limited, chance is vast, and perhaps a lucky accident will be able to do more than knowledge has been able to accomplish, and he will find a remedy for his deafness.

I grow deafer, and consequently more *isolé* from society, every day. I can now say of the world, as the man in Hamlet, *What is Hecuba to me, or I to Hecuba?* My best wishes, however, will attend my friends, though all my hopes have left me. I have in vain tried a thousand things that have done others good in the like case, and will go on trying, having so little to lose, and so much to get. The chapter of knowledge is a very short, but the **chapter of accidents** is a very long one. I will keep dipping in it, for sometimes a concurrence of unknown and unforeseen circumstances, in the medicine and the disease, may produce an unexpected and lucky hit. But no more of myself, that self, as now circumstanced, being but a disagreeable subject to us both.

Charlie is my darling, the young Chevalier

Source: CHARLIE IS MY DARLING
Author: Carolina Oliphant, Baroness Nairne (1766-1845)
First published: c. 1846
Type of work: Lyric poem

Context: One critic notes that "only Shakespeare, Burns and Carolina Oliphant could claim that they wrote so many as three lyrics which after a hundred years or more are still known to everybody. . . ." Baroness Nairne was born in Scotland at Gask, Perthshire, the daughter of an ardent Jacobite who named her Carolina in memory of "Bonnie Prince Charlie." In 1745 Prince Charles Edward, the "Young Pretender," aided by a French declaration of war on England, landed in Scotland in an attempt to lead an uprising which would culminate in his accession to the throne of England. It was a pathetic if heroically romantic attempt, doomed to failure from the start, but for a brief span the Bonnie Prince rode through Scotland raising hearts and hopes for the "good old cause." This lyric commemorates his arrival:

'Twas on a Monday morning,
   Right early in the year,
When Charlie came to our toun,
   The young Chevalier.
     Oh, Charlie is my darling,
     My darling, my darling;
    Oh, **Charlie is my darling,**
     The young Chevalier.
As he came marching up the street,
   The pipes play'd loud and clear,

And a' the folk came running out
　　To meet the Chevalier.
　　　　Oh, Charlie is my darling. . . .

Chaucer, well of English undefiled

Source: THE FAERIE QUEENE (Book IV, Canto 2, stanza 32)
Author: Edmund Spenser (c.1552-1599)
First published: 1590
Type of work: Allegorical poem

Context: Sir Blandamour, riding in company with Paridell, comes upon Sir Ferraugh, who is in the company of the counterfeit Florimell. Sir Blandamour vanquishes Sir Ferraugh in combat and takes Florimell from him. After a time the situation of Florimell's being Sir Blandamour's love irritates Paridell, as Paridell and Blandamour had an agreement to share any prizes they might take. They engage in a fight for the lady, and when both are bleeding freely from their wounds, they are joined by the Squire of Dames, who tells them that there is to be a tournament, the prize to be Florimell's girdle, which Satyran had found and worn until the jealousy of other knights forced him to arrange the contest. As they therefore all go towards the place of the tourney, they are met by the two fast friends, Cambell and Triamond, and their ladies, Canacee and Cambine. There then ensues the stanza in the poem in which Spenser refers to Chaucer as the well of English undefiled. It was a popular Elizabethan idea that Chaucer was the founder of the English language, but Spenser does not say so: what he does say is that Chaucer wrote pure and unblemished English. The stanza containing Spenser's reference to him is as follows (a "beadroll" is a list):

Whylome, as antique stories tellen vs,
Those two were foes the fellonest on ground,
And battell made the dreddest daungerous,
That euer shrilling trumpet did resound;
Though now their acts be no where to be found,
As that renowmed Poet them compyled,
With warlike numbers and Heroicke sound,
Dan Chaucer, well of English vndefyled,
On Fames eternall beadroll worthie to be fyled.

Bur wicked Time, that all good thoughts doth waste,
And workes of noblest wits to nought out weare,
That famous moniment hath quite defaste,
And robd the world of threasure endlesse deare,
The which mote haue enriched all vs heare.

· · ·

139

Chewing the food of sweet and bitter fancy

Source: AS YOU LIKE IT (Act IV, sc. iii, 1. 102)
Author: William Shakespeare (1564-1616)
First published: 1623
Type of work: Dramatic comedy

Context: In the Forest of Arden, Orlando, suitor of Rosalind, discovers and kills a lion ready to attack his cruel brother, Oliver, with whom he becomes reconciled because of this act of bravery and compassion. Wounded, Orlando dispatches Oliver to explain his delay in an appointment with the shepherd lad who instructs him in how to win the hand of Rosalind (actually Rosalind disguised as a shepherd lad as she searches for her father, an exiled Duke).

OLIVER

When last the young Orlando parted from you,
He left a promise to return again
Within an hour, and pacing through the forest,
Chewing the food of sweet and bitter fancy,
Lo what befell. He threw his eye aside,
And mark what object did present itself.
Under an old oak, whose boughs were mossed with age,
And high top bald with dry antiquity,
A wretched ragged man, o'ergrown with hair,
Lay sleeping on his back; about his neck
A green and gilded snake had wreathed itself,
Who with her head, nimble in threats, approached
The opening of his mouth; but suddenly,
Seeing Orlando, it unlinked itself,
And with indented glides did slip away
Into a bush, under which bush's shade
A lioness, with udders all drawn dry,
Lay couching head on ground, with catlike watch
When that the sleeping man should stir; for 'tis
The royal disposition of that beast
To prey on nothing that doth seem as dead.
This seen, Orlando did approach the man,
And found it was his brother, his elder brother.

A chiel's amang you, taking notes

Source: ON THE LATE CAPTAIN GROSE'S PEREGRINATIONS THROUGH SCOTLAND (Stanza 1)
Author: Robert Burns (1759-1796)
First published: 1789
Type of work: Humorous poem

Context: Captain Grose was an antiquarian and friend of Robert Burns, who had published many of his findings on the cultural history of Scotland, including *Antiquities of Scotland* and his *Treatise on Ancient Armor and Weapons.* Burns comments humorously on both the man and his work: of the man, he says it would be better had he fallen in battle than left the army. For his work, Burns has humorous ridicule, commenting that Captain Grose has porridge pots dating from before Noah's Flood, a cinder from Eve's first fire, Tubalcain's fire-shovel and fender, and the Witch of Endor's brass-bound broomstick. Burns even suggests that the antiquary is a colleague of the devil, a man to make ghosts, warlocks, and witches all "quake at his conjuring hammer." In the first stanza the poet warns his fellow Scots that no one is safe from Grose's inquisitive mind, that he takes notes on everything, great or small, significant or of no consequence, in order to get it into print:

> Hear, Land o' Cakes, and brither Scots,
> Frae Maidenkirk to Johnny Groats;—
> If there's a hole in a' your coats,
>   I rede you tent it;
> **A chiel's amang you, taking notes,**
>   And faith, he'll prent it.

Child of misery, baptized in tears

Source: THE COUNTRY JUSTICE, PART ONE, APOLOGY FOR VAGRANTS
Author: John Langhorne (1735-1779)
First published: 1774
Type of work: Didactic poem

Context: The Reverend John Langhorne, D.D., was selected by Dr. Samuel Johnson for a place in his anthology of English poets from Chaucer to Cowper. Langhorne's clergyman father died when the boy was only four; a tender poem commemorates his mother's loving care in his upbringing. Poverty, however, prevented him from continuing his education beyond grammar school. He became first a tutor, then a schoolteacher, always using his spare time writing poetry and studying to become a minister. He continued his religious education as curate to a clergyman. Finally for religious writings, especially his *Genius and Valor: A Scotch Pastoral* he was supposedly given an honorary Doctor of Divinity by the University of Edinburgh in 1766. Some of Langhorne's poetry and prose appeared in *The Monthly Review.* Adding more criticism and fanciful prose, he published a two-volume *Effusions of Friendship and Fancy,* in a flippant style in which critics saw the influence of Sterne. He and his brother published their translation of Plutarch in 1770. Sir Walter Scott and Tobias Smollet were among his admirers. Most of his writing lay

141

in what his son called "the lighter provinces of literature," when he collected his father's verse into two elegant volumes in 1804, twenty-five years after the poet's death. He and his writing are largely forgotten today. Langhorne was never very well off financially, so in 1772 he accepted appointment as Justice of the Peace in Blagdon, Somerset. After carefully considering the duties of his new office, he wrote a three part didactic and satirical poem, called *The Country Justice, a poem by one of Her Majesty's Justices of the Peace for the county of Somerset.* Part I was published in 1774, and the other two parts followed later, a year apart. In the Introduction, the poet praises British laws from King Richard to his own time. The early Saxon serfs gained liberty only by flight, but Edward III did manage to achieve some law and order, and established a system of rural justice. Langhorne describes the ancient Hall of Justice. The stanzas of rhymed couplets that follow are headed by phrases descriptive of their content. In "The Character of a County Justice," the poet writes: "His featur'd soul display'd Honor's strong beam, and Mercy's melting shade." The section "General Motives for Lenity" pleads "Be this, ye rural Magistrates, your plan: / Firm be your justice, but be friends to man." Before sentencing, the magistrate is urged to discover whether vice or nature prompts the deed, and he is adjured to consider "the strong temptations and the need." Bringing up a specific case, Langhorne offers his "Apology for Vagrants."

> For him who, lost to ev'ry hope of life
> Has long with fortune held unequal strife,
> Known to no human love, no human care,
> The friendless, homeless object of despair;
> For the poor vagrant, feel, while he complains,
> Nor from sad freedom sent to sadder chains . . .
>
>   •   •   •
>
> Perhaps on some inhospitable shore
> The houseless wretch a widow'd parent bore,
> Who, then, no more by golden prospects led,
> Of the poor Indian begg'd a leafy bed,
> Cold on Canadian hills, or Minden's plain
> Perhaps that parent mourn'd her soldier slain;
> Bent o'er her babe, her eye dissolv'd in dew,
> The big drops mingling with the milk he drew,
> Gave the sad presage of his future years,
> **The child of misery, baptiz'd in tears!**

The childhood shows the man as morning shows the day

Source: PARADISE REGAINED (Book IV, ll. 220-221)
Author: John Milton (1608-1674)
First published: 1671
Type of work: Epic poem

Context: In offering temptations to Christ, Satan takes Him to the top of a mountain and shows Him all the kingdoms of the world and urges Him to free the tribes of Israel. Christ replies that Jews brought down their own destruction on themselves by departing from the one true God. Satan then shows Him Rome, which spreads its rule over all the earth. With Satan's help, Christ could depose the depraved Tiberius and become the Emperor of Rome, a more exalted position than he would gain by assuming David's throne, which He is prophesied to ascend. Christ scorns the idea, as Rome, although of great magnificence, is also the seat of a wicked, debauched, cruel, blood-thirsty people. Of His kingdom Christ says there is no end. Satan replies that he can give Him any kingdom, as they had all been given to him. He then suggests that Christ should fall down and worship him; this Christ refuses to do. Satan may have tempted Eve but he cannot tempt Christ. Satan then says that perhaps in His disregard for worldly things, Christ is more addicted to contemplation and debate than to the acquisition of material things; when He was only twelve years of age He went to the temple, where He argued learnedly with the priests, and one can tell what a man will be by what he is as a child. Satan says:

> And thou thyself seemst otherwise inclined
> Than to a worldly crown, addicted more
> To contemplation and profound dispute,
> As by that early action may be judged,
> When slipping from thy mother's eye thou went'st
> Alone into the temple; there was found
> Among the gravest rabbis disputant
> On points and questions fitting Moses' chair,
> Teaching, not taught; **the childhood shows the man**
> **As morning shows the day.** Be famous then
> By wisdom; as thy empire must extend,
> So let extend thy mind o'er all the world,
> In knowledge, all things in it comprehend.

A child's a plaything for an hour

Source: PARENTAL RECOLLECTIONS
Author: Mary Ann Lamb (1764-1847)
First published: 1809
Type of work: Children's poem

Context: If it had not been for a writer and publisher disliked by the Lamb family, William Godwin (1756–1836), Mary Lamb might have gone silent to the grave. Her brother Charles Lamb (1775–1834) earned his name in literature by his *Essays of Elia* published in the *London Magazine* between 1820 and 1825, observations on life set down in fa-

143

miliar language and delightful style. His plans for marriage were disrupted by his sister's spell of madness in which she attacked her father and killed her mother. Lamb spent the rest of his life acting as her guardian. He, too, became unbalanced and spent the years 1795-1796 in an asylum, but recovered. So did she, but their acquaintance, Godwin, suggested that to occupy Mary's mind, Charles and she should join in writing children's books for his "Juvenile Library." At that time, most books for children were simple and stupid tales, sure to bore any bright child. Mary Lamb was especially critical of them, so they began writing as a kind of protest, first *King and Queen of Hearts* (1805) and then the volume for which they are best remembered, *Tales from Shakespear* (1807), a prose retelling of his best known plays. Next came a simplified version of the *Adventures of Ulysses* (1808). Since both of the Lambs had written poetry, they collected eighty of their products as *Poetry for Children* (1809). Only internal evidence indicates which author wrote any given poem. One, called "Parental Recollections," is generally attributed to Mary, though some scholars ascribe the authorship to Charles, possibly because he quoted the first line in his Elia essay "The Old and the New Schoolmaster," and because his "Dream Children," is correlated to the whole poem.

A child's a plaything for an hour;
Its pretty tricks we try
For that or for a longer space;
    Then tire, and lay it by.

But I know one, that to itself
    All seasons could controul;
That would have mock'd the sense of pain
    Out of a grievèd soul.

Thou, straggler into loving arms,
    Young climber up of knees,
When I forget thy thousand ways,
    Then life and all shall cease.

The choir invisible

Source: O MAY I JOIN THE CHOIR INVISIBLE (Line 1)
Author: George Eliot (1819-1880)
First published: 1867
Type of work: Lyric poem

Context: Known primarily as a great novelist, George Eliot was also a poet; although it is true that most of her poems are highly personal, she at times touches upon themes and sentiments that are universal. Like many of her more intellectual contemporaries, George Eliot quite early faced the dilemma of Christianity's confrontation with skeptical science. Not only did she radically disagree with the traditional interpretation of Christ, she also translated and made accessible to the English, Straus's *Leben Jesu,* a liberal version of the life of Jesus. But George Eliot was not content to rest with skepticism. Torn by the desire to find a meaningful faith, she came more and more to exalt the basic goodness of man, a humanism that transcended individuals. In this brief poem, she tells of her desire to be a part of the company of men who have made earthly life better; hers was no fuzzy otherworldliness—she searched for a community in which the best of human endeavor formed the highest religion.

O may I join **the choir invisible**
Of those immortal dead who live again
In minds made better by their presence: live
In pulses stirred to generosity,
In deeds of daring rectitude, in scorn
For miserable aims that end with self,
In thoughts sublime that pierce the night like stars,
And with their mild persistence urge man's search
To vaster issues. . . .

The Christless code, that must have life for a blow

Source: MAUD (Part II, sec. i, 11. 26-27)
Author: Alfred, Lord Tennyson (1809-1892)
First published: 1855
Type of work: Narrative poem

Context: When the narrator of this long poem (which Tennyson called a "monodrama") was a small boy, he heard his father and the father of an as yet unborn child agree that, should the baby be a girl, the children shall marry each other when they are grown. But a few years later the narrator's father loses all of his money and dies, perhaps a suicide. Maud's father, on the other hand, grows richer; and the narrator is discarded as a possible husband for Maud because of his poverty—a favorite theme with Tennyson. Maud's brother has found what he considers a better match for her in the person of a newly-made lord, an overdressed, supercilious, and proud young man. The brother, who is politically ambitious, gives a large dinner and ball for his constituents, from which the narrator is pointedly excluded. He and Maud, however, plan that she will meet him in the garden of her house at the conclusion of the dance. But hardly has she entered the garden, in all the splendor of her ballgown and jewels, than her brother arrives, bringing with him the "babefaced lord," and pours out "terms of disgrace" on his sister. The narrator replies with equal anger, until the brother strikes him in the face. This

145

act, according to the code still prevailing as late as the 1850's, demands a challenge, which the narrator immediately gives; and in the duel which takes place within an hour, he kills Maud's brother. Tennyson uses this episode to express his detestation of the code of dueling.

> And he struck me, madman, over the face,
> Struck me before the languid fool,
> Who was gaping and grinning by;
> Struck for himself an evil stroke;
> Wrought for his house an irredeemable woe;
> For front to front in an hour we stood,
> And a million horrible bellowing echoes
>   broke
> From the red-ribb'd hollow behind the wood,
> And thunder'd up into Heaven **the Christless code,**
> **That must have life for a blow.**
> Ever and ever afresh they seem'd to grow.

Christmas comes but once a year

Source: FIVE HUNDRED POINTS OF GOOD HUSBANDRY (Chapter 12, "The Farmer's Daily Diet")
Author: Thomas Tusser (c.1525-1580)
First published: 1557
Type of work: Didactic poem

Context: Thomas Tusser was a gentleman of good birth and a graduate of Eton and Cambridge, who forsook the world of the court and took up farming. He evidently did not prosper at it, for he moved several times and finally died in a debtor's prison; but he nonetheless became the poet of early Elizabethan farm life. His works are composed largely of practical instructions to farmers and housewives, and are written in verse. Much of this material is doggerel, but it is vivid and possesses a homely charm. The result is a faithful and realistic picture of rural England during the middle of the sixteenth century. The first eleven chapters of *Five Hundred Points of Good Husbandry* are short verses which describe husbandry and offer general recommendations; beginning with Chapter Thirteen, Tusser covers the farmer's year month by month, discussing the various activities peculiar to each. Each month is preceded by a brief summary of the matters to be discussed, and various comments on weather, planets and climate are interspersed from time to time. The book is an early forerunner of the farmers' almanacs. Chapter Twelve is entitled "The Farmer's Daily Diet," and describes the plain but solid and substantial fare of the period. Fish is an important staple in the diet, both fresh and salted, as is salt meat. The first three stanzas of the chapter refer to Lent and Easter. "Martilmas beef" is beef dried and smoked in the chimney after the manner of bacon. The couplets which follow refer to Midsummer (St. John's Day), Michaelmas, Hallowmass, and Christmas; these in turn are followed by moral reflections and references to special days. The second and third stanzas and the first five couplets are given below:

Let Lent, well kept, offend not thee,
For March and April breeders be:
Spend herring first, save salt-fish last,
For salt-fish is good, when Lent is past.

When Easter comes, who knows not than
That veal and bacon is the man;
And Martilmas beef doth bear good tack,
When country folks do dainties lack.

When Mackrell ceaseth from the seas,
John Baptist brings grass-beef and pease.

Fresh herring plenty, Mitchell brings,
With fatted crones [old ewes], and such old things.

All Saints do lay for pork and souse,
For sprats and spurlings for their house.

At Christmas play, and make good cheer,
For **Christmas comes, but once a-year.**

Though some then do, as do they would,
Let thrifty do, as do they should.

The Cincinnatus of the West

Source: ODE TO NAPOLEON BONAPARTE (Stanza 19)
Author: George Gordon, Lord Byron (1788-1824)
First published: 1814
Type of work: Satiric ode

Context: Napoleon, in his years of glory, seemed to the British and to many others a supremely dangerous man, and his empire a great shadow into which all Europe would shortly disappear. By the beginning of 1814, however, the tide had turned; and Napoleon's disastrous Russian campaign was the turning point. He invaded Russia with an army of 640,-000 men; the Russians retreated, laying waste the countryside as they retired. When Napoleon entered Moscow it was set afire and burned for

147

five days; his troops had to take refuge in the open, devastated countryside and could not live off the land. It was October, and Napoleon had to retreat. His men, continually harassed by mounted Cossacks, died of hunger, cold, disease, and exhaustion. When the army entered its own territory at last there were but 25,000 men left. No longer thought invincible, Napoleon found all Europe ready to fight him. He still had an army in Germany, and undertook another campaign. A series of victories was followed by utter defeat in the "Battle of the Nations," and his retreat from the Rhine was almost as disastrous as that from Moscow. From Paris he sallied forth once more, but the defeat this time was decisive; Napoleon abdicated on April 6, 1814, and retired to the Island of Elba. Byron was editing a paper called *The Corsair* at the time and had announced his intention to give up the writing of poetry. However, when word was received concerning Napoleon's abdication, Byron broke his resolution and wrote an ode to Bonaparte. In it he excoriates the emperor, who has strewn all Europe with blood and bones and whose only work has been destruction. If Napoleon had been truly great, says Byron, he would have stepped down as soon as France's greatness had been restored. The last portion of the poem is given below; in the final stanza Byron makes an interesting comparison between a leader he deplores and one he admires.

There was a day—there was an hour—
    While earth was Gaul's—Gaul thine—
When that immeasurable power
    Unsated to resign,
Had been an act of purer fame
Than gathers round Marengo's name,
    And gilded thy decline
Through the long twilight of all time,
Despite some passing clouds of crime.

But thou forsooth must be a king . . .
Vain forward child of empire! say,
Are all thy playthings snatch'd away?

Where may the wearied eye repose,
    When gazing on the Great;
Where neither guilty glory glows,
    Nor despicable state?
Yes—one—the first—the last—the best—
The Cincinnatus of the West,
    Whom envy dared not hate,
Bequeath'd the name of Washington,
To make man blush there was but one!

Civility costs nothing and buys everything

Source: LETTER TO THE COUNTESS OF BUTE (30 May 1756)
Author: Lady Mary Wortley Montagu (1689-1762)
First published: 1763
Type of work: Personal letter

Context: The eighteenth century is remembered in part for the excellency of its letter writers such as the Earl of Chesterfield, Thomas Gray, Horace Walpole, and above all Lady Mary Wortley Montagu. The wife of an ambassador, she was provided not only the opportunity for extensive travel but also the access to many of the events which an ordinary traveler would never experience. Her letters, unusually detailed and frank in tone, were written for the most part to her daughter, her sisters, and her intimate friends. Apparently at home in France, Italy, Spain, Germany, Holland, Austria, or Turkey, Lady Mary recorded a vivid and intimate record of the nations and their political institutions. In a letter of May 30, 1756, to her daughter, the Countess of Bute, Lady Mary describes her sorrow upon hearing of the death of an old friend—Sir William Lowther—and, in turn, her anger at the way his estate has been devoured by ravenous inheritors. In this respect she asserts that he died "fortunately," believing "himself blessed in many friends, whom a short time would have shown to be worthless, mercenary, designing scoundrels." The letter is typical of those to her daughter in that it is imbued with moral counsel and earnestness of purpose. In the opening paragraph she urges the countess to be discreet and gracious in her associations with a certain Mr. Prescot who had previously taken offense at her haughty demeanor:

I sent you a long letter very lately, and enclosed one to Lady Jane, and also a second bill for fifty pounds, which I hope you have received, though I fear I cannot prevail on Mr. Prescot to take care of my letters; if he should do it, I beg you would be very obliging to him; remember, **civility costs nothing and buys everything;** your daughters should engrave that maxim in their hearts.

Clean hands and a pure heart

Source: PSALMS 24:4
Author: Unknown
First transcribed: c.400-200 B.C.
Type of work: Religious poetry

Context: Psalm 24 embodies the liturgy for Jehovah's entrance into the Temple. The first two verses are a quiet affirmation of faith, acknowledging God's universal dominion. The next four verses are a liturgy for those who come to worship in Jerusalem, the holy place. In them the need

149

for purity is emphasized: the worshiper must be clean physically and spiritually, he must be humble, and honesty is required of him. Such a person will receive the blessing of the Lord. The serene faith in these lines echoes that in Psalm 23 and is a reflection of the same deep religious feeling. The liturgy ends with a verse stating that the people are spiritually ready to enter the temple. Here there is a gathering sense of anticipation, of a pause before the next act in this sacred drama. The last four verses fulfill that expectation; they celebrate the entrance of Jehovah, as symbolized by the Ark of the Covenant, into the Temple. It is carried in by a procession; members of the procession are singing praises to the Lord, who will be present in the Temple so long as the Ark remains there. This jubilant hymn is a demand that the gates of the Temple may be opened so that the Lord can enter. In accordance with custom, the demand is made twice; twice the identity of "this King of glory" is demanded in return; and twice there is the joyous reply that this King is none other than Jehovah. This brief hymn of four verses is one of the most majestic passages in Scripture; Handel drew upon it for some of the exalted portions of his *Messiah,* giving it music which, in dignity and grandeur, is worthy of it.

The earth is the LORD's, and the fulness thereof; the world, and they that dwell therein.

For he hath founded it upon the seas, and established it upon the floods.

Who shall ascend into the hill of the LORD? or who shall stand in his holy place?

He that hath **clean hands, and a pure heart;** who hath not lifted up his soul unto vanity, nor sworn deceitfully.

He shall receive the blessing from the LORD, and righteousness from the God of his salvation.

This is the generation of them that seek him, that seek thy face, O Jacob. Selah.

Lift up your heads, O ye gates; and be ye lift up, ye everlasting doors; and the King of glory shall come in.

Who is this King of glory? The LORD strong and mighty, the LORD mighty in battle.

Lift up your heads, O ye gates; even lift them up, ye everlasting doors; and the King of glory shall come in.

Who is this King of glory? The LORD of hosts, he is the King of glory. Selah.

Cleave ever to the sunnier side of doubt

Source: THE ANCIENT SAGE (Line 68)
Author: Alfred, Lord Tennyson (1809-1892)
First published: 1885
Type of work: Philosophical poem

Context: A venerable sage a thousand years before the time of Christ speaks to a follower. He points to a gushing spring of water and says that its source is not here, but high up—not merely in the hills, nor yet in the clouds, but in the heavens where the clouds are moulded. The follower has a scroll in which is written a poem, the essence of which is that the things of this earth owe their existence to a nameless power that is never seen nor heard. The Nameless, says the sage, is in all things; if he removed himself, everything would vanish, even though he had never spoken to man. The follower cannot prove the existence of the Nameless; he cannot prove the existence of the world in which he lives; he cannot prove that he is a body, soul, or a combination of the two; he cannot prove that he is either mortal or immortal; he cannot prove that the sage is not another part of himself, holding a dialogue with himself. In fact, since nothing worthy of being proved can be either proved or disproved, he will do well to cleave to the better side of things that he doubts, because faith always sees the best in the world, even though it may be cloaked with the worst.

> Thou canst not prove the Nameless, O my son,
> Nor canst thou prove the world thou movest in,
> Thou canst not prove that thou art body alone,
> Nor canst thou prove that thou art spirit alone,
> Nor canst thou prove that thou art both in one:
> Thou canst not prove thou art immortal, no
> Nor yet that thou art mortal—nay, my son,
> Thou canst not prove that I, who speak with thee,
> Am not thyself in converse with thyself,
> For nothing worthy proving can be proven,
> Nor yet disproven: wherefore thou be wise,
> **Cleave ever to the sunnier side of doubt,**
> And cling to Faith beyond the forms of Faith!

Clever to a fault

Source: BISHOP BLOUGRAM'S APOLOGY (Line 420)
Author: Robert Browning (1812-1889)
First published: 1855
Type of work: Dramatic monologue

Context: Bishop Blougram and a literary acquaintance, Gigadibs, discuss religion over their wine, following Corpus Christi Day supper. Gigadibs, a thirty-year-old magazine writer, appears as a representative of mid-nineteenth century philosophical thought. The bishop, a person with "a soul and body that exact/ A comfortable care in many ways," dominates the discussion with his self-defense. The talk centers on whether it is better to live a life of faith diversified by doubt, as does the bishop, or of doubt diversified by faith, as does Gigadibs. In a skeptical age, the bishop finds his inner-core of faith confronted by his intellectual doubt. He attempts to rationalize his position of a doubting believer whose faith has been questioned by his contemporary intellectuals. His unique position, he claims, is a historical accident. Had he been born three hundred years earlier, no one would have questioned his faith; seventy years later, no one would question his doubt:

> It's through my coming in the tail of time,
> Nicking the minute with a happy tact.
> Had I been born three hundred years ago
> They'd say, "What's strange? Blougram of course believes";
> And, seventy years since, "disbelieves of course."
> But now, "He may believe; and yet, and yet
> How can he?"—All eyes turn with interest.
> Whereas, step off the line on either side—
> You, for example, **clever to a fault,**
> The rough and ready man who writes apace,
> Read somewhat seldomer, think perhaps even less—
> You disbelieve! Who wonders and who cares?

Close thy Byron; open thy Goethe

Source: SARTOR RESARTUS (Book II, chapter 9)
Author: Thomas Carlyle (1795-1881)
First published: 1833-1834
Type of work: Spiritual autobiography

Context: In an involved work with the subtitle "The Life and Opinions of Herr Teufelsdröckh," and written at his wife's farm where they had moved to economize, Carlyle continued his censorship of the highly praised Victorian Era. The title of the work, *Sartor Resartus* (The Tailor Reclothed) was taken from a figure used by Swift in a *Tale of a Tub* (1704). As the father, in Swift's satire, gave garments to his three sons, representing three branches of religion with stipulations that they should not alter the garments, only to have each son change the clothing to suit his ideals, so Carlyle expounded that the material world was merely clothing for the spiritual world. Swift had asked: "What is man himself but a microcoat," living amid surroundings that are like a "large suit of clothes which invests everything?" Carlyle put into the work his own social criticism and transcendental philosophy. And, of course, he worked into it his basic ideas on duty, work, and silence that appear in almost everything he wrote. At the age of 24, Carlyle had begun to study German at a time when few of his countrymen were interested in its philosophy or literature. He translated a number of works not previously available for English readers, such as his 1824 translation of Goethe's *Wilhelm Meister's Apprenticeship and Travels*. He also wrote a biography of Goethe and essays on his works. Not blinded by Romanticism like so many of his contemporaries, he believed that Byron's poetic works were frothy in comparison with the writing of Goethe. In his book, he quotes the imaginary professor and philosophic author Teufelsdröckh, as he utters his "Everlasting No," his bitter and sweeping denunciation of the structure of society. Two chapters later, one entitled "The Everlasting Yea," voices what he does believe: that clothes, and human institutions, and religions of the past should be considered only as an expression of the continuing life of the Soul. Man has the power to design the clothes that he will wear. In urging Englishmen to stop living in the exotic, rebellious world of Byron and Romanticism, and to turn against the love intrigues and irreverent frivolities of *Don Juan* and *Childe Harold,* Carlyle quotes the Professor's stern command: "Love not pleasure; love God. This is the EVERLASTING YEA, wherein all contradiction is solved."

"I asked myself: What is this that, ever since earliest years, thou hast been fretting and fuming, and lamenting and self-tormenting, on account of? Say it in a word: is it not because thou art not HAPPY? Because the THOU (sweet gentleman) is not sufficiently honored, nourished, soft-bedded, and lovingly cared for? Foolish soul! What Act of Legislature was there that *thou* shouldst be Happy? . . . Art thou nothing other than a Vulture, then, that fliest through the Universe seeking after somewhat to *eat;* and shrieking dolefully because carrion enough is not given thee? **Close thy Byron; open thy Goethe."**

Close-lipped patience

Source: THE SCHOLAR-GYPSY (Stanza 20)
Author: Matthew Arnold (1822-1888)
First published: 1853
Type of work: Philosophical poem

Context: The poem is centered around just what its title suggests—a scholar who became a gypsy after being disillusioned with Oxford. This scholar began to learn how gypsies "had arts to rule as they desired/ the workings of men's brains." As time passed, the scholar's great mission in life became to learn this gypsy art completely and then "impart the art" to the world. The scholar-gypsy goes on to say that he must have "heaven-sent moments" to master this skill. Using this legend of the scholar-gypsy and his central mission, the poet Arnold contrasts the gypsy's life with the lives of most men. He says that modern men go first one direction then another, never really knowing what their goal is. And finally after wearing themselves out with their daily insignificant struggles, they wait with "close-lipp'd patience" for death. This in contrast with the scholar-gypsy who waits "for the spark from heaven" so he can carry out his great purpose in life.

153

...and we others pine,
And wish the long unhappy dream would
    end,
And waive all claim to bliss, and try to
    bear;
With **close-lipp'd patience** for our only
    friend,
Sad patience, too near neighbor
    to despair—
But none has hope like thine!

Coat of many colors

Source: GENESIS 37:23
Author: Unknown
First transcribed: c.1000-300 B.C.
Type of work: Religious history and law

Context: Israel has many sons by his wives, Bilhah and Zilpah, but he loves best his son Joseph, because Joseph is the child of his old age. When the other sons see that their father loves Joseph the best, they hate the boy and speak evil of him. Joseph tells his brothers of dreams he has, and these dreams increase their hatred. He tells them that in one dream their sheaves of grain make obeisance to his sheaf and that in another dream "the sun and moon and the eleven stars" make obeisance to him. Later Israel's other sons take their father's flocks to graze in Shechem. While they are away, Israel sends Joseph to ascertain their well-being. Joseph finds they have left Shechem and wandered on with the flocks to Dothan, and he follows them there. When Joseph arrives in their midst, the brothers conspire against him. Lest Joseph be killed, Reuben suggests to the others that Joseph be stripped of the coat their father has given him and be placed in a pit, for Reuben hopes that he may rescue Joseph and return him to their father. But while Reuben is away, the other brothers follow Judah's suggestion to sell Joseph into slavery. To hide their deed they dip Joseph's coat in a kid's blood and send it to Israel, who then believes that a wild beast has killed the boy:

And it came to pass, when Joseph was come unto his brethren, that they stript Joseph out of his coat, his **coat of many colours** that was on him:
And they took him, and cast him into a pit: and the pit was empty, there was no water in it.

· · ·

And they took Joseph's coat, and killed a kid of the goats, and dipped the coat in the blood;
And they sent the **coat of many colours,** and they brought it to their father. . . .

154

And he knew it, and said, It is my son's coat; an evil beast hath devoured him; Joseph is without doubt rent in pieces.

Cock and bull story

Source: THE LIFE AND OPINIONS OF TRISTRAM SHANDY, GENT. (Book IX, chapter 33)
Author: Laurence Sterne (1713-1768)
First published: 1759-1767
Type of work: Novel

Context: Laurence Sterne's novel displays his whimsical nature as an author throughout. He uses such tricks of typography as blank pages, black pages, pointing fingers, and a large assortment of dots, dashes, and asterisks. Even the Preface is at an unusual place, not being found by the reader till he reaches the twentieth chapter of Book III. The very end of the novel is as whimsical as the portions that precede it. The final chapter begins with Mr. Walter Shandy, Tristram's father, discoursing upon idiosyncrasies of man's attitudes toward sex, as compared to those we have about the honor attached to the killing of men, especially in war. While he is speaking he is interrupted by one of his tenants, who has come with a complaint about the bull that Walter Shandy keeps to serve the cows of the parish. The tenant's wife has been brought to bed with a child some six weeks before, but the man's cow, which should have calved at the same time, has not produced an offspring. At the end of the conversation which follows, about the bull and his paternal abilities, Mrs. Shandy asks what the story is all about. Parson Yorick comments to her about the story of the bull, but the ambiguity of his comment goes further, being a statement as well about the novel which Laurence Sterne has laid before the reader.

—Most of the townsmen, an' please your worship, quoth Obadiah, believe that 'tis all the Bull's fault—
—But may not a cow be barren? replied my father, turning to Dr. Slop.
—It never happens: said Dr. Slop, but the man's wife may have come before her time naturally enough—Prithee has the child hair upon his head?—added Dr. Slop—
—It is as hairy as I am; said Obadiah.—Obadiah had not been shaved for three weeks—Wheu—u——u————cried my father; beginning the sentence with an exclamatory whistle—and so, brother Toby, this poor Bull of mine, who is as good a bull as ever p-ssed, and might have done for Europa herself in purer times—had he but two legs less, might have been driven into Doctors' Commons and lost his character—which to a town Bull, brother Toby, is the very same thing as his life—

155

L—d! said my mother, what is this story all about?—

A Cock and a Bull, said Yorick—and one of the best of its kind, I ever heard.

Coiner of sweet words

Source: SOHRAB AND RUSTUM (Line 458)
Author: Matthew Arnold (1822-1888)
First published: 1853
Type of work: Narrative poem

Context: In this long poem, based on an episode in the Persian epic *Shah Namah,* Sohrab, a young Tartar warrior, had been reared by his mother in a province of Persia; because she did not want him to be a warrior, she told his father that the child was a girl. Now, however, Sohrab has grown to manhood and in hopes of finding his father, the famous war chieftain Rustum, challenges the Persian army to send its greatest warrior to fight him in a single combat. Without knowing that the challenger is his son, Rustum comes out of retirement to fight the youth. Although Sohrab at first thinks that the Persian defender is his father, Rustum, who fights incognito, thinks that the hesitant boy wants to back from his challenge and forces him to begin the combat. Just before the quotation, Sohrab again asks the unknown defender if he is Rustum; when Rustum angrily rebukes him, the battle is renewed with such fury that he forgets himself, shouts his battlecry and kills his son, who was too shocked by the cry to defend himself. Early in the combat, Rustum is enraged that the youth has so much skill in arms.

> His breast heaved, his lips foam'd, and twice his voice
> Was choked with rage; at last these words broke way:—
> "Girl! nimble with thy feet, not with thy hands!
> Curl'd minion, dancer, **coiner of sweet words!**
> Fight, let me hear thy hateful voice no more! . . .
> Speak not to me of truce, and pledge, and wine!
> Remember all thy valour; try thy feints
> And cunning! all the pity I had is gone; . . ."

The cold charities of man to man

Source: THE VILLAGE (Line 245)
Author: George Crabbe (1754-1832)
First published: 1783
Type of work: Satiric poem

Context: The poet begins by saying that the usual pastoral poem bears not the faintest resemblance to reality; instead of being based on observation of the country and its folk, it is wholly derived from classical writers, such as Virgil. He gives a description of the land, which is evidently that along the English Channel, in which region Crabbe was born and bred. He finds the soil sandy, thin, and sterile, and covered with the plants that grow only on barren ground. And the people are far different from those in the pastoral idyls. Instead of devoting themselves to happy rural sports and piping gaily, they sweat the long day through in back-breaking toil. Their pains are not the amorous ones of the poets, but actual physical pains of bones, muscles, and sinews. Nor do they sit down to the plain but plentiful repasts of the songs: their diet is sparse and pinching and those who sing of it would not deign to touch it. As a result of what they have to live on, they are highly susceptible to disease. When a man grows old, his miseries increase; he can be useful only in some sedentary labor such as herding sheep. Or he can resort to the poorhouse, truly the dwelling place of misery, where the most enviable inmates are the idiots who do not feel hardships. It is here that the cold charities of man to man are dispensed amidst scenes of unimaginable squalor.

> Here too the sick their final doom receive,
> Here brought, amid the scenes of grief, to grieve,
> Where the loud groans from some sad chamber flow,
> Mix'd with the clamours of the crowd below;
> Here, sorrowing, they each kindred sorrow scan,
> And **the cold charities of man to man:**
> Whose laws indeed for ruin'd age provide,
> And strong compulsion plucks the scrap from pride;
> But still that scrap is bought with many a sigh,
> And pride embitters what it can't deny.

The cold neutrality of an impartial judge

Source: PREFACE TO THE ADDRESS OF M. BRISSOT
Author: Edmund Burke (1729-1797)
First published: 1794
Type of work: Political essay

Context: M. Brissot had addressed the French Constituent Assembly concerning the deterioration of French diplomatic relations with several European nations following the decline into violence of the French Revolution and the attempts of the Concordat to export revolutionary ideas. As a revolutionary himself, he described the horrors in very vivid terms. This address was translated into English by William Burke, a relative and close friend of Edmund. In presenting this *Address* to English readers Edmund Burke prefaced it with an essay in which he described it as the testimony of a revolutionary against his own revolution and therefore of greater force than the opinions of those who opposed the Revolution:

They who are inclined to think favorably of that event will undoubtedly object to every state of facts which comes only from the authority of a royalist. Thus much must be allowed by those who are the most firmly attached to the cause of religion, law, and order, (for of such, and not of friends to despotism, the royal party is composed,)—that their very affection to this generous and manly cause, and their abhorrence of a Revolution not less fatal to liberty than to government, may possibly lead them in some particulars to a more harsh representation of the proceedings of their adversaries than would be allowed by **the cold neutrality of an impartial judge.** This sort of error arises from a source highly laudable; but the exactness of truth may suffer even from the feelings of virtue. History will do justice to the intentions of worthy men, but it will be on its guard against their infirmities; it will examine with great strictness of scrutiny whatever appears from a writer in favour of his own cause. . . .

Coldly profane and impiously gay

Source: THE LIBRARY (Line 265)
Author: George Crabbe (1754-1832)
First published: 1781
Type of work: Satiric poem

Context: The poet begins by saying that books are a refuge for the despondent, as the pains in books are less than those of real life; or they may be so much greater than our own that we are reconciled to our lot. He describes how the books are arranged in the library: first, noble folios, followed by quartos, octavos, and duodecimos. They are also grouped by subject, the first being divinity. These books, however, do not give us the great and important truths by which we could live; instead, they are mainly concerned with religious controversy and hair-splitting distinctions. The writers have been motivated more by spleen than by desire to inform. Sect contends against sect, from the Athanasians against the Arians down to the controversies of modern times. Next to the works on divinity are those on skepticism, which are for the most part of the modern period. The writers of these works lack deep learning, genius, and grace. But what they lack in depth of learning they make up in numbers. Some are serious in their dubious claims; others are more flippant, coldly profane, and impiously gay.

> Near to these seats, behold yon slender frames,
> All closely fill'd and mark'd with modern names;
> Where no fair science ever shows her face,
> Few sparks of genius, and no spark of grace;
> There sceptics rest, a still-increasing throng,
> And stretch their widening wings ten thousand strong;
> Some in close fight their dubious claims maintain;

Some skirmish lightly, fly and fight again;
Coldly profane, and impiously gay,
Their end the same, though various in their way.

Come, gentle Spring, ethereal mildness, come

Source: THE SEASONS: SPRING (Line 1)
Author: James Thomson (1700-1748)
First published: 1728
Type of work: Nature poem

Context: Despite the fact that at the beginning of each new year James Thomson burned what he considered his inferior poetry of the previous year, critics consider his early work inferior to that of most poets, and preserved only because of the excellence of such later efforts as *The Seasons.* After studying theology in Edinburgh, he moved to London where "Winter," the first of his *Seasons,* was published in 1726, followed by "Summer," and, in 1728, by "Spring," dedicated to Frances, Countess of Hertford. Poetry was not a paying profession, and Thomson spent time in a debtors' prison until friends paid the debt. As his poetry became better known, his financial status improved. Yet he always claimed he was too poor to marry, and died a bachelor at forty-eight, boasting "no line which dying he could wish to blot." Part One of the *Seasons,* "Spring," describes the effect of that time of the year on everything from inanimate matter and vegetables to man, and contrasts wild, passionate love with the purer and gentler kind. It begins:

> **Come, gentle Spring, ethereal mildness come;**
> And from the bosom of yon dropping cloud,
> While music wakes around, veil'd in a shower
> Of shadowing roses, on our plains descend.
>   O HERTFORD, fitted or to shine in court
> With unaffected grace, or walk the plain
> With innocence and meditation join'd,
> In soft assemblage, listen to my Song,
> Which thy own season paints; where Nature all
> Is blooming, and benevolent, like thee.
>   And see where surly WINTER passes off,
> Far to the north, and calls his ruffian Blasts;
> While softer gales succeed, at whose kind touch,
> Dissolving snows in livid torrents lost,
> The mountains lift their green heads to the sky.

Come into the garden, Maud

Source: MAUD (Part I, section 22, stanza 1)
Author: Alfred, Lord Tennyson (1809-1892)
First published: 1855
Type of work: Narrative poem

Context: Maud, in its day one of Tennyson's most disputed works, has for many readers lost the appeal which it once had for some. Nonetheless, it is still one of the most readable of all his poems. In form it is a "monodrama"—an extended dramatic monologue divided into episodes, each of which is a soliloquy. The plot, typical of the era in which *Maud* was written, concerns a poor young man; his poverty is a source of great pain to him, for he is proud. He falls in love with the beautiful Maud and struggles to win her in spite of her wealthy family and the rival of their choice; the end is despair, madness, and death. In his first soliloquy the narrator reveals an unstable, or unsettled, mind: he recalls the tragic death of his father, who probably committed suicide; he considers the evils of the world, and says bitterly that war is the best remedy for them. He raves, as his father used to do. In the meantime he notes that the Hall is being refurbished; he has heard of the beauty of Maud, who will live there; he had known her as a child and is eager to see her again. When he does so, his first impression is that she is cold as a stone. After a second meeting, he thinks about her and about the barrier of wealth that lies between them. Later, he hears her sing. Gradually they are drawn together. But the narrator is suddenly convulsed with jealousy: there is a rival, a haughty new-made lord with little to commend him save his money and his title. Maud returns the narrator's love, but he knows he has little chance against Maud's family and the supercilious competitor they have chosen for her. Her love has improved the narrator's mental health, and his nightmare thoughts no longer persecute him. One night there is a huge dinner and dance given at the Hall; Maud will slip away and meet the narrator afterward. He, anticipating her arrival, indulges in a passionate love-song—little dreaming that they will be discovered and that he will kill her brother in a duel:

Come into the garden, Maud,
   For the black bat, night, has flown,
Come into the garden, Maud,
   I am here at the gate alone;
And the woodbine spices are wafted abroad,
   And the musk of the rose is blown.

For a breeze of morning moves,
   And the planet of Love is on high,
Beginning to faint in the light that she loves
   On a bed of daffodil sky,

To faint in the light of the sun she loves,
   To faint in his light, and to die.

      • • •

She is coming, my own, my sweet;
   Were it ever so airy a tread,
My heart would hear it and beat,
   Were it earth in an earthy bed;
My dust would hear her and beat,
   Had I lain for a century dead;
Would start and tremble under her feet,
   And blossom in purple and red.

Come lovely and soothing death

Source: WHEN LILACS LAST IN THE DOORYARD BLOOM'D (Line 135)
Author: Walt Whitman (1819-1892)
First published: 1865
Type of work: Elegy

Context: Walt Whitman wanted to write down-to-earth poetry, unrhymed and with lines of varying length, in order to appeal to the workers. Ironically, few of the common people in his own country knew his works. However, poets all over the world have been influenced by him to experiment with meter and subject matter. Stirred by the Civil War, he wrote patriotic poetry. He traveled to Washington in December, 1862, to look after his brother, wounded in battle; there following the slaughter at Fredericksburg, he found much to do as a volunteer nurse. In Washington he saw President Lincoln many times and was especially moved by his death at the moment of victory. The result was "When Lilacs Last in the Dooryard Bloom'd." Its appearance under such tragic circumstances made over-praise easy. Closer study, however, shows that while the poem contains many lines of rich poetic imagery, much of the poetry is conventional, with stock phrases. The references to Lincoln are so few that the poem might serve as a lament for almost any great man. Actually, Whitman's poem "O Captain! My Captain!" is much more concerned with the national calamity. However, the carol of death, sung by the gray-brown bird, is a poetic statement of Whitman's own attitude toward death. It begins with an echo of Shakespeare's "O amiable lovely death!" (*King John*, III, iv).

Come lovely and soothing death,
Undulate round the world, serenely arriving, arriving,
In the day, in the night, to all, to each,
Sooner or later delicate death.

Prais'd be the fathomless universe,
For life and joy, and for objects and knowledge curious,

161

And for love, sweet love—but praise! praise! praise!
For the sure-enwinding arms of cool-enfolding death.

Come the three corners of the world in arms

Source: KING JOHN (Act V, sc. vii, l. 116)
Author: William Shakespeare (1564-1616)
First published: 1623
Type of work: Historical drama

Context: It is a dark hour in the history of England: the crown is worn by John, a king sadly lacking in grace and grandeur; King Philip of France demands the throne for his nephew, Arthur, son of the deceased older brother of John; the pope excommunicates the king for his refusal to accept the papal choice for the Archbishop of Canterbury; and several powerful English noblemen rebel against their king and join forces with the French. Ironically, though, when the English lords, "her princes," have returned their support to their king, when the breach with the Church has been healed, and when finally the forces of the French have been turned back, it is discovered that King John is dying of poison given to him by a villainous monk. Nevertheless, England has been brought to a firm stand. Henry, the son of King John, receives the crown, and the play ends in a speech of patriotic triumph delivered by Philip Faulconbridge, bastard nephew of King John:

BASTARD
. . .

This England never did, nor never shall
Lie at the proud foot of a conqueror,
But when it first did help to wound itself.
Now these her princes are come home again,
Come the three corners of the world in arms,
And we shall shock them. Naught shall make us rue,
If England to itself do rest but true.

A coming shower your shooting corns presage

Source: A DESCRIPTION OF A CITY SHOWER (Line 9)
Author: Jonathan Swift (1667-1745)
First published: 1710
Type of work: Descriptive poem

Context: Swift's poem realistically describing the coming of a rain shower to eighteenth century London was written in 1710 and published that year in No. 238 of the famous periodical *The Tatler*. Swift describes,

162

in his first verse paragraph, the portents of the coming storm; the second portion of the poem describes people's reactions to the falling rain and their activities during the storm; and the third part describes how the rain, having fallen, runs through the gutters of the London streets to empty into the River Thames. The poem ends with the highly realistic, if somewhat unpoetic, lines that tell what the waters carry away with them: ". . . from butchers' stalls, dung, guts, and blood,/ Drown'd puppies, stinging sprats, all drench'd in mud,/ Dead cats, and turnip-tops, come tumbling down the flood." Readers familiar with Swift's poetry will recognize the technique of this poem, as well as the subject matter, to be akin to his "Description of the Morning," which appeared earlier in *The Tatler.* The quotation above appears in the first verse paragraph, which tells how the approaching storm may be predicted:

Careful observers may foretell the hour
(By sure prognostics) when to dread a show'r.
While rain depends, the pensive cat gives o'er
Her frolics, and pursues her tail no more.
Returning home at night, you'll find the sink
Strikes your offended sense with double stink.
If you be wise, then go not far to dine;
You'll spend in coach-hire more than save in wine.
A coming show'r your shooting corns presage,
Old aches throb, your hollow tooth will rage:
Saunt'ring in coffee-house is Dulman seen;
He damns the climate, and complains of spleen.

Commit the oldest sins the newest kinds of ways

Source: KING HENRY THE FOURTH: PART TWO (Act IV, sc. v, ll. 125-126)
Author: William Shakespeare (1564-1616)
First published: 1600
Type of work: Historical drama

Context: Struck by a fit of apoplexy, King Henry IV is placed on a bed by his courtiers, who have little hope he can survive. Beside him they place the crown, symbol of his kingship. Prince Hal, who has led a riotous life, but who will prove to be one of England's great kings, comes to the sickroom. Dismissing the courtiers, he sits to watch by his father's side. Thinking the old king has died, Hal falls to meditating on the burdens which have come to him. He reaches for the crown, places it upon his head, and, vowing nothing shall keep him from his rightful heritage, steps into another room, to weep. His father, rousing and missing the crown, recalls the young prince to him. Prince Hal defends his action, but the king speaks bitterly of his son and his early, riotous life. He accuses the prince of foolishly stealing what shall be rightfully his within a few hours;

163

and he complains that Hal has never loved him: "Thy life did manifest thou loved'st me not,/ And thou wilt have me die assur'd of it." The dying king continues his complaints, believing that he is leaving England in the hands of a son who will be the ruin of the kingdom. He fears that once he is dead, Hal will dismiss the good officials and repeal all the good decrees. It will be a question when Hal is crowned, laments the king, of elevating vanity and destroying the royal dignity. He fears that England will become "a wilderness again." He prophesies that from every kingdom the worst men will flock to England and his son's court:

HENRY
And to the English court assemble now,
From every region, apes of idleness!
Now, neighbour confines, purge you of your scum.
Have you a ruffian that will swear, drink, dance,
Revel the night, rob, murder, and **commit**
The oldest sins the newest kinds of ways?
Be happy, he will trouble you no more.
England shall double gild his treble guilt,
England shall give him office, honour, might;
For the fifth Harry from curbed license plucks
The muzzle of restraint, and the wild dog
Shall flesh his tooth on every innocent.
O my poor kingdom, sick with civil blows!

Conduct is three-fourths of our life

Source: LITERATURE AND DOGMA (Chapter I, section 3)
Author: Matthew Arnold (1822-1888)
First published: 1873
Type of work: Religious and literary essay

Context: English poet, literary critic, and classical scholar, Matthew Arnold—like John Ruskin—felt himself called as a kind of prophet to the Victorian scene. Son of the Headmaster of Rugby, he had grown up in a stanchly religious, if liberal, home, and he himself had experienced the frustration and spiritual dislocation which resulted from the scientific theories and discoveries of the mid-century. He could not, however, become a convert to science, for science in the final analysis would merely explain the systems under which life exists; it would not replace the inherent psychological needs for the religion it was destroying. Clearly then, to Arnold, with the old religion no longer feasible, a new kind of religion had to be found if man's personality was to remain meaningfully oriented to the principles of human dignity and the value of life. His solution was culture—"the best that has been said and thought in the world." Through education which would inculcate into the new generations the inherent human values as they have been articulated in the great aesthetic creations of the past, man could be taught to respect and sanctify the traditions of his civilization which have been inspired and crystallized under the impetus of religious worship. The Scriptures themselves, for example, quite apart from any divine record, possess valuable human instruction:

> The Old Testament, nobody will ever deny, is filled with the word and thought of righteousness. "In the way of righteousness is life, and in the pathway thereof is no death;" "Righteousness tendeth to life;" "He that pursueth evil pursueth it to his own death;" "The way of transgressors is hard;"—nobody will deny that those texts may stand for the fundamental and ever-recurring idea of the Old Testament. No people ever felt so strongly as those people of the Old Testament, the Hebrew people, that **conduct is three-fourths of our life** and its largest concern. No people ever felt so strongly that succeeding, going right, hitting the mark in this great concern, was the way of peace, the highest possible satisfaction. . . .

The confused jargon of their Babylonian pulpits

Source: REFLECTIONS ON THE REVOLUTION IN FRANCE
Author: Edmund Burke (1729-1797)
First published: 1790
Type of work: Political treatise

Context: Edmund Burke's essay was called "a letter intended to have been sent to a gentleman in Paris." Actually, it was an answer, carefully worked out, from a conservative viewpoint, to the sympathy for the French Revolution which was being expressed in England, written by a man who knew how much he could influence the opinions of his times. As a conservative, and as a man who appreciated the manner by which the history and traditions of Great Britain had evolved as a means to good government, Burke took exception to a suggestion, which he notes, that kings ought to be styled, and to think of themselves, as the servants of the people. That such a notion should be taken seriously, Burke notes, is evidence of a movement to displace solid government in England with the kind of misrule to be found in France during the French Revolution. Burke observes, answering specifically a sermon by Dr. Price, an English clergyman:

> Kings, in one sense, are undoubtedly the servants of the people, because their power has no other rational end than that of the general advantage; but it is not true that they are, in the ordinary sense (by our constitution at least), anything like servants; the essence of whose situation is to obey the commands of some other,

165

and to be removable at pleasure. But the king of Great Britain obeys no other person; all other persons are individually, and collectively too, under him, and owe to him a legal obedience. The law, which knows neither to flatter nor to insult, calls this high magistrate, not our servant, as this humble divine calls him, but *"our sovereign Lord the king;"* and we, on our parts, have learned to speak only the primitive language of the law, and not **the confused jargon of their Babylonian pulpits.**

Congenial horrors, hail!

Source: THE SEASONS: WINTER (Line 6)
Author: James Thomson (1700-1748)
First published: 1726 (*Winter*)
Type of work: Pastoral poem

Context: The first long-sustained poem in English devoted primarily to the description of nature and its changing moods, *The Seasons* broke new ground in several directions. Thomson, a forerunner of the Romantic period, used a number of ideas new at the time—sensuous imagery, fantasy, and a love of nature. He also brought blank verse back into use as a poetic medium, and re-established Milton as a major force in the development of English poetry. He founded the tradition of nature poetry in England. The four parts of *The Seasons* were published over a period of time, from 1726 to 1730, *Winter* being the first; after all the parts were issued they were published with the seasons in their natural order, beginning with spring. *Winter* begins solemnly; Thomson describes the storms, the gloom, the wind, the swelling rivers. But he makes it plain that he enjoys their sublimity to the utmost: "Nature! great parent! whose unceasing hand/ Rolls round the Seasons of the changeful year,/ How mighty, how majestic, are thy works!"

Throughout the scenes of tempest, piled one upon the other, one hears the blast; Thomson's descriptive powers almost provide winter in its actuality. Then the calm descends momentarily; life's vanities are considered a moment; and the storms rage again. We have glimpses of wild creatures and beasts of burden suffering from the elements, and of a belated wanderer lost and freezing in the snow. Thomson dwells for a moment on winter famine and the lot of all who suffer; then he introduces his own snug retreat, "where ruddy fire and beaming tapers join/ To cheer the gloom. There studious let me sit,/ And hold high converse with the mighty Dead. . . ." He considers at some length these great thinkers of the past and the joys they bring the reader. Then he returns to the outside world once more, where at long last the iron grip of winter is gradually relaxing and there are signs of spring. In spite of all its rigors, one is left with the certainty that when another year is past, Thomson will welcome winter once again:

See, Winter comes to rule the varied year,
Sullen, and sad, with all his rising train;
Vapours, and *Clouds,* and *Storms.* Be these my theme,
These, that exalt the soul to solemn thought,
And heavenly musing. Welcome, kindred glooms!
Congenial horrors, hail! with frequent foot,
Pleas'd have I, in my chearful morn of life,
When nurs'd by careless solitude I liv'd,
And sung of Nature with unceasing joy,
Pleas'd have I wander'd thro' your rough domain;
Trod the pure virgin-snows, myself as pure;
Heard the winds roar, and the big torrent burst;
Or seen the deep fermenting tempest brew'd
In the grim evening sky. Thus pass'd the time,
Till thro' the lucid chambers of the south,
Look'd out the joyous Spring, look'd out, and smil'd.

Conscience avant; Richard's himself again

Source: THE TRAGICAL HISTORY OF KING RICHARD III, ALTER'D FROM SHAKE-
SPEARE (Act V, sc. v)
Author: Colley Cibber (1671-1757)
First published: 1699
Type of work: Historical tragedy

Context: Scholars acknowledge that *Richard III,* first performed in 1592 or 1593, is not one of Shakespeare's greatest plays. The dramatist distorted the handsome prince of history into a heartless hunchback, and turned out a "tragedy of blood," so much to the tastes of Elizabethan theater-goers. It deals with Richard's attempt to gain the throne of England, following the death of Edward IV. By craft he gets rid of most of his rivals, then persuades the citizens of London, through their Lord Mayor, to beg him to ascend the throne. However, retribution follows. Henry Tudor, Earl of Richmond and later King Henry VII, invades England. Richard sees the ghosts of his victims appearing on the eve of battle to prophesy his defeat. On Bosworth Field, after having his horse killed from under him and offering his ill-gotten kingdom in exchange for another, he is killed by Richmond. A century after Shakespeare wrote the tragedy, another playwright-actor, Colley Cibber (both of whose names were generally pronounced with a hard "C" during his lifetime), decided he could improve on Shakespeare. Cibber was short, thin, and with a piercing voice, born to be a comic actor, and first achieving recognition in a comedy by Congreve. He was also one of the best comic writers of his age and author of a dozen hits. But he yearned for fame in tragedy. His first attempt, *Xerxes* (1699), lasted one performance; next he decided to "alter" *Richard III.* He changed the order of scenes, cut out scenes where Richard did not appear, brought in lines from other plays by Shakespeare, and

167

added many of his own. The result was a version so much more actable than the original that for nearly two centuries, Cibber's play replaced Shakespeare's. It had fifteen printed editions between 1700 and Cibber's death in 1757. It was the first "Shakespearean" play seen in America, when Edwin Forest toured the colonies with it in 1750. The great Edmund Kean brought it to the independent United States. Even in the twentieth century, it was preferred by Walter Hampton and Robert Mantell. Charles Macready tried to restore Shakespeare in 1821, but in view of audience apathy, had to retreat to Cibber. Not till the time of Sir Henry Irving in the 1870's did the version by Shakespeare make its return to the stage. Audiences complained that Cibber played the sly Richard by slinking about the stage like a pickpocket. He also used the trick of delivering his lines very slowly and deliberately, while the rest of the lines raced with melodramatic speed. But it was effective. And one of the most effective moments closed Act IV, when Catesby (as Cibber renamed Ratcliff) announces the capture of Buckingham. "Off with his head!" cries the king. "So much for Buckingham!" Close to the end of the play, after the ghosts of Richard's victims appear in the dark to curse him, Cibber introduced into Shakespeare's Scene III, what he called Scene V. Of the three speechs quoted, Shakespeare wrote the first; Cibber rearranged words originally written by Shakespeare, in the second; and Cibber was the author of the third dramatic speech that closes the scene.

RICHARD
         . . . , shadows to-night
Have struck more terror to the Soul of Richard
Than can the substance of ten Thousand Soldiers
Arm'd all in Proof, and led by shallow Richmond.

CATESBY
Be more your self, my Lord: consider, sir,
Were it but known a dream had frighted you,
How wou'd your animated Foes Presume on't?

RICHARD
Perish that thought: No, never be it said,
That Fate it self could awe the soul of *Richard*.
Hence, Babling dreams, you threaten here in vain:
Conscience avant; Richard's himself again.
Hark! the shrill Trumpet sounds, to Horse: Away!
  My Soul's in Arms, and eager for the Fray.

168

Conservatism is adherence to the old and tried against the new and untried

Source: ADDRESS AT COOPER UNION, NEW YORK CITY (February 27, 1860)
Author: Abraham Lincoln (1809-1865)
First published: 1860
Type of work: Political speech

Context: John Brown's raid on Harper's Ferry, which the old man hoped would start a general uprising among slaves in the South, was a failure; but it crystallized opinion on both sides of the slavery issue and brought the Civil War a step closer. Brown's raid was a source of embarrassment to the Republican Party. Some abolitionists, feeling that it came closer than any other party to representing their views, flocked to its ranks. The Democrats noted this movement and naturally tried to make the Republicans responsible for the raid. The Republicans went out of their way to deny any connection with John Brown and abolitionism. Lincoln, as leader of the Republican Party, repeated this disavowal in his Cooper Union address. This is not only the most important speech Lincoln had made up to this time but was and is considered one of his greatest. In it he set forth a course and a policy for his party, made his name known throughout the East, and paved his way to the Presidency. The address is basically a reply to the assertion by Stephen A. Douglas that the writers of the Constitution had forbidden the Federal Government to exercise any control over slavery in the territories. Lincoln as Republican spokesman departs from the middle-of-the-road policy his party has hitherto pursued and calls on it to resist strongly any aggressive move by the South to establish slavery in places where it does not yet exist. "Wrong as we think slavery is," says Lincoln, "we can afford to let it alone where it is;" but he does not feel it can be allowed to spread. Denouncing Southern talk of secession from the Union, he concludes with a ringing declaration of purpose: "Neither let us be slandered from our duty by false accusations against us, nor frightened from it by menaces of destruction to the government, nor of dungeons to ourselves. Let us have faith that right makes might, and in that faith let us to the end dare to do our duty as we understand it." It is interesting to note that in replying to the various charges which had been leveled against his party by the Democrats, Lincoln provided what many conservatives still consider the best definition of their viewpoint:

> But you say you are conservative—eminently conservative—while we are revolutionary, destructive, or something of the sort. What is **conservatism? Is** it not **adherence to the old and tried, against the new and untried?** We stick to, contend for, the identical old policy on the point in controversy which was adopted by "our fathers who framed the government under which we live;" while you with one accord reject, and scout, and spit upon that old policy, and insist on substituting something new. . . .

Consider anything, but don't cry

Source: THROUGH THE LOOKING-GLASS (Chapter 5)
Author: Lewis Carroll (Charles Lutwidge Dodgson, 1832-1898)
First published: 1871
Type of work: Imaginative tale for children

Context: How a lecturer in mathematics at Christ Church College, Oxford University, could turn into a writer of fantastic stories for children is as hard to explain as how his pen name "Lewis Carroll," was derived from Lutwidge, Charles. Obviously he had to provide some sort of disguise for a sober mathematician whose college students reported his class lectures as extremely dull; but figuring out the nom de plume by which he is now almost universally known is another sort of problem. He had played with words before. In 1855, while studying Anglo-Saxon poetry, he wrote his famous "Jabberwocky" poem, beginning: " 'Twas brillig, and the slythy toves/ Did gyre and gymble in the wabe." In 1865, he had published *Alice's Adventures in Wonderland,* a work that made him well known. Naturally one success demands another. Queen Victoria, charmed with Alice, had hinted that she would be pleased to have Mr. Dodgson dedicate his next book to her. Unfortunately for Her Majesty, his next book was a mathematical volume with the title *An Elementary Treatise on Determinants.* Not until seven years after the publication of *Alice's Adventures in Wonderland* did he get around to its sequel, *Through the Looking-Glass and What Alice Found There.* It begins with the same sort of illogical logic that is to be found in the original story of Alice. Playing one day with her kitten in the living room, she holds the animal up to the mirror over the fireplace. The game is "Let's Pretend," and Alice is talking about her ideas of what might be in a Looking-glass House, when the mirror turns into mist and she can pass through and jump down on the other side. Here she meets the White Queen, most untidily dressed, who envies Alice.

". . . You must be very happy, living in this wood, and being glad whenever you like!"

"Only it's so very lonely here!" Alice said in a melancholy voice; and at the thought of her loneliness, two large tears came rolling down her cheeks.

"Oh, don't go on like that!" cried the poor Queen, wringing her hands in despair. "Consider what a great girl you are. Consider what a long way you've come today. Consider what o'clock it is. **Consider anything, but don't cry!**"

Alice could not help laughing at this, even in the midst of her tears. "Can you keep from crying by considering things?" she asked.

"That's the way it's done," the Queen said with great decision: "Nobody can do two things at once, you know. . . ."

Consider him as a respectable Hottentot

Source: LETTERS TO HIS SON (Letter 132)
Author: Philip Dormer Stanhope, Lord Chesterfield (1694-1773)
First published: 1774
Type of work: Personal letters

Context: Chesterfield was a proud man and a brilliant one. That he makes a fetish of social graces can be explained in terms of the age in which he lived. Success—that is, statesmanship and a high place in the social and political hierarchy—was dependent upon mastery of all the niceties of etiquette and social behavior. Chesterfield had perfected himself in these matters and had achieved the success he desired. Some critics have accused him, because of his calculating approach to his world, of lacking a heart. This charge is not quite fair to him; he loved his family and had numerous friends he loved and admired. But it is true that he considered the impression one created to be of primary importance. On the other hand, he despised those who possessed the graces and had nothing with which to back them up. His life's ambition, never fully realized, was to make his illegitimate son the finished figure of a polished English gentleman; and his voluminous correspondence with Philip was largely directed toward this end. Although Chesterfield had little use for anyone who had merely acquired the veneer of culture without any solid foundation, he would have probably considered such a person preferable to one who had the good basic qualities and no refinement whatever. To Chesterfield the latter was a mere savage. He might respect and even admire the man, but could not love him: he would lack the sophistication and urbanity Chesterfield considered essential. Chesterfield would never be comfortable in his company. In a letter to Philip written February 28, 1751, Chesterfield makes clear the extent to which he is irked by crudity:

How often have I, in the course of my life, found myself in this situation, with regard to many of my acquaintance, whom I have honored and respected, without being able to love. I did not know why, because, when one is young, one does not take the trouble, nor allow one's self the time, to analyze one's sentiments and trace them up to their source. But subsequent observation and reflection have taught me why. There is a man, whose moral character, deep learning, and superior parts, I acknowledge, admire, and respect; but whom it is so impossible for me to love, that I am almost in a fever whenever I am in his company. His figure (without being deformed) seems made to disgrace or ridicule the common structure of the human body. His legs and arms are never in the position which, according to the situation of his body, they ought to be in, but constantly employed in committing acts of hostility upon the Graces. He throws anywhere, but down his throat, whatever he means to drink, and only mangles what he means to carve. Inattentive to all the regards of social life, he mis-

171

times or misplaces everything. He disputes with heat, and indiscriminately, mindless of the rank, character and situation of those with whom he disputes; absolutely ignorant of the several gradations of familiarity or respect, he is exactly the same to his superiors, his equals, and his inferiors; and therefore, by a necessary consequence, absurd to two of the three. [The person to whom Chesterfield refers is Dr. Samuel Johnson.] Is it possible to love such a man? No. The utmost I can do for him, is to **consider him as a respectable Hottentot.**

A consummation devoutly to be wished

Source: HAMLET (Act III, sc. i, ll. 63-64)
Author: William Shakespeare (1564-1616)
First published: 1603
Type of work: Dramatic tragedy

Context: Hamlet, the meditative, melancholy Prince of Denmark, finds himself with a father dead and a mother taken in an incestuous marriage by his uncle, declared by the Ghost of his father to be the murderer. In his most famous soliloquy, Hamlet, faced with the necessity for revenge, considers his course of action. The idea of the cessation of life through suicide pleases him, but the consequences of the act do not.

HAMLET

To be, or not to be, that is the question—
Whether 'tis nobler in the mind to suffer
The slings and arrows of outrageous fortune,
Or to take arms against a sea of troubles,
And by opposing end them. To die, to sleep—
No more; and by a sleep to say we end
The heart-ache, and the thousand natural shocks
That flesh is heir to; 'tis **a consummation**
Devoutly to be wished. To die, to sleep—
To sleep, perchance to dream, ay there's the rub,
For in that sleep of death what dreams may come
When we have shuffled off this mortal coil,
Must give us pause; . . .

The cool flowery lap of earth

Source: MEMORIAL VERSES: APRIL, 1850 (Line 49)
Author: Matthew Arnold (1822-1888)
First published: 1850
Type of work: Elegy

172

Context: In this poem Arnold laments the deaths of the three greatest poets of the early nineteenth century. Byron, who died in 1824, taught little but enabled men to feel "the strife . . . Of passion with eternal law." Goethe, however, was "Europe's sagest head," and his death in 1832 deprived men of the vision of suffering that might lead to happiness. But Wordsworth, unlike the others, was a healer. Byron and Goethe showed what human life was like and that misery was inescapable; they can be replaced. But after Wordsworth's death in 1850, there can be no other poet to soothe the misery of "doubts, disputes, distractions, fears"; this ability was Wordsworth's greatness— he had neither force nor wisdom, only the ability to make men forget their misery and be young again.

He found us when the age had bound
Our souls in its benumbing round;
He spoke, and loosed our hearts in tears.
He laid us as we lay at birth
On **the cool flowery lap of earth.** . . .
Our youth return'd; for there was shed
On spirits that had long been dead,
Spirits dried up and closely furl'd,
The freshness of the early world.

The coquetry of public opinion

Source: LETTER TO THOMAS BURGH
Author: Edmund Burke (1729–1797)
First published: 1780
Type of work: Open letter

Context: During the mid-eighteenth century Ireland was granted considerable economic concession by England as well as extensive legislative independence. The result was a surge of economic prosperity unprecedented in Irish history. The executive branch of the Irish government remained an English appointment, however, and the millions of Irish Catholics remained subordinated to an Anglican Establishment. Both of these latter conditions displeased Burke, and he worked and hoped consistently for a peaceful reconciliation on all points. Burgh had written to Burke to inform him of the misrepresentation of his Parliamentary position in Ireland, and this letter, which constitutes Burke's reply, was one of his numerous public comments on this issue:

. . . If I had sought popularity in Ireland, when, in the cause of that country, I was ready to sacrifice, and did sacrifice, a much nearer, a much more immediate, and a much more advantageous popularity here, I should find myself perfectly unhappy, because I should be totally disappointed in my expectations, . . . But I acted then, as I act now, and as I hope I shall act always, from a strong impulse of right, and from motives in which popularity, either here or there, has but a very little part.

With the support of that consciousness I can bear a good deal of **the coquetry of public opinion,** which has her caprices, and must have her way. . . . I, too, have had my holiday of popularity in Ireland. . . .

Courage and faith; vain faith, and courage vain

Source: EPITAPH ON A JACOBITE
Author: Thomas Babington Macaulay (1800-1859)
First published: 1845
Type of work: Elegy

Context: Those who sought to restore Roman Catholic James Stuart to the throne of England, after the revolution of 1688 gave it to William III and Mary, were called Jacobites, after the Latin form of James's name, Jacobus. In the struggle for power against the Protestants, some of the Jacobites were imprisoned and killed; others fled to exile on the continent. The movement did not die out with that generation, but had occasional flurries until 1746 when "The Young Pretender," "Bonny Prince Charlie" invaded England on behalf of his father and was defeated at Culloden Moor. The line of Stuarts did not die out, however, until Henry Stuart died in 1807. This brief poem was supposed to have been written for the gravestone of one Jacobite who died in exile in Italy. His "one dear hope" was probably to live in England under a Catholic Stuart ruler, though the romantic reader will suspect it refers to a sweetheart.

To my true king I offered free from stain
Courage and faith; vain faith, and courage vain.
For him, I threw lands, honors, wealth, away,
And one dear hope, that was more prized than they.
For him I languished in a foreign clime,
Grey-haired with sorrow in my manhood's prime;
Heard on Lavernia Scargill's whispering trees,
And pined by Arno for my lovelier Tees;
Beheld each night my home in fevered sleep,
Each morning started from the dream to weep;
Till God who saw me tried too sorely, gave
The resting place I asked, an early grave.
Oh thou, whom chance leads to this nameless stone,
From that proud country which was once mine own,
By those white cliffs I never more must see,
By that dear language which I spake like thee,
Forget all feuds, and shed an English tear
O'er English dust. A broken heart lies here.

174

Courage mounteth with occasion

Source: KING JOHN (Act II, sc. i, l. 82)
Author: William Shakespeare (1564-1616)
First published: 1623
Type of work: Historical drama

Context: Chatillion is sent to John to press the suit of Arthur, John's nephew, for the throne of England. John, at his mother Elinor's urging, tells Chatillion to report to Arthur and his allies, Austria and King Philip of France, that he will fight. Arthur, Philip, and Austria have been fighting against Angiers and are hardly prepared to face John and his forces who arrive practically at Chatillion's heels. Austria, however, urges courage and action.

. . .

CHATILLION

. . .

. . . they are at hand,
To parley or to fight, therefore prepare.

PHILIP

How much unlooked for is this expedition.

AUSTRIA

By how much unexpected, by so much
We must awake endeavour for defence,
For **courage mounteth with occasion.**
Let them be welcome then, we are prepared.

Courtesy is the true Alchemy

Source: THE SONG OF COURTESY (Stanza 4)
Author: George Meredith (1828-1909)
First published: 1859
Type of work: Lyric poem

Context: In this simple little lyric, George Meredith turns to the stories of King Arthur's knights for inspiration and likewise, at least in part, to Chaucer's *Tale of the Wife of Bath.* Sir Gawain, hated by the others because of his purity, is forced to marry an old hag who "was yellow and dry as a snake's old skin," and being the knight of courtesy, a title that roughly means "a perfect gentleman," he cannot hurt the hag's feelings by showing his disgust. Alone with her in the bed chamber, he takes the route of honor: he ignores her loathsomeness and covers her with kisses. Such courtesy, however, is well rewarded, for the hag is miraculously transformed into a beautiful maiden. The quotation occurs in the last stanza of the poem:

175

Of gentle Sir Gawain they had no sport,
When it was morning in Arthur's court;
What think you they cried?
        Now, life and eyes!
This bride is the very Saint's dream of a prize,
        Fresh from the skies!
      See ye not, **Courtesy**
      Is the true Alchemy,
Turning to gold all it touches and tries?

. . .

Cowardly dogs bark loudest

Source: THE WHITE DEVIL (Act III, sc. 1, l. 163)
Author: John Webster (1580?-1625?)
First published: 1612
Type of work: Dramatic tragedy

Context: Paulo Giordano Ursini, Duke of Brachiano, falls in love with Vittoria Corombona and, with the help of her brother, his secretary, the duke pursues her; and she proves willing for the suit to take place. The duke's wife, Isabella, a sister of Francisco de Medicis, Duke of Florence, is thus deserted by her husband; and her brother, with the help of Cardinal Monticelso, seeks to patch up the rift between the married couple. In order to aid his master in having Vittoria Corombona as his mistress, Flamineo, Duke Brachiano's secretary and Vittoria's brother, kills Camillo, Vittoria's husband, making the death look like an accident, giving out that the husband broke his neck jumping a vaulting-horse. At a hearing following Camillo's death, Cardinal Monticelso deals harshly with Vittoria, accusing her of killing her husband that she might more easily have an affair with the Duke of Brachiano. Having had no part in the crime, she asserts her innocence; but the cardinal treats her all the more harshly in his questioning. He asks if she had any visitors the night of her husband's death, and she replies truthfully that she was visited by the duke. The Duke of Brachiano, an observer at the hearing, though uninvited, interferes on her behalf, interrupting the cardinal to say that he had gone to her home to see if he could help her pay off a debt to the cardinal, fearful that the churchman might cheat her. Monticelso then turns on Brachiano:

MONTICELSO
Who made you overseer?

BRACHIANO
Why, my charity, my charity, which should flow
From every generous and noble spirit
To orphans and to widows.

176

Your lust.

BRACHIANO
Cowardly dogs bark loudest: sirrah priest,
I'll talk with you hereafter. Do you hear?
The sword you frame of such an excellent temper
I'll sheathe in your own bowels.
There are a number of thy coat resemble
Your common post-boys.

MONTICELSO
Ha!

BRACHIANO
Your mercenary post-boys:
Your letters carry truth, but 'tis your guise
To fill your mouths with gross and impudent lies.

Cows are my passion

Source: DOMBEY AND SON (Volume I, chapter 21)
Author: Charles Dickens (1812-1870)
First published: 1846-1848
Type of work: Novel

Context: Mr. Dombey, the wealthy London merchant, is at Leamington for a holiday. His hanger-on, Major Joseph Bagstock, has taken him under his wing to acquaint him with the town and to inform him about the current scandals. As they walk down the street, they meet a wheeled chair, in which reclines a faded ancient coquette named Mrs. Skewton. Beside her walks her scornful but beautiful daughter, Mrs. Edith Granger. Mrs. Skewton, who could very well be walking, as there is nothing wrong with her health, invariably rides in one fixed position. Fifty years earlier, when she was a beauty of about twenty years of age, a fashionable artist had sketched her picture as she sat in this posture in a barouche; he had labeled the work "Cleopatra," because the Egyptian queen had taken the same position in her galley. The beauty and the carriage had both disappeared, but the attitude persisted. Mrs. Skewton asks Mr. Dombey if he is fond of nature and explains that she has a passion for seclusion, but society will not permit her to indulge it. She is really an Arcadian at heart, with a burning desire for rural solitude; she is thrown away on society and cows are her passion. What she would like to do is retire to a Swiss farm where she could live entirely surrounded by cows—and china.

   ". . . There is only one change, Mr. Dombey," observed Mrs. Skewton, with a mincing sigh, "for which I really care, and that I fear I shall never be permitted to enjoy. People cannot spare one. But seclusion and contemplation are my what's-his-name—"

"If you mean Paradise, mamma, you had better say so, to render yourself intelligible," said the younger lady.

"My dearest Edith," returned Mrs. Skewton, "you know that I am wholly dependent upon you for those odious names. I assure you, Mr. Dombey, Nature intended me for an Arcadian. I am thrown away in society. **Cows are my passion.** What I have ever sighed for, has been to retreat to a Swiss farm, and live entirely surrounded by cows—and china."

This curious association of objects, suggesting a remembrance of the celebrated bull who got by mistake into a crockery shop, was received with perfect gravity by Mr. Dombey, who intimated his opinion that Nature was, no doubt, a very respectable institution.

Crocodile's tears

Source: ANATOMY OF MELANCHOLY (Part III, sec. 2, memb. 2, subsec. 4)
Author: Robert Burton (1577-1640)
First published: 1621-1651
Type of work: Essays

Context: At about the middle of the introduction to a remarkable book, the author, the Reverend Robert Burton, as "Democritus, Junior," ponders on what his fifth century namesake Democritus would say about behavior in the contemporary world. Burton lists the way man "turns himself into all shades like a chameleon, or as Proteus transforms himself into all that is monstrous." He fawns like a spaniel, rages like a lion, barks like a cur, fights like a tiger, stings like a serpent, grins like a tiger, and weeps like a crocodile. The idea that anything as big and thick-skinned as a crocodile could be so moved by tender emotions as to shed tears from its tiny, deep-sunken eyes, is absurd.

Chapman and Ben Jonson in their 1605 *Eastward Ho!,* and many others who came after Burton, used this phrase. Burton himself used the figure again in Partition III of his anatomical study of morbid psychology. Continuing with a consideration of the causes of Heroical Love, which flourishes most during the conjunction of certain planets, he likewise blames the climate of some places, as well as rich diet and idleness. As more direct causes of the growth of love, he quotes Lucian about the effect of the sight of beauty. Love can also be provoked by artificial stimulants, and increased by opportunity and importunity, including sweet sounds, kisses, dancing, and tears.

. . . When nothing else will serve, the last refuge is their tears. 'Twixt tears and sighs I write this (I take love to witness), saith Chelidonia to Philonius. Those burning torches are now turned to floods of tears. Aretine's Lucretia, when her sweetheart came to

178

Town, wept in his bosom, that he might be persuaded those tears were shed for joy of his return. . . . To these **crocodile's tears,** they will add sobs, fiery sighs, and sorrowful countenance, pale color, leanness, and if you do but stir abroad, these fiends are ready to meet you at every turn, . . .

The cruel crawling foam

Source: ALTON LOCKE, TAILOR AND POET (Chapter 26)
Author: Charles Kingsley (1819-1875)
First published: 1850
Type of work: Novel

Context: The Reverend Charles Kingsley was deeply interested in the workingman and in the labor movement. Labor's militant spirits in the 1840's were the Chartists; this group demanded a Charter which would guarantee certain basic rights to labor. A number of the reforms they agitated for actually took place, and the group then split into the two movements which ensued: coöperatives and trade-unionism. Kingsley supported the Chartist movement, and wrote a number of articles for various radical labor papers. He believed that in order for any labor movement to succeed, it must be based on Christian motives; and he exhorted labor accordingly. In addition to these activities, he wrote one of the first labor novels, *Alton Locke.* This is the story of a young Cockney whose place in society is to be a tailor, but who is determined to surmount all obstacles and become a poet. He is befriended by a Scot,

Sandy Mackaye, who is a Chartist and becomes as a father to him. Alton's mother is a strong Calvinist who does not want him to read anything but Scripture; when he disagrees with her doctrine she casts him out. The story, told in the first person, follows Alton through his encounters with the Chartists, his experiences in the sweatshops, his studies and his trials. He at length goes to an old cathedral town, where he is befriended by Dean Winnstay and falls in love with the Dean's daughter Lillian. At last the long struggle to write poetry while he lives as a hack writer is rewarded: the list of subscribers for his book is complete. Lillian and her father invite Alton to a party where he can meet various literary personages. During the party Lillian plays a haunting air on the piano and asks Alton to write her some verses for it. He obliges with "The Sands o' Dee," which in the novel is untitled:

"O Mary, go and call the cattle home,
    And call the cattle home,
    And call the cattle home,
  Across the sands o' Dee";
The western wind was wild and dank wi' foam,
    And all alone went she.

179

The creeping tide came up along the sand,
    And o'er and o'er the sand,
    And round and round the sand,
    As far as eye could see;
The blinding mist came down and hid the land—
    And never home came she.

"Oh, is it weed, or fish, or floating hair—
    A tress o' golden hair,
    O' drowned maiden's hair,
    Above the nets at sea?
Was never salmon yet that shone so fair,
    Among the stakes on Dee."

They rowed her in across the rolling foam,
    The cruel crawling foam,
    The cruel hungry foam,
    To her grave beside the sea:
But still the boatmen hear her call the cattle home,
    Across the sands o' Dee.

The cruelest lies are often told in silence

Source: VIRGINIBUS PUERISQUE ("Truth of Intercourse")
Author: Robert Louis Stevenson (1850-1894)
First published: 1881
Type of work: Familiar essay

Context: In "The Truth of Intercourse," Stevenson begins by saying that, despite the currency of a proverb to the opposite effect, it is easier to tell a lie than to tell the truth, inasmuch as truth is so hard to ascertain. He notes that "The habitual liar may be a very honest fellow, and live truly with his wife and friends; while another man who never told a formal falsehood in his life may yet be himself one lie—heart and face, from top to bottom." Later in the essay Stevenson tries to show that truth is "something more difficult than to refrain from open lies." For example, one may avoid falsehood and yet not tell the truth; we can speak the truth or avoid it: on the one hand, a man can speak so pithily as to avoid truth; on the other, he can speak at such length as to avoid it:

    The cruelest lies are often told in silence. A man may have sat in a room for hours and not opened his teeth, and yet come out of that room a disloyal friend or a vile calumniator. And how many loves have perished because, from pride, or spite, or diffidence, or that unmanly shame which withholds a man from daring to betray emotion, a lover, at the critical point of the relation, has but hung his head and held his tongue? And again, a lie may be told by a

180

truth, or a truth conveyed through a lie. Truth to facts is not always truth to sentiment; and part of the truth, as often happens in answer to a question, may be the foulest calumny. . . .

A cup of hot wine, with not a drop of allaying Tiber in it

Source: CORIOLANUS (Act II, sc. i, ll. 52-53)
Author: William Shakespeare (1564-1616)
First published: 1623
Type of work: Dramatic tragedy

Context: The renowned Roman general Caius Martius, dubbed Coriolanus for his victory at Corioles, is nevertheless hated by the mobs of Rome, already disgruntled because of famine. Menenius, a popular patrician and friend of Coriolanus, chides Sicinius and Brutus, elected tribunes of the people, for their condemnation of Coriolanus for his pride while they, too, are proud and with little reason. Menenius, dismissing Sicinius and Brutus as "a brace of unmeriting, proud, violent, testy magistrates, alias fools," is told by Sicinius that his reputation is also known in Rome. Menenius then sums up his own reputation:

MENENIUS
I am known to be a humorous patrician, and one that loves **a cup of hot wine, with not a drop of allaying Tiber in't;** said to be something imperfect in favouring the first complaint, hasty and tinder-like upon too trivial motion; one that converses more with the buttock of the night than with the forehead of the morning. What I think I utter, and spend my malice in my breath. . . .

Curse on his virtues! They've undone his country

Source: CATO (Act IV, iv, 35)
Author: Joseph Addison (1672-1719)
First published: 1713
Type of work: Dramatic tragedy

Context: Cato of Utica (95 B.C.–46 B.C.), great-grandson of Cato the Elder, is a symbol of probity in public life. Violently opposed to Julius Caesar and fiercer against the conspiring Cataline than was Cicero, he supported Pompey in his break with Caesar, and even after defeat at Pharsala, fled to Africa to continue resistance. After Caesar crushed Scipio at Thapsus, in 46 B.C., Cato decided on suicide. Addison's excellent classical tragedy in blank verse, following the rules of Aristotle, is only one of many dramatizations of the story. Performed in 1713 and interpreted by the Whigs as an attack on the dominant Tory party, it was a great suc-

181

cess on the stage because of its political implications. It also went through seven printed editions that same year. Throughout Latin America in the nineteenth century, when Spain prohibited local plays about revolution, a Spanish translation of *Cato* was widely used to whip up resistance to Spain. Here is the scene when Cato announces his decision to commit suicide.

LUCIUS

While pride, oppression, and injustice reign,
The world will still demand her Cato's presence.
In pity to mankind, submit to Caesar
And reconcile thy mighty soul to life.

CATO

Would Lucius have me live to swell the number
Of Caesar's slaves, or by a base submission
Give up the cause of Rome, and own a tyrant?

LUCIUS

The victor never will impose on Cato
Ungenerous terms. His enemies confess
The virtues of humanity are Caesar's.

CATO

Curse on his virtues! they've undone his country.
Such popular humanity is treason.

• • •

Custom is the great guide of human life

Source: AN INQUIRY CONCERNING HUMAN UNDERSTANDING (Section V, part 1, 36)
Author: David Hume (1711-1776)
First published: 1748
Type of work: Philosophy

Context: There is a danger, says Hume, that a passion for philosophy, like a passion for religion, may lead us astray; the passion for philosophy may, instead of correcting our manners and relieving our vices, push us toward the very selfishness we are trying to avoid. But nature, maintains Hume, has a means of prevailing upon us, a principle which helps us to avoid our undermining the understanding of common life, that principle being custom, or habit. To judge the happenings about us on the basis of custom enables us to avoid trying to answer the *how* of the happenings and to limit ourselves to that which we know from experience. Reason alone, says Hume, is incapable of variation, but experience tells us there can be variation; so Hume concludes, "All inferences from experience, therefore, are effects of custom, not of reasoning." He continues, in a discussion of custom:

> **Custom, then, is the great guide of human life.** It is that principle alone which renders our experience useful to us; and makes us expect, for the future, a similar train of events with those which have appeared in the past. Without the influence of custom, we should be entirely ignorant of every matter of fact beyond what is immediately present to the memory and senses. We should never know how to adjust means to ends, or to employ our natural powers in the production of any effect. There would be an end at once of all action, as well as of the chief part of speculation.

Cut is the branch that might have grown full straight

Source: THE TRAGICAL HISTORY OF DOCTOR FAUSTUS (Final chorus)
Author: Christopher Marlowe (1564-1593)
First published: 1604
Type of work: Dramatic tragedy

Context: Dr. Faustus, illustrious scholar in divinity, the liberal arts, medicine, and law, in seeking a new field of study succumbs to the fascination of metaphysics and, in a deal with the Devil, sealed with his own blood, sells his soul to Lucifer in exchange for black wisdom, the assurance of twenty-four more years of life, the constant attendance of the demon Mephistophilis, and a life of voluptuousness. The degeneration of Faustus is complete by the end of the years of the bargain; and, amid thunder and the tolling of the midnight bell, devils bear him off to hell, as a final chorus philosophizes for the audience on the tragical fall of Faustus:

CHORUS
Cut is the branch that might have grown full straight,
And burnèd is Apollo's laurel-bough
That sometime grew within this learnèd man.
Faustus is gone: regard his hellish fall,
Whose fiendful fortune may exhort the wise
Only to wonder at unlawful things,
Whose deepness doth entice such forward wits
To practice more than heavenly power permits.

The cynosure of neighboring eyes

Source: L'ALLEGRO (Line 80)
Author: John Milton (1608-1674)
First published: 1645
Type of work: Lyric poem

Context: The poet, bidding Melancholy depart, beseeches blithe and buxom Mirth, daughter perhaps of Venus and Bacchus or perhaps, suggests Milton, of the West Wind and the Dawn, to stay with him, while together they spend the hours from the awakening sights and sounds of morning, through the activities of the day and finally, evening come, through the frolicking tales of the shepherds, the theatrical entertainment of learned Jonson and fanciful Shakespeare, and the sweet sounds of music. The eye of the poet, during the early hours of the morning, would notice the fields with grazing sheep, mountain peaks imbedded in clouds, meadows filled with daisies, and the flowing streams. Looking up, his eye might behold towers above the trees, a source of both beauty and direction for those in the neighborhood:

> Towers and battlements it sees
> Bosomed high in tufted trees,
> Where perhaps some beauty lies,
> **The cynosure of neighboring eyes.**

Daffodils, that come before the swallow dares

Source: THE WINTER'S TALE (Act IV, sc. iv, ll. 118-119)
Author: William Shakespeare (1564-1616)
First published: 1623
Type of work: Tragi-comedy

Context: Banished by her father, King Leontes of Sicilia, Perdita, her mother falsely imprisoned for adultery with King Polixenes of Bohemia and supposedly dead, is reared by a shepherd in a remote section of Bohemia. Since Florizel, son of Polixenes, has fallen in love with the shepherdess (now sixteen), Polixenes and his trusted aide Camillo go disguised to the shepherd's cottage to see and pass judgment on the object of Florizel's affection. With Arcadian charm Perdita pretends she is giving appropriate flowers to her guests and, coming to Florizel, wishes for him daffodils, violets, primrose, oxlips, and lilies:

PERDITA
. . . Now my fair'st friend,
I would I had some flowers o' th' spring that might
Become your time of day; and yours, and yours,
That wear upon your virgin branches yet
Your maidenheads growing. O Proserpina,
For the flowers now, that frighted thou let'st fall
From Dis's wagon; **daffodils,**
That come before the swallow dares, and take
The winds of March with beauty; violets, dim,
But sweeter than the lids of Juno's eyes,

184

Or Cytherea's breath; pale primroses,
That die unmarried, ere they can behold
Bright Phoebus in his strength . . .

Damn with faint praise

Source: EPISTLE TO DR. ARBUTHNOT (Line 201)
Author: Alexander Pope (1688-1744)
First published: 1735
Type of work: Satire

Context: Pope's poetical epistle was written in the form of a dialogue between the poet and his good friend, Dr. Arbuthnot, a physician and contemporary literary figure. The poem is a vehicle for the poet's mordant comments upon other writers of the time, with whom, by his own admission, he found little favor himself. The "Atticus" of the section in which this quotation occurs is Joseph Addison, a quiet and workmanlike man of letters of the period. Pope, however, felt that he had more than one grievance against Addison; in this poem he complains, not quite fairly, that his critic, not being able to stand competition, causes others to sneer at Pope's work to which Addison himself gives less praise than it deserves:

> But were there one whose fires
> True genius kindles and fair fame inspires;
> Blest with each talent and each art to please,
> And born to write, converse, and live with ease:
> Should such a man, too fond to rule alone,
> Bear, like the Turk, no brother near the throne,
> View him with scornful, yet with jealous eyes,
> And hate for arts that caus'd himself to rise;
> **Damn with faint praise,** assent with civil leer,
> And without sneering teach the rest to sneer;
> Willing to wound, and yet afraid to strike,
> Just hint a fault, and hesitate dislike;
>   • • •
> Who but must laugh, if such a man there be?
> Who would not weep, if Atticus were he?

Damned if you do and damned if you don't

Source: REFLECTIONS ON THE LOVE OF GOD (VI, 30, or Chain of Lorenzo)
Author: Lorenzo Dow (1777-1834)
First published: 1836
Type of work: Religious meditation

Context: Lorenzo Dow was an itiner- ant preacher, one of the most remarkable men of his age for his zeal and labor in the cause of religion. A native of Coventry, Conn., he early became impressed with the truths of the Gospel and felt irresistably impelled to devote his life to the preaching of the Word in various parts of the world. He tells about his life between 1777 and 1816 in a four-volume *Journal,* first published in 1836. A fifth edition, published at Wheeling, Va., by John Martin in 1845, includes a number of reflections, sermons, and the "Journey of Life" by his wife, Peggy Dow, telling of their existence together and apart. At the age of four, as Dow testifies in his *Journal,* while playing with a companion, he "fell into a muse about God and heaven and hell," about which he had heard his parents talk. Suddenly he asked his playmate: "Do you ever say your prayers?" When the boy replied: "No," little Lorenzo exclaimed, "You are wicked, and I shall not play with you," and ran into his house. The first chapter records other episodes that served to convince him of his mission in life. At twelve, during a bout with the fever, he had a vision of the prophet Nathan, who told him that he would die at the age of 22. After several more dreams and visions, the arrival of a group of Methodists crystallized Dow's determination, and he made up his mind to become a circuit rider and camp-meeting preacher. Though never formally connected with the society, he was a Methodist in principle. In the beginning of 1796, he did his first preaching. His uncle gave him a horse, and his parents their blessing, and off he went. His eccentric clothes and his forceful sermonizing were both effective. His shrewdness and quick discernment of character gave him considerable influence over the multitudes that attended his ministry. After preaching for several years in the eastern and southern United States, he made the first of two journeys to England and Ireland, where he was just as successful. He then returned to America, and United States. Being a public preacher for more than thirty-five years, Dow probably brought the gospel to more people than any other individual since the days of the Calvinistic preacher George Whitefield (1714–1770). His *Journal* ended with the entry for October 4, 1818, when he was 39; but after that time, on his journeys he rode along jotting down his thoughts and reflections which were published in a number of books such as *The Dealings of God, Man, and the Devil* (Norwich, 1833). In his writings were revealed his purity, integrity, and benevolence. A wanderer through life, he was a sincere Christian Pilgrim in search of a heavenly home. He finally found rest in Georgetown, D.C., on February 2, 1834. As an example of his dramatic style, he wrote concerning "Particular Election" in his "Reflections on the Love of God," an attack on preachers who select for their hearers conflicting opinions and Bible verses, criticizing:

. . . those who preach it up, to make the Bible clash and contradict itself by preaching somewhat like this:
"You can and you can't—You shall and you shan't—
You will and you won't—

186

And you will be **damned if you do**—
And you will be **damned if you don't.**"

Dance an antic hay

Source: THE TROUBLESOME REIGN AND LAMENTABLE DEATH OF EDWARD THE
    SECOND (Act I, sc. i, l. 60)
Author: Christopher Marlowe (1564-1593)
First published: 1594
Type of work: Historical drama

Context: Gaveston, banished from court by old King Edward I because of his bad influence on his son, receives word from King Edward II, the new monarch and his friend, that the old king has died, that he has been crowned, and that he desires the immediate return of his favorite. Returning, Gaveston schemes to control the king by appealing to the weakness of his nature with "wanton poets," musicians, and players:

GAVESTON
Therefore I'll have Italian masks by night,
Sweet speeches, comedies, and pleasing shows.
And in the day, when he shall walk abroad,
Like sylvan nymphs my pages shall be clad;
My men, like satyrs grazing on the lawns,
Shall with their goat-feet **dance an antic hay.**
          • • •
Such things as these best please his majesty,
My lord.

Danger, the spur of all great minds

Source: THE REVENGE OF BUSSY D'AMBOIS (Act V, sc. i, l. 78)
Author: George Chapman (1559-1634)
First published: 1613
Type of work: Dramatic tragedy

Context: Clermont, the brother of the dead Bussy D'Ambois, and the Duke of Guise enter. The duke tells Clermont of a voice that spoke to him in the heat of a battle. Clermont says that it was only a waking dream, as the imaginary power of the mind or the vapors of humors present illusions so convincingly that they seem real. Guise, however, is of the opinion that such things are portents of weighty and secret events to come. The news he has received from abroad convinces him that his plot for the furtherance of Catholicism will prove to be bloody. Upon Clermont's advising him to abandon the plot if there will be so much bloodshed, he replies that to do so would be the abandoning of France. Clermont says to let fall everything that is unlawful and do not in the name of religion indulge in vice. By being virtuous and religious the duke can accumulate grace without running into danger. At this point the ghost of Bussy D'Ambois appears to Clermont alone and remains invisible and inaudible to Guise. He speaks so that only Clermont can hear him:

GHOST
Danger, the spur of all great minds, is ever
The curb to your tame spirits; you respect not,
With all your holiness of life and learning,
More than the present, like illiterate vulgars.
Your mind, you say, kept in your flesh's bounds,
Shows that man's will must ruled be by his power,
When by true doctrine you are taught to live
Rather without the body than within,
And rather to your God still than yourself;
To live to Him is to do all things fitting
His image, in which like Himself we live:
To be His image is to do those things
That make us deathless, which by death is only
Doing those deeds that fit eternity;
And those deeds are the perfecting that justice
That makes the world last, which proportion is
Of punishment and wreak for every wrong,
As well as for right a reward as strong.

   • • •

Dangers by being despised grow great

Source: SPEECH ON THE PETITION OF THE UNITARIANS
Author: Edmund Burke (1729-1797)
First published: 1808
Type of work: Parliamentary address

Context: In May, 1792, a motion was made in the House of Commons to repeal and alter certain acts of Parliament respecting religious opinions. The motion was grounded chiefly upon a petition presented by the Unitarian Society. This motion caused Edmund Burke to make this well-known address in the House of Commons on May 11, 1792. Proclaiming at the beginning of his speech that he is, as always, looking to circumstances, as well as principles, Burke goes on to point out that in a Christian country the church and state are really one, being composed of the same persons; in such a situation, he believes, the magistracy has religion as a part of their care. Burke states as his view, "A reasonable, prudent, provident, and moderate coercion may be a means of preventing acts of extreme ferocity and rigour; for by propagating excessive and extravagant doctrines, such extravagant disorders take place, as require the most perilous and fierce corrections to oppose them." Burke is careful to say that he is looking only at the Unitarians, not at other religious groups, when he says that they represent a danger to the state. He maintains that they are a political faction at that time, as well as a theological sect. He says that they are sympathetic to the French, at a moment when the French Revolution appears as a real threat to the peace of every country in western Europe, including Great Britain. Burke expresses his fear that Unitarians, because of their expressed beliefs, are a danger that cannot be overlooked:

. . . **Dangers by being despised grow great;** so they do by absurd provision against them. . . . Whether an early discovery of evil designs, an early declaration, and an early precaution against them, be more wise than to stifle all inquiry about them, for fear they should declare themselves more early than otherwise they would, and therefore precipitate the evil—all this depends on the reality of the danger. Is it only an unbookish jealousy, as Shakespeare calls it? It is a question of fact. Does a design against the constitution of this country exist? If it does, and if it is carried on with increasing vigour and actively by a restless faction, and if it receives countenance by the most ardent and enthusiastic applauses of its object in the great council of this kingdom, by men of the first parts which this kingdom produces, perhaps by the first it has ever produced, can I think that there is no danger? . . .

Dare to be unhappy

Source: TAMERLANE, A TRAGEDY (Act IV, sc. i, l. 95)
Author: Nicholas Rowe (1674-1718)
First published: 1702
Type of work: Dramatic tragedy

Context: As the play opens, Bajazet, the pagan and dishonorable Emperor of the Turks, has attacked and overrun Greece in violation of a thrice-sworn treaty. In the course of the invasion, Moneses, a Grecian prince and a Christian, and his bride of a few hours, Arpasia, are captured; as a protective device they pretend to be brother and sister. Bajazet, holding Arpasia as hostage, forces Moneses to act as guard to his daughter, Selima, and to conduct her away from the scene of battle. Tamerlane, the pagan but honorable ruler of Asia, has taken the field with his armies to force Bajazet to honor his treaties and restore freedom to Greece; in a preliminary skirmish one of Tamerlane's generals captures Moneses and Selima. After the battle in which the forces of Bajazet are defeated, Moneses is reunited with Arpasia, but she informs him that during their separation Bajazet had forced her into marriage and a consummation of it. She can, therefore, no longer consider herself to be the wife of Moneses but

189

to her great sorrow must remain the wife of the despicable Emperor of the Turks. In the first scene of the fourth act she contemplates suicide, reflects on several classical heroines who preferred death to dishonor, and concludes that as a Christian this course of action is not open to her:

ARPASIA

Oh! Death! thou gentle end of human Sorrows,
Still must my weary Eye-lids vainly wake
In tedious Expectation of thy Peace:
Why stand thy thousand Doors still open,
To take the Wretched in? if stern Religion
Guards every Passage, and forbids my Entrance?—
Lucrece could bleed, and Porcia swallow Fire,
When urg'd with Griefs beyond a mortal Sufferance;
But here it must not be. Think then, Arpasia,
Think on the Sacred Dictates of thy Faith,
And let that arm thy Virtue, to perform
What *Cato*'s Daughter durst not,—Live Arpasia,
And **dare to be unhappy.**

Darkness quieted by hope

Source: SORDELLO (Book I, l. 370)
Author: Robert Browning (1812-1889)
First published: 1840
Type of work: Narrative poem

Context: Long noted for its obscurity, *Sordello,* a study of "the incidents in the development of a soul," is based on the troubadour poet's spiritual growth and the maturation of his poetic genius. The historical background, the Italian civil wars of the late Middle Ages, is so confusing that Browning, who otherwise ignores his audience's lack of historical training, spends several hundred lines describing the political dispute between the Ghibellins and the Guelfs. He places the young Sordello in this world of violence and struggle so that his problems as a poet will take on greater meaning. The quotation occurs toward the end of this long introduction and just before the young poet is first seen as he turns the dreary, war-torn world into a realm of unequalled splendor. As Sordello is presented, Browning compares him to his great follower Dante and points out that, while Dante described the worlds of Hell, Purgatory, and Heaven, Sordello's world was that of ordinary men and women; Browning hopes to bring Sordello from the obscurity into which Dante's greater vision cast him.

. . . what if I approach the august sphere
Named now with only one name, disentwine

190

That under-current soft and argentine
From its fierce mate in the majestic mass
Leavened as the sea whose fire was mixt with glass
In John's transcendent vision,—launch once more
That lustre? Dante, pacer of the shore
Where glutted hell disgorgeth filthiest gloom,
Unbitten by its whirring sulphur-spume—
Or whence the grieved and obscure waters slope
Into a **darkness quieted by hope;**
Plucker of amaranths grown beneath God's eye
In gracious twilights where his chosen lie,—
I would do this! If I should falter now!

The days of our youth are the days of our glory

Source: STANZAS WRITTEN ON THE ROAD BETWEEN FLORENCE AND PISA (Line 2)
Author: George Gordon, Lord Byron (1788-1824)
First published: 1830
Type of work: Lyric poem

Context: The cult of Romanticism is the cult of youth. Too soon young people acquire world weariness. They have seen and experienced all, and there is nothing left to live for. But in their passage through life, they must achieve glory. Of course, the movement had other facets, since each country interpreted Romanticism differently, and there was even a different norm for romantic prose and poetry. Revolt and search for liberty were other characteristics. One of the definitions of Romanticism is "a revolt against everything that Classicism stands for." In English literature, the first generation of Romantic poets, Wordsworth, Coleridge, and Southey, while friends of revolution in their youth, became conservatives by the time the bulk of their work appeared. The second generation of Romantic poets, Byron, Shelley, and Keats, all rebelled so fiercely that their passions wore them out. All died young, before any tendency toward conservatism could develop. It seems unbelievable today, when Byron's poetic gift is considered secondary to that of the other two, that he was formerly widely and admiringly read by people to whom Shelley and Keats were practically unknown. Byron took joy in his youth, and dreaded the approach of old age— which he never knew because when he died of malaria while preparing to help the Greeks in their struggle for liberty against the Turks, he was only thirty-six years old. From the mature age of thirty-three, one day while riding from Florence to Pisa in Italy, he meditated on the significance of Fame and Glory. Probably the resulting poem is a pose, since most Romanticists maintained some sort of pose, but he declares in the four stanzas that he is not ambitious for a name in some future history of literature. He is happy with the lesser crown achieved by a twenty-two-year-old; the more honorable laurel crown is

191

not bestowed until the recipient is too elderly and wrinkled for it to become him. For Byron, the only use of Fame is to realize how it makes him more attractive to the girl beside him, and the sight of love for him in her eyes is his real joy. The final stanza is addressed to Fame.

> Oh, talk not to me of a name great in story;
> **The days of our youth are the days of our glory:**
> And the myrtle and ivy of sweet two-and-twenty
> Are worth all your laurels, though ever so plenty.
>
> What are garlands and crowns to the brow that is wrinkled?
> 'T is but as a dead-flower with May-dew besprinkled.
> Then away with all such from the head that is hoary!
> What care I for the wreaths that can *only* give glory! . . .
>
>   •   •   •
>
> *There* chiefly I sought thee, *there* only I found thee;
> Her glance was the best of the rays that surround thee;
> When it sparkled o'er aught that was bright in my story,
> I knew it was love, and I felt it was glory.

Dead but sceptered sovereigns

Source: MANFRED (Act III, sc. iv, l. 40)
Author: George Gordon, Lord Byron (1788-1824)
First published: 1817
Type of work: Dramatic tragedy

Context: Manfred has been called the perfect expression of Byron's temperament. The first two acts were written during the poet's residence in Switzerland with the Shelleys in 1816. The early lines of incantation over the unconscious Manfred were composed immediately after Byron's unsuccessful attempts at reconciliation with his wife, and are filled with thoughts of her. The final act, completed in Venice the next year, was so adversely criticized by the publisher, that the poet rewrote most of it before publication. However, he explained in the covering letter that he had been ill with a fever when he wrote the original version, and that while he thought the speech of Man-fred to the Sun contained some passable writing, the new version offered some pretty good poetry. He noted that he had changed his characterization of the Abbot and made him a good man. He also brought back the Spirits to be there at Manfred's death. A reader, comparing the two versions, will agree that the changes improved the play, though like most "closet drama," it would be impossible to stage. In this first great poem of revolt by Byron, the parallel to Goethe's *Faust* is obvious. He said he had never read Marlowe's version, but had heard a reading of a translation of the German tragedy. However, he gave his drama originality, and in its field it is excellent, as the story of an individual who cannot find in any external social machinery a remedy for his feeling of isolation. Therefore, he must work out his own solution. Like Dr. Faustus, Manfred is a lonely magician, meditating in his Gothic gallery at midnight about his life. He calls repeatedly upon the spirits of the universe to appear before him, but they do not obey until he commands them in the name of his accursed soul. He demands their aid to help him forget his guilt-haunted past, a former love whose details he will not reveal. They cannot help him. As he falls senseless, there is heard a mysterious, despairing incantation. In the next scene, wandering alone in the Alps, Manfred is befriended by a chamois hunter who suggests he seek the consolation of the Church. A witch offers help in return for obedience to her. Refusing, Manfred returns to his castle where the Abbot of St. Maurice arrives, to save his soul. However, the Abbot confesses he cannot help so noble a man. Later he makes a second attempt, and finds Manfred remembering his thoughts of the past when he stood in the Coliseum, where those who are dead still command. The Abbot, told that a dangerous Spirit is approaching, offers to confront it. Manfred refuses to go with the Spirit to Hell, to which he has no obligation. And so he dies alone and lonely. Nothing except death could conquer him. In his soliloquy in the tower he says:

> I do remember me, that in my youth . . .
> I stood within the Coliseum's wall,
> Midst the chief relics of almighty Rome . . .
> And thou didst shine, thou rolling moon, upon
> All this, and cast a wide and tender light . . .
> Leaving that beautiful which still was so,
> And making that which was not, till the place
> Became religion, and the heart ran o'er
> With silent worship of the great of old,—
> The **dead but sceptred sovereigns,** who still rule
> Our spirits from their urns. . . .

Dead scandals form good subjects for dissection

Source: DON JUAN (Canto I, stanza 31)
Author: George Gordon, Lord Byron (1788-1824)
First published: 1819 (Cantos I and II)
Type of work: Satiric poem

Context: Don Jóse and Donna Inez, proud parents of Don Juan, young hero of Lord Byron's satiric epic, have quarrelled—precisely *why* no one can guess "Though several thousand people chose to try." They live respectably as man and wife while showing to the world a well-bred calm, until at last pent-up anger flares and leaves the world in no doubt as to the true state of affairs between them. Donna Inez tries first to prove that

193

Don Jóse is *mad;* failing this, that he is merely *bad.* When asked on what evidence she is moved to treat him so, she replies only that her conduct is required by her duty to God and man; and, while hinting that she has journals, books and letters which *could* be used should occasion demand, she falls serenely and magnanimously silent. "And then she had all Seville for abettors,/ The hearers of her case became repeaters." Old gossip is dredged up, old rumors brought to life; to the amusement of some, the requital of others, the entertainment of all.

> And then this best and meekest woman bore
>   With such serenity her husband's woes,
> Just as the Spartan ladies did of yore,
>   Who saw their spouses kill'd, and nobly chose
> Never to say a word about them more—
>   Calmly she heard each calumny that rose,
> And saw *his* agonies with such sublimity,
> That all the world exclaim'd, "What magnanimity!"
>
>   . . .
>
> And if our quarrels should rip up old stories,
>   And help them with a lie or two additional,
> *I*'m not to blame, as you well know—no more is
>   Any one else—they were become traditional;
> Besides, their resurrection aids our glories
>   By contrast, which is what we just were wishing all:
> And science profits by this resurrection—
> **Dead scandals form good subjects for dissection.**

Deaf as a door

Source: THE WIL OF WITS (Part IV, "Miseries of Mauillia," The Fifth Miserie)
Author: Nicholas Breton (1545?-1626?)
First published: c.1580
Type of work: Melancholy fiction

Context: Nicholas Breton, from an ancient Essex family, was long believed to have been born in 1555 until modern scholars found a document setting his age at 64 in 1609. Since much of his work was published at Oxford, his wealthy father may have sent him there to study. In his writing, he was influenced by his stepfather, George Gascoigne, from whom he copied his out-of-date verse technique and poetic diction. His *Wil* of Wits, Wits Will, or Wils Wit, chuse you whether was first published in 1580 or 1582, but all copies have been lost, and the earliest surviving edition is 1599. Breton was not as fortunate as some of his contemporaries in choice of patrons; so much of his writing, largely pious tracts, has disappeared. *The Wil of Wits* contains five discourses: 1. A Pretie and Wittie Discourse between Wit and Will; 2. The Authors Dreame; 3.

The Scholler and the Souldiour; 4. The Miseries of Mauillia; 5. The Praise of Vertuous Ladies. In all of them, Breton's fondness for proverbs is apparent. Discourse 4, "The Miseries of Mauillia, the most unfortunate Ladie that ever lived," is divided into five miseries. She begins her suffering when not yet five years old by seeing both her parents stabbed by "bloudie fellowes" pillaging her city. At the child's cries, a poor laundress picks her up, and is rewarded with freedom, since the child pleads for her to one of the captains. However, in the second Miserie Mauillia is kept to sew and clean for him until he decides to send her to a new home, only to have her and her escort attacked by robbers. This time a boy rescues her, and she helps him without bettering her own lot. The author, on the first page, provides a brief biography of poor Mauillia.

> A sweet young soule, in time of tender yeeres,
> In souldiours hands, eskapéd killing neere:
> And growing on, did run through many breers,
> As in the booke, do plainly follow heere.
> Long wandering, in a world of miseries:
> Loathing her life, she lamentably dies.
>
> Her miseries, in number are but five.
> Yet in those five, five thousand haps of hate:
> Which she endurde. whiles that she was alive,
> And dide at last, in miserable state:
> What need more words, the rest here followes on:
> For mourning minds, to sit and muze upon.

The final miserie finds the melancholy narrator in possession of some money, and courted for her wealth, for herself, and for her love. She describes the least attractive suitor, not only (as we say) "deaf as a post," but "an elderly foole who having lately buried his olde Jone, would now fain play the young gentleman." Of him she says:

> . . . the foole will be kissing, and the stubble of his olde shaven beard new come up so pricks mee and tickles my lippes, that I am ready to scratch them after every kisse: but yet his nose is so great that hee hath much a do to kisse kindly; besides, hee hath a stinking breath and a hollow eye.
> Further, I feare by his complexion, hee hath bene a traveller in some lowe countreys. where hee hath been infected with some unholesome ayre: I gesse it the more by his speaking in the nose, and never a good tooth in his head. Hee is as **deafe as a doore;** I must tell him a tale in his eare, that all the town must be privie to, or else hee cannot heare mee.

Dear to maidens are their rivals dead

Source: AMELIA (Line 135)
Author: Coventry Patmore (1823–1896)
First published: 1878
Type of work: Irregular ode

Context: Writing as a man well used to elevate the charms of married love and quite opposed to the lack of sexual restraint that he found in many of his contemporaries, Patmore tells in this poem about the first time he went out alone with his beloved Amelia. Amelia's mother had carefully sheltered her and begs the speaker to remember the girl's honor; with this single warning, she allows her daughter to accompany him to the grave of Millicent, the woman he had once loved. The quiet atmosphere of the cemetery and the speaker's praise of the almost divine Millicent cause Amelia to show her love, but the speaker, being older and recalling the mother's plea, preserves the girl's honor. By restraining himself, he discovers that he will reach the epitome of joy after marriage; thus he finds the hope for a future marriage by taking his sweetheart to the grave of his last love and watching her reactions to his eulogy upon the "rival's" beauty.

> But all my praise
> Amelia thought too slight for Millicent,
> And on my lovelier-freighted arm she leant,
> For more attent;
> And the tea-rose I gave,
> To deck her breast, she dropp'd upon the grave.
> "And this was her's," said I, decoring with a band
> Of mildest pearls Amelia's milder hand.
> "Nay, I will wear it for *her* sake," she said:
> For **dear to maidens are their rivals dead.**

Death has done all death can

Source: AFTER (Line 4)
Author: Robert Browning (1812-1889)
First published: 1855
Type of work: Lyric poem

Context: After is a companion piece to *Before.* In *Before* we see two men in a deadly quarrel because one has wronged the other. The question is, however, who is the wronged and who the wronger? There is no solution for the problem except to fight it out: if the culprit wins, life will take its toll of him; if the wronged man loses, he will have his reward as a martyr in heaven. There can be no question of forgiveness by the wronged man, because wrong must always be resisted and evil not be

196

crowned on earth; God will be the judge. The wronger, obdurate until the end, refuses to admit his wrong, and so the duel takes place. In *After* the winner of the contest looks at the corpse of the victim: death has done all that it can do to him. He is now in a new life in which his wrong and the survivor's vengeance are alike inconsequential. It is only at this place in the poem that the reader learns the victor in the duel is the wronged man: God has shielded the protector of right and has vindicated him, as in the ancient trials by combat. The speaker in the poem concludes by wishing that the two of them were again boys: the victim's outrage, God's patience, and man's scorn would then be easy to bear.

> Take the cloak from his face, and at first
>   Let the corpse do its worst.
>
> How he lies in his rights of a man!
>   **Death has done all death can:**
> And, absorbed in the new life he leads,
>   He recks not, he heeds
> Nor his wrong nor my vengeance—both strike
>   On his senses alike,
> And are lost in the solemn and strange
>   Surprise of the change.
>
> Ha, what avails death to erase
>   His offence, my disgrace?
> I would we were boys as of old
>   In the field, by the fold:
> His outrage, God's patience, man's scorn
>   Were so easily borne.
>
> I stand here now, he lies in his place:
>   Cover the face.

Death is the privilege of human nature

Source: THE FAIR PENITENT (Act V, sc. i, l. 133)
Author: Nicholas Rowe (1674-1718)
First published: 1703
Type of work: Dramatic tragedy

Context: The plot of the first of Rowe's "she-tragedies," concerns Sciolto, a nobleman of Genoa, who has just promised his lovely daughter, Calista, to Altamont, a youth he has befriended since the death of Altamont's parents. Calista secretly loves and has been seduced by Altamont's bitter enemy, "gay Lothario." Lothario forces Calista to meet him on the day of her marriage by threatening to make her shame public. Altamont discovers Lothario and Calista in conference and, having learned their

197

secret, kills Lothario. Sciolto enters and, upon learning of his daughter's shame, attempts to kill her. Altamont prevents this murder, and Sciolto leaves still insisting on justice. In the final act Rowe presents to his audience a scene of appalling melancholy and horror with Calista keeping a deathwatch over the corpse of Lothario. When her father enters, she expresses her wish for death, and he offers his dagger. As she takes the weapon, he announces that his duty as a judge is done and expresses his love for her as a father:

SCIOLTO

I could curse nature and that tyrant, honor,
For making me thy father and thy judge;
Thou art my daughter still.

CALISTA

For that kind word
Thus let me fall, thus humbly to the earth;
Weep on your feet and bless you for this goodness;
Oh! 'tis too much for this offending wretch,
This parricide, that murders with her crimes,
Shortens her father's age and cuts him off
E'er little more than half his years be numbered.

SCIOLTO

Would it were otherwise!—but thou must die.—

CALISTA

That I must die—it is my only comfort;
Death is the privilege of human nature,
And life without it were not worth our taking;
Thither the poor, the pris'ner, and the mourner
Fly for relief and lay their burdens down.
Come then, and take me now to thy cold arms,
Thou meagre shade; here let me breathe my last,
Charmed with my father's pity and forgiveness
More than if angels tuned their golden viols
And sung a requiem to my parting soul.

Death is the veil which those who live call life

Source: PROMETHEUS UNBOUND (Act III, sc. iii, l. 113)
Author: Percy Bysshe Shelley (1792-1822)
First published: 1820
Type of work: Lyric drama

Context: Bound by Jupiter to a rock in the mountains because he refuses to tell the tyrant when he would be overthrown, Prometheus has learned that love is superior to hate, but he still heroically refuses to aid the evil king of the gods. However, the time that Jupiter fears finally comes, and Demogorgon overthrows the monarch, leaving the throne vacant because if any deity seizes it, he might become a tyrant. This heavenly revolt is the sign of a new age of peaceful anarchy during which happiness will come to gods and men alike. Following the fall of Jupiter, Hercules releases Prometheus, who plans to discover how he can further help his beloved race of men, how he can help them escape misery and despair. After he concludes his speech of unlimited love, Asia, the spirit of love and universal brotherhood, and Earth, the great mother, talk of death, the major cause of man's unhappiness. Earth tells why men should not fear it by using the Platonic notion that what men call life is really death, because the body enslaves the soul:

ASIA
Oh, mother! wherefore speak the name of death?
Cease they to love, and move, and breathe, and speak,
Who die?

THE EARTH
It would avail not to reply:
Thou art immortal, and this tongue is known
But to the uncommunicating dead.
Death is the veil which those who live call life:
They sleep, and it is lifted: . . .

Death: the last, best friend

Source: CARMEN NUPTIALE ("The Dream," Stanza 87)
Author: Robert Southey (1774-1843)
First published: 1817
Type of work: Epithalamium

Context: Because he was poet laureate, Southey was called upon to write a commemorative poem to honor Princess Charlotte's royal marriage; however, he was, as he says in the proem to *Carmen Nuptial,* at a loss. He well understood that his talent was limited to themes of vengeance and violence and showed to greatest advantage in poems of epic length. Thus he turned for inspiration to Edmund Spenser and wrote "The Dream," a long poem in the style of his Elizabethan master but lacking both the organization and charm of his source. Southey presents a catalogue of men and personifications who greet the princess and give her gifts. Naturally the last speaker is Death:

"Hear me, O Princess!" said the shadowy form:
"As, in administering this mighty land,

199

Thou with thy best endeavor shalt perform
        The will of Heaven, so shall my faithful hand
Thy great and endless recompense supply:
My name is **DEATH: THE LAST, BEST FRIEND** AM I!"

Death, the poor man's dearest friend

Source: MAN WAS MADE TO MOURN (Stanza 11)
Author: Robert Burns (1759-1796)
First published: 1786
Type of work: Dirge

Context: Robert Burns was rarely a happy man. All his life he knew suffering and disappointment. His youth was harsh and painful. Born on a farm whose tenant farmer, his father, was always in debt because of the poor soil and high rent, Robert spent his early life in a series of moves from one poor farm to another. He tried to better his lot by learning to dress flax, only to have the flax shop burn down. His father's death, when Robert was twenty-five, started the poet on a period of four years of intense labor with his younger brothers in a vain attempt to wrest a living from the soil. In his search for love, he had also been unfortunate. The father of one sweetheart, Jean Armour, refused to consent to their marriage even though the girl was mother of his child. Another girl, Mary Campbell, died while at home preparing to marry him. So Burns could hardly be blamed for writing melancholic poetry. A reader can only admire his spirit when poems of wild fun, satire, and delightful descriptions reveal his fine sense of humor. But certainly "Man Was Made to Mourn" is not of this kind. The poet describes himself walking one chill November evening along the banks of Ayr. He comes upon an eighty-year-old man, with white hair and a face furrowed with care. He inquires of the poet the reason for his roaming, whether it is in search of wealth or fun, or perhaps to join with him in mourning the miseries of mankind. Then he expounds his own philosophy. Every returning winter's sun adds only more proof that most of the inhabitants of the moor toil to support some haughty lord. There is nothing in their future except mourning. Indeed, each stanza of the eleven ends with the melancholic statement that mourning is the lot of most men. Even the major part of those who seem favored by fate, the rich and the great, are not really happy. "Man's inhumanity to man/ Makes countless thousands mourn." The "rev'rend sage" cannot understand why, if designed by Nature to be a slave, he was endowed with ability to form independent desires. His consolation, with which the poem closes, is the most melancholic thought of all: because of his oppressed existence, he has escaped one fear that terrifies so many people. Life for him is so bad that he does not fear Death.

The poor, oppresséd, honest man
   Had never, sure, been born,
Had there not been some recompense
   To comfort those who mourn!

O **Death! the poor man's dearest friend,**
   The kindest and the best!
Welcome the hour my agéd limbs
   Are laid with thee at rest!

The great, the wealthy, fear thy blow,
   From pomp and pleasure torn;
But, Oh! a blest relief to those
   That weary-laden mourn!

The deceiving mirror of self-love

Source: THE PARLIAMENT OF LOVE (Act I, sc. v)
Author: Philip Massinger (1583-1640)
First published: 1805
Type of work: Tragi-comic drama

Context: As the text of *The Parliament of Love* is defective, what we have of the play begins in scene iv of the first act, with Chamont conjuring his former ward, the noble Bellisant, to live a quieter and more decorous life. She is associating herself with unworthy persons, and as a result of her behavior, her reputation will suffer. Bellisant spurns Chamont's advice and says that, since she is entirely virtuous, she will pursue the course that gives her the most amusement; she says that she will disprove the generally accepted idea that chastity can live only in a cottage by living a pure life in the center of court activity. In Act I, scene v, Charles VIII of France returns to his court from his successful military campaign in Italy and finds a universal dullness prevailing. When a courtier attributes the lack of gaity to the cruel behavior of the court ladies, Bellisant says that the fault lies with the courtiers. Formerly, when they desired to woo a lady, they were careful to have to their credit a series of gallant exploits, deep wisdom, and service to the state, and men such as those the ladies could treat with favor. But now, anyone who has traveled enough in Italy to learn a little of the language and can make fashionable grimaces, dance lavoltas, and be rude and saucy and see himself as his self-love would like him to be, thinks there is hardly a woman worthy of him. Bellisant speaks:

   "Ere they durst
Presume to offer service to a lady,
In person they perform'd some gallant acts
The fame of which prepared them gracious hearing,

201

Ere they made their approaches: what coy she, then,
Though great in birth, not to be parallel'd
For nature's liberal bounties, both set off
With fortune's trappings, wealth; but, with delight,
Gladly acknowledged such a man her servant,
To whose heroic courage, and deep wisdom,
The flourishing commonwealth, and thankful king,
Confess'd themselves for debtors? Whereas, now,
If you have traveled Italy, and brought home
Some remnants of the language, and can set
Your faces in some strange and ne'er-seen posture,
Dance a lavolta, and be rude and saucy;
Protest, and swear, and damn, (for these are acts
That most think grace them,) and then view yourselves
In **the deceiving mirror of self-love,**
You do conclude there hardly is a woman
That can be worthy of you."

A deed without a name

Source: MACBETH (Act IV, sc. i, l. 49)
Author: William Shakespeare (1564-1616)
First published: 1623
Type of work: Dramatic tragedy

Context: Macbeth and Banquo are told by three witches that Macbeth will be king and that the descendants of Banquo will be crowned. Driven by his own wicked ambition and that of his wife, Macbeth murders King Duncan and usurps the throne. Worried because the sons of Duncan remain safe in exile and Fleance, son of the recently murdered Banquo, has escaped his assassins, Macbeth visits the den of the weird sisters.

SECOND WITCH
By the pricking of my thumbs,
Something wicked this way comes.
Open locks,
Whoever knocks.

[*Enter* MACBETH.]
MACBETH
How now, you secret, black, and midnight hags?
What is't you do?

ALL
A deed without a name.

MACBETH

I conjure you, by that which you profess,
Howe'er you come to know it, answer me.
Though you untie the winds, and let them fight
Against the churches; though the yesty waves
Confound and swallow navigation up;
Though bladed corn be lodged, and trees blown down;
Though castles topple on their warders' heads;
      · · ·
Even till destruction sicken—answer me
To what I ask you.

The deep damnation of his taking off

Source: MACBETH (Act I, sc. vii, l. 20)
Author: William Shakespeare (1564-1616)
First published: 1623
Type of work: Dramatic tragedy

Context: In a well-known soliloquy, Macbeth, forewarned by the prophecy of three witches that he will be "King hereafter" and spurred on by the determination of Lady Macbeth, debates murdering King Duncan, his kinsman, his king, and, this night, his guest.

MACBETH
   . . . He's here in double trust;
First, as I am his kinsman, and his subject,
Strong both against the deed; then, as his host,
Who should against his murderer shut the door,
Not bear the knife myself. Besides, this Duncan
Hath borne his faculties so meek, hath been
So clear in his great office, that his virtues
Will plead like angels, trumpet-tongued against
The deep damnation of his taking-off.
      · · ·
         . . . I have no spur
To prick the sides of my intent, but only
Vaulting ambition, which o'erleaps itself,
And falls on th'other—

Defaced, deflowered, and now to death devote

Source: PARADISE LOST (Book IX, l. 901)
Author: John Milton (1608-1674)
First published: 1667
Type of work: Epic poem

Context: Eve, deceived by Satan disguised as a serpent, eats the forbidden fruit of the tree of the knowledge of good and evil. The immediate effect upon her is a feeling of intoxication. She soliloquizes that to tell Adam what she has done and to share the fruit with him will be to sacrifice the superiority that she has gained by her daring act. She believes that her new superiority will enhance her charms in Adam's eyes. She then thinks that death, which has not yet appeared, may actually be the result of eating the fruit, and she cannot stand the thought of herself dead and Adam living happily in the garden with a new Eve. She then resolves that Adam will have to eat the fruit and so share her fate, whatever it is to be. When she approaches him, she says that what they had heard about the fruit was not true; it is a remarkable stimulant which made the serpent almost human and her almost a god. Adam is appalled at what she has done, as he fully realizes the immensity of her crime. He drops the garland he had woven for her, and all the roses in it fade and drop their petals. He speaks:

> O fairest of creation, last and best
> Of all God's works, creature in whom excelled
> Whatever can to sight or thought be formed,
> Holy, divine, good, amiable, or sweet!
> How art thou lost, how on a sudden lost,
> **Defaced, deflowered, and now to death devote?**
> Rather how hast thou yielded to transgress
> The strict forbiddance, how to violate
> The sacred fruit forbidden! some cursèd fraud
> Of enemy hath beguiled thee, yet unknown,
> And me with thee hath ruined, for with thee
> Certain my resolution is to die;
> How can I live without thee, how forgo
> Thy sweet converse and love so dearly joined,
> To live again in these wild woods forlorn?
>   •   •   •

Defaming as impure what God declares pure

Source: PARADISE LOST (Book IV, ll. 746-47)
Author: John Milton (1608-1674)
First published: 1667
Type of work: Epic poem

Context: Adam and Eve finish their day's work of cultivating the garden. The time for rest has come, and all the beasts and birds seek repose except the nightingale, which sings throughout the night. Adam explains to Eve that man is dignified by having duties to perform; the lower animals are idle throughout the day. Eve indicates that whatever Adam commands is law to her. She comments on the beautiful evening, the fragrance of the air, and the glittering of the stars. She asks why the stars shine when all are asleep. This question leads Adam into explaining that millions of unseen spirits walk the earth in the starlight. With this explanation, they pass into their blissful bower, which is adorned with flowers; it is closed to the entry of any of the lower creatures. Adam praises the Omnipotent who created all things, and mentions that He has promised them that there will come a race from them to fill the earth, which shall extol the infinite goodness of God.

> This said unanimous, and other rites
> Observing none, but adoration pure
> Which God likes best, into their inmost bower
> Handed they went; and eased the putting off
> These troublesome disguises which we wear,
> Straight side by side were laid, nor turned, I ween,
> Adam from his fair spouse, nor Eve the rites
> Mysterious of connubial love refused:
> Whatever hypocrites austerely talk
> Of purity and place and innocence,
> **Defaming as impure what God declares**
> **Pure,** and commands to some, leaves free to all.
> Our Maker bids increase, who bids abstain
> But our destroyer, foe to God and man?
> Hail, wedded love, mysterious law, true source
> Of human offspring, sole propriety,
> In paradise of all things common else.
>   •   •   •

The demi-Atlas of this earth

Source: ANTONY AND CLEOPATRA (Act I, sc. v, l. 23)
Author: William Shakespeare (1564-1616)
First published: 1623
Type of work: Dramatic tragedy

Context: Once the greatest of generals, Antony has ceased to concern himself with affairs of empire because of his passion for Cleopatra. As one of his friends disgustedly notes, "His captain's heart" "is become the bellows and the fan/To cool a gypsy's lust." But now rebellion and invasion have recalled Antony to Rome, where the other members of the ruling triumvirate—Lepidus and Octavius Caesar—are in great need of his soldierly qualities. In Alexandria, meanwhile, Cleopatra awaits the return of her lover, writing letter after letter to her "demi-Atlas," for if Atlas bore the globe on his shoulders, Antony bears half of it (the other half being borne by Octavius, Lepidus being too ineffectual to matter). As a general, moreover, Antony is the protecter of men, their armor—"arm," and helmet—"burgonet." Thus, the intensity of the conflict within Antony—between his passion for Cleopatra and his Roman sense of duty—is sug- gested unwittingly by Cleopatra her- self:

CLEOPATRA
O Charmian.
Where think'st thou he is now? Stands he, or sits he?
Or does he walk? Or is he on his horse?
O happy horse to bear the weight of Antony!
Do bravely horse, for wot'st thou whom thou mov'st,
The demi-Atlas of this earth, the arm
And burgonet of men? He's speaking now,
Or murmuring Where's my serpent of old Nile—
For so he calls me.

. . .

Deserves to be preached to death by wild curates

Source: A MEMOIR OF THE REVEREND SYDNEY SMITH BY HIS DAUGHTER LADY HOLLAND (Chapter 11)
Author: Sydney Smith (1771-1845)
First published: 1855
Type of work: Biographical memoir

Context: A volume of 268 pages, written by his daughter, Saba (1802–1866), wife of Lord Holland, tells of the life of the Reverend Sydney Smith, and recounts some of the witty sayings for which he was famous. The witticisms are set down one after another, without connection or explanation, rather like the Joe Miller joke book, a volume published in 1739 and many times reprinted, containing jokes supposed to have originated with a famous English comedian, Josiah Miller (1684– 1738). Most of the contents was ac- tually invented by its publisher, John Mottley. In contrast, the amusing comments in Lady Holland's book were the genuine products of her clergyman father's quick mind. The first one obviously originated through a clever twist of the phrase: "tram- pled to death by wild horses."

Oh, the Dean of——**deserves to be preached to death by wild curates.**

. . .

"The advice I sent to the Bishop of New Zealand, when he had to receive the cannibal chiefs there, was to say to them, 'I deeply regret, Sirs, to have nothing on mye own table suited to your tastes, but you will find plenty of cold curate and roasted clergy- man on the sideboard;' and if, in spite of this prudent provision, his visitors should end their repast by eating him likewise, why I should only add, 'I sincerely hope he would disagree with them!' " . . .

206

Destructive, damnable, deceitful woman!

Source: THE ORPHAN (Act III, l. 586)
Author: Thomas Otway (1652-1685)
First published: 1680
Type of work: Domestic tragedy

Context: The leading Restoration writer of comedies was Thomas Otway. One of his best was *The Orphan or The Unhappy Marriage*, a domestic tragedy, distantly following the plot of Shakespeare's *Cymbeline*. Its simple and direct language fits the action. Its psychology is convincing, and its pathos does not distract. It shows Otway's tendency to leave behind the heroic bombast of the Elizabethan period in the direction of pathos and sentimentality. Monimia, an orphan, has been left under the guardianship of Acasto, a Bohemian nobleman, retired from court and living in the country. Both his sons, Castalio and Polydore, love her. She prefers the older Castalio and gives him a password to let him enter her chamber. However, Polydore, overhearing the conversation, arrives first, and when Castalio comes the servant says the lady will not admit him. That news causes Castalio to embark, at the end of Act III, on a tirade to an elderly servant, Ernesto, about all the evil caused by such women as Cleopatra, Helen of Troy, and others:

CASTALIO
My thoughts are full of woman; thou poor
   wretch, art past 'em.

ERNESTO
I hate the sex.

CASTALIO
   Then I'm thy friend, Ernesto.
I'd leave the world for him that hates a woman.
Woman the fountain of all humane frailty!
What mighty ills have not been done by woman?
Who was't betrayed the Capitol? A woman.
          •   •   •
Who was the cause of a long ten years war,
And laid at last old Troy in ashes? Woman.
Destructive, damnable, deceitful woman!
Woman to man first as a blessing giv'n,
When innocence and love were in their prime.

Detested sport, that owes its pleasures to another's pain

Source: THE TASK (Book III, ll. 326-327)
Author: William Cowper (1731-1800)
First published: 1785
Type of work: Meditative poem in blank verse

Context: Cowper, descendant of John Donne, was the last English poet to belong to what has been called the cult of simplicity. He began his adult career in the legal profession and was called to the bar in 1754; however, he was forced into early retirement by attacks of insanity. The first of these made it impossible for him to marry the girl he loved. Another, brought on by the strain of preparing for an examination in 1763, led him to attempt suicide. His convalescence lasted for some time; he then retired to the country and settled eventually at Olney, where he turned to poetry as a serious avocation. He was then fifty years of age. The first volume, *Poems,* was published in 1782; his greatest work, *The Task,* was completed two years later. Its ready sale was ensured by the inclusion of a few other poems to round out the volume, notably his popular humorous ballad *John Gilpin's Ride.* *The Task,* widely praised, brought him lasting renown. It is a lengthy poem in blank verse and explores, quietly and meditatively, the life of seclusion that Cowper leads. He describes the beauty of the countryside, the simple pleasures and routines of the day, and considers the outside world that he has renounced. He dwells at some length on the nature of human existence and upon moral and spiritual problems; his strong Calvinism, a factor in his recurrent periods of depression, encourages him to moralize. The poem is a task given him by his friend Lady Austen, who suggested he write about a sofa. He begins with the sofa and then describes his morning walk and his accompanying thoughts. In the second book he discusses at some length his view of the outside world and its problems. In Book III he takes up the subject of his garden and the pleasure it gives him; but he prefaces this description with some remarks concerning people who visit the country only to disturb the peace and serenity of it: holiday-seekers, hunters, and fishermen. To the mild and gentle Cowper, such people are vandals, utterly lacking in sensibility:

> We persecute, annihilate the tribes
> That draw the sportsman over hill and dale
> Fearless, and rapt away from all his cares;
> Should never game-fowl hatch her eggs again,
> Nor baited hook deceive the fish's eye;
> Could pageantry, and dance, and feast, and song
> Be quell'd in all our summer-months' retreats;
> How many self-deluded nymphs and swains,
> Who dream they have a taste for fields and groves
> Would find them hideous nurs'ries of the spleen,
> And crowd the roads, impatient for the town!

They love the country, and none else, who seek
For their own sake its silence and its shade;
Delights which who would leave, that has a heart
Susceptible of pity, or a mind
Cultured and capable of sober thought,
For all the savage din of the swift pack,
And clamours of the field? **Detested sport,
That owes its pleasures to another's pain,**
That feeds upon the sobs and dying shrieks
Of harmless nature. . . .

The devil watches all opportunities

Source: THE OLD BACHELOR (Act II, sc. ii)
Author: William Congreve (1670-1729)
First published: 1693
Type of work: Dramatic comedy

Context: Araminta teases Belinda for being in love with Bellmour; Belinda strenuously denies the allegation, as loving a man would be unfitting for a lady of quality. The maid announces that Bellmour and Vainlove, with whom Araminta is in love, are waiting on the ladies. Belinda says that she will not stay to receive the gentlemen and calls for her hood, preparatory to leaving the house. Araminta urges the maid, Betty, to put Belinda's hood on her so that she can go, but Belinda takes it off, saying that she has changed her mind and will stay. When Araminta says that Belinda has decided not to let Araminta have all the company to herself, Belinda replies that she is of such a charitable nature that she will not trust Araminta. The devil watches all occasions so as to seize the opportunity to do mischief, and Araminta might be tempted, if alone, to be indiscreet. So Belinda will stay only to protect Araminta's reputation; she contends that she is willing to remain out of pure affection.

BELINDA
. . . Here, take 'em all again, my mind's changed, I won't go.
[*Exit* BETTY *with hoods.*]

ARAMINTA
[*Aside.*] So, this I expected.—[*Aloud.*] You won't oblige me then, cousin, and let me have all the company to myself?

BELINDA
No; upon deliberation, I have too much charity to trust you to yourself. **The devil watches all opportunities;** and, in this favorable disposition of your mind, Heaven knows how far you may be tempted: I am tender of your reputation.

209

I am obliged to you. But who's malicious now, Belinda?

BELINDA
Not I; witness my heart, I stay out of pure affection.

ARAMINTA
In my conscience, I believe you.

Devils are not so black as they be painted

Source: A MARGARITE OF AMERICA
Author: Thomas Lodge (1558?-1625)
First published: 1596
Type of work: Prose romance

Context: Thomas Lodge was a many-sided man. Son of a Lord Mayor of London, he graduated from Oxford in 1577, for which reason he is believed to have been born about 1558. He went on to study law and to make a name for himself in literature with several plays and with euphuistic tales in the style of John Lyly, told in a mingling of extravagant prose and poetry. Shakespeare borrowed from his *Scillaes Metamorphosis* (1589) for *Venus and Adonis,* and from Lodge's best-known *Rosalynde* (1590) for *As You Like It.* Both were planned and partly written during Lodge's voyages to Terceiras and the Canaries in 1588. Later, in 1591–1593, Lodge accompanied Thomas Cavendish on an expedition to South America. During the voyage, he read a Spanish manuscript in a Jesuit library in Santos, Brazil, that he adapted into *A Margarite of America, the Ladies delight and the Ladies honor.* The "America" part of the title came because it was written while passing through the Straits of Magellan. As he indicates in a foreword "To the Gentlemen Readers,"

he found seasickness interfering with composition, so he craved charity from those who perused it. Its elegant and exaggerated style may be traced to Antonio de Guevara (1480–1545) who helped to father Spanish Gongorism. After its completion, Lodge became interested in medicine in which he took two degrees, in Avignon, France, (1598) and at Oxford (1602), after which he practiced medicine for the rest of his life. *A Treatise on the Plague* was one product of his new career. The complicated story of Margarita begins with a flowery description of "blushing morning," as armies under Emperor Protomachus of Mosco and Artofago of Cuzco prepare for combat. Before they join in battle, however, "an old man whose sober looks betokened his severe thoughts and mournful garments shadowed his melancholy mind" takes a position between the armies and delivers a two page speech quoting Plutarch and Plato in a plea not to destroy mankind. He suggests that Arasdachus, heir to the Empire of Cuzco, visit Princess Margarita of Mosco with a view to matrimony.

210

The emperor greets the suitor with a joust. Earl Asaphus gives a party for the knights and ladies. The Cuzcan Prince is a gay deceiver and, as Lodge put it in the 1596 edition: "Margarita (poore princesse) thinking all that golden which glisters, trusted too long." In reporting the earl's speech, Lodge writes (in modernized spelling):

. . . Since therefore (my subjects) you are at my obedience, and upon my direction are to do homage to love, I give you free license to discourse, free liberty to look, the sweets whereof, after you have gathered, come to me, and after the priest hath handfasted you, come touch and spare not, you shall have my patent to take your pleasure. It is a dangerous matter (said Arsadachus) to enter those lists where women will do what they list. Well (said Margarita) **devils are not so black as they be painted** (My Lord), nor women so wayward as they seem. . . . With that they brake up the assembly, for it was supper time, and the prince entreated them to sit down, where they merrily passed the time, laughing heartily at the pleasant and honest mirth wherein they had passed that afternoon.

The devil's in the moon for mischief

Source: DON JUAN (Canto I, stanza 113)
Author: George Gordon, Lord Byron (1788-1824)
First published: 1819 (Cantos I and II)
Type of work: Satiric poem

Context: Don Juan, now growing up, is "Tall, handsome, slender, but well knit: . . ." Since his father's death he has been in the charge of his mother, who, remembering her late lord's frailties, has provided, as his sole companions, the households ancient maids, his tutors and confessor, and, (alas! for ". . . a breeding . . . strictly moral") her lovely friend, Donna Julia, a young wife of twenty-three, who, when Juan was younger ". . . saw, and, as a pretty child,/ Caress'd him often— . . ." But now the pretty child is suddenly sixteen, and a subtle change takes place. Donna Julia is blushingly self-conscious, while Juan broods in the "lonely wood,/ Tormented with a wound he [cannot] know, . . ." One summer's day toward evening, the two find themselves together in a sequestered bower. Donna Julia full of honor, virtue, and resolve never to disgrace the marriage ring she wears; Juan, as is love's way when it is new, tremblingly fearful lest he do wrong as in gratitude he kisses the little hand so carelessly placed on his. And then the moon comes up.

The sun set, and up rose the yellow moon:
The devil's in the moon for mischief; they
Who call'd her CHASTE, methinks, began too soon
Their nomenclature; there is not a day,

211

The longest, not the twenty-first of June,
    Sees half the business in a wicked way,
On which three single hours of moonshine smile—
On them she looks so modest all the while.

There is a dangerous silence in that hour,
    A stillness, which leaves room for the full soul
To open all itself, without the power
    Of calling wholly back its self-control;
The silver light which, hallowing tree and tower,
    Sheds beauty and deep softness o'er the whole,
Breathes also to the heart, and o'er it throws
A loving languor, which is not repose.

The Devil's most devilish when respectable

Source: AURORA LEIGH (Book VII, l. 105).
Author: Elizabeth Barrett Browning (1806-1861)
First published: 1857
Type of work: Romance in blank verse

Context: Marian Erle, a poor but virtuous girl who has had a wretched, poverty-stricken childhood, becomes engaged to marry Romney Leigh, the wealthy, socially conscious cousin of the teller of the tale, Aurora Leigh. A wealthy and beautiful widow, Lady Waldemar, asks Aurora to help her break off Romney's marriage, but Aurora refuses to do so and forms a friendship with Marian. On the wedding day, Marian does not appear at the church, but sends a letter saying that she will not marry Romney. Romney unavailingly searches for Marian for months; finally, he gives up the quest and becomes engaged to marry Lady Waldemar. Later, Aurora, on her way to take up residence in Italy, finds Marian in Paris. Marian is now possessed of a baby boy; the situation at first shocks the somewhat priggish Aurora. According to Marian, Lady Waldemar, under the guise of being Marian's fast friend, convinced her that marriage with Romney would be a mistake. She therefore sent her off with a woman who was supposed to conduct her to Australia to set her up in a new life. Instead, she takes her to France, drugs her, and has her raped. After a period of madness, Marian regains her sanity and gets a position as a lady's maid to a married coquette who is another man's mistress. When the lady finds that Marian is about to give birth to a baby, she disdainfully dismisses her, saying that it would not be reputable to retain her. Aurora meditates that such women are far worse than actual street-walkers— they are most devilish when they put on a cloak of respectability.

For my part,
I'd rather take the wind-side of the stews
Than touch such women with my finger-end!

They top the poor street-walker by their lie
And look the better for being so much worse:
The Devil's most devilish when respectable.

Diana's foresters, gentlemen of the shade, minions of the moon

Source: KING HENRY THE FOURTH: PART ONE (Act I, sc. ii, ll. 25-27)
Author: William Shakespeare (1564-1616)
First published: 1598
Type of work: Historical drama

Context: Sir John Falstaff, jolly old reprobate and friend of Prince Hal, heir to the throne, asks the prince the time of day. Hal, in a jovial mood, declares that, since his old companion spends his life only in napping, eating, and drinking, the hours of the day mean nothing to him. Falstaff, confessing that as a highwayman the night is his time, begs the future king's protection for the men of the night:

FALSTAFF
Marry then sweet wag, when thou art King let not us that are squires of the night's body be called thieves of the day's beauty; let us be **Diana's foresters, gentlemen of the shade, minions of the moon,** and let men say we be men of good government, being governed as the sea is, by our noble and chaste mistress the moon, under whose countenance we steal.

Die to save charges

Source: ANATOMY OF MELANCHOLY (Partition I, sec. 2, memb. 3, subsec. 12)
Author: Robert Burton (1577-1640)
First published: 1621-1651
Type of work: Essays

Context: Some have called this lengthy volume "a literary cosmos, a compendium of everything that caught the fancy of a fine and lusty scholar who lived in an unspecialized age." Science and pseudo-science, history, theology, philosophy, poetry, and politics mingle in this work by a seventeenth century vicar and mathematician whose humor is sly, broad, or earthy by spells. While by his divisions into Partitions, Sections or Paragraphs, Members, and Subsections, he seems to promise a logical development of thought, his continual digressions into any field that comes to his mind make summarization impossible. Partition I begins with a contrast between Adam in Eden and the present-day man who, because of the forbidden fruit, has suffered a universal malady, a melancholy that affects his religion and his knowledge. Burton's idea of this effect of "the hu-

213

mors" is, of course, long out of date, but the mind as a cause of melancholy, the topic of Member 3, is still current. Its twelfth division, Subsection 12, deals with covetousness or miserliness. Burton pictures men as afraid of everything, since anything might impoverish them. They will not spend, for fear of becoming poor, and would hang themselves to avoid poverty, except that ropes cost money. Some even die because of the high cost of remaining well.

> . . . They are afraid of . . . thieves, lest they rob them; they are afraid of war and afraid of peace, afraid of rich and afraid of poor; afraid of all. Last of all, they are afraid of want, that they shall die beggars, which makes them lay up still, and dare not use what they have; (what if a dear year comes, or dearth, or some loss?) and were it not that they are loth to lay out money on a rope, they would be hanged forthwith, and sometimes **die to save charges,** and make away themselves, if their corn and cattle miscarry, though they have abundance left. . . . Valerius makes mention of one that in a famine sold a mouse for 200 pence, and famished himself; such are their cares, griefs, and perpetual fears. . . .

Digestion is the great secret of life

Source: A MEMOIR OF THE REVEREND SYDNEY SMITH BY HIS DAUGHTER LADY HOLLAND
Author: Sydney Smith (1771-1845)
First published: 1855
Type of work: Biographical memoir

Context: Arthur Kinglake probably sent to his neighbor, the Reverend Sydney Smith, a copy of *A Dissertation on Gout* (1804), by his doctor brother, Robert Kinglake (1765–1842). Its idea of the therapeutic value of foods must have fitted in with the dean's own ideas of the effect of diet, in addition to environ-ment, on the life and acts of men, often expressed in his own writing. At any rate, it occasioned one of the witty minister's many letters, full of references from his abundant learning and theories. Timotheus was the famous Court minstrel of Alexander the Great. The letter was sent from Smith's parish.

Dear Sir,   Combe Florey, Sept. 30, 1837
    I am much obliged by the present of your brother's book. I am convinced **digestion is the great secret of life;** and that character, talents, virtues, and qualities are powerfully affected by beef, mutton, pie-crust and rich soups. I have often thought I could feed or starve man into many virtues and vices, and affect them more

214

powerfully with my instruments of cookery than Timotheus could formerly do with his lyre.

Ever yours, very truly   Sydney Smith

Discords make the sweetest airs

Source: HUDIBRAS (Part III, Canto I, l. 919)
Author: Samuel Butler (1612-1680)
First published: First and second parts, 1663; third part, 1678
Type of work: Burlesque poem

Context: The first six cantos of *Hudibras* had been published by 1664. They contained a sarcastic attack upon the enemies of Charles II, ridiculing the Puritans who had beheaded his father. Surely out of gratitude, the Merry Monarch would show the author some sort of favor. Rumor had it that he carried a copy of the poem in his pocket and frequently quoted from it. But the story that Charles settled an annual pension of £100 on the poet must not be true. Butler scribbled in his Common-place Book: "To think how Spenser died, how Crowley mourn'd,/ How Butler's faith and service were return'd." That remark probably explains the lapse of fourteen years between the publication of the Second and Third Parts, and the lack of interest that can be detected in the final section. Two years after it appeared in print, the poet died. If he had had future plans for *Hudibras,* still incomplete, they were never carried out. The poem contains a minimum of action. Actually there are only four episodes: Hudibras' victory over Crowdero; Trulla's victory over Hudibras; Hudibras' victory over Sidrophel, an astrologer; and the Widow's unmasking of Hudibras and his escape through the window. Then the poem drops into religious exposition and attack on the Presbyterians and Independents, whose rivalry had opened the way for the restoration of the throne to Charles II. To parallel the magic scenes in *Don Quixote,* Butler provides one in the first canto of Part III. At the end of the previous canto the angry bickering of the knight and his squire is interrupted by a traveling antique show and violence over a henpecked husband. Hudibras once more tries to attack the sinful crowd until a well-thrown egg discourages him. To discover their future, Ralpho suggests a visit to Sidrophel—under whose name a famous astrologer, William Lilly, is satirized. The episode brings up talk of famous dealers in Black Arts of the past. Hudibras is soon convinced that the conjurer is a fake and sends his servant for a constable while he holds the man and his servant. Afraid that the police will arrest his master for Black Art, Ralpho goes instead to the Widow, confessing his master's trickery. Hudibras, when his prisoners get away, also heads for his lady love. She will not marry him. There are no marriages in Heaven, and she adds: "That's the reason, as some guess,/ There is no heav'n in marriages." But he does not object to quarrels. "The bad in marriages only improves the good."

215

And hearts have been as oft with sullen
As charming looks surpris'd and stolen;
Then why should more bewitching clamor
Some lovers not so much enamour?
For **discords make the sweetest airs,**
And curses are a kind of prayers;
Two slight alloys for all those grand
Felicities by marriage gain'd; . . .

Disease of admiration

Source: WILLIAM PITT, EARL OF CHATHAM
Author: Thomas Babington Macaulay (1800–1859)
First published: January, 1834
Type of work: Biographical essay and book review

Context: Macaulay was well prepared to review an 1827 *History of the Right Honorable William Pitt, Earl of Chatham* by the Reverend Francis Thackeray (1793–1842). Macaulay had long been interested in Parliamentary history and was sympathetic to the spirit of the eighteenth century dominated by Pitt (1708–1778). Like others, he believed Pitt's famous first administration the most glorious in Parliament's history. And so his essay on the Earl of Chatham is one of his best. He drew little upon the two volumes he was supposed to be reviewing. Even in his time, this biography was considered pompous and prolix. Much of his material came from Horace Walpole's *Letters* and his *Memoirs of the Reign of King George the Second.* As a critic, Macaulay speaks, in the very beginning of his essay, of Francis Thackeray's dullness in contrast to his talented nephew, William M. Thackeray (1811–1863), author of *Vanity Fair.* James Boswell (1740–1795) was the admiring biographer of Dr. Samuel Johnson (1709–1784). Macaulay's essay begins:

Almost every mechanical employment, it is said, has a tendency to injure some one or other of the bodily organs of the artisan. Grinders of cuttlery die of consumption; weavers are stunted in their growth; smiths become blear-eyed. In the same manner almost every intellectual employment has a tendency to produce some intellectual malady. Biographers, translators, editors, all, in short, who employ themselves in illustrating the lives or the writings of others, are peculiarly exposed to the *Lues Boswelliana,* or **disease of admiration.** But we scarcely remember ever to have seen a patient so far gone in this distemper as Mr. Thackeray. He is not satisfied with forcing us to confess that Pitt was a great orator, a vigorous minister, an honorable and high-spirited gentleman. He will have it that all virtues and all accomplishments met in his hero. . . .

216

The Dismal Science

Source: LATTER-DAY PAMPHLETS (*The Present Time*)
Author: Thomas Carlyle (1795-1881)
First published: 1850
Type of work: Political essay

Context: These essays on the political problems of his time exhibit Carlyle at his most vehement. He is alarmed by the wave of upheaval that shook all Europe in 1848 with riot and revolution, and by the unrest in England. To Carlyle, the growing trend toward democracy is an evil that must somehow be met and turned into sanity and order. He excoriates the hereditary aristocracy, which he considers least qualified by nature to govern anything; he believes man must be ruled, but that some other group must rule. As for democracy, he considers it no more than "Constituted Anarchy." America cannot serve as a successful example of democracy in action, he points out: with a small population and half a continent to subdue, it could get along with no government at all. When enough time has passed to reverse these conditions, the boasted freedoms will vanish. Here Carlyle pokes fun at suffrage: one cannot change a law of nature, he observes, by voting otherwise. He then turns to one of the great problems of his time, which has also contributed greatly to the revolutionary movements of Europe: the large masses of unemployed and indigent people. The government is spending vast amounts of money keeping these persons alive; some want employment and cannot secure it, others avoid it. Clearly, they and their country cannot be helped in this fashion. They must be put to work, and must be led. The hereditary leaders have already proven themselves incapable of the task; Carlyle suggests that the newly-developed "Captains of Industry" may be better qualified. He then presents an imaginary speech by a hypothetical Prime Minister to these multitudes, pointing out the labor that must be undertaken if all Britain is to be made productive, and the fact that it is better to pay them for work than to pay them for rotting where they sit. At this point there is an interruption from the political and social scientists—"all manner of Economists, Emancipationists, Constitutionalists," and other practitioners of political and social theory; but the Prime Minister quiets them:

"Respectable Professors of **the Dismal Science,** soft you a little. Alas, I know what you would say. For my sins, I have read much in those inimitable volumes of yours,—really I should think, some barrowfuls of them in my time,—and, in these last forty years of theory and practice, have pretty well seized what of Divine Message you were sent with to me. Perhaps as small a message, give me leave to say, as ever there was such a noise made about before. Trust me, I have not forgotten it, shall never forget it. Those Laws of the Shop-till are indisputable to me; and practically useful in certain departments of the Universe, as the multiplication-table it-

217

self. Once I even tried to sail through the Immensities with them, and to front the big coming Eternities with them; but I found it would not do. As the Supreme Rule of Statesmanship, or Government of Men,—since this Universe is not wholly a Shop,—no. You rejoice in my improved tariffs, free-trade movements and the like, on every hand; for which be thankful, and even sing litanies if you choose. But here at last, in the Idle-Workhouse movement, —unexampled yet on Earth or in the waters under the Earth,—I am fairly brought to a stand; and have had to make reflections, of the most alarming, and indeed awful, and as it were religious nature! Professors of **the Dismal Science,** I perceive that the length of your tether is now pretty well run. . . ."

Dispatch is the soul of business

Source: LETTERS TO HIS SON (Letter 104)
Author: Philip Dormer Stanhope, Lord Chesterfield (1694-1773)
First published: 1774
Type of work: Personal letters

Context: In Chesterfield's day it was not possible to become a great statesman or a socially and politically successful person unless one cultivated to perfection the attitudes and graces of the polished gentleman. Chesterfield made every effort to train his son in these attributes; many of his admonitions are simply sound common sense and worth-while advice to anyone. Again, many of them are more applicable to the age in which he lived: great attention to manner, rigid adherence to the many social graces and forms of etiquette, and a carefully calculated and rather cold approach to social relationships. For all the careful training Chesterfield bestowed, Philip never really lived up to his father's expectations. He spent most of his life in Europe, serving the British government; plagued by ill health, he died at thirty-six. Chesterfield corresponded faithfully with him and seldom failed to give him advice. In a letter written February 5, 1750,

he discusses the need to be economical, both of time and money. Quoting the saying, "Take care of the pence, and the pounds will take care of themselves," he points out that the same maxim can be equally well applied to time. The minutes we waste, says Chesterfield, do not amount to much; but if we add them up at the end of a year, it is a different story. One should neglect no opportunity to improve one's time; for example, rather than squandering an idle hour in a coffee-house, it is better to read a good book—not, he hastens to add, "frivolous and idle books, such as the absurd romances . . . where characters, that never existed, are insipidly displayed, and sentiments that were never felt, pompously described." Rather, one should stick to the best established books in any language. Chesterfield then touches on the evils of procrastination and the value of budgeting one's time:

Many people lose a great deal of their time by laziness; they loll and yawn in a great chair, tell themselves that they have not time to begin anything then, and that it will do as well another time. This is a most unfortunate disposition, and the greatest obstruction to both knowledge and business. At your age, you have no right nor claim to laziness; I have, if I please, being *emeritus*. You are but just listed in the world, and must be active, diligent, indefatigable. If ever you propose commanding with dignity, you must serve up to it with diligence. Never put off till tomorrow what you can do today.

Dispatch is the soul of business; and nothing contributes more to dispatch than method. Lay down a method for everything, and stick to it inviolably, as far as unexpected incidents may allow. Fix one certain hour and day in the week for your accounts, and keep them together in their proper order; by which means they will require very little time, and you can never be much cheated. Whatever letters and papers you keep, docket and tie them up in their respective classes, so that you may instantly have recourse to any one. Lay down a method also for your reading. . . .

The divine discontent

Source: HEALTH AND EDUCATION ("The Science of Health")
Author: Charles Kingsley (1819-1875)
First published: 1874
Type of work: Essay

Context: The Reverend Charles Kingsley was a high-minded man whose novels and essays were vehicles for his idealism. In them he tried to work for various kinds of social reform, and he gained a large following. He expressed, among other ideas, his admiration for strength, courage, and good health; and he did so with such effectiveness that these qualities began to be cultivated. An ideal grew up in Victorian England which some persons have since referred to as "muscular Christianity;" its principle was that the youth of England should have the bodies of vikings, with the souls of saints. One of Kingsley's efforts in this direction is his volume of essays, *Health and Education*. In the first essay he observes that the Brit-ish people appear to be less stalwart than they formerly were; and he points out that the reason is that the high mortality rate of earlier times weeded out all but those best equipped to survive. Now that the industrial age is here and advances in human survival have been made, the population is increasing and much of it is less rugged physically. Kingsley adds that instead of longing for a heroic past that was not really so desirable, we must accept the new age and seek to make it better. One factor that has lessened the number of robust Englishmen is the warfare of recent centuries. "War is, without doubt, the most hideous physical curse which fallen man inflicts upon himself; and for this simple reason, that it reverses the very laws of nature, and is more cruel even than pestilence. For instead of issuing in the survival of the fittest, it issues in the survival of the less fit; and therefore, if protracted, must deteriorate generations yet unborn." He then describes the living and working conditions of the poor, noting that these cannot produce healthy children unless they are improved. Intelligence cannot grow properly in an unhealthy body. He then answers those who would rather ignore the problem, or who fear the poor may be made discontented:

> . . . But are not people discontented already, from the lowest to the highest? And ought a man, in such a piecemeal, foolish, greedy, sinful world as this is, and always has been, to be anything but discontented? If he thinks that things are going all right, must he not have a most beggarly conception of what going right means? And if things are not going right, can it be anything but good for him to see that they are not going right? Can truth and fact harm any human being? I shall not believe so, as long as I have a Bible wherein to believe. For my part, I should like to make every man, woman, and child whom I meet discontented with themselves, even as I am discontented with myself. I should like to awaken in them, about their physical, their intellectual, their moral condition, that divine discontent which is the parent, first of upward aspiration and then of self-control, thought, effort to fulfil that aspiration even in part. For to be discontented with **the divine discontent,** and to be ashamed with the noble shame, is the very germ and first upgrowth of all virtue. Men begin at first, as boys begin when they grumble at their school and their schoolmasters, to lay the blame on others; to be discontented with their circumstances. . . . But that way no deliverance lies. That discontent only ends in revolt and rebellion, social or political; and that, again, still in the same worship of circumstances—but this time desperate—which ends, let it disguise itself under what fine names it will, in what the old Greeks called a tyranny; in which . . . all have become the voluntary slaves of one man, because each man fancies that the one man can improve his circumstances for him.

Divine tobacco

Source: THE FAERIE QUEENE (Book, III, Canto 5, stanza 32)
Author: Edmund Spenser (c.1552-1599)
First published: 1590
Type of work: Allegorical poem

Context: The bold and virtuous squire, Timias, pursues a wicked foster, or forester, who had attempted an assault upon the person of the beautiful damsel, Florimell. The foster, knowing the woods, escapes from the pursuit and makes his way to his two brothers, who are as wicked and depraved as he; the three band together to go to meet Timias, with whom they do battle. He finally slays all three of them, but not before he is severely wounded in the thigh by an arrow. The wound and the resultant loss of blood cause him to fall in a faint, almost dead, upon the ground. In the meanwhile the beautiful Belphoebe is ranging the forest in search of a wild beast that she has wounded in the chase. Instead of finding her prey, she comes upon the unconscious Timias, who lies weltering in his blood. Tenderly she removes his armor, and at the sight of his face she falls completely in love with him. She tries for a while unsuccessfully to revive him to consciousness, and then decides that medicines are called for:

> Into the woods thenceforth in hast she went,
> To seeke for hearbes, that mote him remedy;
> For she of hearbes had great intendiment,
> Taught of the Nymphe, which from her infancy
> Her nourced had in trew Nobility;
> There, whether it **diuine Tobacco** were,
> Or *Panachaea,* or *Polygony,*
> She found, and brought it to her patient deare
> Who al this while lay bleeding out his hartbloud neare.

Divinely tall, and most divinely fair

Source: A DREAM OF FAIR WOMEN (Lines 87-88)
Author: Alfred, Lord Tennyson (1809-1892)
First published: 1833
Type of work: Narrative poem

Context: A Dream of Fair Women, in its imagery, shows a certain affinity with Keats. In it the poet tells us he has been reading Chaucer's *Legend of Good Women;* "for a while, the knowledge of his art/ Held me above the subject, as strong gales/ Hold swollen clouds from raining, tho' my heart,/ Brimful of those wild tales,/ Charged both mine eyes with tears. In every land/ I saw, wherever light illumineth,/ Beauty and anguish walking hand in hand/ The downward slope to death." Through his mind there passes a phantasmagoria of scenes occurring throughout the ages in which women have suffered and men have fought over them and for them. There are glimpses of duels and wars, insults, pillage, ruined shrines, dungeons and seraglios. Then the poet falls asleep and finds himself in an ancient forest, where he presently meets a group of beautiful women. These are the famed beauties of legend and history; he sees, among others, Helen of Troy, Cleopatra, and Joan of Arc. Some tell him their stories. The poet is dazzled by these creatures, for some of whom whole armies died; he finds that at least a few wish they had not been born beautiful and that they had not altered the course of empire or of history. Their punishment seems to be that they are forever set aside from

221

men; as Cleopatra expresses it, "I govern'd men by change, and so I sway'd/ All moods . . ./ I have no men to govern in this wood:/ That makes my only woe." The poet, waking, finds himself plunged in melancholy. "With what dull pain/ Com- pass'd, how eagerly I sought to strike/ Into that wondrous track of dreams again!/ But no two dreams are like." The passage in which the poet finds himself in the forest is remarkable for its evocation of stillness and heavy foliage:

> At last methought that I had wander'd far
>   In an old wood: fresh-washed in coolest dew,
> The maiden splendours of the morning star
>   Shook in the steadfast blue.
>
> Enormous elm-tree-boles did stoop and lean
>   Upon the dusky brushwood underneath
> Their broad curved branches, fledged with clearest green,
>   New from its silken sheath.
>   •   •   •
> I knew the flowers, I knew the leaves, I knew
>   The tearful glimmer of the languid dawn
> On those long, rank, dark wood-walks drench'd in dew,
>   Leading from lawn to lawn.
>   •   •   •
> The smell of violets, hidden in the green,
>   Pour'd back into my empty soul and frame
> The times when I remember to have been
>   Joyful and free from blame.
>   •   •   •
> At length I saw a lady within call,
>   Stiller than chisell'd marble, standing there;
> A daughter of the gods, **divinely tall,**
>   **And most divinely fair.**

Do as you would be done by

Source: LETTERS TO HIS SON (Letter 17)
Author: Philip Dormer Stanhope, Lord Chesterfield (1694-1773)
First published: 1774
Type of work: Personal letters

Context: In Lord Chesterfield's letters to his illegitimate son there is a constant emphasizing of the rules by which a young man rises in the world. Due attention is directed to intelligence and ability, but the most important quality a young man can have, according to the earl, is the ability to please. He therefore begins the letter of October 16, 1747, by telling his son to pay constant attention to pleasing; he says that the best way to do so is by observing the Golden Rule. He begins the letter thus:

222

Dear Boy: The art of pleasing is a very necessary one to possess; but a very difficult one to acquire. It can hardly be reduced to rules; and your own good sense and observation will teach you more of it than I can. **Do as you would be done by,** is the surest method that I know of pleasing. Observe carefully what pleases you in others, and probably the same thing in you will please others. If you are pleased with the complaisance and attention of others to your humors, your tastes, or your weaknesses, depend upon it the same complaisance and attention, on your part to theirs, will equally please them. Take the tone of the company that you are in, and do not pretend to give it; be serious, gay, or even trifling, as you find the present humor of the company; this is an attention due from every individual to the majority. . . .

Do other men, for they would do you

Source: MARTIN CHUZZLEWIT (Chapter 11)
Author: Charles Dickens (1812-1870)
First published: 1843-1844
Type of work: Novel

Context: Jonas Chuzzlewit calls upon the Pecksniff sisters, in residence at Todgers', a London boarding house catering to commercial gentlemen, to conduct them to his home for dinner. He walks them until they are thoroughly fatigued and finally brings them to the house occupied by his father, Anthony, and himself. The residence is part of a moldy old office building; the living quarters are strewn with odds and ends of old fabrics and other bits of discarded merchandise; the combination of living room and dining room is filled with office equipment. During the dinner an old retainer, Chuffey, whose wits have been addled, is the target of insulting remarks by Jonas. Even Anthony is not spared, but he seems to enjoy the bitter remarks, as they show that his son is a sharp fellow. In alluding to Mr. Pecksniff, Anthony says that his hypocrisy can be overdone. Jonas replies that a thing not easily overdone is a bargain; one should always try to outdo others:

"There's another thing that's not easily overdone, father," remarked Jonas, after a short silence.
"What's that?" asked the father, grinning already in anticipation.
"A bargain," said the son. "Here's the rule for bargains—**'Do other men, for they would do you.'** That's the true business precept. All others are counterfeits."
The delighted father applauded this sentiment to the echo, and was so much tickled by it, that he was at the pains of imparting the same to his ancient clerk, who rubbed his hands, nodded his palsied head, winked his watery eyes, and cried in his whistling tones, "Good! good! Your own son, Mr. Chuzzlewit!" with every

223

feeble demonstration of delight that he was capable of making. But this old man's enthusiasm had the redeeming quality of being felt in sympathy with the only creature to whom he was linked by ties of long association, and by his present helplessness. . . .

Dog in the manger

Source: FIVE HUNDRED POINTS OF GOOD HUSBANDRY (Chapter 29, "Against Fantastical Scrupleness")
Author: Thomas Tusser (c.1525-1580)
First published: 1557
Type of work: Didactic poem

Context: The expression "dog in the manger" refers of course to Aesop's fable of the dog who, although he had no use for straw, would not allow the ox to have any. Throughout the ages since Aesop this term has been used to describe our common human reluctance to share things we cannot or will not put to use ourselves. Tusser probably did more than any other person to make this expression a popular household saying. His book, *Five Hundred Points of Good Husbandry,* enjoyed a wide and lasting popularity and served to perpetuate many of the proverbs and old sayings contained in it. An early version of the farmer's almanacs, it is made up of verses which give all manner of practical instruction to the farmer. These rhymes also incorporate moral advice, maxims, and observations upon the climate, the planets, and weather. Each month is taken up in its turn, beginning with September, and the work proper to it described at some length. The book thus provides us with an excellent insight into early Elizabethan rural life and farming methods. Tusser was a gentleman of good birth and education who retired to a farm; he obviously had a wide knowledge of husbandry but was unable to make a success of it. After several moves in an effort to improve his condition he at length died in a debtor's prison. In Chapter 29, entitled "Against Fantastical Scrupleness," he encourages hospitality. This chapter is appended to the material for December and refers to the Christmas season. Tusser does not feel that Christmas is a time to be stingy or in any way lacking in generosity. It is easy to see, too, that he prefers a merry soul to a grave one: he is deeply suspicious of the stern and disapproving nature.

> At this time and that time, some make a great matter;
> Some help not, but hinder the poor with their clatter.
> Take custom from feasting, what cometh then last?
> Where one hath a dinner, a hundred shall fast.
>
> To **dog in the manger,** some liken I could,
> That hay will eat none, nor let other that would.
> Some scarce, in a year, give a dinner or two,
> Nor well can abide any other to do.

224

Play thou the good fellow! seek none to misdeem;
Disdain not the honest, though merry they seem;
For oftentimes seen, no more very a knave,
Than he that doth counterfeit most to be grave.

Done those things which we ought not to have done

Source: THE BOOK OF COMMON PRAYER (Page 6)
Author: Traditional; translated and arranged by Archbishop Cranmer (1489–1560)
First published: 1549
Type of work: Prayer of confession

Context: The Order for Daily Morning Prayer is the first service in the Book of Common Prayer and is a direct descendent of a system of worship in practise during the Middle Ages known as the Canonical Hours, which in turn were developed out of Apostolic times from customs of daily instruction, praise, and prayer in use in the early Church. Morning Prayer, evolved principally from the longest of the Canonical Hours, the service of *Matins*, begins in a penitential mood. After a series of opening sentences which set the theme and tone of the service, there follows the *Exhortation* in which the congregation is reminded that no converse with God can be fitting or profitable until the worshiper, in all honesty, lays bare his disobediences to God's Holy Will, and, in all sincerity, seeks reconciliation with His Love. The minister urges the people to accompany him, with pure hearts and humble voices to the very "throne of the heavenly grace" and join with him in a confession of their sins. There follows then the *General Confession,* called "general" because it is said by the minister and all the people and is a confession not only of individual shortcomings but of the corporate guilt of the whole community of worshipers, who have "strayed . . . like lost sheep" from God's holy ways.

Almighty and most merciful Father; We have erred, and strayed from thy ways like lost sheep. We have followed too much the devices and desires of our own hearts. We have offended against thy holy laws. We have left undone those things which we ought to have done; And we have **done those things which we ought not to have done;** And there is no health in us. But thou, O Lord, have mercy upon us, miserable offenders. Spare thou those, O God, who confess their faults. Restore thou those who are penitent; According to thy promises declared unto mankind In Christ Jesus our Lord. And grant, O most merciful Father, for his sake; That we may hereafter live a godly, righteous, and sober life, To the glory of thy holy Name. Amen.

The Dorian pipe, the Dorian strain

Source: THYRSIS (Line 97)
Author: Matthew Arnold (1822-1888)
First published: 1866
Type of work: Elegy

Context: "Thyrsis" was written to commemorate Arnold's close friend Arthur Hugh Clough. The poem is composed in the traditional pastoral form for elegies; shepherds are brought into it, and references to the Doric past are prominent. Arnold brings in the "Dorian" or "Sicilian" by first reminding the reader that ". . . when Sicilian shepherds lost a mate,/ Some good survivor with his flute would go," and of course lament his friend with lyric music. This lovely music would be played directly to Proserpine, daughter of the goddess of vegetation and growth and queen of the world of the dead, who had often "trod Sicilian fields." The goddess cherished the beauty of the countryside and thus also "She loved the Dorian pipe, the Dorian strain."

> O easy access to the hearer's grace
> When Dorian shepherds sang to Proserpine!
> For she herself had trod Sicilian fields,
> She knew the Dorian water's gush divine,
> She knew each lily white which Enna yields,
> Each rose with blushing face;
> She loved **the Dorian pipe, the Dorian strain.**

A double glass o' the inwariable

Source: THE PICKWICK PAPERS (Chapter 33)
Author: Charles Dickens (1812-1870)
First published: 1836-1837
Type of work: Novel

Context: Mr. Pickwick, president of the Pickwick Club, and several companions have agreed to travel to various areas of England, such as Bath and Rochester, and to report of their adventures and travels to the other club members. In the meantime, Mr. Pickwick has an unsolicited adventure: when he rented his present quarters, Mrs. Bardell, his landlady, misunderstood him and concluded that he intended to marry her, and now is suing him for breach of promise. Old Mr. Weller, father of Sam Weller, servant of Mr. Pickwick, meets his son at the Blue Boar to pass along some advice for Mr. Pickwick as he faces trial. As he enters, Mr. Weller is disturbed to find Sam composing a Valentine, this being the thirteenth of February, but, reassured that Sam has no intentions of matrimony, he says in his cockney accent to the waitress:

226

. . . **"A double glass o' the inwariable,** my dear."

"Very well, Sir," replied the girl; who with great quickness appeared, vanished, returned, and disappeared.

"They seem to know your ways here," observed Sam.

"Yes," replied his father, "I've been here before in my time. . . ."

Doubt is Devil-born

Source: IN MEMORIAM (Part XCVI, stanza 1)
Author: Alfred, Lord Tennyson (1809-1892)
First published: 1850
Type of work: Elegy

Context: This elegy was written as a monument to Arthur Henry Hallam, a young man of extraordinary promise and an intimate friend of Tennyson's, who died suddenly in Vienna at the age of twenty-two. The poem records Tennyson's slow spiritual progress from his initial depth of personal sorrow to the gradual healing of grief through a sense of spiritual contact with Hallam in a wider love of God and humanity. Preceding section XCVI, Tennyson describes having fleetingly achieved the reunion in spirit with his friend which he had so earnestly desired. This union in section XCV is one of the climaxes of the elegy. After this mystical experience, Tennyson comes out of his trance and begins to doubt the validity of his experience. In spite of his intellectual doubts, he affirms the certainty of intuitive powers. At the close, he sees darkness and light no longer as two opposing powers but united in a single image of dawn, symbolic of a new faith. Section XCVI is an occasional poem designed to illustrate the change within the poet's mind and soul caused by his experience. Tennyson affirms the value of honest doubting in the search for a stronger faith:

> You say, but with no touch of scorn
> Sweet-hearted, you, whose light-blue eyes
> Are tender over drowning flies,
> You tell me, **doubt is Devil-born.**
>
> I know not: one indeed I knew
> · · ·
> Perplext in faith but pure in deeds,
> At last he beat his music out.
> There lives more faith in honest doubt,
> Believe me, than in half the creeds.

Doubtless God could have made a better berry,
but doubtless God never did

Source: THE COMPLEAT ANGLER (Part I, chapter 5)
Author: Izaak Walton (1593–1683)
First published: 1653
Type of work: Dialogue on fishing

Context: From the third century A.D. Roman rhetorician Claudius Aelianus who first mentioned fly fishing, and Dame Juliana Barnes who first treated the subject in English in her fifteenth century *Treatyse of Fysshynge wyth an Angle* to the present, thousands of fishermen have written of their craft, but few have produced a more enjoyable book than Izaak Walton's *The Compleat Angler.* The first edition appeared in 1653 in a small octavo volume that could be tucked into a fisherman's bulging pocket. It sold for eighteen pence. Previous to that, Walton had written biographies of the Reverend John Donne and Sir Henry Wotton, his friends. "I write not for money but for pleasure," Walton declared. He did not need money, for he had retired after a career in London as ironmonger or hardware merchant. He found in his birthplace of Stafford a refuge from the turmoil of civil war with Royalists and Parliamentarians killing each other. Now aloof from politics, a representative of the seventeenth century search for relief from the world's woes in Nature and the works of God, Walton became a champion for the Christian virtues of friendship and goodness, and for the country joys as opposed to the money-grubbing life of the city. At his age of sixty, when the book appeared, he confessed he was a gentle man wielding "a mild pen, not used to upbraid the world." He wove into its pages anecdotes, poetry, descriptions of nature, and an uncritical choice of quotations from even Pliny with his unnatural *Natural History.* The result may not be a completely trustworthy guide to fishing practices; indeed its author declared that it is hard "to make a man that was none to be an Angler by a book." But the book provides delightful reading for even non-fishermen. The first edition contained thirteen chapters that were later increased to twenty-one, and in the fifth edition of 1676, the last printed during his lifetime, a second part on flymaking and casting was added by his poet friend Charles Cotton (1630–1687). Walton himself preferred "bottom fishing" with worms, grasshoppers, or frogs, using a fifteen-foot pole, a "trembling quill," and a hook tied on by hair leaders. Not until Samuel Pepys (1633–1703) was there mention of the use of gut leaders. Chapter V of *The Compleat Angler* contains a conversation between Piscator (The Fisherman, representing W a l t o n) and Venator (Hunter), who in the first edition, was the scholarly wayfarer, Viator. On their walk in the early dawn to a fishing spot along the river Piscator discourses on the relative merits for trout fishing of flies, worms, caterpillars, and real and artificial minnows; but as he proves by catching fish when his companion is unsuccessful, it is the skill of the fisherman and not the lure that fills the basket. As they walk and later fry their fish under a tree, they discuss Nature. Piscator recites several poems. He also quotes, in modern spelling, from "Dr. Boteler," Doctor William Butler (1535–1618), the Cambridge-trained court physician of King James I, among whose writings was an article on foods and diets.

> . . . No life, my honest Scholar, no life so happy and so pleasant as the life of a well governed Angler; for when the Lawyer is swallowed up with business, and the Statesman is preventing or contriving plots, then we sit on Cowslip-banks, hear the birds sing, and possesse ourselves in as much quietnesse as these Silent silver streams, which we now see glide so quietly by us. Indeed my good Scholar, we may say of Angling, as Dr. Boteler said of Strawberries; **Doubtlesse God could have made a better berry, but doubtlesse God never did:** And so (if I might be Judge) God never did make a more calm, quiet, innocent recreation than Angling.

Down in the mouth

Source: THE OLD BACHELOR (Act IV, sc. iv)
Author: William Congreve (1670-1729)
First published: 1693
Type of work: Dramatic comedy

Context: Araminta and Belinda meet at St. James Park, a favorite gathering place for people of fashion in the seventeenth and eighteenth centuries. Araminta, in love with Vainlove, hopes to meet him on the Mall nearby. She and her beloved have had a disagreement, and she hopes to be able to settle their differences. As they walk along, the two women put on their masks, as women in public often did at the time. As they stroll through the park they are seen by Sir Joseph Wittol, a stupid and cowardly knight, and his favorite companion, Captain Bluffe, a cowardly soldier who pretends to be a bully. Having drunk a bit, the two men approach Araminta and Belinda, hoping to be attractive to them. The two women know the men for what they are and repulse their advances. The reaction of the women causes Captain Bluffe to make his comment.

BLUFFE
Ladies, by these hilts you are well met.

ARAMINTA
We are afraid not.

BLUFFE [*to Belinda.*]
What says my pretty little knapsack carrier?

229

BELINDA

O monstrous filthy fellow! Good slovenly Captain Huffe, Bluffe,
(what is your hideous name?) be gone: you stink of brandy and
tobacco, most soldier-like. Foh! [*Spits.*]

BLUFFE [*aside.*]

Now I am slap dash **down in the mouth,** and have not one word
to say!

Down on flummery

Source: SKETCHES NEW AND OLD ("The Undertaker's Chat")
Author: Mark Twain (1835-1910)
First published: 1875
Type of work: Humorous anecdote

Context: Samuel Langhorne Clemens, more familiarly known to readers as Mark Twain, had many gifts; one of the greatest was his ability to depict character and human feeling through the words of people he created. Another was his mastery of dialect. Combining these with his insight into human nature, he filled his tales with persons who are natural and entirely believable; they seem alive, and we feel that we not only know them, but know them well. All are individuals. Much of Twain's humor derives from the same aspects of his deep understanding: his characters express emotions which are universal, but do so in picturesque and at times outlandish terms. We understand the character, like him, and sympathize with him; at the same time, the humor of the scene is inescapable. Tragedy is sometimes masked with laughter to make it bearable. A brief sketch, "The Undertaker's Chat," provides, a good example. The old undertaker is engaged in readying the body of a friend for burial. He has known and admired this man for many years, and in his conversation reveals deep affection for him. We learn that the dead man was a humble person who deplored ostentation and that he was loved by all. His relatives all wanted to buy him a ruinously expensive coffin, but he refused; he also declined a silver nameplate, observing that "he judged that wher' he was going to a body would find it considerable better to attract attention by a picturesque moral character than a natty burial case with a swell doorplate on it." In his eulogy the undertaker endeavors to camouflage his grief with far-fetched expressions and thereby renders it even more obvious; his apparent irreverence is strangely touching:

"Splendid man, he was. I'd druther do for a corpse like that 'n
any I've tackled in seven year. There's some satisfaction in buryin'
a man like that. You feel that what you're doing is appreciated. . . .

"Well, the relations they wanted a big funeral, but corpse said

230

he was **down on flummery**—didn't want any procession—fill the
hearse full of mourners, and get out a stern line and tow *him* behind. He *was* the most down on style of any remains I ever struck.
A beautiful simple-minded creature—it was what he was, you can
depend on that. He was just set on having things the way he
wanted them, and he took a solid comfort in laying his little
plans. He had me measure him and take a whole raft of directions;
then he had the minister stand up behind a long box with a tablecloth over it, to represent the coffin, and read his funeral sermon,
saying 'Angcore, angcore!' at the good places, and making him
scratch out every bit of brag about him, and all the hifalutin; and
then he made them trot out the choir so's he could help them pick
out the tunes for the occasion, and he got them to sing 'Pop Goes
the Weasel,' because he'd always liked that tune when he was
down-hearted, and solemn music made him sad; and when they
sung that with tears in their eyes (because they all loved him),
and his relations grieving around, he just laid there as happy as a
bug, and trying to beat time and showing all over how much he
enjoyed it; and presently he got worked up and excited, and tried
to join in, for, mind you, he was pretty proud of his abilities in the
singing line; but the first time he opened his mouth and was just
going to spread himself his breath took a walk."

A dream itself is but a shadow

Source: HAMLET (Act II, sc. ii, l. 266)
Author: William Shakespeare (1564-1616)
First published: 1603
Type of work: Dramatic tragedy

Context: As Hamlet probes further
the story told him by his father's
ghost—that his father was murdered
by his Uncle Claudius, the present
king, and that his mother had committed adultery with Claudius—the
young prince feigns madness and is
himself probed by others eager to discover the cause of his madness. The
king and queen send for two of Hamlet's youthful companions, Rosencrantz and Guildenstern, who agree
to scout the melancholy Dane. The
quick-witted Hamlet spars with his
old friends—who wonder whether
ambition may be at the root of his
trouble, that is, disappointment at not
being made king after his father's
death—and manages to keep them interested while avoiding any definite
commitment. Hamlet calls Denmark
a prison; Rosencrantz and Guildenstern protest:

HAMLET

Why then 'tis none to you; for there is nothing either good or bad
but thinking makes it so. To me it is a prison.

231

ROSENCRANTZ

Why then your ambition makes it one; 'tis too narrow for your mind.

HAMLET

O God, I could be bounded in a nutshell, and count myself a king of infinite space, were it not that I have bad dreams.

GUILDENSTERN

Which dreams indeed are ambition, for the very substance of the ambitious is merely the shadow of a dream.

HAMLET

A dream itself is but a shadow.

Dream of London, small, and white, and clean

Source: THE EARTHLY PARADISE ("Prologue: The Wanderers," Line 5)
Author: William Morris (1834-1896)
First published: 1868-1870
Type of work: Narrative poem

Context: English painter, poet, and prose writer, Morris was associated with the Pre-Raphaelite aesthetic movement of the late nineteenth century, an attempt to revive greater freedom of expression for artist and writer alike. This demand for individuality he carried to the production of household furniture, tapestry, and carpet through the foundation of Morris, Marshall, Faulkner, and Company. Later he headed a similar movement in founding the Kelmscott Press to meet the need for quality printing and illustration. As a poet, Morris was primarily interested in the Nordic and Grecian legends, and, in *The Earthly Paradise,* he recounts the tales of a group of Norwegian pilgrims who set sail to find the legendary "earthly paradise" of which they have heard so much. After many years they arrive at a "Western land" where, highly honored by the natives, they pass their remaining years. In establishing his scene at the outset, the author recalls a land unbesmirched by the industrial trade of Victorian England, a land reminiscent of what he imagines Chaucer's England to have been:

Forget six counties overhung with smoke,
Forget the snorting steam and piston stroke,
Forget the spreading of the hideous town;
Think rather of the pack-horse on the down,
And **dream of London, small, and white, and clean,**
The clear Thames bordered by its gardens green;
Think, that below bridge the green lapping waves
Smite some few keels that bear Levantine staves,

232

Cut from the yew-wood on the burnt-up hill,
And pointed jars that Greek hands toiled to fill,
And treasured scanty spice from some far sea. . . .

A nameless city in a distant sea,
White as the changing walls of faerie,
Thronged with much people clad in ancient guise
I now am fain to set before your eyes; . . .

Drink down all unkindness

Source: THE MERRY WIVES OF WINDSOR (Act I, sc. i, l. 203)
Author: William Shakespeare (1564-1616)
First published: 1602
Type of work: Dramatic comedy

Context: Early in the first act of *The Merry Wives of Windsor,* the reader learns that several injustices have been committed against Robert Shallow, Esquire, by Sir John Falstaff and his followers. Master Page, Sir John, and his followers soon enter the scene, and Shallow confronts Falstaff hotly with his list of grievances, which Falstaff acknowledges. When Slender, cousin of Shallow, begins enumerating more in detail what happened to him during his drinking with Falstaff and his men, Sir John calls on his associates to answer the accusations. The words become more heated as Bardolph, Pistol, and Nym deny Slender's charges. The ladies enter the scene, appropriately causing the heated discussion to cease momentarily. Page then urges his wife and the other ladies to invite all the gentlemen inside their house for drink and dinner. He says he hopes that drink will soothe the atmosphere of hostility among them.

PAGE
Wife, bid these gentlemen welcome. Come, we have a hot venison pasty to dinner. Come, gentlemen, I hope we shall **drink down all unkindness.**

Drink fair, whatever you do!

Source: MARTIN CHUZZLEWIT (Chapter 49)
Author: Charles Dickens (1812-1870)
First published: 1843-1844
Type of work: Novel

Context: Dickens was often the conscience of Victorian England, and the theme of *Martin Chuzzlewit* is hypocrisy and selfishness, as exemplified by the various characters; the character of Mrs. Gamp, Sairey she calls herself, is no exception; nor is her erstwhile partner in sickroom care (one cannot call it nursing), Betsey Prig, an exception. On one occasion Mrs. Gamp invites Betsey Prig to tea, hoping to persuade Mrs. Prig to work with her in caring for Mr. Chuffey, a weak-minded man who will require someone's attention twenty-four hours of the day. Since Betsey Prig is difficult to deal with, and does not really like Mrs. Gamp, the latter is careful in her preparations. The little apartment is made neat as it can be, two whole pounds of highly pickled salmon are purchased, and the tea things are laid out carefully. The tea-pot contains spirits, rather than tea, and the two irascible women make frequent application to its contents. Betsey Prig is not much interested in Mrs. Gamp's proposal and reaches frequently for the tea-pot, too frequently to please her hostess. Mrs. Gamp is finally moved to remonstrate with her guest for taking more than her share:

> Here Mrs. Prig, without any abatement of her offensive manner, again counterfeited abstraction of mind, and stretched out her hand to the tea-pot. It was more than Mrs. Gamp could bear. She stopped the hand of Mrs. Prig with her own, and said, with great feeling:
> "No, Betsey! **Drink fair, whatever you do!**"
> Mrs. Prig, thus baffled, threw herself back in her chair, and closing the same eye more emphatically, and folding her arms tighter, suffered her head to roll slowly from side to side, while she surveyed her friend with a contemptuous smile.

A drop of a bucket

Source: ISAIAH 40:15
Author: Isaiah
First transcribed: c.800-200 B.C.
Type of work: Religious prophecy and exhortation

Context: The fortieth chapter of Isaiah is justly considered one of the finest passages in Scripture. Isaiah was both an inspired prophet and a great poet; this chapter is a song of joy resulting from a vision in which he has glimpsed the deliverance of his people. Rejoicing in the greatness of God, he tells his audience that their long suffering is destined to end; and the picture he paints is one of spiritual triumph. Many of these verses were set to music by Handel and incorporated into *Messiah;* the result is a remarkable fusion of genius, in which sublime poetry is enhanced by music of great power and majesty. Chapter 40 forms a prelude to Isaiah's later prophecies, particularly those in chapters 42, 49, 50, 52, and 53, which foretell the coming of the Messiah; Isaiah refers to this figure as the Servant. The early fathers of the Christian Church felt certain, reading these lines, that Isaiah had prophesied the coming of Christ. Later scholars puzzled over the poet's words and considered a number of Jewish leaders, contemporary with Isaiah, who might have fitted the role of deliverer. Later opinion has concluded, however, that a Messiah was precisely what Isaiah had in mind. He begins by saying that the Lord has at last pardoned Israel and that all things shall be made right, and that all men shall see the glory of the Lord. All flesh comes from grass, and men wither away as the grass does, but the word of God endures forever. Men will behold God on earth; and he will rule them, caring for his flock as a shepherd does. Isaiah then emphasizes the greatness of the Lord, beside which the works of man are nothing.

O Zion, that bringest good tidings, get thee up into the high mountain; O Jerusalem, that bringest good tidings, lift up thy voice with strength; lift it up, be not afraid; say unto the cities of Judah, Behold your God!

Behold, the Lord GOD will come with strong hand, and his arm shall rule for him: behold, his reward is with him, and his work before him.

He shall feed his flock like a shepherd: he shall gather the lambs with his arm, and carry them in his bosom, and shall gently lead those that are with young.

Who hath measured the waters in the hollow of his hand, and meted out heaven with the span, and comprehended the dust of the earth in a measure, and weighed the mountains in scales, and the hills in a balance?

Who hath directed the Spirit of the LORD, or being his counselor hath taught him?

With whom took he counsel, and who instructed him, and taught him in the path of judgment, and taught him knowledge, and shewed to him the way of understanding?

Behold, the nations are as **a drop of a bucket,** and are counted as the small dust of the balance: behold, he taketh up the isles as a very little thing.

And Lebanon is not sufficient to burn, nor the beasts thereof sufficient for a burnt offering.

The dust of creeds outworn

Source: PROMETHEUS UNBOUND (Act I, l. 697)
Author: Percy Bysshe Shelley (1792-1822)
First published: 1820
Type of work: Lyric drama

Context: The Titan Prometheus, chained to a precipice in the Indian Caucasus, is tortured by the evil Jupiter because he refused to tell who will overthrow the tyranny of heaven; however, he has suffered so long that he has lost his bitterness and no longer hates his tormenter. Panthea and Ione are seated at his feet when the Phantasm of Jupiter reminds the

235

Titan of his awful curse, and they hear Prometheus repent of his rash anger, but when Mercury comes with the Furies and offers him a life of ignoble ease if he will reveal his dread secret, he refuses to coöperate with evil. As a result, the Furies unleash their worst, but Prometheus, who has learned the secret of suffering love, is able to withstand them until they show him a vision of "a youth/ With patient looks nailed to a crucifix." Such a vision tortures him more than any physical pain could, and as he writhes in agony, Earth calls up the spirits of human thought to comfort him. The quotation is from the First Spirit's song:

> On a battle-trumpet's blast
> I fled hither, fast, fast, fast,
> 'Mid the darkness upward cast.
> From **the dust of creeds outworn,**
> From the tyrant's banner torn,
> Gathering 'round me, onward borne,
> There was mingled many a cry—
> Freedom! Hope! Death! Victory!
> Till they faded through the sky;
> And one sound, above, around,
> One sound beneath, around, above,
> Was moving; 'twas the soul of Love, . . .

Dwindle into a wife

Source: THE WAY OF THE WORLD (Act IV, sc. i)
Author: William Congreve (1670-1729)
First published: 1700
Type of work: Dramatic comedy

Context: Millamant, a beautiful and witty young heiress, falls in love with Mirabell, a gentleman of fashion, who loves her equally. In talking about marriage, Millamant reveals what she expects in matrimony, and as she does, satirizes the views of marriage held by many courtiers at the time. She tells her lover that she could only hate a man who became too assured of her, and that she wants to be assured herself of both her will and pleasure in marriage. She says, too, that she does not want to be called by pet names, as she thinks they are hypocritical. Nor does she want to be openly affectionate or familiar; as she says, "Let us be as strange as if we had been married a great while; and as well bred as if we were not married at all." Mirabell then asks her if she has any other conditions to offer, observing that her demands up to this point seem reasonable. Millamant says more:

MILLAMANT
Trifles—as liberty to pay and receive visits to and from whom

I please; to write and receive letters, without interrogatories or wry faces on your part. To wear what I please; and choose conversation with regard only to my own taste; to have no obligation upon me to converse with wits that I don't like, because they are your acquaintance; or to be intimate with fools, because they may be your relations. Come to dinner when I please, dine in my dressing-room when I'm out of humour, without giving a reason. To have my closet inviolate; to be sole empress of my tea-table, which you must never approach without first asking leave. And lastly, wherever I am, you shall always knock at the door before you come in. These articles subscribed, if I continue to endure you a little longer, I may by degrees **dwindle into a wife.**

Each age is a dream that is dying

Source: ODE (Last stanza)
Author: Arthur William Edgar O'Shaughnessy (1844-1881)
First published: 1874
Type of work: Lyric poem

Context: Arthur William Edgar O'Shaughnessy was himself a man who dreamed a dream; although he was vitally interested in literature and wanted a career as a poet and scholar, he spent his adult life in the natural history department of the British Museum, earning a living by the preserving of fish. Yet from that unpoetic work he emerged as a poet, albeit a minor one, of the Victorian era. Dead at the age of thirty-seven, he did not live long enough to come to grips with great themes in poetry, but he did prove in his short career as a poet that he had a real lyric talent; the *Ode* testifies to that talent. In the poem he tells the reader that he sees history as belonging to men who dream dreams and make music; these men, he says, "are the movers and shakers/ Of the world forever, it seems." One man, he writes, with a dream can conquer a crown; three others with a song can "trample a kingdom down." And he writes in the third and last stanza:

We, in the ages lying
   In the buried past of the earth,
Built Nineveh with one sighing,
   And Babel itself with our mirth;
And o'erthrew them with prophesying
   To the old of the new world's worth;
For **each age is a dream that is dying,**
   Or one that is coming to birth.

Each alike was Greek, alike was free

Source: TO VICTOR HUGO (Line 3)
Author: Algernon Charles Swinburne (1837-1909)
First published: 1866
Type of work: Eulogy

Context: Few major English poets have the power to hypnotize the reader into a state wherein he accepts obscenities because they are given intoxicating rhythms, but Swinburne, a master at turning ugliness into beauty, has just that ability and uses it to create some of the most unforgettable poems in British literature. Perhaps one reason why he was such a shock to his contemporaries was that he learned quite young how to lift his readers into the sound of his verse; such knowledge, of course, came in part, from the other poets he read and loved. A brilliant, searching intellect, he was not content to read only the literature in his own language; in fact, the strongest influences on his style and thought came from French literature of both the Middle Ages and the nineteenth century. Among the French poets that he loved were the romantic writers of the emotional and sensational poetry of the senses—the poetry of men like Victor Hugo, whom he praises in this eulogy. Hugo, like the German and English Romantics, was instrumental in giving the emotions a primary place in poetry that was a mixture of melodious words and sensual content. Such poetry seemed to Swinburne to have the spirit of Greek verse:

> In the fair days when God
> By man as godlike trod,
> And **each alike was Greek, alike was free,**
> God's lightning spared, they said,
> Alone the happier head
> Whose laurels screened it; fruitless grace for thee,
> To whom the high gods gave of right
> Their thunders and their laurels and their light.

Each of us suffers his own hell

Source: THE AENEID (Book VI, as translated by John Jackson)
Author: Virgil (Publius Vergilius Maro, 70-19 B.C.)
First transcribed: c.29-19 B.C.
Type of work: Epic poem

Context: Written with patriotic inspiration, *The Aeneid* attempts to give Rome an origin worthy of her greatness. Aeneas, the son of Venus and a hero of the Trojan War, sails from Troy to Italy, encountering perils reminiscent of those of Ulysses. Upon his arrival in Italy, Aeneas is conducted by a Sybil to the land of the dead where his father Anchises reveals to him his destiny as founder of the Roman Empire, showing him the grandeur of their mutual heirs awaiting their earthly sojourns. Anchises explains to Aeneas that all men bear the taint of guilt and that for this reason *each of us suffers his own hell* before reaching the rewards of the blessed Elysian Fields, or in the translation of Jackson:

. . . Some are hung outspread to the substanceless winds: from others the stain of guilt is washed clean under the waste of waters, or burnt away by fire. **We suffer, each in his proper spirit;** then are sent to the spacious plains of Elysium, where some few abide in the blissful fields; till at length the hoary ages, when time's cycle is run, purge the incarnate stain, and leave but the purified ethereal sense and the unsullied essential flame. . . .

An eagle mewing her mighty youth

Source: AREOPAGITICA
Author: John Milton (1608-1674)
First published: 1644
Type of work: Printed speech

Context: Although Milton had long been one of the most passionate and articulate defenders of Puritanism, he could not agree when the revolutionary Puritan Parliament, on June 14, 1643, ordered that no book, pamphlet, or paper should be printed without a license from the proper authorities. Milton believed implicitly in the individual nature of the search for truth and in the necessity for freedom of speech and conscience. He recognized that such freedoms would, of course, produce differences of opinion. This speech, addressed to Parliament and cast into the form of a classical oration, is Milton's response to the Parliamentary order and is a world-famous defense of freedom of the press. He first demonstrates that none of the great classical states had engaged in such repressive measures and then shows that censorship was invented by the Catholic Church, to the Puritans the greatest symbol of error and heresy. To the often repeated argument that difference of opinions breeds the dangers of sect and schism Milton replies that in their very ability to tolerate such differences and resolve them into truth lies the strength of the English people:

. . . when the cheerfulness of the people is so sprightly up, as that it has not only wherewith to guard well its own freedom and safety, but to spare, and to bestow upon the solidest and sublimest points of controversy and new invention, it betokens us not degenerated, nor drooping to a fatal decay, but casting off the old and wrinkled skin of corruption to outlive these pangs, and wax young again, entering the glorious ways of truth and prosperous

239

virtue, destined to become great and honorable in these latter ages. Methinks I see in my mind a noble and puissant nation rousing herself like a strong man after sleep, and shaking her invincible locks: methinks I see her as **an eagle mewing her mighty youth,** and kindling her undazzled eyes at the full midday beam; purging and unscaling her long-abused sight at the fountain itself of heavenly radiance; while the whole noise of timorous and flocking birds, with those also that love the twilight, flutter about, amazed at what she means, and in their envious gabble would prognosticate a year of sects and schisms.

Earth, with her thousand voices, praises God

Source: HYMN BEFORE SUNRISE, IN THE VALE OF CHAMOUNI (Last line)
Author: Samuel Taylor Coleridge (1772-1834)
First published: 1802
Type of work: Lyric poem

Context: Coleridge, in the Vale of Chamonix, or Chamouni, stands at early dawn before the great mass of Mont Blanc and is so mightily affected by the scene that he is moved to hymn the glory of God, Whose handwork the mountain is. The rivers Arve and Arveiron roar ceaselessly at the base of the mountain, which rises in silence so profound as to make him raise his voice in praise. The wonder of the mighty foundations of the mass, sunk deep into the earth; its face snow-covered, bathed with the rosy light of early morning; its parentage of many streams that perpetually gush forth from its caves of ice; its ice falls, like silent cataracts; all speak to the poet of God. The brilliant blue gentians that flourish up to the edge of the ice, the wild goats leaping upon the crags, the eagles sporting with the mountain storm, and the lightning, like arrows, also proclaim the reality of God. The avalanche that plunges unheard by human ears into the clouds that sometimes veil the mountain, and above all, the great mountain itself, like a kingly spirit enthroned amid the encircling hills, is conjured by the poet to tell the sky, the stars, and the rising sun that the earth in all its forms praises God.

> Thou too, hoar Mount with thy sky-pointing peaks,
> Oft from whose feet the avalance, unheard,
> Shoots downward, glittering through the pure serene
> Into the depth of clouds, that veil thy breast—
> Thou too again, stupendous Mountain! thou
> That as I raise my head, awhile bowed low
> In adoration, upward from thy base
> Slow travelling with dim eyes suffused with tears,
> Solemnly seemest, like a vapory cloud,
> To rise before me—Rise, O ever rise,
> Rise like a cloud of incense from the Earth!

Thou kingly Spirit throned among the hills,
Thou dread ambassador from Earth to Heaven,
Great Hierarch! tell thou the silent sky,
And tell the stars, and tell yon rising sun
Earth, with her thousand voices, praises God.

East of the sun, west of the moon

Source: THE EARTHLY PARADISE ("September")
Author: William Morris (1834-1896)
First published: 1868-1870
Type of work: Narrative poem

Context: In this section of *The Earthly Paradise,* Morris, who is frequently called the last and most excessive of the romantics, tells the tragic love story of a peasant and a queen. Although John, the peasant, loves the queen, he betrays her by telling who she really is. As in the Cupid and Psyche tale, upon which this story is based, John does penance for his betrayal and finally wins back the beautiful queen. However much Morris may have been the romantic, he was also the realist. Where an inferior poet might have ruined the tale, he carefully places the lovers in a world of hard facts and crushing responsibilities so that the reader is never able to wallow in mere sentimentality. The first appearance of the oft-repeated quotation occurs in the queen's speech to her lover, who still sleeps, as she leaves him; as a crushing reminder that the world is indeed real, it is a fitting antidote to the romance of escape.

> Dream not then
> Of named lands, and abodes of men!
> Alas, alas, the loneliest
> Of all such were a land of rest
> When set against the land where I
> Unhelped must note the hours go by! . . .
>   • • •
> My feet, lost Love, shall wander soon
> **East of the Sun, West of the Moon!**
> Tell not old tales of love so strong,
> That all the world with all its wrong
> And heedlessness was weak to part
> The loving heart from loving heart?

Education has for a chief object the formation of character

Source: SOCIAL STATICS (Part II, chapter 17, section 4)
Author: Herbert Spencer (1820-1903)
First published: 1850
Type of work: Scientific treatise

Context: Herbert Spencer, the English social scientist and philosopher, declined the opportunity for a university education. A self-educated man, he was engaged in engineering from 1837–1845, and from 1848–1853 was sub-editor of the *Economist.* His subsequent compositions on psychology, sociology, and ethics did much to apply the Darwinian principles of evolution to philosophy. His first significant title, originally published as *Social Statics: or, the Conditions essential to Human Happiness specified and the first of them developed,* contained various observations on the fundamental purposes and goals of education and the desirability of the state's maintaining and controlling a national educational system. He defends formal education, not as the sole means of proper maturation, but as a system to exercise properly the sentiments through which the savage instincts are checked. At one point he roundly condemns the practice of physical punishment as an inducement to proper behavior. He calls on advocates of "the stern will and the strong hand" to visit Hanwell Asylum and observe the effects of the tolerance practiced by the present management. "Let them contrast (with these horrors) the calmness, the contentment, the tractability, the improved health of mind and body, and the not unfrequent recoveries, that have followed the abandonment of the strait-jacket *regime:* and then let them blush for their creed." And the same principles should be applied to discipline in the classroom:

Education has for a chief object the formation of character. To curb restive propensities, to awaken dormant sentiments, to strengthen the perceptions and cultivate the tastes, to encourage this feeling and repress that, so as finally to develop the child into a man of well-proportioned and harmonious nature—this is alike the aim of parent and teacher. . . . But the power of self government, like all other powers, can be developed only by exercise. Whoso is to rule over his passions in his maturity, must be practised in ruling over his passions during youth. Observe, then, the absurdity of the coercive system. Instead of habituating a boy to be a law to himself, as he is required in after-life to be, it administers the law for him.

Either be wholly slaves, or wholly free

Source: THE HIND AND THE PANTHER (Part II, l. 857)
Author: John Dryden (1631-1700)
First published: 1687
Type of work: Religious allegory

Context: Celebrating his conversion to Roman Catholicism in 1686, England's most noted poet of this period played his part in the quarrel between Protestantism and Catholicism by composing a long allegorical poem about animals, in which the Hind represents the Catholics, the Panther the

Church of England, and the Lion, King James II. Part II of the poem contains a dialogue between the chief animals over religious practices. The Hind upholds church authority and Purgatory, and refuses to concede that everyone should follow "his particular judgment." After the struggle to establish authority of the Bible, it is folly to accept an unauthorized interpretation of it, or argue for a personal hell. Dryden's poetry is superior to his religious exegesis, but he was writing for partisan readers whom he hoped would maintain traditions.

• • •

"Did we a lawful tyranny displace,
To set aloft a bastard of the race?
Why all these wars to win the Book, if we
Must not interpret for ourselves, but she?
Either be wholly slaves, or wholly free.
For *purging* fires traditions must not fight,
But they must prove episcopacy's right.
Thus those led horses are from service freed;
You never mount 'em but in time of need.
Like mercenaries, hir'd for home defense,
They will not serve against their native prince."

• • •

Embarrassment of riches

Source: L'EMBARRAS DES RICHESSES
Author: Abbé Leonore d'Allainval (1700–1753)
First published: 1726
Type of work: Dramatic comedy

Context: To us the expression "An embarrassment of riches" means "Too much to choose from"; that is, the more alternatives we have, the more difficult is our choice. Although a literal translation from the French, it is one in which the meaning does not survive the transition: in its original form it refers to the burden of wealth. Its first appearance in print seems to have been as the title of d'Allainval's comedy, usually given as *L'embarras des richèsses.* The play was popular in France, and an English translation by John Ozell opened at the Haymarket Theater October 9, 1738. In it Harlequin, the stock comic character of French drama, is a gardener. His singing irritates Mr. and Mrs. Midas; Midas is a financier who worships Plutus, the god of wealth. Plutus answers their prayers, and punishes Harlequin by giving him a treasure. Harlequin is utterly corrupted by this gift; he puts on airs, abandons the pastoral Chloe, who loves him, gives himself over to vanity and display, and is in continual terror lest his treasure be stolen from him. He finally gives it up after he has become utterly miserable; the lovers are then reunited, and Harlequin becomes his old self again. The implication here is that wealth is a burden, especially to those who are not born to it; and the play's title had probably

243

become a commonly used figure of speech by the time Voltaire used it in its context in another comedy, *Le Droit du Seigneur,* which was given in Paris in 1762 in five acts under the title *L'Ecueil du Sage (The acquisition of wisdom),* and revived in 1778, after the author's death. In it Mathurin, a farmer who has come into some money, abandons the pastoral Colette and pursues Acante, who is obviously too good for him. Her foster parents agree to let Mathurin marry her, and Acante is desperate. She wishes to take refuge with friends in a ruined château. The lord will be arriving soon, and Acante will appeal to him; she is unaware of "Le droit du seigneur." This "right of the lord" is an old French custom whereby the lord, when one of his vassals marries, spends the wedding night with the bride. In Act II, scene vi, the cavalier is telling Champagne, a servant, that he has been sent ahead by the marquis; his mission is to see that Mathurin does not get to Acante first. He suggests they take advantage of the great man's dignity, gravity, and slowness: they will abduct Acante and take her to a ruined château nearby. Champagne reminisces about the old lady who lives there:

CHAMPAGNE

The old girl was young once.
I remember your madcap of a father
Had a certain affair with her,
Wherein each of them made a poor bargain
Faith, he was a debauched master,
Exactly like you, drinking, loving the girls,
Carrying them off, and then making fools of them;
He devoured everything and left you nothing.

LE CHEVALIER

I have a marquis, and that is a good thing.
With no worries of my own, I live off his bounty.
I want nothing to do with the **responsibility of riches:**
He who can always play is rich enough.
The first good, believe me, is pleasure.

Endless extinction of unhappy hates

Source: MEROPE (Line 102)
Author: Matthew Arnold (1822-1888)
First published: 1858
Type of work: Dramatic tragedy

Context: Twenty years have passed since Polyphontes, now tyrant of Messenia, murdered Cresphontes, the proper king, and forced Merope, the

244

widow of the murdered monarch, to marry him; however, Polyphontes did not kill Merope's youngest son, Aepytus, who mysteriously disappeared. The drama opens as Aepytus, now an adult, returns to Messenia to take vengeance on his father's murderer; he comes with his uncle, Laias, who shows him the kingdom that belongs to him. His plan is to enter the palace as an unknown guest bringing word of his own death; in this way he will be able to kill Polyphontes when he least expects danger. But no sooner does he relate his plan than Merope and Polyphontes enter; she has come to Cresphontes' tomb to honor the twentieth anniversary of his death, but Polyphontes wants her to stop such mourning because her behavior is making the people uneasy. The quotation comes from Polyphontes' speech requesting Merope to stop her mourning:

All this I bear, for, what I seek, I know:
Peace, peace is what I seek, and public calm;
Endless extinction of unhappy hates,
Union cemented for this nation's weal.
And even now, if to behold me here,
This day, amid these rites, this black-robed train,
Wakens, O Queen! remembrance in thy heart
Too wide at variance with the peace I seek—
I will not violate thy noble grief,
The prayer I came to urge I will defer.

Enough to make a deacon swear

Source: THE BIGLOW PAPERS (Second Series, No. 2)
Author: James Russell Lowell (1819-1891)
First published: 1867
Type of work: Satirical poem

Context: This poem, written in the New England dialect, ostensibly by "Squire Biglow," is a commentary on the famous Mason and Slidell incident of the recent Civil War, with a "frame" letter from Homer Wilber, A. M., a fictional person who supposedly forwards the poem from the little town of Jaalam, in Middlesex County, to the editors of the *Atlantic Monthly,* in Boston. Mason and Slidell, appointed by Jefferson Davis as diplomatic representatives of the Confederacy at London and Paris, respectively, had been seized from a British steamer by an American war vessel; this act was of the kind the United States had objected to when England had committed it against Americans prior to the War of 1812. Lowell has Squire Biglow begin by telling how he likes to take a walk in the evening, after the chores are done, "to shake the kinkles out o' back and legs." On one such walk, "round the whale's-back o' Prospect Hill," the squire begins a reverie in which he seems to hear the Concord Bridge, site of the famous battle in the American Revolution, talking to the monument at

Bunker Hill. The bridge, noting that the ghosts of the dead British soldiers buried nearby have been restless in the previous night, asks the Bunker Hill monument what is bothering the long-dead men. The monument says it is Mason and Slidell, the men Captain Wilkes took off the "Trent." The bridge replies that it hopes the authorities have not hanged the two and thus made "a goose a swan." The monument tells the bridge that the English want the release of the two men sent by the Confederacy, to which the bridge replies, thinking the United States has been insulted:

THE BRIDGE
Hev they? Wal, by heaven,
Thet's the wust news I've heered sence Seventy-seven!
By George, I meant to say, though I declare
It's 'most **enough to make a deacon swear.**

Envy keeps no holidays

Source: THE ADVANCEMENT OF LEARNING (Book VI, chapter 3, antitheses, 16)
Author: Sir Francis Bacon (1561-1626)
First published: 1605
Type of work: Philosophy

Context: Sir Francis Bacon was trained in the legal profession and spent much of his active life in politics. He was a member of Parliament for many years, and was careful to associate himself with various royal favorites; one of these was the unfortunate Essex, whom Bacon helped to convict after his fall. Another was George Villiers, Duke of Buckingham. His cultivation of the latter earned for Bacon a series of royal favors which lasted until Buckingham's fall from grace; Bacon was then charged with accepting bribes from various persons who had appeared in his court. Bacon did not deny the truth of these charges, although he insisted that he had not actually perverted justice. He was fined heavily and imprisoned for a brief period, then pardoned. He was forbidden to take part in politics again, however, and entered upon his retirement. His last years were devoted to the voluminous literary and philosophical works for which he is famous; in these writings Bacon concentrated most heavily on the promotion and explanation of his intellectual ideals, and most of them were intended to become a part of *The Great Instauration.* This was planned as a vast work which would reorganize all systems of knowledge along what we would consider more scientific lines. The introduction to it, and a full-length work in itself, is entitled *De Degnitate et Augmentis Scientiarium (Of the Dignity and Advancement of Learning).* Its title is usually shortened. A synopsis and summary of all learning and knowledge current in Bacon's time, it stresses his ideals of objectivity, sound observation, and a critical approach. Its influence upon later philosophical and scientific thought was considerable. Book VI is a discussion of rhetoric, discourse, and argument; in Chapter 3 Bacon gives several examples of fallacious reasoning (sophisms), following with a number of "antitheses"—neatly arranged epigrammatic arguments for and against specific things. An example follows:

XVI. ENVY

For	Against
It is natural for a man to hate that which reproaches to him his own fortunes.	**Envy keeps no holidays.** Nothing but death can reconcile envy to virtue.
Envy in commonwealths is a wholesome kind of ostracism.	Envy puts virtues to laborious tasks, as Juno did Hercules.

Envy, ye great, the dull unlettered small

Source: TRUTH (Line 375)
Author: William Cowper (1731-1800)
First published: 1782
Type of work: Meditative poem

Context: Cowper, a descendant of John Donne, was primarily a poet of rural life; he was the last English poet who belonged to the "cult of simplicity." A deeply religious man, he drew both comfort and despair from his Calvinism: in his writings he moralizes frequently, and most of his poems are to some extent moral essays. His mother died when he was a child, and his life in the public schools was a bitterly unhappy one. He was trained in the legal profession and called to the bar in 1754, but recurring attacks of insanity forced him to abandon his career. His first attack made it impossible for him to marry the cousin he loved; during the second he tried to commit suicide. He suffered from these periods of melancholia, in which his religion played a major role, throughout his later years. Retiring to the country, he eventually settled at Olney. Here, at fifty years of age, he turned to poetry as a serious avocation. The first volume, *Po-ems,* was published in 1782. His humorous poem, *John Gilpin's Ride,* was published the same year and gained wide popularity. *The Task,* his greatest work, appeared in 1785 and ensured his lasting fame. Typical of Cowper at his best, it is a quiet picture of rural life: the beauty of the countryside in winter, the simplicity and the pleasures of his daily routine are vividly and tranquilly presented. He considers, at some length, the nature of life and of moral responsibility; and he examines the world from a comfortable distance. *Truth,* one of the poems in his first volume, is a good example of those works in which Cowper produces a moral commentary akin to a sermon. In it he examines man's moral and spiritual responsibilities and the consolations afforded by Scripture. He concludes that the world and its many activities serve only to alienate man from God, that riches merely compound the problem, and that those who possess little are in reality the   most fortunate:

> Oh bless'd effect of penury and want,
> The seed sown there, how vigorous is the plant!
> No soil like poverty for growth divine,
> As leanest hand supplies the richest wine.
> Earth gives too little, giving only bread,
> To nourish pride, or turn the weakest head;
> To them, the sounding jargon of the schools
> Seems what it is, a cap and bells for fools;
> The light they walk by, kindled from above,
> Shows them the shortest way to life and love:
> They, strangers to the controversial field,
> Where deists always foil'd, yet scorn to yield,
> And never check'd by what impedes the wise,
> Believe, rush forward, and possess the prize.
> **Envy, ye great, the dull unletter'd small;**
> Ye have much cause for envy—but not all;
> We boast some rich ones whom the Gospel sways,
> And one who wears a coronet and prays:
> Like gleanings of an olive-tree they show,
> Here and there one upon the topmost bough.

Ercles' vein

Source: A MIDSUMMER NIGHT'S DREAM (Act I, sc. ii, l. 36)
Author: William Shakespeare (1564-1616)
First published: 1600
Type of work: Dramatic comedy

Context: In Athens the festivities have commenced in celebration of the marriage of Duke Theseus and the fair captive, Hippolyta, Queen of the Amazons. To honor the royal couple, a group of craftsmen rehearse a play based upon the legend of Pyramus and Thisbe. The talkative weaver, Bottom, assigned the role of Pyramus, the lover who gallantly kills himself for love, comments, that, though the part of Pyramus will require acting skill, he would prefer to enact the part of the tyrant familiar to the Elizabethan stage, Hercules:

BOTTOM
That will ask some tears in the true performing of it. If I do it, let the audience look to their eyes. I will move storms. I will condole in some measure. To the rest. Yet my chief humour is for a tyrant. I could play Ercles rarely, or a part to tear a cat in, to make all split.

> The raging rocks,
> And shivering shocks,
> Shall break the locks

248

Of prison gates,
And Phibbus' car
Shall shine from far,
And make and mar
        The foolish Fates.
This was lofty. Now name the rest of the players. This is **Ercles'**
vein, a tyrant's vein. A lover is more condoling.

Erred and strayed like lost sheep

Source: THE BOOK OF COMMON PRAYER (Page 6)
Author: Traditional; translated and arranged by Archbishop Cranmer (1489–
    1560)
First published: 1549
Type of work: Prayer of confession

Context: The Order for Daily Morning Prayer is the first service in the Book of Common Prayer and is a direct descendent of the system of services used during the Middle Ages and known as the Canonical Hours. This system of daily worship was regarded not only as a means of personal edification but as a part of the Church's "bounden duty and service" in a continual offering to God of a corporate act of praise and thanksgiving. Morning Prayer begins with a series of opening sentences which set the theme and tone of the service to come. The Exhortation which follows reminds the worshiper that no converse with God can be fitting or profitable until his sins are laid bare and he has sought reconciliation with God's Love. The minister beseeches the people to accompany him "with a pure heart, and humble voice, unto the throne of heavenly grace," and there to confess their sins unto Almighty God. There follows a General Confession of all the faithful in which they compare themselves to wandering and rebellious sheep the essence of whose sin is self-assertion: the following after their own wills rather than of God's holy ways. The inevitable result of this straying is the loss of the spiritual health which only their merciful and loving shepherd can restore to them.

Almighty and most merciful Father; We have **erred, and**
strayed from thy ways **like lost sheep.** We have followed too
much the devices and desires of our own hearts. We have offended
against thy holy laws. We have left undone those things which
we ought to have done; And we have done those things which
we ought not to have done; And there is no health in us. But
thou, O Lord, have mercy upon us, miserable offenders. Spare
thou those, O God, who confess their faults. Restore thou those
who are penitent; According to thy promises declared unto mankind In Christ Jesus our Lord. And grant, O most merciful Father,
for his sake; That we may hereafter live a godly, righteous, and
sober life, To the glory of thy holy Name. Amen.

The eternal silence of these infinite spaces terrifies me

Source: PENSÉES (Section III, number 206)
Author: Blaise Pascal (1623-1662)
First published: 1670
Type of work: Philosophical commentary

Context: Pascal, a French author and religious thinker, is known for his defenses of the religious reform movement known as Jansenism, named for Cornelius Jansen, who taught the doctrines of original sin, irresistible grace, and man's helplessness before God; in many ways the sect he founded resembled Calvinism. Before his conversion to Jansenism, Pascal was chiefly interested in mathematics; he invented a calculating-machine, did work in probability theory, and is believed by some to have originated the system of calculus. After his religious conversion, he gave most of his attention to theology. His writings are notable for objectivity and rationality, insight, and a graceful style which is at times ironic. *Pensées* (Thoughts) is probably his best-known work today. Found among his belongings after his death, it was considered too unorthodox for publication and did not see the light of print in its entirety until 1844. A collection of religious thoughts and observations, *Pensées* is actually the accumulated notes for an Apologia, or justification, of the Christian religion—a book which Pascal had intended to write. In Section III of *Pensées,* Pascal takes up the subject of eternity and man's relationship to it. Beginning with the ironic comment that "Men despise religion; they hate it and fear it is true," he considers the man who is concerned only with the things of this life. He feels there must be some strange confusion in man's nature that allows him so to concern himself with daily trifles and at the same time remain indifferent to things of vastly greater importance:

For it is not to be doubted that the duration of this life is but a moment; that the state of death is eternal, whatever may be its nature; and that thus all our actions and thoughts must take such different directions, according to the state of that eternity, that it is impossible to take one step with sense and judgement, unless we regulate our course by the truth of that point which ought to be our ultimate end.

. . .

. . . That passion may not harm us, let us act as if we had only eight hours to live.

If we ought to devote eight hours of life, we ought to devote a hundred years.

When I consider the short duration of my life, swallowed up in the eternity before and after, the little space which I fill and even can see, engulfed in the immensity of spaces of which I am ignorant and which know me not, I am frightened and am astonished at being here rather than there; for there is no reason why here rather than there, why now rather than then. Who has put me

250

here? By whose order and direction have this place and time been allotted to me? . . .

The eternal silence of these infinite spaces terrifies me.

Eternity! thou pleasing, dreadful thought!

Source: CATO (Act V, sc. i, l. 10)
Author: Joseph Addison (1672-1719)
First published: 1713
Type of work: Dramatic tragedy

Context: Marcius Porcius Cato (95–46 B.C.) is the hero of Addison's play. Having fought long against Caesar's despotism and espoused the cause of republicanism, Cato is saddened and defeated by the course of events. He has even lost one of his sons in the struggle. He advises Portius, his remaining son, to retire from public life to the Sabine hills, there to live on the land where their great ancestor, Cato the Censor, the present Cato's great-grandfather, had lived. At the beginning of the fifth act of the play Cato is found sitting by a table on which lie a sword and what Addison calls "Plato's Book on the Immortality of the Soul," probably the *Phaedo*. Cato considers what death may bring if he commits suicide, as he later does. He notes that man longs after immortality and shrinks from believing that death is but oblivion. And he asks why man fears death so greatly.

CATO
Why shrinks the soul
Back on herself, and startles at destruction?
'Tis the divinity that stirs within us;
'Tis heaven itself, that points out an hereafter,
And intimates eternity to man.
Eternity! thou pleasing, dreadful thought!
Through what variety of untried being,
Through what new scenes and changes must we pass!
The wide, th' unbounded prospect lies before me;
But shadows, clouds, and darkness, rest upon it.
Here will I hold. If there's a pow'r above us,
(And that there is all nature cries aloud
Through all her works) he must delight in virtue;
And that which he delights in must be happy.
But when! or where!—This world was made for Caesar.
I'm weary of conjectures—This must end 'em.
[*Laying his hand on his sword.*]

251

Eternity was in that moment

Source: THE OLD BACHELOR (Act IV, sc. iii)
Author: William Congreve (1670-1729)
First published: 1693
Type of work: Dramatic comedy

Context: Old Fondlewife, married to the young and beautiful Laetitia, is, as an impotent husband, jealous of the virtue of his lusty wife. He is compelled to be absent on a business matter of £500, and to insure his wife's good behavior, purposes to have a one-eyed Puritanical minister, Tribulation Spintext, sit with her while he is absent. Laetitia had written to Vainlove, whose mistress she had formerly been, and had said that she would so arrange matters that Spintext would not be at her house. Vainlove, who has tired of Laetitia, turns the affair over to his friend, Bellmour, who procures a long black cloak, a broad hat, and an eye-patch and visits Laetitia after her husband departs. At first she is startled to find a stranger in her home, but Bellmour speedily makes an impression upon her with his excellent appearance and bold manners. It is only a matter of moments before she gives him, in return for his importunities, a passionate kiss. As the two part, he says that eternity was in that moment. She admires his agreeable impudence and accedes to his request.

LAETITIA
I hope you are a gentleman;—and since you are privy to a weak woman's failing, won't turn it to the prejudice of her reputation. You look as if you had more honor—

BELLMOUR
And more love, or my face is a false witness, and deserves to be pilloried. No, by Heaven I swear—

LAETITIA
Nay, don't swear if you'd have me believe you; but promise—

BELLMOUR
Well, I promise—A promise is so cold!—give me leave to swear—by those eyes, those killing eyes; by those healing lips.—Oh! press the soft charm close to mine—and seal 'em up for ever.

LAETITIA
Upon that condition.   [*He kisses her.*]

BELLMOUR
Eternity was in that moment! One more upon any condition.

252

Even God cannot change the past

Source: NICHOMACHEAN ETHICS (Book VI, chapter ii)
Author: Agathon (c.477-401 B.C.), attributed by Aristotle (384-322 B.C.)
First transcribed: Fourth century, B.C.
Type of work: Philosophical treatise

Context: Aristotle, in discussing morality, says that in all moral states there is some object which the rational man keeps in view in intensifying or relaxing his activity: this object should be the mean, or the state between two extremes. The intellect, Aristotle says, is divided between the speculative intellect and practical intellect; the function of the speculative intellect is to apprehend truth in conformity with right reason. Thus moral purpose is the origin of action, which implies reason. It then follows that moral purpose is intellectual desire, and it is this intellectual desire which makes a man. Anything that is desired must be something in the future, as it is impossible to desire things in the past. Aristotle explains it thus:

> But nothing which is done and past can be the object of moral choice; for instance, no man chooses to have sacked Troy; because, in fact, no one ever deliberates about what is past but only about that which is future and which may therefore be influenced, whereas what has been cannot not have been: and so Agathon is right in saying,
> **Even God cannot change the past.**

The evening star, love's harbinger

Source: PARADISE LOST (Book XI, ll. 588-589)
Author: John Milton (1608-1674)
First published: 1667
Type of work: Epic poem

Context: Michael, sent down from Heaven by God to instruct Adam in preparation for his expulsion from the garden, takes him to the top of a hill from which can be seen much of the earth and there shows him various forms of death that will kill men as a result of Adam and Eve's wickedness in eating the forbidden fruit. Adam wants to know why man, made in the divine similitude, must suffer these loathesome forms of death. Michael replies that the Maker's image forsook man when his ungoverned appetite led him astray. Man can live a temperate life and drop off easily in old age, but to do so he will have to outlive his youth, his beauty, and his strength. Man should live his life well, whether for a long or a short time, as Heaven decrees. Michael then shows Adam a new sight: a broad plain with tents and grazing cattle; the people are miners and work all sorts of metals. These people are the sons of Lamech: Jabal, Jubel, and Tubal-Cain. The scene then shifts to some dwellers in the hills, just people who worship God in a proper manner. They may be the sons of Seth, who tradition holds were the mysterious "sons of God" (Genesis 6: 2) who took wives of the daughters of men:

> They on the plain
> Long had not walked, when from the tents behold
> A bevy of fair women, richly gay
> In gems and wanton dress; to the harp they sung
> Soft amorous ditties, and in dance came on:
> The men though grave, eyed them, and let their eyes
> Rove without rein, till in the amorous net
> Fast caught, they liked, and each his liking chose;
> And now of love they treat till **the evening star,**
> **Love's harbinger,** appeared; then all in heat
> They light the nuptial torch, and bid invoke
> Hymen, then first to marriage rites invoked;
> With feast and music all the tents resound.
>
> . . .

Every flower enjoys the air it breathes

Source: LINES WRITTEN IN EARLY SPRING (Lines 11-12)
Author: William Wordsworth (1770-1850)
First published: 1798
Type of work: Lyric poem

Context: Reclined in a grove, the poet hears "a thousand blended notes" which lead him to the thought that in the world of external Nature there is a joy in merely being. By contrast, his heart is grieved "to think/ What man has made of man." Whether his belief is heaven-sent, whether it is "Nature's holy plan" that flowers enjoy the air they breathe, the birds their playing, and the twigs their spreading to the air— he knows not. But if it is true, then "Have I not reason to lament/ What man has made of man?" Stanzas 3 and 6 read:

> Through primrose tufts, in that green bower,
> The periwinkle trailed its wreaths;
> And 'tis my faith that **every flower**
> **Enjoys the air it breathes.**
>
> . . .
>
> If this belief from heaven be sent,
> If such be Nature's holy plan,
> Have I not reason to lament
> What man has made of man?

254

Every good servant does not all commands

Source: CYMBELINE (Act V, sc. i, l. 6)
Author: William Shakespeare (1564-1616)
First published: 1623
Type of work: Tragi-comedy

Context: Posthumus orders his servant, Pisanio, in a letter, to slay Imogen, the wife from whom he has been forcibly separated and whom he believes to be untrue to him because of the lies of an Italian, Iachimo. Pisanio, who could not bring himself to kill the lovely and virtuous Imogen, has actually sent her, disguised as a man, to do service as a page to the Roman ambassador. In order to convince Posthumus that he has killed her, however, he sends Posthumus her bloody handkerchief. Posthumus has repented and wishes Pisanio had not followed his orders, for even good servants do not always do as told.

> POSTHUMUS
> Yea, bloody cloth, I'll keep thee, for I wished
> Thou shouldst be colored thus. You married ones,
> If each of you should take this course, how many
> Must murder wives much better than themselves
> For wrying but a little. O Pisanio,
> **Every good servant does not all commands.**
> No bond but to do just ones. Gods, if you
> Should have ta'en vengeance on my faults, I never
> Had lived to put on this; so had you saved
> The noble Imogen to repent, and struck
> Me, wretch, more worth your vengeance. . . .

. . .

Every hero becomes a bore at last

Source: REPRESENTATIVE MEN (Chapter I, "Uses of Great Men")
Author: Ralph Waldo Emerson (1803-1882)
First published: 1850
Type of work: Moral essay

Context: Emerson believed in the importance of great men, and this volume, a collection of seven lectures he gave during the 1840's, illustrates his views on the subject. As representative men he selected Plato, as philosopher; Swedenborg, as mystic; Montaigne, as skeptic; Shakespeare, as poet; Napoleon, as man of the world; and Goethe, as writer. Each of these was, for Emerson, representative of a kind of greatness, and greatness was, for Emerson, a necessary ingredient of the nature of mankind. He says in his opening statement in *Representative Men,* "It is natural to believe in great men." He goes on to comment, "Nature seems to exist for

255

the excellent. The world is upheld by the veracity of good men." And he notes a little later in "Uses of Great Men," "The search after the great man is the dream of youth and the most serious occupation of manhood." But Emerson also warns that we must learn to think for ourselves, that the domination of a great man over others' minds can degenerate into idolatry, and then the influence of the great man becomes evil, rather than good. Nature, suggests Emerson, is a help to us, as she, through death, provides a necessary rotation of great men, so that one is replaced by another of a different kind. The best kind of great man that lives in our own time, suggests Emerson, is one from whom we learn "almost through the pores of our skin, pulling ourselves up to the level, or trying to, of the great one." But though a great man is an indemnification for a whole population of lesser men, there is always some danger from him:

> . . . a new danger appears in the excess of influence of the great man. His attractions warp us from our place. We have become underlings and intellectual suicides. Ah! yonder in the horizon is our help;—other great men, new qualities, counterweights and checks on each other. We cloy of the honey of each peculiar greatness. **Every hero becomes a bore at last.** Perhaps Voltaire was not badhearted, yet he said of the good Jesus, even, "I pray you, let me never hear that man's name again." They cry up the virtues of George Washington,—"Damn George Washington!" is the poor Jacobin's whole speech and confutation. But it is human nature's indispensable defense. The centripetal augments the centrifugence. We balance one man with his opposite, and the health of the state depends on the see-saw.

Every man has his fault, and honesty is his

Source: TIMON OF ATHENS (Act III, sc. i, ll. 28-29)
Author: William Shakespeare (1564-1616)
First published: 1623
Type of work: Dramatic tragedy

Context: Timon, wealthy and generous Athenian nobleman, finally realizing that his indebtedness has become much greater than his wealth, dispatches Flaminius, a trusted servant, to borrow some money to meet the demands of his creditors, from Lucullus, a friend and frequent recipient of Timon's largesse. The refusal of assistance by Lucullus and his condemnation of Timon for too much honesty is typical of the responses Timon receives from his friends. When Flaminius presents the request of his master, "nothing doubting your present assistance therein," Lucullus replies:

LUCULLUS
La, la, la, la! Nothing doubting, says he? Alas good lord! A noble

256

gentleman 'tis, if he would not keep so good a house. Many a time and often I ha' dined with him, and told him on't, and come again to supper to him of purpose to have him spend less, and yet he would embrace no counsel, take no warning by my coming. **Every man has his fault, and honesty is his.** I ha' told him on't, but I could ne'er get him from't.

Every man loves what he is good at

Source: A TRUE WIDOW (Act V)
Author: Thomas Shadwell (1640-1692)
First published: 1679
Type of work: Dramatic comedy

Context: Lady Cheately, a widow with very little capital, comes to London to marry off herself and her two daughters. That each one may marry a rich man, the widow puts on a great show of business affairs, with the aid of a scoundrelly steward. This show is designed to lure wealthy suitors, of course. When the steward threatens to reveal how his mistress is cheating both suitors and business clients, Lady Cheately has one of her suitors, Prig, who thinks of nothing but gaming and sports, act as a clergyman for a mock-marriage. The steward is taken in by the trick and believes he is really married to his employer. Lady Cheately, anxious to be rid of him, tries to have him lured aboard ship and sent out of the country to indentured servitude. But the steward escapes from the ship in time and returns to threaten his "wife." This situation, plus the seduction of her empty-headed daughter, Gertrude, by a fool named Selfish, has Lady Cheately quite disturbed; it seems as though all her planning is to go for nothing. She decides to ask help from Mr. Maggot, another of her suitors, who loves the affairs of business for their own sake:

LADY CHEATELY
. . . Oh Mr. *Maggot!* I have business to communicate to you, of the greatest concernment to me that ever hapned.

MAGGOT
Gad, Madam, do! If any Man in *England* understands Business, or loves it better than I do, I'll be burnt.

LADY CHEATELY
Every Man loves what he is good at; give me a Man of Business for my Friend: the fine Gentlemen of the Town, are like Fidlers, only good at idle hours.

257

Every man meets his Waterloo at last

Source: SPEECHES, FIRST SERIES (Harper's Ferry: Speech delivered at Brooklyn, November 1, 1859)
Author: Wendell Phillips (1811-1884)
First published: 1859
Type of work: Political speech

Context: Wendell Phillips was a confirmed abolitionist and an orator of wide renown. A Harvard graduate and a lawyer, he abandoned the legal profession to identify himself with William Lloyd Garrison's fight against slavery. Forceful, dynamic, pleasant, he abandoned the high-flown oratory of other great speakers and cultivated a natural, familiar style. He soon became one of the country's leading voices in the abolitionist movement. When, in 1859, John Brown and his followers captured the arsenal at Harper's Ferry, Virginia, in an effort to spark a general slave uprising throughout the South, all abolitionists applauded. But Brown's raid was a failure; he and his men were taken after a brief siege, and the revolt failed to materialize. On the evening of November 1, Phillips spoke on "the lesson of the hour" in Henry Ward Beecher's church. "The lesson of the hour," says Phillips, "is insurrection. . . .

Insurrection of thought always precedes insurrection of arms. The last twenty years have been an insurrection of thought. We seem to be entering on a new phase of the great American struggle. . . ." He contrasts Europe with America: "The Old World . . . has always distrusted the average conscience—the common sense of the millions." To Phillips, law is nothing unless public opinion is behind it. And he is not an advocate of passive resistance; "let me say, in passing," he says, "I think you can make a better use of iron than forging it into chains. If you must have the metal, put it into Sharpe's rifles." (The gun made famous by John Brown and his men was invented by Christian Sharpe). Adding that the American public must be made to see things as they are, Philipps praises Brown highly and likens him to the patriots of the Revolution. Though he failed, Brown is no less a hero:

. . . Harper's Ferry is the Lexington of to-day. Up to this moment, Brown's life has been one unmixed success. Prudence, skill, courage, thrift, knowledge of his time, knowledge of his opponents, undaunted daring,—he had all these. He was the man who could leave Kansas, and go into Missouri, and take eleven men, give them liberty, and bring them off on the horses which he carried with him, and two which he took as tribute from their masters in order to facilitate escape. Then, when he had passed his human *protégés* from the vulture of the United States to the safe shelter of the English lion, this is the brave, frank, and sublime truster in God's right and absolute justice, who entered his name in the city of Cleveland, "John Brown, of Kansas," advertised

258

there two horses for sale, and stood in front of the auctioneer's stand, notifying all bidders of—what some would think—the defect in the title. . . . This is the man who, in the face of the nation, avowing his right, and laboring with what strength he had in behalf of the wronged, goes down to Harper's Ferry to follow up his work. Well, men say he failed. Every man has his Moscow. Suppose he did fail, **every man meets his Waterloo at last.** There are two kinds of defeat. Whether in chains or in laurels, LIBERTY knows nothing but victories. Soldiers call Bunker Hill a defeat; but Liberty dates from it, though Warren lay dead on the field. Men say the attempt did not succeed. No man can command success. . . .

Every man's hand against him

Source: GENESIS 16:12
Author: Unknown
First transcribed: c.1000-300 B.C.
Type of work: Religious history and law

Context: One of the famous stories in the Book of Genesis is the story of Hagar and her child, Ishmael. At the time Abram is more than eighty years old, his wife, Sarai, has not given him any children. She gives her maid, Hagar, to Abram, as his concubine, hoping that Hagar will bear children for Abram. Hagar, an Egyptian girl, conceives a child; in her pride at having bested her mistress, she openly despises Sarai. When the wife complains, Abram tells her to deal as she will with the prideful maiden. When Hagar is given harsh treatment for her despising of Sarai, she runs away into the wilderness, where she is visited by an angel of God, who bids the girl return and submit to Sarai. The angel also promises that Hagar shall be rewarded, for her seed will multiply exceedingly. The angel bids Hagar to name her first-born, who will be a son, Ishmael, which means "God hears." But the angel also tells Hagar that her son will be an outcast among men:

And the angel of the LORD said unto her, I will multiply thy seed exceedingly, that it shall not be numbered for the multitude.

And the angel of the LORD said unto her, Behold, thou art with child, and shall bear a son, and shalt call his name Ishmael; because the LORD hath heard thy affliction.

And he will be a wild man; his hand will be against every man, and **every man's hand against him;** and he shall dwell in the presence of all his brethren.

• • •

And Hagar bare Abram a son: and Abram called his son's name, which Hagar bare, Ishmael.

Every schoolboy knows who imprisoned Montezuma

Source: LORD CLIVE
Author: Thomas Babington Macaulay (1800-1859)
First published: January, 1840
Type of work: Biographical essay and book review

Context: An essay on Milton, published in the influential *Edinburgh Review* in 1825, brought Macaulay a reputation as an essayist and biographer. Its smooth elegance and clear prose, with each topic sentence logically developed, made easy reading. The parallels he provided, drawn from the wide scope of his reading, and his phenomenal memory, blinded readers to the real shallowness and sweeping judgments about everything. So Macaulay was frequently assigned books to review, and the result would be very readable and enlightening literary and biographical essays. Since he had become a specialist on Indian affairs, having served in India on the Supreme Council between 1834 and 1838, he was the natural one to review Major-General Sir John Malcolm's three-volume *Life of Robert Lord Clive,* of 1836. While that work is now rarely read, Macaulay's review of it is still the best-known brief account of the early days of the British in India. His review starts with the accusation that the British people know more about the Aztec Emperor Montezuma and Hernán Cortés in sixteenth century Mexico, and about the Inca Emperor Atahualpa and Francisco Pizarro of the same period in Peru than of events in eighteenth century India. Macaulay puts a series of questions to his readers to make them realize how ignorant they are about people and happenings in their wealthiest colony. Still less do the people today know that the British won at Buxar in 1764; Meer Cossim ordered the massacre of 200 British prisoners at Patna; Sujah Dowlah ruled in Oude; and Holkar was a Hindu.

We have always thought it strange that, while the history of the Spanish empire in America is familiarly known to all the nations of Europe, the great actions of our countrymen in the East should, even among ourselves, excite little interest. **Every schoolboy knows who imprisoned Montezuma,** and who strangled Atahualpa. But we doubt whether one in ten, even among English gentlemen of highly cultivated minds, can tell who won the battle of Buxar, who perpetrated the massacre of Patna, whether Sujah Dowlah ruled in Oude or in Travancore, or whether Holkar was a Hindoo or a Mussulman.

. . .

260

Everyone as they like, as the good woman said when she kissed her cow

Source: POLITE CONVERSATION (Dialogue I)
Author: Jonathan Swift (1667-1745)
First published: 1738
Type of work: Dialogue

Context: Under the title *A Complete Collection of Genteel and Ingenious Conversation according to the Most Polite Mode and Method,* and with the author's name given as Simon Wagstaff, Esq., Swift published three dialogues in 1738 from both London and Dublin. The first is in the form of a play with eight characters. Two of them meet in the Mall, from where they go to dine with Lady Smart. Later they have tea and play quadrille (a game for four players and forty cards) until 3 A.M. The expression here quoted is, of course, nonsense. It is sometimes expressed, "There is no accounting for tastes, as the old lady said, . . ." It is merely part of the humor of Dean Swift. At the beginning of the dialogue, Lord Sparkish meets Colonel Atwit in St. James's Park. Mr. Neverout joins them. His protest is humorously taken as a challenge to a duel.

COLONEL
Tom, you must go with me to Lady Smart's for breakfast.

NEVEROUT
Must? Why, Colonel, must's for the King. [*The Colonel offers in jest to draw his sword.*]

COLONEL
Have you spoken with all your friends?

NEVEROUT
Colonel, as you're stout, be merciful.

SPARKISH
Come, agree, agree; the law's costly. [*Colonel taking his hand from the hilt.*]

COLONEL
Well, Tom, you are never the worse man to be afraid of me. Come along.

NEVEROUT
What, do you think I was born in a wood, to be afraid of an owl? I'll wait on you. I hope Miss Notable will be there; 'egad, she's very handsome, and has a wit at will.

261

Why, every one as they like; as the good woman said, when she kissed her cow.

Everyone can master a grief but he that has it

Source: MUCH ADO ABOUT NOTHING (Act III, sc. ii, ll. 28-29)
Author: William Shakespeare (1564-1616)
First published: 1600
Type of work: Dramatic comedy

Context: The principal comic device of this play is an elaborate intrigue in which Don Pedro, Claudio, and Leonato attempt to provoke romantic interest between Benedick and Beatrice, the mocking anti-lovers. By arrangement, each while eavesdropping overhears a declaration of the other's love, and each in turn feels an attraction for the other which he erstwhile has refused to admit to himself, let alone to others. One of the great comic moments comes with this public admission. After all, the jeerers at love have a reputation for barbed wit and cynical jests—directed especially at each other—and difficult indeed is the admission that they who were love's mockers are now love's victims. The comic anticipation is high, then, as Benedick comes on stage for the first time since the eavesdropping scene. His friends, primed for light-hearted taunting, wait to see how he will face down his change of attitude. Ironically, the gallant who has always been the first to accept the gage of verbal combat now finds himself unable to compete, unable even to defend himself against their jibes concerning his cleanshaven, washed face and his well-kempt hair:

DON PEDRO
. . . I will only be bold with Benedick for his company, for from the crown of his head to the sole of his foot, he is all mirth. . . .

BENEDICK
Gallants, I am not as I have been.

LEONATO
So say I, methinks you are sadder.

CLAUDIO
I hope he be in love.

• • •

BENEDICK
I have the toothache.

DON PEDRO
Draw it.

BENEDICK
Hang it.

CLAUDIO
You must hang it first, and draw it afterwards.

DON PEDRO
What? Sigh for the toothache?

LEONATO
Where is but a humour or a worm?

BENEDICK
Well, **every one can master a grief but he that has it.**

CLAUDIO
Yet say I, he is in love.

Everyone lives by selling something

Source: ACROSS THE PLAINS ("Beggars," Section III)
Author: Robert Louis Stevenson (1850-1894)
First published: 1892
Type of work: Familiar essay

Context: Part IX of Stevenson's *Across the Plains* is entitled "Beggars." It opens with reminiscences of two consumptive beggars whom Stevenson had met in his rambles about Scotland. One, an ex-soldier, loved "the romance of language," Keats and Shelley were his favorite poets, and the only books he would borrow from Stevenson—and always return —were volumes of poetry. Recalling this simple lover of literature, Stevenson is led to some random comments on beggars and men who follow other callings. Among the comments are these:

Everyone lives by selling something, whatever be his right to it. The burglar sells at the same time his own skill and courage and my silver plate (the whole at the most moderate figure) to a Jew receiver. The bandit sells the traveller an article of prime necessity: that traveller's life. And as for the old soldier, . . . he dealt in a specialty; for he was the only beggar in the world who ever gave me pleasure for my money. He had learned a school of manner in the barracks and had the sense to cling to it, accosting strangers with a regimental freedom, thanking patrons with a merely

263

regimental difference, sparing you at once the tragedy of his position and the embarrassment of yours. . . .

Everyone soon or late comes round by Rome

Source: THE RING AND THE BOOK (Book V, "Count Guido Franceschini," Line 296)
Author: Robert Browning (1812-1889)
First published: 1868-1869
Type of work: Dramatic monologue

Context: Count Guido Franceschini, the smooth-tongued murderer of his wife and her parents, tells the court about his family's honor and service to the church and state. Arguing that the murder was done with God's blessing, he attempts to create a favorable impression; however, as he speaks, his greed and duplicity frequently creep into his statements so that the reader more and more distrusts his defense. When he describes how his friends advised him to go to Rome in order to live off the corruption in the church, his defense reaches one of its peaks of hypocrisy: he claims that he was too honest to do such a dishonorable thing; instead, he sought a wife who had a large dowry. In effect, he says that the result of his honesty was his marriage to a girl whose "parents" had purchased her from a prostitute and who was not really an heir to the fortune he needed to redeem his family's honor and that he had the right to murder the people who had deceived him.

> I waited thirty years, may it please the Court:
> Saw meanwhile many a denizen o' the dung
> Hop, skip, jump o'er my shoulder, make him wings
> And fly aloft,—succeed, in the usual phrase.
> **Every one soon or late comes round by Rome:**
> Stand still here, you'll see all in turn succeed.
> Why, look you, so and so, the physician here,
> My father's lacquey's son we sent to school,
> Doctored and dosed this Eminence and that,
> Salved the last Pope his certain obstinate sore,
> Soon bought land as became him, names it now: . . .

The evil that men do lives after them

Source: JULIUS CAESAR (Act III, sc. ii, l. 80)
Author: William Shakespeare (1564-1616)
First published: 1623
Type of work: Dramatic tragedy

Context: Julius Caesar has been stabbed to death before the Capitol of

Rome by a group of conspirators. Later, in the Forum, the citizens of Rome are addressed first by Brutus, a friend of Caesar and a conspirator, who explains that the hero has been killed because of his ambition which would lead to the enslavement of free Romans; and then by Mark Antony, who, pretending to agree with Brutus, subtly enrages the throng against the conspirators. Antony speaks:

ANTONY

Friends, Romans, countrymen, lend me your ears.
I come to bury Caesar, not to praise him.
The evil that men do, lives after them,
The good is oft interred with their bones;
So let it be with Caesar. The noble Brutus
Hath told you Caesar was ambitious;
If it were so, it was a grievous fault,
And grievously hath Caesar answered it.
Here, under leave of Brutus, and the rest—
For Brutus is an honourable man,
So are they all, all honourable men—
Come I to speak in Caesar's funeral.

.   .   .

Example is the school of mankind

Source: LETTERS ON A REGICIDE PEACE (Letter I)
Author: Edmund Burke (1729-1797)
First published: 1796-1797
Type of work: Open letter

Context: As Burke's life approached its end so did the life of the French Revolution. In Paris horror succeeded horror, culminating in the execution of the king and queen; the Army moved in, and under the command of Napoleon, protected what was of permanent value in the increasing shambles of the disintegrating Revolution. To the astonishment of many, France, wracked by violent internal conflicts and collapsing credit, was able to break up the European coalition arrayed against her. In England a movement was afoot to make peace with the Revolutionary government, and peace talks were actually opened at one point. Burke, ever a firm and stanch enemy of the French Revolution, was equally firmly opposed to this peace movement. In a series of four open letters he argued his case for France as a menace to all of Europe. Near the end of this first letter he insisted that those led to accept a French monarch's overthrow would soon accept the overthrow of other monarchs:

And is, then example nothing? It is everything. **Example is the school of mankind,** and they will learn at no other. This war is a

265

war against that example. It is not a war for Louis the Eighteenth, or even for the property, virtue, fidelity of France. It is a war for George the Third, for Francis the Second, and for all the dignity, property, honor, virtue, and religion of England, of Germany, and of all nations.

An eye like Mars, to threaten and command

Source: HAMLET (Act III, sc. iv, l. 57)
Author: William Shakespeare (1564-1616)
First published: 1603
Type of work: Dramatic tragedy

Context: Hamlet, Prince of Denmark, robbed by his uncle of a father by murder, of a mother by an incestuous marriage, and a throne by usurpation, confronts his mother and reproaches her in her chamber. Inviting her to compare pictures of her noble first husband and her base second husband, he assesses the two men.

HAMLET
Look here upon this picture, and on this,
The counterfeit presentment of two brothers.
See what a grace was seated on this brow,
Hyperion's curls, the front of Jove himself,
An eye like Mars, to threaten and command,
A station like the herald Mercury,
New lighted on a heaven-kissing hill,
A combination and a form indeed,
Where every god did seem to set his seal
To give the world assurance of a man.
This was your husband, look you now what follows.
Here is your husband like a mildewed ear,
Blasting his wholesome brother. Have you eyes,
Could you on this fair mountain leave to feed,
And batten on this moor? Ha, have you eyes? . . .

Eye of newt

Source: MACBETH (Act IV, sc. i, l. 14)
Author: William Shakespeare (1564-1616)
First published: 1623
Type of work: Dramatic tragedy

Context: Macbeth and Banquo are advised by three witches that Macbeth will become king and that the descendants of Banquo will be monarchs. Macbeth, driven by his own evil ambition and that of his wife, murders Duncan, his king, his cousin, and his over-night guest. Though the

266

crown is given to Macbeth, the new king is worried because the two sons of Duncan remain in exile, and, though Banquo has been murdered, Fleance, his son, has escaped Macbeth's hired assassins. Macbeth prepares to visit the oracles who gave him the former prophecy. In the meantime, the witches fix a charm by preparing a boiling caldron, taking turns casting hideous and venomous objects into the stew and muttering incantations.

SECOND WITCH
Fillet of a fenny snake,
In the caldron boil and bake;
Eye of newt, and toe of frog,
Wool of bat, and tongue of dog,
Adder's fork, and blind-worm's sting,
Lizard's leg, and howlet's wing;
For a charm of powerful trouble,
Like a hell-broth boil and bubble.

ALL
Double, double toil and trouble;
Fire burn, and caldron bubble.

Eyes too expressive to be blue, too lovely to be grey

Source: FADED LEAVES ("On the Rhine," Lines 19-20)
Author: Matthew Arnold (1822-1888)
First published: 1852
Type of work: Lyric poems

Context: Perhaps no other English poet has written with greater serenity and calm about the end of love and the misery of unrequited love than Matthew Arnold; many of his most famous lyrics open with a lovers' quarrel and develop into a speaker's plea for a renewal of the now thwarted love. In these poems he repeats that it is only through the beloved's eyes that the momentarily locked up love can be released. Staring silently into the beloved's eyes causes a bolt deep inside the lover to be thrown back, and he escapes from his sorrow by discovering his true self which has been buried. The group of lyrics in which this quotation appears are descriptive of a romance that has ended because the beloved does not return the poet's love; hoping that if he can gaze into her lovely eyes his sorrow will cease and the romance will again return, he begs his beloved to grant him this final wish. The poem is addressed to Frances Lucy Wightman, his courtship of whom was interrupted because of his poor financial prospects.

So let me lie, and, calm as they,
Let beam upon my inward view
Those eyes of deep, soft, lucent hue—
Eyes too expressive to be blue,
Too lovely to be grey.

Face-flatterer and backbiter are the same

Source: IDYLLS OF THE KING ("Merlin and Vivien," Line 822)
Author: Alfred, Lord Tennyson (1809-1892)
First published: 1859
Type of work: Narrative poem

Context: Vivien, the beautiful, wily, and malignant daughter of a man killed fighting against King Arthur, leaves Tintagel, the court of Mark of Cornwall, to go to Camelot. There she intends to sow seeds of suspicion concerning the honor and purity of Lancelot's devotion to Guinevere. While in Camelot, she sets out to win the heart of the aging wizard, Merlin. Even while doubting Vivien's honesty, Merlin "felt the flattery and at times/ Would flatter his own wish in age for love." Foreseeing the doom poised to fall on Camelot, Merlin leaves the court, consumed with melancholy. Vivien accompanies him to Broceliande where she attempts to extract from him a charm which en-snares its victim forever. Merlin agrees that he owes her a boon for breaking his melancholy, but he asserts that this particular charm should not be shared. He fears that Vivien might, in a sudden fit of anger or jealousy, use the charm against him or one of the Round Table. Mention of the knights irritates Vivien; she accuses them of breaking their vows of chastity. In her spite, she even says Arthur is cowardly and foolishly self-deceived. Merlin proves her accusations to be groundless slander. As a result of Vivien's fit of anger, Merlin swears not to tell her the secret of the charm, in spite of all her previous flattery. He says:

I know the Round Table, my friends of old;
All brave, and many generous, and some chaste.
She cloaks the scar of some repulse with lies.
I will believe she tempted them and failed,
Being so bitter. . . .
     • • •

I will not let her know; nine tithes of times
Face-flatterer and backbiter are the same.
And they, sweet soul, that most impute a crime
Are pronest to it, and impute themselves,
Wanting the mental range, or low desire
Not to feel lowest makes them level all; . . .
     • • •

Facts are facts

Source: THE RING AND THE BOOK (Book II, "Half-Rome," l. 1049)
Author: Robert Browning (1812-1889)
First published: 1868-1869
Type of work: Dramatic monologue

Context: The speaker, defending Guido who has murdered his wife and her parents, sarcastically relates the events that led to the murder. Not believing Pompilia's story of her husband's cruelty and her own innocence, he says that her flight from her husband was an obvious sign of her guilt, especially since she went with a very handsome priest who was not wearing his clerical clothes. That flight had ended in Castelnuovo, just outside Rome, when Guido came upon the pair and demanded the priest's punishment; the court at Rome had disciplined the priest but not as severely as Guido thought it should. The speaker, moreover, agrees with Guido: all of the evidence insinuates that he was grossly wronged, and if future husbands are to have any peace, he must be rewarded for defending his honor. The quotation occurs right after the speaker has described the circumstances under which Guido discovered his wife and the priest in Castlenuovo.

> But **facts are facts** and flinch not; stubborn things,
> And the question "Prithee, friend, how comes my purse
> I' the poke of you?"—admits of no reply.
> Here was a priest found out in masquerade,
> A wife caught playing truant if no more;
> While the Count, mortified in mien enough,
> And, nose to face, an added palm in length,
> Was plain writ "Husband" every piece of him:
> Capture once made, release could hardly be.
> Besides, the prisoners both made appeal,
> "Take us to Rome!"

Faint heart ne'er wan a lady fair

Source: TO DR. BLACKLOCK (Stanza 8)
Author: Robert Burns (1759-1796)
First published: 1789
Type of work: Epistle in verse

Context: Burns, the oldest of seven children of a terribly poor farmer, was encouraged by his father to take up literature. From his mother, he inherited wit and an ability to rhyme. So endowed, at the age of sixteen he wrote his first song, "O, once I loved a bonie lass." But though in subsequent years he added other poems to the manuscripts collected in a table drawer, he did nothing with them until, in 1786, he needed money for passage to Jamaica, where he had been offered a job on a plantation. Then he shipped off the bundle to a publisher who issued them as *Poems, Chiefly in the Scottish Dialect,* in an edition of 600 copies that brought Burns £20. Before he could sail for the West Indies, however, a letter from a certain Dr. Thomas Blacklock reached him, complimenting him on the volume and encouraging him to consider a second edition. From then on, Dr. Blacklock was one of Burns' best friends. A number of Burns' letters to Blacklock have been preserved. However, one, telling how he planned to legitimatize his relationship with Jean Armour by marrying her, was lost in transit. From Edinburgh, on August 24, 1789, Black-lock wrote a rhymed letter beginning "Dear Burns, thou brother of my heart." It inquired about the health of Jean and their children. To this graceful letter, so full of interest and good wishes, Burns replied with another in verse that begins in a light mood, but turns bitter before its conclusion. It is dated at Ellisland Farm, 21st Oct., 1789, and for it the poet used the rhyme scheme now known as "Burns's stanza." It begins: "Wow, but your letter made me vauntie!" In it he apologizes for the non-arrival of the earlier letter. Then Burns mentions his "wife and twa wee laddies," and hopes to provide well for them because it is man's duty to maintain a happy fireside for "weans" (children) and wife. The final three stanzas declare:

Come, Firm Resolve, take thou the van,
Thou stalk o' carl-hemp in man!
And let us mind, **faint heart ne'er wan**
  A lady fair;
Wha does the utmost that he can,
  Will whyles do mair.

But to conclude my silly rhyme,
(I'm scant o' verse, and scant o' time,)
To make a happy fireside clime
  To weans and wife,
That's the true pathos and sublime
  Of human life.

My compliments to sister Beckie;
And eke the same to honest Lucky,
I wat she is a daintie chuckie,
  As e'er tread clay!
And gratefully, my guid auld cockie,
  I'm yours for ay.
          ROBERT BURNS

Fair, fat and forty

Source: SAINT RONAN'S WELL (Chapter 7)
Author: Sir Walter Scott (1771-1832)
First published: 1824
Type of work: Novel

Context: The inhabitants of the new hotel at the watering place of St. Ronan's Well are so devoured by curiosity about the artist, Francis Tyrrel, a lodger at Meg Dods' inn a few miles away from St. Ronan's, that they invite him to dinner and the postprandial activities that enliven the evenings and the resort. After dinner, during the serving of tea and cake, various conversations take place; one recorded at considerable length is between the bachelor Dr. Quackleben and a newcomer to the establishment, Mrs. Blower, the widow of a sea captain. The doctor adds a bit of elixir he carries with him in a flask to Mrs. Blower's tea; the addition of his remedy both improves the taste of the tea and elevates Mrs. Blower's spirits. After the two have discussed the methods of various doctors, Mrs. Blower confides to Dr. Quackleben, to whom she applies a variety of names, that she is a lonely widow whose former husband had left her in very comfortable financial circumstances. The doctor's interest in the fair lady is perceptibly quickened. Scott's expression is an inversion of John O'Keeffe's earlier "fat, fair, and forty." (A carrack is a large ship, or galleon.)

. . . Lady Penelope, the presiding goddess of the region, watchful over all her circle, was not long of observing that the Doctor seemed to be suddenly engaged in close communication with the widow, and that he had even ventured to take hold of her fair plump hand, with a manner which partook at once of the gallant suitor, and of the medical adviser.

"For the love of Heaven," said her ladyship, "who can that comely dame be, on whom our excellent and learned Doctor looks with such uncommon regard?"

"Fair, fat, and forty," said Mr. Winterblossom; "that is all I know of her,—a mercantile person."

"A carrack, Sir President," said the chaplain, "richly laden with colonial produce, by name the Lovely Peggy Bryce—no master—the late John Blower of North Leith having pushed off his boat for the Stygian Creek, and left the vessel without a hand on board."

"The Doctor," said Lady Penelope, turning her glass towards them, "seems willing to play the part of pilot."

"I dare say he will be willing to change her name and register," said Mr. Chatterly.

271

The fair humanities of old religion

Source: THE PICCOLOMINI; OR, THE FIRST PART OF WALLENSTEIN (Act II, sc. ii)
Author: Samuel Taylor Coleridge (1772-1834)
First published: 1800
Type of work: Historical drama

Context: This play is a translation of Schiller's play in German, which was based on a life of Wallenstein, the Duke of Friedland, hero of the Thirty Years' War. Wallenstein, fearful that he may lose his place as the commander of great armies, plots to make his senior officers pledge their loyalty to him alone, and not to the emperor. One officer, Wallenstein fears, may see through the plot; that officer is Lieutenant-General Octavio Piccolomini. To secure the older Piccolomini, Wallenstein uses his daughter, Princess Thekla, who falls in love with the general's son, Max Piccolomini, a colonel of cuirassiers. The two young persons are unaware of the plotting about them; they see only their newly discovered love, found when Max Piccolomini escorts Wallenstein's wife and daughter to the military camp. On the evening of their arrival at the camp, Princess Thekla and Max Piccolomini have a chance to be together, an opportunity arranged for them by Countess Tertsky, the girl's aunt. Princess Thekla tells her aunt and Max of a visit she has just made to the tower where Baptista Seni, an astrologer consulted by her father, consults the stars. Max Piccolomini, a realistic young soldier, states that he will no longer doubt the power of astrology, for love has opened his eyes to something more than "this visible nature, and this common world." He goes on to relate his new-found views:

MAX PICCOLOMINI

For fable is Love's world, his home, his birth-place;
Delightedly dwells he 'mong fays and talismans,
And spirits; and delightedly believes
Divinities, being himself divine.
The intelligible forms of ancient poets,
The fair humanities of old religion,
The Power, the Beauty, and the Majesty,
That had their haunts in dale, or piny mountain,
Or forest by slow stream, or pebbly spring,
Or chasms and wat'ry depths; all these have vanished.
They live no longer in the faith of reason!
But still the heart doth need a language, still
Doth the old instinct bring back the old names. . . .

The fair, the chaste, and unexpressive she

Source: AS YOU LIKE IT (Act III, sc. ii, l. 10)
Author: William Shakespeare (1564-1616)
First published: 1623
Type of work: Dramatic comedy

Context: Safe in the Forest of Arden, the fugitive Orlando has time to remember his love for Rosalind. Daughter of Duke Senior, who has spent many pleasant years of exile in the Forest, Rosalind is now herself a fugitive from court and is in disguise as a young man, having adopted the name Ganymede. Her presence is unknown both to her father and her lover. Orlando festoons the trees of the forest with poems in praise of Rosalind, despite his insistence that she is indescribable, "unexpressive":

ORLANDO
Hang there my verse, in witness of my love,
And thou thrice-crowned queen of night survey
With thy chaste eye, from thy pale sphere above,
Thy huntress' name, that my full life doth sway.
O Rosalind, these trees shall be my books,
And in their barks my thoughts I'll character,
That every eye, which in this forest looks,
Shall see thy virtue witnessed every where.
Run, run, Orlando, carve on every tree
The fair, the chaste, and unexpressive she.

Fair weather cometh out of the north

Source: JOB 37:22
Author: Unknown
First transcribed: c.900-500 B.C.
Type of work: Religious saga

Context: Job, a righteous and God-fearing man of the land of Uz, is put to the test by Satan, with the acquiescence of God. First Satan takes away Job's prosperity and kills Job's seven sons and three daughters. Then Satan visits physical misery on Job, in the form of boils that cover his body from crown to sole. Still Job does not curse God, but neither does he blame himself; he maintains that he is a good man, as he is, and that he has not sinned in any way to justify such miseries and unhappiness. When Eliphaz, Bildad, and Zophar come to visit Job, however, they maintain that he must have done something to deserve his miseries. When the three friends, who give little or no comfort to Job, have finished, Elihu, a fourth man, speaks up. Elihu, too, maintains that God never afflicts a man without cause; he tells Job that God always hears a submissive cry, but that He

273

sends adversity to a man either as a discipline or as a warning. He tells Job that God does great things that mere human beings cannot comprehend. He reminds Job that God causes the snow and the rains, as He causes the winds to blow and the seasons to move in their cycle. And he ends with a terrible warning for Job:

> Hearken unto this, O Job: stand still, and consider the wondrous works of God.
> Dost thou know when God disposed them, and caused the light of his cloud to shine?
> Dost thou know the balancings of the clouds, the wondrous works of him which is perfect in knowledge?
> How thy garments are warm, when he quieteth the earth by the south wind?
> Hast thou with him spread out the sky, which is strong, and as a molten looking glass?
> Teach us what we shall say unto him; for we cannot order our speech by reason of darkness.
> Shall it be told him I speak? if a man speak, surely he shall be swallowed up.
> And now men see not the bright light which is in the clouds: but the wind passeth and cleanseth them.
> **Fair weather cometh out of the north:** with God is terrible majesty.

False, fleeting, perjured Clarence

Source: KING RICHARD THE THIRD (Act I, sc. iv, l. 55)
Author: William Shakespeare (1564-1616)
First published: 1597
Type of work: Historical drama

Context: King Edward the Fourth has sent his brother, George, Duke of Clarence, to the Tower of London, where he will be murdered. Responsible for Clarence's imprisonment is Richard, Duke of Gloucester, the brother of the king and the imprisoned duke. Richard, later to be King Richard the Third, is plotting to remove all obstacles on his path to the throne, and he has persuaded the king that a man whose name begins with "G" will murder the king's sons. Suspicion has fallen, as Richard expected it to fall, on George, the Duke of Clarence, who earlier turned on the Earl of Warwick, his father-in-law, to help King Edward to the English throne. While in prison in the Tower of London, the Duke of Clarence has a terrible dream, in which he sees himself shoved overboard from a ship to his death by his brother Richard. In the dream he sees himself arriving in Hell, having passed over the River Styx in Charon's boat. He dreams he meets the Earl of Warwick, who curses him, and then the ghost of Edward, Prince of Wales, son of Henry the Sixth, whom Clar-

274

ence killed after the Battle of Tewksbury. Prince Edward's ghost also cries out for revenge in Hell. Clarence relates the dream to his keeper at the Tower of London.

CLARENCE
. . . Then came wandring by,
A shadow like an angel, with bright hair
Dabbled in blood; and he shrieked out aloud,
Clarence is come; **false, fleeting, perjur'd Clarence,**
That stabbed me in the field by Tewksbury:
Seize on him, Furies, take him unto torment!
With that, methought, a legion of foul fiends
Environed me, and howled in mine ears
Such hideous cries, that with the very noise
I trembling waked, and for a season after,
Could not believe but that I was in hell,
Such terrible impression made my dream.

Falsehood has a perennial spring

Source: SPEECH ON AMERICAN TAXATION
Author: Edmund Burke (1729-1797)
First published: 1774
Type of work: Political speech

Context: In the second part of his address to Parliament on American taxation, Edmund Burke, who was a foe to its wrongful imposition and a friend to the American Colonies, gives a history of the subject in America. He points out that at the time of the first American Revenue Act, in 1764, the colonists did not object to port duties and that statements made in Parliament itself showed that the colonists had not entered into controversy with the British government on the first excuse, that the colonists had actually been pushed into rebellion by the actions of Parliament. Burke goes on to point out that several falsehoods about the Americans had been widespread, in addition to the lie that they had been looking for controversy. Burke specifically mentions the false story that George Grenville, the author of the Stamp Act, had proposed to the Colonies that they tax themselves and that they had subsequently refused. Burke then proceeds to dispose of another false report— that no one in Parliament had known of the colonists' dislike for port duties:

Thus, Sir, I have disposed of this falsehood. But **falsehood has a perennial spring.** It is said, that no conjecture could be made of the dislike of the Colonies to the principle. This is as untrue as the other. After the resolution of the House, and before the passing of the Stamp Act, the Colonies of Massachusetts Bay and New York did send remonstrances, objecting to this mode of Parliamentary

275

taxation. What was the consequence? They were suppressed; they were put under the table, notwithstanding an Order of Council to the contrary, by the Ministry which composed the very Council that had made the Order: and thus the House proceeded to its business of taxing without the least regular knowledge of the objections that were made to it. . . .

Familiarity begets boldness

Source: THE ANTIQUARY (Act I)
Author: Shackerley Marmion (1603-1639)
First published: 1641
Type of work: Dramatic comedy

Context: With the inconsistent spelling of the seventeenth century, an English dramatist published his first play in 1632 under the name of Schackerley Marmyon, Master of Arts. By the time *The Antiquary* appeared, in 1641, its author was given as Shackerly Mermion, Gent. Actually, the name of the ancient Lancaster family was Shakerly. The dramatist was born in Northampton, in January, 1602 (Old Style). After the usual free-school education, he was sent to Wadham College, out of which he came as gentleman commoner, with a Master of Arts degree in 1624. Lacking a family fortune, for his father was a spendthrift, Shackerley tried the army in the Low Countries, but he found promotion slow, so he returned to England and enlisted in a cavalry troop raised by his friend Sir John Suckling, in 1638, for service against the Scotch Covenanters. However, he became ill during the campaign and returned to London, where he died. His writing, done at intervals, began with two plays, *Holland's Leaguer* (1632), and *A Fine Companion* (1633). A graceful legend of *Cupid and Psyche or An Epic Poem of Cupid and His*

Mistress (1637), on which his poetic fame chiefly rests, was followed by a third play, *The Antiquary* (1641), in imitation of Ben Jonson. A fourth comedy, *The Crafty Merchant or the Soldier'd Citizen,* sometimes attributed to him, was never printed. *The Antiquary* "performed by His Majesty's Servants at the Cock-Pit," was highly admired by Sir Walter Scott and others as one of England's best early dramatic attempts. Scott reprinted it in his *Ancient British Dramas,* as did several other compilers of early plays. The setting of the play is given as Pisa, with the Duke of Pisa as one of the main characters, but the dramatist apparently confused Pisa with Venice, because he mentions "The Rialto" in the first act and "canals" in the third. In the List of Characters he also carelessly called Aemelia "wife to Gasparo" and Lucretia "daughter to Gasparo," where the play shows them as part of the family of elderly Lorenzo. But as Horace observed, even Homer nodded on occasion. The play starts with Lionell, nephew of the wealthy Antiquary Veterano, welcoming Petrutio, Gasparo's stupid son, who is sure his excellent qualities will bring him

276

success at court. Lionell offers, in return for the loan of a hundred ducats, to help him, but now Petrutio is interested only in Lionell's page boy, actually his sister Angelia disguised. Petrutio meets his father in company with Lorenzo, who is seeking a husband for his daughter Lucretia. The fop is not interested in marriage. He declares: "I have chosen Honor as my Mistress upon whose wings I will mount up to heaven where I will fix myself a constellation for all this underworld of mortals to wonder at me." Meanwhile, the Duke of Pisa tells his courtier Leonardo that in order to know his subjects, he has decided to follow the example of Cato, who mingled with the crowds at the Spring Festival to Flora. In Cato's case, his appearance at a public theater amid a licentious festival involving nude women interrupted the spectacle. So the Duke will disguise himself in "mean coverture," or lowly clothing. "Vulgar" refers to the common people. Leonardo suggests that while disguised, they visit the Antiquary, sure to be an excellent companion if he is as expert at wines as at history. At the end of the play, the Duke finds Lionell impersonating him, but arranging justice and happiness for everyone so well that the Duke confirms his decrees. In the first act, planning his walk in disguise among his subjects, the Duke and Leonardo talk. The courtier warns, as many from Aesop and Shakespeare to Mark Twain have done, that "familiarity breeds contempt."

DUKE

. . . I am determin'd to lay by all ensigns of my Royalty for awhile, and walk abroad under a mean coverture. Variety does well; and 't is a great delight, sometimes, to shroud one's head under a coarse roof, as under a rich canopy of gold.

LEONARDO

But what's your intent in this?

DUKE

I have a longing desire to see the fashions of the vulgar; which, should I affect in mine own person, I might divert them from their humors. The face of greatness would affright them, as Cato did the Floralio from the theatre.

LEONARDO

Indeed **familiarity begets boldness.**

DUKE

'T is true, indulgence and flattery take away the benefit of experience from Princes, which ennobles the fortunes of private men.

277

Famous, calm, and dead

Source: A GRAMMARIAN'S FUNERAL (Line 27)
Author: Robert Browning (1812-1889)
First published: 1855
Type of work: Dramatic monologue

Context: The subtitle "Shortly after the revival of learning in Europe" gives the key to this dramatic monologue. It is spoken by one of a group of pupils of the dead grammarian who, with his fellow-students, is carrying the body of his master to burial at the top of a mountain. The pupil describes his late master as a man who has devoted his entire life to scholarship—to the study of the grammatical structure of the Greek language, at that time newly returned to Europe after centuries during which it had been known only in fragments. The grammarian had sacrificed a lifetime to this study; neither illness nor age had halted his work. Now that he is dead, his pupils feel that only burial on a mountain-top, amid the storms and lightnings, is fitting for such a devoted scholar. The poem contains one of Browning's favorite themes: that the important aspect of life is what we *try* to do, not what we accomplish. The man of small mind aims at a low mark and easily attains it. The really great man aims at an impossible goal. This goal he can never reach; yet in his effort to do so, he goes far beyond the reach of the small man. So it was with the dead grammarian: he had tried to master all of the subtleties of the Greek language. He had failed, yet he had been an inspiration to his pupils to whom he had passed on his love of learning for its own sake. So the speaker, who is leading the burial procession, comments:

. . .

Leave we the unlettered plain its herd and crop;
   Seek we sepulture
On a tall mountain, citied to the top,
   Crowded with culture!
All the peaks soar, but one the rest excels;
   Clouds overcome it;
No! yonder sparkle is the citadel's
   Circling its summit.
Thither our path lies; wind we up the heights:
   Wait ye the warning?
Our low life was the level's and the night's;
   He's for the morning.
Step to a tune, square chests, erect each head,
   'Ware the beholders!
This is our master, **famous, calm, and dead,**
   Borne on our shoulders.

Fan spread and streamers out, and a shoal of fools for tenders

Source: THE WAY OF THE WORLD (Act II, sc. ii)
Author: William Congreve (1670-1729)
First published: 1700
Type of work: Dramatic comedy

Context: Mrs. Fainall, formerly the mistress of Mirabell, discusses her situation with Mirabell. When she merely hated her husband, she could tolerate him, but now she despises him and cannot stand him. Mirabell replies that she should have just enough disgust for her husband to give her a relish for her lover. Mirabell explains that he had her marry to save her reputation, as it seemed possible that she might have a child. A better man than her husband should not have been sacrificed to the occasion, and a worse one would not have served the purpose. They then discuss an intrigue they are setting afoot to place Mrs. Fainall's mother, Lady Wishfort, in a compromising position. They are discussing the lady's character when Mrs. Millamant, who loves Mirabell, enters with Witwoud, one of her admirers, and Mincing, her maid. Apparently she makes a rather stately and impressive entrance, for Mirabell likens her to a full-rigged ship; she comes, he says, full sail, with her fan spread and her streamers out, like the ship with its canvas unfurled and all the flags flying:

MRS. FAINALL

Here's your mistress.
[*Enter* MRS. MILLAMANT, WITWOUD, *and* MINCING.]

MIRABELL

Here she comes, i'faith, full sail, with her **fan spread and streamers out, and a shoal of fools for tenders;** ha, no, I cry her mercy!

MRS. FAINALL

I see but one poor empty sculler; and he tows her woman after him.

Fans turn into falchions in fair hands

Source: DON JUAN (Canto I, stanza 21)
Author: George Gordon, Lord Byron (1788-1824)
First published: 1819 (Cantos I and II)
Type of work: Satiric poem

Context: Lord Byron, after selecting "our ancient friend Don Juan" as the protagonist for his satiric epic poem, "begin[s] with the beginning" and goes on to describe the young hero's parents, Don Jóse and Donna Inez, true Gothic aristocrats of Spain without tint of alien blood. Though the learned and witty Donna Inez is virtuous beyond comparison with the saints, she is insipid (as all such perfection must be) as was the garden before the fall, and Don Jóse, a true son of Eve and "a mortal of the careless kind" goes straying after other fruits, never dreaming that she cares. But Donna Inez, for all her merits, has "a devil of a spirit" and repays neglect (the sin to try even a saint!) by getting her lord into many a scrape. And

> This was an easy matter with a man
> Oft in the wrong, and never on his guard;
> And even the wisest, do the best they can,
> Have moments, hours, and days, so unprepared,
> That you might "brain them with their lady's fan;"
> And sometimes ladies hit exceeding hard,
> And **fans turn into falchions in fair hands**
> And why and wherefore no one understands.

> 'Tis pity learned virgins ever wed
> With persons of no sort of education,
> Or gentlemen, who, though well born and bred,
> Grow tired of scientific conversation;
> I don't choose to say much upon this head,
> I'm a plain man, and in a single station,
> But—Oh! ye lords of ladies intellectual,
> Inform us truly, have they not hen-peck'd you all?

Farewell, rewards and fairies!

Source: FAREWELL TO FAIRIES (Line 1)
Author: Bishop Richard Corbet (1582-1635)
First published: 1647
Type of work: Satirical poem

Context: Corbet, in his later days a bishop in the Church of England, and noted for his wit, touches lightly a problem that to him has weighty overtones. Gone from "merry old England," says the poet, are the fairies and the old superstitions countenanced by the Catholics before the coming of Protestantism to the country. If Corbet is critical of the Roman Church for allowing the remnants of paganism to remain among the peasantry, he seems equally critical of the dour-faced Puritans who stamped out the cult of fairies. The first line of the poem supplied Kipling with the title of one of his most famous books for children (1910)

> **"Farewell, rewards and fairies!"**
> Good housewives now may say,
> For now foul sluts in dairies
> Do fare as well as they,

280

And though they sweep their hearths no less
   Than maids were wont to do,
Yet who of late for cleanliness,
   Finds sixpence in her shoe?

Lament, lament, old abbeys,
   The fairies lost command;
They did but change priests' babies,
   But some have changed your land;
And all your children sprung from thence
   Are now grown Puritanes;
Who live as changelings ever since
   For love of your domains.

      • • •

Witness these rings and roundelays
   Of theirs, which yet remain,
Were footed in Queen Mary's days
   On many a grassy plain;
But since of late Elizabeth,
   And later, James came in,
They never danced on any heath
   As when the time hath been.

Fast and furious

Source: TAM O'SHANTER (Line 144)
Author: Robert Burns (1759-1796)
First published: 1791
Type of work: Narrative poem

Context: To persuade Captain Francis Grose (1731?–1791) to sketch Alloway Church, where Burns's father was buried, the poet promised to provide him with a versified ghost story to publish with the picture in *Grose's Antiquities of Scotland* (1791). He finished the poem in twenty-four hours and made an immortal masterpiece. Tam o' Shanter, lazy husband of the shrewish Kate, never came home after market until he had spent all his money in the town tavern, drinking with his crony the Shoemaker Johnny, and the tavern keeper and his ingratiating wife. However, on the day of the story, he finally decides at midnight to dare the furious storm and the night in which "a child might understand/ The Deil (devil) had business on his hand." He rides homeward on Meg, his grey mare, humming a Scotch song, till he comes within sight of Kirk Alloway, about which many frightening stories circulate. He remembers some of the dead people associated with the area. To his amazement, the church is ablaze with light. Too full of liquor to be frightened, because "Wi' usquebae, we'll face the devil," Tammie guides his horse in the direction of the church and cemetery. Here he sees "an unco sight." Warlocks and witches are dancing to the music of hornpipes, jigs, and reels, with Old

Nick himself looking on. On the table before him, in place of holy relics, are bones of murderers, tomahawks, bloodstained "scymitars," and weapons used to commit many barbarous crimes. Here are the meanings of some of the dialectal words: Cleekit —joined hands; ilka carlin—every old woman; swat and reekit—sweat and steamed; Coost her duddies to the wark—stripped off her clothes; linket in her sark—danced in her chemise.

> As Tammie glowr'd, amaz'd, and curious,
> The mirth and fun grew **fast and furious;**
> The piper loud and louder blew;
> The dancers quick and quicker flew;
> They reel'd, they set, they cross'd, they cleekit,
> Till ilka carlin swat and reekit,
> And coost her duddies to the wark,
> And linket at it in her sark!

Fat, fair, and forty

Source: THE IRISH MIMIC, OR BLUNDERS AT BRIGHTON (Act II, sc. iii)
Author: John O'Keeffe (1747-1833)
First published: 1797
Type of work: Farce with music

Context: Called in its time a "contrived piece," *The Irish Mimic* is a musical play put together for light entertainment by an Irish actor and playwright noted for dramatic works of many kinds. His most successful performance was probably *Tony Lumpkin in Town,* produced in 1777. Of his farces, *Wild Oats* had the greatest number of performances. However, it is for a song from his *Merry Sherwood,* "I am a Friar of Orders Gray," that O'Keeffe is chiefly remembered today. A line from his *London Hermit* also survives, though usually misquoted. It announces that general statements are not intended to apply to people hearing them, or as O'Keeffe phrased the assertion: "You should always except the present company." *The Irish Mimic* was intended only for amusement. Farces, unlike comedies, are not to be analyzed for plot or action. Here the audience is supposed to accept a situation in which the two Melcombe ladies, Julia and her Aunt Margaret, can move in society without the realization that there are two of them, and that Julia in regimentals and her aunt in a riding habit might be taken for two young gentlemen. In addition, the story told by Captain Clifford to Mr. Parrots, the Irish Mimic, must seem convincing. To persuade him to whip a rival, he tells of a gentleman who has been insulted by a friend but lacks the spirit to resent the insult himself, but who, dying, will put into his will a legacy of a hundred pounds to anyone who will cane the man "in the public Steine." Part of the complication comes because Clifford tries to spur Mr. Parrots into action by doubting the man's courage. Farces frequently insert characters purely for comic effect, as O'Keeffe did in this play, set at Brighton, England's popular beach resort. It was first performed at the Royal Theatre, Covent Garden, in 1795. Two such characters are Colin, servant to "that voine lady, Miss Melcombe," and his brother Harry, who does not know there are two of the ladies. The chief character is Mr. Parrots, a professional mimic who claims to be able to imitate anybody, and does so in the course of the play, especially in one humorous scene involving Margaret Melcombe and her elderly admirer, Cypress. Since young men admire women "fat, fair and forty," perhaps young women may fall for those men who are "shriveled, sallow, and sixty." In Act II, Parrots comes upon Miss Julia wearing regimentals and talking to Harry.

HARRY

Madam!—Well, ma'am, I've seen variety of lodgings.

JULIA

Hush! How indiscreet!

PARROTS

Madam! I'm sure he did say madam. Oh, oh, this must be the lady Cypress desired me to mimic. Such a beautiful creature, love him! May be so, as the F's, **fat, fair, and forty,** was all the toast of the young men.—Who knows but the S's, shriveled, sallow, and sixty, may become the rage of the young women. [*Aside.*]

JULIA

If Clifford quits Brighton, and carries my aunt off with him, I shall have no occasion to change. [*Exit Harry. Music plays.*]

PARROTS

This Irish music is very fine—Pray, sir, how do you like Planxty Connor?

JULIA

I don't know any such person!

PARROTS

Pardon--Why Sir, it's--'Pon my soul she is a pretty little fellow! Drest herself up for some frolic, I suppose. —When a lady is inclin'd for fun, the gentleman should take half the business on himself.

The fatal gift of beauty

Source: CHILDE HAROLD'S PILGRIMAGE (Canto IV, stanza 42)
Author: George Gordon, Lord Byron (1788-1824)
First published: 1818 (Canto IV)
Type of work: Narrative poem

Context: Byron's *Childe Harold's Pilgrimage* was written and published piecemeal. The poet finished the first two cantos in 1812, and reaped instant glory. Canto III, generally considered the best, with its references to Bonaparte and the Battle of Waterloo, was published in 1816, but Canto IV did not get into print until 1818. Byron wrote it during his stay in Venice in 1817, where gossip reported him living licentiously, yet he had the time to write this canto, the narrative poems *Beppo* and *Mazeppa,* and to begin his famous *Don Juan.* Canto IV is prefaced by a letter to John C. Hobhouse, (1786–1869), who had traveled with Byron on the trip through the Mediterranean that had inspired the first canto. In the preface, Byron declares that Harold the Pilgrim no longer exists for him. His poem has now become his own personal reactions. The canto begins with the famous lines, "I stood in Venice on the Bridge of Sighs,/ A palace and a prison on each hand." Originally he had intended to discuss contemporary Italian Literature and Manners, but the discussion would have made the composition much too long. He sees about him too many great writers who will leave their mark upon their country's literature. So instead, he writes of the loveliness of storied Venice, whose gondoliers used to sing verses by Tasso. The changes in the city remind him of the changes in himself. He pauses to remark that, though he has traveled far and learned many languages, he wants to die in England and be remembered there. Then back to Venice whose history he learned as a child through the plays of many of the world's dramatists. His thoughts expand to include all of Italy. He thinks of Petrarch's tomb in Arqua, and of the "Bards of Hell and Chivalry," that is, Dante and Ariosto. Their homeland whose beauty attracted all the world has, for that reason, lost some of its power and glory, for those attracted to it have sapped its power and wealth. So he exclaims in Stanza 42:

> Italia! oh, Italia! thou who hast
> **The fatal gift of beauty,** which became
> A funeral dower of present woes and past,
> On thy sweet brow is sorrow plough'd by shame,
> And annals graved in characters of flame.
> Oh, God!, that thou wert in thy nakedness
> Less lovely or more powerful, and couldst claim
> Thy right, and awe the robbers back, who press
> To shed thy blood and drink the tears of thy distress.

A faultless monster which the world never saw

Source: AN ESSAY ON POETRY (Line 231)
Author: John Sheffield (1648-1721)
First published: 1682
Type of work: Verse essay

Context: Sheffield was Earl of Mulgrave and later Duke of Buckinghamshire and a member of that group of witty courtly poets which frequented the court of Charles II during the Restoration period. Other members of the group included Sedley, Dorset, Charles Cotton, and the notorious Rochester. The poetry of this group of young noblemen was highly polished and elegant if, at times, somewhat superficial and erotic. Verse was a popular form for the "essay" of criticism in this period, and as Sheffield neared the end of this survey of aesthetic theory he commented that the proper imitation of the classics was appropriate in figures of speech as well as in other features of poetry:

> Their beauties imitate, avoid their faults:
> First, on a plot employ thy careful thoughts;
> Turn it, with time, a thousand several ways;
> This oft, alone, has given success to plays.
> Reject that vulgar errour (which appears
> So fair) of making perfect characters;
> There's no such thing in nature, and you'll draw
> **A faultless monster, which the world ne'er saw.**
> Some faults must be, that his misfortune drew,
> But such as may deserve compassion too.

Fear is the parent of cruelty

Source: SHORT STUDIES ON GREAT SUBJECTS, SERIES III ("Party Politics")
Author: James Anthony Froude (1818-1894)
First published: 1882 (Series III)
Type of work: Political essay

Context: Froude was an English historian of considerable stature, who conceived of history as a great drama; his treatment of British history therefore emphasizes the personal element, and incidents are recounted in a stirring and dramatic manner. His most substantial accomplishment is his *History of England from the Fall of Wolsey to the Defeat of the Spanish Armada.* He also wrote a lengthy biography of Carlyle and a historical novel. His *Short Studies on Great Subjects* include a large variety of essays on various topics. In one of these, "Party Politics," he expresses concern over what he fears is the end of party government. Both parties intend to continue in the same spirit and along the same lines of progress; the only differences between them pertain to the rate at

285

which changes shall take place. As conservatism weakens, it ensures its own doom, talented and ambitious men will join the successful faction, and even when the people desire a change, the materials for a conservative government will no longer exist. Froude then considers the nature of progress, or motion, and points out that it can mean movement toward either growth or decay. He compares expedient social change with the device that captains of slave-ships used to escape their pursuers. They sawed through the bulkheads of their own ships; this trick made the craft more flexible and thus faster. They were safe so long as the wind was behind them, but if they met a head wind the vessel would fall apart and sink. Liberal statesman, in Froude's opinion, act in much the same fashion; for this reason their work can be only destructive in the long run. Froude is suspicious of democracies. "Popular governments have hitherto uniformly glided into democracies, and democracies as uniformly perish of their own excess. If they escape a violent end by faction, they die of a disease which they cannot escape. Men are made by nature unequal." He then considers the necessity of organization, cohesion, and leadership:

> . . . If work is to be productive, the wise must direct and the fool must obey; and as the business of life cannot stand still till the fool is convinced of his folly by argument, direction must take the form of command. Thus gradually the continent of human occupation is trodden into roads, which experience proves to lead most directly to the desired end. Experience teaches slowly, and at the cost of mistakes . . . at any given time the beaten track is safer for the multitude than any independent course which originality may strike out for itself; and if a person who fancies that he is not one of the multitude chooses to act in another direction, he is regarded with natural distrust. In one instance in a thousand he may be right, and if he has the courage to persevere he will earn an exceptional place for himself in the honour of his kind. But the presumption is against him, and penalties are fitly imposed on eccentricity in proportion to the disturbance which it threatens.
>
> As it has been with practice, so it has been with opinion. Surrounded by invisible forces, their destination and their origin alike concealed behind a veil, yet liable at any moment to accidents by which their lives, their fortunes, their happiness might be affected for good or ill, men began early to speculate on the nature of the powers which seemed to envelope their existence. They gave rein to their fears and to their fancy. . . . Ignorance is the dominion of absurdity. **Fear is the parent of cruelty.** Ignorance and fear combined have made the religious annals of mankind the most hideous chapters in history. . . .

Fell death's untimely frost

Source: HIGHLAND MARY (Stanza 3)
Author: Robert Burns (1759-1796)
First published: 1799
Type of work: Song

Context: The year 1786, when Burns was twenty-seven years old, was a most important one for the poet. His poems, written in rapid succession, produced such a body of original work—natural, forcible, and picturesque, and also quaint, sarcastic, humorous, and tender—as had not appeared since the time of Shakespeare. Yet for Burns, misfortunes were also piling up. In 1784, he had met "Bonie Jean" (Jean Armour), and on his side, the acquaintanceship had ripened into passion. Her father had forbidden their marriage. In the spring of 1786 he learned she was about to become a mother. He sent her a written acknowledgment of marriage, a document that by the laws of Scotland made their connection legal. He also wrote a poem beginning "Thou's welcome, wean (child)" and addressed "To His Illegitimate Child." But Mr. Armour still refused to recognize a marriage. He burned the document. Then Burns decided to emigrate as bookkeeper to the estate of Dr. Douglas, in Jamaica. To raise the nine pounds necessary for the voyage, he arranged for the publication of all the poems he had written and tossed into the drawer of his table. About then he became acquainted with Mary Campbell, once servant in the family of Gavin Hamilton and then a dairy maid. They fell in love. She returned to her parents in Argyleshire in May, 1786, to get ready for the marriage, after a tender farewell in which they plighted troth on the banks of the Ayr. While Burns was working on the 600-copy edition of his poems, Mary died. The poet was reticent about her and occupied himself with the preparation of a second edition, at the suggestion of Dr. Blacklock. People thought he had put Mary out of his mind, but years later a number of heartfelt songs proved how much she had meant to him and how deeply and affectionately he remembered her. Besides two songs "To Mary in Heaven," beginning "Thou lingering star with less'ning ray/ That lov'st to greet the early morn," and "To Mary," declaring "could aught of song declare my pains. . ./ The Muse should tell, in labour'd pains/ O Mary, how I love thee," Burns wrote four impassioned stanzas to be sung to the tune of *Katherine Ogie*. He remembers the "banks and braes, and streams around/ The castle of Montgomery" where he "took the last fareweel/ O' my sweet Highland Mary." In the final two stanzas he describes the scene:

> Wi' monie a vow, an' lock'd embrace,
>   Our parting was fu' tender;
> And, pledging aft to meet again,
>   We tore oursels asunder;
> **But oh! fell death's untimely frost,**

287

That nip't my flower sae early!
Now green's the sod, and cauld's the clay,
That wraps my Highland Mary!

O pale, pale now, those rosy lips,
I aft hae kiss'd sae fondly!
And closed for ay the sparkling glance,
That dwelt on me sae kindly!
And mould'ring now in silent dust,
That heart that lo'ed me dearly!
But still within my bosom's core
Shall live my Highland Mary.

A fellow almost damned in a fair wife

Source: OTHELLO (Act I, sc. i, l. 22)
Author: William Shakespeare (1564-1616)
First published: 1622
Type of work: Dramatic tragedy

Context: In the opening scene of the play—in conversation with Roderigo—Iago berates Othello, his military superior, for failure to promote him to second-in-command. Instead, the lieutenancy has been awarded to Cassio, a young Florentine whom Iago denounces as bookish and inexperienced. In his tirade against this new appointee, Iago makes a remark about Cassio's wife which has frequently puzzled readers of the play. "Damned in a fair wife" reflects, of course, a proverbial attitude that a beautiful wife is a source of trouble for her husband. But Shakespeare does not provide Cassio a wife in the play. Perhaps he had originally intended to do so and failed to delete this line when he decided otherwise; in the Italian work by Geraldio Cinthio which served as Shakespeare's source, the captain is indeed married, though not cuckolded. Or perhaps Iago is making a snide remark about the courtesan Bianca and her unsuccessful matrimonial purusit of the lieutenant. In any case, the immediate context is clear. According to Iago, Cassio has neither the experience nor the manliness for his new position. The following lines set the stage for Iago's open declaration of villainy—that he follow Othello but to serve his turn upon him. His subsequent determination to prod Othello into mad jealousy on circumstantial evidence concerning Desdemona's fidelity forms the main action of the plot.

IAGO

• • •

Forsooth, a great arithmetician,
One Michael Cassio, a Florentine,
A fellow almost damned in a fair wife,
That never set a squadron in the field,

288

Nor the division of a battle knows
More than a spinster, unless the bookish theoric,
Wherein the toged consuls can propose
As masterly as he. Mere prattle, without practice
In all his soldiership. But he, sir, had th' election;
And I—of whom his eyes had seen the proof
At Rhodes, at Cyprus, and on other grounds
Christian and heathen—must be be-leed and calmed
By debitor and creditor. This counter-caster,
He, in good time, must his lieutenant be,
And I God bless the mark, his Moorship's ancient.

A fickle thing and changeful is woman always

Source: THE AENEID (Book IV, as translated by John Jackson)
Author: Virgil (Publius Vergilius Maro, 70-19 B.C.)
First transcribed: 29-19 B.C.
Type of work: Epic poem

Context: A true epic is a natural, gradual evolution, about whose author little or nothing is known. So the *Aeneid* (i.e., a poem about Aeneas) is a literary epic, being the result of conscious artistic efforts by Publius Vergilius Maro, product of Rome's Golden Age and friend of its Emperor Augustus. Aeneas, fleeing from burning Troy spends the winter with Queen Dido of Carthage, enjoying her passionate love. Finally details of his delay reach Jove, who has destined Aeneas to found Rome, and he sends his son, Mercury, to order Aeneas to depart. When Queen Dido and her sister Anna beg the Trojan to remain, Mercury again visits him in a vision, to warn him falsely that fickle Dido and her sister are planning to play on his affections and even destroy his ships to prevent his departure. The Greeks are not the only people to have a word for the fickleness of woman. Francis I of France (1494–1547) is supposed to have written with his diamond ring on a window of the Château of Chambord: "Woman often changes; foolish the man who trusts her." The Duke in Verdi's *Rigoletto* sings: "La donna è mobile (Woman is changeable)." As Virgil tells the story:

. . . a vision . . . visited his dreams . . . in all things like to Mercury, voice and color, yellow locks, and the graceful limbs of youth: . . . "Madman, seest not the after-dangers that beset thee? Resolved on death, she is pondering in her heart fell villainy and treachery, and rousing the swirling tide of passion: . . . Anon, thou wilt see the brine a turmoil of shattered timbers, see torches flashing fierce and the strand fervent with fire, if the rays of dawn discover thee tarrying in the land. Up and go!—truce to delay. **A fickle thing and changeful is woman always!**" Thus he said, and mingled with the shadows of night.

289

The final harbor, whence we unmoor no more

Source: MOBY DICK (Chapter 114)
Author: Herman Melville (1819-1891)
First published: 1851
Type of work: Novel

Context: In its search for whales, and with Captain Ahab looking still for Moby Dick, the whaler "Pequod" sails into the relatively calm waters of the Japanese cruising ground. In mild, pleasant weather the boat crews of the whaling-ship seek their prey, often sitting quietly in their frail whale-boats for an hour or more, waiting for whales to rise to the surface. At such times, says Melville, one forgets the tiger heart and remorseless fangs of the ocean, so beautiful and calm it is. On such occasions, "in his whale-boat the rover softly feels a certain filial, confident, land-like feeling towards the sea; that he regards it as so much flowery earth." Even upon Captain Ahab, that tortured soul, the ocean has a soothing effect temporarily. The sea seems almost like land, says Melville, with blue hillsides where play-wearied children sleep in solitude in "some glad Maytime." It is in such a quiet time that a man may think long and deep, to consider not just this life, but the life of his eternal soul, as Melville suggests:

Oh, grassy glades! oh, ever vernal endless landscapes in the soul; in ye,—though long parched by the dead drought of the earthy life,—in ye, men yet may roll, like young horses in new morning clover; and for some few fleeting moments, feel the cool dew of the life immortal on them. Would to God these blessed calms would last. But the mingled, mingling threads of life are woven by warp and woof: calms crossed by storms, a storm for every calm. There is no steady unretracing progress in this life; we do not advance through fixed gradations, and at the last one pause:—through infancy's unconscious spell, boyhood's thoughtless faith, adolescence' doubt (the common doom), then scepticism, then disbelief, resting at last in manhood's pondering repose of If. But once gone through, we trace the round again; and are infants, boys, and men, and Ifs eternally. Where lies **the final harbor, whence we unmoor no more?** In what rapt ether sails the world, of which the weariest will never weary? Where is the foundling's father hidden? Our souls are like those orphans whose unwedded mothers die in bearing them: the secret of our paternity lies in their grave, and we must there to learn it.

A fine puss-gentleman that's all perfume

Source: CONVERSATION (Line 284)
Author: William Cowper (1731-1800)
First published: 1782
Type of work: Essay in verse

Context: Having listed many deterrents to good conversation, such as sound and fury in place of logic, and the smoking of a pipe that not only slows up the story-telling but drives the fair sex from the room, Cowper continues his 908-line discussion of the gift of conversation with attention to another of his pet hatreds, a highly perfumed fine gentleman. His mind travels from the civet out of which perfumes are made to the civet cat from which that secretion is obtained. Accordingly, he calls such persons "puss-gentlemen." Their heavy perfume sickens and even kills some people. The "raree shows" referred to, were peep shows or carnivals, frequented by the unwashed rabble.

> I cannot talk with civet in the room,
> **A fine puss-gentleman that's all perfume;**
> The sight's enough—no need to smell a beau—
> Who thrusts his nose into a raree show?
> His odoriferous attempts to please
> Perhaps might prosper with a swarm of bees;
> But we that make no honey, though we sting,
> Poets, are sometimes apt to maul the thing.
> 'Tis wrong to bring into a mixed resort
> What makes some sick, and others à-la-mort,—
> An argument of cogence, we may say,
> Why such a one should keep himself away.

Fine words butter no parsnips

Source: A LEGEND OF MONTROSE (Chapter 3)
Author: Sir Walter Scott (1771-1832)
First published: 1819
Type of work: Novel

Context: One evening in the decade of the 1640's, when the Royalists of England were fighting the Roundheads, the Earl of Menteith and two servants are traveling up a Scottish glen when a single completely armed man rides towards them. After challenges have been exchanged, the earl says that he is a Royalist and asks the newcomer, Dugald Dalgetty, which side he is on. Dalgetty does not know as yet. He, however, recounts his services on the Continent as a mercenary soldier with various forces: with the Swedes, under Gustavus, the Lion of the North; with Walter Butler's

Irish Regiment, under Wallenstein; with the Spanish; and with the States of Holland. Sometimes he got his full pay and sometimes he did not; but whether he did or not, he usually managed to do well enough by plundering to keep himself satisfied. When Menteith says that he cannot see why Dalgetty does not embrace the cause of King Charles I, he is treated to a discourse on slogans. "Caeteris paribus" is Old Latin for "Other things being equal."

"Ye speak reasonably, my lord," said Dalgetty, "and *caeteris paribus,* I might be induced to see the matter in the same light. But, my lord, there is a southern proverb,—**fine words butter no parsnips.** I have heard enough, since I came here, to satisfy me, that a cavalier of honor is free to take any part in this civil embroilment whilk he may find most convenient for his own peculiar. Loyalty is your pass-word, my lord—Liberty, roars another chield from the other side of the strath—the King, shouts one war-cry—the Parliament roars another—Montrose for ever, cries Donald, waving his bonnet—Argyle and Leven, cries a south-country Saunders, vaporing with his hat and feather—Fight for the bishops, says a priest, with his gown and rochet—stand Stout for the Kirk, cries a minister, in a Geneva cap and band.—Good watchwords all—excellent watchwords. Whilk cause is the best I cannot say. But sure I am, that I have fought knee-deep in blood many a day for one that was ten degrees worse than the worst of them all."

Fingers were made before forks

Source: POLITE CONVERSATION (Dialogue II)
Author: Jonathan Swift (1677-1745)
First published: 1738
Type of work: Satire

Context: English satirist Jonathan Swift, noting that the art of conversation is dying, attempts to enliven it by giving examples of "polite conversation," incidentally filled with clichés, appropriate for ladies and gentlemen at tea, dinner, or other social occasions. At a dinner at the home of Lady Smart, the following dialogue ensues when Miss Notable asks Colonel Atwit for a fritter:

MISS NOTABLE
Pray, colonel, send me some fritters.
[*Colonel takes them out with his hand.*]

COLONEL ATWIT
Here, miss; they say, **fingers were made before forks,** and hands before knives.

292

LADY SMART

Methinks the pudden is too much boil'd.

LADY ANSWERALL

Oh! madam, they say, a pudden is poison when it's too much boil'd.

MR. NEVEROUT

Miss, shall I help you to a pigeon? Here's a pigeon so finely roasted, it cries, Come eat me.

MISS NOTABLE

No, sir; I thank you.

A finished gentleman from top to toe

Source: DON JUAN (Canto XII, stanza 84)
Author: George Gordon, Lord Byron (1788-1824)
First published: 1823-1824 (Cantos XII-XIV)
Type of work: Satirical poem

Context: The parts of *Don Juan* appeared at intervals. Canto I was written in September, 1818 and published with Canto II in 1819; III, IV, and V were printed in 1821; the next nine appeared in groups of three in 1823; XV and XVI were published in March, 1824, and the unfinished Canto XVII, that went to Greece with Byron, was not printed until 1903. After a love affair with the married Donna Julia, a young friend of his mother, Don Juan is sent on a tour of Europe in search of an education in morals. Shipwrecked, he is found by Haidée, the lovely daughter of a pirate and slave-dealer (instead of by the fisherman's daughter as in *Don Juan Tenorio,* a Spanish version). After an amorous interlude, her father ships him to a slave market, and Haidée dies of grief. Sold to the Sultana, the youthful Don Juan is compelled to dress as a dancing maiden to conceal his sex from the Sultan. However, remembering his former sweetheart, Juan refuses to become the Sultana's lover. He escapes, when the armies of Catherine of Russia beseige Ismail. His general bravery and his deed in saving a ten-year-old girl from slaughter by the Cossacks (an actual event of the seige but performed by the Duc de Richelieu), give Don Juan such a reputation that he is chosen to carry news of the victory to the Empress in Russia. In St. Petersburg, with new worlds to conquer, Don Juan quickly becomes a favorite of the Empress. When he is taken ill, Catherine sends him on a diplomatic mission to England which opens another area to the satirical shafts of the poet. As a young, unmarried man, polished and knowledgeable about fashionable etiquette, Juan becomes very popular. Many English ladies make love to him. He is shown the sights of London and introduced to the social world. He also

293

meets "a Prince," actually the Prince Regent, afterward George IV, and about him writes the laudatory stanza quoted below. So slight a thread cannot fill the many stanzas of the long poem. Byron often digresses. He commends Wellington (called Villainton by the French); he excoriates the ministers of England, except Canning; he is ironic about the chastity of English women; he attacks the holiness of the Holy Roman Empire, and criticizes the poetry of numerous contemporaries. As narrator, he introduces many of his own personal likes and dislikes. He even devotes one stanza, number 41 of Canto X, to a rhymed pharmaceutical prescription. But though there are many pages in the poem, there is hardly a dull one.

> There, too he saw (whate'er he may be now)
> A Prince, the prince of princes at the time,
> With fascination in his very bow,
> And full of promise, as the spring of prime.
> Though royalty was written on his brow,
> He had *then* the grace, too, rare in every clime,
> Of being, without alloy of fop or beau,
> **A finish'd gentleman from top to toe.**

The first fine careless rapture

Source: HOME-THOUGHTS, FROM ABROAD (Line 16)
Author: Robert Browning (1812-1889)
First published: 1845
Type of work: Lyric poem

Context: Though it is widely believed that "Home-Thoughts, from Abroad" was written during Browning's first visit to Italy in 1838, W. C. DeVane said that it was probably written in England during April, 1845. (*A Browning Handbook,* 1935, pp. 147–148.) Regardless of place and date of composition, though, the poem is suffused with the poet's love of the sights and sounds of an English spring. In the first stanza he longs to be in England "Now that April's there," to see the tiny leaves "Round the elm-tree bole" and hear the chaffinch sing. In the second stanza he remembers the full spring of May, and at the end he contrasts the gaity of English buttercups with a "gaudy melon-flower" symbolic of spring in Italy. Stanza two follows:

> And after April, when May follows,
> And the whitethroat builds, and all the swallows!
> Hark, where my blossomed pear-tree in the hedge
> Leans to the field and scatters on the clover
> Blossoms and dewdrops—at the bent spray's edge—
> That's the wise thrush; he sings each song twice over,
> Lest you should think he never could recapture
> **The first fine careless rapture!**

294

And though the fields look rough with hoary dew,
All will be gay when noontide wakes anew
The buttercups, the little children's dower
—Far brighter than this gaudy melon-flower!

First follow nature

Source: ESSAY ON CRITICISM (Part I, l. 68)
Author: Alexander Pope (1688-1744)
First published: 1711
Type of work: Satire

Context: Alexander Pope, in his poetic *Essay on Criticism,* warns that to be a bad critic is far worse than to be a bad poet. He notes that few men are born with true taste, and that of these most are led astray by poor education. Two cardinal rules exist for the critic: first, follow nature; second, study the classics. In suggesting nature as a guide for judgment, the poet says:

First follow nature, and your judgment frame
By her just standard, which is still the same:
Unerring nature, still divinely bright,
One clear, unchanged, and universal light,
Life, force, and beauty, must to all impart,
At once the source, and end, and test of art;
Art from that fund each just supply provides;
Works without show, and without pomp presides:
In some fair body thus th' informing soul
With spirits feeds, with vigour fills the whole,
Each motion guides, and every nerve sustains;
Itself unseen, but in th' effects remains.
Some, to whom Heaven in wit has been profuse,
Want as much more, to turn it to its use;
For wit and judgment often are at strife,
Though meant each other's aid, like man and wife.
'Tis more to guide, than spur the muse's steed;
Restrain his fury, than provoke his speed:
The winged courser, like a generous horse,
Shows most true mettle when you check his course.

The first lion thought the last a bore

Source: BOMBASTES FURIOSO (Scene IV)
Author: William Barnes Rhodes (1772-1826)
First published: 1822
Type of work: Burlesque tragic opera

Context: People looking at the short and thick-set Mr. Rhodes, plodding about London, saw nothing in him to indicate humor. There was no twinkle in his eyes. He did his business as Chief Teller in the Bank of England in a serious way. However, in his leisure time, he collected manuscripts of dramas and attended theatrical performances in company with a fellow bank clerk, a tall, gaunt gentleman who ardently admired Siddons and Kemble. Together they beheld Thalia and Melpomene in all their glory at Covent Garden. Between the acts, Rhodes amused himself with extemporaneous parodies on speeches that shortly before had "drowned the stage with tears." Not that he loved Shakespeare less, but he loved burlesque more. And so there came into existence the one-act burlesque tragedy *Bombastes Furioso,* sometimes called *Artaxominous the Great,* performed at the Theatre Royal, London, about 1803, with a noteworthy cast that included Liston as General Bombastes, Liston's diminutive wife as the attractive Distaffina, Mathews as the King, and Taylor as Minister of State Fusbos. The lyrics included in the work are parodies of well-known songs, using familiar melodies. In addition to this work, Rhodes published a mediocre volume of Epigrams, and also supposedly completed two dramatic pieces that were neither performed nor published. The boasting and bombastic soldier provided humor in many a medieval drama under the name of Miles Glorioso or Miles Furioso. Here he is called General Bombastes, commander of the army of cigar-smoking King Artaxominous of Utopia. According to the stage directions, the general wears "a general's military suit—jack boots—comic powdered wig and pigtail—long sword—small cocked hat and plume." The dialog is in a variety of meters. The play opens with His Majesty, in pain after a night of drinking and smoking, uttering such majestic lines as "Get out of my sight, or I'll knock you down." Nevertheless, Minister Fusbos lingers long enough to announce the return of General Bombastes with rich booty after a successful campaign. The king, however, is more concerned wih his problem of how to replace Queen Griskinissa with the charming Distaffina. Upon being consulted, she confesses she loves Bombastes, but a handful of gold coins persuades her to forget the general. Their conversation is interrupted by the sound of the approaching Bombastes. The king flees to a closet, unfortunately leaving his well-known tricorn in sight. At such evidence of Distaffina's inconstancy, furious Bombastes determines to die. To save himself the necessity of suicide, he goes to a woods, fastens his boots to a tree, and displays above them a universal challenge.

"Who dares this pair of boots
  displace
Must meet Bombastes face to
  face,"
Thus do I challenge all the human
  race.

King Artaxominous appears and knocks down the boots with the declaration:

Where'er thou art, with speed prepare to go
Where I shall send thee—to the
  shades below!

Bombastes answers his roar with the

fable of a lion, and is topped by the king's reply. Thereupon he kills the King of Utopia. Into the woods comes Fusbos, and in a duel put to a duet, he slays the regicide. Distaffina then joins Fusbos in a lament, interrupted by the resurrected corpses, and all unite in a jolly final quartet. Here is the fable of the lions:

BOMBASTES
So have I heard on Afric's burning shore,
A hungry lion give a grievous roar;
The grievous roar echoed along the shore.

ARTAXOMINOUS
So have I heard on Afric's burning shore
Another lion give a grievous roar,
And **the first lion thought the last a bore.**

BOMBASTES
Am I then mocked? Now by my fame I swear
You shall soon have it—There!   [*They fight.*]

ARTAXOMINOUS
Where?

BOMBASTES
There,—and there.

The first smith was the first murderer's son

Source: THE TASK (Book V, l. 219)
Author: William Cowper (1731-1800)
First published: 1785
Type of work: Meditative poem in blank verse

Context: Cowper's descriptions of nature in Miltonian blank verse with their re-creation of the sights and sounds of the country anticipated what was later to be called Romanticism. This poem became immediately popular, as did his technique. He used the same meter later in his translations of Homer (1791). Shortly afterward his old melancholia, for which he had several times spent periods in insane asylums, came upon him, and he wrote very little from then until his death. A frosty morning entices the poet to take a walk. He wonders where the song birds have gone, and whether the earthworm is safe under the cold sod. The sight of a frozen water fall recalls to him the Ice Palace of the Russian Empress, Catherine the Great, who ruled from 1762 to 1796. He thinks of her amusements, including war. That reminds him of "the first artificer of death," Tubal-cain, six generations after Cain, who killed his brother.

297

The Bible refers to Tubal-cain as "the forger of every cutting instrument of brass and iron." (Genesis 4:22) Vulcan was the Roman fire god and blacksmith. A falchion is a curved, medieval broadsword.

Cain had already shed a brother's blood;
The Deluge washed it out, but left unquenched
The seeds of murder in the breast of man.
Soon, by a righteous judgment, in the line
Of his descending progeny was found
The first artificer of death: the shrewd
Contriver who first sweated at the forge,
And forced the blunt and yet unbloodied steel
To a keen edge, and made it bright for war.
Him, Tubal named, the Vulcan of old Times
The sword and falchion their inventor claim,
And **the first smith was the first murd'rer's son.**

A flea in his ear

Source: EUPHUES, THE ANATOMY OF WIT
Author: John Lyly (1554?-1606)
First published: 1579
Type of work: Prose romance

Context: "A flea in his ear" is apparently a traditional English expression, meaning either to take umbrage at a speech by someone else or to be highly surprised. An occurrence of the phrase is in *Pilgrimage of the lyf of the manhode* (*c.* 1430): "And manye oothere grete wundres which been fleen in myne eres" (II, xxxix); here the expression means to astonish, but in *De Lisle's Legendarie* (1577) "Sending them away with fleas in their eares, vtterly disappointed of their purpose" (Bvj), it means to be annoyed. John Lyly was the first writer of much note to employ the phrase. In his novel *Euphues, the Anatomy of Wit* Lucilla, a rather light Neapolitan lady, has been the love of Philautus, a pleasure-loving young man of the city of Naples. Philautus introduces a new acquaintance, Euphues, a young scholar from Greece, to Lucilla, and immediately Euphues woos her to such effect that she disdains Philautus. By the time that Philautus has been excluded from her consideration, her father, Ferardo, who has been absent from town, returns and endeavors to effect a marriage between Philautus and his daughter, who treats him with great contempt and refuses to marry him. In the quotation below Ferardo prepares to examine Lucilla to discover why she has so completely changed her mind since the time of his departure from the city. While the interrogation is in progress Philautus stands as though with a flea in his ear, the expression at this point evidently meaning that he is dazed by Lucilla's complete denial of affection for him. After Lyly, Robert Armin (*fl.* 1608) used the expression in *A Nest of Ninnies* (1608): "The fellow knowing himselfe faulty, put up his wrongs, quickly departed, and went to work betimes that morning with a flea in his ear." The quotation from Lyly is as follows:

Ferardo, being a grave and wise gentleman, although he were thoroughly angry, yet he dissembled his fury, to the end he might by craft discover her fancy, and whispering Philautus in the ear (who stood as though he had **a flea in his ear**), desired him to keep silence until he had undermined her by subtlety, . . .

The floor lay paved with broken hearts

Source: GRATIANA, DANCING AND SINGING (Stanza 3)
Author: Richard Lovelace (1618-1657)
First published: 1649
Type of work: Lyric poem

Context: Gay cavaliers of the court of Charles I cultivated the art of light verse, elegant but superficial, addressed to sweethearts whose identity was concealed behind poetic names. Yet some poets also exhibited a serious side, maintaining devotion to the king even at the cost of imprisonment and exile. The poetry of one of the most important of them, Richard Lovelace, exhibits both tendencies. In *To Lucasta, Going to the Wars,* he set out to fight for his king, anticipating death in battle. His poem to Gratiana concerns merely an amorous conflict.

> Each step trod out a Lover's thought
> And the ambitious hopes he brought,
>   Chained to her brave feet with such arts,
> Such sweet command, and gentle awe,
> As when she ceased, we sighing saw
>   **The floor lay pav'd with broken hearts**
>
> So did she move, so did she sing
> Like the Harmonious spheres that bring
>   Unto their rounds their Music's aid;
> Which she performed in such a way
> As all the enamoured world will say
>   The Graces danced, and Apollo played.

The flowery way that leads to the broad gate
and the great fire

Source: ALL'S WELL THAT ENDS WELL (Act IV, sc. v, ll. 56-57)
Author: William Shakespeare (1564-1616)
First published: 1623
Type of work: Dramatic comedy

Context: Bertram, son of the Countess of Rousillon, has rudely rejected Helena as a wife. Forced to marry her by the king's command, he sends her home unkissed and himself renounces his nation to serve the Duke of Florence. In subsequent battles the young count distinguishes himself, but the pining Helena, whose true love will not allow her to remain idle, follows him on a pilgrimage to St. Jaques le Grand. She allows word to be sent both to her husband and to his mother that she has died on the journey. The countess, when she receives this news, is grief-stricken; "If she had partaken of my flesh, and cost me the dearest groans of a mother, I could not have owed her a more rooted love." Lavache, a clown in the Rousillon household, attempts to relieve her sorrow with saucy and impertinent dialogue, by describing bawdily the fool and his bauble, and by averring that—though he serve the Prince of Darkness and though he love a good fire—he has no desire to serve at the Devil's court. But his tricks now begin to jade. Such humor is inappropriate to the occasion, and the fool is peremptorily dismissed by the countess. But, not to be denied, a few lines later the fool reenters to announce the arrival home of the count, her son, with a velvet patch (scar) on his face. He is attended by—and here Lavache gets his final sarcastic gibes at the pomposity and flamboyancy of the aristocrats—". . . a dozen of 'em, with delicate fine hats, and most courteous feathers, which bow the head and nod at every man." His speech about the "great fire" is as follows:

LAVACHE

I am a woodland fellow sir, that always loved a great fire; and the master I speak of ever keeps a good fire. But sure he is the prince of the world, let his nobility remain in's court. I am for the house with the narrow gate, which I take to be too little for pomp to enter. Some that humble themselves may, but the many will be too chill and tender, and they'll be for **the flowery way that leads to the broad gate and the great fire.**

A fool must now and then be right, by chance

Source: CONVERSATION (Line 96)
Author: William Cowper (1731-1800)
First published: 1782
Type of work: Meditative poem

300

Context: This poem was written during the first months of the poet's association with Lady Austen, who encouraged Cowper to extend himself as a poet, telling him that he was capable of writing about any subject he chose. In *Conversation* Cowper suggests that the ability to be a good conversationalist is a gift from the Deity, rather than an art to be learned. The suggestion is not surprising, inasmuch as Cowper was a highly religious man. He notes, however, that a person must be willing to learn, in order to cultivate the heaven-sent gift. He is also of the opinion that talking is not necessarily conversation: "Words learn'd by rote a parrot may rehearse, / But talking is not always to converse." Language, Cowper goes on to say, is a "sacred interpreter of human thought" which few respect or use as carefully as they should. Particularly, he maintains, we should not use the gift of language for adulterous purposes, either in youth or age. In a verse paragraph near the beginning of the poem Cowper asks help of whatever powers there may be who govern human speech:

> Ye pow'rs who rule the tongue, if such there are,
> And make colloquial happiness your care,
> Preserve me from the thing I dread and hate,
> A duel in the form of a debate:
> The clash of arguments and jar of words,
> Worse than the mortal brunt of rival swords,
> Decide no question with their tedious length,
> For opposition gives opinion strength,
> Divert the champions prodigal of breath,
> And put the peacably disposed to death.
> Oh thwart me not, Sir Soph, at ev'ry turn,
> Nor carp at ev'ry flaw you may discern,
> Though syllogisms hang not on my tongue,
> I am not, surely, always in the wrong;
> 'Tis hard if all is false that I advance,
> **A fool must now and then be right, by chance;**
> Not that all freedom of dissent I blame,
> No—there I grant the privilege I claim.

Fools are my theme, let satire be my song

Source: ENGLISH BARDS AND SCOTCH REVIEWERS (Line 6)
Author: George Gordon, Lord Byron (1788-1824)
First published: 1809
Type of work: Satiric poem in couplets

Context: In January, 1808, the *Edinburgh Review,* one of the most influential of literary journals, published a very unfavorable review of Byron's *Hours of Idleness.* The poet believed it the work of the *Review's* founder, Francis Jeffrey (1773–1850), who had blasted Wordsworth's *Excursion* in a devastating criticism beginning, "This will never do!" Later Henry

Peter, Baron Brougham (1778–1868), who afterward became Lord Chancellor, was revealed to have written the article. Previously Byron had written a short satire titled "British Bards," in which he expressed his low opinion of a number of current writers: "simple" Wordsworth because of his commonplace themes and sometimes prosy language; "Obscure" Coleridge; a n d "verbose" Southey. It was set up in type but never offered for sale, because of the poet's hesitation. However, the harsh words of the *Edinburgh Review* decided Byron to revise it, broaden the concept to include the Scotch critic he blamed for the article, and publish it anonymously, in 1,070 lines. Eight months later he reprinted it under his own name. Then in 1810 and 1811 he published other versions, with an additional ninety lines. Finally a fifth attempt had been set in type when Byron began to have doubts about his indiscriminate satire, and he tried to suppress it. But a few copies got out, and the definitive version, included in his complete work, uses this last form. Byron's complaint is that it is silly to expect sensible literary reviews from critics. He calls Jeffrey a "self-constituted judge of poesy." He devotes more than a hundred mocking lines to him, and also makes comment on many other contemporaries now practically forgotten. Though in later years Byron expressed regret at having shot barbed arrows so indiscriminately, many of his judgments are still acceptable today. At the conclusion of the poem, he says he can endure the opinions of the critics, but comes nearer the truth in his boast that he can "break him on the wheel he meant for me." The poem begins with a defense of his "grey goose quill" that he is picking up again to express an uncommon theme. William Thomas Fitzgerald was for thirty years the poetaster who read an original and boring ode at the annual banquet of the Literary Fund. The first six lines of the poem declared:

Still must I hear?—shall hoarse Fitzgerald bawl
His creaking couplets in a tavern hall,
And I not sing, lest, haply, Scotch reviews
Should dub me scribbler and denounce my muse?
Prepare for rhyme—I'll publish, right or wrong:
Fools are my theme, let satire be my song.

Footprints on the sands of time

Source: A PSALM OF LIFE (Stanza 7)
Author: Henry Wadsworth Longfellow (1807-1882)
First published: 1838
Type of work: Lyric poem

Context: This nineteenth century poem is in striking contrast to much of the defeatist, pessimistic verse of the twentieth century. Its highly optimistic message is that this is a real world in which we live and that we lose it if we spend our time in vain repinings about what might have been or wishful thinking of what may be in the future. We are living in the here and now, and our duty to ourselves is to live each day so fully that we accomplish something that will leave an imprint on the world. We should not merely endure life until death releases us so that we can go to our graves. There is so much to do in the world, and we individually have so little time in which to do it, that we should act in such a manner as to accomplish something worthy every day. The lives of the great should inspire us to such a degree that we ought to make the effort to leave our mark on the world, a mark which may in the future encourage someone else to great achievement. The whole idea of the poem, that here is a world in which we can do fine things if only we put our whole souls into the effort, is, of course, utterly abhorrent to twentieth century paternalism.

> Trust no Future, howe'er pleasant!
> Let the dead Past bury its dead!
> Act,—act in the living Present!
> Heart within, and God o'erhead!
>
> Lives of great men all remind us
> We can make our lives sublime,
> And, departing, leave behind us
> **Footprints on the sands of time;**
>
> Footprints, that perhaps another,
> Sailing o'er life's solemn main,
> A forlorn and shipwrecked brother,
> Seeing, shall take heart again.
>
> Let us, then, be up and doing,
> With a heart for any fate;
> Still achieving, still pursuing,
> Learn to labor and to wait.

For God! for the Cause! for the Church! for the Laws!

Source: THE BATTLE OF NASEBY (Line 19)
Author: Thomas Babington Macaulay (1800-1859)
First published: 1824
Type of work: Narrative poem

Context: This first of Macaulay's two "Songs of the Civil War" (The English, not the American Civil War), was supposedly written by a sergeant in the regiment of Henry Ireton (1611–1651), a general in the Puritan revolution. On June 14, 1645, the Parliamentarians under Fairfax and Cromwell defeated the Royalists under Charles I and his nephew Prince Rupert, born in Germany, at the decisive Battle of Naseby, in Northamptonshire, England. Macaulay's swinging lines, so effective in re-creating ancient Rome, are just as stirring when he writes about battles and events in the history of his own land. In this poem, the sergeant describes t h e enemy under King Charles, "the man of blood with his long essenced hair" in contrast to the close-cropped and unperfumed Roundheads. He also speaks of Prince Rupert (1619–1682), Count Palatine of the Rhine and grandson of James I of England. Because of his bravery he won the name of "The Mad Cavalier." Then the narrator turns to his own army:

> Like a servant of the Lord, with his Bible and his sword,
> The General rode along us to form us to the fight,
> When a murmuring shout broke out, and swell'd into a shout,
> Among the godless horsemen upon the tyrant's right.
>
> And hark! like the roar of the billows on the shore,
> The cry of battle rises along their charging line!
> **For God! for the Cause! for the Church! for the Laws!**
> For Charles King of England and Rupert of the Rhine!

For one restraint, lords of the world besides

Source: PARADISE LOST (Book I, l. 32)
Author: John Milton (1608-1674)
First published: 1667
Type of work: Epic poem

Context: Milton begins *Paradise Lost* with the statement of his theme, man's disobedience to God and the coming of death into the world. Throughout the poem the idea is developed that the death is both physical and spiritual. The idea of the introduction of physical death derives from Genesis 3: 19 and 3: 22, where it is contained both in the curse laid on Adam after he had eaten the forbidden fruit though allowed all the rest, and in the fact that he must be evicted from the garden so that he cannot eat of the tree of life and regain his lost immortality. Milton says that a greater Man will come and restore us; that is, Christ will come down and do away with the necessity for spiritual death. Milton then continues that he is going to do things never before attempted in either prose or poetry; among other things, he will justify the ways of God to man. What is meant here is that he will make clear or explain God's ways, which are sometimes difficult of understanding for the ordinary person. When he has done this, he then makes a direct invocation of the heavenly Muse:

> Say first, for heaven hides nothing from thy view
> Nor the deep tract of hell, say first what cause
> Moved our grandparents in that happy state,
> Favored of heaven so highly, to fall off

From their Creator, and transgress his will
For one restraint, lords of the world besides?
Who first seduced them to that foul revolt?
Th' infernal serpent; he it was, whose guile
Stirred up with envy and revenge, deceived
The mother of mankind, what time his pride
Had cast him out from heaven, with all his host
Of rebel angels, by whose aid aspiring
To set himself in glory above his peers,
He trusted to have equalled the most high,
If he opposed. . . .

For 'tis some virtue, virtue to commend

Source: TO SIR GODFREY KNELLER (Line 42)
Author: William Congreve (1670-1729)
First published: 1710
Type of work: Laudatory epistle in verse

Context: William Congreve, Restoration playwright and wit, gives a new twist to the often-debated superiority of the pen over the sword. He compares the pen to the paint brush in a poem to the fashionable painter of his time, Godfrey Kneller, who, as Gottfried Kniller (1646–1723) came to England in 1675 after having studied art in Amsterdam, Rome, and Venice. Following the death of the court painter of Charles II, Pieter Van der Faes (1618–1680), he joined the royal circle. His predecessor had been knighted as Sir Peter Lely, from a lily over the door of the house where his father was born; the new court painter was renamed Sir Godfrey Kneller. By means of an army of apprentices, Kneller turned out an enormous number of portraits of famous people, including the well-known "Ten Beauties of the Court of William III." His period extended from Charles II to George I, with a brief visit to the court of Louis XIV. Dryden had also accorded Kneller poetic tribute when Congreve wrote. The latter begins his poem with an acknowledgment that Kneller's brush can produce better likenesses of people than can his quill pen. He has been looking at the artist's portrait of L——Y——, using an abbreviation common in English literature, though the real name could probably have been easily discovered by anyone acquainted with Kneller's productions. Though he has often tried, says Congreve, to "trace some image of the much-lov'd fair," only the painter could reproduce her in a way that spoke to the heart. Not only does he catch her likeness, but he "paints her mind." To most people, recognition does not come during their lifetime. "Fame due to vast desert is kept in store, Unpaid, till the deserver is no more." However, Kneller's genius has been recognized during his lifetime, especially by the connoisseurs, and Congreve wants to join them. As Polonius said about virtue in *Hamlet,* "Assume a virtue if you have it not," so there is some virtue in recognizing qualities even if you do not possess

305

them. In the first four and last eight lines of the poem, Congreve writes:

> I yield, O Kneller, to superior skill,
> Thy pencil triumphs o'er the poet's quill:
> If yet my vanquish'd Muse exert her lays,
> It is no more to rival thee, but praise.
>
> . . .
>
> Ev'n Dryden has immortalized thy name;
> Let that alone suffice thee, think that fame.
> Unfit I follow where he led the way,
> And court applause by what I seem to pay.
> Myself I praise, while I thy praise intend,
> **For 'tis some virtue, virtue to commend;**
> And next to deeds which our own honor raise,
> Is to distinguish them who merit praise.

For tyme y-lost may not recovered be

Source: TROILUS AND CRISEYDE (Book IV, stanza 184, l. 1283)
Author: Geoffrey Chaucer (c. 1343-1400)
First transcribed: 1380-1386
Type of work: Narrative poem

Context: As Chaucer got his story of Troilus and Criseyde, involved in the twelfth century B.C. siege of Troy, from Benôit and Boccaccio, so Shakespeare borrowed from Chaucer and Robert Henryson (1430–1506). And as Shakespeare transferred the local color from Troy to the days of the late Renaissance, so he modernized his heroine's name to Cressida. The Criseyde of Chaucer is a Trojan widow, attracted by a gallant young warrior who rides past her house to do battle with the Greeks besieging Troy. When her uncle Pandarus tells her that the young hero is dying of love for her, though she suspects there is nothing honorable about his intentions, she allows herself to attend a dinner with him, and with all the ceremony of a medieval court of love, gives him permission to adore her. Next her pandering uncle ma-neuvres her into spending the night at his house, where he brings the lovers together, without much resistance from her. Afterward she even gives Troilus a brooch as token of their eternal love. Book IV shows how eternal it was. In a battle, some of the Greek leaders are captured, including Antenor. Calchas, a Trojan prophet who has fled to the Greeks, arranges that Antenor will be released on condition that Criseyde, his daughter, be allowed to leave Troy and join him in the Greek camp. In the part from which this quotation comes, Criseyde and Troilus spend the last night together, and once more she promises to remain true, and to rejoin him shortly. However, her Greek escort, Diomedes, is too attractive. The change of affection of this girl of old Troy demonstrates that Greek women were as fickle as a Roman woman was proclaimed to be by the Duke of Mantua in *Rigoletto*. She gives Diomedes another of her brooches. Troilus, seeing it, tries to kill her new sweetheart on the battlefield, only to fall beneath the sword of the mighty Achilles. Chaucer does not chide or criticize her; rather, in his well-rounded characterization, he shows that he understands her. As a result, he has produced a very early example of what we now call the psychological novel. In the bedroom scene, she promises:

> For dredelees within a week or two
> I shall ben here! . . .

> For which I wol not make long sermoun,
> **For tyme y-lost may not recovered be;**
> But I will gon to my conclusioun
> (And to the best, in ought that I can see).
> And for the love of God, for-yeve it me
> If I speke ought against your hertes reste,
> For trewely, I speak it for the beste.

For what can war but endless war still breed?

Source: SONNET XV ("On the Lord General Fairfax at the siege of Colchester," Line 10)
Author: John Milton (1608-1674)
First published: 1694
Type of work: Sonnet

Context: This is one of the four sonnets by Milton not published during the poet's lifetime; the text is from the Cambridge Manuscript of Milton's poems. Sir Thomas Fairfax was early one of the most important of the Puritan generals in the Civil War. He won decisive victories over the royalist forces at Marston Moor on July 2, 1644, and at Naseby on June 14, 1645. He captured Colchester in August, 1648, after a siege of seventy-five days. When the march of events passed what Fairfax considered the point of moderation, he resigned his command of the Parliamentary armies, yielding to Oliver Cromwell. In this poem the poet urges the general to turn his energies to the problems of peace.

• • •

> Thy firm unshak'n vertue ever brings
>   Victory home, though new rebellions raise
>   Thir Hydra heads, & the fals North displaies
>   Her brok'n league, to impe their serpent wings,
> O yet a nobler task awaites thy hand;
>   **For what can Warr, but endless warr still breed,**
>   Till Truth, & Right from Violence be freed,
> And Public Faith cleard from the shamefull brand

Of Public Fraud. In vain doth Valour bleed
While Avarice, & Rapine share the land.

Forever most divinely in the wrong

Source: LOVE OF FAME, ON WOMEN (Satire VI, l. 106)
Author: Edward Young (1683-1765)
First published: 1725-1728
Type of work: Satirical poem

Context: In this poem Young satirizes various forms of female behavior. The first person to meet his censure is Lavinia, who is constant in her attendance at church; as silence is more than she can bear, she talks away to God: but when women are proud of praying well, Satan himself will summon them to church. Drusa receives her visitors while she is still in bed; when she wishes to rise, she requests them to turn their backs on her while she dresses. Flavia is not on good terms with her former lover, but supports him for old time's sake; she, apparently faithful, maintains the brood of children born to her by other men than her husband. Amasia scorns restraint and is not as good as she might be. Lucia married an idiot, but a rich one. Wisdom is the only maker of happiness, but she is likened to a practitioner of fine needlework: at least she works in gold. The poet then arrives at Tullia:

> If Tullia had been blest with half her sense,
> None could too much admire her excellence:
> But since she can make error shine so bright,
> She thinks it vulgar to defend the right.
> With understanding she is quite o'er-run;
> And by too great accomplishments undone:
> With skill she vibrates her eternal tongue,
> **For ever most divinely in the wrong.**

Fortunate isle, the abode of the blest

Source: THE AENEID (Book VI, as translated by John Jackson)
Author: Virgil (Publius Vergilius Maro, 70-19 B.C.)
First transcribed: c. 29-19 B.C.
Type of work: Epic poem

Context: The *Aeneid,* written to give Rome an origin suited to her glory, portrays the adventures of her founder, Aeneas, son of Venus and hero of the Trojan War, as he seeks to establish a settlement in Italy. Reaching Italy after a tempestuous voyage from Troy, Aeneas is conducted by a Sybil to the land of the dead, where he eventually meets his father in the Elysian Fields and learns of his own great destiny. Approaching the *fortunate isle, abode of the blest,* Aeneas performs the pre-scribed rites and places the Golden Bough on the threshold.

This at length performed and the service of the goddess discharged, they came to the realms of joy—the pleasant lawns of **the Happy Groves,** and the **seats of the Blest.** Here an ampler ether invests the plains in radiance, and they know their own sun and their own stars. Part by their limbs in the verdant lists and, in sportive conflect, wrestle on the yellow sand; part tread the dance and sing. . . .

Fortune's fool

Source: ROMEO AND JULIET (Act III, sc. i, l. 141)
Author: William Shakespeare (1564-1616)
First published: 1597
Type of work: Dramatic tragedy

Context: At a masked ball in Verona, Romeo of the Montague family falls in love with Juliet of the rival Capulet family. The next day Romeo and Juliet are secretly married, hoping to end the feud of the Montague and Capulet families, who would never have condoned the marriage if permission had been sought. Just after the marriage Romeo, who is determined to keep peace, refuses to draw his sword on Juliet's insulting kinsman, Tybalt, until Tybalt slays Mercutio, Romeo's quick-tempered friend and defender. Incited, Romeo kills Tybalt, is warned by his companion Benvolio to flee the wrath of the prince, and exclaims that he is "fortunes's fool."

BENVOLIO
Romeo away, be gone.
The citizens are up, and Tybalt slain.
Stand not amazed, the Prince will doom thee death,
If thou art taken. Hence, be gone, away.

ROMEO
O I am **fortune's fool!**

Founded upon a rock

Source: MATTHEW 7:25
Author: Unknown (traditionally Matthew the Apostle)
First transcribed: c.75-100
Type of work: Gospel

Context: Of the discourses by Jesus which have come down to us, that traditionally known as the Sermon on the Mount is regarded as among the greatest. Matthew quotes a version of the full text in Chapters 5, 6, and 7. He records in Chapter 4 that after Jesus began to gather His disciples He went about Galilee, preaching the gospel and healing the sick, and that His fame spread all over Syria. Great multitudes from the surrounding country followed Him, and when He saw how large their number was He took His disciples up onto a mountain and instructed them in the gospel He wished them to help Him spread. The Sermon on the Mount is an admirable survey and exposition of the basic principles of Christianity. Beginning with the Beatitudes, Jesus continues with an exposition of moral law, emphasizing inner motivations rather than external codes of conduct. He stresses forgiveness of others, even to the point of loving one's enemies, and He illustrates righteousness in various ways. He provides His followers with a model prayer; this, He says in reference to the Lord's Prayer, embodies all that a prayer should be. He then stresses the importance of spiritual considerations over material things. After warning His disciples against base and hypocritical motives and the ease with which they can be rationalized, He states the Golden Rule. This very basic guide to conduct is then illustrated with a number of practical applications. Jesus points out that His way to salvation requires something of those who follow it and warns against false prophets and the barren lives to which they would lead us. Most of Jesus' other sermons are extensions of the rules, maxims, and principles stated in the Sermon on the Mount; and His life was an effort to exemplify them. He concludes with a striking parable drawn from His work as a carpenter. Anything we build, concrete or symbolic, material or spiritual, must have a solid and enduring basis or it is nothing.

Not every one that saith unto me, Lord, Lord, shall enter the kingdom of heaven; but he that doeth the will of my Father which is in heaven.

Many will say to me in that day, Lord, Lord, have we not prophesied in thy name? and in thy name have cast out devils? and in thy name done many wonderful works?

And then will I profess unto them, I never knew you: depart from me, ye that work iniquity.

Therefore whosoever heareth these sayings of mine, and doeth them, I will liken him unto a wise man, which built his house upon a rock:

And the rain descended, and the floods came, and the winds blew, and beat upon that house; and it fell not: for it was **founded upon a rock.**

And every one that heareth these sayings of mine, and doeth them not, shall be likened unto a foolish man, which built his house upon the sand:

And the rain descended, and the floods came, and the winds blew, and beat upon that house; and it fell: and great was the fall of it.

And it came to pass, when Jesus had ended these sayings, the people were astonished at his doctrine:

For he taught them as one having authority, and not as the scribes.

France, famed in all great arts, in none supreme

Source: TO A REPUBLICAN FRIEND ("Continued," Line 4)
Author: Matthew Arnold (1822-1888)
First published: 1849
Type of work: Sonnet

Context: In 1848, the year that Arnold wrote this poem to Arthur Hugh Clough, the overthrow of the French monarchy marked the beginning of a series of revolutions that spread through Europe. At the time liberals like Clough optimistically forecast that an age of equality and freedom was being ushered in, but Arnold had reservations. By nature melancholy and in philosophy a determinist, Arnold does not believe that political revolutions inaugurate ages of peace; instead, he believes that the cry for freedom will be again stifled by tyrants' greed. France had already demonstrated the course of revolutions when a Napoleon stepped in after the monarchy fell; yet France was being praised for repeating its own bloody history. Rather than copy the French, the liberals should, Arnold believes, emulate the English, who had successfully endured ages of tyranny to evolve into a constitutional government; such evolution requires patience, but it is bloodless and more "artistic" than the violent French way of seeking immediate ends.

> . . . when I muse on what life is, I seem
> Rather to patience prompted, than that proud
> Prospect of hope which France proclaims so loud—
> **France, famed in all great arts, in none supreme;**
>
> Seeing this vale, this earth, whereon we dream,
> Is on all sides o'ershadow'd by the high
> Uno'erleap'd Mountains of Necessity,
> Sparing us narrower margin than we deem.

Freedom, and not servitude, is the cure of anarchy

Source: SPEECH ON MOVING HIS RESOLUTIONS FOR RECONCILIATION WITH THE COLONIES
Author: Edmund Burke (1729-1797)
First published: 1775
Type of work: Political Speech

311

Context: America had no more capable or articulate defender in the English Parliament than Burke. When Parliament considered harsh and repressive measures of taxation and military suppression for the unrest in the Colonies, Burke spoke vehemently in protest. Such measures, he argued, could only be costly and temporary if successful, and they could very well be unsuccessful. He urged instead an act of redress and conciliation such as had been offered to Ireland, Wales, and Chester. He quoted at length from the petition of the citizens of Chester in the reign of Henry VIII and cites that benefits that have been derived from Parliament's acceptance of it:

> What did parliament with this audacious address?—Reject it as a libel? Treat it as an affront to government? Spurn it as a derogation from the rights of legislature? Did they toss it over the table? Did they burn it by the hands of the common hangman? They took the petition of grievance, all rugged as it was, without softening or temperament, unpurged of the original bitterness and indignation of complaint; they made it the very preamble to their act of redress; and consecrated its principle to all ages in the sanctuary of legislation.
>
> Here is my third example. It was attended with the success of the two former. Chester, civilized as well as Wales, had demonstrated that **freedom, and not servitude, is the cure of anarchy;** as religion, and not atheism, is the true remedy for superstition. . . .

Freedom and Whisky gang thegither

Source: THE AUTHOR'S EARNEST CRY AND PRAYER (Last stanza)
Author: Robert Burns (1759-1796)
First published: 1786
Type of work: Political protest

Context: Robert Burns, oldest of the seven children of a farmer who spelled his name Burnes, was born in a cottage that blew down a week after his birth. From his father he inherited brains, general superiority, and a tendency to hypochondria. His wit, love of humor, and lyrical ability came from his mother. He was educated in a small school and later by his father, but his acquaintance with Scotch legends and tales of ghosts and devils came from an old lady, Betty Davidson. When Burns was sixteen, the family moved to a larger community. Here the poet attended dancing school, courted the ladies, and soon became acquainted with taverns and, as he said, "scenes of swaggering riot." He also enjoyed adventures with smugglers who frequented the bare and deeply coved coasts, and took a liking to Scotch whisky. Speaking for all who shared his taste, Burns uttered what is called in the 1793 edition "A Simple Poet's Prayer." It is addressed to "The Right Honourable and Honourable the Scotch Representatives in the House of Commons," in protest against the excise laws which he declares favor "the blackguard Smuggler" and the "chuffie Vintner (Fat-faced Wine Seller)" who get wealthy because of the duty charged on whisky. In a later edition, a signed footnote states that the poem "was wrote before the act anent the Scotch Distilleries of Session 1786; for which Scotland and the author return their most grateful thanks." Apparently his plea, or the general Scotch protest, brought a reduction in taxes, which, in 1789, he could accept appointment as exciseman, to help collect. The poem begins with his appeal addressed to the sober and serious representatives of the boroughs and shires on behalf of his Muse, now hoarse from screeching prosaic verse:

> Ye Irish Lords, ye Knights and Squires,
> Who represent our brughs and shires,
> An' doucely manage our affairs
>   In Parliament,
> To you a simple Bardie's prayers
>   Are humbly sent.

He wants them told that "Scotland an' me's in great affliction/ E'er sin' they laid that curst restriction/ On Aquavitae." He provides a new rhyme for "whisky," "pliskie," meaning a trick, as he declares that ever since they "play'd her that pliskie," she's "like to rin red-wud (stark mad) about her Whisky." In the Postscript, Burns concedes that the half-starved slaves in warmer climes may drink their wine, unenvied by Scotland who "blythe an' frisky/ Eyes her free-born martial boys/ Tak aff their Whisky." And in conclusion, Burns writes:

> Sages their solemn een may steek,
> An' raise a philosophic reek,
> An' physically causes seek,
>   In clime an' season;
> But tell me Whisky's name in Greek.
>   I'll tell the reason.

> Scotland, my auld, respected Mither!
> Tho' whyles ye moistify your leather,
> Till whare ye sit, on craps o' heather,
>   Ye tine your dam:
> **Freedom and Whisky gang thegither!**
>   Tak aft your dram!

Freely they stood who stood, and fell who fell

Source: PARADISE LOST (Book III, l. 102)
Author: John Milton (1608-1674)
First published: 1667
Type of work: Epic poem

Context: Milton begins the third book with an address to God as light, and says that he has just worked his way up through the darkness of chaos from hell, where the rebelling Satan and his hosts had been hurled when they lost the battle in heaven. He then reflects upon his blindness, mentioning other blind poets and some blind philosophers. As the acquisition of knowledge on his part is wholly closed to him through the agency of sight, he will have to depend upon his mind: inner light will have to take the place of external light. Milton then turns his attention to God, enthroned in the empyrean; He looks down on earth, where the newly created man and woman live in joy and love in the solitude of the garden. He sees Satan, weary from his arduous journey through chaos, ready to land on the earth to begin the attempt to ruin mankind. God addresses His Son, telling Him that Satan has come to seduce mankind; he will succeed in his attempt, but his revenge will rebound upon himself. He will succeed in perverting mankind, because man will disobey the one command that has been given to him:

> So will fall
> He and his faithless progeny: whose fault?
> Whose but his own? ingrate, he had of me
> All he could have; I made him just and right,
> Sufficient to have stood, though free to fall.
> Such I created all th'ethereal powers
> And spirits, both them who stood and them who failed;
> **Freely they stood who stood, and fell who fell.**
> Not free, what proof could they have given sincere
> Of true allegiance, constant faith or love,
> Where only what they needs must do, appeared,
> Not what they would? What praise could they receive?
> . . .

Freely we serve, because we freely love

Source: PARADISE LOST (Book V, ll. 538-539)
Author: John Milton (1608-1674)
First published: 1667
Type of work: Epic poem

Context: After Adam and Eve have performed their morning devotions, they see through the trees the glorious shape of Raphael approaching them. Adam tells Eve to prepare a meal; Eve does so by collecting all kinds of fruits and pressing out unfermented grape juice. Adam bids Raphael welcome and offers him what Eve has prepared; for a while they talk, and then Raphael explains that angels require food, just as man does. Milton is here considering the angels as a link between God and man in the great chain of being, and therefore composed of rarefied matter instead of pure spirit. Raphael further explains that the angels have all the

314

senses that man has. Finer fruits grow in heaven than on earth, but Raphael will by no means spurn the earthly produce: all things proceed from God, and they are all good until perverted. He explains gradations of being and says that man functions by means of reason and some intuition, the angels by intuition and some reason. He says that man may, through ascending certain steps, become ethereal if he remains obedient. Adam wants to know how he and Eve can possibly become disobedient. Raphael explains that as they are at the moment happy, let them thank God, Who made them so; if they remain happy, they will be so only through obedience: they were made perfect, but not immutable; their wills are free to do whatever they wish, as is true of the angels.

> Our voluntary service He requires,
> Not our necessitated, such with Him
> Finds no acceptance, nor can find, for how
> Can hearts, not free, be tried whether they serve
> Willing or no, who will but what they must
> By destiny, and can no other choose?
> Myself and all th'angelic host that stand
> In sight of God enthroned, our happy state
> Hold, as you yours, while our obedience holds;
> On other surety none; **freely we serve,**
> **Because we freely love,** as in our will
> To love or not; in this we stand or fall:
> And some are fallen, to disobedience fallen,
> And so from heaven to deepest hell; O fall
> From what high state of bliss into what woe!

. . .

A friend may well be reckoned the masterpiece of nature

Source: FRIENDSHIP
Author: Ralph Waldo Emerson (1803-1882)
First published: 1841
Type of work: Moral essay

Context: Friends, says Emerson, cannot be bought, cannot be looked for; they come unsought with the gift of kindliness and affection that produces a metamorphosis in the world. Indeed, says Emerson, "Let the soul be assured that somewhere in the universe it should rejoin its friend, and it would be content and cheerful alone for a thousand years." Friendship, suggests the essayist, is a gift of God, and "like the immortality of the soul, is too good to be believed." With a friend we may be sincere, for one of the two elements of friendship is truth. One may indeed, says Emerson, think aloud in the presence of a friend, putting aside "even those undermost garments of dissimulation, courtesy, and second thought." The other element of friendship, as Emerson sees it, is tenderness. But it is in his discussion of truth as one of the two qualities of friendship that the quotation appears. He says that a man in solitude is sincere, but that except when we are with friends, hypocrisy appears whenever other persons are present. Ordinarily we "parry and fend the approach of our fellow-man by compliments, by gossip, by amusements, by affairs."

Emerson says he once knew a man who "under a certain religious frenzy" put off the drapery of social graces and spoke to the conscience of every person he met; and people thought the man must be insane. Eventually, however, the man's sincerity was met by equal sincerity, and that situation is unusual in the world:

> . . . But to most of us society shows not its face and eye, but its side and its back. . . . Almost every man we meet requires some civility—requires to be humored; he has some fame, some talent, some whim of religion or philanthropy in his head that is not to be questioned, and which spoils all conversation with him. But a friend is a sane man who exercises not my ingenuity, but me. My friend gives me entertainment without requiring any stipulation on my part. A friend therefore is a sort of paradox in nature. I who alone am, I who see nothing in nature whose existence I can affirm with equal evidence to my own, behold now the semblance of my being, in all its height, variety, and curiosity, reiterated in a foreign form; so that **a friend may well be reckoned the masterpiece of nature.**

From a single crime know the nation!

Source: THE AENEID (Book II, as translated by John Jackson)
Author: Virgil (Publius Vergilius Maro, 70-19 B.C.)
First transcribed: 29-19 B.C.
Type of work: Epic poem

Context: Publius Vergilius Maro, heir to a prosperous family of Northern Italy, and born a few decades before the end of Rome's Golden Age, received an excellent education and the friendship of some of Rome's most cultured and powerful leaders. Through their urging, he began at the age of forty to compose an epic Homeric poem honoring Rome and his friend, the Emperor Augustus. In the story, Aeneas, fleeing from Troy, was driven by storms to Carthage, the city favored by his enemy Juno. Venus, to befriend him, made Queen Dido fall in love with him. During a welcoming feast, the queen urged Aeneas to tell of his adventures. In Book II he commences his account of the fall of Troy, at the moment when the Danaans, or Greeks, have sailed away, leaving on the shore, "with Pallas' celestial skill to aid, a horse, mountain-huge, and interwove the flanks with hewn pine—an offering, they feigned for their safe return." Inside were "weaponed soldiery," a treacherous trick, contrary to fair fighting, that destroyed the reputation for honor and chivalry of the Greek warriors who had taken part in the ten years' siege. While the Trojans are debating what to do with the horse, a prisoner is brought before them. He tells them that the Greeks had built the wooden horse, so big that it could not be moved, intending it to remain on the shore while they go home to make sacrifices, after which they will return and conquer Troy. The destruction of the city can be averted only if the Phrygians (Trojans) get the wooden horse inside their city. In this way Virgil describes the arrival of the treacherous bearer of the false proph-ecy about the horse, a young warrior who says he is the escaped victim of the sacrifice demanded by the gods. Achaea, actually land around the Gulf of Corinth, here stands for all of Greece. Its Greek inhabitants, descended from the mythical Danaus, were sometimes called Danaans. Indicative of their well-known treachery, says Aeneas, is this episode of the Trojan horse. This same treachery occasioned another well-known expression, "I fear the Greeks, even though they bring gifts."

But, lo, in the meantime came a band of Dardan shepherds, dragging to their king, amid clamorous outcry, a youth whose hands were bound behind him. A stranger, he had thrown himself of free will in their path, that he might compass this very end and leave Troy naked before Achaea. . . . Now harken to Danaan guile, and **from a single crime know the nation!** For, as he stood in full view, unweaponed, confused, and swept his gaze round the Phrygian lines, "Alas!" he cried, "what land, what sea, now shall give me haven? . . . I have no place amid the Greeks, and the very Trojans, no less, prove foes and cry for the penalty of blood!"

From each according to his abilities, to each according to his needs

Source: CRITIQUE OF THE GOTHA PROGRAM
Author: Karl Marx (1818-1883)
First published: 1891
Type of work: Economic essay

Context: Marx is best known today, of course, as the creator of the philosophical basis of modern communism. In 1875 representatives of the two German workers' organizations met at Gotha and combined to form a single organization. The new union announced its socialistic policies and goals in an elaborate statement known as the Gotha Program. Marx regarded the entire proceeding as a useless waste of energy which should have been diverted to action rather than to talk, and he considered the statement to be vague, ambiguous, and worthless ("Every step of real movement is more important than a dozen programs"). Sick though he was, Marx wrote a searching and ruthlessly severe commentary on the

317

program statement in which he dissected every ambiguity and vagary. The Gotha Programmers had proposed that all wealth derived from labor should be equally divided among the workers who produced it; Marx pointed out that different workers produced differing amounts and had differing needs; therefore, some other method of distribution would be necessary:

> In a higher phase of communist society, after the enslaving subordination of the individual to the division of labour, and therewith also the antithesis between mental and physical labour, has vanished; . . . after the productive forces have also increased with the all-round development of the individual, and all the springs of cooperative wealth flow more abundantly—only then can the narrow horizon of bourgeois right be crossed in its entirety and society inscribe on its banners: **From each according to his ability, to each according to his needs!**

From the cradle to the grave

Source: THE PARISH REGISTER (Part III, "Burials")
Author: George Crabbe (1754-1832)
First published: 1807
Type of work: Didactic poem

Context: Crabbe was an early exponent of realism. He disliked intensely the old pastoral, rustic poetry which idealized village life and doted on rural simplicity; he was at the same time completely opposed to the developing school of romanticism, which treated the same subject in more dramatic and sentimental terms. His first major work, *The Village,* is a satirical reply to Goldsmith's *The Deserted Village;* in it and in the works that followed it, he recreates in poetry the lives and condition of the poor with stark and unflinching bluntness. It is true that he tends to exaggerate the misfortunes of these people into a picture of unrelieved agony at times, but this comes from his determination to tell their story without any coating of romance. In *The Parish Register,* as in his other poems of like nature, he surveys the inhabitants of a rural area and draws their portraits both realistically and psychologically. He characterizes them in a variety of ways: an epigrammatic comment, a skeletonized biography, or a revealing speech. This poem is a chain of connected tales; it begins with a number of births, follows the people through their lives, and ends with their death and burial. In the opening lines Crabbe announces that "The year revolves, and I again explore/ The simple annals of my parish poor." The first story under "Baptisms" is that of a girl whose child is born out of wedlock; its father, a sailor, is killed at sea. The youthful mother is abused by all and cast out by her father. Other stories follow: of those who long for children and cannot have them, and of others who have too many; of children wanted and unwanted; of ignorance, and of strange names conferred on children for incomprehensible reasons. The poem then traces out some of the lives thus inauspiciously begun, and in the third section, "Burials," brings them to a cheerless end. Crabbe begins "Burials" with the following lines:

There was, 'tis said, and I believe, a time
When humble Christians died with views sublime;
When all were ready for their faith to bleed,
But few to write or wrangle for their creed;
When lively Faith upheld the sinking heart,
And friends, assured to meet, prepared to part;
When Love felt hope, when Sorrow grew serene,
And all was comfort in the death-bed scene.
    Alas! when now the gloomy king they wait,
'Tis weakness yielding to resistless fate;
Like wretched men upon the ocean cast,
They labour hard and struggle to the last;
'Hope against hope,' and wildly gaze around,
In search of help that never shall be found:
Nor, till the last strong billow stops the breath,
Will they believe them in the jaws of Death!
    When these my Records I reflecting read,
And find what ills these numerous births succeed;
What powerful griefs these nuptial ties attend,
With what regret these painful journeys end;
When **from the cradle to the grave** I look,
Mine I conceive a melancholy book.

From the great deep to the great deep

Source: IDYLLS OF THE KING ("The Coming of Arthur," Line 410)
Author: Alfred, Lord Tennyson (1809-1892)
First published: 1869
Type of work: Narrative poem

Context: Young King Arthur presumes to seek the hand of fair Guinevere, only child of King Leodgran, who has requested and received Arthur's help in repelling both the Saxon invaders and the beast prevalent in the desolate countryside torn by petty native kings and weak Roman rulers. Bellicent, daughter of Ygerne and Gorlois, tells Leodgran of legends of the mysterious lineage of Arthur: (1) he is the son of Ygerne and Gorlois, (2) he is the son of Ygerne and King Uther, who killed Gorlois and took his wife, and (3) before his death Bleys, master of Merlin (a magician who reared Arthur), told Bellicent that on the night of the death of Uther, who wept because he had no heir, Merlin and Bleys beheld a fiery dragon-winged ship sail down from heaven, leaving a baby, whom they hailed as heir to Uther, and who is the youthful King

319

Arthur. Confronted by this riddle,   riddles:
Merlin had answered Bellicent in

"Rain, rain, and sun! a rainbow in the sky!
A young man will be wiser by and by;
An old man's wit may wander ere he die.

"Rain, rain, and sun! a rainbow on the lea!
And truth is this to me, and that to thee;
And truth or clothed or naked let it be.

"Rain, sun, and rain! and the free blossom blows:
Sun, rain, and sun! and where is he who knows?
From the great deep to the great deep he goes."

Full fathom five

Source: THE TEMPEST (Act I, sc. ii, l. 396)
Author: William Shakespeare (1564-1616)
First published: 1623
Type of work: Tragi-comedy

Context: Duke Prospero of Milan, his throne usurped by his evil brother Antonio, lives in exile on an island with his daughter Miranda and with a spirit, Ariel, and a savage, Caliban, enthralled by his powers as a sorcerer. At Prospero's behest Ariel causes a storm in which the passengers and crew of a ship, Antonio and other noblemen of Milan and Naples, are cast into the sea and then are allowed to reach Prospero's island safely. Disguised as a water nymph, Ariel, singing, bewitches young Prince Ferdinand, bringing him to Prospero and Miranda. Ariel's words—"Full fathom five thy father lies"—Ferdinand construes to mean that his father has drowned. One stanza of Ariel's song goes:

ARIEL *sings.*
Full fathom five *thy father lies,*
Of his bones are coral made.
Those are pearls that were his eyes,
Nothing of him that doth fade
But doth suffer a sea-change
Into something rich and strange.
Sea-nymphs hourly ring his knell:
[Burden within. Ding-dong.]
Hark, now I hear them—Ding-dong bell.

The further off from England the nearer is to France

Source: ALICE'S ADVENTURES IN WONDERLAND (Chapter 10)
Author: Lewis Carroll (Charles Lutwidge Dodgson, 1832-1898)
First published: 1865
Type of work: Imaginative tale for children

Context: Out rowing in 1862 with the three daughters of his dean, the Rev. Charles Dodgson, instructor in Mathematics of Christ Church College, Oxford, entertained the girls with a fantastic story whose heroine he named Alice, for little Alice Liddell. Later he wrote the story out for her, and still later, in 1865, he had it published. Into this story of another Alice, falling down a rabbit hole into a world of the unusual, the learned Oxford don packed adventures for children, and humor and whimsies for adults. A number of parodies of well-known poems are also slipped in. The wider the knowledge of the reader, the more he will get out of this tale on two levels. Some literary people boast of reading it at least once a year, as musicians like periodically to listen to Mozart, to keep their thoughts in tune. Leaving a world of reality for one where she can grow tall or small at will, and where a cheshire cat can fade away to only his grin, Alice goes on her adventures amid puns and parodies. She hears of the minnows in a "school of fish," learning Laughing and Grief, instead of Latin and Greek, after a grounding in Reeling and Writhing, with Drawling and Stretching for extras in Arts. Here under the instruction of a tortoise ("So-called because he taught us," the Gryphon explains), they study ten hours the first day, nine the next, then eight, and less and less'n lesson, all the time; they learn poems. " 'Tis the Voice of the Sluggard," has been transformed into " 'Tis the Voice of the Lobster." She hears "Twinkle, twinkle, little bat,/ How I wonder where you're at." "Beautiful Snow" becomes "Beautiful Soup, so rich and green," and Alice herself recites to the Caterpillar: "You are old, Father William," based on a serious poem, "The Old Man's Comforts," by Robert Southey. The Duchess sings the unforgettable "Speak roughly to your little boy,/ And beat him when he sneezes." At the Lobster-Quadrille, Alice hears the longest poem. The Mock Turtle, who was once a real Turtle, sings and dances, with tears streaming from his eyes, a nonsense poem about the whitings walking on the sand with a porpoise. "Every fish going on a journey," as the Mock Turtle explains in an aside, "should go with some purpose." The first and last stanzas—with the snail in the second stanza protesting that they are being thrown too far into the sea—go like this:

"Will you walk a little faster?" said a whiting to a snail,
"There's a porpoise close behind us, and he's treading on my tail.
See how eagerly the lobsters and the turtles all advance!
They are waiting on the shingle—will you come and join the dance?

Will you, wo'n't you, will you, wo'n't you,
    will you join the dance?
Will you, wo'n't you, will you wo'n't you,
    wo'n't you join the dance?"

     . . .

"What matter it how far we go?" his scaly friend replied.
"There is another shore, you know, upon the other side.
The further off from England the nearer is to France.
Then turn not pale, beloved snail, but come and join the
    dance.
    Will you, wo'n't you, will you, wo'n't you,
        will you join the dance?
    Will you, wo'n't you, will you, wo'n't you,
        will you join the dance?"

The gadding vine

Source: LYCIDAS (Line 40)
Author: John Milton (1608-1674)
First published: 1637
Type of work: Elegiac pastoral poem

Context: Lycidas is an elegy, but the basic subject is Milton, and not the dead person; the poem was written for a volume of verse in honor of Edward King, a Cambridge University student drowned in the Irish Sea. He was not an intimate friend of Milton, and the poem, in its elegiac features, is conventional rather than impassioned; it follows the pattern of the tradition of the classical pastoral elegy. Milton begins his poem by indicating, by references to laurel, myrtle, and ivy, that he is much concerned about his own poetical fame.

He then announces that Lycidas, or Edward King, is dead; he says that Lycidas was also a poet, although King's productions were only a few mediocre Latin verses. Milton indicates that he and King were fellow shepherds, that is, students at Cambridge; he refers to their feeding their sheep in the hills, although the region around Cambridge is remarkably flat. ("Gadding" means wandering.) The poet describes their taking their flocks afield, the music of the oaten pipe, the dancing of the satyrs and fauns—but there has been a change:

But O the heavy change, now thou art gone,
Now thou art gone, and never must return!
Thee shepherd, thee the woods, and desert caves,
With wild thyme and **the gadding vine** o'ergrown,
And all their echoes mourn.
The willows and the hazel copses green
Shall now no more be seen,
Fanning their joyous leaves to thy soft lays.
As killing as the canker to the rose,
Or taint-worm to the weanling herds that graze,

322

Or frost to flowers, that their gay wardrobe wear,
When first the white-thorn blows,
Such, Lycidas, thy loss to shepherd's ear.

A gallant company

Source: THE SIEGE OF CORINTH (Prologue, l. 3)
Author: George Gordon, Lord Byron (1788-1824)
First published: 1816
Type of work: Narrative poem

Context: Evidence of the change in public feeling toward Byron's poetry over a century and a half can be found in the modern attitude toward his group classified as "Tales, Chiefly Oriental." At their publication, they were bought and read by thousands. With their flow of life and magnificent egotism, they represented the revolutionary side of Byron's character, his passion for vivid color and exotic adventure. Works by Shelley and Keats were rated considerably below them by most contemporaries. But with the passing of time, a better knowledge of the East and an increasing sophistication brought realization of the falsity and melodrama of their rhetoric, and nowadays few read them. First came *The Giaour* (1813) about a female slave thrown into the sea for infidelity, and her revenge by her Venetian lover. Then *The Bride of Abydos* (1813) and *The Corsair* (1814) followed. In 1816, Byron published *The Siege of Corinth,* based on history. However, while history does tell of an explosion of 600 barrels of gunpowder in the Turkish camp, the explosion is considered an accident and not an act of vengeance by an outraged father. And Francesca and her renegade lover do not appear on the pages of the history books. The narrator begins the Prologue of his story in 1810, sitting on "Acro-Corinth's brow," the hill from which Corinth could best be seen. He recounts what happened to that city a century earlier when the Turks, who held most of Greece under Sultan Achmet (or Ahmed) III (1673–1736), were determined to capture Morea and the Ionian Islands from the Venetians. The Sultan thought it necessary first to capture the fortified city of Corinth. The protagonist in this thirty-three stanza story told in rhymed couplets of varied meters, is "Alp, the Adrian renegade," once Lanciotto, a Venetian gentleman but now wearing the turban, and eager to capture Corinth because of his love for Francesca, daughter of its governor, Minotti. As Alp paces under the walls against which an attack will soon be made, he sees a shadowy figure beside him, his Francesca, who begs him to give up his treason and return to the side of Venice. When indignantly he refuses to change loyalties again, "He turned, but she is gone! nothing is there but the column stone." Had she been real, or a ghost, or only a figment of his imagination? "Hath she sunk in the earth, or melted in air?/ He saw not––he knew not—but nothing is there." The next morning Corinth falls. Into the city dashes Alp. He finds Minotti and demands to

323

know the whereabouts of Francesca. The grieving father reports her death the previous night. While Alp is reeling from the fatal news, a shot from a nearby church slays the renegade. Minotti hastens to the church. When the Paynim host tries to capture it, "Old Minotti's hand/ Touched with the torch, the train." and the holy building, with friend and foe inside, is destroyed. The Prologue begins:

In the year since Jesus died for men,
Eighteen hundred years and ten,
We were **a gallant company,**
Riding o'er land and sailing o'er sea.
Oh, but we went merrily!
　　　　　．　．　．
Whether we lay in the cave or the shed,
Our sleep fell soft on the hardest bed.
　　　　　．　．　．
Fresh we woke upon the morrow.
　　All our thoughts and words had scope,
　　We had health, and we had hope,
Toil and travel, but no sorrow.

The game is never lost till won

Source: TALES OF THE HALL ("Gretna Green," Line 334)
Author: George Crabbe (1754-1832)
First published: 1819
Type of work: Narrative poem

Context: The Reverend George Crabbe, an early exponent of realism, disliked intensely the old rustic and pastoral poetic convention that idealized village life; he was equally averse to the newer and oversentimentalized approach of romanticism. His revolt took the form of a harsh, starkly cheerless view of rural existence and of those who endured it. At times his reaction to sentimentality is such that the lives he depicts are sagas of unrelieved anguish—an equally unrealistic point of view. His first major work was *The Village,* a satirical reply to Goldsmith's *The Deserted Village,* which emphasizes the condition of the poor. This was followed by *The Parish Register,* a chain of connected tales about the lives, from birth to death, of the poor people in Crabbe's parish. *Tales of the Hall* deals with life on a somewhat higher level of society, but the lives of its characters are for the most part unenviable. The poem is a loosely woven biography of Richard, a man whose older brother George has acquired the Hall at Binning and invited him there. Into this biography are woven the stories of various people who live at the Hall or visit there, or whose lives impinge upon those of George and Richard. In Book XV, entitled "Gretna Green," Richard meets an old friend who seems cool and distant; he asks George why this should be so. George obliges with the story of James Belwood, a young man who wed unwisely. Belwood is both weak and self-indulgent, and the girl he married, Clara, is a spoiled local beauty. To him she is but an expensive new toy; and her only desire is to be envied by other women. He had met her at a school conducted by her father. The inevitable quarrel arises; she wishes to visit her parents and he objects. The parents, meanwhile, are consumed by misgivings. The mother, feeling her daughter is a mere captive, upbraids the father. He replies, truthfully enough, that it was she who encouraged the match:

> "Had you o'erawed and check'd them when in sight,
> They would not then have ventured upon flight—
> Had you"—"Out, serpent! did you not begin?
> What! introduce, and then upbraid the sin?
> For sin it is, as I too well perceive:
> But leave me, woman, to reflection leave;
> Then to your closet fly, and on your knees
> Beg for forgiveness for such sins as these."

> "A moody morning!" with a careless air
> Replied the wife—"Why counsel me to prayer?
> I think the lord and teacher of a school
> Should pray himself, and keep his temper cool."

> Calm grew the husband when the wife was gone—
> **"The game," said he, "is never lost till won:**
> 'Tis true, the rebels fly their proper home,
> They come not nigh, because they fear to come;
> And for my purpose fear will doubtless prove
> Of more importance and effect than love, . . ."

Gates of ivory

Source: THE ODYSSEY (Book XIX, ll. 657-658, as translated by Alexander Pope)
Author: Homer (c.850 B.C.)
First transcribed: Sixth century B.C.
Type of work: Epic poem

Context: Odysseus, disguised as a beggar, finally returns to his home in Ithaca after his long absence in the Trojan War and his subsequent travels. Penelope, his wife, in questioning the dirty man before her concerning her husband's chances of returning, asks for an interpretation of a dream that she has had in which an eagle kills her twenty geese. Odysseus explains that the eagle clearly represents her husband and the geese the suitors who have plagued the seeming widow. Penelope, however, doubts the optimism of the interpretation and comments on dreams that issue from the gate of ivory and those from the gate of horn:

Hard is the task, and rare, the queen rejoin'd,
Impending destinies in dreams to find;
Immured within the silent bower of sleep,
Two portals firm the various phantoms keep:
Of ivory one; whence flit, to mock the brain,
Of winged lies a light fantastic train:
The gate opposed pellucid valves adorn,
And columns fair incased with polish'd horn:
Where images of truth for passage wait,
With visions manifest of future fate.
Not to this troop, I fear, that phantom soar'd,
Which spoke Ulysses to his realm restored:
Delusive semblance!

A gay deceiver

Source: LOVE LAUGHS AT LOCKSMITHS (Act II)
Author: George Colman, the Younger (1762-1836)
First published: 1803
Type of work: Comic opera

Context: The dramas of a hundred fifty years ago sound artificial to modern readers, and their plots are even more exaggerated. Yet they must have appealed to their contemporaries. The dramatist George Colman (or Coleman) was a successful manager of one of London's most popular theaters, the Haymarket, and some of England's most memorable actors of his time performed there. Of course, *Love Laughs at Locksmiths* is a farce, and farces are supposed to move so fast that spectators have no time to judge their logical development or lack of it. In this play, Lydia, an orphan, has been entrusted to the care of the sister of Vigil, an artist. Vigil maintains guard over her. Yet Frederick Beldare, Captain of Grenadiers, has seen her portrait and has fallen in love. He smuggles a letter to her. The captain's servant, Risk, hearing that Solomon Lob, nephew of Vigil's servant, is coming to London to visit his uncle, schemes to take his place and get into Vigil's house. In the course of the farcical action, Risk interpolates a song about a Captain bold of Halifax who deceived a certain Miss Bailey. Thereupon, she hanged herself. As a ghost, she came back to haunt her betrayer. To exorcise her, he gave her a pound note so that she could secure for herself proper burial. The song has nothing to do with the action of the play. Risk's Captain has honorable intentions in his schemes to get word of his love to Lydia. The second stanza of the song goes:

One night, betimes, he went to rest,
For he had caught a fever;
Says he: "I am a handsome man,
But I'm **a gay deceiver**."

326

His candle, just at twelve o'clock,
Began to burn quite palely;
A ghost stepp'd up to his bed-side,
And said, "Behold Miss Bailey!
Oh! Miss Bailey!
Unfortunate Miss Bailey!"

Gay Lothario

Source: THE FAIR PENITENT (Act V, sc. i)
Author: Nicholas Rowe (1674-1718)
First published: 1703
Type of work: Dramatic tragedy

Context: The Fair Penitent is a domestic tragedy; the playwright in his prologue styles it "A melancholy tale of private woes." It is the story of a young woman who is led astray, the first of Nicholas Rowe's "she-tragedies," plays based on man's inhumanity to woman. The woman of this play is beautiful young Calista, a native of Genoa, who falls in love with Lothario. The immoral Lothario, the archetype of the inconstant lover, steals into Calista's chamber and spends a night with her; but when the girl speaks of marriage, Lothario laughs and leaves her. Despite his treatment, Calista continues to be infatuated with him and is forced to allow an interview with him on her wedding day, after her father has given her in marriage to Altamont. Lothario visits her and is discovered by her husband, who has long been Lothario's enemy. In the fight that ensues, Lothario is killed, and Calista, after a scene with her husband and her father, runs out. At the opening of the fifth act of the play, Calista is found in a room hung with black, keeping watch over Lothario's body, which lies on a bier. Though the dead man has ruined her, Calista still loves him. A mournful song is heard, and Calista picks up a devotional book, placed beside her to encourage her penitence. After glancing at it, she throws the book from her, to look at a skull and bones which lie upon a table. From contemplating the bones she turns to the corpse of Lothario, to gaze upon it in awful contemplation:

CALISTA [*throwing away the book.*]
I have more real anguish in my heart
Than all their pedant discipline e'er knew.
What charnel has been rifled for these bones?
Fie! this is pageantry;—they look uncouthly,
But what of that, if he or she that owned 'em
Safe from disquiet sit, and smile to see
The farce their miserable relics play?
But here's a sight is terrible indeed;
Is this the haughty, gallant, **gay Lothario?**

327

That dear perfidious—Ah!—how pale he looks!
How grim with clotted blood, and those dead eyes!

A general flavor of mild decay

Source: THE DEACON'S MASTERPIECE (Stanza 9)
Author: Oliver Wendell Holmes (1809-1894)
First published: 1858
Type of work: Satirical poem

Context: Holmes, who was no admirer of Calvinistic theology, which had played so prominent a role in the history of New England, satirizes the logical structure of the Calvinists in this poem, and, in a way, laughs it out of people's serious thoughts, as it had long since ceased to be a vital force in their lives. Like the fabulous shay, Calvinism had begun in the most logical fashion theologians could devise; no one was ever able to break it down; but like the shay, that logical structure collapsed in importance, leaving the theologians in the dust. The deacon's masterpiece, built of the finest materials for each portion of its structure, lasts for a hundred years; it was finished by its maker on Lisbon Earthquake Day, November 1, 1755, and is still all in one piece on the hundredth anniversary of that date:

Little of all we value here
Wakes on the morn of its hundredth year
Without both feeling and looking queer.
In fact, there's nothing that keeps its youth,
So far as I know, but a tree and truth.
. . .
FIRST OF NOVEMBER,—the Earthquake-day—
There are traces of age in the one-hoss shay,
A general flavor of mild decay,
But nothing local, as one may say,
There couldn't be,—for the Deacon's art
Had made it so like in every part
That there wasn't a chance for one to start.

A general union of total dissent

Source: A FABLE FOR CRITICS (Line 733)
Author: James Russell Lowell (1819-1891)
First published: 1848
Type of work: Satirical poem

Context: Lowell began *A Fable for Critics,* he says in his first Preface, "to please only myself and my own private fancy." Readers have, for several generations now, been pleased with his humorous satire—pleasant

328

enough, and usually true to the mark, of Emerson, Thoreau, Bryant, Whittier, Hawthorne, Cooper, Poe, and others well known at the time who have slipped, unlike those named, into a literary Limbo. Though his own reputation as a poet has diminished in the decades since his death, Lowell's *Fable,* as well as some selections from *The Biglow Papers,* is still, at least in part, often read. The quotation about "general union of total dissent" is found in Lowell's comments about Theodore Parker, whom he calls the "Orson of parsons":

Here comes Parker, the Orson of parsons, a man
Whom the Church undertook to put under her ban
(The Church of Socinus, I mean),—his opinions
Being So-(ultra)-cinian, they shocked the Socinians;
They believed—faith, I'm puzzled—I think I may call
Their belief a believing in nothing at all,
Or something of that sort; I know they all went
For **a general union of total dissent:**
He went a step farther; without cough or hem,
He frankly avowed he believed not in them;
And, before he could be jumbled up or prevented,
From their orthodox kind of dissent he dissented.
There was heresy here, you perceive, for the right
Of privately judging means simply that light
Has been granted to *me,* for deciding on *you;*
And in happier times, before Atheism grew,
The deed contained clauses for cooking you too.

Genius does what it must, and talent does what it can

Source: LAST WORDS OF A SENSITIVE SECOND-RATE POET
Author: Owen Meredith (Edward Robert Bulwer, 1st Earl of Lytton, 1831-1891)
First published: 1868
Type of work: Poetry

Context: The Earl of Lytton played an important part in the British diplomatic world. His father, the first Baron Lytton, is remembered for his novels *Eugene Aram* (1832), *The Last Days of Pompeii* (1834) and *Rienzi* (1835). The son got his early education at Harrow, where he wrote his first poetry at the age of twelve. After Harrow, instead of going on to a university, he was privately educated by tutors, with emphasis on languages, fortunately, because he later represented his country in such places as Paris, Athens, Florence, Vienna, and Madrid. He began as secretary to his uncle in the embassy at Washington, where he wrote most of his poetry, though none was published until 1860. Since it was not appropriate for a diplomat to write poetry, he signed his work "Owen Meredith," a concoction of Christian names of earlier members of his family. In 1874 he achieved a literary reputation with the publication of *Fables in Song*. Then he revised and added poems for two more collections, one in 1885 and a posthumous collection in 1892. In the meantime, he had been Secretary of the British Legation in Copenhagen (1863), British Minister to Lisbon (1872), Viceroy of India (1876–1880), and finally Ambassador to Paris (1887–1891). During his lifetime, critics ad-mired his poetry for its brilliancy of idea, phrase, and description, but complained that such brilliancy eventually became tiring. One critic lamented that, in spite of being appointed Viceroy of India by Disraeli, Lord Lytton is chiefly remembered for his poem *Lucile* (1860), which the critic rated as "a vast, stale, Victorian piece of poetry." Perhaps it lives in memory for the couplet:

> We may live without friends; we may live without books;
> But a civilized man cannot live without cooks.

Considerably different is his "Last Words of a Sensitive Second-Rate Poet," that appeared in Book IX, "Here and There: Romances and Ballads," of his *Chronicles and Characters* (London, 1868). In it, the poet is dying with only his faithful friend, Will, beside him, weary from three days of vigil. The poet thinks of their youth together, their days of girl-courting, and is reminded of one girl who used the poet and left him. But he must not think bitterly of her.

> There can be no space for the ghost of her face down in this
>   narrow room,
> And the mole is blind, and the worm is mute, and there must be
>   rest in the tomb.

In his youth, the poet was optimistic and confident, with hopes of moving the world, though unable himself to stand firm. Now he begs his friend to burn everything he has written. Perhaps he would have been more popular and successful if his poetry had been less melancholic. All he knows is that he has failed, so he waits patiently for death.

> . . . The world, that had paused to listen awhile, because the first
>   notes were gay,
> Pass'd on its way with a sneer in a smile: "Has he nothing fresher
>   to say?
> This poet's mind was a weedy flower that presently comes to
>   nought!"
> For the world was not so sad but what my song was sadder, it
>   thought.
> Comfort me not. For if aught be worst than failure from over-
>   stress
> Of a life's prime purpose, it is to sit down content with a little
>   success.

Talk not of genius baffled. Genius is master of man.
Genius does what it must, and Talent does what it can.
Blot out my name, that the spirits of Shakspeare and Milton and
 Burns
Look not down on the praises of fools with a pity my soul yet
 spurns.
And yet, had I only the trick of an aptitude shrewd of its kind,
 I should have lived longer, I think, more merry of heart and of
 mind.

Genius is of no country

Source: THE ROSCIAD (Line 207)
Author: Charles Churchill (1731-1764)
First published: 1761
Type of work: Satiric poem

Context: A dissipated clergyman, Churchill won both fame and notoriety as a satiric poet during the last four years of his life. He was associated with and defended John Wilkes, the unscrupulous editor of the *North-Briton.* Much of the harsh and vitriolic nature of Churchill's satire seems to have been formed by this association. In *The Rosciad,* his first important poem, Churchill attacked a number of theatrical personalities with such witty satire that it was at one time regarded as the most important satiric work between those of Pope and Byron. Early in the poem a youth representing Churchill's friend Robert Lloyd speaks forth against the faddish praise of classical culture to the exclusion of native English arts:

"But more than just to other countries grown,
Must we turn base apostates to our own?
Where do these words of Greece and Rome excell,
That England may not please the ear as well?
What mighty magic's in the place or air,
That all perfection needs must center there?
In states, let strangers blindly be preferr'd;
In state of letters, Merit should be heard.
Genius is of no country, her pure ray
Spreads all abroad, as gen'ral as the day:
Foe to restraint, from place to place she flies,
And may hereafter e'en in Holland rise."

Gentle dullness ever loves a joke

Source: THE DUNCIAD (Book II, l. 34)
Author: Alexander Pope (1688-1744)
First published: 1728-1743
Type of work: Satiric poem

331

Context: This long, satiric mock-epic describes the establishment of the kingdom of dullness ruled over by the King of the Dunces. In various stages of the revision of the poem over a number of years Pope appointed several different scribblers to the throne of dullness, depending upon whom he was most irritated with at the moment. Dozens of other minor Grub Street scribblers and hacks come under Pope's withering satiric fire in the course of the poem. Book I invokes the Goddess of Dullness, describes her great empire and her college within the city of London, and closes with her proclamation of Cibber, in the 1742 version, as the new King of the Dunces. In Book II the newly proclaimed king is honored with public games and sports, all in satiric imitation of Virgil's *Aeneid.* As this Book opens, the king on his throne is surrounded by admiring spectators:

> Amid that area wide they took their stand,
> Where the tall may-pole once o'er-look'd the Strand;
> But now (so ANNE and Piety ordain)
> A Church collects the saints of Drury-lane.
>   With Authors, Stationers obey'd the call,
> (The field of glory is a field for all.)
> Glory, and gain, th' industrious tribe provoke;
> And **gentle Dulness ever loves a joke.**
> A Poet's form she plac'd before their eyes,
> And bade the nimblest racer seize the prize;
> No meagre, muse-rid mope, adust and thin,
> In a dun night-gown of his own loose skin;
> But such a bulk as no twelve bards could raise,
> Twelve starv'ling bards of these degen'rate days.

The gentle mind by gentle deeds is known

Source: THE FAERIE QUEENE (Book VI, Canto 3, stanza 1)
Author: Edmund Spenser (c.1552-1599)
First published: 1590
Type of work: Allegorical poem

Context: The concept of courtesy is the major theme of Book VI. In the first portion of this book, courtesy is exemplified in the actions of Calidore, the knight of Courtesy. While on his search for the Blatant Beast, Slander, he finds Priscilla weeping beside her wounded knight, Aladine. A lustful knight had attacked the unarmed Aladine while he and Priscilla were making love; she had escaped by hiding quickly. Calidore assures her that their attacker has already been slain by Tristram. Calidore then straps Aladine on his shield; he and Priscilla carry the wounded knight in this manner to the nearby castle of Aldus, Aladine's father. Spenser then comments that Calidore's actions have been an excellent example of true courtesy. The theme of this episode is expressed in Spenser's quotation from Chaucer (*Canterbury Tales,* "Wife of Bath's Tale," 1. 1170):

True is, that whilome that good Poet sayd,
The gentle minde by gentle deeds is knowne:
For a man by nothing is so well betrayd,
As by his manners, in which plaine is showne
Of what degree and what race he is growne.
For seldom seene, a trotting Stalion get
An ambling Colt, that is his proper owne:
So seldome seene, that one in baseness set
Doth noble courage shew, with courteous manners met.

The gift of gab

Source: THE OLD NAVY (Stanza 1)
Author: Frederick Marryat (1792-1848)
First published: 1837
Type of work: Sea chantey

Context: A much-quoted poem by Capt. Marryat appears most frequently with its first line as title. It describes a battle between the British and the French, perhaps just such a battle as midshipman Marryat experienced when he ran away from his family in 1806 and shipped aboard the frigate *Impérieuse* under Lord Cochrane (1775–1860), who later fought for Chilean independence. Marryat described another such naval battle in a famous chapter of *The King's Own* (1830). A carronade, getting its name from Carron in Scotland where it was first forged, was a mortar-like cannon, carried on the ship's upper deck for use at short range. "Gab," from Middle English *gabben,* "to mock or talk foolishly," is colloquial for "babbling." Whether it is a gift or a curse depends on whether one is uttering it or listening to it. "Odds bobs" is a euphemism for the oath "God's body!" The poem begins and ends, after the sea-fight, as follows:

The captain stood on the carronade—"First lieutenant," says he,
"Send all my merry men aft here, for they must list to me:
I haven't **the gift of the gab,** my sons—because I'm bred to the
    sea;
That ship there is a Frenchman, who means to fight with we. . . ."
           • • •
Our captain sent for all of us; "My merry men," said he,
"I haven't **the gift of the gab,** my lads, but yet I thankful be;
You've done your duty handsomely, each man stood to his gun;
If you hadn't, you villains, as sure as day, I'd have flogged each
    mother's son.
Odds bobs, hammer and tongs, as long as I'm at sea,
I'll fight 'gainst every odds—and I'll gain the victory!"

Gird up thy loins

Source: JOB 38:3
Author: Unknown
First transcribed: c.900-500 B.C.
Type of work: Religious saga

Context: Job, a good man who enjoys prosperity and many sons and daughters, is said to be a fine example of the God-fearing and God-worshiping man. But Satan says that Job is good only because he has always enjoyed good fortune, that he will turn against God if he is visited by adversity. Responding to Satan's challenge, God permits Satan to take away Job's wealth and to slay his sons and daughters; still Job does not turn against God. Next Satan, with God's agreement, visits physical misery upon Job; still Job refuses to turn against God and curse Him. Job is visited by men who claim that he must have been a great sinner in the past, inasmuch as God does not afflict a man without cause. But Job maintains, truthfully, that he is a good man, that there is no reason for him to receive this treatment as punishment. He is patient and enduring, but he does not understand. Elihu, one of the men who visit him, speaks of God's great power, which controls the winds, the snow, the rain, even the passing cycle of the seasons. He warns Job that man cannot understand God, although God will listen to the cry of the submissive man. He also warns that God will not afflict a man without cause. When Elihu finishes speaking, God Himself, out of a whirlwind, speaks to Job; when Job replies submissively after God is finished, God grants him his well-being and prosperity once again:

> Then the LORD answered Job out of the whirlwind, and said,
> Who is this that darkeneth counsel by words without knowledge?
> **Gird up** now **thy loins** like a man; for I will demand of thee, and answer thou me.
> Where wast thou when I laid the foundations of the earth? declare, if thou hast understanding
> Who hath laid the measures thereof, if thou knowest? or who hath stretched the line upon it?
> Whereupon are the foundations thereof fastened? or who laid the corner stone thereof;
> When the morning stars sang together, and all the sons of God shouted for joy?

Give him a little earth for charity

Source: KING HENRY THE EIGHTH (Act IV, sc. ii, l.23)
Author: William Shakespeare (1564-1616)
First published: 1623
Type of work: Historical drama

Context: Cardinal Wolsey, the son of a butcher, has risen in the Church and claims the ear of King Henry VIII. In his duties as Lord Chancellor he has sent far away from Henry all those who oppose his ideas and of whom he is jealous or afraid. He has made himself enormously wealthy, and he even desires to rise to Pope. He sends Buckingham to his death and also rouses Henry against Queen Katharine. She, however, sees through his designs. Henry begins to be conscience-stricken about his marriage to Katharine, his brother's widow. He has met Anne Bullen at a party given by Wolsey and desires to marry her. Wolsey has other plans, but Henry desires Anne and marries her in spite of Wolsey. Through an error, Henry finds papers tallying Wolsey's vast wealth and revealing his desires in the Church. He denounces the cardinal, who, seeing his imminent downfall, only wishes he had been a true churchman. Northumberland arrests him; he goes to the abbey at Leicester, and there, after his overthrow, finds himself, and, as a penitent, dies, forgiven by Katharine.

• • •

KATHARINE

Did'st thou not tell me Griffith, as thou led'st me,
That the great child of honor, Cardinal Wolsey,
Was dead?

• • •

GRIFFITH

He fell sick suddenly, and grew so ill
He could not sit his mule.

• • •

At last, with easy roads, he came to Leicester,
Lodged in the abbey; where the reverend abbot
With all his covent honourably received him;
To whom he gave these words, o, Father Abbot,
An old man, broken with the storms of state
Is come to lay his weary bones among ye;
Give him a little earth for charity.

Give me man as he is not to be

Source: MY FIRST ACQUAINTANCE WITH POETS, BY WILLIAM HAZLITT
Author: Charles Lamb (1775-1834)
First published: 1823
Type of work: Attributed comment

Context: Hazlitt was a harsh and bitter man, badly maladjusted socially, and he quarreled with both enemies and friends; there were many of the former, few of the latter. It appears that he disliked nearly everyone and that the sentiment was repaid in kind. In spite of his social handicap he had a keen mind, was a brilliant essayist, and had a deep appreciation of beauty. He tried first to become a painter, studying in France, and this background made him one of the first aesthetic critics. He was a sensitive man; his reactions to the objects of his literary and dramatic criticism were usually sound and just. Although he later became somewhat estranged from the poets, he was at one time very close to them. His essay, "My First Acquaintance with Poets," reveals the deep respect, even reverence, with which he regarded those he admired. In it he describes his meeting with Coleridge and Wordsworth. The vivid picture he gives of these two great poets at the beginning of their fame is of considerable value in gaining an understanding of them. Hazlitt tells us that he walked ten miles through freezing mud in January, 1798, to hear Coleridge preach, and that he was transfixed by the power of the man's imagination and imagery; so impressed was he that he arranged a meeting and a visit at the poet's home. He recounts their conversations and his subsequent introduction to Wordsworth. It is evident that these days with Coleridge are unforgettable and that they have furnished an inspiration for the literary life Hazlitt is to undertake.

In a day or two after we arrived at Stowey, we set out, I on my return home, and he for Germany. It was a Sunday morning, and he was to preach that day for Dr. Toulmin of Taunton. I asked him if he had prepared anything for the occasion? He said he had not even thought of the text, but should as soon as we parted. I did not go to hear him,—this was a fault,—but we met in the evening at Bridgewater. The next day we had a long day's walk to Bristol, and sat down, I recollect, by a well-side on the road, to cool ourselves and satisfy our thirst, when Coleridge repeated to me some descriptive lines from his tragedy of *Remorse;* which I must say became his mouth and that occasion better than they, some years after, did Mr. Elliston's and the Drury-lane boards. . . .

I saw no more of him for a year or two, during which period he had been wandering in the Hartz Forest in Germany; and his return was cometary, meteorous, unlike his setting out. It was not till some time after that I knew his friends Lamb and Southey. The last always appears to me (as I first saw him) with a commonplace-book under his arm, and the first with a *bon-mot* in his mouth. It was at Godwin's that I met him with Holcroft and Coleridge, where they were disputing fiercely which was the best— *Man as he was, or man as he is to be.* **"Give me,"** says Lamb, **"man as he is not to be."** This saying was the beginning of a friendship between us, which I believe still continues. . . .

Glad confident morning

Source: THE LOST LEADER (Stanza 2)
Author: Robert Browning (1812-1889)
First published: 1845
Type of work: Lyric poem

Context: "The Lost Leader" is gen-   erally thought of as referring in its

336

first two lines—"Just for a handful of silver he left us,/ Just for a riband to stick in his coat"—to two events in William Wordsworth's life: his acceptance of a pension in 1842 and of the Laureateship in 1843. Whether or not it is associated with Wordsworth's shift from fiery liberalism in youth to staid political conservatism in old age, the whole poem shows Browning's scorn for any desertion of principles for gain. John Greenleaf Whittier's "Ichabod" is a similar poem inspired by Daniel Webster's seeming political opportunism when he supported the Missouri Compromise and the Fugitive Slave Bill in 1850. In "The Lost Leader" Browning's first stanza shows the poet's shock and sense of loss at his leader's apostasy. The closing lines of the second stanza contrast the present symbolic darkness with the brightness of an earlier day:

Life's night begins: let him never come back to us!
  There would be doubt, hesitation and pain,
Forced praise on our part—the glimmer of twilight,
  Never **glad confident morning** again!
Best fight on well, for we taught him—strike gallantly,
  Menace our heart ere we master his own;
Then let him receive the new knowledge and wait us,
  Pardoned in heaven, the first by the throne!

Gladly would he learn and gladly teach

Source: THE CANTERBURY TALES (Prologue, l. 308)
Author: Geoffrey Chaucer (1343?-1400)
First transcribed: c.1387-1392
Type of work: Collection of tales

Context: The Canterbury pilgrims, having met by chance at the Tabard Inn in Southwark on their way to the shrine of Thomas à Becket at Canterbury, decide to tell tales to make the journey less boring. In the Prologue, Chaucer, to establish the tale-telling framework and to identify the participants of his work, describes vividly his pilgrims. Among the memorable characters is a clerk, or student, noted for his dedication to acquiring and sharing knowledge.

A CLERK ther was of Oxenford also,
That unto logyk hadde longe ygo.
As leene was his hors as is a rake,
And he nas nat right fat, I undertake,
But looked holwe, and therto sobrely.

· · ·

Noght a word spak he moore than was neede,
And that was seyed in forme and reverence,
And short and quyk and ful of hy sentence;

337

Sownynge in moral vertu was his speche,
And **gladly wolde he lerne and gladly teche.**

The gladsome light of jurisprudence

Source: INSTITUTES: COMMENTARY UPON LITTLETON (First Institute, Epilogue)
Author: Sir Edward Coke (1552-1634)
First published: 1628
Type of work: Legal commentary

Context: Perhaps remembering his own perplexity as a young legal student preparing to become a lawyer, over the jargon of the profession, Edward Coke took time, after he rose to be the first man to be called Lord Chief Justice of England, to take a second look at one of the principle textbooks. Thomas Littleton (1422–1481) was a jurist whose experiences as Justice of the Assize and Judge of Common Pleas gave him experience from which to compile the earliest treatise on the English Law ever printed (1481), the volume *Tenures,* which provided in legal French a complete coverage of English land laws and which became fundamental in legal education in England. Coke reissued the classic volume with Littleton's French version in one column, a second column with an English rendering of the points of law, and a third column of his own comments, explanations, and clarifications. In his Introduction Lord Coke encouraged the young student by remarking that if he did not understand the point of the original author or the commentator on his first reading, he should try the difficult passage again at a later date. After 749 sections, with commentaries, Coke ended with an Epilogue of encouragement and stimulus. Like any teacher, he comments that he might have provided an index or tables to help students more quickly find some particular section, but he thought they would remember the material better if they compiled their own. Either he had a second thought or someone else took pity on students, because the second edition, in 1633, includes a complete index. Here are Coke's closing words:

I had once intended, for the ease of our Student, to have made a table to these Institutes; but when I considered that Tables and Abridgements are most profitable to them that make them, I have left that worke to every Studious Reader. And for a Farewell to our jurisprudent, I wish unto him **the gladsome light of Jurisprudence,** the loveliness of temperance, the stability of fortitude and the soliditie of Justice.

The glass of fashion

Source: HAMLET (Act III, sc. i, l. 161)
Author: William Shakespeare (1564-1616)
First published: 1603
Type of work: Dramatic tragedy

Context: Hamlet, Prince of Denmark, in the position of having to avenge the death of his murdered father, feels himself oppressed by the whole court. Even Ophelia, his love, seems to be a part of the plot against him. Consequently, he berates her in such a vicious manner that when he leaves she can only think that he, the very mirror of the ideal, is mad. Her description of Hamlet as he was before the death of his father is the picture of the idealized Renaissance Prince.

OPHELIA

O what a noble mind is here o'erthrown!
The courtier's, soldier's, scholar's, eye, tongue, sword,
Th' expectancy and rose of the fair state,
The glass of fashion, and the mould of form,
The observed of all observers, quite, quite down,
And I of ladies most deject and wretched,
That sucked the honey of his musicked vows,
Now see that noble and most sovereign reason,
Like sweet bells jangled, out of tune and harsh;
That unmatched form and feature of blown youth
Blasted with ecstasy. O woe is me
T' have seen what I have seen, see what I see.

The glory and the nothing of a name

Source: CHURCHILL'S GRAVE (Line 43)
Author: George Gordon, Lord Byron (1788-1824)
First published: 1816
Type of work: Elegiac poem

Context: Charles Churchill (1731–1764) must have won the admiration of satirical Byron by his biting wit. Though he had died long before Byron's time, his writings, especially his political satires, were still admired. As a young man, son of a Westminster curate, Churchill was refused admittance to Oxford and Cambridge, probably because he had married at the age of seventeen. He tried for the position of postmaster at Merton, but was turned down, allegedly because of lack of a classical training. However, he was ordained a priest in 1756. His was a riotous life. From his acquaintance with the theater and its performers, he published the anonymous *Rosciad* (1761), influenced by Pope's *Dunciad*. In it he lauded Garrick and several of the actresses, but unmercifully criticized many contemporary actors with such lines as "He mouths a sentence as curs mouth a bone." Divorced in 1761, Churchill led a life of dissipation. He gave up his Church offices in 1763 to write campaign literature for John Wilkes (1727–1797), an English political reformer, the idol of the mobs. Wilkes was expelled from Parliament in 1764 and exiled to France. On his trip to visit his friend, Churchill died in Boulogne of a fever. His body was brought back across the Channel to Dover and buried in St. Martin Cemetery, beneath an inscription: "Life to the last enjoyed, here Churchill lies." About to leave England for the last time, Byron visited his grave. Then he tried to write a poem to him in imitation of Churchill's style, with its beauties and its defects. He also included some touches mocking Wordsworth. At the ill-kept tomb, Byron sees a gardener who tells him he does not know who is buried there. The death happened before the gardener's time, and he cannot read the name. But he does know that strangers come to pay their respects to the dead man and pay to the sexton a few pennies, and that some have said the dead man was the most famous writer of his day. So Churchill has both glory and namelessness. Byron gives the sexton a few silver coins he can scarcely spare, and writes: "Let profane ones smile because my homely phrase the truth would tell." Here is the beginning and the conclusion of the forty-three-line poem.

> I stood beside the grave of him who blazed
>   The comet of a season, and I saw
> The humblest of all sepulchres, and gazed
>   With not the less of sorrow and of awe
> On that neglected turf and quiet stone . . .
>   • • •
> You are the fools, not I—for I did dwell
> With a deep thought, and with a soften'd eye,
> On that Old Sexton's natural homily,
> In which there was Obscurity and Fame,—
> **The Glory and the Nothing of a Name.**

The glory, jest, and riddle of the world

Source: AN ESSAY ON MAN (Epistle II, l. 18)
Author: Alexander Pope (1688-1744)
First published: 1733-1734
Type of work: Philosophical poem

Context: An Essay on Man is a philosophical poem which Pope addressed to Henry St. John, Lord Bolingbroke. The subject of Epistle II of the poem is the nature of man and his place in the universe. Like many of his contemporaries in the eighteenth century, Pope saw man as one link in the great chain of being, holding a middle place in that chain. Since man cannot know or understand the states of being above himself, he should

340

study himself; or, as Pope puts it, "The proper study of mankind is man." In this epistle Pope, following his own advice, examines man and his nature. He sees that man has greatness and power on the one hand, but weakness and ignorance upon the other. He is governed by two principles, self-love and reason, both necessary to his place in the scale of being. Self-love is the principle which motivates man; reason is the principle which restrains him. The first verse paragraph of this epistle celebrates the duality of mankind and shows Pope's reasons for his conclusion that man's proper study is himself, that man should not try to pry into the nature, the knowledge, or the actions of God:

> Know then thyself, presume not God to scan:
> The proper study of mankind is man.
> Plac'd on this isthmus of a middle state,
> A being darkly wise, and rudely great:
> With too much knowledge for the sceptic side,
> With too much weakness for the Stoic's pride,
> He hangs between; in doubt to act, or rest;
> In doubt to deem himself a god or beast;
> In doubt his mind or body to prefer;
> Born but to die, and reas'ning but to err;
> Alike in ignorance, his reason such,
> Whether he thinks too little, or too much:
> Chaos of thought and passion, all confus'd;
> Still by himself abus'd, or disabus'd;
> Created half to rise, and half to fall;
> Great lord of all things, yet a prey to all;
> Sole judge of truth, in endless error hurl'd:
> **The glory, jest, and riddle of the world!**

Glory of youth glowed in his soul

Source: SONGS OF TRAVEL (XLIV, stanza 2)
Author: Robert Louis Stevenson (1850-1894)
First published: 1896
Type of work: Lyric poem

Context: Robert Louis Stevenson was a gay and radiant personality whose whole life was a courageous battle for health. Scottish by birth, Stevenson was a novelist, short-story writer, essayist, and poet; today he is best known for his tales of adventure and for *A Child's Garden of Verses.* The sense of adventure was keen in Stevenson and helped him through his illnesses, though it was at the same time a contributing factor to them. Suffering in 1873 from exhaustion, he spent some time in southern Europe; while there he met an American lady, Mrs. Osbourne. She was unhappily married. When Stevenson learned in 1879 that she was obtaining a divorce, he went to America to see her. He had little money, and the trip to

California further undermined his health. He married Mrs. Osbourne and they returned to England in 1880. His physical condition was poor; he had tuberculosis and was subject to severe hemorrhages. When he wrote *A Child's Garden of Verses* he was confined to his bed; his right arm was strapped to his side to lessen the danger of hemorrhage, and an eye infection made total darkness necessary. The poems were written with his left hand on large sheets of paper tacked to a board which he had arranged above him. His father died in 1887; he and his wife then moved to America, residing first at Saranac Lake and then at San Francisco. He spent the next few years roaming the South Seas, and settled at Samoa, where he remained until his death. Death was always an imminent possibility to Stevenson, and he was on intimate terms with it. Though he was always outwardly cheerful, an inevitable melancholy must have lurked in him much of the time; it is quite apparent in *Songs of Travel,* a group of poems written mostly in the South Seas between 1888 and 1894. One of these, untitled, speaks for itself:

> Sing me a song of a lad that is gone,
>> Say, could that lad be I?
> Merry of soul he sailed on a day
>> Over the sea to Skye.
>
> Mull was astern, Rum on the port,
>> Egg on the starboard bow;
> **Glory of youth glowed in his soul:**
>> Where is that glory now?
>> . . .
>
> Give me again all that was there,
>> Give me the sun that shone!
> Give me the eyes, give me the soul,
>> Give me the lad that's gone!
>
> Sing me a song of a lad that is gone,
>> Say, could that lad be I?
> Merry of soul he sailed on a day
>> Over the sea to Skye.
>
> Billow and breeze, islands and seas,
>> Mountains of rain and sun,
> All that was good, all that was fair,
>> All that was me is gone.

Go not, like the quarry-slave at night

Source: THANATOPSIS (Line 77)
Author: William Cullen Bryant (1794–1878)
First published: 1821
Type of work: Lyric poem

Context: The well-known 1821 version of "Thanatopsis" is a revision and expansion of a poem written in Bryant's seventeenth year but not published until 1817. The title, meaning "a view of death," was supplied by the editor who published the 1817 version. This earlier poem began, "Yet a few days, and thee,/ The all-beholding sun, shall see no more ..." (lines 17-18 of the 1821 version) and ended, "And make their bed with thee!"—(line 66 of the 1821 version). The opening lines which Bryant added in 1821 are Wordsworthian in the poet's view of Nature, but the phrasing of much of the poem is marked by eighteenth century "poetic diction" resembling that in the poems of the "graveyard" poets—Edward Young, Robert Blair, and Thomas Gray—whom Bryant had read and enjoyed in youth. In "Thanatopsis" Bryant says to the reader who may now and then muse on the fact that he will someday die: when such thoughts come, listen to the still, comforting voice of Nature. Nature says to man: in a brief time earth, that nourished you, will receive your body which will then be no more than "the insensible rock" or a clod of earth a farmer plows through. Oak roots will "pierce thy mould." Yet when you die you will not rest alone but with the infinite number of others who have lain down in "one mighty sepulchre." Hills, vales, rivers, brooks, ocean—these "Are but the solemn decorations all/ Of the great tomb of man." For ages the heavenly bodies have shone on "the sad abodes of death." Those men who live now "are but a handful" to those who are dead. You shall rest as they do. Though your own passing may be unnoted, "All that breathe/ Will share thy destiny." Through the ages to come you will be joined by infants, youths, men, and women in "the full strength of years," and old people who "Shall one by one be gathered to thy side,/ By those, who in their turn shall follow them." In his later life Bryant was to believe in a personal immortality of the soul and a rejoining of those separated on earth by death. But in "Thanatopsis" there is no hint of this belief. Through the voice of Nature, Bryant counsels man: live so that when death approaches, you will face it not in fear but in the faith that no harm will come to you afterward. Regard death as only an untroubled, but eternal, sleep. This advice is found in the noble lines which close the poem:

So live, that when thy summons comes to join
The innumerable caravan, which moves
To that mysterious realm, where each shall take
His chamber in the silent halls of death,
Thou **go not, like the quarry-slave at night,**
Scourged to his dungeon, but, sustained and soothed
By an unfaltering trust, approach thy grave,
Like one who wraps the drapery of his couch
About him, and lies down to pleasant dreams.

Go, tell the Spartans

Source: PALATINE MANUSCRIPT
Author: Simonides of Ceos (556-468 B.C.)
First transcribed: Fifth century B.C.
Type of work: Poetic epitaph

Context: In 480 B.C. Xerxes, seeking revenge for Darius' defeat at Marathon in 490 B.C., invaded Greece. The Pass of Thermopylae was defended by 300 Spartans under their King Leonidas and by 7,500 other Greeks, who held out for three days until a traitor revealed to the Persians a back path. Then many of the Greeks retreated, but Leonidas and his Spartans died trying to hold the pass. A contest was held to choose a fitting inscription for a monument to their memory. It was won by Simonides of Ceos who had beaten Aeschylus for a similar epitaph for those killed at Marathon. He submitted a two-line epigram, a poetic form that sums up a situation or makes some terse or apt comment, or is antithetical. This poetic form, of which Simonides is recognized as the greatest Greek writer, went into Latin literature with Catullus, Martial, and others, where it was often accompanied by a barb of satire, as later in the epigrams of Voltaire. With Alexander Pope and his heroic couplets, it appeared in English literature. The epigram of Simonides was engraved on the monument, which has since disappeared, but the words have survived. Strabo (c.63 B.C.–c. A.D. 21), who saw it on the column, quoted it. So did Herodotus (VII, 228), Cicero, Plutarch, and others. About 90 other epigrams remain of those written by Simonides, greatest Greek lyric poet before the Persian invasion. Many are contained in a tenth century Byzantine Greek anthology found in 1606 in the library of the Counts Palatine. Others have been discovered in an anthology compiled by Maximus Planidus, and printed in Florence in 1484. Literally the two lines declare:

Oh passerby, tell the Lacedaemonians
That we lie here, obeying their orders.

God forbid

Source: ROMANS 3:31
Author: Paul
First transcribed: c.50-60
Type of work: Religious epistle

Context: Paul's letter to the church in Rome was a letter to strangers; he had never visited it and had had no part in its founding. For this reason the epistle is more a treatise on the nature and principles of Christianity than it is a letter. In it his principal purpose is to declare to all men the greatness of God's mercy through Christ, and to persuade them that salvation depends on faith in the grace of God, as it is expressed through Christ. His primary consideration in the first eight chapters of the epistle is the problem which lies in convincing members of the Jewish faith. In his own missionary work he has found them extremely resistant to his teachings, and now he lists every objection he can think of which they might have, answering each in turn. This portion of the epistle was probably intended to be a handbook containing material for use in obtaining conversions, and Paul doubtless hoped that converted Romans would gain a deeper insight into Jewish ideology from it. He begins the epistle by stating his qualifications and his gospel, reminding his readers that God offers salvation to all who believe in this gospel regardless of their origin. God, he adds, is angered by sin; here Paul enumerates a number of examples. His next major point is that all men are sinners and that mere observance of outward requirements will not help them unless their purity is internal and genuine. In Chapter 3 he goes on to say that observance of the law is good, but that faith in God is more important: by observance of laws alone man cannot hope for salvation. Faith in the gospel of redemption through Christ will save men without the law, and the law will be given meaning by it. Laws differ with men, but Christ's doctrine applies to all. In the fourth, sixth, and thirty-first verses, Paul emphasizes his point with the expression, "God forbid." The last is perhaps most effective.

But now the righteousness of God without the law is manifested, being witnessed by the law and the prophets;

Even the righteousness of God which is by faith of Jesus Christ unto all and upon all them that believe: for there is no difference:

For all have sinned, and come short of the glory of God;

Being justified freely by his grace through the redemption that is in Christ Jesus:

Whom God hath set forth to be a propitiation through faith in his blood, to declare his righteousness for the remission of sins that are past, through the forbearance of God;

To declare, I say, at this time his righteousness: that he might be just, and the justifier of him which believeth in Jesus.

Where is boasting then? It is excluded. By what law? of works? Nay: but by the law of faith.

Therefore we conclude that a man is justified by faith without the deeds of the law.

Is he the God of the Jews only? is he not also of the Gentiles? Yes, of the Gentiles also:

Seeing it is one God, which shall justify the circumcision by faith, and uncircumcision through faith.

Do we then make void the law through faith? **God forbid:** yea, we establish the law.

God is always for the big battalions

Source: LETTER TO FRANÇOIS LOUIS HENRI LERICHE (February 6, 1770)
Author: Voltaire (François Marie Arouet, 1694–1778)
First published: 1785–1789, in *Oeuvres Completes de Voltaire*
Type of work: Personal letter

Context: Voltaire, the outspoken champion of freedom, was a master of the effective phrase. In some cases the thought did not originate with him, but was transformed by his own inspiration into an epigram of such forceful insight that, once read, it cannot be forgotten. At other times he might use a popular expression, but in such a way that it was given a new freshness and permanence. Voltaire's correspondence was enormous; but this ability seldom failed him, and even in a short letter dashed off in a hurry it frequently stands out. The lines are direct and pungent: they bite into the mind. The note which follows is a good example. It was written to M. Leriche, *Receveur des Domaines* at Besançon, when Voltaire was seventy-six years of age and living in exile near Geneva. His violent criticisms of Christianity and priestcraft had made it unsafe for him to live in France, but his creative activities continued unabated, and his influence upon the thought of his time did not lessen. Voltaire had long since learned how to achieve a maximum of communication through economy of means. In this letter he replies to a well-wisher who has evidently switched political parties or schools of thought in an effort to get away from attitudes which disgust him and to find something more acceptable. Voltaire warns him that he is not likely to find it. In a letter written October 18, 1677, Roger de Rabutin, Comte de Bussy (1618–1693) had remarked, "God is generally for the big squadrons against the little ones (*Dieu est d'ordinaire pour les gros escadrons contre les petits*)." Bussy-Rabutin, as he is commonly known, was a member of the French lesser nobility; a notorious rake, whose licentious sketches of the ladies of the court (*Histoire Amoureuse des Gaules*) landed him in the Bastille, he was gifted with considerable literary power. Voltaire, however, expresses the same thought far more effectively (*dieu est toujours pour les gros bataillons*):

6th February 1770

You, sir, have left the Welsh for the Welsh. You will find these stubborn barbarians everywhere. The number of the sages will always be small. It is true that it is growing; however, its increase is nothing in comparison with that of blockheads, and unfortunately it is said that **God is always for the big battalions.** Men of integrity must close ranks and stay under cover: it is impossible for their little band to attack this party of fanatics in the open.

I have been very ill: I have been near death all winter: it is because of this, sir, that I am so late in answering. I am nonetheless touched by your remembrance. Continue your friendship toward me: that will console me for my ills and for the stupidities of the human race.

Receive the assurances, . . .

God is the perfect poet

Source: PARACELSUS (Part II)
Author: Robert Browning (1812-1889)
First published: 1835
Type of work: Poetic drama

Context: In this long poetic drama, Browning's second publication, the poet turns to the German Renaissance in order to dramatize the aspirations and failures of the famous Paracelsus, alchemist, fraud, and last great practitioner of the occult sciences. In the beginning of this remarkable work, Paracelsus decides that he is tired of teaching, and he tells his friend Festus that he aspires to know all things. Believing that knowledge is the result of experience, and rejecting the soul, he hopes to know infinitely in order to overthrow God, but, as Festus warns, his search is doomed from the beginning because he ignores love that springs from the soul. At his lowest moment of failure, however, he meets the wild-eyed Aprile, a poet who has attempted to love infinitely. While the poet has not the knowledge to discriminate between different kinds of beauty, the alchemist can see no beauty at all because he has become a monster that does not know love. Paracelsus realizes that they are "halves of one dissevered world," but before he can learn Aprile's secret, the poet dies, leaving in the cold alchemist the desire to love. The quotation comes from Aprile's dying vision of the goal he had sought and his discovery that by not learning what the alchemist offers he has failed.

APRILE
Ha! go you ever girt about
With phantoms, powers? I have created such,
But these seem real as I.

PARACELSUS
Whom can you see
Through the accursed darkness?

APRILE
Stay; I know,
I know them: who should know them well as I?
White brows, lit up with glory; poets all!

PARACELSUS
Let him but live, and I have my reward!

347

Yes; I see now. **God is the perfect poet,**
Who in his person acts his own creations.
Had you but told me this at first! . . .

God is thy law, thou mine

Source: PARADISE LOST (Book IV, l. 637)
Author: John Milton (1608-1674)
First published: 1667
Type of work: Epic poem

Context: The angels keep watch over the garden, but Satan enters it by overleaping the wall. Uriel tells Adam that he will seek out the alien spirit the next morning; he then slides down a sunbeam to the sun, which has descended below the earth. Evening comes on, and all the birds and beasts go to their beds except the nightingale, which sings throughout the night. Adam tells Eve that all things seek their rest; other creatures, except man, are idle through the day, as they have no specific duties to perform; therefore they need rest less than does man, who has his daily work, either physical or mental; it is this duty that dignifies man above the beasts. Adam says that he and Eve will have to be up at dawn to perform their pleasant work in the garden. He adds that there is more work than they can do to cultivate the garden, as there is a wanton growth that they have to hold in check; also they have to clean up the dropped blossoms and gums so that they can tread at ease. Meanwhile, night bids them take their rest. Eve, calling Adam her "author," since she was created from his rib, says that as God commands Adam, so man commands woman.

>   Those blossoms also, and those dropping gums,
> That lie bestrown unsightly and unsmooth,
> Ask riddance, if we mean to tread with ease;
> Meanwhile, as Nature wills, night bids us rest.
>   To whom thus Eve with perfect beauty adorned.
> My author and disposer, what thou biddest
> Unargued I obey; so God ordains,
> **God is thy law, thou mine;** to know no more
> Is woman's happiest knowledge and her praise.
> With thee conversing I forget all time,
> All seasons and their change, all please alike.
> Sweet is the breath of morn, her rising sweet,
> With charm of earliest birds; pleasant the sun
> When first on this delightful land he spreads
> His orient beams, on herb, tree, fruit, and flower,
> Glist'ring with dew. . . .

God keeps a niche in heaven to hold our idols

Source: FUTURITY (Lines 8-9)
Author: Elizabeth Barrett Browning (1806-1861)
First published: 1844
Type of work: Sonnet

Context: This sonnet is typical of Elizabeth Barrett Browning in that it reflects her theme of social consciousness. In beginning the poem "O beloved voices," she is addressing the people who have already died or broken off "in the middle of that song we sang together softly." These people with whom she "sang" are those who tried, along with Mrs. Browning, "to enrich the poor world with the sense of love." Though these companions have now died, the poetess reaffirms her faith in an afterlife and in the fact that she will meet her "idols" in heaven. She goes on to state that these "idols" will be especially recognized by God and "glorified."

And O belovèd voices, upon which
Ours passionately call, because ere-long
Ye brake off in the middle of that song
We sang together softly, to enrich
The poor world with the sense of love, and witch
The heart out of things evil,—I am strong,
Knowing ye are not lost for aye among
The hills with last year's thrush. **God keeps a niche**
In heaven to hold our idols; and albeit
He brake them to our faces, and denied
That our close kisses should impair their white,
I know we shall behold them raised, complete,
The dust swept from their beauty,—glorified
New Memnons singing in the great God-light.

God the first garden made, and the first city, Cain

Source: THE GARDEN (Stanza 3)
Author: Abraham Cowley (1618-1667)
First published: 1668
Type of work: Ode

Context: Disappointed with his lack of success in life, Abraham Cowley retired from what he termed "the tumult and business of the world" to become one of the best essayists of his time. His essays often contain poetry, sometimes his own, which becomes an integral part of the essay. His poem entitled "The Garden" is really part of such an essay, the first part of which is an epistle to John Evelyn, Cowley's friend and fellow member of the Royal Society, who had dedicated his *Kalendarium Hor-*

tense to Cowley. In the prose portion of Cowley's essay, as well as in the poetical portion, the writer displays the epicureanism so often associated with the neoclassical period. He begins by saying, "I never had any other desire so strong and so like to covetousness as that one which I have always had, that I might be master at last of a small house and a large garden. . . ." As a typical neoclassical epicurean, Cowley believed a quiet country life taken up with books, a garden, and domestic tasks was far the best for man. He points out that God gave man a garden even before He gave man a wife. He goes on to say that it was out of His wisdom that God placed man in the Garden of Eden:

> For God, the Universal Architect,
>   'T had been as easy to erect
> A Louvre or Escurial, or a tow'r
> That might with Heav'n communication hold,
> As Babel vainly thought to do of old:
>   He wanted not the skill or pow'r;
>   In the world's fabric those were shown,
> And the materials were all His own.
> But well He knew what place would best agree
> With innocence, and with felicity:
> And we elsewhere still seek for them in vain.
> If any part of either yet remain,
> If any part of either we expect,
> This may our judgment in the search direct;
> **God the first Garden made, and the first city, Cain.**

A godly righteous and sober life

Source: THE BOOK OF COMMON PRAYER (Page 6)
Author: Traditional; translated and arranged by Archbishop Cranmer (1489–1560)
First published: 1549
Type of work: Prayer of confession

Context: The Order for Daily Morning Prayer, the first service in the Book of Common Prayer, is a direct descendent of *Matins,* one of the services in the medieval system of daily devotions known as the Canonical Hours or Daily Offices. These Offices were in turn developed out of customs of regular instruction, prayer, and praise in practice in the early Church and beyond these from the devotional practices of pious Jews at the time of the birth of Christ. Morning Prayer begins in a penitential mood. After a series of opening sentences of Biblical origin which set the theme of the service to come, the faithful are reminded, in the *Exhortation,* that no converse with God can be fitting or profitable until the worshiper has laid bare his disobediences to God's will and has sought reconciliation with His love. The minister beseeches the congregation to go with him to the very "throne of the heavenly grace" and there humbly to confess their sins in the words of the *General Confession*—called "general" because it is said by the minister and all the people together, and refers not only to individual shortcomings but to the guilt of the whole community of believers. Based in general on St. Paul's analysis of sin in Romans 7:8–25, the prayer asserts that the essence of sin is self-assertion and asks that the penitent sinner be restored to the spiritual health which he has forfeited by his offenses against God's holy laws.

Almighty and most merciful Father; we have erred, and strayed from thy ways like lost sheep. We have followed too much the devices and desires of our own hearts. We have offended against thy holy laws. We have left undone those things which we ought to have done; And we have done those things which we ought not to have done; And there is no health in us. But thou, O Lord, have mercy upon us, miserable offenders. Spare thou those, O God, who confess their faults. Restore thou those who are penitent; According to thy promises declared unto mankind in Christ Jesus our Lord. And grant, O most merciful Father, for his sake; That we may hereafter live **a godly, righteous, and sober life,** To the glory of thy holy Name. Amen.

The Gods are just, and of our pleasant vices make instruments to plague us

Source: KING LEAR (Act V, sc. iii, ll. 170-171)
Author: William Shakespeare (1564-1616)
First published: 1608
Type of work: Dramatic tragedy

Context: The subplot of *King Lear,* that of Gloucester and his two sons, Edgar and Edmund, parallels the story of Lear and his three daughters. Edmund, the bastard son, convinces his father by a forged letter that Edgar, the legitimate son, is, in truth, planning to murder his father. When Edmund's treachery has, among other things, cost Gloucester his eyes, Edgar confronts his brother and they fight. Dying, Edmund confesses his evil designs, and Edgar comments on Gloucester's pleasant begetting of the bastard son.

EDMUND
What you have charged me with, that have I done,
And more, much more; the time will bring it out.
'Tis past, and so am I. But what art thou
That hast this fortune on me? If thou'rt noble,
I do forgive thee.

351

EDGAR

Let's exchange charity.
I am no less in blood than thou art, Edmund;
If more, the more th' hast wronged me.
My name is Edgar, and thy father's son.
The gods are just, and of our pleasant vices
Make instruments to plague us.
The dark and vicious place where thee he got
Cost him his eyes.

God's finger touched him and he slept

Source: IN MEMORIAM (Part LXXXV, stanza 5)
Author: Alfred, Lord Tennyson (1809-1892)
First published: 1850
Type of work: Elegy

Context: This elegy was written as a monument to Arthur Henry Hallam, a young man of extraordinary promise and an intimate friend of Tennyson, who died suddenly in Vienna at the age of twenty-two. The poem records Tennyson's slow spiritual progress from his initial depth of personal sorrow to the gradual healing of grief through a sense of spiritual contact with Hallam in a wider love of God and humanity. Section LXXXV is one of the important spiritual turning points of the elegy: from despair to renewed hope. The section looks in both directions, giving a résumé of the earlier grief and showing the stage at which Tennyson has arrived and how he seeks new friendships even though he cannot replace the old. A look at what might have been if Hallam had lived to marry the poet's sister, Emily, only stirs the old bitterness and threatens the poet's "low beginning of content." His friend, Edmund Lushington, asks what sort of life he now leads—if his great sorrow has dimmed or sustained his faith in God; if the loss of Hallam has drained his capacity for love. As he begins to answer these questions, Tennyson admits how deeply Hallam's death has affected him:

My blood an even tenor kept,
    Till on mine ear this message falls
    That in Vienna's fatal walls
God's finger touched him, and he slept.

The great Intelligences fair
    That range above our mortal state,
    In circle round the blessed gate,
Received and gave him welcome there;
                    •   •   •
But I remain'd, whose hopes were dim
    Whose life, whose thoughts were little worth,

352

To wander on a darken'd earth,
Where all things round me breathed of him.

God's gifts put man's best dreams to shame

Source: SONNETS FROM THE PORTUGUESE (Sonnet 26)
Author: Elizabeth Barrett Browning (1806-1861)
First published: 1850
Type of work: Sonnet

Context: In the octave of this autobiographical love sonnet, Mrs. Browning portrays her companions during her years of invalidism as being "visions" rather than actual people. She says that these images satisfied her for a while. But the "visions" began to fade as years passed, and her senses began to dull from lack of contact with people. Then her lover, Robert Browning, whom she married in 1846, came into her life "to be . . . what they seemed." He fulfilled the greatest dreams of her "soul" and gave even more soul satisfaction than her visions. Thus, she reflects, "God's gifts put man's best dreams to shame."

I lived with visions for my company
Instead of men and women, years ago,
And found them gentle mates, nor thought to know
A sweeter music than they played to me.
But soon their trailing purple was not free
Of this world's dust, their lutes did silent grow,
And I myself grew faint and blind below
Their vanishing eyes. Then THOU didst come—to be,
Belovèd, what they seemed, Their shining fronts,
Their songs, their splendors (better, yet the same,
As river-water hallowed into fonts),
Met in thee, and from out thee overcame
My soul with satisfaction of all wants:
Because **God's gifts put man's best dreams to shame.**

God's soldier be he

Source: MACBETH (Act V, sc. ix, l. 13)
Author: William Shakespeare (1564-1616)
First published: 1623
Type of work: Dramatic tragedy

Context: In the final act of the drama, Macbeth, who has usurped the crown of Scotland and established himself as a bloody tyrant, is besieged in his castle at Dunsinane by an English army under the command of Siward, Earl of Northumberland. Macbeth, however, feels secure by

353

reason of the promises given him by the three witches that he cannot be defeated "until/Great Birnam wood to high Dunsinane hill/Shall come against him," and that "none of woman born" can harm him. The first of these assurances is destroyed when Malcolm, rightful heir to the Scottish throne, orders each soldier in the English army to hew a branch from the trees in Birnam wood and carry it before him so that the size of the attacking forces may be concealed. As a result of this stratagem, the watchers on the castle walls are given the impression that the forest is indeed moving towards "high Dunsinane hill." In a last desperate attempt, although he has grown weary of life, Macbeth orders a sortie, and the battle is joined. The first of his enemies to confront him is young Siward, son of the English commander, who is killed in a hand-to-hand fight with the usurper. When the old earl receives this news, he is concerned only with knowing whether his son fought and died bravely, as a soldier should. His conversation with Ross is as follows:

ROSS

Your son my lord, has paid a soldier's debt.
He only lived but till he was a man,
The which no sooner had his prowess confirmed
In the unshrinking station where he fought,
But like a man he died. • • •

SIWARD

Had he his hurts before?

ROSS

Ay, on the front.

SIWARD

Why then, **God's soldier be he.**
Had I as many sons as I have hairs,
I would not wish them to a fairer death.
And so his knell is knolled.

The gods themselves cannot recall their gifts

Source: TITHONUS (Line 49)
Author: Alfred, Lord Tennyson (1809-1892)
First published: 1860
Type of work: Dramatic monologue

Context: Tithonus was the husband of Aurora, goddess of the dawn, and the son of Laomedan, King of Troy. He asked his wife to grant him immortality, but he neglected to ask also for eternal youth. She granted his wish, and the results were disastrous. While Aurora remained immortally young and lovely, Tithonus became withered and ugly. In this poem he la-

354

ments his immortality, wishing that he had never tried to transcend the bounds of what was intended for mortal men. He alone is set apart, unable to participate in the cycle of life:

> The woods decay, the woods decay and fall,
> The vapors weep their burthen to the ground,
> Man comes and tills the fields and lies beneath,
>
>   .   .   .
>
> Me only cruel immortality
> Consumes. . . .

However, his desire for the beautiful Aurora has not waned, and he is all the more desolate when he reflects upon his present impotence. He asks Aurora:

> Let me go; take back thy gift.
> Why should a man desire in any way
> To vary from the kindly race of men,
> Or pass beyond the goal of ordinance
> Where all should pause, as is most meet for all?
>
>   .   .   .
>
> Why wilt thou ever scare me with thy tears,
> And make me tremble lest a saying learnt,
> In days far-off, on that dark earth, be true?
> **"The Gods themselves cannot recall their gifts."**

Goes to grass

Source: THE KNIGHT OF THE BURNING PESTLE (Act IV, sc. v, l. 107)
Author: Francis Beaumont (1585?-1616)
First published: 1613
Type of work: Dramatic comedy

Context: Before the play gets well started, a citizen grocer and his naïve wife speak up to the actors to say that they want a different play from the one scheduled. What is more, they want their apprentice, Ralph, to take a part in it. Throughout the course of the play they interject their comments and interrupt the action. After Ralph is admitted to the cast, two plots develop: one has to do with Jasper, apprentice to the merchant Venturewell, and his love for Venturewell's daughter. Intertwined in this plot are the affairs of the Merrythought family. Old Merrythought, Jasper's father, who lives a happy life of eating, drinking, and singing, with no thought about how to provide these pleasures, is left alone by the departure of Mistress Merrythought, who is disgusted with her husband's improvidence. Ralph, taking to himself a squire and a dwarf, wanders the world as a knight errant, bent on righting wrongs and rescuing distressed damsels. Finally he abandons his role as a knight and appears as a May-lord, giving a long speech about his own antecedents and the glories of the spring. Among other features of that season, little fishes spawn, snails creep out of their shells, streams become warm, and steeds go out to pasture.

RALPH

The lords and ladies now abroad, for their disport and play
Do kiss sometimes upon the grass, and sometimes in the hay;
Now butter with a leaf of sage is good to purge the blood;
Fly Venus and phlebotomy, for they are neither good;
Now little fish on tender stone begin to cast their bellies,
And sluggish snails, that erst were mewed, do creep out of their
  shellies;
The rumbling rivers now do warm, for little boys to paddle;
The sturdy steed now **goes to grass,** and up they hang his saddle;
The heavy hart, the bellowing buck, the rascal, and the pricket,
Are now among the yeoman's peas, and leave the fearful thicket;
And be like them, O, you, I say, of this same noble town,
And lift aloft your velvet heads, and slipping off your gown,
With bells on legs, and napkins clean unto your shoulders tied,
With scarfs and garters as you please, and "Hey for our town!"
  cried,
March out. . . .

The golden bowl

Source: ECCLESIASTES 12:6
Author: Unknown
First transcribed: c.250-200 B.C.
Type of work: Religious confession

Context: This quotation is the title of a novel by Henry James wherein the breaking of a golden bowl symbolizes the end of a strained family relationship. The writer of Ecclesiastes, the preacher, speaks of the futility of this life, where everything—wisdom, pleasure, labor, hope, and desire— ends with death and the grave. Even before death, in this life, the wicked prosper and the righteous suffer; the ways of God are beyond human understanding. All one can do, "the conclusion of the whole matter," is to "Fear God, and keep his command- ments: for this is the whole duty of man." Particularly in youth, says the preacher, must man remember his creator and rejoice in life as youth knows it. He warns that old age and death inevitably come to every generation, and he remarks upon the end of life, when every man must fear the judgment of God upon his actions, when life and its infirmities become a burden, and when the mourners will soon be in the street. The days of this life are short, but the days in the grave, our "long home," are long and many. Of death itself the writer of Ec-

356

clesiastes writes symbolically, noting it comes in many ways: as the loosening of a cord, the breaking of a bowl, the breaking of a pitcher, or the breaking of a wheel at a cistern:

> Or ever the silver cord be loosed, or **the golden bowl** be broken, or the pitcher be broken at the fountain, or the wheel broken at the cistern.
> Then shall the dust return to the earth as it was: and the spirit shall return unto God who gave it.
> Vanity of vanities, saith the preacher; all is vanity.

Good Americans, when they die, go to Paris

Source: THE AUTOCRAT OF THE BREAKFAST-TABLE (Chapter VI)
Author: Oliver Wendell Holmes (1809-1894)
First published: 1858
Type of work: Essay

Context: The Autocrat of the Breakfast-Table purports to be a series of monologues delivered by a persona who does not identify himself otherwise than by admitting that he dominates the conversation at the breakfast table of his Boston boarding house. His audience is composed of such people as the landlady, the landlady's daughter, the divinity student, the young girl attending finishing school, the schoolmistress, the old man, and the brash young man. The subject of discussion at the beginning of Chapter VI of *The Autocrat* is the bright sayings of the Seven Wise Men of Boston. The first is by Benjamin Franklin: "He that has once done you a kindness will be more ready to do you another than he whom you yourself have obliged." Another saying, this by the Historian, probably John Lothrop Motley, is, "Give us the luxuries of life, and we will dispense with its necessaries." This one leads up to the following, which may be by Thomas Appleton:

> To these must certainly be added that other saying of one of the wittiest of men:—
> **"Good Americans, when they die, go to Paris."**
> —The divinity-student looked grave at this, but said nothing.
> The schoolmistress spoke out, and said she didn't think the wit meant any irreverence. It was only another way of saying, Paris is a heavenly place after New York or Boston.

A good book is the purest essence of a human soul

Source: SPEECH IN SUPPORT OF THE LONDON LIBRARY
Author: Thomas Carlyle (1795-1881)
First delivered: 1840
Type of work: Speech

Context: The greatest library in London, and one of the greatest in the world, is of course the British Museum. Its holdings, however, do not constitute a lending collection for the general reader but a research collection for the scholar. In 1840 Thomas Carlyle had finished his great work on the French Revolution and was beginning his study of Oliver Cromwell. He felt the need, for himself and for the citizens of London, for the establishment of a general lending library. He marshaled all of his influence among persons of political or financial importance and pushed the project to fruition. His contributions included plans, enthusiasm, and one powerful speech. Today the London library stands as one of his finest monuments. In his speech he emphasized the need of the common people of London for a library:

We will leave the British Museum standing on its own basis, and be very thankful that such a Library exists in this country. But supposing it to be managed with the most perfect skill and success, even according to the ideal of such an Institution, still I will assert that this other Library of ours is requisite also. In the first place by the very nature of the thing, a great quantity of people are excluded altogether from the British Museum as a reading room. Every man engaged in business is occupied during the hours it is kept open; and innumerable classes of persons find it extremely inconvenient to attend the British Museum Library at all. But granting that they all could go there, I would ask any literary man, any reader of books, any man intimately acquainted with the reading of books, whether he can read them to any purpose in the British Museum? A book is a kind of thing that requires a man to be self-collected. He must be alone with it. **A good book is the purest essence of a human soul.** How could a man take it into a crowd, with bustle of all sorts going on around him? The good of a book is not the facts that can be got out of it, but the kind of resonance that it awakens in our own minds.

Good digestion wait on appetite

Source: MACBETH (Act III, sc. iv, l. 38)
Author: William Shakespeare (1564-1616)
First published: 1623
Type of work: Dramatic tragedy

Context: Three witches intercept Macbeth and Banquo along a heath and disclose to the warriors that Macbeth will rise in power until finally he becomes king, but that the heirs of Banquo will eventually receive the throne. Driven by his own ambition and that of his wife, Macbeth murders King Duncan of Scotland and usurps the throne. Since Banquo and his son Fleance stand in the way of the new king, Macbeth plans a banquet to which they will be invited, secretly hiring assassins to murder them before the banquet takes place. After the guests have assembled, one of the murderers draws Macbeth aside and informs him that Banquo has been killed but that Fleance has escaped. The whispered conversation between Macbeth and the murderer lasts so long a time that Lady Macbeth, in order to allay any suspicion on the part of the guests, has to remind her husband that he has forgotten his duties as a host.

LADY MACBETH
My royal lord,
You do not give the cheer. The feast is sold
That is not often vouched, while 'tis a-making,
'Tis given with welcome. To feed were best at home;
From thence, the sauce to meat is ceremony,
Meeting were bare without it.
    [*Enter* GHOST OF BANQUO *and sits in* MACBETH'S *seat.*]

MACBETH
Sweet remembrancer!
Now **good digestion wait on appetite,**
And health on both.

LENNOX
May't please your Highness sit.

MACBETH
Here had we now our country's honour roofed,
Were the graced person of our Banquo present; . . .

A good face is a letter of recommendation

Source: THE SPECTATOR (No. 221)
Author: Joseph Addison (1672-1719)
First published: November 13, 1711
Type of work: Essay

Context: In the five hundred and fifty-five regular issues of the *Spectator,* Joseph Addison and Richard Steele brought popular essay journalism to a height of perfection never achieved before and seldom since. For a large middle-class reading public they created an interest in public affairs, literary and dramatic criticism, public morality, and manners. In this essay Addison, behind the mask of Mr. Spectator, amuses himself in an editorial vein by discussing with great mock seriousness the importance of the Latin motto which appeared at the beginning of each issue of the periodical. This selection from a great classical author, he says, is the "good face" which recommends the essay for the day:

It was a saying of an ancient philosopher, which I find some of our writers have ascribed to Queen Elizabeth, who perhaps might have taken occasion to repeat it, that **a good face is a letter of recommendation.** It naturally makes the beholders inquisitive into the person who is the owner of it, and generally prepossesses them in his favour. A handsome motto has the same effect. Besides that, it always gives a supernumerary beauty to a paper, and is sometimes in a manner necessary when the writer is engaged in what may appear a paradox to vulgar minds, as it shows that he is supported by good authorities, and is not singular in his opinion.

A good honest and painful sermon

Source: DIARY (17 March, 1661)
Author: Samuel Pepys (1633-1793)
First published: 1825
Type of work: Diary

Context: From January, 1660, until eye trouble forced him to stop, after May, 1669, an impoverished clerk in London, Samuel Pepys, kept a daily record of his activities, important as well as trivial. Set down in shorthand, the Diary was not completely deciphered and published until 1893. It begins at the time of the Restoration of Charles II to the throne of the Stuarts, when Pepys became a minor clerk in the Admiralty. Before he died, he had twice served as Secretary of the Admiralty and was recognized as the foremost naval authority in England. His Diary covers only nine of the seventy years of his life, including, however, the end of his period of poverty and the beginning of his ability to engage in his favorite diversions, wine and the theater. He was also associating with important people. William Batten, an obscure but excellent seaman, had been knighted and made a rear admiral by Prince Charles for defecting from Parliament and taking his ship, the *Constant Warwick,* to Holland. After the Restoration, Batten was made Commissioner of the Navy and a member of Parliament for Rochester. Here are entries for three days of March, 1661. *The Spanish Curate* was a play by Beaumont and Fletcher. A "chine of beef" is a cut containing part of the backbone. Apparently a sermon, like medicine, must be distasteful to accomplish results.

16th. To Whitefriars, and there saw "The Spanish Curate," in which I had no great content.
17th. (Lord's Day). At church in the morning a stranger preached **a good honest and painful sermon.** My wife and I dined upon a chine of beef at Sir W. Batten's, so to church again. Then to supper at Sir W. Batten's again, where my wife by chance fell down and hurt her knees exceedingly.
18th. This morning early Sir William Batten went to Rochester, where he expects to be chosen Parliament-man. This day an ambassador from Florence was brought into the town in state. . . .

Good order is the foundation of all good things

Source: REFLECTIONS ON THE REVOLUTION IN FRANCE
Author: Edmund Burke (1729-1797)
First published: 1790
Type of work: Political treatise

Context: Burke, one of the greatest political philosophers England has ever produced, steadfastly defended traditional and established rights and privileges throughout his long tenure in Parliament. In the French Revolution, which gained much sympathy in England, he saw a gross and danger- ous perversion of the normal, grad- ual, and orderly evolution of political concepts. Toward the end of this trea- tise he speaks out strongly against the violence and chaos of revolutionary measures and expresses his sympathy for order and regulation:

. . . To keep a balance between the power of acquisition on the part of the subject, and the demands he is to answer on the part of the State, is a fundamental part of the skill of a true poli- tician. The means of acquisition are prior in time and in arrange- ment. **Good order is the foundation of all good things.** To be enabled to acquire, the people, without being servile, must be tractable and obedient. The magistrate must have his reverence, the laws their authority. The body of the people must not find the principles of natural subordination by art rooted out of their minds. They must respect that property of which they cannot partake. . . .

The good received, the giver is forgot

Source: EPISTLE TO LORD HALIFAX (Line 40)
Author: William Congreve (1670-1729)
First published: 1710
Type of work: Epistle in verse

Context: When Congreve was driven from Ireland to England by the Revo- lution, he determined to become a writer. During an illness, he wrote his first play, *The Old Bachelor* (per- formed 1693). When he read it to the players, he pronounced English so badly that the play was almost re- jected. Its successful production won for him the patronage of Charles Montagu (1661–1715), first Earl of Halifax, a wit and patron of such lit- erary men as Addison and Steele. Halifax made Congreve one of the commissioners for leasing coaches, then got him a place in the Pipe-office, and finally nominated him in the Customs House service at six hun- dred pounds a year. Congreve dedi- cated to Halifax his next comedy, *The Double Dealer*. Eventually he gave up playwriting, angry at the re- ception given some of his plays, and he retired to private life, writing poetry and engaging in conversation with his many friends. However, Lord Halifax had given him his start, and he was not one to be ungrateful, so he prefaced his collection of verse with a poetic letter to his patron, flattering him by the statement that the earl might well have been so great a poet that England could have competed with Greece. Unfortunately for literature, he said, Lord Halifax was too busy encouraging other literary men, and founding the Bank of England (1694), and serving as First Lord of the Treasury, to be able to devote time to his own writing. In fact, he is chiefly remembered for a parody on Dryden's *Hind and the Panther* (1687) which he and Matthew Prior wrote the same year under the title *The Town and the Country Mouse*. The reference in Congreve's poem is to Homer whose place of birth was claimed by seven cities of Greece. Halifax was a product of all of England.

> O had your genius been to leisure born,
> And not more bound to aid us than adorn!
> Albion in verse with ancient Greece had vy'd,
> And gain'd alone a fame which, there, seven states divide.
> But such, ev'n such renoun, too dear had cost,
> Had we the patriot in the poet lost.
> A true poetic state we had deplor'd
> Had not your ministry our coin restor'd . . .
>
> · · ·
>
> How oft a patriot's best laid schemes we find
> By party cross'd, or faction undermin'd.
> If he succeed, he undergoes this lot,
> **The good receiv'd, the giver is forgot.—**
> But honors, which from verse their source derive,
> Shall both surmount detraction, and survive:
> And poets have unquestion'd right to claim,
> If not the greatest, the most lasting name.

Good sense, which only is the gift of heaven

Source: MORAL ESSAYS (Epistle IV, l. 43)
Author: Alexander Pope (1688-1744)
First published: 1731-1735
Type of work: Satiric poem

Context: Pope's fourth epistle of the *Moral Essays* was addressed to Richard Boyle, the Earl of Burlington; the poem's topic is "Of the Use of Riches." Pope admires the earl for what he is doing with his wealth: "You shew us, Rome was glorious, not profuse,/ And pompous buildings once were things of Use./ Yet shall, my Lord, your just, your noble rules/ Fill half the land with Imitating-Fools." It is those who have wealth, but not taste, that Pope wishes to correct; too often, he thinks, people of

362

wealth and noble birth abuse the word "taste." In the use of riches, says the poet, the "first principle and foundation" is good sense, as it is in everything: to spend one's wealth is not enough in itself. Good sense, he says, is almost worth all the seven branches of knowledge, and fortunately this quality, he adds, is possessed by the Earl of Burlington. If one does not have the quality, however, not even such a great architect as Inigo Jones, or such a landscape and garden designer as Le Nôtre, of France, can give it:

> Oft have you hinted to your brother Peer
> A certain truth, which many buy too dear:
> Something there is more needful than Expence,
> And something previous even to Taste—'tis Sense:
> **Good Sense, which only is the gift of Heaven,**
> And though no Science, fairly worth the seven:
> A Light, which in yourself you must perceive;
> Jones and Le Nôtre have it not to give.

Good wine needs no bush

Source: AS YOU LIKE IT (Epilogue)
Author: William Shakespeare (1564-1616)
First published: 1623
Type of work: Dramatic comedy

Context: The play ends with two restorations and four marriages. The usurper Duke Frederick is converted to a life of religion and returns the crown to Duke Senior, who has spent many happy years of exile in the Forest of Arden; Oliver, who had tyrannized over his brother, Orlando, decides to retire as a shepherd to the Forest of Arden and turns over house and estate to Orlando. Orlando marries Rosalind, daughter of Duke Senior; Oliver marries Celia, daughter of Duke Frederick; the court jester Touchstone marries the rustic Audrey; the shepherd Silvius marries the shepherdess Phebe. Finally, after a closing dance, Rosalind makes a curtain speech, asking for the audience's applause, and alluding to the fact that female roles in Shakespeare's day were played by boys in women's dress: "If I were a woman. . . ." The comment reminds the audience that the boy actor has, in the play proper, performed the part of a woman disguised as a man. Rosalind suggests that if the play were a good one, it would scarcely need an apologetic epilogue, just as "good wine needs no bush"—that is, a good vintner would need no bush of evergreen hung over his door to draw trade, such bushes being the common sign on the wine trade. A good product needs no advertisement.

363

If it be true that **good wine needs no bush,** 'tis true that a good play needs no epilogue. Yet to good wine they use good bushes; and good plays prove the better by the help of good epilogues. What a case am I in then, that am neither a good epilogue, nor cannot insinuate with you in the behalf of a good play. I am not furnished like a beggar, therefore to beg will not become me. My way is to conjure you, and I'll begin with the women. I charge you, o women, for the love you bear to men, to like as much of the play as please you. And I charge you, o men, for the love you bear to women—as I perceive by your simpering, none of you hates them—that between you and the women the play may please. If I were a woman, I would kiss as many of you as had beards that pleased me, complexions that liked me, and breaths that I defied not. And I am sure, as many as have good beards, or good faces, or sweet breaths, will for my kind offer, when I make curtsy, bid me farewell. [*Exeunt.*]

A grain of manhood

Source: SAMSON AGONISTES (Line 408)
Author: John Milton (1608-1674)
First published: 1671
Type of work: Dramatic tragedy

Context: The hope of deliverance of Israel from her enemies according to prophecy pronounced before his birth, Samson is betrayed by his beloved Dalila, and captured and blinded by the Philistines. On the feast day of Dagon, when the Philistines honor their god for allowing Samson to fall into their hands, the blind strong man, resting from his toil as he sits on the steps of the Gaza prison, is visited first by Danites, men of his tribe who form a chorus for the drama, and then by Manoa, his father. Refusing to accept the excuses offered him by his friends and father, Samson says he deserves his punishment because of his folly in loving Dalila and in revealing to her the secret of his strength. Samson recounts his shame:

> At times when men seek most repose and rest,
> I yielded, and unlock'd her all my heart,
> Who with **a grain of manhood,** well resolv'd
> Might easily have shook off all her snares:
> But foul effeminacy held me yok't
> Her Bond-slave; O indignity, O blot
> To Honour and Religion! servil mind
> Rewarded well with servil punishment!
> The base degree to which I now am fall'n,
> These rags, this grinding, is not yet so base
> As was my former servitude, ignoble,

Unmanly, ignominious, infamous,
True slavery, and that blindness worse then this,
That saw not how degenerately I serv'd.

The grand instructor, Time

Source: LETTER TO SIR H. LANGRISHE (May 26, 1795)
Author: Edmund Burke (1729-1797)
First published: 1844
Type of work: Open letter

Context: Burke was born in Ireland, and although his entire adult life was spent in England he took an active interest in Irish affairs throughout his life. As a member of Parliament he frequently defended the Irish, and he always felt the Anglican domination of the millions of Irish Catholics constituted a sort of tyranny. In 1792 he had published an open letter to Sir Hercules Langrishe which had helped persuade Parliament to extend some degree of legislative franchise to the Catholics. Three years later Langrishe again spoke in defense of the Irish Catholics, and again Burke responded with a sympathetic open letter:

> Your speech on the Catholic question I read with much satisfaction. It is solid; . . . and it ought, on the spot, to have produced that effect which its reason, and that contained in the other excellent speeches on the same side of the question, cannot possibly fail (though with less pleasant consequences) to produce hereafter. What a sad thing it is, that **the grand instructor, Time,** has not yet been able to teach the grand lesson of his own value, and that, in every question of moral and political prudence, it is the choice of the moment which renders the measure serviceable or useless, noxious or salutary!

A grand memory for forgetting

Source: KIDNAPPED (Chapter 18)
Author: Robert Louis Stevenson (1850-1894)
First published: 1886
Type of work: Novel

Context: David Balfour, a Scots lad who is shipped off to enforced labor in the American Colonies by a rascally uncle, is rescued by a Jacobite adventurer named Alan Breck, a Highlander. The two make their way ashore on the Scottish coast and fall into a series of adventures and narrow escapes. A man named Glenure is killed by an unknown murderer, and the blame falls on David Balfour and Alan Breck. The two, pursued by

365

the sheriff and a detachment of British soldiers, escape by speed and cunning. When they are safe, David Balfour finds himself thinking that Alan Breck had a hand in the murder, as an act of revenge. The older man assures the boy that he had no part in the act, but Breck knows who the murderer is. However, like the good Highlander he is, he has used himself and the boy to draw the authorities off on a wild-goose chase. David has difficulty understanding the Highland mind and its workings, but his friend is persuasive:

> ". . . And do you know who did it?" I added. "Do you know that man in the black coat?"
> "I have nae clear mind about his coat," said Alan, cunningly, "but it sticks in my head that it was blue."
> "Blue or black, did ye know him?" said I.
> "I could nae just conscientiously swear to him," says Alan. "He gaed very close by me, to be sure, but it's a strange thing that I should just have been tying my brogues."
> "Can you swear that you don't know him, Alan?" I cried, half angered, half in a mind to laugh at his evasions.
> "Not yet," says he; "but I've **a grand memory for forgetting,** David."

The grand, old, fortifying classical curriculum

Source: FRIENDSHIP'S GARLAND (Part I, letter vi)
Author: Matthew Arnold (1822-1888)
First published: 1871
Type of work: Humorous letters

Context: Matthew Arnold, caught in the Victorian world of shifting values, believed firmly in the continuity of human experience and, above all, in the transcendent emotional values transmitted to his generation by the Christian ideals which had prevailed in the centuries past. Thus, as a patient mediator between the old and the new, he devoted himself to the articulation of the values of the past in language that would be contemporary and meaningful. Between 1866 and 1870 he contributed a series of humorous epistles to the *Pall-Mall Gazette* which, along with the essay *My Countrymen,* previously appearing in *Cornhill Magazine,* was published as *Friendship's Garland.* Expressive of the same social and ethical doctrines as the earlier *Culture and Anarchy,* this essay sets forth with light mockery the "Conversations, Letters, and Opinions of the late Arminius, Baron von Thunder-Ten-Tronckh" concerning his observations on the English scene. At one point Arminius questions the training and intelligence of two magistrates, "Viscount Lumpington" and "Reverend Esau Hittall," the latter recommended highly by his uncle, a prelate:

366

. . . "But I want to know what his nephew learnt [in his education]," interrupted Arminius, "and what Lord Lumpington learnt at Eton." "They followed," said I, **the grand, old, fortifying classical curriculum.** "Did they know anything when they left?" asked Arminius. "I have seen some longs and shorts of Hittall's," said I, "about the Calydonian Boar, which were not bad. But you surely don't need me to tell you, Arminius, that it is rather in training and bracing the mind for future acquisition,—a course of mental gymnastics we call it,—than in teaching any set thing, that the classical curriculum is so valuable. . . . But for my part I have always thought that their both getting their degree at last with flying colours, after three weeks of a famous coach for fast men, four nights without going to bed, and an incredible consumption of wet towels, strong cigars, and brandy-and-water, was one of the most astonishing feats of mental gymnastics I ever heard of."

The grand Perhaps

Source: BISHOP BLOUGRAM'S APOLOGY (Line 190)
Author: Robert Browning (1812-1889)
First published: 1855
Type of work: Dramatic monologue

Context: Bishop Blougram entertains at dinner a young writer who has questioned the bishop's faith and belief and the manner in which he lives. The bishop, who is modeled on Cardinal Wiseman, who reviewed the poem and found it very bad, begins the explanation of his life by saying that this dinner will be the writer's chief claim to fame in time to come, even though he insists that he despises the bishop for his luxurious manner of living and his lack of belief in the Catholic dogmas. The bishop contends that this feeling of the writer's is mere envy, and likens life to a long voyage on a ship: some of the passengers have well-equipped staterooms and others bare cells, but those who have the bare cells could, if they exerted themselves, have comfortable quarters. The bishop admits that he cannot always believe in all the dogmas of the Church—any more than the writer can. Belief and disbelief come and go. But occasionally, when in a period of disbelief, the man experiences something that makes him tend towards belief; *perhaps*—the grand Perhaps—there is a truth in the dogmas. Browning here uses the term in a somewhat similar way to the manner Rabelais, according to Peter Anthony Motteux, who first translated Rabelais into English, is supposed to have used it. According to Motteux, Rabelais, when dying, said, "I am going away in search of a great perhaps."

367

How can we guard our unbelief,
Make it bear fruit to us?—the problem here.
Just when we are safest, there's a sunset-touch,
A fancy from a flower-bell, some one's death,
A chorus-ending from Euripides,—
And that's enough for fifty hopes and fears
As old and new at once as Nature's self,
To rap and knock and enter in our soul,
Take hands and dance, there, a fantastic ring,
Round the ancient idol, on his base again,—
The grand Perhaps! We look on helplessly.
There the old misgivings, crooked questions are—
This good God,—what He could do, if He would,
Would, if He could—then must have done long since:
If so, when, where, and how? some way must be,—
Once feel about, and soon or late you hit
Some sense, in which it might be, after all.
Why not, "The Way, the Truth, the Life"?

The grand style

Source: ON TRANSLATING HOMER ("Last Words")
Author: Matthew Arnold (1822-1888)
First published: 1861
Type of work: Literary essay

Context: Matthew Arnold, like so many of his contemporaries, was caught in the agonizing throes of the intense religious and social transition of the Victorian era. Yet, unlike Newman on the one hand—who rejected the present and took refuge in the dogma of the past—and Huxley on the other—who rejected the past and became an ardent disciple of the New Science—Arnold accepted the modern age with full recognition of its scientific bias and worldly preoccupations. He saw and felt the social crudeness and the spiritual dislocation of his society, but he had a firm faith in the instincts and ideals which the human race had developed. Thus, in the work of his later life, he became a prophet of a new religion, culture—"the best that has been thought and said in the world." Through proper education he would envision a cultured middle-class cognizant of the values of human dignity as they have been articulated in the great aesthetic creations of the past. In 1860, as Professor of Poetry at Oxford, he delivered a series of three lectures in which, as he described it, "I shall try to lay down the true principles on which a translation of Homer should be founded." Among other matters, his lectures criticized a recent translation of the *Iliad* by Francis W. Newman, who printed a rebuttal to the charges. Arnold replied to Newman with an additional lecture, dealing primarily with the style and tone proper to the cultural values of the Greek epic:

368

. . . Nothing has raised more questioning among my critics than these words, "noble, **the grand style.**" People complain that I do not define these words sufficiently, that I do not tell them enough about them. "The grand style, but what is the grand style?" they cry; some with an inclination to believe in it, but puzzled; others mockingly and with incredulity. Alas! the grand style is the last matter in the world for verbal definition to deal with adequately.

. . .

I think it will be found that the grand style arises in poetry, "when a noble nature, poetically gifted, treats with simplicity or with severity a serious subject." I think this definition will be found to cover all instances of the grand style in poetry which present themselves.

The grasshopper shall be a burden

Source: ECCLESIASTES 12.5
Author: Unknown
First transcribed: c. 250-200 B.C.
Type of work: Religious confession

Context: The preacher in Ecclesiastes warns against vanity; all of this life is sheer vanity, he says: "Vanity of vanities . . . vanity of vanities; all is vanity." The search after wisdom or pleasure, fame or wealth, leads but to the grave for each and every generation. He sees that the worthy are defeated, and that the wicked prosper in this life. But some peace we may have, he suggests, and he advises that we subscribe to charity, duty, and faith. These will bring some measure of peace, even though in this life man is condemned never to understand the ways of God. To obey God, not to understand Him, is the lot of man: "Let us hear the conclusion of the whole matter: Fear God, and keep his commandments: for this is the whole duty of man. For God shall bring every work into judgment, with every secret thing, whether it be good, or whether it be evil." The writer of Ecclesiastes advises the young person to rejoice in his youth, but also to remember God the Creator and the judgment of life that must come. The time will come, he warns, when the spirit of man must return to the Creator:

And the doors shall be shut in the streets, when the sound of the grinding is low, and he shall rise up at the voice of the bird, and all the daughters of musick shall be brought low;
Also when they shall be afraid of that which is high, and fears shall be in the way, and the almond tree shall flourish, and **the grasshopper shall be a burden,** and desire shall fail: because man goeth to his long home, and the mourners go about the streets:

. . .

Then shall the dust return to the earth as it was: and the spirit shall return unto God who gave it.

Vanity of vanities, saith the preacher; all is vanity.

A great empire and little minds go ill together

Source: SPEECH ON MOVING HIS RESOLUTIONS FOR RECONCILIATION WITH THE COLONIES
Author: Edmund Burke (1729-1797)
First published: 1775
Type of work: Political speech

Context: As a member of the English Parliament Burke defended the American Colonies with great vigor and vehemence when that body considered harsh taxation and military suppression in response to unrest. England, he argued, was a great country and could well afford to be magnanimous in this instance as she had with such beneficial results in the cases of Ireland, Wales, and Chester. Conciliation, he insisted, would produce more loyal colonists; but he recognized that the narrow politicians would not understand his arguments:

All this, I know well enough, will sound wild and chimerical to the profane herd of those vulgar and mechanical politicians, who have no place among us; a sort of people who think that nothing exists but what is gross and material; and who therefore, far from being qualified to be directors of the great movement of empire, are not fit to turn a wheel in the machine. But to men truly initiated and rightly taught, these ruling and master principles, which, in the opinion of such men as I have mentioned, have no substantial existence, are in truth everything, and all in all. Magnanimity in politics is not seldom the truest wisdom; and **a great empire and little minds go ill together.** If we are conscious of our situation and glow with zeal to fill our place as becomes our station and ourselves, we ought to auspicate all our public proceedings on America with the old warning of the church, *Sursum corda* (Lift up your hearts)!

Great griefs I see medicine the less

Source: CYMBELINE (Act IV, sc. ii, l. 243)
Author: William Shakespeare (1564-1616)
First published: 1623
Type of work: Tragi-comedy

Context: Imogen's husband, Posthumus, who has been banished by King Cymbeline and the queen, sends for her to meet him. Actually, he plans to have her slain by the faithful Pisanio, because through the treachery of an Italian, Iachimo, he believes her to be a strumpet and untrue to him. Pisanio, who knows she is virtuous, cannot bring himself to kill her, but sends her on her way dressed as a man and carrying pills, given to him by the deceitful queen, supposedly to aid her in time of sickness. She meets two woodsmen and their father Belarius. They give her shelter, and being tired and ill she takes the pills and falls into a deathlike coma. Her hosts, meanwhile, have gone out to hunt, only to meet the revenge-thirsty Cloten, the queen's son, who wants to kill Posthumus and rape Imogen for spurning him for Posthumus. The woodsman Guiderius, challenged, beheads Cloten. Arviragus, his brother, finds Imogen and believes her to be dead. The brothers forget Cloten in their grief over the disguised Imogen, but Belarius entreats them to remember that he was a queen's son and that his body deserves respect.

BELARIUS
Great griefs I see medicine the less, for Cloten
Is quite forgot. He was a Queen's son, boys;
And though he came our enemy, remember
He was paid for that. Though mean and mighty rotting
Together have one dust, yet reverence,
That angel of the world, doth make distinction
Of place 'tween high and low. Our foe was princely,
And though you took his life as being our foe,
Yet bury him as a Prince.

Great is Diana of the Ephesians

Source: ACTS 19:34
Author: Unknown (traditionally Luke)
First transcribed: 60-150 (probably c.80-90)
Type of work: Religious history and tradition

Context: The Acts of the Apostles is the only contemporary account of the early Christian Church and its beginnings which remains to us. Although Acts and the third Gospel were evidently written by the same person, there is some doubt that he was actually Luke the physician; in any case, Luke probably provided much of the material. Acts is an epic recital of the apostles' lives, and forms a stirring record of the faith and moral courage that were required to build a new and independent religion. Luke begins with the Resurrection and the commission which Jesus laid upon His apostles, then proceeds with the history of their missionary work in Asia Minor, Syria, Jerusalem, and other portions of the Roman Empire. Chapters 15 through 28 follow the career of Paul, who moves from one place to another and preaches the gospel to people who are often deeply hostile to it. Crossing Syria, he wanders through Greece; he gathers a few

371

converts along the way and is occasionally the excuse for riots. One of these occurs at Thessalonica, where ruffians are persuaded or hired to create scenes of disorder. The Christians are blamed for the uproar, and Paul's congregation takes him to Berea. Here he gains some converts; but the hecklers follow from Thessalonica, and he moves on to Athens. In the latter city he preaches his new doctrine to curious philosophers and wins additional converts, though not many. From Athens he goes to Corinth, where he works as a tentmaker and on the Sabbath argues Scripture in the synagogue. Here he is brought to judgement and released. Later wanderings take him to Ephesus. After more than two years in the city his work makes itself felt: the converts multiply, and the worship of Diana in her great temple enters upon a decline. A riot follows, and Luke's account of it gives us an excellent case study of agitation and the genesis of civil disorder. The confusion and uproar are rendered vividly.

And the same time there arose no small stir about that way.

For a certain man named Demetrius, a silversmith, which made silver shrines for Diana, brought no small gain unto the craftsmen;

Whom he called together with the workmen of like occupation, and said, Sirs, ye know that by this craft we have our wealth.

Moreover ye see and hear, that not alone at Ephesus, but almost throughout all Asia, this Paul hath persuaded and turned away much people, saying that they be no gods, which are made with hands:

So that not only this our craft is in danger to be set at nought; but also that the temple of the great goddess Diana should be despised, and her magnificence should be destroyed, whom all Asia and the world worshippeth.

And when they heard these sayings, they were full of wrath, and cried out, saying, **Great is Diana of the Ephesians.**

And the whole city was filled with confusion: and having caught Gaius and Aristarchus, men of Macedonia, Paul's companions in travel, they rushed with one accord into the theatre.

And when Paul would have entered in unto the people, the disciples suffered him not.

And certain of the chief of Asia, which were his friends, sent unto him, desiring him that he would not adventure himself into the theatre.

Some therefore cried one thing, and some another: for the assembly was confused; and the more part knew not wherefore they were come together.

Great joys, like griefs, are silent

Source: HOLLAND'S LEAGUER (Act V, sc. i)
Author: Shackerley Marmion (1603-1639)
First published: 1632
Type of work: Dramatic comedy

Context: In 1624 an English dramatist who spelled his name in various ways came penniless out of the university because his father had squandered the family fortune. One way to earn a living was to fight with Gustavus Adolphus' army in the Lowlands, but Marmion thought promotion and wealth lay too far in the future, so after brief service, he put aside his pike and returned to London to make a living with his pen. His first attempt at drama, *Holland's Leaguer,* was often performed, according to the published copy, "with great applause by Prince Charles his servants, at the private house in Salisbury Court." The "Holland" has no connection with the country of Marmion's military service, but was the name of a "leaguer," or brothel in London's Holland Street, in Blackfriars. In cataloguing a copy of the play's first edition for sale, Bernard Quaritch called it "Holland's Leaguer, or a historical discourse of the life and action of Dona Britanica Hollandia, the arch-mistris of the wicked women of Eutopia, wherein is detected the notorious sinne of Pandarisme and the execrable life of the luxurious Impudent." A later commentator, Geneste, summarized the plot: "The Lord Philautus is self-conceited to the last degree; he is encouraged in his folly by Ardelio, his steward and parasite. Philautus is brought to his sober senses by Faustina. She turns out to be his sister. The bulk of the play consists of an underplot with comic characters; the fourth act passes chiefly before a brothel, which is repeatedly called the Leaguer and sometimes a castle or fort. Trimalchio and Caprito, two gulls with the tutor of the latter are taken up [arrested] by a pretended constable and watchman, as they are coming from the Leaguer." The use of names like Philautus [lover of himself] and Trimalchio bear witness to the author's classical training. "Snarl," as one of the characters is called, comes from the practice of bestowing names according to characteristics. The names of actors appearing in the roles are given in the 1632 edition, but none can be found in lists of players of the period. Philautus was performed by William Browne, and Richard Godwin was Faustina, the sister. At the beginning of the final act, Philautus, back from the war, talks with Faustina whom he does not recognize, and with his acquaintance Fidelio, who is engaged to her. Philautus thanks her for showing him his follies. Fidelio supplies the explanation.

FIDELIO
But, when you know the author of your freedom,
You'll thank her more.

PHILAUTUS
Why, who is it?

FIDELIO
Your sister.

373

PHILAUTUS

Who? Not Faustina? She told me so indeed,
Her name was Faustina . . . I knew her not;
I am glad there is a scion of our stock
Can bear such fruit as this, so ripe in virtue.
Where have you lived recluse? You were betrothed
To one Fidelio, but crossèd by your father;
I have heard good reports of the gentleman.

FAUSTINA

I never knew you flatter any man
Unto his face before.

PHILAUTUS
Unto his face?

Where is he?

FIDELIO
My name's Fidelio.

PHILAUTUS

I am transported, ravished! Give me leave,
God Gods, to entertain with reverence
So great a comfort. First let me embrace you.
Great joys, like griefs, are silent. Loose me now
And let me make you fast. Here join your hands
Which no age shall untie.

Great men are the guide-posts and landmarks in the state

Source: SPEECH ON AMERICAN TAXATION
Author: Edmund Burke (1729-1797)
First published: 1774
Type of work: Political speech

Context: Edmund Burke made this address in the hope of quieting the antagonism that had arisen between Great Britain and the American colonies because of the duty imposed by Parliament on tea imported into America. The second part of the speech delineates the history of taxation in the American Colonies, with particular emphasis on the events from 1763 to 1774. In relating the account of taxation in the Colonies, Burke was led inevitably to recite the positions taken by various prime ministers in Great Britain, including Charles Townshend. In addition to commenting on the events of the ministries, Burke also, and consciously, speaks about the characters of the ministers themselves. Following his comments about the character of Charles Townshend, he makes these observations:

I beg pardon, sir, if, when I speak of this and of other great men, I appear to digress in saying something of their characters. In this eventful history of the revolutions of America, the characters of such men are of much importance. **Great men are the guide-posts and landmarks in the state.** The credit of such men at court, or in the nation, is the sole cause of all the public measures. It would be an invidious thing (most foreign, I trust, to what you think my disposition) to remark the errors into which the authority of great names has brought the nation without doing justice, at the same time, to the great qualities whence that authority arose. The subject is instructive to those who wish to form themselves on whatever excellence has gone before them.

The great ones eat up the little ones

Source: PERICLES, PRINCE OF TYRE (Act II, sc. i, ll. 31-32)
Author: William Shakespeare (1564-1616)
First published: 1609
Type of work: Tragi-comedy

Context: Pericles, Prince of Tyre, has gone to the court of Antiochus, King of Antioch, to woo his daughter. The hand of the princess can, however, be won only by the man who solves a riddle propounded by her father. The failure to do so brings death to the suitor. Pericles is able to solve the riddle; but in so doing, he uncovers the terrible secret of incest between Antiochus and his daughter. The king knows that Pericles has discovered this secret and resolves upon the prince's death, but Pericles escapes from Antioch and returns to Tyre. But even in his own palace he is not safe from the vengeance of Antiochus, and he is advised by a faithful nobleman, Helicanus, to travel incog-nito until Antiochus either forgets his anger or dies. Pericles accepts the advice and starts on a voyage, just in time to escape Thaliard, an agent sent by Antiochus to murder him. The prince stops for a while at Tarsus; but he is not safe even there, so he resumes his voyage. His ship is wrecked in a storm, and Pericles is the only survivor. As he wanders by the seashore, he meets three fishermen who are discussing the storm and the shipwreck and the dangers of the sea. Their comments on the struggle for survival among the fish are a satirical description of the struggle among men, even among such rulers as Antiochus and Pericles:

PATCH-BREECH
. . . Master, I marvel how the fishes live in the sea.

FIRST FISHERMAN
Why, as men do a-land; **the great ones eat up the little ones.** I can compare our rich misers to nothing so fitly as to a whale; 'a plays and tumbles, driving the poor fry before him, and at last devours

375

them all at a mouthful. Such whales have I heard on a th' land, who never leave gaping till they've swallowed the whole parish, church, steeple, bells and all.

PERICLES [*aside*]

A pretty moral.

Great princes have great playthings

Source: THE TASK (Book V, l. 177)
Author: William Cowper (1731-1800)
First published: 1785
Type of work: Meditative poem in blank verse

Context: This quotation appears in the fifth book of *The Task,* entitled "The Winter's Morning Walk." *The Task* is a long poem, fitting the taste of the time in which it was written. The structure of the poem is discursive and rambling, so that it can contain meditative passages on all sorts of subjects, as well as many remarkable descriptions of nature. In "A Winter's Morning Walk," the poet discusses many topics: the foddering of cattle, man's slavish nature, the respective merits of martyrs and patriots, the Bastille, the whimsical effects of frost at a waterfall, the perishable nature of human institutions, and, among others, the amusements of monarchs. In this passage the poet speaks of war itself as one of the amusements of kings, and he decries the fact that kings can spoil the world by making war. Wise subjects, Cowper comments, would not allow monarchs to "make the sorrows of mankind their sport." The verse paragraph in which the quotation appears is this:

Great princes have great playthings. Some have play'd
At hewing mountains into men, and some
At building human wonders mountain-high.
Some have amused the dull sad years of life
(Life spent in indolence, and therefore sad)
With schemes of monumental fame, and sought
By pyramids and mausolean pomp,
Short-lived themselves, t'immortalize their bones.
Some seek diversion in the tented field,
And make the sorrows of mankind their sport.
But war's a game, which, were their subjects wise,
Kings should not play at. Nations would do well
T'extort their truncheons from the puny hands
Of heroes, whose infirm and baby minds
Are gratified with mischief, and who spoil,
Because men suffer it, their toy the world.

The great refusal

Source: THE DIVINE COMEDY, INFERNO (Canto III, l. 60, as translated by Henry Wadsworth Longfellow)
Author: Dante Alighieri (1265-1321)
First transcribed: c.1314
Type of work: Christian allegory

Context: Dante, in the first chamber of hell, sees the trimmers, or those who did nothing, either good or bad. Here are found the legions of the angels who took neither God's nor Satan's side during the war in heaven. Among these neutral folk, Dante sees the man who through cowardice made "the great refusal." Although there are a few critics who hold this person to be Esau, the great majority consider him to be Pierro Morrone, who was taken from his hermitage when he was eighty years of age and was made pope in 1294. He assumed the name of Celestine V and resigned but five months after he assumed the papal office; he was succeeded by Boniface VIII, to whom Dante ascribes much of the evil of the times. The abdication of Celestine V caused great wonder and wide contemporary comment even as far away as Iceland.

> And I, who looked again, beheld a banner,
>   Which, whirling round, ran on so rapidly,
>   That of all pause it seemed to me indignant;
> And after it there came so long a train
>   Of people, that I ne'er would have believed
>   That ever Death so many had undone.
> When some among them I had recognised,
>   I looked, and I beheld the shade of him
>   Who made through cowardice **the great refusal.**
> Forthwith I comprehended, and was certain,
>   That this the sect was of the caitifi wretches
>   Hateful to God and to his enemies.
> These miscreants, who never were alive,
>   Were naked, and were stung exceedingly
>   By gadflies and by hornets that were there.

The greater the man the greater courtesy

Source: IDYLLS OF THE KING ("The Last Tournament," Line 628)
Author: Alfred, Lord Tennyson (1809-1892)
First published: 1871
Type of work: Narrative poem

Context: "The Last Tournament" is the transitional poem of the *Idylls,* depicting the degeneration of a great civilization. Here is seen the passing of honor, loyalty, and purity. The Tournament of Dead Innocence, the last tournament held at Arthur's court, occurs on a wet and windy autumn day. The weary, disillusioned Lancelot presides. Tristram, just returned from his marriage in Brittany, wins the prize of innocence, a ruby carcanet. Instead of taking the prize to his wife, Iseult of the White Hands, Tristram carries it to his paramour, Queen Iseult, the wife of Mark of Cornwall. Tristram finds Queen Iseult alone at Tintagel castle. She warns him that her husband plans to kill him by guile, perhaps by an ambush or poison. Iseult accuses Tristram of infidelity to her in his marriage to Iseult of Brittany. His lack of honor would stir her hate, she tells him, if she were not married to Mark, compared to whom all men seem noble. Tristram seeks to mollify her, claiming that he loved only the name of his new bride, not her person: "patient, and prayerful, meek,/ Pale blooded, she will yield herself to God." In the give and take of the argument, Tristram angers Queen Iseult. She strikes back, comparing Tristram unfavorably with Lancelot, his old companion in knightly deeds of purity and honor, who has himself fallen into adulterous ways of late:

> Then Tristram, ever dallying with her hand,
> "May God be with thee, sweet, when old and gray,
> And past desire!" a saying that anger'd her.
> " 'May God be with thee sweet when thou art old
> And sweet no more to me!' I need Him now.
> For when had Lancelot utter'd aught so gross
> Even to the swineherd's malkin in the mast?
> **The greater the man the greater courtesy."**

The greater the power, the more dangerous the abuse

Source: SPEECH ON THE MIDDLESEX ELECTION
Author: Edmund Burke (1729-1797)
First published: 1808
Type of work: Parliamentary address

Context: In 1768 one John Wilkes was elected to the House of Commons for Middlesex. At the time of his election he was still outlawed by a court conviction, for, as something of a demagogue, he had been in difficulty in 1764 over political publications. As a result of his unsavory past, in which pornography also figured, the House of Commons voted to expel Wilkes as morally unfit to serve in Parliament. His constituency re-elected him four times. Three of those times he was expelled; on the fourth occasion the House of Commons declared his opponent duly elected, contrary to the actual vote of the people. Although he had no regard for John Wilkes, Edmund Burke spoke up in Parliament in opposition to the action of the House, an action he declared to be unconstitutional. As usual, Burke was speaking as a conservative who believed that order and liberty could be had only by limiting personal and group action to what is within the

378

law. For the House of Commons to deviate from their constitutional powers was, in Burke's view, a threat to the whole fabric of the British system of government. And so he spoke against that action to his fellow members of the House of Commons:

> . . . The substance of the question is, to put bounds to your own power by the rules and principles of law. This is, I am sensible, a difficult thing to the corrupt, grasping, and ambitious part of human nature. But the very difficulty argues and enforces the necessity of it. First, because **the greater the power, the more dangerous the abuse.** Since the Revolution, at least, the power of the nation has all flowed with a full tide into the House of Commons. Secondly, because the House of Commons, as it is the most powerful, is the most corruptible part of the whole Constitution. Our public wounds cannot be concealed; to be cured they must be laid open. . . .

The greatest clerks are not the wisest men

Source: THE CANTERBURY TALES ("The Reeve's Tale," Line 4054)
Author: Geoffrey Chaucer (1343?-1400)
First transcribed: c.1387-1392
Type of work: Collection of tales

Context: In the fabliau "The Reeve's Tale," Chaucer tells the story of the outwitting of a dishonest miller by two students from Cambridge, who have determined that all of the grain of their college sent to be ground shall be returned. When the young men declare that they will watch the grinding of the grain, the miller, certain of his ability to steal a portion of it, muses on their caution and finally quotes a proverb of the time.

> This millere smyled of hir nycetee,
> And thoghte, "Al this nys doon but for a wyle.
> They wene that no man may hem bigyle,
> But by my thrift, yet shal I blere hir ye,
> For al the sleighte in hir philosophye.
> The moore queynte crekes that they make,
> The moore wol I stele whan I take.
> In stide of flour yet wol I yeve hem bren.
> **"The gretteste clerkes been noght the wisest men, . . ."**

The greatest fool may ask more than the wisest man can answer

Source: LACON (Volume I, number 322)
Author: Charles Caleb Colton (1780?-1832)
First published: 1820
Type of work: Aphoristic commentary

Context: An English clergyman, sportsman, and wine merchant, educated at Eton and Kings College, Cambridge, Colton occupied his spare time by collecting two volumes of aphorisms. He had previously published what was called a "sermon," under the title *Plain and Authentic Narrative of the Sampford Ghost* (1810). He had also embarked on a work that he called *Hypocrisy: a Satire in Three Books* (1812), of which only one volume appeared. In 1820, Colton completed the first volume of *Lacon, or Many Things in Few Words addressed to Those who Think,* named from the trait of brevity of Laconian Sparta, that gave the word "laconic" to the English language. The book enjoyed such a sale that the first year saw six editions, and so, in 1822, volume II came out. The Reverend Mr. Colton was a man of many talents, but despite his early inclination toward the Church, few of his gifts fitted him to become a member of the clergy. Though unconnected with the army, he liked to appear in military attire. Hoping to better his estate, he frequently gambled, once winning as much as 25,-000 louis at a session in the Palais Royal, only to go bankrupt through speculation in Spanish bonds. He was forced to flee to America to escape his creditors. Later he returned to France where, unwilling to submit to a surgical operation for a cancer, he committed suicide. Stating his ambition "to combine profundity with perspicacity, wit with judgment, solidity with vivacity, truth with novelty, and all of them with liberality," he collected 578 paragraphs, the result of his reading and reflection. He said that by addressing his work to "those who think" he could increase the number of purchasers, "since every individual flatters himself that he is one of that number." The success of the book, not only in England where it first appeared, but in the United States where the first of many editions appeared in 1824, proved him right. Most of the maxims, Colton declared, are founded on two simple truths; that men are the same and that the passions are the powerful and disturbing forces, the greater or the less prevalence of which gives individuality to character. Some of the maxims are only a few lines long; others occupy several pages of the small book in which they were printed. For instance, here are two examples. The first is a thought that has certainly entered the minds of many students at examination time.

322

Examinations are formidable, even to the best prepared, for **the greatest fool may ask more than the wisest man can answer.**

It is better to have recourse to a quack, if he can cure our disorder, although he cannot explain it, than to a physician, if he can explain our disease, but cannot cure it. In a certain consultation of physicians in a kingdom, they all differed about the nature of an intermittent, and all of them were ready to define the disorder. The patient was a king. At length an empiric, who had been called in, thus interposed: Gentlemen, you all seem to differ about the nature of an intermittent, permit me to explain it: an intermittent, gentlemen, is a disorder which I can cure, and which you cannot.

The greatest of faults is to be conscious of none

Source: HEROES AND HERO-WORSHIP ("The Hero as Prophet")
Author: Thomas Carlyle (1795-1881)
First published: 1841
Type of work: Moral essay

Context: Having shown the first hero to have been Odin, made into a god, Carlyle, in the second of his series of six lectures "On Heroes, Hero-Worship, and the Heroic in History," considers "The Hero as a Prophet." After the transformation of some Norse thinker and man of genius into the Teutonic god Odin, development came next among the Arabs. Men, now more sophisticated, were no longer willing to concede God-like qualities to their leaders; all they would grant was that the leaders were prophets, God-inspired. Basically every great man, as he comes from the hand of Nature, has similar qualities. Odin, Luther, Dr. Johnson, Burns, "are all originally of the same stuff." They are all "men of genius," the Soul of a man actually sent down from the skies with a God's-message for us. As example of a prophet, "we have chosen Mahomet, not as the most eminent, but as the one we are freest to speak of." Carlyle says that he is willing to call Mahomet a true Prophet, since 180,000,000 men during 1,200 years have listened to him. That fact could not have happened unless he had been sincere. His words as a prophet were unlike any other man's words,—direct from the Inner Fact of Things. And his rude message was a real one, an earnest, confused voice from the unknown Deep. Perhaps he had faults, but Carlyle goes on:

. . . Neither can the faults, imperfections, insincerities even, of Mahomet, if such were never so well proved against him, shake the primary facts about him.
On the whole, we make too much of faults; the details of the business hide the real center of it. Faults? **The greatest of faults, I should say, is to be conscious of none.** Readers of the Bible above all, one would think, might know better. Who was called there "the man according to God's own heart?" David, the Hebrew King, had fallen into sins enough; blackest crimes; there was no

want of sins. . . . David's life and history, as written for us in those Psalms of his, I consider to be the truest emblem ever given of a man's moral progress and warfare here below. . . .

Greet as angels greet

Source: TO LUCASTA, GOING BEYOND THE SEAS (Line 18)
Author: Richard Lovelace (1618-1657)
First published: 1649
Type of work: Lyric poem

Context: Since the Puritans did not approve of poetry, much of the verse of the seventeenth century was written by men of the king's party. These Cavalier Poets wrote gay, clever, but superficial poems, in which they paid court to sweethearts or boasted of their own triumphs. After Robert Herrick (1591–1674), the best of the group were Sir John Suckling (1609–1642), Richard Lovelace, and others. Lovelace was renowned for his physical beauty as well as for his loyalty to Charles I. For carrying to Parliament a protest in favor of his monarch, he was imprisoned in 1648, where he wrote his celebrated "To Althea from Prison." From prison he also published his verses in a volume called *Lucasta.* In it appeared the well-known "To Lucasta, Going to the Wars." It was formerly believed that the lady Lucy Sacheverell, concealed behind her poetic name "Lux casta" (Chaste Light), inspired these poems. "To Lucasta, Going Beyond the Seas," was written as Lovelace was about to depart for France, in 1646, to serve with Louis XIV. The lines seemed prophetic, for—so it was thought—hearing he had died at Dunkirk fighting, the "Chaste Lucy" quickly married his rival and probably never thought of him again until they met, as he foresaw, in heaven as disembodied spirits. More modern scholars, however, feel that a member of the family of Sir Charles Lucas was the lady to whom the poems were addressed. These are the last two stanzas.

Though seas and land betwixt us both,
　　Our faith and troth,
　Like separated souls,
　All time and space controls;
Above the highest sphere we meet,
Unseen, unknown, and **greet as angels greet.**

So then we do anticipate
　　Our after fate,
　And are alive in the skies,
　If thus our lips and eyes
Can speak like spirits unconfined
In heaven, their earthly bodies left behind.

Grief is itself a medicine

Source: CHARITY (Line 159)
Author: William Cowper (1731-1800)
First published: 1782
Type of work: Verse essay

Context: Having in the first part of this poem discussed charity or love of one's fellow men, comparing Capt. Cook in the South Seas with Hernán Cortez in Mexico, Cowper indicates how commerce links nations together. Then he talks of art, music, and literature which "thrive most/ Where Commerce has enriched the busy coast." He notes the reciprocal effect of trade upon people and the growth of charity as they learn and teach. But the slave-trade is a most cruel and inhuman commerce, causing endless pain and unendurable sorrow, that no amount of patience can make bearable.

Oh, most degrading of all ills, that wait
On man, a mourner in his best estate!
All other sorrows virtue may endure,
And find submission more than half a cure;
Grief is itself a medicine, and bestowed
T' improve the fortitude that bears the load,
To teach the wanderer, as his woes increase,
The path of wisdom, all whose paths are peace;
But slavery!—Virtue dreads it as her grave. . . .

The guardian Naiad of the strand

Source: THE LADY OF THE LAKE (Canto I, stanza 17, l. 24)
Author: Sir Walter Scott (1771-1832)
First published: 1810
Type of work: Narrative poem

Context: When the stag at eve had drunk his fill, he had made his bed in a wood in Glenartney, but with the dawn a hunt begins. A hundred hounds and mounted riders pursue the stag all day. Finally only one rider and two hounds are still in the chase. At evening, when it seems that the stag is cornered and will have to stand at bay, it eludes the hounds and slips off into safety in the wildest part of the Trosachs. When this event oc- curs, the huntsman's gallant gray horse falls to the ground and dies. The hunter then blows the horn to recall the hounds, which limp back to him, slow, crippled, and sullen. The hunter finds himself upon the shore of Loch Katrine; the scenery is so beautiful that it seems like a fairy dream rather than reality. He enjoys the view for a while and imagines what a magnificent site it would be for a nobleman's or proud churchman's tower, a lady's

383

bower, or a cloister. As, however, he is hopelessly lost in strange territory, he blows his hunting horn again to see if help might be forthcoming. The blast of the horn causes a little skiff to issue from a bay. The occupant of the boat, a young woman of exceeding beauty, comparable only to a Greek deity, actually the Lady of the Lake, like the guardian Naiad of the shore, pauses to listen to the echoes of the horn.

. . .

The boat had touched this silver strand,
Just as the Hunter left his stand,
And stood concealed amid the brake,
To view this Lady of the Lake.
The maiden paused, as if again
She thought to catch the distant strain.
With head upraised, and look intent,
And eye and ear attentive bent,
And locks flung back, and lips apart,
Like monument of Grecian art,
In listening mood, she seemed to stand,
The guardian Naiad of the strand.

Gunpowder, printing, and the Protestant religion

Source: CRITICAL AND MISCELLANEOUS ESSAYS, (Vol. I, "State of German Literature")
Author: Thomas Carlyle (1795-1881)
First published: 1827
Type of work: Book review

Context: Because of his knowledge of the German language, unusual among the British, and his familiarity with its literature and philosophy, Carlyle was frequently asked by editors to review books in German. In 1827, the editor of the *Edinburgh Review* sent him four books by Franz Horn that Carlyle bracketed in a single article in issue No. 92, in 1827. It was reprinted in the first volume of his collected essays. One title was a single volume, *Outlines for the history and Criticism of Polite Literature in Germany during the Years 1790–1818* (Berlin, 1819). The other, in three volumes, was *The Po-* *etry and Oratory of the Germans from Luther's Time to the Present* (Berlin, 1822–1824). As was his custom, Carlyle used the books as the basis for his own essay on the subject. But he was sufficiently faithful to his duties as reviewer to comment that the author's poor arrangement made the studies more a sketch of poets than of poetry. He also objected to Horn's belief that no mortal can be a poet unless he is a Christian, and criticized the author's affected style that forced epigrams like a "perpetual giggle." He remarked that the books were written in a style of "witty and conceited mirth." Johannes Kepler

384

(1571–1630), whom he mentions, was a German mathematician and astronomer, and Baron Gottfried Leibnitz (1646–1716) was a universal genius excelling in philosophy and mathematics. After his brief, preliminary comment, Carlyle gets to his essay.

But our chief business at present is not with Franz Horn, or his book. . . . We have a word or two to say on that strange Literature itself; concerning which our readers probably feel more curious to learn what it is, than with what skill it has been judged of.

Above a century ago, the Père Bouhours propounded to himself the pregnant question: *Si un Allemand peut avoir de l'esprit?* Had the Père Bouhours bethought him of what country Kepler and Leibnitz were, or who it was that gave to mankind the three great elements of modern civilisation, **Gunpowder, Printing, and the Protestant Religion,** it might have thrown light on his inquiry. Had he known the *Nibelungen Lied,* and where *Reinecke Fuchs* and *Faust* and *The Ship of Fools* . . . took its rise, . . . who knows but what he might have found, with whatever amazement, that a German *could* actually have a little *esprit,* or perhaps something even better? . . .

Had I but served my God, with half the zeal I served my King

Source: KING HENRY THE EIGHTH (Act III, sc. ii, ll. 455-456)
Author: William Shakespeare (1564-1616)
First published: 1623
Type of work: Historical drama

Context: Ambitious and wealthy Cardinal Wolsey, long a favorite and influential adviser of King Henry the Eighth, has lost the king's favor because of two errors: he has withdrawn his assistance to Henry VIII in getting a divorce when it has become obvious that the king intends to marry Anne Bullen, only a lady-in-waiting, instead of making a politically judicious alliance with France, and he has inadvertantly allowed a statement of his personal wealth to reach the attention of the king. Wolsey, stripped of his power and his wealth by his liege, talks to Cromwell, his only remaining friend:

WOLSEY
. . .
There take an inventory of all I have,
To the last penny, 'tis the King's. My robe,
And my integrity to heaven, is all
I dare now call mine own. O Cromwell, Cromwell,
Had I but served my God, with half the zeal
I served my King, he would not in mine age
Have left me naked to mine enemies.

385

CROMWELL
Good sir, have patience.

WOLSEY
So I have. Farewell
The hopes of Court, my hopes in heaven do dwell.

Hail, Imperator, those about to die salute thee

Source: LIVES OF THE CAESARS (Book V, "The Deified Claudius")
Author: Suetonius (Gaius Suetonius Tranquillus, c. 70-c. 140)
First transcribed: c. 120
Type of work: Biography

Context: Suetonius, Roman biographer, collected trivia to make his writing interesting as well as informative. Almost all of his *Concerning the Lives of the Caesars* has been preserved, as well as many fragments of an even larger collection of biographies, *Concerning Famous Men.* Book V of the former is devoted to the Deified Claudius, and Part 21 describes the shows Claudius sponsored for the populace. He restored Pompey's Theatre, damaged by fire, and gave magnificent games at the Vatican Circus. They included chariot racing, with bull baiting between every five races, panther hunts, and gladiator shows. In his account, Suetonius includes one of Claudius's feeble attempts at humor that misfired. After the combatants in the arena shouted the traditional: "Ave Imperator, morituri te salutant," they pretended to understand his "Aut non," as meaning that they need not risk their lives in the fight. As Suetonius describes the episode Claudius sponsored:

. . . representations in the Campus Martius of the storming and sacking of a town in the manner of real warfare, as well as of the surrender of the Kings of the Britons, and presided clad in a general's cloak. Even when he was on the point of letting out the water from Lake Fucinus, he gave a sham sea-fight first. But when the combatants cried out: **"Hail, Imperator, those about to die salute thee,"** he replied: "Or not," and after that, all of them refused to fight, maintaining that they had been pardoned.

Hail, wedded love

Source: PARADISE LOST (Book IV, l. 750)
Author: John Milton (1608-1674)
First published: 1667
Type of work: Epic poem

386

Context: Uriel, one of the heavenly guards, indicates to Adam that an alien spirit may have made his way from hell to earth, but promises to seek him out next morning; he then departs by sliding down a sunbeam to the sun, which has sunk beneath the world. Adam explains to Eve that all things must rest at night, especially man, who has specific duties to perform which distinguish him from the lower animals, which idle through the day with no ordained work to do. Adam and Eve have to keep the growth of the garden under control and keep their paths unencumbered. Eve says that whatever Adam commands is law to her, as God is law to Adam. Whenever she is with Adam, she forgets everything but him. She then praises the glories of the garden in which they live. Adam explains to her the stellar virtue that is shed alike on them and on the millions of unseen spirits that walk the earth. They then go to their bower, which is adorned with flowers; it is closed to the entrance of all the lower animals, which stand in awe of man. Adam praises God, Who made all things, and refers to the fact that a race is to come from them to fill the earth:

> This said unanimous, and other rites
> Observing none, but adoration pure
> Which God likes best, into their inmost bower
> Handed they went; and eased the putting off
> These troublesome disguises which we wear,
> Straight side by side were laid, nor turned, I ween,
> Adam from his fair spouse, nor Eve the rites
> Mysterious of connubial love refused:
> Whatever hypocrites austerely talk
> Of purity and place and innocence,
> Defaming as impure what God declares
> Pure, and commands to some, leaves free to all.
> Our Maker bids increase, who bids abstain
> But our destroyer, foe to God and man?
> **Hail, wedded love,** mysterious law, true source
> Of human offspring, sole propriety,
> In paradise of all things common else.

      • • •

Half seas over

Source: THE TRAGEDY OF TRAGEDIES; OR, THE LIFE AND DEATH OF TOM THUMB THE GREAT (Act I, sc. ii, l. 19)
Author: Henry Fielding (1707-1754)
First published: 1730
Type of work: Burlesque tragic drama

Context: Henry Fielding, certainly one of the great comic writers of all time, is probably best known for *Tom Jones,* but before he was a novelist he was a dramatist. Most of his dramas are farces, several containing biting

387

satire of contemporary political figures. *Tom Thumb,* however, is a parody of the absurdly bombastic heroic tragedy of the Restoration and early eighteenth century. Here Fielding burlesques not only hundreds of verbal absurdities from serious tragedies, but he also appends a set of comic footnotes by "H. Scriblerus Secundus," extending the burlesque to criticism as well. The play concerns the doings at the court of King Arthur and his queen, Dollallolla, "a woman entirely faultless, saving that she is a little given to drink, a little too much a virago towards her husband, and in love with Tom Thumb." Thumb, the miniature hero, loves the princess Huncamunca, who loves both him and Lord Grizzle. The play opens with a celebration because Thumb is returning from defeating the giants and brings as a captive their queen, Glumdalca, who has fallen in love with Tom and with whom the king immediately falls in love. In the second scene the king is proclaiming the celebration when the courtier, Doodle, brings a petition:

KING
Petition me no petitions, Sir, to-day;
Let other hours be set apart for business.
To-day it is our pleasure to be drunk,
And this our queen shall be as drunk as we.

QUEEN
(Though I already **half seas over** am)
If the capacious goblet overflow
With arrack punch—'fore George! I'll see it out:
Of rum, and brandy, I'll not taste a drop.

KING
Though rack, in punch, eight shillings be a quart,
And rum and brandy be no more than six,
Rather than quarrel you shall have your will.

Hand open as day

Source: KING HENRY THE FOURTH: PART TWO (Act IV, sc. iv, ll. 31-32)
Author: William Shakespeare (1564-1616)
First published: 1600
Type of work: Historical drama

Context: Clearly death is near for King Henry IV, who has known ill-health and civil strife. The ailing king is surrounded by several close followers, including his sons Thomas of Clarence and Humphrey of Glouces- ter. Addressing Clarence, the king inquires about his eldest son and heir Prince Henry and commands Clarence, whom the prince loves the most of all his brothers, to appreciate this affection, to act as a go-between for

388

Prince Henry and his brothers, and to Prince of Wales:
acknowledge certain qualities of the

KING HENRY

. . .

How chance thou art not with the Prince thy brother?
He loves thee, and thou dost neglect him, Thomas.
Thou hast a better place in his affection
Than all thy brothers, cherish it my boy,
And noble offices thou mayst effect
Of mediation after I am dead,
Between his greatness and thy other brethren.
Therefore omit him not, blunt not his love,
Nor lose the good advantage of his grace,
By seeming cold, or careless of his will,
For he is gracious, if he be observed.
He hath a tear for pity, and a **hand**
Open as day for melting charity,
Yet notwithstanding, being incensed, he's flint,
As humorous as winter, and as sudden
As flaws congealed in the spring of day. . . .

A happy bridesmaid makes a happy bride

Source: THE BRIDESMAID (Line 4)
Author: Alfred, Lord Tennyson (1809-1892)
First published: 1872
Type of work: Sonnet

Context: During the wedding service the bridesmaid wept so hard that she could not see. Her sister, the bride, told her not to weep for her, as a happy bridesmaid makes a happy bride. Love himself came down between the couple at the altar and laughed at the bridesmaid, repeating what the bride had said. The speaker of the poem suddenly learns an important truth: that it was tenderness of heart that made the bridesmaid dissolve into tears. He presses her hand and his is pressed in return, and he knows that henceforth the single life is not for him. The bridesmaid was Emily Sellwood, whom Tennyson married in 1850. The wedding that inspired the poem was that of the poet's brother Charles in 1836.

O bridesmaid, ere the happy knot was tied,
Thine eyes so wept that they could hardly see;
Thy sister smiled and said, "No tears for me!
A happy bridesmaid makes a happy bride!"
And then, the couple standing side by side,
Love lighted down between them full of glee,
And over his left shoulder laughed at thee,

389

"O happy bridesmaid, make a happy bride."
And all at once a pleasant truth I learned,
For while the tender service made thee weep,
I loved thee for the tear thou couldst not hide,
And prest thy hand, and knew the press returned,
And thought, "My life is sick of single sleep;
O happy bridesmaid, make a happy bride!"

A happy child of earth

Source: RESOLUTION AND INDEPENDENCE (Stanza 5)
Author: William Wordsworth (1770–1850)
First published: 1807
Type of work: Didactic poem

Context: After 1800 a note of disillusionment began to appear in Wordsworth's poetry, and this note is quite obvious in "Resolution and Independence," the sentimentality of which made it fair game for the parodists Edward Lear and Lewis Carroll. The poem had its origin in an experience encountered by the poet and his sister in one of their walks in the Lake District: a meeting with an old leech-gatherer, badly crippled by an accident yet eking out a living at his difficult trade. The poet's conversation with the old man—which occupies the second half of the poem—is the sentimental part that became the butt of the parodists. But from this conversation with a man whom Wordsworth described as "carrying with him his own fortitude, and the necessities which our unjust state of society has laid upon him," the poet derived both inspiration and comfort. In the earlier and more cheerful section of the poem, Wordsworth describes a heavy storm at night that ended in a beautiful morning. The poet, in his familiar vein, then tells of his identification with nature and his happiness in it. Yet he is keenly aware that after such moments of joy comes a corresponding dejection of mind, during which the sensitive man is conscious of the tragedies that life will inevitably bring to him. It is in this realization that he writes, in the early part of the poem:

> But, as it sometimes chanceth, from the might
> Of joy in minds that can no further go,
> As high as we have mounted in delight
> In our dejection do we sink as low,
> To me that morning did it happen so;
> And fears, and fancies, thick upon me came;
> Dim sadness—and blind thoughts, I know not, nor could
> name.
>
> I heard the skylark warbling in the sky;
> And I bethought me of the playful hare:
> Even such **a happy child of earth** am I;

Even as these blissful creatures do I fare;
Far from the world I walk, and from all care;
But there may come another day to me—
Solitude, pain of heart, distress, and poverty.

Happy is the city which in time of peace thinks of war

Source: ANATOMY OF MELANCHOLY (Partition II, sec. 3, memb. 6)
Author: Robert Burton (1577-1640)
First published: 1621-1651
Type of work: Essays

Context: The only published work by Robert Burton, after a lifetime of scholarly labor, was *The Anatomy of Melancholy,* a pseudoscientific and philosophic treatise on human happiness. It went into a number of revisions, beginning in 1624. The title page of the first printing gave as the author's name "Democritus, Jr." But a note to the reader revealed the real identity of the author. Partition II discusses remedies for the various causes of melancholy. For instance, a philosophic look at the situation can cure discontent. In the next Member, Burton declares that the best cure for most of man's other passions and feelings is foresight and preparedness. Meditate ahead of time about what is likely to come! He preaches the doctrine of preparedness both by man and by a nation against the woes of life that are bound to occur. Then the calamity will be less painful and troublesome. He cites classical authors, Virgil and Seneca, to prove his point. The couplets that in Burton's original appeared in Latin, have been translated into English.

No labor comes at unawares to me,
For I have long before cast what may be.   (Virgil)

'T is not the first, this wound so sore;
I have suffered worse before.   (Seneca)

The Commonwealth of Venice in their Armoury have this inscription, **Happy is the city which in time of peace thinks of war;** a fit Motto for every man's private home, happy is the man that provides for a future assault. . . .

Hard is to teach an old horse amble true

Source: THE FAERIE QUEENE (Book III, Canto 8, stanza 26)
Author: Edmund Spenser (c. 1552-1599)
First published: 1590
Type of work: Allegorical poem

Context: Florimell, beset by a villainous forester in the woods, escapes his clutches and flees, eventually taking refuge in the hut of a witch and her loutish son. The son becomes enamored of Florimell, who decides to fly before his love becomes too violent for her to control. She therefore decamps early one morning. The witch, upon discovering her departure, sets on her trail a savage beast much like a hyena; the beast pursues her until her horse falls from weariness on the seashore. Florimell had thought to drown herself in the sea to escape being devoured by the beast, but finding a small boat occupied by an old sleeping fisherman drawn up on the shore, she enters it and poles her way out into the water. The beast does not follow; instead, it eviscerates her horse. Florimell's movement of the boat wakes the old fisherman, who at first is dazed by her beauty. The old man finally becomes fully awake and leers horribly at Florimell; although aged, he begins to feel the stirrings of foul lust. He leaps at her, but she scornfully repulses his madness. He, however, pays scant attention to her rebuff. Today we say: You can't teach an old dog new tricks.

> But he, that neuer good nor maners knew,
>> Her sharpe rebuke full litle did esteeme;
>> **Hard is to teach an old horse amble trew.**
>> The inward smoke, that did before but steeme,
>> Broke into open fire and rage extreme;
>> And now he strength gan adde vnto his will,
>> Forcing to doe, that did him fowle misseeme:
> Beastly he threw her downe, ne cared to spill
> Her garments gay with scales of fish, that all did fill.

Hark! the Gaul is at her gates!

Source: BOADICEA (Line 20)
Author: William Cowper (1731-1800)
First published: 1782
Type of work: Ode

Context: The happy youth of William Cowper, was followed by long years of mental disorganization, some of them spent in an insane asylum. Between attacks, he wrote simple, but popular, poetry and many letters that are among the most brilliant in English literature. Following one attack, he was sent to the country, to the home of the Reverend William C. Unwin. As a therepeutic measure, Mrs. Unwin suggested that Cowper resume poetry writing and complete a volume. It was published when he was fifty years old. One poem was "Boadicea," an ode to the heroine of the last British uprising against the Romans, about A.D. 60. In this poem when Queen Boadicea asks advice, a Druid foretells the invasion of Italy by Alaric I in 410, and others that would cause the downfall of Rome. He also prophesies the coming of later Italians, famous for music or, like Dante, renowned for words, not arms. He concludes by predicting the future greatness of Britain. Says the Druid:

> Rome shall perish—write that word
>   In the blood that she has spilt;
> Perish, helpless and abhorred,
>   Deep in ruin as in guilt.
>
> Rome, for empire far renowned,
>   Tramples on a thousand states;
> Soon her pride shall kiss the ground,—
>   **Hark! the Gaul is at her gates!**
>
> Other Romans shall arise,
>   Heedless of a soldier's name.
> Sounds, not arms, shall win the prize,
>   Harmony the path to fame.

The harlot's cry from street to street

Source: AUGURIES OF INNOCENCE (Line 115)
Author: William Blake (1757-1827)
First published: 1863
Type of work: Poetic fragment

Context: In the first half of *Auguries of Innocence* Blake attacks man's cruelty to the various creatures with which he shares the earth—wild and domestic animals and birds, even insects. The poem, a series of couplets never polished by Blake and remaining in manuscript at his death, contains many comments of aphoristic nature; those concerning human relationships are often telling. For example, "A truth that's told with bad intent/ Beats all the Lies you can invent;" or "Tools were made & Born were hands." Blake's attention, in the last half of the poem, is directed to man's cruelty to his own species. He lists certain unsavory human characteristics and habits—slander, envy, jealousy, avarice, and lies. He speaks of the beauty of holiness and of the innocence of little children. He turns from this subject, however, to his basic purpose of depicting human cruelty, and castigates those who beat children. Horrified at the existence of such people as beggars and soldiers, he considers both an insult to the heavens. The meager belongings of the poor and labor's small reward are more to be valued than the wealth of nations. Blake then devotes a number of lines to what he seems to consider the worst crime of all: sowing doubt in the minds of the young. Doubt is evil enough in itself, but to mock the beliefs of children is unspeakable. Throughout the poem he implies that if men could only see what is holy and reverence it, many of the sorrows they are born to would cease. Although *Auguries of Innocence* is the outcry of a devout and compassionate man, there is a sort of grim humor in the following excerpt:

393

A Riddle or the Cricket's Cry
Is to Doubt a fit Reply
The Emmet's Inch & Eagle's Mile
Make Lame Philosophy to smile.
He who Doubts from what he sees
Will neer Believe, do what you Please.
If the Sun & Moon should doubt
They'd immediately Go out
To be in a Passion you Good may do
But no Good if a Passion is in you.
The Whore & Gambler by the State
Licencd build that Nation's Fate
The Harlot's cry from Street to Street
Shall weave Old Englands winding Sheet. . . .

A harmless necessary cat

Source: THE MERCHANT OF VENICE (Act IV, sc. i, l. 55)
Author: William Shakespeare (1564-1616)
First published: 1600
Type of work: Dramatic comedy

Context: Antonio's friend, Bassanio, seems to have lost heavily in commercial investments, and Antonio goes to the rich and usurious Jew, Shylock, to borrow enough money to save his friend. Shylock, pretending a jest, persuades Antonio to pledge a pound of his flesh nearest his heart as surety for the loan. When Antonio's investments seem to miscarry, Shylock appears to demand his due, and when the case comes up in the court of justice, the Duke, as judge, instructs Shylock to show mercy to Antonio. The Jew insists that he have his due and refuses to explain his cruelty:

SHYLOCK

· · ·

You'll ask me why I rather choose to have
A weight of carrion flesh, than to receive
Three thousand ducats. I'll not answer that,
But say it is my humour; is it answered?
What if my house be troubled with a rat,
And I be pleased to give ten thousand ducats
To have it baned. What, are you answered yet?
Some men there are love not a gaping pig;
Some that are mad if they behold a cat;
And others when the bagpipe sings i' th' nose,
Cannot contain their urine; for affection,
Mistress of passion, sways it to the mood
Of what it likes or loathes. Now for your answer.
As there is no firm reason to be rendered
Why he cannot abide a gaping pig;

394

Why he—**a harmless necessary cat;**
Why he—a woollen bag-pipe; but of force
Must yield to such inevitable shame,
As to offend himself being offended;
So can I give no reason, nor I will not,
More than a lodged hate, and a certain loathing
I bear Antonio, that I follow thus
A losing suit against him. Are you answered?

Hast thou named all the birds without a gun?

Source: FORBEARANCE (Line 1)
Author: Ralph Waldo Emerson (1803-1882)
First published: 1842
Type of work: Philosophical poem

Context: The question the poet asks is one of a series in the poem which results in a poetic definition of the man who is noble of soul. Emerson wrote this line, of course, at a time when both amateur birdwatchers and professional ornithologists still clung to the notion that the identification of a bird was truly done, as they said, only down the barrel of a shotgun. Emerson, ahead of his time, and in keeping with his idea that the crea- tures and things of Nature are best seen in their environment, suggests that the good man simply observes the bird, as he observes the wild wood-rose and leaves it on its stalk. Such a person, adds Emerson, is the kind who has courage and knows how to respect nobility of character, and as such is the sort of man the poet will value as a friend. The quotation is the opening line of the poem:

Hast thou named all the birds without a gun?
Loved the wood-rose, and left it on its stalk?
At rich men's tables eaten bread and pulse?
Unarmed, faced danger with a heart of trust?
And loved so well a high behavior,
In man or maid, that thou from speech refrained,
Nobility more nobly to repay?
O, be my friend, and teach me to be thine!

Hath not a Jew eyes?

Source: THE MERCHANT OF VENICE (Act III, sc. i, ll. 57-58)
Author: William Shakespeare (1564-1616)
First published: 1600
Type of work: Dramatic comedy

Context: Shylock, a wealthy Jew of Venice, lends Bassanio three thousand ducats to aid in his quest of the hand of the fair Portia. Antonio, "the merchant of Venice," agrees to stand bond for Bassanio and promises Shylock a pound of his flesh if, by chance, his many ships fail to produce the expected revenue. With apprehension Salanio and Salerio, friends of Bassanio, note the failure of one after another of Antonio's vessels. Hence they query Shylock.

SALERIO

Why I am sure, if he forfeit, thou wilt not take his flesh, what's that good for?

SHYLOCK

To bait fish withal. If it will feed nothing else, it will feed my revenge. He hath disgraced me, and hindered me half a million, laughed at my losses, mocked at my gains, scorned my nation, thwarted my bargains, cooled my friends, heated mine enemies, and what's his reason? I am a Jew. **Hath not a Jew eyes?** Hath not a Jew hands, organs, dimensions, senses, affections, passions? Fed with the same food, hurt with the same weapons, subject to the same diseases, healed by the same means, warmed and cooled by the same winter and summer, as a Christian is? . . .

A haunt of ancient peace

Source: THE PALACE OF ART (Line 88)
Author: Alfred, Lord Tennyson (1809-1892)
First published: 1842
Type of work: Allegorical poem

Context: As a young man, Tennyson was torn between writing poetry that was merely beautiful and sensual and becoming a poet who was regarded as a profound ethical teacher. Under the influence of the Cambridge Apostles, a society of earnest and sincere college students, he came to see that the best poetry was moral and the best qualities in men become ignoble unless they are shared. In this poem, he describes the type of poetry that he had earlier written for his own pleasure and shows how the beauty becomes sterile and finally terrifying as the poet turns more and more from other men and from his social role; when the poet is compelled to leave his selfish world of art and to enter the world of men, he is able to purge his guilt and to discover the true nature of humble but morally sound poetry and beauty. The rich imagery of the poem is a description of art, the soul's "lordly pleasure-house," and is presented as a series of individual pictures of the different parts of the palace where the soul can wander in its selfish loneliness. The quotation comes from the description of the rooms, each fitted to create a particular mood.

396

Full of great rooms and small the palace stood,
   All various, each a perfect whole
From living Nature, fit for every mood
   And change of my still soul.
         . . .

And one, an English home—gray twilight pour'd
   On dewy pastures, dewy trees,
Softer than sleep—all things in order stored,
   A haunt of ancient Peace.

Have a care of the main chance

Source: HUDIBRAS (Part II, Canto 2, l. 502)
Author: Samuel Butler (1612-1680)
First published: First and second parts, 1663; third part, 1678
Type of work: Burlesque poem

Context: Much of the Second Part of Hudibras deals with a whipping. In his attempt to ridicule the Dissenters, Presbyterians, and others who fought against the Royalists in the civil war between Cromwell and Charles I, Butler wrote a satirical poem about two representative Puritans, the knight Sir Hudibras, and his squire Ralpho. As they are obnoxious, hypocritical, and absurd, the author implies, so were the enemies of royalty. If he expected to be rewarded by Charles II, who had been restored to the throne four years before the poem was published, apparently he was disappointed, for Butler complained several times about how poorly he had been rewarded for his services to the crown. In one of the few bits of action in this loquacious composition, the knight is captured by an enraged populace, angered by his crusade against what he considers sin, and is put into the stocks. A wealthy Widow, whom Hudibras would like to marry, hears of his plight and in a visit convinces him that whipping should be part of courtship. She will

get him freed if he will swear an oath to accept a lashing. Because of approaching night, the beating will be postponed till the next day. Then come nearly five hundred lines of argument between the knight and his squire about whether he must keep his oath. Ralpho thinks the idea of a beating is heathenish, and insists that oaths are taken only to be broken. "Quoth Ralpho, Honor's but a word/ To swear by only in a Lord;/ In other men 'tis but a huff/ To vapor with, instead of proof." The followers of Cromwell often broke their oaths, even the leader himself, when he kept Charles I in close confinement, and explained, "The Spirit would not let me keep my word." Later, when his followers broke faith and murdered the king, they protested that "they could not resist the motions of the Spirit." Besides, the knight and his squire decide that if three Jews, according to Scripture, can free another Jew from his obligations, surely two Christians can. With many proverbs, like those of his Spanish counterpart, Sancho Panza, Ralpho tells Hudibras to seize his opportunity. "The main chance" was a common phrase for a long time as something to keep one's eyes on. However, Hudibras suggests that perhaps he ought to beat Ralpho, to avoid the need for a lie. His servant, with his eye on the main chance, insists that the spirit of their oath requires that he beat his master. But no one beats anybody. The servant hurries to the Widow to warn her that Hudibras is going to lie to her about his beating.

> Y'had best (quoth Ralpho), as the Ancients
> Say wisely, **Have a care o' th' main chance,**
> And Look before you ere you leap;
> For As you sow, y'are like to reap;
> And were y'as good as George-a-Green,
> I should make bold to turn agen;
> Nor am I doubtful of the issue
> In a just quarrel, and mine is so.

He bears the seed of ruin in himself

Source: MEROPE (Line 856)
Author: Matthew Arnold (1822-1888)
First published: 1858
Type of work: Dramatic tragedy

Context: Polyphontes slays Cresphontes, the King of Messenia, and two of the latter's sons, to seize the throne of Messenia. He also makes the widow of Cresphontes, Merope, his unwilling wife. Merope sends away her surviving infant son, Aepytus, her third child by Cresphontes, to be reared in safety by his grandfather and Laias, her brother. Twenty years pass, and Aepytus grows to manhood. Accompanied by the uncle who reared him, the young man returns to Messenia to avenge the deaths of his father and brothers, and to make his claim to the kingdom. He goes to the royal palace and asks to see Polyphontes, the usurper. Given an interview by the king, Aepytus passes himself off as an Arcadian nobleman who has come to Messenia as a messenger to bring news of Aepytus' death. Polyphontes, eager to learn of the death of the young man who has a better right than he to the throne of Messenia, asks how Aepytus met his death. The disguised Aepytus says that he died while hunting, that while chasing a stag Aepytus followed the beast into the waters of a lake and was swept to his death by a swift current. He ends by saying that the king of Arcadia bade him bring the news, hoping that the death of the young man would end the suspicion between the Arcadian and Messenian kingdoms:

AEPYTUS
He to thee sends me on, in one thing glad,

398

While all else grieves him, that his grandchild's death
Extinguishes distrust 'twixt him and thee.
But I from our deplored mischance learn this:
The man who to untimely death is doom'd,
Vainly you hedge him from the assault of harm;
He bears the seed of ruin in himself.

He found it inconvenient to be poor

Source: CHARITY (Line 189)
Author: William Cowper (1731-1800)
First published: 1782
Type of work: Verse essay

Context: Having talked about the humane treatment of savages by Captain Cook during his explorations in the Pacific, in contrast to the inhumane treatment of Montezuma and his Indians in Mexico by Cortez, Cowper discusses commerce as one means of knitting the world more closely. However, the slave trade reveals no charity, or love of one's fellow men, but only cruelty. He castigates those who trade in slaves to work the sugar plantations. The fact that slavery brings them money, he says, is no more an excuse than for a burglar to break into a house because he is poor. Only those blinded by greed see no wrong in it.

> Canst thou, and honored with a Christian name,
> Buy what is woman-born, and feel no shame?
> Trade in the blood of innocence, and plead
> Expedience as a warrant for the deed?
> . . .
> So may the ruffian, who with ghostly glide,
> Dagger in hand, steals close to your bedside:
> Not he, but his emergence forced the door,
> **He found it inconvenient to be poor.**
> Had God then given its sweetness to the cane
> Unless his laws be trampled on—in vain?
> Built a brave world, which cannot yet subsist,
> Unless his right to rule it be dismissed?
> Impudent blasphemy! So folly pleads,
> And, avarice being judge, with ease succeeds.

He giveth his beloved sleep

Source: PSALMS 127:2
Author: Unknown
First transcribed: c. 400-200 B.C.
Type of work: Religious poetry

Context: Psalm 127 is a brief expression of man's complete dependence upon God, and is put with deceptive simplicity. The poet emphasizes that God must be a part of everyday undertakings if they are to have any meaning. A house built without spiritual considerations is a sterile and disappointing place, a mere shelter; when faith enters into the construction, integrity and meaning are embodied in it. The poet then elaborates his point: there is little use in guarding a city, he continues, unless there is the firm belief that God is guarding it too. Implied but not stated is the point that if we are convinced that God is *not* guarding the city we immediately become ineffectual protectors. Lack of faith in the undertaking, whatever its nature, is destructive to accomplishment. There is much hard labor in life, but there is comfort even in this fact; for man was not made to spend all his time thus, and the Lord has provided him with rest, that he may have relief from toil. The lines may also have another meaning: that men are prone to fretfulness and worry, and dwell upon their sorrows; and that God has provided comfort and forgetfulness in the form of sleep. In the last half of the poem, the psalmist takes up one of the most important of God's many blessings. Children, he tells us, are a heritage from God and his reward to man. Not only are they the joy of their father; they are his strength in time of need, upholding and supporting him. They give him recognition and honor. The man who has many children is fortunate, for in addition to the devotion they give, they will be his defense against his enemies.

> Except the LORD build the house, they labour in vain that build it: except the LORD keep the city, the watchman waketh but in vain.
> It is vain for you to rise up early, to sit up late, to eat the bread of sorrows: for so **he giveth his beloved sleep.**
> Lo, children are an heritage of the LORD: and the fruit of the womb is his reward.
> As arrows are in the hand of a mighty man; so are children of the youth.
> Happy is the man that hath his quiver full of them: they shall not be ashamed, but they shall speak with the enemies in the gate.

He has joined the great majority

Source: SATYRICON (Section 42)
Author: Petronius (died c. 66)
First transcribed: c. 60
Type of work: Prose satirical romance

Context: Titus Petronius Arbiter was a favorite and intimate of Nero; he served as leading authority on matters of style and taste in the latter's court and thereby earned for himself an unsavory reputation. In Nero's court vice was a fine art: the "arbiter of elegance" was an authority on the

400

subject and doubtless assisted his emperor in creating new forms of it. Tigellinus, another expert in debauchery, saw Petronius as a possible rival and decided to eliminate him. This act was done by playing on the emperor's love of cruelty; Tigellinus persuaded him to charge Petronius with treason, and Nero doubtless thought the whole thing a hilarious joke. Petronius, knowing full well the emperor's inventive genius regarding forms of death, committed suicide rather than wait for execution. His chief work, *The Satyricon,* is a satire on the social life of the time and a disturbing view of the decadence to which Rome had sunk. The first portion of the work is an elaborate account of Trimalchio's banquet. Trimalchio is a vulgar, newly-rich freedman who loves ostentation and has the means to satisfy his desires. The guests are overwhelmed with a little too much of everything—sumptuous surroundings, the very latest advances in sanitary and other facilities, an almost endless meal. Petronius has a considerable gift for vivid and picturesque writing: after reading the mottoes on the walls, taking part in the orgy, and listening to scraps of incidental chatter among the guests, we feel we have actually been in attendance. Seleucus, in his anecdote about a funeral, says of the departed: *"Tamen abiit ad plures."* This is variously interpreted by translators, ranging from the matter-of-fact "Well, he is gone," to the sententious *"He has joined the great majority."* The following version, however, is much truer to the witty spirit of the original:

Seleucus took up the tale and said: "I do not wash every day; the bathman pulls you to pieces like a fuller, the water bites, and the heart of man melts away daily. But when I have put down some draughts of mead I let the cold go to the devil. Besides, I could not wash; I was at a funeral to-day. A fine fellow, the excellent Chrysanthus, has breathed his last. It was but the other day he greeted me. I feel as if I were speaking with him now. Dear, dear, how we bladders of wind strut about. We are meaner than flies; flies have their virtues, we are nothing but bubbles. And what would have happened if he had not tried the fasting cure? No water touched his lips for five days, not a morsel of bread. **Yet he went over to the majority.** The doctors killed him—no, it was his unhappy destiny; a doctor is nothing but a stop to conscience. Still, he was carried out in fine style on a bier covered with a good pall. The mourning was very good too—he had freed a number of slaves—even though his own wife was very grudging over her tears. I daresay he did not treat her particularly kindly. But women one and all are a set of vultures. It is no use doing anyone a kindness; it is all the same as if you put your kindness in a well. But an old love pinches like a crab."

401

He has no hope who never had a fear

Source: TRUTH (Line 298)
Author: William Cowper (1731-1800)
First published: 1782
Type of work: Verse essay

Context: Only God's grace, says the religious Cowper whose occasional mental disorganization and mania of persecution several times caused his confinement to insane asylums, can lead man safely on his journey through life. So he will learn the truth. Such a journey need not be mournful. A saint is not necessarily a Niobe, "all tears." "True piety is cheerful as the day," and Cowper also points out that the only chains of a free-born Christian are "the golden ones of love." A man who is sure has no need of hope. Only to one in uncertainty is fear created and hope necessary. The average man, conscious of his misdeeds, may well fear that his sins will never receive forgiveness. On that account, he will not accept God's promise. He may feel, too, like turning from the Bible, despite the assurance: "The remedy you want I freely give/ The book shall teach you; read, believe, and live!" Such a disbeliever, however, may actually be more fortunate than his fellow who is so sure about the reward for his exemplary existence that he does nothing to insure his future life in heaven. For both of them, the poet has some advice.

> Come then—a still, small whisper in your ear—
> **He has no hope who never had a fear;**
> And he that never doubted of his state,
> He may perhaps—perhaps he may—too late.

He has shook hands with time

Source: THE BROKEN HEART (Act V, sc. ii)
Author: John Ford (1586-1639?)
First published: 1633
Type of work: Dramatic tragedy

Context: At a dance Calantha learns from Armostes that by her father's death, just occurred, she is now Queen of Sparta. Within a few moments she also learns, from Bassanes, that his wife is dead, and from Orgilus that Ithocles, a favorite, has been murdered. Calantha takes all this news calmly; when Orgilus boasts that it was he who murdered Ithocles, for revenge, she coolly tells him that he must die, with the mode of execution his own choice. Orgilus chooses to be his own executioner by cutting his veins. He props himself upon a staff and cuts the veins in one arm; then he asks Bassanes, as a favor, to cut the veins in the other arm. As he stands with his life running out, he recalls that Tecnicus, moved by the power of Apollo, has foretold that revenge would prove its own executioner. Even to the moment of his death Orgilus retains his courage and his presence of mind:

ORGILUS
So falls the standard
Of my prerogative in being a creature!
A mist hangs o'er mine eyes, the sun's bright splendour
Is clouded in an everlasting shadow:
Welcome, thou ice, that sitt'st about my heart!
No heat can ever thaw thee.

[*Dies.*]

NEARCHUS
Speech hath left him.

BASSANES
He has shook hands with time; his funeral urn
Shall be my charge: remove the bloodless body.
The coronation must require attendance;
That past, my few days can be but one mourning.

He in twelve, found truth in all, but one

Source: KING RICHARD THE SECOND (Act IV, sc. i, ll. 170-171)
Author: William Shakespeare (1564-1616)
First published: 1597
Type of work: Historical drama

Context: Richard II, who has banished Henry Bolingbroke on charge of treason and has seized his inheritance on the death of John of Gaunt, father of Bolingbroke and uncle of the king, returns to England from the Irish wars. Bolingbroke, who has invaded England to claim his inheritance, confronts Richard with turncoat accusers and demands a confession of guilt and finally the crown itself from the monarch. The Duke of York, weak and aged uncle of both Richard and Henry Bolingbroke, announces the abdication of Richard and the accession of Bolingbroke, as Henry IV, to the throne. Richard, summoned before the new king, claims that the accusers assembled here have previously pledged to him their allegiance even as the traitor Judas had originally pledged his faith to Christ:

RICHARD
. . . Yet I well remember
The favours of these men: were they not mine?
Did they not sometime cry all hail to me?

403

So Judas did to Christ: but **he in twelve,**
Found truth in all, but one; I, in twelve thousand, none.
God save the King! Will no man say, amen?
Am I both priest, and clerk? Well then, amen.
God save the King, although I be not he,
And yet, amen, if heaven do think him me.
To do what service am I sent for hither?

He is the freeman whom the truth makes free

Source: THE TASK (Book V, l. 733)
Author: William Cowper (1731-1800)
First published: 1785
Type of work: Meditative poem in blank verse

Context: Persuaded to take a walk by the beauty of a frosty winter morning, the English poet Cowper writes pictures in blank verse of the loveliness of the countryside, then digresses into a consideration of royalty, its amusements and diversions, and its likelihood to take itself so seriously as to believe the world made for its use. That idea leads the poet to a consideration that a king is only a human being, and therefore has no right to expect other humans to "bear his burdens" and "sweat in his service." With King George III in mind, about whom he had previously written in admiration, here Cowper continues in further tribute to him for lacking the qualities of a tyrant. "We love the king/ Who loves the laws, respects his bounds,/ And reigns content within them; him we serve/ Freely and with delight, who leaves us free." However, the only true liberty, the one that cannot be taken away, regardless of who tries, is "the liberty of heart, derived from heaven." The reference to mighty Samson who cast off his fetters, is obvious. The reference to knowing the truth and the truth shall make you free, is also Biblical. "Confederate" is taken in its literal meaning, "joined together."

> **He is the freeman whom the truth makes free,**
> And all are slaves beside. There's not a chain
> That hellish foes, confederate for his harm,
> Can wind around him, but he casts it off
> With as much ease as Samson his green withes.

He makes a solitude and calls it—peace!

Source: THE BRIDE OF ABYDOS (Canto II, XX, l. 67)
Author: George Gordon, Lord Byron (1788-1824)
First published: 1813
Type of work: Narrative poem

Context: This "Turkish Tale" by Lord Byron has as chief character one of the "Byronic heroes," satiated with pleasure and with civilized society. Though deeply loving a woman, he tries to suppress all tender feeling, along with an equal feeling of guilt for some youthful sin. Byron's half-dozen similar poems take place in the romantic Orient. This one by its title localizes the story on the Dardanelles. Zuleika, daughter of Pasha Giaffir, is supposed to marry the son of Bey Oglou, but suddenly Selim, long thought to be her brother and the Pasha's cowardly son, reveals himself in romantic fashion as leader of a band of pirates who believe it is human nature to prey on their enemies. Only when the foes are wiped out can peace come. Madly in love with her, Selim urges her to flee with him. He promises that "the spoils of nations shall bedeck her," and paints their joys, promising, in words that echo the phrase of Tacitus: "When they make a wilderness, they call it peace":

> To sooth each sorrow; share in each delight,
> Blend every thought, do all—but disunite!
> Once free, 't is mine our horde again to guide;
> Friends to each other, foes to aught beside;
> Yet there we follow but the bent assign'd
> By fatal Nature to man's warring kind;
> Mark! where his courage and his conquests cease!
> **He makes a solitude, and calls it—peace!**

He passed the flaming bounds of place and time

Source: PROGRESS OF POESY (III, 2, l. 4)
Author: Thomas Gray (1716-1771)
First published: 1757
Type of work: Pindaric ode

Context: Charles Dickens once declared, apropos of the slim output of poetry by Gray: "No other poet ever gained a place among the immortals with so small a volume under his arm." But Gray wrote chiefly for himself and his friends. Publication occurred only at their insistence or at the demands of booksellers. Spenser, Dryden, and Milton were his models, but his study of Greek, when few of his countrymen were interested in that language, provided the stanza form of his greatest work, "Progress of Poesy," originally called "Ode in the Greek Style." Having traced the progress of poetry from Greece to Italy and to Shakespeare in England, Gray refers in the second stanza of Part III to John Milton (1608–1674), and to his flight of poetry in *Paradise Lost.* Gray considers him almost on a par with Shakespeare, and since he wrote of Heaven and Hell, and of times past and future, Grey declares that Milton was not limited in his choice of themes by place or time.

Nor second He, that rode sublime
    Upon the seraph-wings of Ecstasy,
The secrets of th' Abyss to spy,
    He pass'd the flaming bounds of Place and Time;
The living Throne, the sapphire-blaze,
Where Angels tremble, while they gaze,
    He saw; . . .

He serves me most, who serves his country best

Source: THE ILIAD (Book X, l. 201, as translated by Alexander Pope)
Author: Homer (c.850 B.C.)
First transcribed: Sixth century, B.C.
Type of work: Epic poem

Context: Temporarily beaten by the Trojans, as Jupiter wills, the Greeks petition Achilles to return to the fighting to help them. But Achilles, still angry over the staining of his honor by Agamemnon, who demanded the girl Briseis as his prize, refuses to rejoin the fighting to help his fellows-in-arms. Agamemnon, when he is told of Achilles' refusal, is quite disturbed by the seriousness of his situation and, with the help of other Greek leaders, awakens the warriors, lest they be surprised during the night by an attack from the Trojans. Nestor, an aged and wise Greek king, is one who goes about the camp helping Agamemnon alert the Greek forces. He wakens, among others, Diomed, who says that such activity during the night ill fits the advanced age of Nestor, who ought to be allowed to rest. But Nestor replies to Diomed that the situation is so grave that despair has overtaken the Greek camp, that everyone, including such an old man as himself, must be alert and active; but Nestor also tells Diomed he may take over waking the others:

> My friend, (he answered,) generous is thy care;
> These toils, my subjects and my sons might bear;
> Their loyal thoughts and pious loves conspire
> To ease a sovereign and relieve a sire:
> But now the last despair surrounds our host;
> No hour must pass, no moment must be lost;
> Each single Greek, in this conclusive strife,
> Stands on the sharpest edge of death or life:
> Yet, if my years thy kind regard engage,
> Employ thy youth as I employ my age;
> Succeed to these my cares, and rouse the rest;
> **He serves me most, who serves his country best.**

He shall not live; look, with a spot I damn him

Source: JULIUS CAESAR (Act IV, sc. i, 1. 6)
Author: William Shakespeare (1564-1616)
First published: 1623
Type of work: Dramatic tragedy

Context: Julius Caesar has paid the debt of ambition. Returning to Rome amidst great glory following his victory over Pompey, he was hailed by many of the common people as emperor, and his growing ambition was reflected in his being offered the crown on three occasions by his colleague Mark Antony at the feast of Lupercalia. The very thought that Caesar might accept the crown and thus subordinate the law of the Republic to the rule of a single man motivates dissension in Brutus, an idealist who loves Caesar as a man but loves his country more. Consequently, Brutus joined with others of less lofty motivation in a conspiracy to slay Caesar on his way to the Forum during the Ides of March. Following the murder the city, of course, is thrown into political turmoil as factions in defense both of the rebels and the slain Caesar begin to emerge. Antony, Octavius, and Lepidus organize the major opposition to Brutus and his followers. As is the case with any civil war, families and friends are divided in allegiance. Antony, Octavius, and Lepidus, in a council of state, consider those—friend or foe alike—who must be destroyed for the sake of the cause:

ANTONY
These many then shall die; their names are pricked.

OCTAVIUS
Your brother too must die; consent you Lepidus?

LEPIDUS
I do consent.

OCTAVIUS
Prick him down, Antony.

LEPIDUS
Upon condition Publius shall not live,
Who is your sister's son, Mark Antony.

ANTONY
He shall not live; look, with a spot I damn him.
But Lepidus, go you to Caesar's house.
Fetch the will hither, and we shall determine
How to cut off some charge in legacies.

407

LEPIDUS
What, shall I find you here?

OCTAVIUS
Or here, or at the Capitol.

He shared in the plunder, but pitied the man

Source: PITY FOR POOR AFRICANS (Stanza 11)
Author: William Cowper (1731–1800)
First published: 1800
Type of work: Satirical ballad

Context: William Cowper was the last English poet who belonged to what has been called the cult of simplicity; most of his work consists of quiet meditation and reflection, together with vivid though tranquil descriptions of rural life and the countryside. His Calvinism, although it comforted him, was also a source of despair and was a major factor in the attacks of insanity from which he suffered. He was trained in the law, and was called to the bar in 1754. He fell in love with his cousin but emotional stress brought on a breakdown and he was forbidden to see or marry her. Another breakdown occurred in 1763, while he was preparing for an examination, and he attempted suicide. A lengthy convalescence followed, after which he retired to the country and lived with friends, first at Huntingdon and later at Olney. He never married. He had written some verse in his youth but did not turn seriously to the writing of poetry until he was fifty; the first volume, *Poems,* appeared in 1782. His greatest work, *The Task,* was published three years later. Its theme, a sofa, had been suggested to him by his friend Lady Austen. Cowper expanded the theme into a long and tranquil poem on the beauties of the winter countryside, the simple pleasures and routines of daily life, and his own meditations on human existence and the outside world. Another collection of poems was published in 1798; his other works include an edition of Milton and a translation of Homer. He wrote a number of hymns. Little of his spiritual and emotional suffering appears in his work, though he moralizes frequently. He had a sweet disposition and a good though quiet sense of humor; one of his humorous poems, "John Gilpin's Ride," was enormously popular and is still famous. He was also satirical upon occasion; an example, "Pity for Poor Africans," comments both on the frailty of human nature and upon the evils of slavery: decent people react to the latter as does the boy invited to rob a poor man's orchard:

They spoke, and Tom pondered—"I see they will go;
Poor man! what a pity to injure him so!

Poor man! I would save him his fruit if I could,
But staying behind will do him no good.

"If the matter depended alone upon me,
His apples might hang till they dropped from the tree;
But since they will take them, I think I'll go too;
He will lose none by me, though I get a few."

His scruples thus silenced, Tom felt more at ease,
And went with his comrades the apples to seize;
He blamed and protested, but joined in the plan;
He shared in the plunder, but pitied the man.

He stands the shadow of a mighty name

Source: THE CIVIL WAR (*Pharsalia*) (Book I, l. 257)
Author: Lucan (39-65)
First transcribed: c. 54-65
Type of work: Epic poem

Context: Pharsalia, Lucan's epic account of the civil war in Rome, depicts the struggle for power between Caesar and Pompey, though many other historic figures appear in the poem. Cato, for instance, the incompetent chief of the opposition party when Caesar returns to Rome because of internal affairs, stands as an old soldier, enjoying the plaudits of his past. Rowe's translation reads:

Victorious Caesar by the gods was crown'd,
The vanquish'd party was by Cato own'd.
Nor came the rivals equal to the field;
One to increasing years began to yield,
Old age come creeping in the peaceful gown,
And civil functions weigh'd the soldier down;
Disus'd to arms, he turn'd him to the laws,
And pleased himself with popular applause;
With gifts and liberal bounty sought for fame,
And lov'd to hear the vulgar shout his name;
In his own theatre rejoic'd to sit,
Amidst the noisy praises of the pit.
Careless of future ills that might betide,
No aid he sought to prop his failing side,
But on his former fortune much rely'd.
Still seem'd he to possess, and fill his place;
But stood the shadow of what once he was.

409

He still remembered that he once was young

Source: THE ART OF PRESERVING HEALTH (Book IV, l. 227)
Author: John Armstrong (1709-1779)
First published: 1744
Type of work: Didactic poem

Context: John Armstrong, a physician, wrote *The Art of Preserving Health* in four books: Air, Diet, Exercise, and The Passions. Book IV, on The Passions, is a treatment of those internal factors that influence health, the first three books being on externals. After, however, stating that the passions should be kept in moderation, the author treats the subject of love. An unfortunate result of disappointed love is often the resort to inordinate wine-drinking. Armstrong by no means advocates total abstinence from wine, as he has high regard for the virtues of port, champagne, Burgundy, and Rhine wine; but he does deplore drunkenness. While intoxicated, a person can say a word that will lose a friend; he can perform a deed that will haunt him to the grave. Drink will cause the means, the health, the talents to decay and will produce a brutishness that will cause a man to be unrecognizable to those who know him. The author then says that he will give precepts for a happy life, enunciated by a certain virtuous old man:

> How to live happiest; how avoid the pains,
> The disappointments, and disgusts of those
> Who would in pleasure all their hours employ;
> The precepts here of a divine old man
> I could recite. Though old, he still retained
> His manly sense, and energy of mind.
> Virtuous and wise he was, but not severe;
> **He still remembered that he once was young;**
> His easy presence checked no decent joy.
> Him even the dissolute admired; for he
> A graceful looseness when he pleased put on,
> And laughing could instruct. Much had he read,
> Much more had seen; he studied from the life,
> And in th' original perused mankind.
> . . .

He that first cries out stop thief, is often he that has stolen the treasure

Source: LOVE FOR LOVE (Act III, sc. iv)
Author: William Congreve (1670-1729)
First published: 1695
Type of work: Dramatic comedy

410

Context: Samuel Johnson, who had little admiration for Congreve as a dramatist, considered *Love for Love* a comedy closely allied to life, and with more real manners than his previous attempts. It was performed under the direction of Thomas Betterton to open the New Theatre. Johnson admired the regularity of versification (which is almost entirely in the prologue and epilogue) and commented that there is in it "more bustle than sentiment." The plot is busy and intricate, and the events hold the attention of the audience but more because it is perplexed with stratagems and amused with noise than entertained with any real delineation of character. It was Congreve's third play, written by a dramatist not yet twenty-five. In an attack on the English stage in 1698 the Non-conformist clergyman, Jeremy Collier, with plays like this in mind, used the adjective "licentious." It is true that its chief theme is the intimate relation between men and women, but actually Restoration drama, written between 1660 and 1700, deals rather coldly with human love and lust. Following the Puritanical era, people were trying to readjust their values. One defender of the plays commented that scenes in *Pericles* and *Romeo and Juliet* go farther in that direction than anything in the Restoration drama that was trying to cure excess, to exaggerate in order to laugh vice out of existence. Like most Restoration comedies, *Love for Love* has an involved plot, though less so than Congreve's two preceding attempts. It makes an excellent acting vehicle. Wealthy Sir Sampson Legend has two sons, the sailor Ben and a spendthrift gallant, Valentine, now deeply in debt. He is in love with Angelica, an heiress, niece of the astrologer Foresight. Sir Sampson sends his steward to urge Valentine to sign over his inheritance to the favorite Ben (the first realistic sailor in English literature), in return for four thousand pounds in cash to pay his bills. Foresight, learning the offer, schemes for a marriage between Ben and his silly, awkward daughter, Prue (the first country hoyden in English drama). Sampson approves, but Ben, home from a three years' sea voyage, finds greater charm in Mistress Frail, sister of the second Mrs. Foresight, and well-named because of her easy virtue. Scandal, Valentine's friend, who wants to preserve Valentine's inheritance, enlists the help of a half-witted beau, Tattle. Valentine pretends madness to avoid signing the release, but confesses the truth to Angelica, now courted by Sampson to provide a new heir whom the old man can manipulate. But she marries Valentine, and Tattle is fobbed off on the frail Mistress Frail. Ben is left without the money and Prue without a husband. But the ending convinces Foresight and Sir Sampson that they are "illiterate old fools." In the third act, Scandal has pretended a knowledge of astrology to hoodwink Foresight and make love to his young wife. In one of those frank conversations of Restoration comedy, he confesses his designs upon her. He tells her that some women are virtuous, as men are valiant, because of fear. But faced with pleasure, women should regard Honor as a public enemy and Conscience a domestic thief. In reply, she confesses that she is not entirely displeased with him, but adds:

411

MRS. FORESIGHT

You have a villainous Character; you are a Libertine in Speech, as well as Practice.

SCANDAL

Come, I know what you wou'd say,—you think it more dangerous to be seen in Conversation with me, than to allow some other Men the last Favor; you mistake, the Liberty I take in talking, is purely affected, for the service of your Sex. **He that first cries out stop Thief, is often he that has stol'n the Treasure.** I am a Jugler, that act by Confederacy; and if you please, we'll put a Trick upon the World.

. . .

MRS. FORESIGHT

Oh, fie—I'll swear you're impudent.

SCANDAL

I'll swear you're handsome.

He that is not with me is against me

Source: MATTHEW 12:30
Author: Unknown (traditionally Matthew the Apostle)
First transcribed: c. 75-100
Type of work: Gospel

Context: In Chapter 12 of his Gospel, Matthew tells of a time when Jesus and His disciples go abroad on the Sabbath day and walk among the cornfields. The disciples are hungry; they are picking the grains of corn and eating them. The Pharisees, always eager to trap Jesus, point out that it is not lawful to do such an act on the Sabbath. Jesus replies by reminding them that David took bread from the altar on the Sabbath when he and his companions were hungry, and tells the Pharisees that mercy is more important than sacrifice. "The Son of man," He informs them, "is Lord even of the sabbath day." A man with a withered hand approaches and the Pharisees, in another effort to trap Jesus, ask Him whether it is lawful to heal on the Sabbath. Jesus points out that if any of them had a sheep which fell into a pit on the Sabbath, the sheep would be pulled out —and that surely a sheep is less important than a man. He then heals the cripple and sends him away rejoicing. The Pharisees are infuriated; their laws have been turned upon them in a most uncomfortable way, and it seems this opponent has an answer for everything they bring against Him. All too frequently His answers leave them with none of their own. They retire from His presence and hold a conference, trying to plan some way to destroy Him. While they are doing so, Jesus quietly goes forth among the multitudes that follow Him and as He heals them requests that they not make Him known. Matthew links this episode to

412

one of the prophecies of Isaiah: that the Servant (that is, Messiah) will teach the new religion quietly and gently that it may spread across the earth. The Pharisees' next move is to accuse Jesus of being in league with Beelzebub; in His reply He states firmly that in man's acceptance of Christ, there is no middle ground.

Then was brought unto him one possessed with a devil, blind and dumb: and he healed him, insomuch that the blind and dumb both spake and saw.

And all the people were amazed, and said, Is not this the son of David?

But when the Pharisees heard it, they said, This fellow doth not cast out devils, but by Beelzebub the prince of devils.

And Jesus knew their thoughts, and said unto them, Every kingdom divided against itself is brought to desolation; and every city or house divided against itself shall not stand:

And if Satan cast out Satan, he is divided against himself; how then shall his kingdom stand?

And if I by Beelzebub cast out devils, by whom do your children cast them out? therefore they shall be your judges.

But if I cast out devils by the Spirit of God, then the kingdom of God is come unto you.

Or else how can one enter into a strong man's house, and spoil his goods, except he first bind the strong man? and then he will spoil his house.

He that is not with me, is against me; and he that gathereth not with me, scattereth abroad.

Wherefore I say unto you, All manner of sin and blasphemy shall be forgiven unto men: but the blasphemy against the Holy Ghost shall not be forgiven unto men.

He that strives to touch the stars, oft stumbles at a straw

Source: THE SHEPHEARDES CALENDER (July, ll. 99-100)
Author: Edmund Spenser (c. 1552-1599)
First published: 1579
Type of work: Pastoral eclogue

Context: The Shepheardes Calender was Spenser's first poetical work of any note; it is a series of unconnected pastoral idyls unified only by the device of giving each one the name of a month. The language is consciously archaic, imitative of Chaucer's work, although the spelling and the grammar often depart from strict Middle English usage. There is also a great deal of alliteration, which Chaucer avoids. The argument of the eclogue is conducted by Thomalin, a good shepherd, and Morrell, a proud and ambitious goatherd. Morrell tells Thomalin to ascend the mount upon which he is seated, but Thomalin replies that he has no desire to climb. Morrell thereupon recites the names of a number of saints and other holy

413

men who have dwelt on mounts, but Thomalin still refuses to leave his accustomed ground. The eclogue probably was written to show the virtue of the Protestant clergy, represented by Thomalin, as contrasted with the proud Catholic divines, as represented by Morrell; Spenser himself was an ardent Protestant. Says the quoted proverb: The nearer to the church, the farther from God. When in the eclogue Morrell says that hills are nearer heaven than are the lowlands, Thomalin replies:

Syker, thou speakes lyke a lewde lorrell,
　　Of Heauen to demen so:
How be I am but rude and borrell,
　　Yet nearer wayes I knowe.
To Kerke the narre, from God more farre,
　　Has bene an old sayd sawe.
And **he that striues to touch the starres,**
　　Oft stombles at a strawe,
Alsoone may shepheard clyme to skye,
　　That leades in lowly dales,
As Goteherd prowd that sitting hye,
　　Vpon the Mountaine sayles.

He thought I thought he thought I slept

Source: THE ANGEL IN THE HOUSE (Book II, canto viii, prelude 3, "The Kiss")
Author: Coventry Patmore (1823-1896)
First published: 1856
Type of work: Lyric poem

Context: Although condemned today because of its monotony and bathos, Patmore's sequence of odes and various stanzas was immensely popular when it was published, earning the author the honorific title "Poet Laureate of Nuptial Love." Unlike most poets who write of either courtship or adultery, Patmore celebrated the state of marriage with an ardor that has become quaint in the cynicism of the twentieth century. By combining erotic passion and the code of domestic virtue popular a century ago, he develops the theme that marriage is the route to spiritual truth. In bursts of Platonism, Christianity, and mid-Victorian sentiment, he shows that love within an ideal marriage is a way to God, thereby making marriage a sacred state in which Honoria, the wife, is a guiding angel to Felix, leading him through the commonplace incidents of life to a final apotheosis. In the quotation, which comes from the final part of the courtship, Honoria speaks to a friend who saw Felix kiss her; as a proper young lady she cannot let him know that she was awake for such would be a sign of immodesty.

414

"I saw you take his kiss!" " 'Tis true."
"O, modesty!" " 'Twas strictly kept:
He thought me asleep; at least, I knew
He thought I thought he thought I slept."

He was a bold man, that first ate an oyster

Source: POLITE CONVERSATION (Dialogue II)
Author: Jonathan Swift (1667-1745)
First published: 1738
Type of work: Satire

Context: Since, says Swift, noted satirist and Dean of St. Patrick's Cathedral in Dublin, the art of conversation is dying in England, with aplomb he takes it upon himself in his three-dialogue work entitled *Polite Conversation* to enlighten his countrymen by the examples of the conversation of the characters in the work. At the home of Lady Smart oysters are served as an appetizer before dinner, and the following conversation ensues:

LADY SMART
Ladies and gentlemen, will you eat any oysters before dinner?

COLONEL ATWIT
With all my heart. [*Takes an oyster.*] **He was a bold man, that first eat an oyster.**

LADY SMART
They say, oysters are a cruel meat, because we eat them alive: Then they are an uncharitable meat for we leave nothing to the poor; and they are an ungodly meat, because we never say grace.

MR. NEVEROUT
Faith, that's as well said, as if I had said it myself.

He was a rake among scholars and a scholar among rakes

Source: AIKIN'S LIFE OF ADDISON
Author: Thomas Babington Macaulay (1800-1859)
First published: July, 1843
Type of work: Biographical essay and book review

Context: Even while writing the *History of England,* which was to be his masterpiece, Lord Macaulay was always willing to take time out for essay reviews of new books for the *Edinburgh Review. The Life of Joseph*

Addison in two volumes had just been published by Macaulay's own London firm, Longmans. Its author, Miss Lucy Aikin (1781–1864) had published three earlier historical studies. At the request of the publisher, Macaulay had looked over some of the proof of the Addison volume and had indicated to the elderly author about forty errors. Her bitter reception of his criticism provoked Macaulay, and his essay began with a rebuke for her many examples of carelessness. Of course, to discuss the life of Addison, Sir Richard Steele, who was his associate in the publication of the news sheets, *The Tatler* (1709) and *The Spectator* (1711) had to be mentioned. Unlike Addison, who had lived a life of sobriety, Steele left Oxford to join the army, where he earned a bad reputation for his life of excesses. The news sheets, containing something of interest for both men and women, included essays on customs, social notes, news from the war, and comments on life and philosophy. Macaulay says that one who, like Steele, crossed the barriers and could interpose Latin phrases from Horace into gossip from the Coffee Houses and from even lower circles of London society, was a logical writer for the three-times-a-week *Tatler,* since he combined the knowledge of a scholar with the experiences of a dissolute man. "Rake" is a shortened form of "rakehell," "one who explores evil." "Intelligence" means "news." Lord Macaulay commented about Sir Richard Steele thus:

. . . He was not ill qualified to conduct the work which he had planned. His public intelligence he drew from the best sources. He knew the town and had paid dear for his knowledge. He had read much more than the dissipated men of that time were in the habit of reading. **He was a rake among scholars and a scholar among rakes.** His style was easy and not incorrect; . . . His writings have been well compared to those light wines which, though deficient in body and flavor, are yet a pleasant small drink, if not kept too long or carried too far.

He wears the rose of youth upon him

Source: ANTONY AND CLEOPATRA (Act III, sc. xiii, ll. 20-21)
Author: William Shakespeare (1564-1616)
First published: 1623
Type of work: Dramatic tragedy

Context: The vast Roman empire is ruled by Antony, Octavius Caesar, and Lepidus, a shaky triumvirate, filled with friction and disputes of power. Antony, enamored of Cleopatra, the bewitching Queen of Egypt, makes such a fool of himself that he loses his power in the empire to young Caesar. Antony attempts to negotiate a treaty with Caesar. Caesar refuses to consider his bargain, but does agree to a bargain sought by Cleopatra—that she be granted the crown of the Ptolemies—on the con-

dition that she have Antony beheaded. In his extremity, Antony, de-
riding his opponent for youthfulness
and cowardice, vowing that he will
challenge Caesar to a duel, conveys
to Cleopatra the message that she
must send his head to Caesar in exchange for the power she seeks.

ANTONY
. . .

To the boy Caesar send this grizzled head,
And he will fill thy wishes to the brim
With principalities.

CLEOPATRA
That head, my lord?

ANTONY
To him again, tell him **he wears the rose
Of youth upon him;** from which the world should note
Something particular. His coin, ships, legions,
May be a coward's, whose ministers should prevail
Under the service of a child as soon
As i' th' command of Caesar. I dare him therefore
To lay his gay comparisons apart,
And answer me declined, sword against sword,
Ourselves alone. . . .

He who turns and runs away, lives to fight another day

Source: DE FUGA IN PERSECUTIONE (On Flight in Persecution, 10)
Author: Tertullian (160-240)
First transcribed: Third century
Type of work: Moral and ethical treatise

Context: In answer to Fabius, who
asks whether or not the Christian
should flee from persecution, Tertullian replies with this treatise in which
he sets forth the responsibilities of the
persecuted. After examining the demands of God on those who would be
soldiers of Christ, the writer comes to
the conclusion that those who have
received Him as Lord will not choose
the broad way of flight from their
persecutors but the narrow way of
suffering for His sake. However, Tertullian admits that there are those
who, rather than obey the exhortations of God, would argue themselves
out of standing fast by applying to
themselves from the ancient worldly
wisdom of the Greeks, a proverb that
is found again in English in rhymed
form as early as the seventeenth century.

But some, paying no attention to the exhortations of God, are
readier to apply to themselves that Greek versicle of worldly wis-

dom, **"He who fled will fight again;"** perhaps also in the battle to flee again. And when will he who, as a fugitive, is a defeated man, be conqueror? A worthy soldier he furnishes to his commander Christ, who, so amply armed by the apostle, as soon as he hears persecution's trumpet, runs off from the day of persecution. I also will produce in answer a quotation taken from the world: "Is it a thing so very sad to die?" He must die, in whatever way of it, either as conquered or as conqueror. But although he has succumbed in denying, he has yet faced and battled with the torture. I had rather be one to be pitied than to be blushed for. More glorious is the soldier pierced with the javelin in battle, than he who has a safe skin as a fugitive.

He would love, and she would not

Source: PHYLLIDA AND CORYDON (Line 8)
Author: Nicholas Breton (1545?-1626?)
First published: 1591
Type of work: Pastoral poem

Context: Nicholas Breton was a versatile poet, from an old Essex family. His birthdate has only recently been ascertained. He probably attended Oxford, since some of his work was published there. His most ambitious volume was *The Wil of Wits* (1580), but he also wrote considerable satirical and romantic poetry. His sympathy with country life and rural scenery may be found in his pastoral lyrics, in which he shows a delicate and refined touch. In his period, Breton was classified among the greatest writers of all time. Suckling, the Cavalier poet, linked his name with that of Shakespeare. Lyrics about shepherds, or a nymph and a shepherd, courting in the Spring, were very common at the beginning of the seventeenth century. Generally, as in this poem, by convention they were given Greek-sounding names, yet most of them acted no differently from young people today with more modern names. This universality is one reason why this poem still survives, reprinted in twentieth century anthologies. Sometimes the names are written Phillida and Coridon.

In the Merry month of May,
In a morn by break of day,
Forth I walk'd by the wood-side,
Whenas May was in his pride;
There I spièd all alone,
Phyllida and Corydon.
Much ado there was, God wot!
He would love, and she would not.
She said, never man was true:
He said, none was false to you.
He said, he had loved her long,
She said, love should have no wrong.

418

Corydon would kiss her then:
She said, maids must kiss no men
Till they did for good and all;
Then she made the shepherd call
All the heavens to witness truth:
Never loved a truer youth.
Thus with many a pretty oath—
Yea and nay, and faith and troth,
Such as silly shepherds use
When they would not love abuse,
Love which had been long deluded
Was with kisses sweet concluded:
And Phyllida with garlands gay,
Was made the Lady of the May.

Heads I win, tails you lose

Source: CROKER PAPERS (III, 61)
Author: John Wilson Croker (1780-1857)
First published: 1884
Type of work: Letter

Context: John Wilson Croker, a British politician and author, and member of Parliament between 1807 and 1832, took part, as a contributor to the *Quarterly Review,* in frequent literary feuds, such as his attack on Keats' *Endymion,* in 1818. His many writings were collected after his death. During the debates about the Corn Laws in England in 1846, Sir Robert Peel wanted to repeal them gradually, establish Free Trade, and help reduce the cost of living. One of his opponents was Lord Granby, son of the Duke of Rutland, who resigned his government post to oppose the repeal. His father wrote to Croker, who also was opposed to the total repeal of the Laws. The letter is dated Belvoir Castle, January 25, 1846. The duke begins by thanking Croker for his good opinion of his son's speech. He also talks about the "mess" in which England finds itself in India with its call for soldiers to fight the Sikhs. Then in mentioning the unfairness of the French position, he speaks of a game, or a phrase in it, which leaves the speaker the winner, no matter how the coin falls. The expression, at least, is still used among children. Here is the final paragraph of the letter:

Périer [Périer is Auguste Casimir Périer (1811-1878), a French politician and Minister.] has sent in the French Corn Protecting Duties, which seem very stringent. If they close their arms to us, while we open ours to them, we shall play at a game which a sharper once played with a dupe, intituled, **"Heads I win, and tails you lose."** I cautiously avoid forming my final opinion on the

419

whole subject till the measure is in the House of Lords in the shape of a Bill.

Ever, my dear Croker, Most truly yours,
Rutland.

A healthy hatred of scoundrels

Source: LATTER-DAY PAMPHLETS (Number 2, "Model Prisons")
Author: Thomas Carlyle (1795-1881)
First published: 1850
Type of work: Essay of social criticism

Context: The Victorian Age, bringing the world closer together, also increased the difficulties of the lower classes. Some writers, like Carlyle, thought such progress would prove suicidal in the end. He was sick about the sordid lives of the workers in the factories, and the additional crimes occurring with increasing poverty. Since he had known poverty as a child in Scotland, he was sympathetic with the plight of the poor, and began writing attacks on current social evils. His trouble—as one critic pointed out —was that, as a philosopher, he had no system. Some of his conclusions about the social order have proved impractical and dangerous. He believed in a strong paternalistic government because of his sympathy with the unprotected poor, and was convinced that because society changes, it ought to do so intelligently, directed by its best men, "its Heroes." His essay on "Model Prisons" was written following a visit with a friend to an exemplary or model prison in London. There, he says, twelve hundred prisoners are housed in clean buildings where they are well fed and given opportunity to learn in good schools under intelligent teachers. By the "Methods of Kindness," the Captain of the prisoners is training thieves and murderers to do nothing. Yet Carlyle asserts that this system is the worst investment of benevolence that human ingenuity can devise. It is impossible to bestow benevolence on an unworthy man without withdrawing it from a worthy recipient. Around the collection of attractive buildings cluster hundreds of dingy, poor, and dirty dwellings, where nonsinners, not yet a part of the "Devil's regiment," are forced to live. If Carlyle were doing the job, he would sweep the scoundrels somewhere out of the way, and provide good food and good teachers for those who were not criminally inclined. He declares himself sick of the "sugary, disastrous jargon of philanthrophy, the reign of love, the new era of universal brotherhood, that provides, not a Paradise to the well-deserving, but a Paradise to all-and-sundry." It operates under the guise of religion. Then he goes on to say:

Not the least disgusting feature of this Gospel according to the Platform is its reference to religion, and even to the Christian Religion, as an authority and mandate for what it does. Christian Religion? Does the Christian or any religion prescribe love of scoundrels, then? I hope it prescribes **a healthy hatred of scoundrels;** —otherwise what am I, in Heaven's name, to make of it? Me, for one, it will not serve as a religion on those strange terms. Just hatred of scoundrels, I say; fixed, irreconcilable, inexorable enmity to the enemies of God; this, and not love for them, and incessant whitewashing, and dressing and cockering of them, must, if you look into it, be the backbone of any human religion whatsoever.

Hearts of oak

Source: HEART OF OAK (Stanza I)
Author: David Garrick (1717-1779)
First published: 1759
Type of work: Song lyric

Context: The phrase "hearts of oak" is an ancient one and traditionally denotes strength, stoutness of heart, toughness, and unyielding determination. It occurs in Aristophanes' *The Wasps* (422 B.C.): "We'll summon our hearts of oak"; Horace uses a related expression; it appears in the anonymous *Old Meg of Herefordshire* (1609), "Here is a dozen of yonkers that have hearts of oake at fourscore yeares." Cervantes employed the term in *Don Quixote de la Mancha* in 1615 ("Soul of fibre and heart of oak") and Susanna Centlivre, in the epilogue to her play *The Cruel Gift* (1717) asks, "Where are the rough brave Britons to be found/ With Hearts of Oak, so much of old renowned?" More familiar than these, perhaps, are two songs which both contain the expression. One, by David Garrick, appeared in 1759; the other, by Samuel James Arnold, in 1811. Garrick was a great actor who also possessed considerable literary ability; Arnold (1774–1852) was a British dramatist who wrote and produced popular operas. One of these, *The Americans,* contains a song entitled "The Death of Nelson;" the music for it was composed by the famous tenor John Braham, whose rich and powerful voice could span nearly three octaves. He wrote part or all of the music for many operas in which he performed. "The Death of Nelson" became a well-known popular song and so remained for many years. In it appear the following lines: "Our ships were British oak,/ And hearts of oak our men." The song by Garrick, however, has probably enjoyed a wider fame. It was set to music by William Boyce (c.1710–1779), one of England's finest native composers, and was first performed in *The Harlequin's Invasion, or A Christmas Gambol,* given at Drury Lane Theatre on December 31, 1759. This festive affair included a pantomime by Garrick. The song achieved immediate fame, becoming one of England's great national airs and ranking in popularity with "Rule, Britannia." To this day it remains a standard patriotic number. The first and last stanzas are given below; the chorus as quoted for the first stanza is the original. The second chorus quoted is a variant, and perhaps more familiar version:

421

Come, cheer up, my lads! 'tis to glory we steer,
To add something more to this wonderful year:
To honor we call you, not press you like slaves;
For who are so free as the sons of the waves?
   Heart of oak are our ships,
   Heart of oak are our men,
     We always are ready:
     Steady, boys, steady!
We'll fight and we'll conquer again and again.

. . .

Britannia triumphant, her ships sweep the sea;
Her standard is Justice—her watchword, "Be free."
Then cheer up, my lads! with one heart let us sing,
"Our soldiers, our sailors, our statesmen, our King,"
   Hearts of oak are our ships,
   Hearts of oak are our men,
     We always are ready,
     Steady, boys, steady,
We'll fight and will conquer again and again.

Heaven first taught letters for some wretch's aid

Source: ELOISA TO ABELARD (Line 51)
Author: Alexander Pope (1688-1744)
First published: 1717
Type of work: Poetic monologue

Context: Pope is here giving verse form to John Hughes' translation of the letters of the famous medieval lovers. Abelard was the learned clergyman, philosopher, and theologian who fell in love with the daughter of a friend. The intensely passionate love affair was discovered by the authorities, who confined Abelard to a monastery and Eloisa to a convent. The present poem supposes that after many years separation Eloisa accidentally comes upon a letter written by Abelard to a friend in which he recounts his misfortune. This letter reawakens in Eloisa the old emotions, and she speaks to herself as if she were addressing her lost lover:

   Yet write, oh write me all, that I may join
Griefs to thy griefs, and echo sighs to thine.
Nor foes nor fortune take this pow'r away.
And is my Abelard less kind than they?
Tears still are mine, and those I need not spare,
Love but demands what else were shed in pray'r;
No happier task these faded eyes pursue,
To read and weep is all they now can do.
   Then share thy pain, allow that sad relief;
Ah more than share it! give me all thy grief.
Heav'n first taught letters for some wretch's aid,

422

Some banish'd lover, or some captive maid;
They live, they speak, they breathe what love inspires,
Warm from the soul, and faithful to its fires,
The virgin's wish without her fears impart,
Excuse the blush, and pour out all the heart,
Speed the soft intercourse from soul to soul,
And waft a sigh from Indus to the Pole.

Heaven has no rage like love to hatred turned

Source: THE MOURNING BRIDE (Act III, sc. ii)
Author: William Congreve (1670-1729)
First published: 1697
Type of work: Dramatic tragedy

Context: The Mourning Bride, first performed at the New Theatre, where Congreve's *Love for Love* brought up its curtain for the first time two years before, was Congreve's only tragedy, but except for Shakespeare's work it was the most frequently performed of any English tragedy for a century. It gains part of its effect from the dramatist's choice of blank verse to tell its improbable story. Few read it today but fewer will fail to recognize the line spoken by Almeria, Princess of Granada, first played by the famous Mrs. Bracegirdle, as the curtain rises: "Music has Charms to soothe a savage Breast," and, she adds, "to soften rocks, or bend a knotted oak." The Spanish scene was popular with Restoration theatre-goers because the complicated plots of Spain provided a model for intrigues. Dryden, driven by financial necessity, devoted twenty years to turning out plays for "The Merry Monarch," Charles II and his successors. In selecting themes he hoped would be popular, he wrote *The Conquest of Granada* (1669), *The Spanish Friar* (1691), and *Don Sebastian* (1690). So Congreve, eager for a comeback after an unpopular play, chose a situation used in scores of plays and stories of Spain, the reappearance of someone shipwrecked and thought lost forever. The decision of critics was that while the tragedy engaged the attention, pleased the ear, and charmed the eye, it never touched the heart. Yet Mrs. Sarah Kemble Siddons (1775–1831) increased her Shakespearean reputation with the role of Zara, and other actresses delighted in it. Actors, however, were not so happy about the chief male character, Osmyn-Alphonso. Though given lines to start Act II: "How rev'rend is the face of this tall pile . . . and shoot a chillness to my trembling heart," which Samuel Johnson called the most poetical image in the English language, neither Garrick nor Kemble could bring the part to life. From audiences, it had a mixed reception at first. Here was the most important comic writer of his era offering a tragedy. Dryden, at the first night, declared himself enraptured, but he must have had trouble following the plot. Some years before the play begins, Almeria, daughter of King Manuel of Granada, fell in love with Alphonso, a noble subject of King Anselmo of Valencia. They were married aboard a ship just before it wrecked on an African shore. As the play starts, Manuel returns after a victorious war with captives, Queen Zara and Osmyn, a nobleman who turns out to be Alphonso. Complications begin. Almeria must conceal the identity of her restored husband. Zara, in love with Osmyn, must let King Manuel think she loves him, to save herself and Osmyn; and Osmyn must pretend to love Zara to save himself and Almeria. Meanwhile, the king's favorite, the villainous Gonzalez, schemes for a marriage between his son Garcia and Almeria, to win the throne. The denouement of this typical Elizabethan "drama of blood" is swift and simple. Everybody discovers the secrets of the others. The king takes Osmyn's place in prison to catch Zara. Gonzalez gets there first and stabs the disguised king. Zara finds the body and, thinking it Osmyn, drinks poison. Almeria enters, and seeing the double tragedy, is about to drink the same potion when Alphonso and his retinue appear to provide a happy ending. Though an abrupt change of tone, it helped the popularity of the play. In the dramatic close of Act III, Zara has one of the fine poetic speeches that gave actresses of the early eighteenth century their big moments. Having left Osmyn in his dungeon and preparing to sacrifice and scheme for his release, Zara returns and finds him embracing Almeria.

ZARA

Vile and ingrate! too late thou shalt repent
The base injustice thou hast done my love.
Yes, thou shalt know, spite of thy past Distress,
And all those ills which thou so long hast mourn'd;
Heav'n has no Rage like Love to hatred turn'd,
Nor Hell a Fury like a Woman scorn'd.

The heavenly rhetoric of thine eye

Source: LOVE'S LABOUR'S LOST (Act IV, sc. iii, l. 60)
Author: William Shakespeare (1564-1616)
First published: 1598
Type of work: Dramatic comedy

Context: Berowne enters this scene with a paper in his hand which is a second poem he has written for his love. While he stands in the park, the king enters, also holding a paper. As the king begins reading, unaware of the other's presence, Berowne realizes that he also is reading a love poem. But as the king is considering sending the poem to his love, he hears Longaville approaching and quickly steps out of sight. Longaville is carrying a paper with a love poem which he too begins reading aloud. Each man expresses doubt that his poem is an effective expression of his passion. The first line of Longaville's poem asks, "Did not" the alluring and expressive eyes of his lover lead him to break his vow not to associate with women. He goes on to explain that he did not break his vow, because his love is a goddess; it is an earthly woman to whom his vow applies.

LONGAVILLE
Did not **the heavenly rhetoric of thine eye,**
'Gainst whom the world cannot hold argument,
Persuade my heart to this false perjury?
Vows for thee broke deserve not punishment.
A woman I forswore, but I will prove,
Thou being a goddess, I forswore not thee.
My vow was earthly, thou a heavenly love.
Thy grace being gained cures all disgrace in me.
Vows are but breath, and breath a vapour is.
Then thou, fair sun, which on my earth dost shine,
Exhalest this vapour-vow; in thee it is.
If broken then, it is no fault of mine:
If by me broke, what fool is not so wise
To lose an oath to win a paradise?

Heaven's gift takes earth's abatement

Source: ONE WORD MORE (IX, Line 73)
Author: Robert Browning (1812-1889)
First published: 1855
Type of work: Dedicatory epilogue

Context: Browning wrote this poem as an epilogue to dedicate a volume of poetry to his wife, Elizabeth Browning. In it, he discusses the importance of a private existence for the artist apart from his public personage. "God be thanked, the meanest of his creatures/ Boasts two soul-sides, one to face the world with,/ One to show a woman he loves her!" The poet wishes he could turn to a new medium to express his love for a woman as did Dante, who painted to honor Beatrice, or as did Rafael, who wrote a century of sonnets for his love. These evidences of love are more precious to other lovers than are all the masterpieces that the artists created in their fields. An artist wishes, at least once, to be only a man and to be judged for the joy of his love and not by the critical standards applicable to his public performance. There follows a lengthy comparison between the poet and the prophet. Both Moses and the poet live with heaven-sent gifts which, at times, they may wish to ignore but cannot:

. . . no artist lives and loves, that longs not
Once, and only once, for one only
(Ah the prize!), to find his love a language
Fit and fair and simple and sufficient—

425

Using nature that's an art to others,
Not, this one time, art that's turned his nature.

      .   .   .

So to be the man and leave the artist,
Gain the man's joy, miss the artist's sorrow.

Wherefore? **Heaven's gift takes earth's abatement!**
He who smites the rock and spreads the water,

      .   .   .

Even he, the minute makes immortal,
Proves, perchance, but mortal in the minute,
Desecrates, belike, the deed in doing.

The heavens themselves blaze forth the death of princes

Source: JULIUS CAESAR (Act II, sc. ii, l. 31)
Author: William Shakespeare (1564-1616)
First published: 1623
Type of work: Dramatic tragedy

Context: In his home in Rome, Julius Caesar arises early, and, still in his nightgown, discusses with Calphurnia, his wife, whether to go to the Senate as he has intended, since this is the Ides of March, the day against which a soothsayer has warned him. Calphurnia pleads with him to stay at home, recounting the ominous events of the night reported by a watchman —in addition to thunder and lightning, a lion has whelped in the street, graves have opened for the dead to escape, fiery soldiers have battled in the clouds, raining blood upon the Capitol, and the streets have been filled with the sounds of horses whinnying, of the dying groaning, and of ghosts shrieking. Caesar, contending that the portents of the night are directed at all the world as much as at him, continues the discussion:

CAESAR
What can be avoided
Whose end is purposed by the mighty gods?
Yet Caesar shall go forth; for these predictions
Are to the world in general, as to Caesar.

CALPHURNIA
When beggars die, there are no comets seen;
The heavens themselves blaze forth the death of princes.

The heir of all ages, in the foremost files of time

Source: LOCKSLEY HALL (Line 178)
Author: Alfred, Lord Tennyson (1809-1892)
First published: 1842
Type of work: Dramatic monologue

Context: Locksley Hall is Tennyson's first poem of social protest; but it is also an interesting prophecy of the world to come, all the more remarkable when the date of its composition is considered. As the poem opens, the poet stands on the beach near his home, Locksley Hall. He is bidding farewell to the scenes of his boyhood, where he had ranged the moors and beaches, "nourishing a youth sublime/ With the fairy tales of science, and the long result of Time." Here he had glimpsed the wonders of the future; here also he had loved his cousin Amy. She, obeying the customs of the day, had abided by the decision of her parents and married a country gentleman they had chosen for her. The forsaken poet calls her shallow-hearted, "Puppet to a father's threat, and servile to a shrewish tongue." The forecast he gives of her married life is bleak and pitiless: "thou shalt lower to his level day by day,/ What is fine within thee growing coarse to sympathize with clay./ As the husband is, the wife is: thou art mated with a clown,/ And the grossness of his nature will have weight to drag thee down./ He will hold thee, when his passion shall have spent its novel force,/ Something better than his dog, a little dearer than his horse." Torturing himself in this fashion, and feeling it would be better if she were dead, the poet foresees that she will in time be ignored or tolerated by her husband, but will be compensated in some measure by a child. The poet feels he "must mix with action, lest I wither by despair." He yearns for the past, but cannot recapture it: "Knowledge comes, but wisdom lingers, and I linger on the shore,/ And the individual withers, and the world is more and more." He thinks of renouncing civilization completely, going to some island in the South Seas and taking a savage wife who will "rear my dusky race." But even as he considers this course, he knows he cannot follow it:

Iron-jointed, supple-sinew'd, they shall dive, and they shall run,
Catch the wild goat by the hair, and hurl their lances in the sun;

Whistle back the parrot's call, and leap the rainbows of the brooks,
Not with blinded eyesight poring over miserable books—

Fool, again the dream, the fancy! but I *know* my words are wild,
But I count the grey barbarian lower than the Christian child.

I, to herd with narrow foreheads, vacant of our glorious gains,
Like a beast with lower pleasures, like a beast with lower pains!

427

Mated with a squalid savage—what to me were sun or clime?
I the heir of all the ages, in the foremost files of time—

I that rather held it better men should perish one by one,
Than that earth should stand at gaze like Joshua's moon in Ajalon!

Heirs of all eternity

Source: LOVE'S LABOUR'S LOST (Act I, sc. i, l. 7)
Author: William Shakespeare (1564-1616)
First published: 1598
Type of work: Dramatic comedy

Context: King Ferdinand of Navarre and his lords in attendance, Berowne, Longaville, and Dumaine, take an oath to forsake courtly pleasures and to devote three years to studying and fasting, thus making of Navarre "a little Academe." Ferdinand suggests that fame will defeat death's devouring disgrace, and make of the scholars "heirs of all eternity."

> KING
>
> Let fame, that all hunt after in their lives,
> Live registered upon our brazen tombs,
> And then grace us, in the disgrace of death;
> When, spite of cormorant devouring Time,
> Th' endeavour of this present breath may buy
> That honour which shall bate his scythe's keen edge,
> And make us **heirs of all eternity.**
> Therefore, brave conquerors—for so you are,
> That war against your own affections,
> And the huge Army of the world's desires—
> Our late edict shall strongly stand in force.
> Navarre shall be the wonder of the world.
> Our court shall be a little Academe,
> Still and contemplative in living art.

• • •

The Hell within him

Source: PARADISE LOST (Book IV, l. 20)
Author: John Milton (1608-1674)
First published: 1667
Type of work: Epic poem

Context: Satan and other angels, unsuccessful in their attempt to snatch from God the control of Heaven, are cast into the burning lake of Hell. The fallen angels meet in council to discuss making another attempt to gain Heaven, but decide instead to explore an alternate course of ven-

428

geance. Since they have heard of the creation of the Earth, Satan's offer to attempt revenge in this sphere is agreed upon, but as Satan approaches the Garden of Eden and envisions the corruption of the innocence of Adam and Eve, he is torn by doubt and despair:

> . . . horror and doubt distract
> His troubl'd thoughts, and from the bottom stirr
> **The Hell within him,** for within him Hell
> He brings, and round about him, nor from Hell
> One step no more then from himself can fly
> By change of place: Now conscience wakes despair
> That slumbered, wakes the bitter memorie
> Of what he was, what is, and what must be
> Worse; of worse deeds worse sufferings must ensue.
> Sometimes towards Eden which now in his view
> Lay pleasant, his grieved look he fixes sad,
> Sometimes towards Heav'n and the full-blazing Sun,
> Which now sat high in his Meridian Towre:
> Then much revolving, thus in sighs began.

Hence, O hence ye that are uninitiate

Source: THE AENEID (Book VI, as translated by John Jackson)
Author: Virgil (Publius Vergilius Maro, 70-19 B.C.)
First transcribed: 29-19 B.C.
Type of work: Epic poem

Context: Virgil died while making the final revisions of his Homeric epic about Aeneas, the legendary founder of Rome. Augustus Caesar, in whose honor it had been composed, ordered the work preserved. In the early books, Aeneas, who had fled from burning Troy carrying his aged father Anchises, tells the story of his flight to Dido, Queen of Carthage. Warned in a dream by Mercury that the queen intends to keep him in Carthage, Aeneas resumes his journey. At Sicily, Anchises dies and is buried. Finally in Book VI Aeneas reaches the shores of Italy at Cumae, famous for its Sibyl or prophetess. She grants Aeneas the privilege of visiting his father in the underworld, and counsels him about the proper religious ceremonies at the Cavern that marks the descent to Avernus. Proserpine or Persephone, the goddess of fertility, wife of Pluto or Hades, is compelled to remain underground part of each year because of the four pomegranate seeds she had eaten when kidnaped and taken there. Hecate, the moon goddess, is her attendant in the lower world, beyond the River Styx, the realm of the Stygian king. The Furies or Erinyes or goddesses of vengeance are the daughters of Earth or Uranius. Night is Earth's sister. When all is ready at the Cavern entrance, about sunrise, the uninitiated, that is, not instructed in the religious mysteries, are ordered to leave the holy forest. The Sibyl has provided four black steers and a lamb whose fleece is

429

black. She has been:

> . . . calling the while on Hecate, queen alike in Heaven and Hell. Others set the knife to the throat and caught the warm blood in vessels. Himself, Aeneas, smote with the sword a ewe-lamb of sable fleece to the mother of the Furies and her mighty sister, and to thee, Prosperpine, a barren heifer. Then to the Stygian king he reared altars by night and placed on the flames whole carcasses of bulls, pouring rich oil over the burning flesh. But, lo, about the first rays of the orient sun, earth began to moan under foot, and the ridges of forest to tremble, and hounds seemed to bay through the twilight as the goddess drew nigh. **"Hence, O hence,"** cried the prophetess, **"ye that are uninitiate!** Withdraw ye from all the grove!" . . .

Hence these tears

Source: THE LADY OF ANDROS (Act I, sc. i)
Author: Terence (Publius Terentius Afer, c. 190-159 B.C.)
First transcribed: Second century, B.C.
Type of work: Dramatic comedy

Context: Andria (The Lady of Andros), Terence's first play, was produced in 166 B.C., when the playwright was on the threshold of his career. In the drama Pamphilus, a young man of good family, is deeply in love with Glycerium, a girl from Andros. Gino, Pamphilus' father, recently returned home, fears that his son, despite the lad's excellent reputation, has fallen in love with Glycerium's sister, the courtesan Chrysis. When the father attends Chrysis' funeral he discovers the truth. His discovery makes him very unhappy, for he wishes Pamphilus to marry another, the daughter of his friend Chremes, a girl with a good dowry and a good family. All turns out well, as it does in comedy, for in the end Glycerium proves to be a long-lost daughter of the same Chremes. In the first scene of Act I, Simo tells his servant, Sosia, how he discovered that his son loves Glycerium. What he learns is given added proof when Pamphilus prevents the girl from throwing herself on her sister's funeral pyre. The quotation, "hinc illae lacrumae" in the original Latin, has been variously translated, as the following context illustrates:

SIMO
 . . . In short, out of feeling for him I went to the funeral myself, still without suspicion of anything being amiss.

SOSIA
Bless me, Sir, what do you mean?

430

You shall be told. The body was brought out and we followed. Presently among the women in attendance I caught sight of one girl whose figure was—

SOSIA

Not bad, perhaps?

SIMO

—and her face, Sosia, so modest and so charming, it couldn't be beaten. As her grief seemed to me deeper than the others' and her figure was more elegant and ladylike than the others', I went up to the waiting-women and asked who she was. They told me she was Chrysis' sister. It struck me at once. Ha, that's the secret, **that's the source of his tears,** that's his compassion.

Hercules is not only known by his foot

Source: HYDRIOTAPHIA: URN BURIAL (Chapter 3)
Author: Sir Thomas Browne (1605-1682)
First published: 1658
Type of work: Philosophy

Context: This philosophical physician and scientist set out to write a report concerning some forty or fifty Roman funeral urns which were exhumed near Norwich. His speculative nature led him beyond the bounds of a mere scientific treatise to a disquisition on burial customs in general, ranging of course through his vast knowledge of classical literature. In Chapter 3 he discusses not only the effects of burial on the remains discovered but digresses to consider generally the information to be derived from exhumed remains, and reflects upon some classical examples:

. . . When Alexander opened the Tomb of Cyrus, the remaining bones discovered his proportion, whereof urnall fragments afford but a bad conjecture, and have this disadvantage of grave enterrments, that they leave us ignorant of most personal discoveries. For since bones afford not only rectitude and stability, but figure unto the body; it is no impossible physiognomy to conjecture at fleshy appendencies; and after what shape the muscles and carnous parts might hang in their full consistences. A full spread Cariola shews a well-shaped horse behind, handsome formed skulls give some analogy of fleshy resemblance. A critical view of bones makes a good distinction of sexes. Even colour is not beyond conjecture; since it is hard to be deceived in the distinction of Negro's skulls. Dante's characters are to be found in skulls as well as faces. **Hercules is not only known by his foot.** Other parts make out their comproportions, and inferences upon the whole or parts.

And since the dimensions of the head measure the whole body, and the figure thereof gives conjecture of the principal faculties; physiognomy outlives our selves, and ends not in our graves.

Herded wolves, bold only to pursue

Source: ADONAIS (Stanza 28)
Author: Percy Bysshe Shelley (1792-1822)
First published: 1821
Type of work: Elegy

Context: In his elegy on the death of John Keats (1795–1821), who died of tuberculosis in Rome at the age of twenty-six years, Shelley severely blames the reviewer of Keats' *Endymion* for inflicting a wound on the spirit of the young poet that led to the bursting of a blood-vessel in his lung and his subsequent death. Shelley says that everything in nature renews itself with the coming of spring: the ants, the bees, the swallows reappear; fresh leaves and flowers deck dead winter's bier; the lizard and the snake awake from their trance: only Adonais, or Keats, cannot come back; he will awake no more. Misery invokes Urania, the mother Muse of Adonais, to arise and go to the mournful place where Adonais lies. She flees to him and begs him to revive to comfort her; in her grief she exclaims that she would gladly die, as he did, but as an immortal she is chained to time and cannot depart from this world. She says that he was defenseless against the world; he should have waited until the time when wisdom and scorn would have made him impervious to envious thrusts. Wolves in bands, with courage only to pursue that which flees from them, the obscene raven, and the vultures dare not attack the Pythian of the age, Lord Byron, who treated his critics with the contempt they deserved in *English Bards and Scotch Reviewers.*

"The **herded wolves, bold only to pursue;**
The obscene ravens, clamorous o'er the dead;
The vultures to the conqueror's banner true
Who feed where Desolation first has fed,
And whose wings rain contagion;—how they fled,
When, like Apollo, from his golden bow
The Pythian of the age one arrow sped
And smiled!—The spoilers tempt no second blow,
They fawn on the proud feet that spurn them lying low."

Here today and gone tomorrow

Source: THE LUCKY CHANCE, OR AN ALDERMAN'S BARGAIN (Act IV)
Author: Aphra Behn (1640-1689)
First published: 1687
Type of work: Dramatic comedy

Context: Lady Fulbank, who has spent a night with Gayman without his knowing her identity, asks him why he was so quick to leave her at a party the night before. Gayman tells her he loves her and offers a token of his esteem and affection: a ring which she, in her unknown identity gave him while his bedroom companion! When she asks about the ring, telling him she knows he is without money, he tells her that he had it the night before from a female devil who entertained him in a bedroom; he describes the "female devil" as like a "canvas bag full of wooden ladles." Lady Ful- bank says to herself that she would be insulted at such a description of her- self, except that she knows it is un- true. As they talk, her husband, Sir Cautious, comes in, suspicious that Gayman is about to make (or al- ready has made) him a cuckold. Lady Fulbank leaves, and Gayman tells Sir Cautious about the "female devil." They also argue about money that Gayman has lost through Sir Cautious and a mortgage on his lands. Noysey and Bearjest join them; when Gayman leaves, they speak about him and his way of life, using his real name, Wastall:

SIR CAUTIOUS
Do you know this Wastall, Sir!—[*to Noysey.*]

NOYSEY
Know him sir, Ay too well—

BEARJEST
The World's well amended with him Captain, since I lost my money to him and you at the George in *White Fryars*.

NOYSEY
Ay poor fellow—he's sometimes up and sometime down, as the Dice favour him.—

BEARJEST
Faith and that's pity; but how came he so fine o' th' sudden: but last Week he borrowed eighteen pence of me on his Wast Belt to pay his dinner in an Ordinary.

BELMOUR
Were you so cruel Sir to take it?

433

We are not all one Mans Children; faith Sir; we are **here to Day
and gone to Morrow**—

He's for the morning

Source: A GRAMMARIAN'S FUNERAL (Line 24)
Author: Robert Browning (1812-1889)
First published: 1855
Type of work: Dramatic monologue

Context: This poem is the final tribute of a group of students to their dead master, a Greek scholar. As day breaks, they carry his corpse to the mountain top for burial. Their song catches the spirit of those scholars who thirsted after knowledge in the early Renaissance, but they inadvertently reveal that their master chose Knowledge to the exclusion of Life. This unknowing admission by his students shows that the scholar had, in effect, denied the very premise of Renaissance humanism, which originally motivated his search for knowledge. The students praise their master's choice: "That before living he'd learn how to live—No end to learning." They never realize the implications of his withdrawal from both life and humanity. Triumphantly, they bear him to his resting place, isolated from common man:

> That's the appropriate country; there, man's thought,
>> Rarer, intenser,
> Self-gathered for an outbreak, as it ought,
>> Chafes in the censer.
> Leave we the unlettered plain its herd and crop;
>> Seek we a sepulture
> On a tall mountain, citied to the top,
>> Crowded with culture!
>>   • • •
> Our low life was the level's and the night's;
>> **He's for the morning.**
> Step to a tune, square chests, erect each head,
>> 'Ware the beholders!
> This is our master, famous, calm and dead,
>> Borne on our shoulders.

He's only a pauper, whom nobody owns

Source: THE PAUPER'S DRIVE
Author: Thomas Noel (1799-1861)
First published: 1841
Type of work: Humanitarian poem

Context: Though Thomas Noel, the English poet, published a volume of poetry, *Rhymes and Roundelays,* in 1841, only one of its ·contents survives today, "Rocked in the Cradle of the Deep," set to music for the delight of a basso profundo. He also included in the volume a melancholic picture of a pauper driven unaccompanied to a churchyard for burial. Only at his death, says the poet, did the poor man make a noise in the world, as the rickety hearse clattered over the cobbles. At only this moment, writes Noel ironically, did he approach gentility, for at last he rode through London streets in a coach. The poet adds a satirical reminder to other bums that they, too, will have their chance to be a "gemman" (gentleman). It is a poem of six stanzas, each of which has as refrain, the quoted line.

> There's a grim one-horse hearse in a jolly round trot,—
> To the churchyard a pauper is going, I wot;
> The road it is rough, and the hearse has no springs,
> And hark to the dirge which the mad driver sings:
> 　　Rattle his bones over the stones!
> 　　**He's only a pauper whom nobody owns!**
>
> O, where are the mourners? Alas! there are none;
> He has left not a gap in the world, now he's gone,—
> Not a tear in the eye of child, woman, or man,
> To the grave with his carcass as fast as you can:
> 　　Rattle his bones over the stones!
> 　　**He's only a pauper whom nobody owns!**
> 　　　　·　·　·
> You bumpkins! who stare at your brother conveyed,
> Behold what respect to a cloddy is paid!
> And be joyful to think, when by death you're laid low,
> You've a chance to the grave like a gemman to go.
> 　　Rattle his bones over the stones!
> 　　**He's only a pauper whom nobody owns!**

High Heaven rejects the lore of nicely-calculated less or more

Source: ECCLESIASTICAL SONNETS (Part III, 43, "Inside of King's College Chapel, Cambridge")
Author: William Wordsworth (1770-1850)
First published: 1822
Type of work: Religious sonnet

Context: One of the most beautiful buildings at Cambridge University is King's College Chapel, a Gothic church commissioned by Henry VI (1422–1461); however, the chapel cost so much to construct that many of the more critical minds, both while it was being built and later, felt that the expense was disproportionate to its use, for rather than being a public

435

place of worship, it was designed only for the students. Wordsworth, being by nature opposed to the type of thought that measures beauty by practicability, had no patience with these critics; though deeply concerned with the plight of his fellow men, he became more and more conservative as he grew older. Seeing religion as a means whereby men can find the stoic endurance that enables them to withstand great suffering, he expresses his belief in the ability of great beauty, especially that of Christian art, to uplift the worshiper. Such beauty cannot be reckoned in money, only in the spiritual peace that comes to the beholder.

> Give all thou canst; **high Heaven rejects the lore**
> **Of nicely-calculated less or more;**
> So deemed the man who fashioned for the sense
> These lofty pillars, spread that branching roof
> Self-poised, and scooped into ten thousand cells,
> Where light and shade repose, where music dwells
> Lingering—and wandering on as loth to die;
> Like thoughts whose very sweetness yieldeth proof
> That they were born for immortality.

Him first, Him last, Him midst, and without end

Source: PARADISE LOST (Book V, l. 165)
Author: John Milton (1608-1674)
First published: 1667
Type of work: Epic poem

Context: Morning comes and Adam wonders to find Eve still asleep, looking as if she had had an unquiet night. He gently wakens her, saying that they have their work to do. Eve says that she has had a disturbing dream. She thought that as she slept, Adam called to her; in trying to find him, she arrived at the tree of prohibited knowledge. By the tree was a figure like the angels that inhabit the garden by day. The spirit wondered why knowledge was so despised that no one ate of the tree. He plucked a fruit and tasted it, much to Eve's horror; he was, however, delighted with the taste; the fruit, he said, makes gods of men. He then urged Eve to eat, as it would make her a goddess. He pressed the food to her mouth so that she had to taste it. The result was that she flew up to the clouds in exultation. The guide disappeared, and Eve sank down and fell asleep. Adam says that he believes the dream to be of evil origin, but evil thoughts can enter the minds of the most pure and leave no spot behind. They go to the field and begin their morning prayer, praising their Maker in umpremeditated song:

> These are thy glorious works, Parent of good,
> Almighty, thine this universal frame,
> Thus wondrous fair; Thyself how wondrous then!

436

Unspeakable, who sit'st above these heavens
To us invisible or dimly seen
In these thy lowest works, yet these declare
Thy goodness beyond thought, and power divine:
Speak ye who best can tell, ye sons of light,
Angels, for ye behold Him, and with songs
And choral symphonies, day without night,
Circle His throne rejoicing, ye in heaven,
On earth join all ye creatures to extol
Him first, Him last, Him midst, and without end.

Him that makes shoes go barefoot himself

Source: ANATOMY OF MELANCHOLY (Democritus Junior to the Reader)
Author: Robert Burton (1577-1640)
First published: 1621-1651
Type of work: Essays

Context: Robert Burton was an amazing early English writer. Born at Lindley, Leicestershire, he entered Brasenose College, Oxford, at the age of sixteen, and after twenty years got his Bachelor of Divinity degree from Christ College. He remained associated with Oxford University until his death, while, at the same time, filling several positions as a clergyman. In thirty years as a scholar he read widely in a variety of fields, striving to become a universal man. In 1621, seven years after getting his B.D. degree, he published the first edition of what he ironically called *The Anatomy of Melancholy,* intending in three Partitions or Parts to analyze the causes, species, symptoms, and cure of melancholia. The first edition was published under the pseudonym of "Democritus Junior," but a final "Note to the Reader," dated "At my Study in Christ Church, Oxon., Dec. 5, 1620," revealed the secret by his signature of Robert Burton. Other editions with corrections and additions appeared during his lifetime, the sixth of which, the last published before his death, was dedicated to his patron, Lord George Berkeley, who got him appointed vicar of Segrave, Leicestershire, in 1630. The original Democritus was the greatest of the Greek physical philosophers. He flourished in the late fifth century B.C., and was known as the "Laughing Philosopher." However, in Burton's description he was "a little wearish old man, very melancholic by nature, and much given to solitariness." And so Burton, as "Democritus Junior," "writ of melancholy by being busy to avoid melancholy." For most of his statements, he quotes some classical author, "serving a warmed-over dish," yet the result inspired Milton, Sterne, Thackeray, and Lamb, while Samuel Johnson declared it was the only book capable of forcing him to get out of bed two hours ahead of time to read it. In the book's hundred-page introduction, the author is led from one topic to another, telling anecdotes and quoting classical and modern authors, making it a pleasure to read, but impossible to summarize afterward. In one paragraph, the author looks about him and wonders how the Democritus of twenty-two centuries earlier would react to cruelties of seventeenth century man. He mentions the slaughter of war, and the difference between punishment accorded a poor sheep stealer, hanged for appropriating the property of others, and the honor given a general who robs a whole province. Then in catalog form, Burton lists some of the sights that would disgust the Greek philosopher. To these sights he adds others, giving an earlier form of our current proverb about cobblers' children going shoeless.

> To see a servant able to buy out his master, him that carries the mace worth more than the magistrate, which Plato absolutely forbids, Epictetus abhors; . . . **him that makes shoes go barefoot himself;** . . . a toiling drudge starve, a drone flourish!

Hireling wolves, whose gospel is their maw

Source: SONNET XVI ("To the Lord General Cromwell, May 1652," Last line)
Author: John Milton (1608-1674)
First published: 1694
Type of work: Sonnet

Context: One proposal made to the Parliamentary Committee for the Propagation of the Gospel was that no one should be allowed to speak from a pulpit who had not been certified by two or more "godly and orthodox ministers." It was in protest to this proposed restriction on freedom of speech, in which Milton believed intensely, that the poet addressed this sonnet to Oliver Cromwell, then General of the Parliamentary armies and soon to be named Lord Protector of the Commonwealth of England. Milton praised first Cromwell's military achievements and then appealed to him to secure the victories of peace and to protect freedom of conscience.

> Cromwell, our cheif of men, who through a cloud
> Not of warr onely, but detractions rude,
> Guided by faith & matchless Fortitude
> To peace & truth thy glorious way hast plough'd,
> And on the neck of crowned Fortune proud
> Hast reard Gods Trophies, & his work pursu'd,
> While Darwen stream with blood of Scotts imbru'd,
> And Dunbarr feild resounds thy praises loud,
> And Worsters laureat wreath; yet much remaines
> To conquer still; peace hath her victories

No less renownd then warr, new foes aries
Threatning to bind our soules with secular chaines:
Helpe us to save free Conscience from the paw
Of hireling wolves whose Gospell is their maw.

His heart runs away with his head

Source: WHO WANTS A GUINEA (Act I, sc. i)
Author: George Colman the Younger (1762-1836)
First published: 1805
Type of work: Dramatic comedy

Context: Mrs. Elizabeth Inchbald (1753–1821), whose maiden name was Sampson (or Simpson), turned from acting to publishing, not only her own plays and novels, but two valuable collections of plays, *The British Theatre* (1806–1809) and *The Modern Theatre* (1809–1812). She used the original stage prompt-books. It is in volume III of the latter that George Colman's five-act comedy appears, as performed at the Theatre-Royal, Covent Garden. It was immensely popular, running for a long time at its initial appearance, and was later revised as *Jonathan in England* (1829) by the American actor James H. Hackett (1800–1871). A critic in 1839 declared "Colman's comedies satirize past ages whose gentry had more character than at present." Action begins at Heartly's house in Yorkshire, near the coast. The day is supposed to be an object lesson of the superiority of "thinking benevolence" over "haste in charity." The logic of the head is better at making decisions than the sentiment of the heart. The village has suffered a terrible fire that consumed two-thirds of the houses. John Torrent, who has just bought the manor house, has come to town. In the opening conversation, Heartly represents the people eager to help those in need but intending to do so judiciously. By contrast, miserly Hogmore will not take fuel needed for his fireside to warm others. And Torrent is typical of those who have money and are spendthrift in their use of it. Solomon Gundy whose every sentence is scarred by badly-pronounced French, has just appeared with a letter from the new landowner.

SOLOMON
His carriage broke into twenty *morso's*. He wanted to send you a *billy*—no messenger at hand—I've brought it. He gave me a guinea; I called him an angel; he bid me run like a devil; I told him I would; so I have, and there's the contention [*Gives a letter.*]

HEARTLY [*reading the letter.*]
"Dear Heartly, I have just *tumbled* into my estate. Let none of the villagers know who I am till I get to my house. I hate fuss—Don't say I am a rich man. Come to me in the alehouse. JOHN

439

TORRENT."

[*Speaking*.] He arrives just in time to assist his tenants in distress; but I dread his impetuosity, and carelessness of discrimination. Even in haste to make people happy, he defeats his own purpose. **His heart runs away with his head,** and he often produces most harm when he shows most benevolence. I'll wait on the gentleman, Solomon, directly.

His helmet now shall make a hive for bees

Source: POLYHYMNIA ("A Sonnet," Line 7)
Author: George Peele (1558?-1597)
First published: 1590
Type of work: Song lyric

Context: During the reign of Queen Elizabeth I, it became customary to entertain her with a grand military pageant and tournament every seventeenth of November. Feats of arms were performed by noblemen of prowess; music and various tableaux added to the glittering displays of costume and armor. One outstanding feature of the "Triumph at Tylt" for 1590 was a song in honor of Sir Henry Lea, performed by one Mr. Hales. Sir Henry had originated the annual tourney some thirty years before and had competed in it every year; now, because of advancing age, he was retiring from the lists. The lyric for his farewell song was written by George Peele and set to music by John Dowland, eminent English composer. Peele, an English playwright and poet, was the author of numerous dramas, pageants, lyrics for songs in his own plays, and considerable verse celebrating important personages and events. It is likely that he had a part in designing the pageant for the 1590 tournament, in addition to providing a song; in a poem of moderate length, *Polyhymnia,* he describes the event and its participants in laudatory terms. To *Polyhymnia* is appended the song that had been so well received. Entitled simply "A Sonnet," though not written in one of the two regular sonnet forms, it voices the loyal sentiments of a warrior grown old in service to his queen and country:

> His golden locks time hath to silver turn'd;
>   O time too swift, O swiftness never ceasing!
> His youth 'gainst time and age hath ever spurn'd,
>   But spurn'd in vain; youth waneth by increasing:
> Beauty, strength, youth, are flowers but fading seen;
> Duty, faith, love, are roots, and ever green.
>
> **His helmet now shall make a hive for bees,**
>   And, lovers' sonnets turn'd to holy psalms,
> A man-at-arms must now serve on his knees,
>   And feed on prayers, which are age his alms:

440

But though from court to cottage he depart,
His saint is sure of his unspotted heart.

And when he saddest sits in homely cell,
   He'll teach his swains this carol for a song,—
"Bless'd be the hearts that wish my sovereign well,
   Cursed be the souls that think her any wrong!"
Goddess, allow this agèd man his right,
To be your beadsman now that was your knight.

His looks do menace heaven and dare the gods

Source: TAMBURLAINE THE GREAT (Part I, Act I, sc. ii, l. 352)
Author: Christopher Marlowe (1564-1593)
First published: 1590
Type of work: Dramatic tragedy

Context: Mycetes, newly crowned as King of Persia, becomes concerned about the raids of Tamburlaine, a former Scythian shepherd, upon his kingdom, as it is rumored that Tamburlaine seeks to rule all of the East. Mycetes sends Theridamas, in command of a thousand cavalrymen, to defeat Tamburlaine and destroy the menace. When news comes to Tamburlaine that the richly clad and armored Persian force is near, he bids Techelles, one of his subordinate leaders, to ask for a parley between the Persian commander and himself. Tamburlaine also bids his men make ready to fight, if the need arises, and to display their treasure so the Persians can see it. Theridamas comes to speak with Tamburlaine, and he is mightily impressed by the Scythian, so much so that he becomes Tamburlaine's ally:

THERIDAMAS
Where is this Scythian *Tamberlaine?*

TAMBURLAINE
Whom seekest thou, Persian? I am Tamburlain.

THERIDAMAS
Tamburlaine? A Scythian Shepheard so imbellished
With Nature's pride, and richest furniture,
His looks do menace heauen and dare the Gods,
His fierie eies are fixt upon the earth,
As if he now devis'd some Strategeme:
Or meant to pierce *Avernas* darksome vaults,
To pull the triple headed dog from hell.

441

His mind his kingdom, and his will his law

Source: TRUTH (Line 406)
Author: William Cowper (1731-1800)
First published: 1782
Type of work: Essay in verse

Context: Maintaining that the basic and only Truth is God's truth, the English poet Cowper believes that a humble cottage-dweller, weaving at her doorway and going to bed at dark, light of heart, knows more about Truth than the recently-deceased French skeptic Voltaire (1694–1778), who scoffed at the Bible. He reflects that many more poor people than those wealthy or learned gain Heaven. It is not that the rich, noble, and thoroughly versed in science are not wanted there, but that in their journey toward Heaven, their possessions are "a dead, preponderating weight." However, Cowper, admits that some rich people, and at least one man who wears a coronet, are seekers after truth. In the latter, he refers to William, second Earl of Dartmouth, a prominent figure in the Evangelistic movement of which Cowper was a part. This thought brings the poet to a consideration of the Biblical question: What is a man? He cites one answer, far from the truth, an answer provided by a man who is proud of his own power and heedless of the God Who made him. He considers himself supreme and, except that he lacks power over the elements, a god-like being, attractive in person and supreme over the world around him.

> But what is man in his own proud esteem?
> Hear him—himself the poet and the theme;
> A monarch, clothed with majesty and awe,
> **His mind his kingdom, and his will his law,**
> Grace in his mien, and glory in his eyes,
> Supreme on earth, and worthy of the skies,
> Strength in his heart, dominion in his nod,
> And, thunderbolts excepted, quite a god!

His six days' work, a world

Source: PARADISE LOST (Book VII, l. 568)
Author: John Milton (1608-1674)
First published: 1667
Type of work: Epic poem

Context: Raphael was sent down to earth by God to instruct Adam in his duty so that he cannot plead ignorance when he falls from grace, as God knows that he will fall. Adam asks how the world began; Raphael answers that he will instruct him in what he ought to know, but there are some things that the Omniscient keeps hidden. He begins his account by saying that after Lucifer, which was Satan's name while he was still an angel, and his rebel host of angels had been expelled from heaven, God decided to create a new world that would in time fill up the population of heaven that had been diminished by the expulsion of the rebels. It was Milton's belief that if man had not fallen, he would by degrees have ascended over the ages until he became a being like the angels: this idea is the reverse of the process by which the fallen angels regress from spiritual substance to an earthy consistency. Raphael then retells the story of creation as it is given in the first chapter of *Genesis;* Milton's account is, however, much fuller and more elaborate than the Biblical one. He finishes his account by telling Adam that he is to have dominion over all things; all things are for his use except the fruit of the one tree that he is warned not to taste. When God had inspected all His work and had found it good, He ascended to His abode in heaven:

> Up He rode
> Followed with acclamation and the sound
> Symphonious of ten thousand harps that tuned
> Angelic harmonies: the earth, the air
> Resounded, (thou remember'st, for thou heard'st)
> The heavens and all the constellations rung,
> The planets in their stations list'ning stood
> While the bright pomp ascended jubilant.
> Open, ye everlasting gates, they sung,
> Open, ye heavens, your living doors; let in
> The great Creator from his work returned
> Magnificent, **His six days' work, a world;**
> Open and henceforth oft; for God will deign
> To visit oft the dwellings of just men
> Delighted, and with frequent intercourse
> Thither will send his wingéd messengers
> On errands of supernal grace. . . .

His truth is marching on

Source: THE BATTLE-HYMN OF THE REPUBLIC (Stanza 1)
Author: Julia Ward Howe (1819-1910)
First published: 1862
Type of work: Hymn

Context: To a tune usually ascribed to a Southern writer of Sunday School songs, William Steffe, a woman suffragette and social reformer, wrote several patriotic stanzas at the suggestion of James Freeman Clarke (1810–1868). The two were in Washington at the time (1861), watching McClellan's army marching past, singing other words put to that same tune and called *John Brown's Body,* with its stirring refrain of "Glory, Glory, Hallelujah." There is a different story: that Mrs. Howe was inspired to write the patriotic stanzas by watching the 12th Massachusetts Regiment swinging by, on its way to the train, and singing that same song. From chronology, either version can be true. But both show how popular among the soldiers was the melodic ballad about the American abolitionist, John Brown (1800–1859), who tried to capture Harper's Ferry, West Virginia, to get a place for the protection of fugitive slaves. Defeated and captured, he was hanged, but by his martyrdom he attracted many to the defense of the slaves so that his soul went marching on. James T. Fields (1817–1881) gave Mrs. Howe's words their present title when publishing them in the *Atlantic Monthly,* in February 1862. They became immediately popular as a war song. Since they were intended to inspire patriotic fervor, and not as a work of great literature, only a carping critic would notice that "evening dews and damps" was a prosy phrase dragged in by the rhyme and that Christ was not born "in the beauty of the lilies," but in the chill of winter. Here are four of the five stanzas, the third one being omitted.

Mine eyes have seen the glory of the coming of the Lord,
He is trampling out the vintage where the grapes of wrath are
    stored;
He hath loosed the fateful lightning of His terrible, swift
    sword,
        His truth is marching on.
Glory! Glory! Hallelujah!
Glory! Glory! Hallelujah!
Glory! Glory! Hallelujah!
        His truth is marching on!

I have seen Him in the watch-fires of a hundred circling
    camps,
They have builded Him an altar in the evening dews and
    damps;
I can read His righteous sentence by the dim and flaring
    lamps;
        His day is marching on.
            • • •

He has sounded forth the trumpet that shall never call retreat;
He is sifting out the hearts of men before His judgment-seat;
Oh, be swift, my soul, to answer Him! Be jubilant, my feet!
    Our God is marching on.

In the beauty of the lilies Christ was born across the sea,
With a glory in His bosom that transfigures you and me:
As He died to make men holy, let us die to make men free,
    While God is marching on.

History is little more than the register of the crimes, follies, and misfortunes of mankind

Source: THE DECLINE AND FALL OF THE ROMAN EMPIRE (Chapter 3)
Author: Edward Gibbon (1737-1794)
First published: 1776-1788
Type of work: History

Context: Perhaps no one in his age was better acquainted with the course of history than Edward Gibbon, whose vast study of Roman history has become a classic work in historiography. And to read that work is to understand the force of Gibbon's comment upon the nature of history; his recitation of the events and personalities of the Roman Empire show the truth of his observation, and Gibbon makes it clear that he has glossed over some of the more lurid and notorious aspects of the Roman story, though he notes in passing that they existed. The chapter in which his comment occurs is entitled "Of the Constitution of the Roman Empire in the Age of the Antonines." The chapter begins with what the writer calls "the obvious definition of a monarchy" and proceeds to narrate the progress of the Roman Empire from Augustus, including an account of how he solidified his position, through the reign of Hadrian, to Titus Antoninus Pius and his successor, Marcus. The two Antonines ruled the Roman world for forty-two years, with, in Gibbon's words, "the same invariable spirit of wisdom and virtue." The comment about the nature of history is found in a paragraph describing the reign of the earlier Antonine:

Titus Antoninus Pius has been justly denominated a second Numa. The same love of religion, justice, and peace, was the distinguishing characteristic of both princes. But the situation of the latter opened a much larger field for the exercise of those virtues. Numa could only prevent a few neighbouring villages from plundering each other's harvests. Antoninus diffused order and tranquillity over the greatest part of the earth. His reign is marked by the rare advantage of furnishing very few materials for **history; which is,** indeed, **little more than the register of the crimes, follies, and misfortunes of mankind.** In private life, he was an amiable as well as a good man. The native simplicity of his virtue was a stranger to vanity or affectation. He enjoyed with moderation the conveniences of his fortune, and the innocent pleasures of society: and the benevolence of his soul displayed itself in a cheerful serenity of temper.

History is past politics, and politics present history

Source: THE GROWTH OF BRITISH POLICY (Volume I, p. xii)
Author: Sir John Robert Seeley (1834-1895)
First published: 1895
Type of work: History

Context: A brilliant product of the classical tripos at Cambridge University in 1857, John R. Seeley soon abandoned the classics for his greater interests in religion and history. His most widely read and remarkable work was *Ecce Homo* (1865), which dealt with the humanity of Christ, appeared anonymously, and provoked stormy replies. Seeley was Professor of Modern History at Cambridge, 1869–1895. From the beginning his lectures stressed the subordination of history to politics. Reflecting the critical scholarship of the "scientific" historians of the late nineteenth century, Seeley disparaged the essentially literary works of Macaulay and Carlyle. The importance of history was its utility as a school for statesmen. Thus, for Seeley historical narrative was of little value without generalizations, and generalizations were primarily important for their application to current political problems. He adopted in his lectures, though he did not formulate, the view that *"history is past politics, and politics present history."* Yet the political history which concerned Seeley most was not the domestic and constitutional themes of most previous British historians but the history of states acting and reacting on an international scale. Seeley's *The Expansion of England* (1883) dealt with the colonial and commercial aspects of Britain's struggle with France, 1688–1815. What was to have been a parallel study of Britain's foreign policy became instead a major survey of the foundations of the British empire from the reign of Elizabeth I to that of William III. *The Growth of British Policy* was published in 1895, the year of his death. Both works reflected and contributed to the enthusiasm for empire which characterized the British mood at the end of the nineteenth century. Seeley, however, apparently did not coin the phrase which is associated with his name, for in the Memoir prefixed to his book G. W. Prothero says:

. . . In his lecture [his Innaugural Lecture at Cambridge] he laid down the lines which he constantly followed throughout the whole tenure of his professorship. Though he did not coin the phrase **"History is past politics, and politics present history,"** it is perhaps more strictly applicable to his own view of history than to that of its author. . . .

History is the essence of innumerable biographies

Source: CRITICAL AND MISCELLANEOUS ESSAYS (Vol. II, "On History")
Author: Thomas Carlyle (1795-1881)
First published: 1830
Type of work: Essay

Context: In this essay, first published in *Frazer's Magazine,* No. 10, in 1830, the great historian of the French Revolution and of the six-volume history of Frederick II of Prussia gives his ideas on history. Carlyle begins with the assertion that a talent for history is born in everybody, as our chief inheritance. As we *do* nothing but enact History, so likewise we *say* little but recite it. However, the living, actual History of Humanity consists of far different and more fruitful activities than those recorded in the history books. There is an infinite complexity in the simplest facts that constitute the Experience of Life. And the author points out the pitfalls ahead of Historians who produce Artists in history as well as Artisans in history who labor mechanically, without an eye for the whole, or even knowledge that there is a whole. He comments on some of the different sorts of Historians; the Ecclesiastical Historian, like the Political Historian, spends more time on outward mechanics than on essentials. Other Historians concentrate on separate provinces of human action: Sciences, Practical Arts, or Institutions. Carlyle ends with the expressed hope that a Philosophy of History may some day be evolved. As to the difficulties ahead, he has this to say:

> . . . Before Philosophy can teach by Experience, the Philosophy has to be in readiness, the Experience must be gathered and intelligently recorded. . . . let anyone who has examined the current of human affairs, and how intricate, perplexed, unfathomable, even when seen into with our own eyes, are their thousandfold blending movements, say whether the true representing of it is easy or impossible. Social Life is the aggregate of all the individual men's Lives who constitute Society; **History is the essence of innumerable biographies.** But if one Biography, nay, our own Biography, study and recapitulate it as we may, remains in so many points unintelligible to us; how much more must these million, the very facts of which, to say nothing of the purport of them, we know not, and cannot know!

A holiday humour

Source: AS YOU LIKE IT (Act IV, sc. i, ll. 68-69)
Author: William Shakespeare (1564-1616)
First published: 1623
Type of work: Dramatic comedy

Context: Passionately in love with each other, Rosalind and Orlando have never spoken to each other of their love. Both are now in the Forest of Arden, where Rosalind is in disguise as a young man named Ganymede. Orlando does not see through her disguise, and Rosalind wittily takes advantage of the situation. She offers to pose as Rosalind, so that Orlando may know what he is in for. Thus, thinking he is making love to a proxy, Orlando actually woos the genuine Rosalind, who, indeed in a holiday humor, may jest as she pleases. When Orlando is late to a meeting, she tells him she would rather be wooed by a snail, who "brings his destiny with him," that is, the horns the cuckold is proverbially supposed to wear. To Rosalind's vast satisfaction, Orlando replies that "virtue is no horn-maker; and my Rosalind is virtuous." The jest continues:

ROSALIND

Come, woo me, woo me; for now I am in **a holiday humour,** and like enough to consent. What would you say to me now, an I were your very, very Rosalind?

ORLANDO

I would kiss before I spoke.

ROSALIND

Nay, you were better speak first, and when you were gravelled for lack of matter, you might take occasion to kiss.

· · ·

The hollow crown

Source: KING RICHARD THE SECOND (Act III, sc. ii, l. 160)
Author: William Shakespeare (1564-1616)
First published: 1597
Type of work: Historical drama

Context: King Richard returns to England from the Irish wars to find that Bolingbroke, his exiled cousin, has returned to England to claim his inheritance seized by Richard on the death of his uncle, John of Gaunt, father of the exiled Bolingbroke, and that the companions of Richard charged with the responsibility of Bristol castle have been executed. The downcast king suggests to his companions that they sit down and talk of the deaths of kings:

RICHARD
. . . For within **the hollow crown**
That rounds the mortal temples of a king
Keeps Death his court, and there the antic sits,

448

Scoffing his state and grinning at his pomp,
Allowing him a breath, a little scene,
To monarchize, be feared, and kill with looks,
Infusing him with self and vain conceit,
As if this flesh which walls about our life,
Were brass impregnable; and humoured thus,
Comes at the last and with a little pin
Bores through his castle wall, and farewell king!
Cover your heads, and mock not flesh and blood,
With solemn reverence; throw away respect,
Tradition, form, and ceremonious duty,
For you have but mistook me all this while.
I live with bread like you, feel want,
Taste grief, need friends; subjected thus,
How can you say to me, I am a King?

Home-keeping hearts are happiest

Source: BIRDS OF PASSAGE (Flight the Fifth. Song, Stanza 1)
Author: Henry Wadsworth Longfellow (1807-1882)
First published: 1878
Type of work: Lyric poem

Context: One of the characteristics that made Longfellow so popular with his audience was his ability to render scenes of contentment and domestic happiness, of comfort and quiet reflection. Such verses can scarcely be otherwise than sentimental, and this effect of sentimentality now finds less favor with critics than it once did. Nonetheless, his easy versification and the graceful melody of his lines possess an undeniable charm. The following brief lyric of three stanzas depicts home as many visualize it: a place where one may find rest and peace, a place of refuge and safety. It may be significant that Longfellow included it in one of his *Birds of Passage* collections, which consist largely of verse tales about far-off times and places. Although he had traveled extensively in Europe, Longfellow enjoyed the comforts of home, and this desire to remain at home naturally increased with advancing age. In this poem he tells us that at home our cares and troubles seem less serious than they do elsewhere, and doubts cease to trouble us; we enjoy a security which those who have cast loose such ties cannot have. There is a soothing, almost drowsy effect in the verses—as though the poet had just returned from a long, weary journey and knows that at last he will sleep in his own bed again:

Stay, stay at home, my heart, and rest;
Home-keeping hearts are happiest,
For those that wander they know not where
Are full of trouble and full of care;
To stay at home is best.

449

Weary and homesick and distressed,
They wander east, they wander west,
And are baffled and beaten and blown about
By the winds of the wilderness of doubt;
    To stay at home is best.

Then stay at home, my heart, and rest;
The bird is safest in its nest;
O'er all that flutter their wings and fly
A hawk is hovering in the sky;
    To stay at home is best.

Home-made dishes that drive one from home

Source: MISS KILMANSEGG AND HER PRECIOUS LEG ("Her Misery," stanza 1)
Author: Thomas Hood (1799-1845)
First published: 1840-1841
Type of work: Satiric poem

Context: This long narrative poem is both humorous and satirical. The humorously grotesque story of Miss Kilmansegg has a serious interest: the satirization of man's pursuit of wealth. The heroine comes from a long line of persons who have wealth in great quantities. Indeed, Miss Kilmansegg's ancestors owned, among other possessions, geese that laid golden eggs, Colchian sheep with golden fleeces, and the Golden Ass. Miss Kilmansegg is born and reared in a golden atmosphere: everything in her surroundings is gold. But one day her horse, a bay named Banker, runs away while she is riding in London; when horse and rider fall upon the street, Miss Kilmansegg suffers a compound fracture of her right leg; when the leg has to be amputated, she insists upon its being replaced by an artificial leg of gold. Despite her artificial leg, the young woman gets about. She learns how to walk, even how to dance. She is courted by a foreign count and marries him, but, alas, the foreign count proves to be a counterfeit, and Miss Kilmansegg dreams one night she is really married to the Devil. Her misery is compared to all sorts of things, including being forced out of courtesy to eat all sorts of dishes, poorly prepared home-made food and drink, when she is a guest:

Who hath not met with home-made bread,
A heavy compound of putty and lead—
And home-made wines that rack the head,
    And home-made liqueurs and waters?
Home-made pop that will not foam,
And **home-made dishes that drive one from home,**
    Not to name each mess,
    For the face or dress,
Home-made by the homely daughters?

450

Homesickness for the mud

Source: LE MARIAGE D'OLYMPE (Act I)
Author: Guillaume Victor Émile Augier (1820-1899)
First published: 1854
Type of work: Dramatic tragedy

Context: Émile Augier, a French playwright, was outraged at the romanticists' applause of the younger Alexandre Dumas' *La Dame aux camélias,* known as *Camille* in English. The idea that a prostitute is to be forgiven her filthy life because she has loved deeply, so revolted Augier that he wrote *Le Mariage d'Olympe.* This is the story of a courtesan, Olympe Taverny, who had had a notorious career in Paris; she entraps the innocent and inexperienced young son of a high-born family into marriage and gains wealth and a title. Although Olympe glories in being a wealthy countess, a year's virtuous living in small-town hotels far removed from the gaiety of Paris brings her to the verge of distraction from pure boredom; she has been in the company of no one but her husband, Henri de Puygiron, who is too tame for her tastes. She arranges matters so that she and Henri join the de Puygiron family in Vienna, where she soon enters into an affair with a rich young man of common antecedents, the ultimate end of the affair being her death by shooting at the hands of her husband—a conclusion very different from that of *Camille.* As the play opens, the Baron de Montrichard, the Marquis de Puygiron, and Baudel de Beauséjour are discussing the reported death of Olympe Taverny in California. Montrichard says that times are changing, and that such creatures as Olympe are marrying the sons of good families. The marquis suggests that such women should not be allowed to keep the names they gain by their trickery. Baudel takes a romantic view:

BAUDEL
But, M. le Marquis, suppose the woman in question does not drag her stolen plumage in the gutter?

MARQUIS
I cannot admit the hypothesis, Monsieur.

BAUDEL
Is it not possible that she should like to give up her former life and want to lead a quiet and pure existence—?

MARQUIS
Put a duck on a lake among swans, and you will observe that the duck regrets its mire, and will end by returning there.

MONTRICHARD
Homesickness for the mud!

451

An honest exceeding poor man

Source: THE MERCHANT OF VENICE (Act II, sc. ii, l. 52)
Author: William Shakespeare (1564-1616)
First published: 1600
Type of work: Dramatic comedy

Context: Gobbo, old and blind, stumbles along a street in Venice, searching for his son, Lancelot Gobbo, who is employed by the wealthy Jew, Shylock. Lancelot is also walking along the same street, debating with his conscience whether to quit the service of Shylock in favor of the service of the young gentleman Bassanio. Old Gobbo comes upon Lancelot, but, because he is blind and because Lancelot has matured, does not recognize his son, who jests with his father, suggesting that Gobbo must be seeking "Master Lancelot" rather than a menial.

GOBBO

Be God's sonties, 'twill be a hard way to hit. Can you tell me whether one Lancelot that dwells with him, dwell with him or no?

LANCELOT

Talk you of young Master Lancelot? [*aside.*] Mark me now, now will I raise the waters. —Talk you of young Master Lancelot?

GOBBO

No master sir, but a poor man's son. His father though I say it is **an honest exceeding poor man,** and God be thanked well to live.

LANCELOT

Well, let his father be what 'a will, we talk of young Master Lancelot.

An honest man's the noblest work of God

Source: AN ESSAY ON MAN (Epistle IV, l. 248)
Author: Alexander Pope (1688-1744)
First published: 1733-1734
Type of work: Philosophical poem

Context: The fourth, and last, epistle in Pope's *Essay on Man* is a discussion of man's happiness and his struggle to achieve it. Man is destined, says Pope, to search for happiness; he calls the search "our being's end and aim." However, he often fails in this search, but the failure, says Pope, is in himself; he errs in the ways he seeks happiness and so is deprived by his own actions of the felicity intended by God for all. Real happiness, says the poet, can be summed up in three words: "health, peace,

452

and competence." Man's troubles stem from various courses of action, some which Pope examines in detail. Man chases fruitlessly after worldly goods, honor, fame, little guessing that happiness is to be found in virtue. Fame, for example, is not real, but "a fancied life in others' breath." Fame, living in others, is beyond our control, in this life or after death. Pope goes on to examine further the weaknesses of fame:

All that we feel of it begins and ends
In the small circle of our foes or friends;
To all beside as much an empty shade
An Eugene living, as a Caesar dead;
Alike or when, or where, they shone, or shine,
Or on the Rubicon, or on the Rhine.
A wit's a feather, and a chief a rod;
An honest man's the noblest work of God.
Fame but from death a villain's name can save,
As justice tears his body from the grave;
When what t' oblivion better were resign'd,
Is hung on high, to poison half mankind.
All fame is foreign, but of true desert;
Plays round the head, but comes not to the heart:
One self-approving hour whole years outweighs
Of stupid starers, and of loud huzzas.

A hooded eagle among blinking owls

Source: LETTER TO MARIA GISBORNE (Line 208)
Author: Percy Bysshe Shelley (1792-1822)
First published: 1824
Type of work: Verse letter

Context: This poem is a verse letter to Shelley's friend, Maria Gisborne, who is residing at the moment in London; the poet is living in the Gisborne residence in Leghorn. Shelley begins by saying that, like the spider in its web and the silkworm in its cocoon, he sits spinning a cell of rare and subtle thoughts that will, after his death, preserve his memory in the minds of those who love him. He then describes the room in which he is composing his letter: it is crowded with a large number of strange mechanical devices and apparatus for performing experiments in natural philosophy that the poet does not fully comprehend; and there are also books, broken teacups, and all the other odds and ends that accumulate in a man's study. In such a room sits the poet while the elements rage in a thunderstorm outside the house. The poet then falls into reminiscence about the time that Maria and he were together in this region: how they picnicked in the country and how the poet expounded his ideas to Maria. But now Maria is in London, a huge sea that casts up its human wreckage on its shores, but the depths of which contain great treasures, such

453

as William Godwin, the philosopher who did much to shape Shelley's political views and who was, in general, influential in shaping his intellect; and Samuel Taylor Coleridge, whose days of intellectual greatness had passed. Coleridge, he says, is like a captive eagle blindfolded by the falconer's hood and surrounded by a crowd of lesser men who are like a flock of owls. The comparison is between Coleridge, who in his great days, could, like the eagle, stare into the sun of truth, and lesser men, who, like owls, cannot tolerate such bright light.

You will see
That which was Godwin—greater none than he
Though fallen—and fallen on evil times—to stand
Among the spirits of our age and land,
Before the dread tribunal of *to come*
The foremost,—while Rebuke cowers pale and dumb.
You will see Coleridge—he who sits obscure
In the exceeding lustre and the pure
Intense irradiation of a mind,
Which, with its own internal lightning blind,
Flags wearily through darkness and despair—
A cloud-encircled meteor of the air,
A hooded eagle among blinking owls—
You will see Hunt—one of those happy souls
Which are the salt of the earth, and without whom
This world would smell like what it is—a tomb.

Hope thou not much, and fear thou not at all

Source: HOPE AND FEAR (Line 14)
Author: Algernon Charles Swinburne (1837-1909)
First published: 1882
Type of work: Sonnet

Context: Man's life, according to Swinburne, is a progression from the innocence and hope of youth to the corruption and despair of adulthood. Having rebelled against conventional customs and morality, Swinburne found that his fame was more often a notoriety that led to public denouncement than an admiration that led to an acceptance of his works; however, he attempted to live up to his bad reputation, although his weak physical condition turned such dissipation into long, very severe illnesses. By 1879 he was so near to death that only the paternal care of his friend Theodore Watts-Dunton was able to save his life. Under Watts-Dunton's care the wild young man who pursued dissipation to its bitter end became a quiet and conventional old man. In this poem, he describes youth from the vantage point of adulthood; while youth may hope and dream, the adult knows that such hopes will end in disappointment when the individual finally faces reality, an inevitable loss of dreams that no one should fear.

454

Then, when the soul leaves off to dream and yearn,
May truth first purge her eyesight to discern
    What once being known leaves time no power to appal;
Till youth at last, ere yet youth be not, learn
    The kind wise word that falls from years that fall—
"Hope thou not much, and fear thou not at all."

Hopeless grief is passionless

Source: GRIEF (Line 1)
Author: Elizabeth Barrett Browning (1806–1861)
First published: 1844
Type of work: Sonnet

Context: In this sonnet, Elizabeth Barrett Browning contrasts two reactions to death. On one hand, men without the experience or knowledge of death "Beat upward to God's throne in loud access/ Of shrieking and reproach." But the reaction of the "deephearted man" is compared to a "monumental statue set/ In everlasting watch and moveless woe." This "deephearted man" knows that anguish is pointless. Thus Mrs. Browning's contention is that "hopeless grief is passionless" and that there is no escape from it.

I tell you **hopeless grief is passionless;**
That only men incredulous of despair,
Half-taught in anguish, through the midnight air
Beat upward to God's throne in loud access
Of shrieking and reproach. Full desertness,
In souls as countries, lieth silent-bare
Under the blanching, vertical eye-glare
Of the absolute heavens. Deep-hearted man, express
Grief for thy dead in silence like to death—
Most like a monumental statue set
In everlasting watch and moveless woe
Till itself crumble to the dust beneath.
Touch it; the marble eyelids are not wet:
If it could weep, it could arise and go.

Horribly stuffed with epithets of war

Source: OTHELLO (Act I, sc. i, l. 14)
Author: William Shakespeare (1564-1616)
First published: 1622
Type of work: Dramatic tragedy

Context: Iago, at the opening of the play, complains to Roderigo that

Othello, his military commander, has passed over him in naming the second-in-command. Thus, Cassio ". . . must his lieutenant be,/ And I God bless the mark, his Moorship's ancient." Here are the seeds of rancor which will shortly produce Iago's devastating hatred for the Moor and his bride Desdemona. These seeds spring from the perennial competition between the enlisted man with long years of service and practical experience and the young officer commissioned after a relatively brief period of specialized training. Iago, much of his twenty-eight years spent in the military is now to be commanded by "one Michael Cassio, a Florentine," "a great arithmetician, . . . that never set a squadron in the field," one who knows nothing of the "division of a battle" except by "bookish theoric." "Mere prattle, without practice is all his soldiership." Iago's failure to receive this promotion is all the more galling because he has actively sought it; he personally had secured the good offices of various important men of the city to speak to Othello in his behalf. But to no avail, for the Moor rebuffs them, according to Iago, with the specious bombast of military rhetoric. In the remaining portion of the scene, Iago, in order to gain a measure of revenge upon Othello, persuades Roderigo to go with him to Brabantio—Desdemona's father—in an attempt to destroy the Moor's recent marriage.

IAGO

    . . . Three great ones of the city,
In personal suit to make me his lieutenant,
Off-capped to him—and by the faith of man,
I know my price, I am worth no worse a place.
But he, as loving his own pride and purposes,
Evades them, with a bombast circumstance,
Horribly stuffed with epithets of war,
And in conclusion,
Nonsuits my mediators. For certes, says he,
I have already chose my officer.

• • •

How beautiful upon the mountains

Source: ISAIAH 52:7
Author: Isaiah
First transcribed: c.800-200 B.C.
Type of work: Religious prophecy and exhortation

Context: Chapter 52 is one of several in which the poet foretells, or seems to foretell, the coming of the Messiah. Early Christian scholars were convinced that this coming is the proper interpretation of the lines and that Isaiah prophesied accurately the life and ministry of Jesus and the growth of the Church. Later scholarship puzzled over these passages and consid-

456

ered several Jewish leaders of the period, to whom Isaiah might have assigned the role of deliverer. More recently scholarship has tended to the opinion that a true Messiah, as later exemplified by Christ, is what Isaiah does refer to. Chapter 40 serves as a prelude, announcing that the suffering of Israel will presently end and that at last the glory of God will descend upon its people. In Chapter 42 Isaiah describes one he calls the Servant, who has been prepared by the Lord, and who will bring God's religion to the people that it may be spread abroad in the world; his coming will be quiet and without fanfare; his teaching will be gentle. In Chapter 49 another of these evangelistic hymns announces the Servant and portrays him speaking to the nations and explaining his mission to them; in the following chapter he describes his own suffering and the strength that upholds him in it. Chapter 52 begins with Isaiah's jubilant announcement that Babylonian oppression is at an end; Jerusalem the holy city will no longer be defiled by the unclean. In the words of the Lord, the people have sold themselves into captivity for nothing, and will be redeemed in the same way; for they have been oppressed without just cause in the past. Past suffering has paid for present folly. The people return from exile and Jerusalem, in celebration, arrays itself as a bride. A herald now proclaims that God is king and that His kingdom will endure forever.

How beautiful upon the mountains are the feet of him that bringeth good tidings, that publisheth peace; that bringeth good tidings of good, that publisheth salvation; that saith unto Zion, Thy God reigneth!

Thy watchmen shall lift up the voice; with the voice together shall they sing: for they shall see eye to eye, when the Lord shall bring again Zion.

Break forth into joy, sing together, ye waste places of Jerusalem: for the Lord hath comforted his people, he hath redeemed Jerusalem.

The Lord hath made bare his holy arm in the eyes of all the nations; and all the ends of the earth shall see the salvation of our God.

Depart ye, depart ye, go ye out from thence, touch no unclean thing; go ye out of the midst of her; be ye clean, that bear the vessels of the Lord.

For ye shall not go out with haste, nor go by flight: for the Lord will go before you; and the God of Israel will be your rearward.

Behold, my servant shall deal prudently, he shall be exalted and extolled, and be very high.

As many were astonished at thee; his visage was so marred more than any man, and his form more than the sons of men:

So shall he sprinkle many nations; the kings shall shut their mouths at him: for that which had not been told them shall they see; and that which they had not heard shall they consider.

457

How far that little candle throws his beams

Source: THE MERCHANT OF VENICE (Act V, sc. i, l. 90)
Author: William Shakespeare (1564-1616)
First published: 1600
Type of work: Dramatic comedy

Context: The heiress Portia, wife of Bassanio, returns to her home, Belmont, after disguising herself as a wise young judge and freeing Antonio, benefactor of Bassanio, from the forefeiture of Shylock's wicked bond —the payment of a pound of flesh since Antonio's ships had failed to come to port. As Portia and her handmaiden, Nerissa, near Belmont, Portia speaks.

PORTIA
That light we see is burning in my hall.
How far that little candle throws his beams,
So shines a good deed in a naughty world.

NERISSA
When the moon shone we did not see the candle.

PORTIA
So doth the greater glory dim the less.
A substitute shines brightly as a king
Until a king be by, and then his state
Empties itself, as doth an inland brook
Into the main of waters. . . .

How ill white hairs become a fool and jester

Source: KING HENRY THE FOURTH: PART TWO (Act V, sc. v. l. 52)
Author: William Shakespeare (1564-1616)
First published: 1600
Type of work: Historical drama

Context: With King Henry IV dead, the responsibilities of the crown have fallen upon his eldest son, the carousing and reckless youth, Prince Henry. The new monarch, now Henry V, wastes no time in letting it be known that he is changed. When his old drinking companion, the roguish Sir John Falstaff, approaches the new king in a "public place," expecting a boon, Henry casts him off in the following speech:

KING HENRY THE FIFTH
I know thee not old man, fall to thy prayers.
How ill white hairs become a fool and jester.

458

I have long dreamed of such a kind of man,
So surfeit-swelled, so old, and so profane;
But being awaked, I do despise my dream.
Make less thy body hence, and more thy grace,
Leave gormandizing, know the grave doth gape
For thee thrice wider than for other men.
Reply not to me with a fool-born jest,
Presume not that I am the thing I was;
For God doth know, so shall the world perceive,
That I have turned away my former self,
So will I those that kept me company.

                    •   •   •

How long a time lies in one little word

Source: KING RICHARD THE SECOND (Act I, sc. iii, l. 213)
Author: William Shakespeare (1564-1616)
First published: 1597
Type of work: Historical drama

Context: At the lists of Coventry preparations are complete for the joust between Henry Bolingbroke and Thomas Mowbray to settle with swords a dispute which King Richard II has not settled with arbitration— Bolingbroke and Mowbray have each accused the other with treason against his liege. Just as the trumpets sound, Richard motions the combatants to return to their seats and to hear his decree that the joust is forbidden, and exile is pronounced as punishment for the offending knights, Bolingbroke for ten years, and Mowbray for life. Richard, noting the saddened countenance of his revered uncle, John of Gaunt, father of Bolingbroke, in a word reduces the sentence for Bolingbroke from ten to six years:

RICHARD
Uncle, even in the glasses of thine eyes
I see thy grieved heart. Thy sad aspect
Hath from the number of his banished years
Plucked four away. [*to* BOI INGBROKE.] Six
        frozen winters spent,
Return with welcome home from banishment.

BOLINGBROKE
How long a time lies in one little word.
Four lagging winters and four wanton springs,
End in a word; such is the breath of kings.

459

How much more elder art thou than thy looks

Source: THE MERCHANT OF VENICE (Act IV, sc. i, l. 251)
Author: William Shakespeare (1564-1616)
First published: 1600
Type of work: Dramatic comedy

Context: In a Venetian court Portia, the fair bride of Bassanio, in disguise as a young judge, rescues Antonio, Bassanio's friend, from the fate of having the venomous Jew, Shylock, cut one pound of his flesh as forfeiture of a bond which the merchant Antonio has stood for Bassanio to aid in his suit of Portia. As the trial begins, Shylock interprets the words of the judge to mean that, according to the bargain, Shylock may rightfully claim the heart of Antonio. Antonio demands to hear the sentence, Portia speaks, and Shylock, joyously assuming that he has won the case, pronounces the wisdom of the youthful justice.

ANTONIO
Most heartily I do beseech the court
To give the judgment.

PORTIA
Why then thus it is,
You must prepare your bosom for his knife.

SHYLOCK
O noble judge, o excellent young man!

PORTIA
For the intent and purpose of the law
Hath full relation to the penalty,
Which here appeareth due upon the bond.

SHYLOCK
'Tis very true. O wise and upright judge,
How much more elder art thou than thy looks.

How pleasant it is to have money, heigh ho!

Source: DIPSYCHUS (Part II, sc. ii)
Author: Arthur Hugh Clough (1819-1861)
First published: 1862
Type of work: Satiric poem

Context: This poetic dialogue, like so much of Clough's poetry, illustrates his love of melancholy and his religious conflicts. In the poem we find a

460

Faustian hero, with some touches of Lord Byron, speaking on a series of occasions with a somewhat Satan-like spirit. The poem, begun in 1850, while Clough was in Venice, was left unfinished at the time of his death. Echoes of the poetry of both Byron and Goethe abound in it. The Spirit of the dialogue, though at times Satanic, seems more often to be rather the worldly common-sense, while the figure of Dispsychus tends to speak for the poet's idealism; in a sense the dialogue is autobiographical, for Clough himself struggled inwardly, torn between idealism and worldliness. In this section of the poem the Spirit and Dipsychus converse as they slide along the Grand Canal in Venice; the smooth passage of the craft causes Dipsychus to lament that life cannot go as unvexed as their gondola; he decries the struggles over "quarrels, aims, and cares,/ And moral duties and affairs." After some exchange of comments about its being a pity that the gondoliers do not enjoy life more, the Spirit speaks up on behalf of the enjoyment of life, his speech going on through a dozen verses. At the end of each verse he comments (and one thinks of Iago's advice to Roderigo before they leave Venice, "Put money in thy purse.") in a refrain about the advantages of ready wealth:

SPIRIT

As I sat at the café, I said to myself,
They may talk as they please about what they call pelf,
They may sneer as they like about eating and drinking,
But help it I cannot, I cannot help thinking,
 How pleasant it is to have money, heigh ho!
 How pleasant it is to have money.

I sit at my table *en grand seigneur,*
And when I have done, throw a crust to the poor;
Not only the pleasure, one's self, of good living,
But also the pleasure of now and then giving.
 So pleasant it is to have money, heigh ho!
 So pleasant it is to have money.

How the world wags

Source: AS YOU LIKE IT (Act II, sc. vii, l. 23)
Author: William Shakespeare (1564-1616)
First published: 1623
Type of work: Dramatic comedy

Context: His throne usurped by his brother, a Duke of France lives a peaceful, rustic life in exile with a group of followers in the Forest of Arden. However, one of his lords, Jaques, who does not become adapted to the silvan life, weeps when a deer is shot for food and wanders off alone. The Duke searches all day for his doleful companion, but, when Jaques finally appears, he is in a gay mood because of a fool he met in the

461

forest. He repeats the dialogue for the　Duke and his lords:

JAQUES
. . .

> Good morrow, fool, quoth I. No sir, quoth he,
> Call me not fool till heaven hath sent me fortune.
> And then he drew a dial from his poke,
> And looking on it, with lack-lustre eye,
> Says very wisely, it is ten o'clock:
> Thus we may see, quoth he, **how the world wags**
> 'Tis but an hour ago since it was nine,
> And after one hour more, 'twill be eleven;
> And so from hour to hour we ripe, and ripe,
> And then from hour to hour we rot, and rot;
> And thereby hangs a tale. . . .

The huntsmen are up in America

Source: THE GARDEN OF CYRUS (Chapter 5)
Author: Sir Thomas Browne (1605-1682)
First published: 1658
Type of work: Philosophy

Context: Browne, in his five-chapter tract, *The Garden of Cyrus,* has two particular interests: ancient gardens with special interest in the garden of King Cyrus, and the power of five or the quincunx. The quincunx, notes Browne, appears frequently in the arrangement of gardens, as well as in the formations of nature (leaves with five sections, hands and claws with five digits, are examples), a power recognized by both pagan and Christian cultures. As he concludes his treatise the hour is midnight and, rather than "act our Antipodes" or the inhabitants of the opposite side of the globe, he brings his work to a close:

> Though Somnus in Homer be sent to rouse up Agamemnon, I find no such effects in these drowsy approaches of sleep. To keep our eyes open longer, were but to act our Antipodes. **The huntsmen are up in America,** and they are already past their first sleep in Persia. But who can be drowsy at that hour which freed us from everlasting sleep? or have slumbering thoughts at that time, when sleep itself must end, and as some conjecture all shall awake again.

462

I accept the Universe

Source: COMMENT TO THOMAS CARLYLE (as reported by D. A. Wilson)
Author: Margaret Fuller (Ossoli) (1810-1850)
First spoken: 1846
Type of work: Biographical anecdote

Context: A minor New England writer of the nineteenth century, Margaret Fuller was a homely, brilliant, talkative eccentric who edited the transcendentalist magazine *The Dial* and published several books. In the summer of 1846 she traveled to Europe with a family named Spring, sending back gossipy letters which were published in the New York *Tribune.* Among the famous people she met was Thomas Carlyle, in whose home she visited. Emerson had recommended her to Carlyle as "this wise, sincere, accomplished, and most entertaining of women." Carlyle was later to write to Emerson that he had found her a "high-soaring, clear, enthusiast soul" and to his brother John Carlyle that she was "a strange, *lilting* lean old maid, not nearly such a bore as I had expected." Margaret's most famous reported remark is, "I accept the Universe!" To this, Carlyle is supposed to have said, "By god! she'd better" or "Gad! she'd better!" D. A. Wilson, one of Carlyle's biographers, believes that Carlyle's remark was made in Margaret's presence during a visit that Jane and Thomas Carlyle made to Margaret and her friends the Springs. Says Wilson:

It may have been on the same night that Margaret perorated picturesquely, to the admiration of all her listeners but one,—"**I accept the Universe!**"
"Gad, you'd better!" said Carlyle.

I am a feather for each wind that blows

Source: THE WINTER'S TALE (Act II, sc. iii, l. 154)
Author: William Shakespeare (1564-1616)
First published: 1623
Type of work: Tragi-comedy

Context: King Leontes of Sicilia, falsely accusing his wife, Hermione, great with child, of adultery with his friend Polixenes, King of Bohemia, brutally sentences her to imprisonment. A daughter, born to Hermione in prison, is carried by Paulina, a lady-in-waiting of Hermione and wife of Antigonus, to Leontes with the hope that seeing his baby will cause the jealous monarch to reprieve his wife. Beholding the child, Leontes commands that she be burned to death, but then, weakening, commands Antigonus to bear the baby to some desert and abandon her. Recognizing his indecision, Leontes says:

I am a feather for each wind that blows.
Shall I live on, to see this bastard kneel,
And call me father? Better burn it now,
Than curse it then. But be it; let it live.
It shall not neither. [*To* ANTIGONUS.] You sir, come
    you hither;
You that have been so tenderly officious
With Lady Margery, your midwife there,
To save this bastard's life—for 'tis a bastard,
So sure as this beard's gray—what will you adventure
To save this brat's life?

ANITIGONUS
Any thing, my lord,
That my ability may undergo, . . .

I am a part of all that I have met

Source: ULYSSES (Line 18)
Author: Alfred, Lord Tennyson (1809-1892)
First published: 1842
Type of work: Lyric poem

Context: Following Dante (*Inferno,* XXVI), Tennyson imagines Ulysses many years after his return home to Ithaca from the Trojan War. Though aged he is restless and he longs to set out with a band of mariners on a voyage of exploration and adventure like those he remembers from past years. He will leave his son Telemachus, a prudent administrator, to govern the kingdom in his absence. "He works his work," says Ulysses, "I mine." Though the whole poem is a dramatic monologue addressed to his mariners before the voyage begins, the first half seems more a soliloquy in which Ulysses muses on his present boredom with "an aged wife" and the dull business of ruling "a savage race,/ That hoard, and sleep, and feed, and know not me." This existence is a waste of time, it seems, to a man who, though old, would still drink "Life to the lees." Then he reviews his past and proudly recalls his travels and his fame:

    All times I have enjoyed
Greatly, have suffered greatly, both with those
That loved me, and alone; on shore, and when
Through scudding drifts the rainy Hyades
Vexed the dim sea. I am become a name;
For always roaming with a hungry heart
Much have I seen and known—cities of men
And manners, climates, councils, governments,
Myself not least, but honored of them all—

And drunk delight of battle with my peers,
Far on the ringing plains of windy Troy.
I am a part of all that I have met; . . .

I am a Roman citizen

Source: IN VERREM (II, v, lvii, 147)
Author: Marcus Tullius Cicero (106-43 B.C.)
First transcribed: 70 B.C.
Type of work: Denunciatory oration

Context: In the summer of 70 B.C., Cicero prosecuted Gaius Verres for extortion, misgovernment, and oppression. During his three years as Governor of the Sicilian people, Verres had used all sorts of legal trickery to avoid a fine and the loss of his Roman citizenship. The trial and verdict were tied up with the passage of a bill to take the complete control of criminal courts away from the Senate, and to give it only a third of the total vote. The criminal confessed his guilt by flight from Rome, and the bill passed. Cicero's second speech against Verres occupies five books. Close to its conclusion, he describes the governor's schemes for enriching himself. He would order the crews of ships arriving at Syracuse seized and flung into a prison called The Stone Quarries. Their claims to Roman citizenship ("Civis Romanus sum"), that granted them the right to be tried in Roman courts, did no good. The governor maintained that they were really fugitives from the army of Sertorius, in revolt, or traders with Mediterranean pirates, and confiscated their possessions, which he kept. Cicero tells about the situation:

These methods presently crowded the prison with honest traders; and then those things began to happen of which you have heard from Lucius Suettius, a Roman knight and most excellent man, and of which you shall hear from others likewise. There, in that prison, guiltless Roman citizens were most shamefully strangled. Now at last the cry, **"I am a Roman Citizen,"** the famous appeal that has so often brought men help and rescue among savage races in the furthest corners of the earth, was to hasten the affliction and increase the agony of these men's death. . . .

I am never merry when I hear sweet music

Source: THE MERCHANT OF VENICE (Act V, sc. i, l. 69)
Author: William Shakespeare (1564-1616)
First published: 1600
Type of work: Dramatic comedy

465

Context: Lorenzo, friend of Bassanio, and his bride Jessica, daughter of the Jew Shylock, talk tenderly on a moonlit night along the avenue to Belmont, home of the heiress Portia and her husband Bassanio. Though messengers inform the pair of the return of Portia and Bassanio, Lorenzo and Jessica delay the preparations for the home-coming of the master and mistress of the house. Lorenzo orders music, commenting that on such a night the soul can almost hear the harmony of the spheres. In a light mood, Lorenzo greets the musicians, but Jessica replies that she is not merry when she hears sweet music.

LORENZO
. . .

Come ho, and wake Diana with a hymn,
With sweetest touches pierce your mistress' ear,
And draw her home with music. [*Music plays.*]

JESSICA
I am never merry when I hear sweet music.

LORENZO
The reason is, your spirits are attentive. . . .

I am not arguing with you—I am telling you

Source: THE GENTLE ART OF MAKING ENEMIES
Author: James McNeill Whistler (1834–1903)
First published: 1890
Type of work: Literary record

Context: James McNeill Whistler was often stung to the quick by opinions other artists, art critics, and the general public expressed about his work, as the famous libel suit he brought against John Ruskin testifies. Among the comments which prompted a reply from Whistler was an article that appeared in *The World of London* on December 8, 1880. In that article an anonymous writer belittles an exhibition of twelve etchings by Whistler, saying that the etchings are of slight workmanship and "unimportant dimensions," without either value of originality. The unknown writer says that the etchings are like the sketches, unfinished, such as every artist brings back from a visit to Venice. These comments called forth the following reply from Whistler:

A PROPOSAL

Atlas, *mon bon, méfiez-vous de vos gens!* Your art gentleman says that Mr. Whistler exhibits twelve etchings, "slight in execution and unimportant in size." Now the private assassin you keep, for us, need not be hampered by mere connoisseurship in the perpe-

466

tration of his duty—therefore, *passe,* for the execution—but he should not compromise his master's reputation for brilliancy, and print things that he who runs may scoff at.

Seriously, then, my Atlas, an etching does not depend for its importance, upon its size. **"I am not arguing with you—I am telling you."** As well speak of one of your own charming *mots* as unimportant in length!

Look to it, Atlas. Be severe with your man. Tell him his "job" should be "neatly done." I could cut my own throat better; and if need be, in case of his dismissal, I offer my services.

I am not in the giving vein to-day

Source: KING RICHARD THE THIRD (Act IV, sc. ii, l. 119)
Author: William Shakespeare (1564-1616)
First published: 1597
Type of work: Historical drama

Context: Richard, having determined to "prove a villain" and to secure for himself the throne of England at any cost, finds the Duke of Buckingham a convenient and profitable ally in his schemes. Following the execution of his brother George, Duke of Clarence, and the death of his brother Edward IV, Richard uses the ambitious Buckingham to create dissension between powerful nobles such as Lord Hastings and Earl Rivers. When the Lord Mayor of London and a representative group of citizens are persuaded to request that Richard assume the protectorate following the king's death, again it is Buckingham who directs the scene, planting men in the crowd who call for Richard at various times and himself describing the holy devotion of Richard as the Duke of Gloucester is disclosed studying the Scripture. As Richard's desire to gain full control grows more desperate, he informs Buckingham that he "would be king," that he would have "the bastards [Edward's sons] dead." Buckingham's hesitation in agreeing to carry out this act is fatal, for Richard perceives in it a moral squeamishness which renders him useless as a henchman. A few lines later Buckingham, requesting the earldom he had earlier been promised, is rebuffed in a despotic fit of whimsicality which illustrates graphically the tenuousness of Richard's favor and foreshadows the ultimate fate which awaits Buckingham:

BUCKINGHAM
My lord, your promise for the earldom—

RICHARD
Richmond! When last I was at Exeter,
The mayor in courtesy showed me the castle,
And called it Rougemont, at which name I started,
Because a bard of Ireland told me once

I should not live long after I saw Richmond.

BUCKINGHAM

My lord—

RICHARD

Ay, what's a clock?

BUCKINGHAM

I am thus bold to put your Grace in mind
Of what you promised me.

RICHARD

Well, but what's a clock?

BUCKINGHAM

Upon the stroke of ten.

RICHARD

Well, let it strike.

BUCKINGHAM

Why let it strike?

RICHARD

Because that like a Jack thou keep'st the stroke
Betwixt thy begging and my meditation.
I am not in the giving vein to-day.

BUCKINGHAM

Why then resolve me whether you will or no.

RICHARD

Thou troublest me, I am not in the vein.

I am not the less human for being devout

Source: TARTUFFE (Act III, sc. iii)
Author: Molière (Jean Baptiste Poquelin, 1622-1673)
First published: 1669
Type of work: Tragi-comic drama

Context: The hypocritical Tartuffe makes rapid progress in undermining the happy home of Orgon, his gullible friend. Having already attempted to get himself married to Orgon's daughter Mariane, Tartuffe, in Act III, reveals his designs also upon Orgon's beautiful wife Elmire. He pretends

468

that his love of God has led him to love Elmire, one of God's most beau- tiful creations, and in a long, flattering speech he declares this love:

ELMIRE

The declaration is most gallant, but, to tell the truth, it is a bit surprising. I think you should better guard your heart, and reflect a little on such a design. A devout man like you, one who is everywhere called. . . .

TARTUFFE

Ah! **I am not the less human for being devout;** and when one sees your heavenly allurements the heart surrenders, and does not reflect. I know that such language from me appears strange; but, Madam, after all, I am no angel; and if you condemn the avowal I have made, you must blame your own lovely charms. . . .

I am Sir Oracle

Source: THE MERCHANT OF VENICE (Act I, sc. i, l. 93)
Author: William Shakespeare (1564-1616)
First published: 1600
Type of work: Dramatic comedy

Context: Antonio, "the merchant of Venice," confesses to his friends, Salerio and Salanio, that he is plagued with sadness, not over his trading business, since his fortune rests with many vessels, nor over his love affairs. Salerio and Salanio, having tried in vain to cheer Antonio, leave when Antonio is joined by his close friend, Bassanio, and his companions, Lorenzo and Gratiano. Gratiano, noted for his loquaciousness, also tries to convince Antonio to leave off his sadness, pointing out the folly of those who vainly feign wisdom by a dour countenance:

GRATIANO

There are a sort of men whose visages
Do cream and mantle like a standing pond,
And do a wilful stillness entertain,
With purpose to be dressed in an opinion
Of wisdom, gravity, profound conceit,
As who should say, **I am Sir Oracle,**
And when I ope my lips, let no dog bark!

469

I appeal unto Caesar

Source: ACTS 25:11
Author: Unknown (traditionally Luke)
First transcribed: 60-150 (probably c.80-90)
Type of work: Religious history and tradition

Context: In The Acts of the Apostles we have the only extant contemporary account of the Christian Church in its beginning and early growth. Acts was evidently written by the same person who wrote Luke; he may or may not have been Luke the physician. In any case it is probable that Luke supplied much of the author's information. The book is a memorable record of hardship and devotion to an ideal, and it records the evolution of Christianity from a sect of Judaism to an independent religion. The story of Paul and his missionary work is given in Chapters 15 through 28. His travels in Syria, Greece, Asia Minor and Israel are covered. He faces many difficulties, and is twice the focal point of riots, in Thessalonica and Ephesus. At length he feels he must go to Jerusalem, and, in spite of warnings, makes the journey. Arrived there, he goes to the temple and is recognized and accused by people who have seen him in Asia Minor. Manhandled by a mob, he is turned over to the centurions. Asking the captain for leave to speak, he tells the people how he became a Christian; they are not receptive, and he is saved from a scourging only because he is a Roman citizen. He is released the next day and examined before his accusers. Another scene of disorder results, and the captain is forced to return Paul to prison in order to save his life. On the following day forty of the Pharisees swear to kill him the next time he is brought before them. The captain, warned, sends Paul under guard to Felix, Roman governor in Cæsarea. The latter postpones judgment, and presently Ananias and his elders appear with an orator named Tertullus who accuses Paul again. Judgment is again postponed; Paul is well treated but confined to the premises. Eventually Felix's term of office expires, and his successor, Festus, inherits the prisoner. The accusations are renewed, and Paul is once more commanded to appear before the seat of judgment.

And when he had tarried among them more than ten days, he went down unto Cæsarea; and the next day sitting on the judgment seat commanded Paul to be brought.

And when he was come, the Jews which came down from Jerusalem stood round about, and laid many grievous complaints against Paul, which they could not prove.

While he answered for himself, Neither against the law of the Jews, neither against the temple, nor yet against Cæsar, have I offended any thing at all.

But Festus, willing to do the Jews a pleasure, answered Paul, and said, Wilt thou go up to Jerusalem, and there be judged of these things before me?

Then said Paul, I stand at Cæsar's judgment seat, where I ought to be judged: to the Jews have I done no wrong, as thou very well knowest.

For if I be an offender, or have committed any thing worthy of death, I refuse not to die: but if there be none of these things whereof these accuse me, no man may deliver me unto them. **I appeal unto Cæsar.**

Then Festus, when he had conferred with the council, answered, Hast thou appealed unto Cæsar? unto Cæsar shalt thou go.

And after certain days king Agrippa and Bernice came unto Cæsarea to salute Festus.

And when they had been there many days, Festus declared Paul's cause unto the king, . . .

I awoke, and behold it was a dream

Source: THE PILGRIM'S PROGRESS (Part I)
Author: John Bunyan (1628-1688)
First published: 1678
Type of work: Religious allegory

Context: The narrator of this dream allegory has witnessed, in his dream, the long and arduous struggles of Christian to overcome the snares and deceits of temptation in his journey to the Heavenly City. Finally, at the end of Part I, Christian and his companion, Hopeful, reach the gate where they are met by shining angels, who first describe and then admit them to the heavenly Jerusalem. Shortly thereafter, Ignorance, who had accompanied Christian and Hopeful on a portion of their journey, assisted by Vain-hope, approaches the gate. The gatekeepers do not admit him; instead, they demand from over the gate to see his certificate which would merit him admission. But Ignorance has no certificate. The dreamer's final vision is of the terrible fate of Ignorance:

> So they told the King, but he would not come down to see him, but commanded the two Shining Ones that conducted Christian and Hopeful to the City, to go out and take Ignorance, and bind him hand and foot, and have him away. Then they took him up, and carried him through the air to the door that I saw in the side of the hill, and upt him in there. Then I saw that there was a way to hell, even from the gates of heaven, as well as from the City of Destruction. So **I awoke, and behold it was a dream.**

I awoke one morning and found myself famous

Source: LETTERS AND JOURNAL OF LORD BYRON (Chapter 14)
Author: Thomas Moore (1779-1852)
First published: 1830
Type of work: Biography

Context: Thomas Moore, the Irish poet and writer of sentimental songs, the best remembered of which are "The Last Rose of Summer" and "Believe Me, If All Those Endearing Young Charms," was one of Byron's closest friends. It was to him that Byron, in a characteristically impulsive and indiscreet gesture, had given the MS of His Memoirs to do with as he pleased. Moore, who was chronically in debt, had assigned the MS to the publisher Murray for two thousand guineas. Shortly after the news of Byron's death had reached England, at a meeting in London attended by those concerned with the fate of the Memoirs, the MS was burned; and, for better or for worse, whatever Byron may have said about his own life vanished forever. Because of the notoriety—in fact, scandal—associated with the late poet, no sooner was he dead than inaccurate and highly-colored biographical notes began to appear. Moore, who had known Byron intimately, made the first attempt to write a biography that was factually accurate and that was based upon careful research. In spite of the opposition of many of the poet's other friends, he completed the work in 1830; and it still remains a cornerstone in any study of Byron's life. The quotation above sprang from the phenomenal success of the first two cantos of "Childe Harold," which appeared in March of 1812. Within three days the first edition had been sold out. Byron had already created a commotion with "English Bards and Scotch Reviewers" in 1809; now he was suddenly the most talked-about poet in England. Moore's account of the effect of the new poem is as follows:

> . . . never did there exist before, and it is most probable, never will exist again, a combination of such vast mental power and surpassing genius, with so many other of those advantages and attractions, by which the world is, in general, dazzled and captivated. The effect was, accordingly, electric;—his had not to wait for any of the ordinary gradations, but seemed to spring up, like the palace of a fairy tale, in a night. As he himself briefly described it in his Memoranda,—**"I awoke one morning and found myself famous."** The first edition of his work was disposed of instantly; and, as the echoes of its reputation multiplied on all sides, "Childe Harold" and "Lord Byron" became the theme of every tongue. . . .

I can suck melancholy out of a song, as a weasel sucks eggs

Source: AS YOU LIKE IT (Act II, sc. v, ll. 11-12)
Author: William Shakespeare (1564-1616)
First published: 1623
Type of work: Dramatic comedy

Context: Duke Senior, exiled by his usurping brother, is, together with his followers, having a thoroughly pleasurable time in the paradisal Forest of

Arden. "Sweet are the uses of adversity," says the Duke. One of his followers, however, seems constitutionally unable to take pleasure in anything, unless it is in his own melancholy; he is the "melancholy Jaques." After one of the Duke's men, Lord Amiens, sings a verse of the delightful song, "Under the greenwood tree," Jaques begs him to continue:

JAQUES
More, more, I prithee more.

AMIENS
It will make you melancholy Monsieur Jaques.

JAQUES
I thank it. More, I prithee more. **I can suck melancholy out of a song, as a weasel sucks eggs.** More, I prithee more.

AMIENS
My voice is ragged. I know I cannot please you.

JAQUES
I do not desire you to please me, I do desire you to sing. Come, more; another stanzo. . . .

I care not two-pence

Source: THE COXCOMB (Act V, sc. i)
Authors: Francis Beaumont (1585?-1616) and John Fletcher (1579-1625)
First published: 1647
Type of work: Dramatic comedy

Context: Of the thirty-four plays making up the First Folio of the plays of Beaumont and Fletcher, scholars believe Fletcher to be part or complete author of all but two. "Judicious Beaumont" helped with a maximum of ten—the best among them—and another Elizabethan master of stagecraft, Philip Massinger (1583–1640), collaborated in so many that his name should have appeared among the authors. Most critics agree that Beaumont was certainly a collaborator in *The Coxcomb,* performed by the King's Men (Shakespeare's group), at the Blackfriars Theatre, London, in October, 1612. The next year Beaumont married, moved to his country estate, and gave up playwriting, as had Shakespeare by this time. Fletcher continued by himself and with Massinger to supply the King's Men with dramas until the plague killed him in 1625. Massinger wrote plays until he died, when, according to tradition, he was buried in the same grave as Fletcher. The Stuart world of the mid-seventeenth century considered Fletcher the master of comedy, and the poet Beaumont excellent in Tragedy. *The Coxcomb* is all comedy, but with examples of excellent poetic speeches along with its prose. Its plot is complicated and improbable, but to its audiences "good theatre" and a chance to laugh were more important than a credible plot. Antonio, the foppish Coxcomb, has just returned to his wife, Maria, from several years of travel with his companion, Mercury, who has become bored with him. Mercury is smitten by Maria but decides to run away to escape temptation. However, Antonio assures him that friendship is more valuable than a wife's love, and if Maria and Mercury love each other, Antonio will not stand in their way He even disguises himself as an Irish servant to carry to her a false love letter from Mercury. The wife pierces the disguise, orders her servants to beat and lock up her husband, and goes searching for Mercury. Mercury brings her to his mother's house about the time that the continued absence of Antonio, helped by his babbling while disguised as a servant, has created the suspicion that Maria and Mercury murdered Antonio. In search of them come Antonio's kinsman, Curio, and a Justice whose description by the dramatist as "a shallow one," indicates his descent from Shakespeare's Justice Shallow of *Henry IV* and *The Merry Wives of Windsor*. In Act V, the Justice comes to the house where Mercury and Maria are lodging. His bumbling language confirms Curio's comment that he had sought out the Justice as the nearest official, though certainly not the wisest one.

JUSTICE

It shall not be i' faith friend, here I have it,
That one Antonio a Gentleman, I take it so,
Yes, it is so, a Gentleman is lately thought to
Have been made away, and by my faith, upon a
Pearls ground too, if you consider; well, there's
Knavery in't, I see that without spectacles . . .

. . .

And now I have consider'd, I believe it.

CURIO

What Sir?

JUSTICE

That he was murdered.

CURIO

Did you know him?

JUSTICE

No.

CURIO

Nor how it is suppos'd.

474

No, nor **I care not two-pence,** those are toys, and yet I verily believe he was murder'd, as sure as I believe thou art a man, I have never fail'd in these things yet, w'are a man that's beaten to these matters, experience is a certain conceal'd thing that fails not. . . .

I did not weep, they wept

Source: THE DIVINE COMEDY, INFERNO (Canto XXXIII, ll. 46-47, as translated by H. F. Cary)
Author: Dante Alighieri (1265-1321)
First transcribed: c.1314
Type of work: Christian allegory

Context: Dante's great poem takes its name from the poet's definitions of tragedy and comedy. To Dante, a tragedy begins with pleasant scenes and ends in those of a painful or terrible nature; comedy begins painfully and ends in happiness. Thus, for his poem which begins with the terrible scenes of Hell and ascends through Purgatory to the glory of Paradise, he chose the title *Divine Comedy.* At the midway point of his life (that is, in his thirty-fifth year), the poet finds himself in a dark wood; here he meets the Roman poet Virgil, who offers to conduct him through the underworld. Beatrice, Dante's ideal of womanhood, will then accompany the poet through Purgatory and Paradise. Dante and Virgil accordingly begin their journey; as they progress Dante singles out for description the various great criminals of history. The crimes and corresponding punishments increase in horror as the two travelers progress from one circle to the next. The ninth and lowest circle of Hell is reserved for traitors; it is divided into four rounds, in which the sufferers are buried to various depths in solid ice. The first of these rounds, called Caïna, contains those who have betrayed their kindred; the second round, Antenora, those who have betrayed their country. In crossing this round, Dante encounters a spirit who is engaged in gnawing at the skull of another imprisoned with him, and expresses curiosity. The spirit is that of Count Ugolino, leader of one of three factions seeking control of Pisa in the thirteenth century. He and the Archbishop Ruggieri, leader of a second faction, had combined forces in order to destroy the remaining party. The archbishop then betrayed Ugolino. Ultimately the latter, with two sons and two grandsons, was shut up in the tower and killed by starvation; priests were not allowed to enter, even after he repented, and he died unshriven. Now the spirits of Ugolino and Ruggieri are prisoned together in the ice for eternity, and Ugolino tears at the skull of the archbishop. Ugolino tells Dante of his suffering in the tower:

   . . . When I awoke,
Before the dawn, amid their sleep I heard
My sons (for they were with me) weep and ask
For bread. Right cruel art thou, if no pang
Thou feel at thinking what my heart foretold;
And if not now, why use thy tears to flow?
Now had they waken'd; and the hour drew near
When they were wont to bring us food; the mind
Of each misgave him through his dream, and I
Heard, at its outlet underneath lock'd up
The horrible tower: whence, uttering not a word,
I look'd upon the visage of my sons.
I wept not: so all stone I felt within,
They wept: and one, my little Anselm, cried,
'Thou lookest so! Father, what ails thee?' Yet
I shed no tear, nor answer'd all that day
Nor the next night, until another sun
Came out upon the world. When a faint beam
Had to our doleful prison made its way,
And in four countenances I descried
The image of my own, on either hand
Through agony I bit. . . .

I do not choose to run

Source: PRESS REPORT
Author: Calvin Coolidge (1872-1933)
First published: August 2, 1927
Type of work: Presidential statement

Context: The taciturnity of the thirtieth President of the United States caused him to be nicknamed "Silent Cal," and during his presidency many of the jokes about him played upon his habit of wasting no words. His most famous remark was made in answer to the question of whether he would run for a second full term. As vice-president, he had finished out the term of President Harding, who had died in 1923; he had then been elected to one full term as president on his own. The written statement which Coolidge issued to the press on August 2, 1927, read: "I do not choose to run for President in nineteen twenty-eight." Though many people for a while thought the statement equivocal, Coolidge meant what he said. The Republicans then chose Herbert Hoover who won the election overwhelmingly against the Democratic candidate, Alfred E. Smith.

I do not choose to run.

I do not know the method of drawing up an indictment against a whole people

Source: SPEECH ON CONCILIATION WITH AMERICA (March 22, 1775)
Author: Edmund Burke (1729-1797)
First published: 1775
Type of work: Parliamentary address

Context: When he gave this speech in the House of Commons, Edmund Burke believed that it was possible to frame legislation which would end the distrust of the American colonists and bring peace between The Colonies and Great Britain. He points out that he is not searching for anything but simple peace, and that he is speaking with good intentions and genuine simplicity of heart. He states that the number of persons living in the American Colonies has been growing rapidly, and he cites the extent of the trade between The Colonies and Great Britain, illustrating its growth between 1704 and 1772. He suggests that to use force on the colonists will be but temporary and uncertain in its results; that the American colonists are the descendants of Englishmen, "not only devoted to liberty, but to liberty according to English ideas, and on English principles," and he notes that one Englishman is the unfittest person in the world to try to argue another Englishman into slavery. He tries to make the point that the British government, in any attempt to conciliate the Americans, must be willing to admit past mistakes and must cease to regard rebellious colonists as criminals:

At this proposition I must pause a moment. The thing seems a great deal too big for my ideas of jurisprudence. It would seem to my way of conceiving such matters, that there is a very wide difference in reason and policy, between the mode of proceeding on the irregular conduct of scattered individuals, or even of bands of men, who disturb order within the state, and the civil dissensions which may, from time to time, on great questions, agitate the several communities which compose a great empire. It looks to me to be narrow and pedantic, to apply the ordinary ideas of criminal justice to this great public contest. **I do not know the method of drawing up an indictment against a whole people. . . .** I hope I am not ripe to pass sentence on the gravest public bodies, intrusted with magistracies of great authority and dignity, and charged with the safety of their fellow-citizens, upon the very same title that I am. I really think, that for wise men this is not judicious; for sober men, not decent; for minds tinctured with humanity, not mild and merciful.

I dreamt that I dwelt in marble halls

Source: THE BOHEMIAN GIRL (Act II, "The Gipsy-Girl's Dream")
Author: Alfred Bunn (1796?-1860)
First published: 1843
Type of work: Operatic aria

Context: One aria in Michael William Balfe's *The Bohemian Girl,* with a libretto by Alfred Bunn, is known to millions of listeners who have never attended a performance of the opera and who know none of the remaining music in it. The aria is sung in Act II by Count Arnheim's daughter Arline, who was abducted as a child by Devilshoof, a gipsy chieftain, and who has lived with a gipsy band for twelve years. Waking from a deep sleep, Arline reveals a beautiful dream she had to Thaddeus, an exiled Pole who has joined the gipsy band and has fallen in love with Arline. Having saved her from a fierce stag shortly before her abduction, Thaddeus knows her identity, but she herself does not learn it until after her gipsy marriage to her rescuer. The first stanza of the aria reads:

I dreamt that I dwelt in marble halls,
   With vassals and serfs at my side,
And of all who assembled within those walls,
   That I was the hope and the pride.
I had riches too great to count—could boast
   Of a high ancestral name;
And I also dreamt, which pleased me most,
   That you loved me still the same.

I find the medicine worse than the malady

Source: LOVE'S CURE; OR, THE MARTIAL MAID (Act III, sc. ii)
Author: John Fletcher (1579-1625)
First published: 1647
Type of work: Dramatic comedy

Context: Fernando de Alvarez, during a twenty-year enforced absence from his wife Eugenia, has reared their daughter Clara as a boy and later as a soldier. At home, Eugenia has reared her son Lucio as a girl. When Alvarez returns from his long exile he brings the mannish Clara who must now learn to be a woman, just as effeminate Lucio must be taught to be a man. Piorato, a swordsman, is to aid in the curing of Lucio's womanish character. He informs Alvarez's steward Bobadilla of the method he once used to develop manhood in a cowardly milksop. He starved him before a loaded table until he drew a knife to cut meat. Then he dieted him on special food and drink, and rigorously trained him in the use of gun and sword. Bobadilla wonders if perhaps Piorato

478

could use a reverse kind of training to cure him of an ailment. The idea is, of course, more familiar to us in the words of Francis Bacon, "The remedy is worse than the disease."

BOBADILLA

Could you not cure one, sir, of being too rash
And over-daring?—there now's my disease—
Fool-hardy, as they say? for that in sooth
I am.

PIORATO

Most easily.

BOBADILLA

How?

PIORATO

To make you drunk, sir,
With small beer once a-day, and beat you twice,
Till you be bruis'd all over; if that help not,
Knock out your brains.

BOBADILLA

This is strong physic, signior,
And never will agree with my weak body:
I find the medicine worse than the malady,
And therefore will remain fool-hardy still.

.   .   .

I had a soul above buttons

Source: SYLVESTER DAGGERWOOD (Scene x)
Author: George Colman the Younger (1762-1836)
First published: 1795
Type of work: Farce

Context: Sylvester Daggerwood or New Hay at the Old Market is a one-act picture of London theatrical life written by George Colman (or Coleman) a graduate of Christ College, Oxford, and King's College, Aberdeen. He took over management of the Haymarket Theatre when his father, another playwright, went mad. At the beginning of this farce, Fustian, a writer of tragedies, and Daggerwood, a strolling player of the Dunstable Company, sit in the manager's office at the Haymarket Theatre, looking for employment. The skit recounts the difficulties in mounting a theatrical performance, and ends with a song. Fustian seeks details about Daggerwood, whom he takes for some rustic barnstormer. He gets an

479

autobiographical answer. Daggerwood feels himself born for something above a commercial or manufacturing life. He is an artist, though an improverished one. He laments the fact that his wife stutters and therefore cannot help him in a stage career. As for his possessions, he says he has three shirts, and:

DAGGERWOOD

Children too young to make a *debut*—except my eldest, Master Apollo Daggerwood; a youth of only eight years old; who has twice made his appearance in Tom Thumb, to an overflowing and brilliant barn—house, I mean—with unbounded and universal applause.

FUSTIAN

Have you been long upon the stage, Mr. Daggerwood?

DAGGERWOOD

Fifteen years since I first smelt the lamp, Sir. My father was an eminent Button-Maker at Birmingham; . . . but **I had a soul above buttons,** and abhorred the idea of mercenary marriage. I panted for a liberal profession—so ran away from my father, and engaged with a travelling company of Comedians.

I had had an affair with the moon

Source: A SENTIMENTAL JOURNEY THROUGH FRANCE AND ITALY ("The Monk. Calais")
Author: Laurence Sterne (1713-1768)
First published: 1768
Type of work: Travel miscellany

Context: In 1765 Sterne traveled through France and Italy; his decision to describe the journey from a "sentimental" point of view probably resulted from his previous account of a stay in France (in *Tristram Shandy*). The present work was intended to reach four volumes; but Sterne completed only two, dying a little less than a month after their publication. His style is best described as chaotic. An effervescent person, Sterne seems in his writings to have approached all aspects of life gleefully. There is little continuity or progress to his books; they are gossipy, haphazard, funny, at times hilarious. They are also full of surprises, vivid snapshots, color and variety. They digress, as Sterne intended: to him digression was an art, and it is obvious that he delighted in it. *A Sentimental Journey* begins with a conversation between Yorick (Sterne) and a gentleman who has been to France and as a result is an immeasurably superior person. Yorick decides that if a mere twenty miles can make that much difference he may as well go himself—so he grabs up his portmanteau and departs. In no time at all he is in Calais and enjoying an excellent dinner. The wine is outstanding; Yorick's heart swells with love for his fellow man. He finds himself overflowing with benevolence and generosity. He kicks his portmanteau: mere possessions are paltry things. Taking out his purse, he wishes he had someone to share it with. His wish is unexpectedly granted, as is told below; but be it said to Yorick's credit that he later repents of his sudden change of heart and actually does reward the supplicant. To return: Yorick, glowing with wine and his own burgeoning humanity, has just declared himself King of France and wants to present his portmanteau to the first beggar who desires it:

I had scarce uttered the words, when a poor monk of the order of St. Francis came into the room to beg something for his convent. No man cares to have his virtues the sport of contingencies —or one man may be generous, as another man is puissant—*sed non quo ad hanc*—or be it as it may—for there is no regular reasoning upon the ebbs and flows of our humours; they may depend upon the same causes, for aught I know, which influence the tides themselves—'twould oft be no discredit to us, to suppose it was so: I'm sure at least for myself, that in many a case I should be more highly satisfied, to have it said by the world, **"I had had an affair with the moon,** in which there was neither sin nor shame," than have it pass altogether as my own act and deed, wherein there was so much of both.
But be this as it may. The moment I cast my eyes upon him, I was predetermined not to give him a single sous; and accordingly I put my purse into my pocket—button'd it up—set myself a little more upon my center, and advanced up gravely to him: there was something, I fear, forbidding in my look: I have his figure this moment before my eyes, and think there was that in it which deserved better.

I have a kind of alacrity in sinking

Source: THE MERRY WIVES OF WINDSOR (Act III, sc. v, l. 14)
Author: William Shakespeare (1564-1616)
First published: 1602
Type of work: Dramatic comedy

Context: As the play progresses, Sir John Falstaff sees himself as a great lover and decides to have affairs with the wives of both Master Ford and Master Page in order to get at the family purses. The two ladies talk and discover that Falstaff has sent each identical love notes. The two are not at all interested in his propositions, but they decide to have some fun at the fat knight's expense. Of course, neither husband is told what is being planned, but an informer tells both of them that the wives are going

481

to be unfaithful and thereby cuckold the two men. After the two ladies plot their scheme, Mistress Ford decides the meeting time and sends word to Falstaff. Master Ford is also informed of the rendezvous by one of Sir John's followers. Mistress Ford and Mistress Page had plotted for Mistress Page to come in just after Falstaff arrives, and Mistress Ford would hide him in a dirty clothes basket. Mistress Ford had previously instructed two servants to carry out the basket and dump Falstaff into the river. Not only does Mistress Page appear but also Master Ford and several of his friends; thus Falstaff is doubly ready to hide in the laundry basket. Being so obese, he of course sinks rapidly to the river bottom when dumped by the servants.

FALSTAFF
• • •

. . . The rogues slighted me into the river with as little remorse, as they would have drowned a bitch's blind puppies, fifteen i' th' litter; and you may know by my size, that **I have a kind of alacrity in sinking.** If the bottom were as deep as hell, I should down. I had been drowned, but that the shore was shelvy and shallow. A death that I abhor. For the water swells a man; and what a thing should I have been, when I had been swelled! I should have been a mountain of mummy.

I have not slept one wink

Source: CYMBELINE (Act III, sc. iv, l. 102)
Author: William Shakespeare (1564-1616)
First published: 1623
Type of work: Tragi-comedy

Context: Imogen, daughter of King Cymbeline, marries Posthumus against the wishes of the king and her stepmother, who wants her to marry the latter's son, Cloton. Cymbeline banishes Posthumus, who, in Italy, makes a bet with an Italian, Iachimo, on the purity and faithfulness of the wife from whom he is forcibly separated. Through treachery on the part of the Italian, Posthumus is led to believe that Imogen has been untrue to him. Posthumus has ordered, by letter, his servant Pisanio, to kill her. Pisanio, however, knows of Imogen's faithfulness and the suffering she has gone through for her husband. He reveals to her his orders, and she, feeling life is worthless if Posthumus believes her to be an adultress, pleads with Pisanio: "I draw the sword myself. Take it, and hit/ The innocent mansion of my love, my heart."

• • •

IMOGEN
. . . Where's thy knife?
Thou art too slow to do thy master's bidding

482

When I desire it too.

PISANIO
O gracious lady,
Since I received command to do this business,
I have not slept one wink.

IMOGEN
Do't and to bed then.

PISANO
I'll wake mine eyeballs out first.

I have nothing to declare except my genius

Source: COMMENT TO CUSTOMS OFFICERS (as reported by Frank Harris)
Author: Oscar Wilde (1856-1900)
First spoken: 1881
Type of work: Biographical anecdote

Context: No one ever characterized the Dublin-born wit Oscar Wilde as a modest person. Friends continually quoted his boasting, sometimes with a basis in fact. Said E. F. Benson: "How like was his talk to the play of a sunlit fountain." Once, along with an invitation to dinner, the host expressed uncertainty about what would be served. "Oh, anything," Wilde assured him. "I have the simplest tastes. I am always satisfied with the best." About his writing, he declared: "Would you like to know the grand drama of my life? It is that I have put my genius into my life—I have put only my talent into my works." One of his most-quoted quips came at the end of his voyage to New York in 1881 to lecture and press for a production of his drama *Vera*. As his friend Frank Harris described the episode:

It was on the cards that he might succeed in his new adventure. The taste of America in letters and art is still strongly influenced, if not formed, by English taste, and, if Oscar Wilde had been properly accredited, it is probable that his extraordinary gift of speech would have won him success in America as a lecturer.

His phrase to the Revenue Officers on landing: **"I have nothing to declare except my genius,"** turned the limelight full upon him and excited comment and discussion all over the country. But the fuglemen of his caste whose praise had brought him to the front in England were almost unrepresented in the States, and never bold enough to be partisan. . . .

483

I have set my life upon a cast

Source: KING RICHARD THE THIRD (Act V, sc. iv, l. 9)
Author: William Shakespeare (1564-1616)
First published: 1597
Type of work: Historical drama

Context: Richard III, a deformed hunch-back, has usurped the throne of England by hypocrisy, dissemblance, and murder. The Earl of Richmond, later King Henry VII, leads a revolt against the villainous king, in which the opposing armies meet at Bosworth Field. In desperation Richard vainly seeks a replacement for his slain horse. In a final speech, directed to a supporter, before his death at the hand of Richmond, Richard refuses to withdraw from the fray, saying that the die that determines his fate has already been cast, and he will await his fortune:

RICHARD

Slave, **I have set my life upon a cast,**
And I will stand the hazard of the die.
I think there be six Richmonds in the field;
Five have I slain to-day instead of him.
A horse, a horse, my kingdom for a horse!

[*Exeunt.*]

I have taken all knowledge to be my province

Source: LETTER TO LORD BURGHLEY (1592)
Author: Sir Francis Bacon (1561–1626)
First published: 1734
Type of work: Personal letter

Context: Famous English philosopher and statesman Francis Bacon was appointed Lord Chancellor under James I in 1618 and was created Baron Verulam in 1618 and Viscount St. Albans in 1621. These were the crowning political and social achievements for a man who possessed unquestioned abilities and a rather crass determination to exploit them. Without doubt he was one of the most brilliant men of his day. He carried on scientific and philosophic investigations and planned to reorganize the epistemological systems of his time on an experimental inductive basis. He was stubbornly opposed to reasoning from authority and the syllogistic quibbling to which the Scholastic philosophy had declined in the early seventeenth century. Much of his philosophic work was written in Latin, most significant of which are *Novum Organum* and *De Augmentis Scientarium*. In literature he is, of course, best known for his essays. At the age of thirty-one ("I wax somewhat ancient; one and thirty years is a great deal of sand in the hourglass"), in good health, and with as-

484

piring ambitions, he writes in 1592 to Lord Burghley to request a place and opportunity for service to his lordship and the crown:

> Again, the meanness of my estate doth somewhat move me: for though I cannot accuse myself that I am either prodigal or slothful, yet my health is not to spend, nor my course to get. Lastly, I confess that I have as vast contemplative ends, as I have moderate civil ends: for **I have taken all knowledge to be my province;** and if I could purge it of two sorts of rovers, whereof the one with frivolous disputations, confutations, and verbosities, the other with blind experiments and auricular traditions and impostures, hath committed so many spoils, I hope I should bring in industrious observations, grounded conclusions, and profitable inventions and discoveries; the best state of that province.

I hear America singing

Source: LEAVES OF GRASS ("I hear America Singing," Line 1)
Author: Walt Whitman (1819-1892)
First published: 1860
Type of work: Lyric poem

Context: When *Leaves of Grass* was first published, it met with a storm of abuse due in part to the originality of Whitman's style; his poems were a radical departure from previous metrical conventions. Cast in the form of inspired chants, they are not quite blank verse but a verse-prose combination, exciting and full of vitality. Whitman's ideal was to depict America in its entirety, as he saw it, leaving out nothing and glossing nothing over. He loved the common man and had toured the country on foot, working his way from place to place as carpenter and builder. He felt an intense personal relationship to all Creation—to God, to nature, to mankind, to life itself. This idealist who vowed to be a realist found his work despised. He dealt with social and moral topics with a freedom unknown in the 1850's, and to many his work was at best shocking, at worst depraved. It was only gradually that he was recognized for the original genius that he was. Whitman's vitality and enthusiasm, and his ability to see the individual elements of his vast subject with objective and comprehensive clarity and so to present them, are qualities for which he is widely appreciated today, as is the rugged beauty of his lines. In the first portion of *Leaves of Grass,* a number of poems are given under the general heading "Inscriptions," a suggestive and appropriate term; all are brief and intense, and each is in its way a tribute to some aspect of life. The poem entitled "I Hear America Singing" is the eighteenth of these. In it Whitman celebrates his love for the workingman, which he frequently re-emphasizes throughout his poetry; at the same time he gives a vivid picture of a young and bustling country, enthusiastically building itself toward

485

greatness.

> **I hear America singing,** the varied carols I hear,
> Those of mechanics, each one singing his as it should be blithe
>   and strong,
> The carpenter singing his as he measures his plank or beam,
> The mason singing his as he makes ready for work, or leaves off
>   work,
> The boatman singing what belongs to him in his boat, the deck-
>   hand singing on the steamboat deck,
> The shoemaker singing as he sits on his bench, the hatter singing
>   as he stands,
> The wood-cutter's song, the ploughboy's on his way in the morn-
>   ing, or at noon intermission or at sundown,
> The delicious singing of the mother, or of the young wife at work,
>   or of the girl sewing or washing,
> Each singing what belongs to him or her and to none else,
> The day what belongs to the day—at night the party of young fel-
>   lows, robust, friendly,
> Singing with open mouths their strong melodious songs.

I know a bank where the wild thyme blows

Source: A MIDSUMMER NIGHT'S DREAM (Act II, sc. i, l. 249)
Author: William Shakespeare (1564-1616)
First published: 1600
Type of work: Dramatic comedy

Context: Excitement prevails in Athens over the marriage of Duke Theseus and Hippolyta, his fair captive Queen of the Amazons. Even the fairies of India, including King Oberon and Queen Titania, have come to celebrate. Oberon and Titania, however, argue over a changeling boy that Titania refuses to give to Oberon. Vowing vengeance, Oberon sends Puck to secure a love potion that will make Titania fall foolishly in love with whatever her eyes behold, even a beast. As Puck appears with the herb, Oberon says:

OBERON

. . .

> **I know a bank where the wild thyme blows,**
> Where oxlips and the nodding violet grows,
> Quite over-canopied with lush woodbine,
> With sweet musk-roses, and with eglantine.
> There sleeps Titania sometime of the night,
> Lulled in these flowers with dances and delight.
> And there the snake throws her enamelled skin,
> Weed wide enough to wrap a fairy in.
> And with the juice of this I'll streak her eyes,

486

And make her full of hateful fantasies.

. . .

I know a hawk from a handsaw

Source: HAMLET (Act II, sc. ii, l. 396)
Author: William Shakespeare (1564-1616)
First published: 1603
Type of work: Dramatic tragedy

Context: Hamlet is playing a very dangerous game. After having been told by his father's ghost that his Uncle Claudius, the present king, is the murderer of his father, Hamlet feigns madness while he feels his way. Two old schoolmates, Rosencrantz and Guildenstern, have been set the task of determining the cause of Hamlet's madness. Hamlet lures them on, teasingly suggesting a number of possibilities. Finally, he almost, but not quite, admits his sanity. The proverb, "I know a hawk from a handsaw," means simply that he still has sense enough to distinguish obvious dissimilarities, and may be intended as an ironic attack on Rosencrantz and Guildenstern, who pretend loyalty and friendship. "Handsaw" is usually explained as a North Country word meaning "heron."

HAMLET

. . .

You are welcome; but my uncle-father, and aunt-mother, are
  deceiv'd.

GUILDENSTERN

In what, my dear lord?

HAMLET

I am but mad north-north-west; when the wind is southerly
I know a hawk from a handsaw.

I know a trick worth two of that

Source: KING HENRY THE FOURTH, PART ONE (Act II, sc. i, ll. 40–41)
Author: William Shakespeare (1564-1616)
First published: 1598
Type of work: Historical drama

Context: King Henry IV, beset with political problems as rebellion breaks out in the north and in the west, is also plagued by what he assumes to be the utter dissipation of his son and heir apparent, Prince Hal. Actually, Hal perceives his role quite clearly; in anticipation of the time when he will

487

ascend the throne, he is determined to mingle with all classes of people in order that his rule might be more efficient. Moreover, there can be no doubt of Hal's affection for his old companion in fun, Falstaff, that "huge bombard of wit." The group of Eastcheap rowdies with whom the Prince consorts plans to rob the king's retainers at Gads Hill. Secretly Hal and Poins have contrived an elaborate scheme to counter-rob the robbers in order to force Falstaff to display his true colors. Effecting the plan awaits now only the confirmation of the specific time the gold will be in transit. This information is to be secured by one of the prince's companions, Gadshill, who has an agreement with the chamberlain of the inn. In the early morning hours Gadshill mingles with the carriers both to gain their confidence and to pick up any information which might be useful to the robbers. But the carriers are a wary lot; quick with an evasive retort, they effectively parry Gadshill's leading questions:

GADSHILL

Good morrow, carriers. What's a clock?

FIRST CARRIER

I think it be two a clock.

GADSHILL

I prithee lend me thy lantern, to see my gelding in the stable.

FIRST CARRIER

Nay by God soft, **I know a trick worth two of that,** i' faith.

GADSHILL

I pray thee lend me thine.

SECOND CARRIER

Ay when? Canst tell? Lend me thy lantern quotha? Marry I'll see thee hang'd first.

GADSHILL

Sirrah carrier, what time do you mean to come to London?

SECOND CARRIER

Time enough to go to bed with a candle, I warrant thee. Come neighbor Mugs, we'll call up the gentlemen; they will along with company, for they have great charge.

I know thee who thou art

Source: PARADISE LOST (Book II, l. 990)
Author: John Milton (1608-1674)
First published: 1667
Type of work: Epic poem

Context: Satan, once the bright angel named Lucifer, has been plunged into Hell after the civil war in Heaven, preciptated by his ambition to rebel against God's authority. Following their fall, Satan and his fellow rebels hold a conclave in Hell to decide what action to take. Some of the fallen angels urge another battle with the heavenly host, to be undertaken with the goal of regaining Heaven; others urge against renewing the combat. A suggestion by Satan is reviewed, a third proposal. It is to search out the world and man, whose creation by God has been prophesied. This course of action is chosen, and Satan himself undertakes the difficult mission. He passes out of Hell to "the hoary deep, a dark/ Illimitable ocean without bound,/ Without dimension, where length, breadth, and height,/ And time and place are lost." Passing through this void, Satan comes to the throne of Chaos, the ruling spirit, who holds court with Night, his consort, and other spirits: Orcus, Ades, Demogorgon, Rumor, Chance, Tumult, Confusion, and Discord. Satan offers to return the newly created universe to its original darkness, if the spirit Chaos will tell him where it is. Chaos replies to Satan:

> . . . him thus the anarch old
> With faltering speech and visage incomposed
> Answered. "**I know thee,** stranger, **who thou art,**
> That mighty leading angel, who of late
> Made head against heaven's king, though overthrown.
> I saw and heard, for such a numerous host
> Fled not in silence through the frighted deep
> With ruin upon ruin, rout on rout,
> Confusion worse confounded; and heaven gates
> Poured out by millions her victorious bands
> Pursuing."

I lisped in numbers, for the numbers came

Source: EPISTLE TO DR. ARBUTHNOT (Line 128)
Author: Alexander Pope (1688-1744)
First published: 1735
Type of work: Satire

Context: According to the advertisement of the first publication of this work, which was written by the poet himself, the epistle is a complaint against persons who had in one way or another attacked Pope, not only through his person, but also through his family and morals. The epistle takes the form of a dialogue between Dr. John Arbuthnot, the poet's friend, and the poet. Arbuthnot, in addition to being Pope's intimate, was physician to Queen Anne and a well-known literary figure of the time. In the dialogue Pope complains that he gets no rest from flatterers, foes, and would-be writers—all of whom besiege his door. The flatterers, he says, are the worst, for what the flatterer intends as praise proves ridicule in its exaggeration. Others, complains Pope, comment ridiculously that he coughs like Horace, has Ovid's nose, and holds his head in illness like Virgil. He goes on, answering a rhetorical question he puts to himself:

> Why did I write? what sin to me unknown
> Dipp'd me in ink, my parents', or my own?
> As yet a child, nor yet a fool to fame,
> **I lisp'd in numbers, for the numbers came.**
> I left no calling for this idle trade,
> No duty broke, no father disobey'd.
> The Muse but serv'd to ease some friend, not wife,
> To help me through this long disease, my life;
> To second, Arbuthnot! thy art and care,
> And teach the being you preserv'd, to bear.

I must be about my Father's business

Source: LUKE 2:49
Author: Unknown (Traditionally Luke the Apostle)
First transcribed: c.80-100
Type of work: Gospel

Context: The authorship of this Gospel is a matter of some dispute. Both Luke and Acts were evidently written by the same man. Some scholars find internal evidence indicating that the writer must have been a physician; and since Luke the physician was a friend and companion of the Apostle Paul, the traditional attribution of this Gospel to him would seem logical. In any case, the author is at some pains in the beginning of the work to indicate that many are writing gospels, and that he has gathered his own material from people still living who were present when many of these events occurred. The rest of Chapter I discusses the various events which foretold the birth of Christ. In the second chapter he tells the story of the Nativity in terms of quiet and moving simplicity; this is the account which is, because of its poetic beauty, most familiar to us. It has long been a favorite passage for use in the celebration of Christmas. Luke then records the significant events that occurred during the infancy of Jesus: circumcision and purification according to the law, the presentation in the Temple, and the prophecies of Simeon and Anna. Simeon was an old man, who had been told by the Holy Ghost that he would see Christ before his death. Led by the Spirit, he enters the Temple and takes the child up in his arms, saying He will be the glory of Israel. Anna, a prophetess, also enters the Temple at this time and confirms what Simeon has said. When all customary religious observances have been completed, Jesus' parents return with him to Nazareth. Luke tells very little more about the childhood of Jesus, save that He was wise beyond his years. He supports this statement with a memorable picture of the group of old scholars, who are delighted with the boy's eagerness and precocity:

> And the child grew, and waxed strong in spirit, filled with wisdom: and the grace of God was upon him.
> Now his parents went to Jerusalem every year at the feast of the passover.
> And when he was twelve years old, they went up to Jerusalem after the custom of the feast.
> And when they had fulfilled the days, as they returned, the child Jesus tarried behind in Jerusalem; and Joseph and his mother knew not of it.
> But they, supposing him to have been in the company, went a day's journey; and they sought him among their kinsfolk and acquaintance.
> And when they found him not, they turned back again to Jerusalem, seeking him.
> And it came to pass, that after three days they found him in the temple, sitting in the midst of the doctors, both hearing them, and asking them questions.
> And all that heard him were astonished at his understanding and answers.
> And when they saw him, they were amazed: and his mother said unto him, Son, why hast thou thus dealt with us? behold, thy father and I have sought thee sorrowing.
> And he said unto them, How is it that ye sought me? wist ye not that **I must be about my Father's business?**

I must be cruel only to be kind

Source: HAMLET (Act III, sc. iv, l. 178)
Author: William Shakespeare (1564-1616)
First published: 1603
Type of work: Dramatic tragedy

Context: Confronting his mother, Queen Gertrude, who has joined in an incestuous marriage with his uncle, Hamlet kills the evesdropping Polonius and reproaches his mother for the bestiality of her nature and begs her to repent. For his quickness to kill and his harshness with her, he asks forgiveness and explains the reason for his cruelty.

491

. . . Once more good night,
And when you are desirous to be blessed,
I'll blessing beg of you. For this same lord,
I do repent; but heaven hath pleased it so
To punish me with this, and this with me,
That I must be their scourge and minister.
I will bestow him, and will answer well
The death I gave him. So again good night.
I must be cruel only to be kind.
Thus bad begins, and worse remains behind. . . .

I must become a borrower of the night

Source: MACBETH (Act III, sc. i, l. 27)
Author: William Shakespeare (1564-1616)
First published: 1623
Type of work: Dramatic tragedy

Context: Duncan has been murdered, and Macbeth, on the disappearance of Malcolm and Donalbain, sons of the dead king, has been named sovereign. Nature is in a turmoil, but Macbeth has ordered a feast at which he wishes Banquo's presence. Banquo, however, in a short soliloquy, reveals his suspicions of foul play on Macbeth's part. He also reminds himself of the witches' prophecy that he shall be "the root and father/ Of many kings." He has to leave with his son, Fleance, but he hopes to be back in time for Macbeth's festivities. Macbeth has other plans, however, for he is afraid of Banquo and Banquo's knowledge of the old hags' words.

MACBETH
Ride you this afternoon?

BANQUO
Aye, my good lord.

MACBETH
We should have else desired your good advice,
Which still hath been both grave and prosperous,
In this day's council; but we'll take tomorrow.
Is't far you ride?

BANQUO
As far, my lord, as will fill up the time
'Twixt this and supper. Go not my horse the better,
I must become a borrower of the night
For a dark hour or twain.

492

I own the soft impeachment

Source: THE RIVALS (Act V, sc. iii)
Author: Richard Brinsley Sheridan (1751-1816)
First published: 1775
Type of work: Dramatic comedy

Context: In this last scene of Sheridan's play each of the several strands of the plot is unwoven. Captain Absolute is revealed to be also the fictitious "Ensign Beverley," his own rival for the hand of Lydia Languish in marriage. He is accepted in his true identity by her, to be her husband. One of his real rivals, Acres, a bumpkin from the country, refuses to fight a duel with "Ensign Beverley" when he discovers who the "ensign" really is, his old friend Captain Absolute; young Acres gives up any claim he might have for Lydia in marriage, accepting the girl's decision. But Sir Lucius O'Trigger, another rival suitor, refuses to abdicate his suit for Lydia's hand, being a man of action and honor. He produces letters from "Delia," who is, he assumes, really Lydia Languish. However, it turns out that "Delia" is actually Mrs. Malaprop, Lydia's elderly guardian, who has been writing love letters to Sir Lucius. When Sir Lucius produces the letters, Mrs. Malaprop is forced to confess:

MRS. MALAPROP
O, he will dissolve my mystery!—Sir Lucius, perhaps there's some mistake—perhaps I can illuminate——

SIR LUCIUS
Pray, old gentlewoman, don't interfere where you have no business. —Miss Languish, are you my Delia or not?

LYDIA
Indeed, Sir Lucius, I am not. [*Walks aside with Capt. Absolute.*]

MRS. MALAPROP
Sir Lucius O'Trigger—ungrateful as you are—**I own the soft impeachment**—pardon my blushes, I am Delia.

SIR LUCIUS
You Delia—pho! pho! be easy.

MRS. MALAPROP
Why, thou barbarous Vandyke—those letters are mine. —When you are more sensible of my benignity—perhaps I may be brought to encourage your addresses.

493

Mrs. Malaprop, I am extremely sensible of your condescension; and whether you or Lucy have put this trick on me, I am equally beholden to you. —And, to show you I am not ungrateful, Captain Absolute, since you have taken that lady from me, I'll give you my Delia into the bargain.

I rose the wrong way today

Source: THE TOWN-FOP; OR, SIR TIMOTHY TAWDREY (Act V, sc. i)
Author: Aphra Behn (1640-1689)
First published: 1676
Type of work: Dramatic comedy

Context: Betty Flauntit is a common prostitute who is ambitious to rise in her world. As a first step she has become the kept woman of Sir Timothy Tawdrey, a London fop. Her new status, however, does not prevent her from plying her trade in the bawdyhouse kept by Mrs. Driver. Nor does his keeping of Betty Flauntit prevent Sir Timothy from visiting bawdyhouses, including Mrs. Driver's establishment. On the night of his forced marriage to his cousin, Lady Diana, Bellmour escapes from the bridal chamber and, beside himself with grief over being unable to marry Celinda, the girl he loves, goes to Mrs. Driver's place of business with Sir Timothy. Bellmour, emotionally upset, drinks considerably and loses large sums of money to Sir Timothy and the latter's hangers-on. Mrs. Driver, thinking Bellmour an easy mark, sends Betty Flauntit, along with two other girls, when Sir Timothy calls for women. Betty Flauntit expects, one way or another, to make Bellmour her victim. But her intentions are first prevented by Sir Timothy's recognition of her and, later, by the appearance of Charles, Bellmour's younger brother, who comes to rescue the distraught Bellmour from the rogues who are trying to fleece him. To make matters worse for Betty Flauntit, Mrs. Driver tells Sir Timothy that Betty is not being "true" to her lover. Escaping from the bawdy-house when a brawl breaks out, she walks in Covent Garden, musing over her ill luck:

BETTY FLAUNTIT

Sure **I rose the wrong way to day,** I have had such damn'd ill luck every way: First, to be sent for to such a Man as this Bellmour, and, as the Devil wou'd have it, to find my Knight there; then to be just upon the Point of making my Fortune, and to be interrupted by that virtuous Brother of his; then to have a Quarrel happen, that (before I could whisper him in the Ear, to say so much as, Meet me here again—anon) forc'd me to quit the House, lest the Constable had done it for me; then that silly Baud should discover all to my Cully. If this be not ill Luck, the Devil's in't. . . .

494

I saw the iron enter into his soul

Source: A SENTIMENTAL JOURNEY THROUGH FRANCE AND ITALY ("The Captive. Paris")
Author: Laurence Sterne (1713-1768)
First published: 1768
Type of work: Travel miscellany

Context: Yorick (Sterne) has rushed off to France at a moment's notice because he has discovered in conversation that a trip to that country makes one immeasurably superior; as he observes, if a mere journey of twenty miles can accomplish this result, he may as well go. Arrived in France, he proceeds in a leisurely fashion toward Paris; on the road he flirts with women, hires a servant named La Fleur, and has a fine time in an aimless, harmless way. In Paris he is so overcome by a female shopkeeper that he buys several pairs of gloves, all the wrong size; he is blissfully unaware that she may be available for an altogether different kind of relationship. He attends the opera, learns to his astonishment that the French have a ribald sense of humor, and ponders the fact. Two women have been seated in the same box with a clergyman, and the crowd heckles him, enjoining him to keep his hands in the air. Yorick also notes a dwarf who cannot see the stage because a huge German is standing in front of him. French justice triumphs: a Gendarme places the dwarf in front of the German. Wandering about the city later, Yorick flirts with a chambermaid. Then he learns the police are looking for him. It seems that in his haste to leave England he had forgotten that England and France are at war; moreover, he has no passport. In a sudden access of contrition, Yorick decides to turn himself in; but, hearing a voice, he looks around and spies a starling in a cage. The bird is repeating, in English, "I can't get out." Yorick purchases the feathered prisoner and then begins to reconsider his legal duty; he ponders in his mind the horrors of imprisonment. Giving his imagination free rein, he pictures the victim in the cell:

I beheld his body half wasted away with long expectation and confinement, and felt what kind of sickness of the heart it was which arises from hope deferr'd. Upon looking nearer I saw him pale and feverish: in thirty years the western breeze had not once fann'd his blood—he had seen no sun, no moon, in all that time— nor had the voice of friend or kinsman breathed through his lattice:—his children—

But here my heart began to bleed—and I was forced to go on with another part of the portrait.

He was sitting upon the ground upon a little straw, in the furthest corner of his dungeon, which was alternately his chair and bed: a little calendar of small sticks were laid at the head, notch'd all over with the dismal days and nights he had passed there—he had one of these little sticks in his hand, and with a rusty nail he was etching another day of misery to add to the heap. As I darkened the little light he had, he lifted up a hopeless eye towards the door, then cast it down—shook his head, and went on with his work of affliction. I heard his chains upon his legs, as he turned his body to lay his little stick upon the bundle. —He gave a deep sigh—**I saw the iron enter into his soul**—I burst into tears—I could not sustain the picture of confinement which my fancy had drawn—I started up from my chair, and called La Fleur—I bid him bespeak me a *remise,* and have it ready at the door of the hotel by nine in the morning.

I seem to tread on Classic ground

Source: A LETTER FROM ITALY (Line 12)
Author: Joseph Addison (1672-1719)
First published: 1703
Type of work: Literary dedication

Context: Having studied Latin and Greek at Queens College, Oxford, Addison was eager to visit the continent. Through the kindness of Lord Chancellor Somers in 1700, he was given a yearly grant of three hundred pounds to spend four years abroad. His first report of activities came in his rhymed *A Letter from Italy,* dedicated to Charles, Lord Halifax, dated Feb. 19, 1701, and published two years later. His travel book, *Remarks on Italy* (1705) dedicated to Somers, was an elaboration on the *Letter,* disappointing to readers who wanted a comment on Italian customs and policies, but delightful in its poetic comparison between the Italy he saw and that drawn by classical writers. In the first stanza, the poet comments on the life of retirement enjoyed by Lord Halifax, while Addison is traveling through balmy Italy a land which has inspired so many to write poetry:

> For wheresoe'er I turn my ravished eyes
> Gay gilded scenes and shining prospects rise,
> Poetic fields encompass me around,
> And still **I seem to tread on Classic ground;**
> For here the Muse so oft her harp has strung
> That not a mountain rears its head unsung,
> Renowned in verse each shady thicket grows
> And every stream in heavenly numbers flows.

I shall sleep like a top

Source: THE RIVALS (Act III)
Author: Sir William Davenant (1606-1668)
First published: 1668
Type of work: Tragi-comedy

Context: Sir William Davenant or D'Avenant, was the godson of William Shakespeare. Many suspect that he was an actual son of the great playwright, a belief that Davenant made no effort to deny. But, though he was governor of the King and Queen's Company of Players (1635), he could not equal the dramatic skill of his godfather. With John Dryden (1631–1700), he adapted Shakespeare's *The Tempest,* without improving it. He wrote a number of plays by himself before the closing of the English theaters by Cromwell in 1642; and when he returned from exile in France he formed another acting group for his friend, William Beeston. The theater-loving King Charles II knighted him. Davenant wrote both heroic tragedies and Restoration comedies. *The Rivals* has no connection with the more famous comedy of a century later by Richard B. Sheridan (1751–1816). Davenant's play is a drastically changed rewriting of the earlier *The Two Noble Kinsmen* (1613), thought by many to represent the collaboration of Shakespeare and Fletcher, that, in turn was based on "The Knight's Tale," from Chaucer's *The Canterbury Tales.* The characters have been rechristened. Theocles and Philander are both in love with star-crossed Celania, daughter of the Provost of Prince Arcon of Arcadia. Thwarted in her love for Philander, Celania has gone mad. Perhaps with memories of Ophelia, Davenant presents her in the forest, accompanied by her maid, Leucippe, singing a song born of her insanity. She plans to dress like a man and go searching for her absent love. She will ride a stick like a witch, or pause and sleep. But why "like a top?" The phrase was not forced by the rhyme. The rest of it, the nightingale and the hawthorn, is a poetic figure. A spinning top seems motionless, but it does have a humming sound which may, perhaps, give origin to the expression paraphrased as "to sleep sound." But even granting Celania her madness, it is hard to explain her choice of this figure. Here is her song, with its meaningless refrain.

For straight my green gown into breeches I'll make,
And my long yellow locks much shorter I'll take,
   Sing down a, down, down a, down a.
Then I'll cut me a switch, and on that ride about,
And wander and wander till I find him out,
   With a heigh down, down a, down, down a,
O for a hawthorn; like a nightingale
To lean my breast against, or else **I shall sleep like a top.**

I sighed as a lover, I obeyed as a son

Source: AUTOBIOGRAPHY (World Classics edition, p. 83)
Author: Edward Gibbon (1737-1794)
First published: 1796
Type of work: Autobiography

Context: Edward Gibbon spent most of his life studying and writing. He was a sickly child with a strong scholarly bent; his life was frequently despaired of until he began to show improved health in his sixteenth year. He was the only one of his father's seven children to reach maturity—a good illustration of the mortality rate at that time. Gibbon went to Oxford in 1752 and while there joined the Roman Catholic Church. He felt the courses at Oxford were a waste of time, and his exasperated father sent him to Lausanne to live with a Calvinist minister, M. Pavilliard. Gibbon learned French through necessity and was soon able to think in that language; his writing, from that time on, exhibited a strong French influence. While there he studied the logic of Crousaz, and as a result returned to Protestantism. He pursued his studies avidly and in 1755 traveled about Switzerland. In 1757 he met Voltaire. It was in this year that he met a girl named Suzanne Curchod, daughter of the pastor of Crassier, and fell in love with her. Gibbon's father, who had just remarried, objected to the marriage of his son. Gibbon complied with his father's wishes in the matter, and did not allow himself to fall in love again. Instead, he continued his studies. During the next few years he determined to write a history, but it was some time before he settled on a topic. Finally, in 1772, he began his *Decline and Fall of the Roman Empire,* a monumental work which took him fifteen years to complete. It may be said to be his life's work; all his studies led up to it, and he wrote little else of consequence. He was interested in his own life history, and a curious fact about this interest is that Gibbon wrote no less than six autobiographical sketches or memoirs. After his death, these were carefully edited by Lord Sheffield and published as a single narrative containing what was considered the best material from each. The third memoir, written about 1789, contains the following wistful account of Gibbon's student friendship and first love:

I should be ashamed if the warm season of youth had passed away without any sense of friendship or love; and in the choice of their objects I may applaud the discernment of my head or heart. Mr. George Deyverdun, of Lausanne, was a young Gentleman of high honour and quick feelings, of an elegant taste and a liberal understanding: he became the companion of my studies and pleasures; every idea, every sentiment, was poured into each other's bosom; and our schemes of ambition or retirement always terminated in the prospect of our final and inseparable union. The beauty of Mademoiselle Curchod, the daughter of a country clergyman, was adorned with science and virtue: she listened to the tenderness which she had inspired; but the romantic hopes of youth and passion were crushed, on my return, by the prejudice or prudence of an English parent. **I sighed as a lover, I obeyed as a son;** my wound was insensibly healed by time, absence, and the habits of a new life; and my cure was accelerated by a faithful report of the tranquillity and chearfulness of the Lady herself. Her equal behaviour under the tryals of indigence and prosperity has displayed the firmness of her character. A citizen of Geneva, a rich banker of Paris, made himself happy by rewarding her merit; the genius of her husband has raised him to a perilous eminence; and Madame Necker now divides and alleviates the cares of the first minister of the finances of France.

I 'spect I growed

Source: UNCLE TOM'S CABIN (Chapter 20)
Author: Harriet Beecher Stowe (1811-1896)
First published: 1852
Type of work: Novel

Context: Like all the Beechers of New England, the daughter of the Reverend Lyman Beecher was enthusiastic about religious matters and the improvement of humanity. In 1836, she married Professor Calvin Stowe, and aided runaway slaves through her Cincinnati, Ohio, station of the "Underground Railroad." From these fugitives and from her brothers in New Orleans, she learned of the cruelty of slavery. So she wrote *Uncle Tom's Cabin or Life Among the Lowly,* published serially in an abolitionist newspaper, *The National Era* (June, 1851– April 1852). The work appeared as a novel in 1852 with 300,000 copies sold the first year. Immediately dramatized by G. L. Aikin, and by many others, it was continually performed for almost a century. Though lacking in literary merit, and absurdly sentimental, the novel played an important part in preparing for the American Civil War, and was a powerful factor in preventing the Confederacy from obtaining in Europe full recognition as an independent nation. President Lincoln, meeting her for the first time, exclaimed: "Is this the little woman that sparked this great war?" Topsy, who supplies much of the comedy in the many stage versions, is introduced in Chapter 20. She is an eight-year-old Negress whom St. Clare has bought for Miss Ophelia to educate. Her new mistress starts questioning the slave, whose name may have been suggested by the expression "topsy turvy."

"Have you ever heard anything about God, Topsy?"
The child looked bewildered, but grinned, as usual.
"Do you know who made you?"
"Nobody as I knows on," said the child, with a short laugh.
The idea appeared to amuse her considerably; for her eyes twinkled, and she added.
"I 'spect I grow'd. Don't think nobody never made me."

I stumbled when I saw

Source: KING LEAR (Act IV, sc. i, l. 19)
Author: William Shakespeare (1564-1616)
First published: 1608
Type of work: Dramatic tragedy

Context: Believing in the wrong son as King Lear believed in the wrong daughters, the Earl of Gloucester has been betrayed by his bastard, Edmund. Gloucester secretly helps the maddened king and receives a letter telling him that Lear's daughter Cordelia, still faithful despite Lear's banishment of her, is landing at Dover with a French army. All this, Edmund reveals to one of Lear's evil daughters, Regan, and her vicious husband, the Duke of Cornwall. Cornwall blinds Gloucester and turns him out of doors, where he is discovered by his legitimate son, Edgar, falsely denounced by Edmund as a would-be murderer of his father. Edgar has adopted the disguise of a "bedlam beggar," one who is mad or pretends madness to secure charity. Gloucester, who has finally learned the truth about his sons, wishes to be led to the cliffs of Dover in order to commit suicide, and he asks the presumed Bedlamite to lead him. In a speech reminiscent of Oedipus' assertion that he blinded himself because of his disgust with what he could see, Gloucester tells an old retainer that when he had eyes he felt too sure of himself—his "means" made him feel secure; he is better off with his present "defects."

OLD MAN
You cannot see your way.

GLOUCESTER
I have no way, and therefore want no eyes.
I stumbled when I saw. Full oft 'tis seen,
Our means secure us, and our mere defects
Prove our commodities. O dear son Edgar,
The food of thy abused father's wrath;
Might I but live to see thee in my touch,
I'd say I had eyes again.

I was a king in Babylon and you were a Christian slave

Source: ECHOES (xxxvii, to W.A., ll. 3-4)
Author: William Ernest Henley (1849-1903)
First published: 1884
Type of work: Ballad

Context: Crippled by tuberculosis of the bone, this tall English poet on crutches was the model for Long John Silver, of *Treasure Island.* He fought hard, as a critic, against Victorian prudery and in favor of realism. As editor of a magazine, he gave their start to Kipling, Conrad, and Yeats. His own poetry, first collected in *A Book of Verse* (1888), was aggressively masculine. Perhaps "Invictus" from that volume is the best known. His attempt to be "unpoetic" in vocabulary is evident in his Ballad to W.A. (William Archer), number 37 in the division: "Echoes 1872-1889." It is the poem of which the author was proudest. But though even an unimaginative person can understand being "master of my fate" and "captain of my soul," he may not comprehend the theory of transmigration of souls and the parallel existences of the King of Babylon and his Christian slave, described in the five stanzas of this ballad. So he will prefer "Invictus." "Or ever," that is, before the romantic period of chivalry ended, I was King in Babylon and loved a Christian slave. After loving her, I cast her aside, but upon her death, built her a tomb. Now in a new existence, we are together, but there is still a barrier between us. . . . Expressed poetically:

Or ever the knightly years were gone
　　With the old world to the grave,
I was a King in Babylon
And you were a Christian Slave.

I saw, I took, I cast you by,
　　I bent and broke your pride.
You loved me well, or I heard them lie,
　　But your longing was denied.
Surely I knew that by and by
　　You cursed your gods and died.

And a myriad suns have set and shone
　　Since then upon the grave
Decreed by the King of Babylon
　　To her that had been his Slave.

I was all ear

Source: COMUS (Line 559)
Author: John Milton (1608-1674)
First published: 1637
Type of work: Masque

Context: The Earl of Bridgewater's installation as President of Wales was the occasion for the composition of *Comus* and its presentation in the great hall of Ludlow Castle. The earl's daughter and two sons acted leading roles. As the three seek to make their way through a tangled wood, the daughter, known as the Lady, becomes wearied, and the two brothers separate from her to find fruits and berries with which to restore her strength. They become lost in the forest and are met by the attendant Spirit of the Woods, who is disguised as a shepherd. He tells the brothers that they are in the domain of the great sorcerer Comus, son of Bacchus and Circe, who gives wanderers in the forest an enchanted drink that transforms their faces into those of beasts and undermines their reason. The supposed shepherd had listened this very evening to the roar of the wizard's followers that customarily filled the night woods with bar-

501

barous dissonance; he had noted a sudden cessation of the noise which he considered significant. At last he heard a most pleasing sound, a sound which he perceived was the Lady's voice. When he listened intently and discovered that she was in conversation with Comus, he sped through the woods to find the brothers:

> At last a soft and solemn breathing sound
> Rose like a steam of rich distilled perfumes,
> And stole upon the air, that even silence
> Was took ere she was ware, and wished she might
> Deny her nature, and be never more,
> Still to be so displaced. **I was all ear,**
> And took in strains that might create a soul
> Under the ribs of death; but O ere long
> Too well I did perceive it was the voice
> Of my most honored lady, your dear sister.
> Amazed I stood, harrowed with grief and fear,
> And O poor hapless nightingale, thought I,
> How sweet thou singest, how near the deadly snare!

I will make a Star-Chamber matter of it

Source: THE MERRY WIVES OF WINDSOR (Act I, sc. i, ll. 1-2)
Author: William Shakespeare (1564-1616)
First published: 1602
Type of work: Dramatic comedy

Context: As the play opens, Robert Shallow, a country justice, is proclaiming that he has been wronged by Sir John Falstaff. Shallow will not be appeased by Parson Hugh Evans, who recognizes that Falstaff is of noble rank and, being on a hunting trip, does not wish to be bothered. But Shallow knows that Falstaff and his men had "beaten" his associates, "kill'd" his deer, and "broke open" his lodge. Thus he says at the first of the play that despite the fact that Sir John is of the nobility, he will take his charges before a court and "make a Star-Chamber matter of it." The Star-Chamber (so called because of the stars on the ceiling of the room where it sat) was a high court exercising very wide powers.

SHALLOW
Sir Hugh, persuade me not. **I will make a Star-Chamber matter of it.** If he were twenty Sir John Falstaffs, he shall not abuse Robert Shallow, Esquire.

I will praise any man that will praise me

Source: ANTONY AND CLEOPATRA (Act II, sc. vi, l. 92)
Author: William Shakespeare (1564-1616)
First published: 1623
Type of work: Dramatic tragedy

Context: The rulers of the Roman Empire—Mark Antony, Octavius Caesar, and Lepidus—force the rebellious Pompey to come to terms, and the four prepare to seal their pact by a round of eating and drinking. In the general euphoria that follows, the delightfully shrewd and cynical Enobarbus, friend and officer of Antony, greets an old acquaintance, the equally shrewd and cynical Menas, friend and officer of Pompey. Their conversation is a humorous foil to the dialogue of the four military leaders:

MENAS
. . . You and I have known, sir.

ENOBARBUS
At sea, I think.

MENAS
We have sir.

ENOBARBUS
You have done well by water.

MENAS
And you by land.

ENOBARBUS
I will praise any man that will praise me, though it cannot be denied what I have done by land.

MENAS
Nor what I have done by water.

ENOBARBUS
Yes, something you can deny for your own safety. You have been a great thief by sea.

MENAS
And you by land.

ENOBARBUS
There I deny my land service. But give me your hand Menas, if our eyes had authority, here they might take two thieves kissing.

503

I would fain die a dry death

Source: THE TEMPEST (Act I, sc. i, ll. 71-72)
Author: William Shakespeare (1564-1616)
First published: 1623
Type of work: Tragi-comedy

Context: A ship bearing noblemen of Milan and Naples, encountering a storm produced by the conjuring of Prospero (the rightful Duke of Milan, whose throne has been usurped by his wicked brother Antonio), is wrecked off the coast of the island occupied by Prospero. As the occupants begin their struggle to reach the island, Gonzalo, an old and trusted friend of Prospero, gasps:

GONZALO

Now would I give a thousand furlongs of sea, for an acre of barren ground. Long heath, brown furze, any thing. The wills above be done, but **I would fain die a dry death.** [*Exit.*]

I would give all my fame for a pot of ale and safety

Source: KING HENRY THE FIFTH (Act III, sc. ii, ll. 13-14)
Author: William Shakespeare (1564-1616)
First published: 1600
Type of work: Historical drama

Context: Henry V, the "mirror of a Christian king," has led his forces into France to press the English claim to the right of the French throne. Having intercepted at Southampton the English traitors Grey, Scroop, and Cambridge, who planned to betray England, he now lays seige to Harfleur in a determined effort to convince Charles VI and the Dauphin of the superiority of the English forces. Henry is destined to succeed in this venture and to annihilate the French in an amazingly successful display of bravery and skillful tactical maneuvering at Agincourt, a battle which will bring French submission and the arranged royal wedding between Henry and the French princess, Katherine. Much of the success of the English forces can be attributed to their stalwart leader, who with "a touch of Harry in the night" moves among his men to encourage their best efforts as men of England. During the battle of Harfleur he urges them "Once more into the breach, dear friends, . . . / Or close the wall up with our English dead." Among the flurry of soldiers and the bravura of battle, a boy comments with touching irony that—despite the thrill of patriotic endeavor—he would willingly be in England, relaxing at the tavern:

504

BARDOLPH
On, on, on, on, on, to the breach, to the breach, to the breach!

NYM
Pray thee corporal stay, the knocks are too hot; and for mine own part, I have not a case of lives. . . .

PISTOL
· · ·
Knocks go and come; God's vassals drop and die;
And sword and shield,
In bloody field,
Doth win immortal fame.

BOY
Would I were in an alehouse in London! **I would give all my fame for a pot of ale, and safety.**

PISTOL
And I:

If wishes would prevail with me,
My purpose should not fail with me;
But thither would I hie.

I would live to study, and not study to live

Source: LETTER TO KING JAMES I
Author: Sir Francis Bacon (1561-1626)
First published: 1734
Type of work: Personal letter

Context: Bacon, remembered today for his philosophical writings, was an important political figure in his own time. A member of Parliament and a personal friend of James I, a magistrate trained in the legal profession, he acquired an impressive list of titles: Baron of Verulam, Viscount St. Albans, Lord High Chancellor of England. He was careful to attach himself to royal favorites; one was the ill-starred Essex. When the latter attempted rebellion, Bacon helped to convict him. Another such attachment was George Villiers, Duke of Buckingham. This wise relationship brought Bacon numerous royal favors and advancements, until Buckingham's popularity waned. On January 22, 1621, Bacon observed his sixtieth birthday; on January 27, he was made Viscount St. Albans. In March the blow fell: he was charged with accepting bribes from persons who had appeared in his court. Admitting that the charges were true, Bacon nonetheless insisted he had not allowed any gratuities to influence his decisions. Perhaps he had not; however, he had bowed to Buckingham's wishes whenever any of the latter's friends had appeared in court. Early

505

in May he was stripped of his offices, fined forty thousand pounds, and imprisoned briefly in the Tower of London. He was also forbidden to sit in Parliament again and banned from the court. The last two rulings were never lifted entirely; some of the others were eased. Buckingham, still powerful, coveted Bacon's house; Bacon had to sell it to him in order to gain readmission to the court. He now entered upon his retirement, going to live at Gorhambury, and devoted himself to the writing which has won him lasting fame. His *History of Henry VII* was completed in October; he then embarked upon *The Ad-*

vancement of Learning. He appealed to the king for mercy, but with little result. In one letter he pleads his case at some length, pointing out his long service and reminding the king of their old friendship. Apparently undated, it was written when Bacon was "a year and a half old in misery;" this statement would seem to indicate that he wrote the letter during the winter of 1622–23. In it he summarizes his troubles, combining politely veiled rebuke with the lavish flatteries demanded by custom, and ends by begging abjectly that he not be reduced to utter destitution:

. . . Therefore as one that hath had the happiness to know your Majestie near hand, I have (most gracious Sovereign) faith enough for a miracle, much more for a grace, that your Majestie will not suffer your poor creature to be utterly defaced, nor blot that name quite out of your book, upon which your sacred hand hath been so oft for new ornaments and additions.

Unto this degree of compassion, I hope God above . . . will dispose your princely heart, already prepared to all piety. And why should I not think, but that thrice noble Prince . . . will help to pull me (if I may use that homely phrase) out of the mire of an abject and sordid condition in my last days. . . .

But, if it may please your Majestie (for Saints, I shall give them reverence, but no adoration, my address is to your Majestie, the fountain of goodness;) your Majestie shall by the grace of God, not feel that in gift, which I shall extremely feel in help; for my desires are moderate, and my courses measured to a life orderly and reserved, hoping still to do your Majestie honour in my way. Only I most humbly beseech your Majestie to give me leave to conclude with those words which necessity speaketh: help me (*dear Sovereign Lord and Master*) and pity me so far, as I that have born a bag, be not now in my age forced in effect to bear a wallet; **nor I that desire to live to study, may not be driven to study to live.** I most humbly crave pardon of a long letter. . . .

An idiot race to honor lost

Source: ON SEEING STIRLING PALACE IN RUINS
Author: Robert Burns (1759-1796)
First published: 1787
Type of work: Epigram

Context: In 1787 Robert Burns temporarily left Edinburgh where he had been lionized as a literary genius, but generally misunderstood, for a trip through the Highlands, perhaps in memory of Highland Mary. His companion was William Nicol, Master of Edinburgh High School, one of his close friends. They visited Felkirk, Stirling, and the nearby field of Bannockburn where Robert the Bruce in 1314 established himself on the Scotch throne by defeating Edward II of England. On their return to Stirling, with a diamond that he had recently purchased, Burns inscribed some treasonable verses on the window pane of the inn. Six weeks later, worried about what he had written, he returned to Stirling and smashed the glass, but he could not blot out the lines. Too many peopie had seen and copied them. Some of Burns's ancestors had espoused the cause of the Stuarts, a family acting as regents in Scotland as early as the twelfth century. Because of the marriage of James IV of Scotland to Margaret Tudor, eventually James VI of Scotland became James I of England in 1603. After the death of Anne, the last of the Stuarts to rule England, the crown passed to George I of the House of Hanover. However, the Jacobites continued to support various pretenders. Burns himself was not really politically minded. He was a sort of sentimental Jacobite, upheld by his own discontent. While denouncing the rulers of his country, he was really expressing the private ills that he enlarged to include the world. Unfortunately, he was imprudent in his expression of these opinions. He was being feted in Edinburgh and had created a number of enemies. One can see what his detractors, quick to denounce him for his exuberant living, would make of his brief poem about Stirling Palace. Built on the summit of a hill above the city, it had been the birthplace of James II and other rulers. Mary Stuart and James VI were crowned there. It had been damaged during a three-month seige by Edward I in 1304, and further ruined when it was recaptured by the Scots after Bannockburn. The "outlandish race," of course, were the Hanoverians, of another land and another language, and therefore to a Jacobite, even a sentimental one, an "idiot race," and "to honor lost." However, that the better one knew them the more one despised them was certainly poetic license. Here is the entire poem.

> Here Stuarts once in glory reign'd,
> And laws for Scotland's weal ordain'd;
> But now unroof'd their palace stands,
> Their sceptre's sway'd by other hands;
> The injur'd Stuart line is gone,
> A race outlandish fills their throne,
> **An idiot race to honor lost,**
> Who knows them best, despise them most.

Idleness is only the refuge of weak minds

Source: LETTERS TO HIS SON (Letter 75)
Author: Philip Dormer Stanhope, Lord Chesterfield (1694-1773)
First published: 1774
Type of work: Personal letter

Context: Lord Chesterfield was determined to train his son Philip to be an accomplished English Gentleman, statesman, and man of the world; and in his letters he spared no pains to give the young man sound advice. Philip, though illegitimate, was loved by his father, and Chesterfield had great hopes for him. However, the boy did not fulfill his father's hopes; he never became a real devotee of the stylized life of grace, manner, and formula that marked the truly polished and successful gentleman. He died young, leaving a wife and two young sons; Chesterfield, who had not known of their existence, was delighted with all three and undertook their support. The letters Chesterfield wrote to Philip deal for the most part with manners and deportment, the various niceties of social usage, and other habits and accomplishments necessary to success. Philip worked for the British government, his work taking him to various places in Europe; Chesterfield corresponded with him voluminously and faithfully, doing his best to smooth Philip's path and to prepare him for whatever situations he might face. In his letter of July 20, 1749, he chides Philip for neglecting to answer a letter from a friend who is not without influence: "Those attentions ought never to be omitted; they cost little, and please a great deal; but the neglect of them offends more than you can imagine. Great merit, or great failings, will make you respected or despised; but trifles, little attentions, mere nothings, either done, or neglected, will make you either liked or disliked, in the general run of the world. . . . Moral virtues are the foundation of society in general, and of friendship in particular; but attentions, manners, and graces, both adorn and strengthen them." He follows this counsel with an inquiry concerning Philip's health, which has been poor; then tells Philip he has sent a letter of thanks to one Mr. Firmian:

. . . I hope you write to him too, from time to time. The letters of recommendation of a man of his merit and learning will, to be sure, be of great use to you among the learned world in Italy; that is, provided you take care to keep up to the character he gives you in them; otherwise they will only add to your disgrace.

Consider that you have lost a good deal of time by your illness; fetch it up now that you are well. At present you should be a good economist of your moments, of which company and sights will claim a considerable share; so that those which remain for study must be not only attentively, but greedily employed. But indeed I do not suspect you of one single moment's idleness in the whole day. **Idleness is only the refuge of weak minds,** and the holiday of

fools. I do not call good company and liberal pleasures, idleness;
far from it: I recommend to you a good share of both.

If all the pens that ever poets held

Source: TAMBURLAINE THE GREAT (Part I, Act V, sc. i, l. 1942)
Author: Christopher Marlowe (1564-1593)
First published: 1590
Type of work: Dramatic tragedy

Context: Tamburlaine, flushed with many conquests, almost at the zenith of his career in conquering the world he knew, besieges Damascus. This is the city of Zenocrate, the princess Tamburlaine loves. She asks that her father, its ruler, be dealt with kindly, but Tamburlaine refuses, though to refuse causes him sadness, so that he agrees not to put Zenocrate's father to death when the city falls. The ruler of Damascus sends four beautiful young virgins to Tamburlaine, hoping they can persuade him to accept the city's surrender without slaughter and destruction. The great conqueror, melancholy and dressed all in black, receives the four virgins, but he remains unmoved by their appeal; he has them taken out to be killed by a group of charging horsemen and their bodies hung up in sight of the defenders of the city. Even while giving his heartless orders, however, Tamburlaine thinks of his love for Zenocrate and how her pleas for her father, the Sultan of Egypt, cause him emotion:

TAMBURLAINE
. . .
What is beauty saith my sufferings then
If all the pens that ever poets held,
Had fed the feelings of their master's thoughts,
And every sweetnes that suspir'd their hearts,
Their minds, and muses on admired themes:
If all the heavenly Quintessence they still
From their immortall flowers of Poesy,
Wherein, as in a mirror we perceive
The highest reaches of a human wit.
If these had made one Poems' period
And all combin'd in Beauty's worthiness,
Yet should ther hover in their restless heads,
One thought, one grace, one woonder, at the least,
Which into words no virtue can digest.

If God choose, I shall but love thee better after death

Source: SONNETS FROM THE PORTUGUESE (Sonnet XLIII, ll. 13-14)
Author: Elizabeth Barrett Browning (1806–1861)
First published: 1850
Type of work: Sonnet

Context: Elizabeth Barrett, an invalid, made the acquaintance of Robert Browning. The two fell in love as soon as they met, and Elizabeth began the composition of a series of love sonnets, which she kept hidden from Robert until after their marriage, in 1846. The name of the cycle, *Sonnets from the Portuguese,* derives from Browning's having called her "his Portuguese," the name having been suggested by her poem "Caterina to Camoens." The sonnets are probably the most impassioned love poetry in English. In Sonnet XLIII, Elizabeth endeavors to list the many ways in which she loves Robert. She loves him to the length and breadth and height her soul can reach and also on the level of every day's quiet need. She loves him purely and passionately. She loves him as she once did her saints, and with the smiles and tears of her whole life. And if God lets her, she will love him more after death than she does while she is living:

> How do I love thee? Let me count the ways.
> I love thee to the depth and breadth and height
> My soul can reach, when feeling out of sight
> For the ends of Being and ideal Grace.
> I love thee to the level of every day's
> Most quiet need, by sun and candlelight.
> I love thee freely, as men strive for Right;
> I love thee purely, as they turn from Praise.
> I love thee with the passion put to use
> In my old griefs, and with my childhood's faith.
> I love thee with a love I seemed to lose
> With my lost saints—I love thee with the breath,
> Smiles, tears, of all my life!—and, **if God choose,**
> **I shall but love thee better after death.**

If I were dead, you'd sometimes say, Poor Child!

Source: TO THE UNKNOWN EROS (Book I, "If I Were Dead," Line 1)
Author: Coventry Patmore (1823-1896)
First published: 1877
Type of work: Lyric poem

Context: In this collection of poems, written after several years of silence, Patmore creates his most mysterious and transcendental volume; often obscure because of his dependence on the tradition of Roman Catholic mysticism and frequently banal because of his exaltation of the commonplace, these poems occasionally reveal the insights of a man who understood both the problems and the joys of marriage. The fortunate moments when Patmore leaves philosophy and mysticism to describe the small, everyday moments that all married people encounter give the collection a perennial charm that keeps the heavier elements from dominating the volume; this quotation comes from one of these lighter poems, a short lyric in which the parent, after punishing his child, hears the boy's pathetic cry.

> 'If I were dead, you'd sometimes say, Poor Child!'
> The dear lips quiver'd as they spake,
> And the tears brake
> From eyes which, not to grieve me, brightly smiled.
> Poor Child, poor Child!
> I seem to hear your laugh, your talk, your song.
> It is not true that Love will do no wrong.
> Poor Child!
> And did you think, when you so cried and smiled,
> How I, in lonely nights should lie awake,
> And of those words your full avengers make?

If I were not Alexander, I would be Diogenes

Source: PARALLEL LIVES ("Alexander")
Author: Plutarch (c.45-c.125)
First transcribed: 105-115
Type of work: Biography

Context: After Alexander and his Macedonians had destroyed Thebes and razed it to the ground, he was reconciled with the Athenians and treated them mercifully, possibly to compensate for his savagery toward the Thebans. Afterward, in a general assembly, the Greeks voted to join under Alexander's leadership in an expedition against Persia.

Thereupon many statesmen and philosophers came to him with their congratulations, and he expected that Diogenes of Sinope also, who was tarrying in Corinth, would do likewise. But since that philosopher took not the slightest notice of Alexander, and continued to enjoy his leisure in the suburb Craneion, Alexander went in person to see him; and he found him lying in the sun. Diogenes raised himself up a little when he saw so many persons coming towards him, and fixed his eyes upon Alexander. And when that monarch addressed him with greetings, and asked if he wanted anything, "Yes," said Diogenes, "stand a little out of my sun." It is said that Alexander was so struck by this, and admired so much the haughtiness and grandeur of the man who had nothing but scorn for him, that he said to his followers, who were

511

laughing and jesting about the philosopher as they went away,
"But verily, **if I were not Alexander, I would be Diogenes.**"

If it be against reason, it is of no force in law

Source: INSTITUTES: COMMENTARY UPON LITTLETON (First Institute, Book
   I, chapter 10, section 80)
Author: Sir Edward Coke (1552-1634)
First published: 1628
Type of work: Legal commentaries

Context: Lord Coke, who was speaker of the British House of Commons in 1593, made a life-long enemy of Francis Bacon by defeating him for the position of Attorney General, in 1594. He became Chief Justice of the Court of Common Pleas, in 1606, and was the first to be called Lord Chief Justice of England. Like all lawyers Coke got part of his training by poring over legal tomes. One, based on Justinian's "Institutes," was the work of Thomas Littleton (1422–1481), who wrote in French under the title *Tenures* the earliest treatise on English law ever printed (1481). It covered legal procedure dealing with obligations of landholders to their landlords. Though Coke called it "the ornament of Common Law and the most perfect and absolute book that was ever written in any humane Science," he must have found it difficult reading, because when later he published his commentaries on Littleton's treatise, he offered encouragement to other students in his Introduction. "If the Reader does not in one day reach the meaning of our author or our commentaries, let him proceed on some other day, and that doubt will be cleared." Book I deals with "Estates in Lands and Tenements." It is one of four *Institutes of the Lawes of England* written between 1628 and 1644, and it is generally referred to as "Coke Upon Littleton." It was the standard legal text until the nineteenth century. Each page was divided into three columns. One printed the French opinions of Thomas Littleton, the second provided a statement of the law in English, and in the third, Sir Edward Coke, greatest exponent of England's Common Law, explains, interprets, and gives helpful comments for law students. Perhaps his son was one of those for whom he intended it. At least in several sections he starts the comment with "My son." In his interpretation of Section 80 of Chapter 10 (There is a total of 749 sections), Littleton's text is: "And so it is to bee understood, that in divers Lordships, and in divers Manors, there be many and divers customes, in such cases as to take tenements, and as to plead, and as to other things and customes to be done, and whatsoever is not against reason, may well bee admitted and allowed." Coke's comment on the text follows:

This was cautiously set downe, for in respect to the variety of customes in most mannors, it is not possible to set downe any certainty, only this incident inseparable every custome must have, viz., that it be consonant to reason; for how long soever it hath continued, **if it be against reason, it is of no force in law.**

If you are in Rome, live in the Roman style

Source: DUCTOR DUBITANTIUM (Part I, chapter 1, rule 5)
Author: Jeremy Taylor (1613-1667)
First published: 1660
Type of work: Religious guide

Context: The Reverend Jeremy Taylor, son of a churchwarden who was by profession a barber skilled in drugs and surgery, became a brilliant theologian. He was admitted to college at the age of 13, and given a fellowship at Cambridge in 1630, then sent to Oxford for a Master of Arts degree. Though accused of love for the Roman Catholic faith, he did not follow its precepts. He married in 1639, and had three sons. He became chaplain to Charles I, who gave him a Doctor of Divinity degree when he was dispensing honors. Taken prisoner at the fall of the king in 1644, Taylor was soon released. He established a school to earn his living, and wrote tracts and sermons, but because of fear for his safety, his friends urged him to flee to northeastern Ireland. In his study at Portmore in Kilultagh he wrote *Ductor Dubitantium or the Rules of Conscience in all her general Measures, serving as a great Instrument for the Determination of Cases of Conscience.* It was in press when Charles II was restored to the throne, so the author foresightedly hastened to insert a dedication "To the Most Sacred Majesty of Charles II." As a result, he was made bishop of Down, Connor, and Dromore. His writings were noted for their logic and casuistry. His *Ductor Dubitantium* draws its contents from many church leaders. Taylor credits St. Ambrose of Milan (340?–397) for the precept quoted in Latin. St. Ambrose was also a bishop, noted for his justice and concern for the common people, and author of a number of sermons based on the Gospel and the Creed. Some of them spurred the conversion of St. Augustine. Taylor's works were collected in three massive volumes of about 2,800 pages, published in London in 1837. In Rule 5, entitled "All Consciences are to walk by the same Rule, and that which is just to one is so to all, in the like Circumstances," Taylor explains:

If all men were governed by the same laws, and had the same interest, and the same degrees of understanding, they would perceive the truth of this conclusion. But men are infinitely differenced by their own acts and relations, by their understandings and proper economy, by their superinduced differences and orders, by interest and mistake, by ignorance and malice, by sects

513

and deceptions; and this makes that two men may be damned for doing two contradictories: as a Jew may perish for not keeping of his sabbath, and a Christian for keeping it, an iconoclast for breaking images and another for worshipping them; for eating and for not eating. . . .

But this variety is not directly of God's making, but of man's. God commands us to walk by the same rule and to this end . . . "to be of the same mind." . . . He that fasted upon a Saturday in Ionia or Smyrna, was a schismatic; and so was he that did not fast at Milan or Rome upon the same day, both upon the same reason; Cum fueris Romae, Romano vivito more **[When you are in Rome, live in the Roman style]** . . . because he was to conform to the custom of Smyrna, as well as that of Milan, in the respective dioceses.

Ignobly vain, and impotently great

Source: PROLOGUE TO MR. ADDISON'S CATO (Line 29)
Author: Alexander Pope (1688-1744)
First published: 1713
Type of work: Dramatic tragedy

Context: With British political feeling heated between Whigs and Tories in 1712, Joseph Addison was prevailed upon to complete his play *Cato,* a drama emphasizing the heroic qualities of Cato, leader of the unsuccessful party opposed to Caesar during the civil war in Rome. Though Pope disliked Addison, he was willing to write the *Prologue* to *Cato* because of the great publicity the play received. Too late, states Pope in the *Prologue,* Rome realizes that the sword of noble Cato is preferable to the conquering sword of Caesar:

> Ev'n when proud Caesar 'midst triumphal cars,
> The spoils of nations, and the pomp of wars,
> **Ignobly vain, and impotently great**
> Showed Rome her Cato's figure drawn in state,
> As her dead father's rev'rend image past,
> The pomp was darkened, and the day o'ercast,
> The triumph ceased,—tears gushed from ev'ry eye;
> The world's great victor past unheeded by;
> Her last good man dejected Rome adored,
> And honored Caesar's less than Cato's sword.

Ignorance is not innocence but sin

Source: THE INN ALBUM (Section V, l. 2262)
Author: Robert Browning (1812-1889)
First published: 1875
Type of work: Poetic dialogue

514

Context: Like most of the psychological studies of villainy that Browning produced, *The Inn Album* is based to some extent on actual occurrences. In the present instance his chief inspiration was the story of Lord De Ros, a friend of the Duke of Wellington; it had been recounted in Greville's memoirs. Browning adapted this material and added some ideas deriving from the case of the Tichborne Claimant. The plot involves two men. One is a young man who has just inherited a fortune, but who lacks the aristocratic polish and knowledge of the world which would enable him to move easily in a sophisticated society. The other, with whom he has become friendly, is a man of fifty; he has all the refinement and sophistication the young man lacks but is virtually penniless. The young man wants his companion to teach him how to behave in the company to which wealth will admit him; the older man sees the younger as a potential source of funds. As a step toward acquiring the youngster's money, he allows the lat-ter to win at cards and thus indebts himself to the extent of ten thousand pounds. He intends to use the debt as a lever with which to swindle twice its amount from the boy. In an exchange of confidences each man tells the other he has been unhappy in love; the older admits he once seduced and then abandoned a woman, and the younger tells of his love for a girl who would not have him but took a middle-aged rake instead. The drama reaches its climax when the boy discovers that both have been involved with the same woman. She has encountered the older man and is reacting bitterly when the boy intrudes and recognizes her. He denounces both. She tells the boy to renounce his corrupt companion and to marry the cousin who loves him; and she begs the older man to leave, never letting the other girl know "How near came taint of your companionship!" The rake replies ironically that for innocence to be crowned with ignorance is desirable but difficult. She replied:

"**Ignorance is not innocence but sin**—
Witness yourself ignore what after-pangs
Pursue the plague-infected. Merciful
Am I? Perhaps! the more contempt, the less
Hatred; and who so worthy of contempt
As you that rest assured I cooled the spot
I could not cure, by poisoning, forsooth,
Whose hand I pressed there? Understand for once
That, sick, of all the pains corroding me
This burnt the last and nowise least—the need
Of simulating soundness. I resolved—
No matter how the struggle tasked weak flesh—
To hide the truth away as in a grave
From—most of all—my husband: he nor knows
Nor ever shall be made to know your part,
My part, the devil's part,—I trust, God's part
In the foul matter. Saved, I yearn to save
And not destroy: and what destruction like
The abolishing of faith in him, that's faith

515

In me as pure and true? . . . 'Tis God
. . .
Must bear such secrets and disclose them . . ."

I'll cross it, though it blast me

Source: HAMLET (Act I, sc. i, l. 127)
Author: William Shakespeare (1564-1616)
First published: 1603
Type of work: Dramatic tragedy

Context: The ghost of Hamlet's father appears twice in the opening scene of the play. After the first appearance, Hamlet's friend, Horatio, wonders what the apparition might mean—"This bodes some strange eruption to our state"—and notes that "In the most high and palmy state of Rome,/ A little ere the mightiest Julius fell,/ The graves stood tenantless, and the sheeted dead/ Did squeak and gibber in the Roman streets." When the ghost reappears, Horatio performs the dangerous act of moving directly into the path of the spirit. In calling upon the ghost to speak, Horatio lists the causes that may force a spirit to return to earth; he seems about to get a response when the cock crows and the ghost stalks away, for, according to ancient belief, ghosts and other walkers in darkness cannot endure the sunlight. The entire scene is extraordinarily dramatic:

HORATIO
. . .
[*Re-enter* GHOST.]
But soft, behold, lo where it comes again.
[GHOST *spreads its arms.*]
I'll cross it, though it blast me. Stay illusion,
If thou hast any sound or use of voice,
Speak to me.
If there be any good thing to be done
That may to thee do ease, and grace to me,
Speak to me.
If thou art privy to any country's fate
Which happily foreknowing may avoid,
O speak.
Or if thou hast uphoarded in thy life
Extorted treasure in the womb of earth,
For which they say you spirits oft walk in death,
[*Cock crows.*]
Speak of it; stay and speak. Stop it Marcellus.

516

I'll eat my head

Source: OLIVER TWIST (Chapter 14)
Author: Charles Dickens (1812-1870)
First published: 1837-1839
Type of work: Novel

Context: Oliver Twist, accompanying the Artful Dodger and Charlie Bates, the thief-trainer Fagin's assistants, is erroneously thought to have picked the pocket of old Mr. Brownlow. He is pursued, captured, and taken to a police station, where, in spite of all that Mr. Brownlow can do, he is sentenced to three months hard labor. He is saved, however, on the evidence of the bookseller at whose stall Mr. Brownlow was reading when the robbery took place. Upon being released, Oliver faints upon the sidewalk and is picked up and carried home by Mr. Brownlow. For weeks he is unconscious with fever; but when he recovers his health, Mr. Brownlow summons him for a talk in his study. Before the talk gets under way there is a visitor:

At this moment, there walked into the room; supporting himself by a thick stick: a stout old gentleman, rather lame in one leg, who was dressed in a blue coat, striped waistcoat, nankeen breeches and gaiters, and a broad-brimmed white hat, with the sides turned up with green. A very small-plaited shirt frill stuck out from his waistcoat; and a very long steel watch-chain, with nothing but a key at the end, dangled loosely below it. . . . he fixed himself, the moment he made his appearance; and, holding out a small piece of orange-peel at arm's length, exclaimed, in a growling, discontented voice,

"Look here! do you see this! Isn't it a most wonderful and extraordinary thing that I can't call at a man's house but I find a piece of this poor surgeon's-friend on the staircase? I've been lamed with orange-peel once, and I know orange-peel will be my death at last. It will, sir; orange-peel will be my death, or I'll be content to eat my own head, sir!"

This was the handsome offer with which Mr. Grimwig backed and confirmed nearly every assertion that he made. . . . Mr. Grimwig's head was such a particularly large one, that the most sanguine man alive could hardly entertain a hope of being able to get through it at a sitting—to put entirely out of the question, a very thick coating of powder.

"**I'll eat my head,** sir," repeated Mr. Grimwig, striking his stick upon the ground. "Hallo; what's that!" looking at Oliver, and retreating a pace or two.

I'll have a fling

Source: RULE A WIFE AND HAVE A WIFE (Act III, sc. v)
Author: Francis Beaumont (1585?-1616) and John Fletcher (1579-1625)
First published: 1640
Type of work: Dramatic comedy

Context: This play, probably entirely by Fletcher, is on somewhat the same theme as Shakespeare's *Taming of the Shrew,*—wife-taming. Margarita, an exceedingly wealthy and beautiful young woman of Seville, wants to marry a complaisant husband so that she will be free to pursue her amours without damage to her reputation. Altéa, one of her attendants, recommends Leon (who is actually her very knowing brother, in league with her to win Margarita and her wealth), as a simple, unknowing, but handsome young fellow who would admirably serve Margarita's purpose. Margarita has an interview with him and, believing him to be what she desires, marries him and immediately removes for a short time to her country estate. She soon returns to her city house, and immediately preparations are set on foot for a party at which will be present Margarita's admirer, the Duke of Medina. As the arrangements for the party go forward, Leon gives his wife a bit of counsel as to her behavior; she is astonished both at his tone and the tenor of his remarks. The guests, all unaware that Margarita is married, arrive; among them is Cacafogo, a usurer who entertains thoughts of marrying Margarita for her fortune. He muses that winning her would cost him a bit of money, but decides to risk it, to have a fling, as of the dice.

DUKE OF MEDINA
I thank ye, lady. I am bold to visit ye,
Once more to bless mine eyes with your sweet beauty:
'T has been a long night since you left the court,
For, till I saw you now, no day broke to me.

MARGARITA
Bring in the duke's meat!

SANCHIO
She is most excellent.

JUAN DE CASTRO
Most admirable fair as e'er I looked on;
I had rather command her than my regiment.

CACAFOGO
[*aside.*] **I'll have a fling;** 'tis but a thousand ducats,
Which I can cozen up again in ten days,
And some few jewels, to justify my knavery.

518

Say I should marry her, she'll get more money
Than all my usury, put my knavery to it:
She appears the most infallible way of purchase.

I'll put a spoke among your wheels

Source: THE MAD LOVER (Act III, sc. vi)
Author: John Fletcher (1579-1625)
First published: 1647
Type of work: Dramatic comedy

Context: Memnon, a rough soldier, general of the King of Paphos's armies, arrives home after a long absence; he sees the king's sister, Calis, and falls so completely in love with her that he offers his heart to her, an offer she sportively assumes to be literal. Nothing daunted, Memnon makes preparations for delivering it to her. Syphax, also a soldier, sees the princess and also falls madly in love with her; he enlists the aid of Cleanthe, his sister, in the furtherance of his love. She bribes the priestess of Venus to tell the princess on her next visit to the shrine that, to cure the lovesickness that she had contracted for Polydorus, she is to love a man she describes; the man is to be Syphax. Chilax, a merry old soldier, from a position in hiding, hears Cleanthe giving her directions to the priestess and vows to foil the plot; he says that he will put a spoke among her wheels: the imagery is that of thrusting a tough, strong spoke through a pair of wheels and so bringing the vehicle to a halt. This version of the saying gives a clearer picture of what is meant than does the common modern version: "I'll put a spoke in your wheel." Many people in modern times construe this to mean adding a spoke to the construction of a wheel to strengthen it, a meaning not borne out by Fletcher's version.

CLEANTHE
Charge her take the next man she shall meet with,
When she comes out;—you understand me?—

PRIESTESS
                                    Well.

CLEANTHE
Which shall be he attending. This is all,
And easily without suspicion ended;
Nor none dare disobey, 'tis Heaven that does it,
And who dares cross it then, or once suspect it?
The venture is most easy.

PRIESTESS
                        I will do it.

519

As ye shall prosper?

PRIESTESS
As I shall prosper!

CLEANTHE
Take this too, and farewell; but, first, hark hither.

CHILAX
[*aside*.] What a young whore's this to betray her mistress!
A thousand cuckolds shall that husband be
That marries thee, thou art so mischievous.
I'll put a spoke among your wheels.

An ill-favoured thing sir, but mine own

Source: AS YOU LIKE IT (Act V, sc. iv, l. 60)
Author: William Shakespeare (1564-1616)
First published: 1623
Type of work: Dramatic comedy

Context: The Forest of Arden provides refuge to an exiled Duke of France and his followers; to the daughter of the Duke, Rosalind (disguised as the shepherd lad Ganymede) and her cousin and friend, Celia (disguised as the shepherdess Aliena); to Orlando and his cruel brother, Oliver; and to the clown, Touchstone, as well as to a number of native inhabitants of the area. From a general state of confusion, a reconciliation is effected: Rosalind, revealing herself to her father, plans to wed Orlando; Celia intends to marry his repentant brother Oliver; the little shepherdess, Phebe, is reconciled to the love-sick shepherd, Silvius; and even the clown Touchstone, addressing the Duke, announces his intention to marry the goat-girl, Audrey:

TOUCHSTONE
God 'ild you sir, I desire you of the like, I press in here sir, amongst the rest of the country copulatives, to swear and to forswear, according as marriage binds and blood breaks—a poor virgin sir, **an ill-favoured thing sir, but mine own;** a poor humour of mine sir, to take that that no man else will. Rich honesty dwells like a miser sir, in a poor house, as your pearl in your foul oyster.

I'm sickly but sassy

Source: BROTHER RABBIT PRETENDS TO BE POISONED
Author: Joel Chandler Harris (1848-1908)
First published: 1883 in *Nights with Uncle Remus*
Type of work: Short story

Context: The first Uncle Remus stories, supposedly told by an elderly ex-slave in central Georgia to the seven-year-old son of "Miss Sally," appeared in *The Atlanta Constitution* in 1876, where their author, Joel Chandler Harris, was a reporter. Thirty-four of the tales were collected in 1880 into *Uncle Remus, His Songs and His Sayings.* That volume contained the Tar-Baby story and other accounts of the many times that Mr. Rabbit outwitted Mr. Fox. In his Introduction, the author discussed the wide spread of animal stories in folk lore, with the same episode appearing in Planatation tales, in Indian lore, and in anecdotes from the Amazon regions of South America. Three years later appeared another volume, *Nights with Uncle Remus,* containing more stories. In Chapter 50 of this book, called "Brother Rabbit Pretends to be Poisoned," a squinch owl is a screech owl. While the boy is visiting Uncle Remus, hoping to hear a story

> . . . the door opened and Aunt Tempy made her appearance. Her good humor was infectious.
> "Name er goodness!" she exclaimed, "I lef' you all settin' yer, way las' week; I goes off un I does my wuk, un I comes back, un I fin's you settin' right whar I lef' you. Goodness knows I dunner whar you gits yo' vittles. . . ."
> "Yas, Sis Tempy, we er settin' whar you lef' us, en der Lord, he bin a-pervidin'. W'en de vittles don't come in at de do' hit come down de chimbley, en so w'ats de odds? We er sorter po'ly, Sis Tempy, I'm 'bliged ter you. You know w'at de jay-bird say ter der squinch owl: **'I'm sickly but sassy.'** "

The imperial theme

Source: MACBETH (Act I, sc. iii, l. 129)
Author: William Shakespeare (1564-1616)
First published: 1623
Type of work: Dramatic tragedy

Context: Macbeth and Banquo meet the witches who inform them that Macbeth will be Thane of Cawdor and King of Scotland, and that Banquo will beget kings. As the witches vanish, Ross and Angus appear to tell Macbeth of the praises and rewards heaped upon him by King Duncan— one of which is the title of the Thane of Cawdor, stripped from the traitor whom Macbeth had defeated along with Sweno of Norway. Both Macbeth and Banquo are startled at how suddenly the prophecy of the witches comes true. Banquo is dubious of the "instruments of darkness" and their words, for he fears betrayal. Macbeth too is really torn between a feeling of good and evil and cannot understand why he is so stunned and frightened when part of the tidings has already been fulfilled. He becomes deeply absorbed in his own thoughts, which dwell constantly on the last part of the prediction.

MACBETH [*aside*]
                    Two truths are told,
As happy prologues to the swelling act
Of **the imperial theme**. . . .
              . . .

This supernatural soliciting
Cannot be ill, cannot be good. If ill,
Why hath it given me earnest of success,
Commencing in a truth? I am Thane of Cawdor.
If good, why do I yield to that suggestion,
Whose horrid image doth unfix my hair,
And make my seated heart knock at my ribs,
Against the use of nature? . . .
              . . .

In black and white

Source: EVERY MAN IN HIS HUMOUR (Act IV, sc. iv, l. 21)
Author: Ben Jonson (1573?-1637)
First published: 1601
Type of work: Dramatic comedy

Context: At a general gathering of most of the characters of the play at the home of Kitely, a cowardly and jealous husband, Oliver Cob, a water-drawer, falls foul of the braggart soldier, Captain Bobadill, who bitterly resents Cob's derogatory remarks about the smoking of tobacco. So incensed is Bobadill that he roundly beats Cob with a cudgel. Cob repairs to the home of a mad wag of a judge, Justice Clement, to obtain a writ to bind Bobadill to keep the peace. When Justice Clement learns that the quarrel arose over Cob's finding fault with tobacco smoking, he summarily sentences Cob to jail. Cob is horribly frightened, but Justice Clement reprieves him and orders his clerk, Roger Formal, to make out the warrant. Cob returns to his house and tells his wife Tib that Bobadill will pay for the black and blue he administered in the beating, as he has the warrant in his hand, in black and white. Cob admits that the justice put him in great fear for his liberty; he is a fine old fellow, though. Cob then orders his wife to go into the house, lock the door, and admit no one, especially Bobadill:

522

Why, what's the matter, trow!

O, he has basted me rarely, sumptuously! but I have it here **in black and white,** for his black and blue shall pay him. O, the justice! the honestest old brave Trojan in London! I do honor the very flea of his dog. A plague on him though, he put me once in a villainous filthy fear; marry, it vanished away like the smoke of tobacco; but I was smoked soundly first. I thank the devil, and his good angel, my guest. Well, wife, or Tib, which you will, get you in, and lock the door, I charge you let no body in to you, wife; no body in to you; those are my words; not Captain Bob himself, nor the fiend in his likeness. You are a woman, you have flesh and blood enough in you to be tempted; therefore keep the door shut upon all comers.

In every parting there is an image of death

Source: SCENES OF CLERICAL LIFE ("The Sad Fortunes of the Reverend Amos Barton," Chapter X)
Author: George Eliot (Mary Ann Evans, 1819-1880)
First published: 1858
Type of work: Short novel

Context: Amos Barton is one of a group of three short novels, all dealing with the clergy. It traces the career and hardships of Barton during his tenure as curate of Shepperton. Barton is a dedicated man of unprepossessing appearance and is anything but spectacular; he is blessed with a good wife, Milly, and a large family. Their living is meager and genteel poverty their lot. The influential people of the community dislike the clergyman; his sermons are colorless and unpopular, he is a poor teacher, and they fail to see the underlying goodness of the man. He tries vainly to inspire his congregation and the local coal miners, who are a difficult proposition at best. He and his family must borrow money in order to survive, and his wife is not well. A woman, Countess Czerlaski, who passes herself off as a person of means, moves in with the Bartons temporarily and remains for months. Gossip ensues concerning a fancied relationship between Barton and the countess, who is not paying the Bartons any board or helping with any household tasks. The local snobs disapprove of Barton anyway; they feel that he could at least be poor without showing it. Milly is wearing out with the work of caring for her many children, her husband, and her inconsiderate house guest. Eventually the countess is made aware of what is being said about her, and leaves; but the bills she has run up remain, and Milly dies in childbirth. Following this tragedy, the townspeople relent somewhat, but not enough to relieve Barton's suffering. Finally he receives a letter from the vicar: that worthy is

523

coming to Shepperton himself and will reside there. Barton is done out of his curacy, with no prospects of another nearby. The truth is that the vicar wants this post for his own brother-in-law. Barton finds a curacy in a distant county, in a dingy and unattractive manufacturing town, and takes his leave of Shepperton.

. . . There was general regret among the parishioners at his departure: not that any one of them thought his spiritual gifts preeminent, or was conscious of great edification from his ministry. But his recent troubles had called out their better sympathies, and that is always a source of love. Amos failed to touch the spring of goodness by his sermons, but he touched it effectually by his sorrows; and there was now a real bond between him and his flock.

• • •

The sad good-byes had all been said before that last evening; and after all the packing was done and all the arrangements were made, Amos felt the oppression of that blank interval in which one has nothing left to think of but the dreary future—the separation from the loved and familiar, and the chilling entrance on the new and strange. **In every parting there is an image of death.**

In hell they'll roast thee like a herrin'

Source: TAM O'SHANTER (Line 202)
Author: Robert Burns (1759-1796)
First published: 1791
Type of work: Narrative poem

Context: Kirk Alloway was a small church near where Burns spent the last years of his life. As a young man, he had listened to legends of ghosts told him by Betty Davidson, an old lady with the best collection of horror yarns in the surrounding region. In 1789 Burns dug into his memory for some of them. An antiquarian, Captain Francis Grose, was collecting material in the neighborhood for a book to be called *Grose's Antiquities of Scotland.* Burns asked him to sketch the church and cemetery where his father was buried and where he himself expected to have his grave. The author agreed, on condition that Burns would provide him with a legend to be printed along with the sketch. So in one day Burns completed one of his greatest poems, the legend of Tam o' Shanter. Tam is a ne'er-do-well, a drinker who stays away from his nagging wife Kate, on market days, not going home until he has spent most of the money he has taken in. However, on this particular day, eventually he heads homeward through the storm, on his horse Meg. His road leads past Kirk Alloway which, to his amazement, is brightly lighted. Since John Barleycorn gives men courage even to confront the Devil, Tammie spurs his horse close enough that he can look on the revelry. Presided over by Old Nick, warlocks and witches are dancing reels so furiously among the open coffins that

524

the women are discarding their garments. Most of them are so old and ugly that Tam is disgusted, but there is one winsome wench, Nannie, in a cutty sark (short shift), who dances so madly and is so pretty that the onlooker, forgetting the circumstances, calls out, "Well done, Cutty-sark!" Out go the lights! The evil dancers come after Tam, who spurs his horse. Every Scot knows that witches cannot cross a stream of running water, so Tammie heads Meg for the bridge. Once beyond the key stone, in the middle, he will be safe. But Nannie follows swiftly. At the moment she overtakes Tam, everything except the tail of his horse is beyond the middle of the stream, but she seizes that, and off it comes in the witch's grasp, leaving only a stump. In concluding, Burns appends a moral. Before you take a drink or focus your mind on scantily clad women, pause and remember Tam o' Shanter. Here is the conclusion:

Ah, Tam! ah, Tam! thou'll get thy fairin!
In hell they'll roast thee like a herrin'!

In vain thy Kate awaits thy comin!
Kate soon will be a woefu' woman!
Now, do thy speedy utmost, Meg.
And win the key-stane of the brig . . .
Ae spring brought aff her master hale,
But left behind her ain gray tail;
The carlin claught her by the rump,
And left poor Maggie scarce a stump.
Now, wha this tale o' truth shall read,
Ilk man and mother's son, take heed;
Whene'er to drink you are inclin'd,
Or cutty-sarks run in your mind,
Think, ye may buy the joys o'er dear,
Remember Tam o' Shanter's mare.

In married life three is company and two is none

Source: THE IMPORTANCE OF BEING EARNEST (Act I)
Author: Oscar Wilde (1856-1900)
First published: 1895
Type of work: Dramatic comedy

Context: In this comedy by the Dublin-born wit Oscar Fingall O'Flahertie Wills Wilde, Jack Worthing is in love with Gwendolen Fairfax, daughter of Lady Bracknell. His friend Algy is Lady Bracknell's nephew. Algy is a bunburyist, that is, he has invented an invalid friend, Bunbury, whose uncertain health calls Algy from London whenever it is desirable to escape one of his aunt's dull parties. Jack, as a means of occasional relief from his soberness as guardian of a young lady, has invented a reprobate brother called Ernest, who lives in London. He tells Algy that upon marriage, he will get rid of Ernest, and advises his friend to kill off Bun-

bury. Algernon scoffs at the advice.

ALGERNON

Nothing will induce me to part with Bunbury, and if you ever get married, which seems to me extremely problematic, you will be very glad to know Bunbury. A man who marries without knowing Bunbury has a very tedious time of it.

JACK

That is nonsense. If I marry a charming girl like Gwendolen, and she is the only girl I ever saw in my life that I would marry, I certainly won't want to know Bunbury.

ALGERNON

Then your wife will. You don't seem to realise, that **in married life three is company and two is none.**

In nature there is nothing melancholy

Source: THE NIGHTINGALE (Line 15)
Author: Samuel Taylor Coleridge (1772-1834)
First published: 1798
Type of work: A conversation poem

Context: In addition to the many poems by Wordsworth that appeared in *Lyrical Ballads* (1798), which marks the beginning of the English Romantic Movement, there were only two by his friend and collaborator, Coleridge: "The Ancient Mariner," and "The Nightingale," along with fragments of an unpublished drama *Osorio.* The revised edition of 1800 contained a preface by Wordsworth, stating the creed of the romanticists. Breaking with neoclassical theory, they stood for nature worship and— under the influence of Rousseau and Wordsworth's sojourn in France— democracy, and the common man with his simple, natural language. In "The Nightingale," Coleridge speaks to William Wordsworth and his sister Dorothy, and tells them about his in- fant son, whom he intends to make "Nature's playmate." The baby loves the nightingale's song and the evening star, and once the poet hushed him by taking him to the orchard where he could see the moon. For *Lyrical Ballads,* Wordsworth was supposed to supply nature poems, and Coleridge to deal with the supernatural and ex- otic, but in this poem, except for a reference to the mysterious ruins of a castle in an unkempt forest, Coleridge writes about nature. He begins with a description of evening and the sinking sun, and suggests that the hikers rest on an old mossy bridge, amid the still- ness. The spring shower has ended, and the stars can be dimly seen. This is the hour to hear the song of the nightingale, which Milton called "most musical, most melancholy."

526

Coleridge, however, protests that it is really a merry bird, hurrying to fill an April night with delicious notes, as if fearing that dawn would soon appear. Its reputation for melancholy came from some unhappy person who transferred his sorrows to the song of the nightingale; and poets, instead of enjoying the sunshine beside a brook, echoed this idea until everybody came to believe that nightingales were melancholy. There is nothing melancholy in nature unless man makes it so.

> And hark! the Nightingale begins its song,
> "Most musical, most melancholy" bird!
> A melancholy bird? Oh! idle thought!
> **In Nature there is nothing melancholy.**
> But some night-wandering man whose heart was pierced
> With the remembrance of a grievous wrong,
> Or slow distemper, or neglected love,
> (And so, poor wretch! filled all things with himself,
> And made all gentle sounds tell back the tale
> Of his own sorrow) he, and such as he,
> First named these notes a melancholy strain.
> And many a poet echoes the conceit; . . .

In such a night stood Dido

Source: THE MERCHANT OF VENICE (Act V, sc. i, ll. 9-10)
Author: William Shakespeare (1564-1616)
First published: 1600
Type of work: Dramatic comedy

Context: Jessica, daughter of the Jew Shylock, and her husband, Lorenzo, friend of Bassanio, talk poetically on a moonlit night along the avenue to Belmont, home of the heiress Portia, recent bride of Bassanio. The lovers are reminded that on a night such as this Dido, Queen of Carthage, holding a willow branch, symbol of unrequited love, waited vainly for the return of her beloved Æneas.

> LORENZO
> **In such a night**
> **Stood Dido** with a willow in her hand
> Upon the wild sea banks, and waft her love
> To come again to Carthage.
>
> JESSICA
> In such a night
> Medea gathered the enchanted herbs
> That did renew old Æson.

In the brave days of old

Source: LAYS OF ANCIENT ROME ("Horatius," Stanza 31)
Author: Thomas Babington Macaulay (1800-1859)
First published: 1842
Type of work: Narrative poem

Context: "Horatius at the Bridge" is the best-known poem of the volume, *Lays of Ancient Rome.* "In the brave days of old," when schoolboys had to learn poems to recite on Friday afternoon, it was a favorite. Following Livy and Dionysius, it recounts the brave exploit of Rome's legendary hero, Horatius Cocles, who, with two companions, held the Sublician Bridge that connected Rome with the west, against the Etruscan army of Lars Porsena, until the rest of the defenders of the city could destroy the bridge. Horatius then swam to safety back across the Tiber River. For reward, he was given as much land as he could plough in one day. The poem is imagined to have been composed about 360 B.C., concerning events that happened 120 years earlier. It begins: "Lars Porsena of Clusium/ By the Nine Gods he swore/ That the ancient house of Tarquin/ Should suffer wrong no more." Horatius, the Captain of the Gate, offers to keep the bridge, and Spurius Lartius and Titus Herminius volunteer to fight beside him. Stanzas 31 and 32 set the scene:

> "Horatius," quoth the Consul,
> "As thou sayest, so let it be."
> And straight against that great array
> Forth went the dauntless three.
> For Romans in Rome's quarrel
> Spared neither land nor gold,
> Nor sons nor wife, nor limb nor life,
> **In the brave days of old.**
>
> Then none was for a party;
> Then all were for the state;
> Then the great man helped the poor,
> And the poor man loved the great:
> The lands were fairly portioned;
> Then spoils were fairly sold:
> The Romans were like brothers
> **In the brave days of old.**

In this world a man must either be anvil or hammer

Source: HYPERION (Book IV, chapter 7)
Author: Henry Wadsworth Longfellow (1807-1882)
First published: 1839
Type of work: Novel

Context: The idea that a man is either the smiter or the one smitten is an old one. If he does not assert himself, he will be put upon by others. Some writers have varied the expression, to insist that in his lifetime man plays both parts, and must act in either role to his utmost capacity. In the days of Christian martyrdom, the second century Bishop of Antioch, St. Ignatius Theophorus, told his followers: "Stand like an anvil when it is beaten upon." A later religious poet, George Herbert (1593–1633) advised in *Jacula Prudentum* (1640): "When you are an anvil, hold you still;/ When you are a hammer, strike your fill." More recently the American poet, Edward Markham (1852–1940) wrote in "Preparedness":

"When you are the anvil, bear—/ When you are the hammer, strike." Longfellow, in his longest prose work, *Hyperion,* employed the same figure. Based on the New England poet's trip to Europe in 1835–1836 to study at Heidelberg, *Hyperion* embodied Longfellow's own experiences and even used as heroine Frances Appleton, whom he was to marry five years later. About Paul Flemming (representing Longfellow), the hero of this sentimental romance, the novelist declares in Book I, chapter IV: "One half of the world must sweat and groan, that the other half may dream." In Part IV, a priest, after telling Flemming a story, bids him goodbye with the comment:

"I shall not see you in the morning, so goodby, and God bless you. Remember my parting words. Never mind trifles. **In this world a man must either be anvil or hammer.** Care killed a cat!"

"I have heard you say that so often," replied Flemming, laughing, "that I begin to believe it. But I wonder if Care shaved his left eyebrow after doing the deed, as the ancient Egyptians used to do!"

"Aha! now you are sweeping cobwebs from the sky! Good night! Good night!"

In time we hate that which we often fear

Source: ANTONY AND CLEOPATRA (Act I, sc. iii, l. 12)
Author: William Shakespeare (1564-1616)
First published: 1623
Type of work: Dramatic tragedy

Context: From Cleopatra's love and Egypt's luxury, Antony is recalled to a stern sense of duty as one of the three rulers of the Roman Empire. The Parthians have invaded from the East ("These strong Egyptian fetters I must break"); his wife, Fulvia, is dead ("There's a great spirit gone."); rebellion is afoot in the West. "I must from this enchanting queen break off," asserts Antony. Cleopatra, however, has other ideas, and we now see her at work. She tells one of her attendants: "See where he is, who's with him, what he does—/ I did not send you. If you find him sad,/ Say I am dancing; if in mirth, report/ That I am sudden sick. Quick, and return."

But one of her ladies-in-waiting thinks Cleopatra is going about her business in the wrong way:

CHARMIAN

Madam, methinks if you did love him dearly,
You do not hold the method to enforce
The like from him.

CLEOPATRA

What should I do, I do not?

CHARMIAN

In each thing give him way, cross him in nothing.

CLEOPATRA

Thou teachest like a fool—The way to lose him.

CHARMIAN

Tempt him not so too far; ywis forbear,
In time we hate that which we often fear.

The Indian Summer of the heart!

Source: MEMORIES (Last stanza)
Author: John Greenleaf Whittier (1807-1892)
First published: 1843
Type of work: Lyric poem

Context: Among Whittier's *Poems Subjective and Reminiscent* appears his "Memories," with its nine stanzas. After several years of academic training, during which he submitted poems to the *Haverhill* (Mass.) *Gazette,* in 1829 he became editor of a Boston magazine, *American Manufacturer,* in which he published both his prose and his poetry. The poems were collected into a volume in 1857. In "Memories," Whittier thinks back, in later years, to a "Beautiful and happy girl" with whom as a child he used to talk and walk. Whittier's biographer says the poem was written in 1841, when the poet was thirty-four years old, and certainly not in the autumn of his life. Indian Summer is said to come in the fall, after the first frost. Whittier is supposed to have hesitated to publish the poem "because it was so personal and near my heart." Most poets think that that is the stuff of which good poetry is made. The final stanza declares:

Thus, while at times before our eyes
The shadows melt, and fall apart,
And, smiling through them, round us lies
The warm light of our morning skies,—

530

The Indian Summer of the heart!
In secret sympathies of mind,
In founts of feeling which retain
Their pure, fresh flow, we yet may find
Our early dreams not wholly vain!

An indifference closely bordering on aversion

Source: THE NEW ARABIAN NIGHTS ("The Rajah's Diamond": Story of the House with the Green Blinds)
Author: Robert Louis Stevenson (1850-1894)
First published: 1882
Type of work: Fantastic tale

Context: There was a wave of interest in things Oriental during the Victorian era, and Stevenson's *New Arabian Nights* probably reflects this. In this book he turns London into a place of fantasy and mystery, where happenings have the strangeness and vivid illogicality of dreams. "The Rajah's Diamond" is a tale, or series of episodes, following a similar sequence entitled "The Suicide Club"; the Bohemian Prince Florizel, a sort of genie-figure, moves through both. The individual episodes are connected by Stevenson's editorial comments, in which he summarizes whimsically the transitions employed by his "Arabian author." The stories are in a sense modern fairy tales. "The Rajah's Diamond" follows the adventures of a fabulous and unlucky gem from one owner to the next, until finally Prince Florizel acts the good angel and disposes of it forever. It had been obtained by foul means and at the cost of many lives by General Vandeleur when he was in India; he has a fortune in diamonds, but his wife bankrupts him and steals the stones, entrusting them to her manservant. He is to convey them to the general's brother, a connoisseur and collector who is also an accomplished jewel thief. The servant is separated from this fortune by a series of misadventures, and the Rajah's diamond gets into the hands of a clergyman, who immediately falls from grace and joins the underworld in an effort to "fence" the stone. He meets with the general's brother, John, who robs him of it; John's daughter subsequently passes it on to young Francis Scymgeour, who has fallen in love with her. Francis has been given an anonymous but generous monthly allowance, presumably from his unknown father; learning part of the plot, he spies on John and his daughter. From a house next door he sees John drug the clergyman. He has deduced that John is actually his own father and is in some sort of trouble, so he rushes to offer his assistance and reveals himself just as John lifts the diamond from his victim's pocket. His reaction to Francis is anything but cordial:

Then a light seemed to break upon Mr. Vandeleur, and he laughed aloud.

531

"I see," cried he. "It is the Scrymgeour. Very well, Mr. Scrymgeour. Let me tell you in a few words how you stand. You have entered my private residence by force, or perhaps by fraud, but certainly with no encouragement from me; and you come at a moment of some annoyance, a guest having fainted at my table, to besiege me with your protestations. You are no son of mine. You are my brother's bastard by a fishwife, if you want to know. I regard you with **an indifference closely bordering on aversion;** and from what I now see of your conduct, I judge your mind to be exactly suitable to your exterior. . . ."

Indolent vacuity of thought

Source: THE TASK (Book IV, l. 297)
Author: William Cowper (1731-1800)
First published: 1785
Type of work: Meditative poem in blank verse

Context: Writing at the urging of a friend, Lady Austen, to uphold the superiority of "rural ease and leisure" over London life, for people who sought to live in virtue, Cowper was the first eighteenth century poet to relish country life for its own sake. Being a highly moral person, he abhorred the many opportunities for lapses from virtue in a big city, but in addition, the poet loved the country, its landscape, its activities, and, here, its moments for relaxation. This highly autobiographical work foreshadows the kind of poetry Wordsworth was to write. It is Cowper's greatest poem. Written in blank verse, and containing many digressions, it commences in Book I, called "The Sofa," to trace the history of a place to sit, from the early stool to a luxurious sofa. Then come Book II, "The Time Piece," Book III, "The Garden," and Book IV, "The Winter Evening." Following the arrival of the post, and the reading of the newspaper, comes dinner and later relaxation before a fire in the mirrored drawing room. This pleasure can happen only during "Winter, ruler of the inverted year." Staring at the imaginary pictures in the fireplace, the poet wonders, whenever thoughts enter his lazy, inactive brain, whether there are people "that never felt a stupor, know no pause, nor need one." He sees:

> Trees, churches, and strange visages expressed
> In the red cinders, while with poring eye
> I gazed, myself creating what I saw.
> Not less amused have I quiescent watched
> The sooty films that play upon the bars,
>
> • • •
>
> 'T is thus the understanding takes repose
> In **indolent vacuity of thought**
> And sleeps, and is refreshed. . . .

532

Inflaming wine, pernicious to mankind

Source: THE ILIAD (Book VI, l. 330, as translated by Alexander Pope)
Author: Homer (c. 850 B.C.)
First transcribed: Sixth century, B.C.
Type of work: Epic poem

Context: Book VI of *The Iliad* relates how, for a time, the gods leave the field of battle, and the Greeks prevail over the Trojans. Hector, the Trojan leader, advised by Helenus, the chief seer of the Trojans, leaves his men to return to the city. He has a two-fold purpose in taking this course: he wishes to have his mother, Hecuba, Queen of Troy, take her women to the temple of Minerva, there to offer sacrifice to gain the goddess' help in removing Diomed, a great Greek warrior, from the fighting; he also hopes to persuade Paris, his brother, to return to the battles, where he has not been seen since his own luckless battle with Menelaus. During Hector's absence the fighting abates between the armies, and Homer describes how Diomed, a Greek, and Glaucus, a Trojan, meet and talk between the two forces. Hector, returning to the royal palace in Troy, finds his mother. She embraces her son, who is weary from the fighting, and tells him she will bring him wine, partly to be used as an offering to the gods, and partly to be used as a refreshing drink for Hector. But Hector refuses the wine, saying it is bad for men and should be used rather as an offering to the gods. He asks his mother, since his hands are stained with blood, and he is impure, to go make offering on behalf of Troy to Minerva:

> Far hence be Bacchus' gifts; (the chief rejoin'd:)
> **Inflaming wine, pernicious to mankind,**
> Unnerves the limbs, and dulls the noble mind.
> Let chiefs abstain, and spare the sacred juice
> To sprinkle to the gods, its better use.
> By me that holy office were profaned;
> Ill fits it me, with human gore distain'd,
> To the pure skies these horrid hands to raise,
> Or offer heaven's great Sire polluted praise.
> You, with your matrons, go! a spotless train,
> And burn rich odours in Minerva's fane.

An injury is much sooner forgotten than an insult

Source: LETTERS TO HIS SON (Letter I)
Author: Philip Dormer Stanhope, Lord Chesterfield (1694-1773)
First published: 1774
Type of work: Personal letters

Context: In this letter Chesterfield begins by counselling his illegitimate son to try every day to improve his intelligence, as it is the coach in which men ride through the world. He also says that his son is given to laziness, inattention, and indifference, and begs him to cure these faults. If a man wants to succeed in practically anything, he can, with the exception of poetry, which calls for innate ability. In addition to the accomplishments of the mind there are lesser accomplishments necessary for the man who would succeed. He must do such things as dance gracefully and dress well. Above all, he should not be given to fits of absentmindedness when in the company of others. The only minds that can be excused for not paying attention in company are those that are very weak or those which are thinking great thoughts, like Newton's; there are very few of this latter kind of mind. A young man displaying absence of mind in company, especially in a company given to frivolity, is actually insulting those around him by displaying a form of contempt, and there is nothing that offends people more than insults; injuries are much more readily tolerated than contempt; therefore the wise man will flatter his associates by giving ready attention to their little vanities.

. . . However frivolous a company may be, still, while you are among them, do not show them, by your inattention, that you think them so; but rather take their tone, and conform in some degree to their weakness, instead of manifesting your contempt for them. There is nothing that people bear more impatiently, or forgive less, than contempt; and **an injury is much sooner forgotten than an insult.** If, therefore, you would rather please than offend, rather be well than ill spoken of, rather be loved than hated; remember to have that constant attention about you which flatters every man's little vanity; and the want of which, by mortifying his pride, never fails to excite his resentment, or at least his ill will. . . .

Inquisitorious and tyrannical duncery

Source: THE REASON OF CHURCH GOVERNMENT URGED AGAINST PRELATY (Book II, preface)
Author: John Milton (1608-1674)
First published: 1642
Type of work: Theological tract

Context: During the years that immediately preceded the civil war the spokesmen for the Puritan and Anglican churches engaged in a spirited and often bitter pamphlet war. As perhaps the most articulate representative of the Puritan position, Milton contributed several important pamphlets to his party's campaign. The major differences between these two parties were not concerned with doctrine, or belief, but with discipline, or

534

the government of the Church. Since the conventions of pamphlet war at this time were to attack both the opposition's argument as well as any personalities of importance, Milton frequently found occasion to defend not only Puritanism but himself as well. In Book I of this work he argues that the proper form of church government is prescribed in Scripture and attempts to refute specific arguments advanced by the Anglicans. In Book II he shows in detail how "Prelaty opposeth the Reason and End of the Gospel in three Ways," but first he inserts a preface in which he replies to some personal attacks which had been made against his shortcomings as a poet. His intentions as a poet, he says, contrary to those of the "libidinous and ignorant poetasters" of the other party, have always been to inspire wisdom and virtue.

. . . And the accomplishment of them lies not but in a power above man's to promise; but that none hath by more studious ways endeavored, and with more unwearied spirit that none shall, that I dare almost aver of myself, as far as life and free leisure will extend; and that the land had once enfranchised herself from this impertinent yoke of prelaty, under whose **inquisitorious and tyrannical duncery,** no free and splendid wit can flourish. Neither do I think it shame to covenant with any knowing reader, that for some few years yet I may go on trust with him toward the payment of what I am now indebted, as being a work not to be raised from the heat of youth, or the vapors of wine; like that which flows at waste from the pen of some vulgar amorist, of the trencher fury of a rhyming parasite; . . .

The insane root that takes the reason prisoner

Source: MACBETH (Act I, sc. iii, ll. 84-85)
Author: William Shakespeare (1564-1616)
First published: 1623
Type of work: Dramatic tragedy

Context: Macbeth and Banquo, generals in the army of Duncan, King of Scotland, pass along a heath near Forres as they return home after successfully putting down a rebellion against their king. Suddenly three witches appear from the gloom and hail the warriors with the prophecy that Macbeth, Thane of Glamis, will receive the titles Thane of Cawdor and king, and that Banquo, though he will not become king, will beget kings. The fateful words spoken, the witches disappear, leaving Macbeth and Banquo stunned and wondering if they have eaten something to make them have visions, possibly the root of hemlock.

BANQUO
The earth has bubbles, as the water has,

And these are of them. Whither are they vanished?

MACBETH

Into the air; and what seemed corporal melted,
As breath into the wind. Would they had stayed.

BANQUO

Were such things here, as we do speak about?
Or have we eaten on **the insane root**
That takes the reason prisoner?

MACBETH

Your children shall be kings.

BANQUO

You shall be king.

MACBETH

And Thane of Cawdor too—went it not so?

BANQUO

To the selfsame tune and words.

An institution is the lengthened shadow of one man

Source: SELF-RELIANCE
Author: Ralph Waldo Emerson (1803-1882)
First published: 1841
Type of work: Moral essay

Context: Emerson believed every human being is divine insofar as he has a soul. Every man can be self-reliant, then, in the sense that he can trust his own judgment in all matters. Emerson specifically objects in this essay to the individual's conforming to either customs of the past or the cry of the multitude, when these forces are contrary to his judgment; as Emerson writes, "What I must do is all that concerns me, not what people think." He warns that by his nonconformity to mass opinion the individual arouses antagonism, that the individual must be willing to pay the price for nonconformity, for "the world whips you with its displeasure." Somewhat later in the essay Emerson says that the world always misunderstands the great individual, as they misunderstood such heroes of the past as Pythagoras, Socrates, Jesus, Luther, Copernicus, Galileo, and Newton. But the important thing, says Emerson, is to be true to one's self, not to violate one's own nature. To be true to one's nature is to be great, to avoid "the smooth mediocrity and squalid contentment" of the

536

times. Emerson issues a call for us all to be great in this way, leading other people instead of following. He believes that "Character, reality, reminds you of nothing else; it takes the place of the whole creation." The great person, suggests Emerson, is the man who makes all surrounding circumstances indifferent, is a creator not a user, a leader instead of a follower:

> . . . Every true man is a cause, a country, and an age; requires infinite spaces and numbers and time fully to accomplish his design; and posterity seem to follow his steps as a train of clients. A man Caesar is born, and for ages after we have a Roman Empire. Christ is born, and millions of minds so grow and cleave to his genius, that he is confounded with virtue and the possible of man. **An institution is the lengthened shadow of one man;** as Monachism, of the Hermit Antony; the Reformation, of Luther; Quakerism, of Fox; Methodism, of Wesley; Abolition, of Clarkson. Scipio, Milton called "the height of Rome"; and all history resolves itself very easily into the biography of a few stout and earnest persons.

The insupportable labor of doing nothing

Source: THE SPECTATOR (Number 54)
Author: Sir Richard Steele (1672-1729)
First published: May 2, 1711
Type of work: Essay

Context: Sir Richard Steele was a busy and talented man. After dropping out of Oxford he served for a time in the dragoon and foot guards, but his literary aspirations were uppermost. He wrote a number of successful comedies and soon gained some notice as a playwright. An ebullient, witty person, he was always immersed in moneymaking schemes that kept him destitute. His great and lasting contribution to English literature was his founding, in 1709, of the first real English magazine. This was *The Tatler,* which ran two years. He was joined by Joseph Addison, who collaborated in the project and wrote some of the articles. *The Tatler* ceased publication in January, 1711, and was soon succeeded by the more famous *Spectator,* a daily which ran from March 1, 1711, to December 6, 1712. Of its 555 issues, Addison wrote about 274 and Steele about 240, while guest essayists contributed the remainder. These papers were a reaction to the excesses of the Restoration, and their basic purpose was to popularize morality and temper it with wit. They succeeded admirably in their design, their social criticism being witty, urbane, cheerful; and in addition, the papers are an unsurpassed running commentary on the life of the time, and a high literary standard is always upheld in them. Nearly any subject could be treated, with the exception of politics. A number of fictitious characters appeared in these pages, among them Mr. Spectator, the detached observer of human affairs. One literary device employed was the letters to the editor, nearly all of which were of course written by the authors—a practice not unknown to modern journalism. Steele prints a letter in *The Spectator,* for example, which is supposedly from Cambridge and tells of a new sect of philosophers, The Loungers; their fundamental belief, upon which their whole system is built, is "That Time being an implacable Enemy to and Destroyer of all things, ought to be paid in his own coin, and be destroyed and murdered without Mercy . . ." Steele offers a general comment:

> I must be so just as to observe I have formerly seen of this Sect at our other University; tho' not distinguished by the the Appelation which the learned Historian, my Correspondent, reports they bear at *Cambridge.* . . . The *Lowngers* are satisfied with being merely Part of the Number of Mankind, without distinguishing themselves from amongst them. They may be said rather to suffer their Time to pass, than to spend it. . . . When one of this Order happens to be a Man of Fortune, the Expence of his Time is transferred to his Coach and Horses, and his Life is to be measured by their Motion . . . The chief Entertainment one of these Philosophers can possibly propose to himself, is to get a Relish of Dress . . . When the *Lowngers* leave an Academick Life, . . . [and] retire to the Seats of their Ancestors, they usually join a Pack of Dogs, and employ their Days in defending their Poultry from Foxes: I do not know any other Method that any of this Order has ever taken to make a Noise in the World; but I shall inquire into such about this Town as have arrived at the Dignity of being *Lowngers* by the Force of natural Parts, without having ever seen an University; and send my Correspondent, for the Embellishment of his Book, the Names and History of those who pass their Lives without any Incidents at all; and how they shift Coffee-houses and Chocolate-houses from Hour to Hour, to get over **the insupportable Labour of doing nothing.**

Invention breeds invention

Source: SOCIETY AND SOLITUDE (Chapter 7, "Works and Days")
Author: Ralph Waldo Emerson (1803-1882)
First published: 1870
Type of work: Moral essay

Context: Philosophical idealist though he was, Emerson had a great admiration for what man was able to do with the stuff of this life. Emerson was a canny Yankee, as well as a philosopher, and he found his own century to be "an age of tools." He pities earlier generations for not having known all the contrivances which had come into being by his own time. Man's discoveries, such as "steam and galvanism, sulphuric ether and

538

ocean telegraphs, photograph and spectroscope," Emerson says, "open great gates of a future, promising to make the world plastic and to lift human life out of its beggary to a god-like ease and power." He goes on to sound a litany of products and techniques acquired by man during the first three-quarters of the nineteenth century, and he sees the progress mankind is making to be an unfolding of the work of the Deity; he hints that such progress is a better approach to Deity, who seems to be working through mankind. But Emerson warns, later in the essay, that man must be careful lest machinery, which he sees as aggressive, does not begin to use mankind, instead of mankind's using machinery. But, as Emerson sees it, the technical progress is enthralling:

> There does not seem any limit to these new informations of the same Spirit that made the elements at first, and now, through man, works them. Art and power will go on as they have done,—will make day out of night, time out of space, and space out of time.
> **Invention breeds invention.** No sooner is the electric telegraph devised than gutta percha, the very material it requires, is found. The aëronaut is provided with gun-cotton, the very fuel he wants for his balloon. When commerce is vastly enlarged, California and Australia expose the gold it needs. When Europe is over-populated, America and Australia crave to be peopled; and so throughout, every chance is timed, as if Nature, who made the lock, knew where to find the key.

Irrevocably dark, total eclipse without all hope of day!

Source: SAMSON AGONISTES (Lines 81-82)
Author: John Milton (1608-1674)
First published: 1671
Type of work: Dramatic tragedy

Context: Blind Puritan poet John Milton, in writing the dramatic poetic tragedy *Samson Agonistes,* must have felt particular sympathy for Samson, the blind captive strong-man of Israel, as he toiled in the tread mills of the Philistines, the enemy from which, according to prophecy before his birth, he should deliver his people. While the Philistines celebrate the feast of Dagon, their Sea-Idol, Samson, enjoying a brief rest from his labor, sits on the Gaza prison steps in the sunshine and fresh air and bemoans his sad condition, the most tragic phase of which, says Samson, is his blindness:

> O loss of sight, of thee I most complain!
> Blind among enemies, O worse then chains,
> Dungeon, or beggery, or decrepit age!
> Light the prime work of God to me is extinct,
> And all her various objects of delight

Annull'd, which might in part my grief have eas'd,
Inferiour to the vilest now become
Of man or worm; the vilest here excel me,
They creep, yet see, I dark in light expos'd
To daily fraud, contempt, abuse and wrong,
Within doors, or without, still as a fool,
In power of others, never in my own;
Scarce half I seem to live, dead more than half.
O dark, dark, dark, amid the blaze of noon,
Irrevocably dark, total Eclipse
Without all hope of day!

Is <u>must</u> a word to be addressed to princes?

Source: A SHORT HISTORY OF THE ENGLISH PEOPLE, J. R. GREEN (Chapter 7,
  sec. VIII, p. 459)
Author: Elizabeth I, Queen of England (1533-1603)
First published: 1874
Type of work: Biographical anecdote

Context: The last years of the great Queen Elizabeth I were gloomy ones. She had always been a lonely figure, and now she grew lonelier. As sometimes happens, she had outlived the age of which she was a part. The statesmen, counselors, and warriors of her younger days had passed on one by one; those who had followed them were waiting for her to go and already intriguing for a place in the reign that would come next. Lord Essex, her favorite, became involved in a mad attempt at revolution and was executed. The old splendor for which her court had been famous gradually declined and at length disappeared; the nobility avoided her. A brilliant woman, imperious, fanciful, not overly scrupulous, she belonged to the Renaissance—and the Renaissance was gone forever. She had always thoroughly enjoyed life as it had been lived in her youth; now she clung to it. Hunting, dancing, joking and coquetting, scolding, she continued her colorful progresses from one country house to another so long as she was able. These old-fashioned displays of pomp and splendor no longer met with general approval, but she finally gave them up only because her health was failing. Green's recital of the events of her last hours paints a haunting and tragic picture:

  . . . Her face became haggard, and her frame shrank almost to a skeleton. At last her taste for finery disappeared, and she refused to change her dresses for a week together. A strange melancholy settled down on her: "she held in her hand," says one who saw her in her last days, "a golden cup, which she put often to her lips: but in truth her heart seemed too full to need more filling." Gradually her mind gave way. She lost her memory, the violence of her temper became unbearable, her very courage seemed to forsake her.

She called for a sword to lie constantly beside her, and thrust it from time to time through the arras, as if she heard murderers stirring there. Food and rest alike became distasteful. She sate day and night propped up with pillows on a stool, her finger to her lip, her eyes fixed on the floor, without a word. If she once broke the silence, it was with a flash of her old queenliness. When Robert Cecil asserted that she "must" go to bed, the word roused her like a trumpet. "Must!" she exclaimed; **"is must a word to be addressed to princes?** Little man, little man! thy father, if he had been alive, durst not have used that word." Then, as her anger spent itself, she sank into her old dejection. "Thou art so presumptuous," she said, "because thou knowest I shall die." She rallied once more when the ministers beside her bed named Lord Beauchamp, the heir to the Suffolk claim, as a possible successor. "I will have no rogue's son," she cried hoarsely, "in my seat." But she gave no sign, save a motion of the head, at the mention of the King of Scots. She was in fact fast becoming insensible; and early the next morning the life of Elizabeth, a life so great, so strange and lonely in its greatness, passed quietly away.

Is the wind in that door?

Source: LE MORTE D'ARTHUR (Book VII, chapter 34)
Author: Sir Thomas Malory (1400?-1471)
First published: 1485
Type of work: Medieval romance

Context: The story of Gareth and how he became a Knight of the Round Table is an entertaining and rather typical example of the romantic tales which make up a large part of Arthurian legend. Gareth, brother of Sir Gawaine, desires knighthood and presents himself to King Arthur at the King's annual high feast. He does not reveal his identity, wishing to prove himself first; but he has three requests to make of the king. The first of these is for a year's food and lodging, which Arthur grants with his characteristic generosity. Gareth will not reveal his other two requests until the next high feast, and in Arthur's world there is nothing unusual in this action. He welcomes Gareth to the court and turns him over to Sir Kay the steward, who christens him Beaumains (Fair Hands), mocks him, and puts him to work in the kitchen. He is befriended by Sir Gawaine, who does not recognize him, and by Sir Launcelot, but he serves out his twelve months in the scullery. At the next high feast a damsel, Linet, arrives to tell the king that her lady is besieged by a cruel tyrant and desires that a knight come and rescue her. Gareth then makes his other two requests of Arthur: that he be allowed the adventure and that Sir Launcelot make him a knight. He then accompanies the damsel, who has a sharp tongue and dislikes kitchen boys. After a long series of battles and adventures he at length rescues the lady, Dame Liones, and falls in love with her; his affection is returned. The story culminates in a great tournament held at her castle, attended by Arthur and his knights. Gareth and Gawaine fight an epic battle; the damsel Linet intervenes, telling Gawaine he is fighting his own brother. There is a joyful reunion, and Sir Gareth and Dame Liones are then presented to King Arthur:

> . . . And there the king asked his nephew, Sir Gareth, whether he would have that lady as paramour, or to have her to his wife. My lord, wit you well that I love her above all ladies living. Now, fair lady, said King Arthur, what say ye? Most noble King, said Dame Liones, wit you well that my lord, Sir Gareth, is to me more lever to have and welde as my husband, than any king or prince that is christened; and if I may not have him I promise you I will never have none. For, my lord Arthur, said Dame Liones, wit you well he is my first love, and he shall be the last; and if ye will suffer him to have his will and free choice I dare say he will have me. That is truth, said Sir Gareth; an I have not you and welde not you as my wife, there shall never lady nor gentlewoman rejoice me. What, nephew, said the king, **is the wind in that door?**

It can't be nature, for it is not sense

Source: THE FAREWELL (Line 200)
Author: Charles Churchill (1731–1764)
First published: 1764
Type of work: Satiric dialogue

Context: Charles Churchill, whose early ambitions turned toward an ecclesiastical career ran afoul of love for wine, women, and wrangling, wrote toward the end of his short life a poetic conversation about his proposal to leave Europe and go to India. "P" probably stands for the poet, and "F" for his friend, who questions his decision by asking what could some other part of the world offer as better targets for satire than England, where he can find vice and folly aplenty? The poet says he is tired of hearing repeated protests of love for England, despite her faults. The same patriotic utterance has frequently been voiced in the United States, as, for example, when Commander Stephen Decatur (1779–1820) of the U.S. Navy declared at a banquet in 1815 after defeating the Algerian pirates: "Our country! In her intercourse with foreign nations, may she be always in the right, but our country, right or wrong!" And Senator John J. Crittenden (1787–1863) of Kentucky, with one son in the Northern armies and one in the Confederacy, vowed to stand by his country, right or wrong. The Friend in the poem sees no difference in mankind, whether in England or Japan. In a slight shift of thought, the poet agrees that man is usually partial to the land of his birth. To call all lands alike "may be PHILOSOPHY, but can't be SENSE."

However, the friend says that while Nature must receive its due, one should not cloud Reason and argue that the Master Passion for one's country is "fix'd by Nature in the human breast." If one's native land is found by comparison with other places to be a spot of Virtue, Plenty, Honesty in Politics, with sacred Love, and Liberty certain, even a Hottentot would love it. But if the place of one's birth is some barren spot where injustice and slavery exist, nobody would love it, any more than the Devil is enraptured of Hell. However, at the conclusion, the poet gets around to his point. Since Clive and those accompanying him as governor of India had left for the Orient on June 4, 1764, the poet concludes that he will find abundant material for his satires when he reaches India. In saying that a country must offer certain qualities before it will be loved, the Friend declares:

> But if, by Fate's decrees, you owe your birth
> To some more barren and penurious earth,
> Where, ev'ry comfort of this life denied,
> Her real wants are scantily supplied,
> Where Pow'r is Reason, Liberty's a joke,
> Laws never made, or made but to be broke,
> To fix thy love on such a wretched spot . . .
>   • • •
> Is Folly which admits not of defence;
> **It can't be Nature, for it is not Sense.**
> By the same argument which here you hold
> (When Falsehood's insolent, let Truth be bold)
> If Propagation can in torments dwell,
> A Devil must, if born there, love his hell.

It is an honest ghost

Source: HAMLET (Act I, sc. v, l. 138)
Author: William Shakespeare (1564-1616)
First published: 1603
Type of work: Dramatic tragedy

Context: One of Hamlet's basic problems is that of the identity of the ghost who nightly walks at Elsinore. Is it the ghost of his father or a tempting demon in disguise? The problem is stated most clearly at the end of Act II: "The spirit that I have seen/ May be a devil, and the devil hath power/ T' assume a pleasing shape; . . ." The question is raised at the first sighting of the ghost by Horatio and the watchmen, and it is reasserted by Hamlet at his first encounter, when he insists that he will speak to it, "Be thou a spirit of health, or goblin damned." But after the ghost tells Hamlet, in private, that he is his father's spirit, that he was murdered by Hamlet's uncle, Claudius, the present king, and that Claudius and Hamlet's mother, Gertrude, had earlier committed adultery, Hamlet concludes—though only for the moment—that the ghost is genuine—

"honest"—and tells Horatio and the guard as much, though he refuses to disclose anything further:

HAMLET

. . .

Touching this vision here—
It is an honest ghost, that let me tell you—
For your desire to know what is between us,
O'ermaster't as you may.

. . .

It is better to be a fool than to be dead

Source: VIRGINIBUS PUERISQUE ("Crabbed Age and Youth")
Author: Robert Louis Stevenson (1850-1894)
First published: 1881
Type of work: Familiar essay

Context: Stevenson begins the essay entitled "Crabbed Age and Youth" by suggesting that proverbs are invented for mediocre people, to discourage them from overly ambitious attempts and to console them in their mediocrity. He notes that though they are discredited in practice, proverbs hold their own in theory. They are, he suggests, a fine example of how allowances are made for the illusions of youth, but none for the disenchantment of age; seldom do the young quote proverbs to the older generation; it is the older generation who quote proverbs for the edification of youth. Stevenson says that youth should be given credit for what it is, for having enthusiasm; one cannot, he implies, be worth while without having been a youth, with all the faults of youth. Youth, he says, needs to be considered carefully, just as are experience and maturity. He writes pointedly, "It is as natural and as right for a young man to be imprudent and exaggerated, to live in swoops and circles, and beat about his cage like any other wild thing newly captured, as it is for old men to turn gray. . . ." Stevenson is thus making a case for each age to be true to itself, and to live as is natural to it:

. . . All error, not merely verbal, is a strong way of saying that the current truth is incomplete. The follies of youth have a basis in sound reason, just as much as the embarrassing questions put by babes and sucklings. Their most antisocial acts indicate the defects of our society. When the torrent sweeps the man against a boulder, you must expect him to scream, and you need not be surprised if the scream is sometimes a theory. . . . Generous lads irritated at the injustices of society, see nothing for it but the abolishment of

544

everything and Kingdom Come of anarchy. Shelley was a young fool; so are these cocksparrow revolutionaries. But **it is better to be a fool than to be dead.** It is better to emit a scream in the shape of a theory than to be entirely insensible to the jars and incongruities of life and take everything as it comes in a forlorn stupidity. . . .

It is, but hadn't ought to be

Source: MRS. JUDGE JENKINS (Being the only Genuine Sequel to "Maud Muller," Last line)
Author: Bret Harte (1836-1902)
First published: 1870
Type of work: Parody

Context: "Maud Muller," the well-known poem by John Greenleaf Whittier, tells the story of a farm girl and a judge. The judge rides by on his fine horse and asks for a drink of water; Maud brings it and the judge chats pleasantly with her about the haying and other everyday topics, thanks her, and rides on. Each later daydreams about the other. Maud thinks of the happiness and security she and her family could have, and all the good she might do, if the judge were her husband. The judge thinks of Maud and longs for the life of rural simplicity she represents. Each marries within his own station; the judge weds an ambitious woman who drives him up the ladder of success, and Maud marries a farmhand who gives her a large family. As the years pass, they still think wistfully of each other. Whittier concludes with his oft-quoted observation, "Of all the words of tongue or pen,/ The saddest are these: 'It might have been!' " Harte, exponent of a somewhat more hard-boiled view of life than that of Whittier, parodies the original with something less ideal and perhaps more realistic. He begins by assuming that the judge returns for Maud after all; when he arrives, Maud can only stammer ungrammatically and her father requests a small loan. Her brother is drunk at the wedding, and the rest of the family is drunk afterward. In the spring Maud bears the judge a pair of twins, "And the Judge was blest, but thought it strange/ That bearing children made such a change;/For Maud grew broad and red and stout,/ And the waist that his arm once clasped about/ Was more than he now could span; and he/ Sighed as he pondered, ruefully,/ How that which in Maud was native grace/ In Mrs. Jenkins was out of place. . . ." The judge finds himself wishing, now that it is much too late, that his sons could look less like hay-hands and that his wife were better educated:

Alas for maiden! alas for judge!
And the sentimental,—that's one-half "fudge;"

For Maud soon thought the Judge a bore,
With all his learning and all his lore;

And the Judge would have bartered Maud's fair face
For more refinement and social grace.

If, of all words of tongue and pen,
The saddest are, "It might have been,"

Sadder are these, we daily see:
"It is, but hadn't ought to be."

It is certain, because it is impossible

Source: DE CARNE CHRISTI (5)
Author: Tertullian (c. 155-c. 220)
First transcribed: c. 209
Type of work: Religious philosophy

Context: Tertullian, educated in Carthage and in Rome with specialization in law and rhetoric, and later converted to Christianity, was well prepared for his role as defender of the Christian faith. In *De Carne Christi,* Tertullain answers the heretical writings of Marcion, Apelles, Basilides, and Valentinus, who argued that Christ never existed in the flesh. With legalistic logic Tertullain contends that the heresy of his opponents is fallacious because it is the very foolishness, or one may say wisdom, of God that made Him elect to be born as a human, to suffer, and to die:

There are, to be sure, other things also quite as "foolish" [as the birth of Christ], which have reference to the humiliations and sufferings of God. Or else, let them call a crucified God "wisdom." But Marcion will apply the knife to this [doctrine] also, and even with greater reason. For which is more unworthy of God, which is more likely to raise a blush of shame, that [God] should be born, or that He should die? that He should bear the flesh, or the cross? be circumcised, or be crucified? be cradled, or be coffined? be laid in a manger, or in a tomb? [Talk of "wisdom!"] You will show more of that if you refuse to believe this also. But, after all, you will not be "wise" unless you become a "fool" to the world, by believing "the foolish things of God." . . . And He was buried, and rose again; **the fact is certain, because it is impossible.**

It is enough to have perished once

Source: THE AENEID (Book IX, lines 140-141)
Author: Virgil (Publius Vergilius Maro, 70-19 B.C.)
First transcribed: c. 29-19 B.C.
Type of work: Epic poem

Context: Fired by patriotism, Virgil wrote the *Aeneid* to give to Rome an origin suited to her greatness. Aeneas, son of Venus and hero of the Trojan War, encounters difficulties similar to those of Ulysses as he sails from Troy to Italy, but, led on by his destiny, he reaches Italy and overcomes the armies of the inhabitants. The destined union of the Latins and the Trojan invaders is accomplished when the aged King Latinus gives to Aeneas the hand of his daughter Lavinia. Turnus, chief suitor of Lavinia, becomes the arch enemy of Aeneas, and, declaring his intention of fighting until death against the Trojans, exclaims, "It is enough to have perished once." In the translation of Mackail the passage reads:

> . . . In no wise am I dismayed by those divine oracles of doom that the Phrygians insolently advance. Fate and Venus are satisfied, in that the Trojans have touched our fruitful Ausonian fields. I too have my destiny against theirs, to put utterly to the sword the guilty nation who have robbed me of my bride; not the sons of Atreus alone feel that pain, nor may Mycenae alone take arms. **But to have perished once is enough!** . . .

It is hardly necessary to light a candle to the sun

Source: DISCOURSES CONCERNING GOVERNMENT (Chapter II, section 23)
Author: Algernon Sidney (1622-1683)
First published: 1698
Type of work: Political treatise

Context: English Republican leader, grand-nephew of Sir Philip Sidney and son of Robert Sidney, Second Earl of Leicester, Algernon Sidney was wounded at Marston Moor in 1644 while fighting for the Parliamentary side in the Civil War. After the Restoration he was pardoned by Charles II, but upon his return to England he supported the Duke of Monmouth in the affair in which Charles' illegitimate son challenged the right of his uncle, the Duke of York, to be first in the line of succession to the throne. This conspiracy was discovered by the exposure of another one, the Rye House Plot. After an unfair trial under Jeffreys of Wem in which he was condemned without sufficient evidence, Sidney was sentenced to death for treason and executed on Tower Hill. His name was cleared in 1689. His most significant work is *Discourses Concerning Government,* in which he sets forth the philosophy of political self-determination: "God leaves to man the choice of forms in government."

Political power is established for the good of the governed, not for the good of the governor. He maintains that the political structure inevitably decays when absolute power falls into the hands of an individual man. Consequently, no king has the right to confer upon his descendents an automatic guarantee of political authority. It is impossible for a monarch to govern effectively unless his powers are regulated by law. "The contracts made between magistrates and the nations that created them, were real, solemn, and obligatory." Among the imperative duties of government is the encouragement of valiant citizens through the proper recognition of their deeds and accomplishments:

> The same policy that made men valiant and industrious in the service of their country during the first ages, would have the same effect, if it were now in being; and men would have the same love to the public as the Spartans and the Romans had, if there was the same reason for it. We need no other proof of this than what we have seen in our own country, where in a few years good discipline, and a just encouragement given to those who did well, produced more examples of pure, incorruptible, and invincible virtue than Rome or Greece could ever boast. And if more be wanting, they may easily be found among the Swiss, Hollanders, and others: but **it is hardly necessary to light a candle to the sun.**

It is not best to swap horses while crossing the river

Source: REPLY TO A DELEGATION FROM THE NATIONAL UNION LEAGUE (June 9, 1864)
Author: Abraham Lincoln (1809-1865)
First published: 1864
Type of work: Political speech

Context: Between May 4 and June 8, 1864, General Ulysses S. Grant had suffered a number of serious defeats —the Battles of The Wilderness, Spotsylvania, and Cold Harbor, his losses running as high as 55,000 men. Such events, occurring as they did in an election year, could have spelled serious trouble for incumbent President Abraham Lincoln. Moving quickly and before the country had comprehended the full significance of Grant's defeats, the Republican Party (its name changed briefly to National Union Party) met in convention at Baltimore. Lincoln's party had not been solidly behind him; on the contrary, there was considerable opposition to his policies, and the party's more radical element had been giving him trouble. Nonetheless, those meeting at the convention realized that Lincoln had a better chance of winning the election than anyone else they might propose, and he was accordingly nominated for a second term by unanimous vote. Andrew Johnson, War Governor of Tennessee, was named his running mate. Among the various groups lending Lincoln their support was the Union League of America, or National

Union League. This organization had been founded as a secret society during the early days of the war, its purpose being to organize and consolidate loyalty to the Union. Its National Grand Council met in Baltimore at the same time as the National Union convention and stood solidly for Lincoln's re-election. Lincoln, beset by numerous problems, was deeply gratified by the support given him—even though he knew the campaign of 1864 would be a difficult one. His gratitude and relief are evident in his humble, humorous reply to the Union League's delegation:

. . . I am very grateful for the renewed confidence which has been accorded to me both by the convention and by the National League. I am not insensible at all to the personal compliment there is in this, and yet I do not allow myself to believe that any but a small portion of it is to be appropriated as a personal compliment. That really the convention and the Union League assembled with a higher view—that of taking care of the interests of the country for the present and the great future—and that the part I am entitled to appropriate as a compliment is only that part which I may lay hold of as being the opinion of the convention and of the League, that I am not entirely unworthy to be intrusted with the place which I have occupied for the last three years. But I do not allow myself to suppose that either the convention or the League have concluded to decide that I am either the greatest or best man in America, but rather they have concluded that **it is not best to swap horses while crossing the river,** and have further concluded that I am not so poor a horse that they might not make a botch of it in trying to swap.

It is nought good a sleeping hound to wake

Source: TROILUS AND CRISEYDE (Book III, stanza 110, l. 764)
Author: Geoffrey Chaucer (c. 1343-1400)
First transcribed: 1380-1386
Type of work: Narrative poem

Context: The story of Troilus and Criseyde first appeared in Benôit de Sainte-Maure's *Roman de Troie* (1184), which was supposed to be based on narratives by Dictys of Crete, author of a fourth century work translated from an earlier Greek original, and from Dares the Phrygian, of at latest the fifth century. During the Middle Ages this pair was generally believed to have been present at the siege of Troy. Giovanni Boccaccio (1313–1375) had Benôit in mind in his *Il filostrato* (c.1335–1345); and Chaucer used both Boccaccio's and Benôit's versions. He even employed the Rima royal of seven-line stanzas that Boccaccio used. The time is the Trojan War in the Bronze Age, perhaps 1200 B.C., but the Chaucerian version fills it with the customs of a medieval court of love. For modern tastes, its five books and more than 8,000 lines

549

make its reading a bit tedious, especially with the long soliloquys, speeches, and digressions. Yet it has been called an almost perfectly constructed narrative poem, full of a strange sweetness characteristic of Chaucer, especially in his second period. It is the only long poem he completed. Troilus, one of the sons of King Priam of Troy—Hector was another—is presented in the first stanza of the "Proem"; then the narrator in the other seven stanzas asks the gods for help in telling his tale. As the story starts, Calchas, the Trojan prophet, foresees that the Greeks will be successful in their siege of Troy, so he flees to the winning side, leaving his widowed daughter, Criseyde. During the spring festival, joining the celebration, where she stood out in beauty, she attracts Troilus's eyes.

Smitten with her, yet believing his love hopeless, he goes out to attack the Greeks. However, Pandarus (whose name originated the expression "to pander,") offers to act as go-between, an easy task, since he is Criseyde's uncle. She has seen Troilus riding by on his way from the battlefield. When she learns that he is dying for her, she finds nothing dishonorable in encouraging him. In the third Book, to carry further his scheme, Pandarus invites her to dine with him, assuring her that Troilus is out of Troy. However, when a rain storm forces her to spend the night at the house, he comes into the bedroom by a secret trapdoor. When she suggests she awaken one of her women, Pandarus answers with the fourteenth century equivalent of "Let sleeping dogs lie."

> It is nought good a sleping hound to wake,
> Ne yive a wight a cause to devyne,
> Your women sleepen alle, I undertake,
> So that, for hem, the hous men mighte myne;
> And sleepen wolen til the sonne shyne.
> And whan my tale al brought is to an ende,
> Unwist, right as I com, so will I wende.

It is sweet and fitting to die for one's country

Source: ODES (Book III, Ode 2, l. 13)
Author: Horace (65-8 B.C.
First transcribed: 23-13 B.C.
Type of work: Ode

Context: Horace encourages fortitude and fidelity in the young soldier. The poet cites the honor attached to dying for one's country, at the same time noting that death comes alike to hero and to coward. H. V. Macnaghton translated the passage:

> Let every Roman boy be taught to know
> Constraining hardship as a friend, and grow
> Strong in fierce warfare, with dread lance and horse

Encountering the gallant Parthian foe.

Aye, let him live beneath the open sky
In danger. Him from leagured walls should eye
   Mother and daughter of th' insurgent king,
And she for her betrothed, with many a sigh,

Should pray, poor maiden, lest, when hosts engage,
Unversed in arms he face that lion's rage
   So dangerous to trust what time he gluts
His wrath upon the battle's bloody stage.

For country 'tis a sweet and seemly thing
To die. Death ceases not from following
   E'en runaways. Can youth with feeble knees,
That fears to face the battle, scape his wing?

It is the low man thinks the woman low

Source: QUEEN MARY (Act V, sc. ii, l. 251)
Author: Alfred, Lord Tennyson (1809-1892)
First published: 1875
Type of work: Historical drama

Context: During the 1870's there was a reaction against Tennyson's previously unquestioned leadership in British letters, expressed publicly by Swinburne. In those years when his poetry was reaching a relatively indifferent public, Tennyson turned to writing drama, penning three plays concerned with English history: *Queen Mary, Harold,* and *Becket.* Of the three, only the last-named, revised by Sir Henry Irving, had a successful run in the theater. The queen of Tennyson's play is Mary Tudor, daughter of Henry the Eighth, elder half sister of the woman who was to be Elizabeth the First. Mary is portrayed as loving deeply Philip of Spain and fearing, rightfully, that many persons in her kingdom wish to prevent her marriage to the Spanish (and Catholic) monarch. Outside her kingdom, too, Mary learns, through the French ambassador, there is opposition to a union of Spain and England. Despite the opposition, Mary Tudor dotes on Philip, to the point that she falls in trances and sits upon the floor in an unqueenly manner. While the queen is in a trance, Alice, a maid, and Lady Magdalen Dacres, one of the waiting-women, talk to each other:

ALICE
I would I were as tall and strong as you.

LADY MAGDALEN
I seem half-ashamed at times to be so tall.

ALICE

You are the stateliest deer in all the herd—
Beyond his aim—but I am small and scandalous,
And love to hear bad tales of Philip.

LADY MAGDALEN
Why?
I never heard him utter worse of you
Than that you were low-statured.

ALICE

Does he think
Low stature is low nature, or all women's
Low as his own?

LADY MAGDALEN
There you strike in the nail.
This coarseness is a want of phantasy.
It is the low man thinks the woman low;
Sin is too dull to see beyond himself.

It is the nature of all greatness not to be exact

Source: SPEECH ON AMERICAN TAXATION, 1774
Author: Edmund Burke (1729-1797)
First published: 1774
Type of work: Political speech

Context: Edmund Burke was a friend to the American Colonies; he was also a believer in truth and justice. This speech is an example of the man's principles, beliefs, and actions. In it Burke appeals to Parliament to abolish the duty on tea which has created such animosity in America and led to a threat of war. Burke tries to show that there is really no obstacle to repealing the tax, noting that other taxes imposed by the same bill had been repealed already. He further notes that the principle of taxation which some men thought the tea tax represented had been given up by the British government already, citing a letter written by Lord Hillesborough. Turning to the past, Burke then recites the history of taxation in the American Colonies. Coming to George Grenville and the Act of Navigation, he says that this act of Parliament needed to be changed "according to the change of the times and the fluctuation of circumstances." Not to change the act, says Burke, is to fail to realize that great mischief might be done, and the very purpose of the act defeated, by the change in commerce of the American Colonies in the years after the French and Indian War:

After the war, and in the last years of it, the trade of America

552

had encreased far beyond the speculations of the most sanguine imaginations. It swelled out on every side. It filled all its proper channels to the brim. It overflowed with a rich redundance, and breaking its banks on the right and on the left, it spread out upon some places where it was indeed improper, upon others where it was only irregular. **It is the nature of all greatness not to be exact;** and great trade will always be attended with considerable abuses. The contraband will always keep pace in some measure with the fair trade. It should be a fundamental maxim, that no vulgar precaution ought to be employed in the cure of evils, which are closely connected with the cause of our prosperity. . . .

It is the very error of the moon

Source: OTHELLO (Act V, sc. ii, l. 109)
Author: William Shakespeare (1564-1616)
First published: 1622
Type of work: Dramatic tragedy

Context: Because of a plot of vengeance laid by the Machiavellian Iago, Othello, the noble Moor of Venice, smothers his new bride Desdemona, whom he believes to have been unfaithful to him with Cassio, his former friend and lieutenant. The murder, says Othello, is so horrible that one might expect even an eclipse. When Emilia, maid to Desdemona, reports another murder, Othello attributes the acts of man to the irregularity of the moon.

OTHELLO
. . . My wife? My wife—what wife? I have no wife.
O insupportable! O heavy hour!
Methinks it should be now a huge eclipse
Of sun and moon, and that th' affrighted globe
Did yawn at alteration.
                    •   •   •
[*Enter* EMILIA]
                    What's the matter with thee now?

EMILIA
O my good lord, yonder's foul murders done.
                    •   •   •

OTHELLO
It is the very error of the moon;
She comes more nearer earth than she was wont,
And makes men mad.

553

It matters not how a man dies, but how he lives

Source: THE LIFE OF SAMUEL JOHNSON, LL.D. (For 1769)
Author: James Boswell (1740-1795)
First published: 1791
Type of work: Biography

Context: Once when Boswell and Johnson were alone, Boswell introduced into the conversation the subject of death, which he knew Johnson abhorred. Johnson strenuously denied that any sensible person could be unafraid of death: if one pointed a pistol at a dying man, he would be terror-stricken. Although Johnson had, in his poem *The Vanity of Human Wishes*, written that death was a retreat from the world to a happier existence, he very much disliked the idea of passing on to that joyful state. The trouble is that a man has to give up everything he has to achieve it. In answer to Boswell's query as to whether we cannot fortify our minds against the idea of death, Johnson exclaimed that the important thing was not how a man dies but how he lives:

. . . To my question, whether we might not fortify our minds for the approach of death, he answered, in a passion, "No, Sir, let it alone. **It matters not how a man dies, but how he lives.** The act of dying is not of importance, it lasts so short a time." He added (with an earnest look), "A man knows it must be so, and submits. It will do him no good to whine."

It must be right: I've done it from my youth

Source: THE BOROUGH (Letter 3, l. 139)
Author: George Crabbe (1755-1832)
First published: 1810
Type of work: Descriptive poem

Context: *The Borough* is a description of the town and those who inhabit it in the early nineteenth century. The poem consists of a number of "letters," containing descriptions of people, except for the first letter, which is a general picture of the borough. The third letter describes the local clergy, including the vicar and the curate; the quotation is from the portrait of the vicar. Crabbe speaks of the vicar as a man who from his earliest days as a clergyman sought always to offend no one. The poet also says of him: "Fear was his ruling passion." The vicar is never tempted, because he never allows himself near temptation, even in love. His courtship of the one young girl for whom he felt affection was so languid that she turned from him to marry another, realizing that she would always have to take the lead if she were to marry the clergyman. What were the pleasures of such a man? They were simple: "Fiddling and fishing were

554

his arts: at times/ He alter'd sermons, and he aim'd at rhymes;/ And his fair friends, not yet intent on cards,/ Oft, he mused with riddles and charades." In his work the vicar simply dismisses from his mind other sects and their variant views. Crabbe suggests what the vicar stood for:

> These were to him essentials; all things new
> He deem'd superfluous, useless, or untrue;
> To all beside indifferent, easy, cold,
> Here the fire kindled, and the wo [*sic.*] was told.
> Habit with him was all the test of truth,
> **"It must be right: I've done it from my youth."**
> Questions he answer'd in as brief a way,
> "It must be wrong—it was of yesterday."

It's as easy to marry a rich woman as a poor woman

Source: THE HISTORY OF PENDENNIS (Volume I, chapter 28)
Author: William Makepeace Thackeray (1811-1863)
First published: 1848-1850
Type of work: Novel

Context: Arthur Pendennis, after his father's death, is reared by his mother, Helen, with help from Major Arthur Pendennis, the child's uncle. Young Pendennis is something of a snob and tends to follow his uncle, who wants to help the boy rise socially, rather than to follow his mother, who wants to keep her son natural and unspoiled by selfish scheming to rise from the middle-class to the aristocracy. Mrs. Pendennis hopes her son will marry Laura Bell, Mrs. Pendennis' ward, but the snobbery of young Arthur offends Laura's self-respect, even though she loves him and has used a portion of her inheritance to see him through the university. Following Laura's refusal of his suit, young Pendennis goes down to London to study law, to begin a writing career, and to enjoy the social life. One day he is visited by his uncle, Major Pendennis, who inquires if the young man has any new loves and offers this advice to his nephew:

". . . You are heir to a little independence, which everybody fancies is a doosid deal more. You have a good name, good wits, good manners, and a good person—and, begad! I don't see why you shouldn't marry a woman with money—get into Parliament—distinguish yourself, and—and, in fact, that sort of thing. Remember, **it's as easy to marry a rich woman as a poor woman:** and a devilish deal pleasanter to sit down to a good dinner, than to a scrag of mutton in lodgings. Make up your mind to that. A woman with a good jointure is a doosid deal easier a profession than the law, let me tell you. Look out; *I* shall be on the watch for you. . . ."

It's more than a game. It's an institution

Source: TOM BROWN'S SCHOOL DAYS (Part II, chapter 8)
Author: Thomas Hughes (1822-1896)
First published: 1857
Type of work: Reform novel

Context: As a young man of nineteen, Tom Brown spends his last day at Rugby playing cricket against a rival school. It is an important match, and Tom, as befits a senior boy who is a good cricket man, is captain of the Rugby eleven. As the game progresses, he sits with his friend Arthur and a young faculty member who has taken an interest in him. The young master tries to draw an analogy for Tom and Arthur, pointing out that they see much more of the fine technique of cricket than he, because they are interested and have studied it. He goes on to say that Tom, had he spent as much effort on his Greek, could have just as much insight into, say, an Aristophanic comedy like *The Knights* as anyone, and so enjoy his studies much more. Tom takes this observation good-humoredly, as he has learned to like this particular faculty member and has grown up enough to cease regarding his teachers as, at best, friendly enemies. As they watch, the young master learns some of the finer points of the game and comments to Tom and Arthur:

"Come, none of your irony, Brown," answers the master. "I'm beginning to understand the game scientifically. What a noble game it is, too!"

"Isn't it? But **it's more than a game. It's an institution**," said Tom.

"Yes," said Arthur, "the birthright of British boys old and young, as *habeas corpus* and trial by jury are of British men."

"The discipline and reliance on one another which it teaches is so valuable, I think," went on the master, "it ought to be such an unselfish game. It merges the individual in the eleven; he doesn't play that he may win, but that his side may."

"That's very true," said Tom, "and that's why football and cricket . . . are such much better games than fives or hare-and-hounds, or any others where the object is to come in first or to win for one's self, and not that one's side may win."

It's no fish ye're buying—it's men's lives

Source: THE ANTIQUARY (Chapter 11)
Author: Sir Walter Scott (1771-1832)
First published: 1816
Type of work: Novel

Context: Mr. Jonathan Oldbuck, Oldenbuck, or Oldinbuck, known also as Monkbarns, from the name of his estate on the northeastern coast of Scotland, is conducting his young friend, Mr. Lovel, along the seashore to visit Sir Arthur Wardour and his daughter, whom Oldbuck and Lovel had been instrumental in saving from drowning in a storm-driven high tide the previous evening. Unknown to Oldbuck, who has a fanatical love for antiquities of all kinds, Lovel, who had risked his life in the rescue, is in love with Miss Wardour, who does all in her power to discourage his ardor. As the two make their way along the shore, Oldbuck and Lovel come upon a very masculine-looking woman sitting before a cottage and mending a fishing net. Thereupon ensues a bargaining session between Oldbuck and the woman for some fish. At first the two are far apart in their bidding and asking, but eventually they agree on a price. She offers her wares in a strident tone: "What are ye for the day" means "what do you want today?"

. . . "What are ye for the day, your honor?" she said, or rather screamed, to Oldbuck; "caller haddocks and whitings—a bannock-fluke and a cock-padle."

"How much for the bannock-fluke and the cock-padle?" demanded the Antiquary.

"Four white shillings and sixpence," answered the Naiad.

"Four devils and six of their imps!" retorted the Antiquary; "do you think I am mad, Maggie?"

"And div ye think," rejoined the virago, setting her arms a-kimbo, "that my man and my sons are to gae to the sea in weather like yestreen and the day—sic a sea as it's yet outby—and get naething for their fish, and be misca'd into the bargain, Monkbarns? **It's no fish ye're buying—it's men's lives."**

"Well, Maggie, I'll bid you fair—I'll bid you a shilling for the fluke and the cock-padle, or sixpence separately—and if all your fish are as well paid, I think your man, as you call him, and your sons, will make a good voyage."

I've a great fancy to see my own funeral afore I die

Source: CASTLE RACKRENT ("Continuation of Memoirs")
Author: Maria Edgeworth (1767-1849)
First published: 1800
Type of work: Novel

Context: Blessed—or, according to many critics, cursed—by having a father who not only pushed her into writing but also carefully revised her work, Miss Edgeworth presents a strange figure to moderns. With her father she wrote several books on education, a subject that Mr. Edgeworth hoped to reduce to scientifically provable steps, but she was an incurable romantic, not the calculating rationalist that was her father's ideal of the proper female. In strictest secret she wrote this novel and gave it to her father only after it was printed; thus it is unique among her fiction. It

557

is the long monologue of one of her most delightful characters, Thady Quirk, the homely tenant of the Rackrents whose tale he slowly unfolds. Through the creation of this character, Miss Edgeworth often lets her imagination run wild for the sake of comedy. The quotation comes from one of these sections: Thady is describing Sir Condy, the last of the Rackrents, whose triumph was to have his funeral before he died so that he could hear that people said of him at his wake, a triumph that soured because nothing remarkable was said.

> "Thady," says he, "all you've been telling me [about the civil things said of him] brings a strange thought into my head: I've a notion I shall not be long for this world any how, and I've a great fancy to see my own funeral afore I die."

Ivory tower

Source: PENSÉES D'AOÛT (Stanza 3)
Author: Charles Augustin Sainte-Beuve (1804-1869)
First published: 1837
Type of work: Literary criticism

Context: The idea of retiring to a tower, getting away from the world and its temptations, has been frequently expressed since the Syrian hermit Simeon Stylites, who died about 459, spent thirty-five years on top of a tall pillar to escape mankind. What the escape mechanism was made of, did not matter. The "tower of ivory" mentioned in "Song of Solomon" (VII, 4) describing the neck of the poet's sweetheart, was of a different sort—a temptation, not an escape. In the current significance, an ivory tower is an imaginary place in which a recluse can remain aloof from the world. The phrase occurs in the works of many writers. Jules de Gaultier, in the nineteenth century, in his "War and the Destiny of Art," compared "the poet, retired to his Tower of Ivory, isolated, according to his desires, from the world of men" to a lighthouse keeper. Henry James in 1917 started to write a novel *The Ivory Tower.* Thomas Mann (1875–1955), being told in 1937 that his name had been removed from the list of Honorary Doctors of the University of Bonn, said that no one could separate the artistic and intellectual life from the political and social life and isolate himself within the ivory tower of the "culture" proper. It was, however, the literary critic Sainte-Beuve who probably coined the phrase in his poem to Abel François Villemain (1790–1870), French critic and politician, later Minister of Education. It appears in his volume of poems *Pensées d'Août (August Thoughts)*, published in 1837.

> Hugo, stern partisan,
> . . . fought in armor,

And held his banner high in the midst of the tumult:
He still holds it; and Vigny, more reserved,
Retired before the noon-day, as if in his **ivory tower.**

Jacob's ladder

Source: GENESIS 28:12
Author: Unknown
First transcribed: c. 1000-300 B.C.
Type of work: Religious history and law

Context: Esau comes to hate his brother Jacob because their father, Isaac, says that Esau shall serve Jacob. So great is Esau's hatred that he vows he will kill Jacob. Rebekah, their mother, learning of her older son's vow of hate, arranges with Isaac to send the younger son to Padan-aram, to stay for a time with Rebekah's brother, Laban. When Jacob leaves home his father bids him choose a wife from among the daughters of Laban. Jacob sets out with his parents' blessings and instructions, leaving Beersheba to travel toward Haran. When sunset comes he is upon the road, where he stops, makes a pillow of stones, and falls asleep. During the night he has a dream, in which he sees a ladder reaching to heaven, and he hears the voice of God making a prophesy about him:

And he **[Jacob]** dreamed, and behold a **ladder** set up on the earth, and the top of it reached to heaven: and behold the angels of God ascending and descending on it.

And, behold, the LORD stood above it, and said, I am the LORD God of Abraham, thy father, and the God of Isaac: the land whereon thou liest, to thee will I give it, and to thy seed:

And thy seed shall be as the dust of the earth, and thou shalt spread abroad to the west, and to the east, and to the north, and to the south: and in thee and in thy seed shall all the families of the earth be blessed.

And, behold, I am with thee, and will keep thee in all places whither thou goest, and will bring thee again into this land; for I will not leave thee, until I have done that which I have spoken to thee of.

A jest breaks no bones

Source: THE LIFE OF SAMUEL JOHNSON, LL.D. (For 1781)
Author: James Boswell (1740-1795)
First published: 1791
Type of work: Biography

Context: A group of men who practised law in the lower courts of Edin-

559

burgh had obtained a royal charter, In that document they took great care to have their old designation of "procurator" changed to "solicitor," on the foolish basis that the latter title was more genteel. They quickly made great public use of their new title in advertising their meetings. The group's undue emphasis upon their name, plus the other meanings attached to the words "procurer" and "solicitor," gave rise to at least one instance of ridicule: *The Caledonian Mercury,* a Scottish newspaper, printed a paragraph which made the group the butt of its humor. The Society of Solicitors proceeded to prosecute the publisher of the newspaper, a Mr. Robertson, for damages to their reputation. The court dismissed the original action, but the Society of Solicitors petitioned for a new trial in the Court of Session; for the second trial James Boswell was counsel for the defense. Boswell reports that Dr. Johnson, when told of the whole matter by Boswell, offered the following opinion of the case:

> "All injury is either of the person, the fortune, or the fame. Now it is a certain thing, it is proverbially known that **a jest breaks no bones.** They have never gained half-a-crown less in the whole profession since this mischievous paragraph has appeared; and, as to their reputation, What is their reputation but an instrument of getting money? If, therefore, they have lost no money, the question upon reputation may be answered by a very old position,— *De minimis non curat Praetor.*"

A joke's a very serious thing

Source: THE GHOST (Book IV, l. 1386)
Author: Charles Churchill (1731-1764)
First published: 1762-1763
Type of work: Satiric poem

Context: Charles Churchill was a dissipated clergyman who won for himself both fame and notoriety as a satiric poet during the last few years of his life. Much of the character of his verse seems to have been determined by his association with the unscrupulous editor of the *North-Briton,* John Wilkes. The story of the Cock Lane Ghost broke in 1762 when William Kent was accused of having committed adultery with and subsequently murdering his sister-in-law, Fanny Lynes. The accusation was made by Richard Parsons, whom Kent had sued for debt, and the evidence was the testimony of Fanny's ghost given through Parsons' daughter as a medium. Kent appealed to the courts to vindicate his character, and a commission including Dr. Samuel Johnson investigated the affair and pronounced it all a fraud. The affair was a very popular butt for satirists, including the dramatists, and Churchill's somewhat rambling comic treatment extends to four books. Book IV rambles even more discursively, if possible, than Book III, digressing frequently into political satire. One of the bitterest attacks is upon Lewis Bruce, as Crape, who had been given a clerical promotion which Churchill had expected to receive:

> Nor think a joke, CRAPE, a disgrace
> Or to my Person, or my place;
> The wisest of the Sons of Men
> Have deign'd to use them now and then.
>
> • • •
>
> Great Use they have, when in the hands
> Of One, like me, who understands,
> Who understands the time, and place,
> The persons, manner, and the grace,
> Which Fools neglect; so that we find,
> If all the requisites are join'd
> From whence a perfect joke must spring,
> **A joke's a very serious thing.**

Keep up appearances

Source: NIGHT (Line 311)
Author: Charles Churchill (1731-1764)
First published: 1762
Type of work: Satirical poem

Context: Those who have never heard of Charles Churchill will be amazed to learn that his volume of poetical works contains more than 450 pages. The son of a minister and himself intended for the Church he spoiled his chances for a scholarship at Cambridge by an early marriage. Life became difficult. Finally he tried writing poetry to provide an income, and especially to help the political career of his friend in Parliament, John Wilkes (1727–1797). The appearance of his *Rosciad* brought criticisms of his "ingenious and cruel satire." Most people attributed its authorship to a trio of Robert Lloyd, the dramatist George Colman the Elder, and Bonnell Thornton. So in the second edition Churchill put his name onto the title page and wrote "The Apology," that started a lasting quarrel with Tobias Smollett, author of an article about it in the *Critical Review*. Then, still apologetic, Churchill addressed another poem to Lloyd, accused of writing the first one. It was of a different style. The income of the *Rosciad* had lessened restraints put by poverty upon an obscure man. Another reason for taking up his pen again was a poem called "Day," written by an army doctor, John Armstrong (1709–1779), stationed with the forces in Germany. Its manuscript reached John Wilkes, with a request that it be corrected and printed. Churchill imagined himself its target, though he had not been writing long enough to be known, and promptly wrote an answer. It was published in January, 1762, a year after the appearance of "Day." Critics did not think highly of it. Its morality was far

561

removed from that of a Christian, and the careless diction was unworthy of the author of the *Rosciad*. He begins it, "When foes insult, and *prudent* friends dispense,/ In pity's strain, the worst of insolence"; then the poet pays his tribute to his friend Lloyd. In the course of the poem, Churchill brings out his own enmity with Smollet who, because he was a surgeon's mate at the siege of Cartagena in 1741, thought he could set himself up as a physician at Bath. Churchill says he himself leads the sort of life that suits him best. He prefers night life. Punning, he declares: "We, our friends, our foes, ourselves, survey,/ And see by NIGHT what fools we are by DAY." He refuses to court those who appear great. He is "too proud to flatter, too sincere to lie,/ Too plain to please, too honest to be great." Then he quotes an ironic tutor "more read in men than books," a "crafty man, demurely sly," who gives this satirical advice to his favorite pupil:

> Would'st thou, my son, be wise and virtuous deem'd,
> By all mankind a prodigy esteem'd?
> Be this thy rule; be what people *prudent* call;
> PRUDENCE, almighty PRUDENCE gives thee all.
> **Keep up appearances;** there lies the test,
> The world will give thee credit for the rest.
> Outward be fair, however foul within;
> Sin if thou wilt, but then in secret sin.
> This maxim's into common favor grown.
> Vice is no longer vice unless 'tis known.
> Virtue indeed may barefac'd take the field,
> But vice is virtue, when 'tis well conceal'd.

The keys of the kingdom

Source: MATTHEW 16:19
Author: Unknown (traditionally Matthew the Apostle)
First transcribed: c. 75-100
Type of work: Gospel

Context: Jesus, having taught the multitudes and displayed for them His divine power by miracles of healing and of feeding four thousand by the Sea of Galilee, moves up to Caesarea Phillippi with His disciples, concentrating upon making the message of His kingdom clear to them in preparation for the time when they must carry on the work of the kingdom after His ascension. Jesus, asking the disciples who men think He is, is told that He is considered to be a prophet, perhaps John the Baptist, Elias, or Jeremias. The Master then asks who the disciples believe He is:

> And Simon Peter answered and said, Thou art the Christ, the Son of the living God.
> And Jesus answered and said unto him, Blessed art thou, Simon

562

Barjona: for flesh and blood hath not revealed it unto thee, but my Father which is in heaven.

And I say also unto thee, That thou art Peter, and upon this rock I will build my church; and the gates of hell shall not prevail against it.

And I will give unto thee **the keys of the kingdom** of heaven: and whatsoever thou shalt bind on earth shall be bound in heaven: and whatsoever thou shalt loose on earth shall be loosed in heaven.

Kill not the moth nor butterfly

Source: AUGURIES OF INNOCENCE (Line 39)
Author: William Blake (1757-1827)
First published: 1863
Type of work: Poetic fragment

Context: Auguries of Innocence, which Blake never revised for publication, is a lengthy series of couplets concerning human cruelty. This poem is somewhat less difficult to follow than much of Blake's later poetry, which became increasingly mystical and obscure as he grew older. Though it is more or less organized, it is disconnected and quite haphazard in places—obviously a rough draft. Many of the statements in it take the form of aphorisms; and Blake may have simply let the poem grow over a period of time, jotting these thoughts down as they occurred to him. Beginning with the infinity that lies in everything and implying the holiness of all life, he cries out against man's cruelty to animals—a cruelty sometimes deliberate, sometimes merely thoughtless. To Blake, God is in all things and in all creatures, and they deserve consideration and respect. Caged birds, starving dogs, misused horses are all seen as an affront to divinity and a curse to man. After a thorough coverage of man's mistreatment of his fellow-creatures, Blake turns his attentions to man's misuse of man. His conclusion appears to be that although man was made for joy and sorrow, and may in some cases be born to a life of misery and suffering, much of this condition could be alleviated by a concern for other things that share life with him. It is interesting to note that the poet's sympathy is not limited to domestic animals and to wild creatures that are hunted for food or sport; he includes insects in his catalog as well, after presenting a number of maxims about the creatures we are more likely to pity:

> The Lamb misusd breeds Public strife
> And yet forgives the Butchers Knife.
> The Bat that flits at close of Eve
> Has left the Brain that won't Believe.
> The Owl that calls upon the Night
> Speaks the Unbeliever's fright.
> He who shall hurt the little Wren

Shall never be belovd by Men.
He who the Ox to wrath has mov'd
Shall never be by Woman lov'd.
The wanton Boy that kills the Fly
Shall feel the Spider's enmity.
He who torments the Chafer's sprite
Weaves a Bower in endless Night.
The Catterpiller on the Leaf
Repeats to thee thy Mother's grief.
Kill not the Moth nor Butterfly
For the Last Judgment draweth nigh. . . .

The king can do no wrong

Source: COMMENTARIES ON THE LAWS OF ENGLAND (Book III, chapter 17)
Author: Sir William Blackstone (1723-1780)
First published: 1765-1769
Type of work: Legal commentary

Context: Sir William Blackstone was a distinguished student both at school and later at Oxford. He was admitted to the English bar in 1746, but his legal practice was not successful; he lacked elocutionary power, and his personality did not fit him for the role of popular advocate. He abandoned his practice and returned to his fellowship at Oxford. Since there was no provision for any courses dealing with the laws and constitution of the country, Blackstone decided to offer a series of lectures on the subject. So successful were these that they gave Oxford a lasting and enviable distinction; the reputation of the school and the courses grew steadily, and as a result one wealthy patron of the university endowed a school of law there. Blackstone was its first professor. He wrote a number of legal works, but the best known of these is his *Commentaries on the Laws of England.* It is the best work of its type written up to that time, and has kept his name alive since; now considered one of the classics of legal literature, it is still studied, consulted, and cited. In this work Blackstone seeks to cover and to explain in plain terms the whole body of British law. This endeavor not only involves the statement and explanation of individual laws, but careful description of important precedents and historic cases. British law had sufficiently matured by Blackstone's time to allow a methodical treatment of it; Blackstone's work is not only methodical and logically arranged, but possesses remarkable clarity, particularly noticeable in areas of complexity. One important aspect of law in England is its definition of monarchy and of the unique position enjoyed by the king. After discussing "the injuries, or private wrongs, that may be offered by one subject to another, all of which are redressed by the command and authority of the king," Blackstone takes up the matter of injuries committed by the royal personage:

That **the king can do no wrong** is a necessary and fundamental principle of the English constitution: meaning only, as has formerly been observed, that, in the first place, whatever may be amiss in the conduct of public affairs is not chargeable personally on the king, nor is he, but his ministers, accountable for it to the people; and, secondly, that the prerogative of the crown extends not to do any injury; for, being created for the benefit of the people, it cannot be exerted to their prejudice. Whenever, therefore, it happens that, by misinformation or inadvertence, the crown hath been induced to invade the private rights of any of its subjects, though no action will lie against the sovereign (for who shall command the king?), yet the law hath furnished the subject with a decent and respectful mode of removing that invasion, by informing the king of the true state of the matter in dispute; and, as it presumes that to *know of* any injury and to *redress it* are inseparable in the royal breast, it then issues as of course, in the king's own name, his orders to his judges to do justice to the party aggrieved.

The distance between the sovereign and his subjects is such that it rarely can happen that any *personal* injury can immediately and directly proceed from the prince to any private man; and, as it can so seldom happen, the law in decency supposes that it never will or can happen at all. . . . But injuries to the rights of *property* can scarcely be committed by the crown without the intervention of its officers; for whom the law in matters of right entertains no respect or delicacy, but furnishes various methods of detecting the errors or misconduct of those agents, by whom the king has been deceived and induced to do a temporary injustice.

A king may make a nobleman, but he cannot make a gentleman

Source: LETTER TO WILLIAM SMITH (January 29, 1795)
Author: Edmund Burke (1729-1797)
First published: 1844
Type of work: Personal letter

Context: Burke was born in Ireland, and although his entire adult life was spent in England he took an active interest in Irish affairs throughout his career. As a member of Parliament he frequently defended the Irish, and he always felt the Anglican domination of the millions of Irish Catholics constituted a sort of tyranny. William Smith, a member of the Irish Parliament, had spoken in defense of Irish Catholics, and Burke responded with this encouraging letter:

. . . The divisions which formerly prevailed in the Church, with all their overdone zeal, only purified and ventilated our common faith, because there was no common enemy arrayed and embattled to take advantage of their dissensions; but now nothing but inevitable ruin will be the consequence of our quarrels. I think we may dispute, rail, persecute, and provoke the Catholics out of their prejudices; but it is not in ours they will take refuge. If anything is, one more than another, out of the power of man, it is to *create* a prejudice. Somebody has said, that **a king may make a nobleman, but he cannot make a gentleman.**

The king never dies

Source: COMMENTARIES ON THE LAWS OF ENGLAND (Book I, chapter 3)
Author: Sir William Blackstone (1723-1780)
First published: 1765-1769
Type of work: Legal commentary

Context: When Sir William Blackstone published his *Commentaries on the Laws of England,* he did his country and his profession an important service; he also won lasting fame for himself. The work was not only greatly superior to anything of its kind attempted prior to his time; it also became a legal classic and has remained so to the present day. Blackstone is still consulted, still quoted. Educated in law at Oxford, he failed as a lawyer through lack of the elocutionary and other talents which contribute to popular appeal; he therefore returned to Oxford, taking up his fellowship at the university. Since there was no provision for a course in English law at Oxford, Blackstone offered a series of lectures on the subject. These became so popular, and so increased the reputation of the university, that a School of Law was endowed by a benefactor and Blackstone made its first profes-sor. He produced a number of other legal works, but his commentaries are his major contribution to the literature of the profession. In them he discusses and explains the entire body of English law, doing so with admirable clarity. In Book I he undertakes the complex and often confusing problem of royal succession. He discusses the nature of monarchy, and points out that while lands and thrones are not naturally descendible, "the law has thought proper, for the benefit and peace of the public, to establish hereditary succession" in both. He notes the feudal character of the royal succession and describes some of the problems arising from cases wherein rulers have died without issue. If a question arises because of an heir's physical or mental incapacity, any decision rests jointly with Parliament and the king. In any case, the office is the important point, and succession perpetual:

. . . however the crown may be limited or transferred, it still retains its descendible quality, and becomes hereditary in the wearer of it. And hence in our law **the king is said never to die,** in his political capacity; though, in common with other men, he is subject to mortality in his natural: because immediately upon the natural death of Henry, William, or Edward, the king survives in his successor. For the right of the crown vests, *eo instanti* (from that instant) upon his heir; either the *haeres natus* (the heir born), if the course of descent remains unimpeached, or the *haeres factus* (the heir appointed), if the inheritance be under any particular settlement. So that there can be no *interregnum* [the space between two reigns]; but, as Sir Matthew Hale observes, the right of sovereignty is fully invested in the successor by the very descent of the crown. And therefore, however acquired, it becomes in him absolutely hereditary, unless by the rules of the limitation it is otherwise ordered and determined. In the same manner as landed estates, to continue our former comparison, are by the law hereditary, or descendible to the heirs of the owner; but still there exists a power, by which the property of those lands may be transferred to another person. If this transfer be made simply and absolutely, the lands will be hereditary in the new owner, and descend to his heir at law: but if the transfer be clogged with any limitations, conditions, or entails, the lands must descend in that channel, so limited and prescribed, and no other.

King of intimate delights

Source: THE TASK (Book IV, l. 139)
Author: William Cowper (1731-1800)
First published: 1785
Type of work: Meditative poem in blank verse

Context: The quotation is from the fourth book of *The Task,* entitled "The Winter Evening," one of the six books, or divisions, of the poem. Cowper, at the suggestion of Lady Austen, began writing about the simple and uneventful life he was living, a life forced upon him by an earlier, severe mental illness. Lady Austen suggested that he undertake the task (whence the title) of writing a blank verse poem about the sofa, which became the subject of Book I of the poem. Book IV relates the simple pleasures of an eighteenth century winter evening spent drinking tea before a fire in the living room, with curtains drawn to keep out the cold. The poet addresses winter and praises it for the quiet family gatherings it brings:

> Thou hold'st the sun
> A prisoner in the yet undawning east,
> Shortening his journey between morn and noon,
> And hurrying him, impatient of his stay,
> Down to the rosy west; but kindly still
> Compensating his loss with added hours
> Of social converse and instructive ease,
> And gath'ring, at short notice, in one group
> The family dispers'd, and fixing thought,
> Not less dispers'd by day-light and its cares.

567

I crown thee **king of intimate delights,**
Fire-side enjoyments, home-born happiness,
And all the comforts that the lowly roof
Of undisturb'd retirement, and the hours
Of long uninterrupted ev'ning, know.

A king's a king, do fortune what she can

Source: THE BARON'S WARS (Book V, stanza 36)
Author: Michael Drayton (1563-1631)
First published: As *Mortimeriados,* 1596; revised as *The Barons' Wars,* 1603
Type of work: Historical poem

Context: The poem treats of the conflict between King Edward II and his nobles, a subject dramatized by Christopher Marlowe in *Edward the Second.* The barons of England, angered at the king's misrule and insulted by the favoritism shown to Piers Gaveston and to members of the Spencer family, revolted under the Mortimers. Even the much neglected but perhaps not too virtuous queen, Isabella, sister of the King of France, fell away from the king and fled to France to raise a military force, the ostensible purpose of which was to insure her rights and those of her son, Prince Edward, afterwards King Edward III. At first the king's forces were successful in the war, but fortune turned against him and he was captured and imprisoned by the barons. The barons forced Edward to abdicate his throne; he did what he had to, insisting, however, that as an anointed king, he was supreme and the barons had no power over him. His protestations did him no good, and he was taken as a close prisoner from one castle to another. Finally he was set upon by a pair of most odious felons named Gurney and Matrevis, who subjected him to a series of indignities, such as wetting him with pond water, shaving his head and beard, clothing him in rags, depriving him of rest and food, and making him ride on a sorry jade. At this point in the poem the poet addresses the murderers and tells them to keep their unhallowed hands off the king, because he had had the spirit of God infused into him; he was still a king, although fortune had dealt severely with him.

> Vile traitors, hold off your unhallowed hands,
> His brow, upon it majesty still bears;
> Dare ye thus keep your sovereign lord in bands?
> And can your eyes behold th'anointed tears?
> Or if your sight all pity thus withstands,
> Are not your hearts yet pierced through your ears?
>   The mind is free, what ere afflict the man,
>   **A king's a king, do fortune what she can.**

> Dare man take that which God himself hath given?
> Or mortal spill the spirit by him infused,

568

Whose power is subject to the power of heaven?
Wrongs pass not unrevenged, although excused.
Except that thou set all at six and seven,
Rise, majesty, when thou art thus abused;
  Or for thy refuge, which way wilt thou take,
  When in this sort thou dost thyself forsake?

Kissing don't last: cookery do!

Source: THE ORDEAL OF RICHARD FEVEREL (Chapter 28)
Author: George Meredith (1828–1909)
First published: 1859
Type of work: Novel

Context: Richard Feverel is reared according to System by his father, Sir Austin Feverel. The father's personal System involves choosing a wife suitable for the young man, but Richard is attracted by a girl different from the one his father intends. He falls in love with the pretty seventeen-year-old niece of a neighboring farmer. The girl's name is Lucy Desborough. Young Richard arranges, with the help of a friend, Ripton Thompson, to house Lucy in London with a Mrs. Berry, until the arrangements can be made for them to be married. One day just before the marriage, Richard, Lucy, and Ripton meet an uncle of Richard in the park. Ripton, to hide Lucy's identity, introduces her as his sister. The experience is unnerving to the three young persons, especially to Lucy. When she returns to her lodgings, she goes to bed, with what Mrs. Berry calls "the flutters." When Lucy recovers after a few hours, she and Mrs. Berry have a chat, during which Mrs. Berry, who was kicked and deserted by her husband, narrates her unhappy marital experiences. She tries to encourage Lucy about her coming marriage, for Lucy worries about marrying so young. Mrs. Berry tells her about an Irish lady who married at fourteen, three years younger than Lucy, adding that the Irish lady was a grandmother by thirty. Lucy asks Mrs. Berry if the Irish lady's husband always loved her, and receives the following answer:

"In his way, my dear, he did," said Mrs. Berry, coming upon her matrimonial wisdom. "He couldn't help himself. If he left off, he began again. She was so clever, and did make him so comfortable. Cook! there wasn't such a cook out of an Alderman's kitchen; no indeed. And she a born lady! That tells ye it's the duty of all women! She had her saying—'When the parlour fire gets low, put coals on the kitchen fire!' and a good saying it is to treasure. Such is man! no use in havin' their hearts if ye don't have their stomachs."

Perceiving that she grew abstruse, Mrs. Berry added briskly: "You know nothing about that yet, my dear. Only mind me and mark me: don't neglect your cookery. **Kissing don't last: cookery do!**

A knave's religion is the rottenest thing about him

Source: TIME AND TIDE (Letter VIII)
Author: John Ruskin (1819-1900)
First published: 1867
Type of work: Satirical letters

Context: Ruskin's series of letters, twenty-five of them, were addressed to one Thomas Dixon, a cork-cutter of Sutherland, England. The purpose of the letters which make up *Time and Tide* was to urge the working-people to consider, beyond the right to vote, the reform of laws. The tone of the letters, in which Ruskin's prejudices and usual startling proposals are evident, is a passionate one, making the letters seem much like sermons. Letter VIII is about four possible theories respecting the authority of the Bible. Ruskin begins, however, by stating that the political economy he is trying to teach is founded on *"presumably attainable honesty* in men," while the popular political economy of the times is based on man's supposed regard for himself. Ruskin goes on to ask, rhetorically, what basis there can be for the honesty he believes man can attain. He proceeds to answer the question he has posed:

> . . . my answer is—not in any hesitating or diffident way (and you know, my friend, that whatever people may say of me, I do often speak diffidently; though, when I am diffident of things, I like to avoid speaking of them, if it may be; but here I say with no shadow of doubt)—your honesty is *not* to be based either on religion or policy. Both your religion and policy must be based on *it.* Your honesty must be based, as the sun is, in vacant heaven; poised, as the lights in the firmament, which have rule over the day and over the night. If you ask why you are to be honest—you are, in the question itself, dishonoured. 'Because you are a man,' is the only answer; and therefore I said in a former letter that to make your children *capable of honesty* is the beginning of education. Make them men first, and religious men afterwards, and all will be sound; but **a knave's religion is** always **the rottenest thing about him.**

A knock-down argument

Source: AMPHITRYON (Act I, sc. i)
Author: John Dryden (1631-1700)
First published: 1690
Type of work: Dramatic comedy

Context: For the songs of this comedy, the famous English musician Henry Purcell (1659–1695) composed the music. In the Dedicatory

Epistle, Dryden acknowledged his indebtedness to farces by Plautus and Molière, but the first version was of much earlier Greek origin. Produced at the Theatre Royal, in Drury Lane, in October, 1690, it remained constantly on the boards until Nokes, the original Socia, died in 1696. It has often been revived, as recently as 1922. Mercury and Phoebus open the comedy in Thebes, as they discuss marital complications in Olympus. They are interrupted by the appearance of Jupiter, who demands their assistance. He wants to enjoy Amphitryon's wife, Alcmena, that night, by appearing in the likeness of her husband. He says he will beget a future Hercules to conquer monsters and reform the world. The gods are not impressed. It looks as if Jupiter has set up straw men as an excuse to create someone to knock them down. But at least the pair appreciate Jupiter's honesty.

MERCURY

Ay, brother Phoebus; and our father made all those monsters for Hercules to conquer, and contriv'd all those vices on purpose for him to reform, too, there's the jest on it.

PHOEBUS

Since arbitrary pow'r will hear no reason, 't is wisdom to be silent.

MERCURY

Why, that's the point; this same arbitrary power is **a knockdown argument;** 't is but a word and a blow. Now methinks, our father speaks out like an honest bare-fac'd god, as he is.

Know what thou canst work at

Source: SARTOR RESARTUS (Book II, chapter 7, "The Everlasting No")
Author: Thomas Carlyle (1795-1881)
First published: 1833-1834
Type of work: Philosophical essay

Context: Sartor Resartus, the tailor retailored, is supposedly the life and works of a German scholar, entirely fictional, named Teufelsdröckh. As part of the fiction, Carlyle supposedly edited the contents of six paper sacks, the German's writings, which came into his hands. The quotation above is from the chapter entitled "The Everlasting No," Carlyle's term for a bitter and sweeping rejection of European society and its conventions, to be contrasted with Carlyle's idea of The Everlasting Yea, which is a call to the life of the soul. Carlyle, as the editor for his fictional savant, says that Teufelsdröckh is as great when uttering his nay-saying as at any other point, even so far as this: ". . . perhaps at no era of his life was he more decisively the Servant of God, than even now when doubting his God's

571

existence." While wandering, filled with weariness of the world, Teufelsdröckh suffered. He doubted even the great maxim of Western philosophy, from the lips of Socrates, and echoed by Plato, to "Know thyself." Knocking about the world, viewing the emptiness and hypocrisy of materialism, Teufelsdröckh cannot accept the idealistic philosopher's view. He must change it; he must out of it force some workable command for action, inasmuch as he finds the old command too much to ask of humankind:

. . . "The painfullest feeling," writes he, "is that your own Feebleness (*Unkraft*); ever, as the English Milton says, to be weak is the true misery. And yet of your Strength there is and can be no clear feeling, save by what you have prospered in, by what you have done. Between vague wavering Capability and fixed indubitable Performance, what a difference! A certain inarticulate Self-consciousness dwells dimly in us; which only our Works can render articulate and decisively discernible. Our Works are the mirror wherein the spirit first sees its natural lineaments. Hence, too, the folly of that impossible Precept, *Know Thyself;* till it be translated into this partially possible one, **Know what thou canst work at.**"

Knowledge by suffering entereth

Source: A VISION OF POETS ("Conclusion")
Author: Elizabeth Barrett Browning (1806-1861)
First published: 1844
Type of work: Narrative poem

Context: Written as a dream-vision wherein truth is encountered, this poem is an allegorical account of the making of a poet and of his relation to the world of ordinary men. Dreaming that he is unable to sleep, the poet sees a beautiful lady riding upon a white horse; she says that she has come "to crown all poets to their worth," a declaration that the poet does not at first understand because he thinks that poets are never praised in life. However sceptical he might be, he finally follows the strange lady to three fountains of which he must drink in order to become a true poet: world's use, world's love, and world's cruelty. The last fountain causes him to swoon, but upon waking he discovers that the forest has turned into a church and an angel stands before the altar. Soon he is joined by a procession of true poets, each with a bleeding heart, and listens to the angel who tells about the Poet-God that all poets worship in their verse. Allegorically the dream-vision is a journey through death and suffering to the knowledge of God and the acceptance of the poet's role as seer; the "Conclusion" not only makes such an interpretation clear but also shows the adoration of the true poet after his death and the faith that his surviving son has in his father's vision.

"But *thou*," I murmured to engage
The child's speech farther, "hast an age
Too tender for this orphanage."

"Glory to God—to God!" he saith,
"KNOWLEDGE BY SUFFERING ENTERETH,
AND LIFE IS PERFECTED BY DEATH."

Knowledge enormous makes a God of me

Source: HYPERION (Book III, l. 113)
Author: John Keats (1795-1821)
First published: 1820
Type of work: Narrative poem

Context: The Titans, the elder gods, have been overthrown by Jupiter and his brothers and sisters, the younger gods. Saturn, formerly the king of the world, dethroned and defeated in open war by his own children, lies stupefied upon the earth. He is visited by Thea, wife of Hyperion, who leads him to a dark, wild, rock-strewn region where many of the other defeated Titans lie in the dejection of defeat. Meanwhile, Hyperion, a Titan not deprived of his ancient office of driving the sun across the sky, finishes his day's work and repairs to his golden palace in the heavens. He is disturbed at the thought that he, as well as the other Titans, may be deposed. He plunges through the black night and arrives at the spot where the other Titans lie. After a catalogue of the Titans not unlike the catalogue of the devils in Book II of *Paradise Lost,* there is a conference similar to the one in *Paradise Lost* where the devils plot how to regain heaven (Book II). Saturn asks for suggestions on how they can war against the gods. The first to answer is Oceanus, who says that what has happened is in accordance with nature. The Titans are neither the beginning nor the end: they have brought forth a more beautiful race than themselves, and it is proper for the young to succeed to the rule. Then Clymene tells that she heard a far more beautiful music than any that the Titans could produce. But Enceladus is all for open war and revenge for the blows the new gods have dealt them. While the Titans debate, Apollo is wandering about the earth in sadness when he meets Mnemosyne, or Memory, and begs her to fill him with knowledge, because enormous knowledge makes a god of him:

O tell me, lonely Goddess, by thy harp,
That waileth every morn and eventide,
Tell me why thus I rave, about these groves!
Mute thou remainest—Mute! yet I can read
A wondrous lesson in thy silent face:

573

Knowledge enormous makes a God of me.
Names, deeds, grey legends, dire events, rebellions,
Majesties, sovran voices, agonies,
Creations and destroyings, all at once
Pour into the wide hollows of my brain,
And deify me, as if some blithe wine
Or bright elixir peerless I had drunk,
And so become immortal. . . .

The laboring mountain scarce brings forth a mouse

Source: ARS POETICA (Line 168, as translated by the Earl of Roscommon)
Author: Horace (65–8 B.C.)
First transcribed: c.13–8 B.C.
Type of work: Critical essay in form of a letter

Context: In an epistle in which Piso is addressed, which is actually a critical essay on how to write poetry, Horace cautions against either too great a flourish or dullness, suggesting that the style must suit the subject. He advises against originality, in which the aspiring poet may falter, concluding that the writer is more likely to produce a pleasing work of art by following closely the work of another writer whom he admires, but with a style suited to his art as a beginning poet, hence avoiding a ridiculously ostentatious poem:

Begin not as th'old poetaster did,
"Troy's famous war, and Priam's fate I sing;"
In what will all this ostentation end?
The lab'ring mountain scarce brings forth a mouse. . . .

Lady bountiful

Source: THE BEAUX' STRATAGEM (Act I, sc. i)
Author: George Farquhar (1677?–1707)
First published: 1707
Type of work: Dramatic comedy

Context: Farquhar's play is a romantic comedy, with satirical intent being secondary. In his Prologue for this play, the author says that satire is "the Business of the Stage" during times of strife or when society is corrupted by sloth, but that in his time, the reign of Queen Anne, there is no need for satire except to point out fools, who grow, like weeds, in the best cultivated fields. At the beginning of the play the romance is introduced; two young gentlemen, Aimwell and Archer, are looking for wealthy young women to marry. The two aptly named suitors come to Litchfield in their search for wealth and love, with Archer disguised as

574

Aimwell's servant. They stop at an inn owned by Will Bonniface, who tells them how his wife died because she drank some whiskey instead of their own good ale. In telling about his wife the innkeeper mentions Lady Bountiful, the rich and charitable gentlewoman of the locality, who gives of her time and money to help the sick. When asked by Aimwell to tell more about this good woman, Will Bonniface replies:

BONNIFACE

. . . My **Lady Bountyful** is one of the best of Women: Her last Husband Sir Charles Bountyful left her worth a Thousand Pounds a Year; and I believe she lays out one half on't in charitable Uses for the Good of her Neighbors; she cures Rheumatisms, Ruptures, and broken Shins in Men, Green Sickness, Obstructions, and Fits of the Mother in Women;—The King's-Evil, Chin-Cough, and Chilblains in Children; in short, she has cured more People in and about Litchfield within Ten Years than the Doctors have kill'd in Twenty; and that's a bold Word.

A lady in the case

Source: DON JUAN (Canto V, stanza 19)
Author: George Gordon, Lord Byron (1788–1824)
First published: 1821 (Cantos III–V)
Type of work: Satiric poem

Context: While supposedly writing the epic of Don Juan, Byron uses his vehicle for all sorts of digressions, personal reminiscences, tirades against England, and side-slaps at poets. For instance, in Canto IV, commenting on criticisms against licentiousness in his earlier cantos, he says he will skip over certain episodes and "leave them to the purer pages of Smollett, Prior, Ariosto, Fielding." The poem's slender plot follows the adventures of Don Juan, sent by his bluestocking mother on a tour of Europe following discovery of his affair with one of her young married friends, Donna Julia. Sailing from Cadiz to Italy, Juan's ship is wrecked in a storm. After days in a lifeboat without food or water, the young man is washed ashore almost unconscious. He finds a lovely girl bending over him, Haidée, daughter of the island's ruler, the pirate Lambro. Knowing that her father will sell him as a slave, she hides Juan in a cave. Then when Lambro leaves on an expedition, she brings him to her home, lavishes food on him, loads him with jewels, and as a passionate child of Nature, unacquainted with men, gives herself utterly to him. Though trying to think of Donna Julia, he cannot resist Haidée. Interrupting the story for an apostrophe to Greece and a consideration of fame, along with further insults to the Lake Poets, such as a comment that perhaps Homer sometimes nods, but Wordsworth sometimes awakens, Byron returns to the idyl of Juan and Haidée. It is interrupted by the return of her father, the

575

pirate. He discovers Juan, who is wounded resisting capture. As he is taken aboard ship, Haidée loses her mind in grief at her lover's capture, and in the often quoted line, "Whom the gods love, die young," she leaves the story, and Juan never sees her again or knows that she died giving birth to his child. Juan is shipped off to a slave market along with Circassian beauties, Nubians, and others. Byron ends the fourth canto without telling of Juan's fate, "because the Canto has become too long." After a digression about the poet's "passion for the name of Mary," Byron gets back to the slave market where the youthful Juan and a thirty-year-old Englishman are sold to a eunuch from the sultana's palace. She, wanting Juan for a lover, compels him to dress as a dancing maiden, to conceal his sex from the sultan. In a conversation with the Englishman, Juan learns that the man's first wife died, his second one abandoned him, and he ran away from the third. Seeing Juan's pale and melancholic looks, his friend asks about his experiences. Juan replies that he is not deploring his present lot as a slave, for he has borne hardships "which have the hardiest overworn. . . .

> On the rough deep. But this last blow—" and here
>   He stopp'd again, and turn'd away his face.
> "Ay," quoth his friend, "I thought it would appear
>   That there had been **a lady in the case;**
> And these are things which ask a tender tear,
>   Such as I, too, would shed if in your place;
> I cried upon my first wife's dying day,
> And also when my second ran away."

The land of scholars and the nurse of arms

Source: THE TRAVELLER (Line 356)
Author: Oliver Goldsmith (1728–1774)
First published: 1764
Type of work: Descriptive and meditative poem

Context: The poet addresses his work to his brother, who, although poor, has a happy and contented home life. The poet is a traveler in foreign lands, which he characterizes as to their physical features and the nature of their people, from those living in the arctic to those in the tropics. He discovers that the natives of all lands find their own to be the best. Italy, for instance, is blessed with a benign climate that aids in the production of a profusion of fruits and flowers; but the people, though poor, are too much given to a love of luxury; though submissive, they are vain; though grave, they are trifling; though zealous, they are untrue. They suffer greatly from a realization of departed wealth, which produced a host of architectural monuments that still exist to remind them of their past glories. The Swiss, on the other hand, live in a bleak land with a sufficiency of the

576

necessities of life but no luxuries. The people are good and industrious, but lack the graces. France is a country filled with gay and sprightly people, but they pay too much attention to honor. Their desire for honor leads them into lives of vulgar ostentation. Holland, wrested from the sea, is wealthy, but the people are too likely to stoop to unworthy acts in their desire for gold. The result is a land of tyrants and of slaves. Britain is singu-larly blessed in its climate, and freedom flourishes in the land. The British, however, are too independent and tend to keep themselves apart from others. Because of this tendency there is continual faction, and there is also a general lack of affection; these characteristics may lead to the growth of avarice and the decline of the nation which has for ages been famous for scholarship and military prowess.

> Nor this the worst. As nature's ties decay,
> As duty, love, and honor fail to sway,
> Fictitious bonds, the bonds of wealth and law,
> Still gather strength, and force unwilling awe.
> Hence all obedience bows to these alone,
> And talent sinks, and merit weeps unknown:
> Till time may come, when, stript of all her charms,
> **The land of scholars and the nurse of arms,**
> Where noble stems transmit the patriot flame,
> Where kings have toiled and poets wrote for fame,
> One sink of level avarice shall lie,
> And scholars, soldiers, kings, unhonored die.

Language is fossil poetry

Source: THE POET
Author: Ralph Waldo Emerson (1803–1882)
First published: 1844
Type of work: Moral essay

Context: As a transcendentalist, a philosophical idealist, Emerson believed in an ultimate reality, the Oversoul. As early as 1836, in his essay entitled *Nature,* he gave his theories a form, including his theory of language as symbolism. Words, as he saw them, are more than symbols for specific facts on the present level of existence; he saw them as symbols for symbols, the specific facts in their turn being symbols of transcendental facts, or realities, on a higher level of existence. To the poet, with whom Emerson lodges the responsibility for expression, he gives the opportunity for creating language at both levels. The poet is then the ultimate knower, who helps, by his expression in the medium of language, the rest of mankind to see that the universe is "the externalization of the soul." From this standpoint, of course, the poet is the true scientist, giving the best insight to the ultimate nature of things:

577

By virtue of this science the poet is the Namer, or Language-maker, naming things sometimes after their appearance, sometimes after their essence, and giving to every one its own name and not another's, thereby rejoicing the intellect, which delights in detachments or boundary. The poets made all the words, and therefore language is the archives of history, and, if we must say it, a sort of tomb of the muses. For, though the origin of most of our words is forgotten, each word was at first a stroke of genius, and obtained currency because for the moment it symbolized the world to the first speaker and to the hearer. The etymologist finds the deadest word to have been once a brilliant picture. **Language is fossil poetry.** As the limestone of the continent consists of infinite masses of the shells of animalcules, so language is made up of images or tropes, which now, in their secondary use, have long ceased to remind us of their poetic origin. . . .

The last of all the Romans, fare thee well!

Source: JULIUS CAESAR (Act V, sc. iii, l. 99)
Author: William Shakespeare (1564–1616)
First published: 1623
Type of work: Dramatic tragedy

Context: Brutus, the idealist who would protect the Roman Republic from degenerating into a dictatorship, has joined with Cassius, Casca, and others, who from malice and ill-fed ambition would grasp more power for themselves. As a coalition, they have murdered Julius Caesar and consequently thrown the city into political turmoil. The civil war which has resulted has turned friend against friend and kin against kin. Antony, Octavius, and Lepidus—leaders of the faction which supports the cause of the slain Caesar—gather their forces to do battle with Brutus and his followers on the plains of Philippi. When a parley between the opposing generals produces nothing but mutual recriminations, the battle begins in earnest. Brutus enjoys initial success against Octavius but Cassius' forces are pushed back by Antony, and Cassius, ordering his servant to strike, dies like a Roman. Titinius, following the example of his general, also strikes home with Cassius' sword. Dejectedly observing the scene of self-destruction, Brutus avers that Julius Caesar is mighty yet: "Thy spirit walks abroad, and turns our swords in our own proper entrails." Perhaps anticipating his own moment of self-sacrifice, he pauses to speak a brief eulogy over the bodies of his comrades-in-arms:

Are yet two Romans living such as these?
The last of all the Romans, fare thee well!
It is impossible that ever Rome
Should breed thy fellow. Friends, I owe moe tears
To this dead man than you shall see me pay.

578

I shall find time, Cassius; I shall find time.
Come therefore, and to Thasos send his body.
His funerals shall not be in our camp,
Lest it discomfort us. Lucilius come,
And come young Cato, let us to the field.
Labeo and Flavius, set our battles on.
'Tis three a clock; and Romans, yet ere night
We shall try fortune in a second fight.

The last rose of summer, left blooming alone

Source: IRISH MELODIES ("The Last Rose of Summer," Lines 1–2)
Author: Thomas Moore (1779–1852)
First published: 1808
Type of work: Song

Context: Thomas Moore was an Irish poet of the romantic period who tried to do for Ireland what Burns had done for Scotland; he wrote graceful lyrics for traditional and ancient airs of his country, working on the project for nearly twenty years. The results, published over a period of time (1807–1834), were entitled *Irish Melodies.* In some cases Moore composed tunes as well as lyrics, but most of the airs were of great age. He had a good voice and sang these compositions on occasion. Modern critics are likely to feel that his work is too often superficial and oversentimental, but it nonetheless retains considerable charm. In his day Moore was, next to Byron, the most popular poet in Britain. A close friend of Byron, he produced a good biography of the latter and at times defended Byron's memory from critics. Other popular works by him were *Lalla Rookh* and *The Loves of the Angels,* works exploiting the currently stylish Orientalism. He wrote one novel, *The Epicurean,* a *History of Ireland,* and some light satire. Moore came to be regarded as the national poet of Ireland, and it is for his Irish songs that he is remembered today; many are still popular old favorites. Among the best known of these are "Believe Me, If All Those Endearing Young Charms"; "The Minstrel Boy"; "The Harp That Once Through Tara's Halls"; and "The Last Rose of Summer." The last-mentioned was used by Friedrich von Flotow (1812–1883), German composer, in his most successful and still popular opera, *Martha;* here it is used as a theme song, occurring several times during the course of the work. First performed in 1844, it still holds a place in light opera repertoire. The poem merely expresses its writer's sadness upon realizing that the last rose of the season is blooming and that it will be a year before he will see roses again. He likens it to human existence, hoping he will not remain solitary to exist in a bleak world after all his friends are gone into death.

579

'Tis **the last rose of summer,**
　Left blooming alone;
All her lovely companions
　Are faded and gone;
No flower of her kindred,
　No rose-bud is nigh,
To reflect back her blushes,
　Or give sigh for sigh.

I'll not leave thee, thou lone one!
　To pine on the stem;
Since the lovely are sleeping,
　Go, sleep thou with them.
Thus kindly I scatter
　Thy leaves o'er the bed
Where thy mates of the garden
　Lie scentless and dead.

So soon may *I* follow,
　When friendships decay,
And from Love's shining circle
　The gems drop away.
When true hearts are withered,
　And fond ones are flown,
O who would inhabit
　This bleak world alone?

The lasting mansions of the dead

Source: THE LIBRARY (Line 101)
Author: George Crabbe (1754–1832)
First published: 1781
Type of work: Descriptive poem

Context: In 1780–1781 George Crabbe was poverty-stricken, and publishers refused him any help. In despair he wrote to Edmund Burke, whom he did not know personally. Burke, moved by the poet's plight and his appeal, sent money and a promise of influence. As a result of the great man's help, *The Library* was published, and, urged by his benefactor, Crabbe became an Anglican clergyman and received the post of curate at Aldeburgh, his native town in Suffolk. In this poem he discusses many topics related to a library, such as the consolation to the mind afforded by books, an author's hope of speaking through his writings to posterity, the arrangement of books on the shelves, the mode of publishing in pamphlet form, books on medicine and law, and the apprehensions suffered by authors. The quotation is from his discussion of how writers speak to later generations through their works. The poet says, "Delightful prospect! when we leave behind/ A worthy offspring of the fruitful

580

mind!" He goes on to comment, however, that all books are not noble products; some works are better guides than others. He observes that people come to a library and its books for many reasons. Some come to escape their griefs, others to feed their curiosity and assuage its hunger, and still others to find inspiration. The poet then speaks of his own feelings about a library:

> With awe, around these silent walks I tread;
> These are **the lasting mansions of the dead:**—
> "The dead," methinks a thousand tongues reply;
> "These are the tombs of such as cannot die!
> Crown'd with eternal fame, they sit sublime,
> And laugh at all the little strife of time."

Laugh all honesty out of fashion

Source: THE DUCHESS OF MALFI (Act I, sc. ii, ll. 116–117)
Author: John Webster (1580?–1625?)
First published: 1623
Type of work: Dramatic tragedy

Context: The opening scene of this play, the most famous of the post-Shakespearean "tragedies of blood," is in the Presence Chamber of the Duchess' palace at Malfi. Her steward, Antonio, has just returned from France. Early in the first act (which in the older editions is not divided into scenes but is so divided in more modern texts) he answers the questions of his friend Delio concerning the three principal characters of the drama: the Duke of Calabria; his brother, the Cardinal; and their sister, the Duchess of Malfi. Of the Cardinal, Antonio paints the portrait of a "melancholy churchman," a licentious, indeed, a thoroughly wicked man, who missed attaining the Papal Crown only because he scattered bribes too lavishly. The Duke is even worse. Antonio says of the Cardinal "Some good he hath done—," and then breaks off when Delio demands to be told of the Duke. He begins:

> ANTONIO
> The Duke there? A most perverse and turbulent nature.
> What appears in him mirth is merely outside;
> If he laughs heartily, it is to **laugh**
> **All honesty out of fashion.**

581

The laughing queen that caught the world's great hands

Source: THE NILE (Line 8)
Author: Leigh Hunt (1784–1859)
First published: 1818
Type of work: Sonnet

Context: James Henry Leigh Hunt is remembered today for only a few graceful poems. In his day he was poet, critic, and essayist; a friend of Keats, Shelley, and Byron, he influenced Keats' early work to some extent. Keats later outgrew the influence and evolved along lines of his own. In 1822 Byron and Shelley invited Hunt to Italy to edit a new quarterly called *The Liberal;* Hunt took his family there, and four issues of the quarterly appeared. However, Byron lost interest in the project and there was a quarrel; he abandoned the Hunts, who were left without resources in a foreign land. When Hunt managed to return home, in 1825, he found a huge demand for material on Byron, and contributed *Lord Byron and Some of His Contemporaries.* Hunt did not falsify anything in this work but he did take the opportunity to get even with Byron for numerous humiliations to which the latter had subjected him. To show the less attractive side of a public idol, particularly a recently deceased one, is always unwise: Hunt bitterly regretted his criticism afterward. He was vilified; Thomas Moore likened him to a dog attacking a dead lion. Hunt continued with his literary efforts and wrote voluminously until his death, enjoying a measure of success. A good journalist and a man who loved beauty, he nonetheless lacked the sensibility and taste that characterize the great poets. Among the few of Hunt's poems which are still felt to be of lasting value is *The Nile,* a picture of the ancient dreaming river and its vanished civilization, a glimpse of Cleopatra, and a sense of the steadily flowing stream of time. The sonnet was composed in competition with Keats and Shelley, each poet writing a sonnet on the same subject. In fairness to the now almost forgotten Hunt, it should be said that his sonnet was the best of the three. The sonnet is as follows:

It flows through old hushed Egypt and its sands,
   Like some grave mighty thought threading a dream,
   And times and things, as in that vision, seem
Keeping along it their eternal stands,—
Caves, pillars, pyramids, the shepherd bands
     That roamed through the young world, the glory extreme
   Of high Sesostris, and that southern beam,
The laughing queen that caught the world's great hands.

Then comes a mightier silence, stern and strong,
As of a world left empty of its throng,
   And the void weighs on us; and then we wake,
And hear the fruitful stream lapsing along

Twixt villages, and think how we shall take
Our own calm journey on for human sake.

Laughter is nothing else but sudden glory

Source: TRIPOS ("Human Nature," Chapter 9, sec. XIII)
Author: Thomas Hobbes (1588–1679)
First published: 1640
Type of work: Philosophical essay

Context: Thomas Hobbes was a philosopher and political scientist, whose best known work, *Leviathan,* is an analysis of government; it is a strongly materialistic interpretation of political institutions. To Hobbes, man is by nature equal, and self-seeking; competition is basic to him. Every man is the natural enemy of every other: therefore, governments are formed that order may be ensured. In the process, every individual contracts with all other individuals, each giving up his rights to the governing person or body. This sacrifice is made in order to achieve survival, security, and happiness for each individual. The contract is a mutual one among the governed, not between subject and ruler. Thus, to Hobbes, the right of the state or of the sovereign is absolute. He believes also in the separation of church and state: the laws of God are internal, those of man are external, and the two do not conflict. To resist one's government is to sin against the laws of God, since these are the laws of nature. Hobbes' metaphysics also reflects his materialism; he considers the entire universe matter, and things of the spirit, including God, are also matter but somewhat less substantial. His system is actually one of mechanics or physics. Hobbes also explored psychology, concluding that all so-called voluntary actions have necessary causes and are therefore both involuntary and inevitable. *Tripos* is a group of his three most important works on this subject; each is a discourse on certain areas of human psychology and motivation. The first takes up the nature of man; the second examines law and the body politic; and the third explores the relationship between freedom and necessity. In the first essay, *Human Nature,* Hobbes begins with a discussion of the senses, the reasoning process, and the passions. Laughter, representative of a passion which has no name, is subjected to a penetrating analysis:

. . . Men laugh often, especially such as are greedy of applause from every thing they do well, at their *own* actions performed never so little beyond their own expectations; as also at their own *jests:* and in this case it is manifest, that the passion of laughter proceedeth from a *sudden conception* of some *ability* in himself that laugheth. Also men laugh at the *infirmities* of others, by comparison wherewith their own abilities are set off and illustrated. Also men laugh at *jests,* the *wit* whereof always consisteth in the

583

elegant *discovering* and conveying to our minds some *absurdity* of *another:* and in this case also the passion of laughter proceedeth from the *sudden* imagination of our own odds and eminency: for what is else the recommending of ourselves to our own good opinion, by comparison with another man's infirmity or absurdity? For when a jest is broken upon ourselves, or friends of whose dishonour we participate, we never laugh thereat. I may therefore conclude, that the passion of **laughter is nothing else but <u>sudden glory</u>** arising from some sudden *conception* of some *eminency* in ourselves, by *comparison* with the *infirmity* of others, or with our own formerly: for men laugh at the follies of themselves past, when they come suddenly to remembrance, except they bring with them any present dishonour. It is no wonder therefore that men take heinously to be laughed at or derided, that is, triumphed over. Laughter *without offence,* must be at *absurdities* and infirmities *abstracted* from persons, and when all the company may laugh together. . . .

Law is a bottomless pit

Source: THE HISTORY OF JOHN BULL (Title-page and Chapter VI of Pamphlet I)
Author: John Arburthnot (1667–1735)
First published: 1712
Type of work: Political satire

Context: The title page of the first edition of the first installment of this work, which was issued as five pamphlets, reads: *Law is a Bottomless-Pit, Exemplify'd in the Case of the Lord Strutt, John Bull, Nicholas Frog, and Lewis Baboon, Who Spent all they had in a Law-Suit.* In 1727 the collection of pamphlets was reprinted in Pope and Swift's *Miscellanies in Prose and Verse as Law is a Bottomless Pit, or, The History of John Bull,* and since that time it has been known as *The History of John Bull.* It is popularly attributed to John Arburthnot, but whether Jonathan Swift (1667–1745) had a hand in it, or whether he wrote it, is a matter of debate. The work is a satire on the situation that prevailed after the death of Charles II of Spain in 1700.

Charles left the Spanish monarchy to Philip of Anjou, grandson of Louis XIV of France. England and Holland feared that the combining of the two monarchies in one family would injure their trade and in 1702 declared war on Spain and France. The first four chapters of the work give the characters of the various contestants. Chapter VI tells of the Dutch and English military successes during 1702–1709. The victories, however, cost huge sums of money, which were supplied by borrowings. The allegory of the lawsuit means the military campaign; Hocus is the leader of the Dutch and English armies, the Duke of Marlborough; John Bull is England; Lord Strutt is Philip of Spain. Chapter VI begins as follows:

Law is a bottomless pit, it is a cormorant, a Harpy, that devours everything; John Bull was flattered by his lawyers that his suit would not last above a year or two at most; that before that time he would be in quiet possession of his business; yet ten long years did Hocus steer his cause through all the meanders of the law, and all the courts; no skill, no address, was wanting; and to say truth, John did not starve the cause; there wanted not yellow-boys to fee counsel, hire witnesses, and bribe juries. Lord Strutt was generally cast, never had one verdict in his favor; and John was promised, that the next and the next would be the final determination; but alas! that final determination, and happy conclusion was like an enchanted island, the nearer John came to it, the further it went from him: new trials upon new points still arose; new doubts, new matters to be cleared; in short, lawyers seldom part with so good a cause till they have got the oyster, and their clients the shell.

Laws, like houses, lean on one another

Source: TRACT ON THE POPERY LAWS (Chapter III, part 1)
Author: Edmund Burke (1729–1797)
First published: 1865–1867
Type of work: Political treatise

Context: Although he was born in Ireland, Burke spent his adult life in England as a member of Parliament. However, he never lost interest in Irish affairs, and in his official capacity he defended Ireland as strongly against oppression as he did the American Colonies. Although his thoughts on religious toleration were not in advance of his age, he did regard the domination of the millions of Irish Catholics by the Anglican church as a kind of tyranny. His attack on the discriminatory laws directed against the Catholics was never completed. In his third chapter he pauses to comment on the processes of making and changing laws:

In the making of a new law it is undoubtedly the duty of the legislator to see that no injustice be done even to an individual: for there is then nothing to be unsettled, and the matter is under his hands to mould it as he pleases; and if he finds it untractable in the working, he may abandon it without incurring any new inconvenience. But in the question concerning the repeal of an old one, the work is of more difficulty; because **laws, like houses, lean on one another,** and the operation is delicate, and should be necessary: the objection, in such a case, ought not to arise from the natural infirmity of human institutions, but from substantial faults which contradict the nature and end of law itself,—faults not arising from the imperfection, but from the misapplication and abuse of our reason.

Lead apes in hell

Source: THE TAMING OF THE SHREW (Act II, sc. i, l. 34)
Author: William Shakespeare (1564–1616)
First published: 1623
Type of work: Dramatic comedy

Context: Bianca, gentle younger daughter of the rich gentleman of Padua, Baptista, is being wooed by several suitors, but Katharine, the shrewish elder daughter is shunned by every eligible man. In a room in Baptista's house Katharine, trying to discover the suitor preferred by Bianca, ties her sister's hands and strikes her. Baptista comes to the rescue of his daughter, who truthfully says she has not fallen in love, while the spiteful and jealous Katharine regales her father:

BAPTISTA

Why how now dame, whence grows this insolence?
Bianca stand aside. Poor girl, she weeps.
Go ply thy needle, meddle not with her.
For shame thou hilding of a devilish spirit,
Why dost thou wrong her, that did ne'er wrong thee?
When did she cross thee with a bitter word?

KATHARINE

Her silence flouts me, and I'll be revenged.
                              [*Makes for* BIANCA.]

BAPTISTA [*holds her back*]
What, in my sight? Bianca get thee in.
                              [*Exit* BIANCA.]

KATHARINE

What will you not suffer me? Nay now I see
She is your treasure, she must have a husband;
I must dance barefoot on her wedding-day,
And for your love to her, **lead apes in hell.**
Talk not to me, I will go sit and weep,
Till I can find occasion of revenge.

Lean and slippered pantaloon

Source: AS YOU LIKE IT (Act II, sc. vii, l. 158)
Author: William Shakespeare (1564–1616)
First published: 1623
Type of work: Dramatic comedy

Context: For the sixth of his "seven ages" of man, the "melancholy Jaques" refers to a stock figure of Italian comedy, the Pantaloon, usually an old, lean, gullible dotard, clothed precisely as Shakespeare describes him. Jaques presents his cynical description of the seven ages— the infant, schoolboy, lover, soldier, justice, "pantaloon," and senile dodderer—after his master, the exiled Duke Senior, has pointed out that unhappiness may be found, not only in the Forest of Arden, but in the entire world, the "wide and universal theatre." Jaques replies:

JAQUES
All the world's a stage,
And all the men and women merely players.
They have their exits and their entrances,
And one man in his time plays many parts,
His acts being seven ages.
. . .
The sixth age shifts
Into the **lean and slippered pantaloon**,
With spectacles on nose and pouch on side,
His youthful hose, well saved, a world too wide
For his shrunk shank, and his big manly voice,
Turning again toward childish treble pipes
And whistles in his sound.
. . .

Lean, hungry, savage, anti-everythings

Source: A MODEST REQUEST (Line 98)
Author: Oliver Wendell Holmes (1809–1894)
First published: 1849
Type of work: Occasional verse

Context: Holmes wrote this poem on the occasion of the inauguration of President Everett, of Harvard. It humorously recounts a request that comes by mail for him, the poet, to provide a speech, a song, and a toast —all by himself—for the dinner honoring the new college president; the poem includes the poet's responses to the request, done in Holmes' witty fashion. He describes the speaker, looking very red because he is "so very green," embarrassed by the amount of learning in many studies represented by the men at the banquet tables about him. In mimicry of

587

speeches delivered at such functions as the inaugurations of college presidents, Holmes has his speaker give a prophetic utterance about the future of Harvard, punctuated, as he notes, by "three tremendous cheers." The speaker, looking to a splendid future, declaims:

> My eye prophetic, as the depths unfold,
> Sees a new advent of the age of gold;
> While o'er the scene new generations press,
> New heroes rise the coming time to bless,—
> Not such as Homer's, who, we read in Pope,
> Dined without forks and never heard of soap,—
> Not such as May to Marlborough Chapel brings,
> **Lean, hungry, savage, anti-everythings,**
> Copies of Luther in the pasteboard style,—
> But genuine articles,—the true Carlyle;
> While far on high the blazing orb shall shed
> Its central light on Harvard's holy head,
> And Learning's ensigns ever float unfurled
> Here in the focus of the new-born world!

A leap into the dark

Source: LETTERS FROM THE DEAD TO THE LIVING (Part I, number 2)
Author: Thomas Brown (1663–1704)
First published: 1702
Type of work: Satire

Context: The son of a well-to-do Shropshire farmer, Tom Brown, as he usually signed himself, was educated at Oxford. He learned five foreign languages, but it was for his audacity and wildness, rather than his ability to learn, that he became known. The Dean of Christ College, Dr. John Fell, once called him on the carpet to expel him, but because of the student's apparent contrition, agreed to let him stay if he could translate an epigram from Martial, beginning: "Non amo te, Sabidi." Brown's impromptu translation became famous.

"I do not love thee, Doctor Fell,
  The reason why I cannot tell,
  But this I know, and know full well,

I do not love thee, Doctor Fell."

He was allowed to remain. He and the dean became friends, and upon Dr. Fell's death, in 1686, Brown wrote his epitaph. Leaving Oxford without a degree, Brown became a political pamphleteer, one of the best of the Grub Street hacks, and the first to pretend to disguise his victims by replacing the vowels in their name by dashes, as in, Sir Th-m-s T-pt-n. Later he became the protégé of Charles Sackville, sixth Earl of Dorset. However, fonder of jokes than of friends, Brown estranged the earl and died in poverty at the age of forty-one, his last years spent largely in low taverns. Much of Brown's work comprised translations, but he also wrote

London Amusements (1700) and just before his death published *Letters from the Dead to the Living* (1702), of which he composed only a portion. He revised other entries and translated some from the French. The volume begins with "A Letter of News from Mr. Joseph Haines, of Merry Memory, to his Friends at Will's Coffee House." Haines, who died in 1701, was a versatile person who served as Latin secretary to Sir Joseph Williamson, a seventeenth century British diplomat. Then he became a strolling player for whom Dryden and others wrote plays. He turned Catholic when to do so was

expedient, during the reign of James II. Will's Coffee House, at the corner of Bow and Russell Streets, was a favorite with Dryden and his fellow wits. In his letter, Haines tells of his arrival in Hell, and his new job as astrologer and dancing teacher to the Devil's sister. He asks for news from the upper world. A reply "An Answer to Mr. Joseph Haines, High German Astrologer, at the Sign of the Urinal and Cassiopea's Chair," reports discussions in Parliament about a war with France, and the publication of *The Life of the Famous Comedian Jo Haynes,* of unknown authorship, in 1701.

. . . our Grub Street pamphleteers advise the shires and boroughs what sort of members to choose; the shires and boroughs advise their representatives what course to steer in parliament; and the senators, no doubt on't, will advise his majesty what ministers to rely on, and how to behave himself in this present conjuncture. . . . We forgot to tell you, Mr. Haines, that since you left this upper world, your life has been written by a brother player, who pretends he received all his memoirs from your own mouth, a little before you made **a leap into the dark,** and really you are beholden to the fellow, for he makes you a Master of Arts at the university, tho' you never took a degree there. That and a thousand stories of other people, he has fathered upon you, and the truth on't is, the adventures of thy life, if truly set down, are so romantic, that few besides thy acquaintance would be able to distinguish between the history and the fable.

Learn'd without sense, and venerably dull

Source: THE ROSCIAD (Line 592)
Author: Charles Churchill (1731–1764)
First published: 1761
Type of work: Satirical poem

Context: Deprived of remunerative church appointments by an early marriage, Churchill turned to poetry to support his wife and children. The success of *The Actor,* a poem by Robert Lloyd (1733–1764) that had

been published in 1760, made him decide to turn his many nights in the first row seats in London's theaters into a poem. So he wrote *The Rosciad,* named from the Roman actor Quintus Roscius (126?–62 B.C.), friend of Cicero and regarded as Rome's greatest comic actor. He is mentioned in *Hamlet*. Imitating Pope's *Dunciad* (1728–43), Churchill called his work *The Rosciad*. No publisher would pay him the £20 he asked for it. The best offer was £5, so Churchill published it anonymously at his own expense. He had no need to advertise it. The agonizing cries of the theatrical people attacked made hundreds more troop to the book stores. One reviewer called it a well-written, ill-natured, ingenious, abusive poem. Many were the poets suspected of having been its author, but the second edition that same year, with a rise in price to one-and-six, carried his name to end doubts. The public enjoyed the actors' distress. Too many times, the stage folk had poked fun at audiences! Many said that Churchill's criticisms of the performers were repetitions of those heard in the coffee houses, but they were listened to. Among those attacked, Thomas Davis (1712?–1795) retired from the stage. The poet also handed out praise, especially to Kitty Clive (1711–1785), Jane Pope (1742–1818), Mrs. Pritchard (1711–1769), the great tragic actress Mrs. Cibber (1714–1766), and of course to David Garrick (1717–1779). However, today's readers need an annotated edition of the poem, since many stage people mentioned in its 1090 lines have long been forgotten. The poem starts: "Roscius deceas'd, each high aspiring play'r/ Push'd all his int'rest for the vacant chair." But how to choose the best? In London, says Churchill, the way to succeed on the stage is through bribery. S-T-R opens his house and feeds people; Y-T-S offers laughter and fun; F-TE serves tea. But this time they are to be judged by performance on the stage. They refuse to accept the verdict of any judge. J-HNS-N would be too serious; ST-NE, too gay, and F-KL-N appreciates only his own talent. Finally, Lloyd makes the acceptable suggestion of leaving the decision to Shakespeare and Dr. Johnson. Then begins the procession of the contestants, with description and criticism of each. About one, the poet goes into great detail. Apart from all the rest, comes the great M-RP-Y. This was Arthur Murphy (1727–1805) who played *Othello* at Covent Garden in 1754 and declared the next year that he was unsuited to be an actor. "The Shuffling Trade" is priesthood. About Murphy Churchill comments: "In cold-wrought scenes, the lifeless actor flags./ In passion, tears the passion into rags," then adds:

How few are found with real talents bless'd,
Fewer with Nature's gifts contented rest.
Man from his sphere eccentric starts astray;
All hunt for fame, but most mistake the way.
Bred at ST. OMER'S to the Shuffling trade,
The hopeful youth a Jesuit might have made,
With various readings stor'd his empty skull,
Learn'd without sense, and venerably dull;
Or at some Banker's desk, like many more,
Content to tell that two and two make four,
His name had stood in CITY ANNALS fair,
And PRUDENT DULLNESS mark'd him for a Mayor.

Learning, that cobweb of the brain

Source: HUDIBRAS (Part I, Canto 3, l. 1339)
Author: Samuel Butler (1612–1680)
First published: First and second parts, 1663; third part, 1678
Type of work: Burlesque poem

Context: In satirizing the Presbyterians, Dissenters, and others who under Cromwell, opposed Charles I, to make them appear odious and obnoxious, an English poet combined pictures of contemporaries with quotable lines and much learning. By making one of the characters an enthusiastic Presbyterian Justice with a nose for sin, and the other an ignorant Independent squire, Butler could work unending religious debates into his poem. Indeed, there is more talk than action, and one of the criticisms of the poem is its poverty of incident. Some of the human foibles, too, against which the lively sarcasm is directed, no longer exist. Nevertheless, the style and execution have long been admired. Like *Don Quixote,* after which the poem was modeled, the knight and his squire get the worst of every encounter, though once they do appear successful. In their first sally, they put an end to a gay gathering at a bear baiting and set the fiddler Crowdero into the stocks. But later the vanquished crowd returns, when the crusaders leave the palace of a wealthy Widow, to do battle again. One Amazonian member, Trulla, attacks Hudibras from behind, and he and his squire occupy the stocks instead of Crowdero, to meditate upon their situation. Ralpho, blaming their predicament upon his master's bad conduct, satirizes Sir Hudibras' religion, and that act starts an argument about Synods, neither pertinent nor interesting to modern readers, that lasts 300 lines to the end of the canto. *Hudibras* is not a story to be read in its entirety, but rather to be dipped into. In the religious debate, Ralpho accuses his master of getting his arguments from the Ranters, a sect that denied Heaven and Hell, and insisted that John the Baptist and Christ were impostors, and that people should learn only from God, directly. Ralpho makes an attack on learning until Sir Hudibras stops him with a plea to take it up later. During his attack on the learning that brought them to their present trouble, Ralpho says:

> The self-same cavils then I heard,
> When b'ing in hot dispute about
> This controversy, we fell out;
> And what thou know'st I answer'd then
> Will serve to answer thee agen.
>   Quoth Ralpho, Nothing but th' abuse
> Of human learning you produce,
> **Learning, that cobweb of the brain,**
> Profane, erroneous, and vain;
> A trade of knowledge as replete
> As others are with fraud and cheat; . . .

591

Leave Now for dogs and apes! Man has Forever

Source: A GRAMMARIAN'S FUNERAL (Lines 83–84)
Author: Robert Browning (1812–1889)
First published: 1855
Type of work: Dramatic monologue

Context: In this poem Robert Browning expresses one of his favorite ideas: that man is finest when he strives mightily, no matter what his actual achievements may be. In the poem, a group of disciples are carrying their dead master, a Renaissance grammarian, to his last resting place upon a high mountain at the top of which shines a citadel. The dead master was born with the face of Apollo, but instead of living a life of pleasure and self-gratification, he devoted himself to learning. He wanted to know all that the poets and sages had learned about man, and so he doggedly ground away at his studies. When his disciples first gathered around him, they found him profoundly learned, but they also found him bald and leaden-eyed, with his youthful handsomeness gone. He wanted to eat even the crumbs of intellectual life. He was going to live when he had learned all about life that books could tell him, but not until then. He would learn to live before living, but as there was no end to learning he decided to leave the present moment to the lower animals, who cannot communicate what they learn; man—the race, not the individual—has the ability to communicate, and so he has forever.

> Yea, this in him was the peculiar grace
>> (Hearten our chorus!)
> That before living he'd learn how to live—
>> No end to learning;
> Earn the means first—God surely will contrive
>> Use for our earning.
> Others mistrust and say—"But time escapes!
>> Live now or never!"
> He said, "What's time? **leave Now for dogs and apes!**
> **Man has Forever."**
> Back to his book then: deeper drooped his head;
>> *Calculus* racked him:
> Leaden before, his eyes grew dross of lead:
>> *Tussis* attacked him.

Leave us leisure to be good

Source: HYMN TO ADVERSITY (Line 20)
Author: Thomas Gray (1716–1771)
First published: 1753
Type of work: Pindaric ode

After returning from two years in France and Italy, where he wrote only a few poems in Latin, Gray began in 1742 to write poetry in English. In the spring, he completed "Hymn to Adversity," and in the fall began "An Elegy Wrote in a Country Churchyard," for which he is best known. It was not completed until 1750. His noble friend Horace Walpole issued the "Elegy" in a quarto pamphlet in 1751. Walpole was also responsible for the publication the next year of "Hymn to Adversity," with illustrations by Richard Bentley. The poem bears a motto in Greek from Aeschylus: "It profits to learn discretion through suffering," which is reminiscent of Shakespeare's "Sweet are the uses of adversity," from *As You Like It*. Gray's ambitions in life, he says at its conclusion, are to examine himself, learn about others, and "to feel and know myself as a Man." *Paradise Lost* by Milton seems to be the inspiration of part of this Hymn. Addressing the daughter of Jove, who gives a taste of pain to even the proud and frightens away frivolity and temptation which so involve a man that he has little time to practice goodness, Gray writes in the third stanza:

> Scared at thy frown terrific, fly
>   Self-pleasing Folly's idle brood,
> Wild Laughter, Noise, and thoughtless Joy,
>   And **leave us leisure to be good.**
> Light they disperse, and with them go
>   The summer friend, the flattering foe;
> By vain Prosperity received
> To her they vow the truth, and are again believed.

A leper once he lost and gained a king

Source: PARADISE LOST (Book I, l. 471)
Author: John Milton (1608–1674)
First published: 1667
Type of work: Epic poem

Context: In giving a catalogue of the devils in imitation of Homer's catalogue of the ships in Book II of the *Iliad,* Milton makes a reference to Rimmon's losing a leper; the story is told in II Kings 5: Naaman, a famous Syrian general, is a leper. A little captive maid from the land of Israel who waits on Naaman's wife says that he could be cured of his disease if he would consult the prophet in Samaria. The King of Syria sent a letter to the King of Israel, requesting a cure for Naaman's illness. The king, being powerless to effect a cure, was greatly troubled lest the King of Syria was seeking a quarrel with him, but the prophet Elisha took the matter upon himself. He commanded Naaman to wash seven times in the Jordan; this advice greatly angered Naaman, who said that the rivers of Damascus were superior to the Jordan. He was about to return home, but his servants prevailed upon him to follow Elisha's advice. He did so and was cured, and, as a result, became a believer in the one true God. The reference in the quotation to the gaining of a king concerns Ahaz, King of Judah, who allied himself with Assyria and encompassed the total destruction of the kingdom of Israel. "Grunsel," modern "ground sill," is part of a foundation.

> Next came one
> Who mourned in earnest, when the captive ark
> Maimed his brute image, head and hands lopped off
> In his own temple, on the grunsel edge,
> Where he fell flat, and shamed his worshippers:
> Dagon his name, sea monster, upward man
> And downward fish: yet had his temple high
> Reared in Azotus, dreaded through the coast
> Of Palestine, in Gath and Ascalon,
> And Accaron and Gaza's frontier bounds.
> Him followed Rimmon, whose delightful seat
> Was fair Damascus, on the fertile banks
> Of Abbana and Pharphar, lucid streams.
> He also against the house of God was bold:
> **A leper once he lost and gained a king,**
> Ahaz his sottish conqueror, whom he drew
> God's altar to disparage and displace
> For one of Syrian mode, whereon to burn
> His odious offerings, and adore the gods
> Whom he had vanquished.

Let dogs delight to bark and bite

Source: DIVINE SONGS (XVI)
Author: Isaac Watts (1674–1748)
First published: 1720
Type of work: Didactic poem

Context: Isaac Watts, concerned about the importance of proper moral education for young children and convinced that instruction carried by the vehicle of verse was more easily remembered than prose instruction, wrote *Divine Songs.* In Song XVI, the poet notes that it is the nature of dogs to bark and bite and for bears and lions to growl and fight, but children, he says, should follow the example of the Christ child and be gentle as lambs. The poem begins:

> **Let dogs delight to bark and bite,**
> For God has made them so,
> Let bears and lions growl and fight,
> For 'tis their nature too.

But, children, you should never let
   Such angry passions rise:
Your little hands were never made
   To tear each others' eyes.

Let love through all your actions run,
   And all your words be mild:
Live like the Blessed Virgin's Son,
   That sweet and lowly child.

His soul was gentle as a lamb;
   And, as his stature grew,
He grew in favour both with man
   And God his Father too.

Let Grill be Grill and have his hoggish mind

Source: THE FAERIE QUEENE (Book II, Canto 12, stanza 87)
Author: Edmund Spenser (c. 1552–1599)
First published: 1590
Type of work: Allegorical poem

Context: The theme of temperance is paramount in the Book II of the epic. Guyon, the Knight of Moral Reason, assays to destroy the Bower of Bliss and to overthrow its mistress, Acrasie, who represents Intemperance and who prevents man from attaining his best self. Guyon is guided in his effort by the Palmer, who exemplifies the intellectual virtue of Prudence. Guyon attains the proper balance between his natural, rational soul and his physical actions through theoretical education and physical training at Alma's Castle, the House of Temperance. Having attained this balance, Guyon and the Palmer are able to fight their way through the Bower of Bliss where they find Acrasie with her new lover, Verdant. Casting unbreakable nets over the two, Guyon and the Palmer mercilessly destroy the palace and its garden. There they find men whom Acrasie has turned into wild beasts. The Palmer returns these to their former state. Some are shamed, others angry. Grill, who had been turned into a hog, even berates his saviors for rescuing him. Guyon remarks how quickly this man has forgotten the divine grace which ordains all men to a higher end. The Palmer's answer points out that the saving of all men is not within the power of one man; there are those who will resist all attempts to save them and are best left to their own desires.

Said Guyon, "See the mind of beastly man,
That hath so soone forgot the excellence
Of his creation, when he life began,
That now he chooseth, with vile difference,
To be a beast, and lacke intelligence."

595

To whom the Palmer thus, "The donghill kind
Delights in filth and foule incontinence:
Let <u>Grill</u> be <u>Grill</u>, and have his hoggish mind;
But let us hence depart, whilest wether serves and wind."

Let him not boast who puts his armor on

Source: MORITURI SALUTAMUS (Stanza 9)
Author: Henry Wadsworth Longfellow (1807–1882)
First published: 1875
Type of work: Philosophical poem

Context: Longfellow graduated from Bowdoin College in 1825. In October, 1874, he was urged to write a poem for the fiftieth anniversary of his graduating class, the reunion of which was to take place the following summer. Longfellow felt a strong aversion to writing poems for special occasions, and at first said he could not undertake this one. However, an inspiration evidently came to him; it has been suggested that he may have seen a representation of the painting by Gerome which depicts the Roman gladiators hailing Caesar. At any rate, he not only wrote the poem, but read it for the occasion—a performance he very rarely undertook. The poem begins with a translation of its title: " 'O Caesar, we who are about to die/ Salute you!' was the gladiators' cry/ In the arena, standing face to face/ With death and with the Roman populace." Longfellow then describes the natural beauties of the college and its setting, and adds, "we who are about to die,/ Salute you." The college is the same, but he and his companions are one with the vanished past; they are old and their lives are nearly over; the college, however old it may become, will always be the world of youth. The teachers he and his companions knew are all gone save one, to whom Longfellow pays tribute. He then tells of Dante finding his old teacher among the shades and of Dante's reverence for this man who had instructed him in his youth. "To-day," says Longfellow, "we make the poet's words our own." He then applies them to the teachers he and his companions knew: "Nor to the living only be they said,/ But to the other living called the dead,/ Whose dear, paternal images appear/ Not wrapped in gloom, but robed in sunshine here;/ Whose simple lives, complete and without flaw,/ Were part and parcel of great Nature's law." Finally he addresses another generation which still has most of life before it:

And ye who fill the places we once filled,
And follow in the furrows that we tilled,
Young men, whose generous hearts are beating high,
We who are old, and are about to die,
Salute you; . . .

. . .

596

How beautiful is youth! how bright it gleams
With its illusions, aspirations, dreams!
Book of Beginnings, Story without End,
Each maid a heroine, and each man a friend!
Aladdin's Lamp, and Fortunatus' Purse,
That holds the treasures of the universe!
All possibilities are in its hands,
No danger daunts it, and no foe withstands;
In its sublime audacity of faith,
"Be thou removed!" it to the mountain saith,
And with ambitious feet, secure and proud,
Ascends the ladder leaning on the cloud!

           .   .   .

Let him not boast who puts his armor on
As he who puts it off, the battle done.
Study yourselves; and most of all note well
Wherein kind Nature meant you to excel.
Not every blossom ripens into fruit; . . .

Let joy be unconfined

Source: CHILDE HAROLD'S PILGRIMAGE (Canto III, stanza 22)
Author: George Gordon, Lord Byron (1788–1824)
First published: 1816 (Canto III)
Type of work: Narrative poem

Context: Though the first two cantos of *Childe Harold's Pilgrimage* brought Byron his great fame when published in 1812, it was the third canto, which did not appear until 1816, that is universally considered the finest part of the poem. It begins with words for his daughter Ada, not seen since he angrily left his wife fifteen months after their marriage. Then he ponders the effect of time on his hero who, too proud to be dominated by others, has sought independence in travel. In the course of his wanderings, Harold reaches the battlefield of Waterloo, "the grave of France," where in June, 1815, Wellington ended the power of Napoleon I. Thackeray, too, incorporated the battle into his *Vanity Fair,* but Byron gives it a different twist. He sees the struggle as the effort of enemies of liberty to tear to pieces the eagle of freedom. Though it resulted in the fall of one despot, it gave increased power to many rulers. Napoleon was a composite of mighty ambitions, as well as petty ones, but they were so extreme that they caused the overthrow of a great man. Stanza 21 begins on the eve of the battle, with a well-known line: "There was a sound of revelry by night." It came from the Duchess of Richmond's ball, on the night of the 15th of June. Byron describes the "fair women and brave men" dancing in Brussels, Belgium's capital. Suddenly they hear a cannon shot, "a deep sound strikes like a rising knell." Byron's description of the heedlessness of the gay dancers in the great ballroom and the sudden shock of their realization of the approaching   battle, fills Stanza 22.

> Did ye not hear it?—No; 't was but the wind.
> Or the car rattling o'er the stony street;
> On with the dance! **let joy be unconfined;**
> No sleep till morn, when Youth and Pleasure meet
> To chase the glowing Hours with flying feet—
> But hark!—that heavy sound breaks in once more,
> As if the clouds its echo would repeat;
> And nearer, clearer, deadlier than before!
> Arm! Arm! it is—it is—the cannon's opening roar!

Let them hate, so that they fear

Source: PHILIPPICS (I, 14)
Author: Marcus Tullius Cicero (106–43 B.C.)
First transcribed: 44–43 B.C.
Type of work: Oration

Context: Julius Caesar was assassinated on March 15th, 44 B.C. Three days later the Roman Senate ratified a number of his acts, as presented by Mark Antony, in the interest of public peace and safety. In June of the same year Antony summoned the Senate to the Temple of Concord, where they were held under armed guard, and forced them to ratify a number of apparently fictitious acts of Caesar. Cicero, discouraged by the train of events, left Rome for Greece. He abandoned his trip, however, and returned to Rome on August 31st. The next day, September 1st, Mark Antony attacked Cicero with a speech before the Senate, decrying Cicero's absence. The following day, Cicero went to the Senate to make his reply, which was not only a defense of his own conduct, but an attack on Mark Antony. In this speech, his first *Philippic,* Cicero first tells why he left and why he returned to Rome; he proceeds to protest the honors paid to Julius Caesar's memory, as being impious; he then says he agrees to the ratification of Caesar's acts, but states that mere promises and memoranda are not acts. Most of all, Cicero complains that certain acts of Caesar should not have been ratified because they abrogate positive laws. He then makes an appeal, which is also an attack on Mark Antony and Dolabella, for them to seek real glory, not mere domination of their fellow Romans. In so doing, Cicero uses a line from an old play, Accius' *Atreus,* which is no longer extant; the line, the quotation above, reads in Latin "Oderint, dum metuant."

What I more fear is this—that, blind to glory's true path, you may think it glorious to possess in your single self more power than all, and to be feared by your fellow-citizens. If you think so, you are totally blind to the true way of glory. To be a citizen dear to all, to deserve well of the State, to be praised, courted, loved, is glorious; but to be feared and an object of hatred is invidious, detestable, a proof of weakness and decay. We see this even in the play: the very man who said **"Let them hate, so that they fear,"** found that it was fatal. Would, Marcus Antonius, you had remembered your grandfather! though of him you have heard much from me, and that very often. Do you think that he would have wished to earn immortality by being feared for his ability to keep an armed guard? To him life, to him prosperous fortune, was equality in liberty with the rest, the first place in honour.

Let there be light

Source: GENESIS 1:3
Author: Unknown
First transcribed: c.1000–300 B.C.
Type of work: Religious history and law

Context: The Book of Genesis, first book of the Old Testament, gives the Hebrews' version of the creation of the universe. It describes how God created both heavens and earth, though the earth was at first without form. It was also without light, but God's Spirit moved upon the waters, and then He created light, dividing darkness from light, thus creating night and day. The first chapter of Genesis goes on to describe how the waters of the firmament were divided into the heavens and earth, and then how the dry land was created and, upon it, the vegetation and animal life. The passage is one of the most significant in the Bible historically, for the Hebrews and Christians, until relatively recent times, believed in the description, not as a legend, but as the factual account of how there came about the origin of the universe in which mankind finds itself. The Book of Genesis, one of the books called the Pentateuch, is the first of the Five Books of Moses.

In the beginning God created the heaven and the earth.
And the earth was without form, and void; and darkness was upon the face of the deep. And the Spirit of God moved upon the face of the waters.
And God said, **Let there be light:** and there was light.
And God saw the light, that it was good: and God divided the light from the darkness.
And God called the light Day, and the darkness he called Night. And the evening and the morning were the first day.

599

Let us be moral. Let us contemplate existence

Source: MARTIN CHUZZLEWIT (Chapter 9)
Author: Charles Dickens (1812–1870)
First published: 1843–1844
Type of work: Novel

Context: The Pecksniff family removes to London, where they put up at the boarding house of Mrs. Todgers. After a highly patronizing visit to Tom Pinch's sister, Ruth, by the Pecksniffs, plans are formed at Todgers' to have the Pecksniff family dine with the resident commercial gentlemen on Sunday afternoon. The dinner is a great success, with speeches, songs, toasts, and a great deal of other drinking. After dinner the ladies retire, and the gentlemen continue drinking until it is time to rejoin them. During the ensuing jollity, Mr. Pecksniff, who contends that he has a mysterious chronic condition, collapses into the fireplace. He is dragged out and put to bed; when he calls for one last drink a young gentleman suggests water, the idea of which arouses Mr. Pecksniff's ire. As the guests leave, Mr. Pecksniff appears at the head of the stairs in a shaky condition and addresses the company. The "voice of the sluggard" is a quotation from Isaac Watts, later parodied by Lewis Carroll.

"My friends," cried Mr. Pecksniff, looking over the banisters, "let us improve our minds by mutual inquiry and discussion. **Let us be moral. Let us contemplate existence.** Where is Jinkins?"

"Here," cried that gentleman. "Go to bed again!"

"To bed!" said Mr. Pecksniff. "Bed! 'Tis the voice of the sluggard; I hear him complain; you have woke me too soon; I must slumber again. If any young orphan will repeat the remainder of that simple piece from Dr. Watts's collection, an eligible opportunity now offers."

Nobody volunteered.

"This is very soothing," said Mr. Pecksniff, after a pause. "Extremely so. Cool and refreshing; particularly to the legs! The legs of the human subject, my friends, are a beautiful production. Compare them with wooden legs, and observe the difference between the anatomy of nature and the anatomy of art. Do you know," said Mr. Pecksniff, leaning over the banisters, with an odd recollection of his familiar manner among new pupils at home, "that I should very much like to see Mrs. Todgers' notion of a wooden leg, if perfectly agreeable to herself."

Let us hob-and-nob with Death

Source: THE VISION OF SIN (Line 74)
Author: Alfred, Lord Tennyson (1809–1892)
First published: 1842
Type of work: Allegorical poem

Context: In this dream-vision, Tennyson, who was greatly concerned with the doctrine of art-for-art's-sake, shows that the poet interested only in immorality and thus turning from the true calling of the soul is consumed by his own desire. The poem is presented in two parts and a cryptic summary. The young poet rides into a drunken orgy in a palace where the sensual music finally becomes so frenzied that his ability to sing is killed. Then the vision shifts to a senile debauch in a ruined tavern where self-inflicted misery leads to the desire to die. Both selfish pathways end in emotional frenzy, not happiness or peace. At the end of the poem Tennyson insinuates that the only way to true art and thus to genuine joy is through God; however, this way is often obscure because the voice of God cannot always be clearly understood. The quotation comes from the tavern scene where the old man sings of his search for sensation and his disillusionment.

> Slip-shod waiter, lank and sour,
>   At the Dragon on the heath!
> Let us have a quiet hour,
>   **Let us hob-and-nob with Death.**
>
> I am old, but let me drink;
>   Bring me spices, bring me wine;
> I remember, when I think,
>   That my youth was half divine.

Let us reason together

Source: ISAIAH 1:18
Author: Isaiah
First transcribed: c.800–200 B.C.
Type of work: Religious prophecy and exhortation

Context: Isaiah lived in times that were tragic for Israel; and though he had no difficulty in seeing that his country was about to be overrun, he was powerless to save it. Israel had split into two nations after Solomon's reign, Israel and Judah. These and the other small nations of western Asia were no match for any really strong aggressor that might arise, and they had descended to intriguing and fighting among themselves. Meanwhile Assyria was growing steadily in strength and ambition. Israel and

601

Judah were by this time wealthy countries and tempting prizes, and the people had become indolent and corrupt. The leaders of both countries were unable to see any danger in the Assyrians. When the kings of Israel and of the Aramaeans conspired to plunder Judah, the Judean king called on the Assyrians for help. Invasion followed immediately and as a result both Israel and Judah became Assyrian satellites, doomed to pay heavy tribute thereafter. Assyria had of course been ready for some time to extend its sphere of influence, and its leaders were probably both astonished and delighted when they were given an invitation to attack. Isaiah had seen already the evil that a few greedy and blundering rulers were inviting; now he undoubtedly foresaw that this result was only the beginning of a long and bitter oppression. In terms of reproach that betray his exasperation and his sorrow, Isaiah points out the ruin which all this madness has brought about. He tells his people this is just punishment for allowing themselves to become corrupt and for turning away from God. Now their country is desolate and their cities burnt, and their land is devoured by strangers. "Hear the word of the Lord, ye rulers of Sodom," says Isaiah with bitter sarcasm; "give ear unto the law of our God, ye people of Gomorrah." Then he quotes God's willingness to forgive if they will repent:

To what purpose is the multitude of your sacrifices unto me? saith the Lord: I am full of the burnt offerings of rams, and the fat of fed beasts; and I delight not in the blood of bullocks, or of lambs, or of he goats.

When ye come to appear before me, who hath required this at your hand, to tread my courts?

Bring no more vain oblations; incense is an abomination unto me; the new moons and sabbaths, the calling of assemblies, I cannot away with; it is iniquity, even the solemn meeting.

Your new moons and your appointed feasts my soul hateth: they are a trouble unto me; I am weary to bear them.

And when ye spread forth your hands, I will hide mine eyes from you: yea, when ye make many prayers, I will not hear: your hands are full of blood.

Wash you, make you clean; put away the evil of your doings from before mine eyes; cease to do evil;

Learn to do well; seek judgment, relieve the oppressed, judge the fatherless, plead for the widow.

Come now, and **let us reason together,** saith the Lord: though your sins be as scarlet, they shall be as white as snow; though they be red like crimson, they shall be as wool.

If ye be willing and obedient, ye shall eat the good of the land: . . .

Let's have one other gaudy night

Source: ANTONY AND CLEOPATRA (Act III, sc. xiii, l. 184)
Author: William Shakespeare (1564–1616)
First published: 1623
Type of work: Dramatic tragedy

Context: Mark Antony, co-ruler of the Roman Empire, falls in love with Cleopatra, Queen of Egypt. Through a series of circumstances he ends his friendship with Octavius, his fellow-ruler, and the opposing forces of Octavius and Antony meet at the Battle of Actium, in which Antony is defeated. He is defeated because, at a crucial point in the sea-battle, Cleopatra and her fleet desert him. Antony, who can think only of Cleopatra, leaves the fighting to follow her, thus losing the battle, the empire, and his honor. The lovers meet at Alexandria, some time after the battle, in Cleopatra's palace. At this meeting Antony tells Cleopatra that he knows his whole cause is lost; he says, "Alack, our terrene moon/ Is now eclipsed, and it portends alone/ The fall of Antony." Reassured by Cleopatra that she still loves him, Antony recalls his courage, and resolves to try once more, with his land forces, to seek the defeat of Octavius, after a celebration. Cleopatra, in her reply to him, reveals the selfishness that is part and parcel of her nature. She thinks and speaks, not of Antony and his future, but of the fact that the present day is her birthday. The quotation supplied the title of a famous mystery story by Dorothy Sayers.

ANTONY
I will be treble-sinewed, hearted, breathed,
And fight maliciously; for when mine hours
Were nice and lucky, men did ransom lives
Of me for jests. But now I'll set my teeth,
And send to darkness all that stop me. Come,
Let's have one other gaudy night. Call to me
All my sad captains, fill our bowls once more.
Let's mock the midnight bell.

CLEOPATRA
    It is my birthday.
I had thought t'have held it poor. But since my lord
Is Antony again, I will be Cleopatra.

ANTONY
We will yet do well.

603

Letting I dare not wait upon I would

Source: MACBETH (Act I, sc. vii, l. 44)
Author: William Shakespeare (1564–1616)
First published: 1623
Type of work: Dramatic tragedy

Context: Macbeth, destined to become King of Scotland according to the prophecy of three witches, wavers in his determination to usurp the throne by murdering King Duncan, his liege, his cousin, and his guest for the night. Lady Macbeth chides her husband for his cowardice, comparing him to the cat, in an adage of Heywood, which would like to eat fish, but does not want to get his feet wet.

MACBETH
We will proceed no further in this business.
He hath honoured me of late, and I have bought
Golden opinions from all sorts of people,
Which would be worn now in their newest gloss,
Not cast aside so soon. . . .

LADY MACBETH
. . . Wouldst thou have that
Which thou esteem'st the ornament of life,
And live a coward in thine own esteem,
Letting I dare not wait upon I would,
Like the poor cat i' th' adage?

Letting the rank tongue blossom into speech

Source: CALIBAN UPON SETEBOS (Line 23)
Author: Robert Browning (1812–1889)
First published: 1864
Type of work: Dramatic monologue

Context: Caliban—a subhuman monster, half man, half beast—is the unwilling servant of the magician Prospero and his daughter, Miranda. (Shakespeare: *The Tempest*) We hear Caliban speaking literally and morally from the bottom of a swamp as he muses on the nature of Setebos, the god of his witch-mother, Sycorax. He identifies Setebos with the aching unpleasantness of cold and therefore believes that it is safer to talk about him in the summer's warmth and safety. The key to Caliban's interpretation is found in the motto that prefixes the poem: "Thou thoughtest that I was altogether such an one as thyself." Thus Caliban attempts to deduce the character of God from the evidence he sees in nature around him and creates a god made in his own image. Caliban believes that Setebos made the world out of spite, envy, listlessness, or sport. Man can only hope that Setebos will tire of this world and ignore it or that Setebos will evolve into a more beneficent god. The opening lines of the poem describe the physical setting and begin Caliban's philosophical musings:

He looks out o'er yon sea. . . .

. . .

And talks to his own self, howe'er he please,
Touching that other, whom his dam called God.
Because to talk about Him, vexes—ha,
Could He but know! and time to vex is now,
When talk is safer than in winter time.
Moreover Prospero and Miranda sleep
In confidence he drudges at their task;
And it is good to cheat the pair, and gibe,
Letting the rank tongue blossom into speech.

Setebos, Setebos, Setebos!
'Thinketh He dwelleth i' the cold o' the moon.

Liberty consists in doing what one desires

Source: ON LIBERTY (Chapter 5, "Applications")
Author: John Stuart Mill (1806–1873)
First published: 1859
Type of work: Philosophical essay

Context: John Stuart Mill bases the fifth chapter of his essay on liberty on two maxims: the first is that the individual is not accountable to society for those of his actions which concern only himself, and the second is that the individual is accountable to society for those actions which are prejudicial to others, indeed may for those actions be subjected to legal or social punishments. Mill applies these maxims to the concept of free trade, pointing out that restrictions on trade at least endanger, if not destroy, the liberty of the buyer. Any such infringement, or its danger, seems to Mill objectionable. The sale of poisons, he suggests, is an example of how the limits of police powers and the limits of liberty may be open to question. In his discussion he states that while it is the function of government to prevent crime, this preventive action is liable to abuse by officials. He goes on to say that it is a function of public authority to prevent accidents, and it is here that his definition of liberty occurs:

. . . it is a proper office of public authority to guard against accidents. If either a public officer or any one else saw a person attempting to cross a bridge which had been ascertained to be unsafe, and there were no time to warn him of his danger, they might seize him and turn him back without any real infringement of his liberty; for **liberty consists in doing what one desires,** and he does not desire to fall into the river. Nevertheless, when there is not a certainty, but only a danger of mischief, no one but the person himself can judge of the sufficiency of the motive which may prompt him to incur the risk; in this case, therefore, (unless he is a child, or delirious, or in some state of excitement or absorption incompatible with the full use of the reflecting faculty,) he ought, I conceive, to be only warned of the danger; not forcibly prevented from exposing himself to it. . . .

Liberty must be limited in order to be possessed

Source: LETTER TO THE SHERIFFS OF BRISTOL
Author: Edmund Burke (1729–1797)
First published: 1777
Type of work: Political treatise

Context: Edmund Burke wrote to the sheriffs of Bristol, as their representative in the House of Commons, to relate to them some recent acts of the British Parliament and his reasons for not supporting those acts. Burke was a conservative, but he was also a man who thought that human beings come before abstract principles. He earnestly believed that the British government was, for reasons which could not be defended, mistreating the American colonists. He points out in this letter that the colonists want a free government according to their definition. Burke states, in discussing civil freedom, that liberty "is a blessing and a benefit, not an abstract speculation." He goes on to give his opinion that liberty, like all else in life, is unlike a proposition in geometry or metaphysics; that in life we find not simply right and wrong, but many degrees and shades of events. He continues to comment specifically on the nature of liberty and how it can be enjoyed:

. . . The *extreme* of liberty (which is its abstract perfection, but its real fault) obtains nowhere, nor ought to obtain anywhere. Because extremes, as we all know, in every point which relates either to our duties or satisfactions in life are destructive both to virtue and enjoyment. **Liberty, too, must be limited in order to be possessed.** The degree of restraint it is impossible in any case to settle precisely. But it ought to be the constant aim of every wise public council to find out by cautious experiments and rational cool endeavours with how little, not how much, of this restraint the community can subsist. For liberty is a good to be improved, and not an evil to be lessened. It is not only a private blessing of the first order, but the vital spring and energy of the state itself, which has just so much life and vigour as there is liberty in it. . . .

606

Liberty passes into the harshest and bitterest form of slavery

Source: THE REPUBLIC (Book VIII, 569, as translated by Benjamin Jowett)
Author: Plato (427–347 B.C.)
First transcribed: Fourth century B.C.
Type of work: Political philosophy

Context: Plato, Greek philosopher, a disciple of Socrates and teacher of Aristotle, wrote in the form of dialogues in which Socrates through interrogation leads others to perceive the truth. Probably his greatest work, *The Republic* describes the workings of an imaginary ideal state. This first Utopia was based on justice and a division of labor whereby each class in society happily performed the functions and duties for which it was best suited. Under such a system the philosopher ruled, the soldier fought, the worker tended the field—and all enjoyed the fruits of their common labor. Plato's proposal of communism was not based on the assumption that equality *per se* was the highest good, but that only this form of government could insulate man from the temptations and distractions which more extensive public power inevitably generates. Thus, in Book VIII, Socrates, Glaucon, and Adeimantus consider the various features of timocracy, oligarchy, democracy, and tyranny or despotism. In a democracy three classes emerge: the drones or spendthrifts, the orderly or wealthy, and the workers. The desire of the worker to gain the wealth and status of the orderly leads him to raise a protector who, once he has tasted blood, is converted into a tyrant. As long as the tyrant is able to live off the spoils of his rebellion, he rules with tolerance; but, when necessary, he exploits the very parents (the people) who fostered him:

By heaven, he said, then the parent will discover what a monster he has been fostering in his bosom; and, when he wants to drive him out, he will find that he is weak and his son strong. . . . Then he is a parricide, and a cruel guardian of an aged parent; and this is real tyranny, about which there can be no longer a mistake: as the saying is, the people who would escape the smoke which is the slavery of freemen, have fallen into the fire which is the tyranny of slaves. Thus **liberty,** getting out of all order and reason, **passes into the harshest and bitterest form of slavery.**

Liberty's a glorious feast!

Source: THE JOLLY BEGGARS (Line 299)
Author: Robert Burns (1759–1796)
First published: 1799
Type of work: Cantata

Context: Gossip did its best to obscure the facts of Burns' life. He was

607

falsely described as a debauched drunkard, chiefly by enemies who fought his strong republicanism by slandering him as a man. There is truth in the accusation that he drank a great deal, but drink was a vice of his time, which he developed while being lionized by high society. *The Jolly Beggars,* devoted to the celebration of drinking, takes the form of a cantata, and was started about 1785. This zestful pagan work is at times serious, at times satirical. So little interest did the author have in it that he did not believe it worth publication. In 1793, his friend George Thomson, editor of a six-volume *Select Collection of Scottish Airs for the Voice* (1793–1811), who had heard it mentioned, wrote to Burns for a copy. Burns replied that he had forgotten it and doubted whether a copy existed. However, Thomson tracked it down and it was published in Glasgow in 1799, after Burns' death. It had its inception following a visit by Burns and his friend James Smith to the Change House of Poosie Nansie's in Mauchline, a favorite haunt of vagrants. The cantata begins with the description of the gang of loafers drinking in the tavern. Popular tunes of the day provided the music. One man nearest the fire is a soldier in a ragged red uniform, sitting with his sweetheart. He sings to her a stanza beginning: "I am a son of Mars," and boasting of fighting in Quebec, Cuba, and in Gibraltar where he lost his leg and arm. A Recitativo introduces his doxy, who comments on her love life and her final decision to love the "sodger laddie." Next a Merry Andrew tells of his experiences as a clown, and is followed by a "raucle carlin" (brave old woman), a traveling violinist, a tinker, and finally a poet. If, as the legend goes, this poem is based on an actual experience, the poet may represent Burns himself. Begged for a ballad, he sings stanzas for which the crowd provides the chorus. The tune used was *Jolly Mortals, fill your glasses.*

See! the smoking bowl before us,
   Mark our jovial, ragged ring;
Round and round take up the chorus,
   And in raptures let us sing:

CHORUS
A fig for those by law protected!
   Liberty's a glorious feast!
Courts for cowards were erected,
   Churches built to please the priest!

What is title? what is treasure?
   What is reputation's care?
If we lead a life of pleasure,
   'Tis no matter, how or where.
         •   •   •

Here's to budgets, bags, and wallets!
Here's to all the wandering train!

608

License they mean when they cry liberty

Source: SONNET XII ("On the Same," Line 11)
Author: John Milton (1608–1674)
First published: 1673
Type of work: Sonnet

Context: Milton, the great poet and Puritan pamphleteer, wrote four tracts in which he argued in favor of a rational attitude toward divorce and the admission of incompatibility as a basis for it. Although he was an important Puritan spokesman, Milton's views on divorce were widely misinterpreted, and on one occasion a Puritan clergyman denounced them in a sermon to Parliament. In this sonnet, concerned with the public reaction to his views, Milton protests that he only advocates the sanity and reasonableness of the classical virtues and that he has been grossly misunderstood, likening his detractors to those rustics of Greek mythology who jeered at the goddess Latona, refusing to allow her to drink from their fountain, and were turned into frogs for their rudeness. He says:

> I did but prompt the age to quit their cloggs
>   By the known rules of antient libertie,
>   When strait a barbarous noise environs me
>   Of Owles and Cuckoes, Asses, Apes and Doggs.
> As when those Hinds that were transform'd to Froggs
>   Raild at Latona's twin-born progenie
>   Which after held the Sun and Moon in fee.
>   But this is got by casting Pearl to Hoggs;
> That bawle for freedom in their senceless mood,
>   And still revolt when truth would set them free.
>   **Licence they mean when they cry libertie;**
> For who loves that, must first be wise and good;
>   But from that mark how far they roave we see
>   For all this wast of wealth, and loss of blood.

Lick the dust

Source: PSALMS 72:9
Author: Unknown
First transcribed: c. 400–200 B.C.
Type of work: Religious poetry

Context: Psalm 72 is a prayer for Solomon, composed in the early days of that monarch's reign. It is the last in a series of Psalms attributed to David, and in it the poet prays for an enlightened, peaceful, and prosperous reign. He begins by asking for righteousness and judgment on the part of the king, and for attention to the needs of the poor. The reign of Solomon, he believes, will usher in a period of great prosperity; nature will

609

flourish and the fields and mountains will be productive. Again he expresses the hope that this king will have compassion upon the poor and that he will protect his people. It has always been customary for poets to praise new rulers and at the same time to mention those standards which they hope the rulers will uphold: any new ruler is to some extent an unknown quantity. But in this case many of the poet's predictions are accurate, for under Solomon the children of Israel will at last become a nation demanding respect from the nations around it. This king, says the poet, will be a strong ruler, destructive to oppressors; there will be a long period of greatness; his coming will be as welcome as the rain. Rain in a parched land is the greatest of blessings. Solomon, says the poet, will rule the known world and his enemies will humble themselves before him; other nations will pay him tribute. Once again the poet expresses the hope that Solomon will show consideration for the poor, who will repay it by praying for him and giving him everlasting fame. The psalm ends with a moving declaration of faith and optimism.

Give the king thy judgments, O God, and thy righteousness unto the king's son.

He shall judge thy people with righteousness, and thy poor with judgment.

The mountains shall bring peace to the people, and the little hills, by righteousness.

He shall judge the poor of the people, he shall save the children of the needy, and shall break in pieces the oppressor.

They shall fear thee as long as the sun and moon endure, throughout all generations.

He shall come down like rain upon the mown grass: as showers that water the earth.

In his days shall the righteous flourish; and abundance of peace so long as the moon endureth.

He shall have dominion also from sea to sea, and from the river unto the ends of the earth.

They that dwell in the wilderness shall bow before him; and his enemies shall **lick the dust.**

The kings of Tarshish and of the isles shall bring presents: the kings of Sheba and Seba shall offer gifts.

Yea, all kings shall fall down before him: all nations shall serve him.

The lie that flatters I abhor the most

Source: TABLE TALK (Line 88)
Author: William Cowper (1731–1800)
First published: 1782
Type of work: Essay in verse

Context: In publishing his first collection of poetry, Cowper decided to
lead off with the poem "Table Talk,"
because "it will repel the ordinary
reader less than any of the others."
He realized that his purpose in writing, to obtain "a monitor's though not
a poet's praise" would result in somewhat dull verse. Yet he wrote satires
of admonition and sermons in verse,
"with a hope to do good." Though
"Table Talk" is a dialogue, there
seems to be little attempt to differen-
tiate between the two speakers, A and
B, and considerable difficulty in discovering the various subjects of their
discussion. As far as can be discerned, the main theme is the need of
character and integrity in public servants. Beginning with the premise that
only the glory built on unselfish principles is admirable, the two speakers
agree in admiration of wars fought
for justice. This opinion leads to a
discussion of the qualities of an ideal
king, and what results is obviously a
portrait of George III, in which the
poet insists that he is speaking sincerely with no purpose of flattery.
"The patriotic tribe" uses the word in
its eighteenth century political meaning, as Johnson did when saying:
"Patriotism is the last refuge of a
scoundrel." A patriot was one who
upheld the nation, and was opposed
to the king or the court. The following is the way B describes the qualities of King George III:

B. His life a lesson to the land he sways;
To touch the sword with conscientious awe,
Nor draw it but when duty bids him draw;
To sheath it in the peace-restoring close,
With joy beyond what victory bestows—
Blest country, when these kingly glories shine,
Blest England, if this happiness be thine!
A. Guard what you say: the patriotic tribe
Will sneer and charge you with a bribe. *B*. A bribe?
The worth of his three kingdoms I defy
To lure me to the baseness of a lie.
And of all lies (be that one poet's boast),
The lie that flatters I abhore the most.
Those arts be theirs who hate his gentle reign,
But he that loves him has no need to feign.

Life is an incurable disease

Source: PINDARIC ODES ("To Dr. Scarborough," Stanza VI)
Author: Abraham Cowley (1618–1677)
First published: 1656
Type of work: Pindaric ode

Context: Abraham Cowley was a
precocious man: his first volume of
poems was published when he was fifteen. He was given a good education
and had received a Cambridge fellowship when he was dispossessed by
the Puritan commissioners and left on
his own resources. Following his roy-

alist friends to Oxford, he entered the service of the king. He then followed the dispossessed Charles II to France. Cowley, however, had the misfortune to be born into a violent era that he could not cope with; he was a mild and unenthusiastic man, and his nature often placed him in dangerous or ridiculous situations. He was assigned to various secret service activities for which he seems to have been utterly unqualified: Charles II suspected him of treason, and Cromwell put him in prison as a spy. He finally retired to a quiet life in the country, where he studied medicine and botany. At the same time he continued to write poetry and essays. He is again unfortunate in that his unfinished Biblical epic *Davideis* is a failure compared to the *Paradise Lost* of John Milton; and his lyrical poems, inspired by Donne, suffer by comparison with the latter's work. Not a true metaphysical poet, Cowley enjoys intricate metaphors and plays on words; he is sometimes quietly witty and exhibits a cheerful pessimism. In 1656 he published his fifteen *Pindaric Odes.* These established his reputation and exerted a considerable influence for a time. The form he developed retains rhyme but in many ways resembles free verse; it does not actually employ the structure of Pindar's work but is strongly reminiscent of it and is rather impressive. The form enjoyed great popularity for many years, especially for ceremonials and dedications. One of Cowley's "pseudo-Pindaric" odes, honoring Dr. Charles Scarborough, provides a memorable tribute. The closing portion is given below:

And this great race of learning thou hast run,
   Ere that of life be half yet done;
   Thou see'st thyself still fresh and strong,
   And like t' enjoy the conquests long.
The first fam'd aphorism thy great master spoke,
   Did he live now he would revoke,
   And better things of man report;
For thou dost make life long, and art but short.

Ah, learned friend! it grieves me, when I think
   That thou with all thy art must die,
   As certainly as I;
And all thy noble reparations sink
Into the sure-wrought mine of treacherous mortality.
Like Archimedes, honourably in vain,
Thou hold'st out towns that must at last be ta'en,
And thou thyself, their great defender, slain.
Let's e'en compound, and for the present live,
'Tis all the ready-money Fate can give;
   Unbend sometimes thy restless care,
   And let thy friends so happy be
   T' enjoy at once their health and thee:
Some hours, at least, to thine own pleasures spare:
Since the whole stock may soon exhausted be,

Bestow 't not all in charity.
Let Nature and let Art do what they please,
When all 's done, **life's an incurable disease.**

Life is too short for chess

Source: OUR BOYS (Act I)
Author: Henry James Byron (1834–1884)
First published: 1880
Type of work: Dramatic comedy

Context: Byron, an enormously prolific writer for the British theater, turned out innumerable comedies, farces, and burlesques. One chronological list of his works includes 136 titles. Probably the most popular was the three-act comedy, *Our Boys,* that opened in London on January 16th, 1875, and had an unequaled continuous run, according to the first printed edition, of 1,500 nights. With other works by Byron, it was reprinted among the 165 volumes of Lacy's *Acting Editions of Plays, Dramas, Extravaganzas, etc.* as No. 116 (1880), and by Samuel French in England and the United States. For Baker, in 1915, Frank E. Fowle edited "An Acting Copy, containing all the Gags and Stage Business employed by Professional Actors." Surprisingly, the comedy has few sympathetic characters. Sir Geoffrey Champney is father of washed-out Talbot with yellowish-red hair, for whom he dreams of a career in Parliament. Uncouth Perkyn Middlewick, a retired "butter man," with ridiculous language and a belief that money not only makes the mare go, but activates a whole stable, has a handsomer son, Charley. The two young men are bracketed by Sir Geoffrey as "Our Boys," As the comedy opens, the two fathers are await-

ing the return of their sons from a European trip in which only Charley profited. There he meets the heiress Violet Melrose to whom he identifies himself as Mr. Morton. Her penniless cousin, Mary, traveling with her, is attracted by the unattractiveness of Talbot Champney. Sir Geoffrey can scarcely conceal his disapproval of the coarse Middlewick. His sister, Aunt Clarissa, has a kinder attitude, but she is thinking chiefly of the break in the monotony of the manor offered by Talbot's homecoming. Events disappoint her. Complaining that his father would not let him have his fling abroad, like Charley, he scorns an evening of backgammon or chess at home with his aunt. After his taste of life in Paris, he looks forward to the delights of London. Violet and her cousin appear. Violet is angry that Charles lied about his name, and is further disillusioned by a look at her possible father-in-law. To Sir Geoffrey's delight, Mr. Middlewick is no less scornful of "that rich stuck up gal," for Sir Geoffrey anticipates Violet's marriage to Talbot to provide funds for the young man's political career. The second act contains the scene where Sir Geoffrey invites Mr. Middlewick to a game of billiards. He trounces the inexperienced country merchant, whose skill runs to bowl-

613

ing. Middlewick threatens: "He's up to these grand games, but one of these days I'll *loore* him on to *skittles* and astonish him." In the final act, "Our Boys" have left their parents to live in poverty in the big city, but the plotting of Aunt Clarissa and the change of heart of the fathers achieve a happy ending for the young people. Part of the homecoming in Act I includes a scene between Clarissa and Talbot.

AUNT CLARISSA
Talbot, it is so delightful to have you back again. I shall now have such charming evenings with you at chess.

TALBOT
At what?

AUNT CLARISSA
Chess—the king of games.

TALBOT
Do you call that a game? Ha! ha! No, thanks; **life's too short for chess.**

AUNT CLARISSA
Well, well, we'll say backgammon.

TALBOT
I don't mind saying backgammon, but you don't catch me playing backgammon.

AUNT CLARISSA
Well, then, we must even continue our usual cosy evenings. I do my wool work whilst your father reads us the debates. That's our regular evening's program.

TALBOT (*aside*)
They must have had a rollicking time of it. The debates! a dozen columns of dullness filtered through father. Not for Talbot!

The life of man, solitary, poor, nasty, brutish, and short

Source: LEVIATHAN (Part I, chapter 13)
Author: Thomas Hobbes (1588–1679)
First published: 1651
Type of work: Philosophy

Context: When men are not kept in awe by a common power, says English philosopher Thomas Hobbes, a time of war exists for one of three common causes: competition, diffidence, or glory. Describing the condi-

tions during a time of war, he continues:

> Whatsoever therefore is consequent to a time of war, where every man is enemy to every man, the same is consequent to the time wherein men live without other security than what their own strength and their own invention shall furnish them withal. In such condition there is no place for industry, because the fruit thereof is uncertain: and consequently no culture of the earth; no navigation, nor use of the commodities that may be imported by sea; no commodious building; no instruments of moving and removing such things as require much force; no knowledge of the face of the earth; no account of time; no arts; no letters; no society; and which is worst of all, continual fear, and danger of violent death; and **the life of man, solitary, poor, nasty, brutish, and short.**

Life's but a walking shadow

Source: MACBETH (Act V, sc. v, l. 24)
Author: William Shakespeare (1564–1616)
First published: 1623
Type of work: Dramatic tragedy

Context: Macbeth, destined to become King of Scotland according to the prophecy he receives from three witches and urged on by his wife in his ambition to obtain the crown, murders King Duncan and seizes the throne. Insecure in his tenure of power, Macbeth commits additional murders. Lady Macbeth, strong in ambition at first, becomes weak from worry over the foul deeds committed by the pair and finally suffers a complete mental and physical collapse, and dies. Macbeth receives word of her death while he watches the advance of an English army commanded by Malcolm, son of the murdered King Duncan. In a well-known speech Macbeth comments on the brevity and futility of life as he sorrows for his dead queen:

MACBETH
. . .

To-morrow, and to-morrow, and to-morrow,
Creeps in this petty pace from day to day,
To the last syllable of recorded time;
And all our yesterdays have lighted fools
The way to a dusty death. Out, out, brief candle!
Life's but a walking shadow, a poor player,
That struts and frets his hour upon the stage,
And then is heard no more. It is a tale
Told by an idiot, full of sound and fury
Signifying nothing.

Light thickens, and the crow makes wing

Source: MACBETH (Act III, sc. ii, ll. 50–51)
Author: William Shakespeare (1564–1616)
First published: 1623
Type of work: Dramatic tragedy

Context: Macbeth, told by three witches that he shall become king, and driven by a wicked ambition, slays King Duncan and usurps the throne. One evil act leads to another as Macbeth plans the murder of Banquo and his son Fleance to foil the decree of the witches that the heirs of Banquo shall be kings. As evening approaches and the time draws near for his hired assassins to kill Banquo and Fleance, Macbeth notes the atmosphere of evil in the night, and says to Lady Macbeth:

MACBETH

. . .

. . . **Light thickens, and the crow**
Makes wing to th' rooky wood.
Good things of day begin to droop and drowse,
Whiles night's black agents to their preys do rouse.
Thou marvel'st at my words; but hold thee still,
Things bad begun make strong themselves by ill.
So prithee go with me.

[*Exeunt.*]

A light to lighten the Gentiles

Source: LUKE 2:32
Author: Unknown
First transcribed: c. 80–100
Type of work: Gospel

Context: Scholars are not agreed upon the authorship of this gospel. Though it is evident that Luke and Acts were both written by the same person, there is some doubt that he is actually the physician Luke, friend and companion of the Apostle Paul. Some have found internal evidence, in the form of terminology a medical man would have been likely to use, which lends support to the traditional attribution. In Chapter 1 the author comments upon the large number of people who are writing gospels, and makes it clear that he has been careful to obtain much of his own material from eyewitnesses and others who actually took part in the great drama of Christ's ministry. "Theophilus," to whom he dedicates this book, may have been a Roman official sympathetic to Christianity. Chapter 1 is largely introductory, covering those events which led up to the birth of Jesus. In Chapter 2 he gives what has become the most popular and familiar account of the Nativity, telling it with great tenderness and beauty. Luke's version is that which most frequently forms a part of the celebration of Christmas. When Jesus is eight days of age he is circumcised and is named according to instructions given Mary by the angel of the Lord. After Mary's days of purification according to the law are ended, Jesus is taken to Jerusalem that he may be presented to the Lord in the Temple, and that a sacrifice may be offered. This sacrifice is made according to holy law, and consists of a pair of turtle-doves or young pigeons. While Jesus and his parents are in the Temple, two persons who are inspired with prophecy enter and foretell something of the consolation that this child will bring to his people, and to the other nations of the world. The first of these is Simeon, an old man; the second is Anna, who confirms his words.

And behold, there was a man in Jerusalem, whose name was Simeon; and the same man was just and devout, waiting for the consolation of Israel: and the Holy Ghost was upon him.

And it was revealed unto him by the Holy Ghost, that he should not see death, before he had seen the Lord's Christ.

And he came by the Spirit into the temple: and when the parents brought in the child Jesus, to do for him after the custom of the law,

Then took he him up in his arms, and blessed God, and said,

Lord, now lettest thou thy servant depart in peace, according to thy word:

For mine eyes have seen thy salvation,

Which thou hast prepared before the face of all people;

A light to lighten the Gentiles, and the glory of thy people Israel.

And Joseph and his mother marvelled at those things which were spoken of him.

And Simeon blessed them. and said unto Mary his mother, Behold, this child is set for the fall and rising again of many in Israel; and for a sign which shall be spoken against;

(Yea, a sword shall pierce through thy own soul also,) that the thoughts of many hearts may be revealed.

A light wife doth make a heavy husband

Source: THE MERCHANT OF VENICE (Act V, sc. i, l. 130)
Author: William Shakespeare (1564–1616)
First published: 1600
Type of work: Dramatic comedy

Context: In the early action of the play Antonio, the merchant, borrows money from Shylock, the usurious Jew, in order to save his friend Bassanio, whose ships are long overdue and feared lost. Shylock, pretending a jest, persuades Antonio to pledge the pound of flesh nearest his heart as surety for the loan. Antonio's investments also seem to fail, and Shylock brings his claim to court in order to collect his pound of flesh. At the trial Antonio is saved by a brilliant young lawyer who is, unknown to the men, the girl both have wooed and Bassanio has won, Portia, in disguise. After the trial Portia hurries home, where she meets Lorenzo and Jessica and swears them to secrecy concerning her part in the trial. Bassanio, Antonio, and several of their friends follow close behind:

LORENZO
Your husband is at hand, I hear his trumpet.
We are no tell-tales madam, fear you not.

PORTIA
This night methinks is but the daylight sick;
It looks a little paler: 'tis a day,
Such as the day is when the sun is hid.
     Enter BASSANIO, ANTONIO, GRATIANO, *and* SERVANTS.

BASSANIO
We should hold day with the Antipodes,
If you would walk in absence of the sun.

PORTIA
Let me give light, but let me not be light;
For **a light wife doth make a heavy husband,**
And never be Bassanio so for me.
But God sort all. You're welcome home my lord.

BASSANIO
I thank you madam. Give welcome to my friend.

Like a great sea-mark standing every flaw

Source: CORIOLANUS (Act V, sc. iii, l. 74)
Author: William Shakespeare (1564–1616)
First published: 1623
Type of work: Dramatic tragedy

Context: Having been unjustly banished from Rome and his family, Coriolanus has joined forces with his sworn enemy, Aufidius, and the Volscian army. Under the guidance of Coriolanus, this army scores a number of successes and is soon standing before the gates of Rome. Coriolanus has revenge within his reach; Rome is powerless before him. He who was once Rome's savior is now ready to destroy her. The Senate sends an old friend to persuade Coriolanus to spare the city. Coriolanus refuses: "Wife, mother, child, I know not. My affairs/ Are servanted to others.

618

Though I owe/ My revenge properly, my remission lies/ In Volscian breasts." The Roman Senators, in a final effort to hold off the doom that threatens the city, send forth the mother, wife, and child, whom Coriolanus has sworn to "know not." Before his mother's logic and appeal, Coriolanus is faced with an impossible choice. If he denies his own flesh, he will destroy his good name for all history; if he spares Rome, he will probably be killed by the Volscians. Volumnia realizes full well what she is asking, and she begins her attack on her son by presenting him his child:

VOLUMNIA
This is a poor epitome of yours,
Which by th' interpretation of full time
May show like all yourself.

CORIOLANUS
The god of soldiers,
With the consent of supreme Jove, inform
Thy thoughts with nobleness, that thou mayst prove
To shame invulnerable, and stick i' th' wars
Like a great sea-mark standing every flaw,
And saving those that eye thee.

Like Niobe all tears

Source: HAMLET (Act I, sc. ii, l. 149)
Author: William Shakespeare (1564–1616)
First published: 1603
Type of work: Dramatic tragedy

Context: Hamlet, Prince of Denmark, bemoans his noble father's death, the usurpation of the throne by Claudius, his base uncle, and the hasty marriage of his mother, Queen Gertrude, to that same uncle. In his first soliloquy, he laments his mother's frailty and notes that although she wept at the funeral like Niobe whose fourteen children were slain by Apollo, she accepted Claudius in a marriage, which, in Hamlet's eyes, is an incestuous relationship.

HAMLET
 . . . That it should come to this—
But two months dead, nay not so much, not two—
So excellent a King, that was to this
Hyperion to a satyr, so loving to my mother,
That he might not beteem the winds of heaven
Visit her face too roughly. Heaven and earth,
Must I remember? Why she would hang on him

As if increase of appetite had grown
By what it fed on, and yet within a month—
Let me not think on't—frailty, thy name is woman.
A little month or e'er those shoes were old
With which she followed my poor father's body,
Like Niobe all tears, why she, even she—
O God, a beast that wants discourse of reason
Would have mourned longer—married with my uncle,

. . .

The lilies and languors of virtue

Source: DOLORES (Stanza 9)
Author: Algernon Charles Swinburne (1837–1909)
First published: 1866
Type of work: Lyric poem

Context: Written in praise of a prostitute, this poem shows the soul broken by suffering and passion, half-humorously playing with pleasures even as it fully recognizes its pain. The woman of the poem brings the speaker only sorrow, yet he is unwilling and unable to flee from her. As in many of Swinburne's poems, pleasure and pain, freedom and bondage, suffering and joy are strangely joined so that the soul must experience the full extreme of the one in order to enjoy the other. Dolores, "Our Lady of the Seven Sorrows," is a fitting symbol for the idol of such a philosophy. As a prostitute she is the goddess of self-inflicted pain, a deity who makes men willingly exchange the comforts of virtue for the misery of vice. As a woman she suffers from her own sterile life and makes others suffer by desiring her; she turns virtue into vice and now makes vice into an endless state of suffering for whoever desires her because she forces men to love her but cannot return their love.

Could you hurt me, sweet lips, though I hurt you?
 Men touch them, and change in a trice
The lilies and languors of virtue
 For the raptures and roses of vice;
Those lie where thy foot on the floor is,
 These crown and caress thee and chain,
O splendid and sterile Dolores,
 Our Lady of Pain.

Lilies that fester smell far worse than weeds

Source: SONNET 94 (Line 14)
Author: William Shakespeare (1564–1616)
First published: 1609
Type of work: Sonnet

Context: Those people who have within themselves potential greatness or goodness, says the poet, yet who do not excel, are far worse than those with less promise. The final six lines of the sonnet make clear the superiority of a simple, untainted flower or of a simple, untainted person to an infected blossom or a great person, soured by vile deeds, or as the poet states in the closing couplet, decayed lilies smell worse than decayed weeds:

> They that have power to hurt, and will do none,
> That do not do the thing they most do show,
> Who moving others, are themselves as stone,
> Unmoved, cold, and to temptation slow;
> They rightly do inherit heaven's graces,
> And husband nature's riches from expense;
> They are the lords and owners of their faces,
> Others but stewards of their excellence.
> The summer's flower is to the summer sweet,
> Though to itself it only live and die;
> But if that flower with base infection meet,
> The basest weed outbraves his dignity.
>   For sweetest things turn sourest by their deeds;
>   **Lilies that fester smell far worse than weeds.**

A lion among ladies

Source: A MIDSUMMER NIGHT'S DREAM (Act III, sc. i, ll. 31–32)
Author: William Shakespeare (1564–1616)
First published: 1600
Type of work: Dramatic comedy

Context: The celebration of the marriage of Theseus, Duke of Athens, and Hippolyta, fair captive Queen of the Amazons, will take place at the rise of the new moon. Some common craftsmen plan to produce a play based on the story of Pyramus and Thisbe. During a rehearsal fears are voiced that the ladies in the audience will be frightened at the death of Pyramus by his own sword and at the appearance of a lion. The dialogue among the craftsmen proceeds thus:

SNOUT
Will not the ladies be afeard of the lion?

STARVELING
I fear it, I promise you.

BOTTOM
Masters, you ought to consider with yourselves—to bring in, God shield us, **a lion among ladies** is a most dreadful thing. For there is

621

not a more fearful wild-fowl than your lion living; and we ought
to look to't.

SNOUT

Therefore another prologue must tell he is not a lion.

Lips say, "God be pitiful," who never said, "God be praised"

Source: THE CRY OF THE HUMAN (Lines 7–8)
Author: Elizabeth Barrett Browning (1806–1861)
First published: 1844
Type of work: Humanitarian poem

Context: Handicapped by semi-paralysis and confined between 1821 and 1845 in a darkened room, Mrs. Browning was not a self-centered woman; her concern with the suffering of the lower class and with people anywhere in slavery or political oppression enabled her to rise above her own misfortunes to become one of the great poets of social protest. Hearing of children who must go to bed without food and of the increasing wealth of the already prosperous middle class, she attempted to awaken the consciences of her own class, not by advocating particular reforms but by clearly showing the horrible conditions of life that were present in London itself. In this poem she shows how most people have the tenderness to pity the starving children but are blinded by greed until a loved one dies; then the soul discovers the plight of the multitudes and can learn to pray, thus overcoming selfishness. While such a remedy is, perhaps, far-fetched, the poem does clearly portray the need to overcome greed in order to save the poor and also to improve the callous behavior of the thoughtless middle class.

> "There is no God," the foolish saith,
>   But none, "There is no sorrow;"
> And nature oft the cry of faith,
>   In bitter need will borrow:
> Eyes which the preacher could not school,
>   By wayside graves are raised;
> And **lips say, "God be pitiful,"**
>   **Who ne'er said, "God be praised."**
>   Be pitiful, O God.

The little dogs and all, Tray, Blanch, and Sweetheart

Source: KING LEAR (Act III, sc. vi, ll. 65–66)
Author: William Shakespeare (1564–1616)
First published: 1608
Type of work: Dramatic tragedy

Context: The aged King Lear, who has foolishly divided his kingdom between Goneril and Regan, his two unloving daughters, and has disinherited Cordelia, the loving and youngest, but blunt, daughter, finds himself cast out by his heirs. Furious, he rushes into the stormy night. His wits gone, Lear is removed by his old friends Gloucester and Kent, Edgar, disguised as a madman, and his faithful fool, to the shelter of a farmhouse, where in a mock trial he charges his daughters.

LEAR

Arraign her first; 'tis Goneril. I here take my oath before this honourable assembly, she kicked the poor King her father.

. . .

And here's another whose warped looks proclaim
What store her heart is made on. Stop her there!
Arms, arms, sword, fire! Corruption in the place!
False justicer, why hast thou let her 'scape?

. . .

KENT

O pity! Sir, where is the patience now
That you so oft have boasted to retain?

. . .

LEAR

The little dogs and all,
Tray, Blanch, and Sweetheart, see, they bark at me.

The little foxes, that spoil the vines

Source: THE SONG OF SOLOMON 2:15
Author: Unknown
First transcribed: c.300–200 B.C.
Type of work: Lyric poetry

Context: The *Song of Songs* has been interpreted in many ways over the centuries. Read literally, it is a dialogue of endearments between a young girl and her lover; she is a keeper of the vineyards, he a shepherd. The vivid and striking imagery and great literary power of the work, combined with its freedom of expression, make it one of the great love poems of the ages. It was at one time thought by Jewish scholars to be an allegory symbolizing the love between the Lord and his chosen people, and probably became a part of Scripture for this reason. This view was accepted by some of the early Christian scholars; others thought it an allegory of Christ and His church. The chapter headings of the Authorized King James Version represent the latter opinion. The modern tendency among

623

scholars is to accept the literal interpretation, and to consider the text a single love lyric, or more probably a collection of love songs edited and unified by its original compiler. In chapter 2, the girl recalls a time when her lover came to her house in the evening, spoke through the lattice to her, and begged her to go with him. The young man's ardor paints a vivid, idyllic picture of the springtime and its beauty. When she remains silent he adds another inducement: this is the season when foxes nibble at the young grapevines. By referring to this annual problem of the vineyards he is implying that she should come out and guard them; he of course will assist her. It is easy to imagine the girl smiling at this transparent approach; nonetheless she pledges herself to him, though not aloud. When she finally speaks to her suitor, it is only to tell that disappointed youth she will be happy to see him in the morning.

My beloved is like a roe or a young hart: behold, he standeth behind our wall, he looketh forth at the windows, shewing himself through the lattice.

My beloved spake, and said unto me, Rise up, my love, my fair one, and come away.

For, lo, the winter is past, the rain is over and gone;

The flowers appear on the earth; the time of the singing of birds is come, and the voice of the turtle is heard in our land;

The fig tree putteth forth her green figs, and the vines with the tender grape give a good smell. Arise, my love, my fair one, and come away.

O my dove, that art in the clefts of the rock, in the secret places of the stairs, let me see thy countenance, let me hear thy voice; for sweet is thy voice, and thy countenance is comely.

Take us the foxes, **the little foxes, that spoil the vines:** for our vines have tender grapes.

My beloved is mine, and I am his: he feedeth among the lilies.

Until the day break, and the shadows flee away, turn, my beloved, and be thou like a roe or a young hart upon the mountains of Bether.

A little more than kin, and less than kind

Source: HAMLET (Act I, sc. ii, l. 65)
Author: William Shakespeare (1564–1616)
First published: 1603
Type of work: Dramatic tragedy

Context: Claudius, brother to King Hamlet, has secretly murdered his brother, usurped the throne from its rightful owner, Hamlet, Prince of Denmark, and married immediately his former sister-in-law, Queen Gertrude. Young Hamlet, unaware of the fact that Claudius has killed the noble king, but feeling deeply the difference between the two kings, and the hasty marriage of his mother to his uncle, broods about the court. On his first appearance in the play, Claudius acts the role of the good king by attending to the affairs of state and to the personal affairs of Laertes, the son of his Lord Chamberlain. Then he turns to Hamlet and attempts to show fatherly concern for the unhappy prince, who cannot accept the low Claudius as replacing his own noble father. He replies to the words of Claudius, in an aside, in words that may be paraphrased as "I am more closely related to you than cousin (step-son), but little like you in nature." However, he may mean in the second part of the phrase that he cannot be kind to his uncle, that he hates the usurper.

CLAUDIUS
Take thy fair hour Laertes, time be thine,
And thy best graces spend it at thy will.
But now, my cousin Hamlet, and my son.

HAMLET [aside]
A little more than kin, and less than kind.

A little rebellion, now and then, is a good thing

Source: LETTER TO JAMES MADISON (January 30, 1787)
Author: Thomas Jefferson (1743–1826)
First published: 1829
Type of work: Personal letter

Context: When the United States had won its independence from Great Britain and hostilities had ceased in 1781, the new nation found it necessary to establish firm connections with other countries in regard to trade and commerce. The negotiation of such matters was of great importance to the survival of this country. In 1784 Jefferson was sent to France to join John Adams and Benjamin Franklin in these efforts, succeeding Franklin in 1785 as minister plenipotentiary to the French court. Before he returned to America in 1789 he had succeeded in persuading the French government to remove a number of unjust restrictions on American commerce. These restrictions had imposed hardships on the eastern states, and the people had grown rebellious. In a letter to James Madison written January 30, 1787 Jefferson analyzes the situation with his usual insight, outlines the causes of the unrest, and expresses a hope that the governments of those states will not be too hard on the offenders. "A consciousness of those in power that their administration of the public affairs has been honest," he cautions, "may, perhaps, produce too great a degree of indignation; and those characters, wherein fear predominates over hope, may apprehend too much from these instances of irregularity. They may conclude too hastily, that nature has formed man insusceptible of any other government than that of force, a conclusion not founded in truth nor experience." Jefferson then describes what he considers the three basic forms of government and their characteristics:

> . . . Societies exist under three forms, sufficiently distinguishable. 1. Without government, as among our Indians. 2. Under governments, wherein the will of every one has a just influence; as is the case of England, in a slight degree, and in our States, in a great one. 3. Under governments of force; as is the case in all other monarchies, and in most of the other republics. To have an idea of the curse of existence under these last, they must be seen. It is a government of wolves over sheep. It is a problem, not clear in my mind, that the first condition is not the best. But I believe it to be inconsistent with any great degree of population. The second state has a great deal of good in it. The mass of mankind under that, enjoys a precious degree of liberty and happiness. It has its evils, too; the principal of which is the turbulence to which it is subject. But weigh this against the oppressions of monarchy, and it becomes nothing. *Malo periculosam libertatem quam quietam servitutem.* Even this evil is productive of good. It prevents the degeneracy of government, and nourishes a general attention to the public affairs. I hold it, that **a little rebellion, now and then, is a good thing,** and as necessary in the political world as storms in the physical.

A little water clears us of this deed

Source: MACBETH (Act II, sc. ii, l. 67)
Author: William Shakespeare (1564–1616)
First published: 1623
Type of work: Dramatic tragedy

Context: Macbeth has just murdered Duncan, the King of Scotland. He is in a state of shock, and he has not carried out the plan he and Lady Macbeth had made to put the knife in the hands of the drugged and drunken grooms who guarded the king. Lady Macbeth, who could not kill Duncan herself because he reminded her of her father, goes to complete the plan. She is now the strong one, for her husband can no longer even think of what he has done, much less look at it again. She bolsters herself with brave talk and leaves to set the scene. Meanwhile Macbeth stares at his bloody hands in horror, believing that they can never be cleansed. Lady Macbeth, however, whose hands are now as bloody, berates him as a coward and assures him that merely washing their hands will clear them of murder. A knocking at the gates halts their hurried conversation and sends them to their rooms to pretend sleep.

MACBETH
. . .
Will all great Neptune's ocean wash this blood

626

Clean from my hand? No. This my hand will rather
The multitudinous seas incarnadine,
Making the green one red.

LADY MACBETH

My hands are of your colour; but I shame
To wear a heart so white. [*Knock.*] I hear a knocking
At the south entry. Retire we to our chamber.
A little water clears us of this deed.

. . .

Live, and move, and have our being

Source: ACTS 17:28
Author: Unknown (traditionally Luke)
First transcribed: 60–150 (probably c.80–90)
Type of work: Religious history and tradition

Context: The Acts of the Apostles is the only existing account of the beginnings of the Christian Church. It is evident that the writer of Acts and the author of Luke were one and the same, but whether he was actually Luke the physician is not certain. It is likely that if Luke did not write these he was responsible for portions of them. Acts is a biographical and historical record of the various apostles and their work after the death of Jesus; in it can be seen the gradual evolution of Christianity from a branch or sect of Judaism into an independent evangelical faith. Luke begins with the Resurrection and the commission which Jesus lays upon His apostles, then gives an account of their activities in Jerusalem, in Syria and Asia Minor, and in various parts of the Roman Empire. The reader of Acts cannot but be impressed by the religious devotion and moral heroism that it mirrors. This epic account of struggle and suffering, of growth under persecution into an enduring institution, was doubtless written both to provide a record of events and to be an inspiration to its members. Chapters 15 through 28 follow the career of Paul; in Chapter 17 there is an account of his missionary work at Thessalonica. He and Silas stop here, and at the synagogue Paul proclaims his message. He spends three days arguing Scripture with the Jews. A number of ruffians are then persuaded, perhaps hired, to demonstrate against the Christians and incite a riot. The Christians are blamed for the incident; they get Paul out of the city and send him to Berea. Here he is more successful and wins some converts; but the agitators from Thessalonica follow him, and his congregation moves him to Athens, where there are a number of philosophers who, curious about Paul's new doctrine, ask him to tell them about it.

Then Paul stood in the midst of Mars' hill, and said, Ye men of Athens, I perceive that in all things ye are too superstitious.

627

For as I passed by, and beheld your devotions, I found an altar
with this inscription, TO THE UNKNOWN GOD. Whom therefore ye ignorantly worship, him I declare unto you.

God that made the world and all things therein, seeing that he
is Lord of heaven and earth, dwelleth not in temples made with
hands;

Neither is worshipped with men's hands, as though he needed
any thing, seeing he giveth to all life, and breath, and all things;

And hath made of one blood all nations of men for to dwell on
all the face of the earth, and hath determined the times before appointed, and the bounds of their habitation;

That they should seek the Lord, if haply they might feel after
him, and find him, though he be not far from every one of us:

For in him we **live, and move, and have our being;** as certain
also of your own poets have said, For we are also his offspring.

Forasmuch then as we are the offspring of God, we ought not
to think that the Godhead is like unto gold, or silver, or stone,
graven by art and man's device.

Live we how we can, yet die we must

Source: KING HENRY THE SIXTH: PART THREE (Act V, sc. ii, l. 28)
Author: William Shakespeare (1564–1616)
First published: 1623
Type of work: Historical drama

Context: With his last breath, Warwick, maker of kings, dies in the service of the House of Lancaster. From
fast friend of the Duke of York, he
becomes foe when the young King
Edward marries Lady Grey instead of
Bona, sister to the Queen of France.
Warwick switches his allegiance to
King Henry VI after he is told that
Edward, who succeeded his father as
usurper of Henry's throne, has married Lady Grey out of lust, thereby
making a fool of Warwick, who had
gone to France to plead for the hand
of the Lady Bona for his king. Edward has no intention of giving up his
crown, and Warwick is mortally
wounded in battle between the two
Houses and their supporters.

WARWICK
. . .

For who lived king, but I could dig his grave?
And who durst smile when Warwick bent his brow?
Lo, now my glory smeared in dust and blood!
My parks, my walks, my manors that I had,
Even now forsake me; and of all my lands
Is nothing left me, but my body's length.
Why, what is pomp, rule, reign, but earth and dust?
And **live we how we can, yet die we must.**

628

The living need charity more than the dead

Source: THE JOLLY OLD PEDAGOGUE (Stanza 3)
Author: George Arnold (1834–1865)
First published: c.1886
Type of work: Humorous verse

Context: Arnold was born in Bedfordshire in New York and was educated at home. Following a boyhood in the country, he studied painting and wrote a considerable amount of art criticism. His interests turned more from art to writing, and he produced a number of stories, sketches, poems comic and satiric, criticism, and editorials. Much of his writing was published pseudonymously. *The Jolly Old Pedagogue* is a verse character sketch of an elderly and kindly rural schoolmaster. In it Arnold describes the genial and humane philosophy of the old man, his kindly treatment of difficult students, and his peaceful death:

> With the stupidest boys he was kind and cool,
>   Speaking only in gentlest tones;
> The rod was hardly known in his school,—
> Whipping, to him, was a barbarous rule,
>   And too hard work for his poor old bones;
>   "Besides, it is painful," he sometimes said;
>   "We should make life pleasant down here below,
> **The living need charity more than the dead.**"
>   Said the jolly old pedagogue, long ago.

Loathsome canker lives in sweetest bud

Source: SONNET 35 (Line 4)
Author: William Shakespeare (1564–1616)
First published: 1609
Type of work: Sonnet

Context: The poet, wronged by the one to whom the sonnet is addressed, pleads his friend's case (roses have thorns, fountains mud, sun and moon eclipses) until he finds himself an accessory of the loved one who has "robbed," or wronged, him—hence, he has a conflict within himself instead of with his friend. The sonnet begins with an expression of the naturalness of a flaw in what is near perfection:

> No more be griev'd at that which thou hast done:
> Roses have thorns, and silver fountains mud,
> Clouds and eclipses stain both moon and sun,
> And **loathsome canker lives in sweetest bud.**
> All men make faults, and even I in this,

Authorizing thy trespass with compare,
Myself corrupting, salving thy amiss,
Excusing thy sins more than their sins are;
For to thy sensual fault I bring in sense—
Thy adverse party is thy advocate—
And 'gainst myself a lawful plea commence.
Such civil war is in my love and hate,
    That I an accessary needs must be
    To that sweet thief which sourly robs from me.

A local habitation, and a name

Source: A MIDSUMMER NIGHT'S DREAM (Act V, sc. i, l. 17)
Author: William Shakespeare (1564–1616)
First published: 1600
Type of work: Dramatic comedy

Context: As the marriage of Theseus, Duke of Athens, and Hippolyta, the captive Queen of the Amazons, approaches, revelry prevails. A group of craftsmen present, for the amusement of the Athenian court, a play based on the Pyramus and Thisbe legend. At the conclusion of the production, Theseus comments to Hippolyta that the pen of the poet gives the air of reality to legend and fantasy.

THESEUS
The poet's eye, in a fine frenzy rolling,
Doth glance from heaven to earth, from earth to heaven.
And as imagination bodies forth
The forms of things unknown, the poet's pen
Turns them to shapes, and gives to airy nothing
A local habitation, and a name.
Such tricks hath strong imagination,
That if it would but apprehend some joy,
It comprehends some bringer of that joy.
Or in the night, imagining some fear,
How easy is a bush supposed a bear!

Lofty designs must close in like effects

Source: A GRAMMARIAN'S FUNERAL (Line 145)
Author: Robert Browning (1812–1889)
First published: 1855
Type of work: Dramatic monologue

Context: This poem is the final tribute of a group of students to their dead master, a Greek scholar. At daybreak they are carrying his corpse to the mountain top for burial. Their song of praise catches the spirit of those scholars who thirsted after knowledge in the early Renaissance, but they inadvertantly reveal that their master chose Knowledge to the exclusion of Life. This unknowing admission by his students shows that the scholar had, in effect, denied the very premise of Renaissance human-ism, which had originally motivated his search for knowledge. The students praise their master's choice: "That before living he'd learn how to live— No end to learning." They never realize the implications of his withdrawal from life. Triumphantly, they complete the process of separa-tion from humanity which the Gram-marian himself began:

> Here's the top peak; the multitude below
> Live, for they can, there;
> This man decided not to Live but Know—
> Bury this man there?
> Here—here's his place, where meteors shoot, clouds form,
> Lightnings are loosened,
> Stars come and go! Let joy break with the storm,
> Peace let the dew send!
> **Lofty designs must close in like effects;**
> Loftily lying,
> Leave him—still loftier than the world suspects,
> Living and dying.

The long habit of living indisposeth us for dying

Source: HYDRIOTAPHIA: URN BURIAL (Chapter 5)
Author: Sir Thomas Browne (1605–1682)
First published: 1658
Type of work: Philosophy

Context: In his "discourse of the sep-ulchrall urnes lately found in Nor-folk" Browne speculates upon these relics of the unknown dead. He pon-ders the fact that most of us quickly become anonymous—that death con-signs us, together with all we have done and seen, felt, thought, and said, to swift oblivion. As he says, "to pre-serve the living, and make the dead to live, to keep men out of their Urnes, and discourse of humane fragments in them, is not impertinent unto our profession." In Chapter 5 he consid-ers the greatness that is forgotten, and the insignificance that endures. These bones are minor monuments; yet they have outlasted everything built above them and have "quietly rested under the drums and tramplings of three conquests." Browne believes men should strive for the greatness that is in them, that they may hold oblivion at bay for a time—though, as he ob-serves, it is better to have been virtu-ous but unknown than to live in in-famy for ages. Browne's speculations lead him further: even the greatest deeds and names, the noblest monu-ments, cannot last forever; in terms

631

of eternity, even the pyramids are but pillars of snow. He counsels the reader, therefore, to seek other glories than earthly ones. "There is nothing strictly immortall, but immortality; whatever hath no beginning, may be confident of no end—which is the peculiar of that necessary essence that cannot destroy itself; and the highest strain of omnipotency, to be so powerfully constituted as not to suffer even from the power of itself: All others have a dependent being, and within the reach of destruction, but the sufficiency of Christian Immortality frustrates all earthly glory, and the quality of either state after death, makes a folly of posthumous memory." Before passing on to this escape from oblivion and a discussion of it, Browne comments both on man's fear of death and on the latter's inevitability:

In vain we hope to be known by open and visible conservatories, when to be unknown was the means of their continuation and obscurity their protection: If they dyed by violent hands, and were thrust into their Urnes, these bones become considerable, and some old Philosophers would honor them, whose souls they conceived most pure, which were thus snatched from their bodies; and to retain a stranger propension unto them: whereas they weariedly left a languishing corps, and with faint desires of reunion. If they fell by long and aged decay, yet wrapt up in the bundle of time, they fall into indistinction, and make but one blot with Infants. If we begin to die when we live, and long life be but a prolongation of death; our life is a sad composition; We live with death, and die not in a moment . . . Our dayes become considerable, like petty sums by minute accumulations; where numerous fractions make up but small round numbers; and our dayes of a span long make not one little finger.

If the nearnesse of our last necessity, brought a nearer conformity into it, there were a happinesse in hoary hairs, and no calamity in half senses. But **the long habit of living indisposeth us for dying;** . . .

Look before you leap

Source: FIVE HUNDRED POINTS OF GOOD HUSBANDRY (Chapter 57, "Of Wiving and Thriving")
Author: Thomas Tusser (c.1525–1580)
First published: 1562 (Chapter 57)
Type of work: Didactic poem

Context: Like many of our proverbs and familiar sayings, "look before you leap" is very old. John Heywood (1497–1580) included it in his book, Proverbes (1546), the first such collection in English, and it was probably considered ancient then. It has not changed greatly; in Heywood's

632

day it was "look ere ye leap." Thomas Tusser did much to perpetuate familiar sayings through his inclusion of them in such works as *Five Hundred Points of Good Husbandry*. This book is an early form of farmer's almanac, which takes up the months of the year one by one, from September to August. Instructions concerning the farmer's tasks are set forth for each month, together with much general information which includes observations on weather and climate, the planets, and principles of agriculture. The entire work is in verse, much of it doggerel, and is spiced with maxims and proverbs. The result is a practical handbook for the Elizabethan farmer, which gives the reader of today an excellent view of rural life in the early sixteenth century. In addition it is vivid and possesses considerable rustic charm. In later editions Tusser added more material to his book, including hints to housewives and a bit of advice to bachelors entitled "Of wiving and thriving." This admonition is in the form of a dialogue between two single men, one of whom believes marriage is a good idea; his companion, however, remains unconvinced. Most of his objections relate to his unshakable conviction that a wife is an expensive luxury. His companion argues in vain that a man who does not marry spends as much on trifles for himself as he would spend on a wife:

AFFIRMATION
Not so, for now where thou dost spend,
Of this and that, to no good end,
    Which hindreth thee to thrive:
Such vain expences thou should'st save,
And daily then lay more to have,
    As others do that wive.

OBJECTION
Why then do folk, this proverb put,
The black ox near trod on thy foot,
    If that way were to thrive:
Here out a man may soon pick forth,—
Few feeleth what a penny is worth,
    Till such time as they wive.

AFFIRMATION
It may so chance, as thou dost say,
This lesson therefore bear away,
    If thereby thou wilt thrive:
Look ere thou leap, see ere thou go,
It may be for thy profit so,
    For thee to lay to wive.

633

Look in thy heart and write

Source: ASTROPHEL AND STELLA (Sonnet I, 1. 14)
Author: Sir Philip Sidney (1554–1586)
First published: 1591
Type of work: Sonnet

Context: Sir Philip Sidney, in the courtly tradition, writes a sonnet sequence to win the favor of a lady whom he admires, generally thought to be Penelope Devereaux. The poet, searching for words to express his love, studies poetry, vainly reading the verse of others as he strives to write, but his words falter without "Invention," (creative imagination) until the poet "great with child to speak," gives literary birth to his sonnets by following the advice of his Poetic Muse, which tells him to "look in thy heart and write:"

> But words come halting forth, wanting Invention's stay;
> Invention, Nature's child, fled step-dame Study's blows;
> And others' feet still seemed but strangers in my way.
> Thus great with child to speak, and helpless in my throes,
> Biting my truant pen, beating myself for spite:
> "Fool!" said my Muse to me, "**look in thy heart, and write.**"

Looked unutterable things

Source: THE SEASONS: SUMMER
Author: James Thomson (1700–1748)
First published: 1727 ("Summer")
Type of work: Pastoral poem

Context: The Seasons broke a great deal of new ground in English poetry. Thomson was a forerunner of romanticism; and in this first long-sustained poem to deal primarily with nature, he introduced a number of qualities unique at the time. These included love of natural scenery, humanitarianism, and vivid imagery. He is at times sensuous and there is occasionally a certain fantasy in his work. The poem is also important for its reintroduction of blank verse, part of Thomson's successful effort to establish Milton as a leading force in English poetic tradition. *Spring* describes the gradual fading of winter and its replacement by warmth and sunlight, seedtime, new growth, love and the renewal of all things. In *Summer,* Thomson continues his description of the changing world of nature; the gentle air of spring is replaced by the hot sun and brilliant light of summer. The poet observes that he must find himself some shade and seek fresh inspiration there. He considers the short and peaceful night and the early dawn that follows, revealing a world refreshed. "The dripping rock, the mountain's misty top,/ Swell on the sight, and brighten with the dawn./

Blue through the dusk the smoking currents shine;/ And from the bladed field the fearful hare/ Limps, awkward; while along the forest glade/ The wild deer trip, and often turning gaze/ At early passenger. Music awakes/ The native voice of undissembled joy:/ And thick around the woodland hymns arise." Thomson regrets that more people do not awake in time to enjoy "the cool, the fragrant, and the silent hour." The sun rises, flooding the earth with "fluid gold." After a brief hymn to the sun and its creator, Thomson follows this world of the pastoral poem through a day of happiness and frolic, health and rewarding labor. The blistering midday sun, the sultry early afternoon, and the cool forest shade are all a prelude to the summer thundershower, which gathers swiftly and breaks with brief but stunning violence. At this point he introduces Celadon and Amelia, pastoral figures who are unaware of their love for one another until they are caught in the storm:

> Down comes a deluge of sonorous hail,
> Or prone-descending rain. Wide rent, the clouds,
> Pour a whole flood; and yet, its flame unquench'd,
> Th' unconquerable lightning struggles through,
> Ragged and fierce . . .
> And yet not always on the guilty head
> Descends the fated flash. Young Celadon
> And his Amelia were a matchless pair;
> With equal virtue form'd, and equal grace . . .
>   They lov'd: but such the guileless passion was,
> As in the dawn of time inform'd the heart
> Of innocence, and undissembling truth.
> 'Twas friendship heighten'd by the mutual wish;
> Th' inchanting hope, and sympathetic glow,
> Beam'd from the mutual eye. Devoting all
> To love, each was to each a dearer self;
> Supremely happy in th' awaken'd power
> Of giving joy. Alone, amid the shades,
> Still in harmonious intercourse they lived
> The rural day, and talk'd the flowing heart,
> Or sigh'd, and **look'd unutterable things.**

Looking as cheerful as any man could do in that condition

Source: DIARY (13 October 1660)
Author: Samuel Pepys (1633–1703)
First published: 1825
Type of work: Diary

Context: The Diary of Samuel Pepys covers a period from January 1, 1660 to May 31, 1669, when his eyes gave out. Written in a system of shorthand devised by Thomas Shelton, made public in 1641, it contains daily entries for the early period. In three years, working twelve hours a day, the Reverend John Smith deciphered it in 1819, and part was printed in 1825. In complete form, it appeared in 1893–1899. Whatever unity the Diary has is two-fold, the record of the rise by hard work and by the seizing of opportunities of a poor and obscure clerk to a position of wealth and power; and second, the domestic tension between a sensitive man who could not resist a pretty woman and his young and devoted wife incapable of sharing her husband's interests and ambitions. In his Diary, Pepys shows himself an observer of important as well as unimportant moments of history. In this entry he records the hanging of the man appointed by Cromwell to convey Charles I from Windsor Castle to Whitehall, and who also served as one of the judges who tried and sentenced the king to execution.

I went out to Charing Cross to see Major-General [Thomas] Harrison hanged, drawn, and quartered; which was done there, he **looking as cheerful as any man could do in that condition.** He was presently cut down, and his head and heart shown to the people, at which there was great shouts of joy. It is said, that he said he was sure to come shortly at the right hand of Christ to judge them that now had judged him; and that his wife do expect his coming again. Thus it was my chance to see the King beheaded at White Hall, and to see the first blood shed in revenge for the King at Charing Cross. After that I went by water home, where I was angry with my wife for her things lying about, and in my passion kicked the little fine basket, which I bought her in Holland, and broke it, which troubled me after I had done it.

Lord, lord, how this world is given to lying

Source: KING HENRY THE FOURTH: PART ONE (Act V, sc. iv, ll. 148–149)
Author: William Shakespeare (1564–1616)
First published: 1598
Type of work: Historical drama

Context: Sir John Falstaff, the jovial and rotund companion of Prince Hal, heir to the throne, has not comported himself well in the battle between the forces of the king and those of the rebellious Hotspur. While Hal and Hotspur fight a mortal duel, Falstaff fights Douglas. Falling down and pretending death, Falstaff rises from the deserted field of battle, stabs again the already dead Hotspur, and claims a reward for his actions. Hal denies the efforts of his lying friend.

PRINCE HENRY

Why, Percy I killed myself, and saw thee dead.

FALSTAFF

Didst thou? **Lord, lord, how this world is given to lying.** I grant you I was down, and out of breath, and so was he, but we rose both at an instant, and fought a long hour by Shrewsbury clock. If I may be believed, so; if not, let them that should reward valour bear the sin upon their own heads. I'll take it upon my death, I gave him this wound in the thigh. If the man were alive, and would deny it, zounds I would make him eat a piece of my sword.

Lord of thy presence, and no land beside

Source: KING JOHN (Act I, sc. i, l. 137)
Author: William Shakespeare (1564–1616)
First published: 1623
Type of work: Historical drama

Context: Robert Faulconbridge and his bastard brother, Philip, go before King John to plead for their father's inheritance. Robert, who is given the inheritance in his father's will, says Philip was begotten by Richard, John's brother. Queen Elinor and John both think Philip favors Richard in speech and looks, while Robert supposedly looks a good deal like his father, who was in Richard's service. Elinor asks if Philip would rather be like Robert or be the reputed son of Richard Coeur-de-lion, and follow her and John to war with France.

ELINOR

Whether hadst thou rather be a Faulconbridge,
And like thy brother, to enjoy thy land,
Or the reputed son of Cordelion,
Lord of thy presence, and no land beside?

BASTARD

Madam, an if my brother had my shape
And I had his, . . .
    .   .   .
Would I might never stir from off this place,
I'd give it every foot to have this face.
I would not be Sir Nob in any case.

The Lord's anointed temple

Source: MACBETH (Act II, sc. iii, l. 74)
Author: William Shakespeare (1564–1616)
First published: 1623
Type of work: Dramatic tragedy

637

Context: Forewarned by the prophecy of three witches of his destiny to become King of Scotland and spurred on by an ambitious wife, Macbeth murders Duncan, his king, his kinsman, and his over-night guest. The corpse is discovered by Macduff, a nobleman charged with the duty of awakening the king. Referring to the king as "the Lord's anointed temple," Macduff reports the murder.

MACDUFF

O horror, horror, horror! Tongue nor heart
Cannot conceive nor name thee.

MACBETH *and* LENNOX

What's the matter?

MACDUFF

Confusion now hath made his masterpiece.
Most sacrilegious murder hath broke ope
The Lord's anointed temple, and stole thence
The life o' th' building.

MACBETH

What is't you say—the life?

LENNOX

Mean you his Majesty?

MACDUFF

Approach the chamber, and destroy your sight
With a new Gorgon. Do not bid me speak.
See, and then speak yourselves. . . .

Lords are lordliest in their wine

Source: SAMSON AGONISTES (Line 1418)
Author: John Milton (1608–1674)
First published: 1671
Type of work: Dramatic tragedy

Context: The play opens with the last phase of the life of Samson, the Old Testament hero. The Philistines have blinded him and hold him prisoner in Gaza. The play, structured as a Greek tragedy, depicts the restoration of the fallen Samson to the grace of God. Samson has already been tested by God and failed the test. Having been punished and having repented his sin, he now undergoes trials of his will and integrity to prove that he is worthy to be tested a second time. Surmounting these trials, he is summoned to entertain the Philistine nobles at the feast of the pagan god

Dagon. He refuses to follow the summoning officer. While the officer is gone, Samson confides to the chorus that his strength is returning and he will never be forced to perform at the feast of Dagon, although he could go of his own free will. Within him there are strange stirrings, and in recognition of God's Providence he decides to attend the feast. He assures the Chorus that "This day will be remarkable in my life/ By some great act or of my days the last." When the officer returns to demand his attendance, he goes with him quietly. As he leaves, Samson, in his last speech, tells the Chorus:

> Brethren, farewell, your company along
> I will not wish, lest it perhaps offend them
> To see me girt with friends; and how the sight
> Of me as of a common Enemy,
> So dreaded once, may now exasperate them
> I know not. **Lords are Lordliest in their wine;**
> And the well-feasted Priest then soonest fir'd
> With zeal, if aught Religion seem concern'd:
> No less the people on their Holy-days
> Impetuous, insolent, unquenchable;
> Happen what may, of me expect to hear
> Nothing dishonorable, impure, unworthy
> Our God, our Law, my Nation, or my self,
> The last of me or no I cannot warrant.

The lot of man; to suffer, and to die

Source: THE ODYSSEY (Book III, l. 117, as translated by Alexander Pope)
Author: Homer (c. 850 B.C.)
First transcribed: Sixth century, B.C.
Type of work: Epic poem

Context: Accompanied by the goddess Minerva, who is disguised in the shape of Mentor, Telemachus ventures forth from his native Ithaca to search for Ulysses, his father, who has failed to return to Ithaca after the Trojan War, years before. At the opening of Book III, Telemachus' ship nears the shore of Pylos early one morning, as King Nestor and his sons, "At nine green theaters," prepare to sacrifice to Neptune. Telemachus lands, though he is unsure of himself in meeting the elderly and very wise Nestor. Minerva counsels him, however, to have no fear; she advises him to speak up courageously, for the gods will give him help. Telemachus and the disguised Minerva are greeted by Pisistratus, and they are led to Nestor, whom they join in the Pylian sacrifice. Following the ceremonial rites, Nestor invites Telemachus and his companion to join in the feasting. The banquet done, Nestor asks his guests from whence they come, their identity, and the reasons for their adventuring upon the

639

seas. Responding as he was advised to do, Telemachus speaks, inspired by the gods; he tells Nestor that he is the son of King Ulysses of Ithaca, and that he seeks his father, a famous leader in the Trojan War, who has failed to return to his home. Telemachus asks Nestor to tell him what he can, for he knows that Nestor, too, was at the Trojan War. The young man asks for the truth, even if it means word of Ulysses' death:

> Of all the chiefs, this hero's fate alone
> Has Jove reserv'd, unheard of, and unknown;
> Whether in fields by hostile fury slain,
> Or sunk by tempests in the gulfy main?
> Of this to learn, oppress'd with tender fears,
> Lo, at thy knee his suppliant son appears.
> If or thy certain eye, or curious ear,
> Have learnt his fate, the whole dark story clear.
> And, oh! whate'er Heaven destined to betide,
> Let neither flattery soothe, nor pity hide.
> Prepared I stand: he was but born to try
> **The lot of man; to suffer, and to die.**

The loudest wit I ever was deafened with

Source: DON JUAN (Canto XVI, stanza 81)
Author: George Gordon, Lord Byron (1788–1824)
First published: 1824
Type of work: Satiric poem

Context: Between 1818 and 1824, the year of his death, Byron was busy with an epic poem about the great Spanish lover, Don Juan. The plot is slender. Juan, after an affair with one of his mother's friends, is sent on a tour of Europe. A shipwreck during the first stage involves him in a passionate affair with the beautiful daughter of a slave-trader who sells him to a sultana. The attack upon her palace by Russian forces lets him escape her clutches, but he is sent to carry news to the Empress Catherine of Russia, who also wants him for a lover. Because of his illness, she sends him on a diplomatic mission to England. Here his charm and polish bring many opportunities for marriage, with Lady Adeline to point out the advantages of the various ladies. The only one to interest him is prim, melancholic Aurora Raby. Her indifference to him, as she sits beside him at a banquet in Lady Adeline's house, piques him. That evening he sees the ghost of the Black Friar, who had once lived in that house. Thomas Moore, the Irish poet and friend of Byron, in his life of the poet, asserts that Byron himself during a visit to Newstand Abbey in 1814 fancied he saw the ghost of the Black Friar who had haunted the place since the time of the dissolution of the monasteries. The ghost's appearance was supposed to presage a death, a wedding, or a birth. The next morning the guests

640

talk of the ghost, and Adeline sings a song about the Black Friar and warns them all to beware of him. However, that night Juan forgets the warning. When seeing a shadowy figure, he pursues it and discovers "beneath the sable frock and dreary cowl," the voluptuous figure of one of the guests, the Duchess of Fitz-Fulke. This incident ends the narrative. Before Byron could conclude the next canto, he died in Greece, encouraging the Greeks to fight for their independence. In the 1903 edition of Byron's poems, fourteen stanzas of Canto XVII were included, printed from a manuscript in the possession of the family of a close friend, John Hobhouse, to whom the fourth canto of *Childe Harold's Pilgrimage* and *The Siege of Corinth* were dedicated. The final stanza takes up the narrative and reports the appearance next morning of a wan and weary Juan, looking as if he had struggled with ghosts, and of a pale Duchess. How could this slight narrative occupy seventeen cantos, some with more than a hundred stanzas? It could do so because of the constant digressions, flippant comments, ironical opinions about people and history, satire of many great men of the past, and invectives against leading figures of Byron's time. One example comes in the midst of the Black Friar episode. Speaking of the country acres of Lady Adeline Amundeville and Lord Henry, Byron interjects a personal note about his preference for city life over country life, scoffing at those whose choice lies in the other direction. Someone has guessed that this invective is directed against the Reverend Sydney Smith (1771–1845), whose *Peter Pymley Letters* was published in 1807. It takes place during an election banquet given by Sir Henry, with lords and ladies from the city, and also guests from the rural regions.

> There were some country wags too—and, alas!
>   Some exiles from the town, who had been driven
> To gaze, instead of pavements, upon grass,
>   And rise at nine in lieu of long eleven.
> And lo! upon that day it came to pass
>   I sat next that o'erwhelming son of heaven,
> The very powerful parson, Peter Pith,
>   **The loudest wit I e'er was deafen'd with.**

Love and murder will out

Source: THE DOUBLE-DEALER (Act IV, sc. ii)
Author: William Congreve (1670–1729)
First published: 1694
Type of work: Dramatic comedy

Context: Brisk, a pert coxcomb, enters onto the scene and sends Sir Paul Plyant, his daughter Cynthia, and Lady Plyant out of the room to have an opportunity to make advances to Lady Froth, whom he intends to seduce. He soliloquizes upon how engaging she would be if she were not so fond of her stupid husband. He has just begun to practice his speech to her when she enters. Pretending not to see her, he cries out her name several times. She thereupon asks what is wrong with him. Upon his saying that he had merely been in agreeable contemplation, she asks him why he called out her name so loudly. He says that he had not been aware of doing so, but the reason must be that murder and love will out. He thus modifies a quotation from Chaucer's *Prioress's Tale* (line 567): "Mordre wol out, certeyn it wol not faille." In Chaucer's quotation the reference is to a genuine murder.

LADY FROTH

Bless me! why did you call out upon me so loud?

BRISK

O Lord, I, madam? I beseech your ladyship—when?

LADY FROTH

Just now as I came in: bless me! why, don't you know it?

BRISK

Not I, let me perish! But did I? Strange! I confess your ladyship was in my thoughts; and I was in a sort of dream that did in a manner present a very pleasing object to my imagination, but—but did I indeed?—To see how **love and murder will out!** But did I really name my Lady Froth?

LADY FROTH

Three times aloud, as I love letters! . . .

Love, first learned in a lady's eyes

Source: LOVE'S LABOUR'S LOST (Act IV, sc. iii, l. 327)
Author: William Shakespeare (1564–1616)
First published: 1598
Type of work: Dramatic comedy

Context: At the beginning of the play, several lords attending the King of Navarre agree to take an oath with him to engage in serious study and to abstain from any sort of contact with women for three years. One lord, Berowne, expresses doubt over the wisdom of the latter part of the vow but agrees to it since the others do. As the play progresses, all of the men, including the king, come into unavoidable contact with the Princess of France and her court of ladies. All fall in love but seek to hide the fact from one another. Berowne, however, reveals their amorous longings publicly after overhearing each one read a love letter. Always prone to philosophize, he takes the opportunity to point out that love is an excellent

642

teacher because it makes a person sensitive to the beauty and delicacy of the world around him. Furthermore, he says, it is a woman who teaches a man to love.

BEROWNE

• • •

Other slow arts entirely keep the brain,
And therefore finding barren practisers,
Scarce show a harvest of their heavy toil.
But love, first learned in a lady's eyes,
Lives not alone immured in the brain,
But with the motion of all elements,
Courses as swift as thought in every power,
And gives to every power a double power
Above their functions and their offices.

• • •

Love is like linen often changed, the sweeter

Source: SICELIDES, A PISCATORY (Act III, sc. v)
Author: Phineas Fletcher (1582–1650)
First published: 1631
Type of work: Dramatic comedy

Context: The brothers, Giles and Phineas Fletcher, were two of the most devoted followers of Edmund Spenser in the seventeenth century. Their devotion was a disservice, in a sense, to the author of the *Faerie Queene,* for the brothers so exaggerated the allegory and over-refined the melodies of their master that they precipitated a mild reaction against Spenser. In *Sicelides* Phineas, the elder of the two, attempted a romantic comedy on the model of the popular pastoral drama of the period except that, following the Italian Sannazaro, he substituted fishermen for the conventional shepherds. In the play, the conventional roles of the man who continually satirizes women and the woman who constantly makes jeering fun of men and who end up as a romantic pair are played by Pas, a fisherman, and Cosma, a nymph. In Act III they are still bantering each other:

COSMA
I can but smile to thinke how foolish wise
Those women are, that chuse their loves for wisedome.
Wisedome in men's a golden chaine to tie
Poore women in a glorious slavery.

PAS
Hark Heavens! O monstrous! harke: O women, women.

643

Fond men, that blame the love that ever ranges.
To foule and sluttish love, that never changes!
The Muses love by course to change their meeter,
Love is like linnen often chang'd, the sweeter.

PAS

Thus these neate creatures, dead with love and all,
By shunning beastlines, make it beastiall.

The love of liberty consists in the hatred of tyrants

Source: POLITICAL ESSAYS (*The Times Newspaper:* "On the Connexion Between Toad-eaters and Tyrants")
Author: William Hazlitt (1778–1830)
First published: 1817
Type of work: Essay

Context: Hazlitt was very much an individualist, and frequently at odds with the world; often he found himself fighting alone. This situation did not trouble him in the least. Attacked viciously, he retaliated in kind. It is likely that these savage rebuttals rendered at least some of his opponents speechless with fury. Hazlitt's life of adversity and misfortune filled him with anger rather than melancholy; he did not expend his feelings in a useless hatred of life itself, but railed instead at persons and institutions with whom he disagreed. His outbursts were often undisciplined and he nursed grudges. At the same time he was fully dedicated to human rights and to liberty: these were what he actually fought for. He idolized Napoleon because the latter was an enemy of hereditary monarchy, and Hazlitt knew that the emperor's defeat was a gain for the forces of reaction. Though he may have considered the man a tyrant, he still believed that in monarchy lay the worse tyranny.

Hazlitt expended the bulk of his fury in his *Political Essays,* at the same time proving himself to be a brilliant and incisive thinker. Some of these are articles he sent to the *Times;* that concerning the relationship "between toad-eaters and tyrants" is a particularly trenchant example. In it he attacks Burke, who favored the monarchy and was opposed to the French Revolution, and accuses such writers of subordinating human rights and liberty to the "gratification of their literary jealousy." The love of power, Hazlitt believes, is man's most ruinous disease; but "Man is a toad-eating animal. The admiration of power in others is as common to man as the love of it in himself: the one makes him a tyrant, the other a slave." This is the reason why men long for liberty and accept tyranny in its place. Paradoxically enough, tyranny brings about an increased loyalty to itself. Hazlitt then defends a French political club, the Jacobins:

. . . A true Jacobin, then, is one who does not believe in the divine right of kings, or in any other *alias* for it, which implies that they reign 'in contempt of the will of the people'; and he holds all such kings to be tyrants, and their subjects slaves. To be a true Jacobin, a man must be a good hater; but this is the most difficult and the least amiable of all the virtues: the most trying and the most thankless of all tasks. **The love of liberty consists in the hatred of tyrants.** The true Jacobin hates the enemies of liberty as they hate liberty. . . . "The love of truth is a passion in his mind, as the love of power is a passion in the minds of others. Abstract reason, unassisted by passion, is no match for power and prejudice, armed with force and cunning. The love of liberty is the love of others; the love of power is the love of ourselves. The one is real; the other often but an empty dream. Hence the defection of modern apostates. While they are looking about, wavering and distracted, in pursuit of universal good or universal fame, the eye of power is upon them, like the eye of Providence, that neither slumbers nor sleeps, and that watches but for one object, its own good. They take no notice of it at first, but it is still upon them, and never off them. It at length catches theirs, and they bow to its sacred light; and like the poor fluttering bird, quail beneath it, are seized with a vertigo, and drop senseless into its jaws, that close upon them forever, and so we see no more of them, which is well."

Love will still be lord of all

Source: THE LAY OF THE LAST MINSTREL (Canto VI, stanza ii, l. 194)
Author: Sir Walter Scott (1771–1832)
First published: 1805
Type of work: Narrative poem

Context: In Canto VI the old minstrel tells of the marriage feast of Margaret, daughter of the Ladye of Branksome Hall, and Lord Cranstoun. It was said that the Ladye, a powerful magician, would not dare go near the altar, but this statement was a lie, as she was there when her daughter was married. Lord Cranstoun's goblin page, a malignant dwarf whose only joy was in causing pain and trouble to others, was especially active during the festivities attendant upon the wedding. First, he provoked a quarrel between the German, Conrad, Lord of Wolfenstein, and Hunt-hill, known as Dickon Draw-the-sword. Two weeks later Conrad was found dead of stab wounds in a wood, and ever afterwards Hunthill wore a Cologne sword. The goblin then caused uproar in the servants' quarters. He remembered that on a former occasion Tinlinn had shot him through the shoulder with an arrow. He therefore snatched the choicest food off Tinlinn's plate, spilled his drink, and drove a poisoned bodkin into his knee, inflicting a wound that festered for a long time. The minstrels were called into the hall and began their songs. The first to perform is old Albert Graeme, who sings of a Scottish lady who married an English lord, for love will be lord of all. The lady's brother poisoned her and was subsequently slain by the lord, who became, in penance, a Crusader.

It was an English ladye bright,
  (The sun shines fair on Carlisle wall)
And she would marry a Scottish knight,
  For **Love will still be lord of all.**

Blithely they saw the rising sun,
  When he shone fair on Carlisle wall;
But they were sad ere day was done,
  Though Love was still the lord of all.

Her sire gave brooch and jewel fine,
  Where the sun shines fair on Carlisle wall;
Her brother gave but a flask of wine,
  For ire that Love was lord of all.

For she had lands both meadow and lea,
  Where the sun shine on Carlisle wall;
And he swore her death, ere he would see
  A Scottish knight the lord of all!

Loved at home, revered abroad

Source: THE COTTER'S SATURDAY NIGHT (Line 164)
Author: Robert Burns (1759–1796)
First published: 1786
Type of work: Narrative poem

Context: Burns was writing from personal experience about the daily life of the hard-working Scotch farmers, in this description of a weekend. He was born in a clay cottage, and his early life was devoted to the backbreaking labor he describes. The poem itself is a tribute to his own father, the industrious William Burnes, as he spelled his name. Father of seven, always in debt because of unfertile land and high rent, he still managed to provide his children—of whom Robert was the oldest—with some education. The meter is the Spenserian stanza of the sixteenth century Elizabethan poet, Edmund Spenser. It tells of a poor family home together for the Sabbath. The children have returned from working out among the neighbors. Jenny, the oldest, is there to help with the chores. The mother will be ready to mend clothes, and the father, as the head of the family, will provide the religious atmosphere that has made Scotland great. Gilbert, the poet's brother, recorded that this poem grew from Robert's feeling of something particularly venerable in the phrase

"Let us worship God," uttered by a decent, sober head of a family as introduction to family worship. This is the picture painted in stanza 12, as "The cheerfu' supper done, wi' serious face/ They, round the ingle, form a circle wide,/ The sire turns o'er, wi' patriarchal grace,/ The big ha'-Bible, ance his father's pride." Then he picks out a Scriptural passage with judicial care, "And 'Let us worship God!' he says with solemn air." After the Scripture reading and the prayer, the group disbands, each going his separate way. Such scenes, says Burns, are the basis for Scotland's grandeur. To describe their effect upon home folk and foreigners, the poet contrasts their feelings using two verbs. Those at home *feel* love and a personal affection, while the rest of the world *looks* at Scotia (Scotland) with respect and esteem. Quoting Pope's *Essay on Man* that "an honest man is the noblest work of God," Burns believes it is easier to find the road to heaven from a humble cottage than from a palace. The third stanza from the end of the poem declares:

> From scenes like these old Scotia's grandeur springs,
>   That makes her **lov'd at home, rever'd abroad:**
> Princes and lords are but the breath of kings,
>   "An honest man's the noblest work of God:"
> And certes, in fair virtue's heavenly road,
>   The cottage leaves the palace far behind;
> What is a lordling's pomp? a cumbrous load,
>   Disguising oft the wretch of human kind,
> Studied in arts of hell, in wickedness refin'd.

A love-machine

Source: FAUSTINE (Line 142)
Author: Algernon Charles Swinburne (1837–1909)
First published: 1862
Type of work: Lyric poem

Context: Of this poem, Swinburne himself wrote, " 'Faustine' is the reverie of a man gazing on the bitter and vicious loveliness of a face . . . and dreaming of past lives in which this fair face may have held a nobler or fitter station." He says that the idea of the poem is "the transmigration of a single soul, doomed as though by accident from the first to all evil and no good." As the epigraph of the poem suggests, the Faustine of the title is either the notorious wife of Antoninus Pius, the Roman emperor, or her even more notorious daughter of the same name, the wife of Marcus Aurelius. Whenever she lives, suggests the poet, this soul serves but one god, the Lampsacene Priapus, a fertility god. If a man should truly love her, she would give him poison, or some other evil, being herself incapable of love. Faustine is the kind of woman who enjoys games in which men die, as though she is revived by "the slain man's blood and breath."

647

But though she craves love, her own love is but maimed and mean. It is no more than mere lust, perhaps close to hate; the poet says, addressing her:

> You seem a thing that hinges hold,
>   **A love-machine**
> With clockwork joints of supple gold—
>   No more, Faustine.
>
> Not godless, for you serve one God,
>   The Lampsacene,
> Who metes the gardens with his rod;
>   Your lord, Faustine.

Love-quarrels oft in pleasing concord end

Source: SAMSON AGONISTES (Line 1008)
Author: John Milton (1608–1674)
First published: 1671
Type of work: Dramatic tragedy

Context: Samson, blinded and disgraced, is visited while lying on a sunny bank in the city of Gaza, first by his father and then by Delilah, who, according to Milton, was his wife, but who, according to *Judges* 16:4, was merely a woman of Sorek whom he loved. Delilah first tries to explain her betrayal of Samson to the Philistines by saying that she mistakenly did it all because she loved him. When Samson will not accept this excuse, she explains that she was deceived by the Philistines, who averred that they had no evil designs on Samson; she performed her act of treachery for the public good, setting aside for the time her private concerns. Samson will not accept this reason either. He asks her why she married him if she did not intend to be a faithful wife, leaving parents and country to be with him: being his wife, she owed nothing to the Philistines. Delilah still tries to be reconciled with Samson, but he continues to spurn her advances. She then tells him that, although the Jews may hate her for all time, she will be one of the most famous of her own race for having conquered an enemy of her people. When she dies, her tomb will be a shrine. She then departs, but the Chorus says that her beauty may overwhelm him if she returns. To this Samson says that frequently love-quarrels end in joy and satisfaction, but her act was treachery.

CHORUS
She's gone, a manifest serpent by her sting
Discovered in the end, till now concealed.

SAMSON
So let her go; God sent her to debase me,

648

And aggravate my folly who committed
To such a viper his most sacred trust
Of secrecy, my safety, and my life.

CHORUS
Yet beauty, though injurious, hath strange power,
After offence returning, to regain
Love once possessed, nor can be easily
Repulsed, without much inward passion felt
And secret sting of amorous remorse.

SAMSON
Love-quarrels oft in pleasing concord end,
Not wedlock-treachery, endangering life.

A lover's eyes will gaze an eagle blind

Source: LOVE'S LABOUR'S LOST (Act IV, sc. iii, l. 334)
Author: William Shakespeare (1564–1616)
First published: 1598
Type of work: Dramatic comedy

Context: At the first part of the play, several men pledge with the King of Navarre to study for three years and to abstain from any contact with women. Berowne, one of the lords attending the king, is the only one in the group who expresses doubt as to the wisdom of the second part of the vow. Later, after he is proven correct when all of the group have fallen in love, he explains and philosophizes on the benefits of love. He emphasizes repeatedly the fact that love makes all the senses alert "And gives to every power a double power." Thus the eyes of a lover will be increased in their ability to see with more scope and comprehension the world around them.

BEROWNE
. . .
But love, first learned in a lady's eyes,
Lives not alone immured in the brain,
But with the motion of all elements,
Courses as swift as thought in every power,
And gives to every power a double power
Above their functions and their offices.
It adds a precious seeing to the eye:
A lover's eyes will gaze an eagle blind.
A lover's ear will hear the lowest sound,
When the suspicious head of theft is stopped.
. . .

Love's the noblest frailty of the mind

Source: THE INDIAN EMPEROR (Act II, ii)
Author: John Dryden (1631–1700)
First published: 1667
Type of work: Heroic tragedy

Context: Having successfully collaborated with Sir Robert Howard (1628–1698) on *The Indian Queen,* in 1663–1664, Dryden by himself wrote a sequel, *The Indian Emperor or The Conquest of Mexico.* It was well received and held the boards for forty years. It is a gory piece, showing Montezuma and an Indian priest tortured, and two Spaniards and three Indians killing one another. There is abundant romance. Almeria has one wooer, Cydaria two, and Alibach three. Among the other characters are spirits and the ghost of the earlier Indian Queen. Though the action is set only twenty years after the coronation of Montezuma, the dramatist, in his foreword, admits that he does not follow history closely. In Act II, Cydaria, daughter of Montezuma, tries to get Cortez to prevent a battle and further bloodshed between the Spaniards and the Aztecs, but Cortez, though he loves her, declares that he must obey the orders of his king. When, at last, she wins him over, and he is telling his general, Pizarro, that love is more important than honor and fame, and that he will therefore disobey royal orders and end the fighting, Pizarro informs him that it is too late. The order to attack has already been given. (This general is not the Francisco Pizarro who conquered Atahualpa and the Incas.)

CORTEZ
No more, your kindness wounds me to the death,
Honour, be gone, what art thou but a breath?
I'le live, proud of my infamy and shame,
Grac'd by no Triumph but a Lover's name;
Men can but say Love did his reason blind,
And **Love's the noblest frailty of the mind.**
Draw off my Men, the War's already done.

PIZARRO
Your Orders come too late, the Fight's begun, . . .

Lukewarmness I account a sin

Source: THE MISTRESS, OR SEVERAL COPIES OF LOVE-VERSES ("The Request," Stanza IV)
Author: Abraham Cowley (1618–1677)
First published: 1647
Type of work: Lyric poem

650

Context: Cowley had the misfortune to be a mild and rather moderate person living in a robust and even violent age; as a result, he often found himself placed in ridiculous and sometimes very uncomfortable positions. He received a good education and had earned himself a fellowship at Cambridge when the Puritan commissioners dispossessed him and set him adrift. He and his friends espoused the royalist cause and followed the king, first to Oxford and later to Paris, where Charles II elected to spend his exile. During his stay in Paris Cowley was given various secret-service assignments, which he seems to have carried out with a notable lack of enthusiasm. He must have been quite inept at cloak-and-dagger work: Charles II suspected him of treason, and Cromwell had him imprisoned as a spy. Cowley's political convictions were sincere enough but so mildly expressed that they were unconvincing. He eventually retired to the country where he studied medicine and botany, meanwhile writing essays and continuing to compose poems. A precocious poet, he had produced his first volume at the age of fifteen. His work reveals much inventiveness and versatility, but he was again unfortunate in that it must be compared with two giants, Donne and Milton. He produced an unfinished Biblical epic, the *Davideis*, which may have given the latter some ideas for *Paradise Lost*. Another work, *The Mistress*, was inspired by Donne but is not closely imitative. It is a collection of lyric verse detailing the pangs of unrequited love. Cowley sometimes casts these poems in the style of Donne, and occasionally employs intricate and striking metaphors or plays on words; however, his work is not metaphysical in the way that Donne's is. Instead, it possesses a certain cheerful pessimism and is at times either whimsical or mildly witty. It is also characterized by gracefulness and precision. "The Request" is a good example:

If she be coy, and scorn my noble fire;
   If her chill heart I cannot move;
    Why I'll enjoy the very love,
And make a mistress of my own desire.
   Flames their most vigorous heat do hold,
And purest light, if compass'd round with cold:
    So, when sharp Winter means most harm,
The springing plants are by the snow itself kept warm.

But do not touch my heart, and so be gone;
   Strike deep thy burning arrows in!
    Lukewarmness I account a sin,
As great in love as in religion.
   Come arm'd with flames; for I would prove
All the extremities of mighty Love.
    Th' excess of heat is but a fable;
We know the torrid zone is now found habitable.

651

Luve will venture in, where it daur na weel be seen

Source: THE POSIE (Line 1)
Author: Robert Burns (1759–1796)
First published: 1792
Type of work: Lyric poem

Context: Appearing in his 1793 collected poems in two volumes, just ahead of a poem he dated 1787 when sending it to Mr. Ballantine, is a seven-stanza poem about a posie or bouquet of flowers that Burns would collect for his "ain dear May." However, he was a better poet than a botanist because into the Posie "tied round wi' the silken band o' luve," he puts flowers of spring, summer, and autumn. In the verses, Burns reveals the same love of living things that made him write eight "Burns Stanzas" to a mouse whose nest he turned up with a plough in November, 1785. On that occasion, he pointed out the futility of the "beastie's" attempted forethought to provide for the cold winter, and wrote: "But, Mousie, thou art no thy lane (not alone)/ In proving foresight may be vain:/ The best laid plans o' mice an' men/ Gang aft agley (often go astray)/ An' lea'e us nought but grief an' pain/ For promis'd joy." In his desire to "pu'" (pull or pluck) flowers for May, he says he will gather some of the hawthorn, "but the songster's nest within the bush/ I winna tak away." In the first stanza of the poem, with its three lines rhyming somewhat more closely than frequently happens in Burns' poetry, and with an unrhymed fourth line that appears in variations like a chorus in the other six stanzas, Burns tells how a lover ventures into spots where he dare not be seen, and where Wisdom knows enough not to return, in order to collect a bouquet for his true love.

O luve will venture in, where it daur na weel be seen,
O luve will venture in, where wisdom ance hath been;
But I will down yon river rove, amang the wood sae green,
    And a' to pu' a Posie to my ain dear May . . .

I'll tie the Posie round wi' the silken band o' luve,
And I'll place it in her breast, and I'll swear by a' above,
That to my latest draught o' life the band shall ne'er remuve,
    And this will be a Posie to my ain dear May.

The luxury of doing good

Source: TALES OF THE HALL (III, "Boys at School," Line 139)
Author: George Crabbe (1754–1832)
First published: 1819
Type of work: Narrative poem

Context: Book III of *Tales of the Hall* is a discussion of boys, school-life, and the effects of schooling on the men who the boys become. In this section the rector tells Richard and Jacques, about whom the poem centers, of the patronized schoolboy and his career. The boy has as his patron a great nobleman, whose patronage affects the lad's whole life and even his death. The quotation is from the beginning of the rector's account. The lad is a "boy with pensive look,/ Whom some great patron order'd to his book,/ Who from his mother's cot reluctant came,/ And gave *my lord,* for his compassion, fame." The rector obviously does not consider the nobleman's effort one to reflect either great significance or praise on the great man. The nobleman in truth deserves but little credit.

> This noble lord was one disposed to try
> And weigh the worth of each new luxury;
> Now, at a certain time, in pleasant mood,
> He tried **the luxury of doing good;**
> For this he chose a widow's handsome boy,
> Whom he would first improve, and then employ.
>
> • • •
>
> Him sent my lord to school, and this became
> A theme for praise, and gave his lordship fame;
> But when the boy was told how great his debt,
> He proudly ask'd, "is it contracted yet?"

Lying becomes none but tradesmen

Source: THE WINTER'S TALE (Act IV, sc. iv, ll. 741–742)
Author: William Shakespeare (1564–1616)
First published: 1623
Type of work: Tragi-comedy

Context: Perdita, banished to a desert as a bastard by her father King Leontes of Sicilia, is reared by a shepherd in Bohemia. Now sixteen, Perdita is courted by Florizel, son of Polixenes, King of Bohemia and one-time friend of Leontes who falsely accused him of adultery with Queen Hermione of Sicilia. Since Polixenes is incensed at the idea of the marriage of the shepherdess Perdita and his son Florizel, the youth plans to elope with Perdita, disguising himself by exchanging clothes with Autolycus, a vender. Perdita's guardian shepherd, fearing for his life, goes to Polixenes with a bundle, containing evidence of Perdita's royal birth, but he and the clown who accompanies him are accosted by Autolycus:

AUTOLYCUS

Your affairs there? What? With whom? The condition of that fardel? The place of your dwelling? Your names, your ages, of what having, breeding, and any thing that is fitting to be known—discover.

CLOWN

We are but plain fellows, sir.

AUTOLYCUS

A lie; you are rough, and hairy. Let me have no **lying.** It **becomes none but tradesmen,** and they often give us soldiers the lie: but we pay them for it with stamped coin, not stabbing steel, therefore they do not give us the lie.

Mad world, mad kings, mad composition!

Source: KING JOHN (Act II, sc. i, l. 561)
Author: William Shakespeare (1564–1616)
First published: 1623
Type of work: Historical drama

Context: The Bastard, who has been making intermittent comments in the battle between Arthur and Philip of France and King John of England, comments on the madness of what he has witnessed. The enemies have just taken the suggestion of the surrounded town of Angiers to marry John's niece, Blanch of Spain, to Lewis, the dauphin of France, there- by pledging their loyalty to one another. These two, who have come from the bloody field of battle as enemies, agree, and the match is made. As Blanch's dowry, John gives exactly those provinces which have been fought over from the beginning of the play. Arthur is to be pacified with a dukedom and an earldom.

BASTARD

Mad world, mad kings, mad composition!
John, to stop Arthur's title in the whole,
Hath willingly departed with a part;
And France, whose armour conscience buckled on,

. . .

Hath drawn him from his own determined aid,
From a resolved and honorable war,
To a most base and vile-concluded peace.

. . .

Made almost a sin of abstinence

Source: FABLES ANCIENT AND MODERN ("The Character of a Good Parson," Line 11)
Author: John Dryden (1631–1700)
First published: 1700
Type of work: Narrative poem

654

Context: Proclaimed as "Imitated from Chaucer, and inlarg'd," Dryden included a portrait of a godly parson in his *Fables Ancient and Modern,* published in 1700, the year of his death. In 1698 the diary writer Samuel Pepys (1633–1703), while dining with Dryden, suggested that the poet bring some of Geoffrey Chaucer (c. 1340–1400) up to date, and that he write a modern version of Chaucer's "Good Parson." The following year Dryden completed his "Character of a Good Parson" and sent a copy to Pepys. Dryden looked on the poem, perhaps, as a sort of apology for the many scathing and satirical remarks he had made about ministers in his writings. From its Preface, one might expect the fable to be a rewriting of the portrait of the parson in the Pro-logue of *The Canterbury Tales* (lines 477–528), even though Dryden used the rhymed couplets and occasional triplets, instead of Chaucer's meter. However, a comparison of the two passages indicates that they must be parsons from different dioceses. Dryden's version begins: "A parish priest was of the pilgrim train;/ An awful, reverend, and religious man." It gives his age as sixty years, with the possibility of another sixty unless his severe and rigid mode of living kills him before his time. He wears shabby clothes, as Jesus did on earth, and is so pious and abstemious that he carries his virtues to excess and almost makes sins of them. Yet obviously, the poet admires the parson and thinks him as sincere as he appears.

· · ·

Rich was his soul, tho' his attire was poor,
(As God had cloth'd his own ambassador;)
For such, on earth, his blest Redeemer bore.
Of sixty years he seem'd; and well might last
To sixty more, but that he lived too fast;
Refin'd himself to soul, to curb the sense;
And **made almost a sin of abstinence.**
Yet had his aspect nothing of severe,
But such a face as promis'd him sincere.
Nothing reserved or sullen was to see,
But sweet regards and pleasing sanctity;
Mild was his accent, and his action free.

· · ·

Made his mouth water

Source: HUDIBRAS (Part I, Canto 3, l. 379)
Author: Samuel Butler (1612–1680)
First published: First and second parts, 1663; third part, 1678
Type of work: Burlesque poem

Context: A self-taught English poet decided to write a mock romance to poke fun at the hypocrisy of the Puritans, now that they had been driven out of power with the restoration to the English throne of Charles II, in

1660. In imitation of the Spanish *Don Quixote,* well known in England through several translations, Butler sends Sir Hudibras, a Presbyterian Justice of the Peace, roaming the land to put down abuses. The hero gets his name from a character of Spenser's *Faerie Queene,* II, ii, 17: "He that made love unto the eldest dame/ Was hight Sir Hudibras, an hardy man." It is probably a contraction of Hugh de Bras. He was accompanied by his squire, Ralpho, in religion an Independent, one of the more than 200 sects of the time. Through the pair, the author makes both Presbyterians and Independents odious. It is a poem in which more is said than done. The wit of the author provides a never-failing sequence of aphorisms and most unusual poetic images. In Part I, in three cantos expressed in lively rhythm suited, as Dr. Johnson commented, "to the vulgarity of the words," the author tells of the initial exploits of the pair. Equating enjoyment with sin, they attack a holiday crowd amused by bear baiting and fiddling. They put the musician into the stocks and in the confusion caused by the escape of the bear, get away. The crusading Hudibras, continuing on his journey to reform the world's sinners, meets a wealthy Widow living in a castle on the edge of the town. He begs rest for his body and medicine for his bruises. But in her company he gets another hurt, as Butler describes it, "of a deadlier sort, by Cupid made." Her land and possessions render her additionally attractive to Hudibras. However, she makes no secret of her disdain for him. He thinks that perhaps a display of his bravery and valor may make her change her mind.

> But being brought so nigh by Fate,
> The vict'ry he achiev'd so late
> Did set his thoughts agog, and ope
> A door to discontinu'd hope,
> That seem'd to promise he might win
> His dame too, now his hand was in;
> And that his valor and the honor
> H'had newly gain'd, might work upon her,
> These reasons **made his mouth to water**
> With am'rous longings to be at her.

Madman or slave, must man be one?

Source: A SUMMER NIGHT (Line 75)
Author: Matthew Arnold (1822–1888)
First published: 1852
Type of work: Lyric poem

Context: "A Summer Night" is Arnold's lyric portrayal of what he sees as most men's status in life. On the one hand there are men who "in a brazen prison live" and give their lives "to some unmeaning taskwork" until "Gloom settles slowly down over their breast." The next twenty-three lines of the poem discuss the second group, the madmen. In this stanza a sea motif is used to picture man as a "freed prisoner" determined to go somewhere but losing all direction because of the lack of a definite or tangible goal. In reaction to both ways of life, Arnold voices the question, "Is there no life, but these alone?" The final stanza contains an answer. Close contact with and the study of nature are the means by which men can realize direction and purpose and find fulfillment.

Is there no life, but these alone?
Madman or slave, must man be one?

Plainness and clearness without shadow of stain!
Clearness divine!
Ye heavens, whose pure dark regions have no sign
Of languor, though so calm, and, though so great,
Are yet untroubled and unpassionate;
Who, though so noble, share in the world's toil,
And, though so task'd, keep free from dust and soil!

Maggots in your brains

Source: WOMEN PLEASED (Act III, sc. iv)
Authors: Francis Beaumont (1585?–1616) and John Fletcher (1579–1625)
First published: 1647
Type of work: Tragi-comedy

Context: While Lopez, an odious old miser who much neglects his beautiful young wife, Isabella, is absent from home, his wife arranges a meeting with a lover, Claudio. She fastens a string to her finger and runs it out of her apartment so that Claudio, when he arrives, can pull it and waken her. While she is asleep, Lopez comes home, discovers the device, gently disengages the string from her hand, and waits for the lover to appear on the scene. When the tug comes on the string, he gives chase to the lover, but loses him. In the meantime Isabella wakes, finds out what has happened, and bribes her maid Jaquenette to await the return of Lopez, who in the dark gives the servant a sound beating and scratches her face. He departs to get witnesses to the perfidy of his wife, as will be evidenced by the scratched face. Isabella, wholly unmarked, is there in the place of the injured Jaquenette. The witnesses ask Lopz if he is not under an illusion caused by the moon and suggest that he has maggots, or whims, in his brains, like "bats in his belfry."

GENTLEMAN
Here walks my cousin full of meditation,
Armed with religious thoughts.

657

BARTELLO

Is this the monster?

FIRST GENTLEWOMAN

Is this the subject of that rage you talked of? . . .

. . .

Are not you mad, my friend? What time o' th' moon is't?
Have not you **maggots in your brains?**

LOPEZ

'Tis she, sure.

GENTLEMAN

Where's the scratched face ye spoke of, the torn garments,
And all the hair plucked off her head?

Maiden meditation, fancy-free

Source: A MIDSUMMER NIGHT'S DREAM (Act II, sc. i, l. 164)
Author: William Shakespeare (1564–1616)
First published: 1600
Type of work: Dramatic comedy

Context: There is great excitement at the approach of the marriage of Theseus, Duke of Athens, and the captive Queen of the Amazons, Hippolyta. The romantic time is shared even by fairies from India, including, Oberon, their king, and Titania, their queen. Oberon, however, angry with Titania because she refuses to relinquish a changeling child, orders Puck to secure for him an herb used as a love potion so that he can play a trick upon Titania. In a poetic speech, possibly directed at Queen Elizabeth, Oberon explains to Puck the origin of the magical qualities of the flower: once upon a time Cupid, flying between the moon and earth, directed at a virgin a dart, not visible to mortal eyes; but the beams of the moon, "the imperial vot'ress," averted the course of the arrow so that it missed its target and hit instead the flower, giving it power to influence love.

OBERON

. . .

But I might see young Cupid's fiery shaft
Quenched in the chaste beams of the watery moon,
And the imperial vot'ress passed on,
In **maiden meditation, fancy-free.**
Yet marked I where the bolt of Cupid fell.
It fell upon a little western flower;
Before, milk-white; now purple with love's wound,
And maidens call it, love-in-idleness.

Fetch me that flower; the herb I shewed thee once.
The juice of it on sleeping eyelids laid,
Will make or man or woman madly dote
Upon the next live creature that it sees.

. . .

Make assurance double sure

Source: MACBETH (Act IV, sc. i, l. 83)
Author: William Shakespeare (1564–1616)
First published: 1623
Type of work: Dramatic tragedy

Context: Macbeth is extremely unhappy and unsure as king. He revisits the old witches to ask for more prophecy so he may know what to expect. The witches call upon their masters. The first apparition, an armed Head, tells Macbeth to beware of Macduff, whom he had already suspected and feared. An apparition of a bloody child tells him not to fear, for no man of woman born can harm him. Somewhat pacified for a moment, Macbeth almost decides to let Macduff live. However, his usual fear and suspicion overcome him, and he quickly changes his mind and plans for Macduff's death so that he may hopefully sleep in peace once again— as he did before he murdered Duncan.

SECOND APPARITION
Be bloody, bold, and resolute, laugh to scorn
The power of man, for none of woman born
Shall harm Macbeth.

[*Descends.*]

MACBETH
Then live Macduff, what need I fear of thee?
But yet I'll **make assurance double sure,**
And take a bond of fate. Thou shalt not live;
That I may tell pale-hearted fear it lies,
And sleep in spite of thunder.

Make haste slowly

Source: LIVES OF THE CAESARS (Book II, chapter 25)
Author: Suetonius (Gaius Suetonius Tranquillus, c. 70-c. 140)
First transcribed: Second century
Type of work: Biography

Context: Gaius Suetonius Tranquil-   lus, Roman biographer and private secretary to Emperor Hadrian, gathered all sorts of inconsequential items, as well as those of historical importance to incorporate into the biographies he wrote. His work was a model for many subsequent biographers. In his *Lives of the Caesars,* which includes a biography of Caesar Augustus, the historian tells of Rome's leaders. The section about Augustus gets the title of Divus Augustus because later the ruler was deified. It recounts his innovations in warfare, largely a cataloguing of them written without unity. He tried to avoid familiarity by requiring that troops be addressed as "soldiers," never as "Fellow soldiers." He refused to admit freed slaves into the ranks, since being a soldier of Rome was too high an honor for their low estate. He did not especially reward officers who had taken part in his victories, because they themselves could grant such recognition to any one whom they chose. Here is one paragraph of Suetonius's catalog of Augustus Caesar's customs. "Festina lente (Make haste slowly)" was a common Greek and Latin proverb, an expression certainly not originated by Augustus.

He thought nothing more derogatory to the character of an accomplished general than precipitancy and rashness; on which account he had frequently in his mouth those proverbs: **"Make haste slowly,"** and "The cautious captain's better than the bold," and "That is done fast enough which is done well enough."

Make the fur fly

Source: HUDIBRAS (Part I, Canto 3, l. 277)
Author: Samuel Butler (1612–1680)
First published: First and second parts, 1663; third part, 1678
Type of work: Burlesque poem

Context: The Puritan Revolution was the name given to the struggle during the first half of the seventeenth century between the subjects of James I and Charles I and their rulers. Actually there were more than religious factors involved. In the final defeat of royalist Cavaliers by Cromwell's Puritan Roundheads, nonreligious country gentry and city merchants had a hand. This was the period selected by the Bristish satirical poet Butler for a long mock romance that begins: "When civil dudgeon first grew high/ And men fell out they knew not why." Butler, son of a poor farmer, received a grammar-school education, but despite his claims of further study at Cambridge and Oxford, modern scholars doubt that he attended either. He worked as clerk for an eminent Justice of the Peace, Mr. Jefferys, where he had time for reading and studying music and painting. Later he became secretary of the Countess of Kent, where he had access to a good library. He left her to serve Sir Samuel Luke, a rigid Pres-

660

byterian who had been one of Cromwell's officers. The household was a stronghold of Puritanism, and many believe Sir Samuel the model for Sir Hudibras in the long poem Butler began writing there. Since 1612, people in England had been able to read the Spanish novel *Don Quixote* (1605) in their language, and in 1652 another popular translation appeared. Butler got the idea of writing an English *Don Quixote* in verse, with an ignorant Presbyterian Justice and his Independent squire riding through the land to suppress superstition and correct abuses. Part I, containing three cantos, was published in 1663, when the author was more than fifty years old. In it, Sir Hudibras starts on his quest, full of learned conversation, loaded with classical references. As his Rocinante, he rides a horse so skinny that "his strutting

ribs on both sides show'd/ Like furrows he himself had plough'd." In Canto 2, they run into a crowd of people enjoying themselves, a sure sign to the knight that he had discovered an abode of sin. They see peg-leg Crowdero, a fiddler, and Orsin, owner of a bear used for bear baiting. Though Talgol, the butcher, and others fight bravely, Hudibras and his squire Ralpho capture Crowdero, breaking his wooden leg, and putting him in the stocks. In the final canto, Part I, the knight-errant visits a Widow with whom he falls in love. But meanwhile his vanquished victims have rallied. Crowdero is released. They all determine on revenge, and start after Hudibras and Ralpho. Orsin vows to make them regret their deeds, and Cerdon, another in the crowd, agrees.

> Quoth Cerdon, Noble Orsin, th'hast
> Great reason to do as thou say'st,
> And so has ev'ry body here,
> As well as thou hast, or thy Bear;
> Others may do as they see good;
> But if this twig be made of wood
> That will hold tack, I'll **make the fur**
> **Fly** 'bout the ears of that old cur,
> And th' other mungrel vermin, Ralph,
> That brav'd us all in his behalf.

A man cannot be too careful in the choice of his enemies

Source: THE PICTURE OF DORIAN GRAY (Chapter 1)
Author: Oscar Wilde (1856–1900)
First published: 1891
Type of work: Novel

Context: Supposedly inspired by the novel *Vivian Gray* (1826) of Benjamin Disraeli (1804–1881), that treats of the delusions and desires of

youth and their change on the road to old age, the wit Oscar Wilde wrote *A Picture of Dorian Gray,* epitomizing the decadence of his epoch and ex-

661

pressing his own exaggerated hedonism. To some extent, the relation of Dorian Gray to Lord Henry Wotton anticipates the novelist's relationship with Lord Alfred Douglas. In its Preface, Wilde declares: "There is no such thing as a moral or an immoral book. Books are well written or badly written. That is all." This one is carefully plotted, and its writing combines paradox and poetry. At its start, the artist Basil Hallward is painting a portrait of his handsome Faustian friend, Dorian Gray, when Lord Henry Wotton expresses a desire to meet the young man. The request begins a discussion of friendship. Hallward accuses Lord Henry of understanding neither friendship nor enmity, and of being indifferent to everybody.

"How horribly unjust of you!" cried Lord Henry, tilting his hat back, and looking up at the little clouds that, like ravelled skeins of glossy white silk, were drifting across the hollowed turquoise of the summer sky. "Yes, horribly unjust of you. I make a great difference between people. I choose my friends for their good looks, my acquaintances for their good characters, and my enemies for their good intellects. **A man cannot be too careful in the choice of his enemies.** I have not got one who is a fool. They are all men of some intellectual power, and consequently they all appreciate me. . . ."

Man dreams of fame while woman wakes to love

Source: IDYLLS OF THE KING ("Merlin and Vivien," Line 458)
Author: Alfred, Lord Tennyson (1809–1892)
First published: 1859
Type of work: Narrative poem

Context: Vivien, the beautiful, wily, and malignant daughter of a man killed fighting against King Arthur, leaves Tintagel, the court of Mark of Cornwall, to go to Camelot. There she intends to sow seeds of suspicion concerning the honor and purity of Lancelot's devotion to Guinevere. Vivien swears to return with the hearts of all the Round Table in her hand and perhaps a curl from Arthur's beard. Gaining access to Arthur's castle, she spreads her vicious rumors and then steals away "as an enemy that has left/ Death in living waters and withdrawn." Her next project is to win the heart of the aging wizard, Merlin. Even while doubting Vivien's honesty, Merlin "felt the flattery and at times/ Would flatter his own wish in age for love." Foreseeing the doom poised to fall on Camelot, Merlin leaves the court consumed with melancholy. Vivien accompanies him to Broceliande where she attempts to extract from him a charm which ensnares its victim forever, invisible to all but the enchanter. Merlin agrees that he owes her a boon for breaking his melancholy, but he asserts that this particular charm should not be shared. Vivien replies that

662

Merlin should trust her "not at all or all in all," a line from a song she once heard Lancelot sing. Making a strong plea for her wish, she sings the whole song to Merlin, who replies:

"But, Vivien, when you sang me that sweet rhyme,
I felt as tho' you knew this cursed charm,
Were proving it on me, and that I lay
And felt them slowly ebbing, name and fame."
And Vivien answer'd smiling mournfully:
"O, mine have ebb'd away for evermore
And all for following you to this wild wood
. . .
—So is it with this rhyme—
. . .
It lives dispersedly in many hands
And every minstrel sings it differently;
Yet is there one true line, the pearl of pearls:
'Man dreams of fame while woman wakes to love.' "

Man: false man

Source: THEODOSIUS (Act III, sc. ii, line 67)
Author: Nathaniel Lee (1655?–1692)
First published: 1680
Type of work: Dramatic tragedy

Context: Little is known about the English dramatist Nathaniel Lee. Neither the place nor the year of his birth is certain. He may have been born as early as 1649. His minister father changed religious belief according to political changes, but retained his rectory at Hatfield, where Nathaniel was brought up. Like Otway, stage fright prevented his becoming an actor, so he started writing plays, beginning with *Nero* in 1674. Critics lampooned its plotting and characterization, but he learned from it, and in *Sophonisba* (1675) glorifying heroic love, he scored a hit. He became friendly with Dryden, with whom he collaborated on *Oedipus* (1678) that ran ten nights. Lee's *Rival Queens* was his most popular success, but he considered *Mithri-* dates (1678) his best play. Then, for political and religious reasons, his popularity waned, and he tried to regain his public with *Theodosius or The Force of Love,* based on *Pharamond* (1661) by the French dramatist Gautier de la Calprenède (1609–1663). For its eight songs, the English composer Henry Purcell provided music. As a tender heroic drama, with a love-honor conflict, its sentiments appealed to the ladies. He dedicated it to "La Belle Stuart," the Duchess of Richmond, the king's favorite. It won back his popularity. However, Lee's sympathies for the Whigs appeared in his last two plays, and they were suppressed. The dramatist went mad and was committed to Bedlam in 1684. Though finally released, he remained ill and in poverty. No one knows the actual cause of his death, and no trace of his grave remains today. For his times, Lee's characters are unusually complex and reveal understanding of human passions and motivations. Though not a major dramatist, he did express the dignity and nobility of man. In this tragedy, set in Persia, Theodosius sees Athenais bathing and falls in love with her. She, however, has long been in love with his friend Prince Varanes. (In the French drama she loves no one and is quite willing to marry Theodosius while Varanes, refused by Rosamond, is content with the Princess Sydemiris, but Lee omits both these women.) By stressing the eternal love of Athenais and Varanes, he produced a tragedy which ends with the death of both lovers. There is a subplot in which Princess Pulcheria, in love with a commoner, General Marcian, banishes him to test his love for her. Addison declared that, though it may lack the strength of some of Lee's other plays, *Theodosius* also lacks their extravagance, violence, and occasional repugnance. While it may not be Lee's greatest work, yet because of its warmth, tenderness, and emotional appeal, it is certainly his most charming. At the end of Act II, Varanes, heir to the throne of Persia, cannot persuade himself to marry the daughter of a commoner philosopher, so he spurns her. In Act III, after a torturing night in which Love and Glory struggle, his love for Athenais conquers, but too late. She has taken her final vows. Here she rages to her friend, Princess Pulcheria, about the fickleness and evil in man. (The old spellings have been modernized.)

ATHENAIS

Drive me! O drive me from the traitor man:
So I might 'scape that monster, let me dwell
In lions' haunts or in some tiger's den;
Place me on some steep, craggy, ruin'd rock,
That bellies out, just dropping in the ocean;
Bury me in the hollow of its womb;
Where, starving on my cold and flinty bed,
I may from far, with giddy apprehension,
See infinite fathoms down the rumbling deep!
Yet not ev'n there, in that vast whirl of death,
Can there be found so terrible a ruin
As **man: false man,** smiling, destructive man.

A man has shop to mind

Source: SHOP (Line 96)
Author: Robert Browning (1812–1889)
First published: 1876
Type of work: Dramatic monologue

Context: All men, whether poets or butchers, have the right and duty to a private existence behind the everyday façade that they show the world. A

664

man's inner being, the home of his soul and intellect, is like the house he physically inhabits. Each man's mind should contain diverse interests and ideas, just as his physical house should not be entirely devoted to the occupation by which the man earns his living. The house which outwardly appears so interesting may on the inside lack all diversity. So may it be with a man's mind as well. The speaker is amazed to discover that a man's shop could so dominate his house that he retains for himself only "A hole, the wall where, heel by head,/ The owner couched, his ware behind,/ -In cupboard suited to his mind." In the same way that a man's house may be all shop, a man's inner being may gradually move away from all interests, ideas, and people, shutting the door on real living. The speaker protests:

> Because **a man has shop to mind**
>   In time and place, since flesh must live,
> Needs spirit lack all life behind,
>   All stray thoughts, fancies fugitive
>   All loves except what trade can give?
>   . . .
> But—shop each day and all night long!
>   Friend, your good angel slept, your star
> Suffered eclipse, fate did you wrong;
>   From where these sorts of treasures are,
>   There should our hearts be—Christ, how far!

Man hath all which Nature hath, but more

Source: IN HARMONY WITH NATURE: TO A PREACHER (Line 5)
Author: Matthew Arnold (1822–1888)
First published: 1849
Type of work: Sonnet

Context: One of the popular notions to emerge from the late eighteenth century, especially from writers like Rousseau and Wordsworth, was that men could be happy only when they left cities and lived in harmony with nature; from its conception, this notion was bandied about by men who sought a romantic escape from the problems of human life. By the middle of the nineteenth century, however, the notion was becoming passé. Arnold, who wrote this poem after he heard a preacher urge his congregation to live in harmony with nature, violently disliked such an easy solution to the suffering he found in his contemporaries. A stanch believer in humanistic culture, Arnold thought that nature. was cruel, stubborn, fickle, and antagonistic to man, and that the spiritual values that men should seek are opposed to such savagery. The only way to meet the problems of modern society was, according to Arnold, to face them squarely and, by using the best thoughts of the best men, to seek solutions that were practicable:

"In harmony with Nature?" Restless fool,
Who with such heat dost preach what were to thee,
When true, the last impossibility—
To be like Nature strong, like Nature cool!

Know, **man hath all which Nature hath, but more,**
And in that *more* lie all his hopes of good. . . .

Man must begin, know this, where Nature ends;
Nature and man can never be fast friends.
Fool, if thou canst not pass her, rest her slave!

A man in armor is his armor's slave

Source: ARISTOPHANES' APOLOGY (*Herakles,* Line 206)
Author: Robert Browning (1812–1889)
First published: 1875
Type of work: Poetic drama

Context: In 1871 Browning began to explore classical mythology and to cultivate it diligently. The first result of this work was *Balaustion's Adventure,* an offshoot from Euripides with Alcestis for its theme. Browning was particularly fond of Euripides, who was currently being neglected by scholars and critics in favor of Aeschylus; hence, Browning wrote a number of works that attempted to vindicate his favorite. The second of these, *Aristophanes' Apology,* is a sequel to *Balaustion's Adventure.* Its form is Browning's usual grouping of monologues to form a drama; in this case the poem is an extended conversation in which the Greek classic dramatists are discussed by some of their contemporaries. To prove a point, one of the speakers reads a dramatic piece by Euripides, entitled *Herakles,* to the others. When the play opens, Herakles (Hercules) has completed all but one of the twelve great labors assigned to him by Eurystheus. Eight of these tasks have involved the capture, or the slaying, of fabled animals; in addition, he has cleaned the Augean stables, taken a girdle belonging to the Queen of the Amazons, and gained the golden apples of the Hesperides. Now he has departed on the final task. To fulfill it he must descend to Hades and return, bringing the three-headed dog Cerberus, guardian of the infernal regions, back with him. His father, Amphitruon, keeps vigil at the altar of Zeus in Herakles' absence; he is worried because Lukos wishes to destroy Herakles' wife Megara and her children. Lukos had killed Megara's father Kreon, and now holds his seat: if the children grow up, they will be a danger to him. He tells Amphitruon and Megara as much, and implies that Herakles is not really a great fighter; only a coward would rely on the weapons of the archer—the real warrior wears armor and wields a sword. Amphitruon replies indignantly:

Amphitruon. As to the part of Zeus in his own child,
Let Zeus defend that! As to mine, 't is me
The care concerns to show by argument
The folly of this fellow,—Herakles,
Whom I stand up for! since to hear thee styled—
Cowardly—that is unendurable.

                    . . .

Go ask at Pholoé, vilest thou of kings,
Whom they would pick out and pronounce best man,
If not my son, "the seeming-brave," say'st thou!
But Dirphus, thy Abantid mother-town,
Question her, and she would not praise, I think!
For there's no spot, where having done some good,
Thy country thou might'st call to witness worth.
Now, that allwise invention, archer's-gear,
Thou blamest: hear my teaching and grow sage!
A man in armor is his armor's slave,
And, mixed with rank and file that want to run,
He dies because his neighbors have lost heart.
Then, should he break his spear, no way remains
Of warding death off,—gone that body-guard,
His one and only; . . .

Man is a carnivorous production

Source: DON JUAN (Canto II, stanza 67)
Author: George Gordon, Lord Byron (1788–1824)
First published: 1819 (Cantos I and II)
Type of work: Satiric poem

Context: Don Juan, at sixteen, has succeeded in causing a divorce and one of the liveliest scandals in all Spain. As a remedy for his waywardness, the precocious offender has been packed off to sea "As if a Spanish ship were Noah's ark,/ To wean him from the wickedness of earth,/ And send him like a dove of promise forth." The repentent exile stands on the deck of the departing vessel, his eyes overflowing with tears as the shoreline of his homeland recedes into the distance, and the memory of his mother and his forbidden love weighs heavily on his heart. But both love and country are soon forgotten as the young hero is assailed by the pangs of seasickness, and, later, by the great storm that batters vessel and crew until the ship founders and sinks. With it go two hundred souls, leaving thirty survivors, including Don Juan, afloat in the long-boat. As the storm continues to rage, the castaways, for love of life ". . . stand like rocks the tempest's wear and tear;" but, alas! hunger proves stronger than fortitude and leads to deadly folly, for

> . . . **man is a carnivorous production,**
> And must have meals, at least one meal a day;

667

He cannot live, like woodcocks upon suction,
  But, like the shark and tiger, must have prey;
Although his anatomical construction
  Bears vegetables, in a grumbling way,
Your labouring people think beyond all question
Beef, veal, and mutton, better for digestion.

And thus it was with this our hapless crew;
  For on the third day there came on a calm,
And though at first their strength it might renew,
  And lying on their weariness like balm,
Lull'd them like turtles sleeping on the blue
  Of ocean, when they woke they felt a qualm,
And fell all ravenously on their provision,
Instead of hording it with due precision.

Man is a noble animal, splendid in ashes, pompous in the grave

Source: HYDRIOTAPHIA: URN BURIAL (Chapter 5)
Author: Sir Thomas Browne (1605–1682)
First published: 1658
Type of work: Philosophy

Context: This philosophical physician and scientist set out to write a report concerning some forty or fifty Roman funeral urns which were exhumed near Norwich. His speculative nature led him beyond the bounds of a mere scientific report to a disquisition on burial customs in general, ranging, of course, through his vast knowledge of classical literature. In his final chapter Browne speculates on death and the brevity of human life. It is but vanity, he says, to "hope for immortality, or any patent from oblivion" in this world.

There is nothing strictly immortal, but immortality. Whatever hath no beginning may be confident of no end (all others have a dependent being, and within the reach of destruction) which is the peculiar of that necessary essence that cannot destroy itself; And the highest strain of omnipotency to be so powerfully constituted, as not to suffer even from the power of itself. But the sufficiency of Christian Immortality frustrates all earthly glory, and the quality of either state after death makes a folly of posthumous memory. God who only can destroy our souls, and hath assured our resurrection, either of our bodies or names hath directly promised no duration. Wherein there is so much chance that the boldest expectants have found unhappy frustration; and to hold long subsistence, seems but a scape in oblivion. But **man is a noble animal, splendid in ashes, and pompous in the grave,** solemnizing nativities and Deaths with equall lustre, nor omitting ceremonies of bravery, in the infamy of his nature.

668

Life is a pure flame, and we live by an invisible sun within us. A small fire sufficeth for life, great flames seemed too little after death. . . .

Man is a religious animal

Source: REFLECTIONS ON THE REVOLUTION IN FRANCE
Author: Edmund Burke (1729–1797)
First published: 1790
Type of work: Political treatise

Context: As a conservative, albeit one of originality and relatively liberal views, Edmund Burke deplored the French Revolution. He believed that it would do more to injure mankind and society than it could do good. He believed in the slow accretion of culture, and so he hated to see institutions which had been brought into being over centuries erased within a few days or weeks, to be supplanted by theories which could be used or abused by persons in power. Specifically, he felt that religion is important to mankind as "the basis of civil society, and the source of all good and of all comfort." Realizing that others might argue that England had undergone a religious revolution in parting from the Roman Church, Burke defends the Anglican Church, saying that the British have chosen it from zeal, not apathy, and that it has more of Christian principle in it, rather than less. He also defends it as part of a social fabric which, along with its success, contains established monarchy, established aristocracy, and an established democracy, as well. What is happening to religion during the French Revolution he sees as a surge of atheism which cannot last long:

We know, and it is our pride to know, that **man is** by his constitution **a religious animal;** that atheism is against, not only our reason, but our instincts; and that it cannot prevail long. But if, in the moment of riot, and in a drunken delirium from the hot spirit drawn out of the alembic of hell, which in France is now so furiously boiling, we should uncover our nakedness, by throwing off that Christian religion which has hitherto been our boast and comfort, and one great source of civilization amongst us, and among many other nations, we are apprehensive (being well aware that the mind will not endure a void) that some uncouth, pernicious, and degrading superstition might take the place of it.

Man is a tool-making animal

Source: THE LIFE OF SAMUEL JOHNSON, LL.D. (For 1778)
Author: James Boswell (1740–1795)
First published: 1791
Type of work: Biography

Context: On Tuesday, April 7, 1778, Boswell ate breakfast with Dr. Johnson at the latter's house in London, and the conversation was varied. For example, Johnson mentioned that he had once bought a flageolet, but had never been able to play a tune upon it; to this comment Boswell retorted that the size and sounds of a cello made it a fitter instrument for a man of Johnson's size and character. The talk also was, in part, about people. Dr. Johnson pointed out that Dr. John Campbell, who was accurate with his pen in hand, was unreliable in conversation for the handling of the truth. Comments were also made by the two men on Mrs. Montagu and Mr. Harris, with Johnson saying that the latter was "a prig and a bad prig," which observation led to the following exchange, in which Boswell attributed the definition of man as a tool-making animal to Benjamin Franklin:

BOSWELL

. . . He [Mr. Harris] says plain things in a formal and abstract way, to be sure: but his method is good: for to have clear notions upon any subject, we must have recourse to analytick arrangement.

JOHNSON

Sir, it is what every body does, whether they will or no. But sometimes things may be made darker by definition. I see a *cow,* I define her, *Animal quadrupes ruminians cornutum.* But a goat ruminates, and a cow may have no horns. *Cow* is plainer.

BOSWELL

I think Dr. Franklin's definition of **Man [is]** a good one— **"A tool-making animal."**

JOHNSON

But many a man never made a tool; and suppose a man without arms, he could not make a tool.

Man is an embodied paradox

Source: LACON (Volume I, number 408)
Author: Charles Caleb Colton (1780?–1832)
First published: 1820
Type of work: Aphoristic commentary

Context: Colton, a product of Eton and Kings College, Cambridge, was known as an eccentric. Though given quarters at the university, he preferred lodgings over a marine store in London, which he furnished with books such as Defoe's *History of the Devil,* manuscripts, fishing rods, and, as one caller reported after visiting him to enjoy his sparkling conversations, two bottles of excellent wine. One of these manuscripts turned into *Lacon, or Many Things in Few Words for Those who Think,* a collection of aphorisms of an edifying kind, usually forcefully expressed. Many came from Bacon's *Essays* and from *Material for Thinking* (1803–1815) by William Burdon (1764–1818). But who could expect complete originality in such an undertaking? The book was so popular when it came out in 1820 that six editions had to be printed the first year, and the author was encouraged to produce Volume II in 1822. After losing his fortune through speculations in Spanish bonds, the Reverend Mr. Colton thought it wise to flee to America and later to Paris, but in 1827 he returned to England to claim his university privileges, only to find that a successor had been appointed. After another visit to America, he settled permanently in France, putting in his time gambling. One report tells of a winning of 25,000 louis in one session; however, usually his luck was bad, and the story went that he was being supported by "his aged mother." Suffering from a painful disease and afraid of surgery, he ran counter to one of the maxims in *Lacon* that "No one ever committed suicide from bodily anguish, though thousands have done so from mental anguish," by killing himself. In the first volume, Colton published 588 aphorisms, from No. 1, beginning with: "It is almost as difficult to make a man unlearn his errors as his knowledge," and ending with: "Time is the most undefinable yet paradoxical of things, the past is gone, the future is not come, and the present becomes the past, even while we attempt to define it." Number 408 was inspired, as a footnote declares, by a faker, Joanna Southcote, who set herself up as a fortuneteller and made a profitable living among the gullible of London, "the first metropolis of the world." The author cannot understand how she gained so many wealthy proselytes "in an era of general illumination." But he decides that no one except a philosopher can talk with sanity on the folly of mankind.

408

Man is an embodied paradox, a bundle of contradictions; and some set off against the marvellous things that he has done, we might fairly adduce the monstrous things that he has believed. The more gross the fraud, the more glibly will it go down, and the more greedily will it be swallowed, since folly will always find faith wherever impostors will find imprudence.

A man is as old as he's feeling, a woman as old as she looks

Source: THE UNKNOWN QUANTITY
Author: Mortimer Collins (1827–1876)
First published: 1860
Type of work: Light verse

671

Context: The idea that physical decline is not dependent on chronology has frequently been expressed. One version was the punning comment: "Whether life is worth living or not depends on the liver." In 1806, Dr. Pierre J. G. Cabanis (1757–1808), the French physician and philosopher, published the medical epigram: "A man is as old as his arteries." The American man of letters George William Curtis (1824–1892) wrote in *Prue and I* (1857): "Age . . . is a matter of feelings, not of years." However, it remained for a British teacher of mathematics to figure out the best formula for determining the age of both men and women. As a pastime, Mortimer Collins wrote and published a quantity of light verse which appeared in magazines, and the works were published in four volumes: *Idylls and Rhymes* (1855), *Summer Songs* (1860), *The Inn of Strange Meetings* (1870) and a posthumous *Selections from the Poetical Works of Mortimer Collins* (1886), edited by Collins's wife's cousin, F. Percy Cotton, who provided musical settings for a number of them. Collins was also editor of a satirical poem, *The British Birds, a Communication from the Ghost of Aristophanes* (1872), and several novels, including *Sweet Anne Page* (1868). All of them might have been forgotten along with the name of the author, in the passing of time, had Collins not written one brief poem known both by its mathematical-sounding title, *The Unknown Quantity,* and by the simpler *How Old Are You?*

> O wherefore our age be revealing?
> Leave that to the registry books!
> **A man is as old as he's feeling,**
> **A woman as old as she looks.**

Man is not Man as yet

Source: PARACELSUS (Part V)
Author: Robert Browning (1812–1889)
First published: 1835
Type of work: Poetic drama

Context: Having aspired to know infinitely, Paracelsus discovers that he had relied too much on intellect and consequently had forgotten how to love or to recognize beauty. After a period of melancholy, Festus, his close friend and only associate, gives him the confidence to aspire a second time; this time to love infinitely, a desire that is just as futile as his first aspiration. Defeated because he cannot join the drive to know and the urge to love, he loses his mind as he dies. In his final ravings, however, he discovers the truth of the human condition: man's nature is twofold, consisting of the mutually exclusive drives of the emotions and the intellect, and man, torn by these drives, can find no peace on earth. But he also sees the ultimate hope of suffering man: as he continues to evolve, he will slowly

672

progress closer to the harmony of God, the full union of contrary drives that was shown in the Incarnation. Paracelsus thus dies knowing that he has failed but confident that failure such as his will help mankind reach the final stage of evolution.

—And this to fill us with regard for man,
With apprehension of his passing worth,
Desire to work his proper nature out,
And ascertain his rank and final place,
For these things tend still upward, progress is
The law of life, **man is not Man as yet.**
Nor shall I deem his object served, his end
Attained, his genuine strength put fairly forth,
While only here and there a star dispels
The darkness, here and there a towering mind
O'erlooks its prostrate fellows: when the host
Is out at once to the despair of night,
When all mankind alike is perfected,
Equal in full blown powers—then, not till then,
I say, begins man's general infancy.

Man is the measure of all things

Source: THEAETETUS (152, as translated by Benjamin Jowett)
Author: Plato (427–347 B.C.)
First transcribed: Fourth century B.C.
Type of work: Socratic dialogue

Context: In the dialogue known as *Theaetetus,* Socrates and Theaetetus discuss the nature of knowledge, seeking to find the true definition of it. After some false starts at answering by his friend, Socrates once again puts his question, "What is knowledge?" Theaetetus begins again by stating that knowledge is perception. Socrates notes that this doctrine is an old and honorable one that was expounded by the famous Protagoras, a Greek philosopher of an earlier generation. Socrates notes, too, that the obvious meaning for Protagoras' statement is that things are actually what they appear to be at any given moment in time. Such a statement, suggests Socrates, is true only in some cases; that Protagoras must have had a deeper meaning. He suggests that Protagoras meant that all things are relative and in motion. Socrates adds that many of the ancients, including Heracleitus and Empedocles, were in agreement with such a statement. Both Socrates and Plato, however, do not believe in the relativity of truth and knowledge. As philosophical idealists they believe in ultimate, immutable, and absolute truth. Plato has Socrates go on to question Theaetetus until both are satisfied that even the statement of such a great thinker as Protagoras is wrong when it attempts to exchange transient and mutable perception for knowledge of truth. Following Socrates' question,

673

asking for a statement of the nature of knowledge, Theaetetus begins:

THEAETETUS

. . . Now he who knows perceives what he knows, and, as far as I can see at present, knowledge is perception.

SOCRATES

Bravely said, boy; that is the way in which you should express your opinion. And now, let us examine together this conception of yours, and see whether it is a true birth or a mere wind-egg: —You say that knowledge is perception?

THEAETETUS

Yes.

SOCRATES

Well, you have delivered yourself of a very important doctrine about knowledge; it is indeed the opinion of Protagoras, who has another way of expressing it. **Man,** he says, **is the measure of all things,** of the existence of things that are, and of the nonexistence of things that are not:—You have read him?

THEAETETUS

O yes, again and again.

SOCRATES

Does he not say that things are to you such as they appear to you, and to me such as they appear to me, and that you and I are men?

THEAETETUS

Yes, he says so.

A man of sorrows

Source: ISAIAH 53:3
Author: Isaiah
First transcribed: c. 800–200 B.C.
Type of work: Religious prophecy and exhortation

Context: That Isaiah, poet and prophet of the Old Testament, foretold the life and ministry of Jesus has been acknowledged for centuries. The early fathers of the Christian Church were of this opinion; later scholars puzzled over the prophetic verses and considered a number of contemporary figures Isaiah may have wished to cast in the role of deliverer. More recently it has become the belief of scholars that Isaiah's thoughts were

674

not concerned with ordinary heroes and that he believed a Messiah would come from God to save the people of Israel in a spiritual rather than physical sense. He refers to this Messiah as the Servant, and the passages in which the Servant appears take the form of evangelical hymns. The various Messiah prophecies occur in chapters 40, 42, 49, 50, 52 and 53. The first of these chapters is a form of prelude to the other passages; here Isaiah announces in a hymn of great sublimity that Israel's suffering under foreign oppression is at an end, and that the Lord and his glory will descend on the people. He first refers to the Servant in Chapter 42: one prepared by the Lord, who will arrive quietly and teach God's religion in a gentle way; his teaching will reach everyone and be spread throughout the world. In Chapter 49 the Servant is announced dramatically as speaking to the nations, explaining his mission and exhorting them. His suffering, and the patience and determination with which he endures it, are mentioned in Chapter 50; and in Chapter 52 it is prophesied that out of this suffering will come a triumph that will astonish the nations of the earth. In Chapter 53, perhaps the most striking of the Messiah passages, it is revealed that he will suffer for the sins of others, who will be forgiven thereby, and that he will die for others as well.

He is despised and rejected of men; **a man of sorrows,** and acquainted with grief: and we hid as it were our faces from him; he was despised, and we esteemed him not.

Surely he hath borne our griefs, and carried our sorrows: yet we did esteem him stricken, smitten of God, and afflicted.

But he was wounded for our transgressions, he was bruised for our iniquities: the chastisement of our peace was upon him; and with his stripes we are healed.

All we like sheep have gone astray; we have turned every one to his own way; and the LORD hath laid on him the iniquity of us all.

He was oppressed, and he was afflicted, yet he opened not his mouth: he is brought as a lamb to the slaughter, and as a sheep before her shearers is dumb, so he openeth not his mouth.

He was taken from prison and from judgment: and who shall declare his generation? for he was cut off out of the land of the living: for the transgression of my people was he stricken.

And he made his grave with the wicked, and with the rich in his death; because he had done no violence, neither was any deceit in his mouth.

Yet it pleased the LORD to bruise him; he hath put him to grief: when thou shalt make his soul an offering for sin, he shall see his seed, he shall prolong his days, and the pleasure of the LORD shall prosper in his hand.

675

Man partly is and wholly hopes to be

Source: A DEATH IN THE DESERT (Line 588)
Author: Robert Browning (1812–1889)
First published: 1864
Type of work: Narrative poem

Context: In this long poem, supposedly an account of the death of St. John written by a first century Christian, Browning sets forth several of his favorite religious and philosophical concepts. Among such concepts the one repeated most frequently in his other poems is that man is unique in the universe because he alone strives to better himself; this unique quality is man's blessing but also his curse, for he will never be satisfied with what he thinks he wants. The process is, therefore, an eternal striving for an unattainable goal, but neither Browning nor St. John, his spokesman, despairs over the futility implied in this struggle. Quite the contrary: the struggle, not the goal, should give man the greatest degree of available happiness; a man who sets such a low goal that he can attain it will earn only the misery of not being able to strive for a higher.

> . . . man knows partly but conceives beside,
> Creeps ever on from fancies to the fact,
> And in this striving, this converting air
> Into a solid he may grasp and use,
> Finds progress, man's distinctive mark alone,
> Not God's, and not the beasts': God is, they are,
> **Man partly is and wholly hopes to be.** . . .
> Man, therefore, thus conditioned, must expect
> He could not, what he knows now, know at first;
> What he considers that he knows to-day,
> Come but to-morrow, he will find misknown. . . .

Man wants but little; nor that little, long

Source: THE COMPLAINT: OR, NIGHT THOUGHTS ("Night the Fourth," l. 118)
Author: Edward Young (1683–1765)
First published: 1742
Type of work: Philosophical poem

Context: Night IV attempts to combat the fear of death, which, the poet contends, is not the horrible bugbear that man imagines. The knell, the shroud, the mattock, the grave, the darkness, and the worm are things that terrorize the living, not the dead. But even if death were frightful, what have the aged to fear from it? They see the world for what it is, a very wretched place, and should not repine at leaving it. Even if we admit that life has some joys, we outlive our ability to appreciate them: new people spring up, our neighbors are strangers to us, we accumulate wealth only that we may die rich. We work mightily during our little hour here on earth to achieve fame and wealth, even forming schemes for our future glory when we lie on our death-beds, but the end for everybody is the inscription, "Here he lies." As men grow old, they become pitiful remnants of what they once were, and they are foolish to cling stubbornly to earth like ancient trees ever sinking their roots deeper into the earth. Man needs but little here in this world, and that little he needs for but a short time; nature, which is economical of its resources, only lends him what he has. Man spends his existence acquiring the key of life, which, as soon as he gets it, opens the gates of death. Oliver Goldsmith echoed the line in the Ballad in Chapter 8 of *The Vicar of Wakefield.*

O my coevals! remnants of yourselves!
Poor human ruins, tottering o'er the grave!
Shall we, shall aged men, like aged trees,
Strike deeper their vile root, and closer cling,
Still more enamored of this wretched soil?
Shall our pale, withered hands be still stretched out,
Trembling, at once, with eagerness and age?
With avarice and convulsions, grasping hard?
Grasping at air! for what has earth beside?
Man wants but little; nor that little, long:
How soon must he resign his very dust,
Which frugal nature lent him for an hour!
Years unexperienced rush on numerous ills;
And soon as man, expert from time, has found
The key of life, it opes the gates of death.

Manifest destiny

Source: U.S. NEWS AND DEMOCRATIC REVIEW (Volume XVII, p. 5)
Author: John Louis O'Sullivan (1813–1875)
First published: August-September, 1845
Type of work: Patriotic editorial

Context: In 1837, John O'Sullivan and S. D. Langtree founded in Washington the *U.S. News and Democratic Review* (better known as the *Democratic Review*) as a mouthpiece for nationalism. They predicted the expansion of the United States to include Mexico and Cuba. In 1841, O'Sullivan bought out his partner and moved the publication to New York. In a six-page patriotic article, "Annexation," the editor opened the seventeenth volume, with an appeal to his countrymen to forget the dissention that discussions of the annexation of Texas had caused between friends and foes of slavery. Now that the Texas Congress and Convention had accepted the proffered invitation by the United States to join the Union, annexation had come about. "Her star and her stripe may already be said to have taken their place in the glorious blazon of our common nationality. She comes within the dear and sacred designation of Our Country." So let opposition cease. If there must be party differences, let them grow out of other problems. O'Sullivan reminds his readers that the move was not one of spoliation or revenge against Mexico. Nor was it a military conquest or territorial aggrandizement at the expense of justice. Objections by England or France are to be disregarded. Because of the acts and faults of Mexico. Texas had become free, and by the great divine plan was fated to become part of the United States. From early times, people believed that God or Providence looked after the development of nations. The British sovereigns were such "by the grace of God," and during the Revolution, countless divines in the Colonies proclaimed Americans to be God's chosen people. It was the fate or destiny of a nation to achieve whatever success came to it. So Lowell could write of "the destiny of the free republics of America," and Churchill could extend the idea to "the destiny of mankind," controlled by something beyond space and time. Even the homespun philosopher "Josh Billings" (1818–1885) wrote an entire article on "Manifest Destiny," which he defined as "the science ov going tew bust or enny other place before yer get there." O'Sullivan saw the need for the United States to make space "for the two hundred and fifty or three hundred millions—and American millions—destined to gather beneath the flutter of the stars and stripes, in the fast hastening year of the Lord 1945." O'Sullivan was somewhat optimistic about the growth of his country in the course of a century, but he did foresee its "manifest destiny," and was the first to use the phrase.

Were other reasons wanting, in favor of now elevating this question of the reception of Texas into the Union, out of the lower region of our past party dissentions, up to its proper level of a high and broad nationality, it surely is to be found, found abundantly, in the manner in which other nations have undertaken to intrude themselves into it, between us and the proper parties to the case, in a spirit of hostile interference against us, for the avowed object of thwarting our policy and hampering our power, limiting our greatness and checking the fulfilment of our **manifest destiny** to overspread the continent allotted by Providence for the free development of our yearly multiplying millions.

A manly, moral, regulated liberty

Source: REFLECTIONS ON THE REVOLUTION IN FRANCE
Author: Edmund Burke (1729–1797)
First published: 1790
Type of work: Political treatise

Context: Burke was certainly one of   the   greatest   political   philosophers

England has ever produced. Though he was for some time a member of the English Parliament and influenced extensively the political thinking of an entire era, he never rose to high political office. The American Revolution he lamented but considered it to be a justifiable defense of traditional liberties; the French Revolution, on the other hand, he regarded as a dangerous and vicious repudiation of all sane principles of liberty and just government. Because of extensive sympathy in England for the revolution in France he was led to the publication of these *Reflections*. The immediate quotation is from a discussion concerning an unsigned defense of the revolution in highly general and abstract terms issued by a society of English sympathizers:

> I flatter myself that I love **a manly, moral, regulated liberty** as well as any gentleman of that society, be he who he will; and perhaps I have given as good proofs of my attachment to that cause, in the whole course of my public conduct. I think I envy liberty as little as they do, to any other nation. But I cannot stand forward, and give praise or blame to anything which relates to human actions and human concerns, on a simple view of the object, as it stands stripped of every relation, in all the nakedness and solitude of metaphysical abstraction. Circumstances (which with some gentlemen pass for nothing) give in reality to every political principle its distinguishing colour, and discriminating effect. The circumstances are what render every civil and political scheme beneficial or noxious to mankind. . . .

A man's a man for a' that

Source: FOR A' THAT (Stanza 2)
Author: Robert Burns (1759–1796)
First published: 1795
Type of work: Didactic poem

Context: In January, 1795, Robert Burns wrote to his friend, George Thomson, who was publishing Burns' songs in his six volume *Collection of Original Scotch Airs for the Voice* (1793–1811), that their common friend, the critic Robert Aiken, had declared love and wine to be the exclusive themes for song writing. However, adds the poet, "The following is on neither subject, and consequently is no song; but will be allowed, I think, to be two or three pretty good prose thoughts converted into rhyme." In it, Burns expresses the ideal of future republicanism with a democratic confidence. The poem does not show him as an original thinker, but the lines indicate his ethical code and absolute sincerity. In his thinking, man represents the basic gold. Any rank or position he may acquire is only the mark put upon him by the mint, stamping out the coinage. Having been brought up on Alexander Pope (1688–1744) from an early age, Burns repeats the essence of Pope's lines from his *Essay on Man,* Epistle IV, "An honest man's the noblest work of God." (In "The Cotter's Saturday Night," he quotes this line directly.) In another place, in his "Jolly Beggar," published posthumously in 1801, one of the songs is to be sung to the tune of "For a' that and a' that." In the first two of the five stanzas, Burns counsels no man to hide his head in shame because he is poor but honest. Let him consider his homely fare and drab clothes the equivalent of the rich wines and colorful silks of a king's palace. At the conclusion of the poem, he prays for the time to come when "man to man, the world o'er/ Shall brothers be for a' that." The poem begins:

> Is there, for honest poverty,
>   That hings his head, and a' that?
> The coward-slave, we pass him by,
>   We dare be poor for a' that!
>   For a' that, and a' that,
>   Our toils obscure, and a' that;
>   The rank is but the guinea's stamp;
>   The man's the gowd for a' that.

> What tho' on hamely fare we dine,
>   Wear hodden-grey, and a' that;
> Gie fools their silks, and knaves their wine,
>   **A man's a man for a' that.**
>   For a' that, and a' that,
>   Their tinsel show, and a' that;
>   The honest man, tho' e'er sae poor,
>   Is King o' men for a' that.

A man's house is his castle

Source: COKE'S REPORTS, SEMAYNE'S CASE (5 Co. Rep. 91b, 77 Eng. Rep. 194)
Author: Sir Edward Coke (1552–1634)
First published: 1604
Type of work: Legal codification

Context: The idea of a man's house being his castle lies at the heart of English psychology and jurisprudence. It was proverbial by the middle of the seventeenth century. John Ray, in his *English Proverbs* (1670) says: "A man's house is his castle. This is a kind of law proverb, *Jura publica favent privato domus.*" Ralph Waldo Emerson, in America, said (*Works,* VII, 132): "The language of a ruder age has given to common law the maxim that every man's house is his castle." Thus the belief that a man and his property were safe against invasion and seizure was ingrained in the sophisticated as well as the popular mind long before Sir Edward Coke's codification. He states the proverb thus:

For **a man's house is his castle,** *et domus sua cuique tutissimum refugium* . . . and Fortresse, as well for his defence against injury and violence as for his repose . . . Resolved: The house of every man is his castle, and if thieves come to a man's house to rob or murder, and the owner or his servants kill any of the thieves in defence of himself and his house, it is no felony and he lose nothing. . . .

Man's unhappiness comes of his greatness

Source: SARTOR RESARTUS (Book II, chapter 9)
Author: Thomas Carlyle (1795–1881)
First published: 1833–1834
Type of work: Spiritual autobiography

Context: After years of the study of German philosophy and literature, a Scotsman, whose religious doubts turned him from the ministry, produced his first important book, and many believe his greatest, out of his profound disgust with the materialism of his age. *Sartor Resartus* first appeared in installments in *Frazer's Magazine* in 1833–1834. It was published in book form in Boston in 1836, and in England in 1838. Carlyle described it to his brother as: "a very singular book, I assure you. It glances from Heaven to Earth, and back again in a strange and satirical frenzy." And the language is even stranger. The author attempted to work into his English sentences, a structure peculiar to German prose. It resulted in un-English inversions, and unusual coined words and combinations of words. The style keeps changing from pedestrian, earthy paragraphs to poetic flights. He confessed he used the abrupt changes to shock the self-complacency of the reader and compel his close attention. Borrowing an idea from Swift's *Tale of a Tub,* Carlyle named his book *Sartor Resartus* (The Tailor Re-clothed), using the figure that the material world is only clothing for the soul. The author claims to be explaining and commenting on the philosophy of an eccentric German Professor, Diogenes Teufelsdröckh (Born-of-God Devil-Dung) who lectures at the University of Weissnichtwo (No-body-knows-where). He has sent six bags of his papers to an English editor to be turned into a book about his life and philosophic theory. The theme is a contrast between the way things seem to be and really are. Behind its robes of civilization, he believes, the world conceals its soul. To deny God, to lose faith in spiritual values, is to give the "Everlasting No" to life; but to say the "Everlasting Yea" is to face life with spiritual courage and a willingness to work. In one chapter, the professor describes himself in his skyey tent, musing in front of the mountains, looking down at the towns and villages below. He sees the beauty of Nature, which he declares is God. He can look with pity on his fellow men, who are usually involved in some controversy touching on the Origin of Evil or some other problem.

681

. . . For it is man's nature to change his Dialect from century to century; he cannot help it though he would. The authentic Church-Catechism of our present century had not yet fallen into my hands: meanwhile, for my own private behoof, I attempt to elucidate the matter so. **Man's Unhappiness,** as I construe, **comes of his Greatness;** it is because there is an Infinite in him, which with all his cunning he cannot quite bury under the Finite. Will the whole Finance Ministers and Upholsterers and Confectioners of modern Europe undertake, in jointstock company, to make one Shoeblack HAPPY? . . .

Man's word is God in man

Source: IDYLLS OF THE KING ("The Coming of Arthur," Line 132)
Author: Alfred, Lord Tennyson (1809–1892)
First published: 1869
Type of work: Narrative poem

Context: Before the coming of King Arthur, England was torn by internal dissention and invasion by foreign kings. The cultivated land decreased in area, and the wilderness increased; men became fewer, and wild beasts grew in number. The land of Cameliard, King Leodogran's domain, was in such a deplorably lawless state that the king asked Arthur's aid. There were those who said that Arthur was not Uther's son, and Arthur had as yet done no memorable deeds, but he answered the call. At Leodogran's castle he first saw Princess Guinevere and felt her enter his life, although she did not seem to notice him. Arthur knew himself to be nothing, but felt that he and Guinevere together would be able to bring life into this dead world. The battle began between Arthur's force and that of a powerful coalition of kings; the tide of battle ran back and forth between the two hosts, but finally Arthur prevailed. He called to him the man he loved and honored most, and they two swore a deathless love. Arthur said that a man's promise is like God in him, and come what may, Arthur will trust his friend even till death.

> He laughed upon his warrior whom he loved
> And honored most. "Thou dost not doubt me King,
> So well thine arm hath wrought for me to-day."
> "Sir and my liege," he cried, "the fire of God
> Descends upon thee in the battle-field:
> I know thee for my King!" Whereat the two,
> For each had warded either in the fight,
> Sware on the field of death a deathless love.
> And Arthur said, **"Man's word is God in man:**
> Let chance what will, I trust thee to the death."

682

Many a good hanging prevents a bad marriage

Source: TWELFTH NIGHT (Act I, sc. v, ll. 20–21)
Author: William Shakespeare (1564–1616)
First published: 1623
Type of work: Dramatic comedy

Context: Maria, Countess Olivia's waiting woman, is quarreling with Feste, the Clown, another of Olivia's servants, and he returns her some saucy answers:

MARIA
Nay, either tell me where thou hast been, or I will not open my lips so wide as a bristle may enter, in way of thy excuse. My lady will hang thee for thy absence.

FESTE
Let her hang me. He that is well hanged in this world needs to fear no colours.

MARIA
Make that good.

FESTE
He shall see none to fear.

. . .

MARIA
Yet you will be hanged for being so long absent, or, to be turned away. Is not that as good as a hanging to you?

FESTE
Many a good hanging prevents a bad marriage; . . .

The march of the human mind is slow

Source: SPEECH ON CONCILIATION WITH AMERICA (March 22, 1775)
Author: Edmund Burke (1729–1797)
First published: 1775
Type of work: Parliamentary address

Context: Edmund Burke thought it best for Great Britain to conciliate the American colonists; he also thought that, at the time he gave this speech in the House of Commons, conciliation was possible, on both sides, between the colonists and the British government. In an effort to show the advantages of conciliation to British commerce, he points out

683

the increasing population of the Colonies and the growth of trade between them and the mother country. He pleads for admitting the people of the Colonies to full rights and privileges as Englishmen. He also turns to British history, to give an account of Great Britain's policies in Ireland, to show that Ireland was made, by constitutional means, "a principal part of the strength of Great Britain." He cites also the history of Wales. By comparison, he says, Wales was kept in a state of war with England for many years. He notes that the laws passed with respect to the Welsh in a bygone era could well be used as precedents for new laws against the American colonists, but he also reminds his fellow members of the House of Commons of the unfavorable results which followed the passage of those laws:

Here we rub our hands—A fine body of precedents for the authority of parliament and the use of it!—I admit it fully; and pray add likewise to these precedents, that all the while, Wales rid this kingdom like an *incubus;* that it was an unprofitable and oppressive burthen; and that an Englishman travelling in that country could not go six yards from the high road without being murdered.

The march of the human mind is slow. Sir, it was not, until after two hundred years, discovered, that, by an eternal law, Providence had decreed vexation to violence, and poverty to rapine. Your ancestors did however at length open their eyes to the ill husbandry of injustice. They found that the tyranny of a free people could of all tyrannies the least be endured; and that laws made against a whole nation were not the most effectual methods for securing its obedience. . . .

Mark Hopkins on one end and I on the other

Source: PRESIDENT GARFIELD AND EDUCATION (Page 43)
Author: James A. Garfield (1831–1881), attributed by Burke A. Hinsdale
First published: 1882
Type of work: Biography

Context: Burke A. Hinsdale, president of Hiram College, describes James A. Garfield's career at the newly founded Eclectic Institute, a preparatory school that later became Hiram College, at Hiram, Ohio. Before entering the Institute, Garfield had taught grade school, and as a student he also acted as a teacher at the Institute. After three years at Hiram he went to Williams College, at Williamstown, Massachusetts; Mark Hopkins was president of the college at the time. After graduation from Williams, Garfield returned to take up teaching again at Hiram, at the age of twenty-three years. He became well known throughout the region as a public speaker, and the question in the minds of those who knew him was whether he should enter the ministry or the law. Garfield always had great affection for small schools in out-of-the-way places. He believed that in

684

such schools the personal element in teaching operated with more power than in larger institutions. He believed in having adequate physical equipment for schools but also believed that good teachers were more important than apparatus. Later in life he said:

> To all that has been said, I most heartily assent. No words of mine shall in any way detract from the importance of everything that has been urged; but I am not willing that this discussion should close without mention of the value of a true teacher. Give me a log hut, with only a simple bench, **Mark Hopkins on one end and I on the other,** and you may have all the buildings, apparatus, and libraries without him.

Marriage is nothing but a civil contract

Source: TABLE TALK (Marriage)
Author: John Selden (1584–1654)
First published: 1689
Type of work: Recorded conversation

Context: Contemporaries of tall John Selden, of the gray eyes and long nose in a thin, oval face, believed him a bachelor jurist who lived alone without servants, among his books, except for visits to widowed Lady Kent in Bedfordshire and London, to console her for the death of the Earl of Kent, in 1639. Not till after her death, in 1651, leaving him her heir and executor, was it discovered that all the time they had been married secretly, "upon some law account." After his graduation from Oxford, in 1602, Selden had been admitted to the bar, imprisoned briefly for political activities, elected member of Parliament in 1623, and then imprisoned again for five years for his activities against the crown. Later he served in the Long Parliament as representative of his Alma Mater, then retired to private life to devote himself to writing. John Selden was considered one of the most learned men of his time, a writer who displayed his knowledge in abstruse books written in a harsh style and archaic vocabulary that dealt with topics such as British and rabbinical law, and England's rights of sovereignty over the waters of the English Channel. However, there was another side to him. As a young man, Selden had been part of a brilliant conversational group at the Mermaid Tavern that included Sir Walter Raleigh, Drayton, Ben Jonson, and Shakespeare. Later, with money left him by Lady Kent, he set a bounteous table for his intellectual friends. His amanuensis, the Reverend Richard Milward (1609–1680), carefully set down his comments and quips; and after his employer's death, the secretary published his accumulation as *Table Talk,* sorted into 125 headings, from "Abbeys and Priories" to "Zealots." Samuel Johnson, though on the other side of the fence politically, spurned a French book of aphorisms

685

with the comment: "A few in it are good, but we have one book of that kind better than any of them, Selden's *Table Talk*." Coleridge declared: "There is more weighty bullion sense in this book than I ever found in the same number of pages of any uninspired writer." Selden's views on marriage run counter to the often-repeated lines of John Lyly, "Marriage is Destiny, made in Heaven," and Tennyson's "Marriages are made in heaven." They are nearer to Southerne's cynical "If marriages are made in heaven, they should be happier." Perhaps the difficulties of Selden's own secret marriage motivated his views on the subject that fill one page of his small book.

1. Of all actions of a man's life, his marriage does least concern other people, yet of all actions of our life 't is most meddled with by other people.

2. **Marriage is nothing but a civil contract.** 'T is true, 't is an ordinance of God; so is every other contract; God commands me to keep it when I make it.

3. Marriage is a desperate thing. The frogs in Aesop were extreme wise; they had a great mind to some water, but they would not leap into the well, because they could not get out again.

4. We single out particulars, and apply God's Providence to them. Thus when two are married and have undone one another, they cry it was God's Providence we should come together, when God's Providence does equally concur to every thing.

The marriage of true minds

Source: SONNET 116 (Line 1)
Author: William Shakespeare (1564–1616)
First published: 1609
Type of work: Sonnet

Context: There exists no impediment, says the poet, to the union of minds through love. True love, constant as the star which safely guides sailors to port, does not change, though it encounters change, nor does it lessen with the passage of time and the subsequent physical changes. The entire familiar sonnet reads:

Let me not to **the marriage of true minds**
Admit impediments. Love is not love
Which alters when it alteration finds,
Or bends with the remover to remove.
O no, it is an ever-fixed mark
That looks on tempests and is never shaken;
It is the star to every wand'ring bark,
Whose worth's unknown, although his height be taken.
Love's not Time's fool, though rosy lip and cheeks

686

Within his bending sickle's compass come.
Love alters not with his brief hours and weeks,
But bears it out even to the edge of doom.
   If this be error and upon me proved,
   I never writ, nor no man ever loved.

Married in haste, we may repent at leisure

Source: THE OLD BACHELOR (Act V, sc. iii)
Author: William Congreve (1670–1729)
First published: 1693
Type of work: Dramatic comedy

Context: The old bachelor, Heartwell, who professes to despise all womankind, is secretly in love with Sylvia, who is Vainlove's castoff mistress. Heartwell tries to seduce Sylvia, but she plays upon him to the extent that he agrees to marry her. Vainlove, however, has other plans for her. Heartwell turns up at her house to marry her, and mistakes Bellmour, dressed as Tribulation Spintext, a Puritan minister, for a genuine minister; Bellmour is on his way home from an unsuccessful attempt to seduce Laetitia, old Fondlewife's wife. He, aware of Vainlove's intention to marry Sylvia to Sir Joseph Wittol, a simple Knight, goes through with the performing of a marriage ceremony between Sylvia and Heartwell. Sharper, two hours after the supposed marriage, indicates to Heartwell that Sylvia's character is highly questionable. Pretending ignorance of the mock marriage, Sharper says that he will go to visit Sylvia himself. But Heartwell warns him to stay away from his house, admitting that he has been married to Sylvia for two hours. Sharper, in soliloquy at the end of the scene, says that people marry in haste and repent at leisure.

HEARTWELL

Oh, an age, an age! I have been married these two hours.

SHARPER

My old bachelor married! that were a jest! ha! ha! ha!

HEARTWELL

Death! d'ye mock me! Hark ye, if either you esteem my friendship or your own safety, come not near that house—that corner house—that hot brothel; ask no questions.   [*Exit.*]

SHARPER

Mad, by this light!
Thus grief still treads upon the heels of pleasure;
Married in haste, we may repent at leisure.

The Master of those who know

Source: THE DIVINE COMEDY, INFERNO (Canto IV, line 131, as translated by Henry Wadsworth Longfellow)
Author: Dante Alighieri (1265–1321)
First transcribed: c. 1314
Type of work: Christian allegory

Context: Dante, in Limbo, where the good people who died unbaptised dwell, sees the noble poets Homer, Horace, Ovid, and Lucan. They hail the newly returned Virgil and admit Dante to their company. The travelers then pass a seven-walled castle with seven gates, the castle probably symbolizing philosophy, the seven walls the liberal virtues (prudence, justice, fortitude, temperance, wisdom, knowledge, and understanding), and the seven gates the liberal arts (grammar, logic, rhetoric, music, arithmetic, geometry, and astronomy). There is a green inside the castle peopled with Trojans and great Romans. Dante then sees the great master of those who know, Aristotle. Surrounding him are the representatives of the major schools of philosophy, many of which stem from Aristotelian teaching. Aristotle is chosen by Dante as the grand master because his philosophy was dominant in medieval scholastic thought; Plato did not become popular until the Renaissance. The Spanish-Arabian philosopher Averroes (1126–1198) wrote a commentary on Aristotle.

When I had lifted up my brows a little,
 The Master I beheld **of those who know,**
Sit with his philosophic family.
All gaze upon him, and all do him honor.
 There I beheld both Socrates and Plato,
 Who nearer him before the others stand;
Democritus, who puts the world on chance,
 Diogenes, Anaxagoras, and Thales,
 Zeno, Empedocles, and Heraclitus;
Of qualities I saw the good collector,
 Hight Dioscorides; and Orpheus saw I,
 Tully and Livy, and moral Seneca,
Euclid, geometrician, and Ptolemy,
 Galen, Hippocrates, and Avicenna,
Averroes, who the great Comment made.

A master-passion is the love of news

Source: THE NEWSPAPER (Line 279)
Author: George Crabbe (1754–1832)
First published: 1785
Type of work: Satiric poem

Context: The poet, in examining what is wrong with newspapers, says that the man who owns a hut and is possessed of an income of forty shillings a year (which annual income entitled him to vote) reads his newspapers and cries out that all that the venal candidates care for is getting elected; at the same time he feels joy that he can sell his vote at the usual price. The papers are filled with scandal, fraud, falsehood, and folly; and it is to them that the populace looks for guidance. But the poet, who longs for lasting fame and who with patient care refines every line of his work, finally publishes it, only to be greeted by censure or neglect. Writers for the newspapers, however, meet a happier fate, getting the praise that should go to worthier works. The newspaper writers are interested only in how many words make up a line, how many lines make up a column, and how many columns make up a sheet. And the readers, who abhor a book, are delighted with a paper; those who would never think of reading the Bible consider it a hardship to be deprived of their daily news. Newspapers are like public inns: there is something for everyone, and all for some. The politician looks for fact alone; gay ladies neglect fact for songs and accounts of birthdays and balls; financial advertisements are the study of the business man. When people are in the country and the paper does not arrive on time, they are completely out of sorts. In fact, a mastering passion of the human race is the love of news.

> So charm the News; but we, who far from town
> Wait till the postman brings the packet down,
> Once in the week, a vacant day behold,
> And stay for tidings, till they're three days old:
> That day arrives; no welcome post appears,
> But the dull morn a sullen aspect wears:
> We meet, but ah! without our wonted smile,
> To talk of headachs, and complain of bile;
> Sullen we ponder o'er a dull repast,
> Nor feast the body while the mind must fast.
> **A master-passion is the love of news,**
> Not music so commands, nor so the Muse:
> Give poets claret, they grow idle soon;
> Feed the musician, and he's out of tune;
> But the sick mind, of this disease possess'd,
> Flies from all cure, and sickness when at rest.

May we never want a friend in need, nor a bottle to give him

Source: DOMBEY AND SON (Volume I, chapter 15)
Author: Charles Dickens (1812–1870)
First published: 1846–1848
Type of work: Novel

Context: Near the offices of Dombey   and Son is the shop of Solomon Gills, dealer in navigational instruments; with him lives his beloved nephew, Walter Gay, who secures employment at Dombey and Son as a minor clerk. A friend of Mr. Gills is Captain Cuttle, a retired sea captain. Florence Dombey, because of the momentary carelessness of her brother Paul's nurse, becomes lost in the streets of London, and Walter finds her and returns her to her home; this act of Walter produces an intense dislike for him on the part of Mr. Dombey. As Sol Gills' business withers away until he is desperate for money, Walter approaches Mr. Dombey for a loan, which young Paul urges, and so it is granted. Mr. Dombey and his manager, Mr. Carker, arrange to transfer Walter to a vacant post in Barbados, largely so that he and Florence cannot see each other. Walter, aware that the post is a bad one, is in great doubt how to break the news of his imminent departure from London to his uncle. He asks Captain Cuttle for advice, and the Captain offers two complete non-sequiturs as a solution of the problem. Walter explains the situation:

". . . I am sorry to say, I am not a favorite with Mr. Dombey. I have always tried to do my best, and I have always done it; but he does not like me. He can't help his likings and dislikings, perhaps. I say nothing of that. I only say that I am certain he does not like me. He does not send me to this post as a good one; he disdains to represent it as being better than it is; and I doubt very much if it will ever lead me to advancement in the House—whether it does not, on the contrary, dispose of me for ever, and put me out of the way. Now, we must not say anything of this to my uncle, Captain Cuttle, but must make it out to be as favorable and promising as we can; and when I tell you what it really is, I only do so, that in case any means should ever arise of lending me a hand, so far off, I may have one friend at home who knows my real situation."

"Wal'r, my boy," replied the captain, "in the Proverbs of Solomon you will find the following words, **'May we never want a friend in need, nor a bottle to give him!'** When found, make a note of."

Measure your mind's height by the shade it casts!

Source: PARACELSUS (Part III)
Author: Robert Browning (1812–1889)
First published: 1835
Type of work: Poetic drama

Context: Fourteen years after Paracelsus, the German alchemist, left his friend Festus in his search for total knowledge, he pauses long enough to tell about his aspiration and failure. Festus, who has chosen a life of happy obscurity and has reared a family, had warned Paracelsus against trying to ignore human limitations; still, he admires the alchemist so much that he asks to hear about the struggle. Describing how he sought to know infinitely and thereby ignored God, Paracelsus tells that he could not love or recognize beauty; when he met the dying poet Aprile, he discovered his mistake, saw that he was a failure, and sank into a passive melancholy. He has publicly denounced the philosophers of Roman Catholicism and has loudly opposed Luther; he stands completely alone, having no one he can turn to or follow. But the memory of Aprile haunts him so that, as Festus attempts to raise him from his wretchedness, he slowly comes to see that he can aspire to be what the poet was— a man who loves infinitely. The quotation is from Festus' speech encouraging him to overcome his despair.

> I know you and the lofty spirit you bear,
> And easily ravel out a clue to all.
> These are the trials meet for such as you,
> Nor must you hope exemption: to be mortal
> Is to be plied with trials manifold. . . .
>   Since
> The rabbit has his shade to frighten him,
> The fawn a rustling bough, mortals their cares,
> And higher natures yet would slight and laugh
> At these entangling fantasies, as you
> At rammels of a weaker intellect,—
> **Measure your mind's height by the shade it casts!**

Medicines to make me love him

Source: KING HENRY THE FOURTH: PART ONE (Act II, sc. ii, l. 19)
Author: William Shakespeare (1564–1616)
First published: 1598
Type of work: Historical drama

Context: Prince Hal, heir to the throne, and Poins, his low companion, set out to frustrate their friends Falstaff, Gadshill, Bardolph, and Peto, who plan to rob a traveling group. Pretending to take part in the robbery, Poins, with Hal's knowledge, hides the rotund Falstaff's horse. Falstaff, unaccustomed to walking, rages at his supposed brother in banditry:

FALSTAFF

. . . If I travel but four foot by the squier further afoot, I shall break my wind. Well, I doubt not but to die a fair death for all this, if I 'scape hanging for killing that rogue. I have forsworn his company hourly any time this two and twenty years, and yet I am bewitched with the rogue's company. If the rascal have not given me **medicines to make me love him,** I'll be hanged. It could not be else; I have drunk medicines. Poins, Hal, a plague upon you both!

691

Melancholy as an unbraced drum

Source: THE WONDER! (Act II, sc. i)
Author: Sussanah Centlivre (1667?–1723)
First published: 1761
Type of work: Dramatic comedy

Context: The English actress and compiler of anthologies of early English plays, Mrs. Inchbald, puts Mrs. Centlivre in the first rank of her country's comic dramatists, for her handling of plots and characters. Though her weakness in dialogue puts her below Congreve, Wycherley, and even Farquhar, Congreve gave up his career as a dramatist because his *The Way of the World* (1700) was so coldly received by the public at a time when Mrs. Centlivre's *Busy Body* was breaking records with a run of thirteen performances. Sussanah Freeman was driven to playwriting by necessity. Her father was a dissenter whose estates were confiscated, and he and his family driven to exile in Ireland. Here Sussanah found herself an orphan at the age of twelve. Impoverished and pursued for her beauty, she started for London. Tradition says she met a young man who later became "Silver Tongued Anthony Hammond, Commissioner of the Navy," who persuaded her to put on masculine attire and accompany him to college. After one such experience, she demanded marriage of her next sweetheart, but was widowed before she was eighteen. In a third matrimonial episode, she became Mrs. Carroll, only to be left a widow again. The only comment on this period in her biography declares, "After several gay adventures over which we shall draw a veil," she turned to the theatre as a not very successful actress but an increasingly popular playwright with her nineteen plays, fifteen of which were successful. She performed on tour in her comedy, *At a Venture,* including an appearance at Windsor Castle in 1706, where Queen Anne's pastry cook, Joseph Centlivre, fell in love with and married her. This time she was the one who died first. The best comedy by this matrimonial risk was *The Wonder! A Woman Keeps a Secret,* suggested by Ravencroft's *The Wrangling Lovers.* It appealed to some of the best actors of England. Garrick found the jealous Don Felix one of his favorite roles. He declared that here was a play that entertained without recourse to either drollery or sentiment. It roused the expectations of an audience and maintained them without disappointment. The famous Mrs. Glover introduced the part of Violante. It was no novelty for a heroine to kill a tyrant or to be a raging virago and kill herself, but the cool deliberateness of Violante in holding her tongue caused her to be regarded as the "Wonder" of the title. The action of the play takes place in Lisbon, when that city was part of Spain's empire. Don López has two children, Felix and Isabel. Because of a duel over his projected marriage, Felix has to flee, supposedly to England. This episode gives the dramatist a chance to include speeches of admiration for the English love of liberty. López intends to curb Isabel's love of liberty by marrying her to elderly Don Guzmán, whose only merits are money and noble blood. Isabel tells her servant Inis that she would perfer a convent. Her father, overhearing, reminds her of a Spanish child's duty of parental obedience. Felix loves Violante, daughter of Don Pedro. To her, Felix's servant, Lissardo, brings a letter saying his master has not fled, but is returning to see her. At the conclusion, in the style of Spanish plays, everybody is properly married, Violante with her Felix, and Isabel with an English Colonel Briton. The servants of the sweethearts are also paired off, Flora to Lissardo and Inis to Scottish Gibby, the colonel's batman. Receiving Don Felix's letter in Act II, Violante questions the messenger, Lissardo, who insists that his master is wasting away in his melancholy for her. An "unbraced drum," (meaning the drumhead is not tightened) makes a most melancholy sound. Violante is suspicious.

VIOLANTE

You live very merrily then, it seems. . . . Had ye treats and balls?

LISSARDO

Oh, yes, yes, madam, several. [*He is kissing the hand of Flora, her servant.*]

FLORA [*aside*]

You are mad, Lissardo; you don't mind what my lady says to you.

VIOLANTE

Ha! Balls!—Is he so merry in my absence? And did your master dance, Lissardo?

LISSARDO

Dance, madam! Where, madam?

VIOLANTE

Why, sure you are in love, Lissardo; did you not say but now, you had balls where you have been?

LISSARDO

Balls, madam! Odslife, I beg your pardon, madam! I, I, I had mislaid some wash-balls of my master's t'other day; and because I could not think where I had mislaid them just when he asked for them, he fairly broke my head, madam; and now, it seems, I can think of nothing else. Alas, he dance, madam! No, no, poor gentleman! he is as **melancholy as an unbraced drum.**

693

Melancholy, long, withdrawing roar

Source: DOVER BEACH (Stanza 4)
Author: Matthew Arnold (1822–1888)
First published: 1867
Type of work: Lyric poem

Context: With a loved one, the poet looks out across the Straits of Dover toward the French coast and listens to the endless washing movement, landward and seaward, of the waves which seem to him to "bring/ The eternal note of sadness in." In ancient Greece, Sophocles heard the sound and was reminded of "the turbid ebb and flow/ Of human misery. . . ." To Arnold, whose religious faith— like that of many of his contemporaries—had been weakened by the influence of such scientific ideas as those of Charles Darwin and Herbert Spencer, the waves' sound has a very different meaning, and he sadly comments:

> The Sea of Faith
> Was once, too, at the full, and round earth's shore
> Lay like the folds of a bright girdle furled.
> But now I only hear
> Its **melancholy, long, withdrawing roar,**
> Retreating, to the breath
> Of the night-wind, down the vast edges drear
> And naked shingles of the world.

The mellow glory of the Attic stage

Source: TO A REPUBLICAN FRIEND (Line 13)
Author: Matthew Arnold (1822–1888)
First published: 1849
Type of work: Sonnet

Context: When asked by a friend how he was able to preserve his mental stability in an age of doubt and uncertainty, Arnold replied that his familiarity with classical literature had taught him that man's suffering was never-ending and that from misery men may learn to be wise. Indebted throughout his life to the classical view of joy through tragedy, Arnold cultivated a stoic endurance that enabled him to transcend the clashes of opinion that had grown frenzied and loud by the middle of the nineteenth century. Through his stoicism he became a detached critic of his society and found that tragic joy was possible even in a dreary and bleak age. Of all the classical writers, Sophocles (496– 406 B.C.) was the one he most often turned to. Born near Colonus and writing for the Attic or Athenian stage, Sophocles wrote with brilliant serenity of the suffering of man and the wisdom that grows from it; in his play *Oedipus at Colonus,* for example, he portrays the old blind king who has risen above the comn on pursuits of life to the wisdom of the prophet who knows the meaning of endured suffering.

> . . . be his
> My special thanks, whose even-balanced soul,
> From first youth tested up to extreme old age,
> Business could not make dull, nor passion wild;
> Who saw life steadily, and saw it whole;
> **The mellow glory of the Attic stage,**
> Singer of sweet Colonus, and its child.

Memorize another Golgotha

Source: MACBETH (Act I, sc. ii, l. 40)
Author: William Shakespeare (1564–1616)
First published: 1623
Type of work: Dramatic tragedy

Context: A bleeding captain enters early in the second scene of the play to report to Duncan, King of Scotland, and his supporters the progress in the war with "the merciless Macdonwald." Macdonwald is a worthy foe and fights to the last with valor. Macbeth, however, with Banquo's aid, triumphs. The battlefield is indeed a bloody one and would be as memorable as Golgotha where Christ was crucified. Macbeth then goes on to defeat Sweno of Norway and the rebellious Thane of Cawdor.

CAPTAIN
But the Norweyan lord . . .
. . .
Began a fresh assault.

DUNCAN
Dismayed not this
Our captains, Macbeth and Banquo?

CAPTAIN
Yes,
As sparrows eagles, or the hare the lion.
If I say sooth, I must report they were
As cannons overcharged with double cracks, so they
Doubly redoubled strokes upon the foe.
Except they meant to bathe in reeking wounds,
Or **memorize another Golgotha,**
I cannot tell—
. . .

695

The memory of man runneth not to the contrary

Source: INSTITUTES; COMMENTARY UPON LITTLETON (Section 170, "Of Tenure in Burgage")
Author: Sir Edward Coke (1552–1634)
First published: 1628
Type of work: Legal commentary

Context: Edward Coke, Lord Chief Justice of England, got part of his legal training, as did most would-be lawyers of the day, by reading earlier court decisions and opinions. One of the standard volumes was *Tenures,* written in French by Sir Thomas Littleton (1422–1481), which when printed in 1481 represented the earliest published treatise on English law. Coke must have found it difficult to understand because after he was settled in his profession and had become an authority of English Common Law, he prepared a new edition with three columns on each page: Littleton's French version, its English translation, and Coke's annotations and commentary. He called it "Institutes" because, as he said, it was "intended to institute and instruct the student and guide him in a ready way to the knowledge of the National Laws of England." So well did Sir Edward do his task that his annotated edition remained a standard legal text from 1628 when the first edition was published up to the nineteenth century. Various times in his discussions, Coke stresses the reasons back of law; and in Section 170 he discusses how law maintains a situation that has always existed, or has existed as long as the memory of the oldest citizen. This section concerns burgage, a form of privileged tenure of real property in boroughs by which lands are held by kings or lords who receive a certain yearly rent in money or goods. If the system had been set up in the distant past, says Littleton as Coke explains him, as far back as man can remember, the arrangement is still legal. As he comments:

No custom is to be allowed, but such custom as hath been used by title of prescription, that is to say, from time out of mind . . . some have said that time out of mind should be said from time of limitation in a Writ of rights, that is to say from the time of King Richard the first after the Conquest, as is given by the Statute of Westminster . . . And by such a writ, a man may recover his right of the possession of his ancestors, of the most ancient time that any man may by any writ by the law, etc. . . . But they have said that there is also another title of prescription, that was at the Common Law, before any statute of limitation of Writs, etc. And that it was where a custom or usage or other thing hath been used for time whereof mind of man runneth not to the contrary. . . . Where a man will plead a title of prescription of custom. He shall say that such custom hath been used from time whereof **the memory of man runneth not to the contrary,** that is as much as to say, no man then alive hath heard any proof to the contrary.

Men are April when they woo, December when they wed

Source: AS YOU LIKE IT (Act IV, sc. i, ll. 147–148)
Author: William Shakespeare (1564–1616)
First published: 1623
Type of work: Dramatic comedy

Context: A French Duke, his throne usurped by his brother Duke Frederick, lives with his followers in exile in Arden Forest. His daughter Rosalind, who lives at the court as a companion for Celia, Frederick's daughter, becomes enamored of Orlando. Mistreated in Frederick's court, Rosalind and Celia flee to the Forest of Arden in search of Duke Senior, posing as a shepherd and shepherdess, Ganymede and Aliena. Rosalind discovers Orlando in the forest and playfully, as the shepherd Ganymede, gives him lessons in how to woo his Rosalind. At last she brings Orlando to the point of proposing to his beloved, but then she chides him for man's inconstancy:

ROSALIND
Now tell me how long you would have her, after you have possessed her.

ORLANDO
For ever, and a day.

ROSALIND
Say a day, without the ever. No, no, Orlando, **men are April when they woo, December when they wed.** Maids are May when they are maids, but the sky changes when they are wives.

Men are but children of a larger growth

Source: ALL FOR LOVE (Act IV, l. 43)
Author: John Dryden (1631–1700)
First published: 1678
Type of work: Dramatic tragedy

Context: Dryden's greatest tragedy, for which he borrowed from Shakespeare's *Antony and Cleopatra* was performed and published almost immediately. Dryden made changes in his model to preserve the classical unities, and therefore had to invent action not in his source, with psychological analysis substituted for action. In Act IV, after Octavia, wife of Caesar, has told Cleopatra that every evil suffered by Caesar has been the fault of the Egyptian Queen, Antony tries to persuade his friend Dollabella to carry his farewell to Cleopatra while he goes to Caesar in an attempt to save her and some of her possessions for her. He is afraid that if he looks at

697

Cleopatra again, his love will make him change his mind and ruin her as well as himself. After his departure, Dollabella ponders on the lack of maturity of men. They are only children a few years older, and frequently act like children. They lack introspection. Dollabella thinks his friend is like that, and pities him for his blind infatuation with the lovely Cleopatra; yet at the same time, he envies Antony.

DOLLABELLA

Men are but children of a larger growth;
Our appetites as apt to change as theirs,
And full as craving too, and full as vain.
And yet the soul, shut up in her dark room,
Viewing so clear abroad, at home sees nothing;
But, like a mole in earth, busy and blind,
Works all her folly up, and casts it outward
To the world's open view; thus I discover'd,
And blam'd the love of ruin'd Antony;
Yet wish that I were he, to be so ruin'd.

Men are never so good or so bad as their opinions

Source: DISSERTATION ON THE PROGRESS OF ETHICAL PHILOSOPHY (Section VI, "Bentham")
Author: Sir James Mackintosh (1765–1832)
First published: 1830
Type of work: History and criticism of philosophy

Context: Sir James Mackintosh was a Scottish historian and philosophical writer with an impressive record of service to his country. Educated at Aberdeen and Edinburgh, he studied medicine and took his degree in 1787. Shortly thereafter he published *Vindiciae Gallicae,* a reply to Burke's writings on the French Revolution. He then left medicine for law, being called to the bar in 1795. Brilliant lectures and work as defense counsel won him fame; in 1804 he was knighted and received a government post in India. After an honorable career in that country he returned to England and served twice in Parliament, was professor of law at Haileybury College, and held other positions in the government. His writings include a history of England up to the reign of Elizabeth I and an unfinished work on the Revolution of 1688. His other works include a life of Sir Thomas More, written for Lardner's *Cyclopaedia* and his *Dissertation on the Progress of Ethical Philosophy,* for the *Britannica.* When the seventh edition of the *Encyclopeadia Britannica* was projected, it was decided that the first volume should be a general history of the arts and sciences— a record of progress. A number of dissertations on various fields had already been published as supplements, and would now be included. Mackintosh was asked to write on ethical philosophy, a subject of great interest to him. The seventh edition of the *Britannica* was published from 1830 to 1842; Mackintosh's dissertation was published as an independent work in 1836. In his review of Jeremy Betham, Mackintosh tries to strike a balance between the violent partisans and rabid detractors, pointing out the philosopher's real contributions. Mackintosh feels that too often social and ethical philosophers fail to allow for emotional considerations; to him the principle of utility as a standard of action is both a mechanical device and a cynical or hypocritical one.

. . . It was said of Andrew Fletcher, "he would lose his life to *serve* his country, but would not do a base thing to *save* it." Let those preachers of utility who suppose that such a man sacrifices *ends* to *means,* consider whether the scorn of baseness be not akin to the contempt of danger, and whether a nation composed of such men would not be invincible. But theoretical principles are counteracted by a thousand causes, which confine their mischief as well as circumscribe their benefits. **Men are never so good or so bad as their opinions.** All that can be with reason apprehended is, that they may always produce some part of their natural evil, and that the mischief will be greatest among the many who seek excuses for these passions. Aristippus found in the Socratic representation of the union of virtue and happiness a pretext for sensuality; and many Epicureans became voluptuaries in spite of the example of their master; easily dropping by degrees the limitations by which he guarded his doctrines. In proportion as a man accustoms himself to be influenced by the utility of particular acts, without regard to rules, he approaches to the casuistry of the Jesuits, and to the practical maxims of Caesar Borgia.

Men have lost their reason in nothing so much as their religion

Source: HYDRIOTAPHIA: URN BURIAL (Chapter 4)
Author: Sir Thomas Browne (1605–1682)
First published: 1658
Type of work: Philosophy

Context: This philosophical physician and scientist set out to write a report concerning some forty or fifty Roman funeral urns which were exhumed near Norwich. His speculative nature led him beyond the bounds of a mere scientific report to a disquisition on burial customs in general, ranging, of course, through his vast knowledge of classical literature. In Chapter IV Browne discusses both modern and antique funeral rites and the improper doctrinal implications of undue emphasis on the physical remains and worldly fame:

Christian invention hath chiefly driven at rites, which speak hopes of another life, and hints of a Resurrection. And if the ancient Gentiles held not the immortality of their better part, and some subsistence after death; in several rites, customs, actions and expressions, they contradicted their own opinions: . . . Lucian spoke much truth in jest, when he said, that part of Hercules which proceeded from Alchmena perished, that from Jupiter remained immortal. Thus Socrates was content that his friends should bury his body, so they would not think they buried Socrates, and regarding only his immortal part, was indifferent to be burnt or buried. . . .

Men have lost their reason in nothing so much as their religion, wherein stones and clouts make martyrs; and since the religion of one seems madness unto another, to afford an account or rational of old rites, requires no rigid reader; That they kindled the pyre aversly, or turning their face from it, was an handsome symbol of unwilling ministration; That they washed their bones with wine and milk, that the mother wrapt them in linen, and dryed them in her bosom, the first fostering part, and place of their nourishment; That they opened their eyes towards heaven, before they kindled the fire, as the place of their hopes or original, were no improper ceremonies. . . .

Men must be knaves; 'tis in their own defense

Source: A SATYR AGAINST MANKIND (Line 158)
Author: John Wilmot (Second Earl of Rochester, 1647–1680)
First published: 1675
Type of work: Verse satire

Context: Rochester was an only son; his father was a cavalier and his mother a Puritan. A cavalier himself, he traveled abroad, fought in the Dutch War, and became a courtier under Charles II. He was one of a group of court poets who flourished during the Restoration, and ended as one of the most notorius rakes of the period. He was selfish, ruthless, cynical, and talented. Socially, he devoted himself to the sensual pleasures provided by wine and women; intellectually, he allied himself with the materialistic philosophy of Thomas Hobbes. Worn out by dissipation and venereal disease, he died in his thirty-third year, undergoing a religious conversion on his deathbed. He was briefly a patron to several other poets, Dryden among them, but delighted in abusing them after one or two gestures of encouragement. Much of his own poetry derives from his debaucheries, and some of it is obscene; the remainder is of a high order. His specialty lay in wit and the resulting satires are clever, penetrating, and savage. His lampoons of the king lost him royal favor; he then shifted his attack and burlesqued the science of his day. *A Satyr Against Mankind* is his assault upon wit and reason. It is based upon the eighth satire of Boileau, who had complained that man the rational animal is at times unreasonable. Rochester, however, attacks the reasoning faculty itself. Reason, he believes, has brought man more trouble than it has ever saved him from. He adds that if he could be any creature in existence he would not choose to be human. Anti-rationalists were not uncommon in Rochester's time, but none were so vehement as he. After describing the myriad follies that man's reason has brought about, Rochester declares that all such reasoning is false; that true reason is guided by the senses; and that he at least will live only by his appetites. In conclusion he points out that all of man's good actions are mere disguises and that, in every case, the underlying motivation is fear:

Look to the Bottom of his vast Design,
Wherein Man's Wisdom, Pow'r, and Glory join;
The Good he acts, the Ill he does endure,
'Tis all from Fear, to make himself secure.
Meerly for Safety, after Fame they thirst;
For all Men would be Cowards if they durst:
And Honesty's against all common Sense:
Men must be Knaves; 'tis in their own Defence,
Mankind's dishonest; if you think it fair,
Amongst known Cheats, to play upon the square,
You'll be undone—
Nor can weak Truth your Reputation save;
The Knaves will all agree to call you Knave.
Wrong'd shall he live, insulted o'er, opprest,
Who dares be less a Villain than the rest.
Thus here you see what Human Nature craves,
Most Men are Cowards, all Men shou'd be Knaves.
The Difference lies, as far as I can see,
Not in the Thing it self, but the Degree;
And all the Subject Matter of Debate,
Is only who's a Knave of the First Rate.

Men must work, and women must weep

Source: THE THREE FISHERS (Stanza 1)
Author: Charles Kingsley (1819–1875)
First published: 1851
Type of work: Ballad

Context: Besides his religious tracts, the Reverend Charles Kingsley wrote poetry and historical novels. *Water-Babies* (1863) was his contribution to children's literature. His poem, "Sands of Dee," is the one best remembered today. "The Three Fishers," published in *Andromeda and Other Poems*, which inspired Tennyson's "Crossing the Bar," grew out of an incident in Kingsley's life as a preacher. Asked to preach a sermon to working men, he chose as his topic "The Message of the Church to Laboring Men." He stressed the equality of man and the brotherhood of rich and poor. At the conclusion, one of the congregation rose to voice his be-

701

lief that there is a wide gap between classes. That evening, Kingsley wrote this tragic poem of three fishermen who went out to earn for their families, only to be caught in a squall and rolled up dead on the beach the next morning. Each stanza ends with the refrain, applicable to all classes, that man must labor and that sorrows come to the woman. It begins:

Three fishers went sailing away to the West,
    Away to the West as the sun went down;
Each thought on the woman who loved him the best;
    And the children stood watching them out of the town;
    For **men must work, and women must weep,**
    And there's little to earn, and many to keep,
        Though the harbor bar be moaning.

Men of culture are the true apostles of equality

Source: CULTURE AND ANARCHY (Chapter I)
Author: Matthew Arnold (1822–1888)
First published: 1869
Type of work: Social and moral essay

Context: The collection of essays on political and social conditions which comprises *Culture and Anarchy* includes many of Arnold's most famous utterances on his evaluation of the Victorian scene. Dislocated spiritually on the one hand as a result of the scientific discoveries which undermined religion and exploited economically on the other hand as a result of the *laissez faire* policies of the money lords who controlled the industrial revolution, England—as Arnold saw it—desperately needed a new direction and new values. He saw this need not merely as a call for a new religion or extensive economic legislation; both religion and business, in the form of their human institutions, could be and had been previously perverted to serve the purposes of individual ambition. What was vitally needed was a basic alteration of the human personality—and, if human nature is basically unchangeable, the complete fulfillment of the human personality through sound education was a factor over which man exercised some control. Thus, Arnold's goal, the achievement through proper education of a cultured middle class, emerged as his dominant thesis for the rest of his life. Fully realized, such culture would eliminate classes by eliminating man's desire for exploitation of his fellow man:

. . . It seeks to do away with classes; to make the best that has been thought and known in the world current everywhere; to make all men live in an atmosphere of sweetness and light, where they may use ideas, as it uses them itself, freely,—nourished, and not bound by them.

702

This is the social idea; and the **men of culture are the true apostles of equality.** The great men of culture are those who have had a passion for diffusing, for making prevail, for carrying from one end of society to another, the best knowledge, the best ideas of their time; . . .

Men of few words are the best men

Source: KING HENRY THE FIFTH (Act III, sc. ii, ll. 38–39)
Author: William Shakespeare (1564–1616)
First published: 1600
Type of work: Historical drama

Context: Henry V and his English forces, convinced of the validity of their claim to the French throne, have invaded the kingdom of France. Charles VI, the French king, and Lewis, the Dauphin, have scoffed at the English claims, the Dauphin earlier having sent Henry a set of tennis balls in mock recollection of Hal's previous days as a bounder at the Boar's Head in Eastcheap. Henry, the "mirror of a Christian king," is now determined to prove through his military adventures both the might and vigor of the English forces and his own maturity as a ruler. The first real test of strength is at Harfleur, a walled city which has refused to surrender. During the battle Henry encourages his men to expend their best efforts as patriots of their country. Among the soldiers are Bardolph, Falstaff's associate from the Henry IV plays; Pistol, a rowdy braggadocio; and Nym, a foolish and naïve soul whose bravery is qualified by a Falstaffian discretion. The conversations of these common soldiers provide a constant reminder of the differences between the florid and eloquent martial oratory of the nation's leaders and the realistic and earthy dialogue of the foot soldiers engaged in actual battle. A young boy who has accompanied them to battle sees through the façade of their bravura and decides to part from them at his first opportunity:

BOY

As young as I am, I have observed these three swashers. I am boy to them all three, but all they three, though they would serve me, could not be man to me; for indeed three such antics do not amount to a man. For Bardolph, he is white-livered, and red-faced; by the means whereof 'a faces it out, but fights not. For Pistol, he hath a killing tongue, and a quiet sword; by the means whereof, 'a breaks words, and keeps whole weapons. For Nym, he hath heard that **men of few words are the best men,** and therefore he scorns to say his prayers, lest 'a should be thought a coward: but his few bad words are matched with as few good deeds; for 'a never broke any man's head but his own, and that was against a post when he was drunk.

• • •

703

Mighty-mouth'd inventor of harmonies

Source: EXPERIMENTS. MILTON. ALCAICS (Line 1)
Author: Alfred, Lord Tennyson (1809–1892)
First published: 1863
Type of work: Metrical experiment

Context: Like many poets, Tennyson was fascinated by the technique as well as by the content of poetry; thus, while he praises Milton for his inventions in prosody, he imitates the classical form of poetry invented by the Greek lyric poet Alcaeus (fl. 600 B.C.). This form is quantitative, the metrical foot being measured by the duration of sound, whereas the usual English poem has been qualitative or syllabic. Ranking Milton as the superior stylist whom no other English poet has matched, Tennyson fittingly praises the master in this experimental poem. By combining eulogy and metrical experimentation, he achieves one of his remarkable poems in which form and content completely join and illustrate not only Milton's greatness but also Tennyson's own ear for the music of verse.

> O **mighty-mouth'd inventor of harmonies,**
> O skill'd to sing of Time or Eternity,
>   God-gifted organ-voice of England,
>   Milton, a name to resound for ages;
> Whose Titan angels, Gabriel, Abdiel,
> Starr'd from Jehovah's gorgeous armories,
>   Tower, as the deep-domed empyrean
>   Rings to the roar of an angel onset! . . .

Milk-soup men call domestic bliss

Source: OLYMPUS (Line 15)
Author: Coventry Patmore (1823–1896)
First published: 1861
Type of work: Lyric poem

Context: One of the few poets who was not only happily married but who also dedicated his career to the singing of domestic bliss, Patmore is unique; while his verse has been scorned by twentieth century cynics and has been called neurotic by modern arm-chair psychologists, his poetic world, narrowed to the confines of the Victorian home, draws upon social, philosophical, and theological sources to exalt its simple, unpretentious joys. In this short poem Patmore shows the gracious wife who understands the custom of the husband's night on the town; in fact, she provides everything necessary for him to "get away" from the home and spend an evening with his literary friends at the local coffeehouse. But the husband very quickly discovers that such freedom is painful; as soon

704

as he realizes that true happiness consists of the companionship of his wife and a quiet evening at home, he excuses himself from his friend's "Olympian feast" and returns to his wife, appreciating her more after his short absence than he had before.

> And I,
> Who inly murmur'd, "I will try
> Some dish more sharply spiced than this
> **Milk-soup men call domestic bliss,"**
> Took, as she, laughing, bade me take,
> Our eldest boy's brown wide-awake
> And straw box of cigars, and went
> Where, like a careless parliament
> Of gods olympic, six or eight
> Author and else, reputed great,
> Were met in council jocular. . . .

A mind conscious of virtue may bring to thee suitable rewards

Source: THE AENEID (Book I, l. 604)
Author: Virgil (Publius Vergilius Maro, 70–19 B.C.)
First transcribed: c. 29–19 B.C.
Type of work: Epic poem

Context: Virgil, with great patriotism, influenced by Homer, sought to proclaim an origin suitable to the glory of Rome in his epic *The Aeneid*. Aeneas, son of Venus and a hero of the Trojan War, leader of a company attempting to establish a kingdom in Italy, is confronted with perils similar to those of Ulysses as he and his men sail from Troy to Italy. Shipwrecked near Carthage, Aeneas and Achates, a companion, become separated from the other voyagers, who are rescued and sustained by Dido, Queen of Carthage. Shrouded by a cloud provided by his mother Venus, Aeneas suddenly becomes visible to Dido and, to the amazement of all of the beholders, declares that he is Aeneas, whom they seek. Expressing his gratitude to Dido for the safety of his men, he states that a mind conscious of virtue may bring to thee suitable rewards, or in the translation of Davidson:

. . . I, whom you seek, am present before you; Trojan Aeneas, snatched from the Libyan waves. O thou, who alone hast commiserated Troy's unutterable calamities! who in thy town and palace dost associate us, a remnant saved from the Greeks, who have now been worn out by woes in every shape . . . to repay thee due thanks, great queen, exceeds the power not only of us, but of all the Dardan race, wherever dispersed over the world. The gods (if any powers divine regard the pious, if justice anywhere exists, and **a mind conscious of its own virtue) shall yield thee a just recompence.** . . .

705

A mind quite vacant is a mind distressed

Source: RETIREMENT (Line 624)
Author: William Cowper (1731–1800)
First published: 1782
Type of work: Meditative poem

Context: Cowper, descendant of John Donne and the last English poet who belonged to what has been called the cult of simplicity, began his adult life in the legal profession. He was called to the bar in 1754. His early retirement from this career was forced upon him by attacks of insanity, the first of which prevented him from marrying. During the second, in 1763, he attempted to commit suicide. Following a long convalescence, he retired to the country. After living for a time at Huntingdon he settled at Olney. Here, at the age of fifty, he turned seriously to the writing of poetry; the first volume, *Poems,* appeared in 1782. Cowper's poetry is quiet and meditative; in it he reflects upon the serene beauty of the countryside and upon the simplicity and peace of rural existence. He considers the nature of conditions and events in the outside world, but it is remote. Deeply religious, he tends to moralize; although his Calvinism was an important factor in the recurrent periods of despair it was also a source of comfort, and it is the comfort rather than the despair which is most apparent in his work. *The Task,* his greatest poem, is most eloquent of Cowper's powers at their best. He also produced a new edition of Milton, translated Homer and a number of minor works, wrote nearly seventy hymns, and produced a few humorous verses. Some of his poems are akin to sermons. *Retirement,* for example, meditates upon the destructive qualities of everyday life in the competitive urban world. Cowper considers the moral dangers and the dreary labor, the temptations and the problems; and he notes also the universal dream of a place to which one can escape. Describing the various walks of life and their stresses, he prescribes God's handiwork in nature as the best cure—beneficial even when enforced. He also notes, shrewdly enough, that retirement and inactivity are a deadly combination:

> Lucrative offices are seldom lost
> For want of pow'rs proportion'd to the post:
> Give ev'n a dunce th' employment he desires,
> And he soon finds the talent it requires;
> A business, with an income at its heels,
> Furnishes always oil for its own wheels.
> But in his arduous enterprise to close
> His active years with indolent repose,
> He finds the labors of that state exceed
> His utmost faculties, severe indeed.
> 'Tis easy to resign a toilsome place,
> But not to manage leisure with a grace;

Absence of occupation is not rest,
A mind quite vacant is a mind distress'd.
The vet'ran steed, excused his task at length
In kind compassion of his failing strength,
And turn'd into the park or mead to graze,
Exempt from future service all his days,
There feels a pleasure perfect in its kind,
Ranges at liberty, and snuffs the wind.
But when his lord would quit the busy road,
To taste a joy like that he has bestow'd,
He proves, less happy than his favour'd brute,
A life of ease a difficult pursuit.

Mindful of the unhonored dead

Source: ELEGY WRITTEN IN A COUNTRY CHURCHYARD (Line 93)
Author: Thomas Gray (1716–1771)
First published: 1751
Type of work: Didactic elegy

Context: The "Elegy" was written to commemorate the humble dead, who are buried in the churchyard; the high-born are customarily buried in the church itself. The churchyard referred to was that of Stoke Poges, and the scene as described by Gray has apparently remained unaltered until this day. The poet sets his description in the evening, when the day's work is done; morning, with all of its activity, will never come to these people again. These folk lived lives of honest toil, seasoned by homely joys. Those who live on a higher social stratum have no reason to look down upon these simple folk, as their end will be the same: the paths of glory lead but to the grave. Penury kept these humble folk ignorant, but perhaps some of them may have had great potentialities that were never realized. Perhaps a Milton, who was forced into muteness by his situation in life, lies here. And as their opportunities for doing good were restricted, so were their chances for committing crimes; they did not wade through blood to thrones. In quietness they lived their lives far from the madding crowd, but their rude memorials still exist in the churchyard.

> On some fond breast the parting soul relies,
>   Some pious drops the closing eye requires;
> Ev'n from the tomb the voice of Nature cries,
>   Ev'n in our ashes live their wonted fires.
>
> For thee, who **mindful of th' unhonored dead**
>   Dost in these lines their artless tale relate;
> If chance, by lonely Contemplation led,
>   Some kindred spirit shall inquire thy fate,

707

Haply some hoary-headed swain may say,
  "Oft have we seen him at the peep of dawn
Brushing with hasty steps the dews away
  To meet the sun upon the upland lawn.

There at the foot of yonder nodding beech
  That wreathes its old fantastic roots so high,
His listless length at noontide would he stretch,
  And pore upon the brook that babbles by."

Minister to a mind diseased

Source: MACBETH (Act V, sc. iii, l. 40)
Author: William Shakespeare (1564–1616)
First published: 1623
Type of work: Dramatic tragedy

Context: Macbeth, receiving the prophecy of three witches that he will become king, murders King Duncan of Scotland and usurps the throne. In all this and in additional murders Macbeth is abetted by his wife until finally Lady Macbeth lapses into insanity. Macbeth then has two deep concerns: First, an English army is advancing against his forces with the intention of giving the crown to Malcolm, son of the murdered king, and second, Lady Macbeth is critically ill. While receiving reports on the approach of the English army, Macbeth also confers with Lady Macbeth's doctor:

MACBETH
. . .
How does your patient, doctor?

DOCTOR
           Not so sick my lord,
As she is troubled with thick-coming fancies
That keep her from her rest.

MACBETH
           Cure her of that.
Canst thou not **minister to a mind diseased,**
Pluck from the memory a rooted sorrow,
Raze out the written troubles of the brain,
And with some sweet oblivious antidote
Cleanse the stuffed bosom of that perilous stuff
Which weighs upon the heart?

DOCTOR
           Therein the patient
Must minister to himself.

708

The minority is always in the right

Source: AN ENEMY OF THE PEOPLE (Act IV)
Author: Henrik Ibsen (1828–1906)
First published: 1882
Type of work: Social drama

Context: Dr. Thomas Stockmann, medical officer of the municipal baths in a coastal town in southern Norway, tries to warn his fellow townsmen that the water supply of the baths is impure and that the baths themselves are built upon pestiferous ground. The officials of the town, including his brother Peter, the mayor and also the chairman of the bath committee, refuse to do anything about the matter; the local newspaper, *The People's Messenger,* sides against the doctor and truth; even the townspeople themselves, who do not wish the news to get abroad to sully the town's reputation, and who have no desire to pay higher tax rates to solve the sanitary problems, side against the doctor. Dr. Stockmann finally calls a public meeting at a private home, no public place being open to him, to deliver a lecture. His enemies come, but when he says he wants to speak about a matter other than the municipal baths, they agree to hear him. He tells them that the problems of the baths are not to be laid upon officialdom alone; he places the blame on the majority of the people of the town, saying they are unwilling to face the truth. When some of the audience protest this statement, he goes on to exclaim his bitterness over their behavior:

DR. STOCKMANN

The majority *never* has right on its side. Never, I say. That is one of these social lies against which an independent, intelligent man must wage war. Who is it that constitute the majority of the population in a country? Is it the clever folk or the stupid? I don't imagine you will dispute the fact that at present the stupid people are in an overwhelming majority all the world over. But, good Lord!—you can never pretend that it is right that the stupid folk should govern the clever ones! . . . The majority has *might* on its side—unfortunately; but *right* it has *not.* I am in the right—I and a few other scattered individuals. **The minority is always in the right.**

A minute's success pays the failure of years

Source: APOLLO AND THE FATES. A PROLOGUE (Stanza 42)
Author: Robert Browning (1812–1889)
First published: 1887
Type of work: Poetic dialogue

Context: This poem, the prologue to   one of Browning's last volumes of verse, is an elaborate discussion of the meaning that can be found in human life. Apollo, god of music and harmony, flies to the cave of the Three Fates, Clotho, Lachesis and Atropos, in order to save the life of Admetus. The Fates, not wanting to release the mortal from their grasp, argue with their unwelcome visitor by saying that a man's life can have meaning only because he will die. Actually Browning puts much of his own philosophy into the mouths of the Fates, for he makes them defend

his own "doctrine of imperfection": viewed objectively, a man's life is a series of failures, because he has never done really what he hoped to do, and in these failures there is the sign of his aspirations; since life is essentially a series of such aspirations and failures, the worth of a man lies in what he hopes, not in what he does. When Clotho reveals this outlook to Apollo, she has described the secret of human happiness—triumph in defeat.

> Infancy? What if the rose-streak of morning
> Pale and depart in a passion of tears?
> Once to have hoped is no matter for scorning!
> Love once—e'en love's disappointment endears!
> **A minute's success pays the failure of years.**
>
> Manhood—the actual? Nay, praise the potential!
> (Bound upon bound, foot it around!)
> What *is*? No, what *may* be—sing! that's Man's essential!
> . . .

A miss for pleasure, and a wife for breed

Source: THE TOILETTE (Line 86)
Author: John Gay (1685–1732)
First published: 1720
Type of work: Satiric poem

Context: Gay's satire is about a woman of thirty-five, a lady of fashion, who has lost her lover to a much younger woman. Gay catches the victim of age and love as she dresses in the morning, surrounded by her parrot, her lapdog, and all the other paraphernalia of a lady of fashion's dressing-room at the time. Lydia mourns not only the loss of her lover,

Damon; she mourns as well the loss of her youth and the inconsistency of love. Life seems suddenly empty to her, and she wonders what to do with her time; she thinks of going shopping at the Exchange, but she knows that shopping will only remind her of similar times spent with her faithless lover in the past. Such considerations lead the unhappy woman to raving:

> "O happy Poll, in wiry prison pent;
> Thou ne'er hast known what love or rivals meant,

And Pug with pleasure can his fetters bear,
Who ne'er believed the vows that lovers swear!
How am I curst! (unhappy and forlorn)
With perjury, with love, and rival's scorn!
False are the loose coquet's inveigling airs,
False is the pompous grief of youthful heirs,
False is the cringing courtier's plighted word,
False are the dice when gamesters stamp the board,
False is the sprightly widow's public tear;
Yet these to Damon's oaths are all sincere.
  "Fly from perfidious man, the sex disdain;
Let servile Chloe wear the nuptial chain.
Damon is practis'd in the modish life,
Can hate, and yet be civil to a wife;
He games; he swears; he drinks; he fights; he roves;
Yet Chloe can believe he fondly loves.
Mistress and wife can well supply his need,
A miss for pleasure, and a wife for breed."

Monday is parson's holiday

Source: JOURNAL TO STELLA (March 3, 1712)
Author: Jonathan Swift (1667–1745)
First published: 1766–1768
Type of work: Letters

Context: Going to London in 1710, Swift left behind two dear friends, Esther Johnson, whom he called Stella, and Rebecca Dingley. At that period, mature women even though unmarried were usually referred to as Mistress, or Mrs. Swift kept these friends informed of his doings in London by sending them his diary, in installments. In Letter XLI, covering part of February and March, 1711/1712 (Julian/Gregorian), he includes items of business and gossip. He comments that on the day after the Sunday sermon, the minister has the right to a day of relaxation. Part of the rest of the entry is set down in a sort of baby talk, perhaps the dean's idea of humor, though it does not occur very often in the Journal. "Deelest logues" must be "dearest loves," "oo" is used for "you," and the letters "z" and "s" replace "th." Having mentioned the pension of a friend, he continues:

. . . but oo must not know zees sings, zey are secrets; and we must keep them from nauty dallars. I dined in the city with my printer, with whom I had some small affair. I have no large work on my hands now. I was with Lord-Treasurer this morning and hat (what) care oo for zat? You dined with the Dean today. **Monday is parson's holiday.** And oo lost oo money at cards and dice; ze Givars' (Devil's) device. So I'll go to bed. Nite, my two deelest logues.

Moon-struck madness

Source: PARADISE LOST (Book XI, l. 486)
Author: John Milton (1608–1674)
First published: 1667
Type of work: Epic poem

Context: Michael is sent down from heaven by God to tell Adam what will happen in the world in the future. The garden would have been the capital of the world if Adam had not sinned and so lost it. As things are to be, other great cities will arise. Michael and Adam ascend a hill of paradise, from the top of which they can see much of the earth, as far as from Mexico and Peru to China. Michael shows Adam what will come, beginning with the murder of Abel by Cain. Adam thus witnesses the death that his own sinful act brought into the world. Adam is mightily impressed, but Michael tells him that this is only one form of death, and there are many other kinds, all dismal. Some men shall fall by violence, others by the intemperate use of food and drink, which shall produce dire diseases in man. He says that he will present to Adam's eyes a monstrous crew of them so that he will know what Eve's intemperance brought into an otherwise good world: A lazar-house is a hospital for pestilence victims. It was a medieval belief that insanity (lunacy) was caused by moonlight.

> Immediately a place
> Before his eyes appeared, sad, noisome, dark,
> A lazar-house it seemed, wherein were laid
> Numbers of all diseased, all maladies
> Of ghastly spasm, or racking torture, qualms
> Of heart-sick agony, all feverous kinds,
> Convulsions, epilepsies, fierce catarrhs,
> Intestine stone and ulcer, colic pangs,
> Daemonic phrenzy, moping melancholy
> And **moon-struck madness,** pining atrophy,
> Marasmus, and wide-wasting pestilence,
> Dropsies, and asthmas, and joint-racking rheums.
> Dire was the tossing, deep the groans, despair
> Tended the sick busiest from couch to couch;
> And over them triumphant death his dart
> Shook, but delayed to strike, though oft invoked
> With vows, as their chief good, and final hope.
> . . .

More an antique Roman than a Dane

Source: HAMLET (Act V, sc. ii, l. 352)
Author: William Shakespeare (1564–1616)
First published: 1603
Type of work: Dramatic tragedy

712

Context: To assure Hamlet's death, Claudius and Laertes plan a fencing match in which Laertes is to use an unblunted and poisoned sword against Hamlet. To make doubly sure of the death, Claudius prepares a poisoned cup which the prince will take during a respite in the seemingly friendly fight. After Queen Gertrude drinks from the cup and Claudius and Laertes die from the poisoned sword, Hamlet, mortally wounded by the same sword, asks Horatio, his friend, to explain to the world the rightness of his actions. Horatio seeks to follow his prince through suicide into death, as would a Roman, with the poisoned cup, but Hamlet urges him to live.

HAMLET
. . . Horatio, I am dead,
Thou livest; report me and my cause aright
To the unsatisfied.

HORATIO
· · ·
I am **more an antique Roman than a Dane.**
Here's yet some liquor left.

HAMLET
As th' art a man,
Give me the cup—let go, by heaven I'll ha't.
O God, Horatio, what a wounded name,
Things standing thus unknown, shall live behind me.
If thou didst ever hold me in thy heart,
Absent thee from felicity awhile,
And in this harsh world draw thy breath in pain,
To tell my story. . . .

More needs she the divine than the physician

Source: MACBETH (Act V, sc. i, l. 79)
Author: William Shakespeare (1564–1616)
First published: 1623
Type of work: Dramatic tragedy

Context: Lady Macbeth has been ailing and walking in her sleep since Macbeth went to war with England, Malcolm, Macduff, and Siward. A doctor is called, and while one of Lady Macbeth's women is describing her condition to him, Lady Macbeth herself suddenly appears with a taper, sleepwalking. She rubs her hands, trying to remove the imaginary blood from them and speaks of both Duncan's and Banquo's murders. The doctor is shocked, but he is both personally and professionally touched at her sighing laments. He realizes that she is beyond his help as a doctor and commends her to God. His only prescription is that she be constantly

713

watched and kept from harming her- self.

DOCTOR

Foul whisperings are abroad. Unnatural deeds
Do breed unnatural troubles; infected minds
To their deaf pillows will discharge their secrets.
More needs she the divine than the physician.
God, God forgive us all. Look after her,
Remove from her the means of annoyance,
And still keep eyes upon her. So good night.
My mind she has mated, and amazed my sight.
I think, but dare not speak.

More people are flattered into virtue than bullied out of vice

Source: THE ANALYSIS OF THE HUNTING FIELD (Chapter 1)
Author: Robert Smith Surtees (1803–1864)
First published: 1846
Type of work: Humorous treatise on fox-hunting

Context: Robert Surtees came of an ancient family and started his adult life as a solicitor in London. He was unsuccessful in this occupation and turned his talents to journalism, where he found his proper medium in sporting events. In 1831 he became editor of *The New Sporting Magazine.* He wrote a number of humorous sketches for its columns, in which he developed the character named John Jorrocks. Jorrocks, a London grocer, wishes more than anything else to become a Master of Foxhounds. Surtees published a collection of these sketches in 1838 under the title *Jorrocks' Jaunts and Jollities.* An influential writer of the day, John Gibson Lockhart, was impressed and suggested that Surtees write a novel. Dickens used the book as a basis for the arrangement of his own *Pickwick Papers.* By this time Surtees had inherited his ancestral estate, and was free to write. He produced a number of sporting novels and other books.

These are all jovial, rollicking, and irrepressible; at one time they were considered rather vulgar. They are at times incomprehensible to one who is not an enthusiastic fox hunter. *The Analysis of the Hunting Field* is a humorous series of sketches in which a great deal of information on the subject is presented; it is based on a review of the 1845–1846 sporting season. Surtees opens the first chapter with a Meeting of Foxhounds, so that he can describe the various people who take part in one. He portrays the Master of Hounds at length and describes some of the ordeals this stalwart individual must endure, not the least of which is the dinner party. Since hunting is an expensive sport, it is often financed by people such as Mr. Cottonwool, who employ the Master for prestige purposes. Mr. Cottonwool is obviously in need of education; Surtees tells us how his education is acquired:

714

. . . the best hounds in the world, with the "best fellow under the sun" at the head of them, are useless without foxes, and fox or no fox is in the caprice of such creatures as Cottonwool. Some Cottonwools are apt to "keep the word of promise to the ear and break it to the hope," giving their keepers orders perhaps not to shoot foxes, but at the same time not to let a vixen lie up on the estate. There are many ways of preserving foxes—at all events of salving a not troublesomely fastidious conscience. If our "best fellow under the sun" suspects anything like foul play, he will lead old Wool unto the ice, get him to talk big about hunting, the pleasures of the morning, the delights of a find, the certainty of sport, the abundance of foxes—our Master slyly exclaiming to old Pigskin or anyone furthest off, so that every one must hear, "Ah, Mr. Pigskin, I wish all people were like our worthy host Mr. Cottonwool! There would be no lack of foxes—no fear of sport then." He may then observe, almost to "Wool" himself, "I'm sure all here will bear me out in saying that I always hold our excellent friend Mr. Cottonwool up as a perfect specimen of what an English gentleman ought to be." Now, that is good, wholesome, unadulterated flattery—all Wool's own too, and the odds are that thinking he has not committed himself, he will retract the qualifying order about the vixens, and show himself at the next cattle show as a perfect specimen of what an English gentleman ought to be. **More people are flattered into virtue than bullied out of vice.**

More ways of killing a cat than choking her with cream

Source: WESTWARD HO! (Chapter 20)
Author: Charles Kingsley (1819–1875)
First published: 1855
Type of work: Novel

Context: Besides his religious tracts, the Rev. Charles Kingsley wrote three historical novels: *Hypatia* (1853), *Westward Ho!,* and *Hereward the Wake* (1866) about Anglo-Saxon courage against the conquering Normans. The breezy tale of *Westward Ho!* is the most interesting of the trio. Against the background of Elizabethan adventure on the sea, the author defends the principles of the nineteenth century Broad Church movement for which he jousted against Cardinal John Henry Newman (1801–1890). The great character of Salvation Yeo contrasts with the Spanish-American Jesuits and inquisitors. Most of Kingsley's local color came from Hakluyt's *Voyages,* and while there are occasions where his lack of sea knowledge caused slips, most critics believe that Kingsley expressed well the feelings of the age of Good Queen Bess. In the story, Amyas Leigh, his brother Frank, and villainous Cousin Eustace are brought up in Bideford, along with Rose Salterne, the Mayor's daughter. The boys go to sea, around the world with Sir Francis Drake. Following the victory over the Spanish Armada in 1588, among the Spanish prisoners

715

brought to the village to await ransom money is the nobleman Guzmán de Soto. When Rose later disappears, the young men suspect that the ransomed Spaniard has abducted her. So in a ship *The Rose* they sail Westward Ho! to La Guayra, Venezuela, where Guzmán has been sent as Governor. Roman Catholic Eustace warns the Spaniards, so a Spanish vessel is waiting their arrival. As for the colloquial phrase, though the proverbial cat has nine lives, there are many ways of killing it. "Care killed a cat" and "Cat killed by kindness," come to mind, as well as "Skinning the cat," and this method, the most inappropriate of all. Here is Kingsley's account of the sea fight:

> Bang went one of the Spaniard's bow guns, and the shot went wide. Then another and another, while the men [of Amyas] fidgeted about, looking at the priming of their muskets, and loosened their arrows in the sheaf.
>
> "Lie down, men, and sing a psalm. When I want you, I'll call you. Closer still, if you can, helmsman, and we will try a short ship against a long one. We can sail two points nearer the wind than he."
>
> As Amyas had calculated, the Spaniard would gladly enough have stood across the *Rose*'s bow, but, knowing the English readiness, dare not for fear of being raked; so her only plan, if she did not intend to shoot past her foe down to leeward, was to put her head close to the wind, and wait for her on the same tack.
>
> Amyas laughed to himself. "Hold on yet awhile. **More ways of killing a cat than choking her with cream.** Drew, there, are your men ready?"
>
> "Ay, ay, sir!" and on they went, closing fast with the Spaniard, till within a pistol-shot.

Mother and lover of men, the sea

Source: THE TRIUMPH OF TIME (Line 258)
Author: Algernon Charles Swinburne (1837–1909)
First published: 1866
Type of work: Lyric poem

Context: Writing shortly after he had been rejected by a girl whom he loved, Swinburne pours out his misery in this long, rambling, and emotional poem. Because the girl did not love him, he mourns that youth and dreams will be forever dead to him and that nature, once beautiful and full of life, will be now filled with grief. Only the barren sea, the "mother of loves that are swift to fade," remains without change because, unlike humans, it is beyond the touch of time. The image of the sea, one of Swinburne's favorite symbols, is a complex union of love and the death that inevitably comes from love, of birth and the sterile life that follows birth. Whereas the girl has rejected him, the sea will embrace him,

716

an embrace that is death. The quotation comes from Swinburne's suicidal ravings that death is better than a life of continued misery, especially a death by drowning because by this death his decayed body will join the sea itself and enable him to transcend the earth.

> I will go back to the great sweet mother,
> **Mother and lover of men, the sea.**
> I will go down to her, I and none other,
>   Close with her, kiss her, and mix her with me;
> Cling to her, strive with her, hold her fast:
> O fair white mother, in days long past
> Born without sister, born without brother,
>   Set free my soul as thy soul is free.

A mother's pride, a father's joy!

Source: ROKEBY (Canto III, stanza 15, l. 368)
Author: Sir Walter Scott (1771–1832)
First published: 1815
Type of work: Narrative poem

Context: Immediately after the battle of Marston Moor (July 3, 1644), Bertram Risingham, a villainous fortune-hunter who had murdered his way from Europe to Peru and back again, arrives at the home of Oswald Wycliffe to announce that he has killed his leader, Philip of Mortham, during the heat of the battle. He had done this act because Mortham, his former comrade in arms, had cast him off, and because Oswald, Mortham's heir, had promised to divide with him the wealth that Mortham had plundered from the Americas. Wilfred, Oswald's soft, gentle, dreaming son, accompanies Bertram to Mortham's home, as Bertram believes that the riches are concealed in the tomb of Mortham's wife. Before the tomb, Bertram admits that he had murdered Mortham. Wilfred, weak as he is, draws his sword to inflict vengeance on the rogue; as Bertram is about to strike him down with his sword, the ghost of Mortham interposes to save the lad. At this point Oswald arrives, with a company of men who immediately pursue Bertram. He escapes and while resting, is greeted by a criminal as bad as he, who offers him the leadership of an outlaw band. He accompanies the newcomer, Guy Denzil, to the cave of the robbers:

> Hark! the loud revel wakes again
> To greet the leader of the train.
> Behold the group by the pale lamp
> That struggles with the earthy damp.
> By what strange features Vice hath known
> To single out and mark her own!
> Yet some there are whose brows retain
> Less deeply stamped her brand and stain.

717

See yond pale stripling! when a boy,
A mother's pride, a father's joy!
Now, 'gainst the vault's rude walls reclined,
An early image fills his mind:
The cottage, once his sire's, he sees,
Embowered upon the banks of Tees;
He views sweet Winston's woodland scene,
And shares the dance on Gainford-green.

Motley's the only wear

Source: AS YOU LIKE IT (Act II, sc. vii, l. 34)
Author: William Shakespeare (1564–1616)
First published: 1623
Type of work: Dramatic comedy

Context: A Duke of France, his throne usurped by his brother, lives with a number of his followers in exile in the Forest of Arden. The Duke and all his lords except Jaques enjoy the simplicity of their sylvan existence. Jaques, however, is usually sad, weeping when a deer is shot for food and wandering alone in the forest. The Duke, concerned, searches all day for Jaques, only to find his doleful follower in a gay mood. Jaques tells his friends that in the forest he encountered a fool with a watch and that the fool's crude philosophy about time has made him merry.

JACQUES
. . .

And then he drew a dial from his poke,
And looking on it, with lack-lustre eye,
Says very wisely, it is ten o'clock:
Thus we may see, quoth he, how the world wags.
'Tis but an hour ago since it was nine,
And after one hour more, 'twill be eleven;
And so from hour to hour we ripe, and ripe,
And then from hour to hour we rot, and rot;
And thereby hangs a tale. When I did hear
The motley fool thus moral on the time,
My lungs began to crow like chanticleer,
That fools should be so deep contemplative.
And I did laugh sans intermission
An hour by his dial. O noble fool,
A worthy fool. **Motley's the only wear.**

Mountains of Necessity

Source: TO A REPUBLICAN FRIEND ("Continued," Line 7)
Author: Matthew Arnold (1822–1888)
First published: 1849
Type of work: Sonnet

Context: After Arthur Hugh Clough had optimistically argued that the series of revolutions shaking Europe in 1848 would usher in an age of equality and freedom, Arnold addressed this poem to him. According to Arnold's determinism, man is not free to make a heaven on earth; quite the contrary, history shows that the violence of revolution most often ends in an avaricious tyrant's using the cry for freedom to further his own selfish ends. In fact, the essential condition of human life, according to Arnold in other poems, is suffering: the individual is trapped in a world that he neither wants nor understands. This condition makes men slaves to themselves; regardless of their desire for freedom, they cannot make the dream into reality. This quotation, therefore, refers both to the limitations of history that no group of men can alter and to individual limitations that make men incapable of realizing their fondest dreams.

> . . . when I muse on what life is, I seem
> Rather to patience prompted, than that proud
> Prospect of hope which France proclaims so loud—
> France, famed in all great arts, in none supreme;
>
> Seeing this vale, this earth, whereon we dream,
> Is on all sides o'ershadow'd by the high
> Uno'erleap'd **Mountains of Necessity,**
> Sparing us narrower margin than we deem.

The moving finger writes

Source: THE RUBÁIYÁT OF OMAR KHAYYÁM (Stanza 71)
Author: Omar Khayyám (died c.1123)
Translator and adapter: Edward FitzGerald (1809–1883)
First published: 1859
Type of work: Translation and poetic adaptation of Persian poetry

Context: Edward FitzGerald was a gentle, placid recluse of considerable intellectual powers; he had a small permanent income which enabled him to lead a quietly happy rural life and to do just as he pleased. Though he did visit London to enjoy music and the theater, he spent most of his time alone with his books and his garden. His marriage ended in a separation, but this apparently left no scars with him. His must have been a charming personality, if the whimsical intimacy of his letters is any indication; and he was something of a hedonist. In this and in his religious skepticism he was part of the growing movement of his age. At one point he took up the study of Persian and presently encountered the quatrains written by Omar Khayyám. These he translated —transmuted might be a better term —into a poem of great sensitivity and beauty: a poem better known today

719

than any other of the Victorian era. In it two principal themes are interwoven; first, the idea that life is fleeting and must be enjoyed before the opportunity is lost; and second, the feeling of resentment against a Power that holds men responsible for a nature they cannot determine. FitzGerald, unsatisfied with the first version of his work, polished it again and again, carrying it to five editions. The last of these is considered the definitive one, but there is some question whether certain lines in the first are not bolder and more effective. The poem begins with the sunrise and the opening of the tavern. The poet ponders on the unknown purposes of destiny, and on the brevity of human life; the philosophers who had all the answers to the universe have been ignored by it and are dust; the poet and his love will soon be dust in their turn. To enjoy what one has, while one can, is the poet's solution. He considers the inexorable nature of destiny and man's helplessness in the face of it:

> We are no other than a moving row
> Of Magic Shadow-shapes that come and go
>   Round with the Sun-illumined Lantern held
> In Midnight by the Master of the Show;
>
> But helpless Pieces of the Game He plays
> Upon this Chequer-board of Nights and Days;
>   Hither and thither moves, and checks, and slays,
> And one by one back in the Closet lays.
>   .   .   .
>
> **The Moving Finger writes;** and, having writ,
> Moves on: nor all your Piety nor Wit
>   Shall lure it back to cancel half a Line,
> Nor all your Tears wash out a Word of it.
>
> And that inverted Bowl they call the Sky,
> Whereunder crawling coop'd we live and die,
>   Lift not your hands to *It* for help—for It
> As impotently moves as you or I.
>   .   .   .
>
> YESTERDAY *This* Day's Madness did prepare;
> TOMORROW'S Silence, Triumph, or Despair:
>   Drink! for you know not whence you came, nor why:
> Drink! for you know not why you go, nor where.

Much malice mingled with a little wit

Source: THE HIND AND THE PANTHER (Part III, l. 1295)
Author: John Dryden (1631–1700)
First published: 1687
Type of work: Religious allegory

Context: A 2,592-line poem in three parts followed Dryden's conversion

720

to Roman Catholicism. In it, various animals represent the conflicting religious bodies of England, with the White Hind symbolizing the Roman Catholics, and the Panther the Church of England. In the second part, the Hind and the Panther, journeying through the woods together, reach the Hind's den into which she invites the Panther. She is amazed at its attractiveness. The Hind suggests that her guest might well make the den her "dwelling place of everlasting rest." At the beginning of the third part, the poet makes his defense for using in his allegory "foreign animals" that do not exist in England. He cites Spenser's *Mother Hubbard's* *Tale* where "Mother Hubbard in her homely dress, Has sharply blam'd a British Lioness/ . . . Expos'd obscenely naked and asleep." Dryden protests that if Aesop in his fables could introduce animals nonexistent in Greece, why can he not do the same for England? The first line of the defense quoted was used by Montagu and Prior, "Much Malice and Little Wit," as title for their satire on Dryden's poem. Caledon, the name of Scotland, is used poetically for all the British Isles. Dryden protests that people of ill will but some cleverness may attack what he has written. He calls his work "mysterious" because it was first published anonymously.

Much malice mingled with a little wit,
Perhaps, may censure this mysterious writ;
Because the Muse has peopled Caledon
With Panthers, Bears, and Wolves, and beasts unknown,
As if we were not stock'd with monsters of our own.
Let Aesop answer, he who set to view
Such kinds as Greece and Phrygia never knew.

. . .

Led by those great examples, may not I
The wanted organs of their words supply?
If men transact like brutes, 't is equal then
For brutes to claim the privilege of men.

. . .

The muddy ecstasies of beer

Source: INEBRIETY (Line 120)
Author: George Crabbe (1754–1832)
First published: 1775
Type of work: Didactic poem

Context: While he was apprenticed to a surgeon at Woodbridge, Crabbe wrote a number of poems which he later wished to suppress. *Inebriety,* first published in pamphlet form, was one of them. As a surgeon's apprentice, the poet had had opportunity to observe many cases of intemperance, and he drew upon those observations to describe the vice of drunkenness. The poem is, deliberately, in imitation of Alexander Pope's satires earlier in the century, as Crabbe observed for the reader in the Preface to

721

the poem. At the beginning of the work Crabbe announces his subject in mock-heroic fashion, echoing both Virgil and Pope: "The mighty spirit, and its power, which stains/ The bloodless cheek, and vivifies the brains,/ I sing." The poet goes on to describe the varieties of liquors popular among the different classes and the pseudo peace of mind alcohol brings to its devotees. He describes the clergyman addicted to alcohol and then the ordinary man, a drinker of ale, in words reminiscent of Pope's lines on the Indian:

> Lo! the poor toper whose untutor'd sense,
> Sees bliss in ale, and can with wine dispense;
> Whose head proud fancy never taught to steer,
> Beyond **the muddy ecstacies of beer;**
> But simple nature can her longing quench,
> Behind the settle's curve, or humbler bench:
> Some kitchen fire diffusing warmth around,
> The semi-globe of hieroglyphics crown'd;
> Where canvass purse displays the brass enroll'd,
> Nor waiters rave, nor landlord thirst for gold;
> Ale and content his fancy's bounds confine,
> He asks no limpid punch, no rosy wine;
> But sees, admitted to an equal share,
> Each faithful swain the heady potion bear:
> Go wiser thou! and in thy scale of taste,
> Weigh gout and gravel against ale and rest.

The multitude is always in the wrong

Source: ESSAY ON TRANSLATED VERSE (Line 184)
Author: Wentworth Dillon (Earl of Roscommon, 1633?–1685)
First published: 1684
Type of work: Verse essay

Context: To produce a good translation of verse, says the Earl of Roscommon, the translator must select a worthy piece of poetry to work on: it must have sufficiently exalted subject matter to make the project of translating it worth while. Moreover, it must fit the taste and inclinations of the translator so that he will be sympathetic towards it. The piece should be of acceptable morality, as there is no justification for recording improper and indecent matter or using coarse words, when there is so much worthy poetry available. Also, men of sense despise a trivial choice of subject. Foul descriptions offend people of taste and judgment, either by being like their originals or, on the other hand, by the falsity of being unlike them. The translator should employ the greatest symmetry in the formation of his work; and, although the composition of a great original poem requires genius, a good translation also calls for a high degree of talent and poetic skill. The better the original is. the more difficult it will be to translate in an understandable manner: Virgil, for instance, wrote ages

722

ago, but he is still only slenderly understood by the ordinary reader. In translating him, a talent almost as great as his is necessary. Roscommon proceeds thus:

> What I have instanced only in the best,
> Is, in proportion, true of all the rest.
> Take pains the genuine meaning to explore;
> There sweat, there strain, tug the laborious oar:
> Search every comment that your care can find,
> Some here, some there, may hit the poet's mind;
> Yet be not blindly guided by the throng;
> **The multitude is always in the wrong.**

The murmuring poor, who will not fast in peace

Source: THE NEWSPAPER (Line 158)
Author: George Crabbe (1754–1832)
First published: 1785
Type of work: Satiric poem

Context: The poem begins by saying that poetry is not in a thriving condition, as it cannot find a market. The only poets who are doing well are those connected with newspapers, which have a virtual monopoly on the reading public. There is a multitude of newspapers: some are published daily, some thrice a week, some twice, and some weekly. They are of every shade of opinion: some support the ministry, some oppose it, and some shift from one side to the other as advantage seems to indicate. There is even one impartial newspaper. They come out in the morning, in the evening, and in the intervening hours; they are ephemera, lasting less than a day; like ephemeral insects, they die before the morning after the day on which they are born. Some papers are frankly scurrilous, some ostensibly moral, but even these contain their quota of filth in the back pages. Because of their inaccuracy, everyone is ill informed upon the truth; the papers cannot lie as fast as the public will believe. The poet asks the papers not to get their news about such things as rising taxes, the hungry poor that complain about their poverty, political gossip, and foreign affairs from ill-informed sources:

> But oh! ye Muses, keep your votary's feet
> From tavern-haunts where politicians meet;
> Where rector, doctor, and attorney pause,
> First on each parish, then each public cause:
> Indited roads, and rates that still increase;
> **The murmuring poor, who will not fast in peace;**
> Election zeal and friendship, since declined;
> A tax commuted, or a tithe in kind;
> The Dutch and Germans kindling into strife;
> Dull port and poachers vile! the serious ills of life.

723

Music, the greatest good that mortals know

Source: SONG FOR ST. CECILIA'S DAY (Stanza 3)
Author: Joseph Addison (1672–1719)
First published: 1694
Type of work: Ode

Context: Remaining in Oxford after his graduation in 1693, Addison worked on classical translations. He was also called upon for occasional verse, as for a celebration of St. Cecilia's Day, Nov. 22, 1694. This martyr of the third or fourth century refused to consummate a marriage, but sat apart during the wedding ceremony "singing to herself praises of God." Therefore she became patron saint of musicians. Addison seized the opportunity of a celebration to her, to hymn music in general, with only one reference to the martyr. The poem is but one among many written in imitation of Dryden's *Alexander's Feast* and *A Song for St. Cecilia's Day.*

> Forever consecrate the day
> To Music and Cecilia;
> **Music, the greatest good that mortals know,**
> And all of heaven we have below.
> Music can noble hints impart,
> Engender fury, kindle love;
> With unsuspecting eloquence can move
> And manage all the man with secret art.
> When Orpheus strikes the trembling Lyre,
> The streams stand still, the stones admire; . . .

The music, yearning like a God in pain

Source: THE EVE OF SAINT AGNES (Stanza 7)
Author: John Keats (1795–1821)
First published: 1820
Type of work: Narrative poem

Context: It is the Eve of St. Agnes, January 20, and bitter cold. The owl, with ruffled-up feathers, is cold, and the hare limps through the frozen grass. A priest in the chapel, telling his rosary with numb fingers, breathes out a cloud that rises like incense. His prayers finished, he takes his way out of the chapel and hears the music for the great party for a thousand guests. A member of the household, however, the Lady Madeline, daughter of the Lord of the castle, has her mind not upon revelry but upon the sacred rites of St. Agnes' Eve. It had been told her that if young virgins followed the ritual faithfully they would have visions of their lovers. They had to go supperless to bed and lie upon their backs, looking neither to one side or the other, but straight up. As Madeline prepares to go through the ceremonies she scarcely hears the music, yearning like a god in pain; she goes through the throng assembled for the party without noting the guests. Her downcast eyes see only sweeping trains upon the floor. Amorous youths come up to her to pay their court, but she does not see them: her heart is elsewhere.

Full of this whim was thoughtful Madeline:
The music, yearning like a God in pain,
She scarcely heard: her maiden eyes divine,
Fixed on the floor, saw many a sweeping train
Pass by—she heeded not at all: in vain
Came many a tiptoe, amorous cavalier,
And back retired; not cooled by high disdain,
But she saw not: her heart was otherwhere:
She sighes for Agnes' dreams, the sweetest of the year.

The mutable, rank-scented many

Source: CORIOLANUS (Act III, sc. i, l. 66)
Author: William Shakespeare (1564–1616)
First published: 1623
Type of work: Dramatic tragedy

Context: Coriolanus has returned to Rome fresh from his astounding feats at the battle of Corioli, where, single-handed, he captured the enemy town. The Roman Senate rewards him with the office of Consul. However, in order to be confirmed in the office, Coroilanus must perform the ceremony of seeking the confirmation of the plebeians. From his very birth Coriolanus has been bred to fight, to be proud, and to despise the plebeians. He seeks the consulship because his mother, Volumnia, wishes him to do so. Reluctantly he goes through the degrading process of begging the masses for their support. His aristocratic pride, which is his virtue, is here a weakness which leaves him at the mercy of his enemies. Although he is elected according to the custom, his enemies arouse the masses to revoke the election before it is confirmed. When urged by his friends to curb his pride, Coriolanus will not back down. He tells his friends:

   . . . My nobler friends,
I crave their pardons.
For **the mutable, rank-scented many,** let them
Regard me as I do not flatter, and
Therein behold themselves. I say again,
In soothing them, we nourish 'gainst our senate
The cockle of rebellion, insolence, sedition,
Which we ourselves have ploughed for, sowed, and scattered,
By mingling them with us, the honoured number,
Who lack not virtue, no, nor power, but that
Which they have given to beggars.

725

A mutilated curtsey

Source: THE VICAR OF WAKEFIELD (Chapter I)
Author: Oliver Goldsmith (1728–1774)
First published: 1766
Type of work: Novel

Context: The events of this work are related in the first person. The writer begins by telling how he, a vicar, married a good wife who could read, pickle, preserve, and work. He and his wife loved each other tenderly; they lived in an elegant house and filled in their vacant time with rural amusements, visiting their rich neighbors, and relieving the wants of the poor; their life was easy and pleasant. As they dwelt near the highroad, they had a great deal of company, especially relatives, some of whom were not very creditable representatives of the family. As, however, the wife insisted that they were of the same flesh and blood, they were all entertained in the best possible manner. When anyone turned up who was actually unwelcome, the vicar and his wife entertained him as well as they did anyone else; but at his departing they lent him a riding coat, a pair of boots, or a horse of small value, and as he never came back to return what he had borrowed, they were spared his company in the future. Thus they lived in happiness, although sometimes their orchard was plundered or the wife's custards purloined; sometimes the squire would fall asleep during the best part of the sermon, or the squire's lady would greet the vicar's wife's civilities with small politeness —with a mutilated curtsey:

> Thus we lived several years in a state of much happiness, not but that we sometimes had those little rubs which Providence sends to enhance the value of its favors. My orchard was often robbed by schoolboys, and my wife's custards plundered by the cats or the children. The Squire would sometimes fall asleep in the most pathetic parts of my sermon, or his lady return my wife's civilities at church with **a mutilated curtsey.** But we soon got over the uneasiness caused by such accidents, and usually in three or four days began to wonder how they vexed us.

My age is as a lusty winter, frosty, but kindly

Source: AS YOU LIKE IT (Act II, sc. iii, ll. 52–53)
Author: William Shakespeare (1564–1616)
First published: 1623
Type of work: Dramatic comedy

Context: Kept in penury, uneducated, and refused his share of an inheritance by his evil older brother, the young gentleman Orlando now discovers that the older brother, Oliver, intends to murder him. He is warned that he must run away by a faithful old retainer, Adam, who offers his life savings and asks only that he be permitted to serve his young master:

ADAM

. . .

Here is the gold;
All this I give you. Let me be your servant.
Though I look old, yet I am strong and lusty.
For in my youth I never did apply
Hot and rebellious liquors in my blood,
Nor did not with unbashful forehead woo
The means of weakness and debility.
Therefore **my age is as a lusty winter,
Frosty, but kindly.** Let me go with you;
I'll do the service of a younger man
In all your business and necessities.

ORLANDO

O good old man, how well in thee appears
The constant service of the antique world,
When service sweat for duty, not for meed.

. . .

My banks they are furnished with bees

Source: A PASTORAL BALLARD, IN FOUR PARTS (Part II, "Hope," l. 1)
Author: William Shenstone (1714–1763)
First published: 1755
Type of work: Pastoral ballad

Context: Shenstone's poem in the traditional pastoral manner is about the unrequited love of a shepherd named Corydon for the beautiful Phyllis. The poem is in four parts: the first, entitled "Absence," tells of Corydon's love for the young woman, his memories of her, and his sorrow while she is gone from him; Part Two, from which the quotation is taken, tells of the shepherd's hope that Phyllis will return to share the grove and bower and gifts he has prepared for her; Part Three, "Solicitude," tells, as the title indicates, of Corydon's solicitude for his beloved and his fears that another shepherd, named Paridel, will seduce her with mock passion from Corydon's real love; the last part of the poem, "Disappointment," rings with Corydon's complaint, "She is faithless—and I am undone," as he learns that the lovely Phyllis has proved fickle and left him for all time, leaving him only this "same sad complaint." The quotation is from the opening stanza of Part Two, one of two stanzas that describe the bower Corydon has labored to rear:

727

My banks they are furnish'd with bees,
Whose murmur invites one to sleep;
My grottoes are shaded with trees,
And my hills are white-over with sheep.
I seldom have met with a loss,
Such health do my fountains bestow;
My fountains all border'd with moss,
Where the hare-bells and violets grow.

Not a pine in my grove is there seen,
But with tendrils of woodbine is bound:
Not a beech's more beautiful green,
But a sweet-briar entwines it around.
Not my fields in the prime of the year,
More charms than my cattle unfold:
Not a brook that is limpid and clear,
But it glitters with fishes of gold.

My dear Lady Disdain

Source: MUCH ADO ABOUT NOTHING (Act I, sc. i, l. 118)
Author: William Shakespeare (1564–1616)
First published: 1600
Type of work: Dramatic comedy

Context: As the play opens, the victorious forces of Don Pedro are returning to Messina. Among them is a young gallant named Benedick, with whom Beatrice—the niece of Leonato, Governor of Messina—has engaged in a rhetorical war of comic badinage in action antecedent to the play. Before the soldiers return, she mockingly asks a messenger whether "Signior Mountanto [thruster]" has returned from the wars and how many he has killed ("for indeed I promised to eat all of his killing"). Leonato explains to the confused messenger that "there is a kind of merry war betwixt Signior Benedick and her. They never meet but there's a skirmish of wit between them."

Their repartee forms a major thread of the comedy throughout the play. Moreover, with each claiming to be invulnerable to Cupid and with each supposedly holding the other in utter disdain, they are primed for falling in love despite their articulations to the contrary. Don Pedro, Leonato, and Claudio scheme to let each overhear a conversation in which the other's love is described as strong but reticent in the face of mockery. The bait takes, and the comedy concludes with a wedding of these anti-lovers. As predicted in the first scene, when Benedick and other soldiers enter, their war of words begins almost immediately. She tartly interrupts Benedick's conversation with Don Pedro:

728

BEATRICE
I wonder that you will still be talking, Signior Benedick. Nobody marks you.

BENEDICK
What **my dear Lady Disdain!** Are you yet living?

BEATRICE
Is it possible disdain should die, while she hath such food to feed it, as Signior Benedick? Courtesy itself must convert to disdain, if you come in her presence.

BENEDICK
Then is courtesy a turncoat. But it is certain I am loved of all ladies, only you excepted. And I would I could find it in my heart that I had not a hard heart, for truly I love none.

BEATRICE
A dear happiness to women, they would else have been troubled with a pernicious suitor. I thank God and my cold blood, I am of your humour for that. I had rather hear my dog bark at a crow, than a man swear he loves me.

My great taskmaster's eye

Source: SONNET VII, ON HIS HAVING ARRIVED AT THE AGE OF TWENTY-THREE (Line 14)
Author: John Milton (1608–1674)
First published: 1645
Type of work: Sonnet

Context: Milton, having attained the age of twenty-three, takes stock of himself. His physical appearance might indicate that the poet is younger than Time would admit, nor does he have any accomplishments of which to be proud at this stage in his life, his late youth. In the closing sestet of the sonnet, Milton resolves the problem by stating that the pattern of his life is in the hand of God; hence, his development and his accomplishments rest with the will of God, and he but asks the grace to fulfill the behests of his "Taskmaster." The entire sonnet appears:

> How soon hath Time, the subtle thief of youth,
>   Stoln on his wing my three and twentieth year!
>   My hasting days fly on with full career,
>   But my late spring no bud or blossom show'th.
> Perhaps my semblance might deceive the truth,
>   That I to manhood am arrived so near,
>   And inward ripeness doth much less appear,

That some more timely-happy spirits endu'th.
Yet be it less or more, or soon or slow,
  It shall be still in strictest measure even
  To that same lot, however mean or high,
Toward which Time leads me, and the will of Heaven;
  All is, if I have grace to use it so,
  As ever in **my great Taskmaster's eye.**

My griefs; still am I King of those

Source: KING RICHARD THE SECOND (Act IV, sc. i, l. 193)
Author: William Shakespeare (1564–1616)
First published: 1597
Type of work: Historical drama

Context: Richard II, forced to abdicate by his cousin Henry Bolingbroke, who succeeds him as Henry IV of England, is summoned to the presence of the new monarch. Bolingbroke expresses surprise as Richard bemoans his fate:

BOLINGBROKE
I thought you had been willing to resign.

RICHARD
My crown I am, but still my griefs are mine.
You may my glories and my state depose,
But not **my griefs; still am I King of those.**

BOLINGBROKE
Part of your cares you give me with your crown.

RICHARD
Your cares set up do not pluck my cares down.
My care, is loss of care, by old care done;
Your care, is gain of care, by new care won.
The cares I give, I have, though given away,
They tend the crown, yet still with me they stay.

My late espoused saint

Source: SONNET XXIII (Line 1)
Author: John Milton (1608–1674)
First published: 1673
Type of work: Sonnet

Context: John Milton, scholarly poet of Puritan England, is noted not only

730

for his ponderously impressive *Paradise Lost,* but also for his sonnets of both public and personal nature. In sonnet XXIII the poet in a dream beholds again the veiled visage of his second wife, Catherine Woodstock Milton, who has died in childbirth. As Hercules, son of Jove, brought back from the land of the dead Alcestis, wife of Greek King Admetus, according to legend and a play of Euripides, even so in Milton's dream is his deceased wife returned to the poet, until, reaching to embrace her, he awakens and she is not there. The entire sonnet reads:

> Methought I saw **my late espousèd saint**
>> Brought to me like Alcestis from the grave,
>> When Joves great Son to her glad Husband gave,
> Rescu'd from death by force though pale and faint.
> Mine, as whom washt from spot of child-bed taint,
>> Purification in the old Law did save,
>> And such, as yet once more I trust to have
> Full sight of her in Heaven without restraint,
>> Came vested all in white, pure as her mind:
>> Her face was veil'd, yet to my fancied sight,
>> Love, sweetness, goodness, in her person shin'd
> So clear, as in no face with more delight.
>> But O as to embrace me she enclin'd
>> I wak'd, she fled, and day brought back my night.

My life is like the summer rose

Source: LAMENT OF THE CAPTIVE (Stanza 1)
Author: Richard Henry Wilde (1789–1847)
First published: 1819
Type of work: Lyric poem

Context: To the Honorable Richard Henry Wilde, poetry writing was an avocation. Born in Dublin, the son of an Irish hardware dealer and a Tory refugee mother from America, he was brought to Baltimore at the age of eight. Upon the death of his father, his mother moved to Augusta, Georgia, and opened a store. Wilde was completely self-taught, yet he was admitted to the Georgia bar at the age of twenty, and had a career as State Attorney General and U.S. Congressman, until ill health sent him to Italy. In Florence he completed a study of the poet Torquato Tasso (1544–1595) including translation of eighteen of his sonnets which Longfellow later reprinted. Wilde never finished his research into Dante, but the Tasso book was published in 1842 upon his return to the United States. Stories told by his brother James, an officer in a military expedition against the Seminoles in Florida, so interested Richard that for the amusement of the family he started an epic poem about them. The death of his brother in a duel took the pleasure out of the project after the completion of several fragments, including narration and description. Wilde did not believe that great poetry could be composed in the United States because life was too commonplace. Though its scenery was beautiful, it lacked historical and literary associations to humanize it. However, the fourth fragment included a three-stanza unit, quoted by the Seminole chief in describing the sorrows of a white captive of the tribe "many moons ago." This person was probably intended to be the Spaniard Juan Ortiz who, in 1542, was to guide Hernando De Soto to the Mississippi River. This "Lament of the Captive" is the only Wilde poem much remembered. It was published anonymously in the *Analectic Magazine,* for April, 1819, set to music by Charles Thibault, Sydney Lanier, and others, and not claimed by Wilde until 1834. Here are two of its stanzas, with the middle one omitted.

My life is like the summer rose
That opens to the morning sky,
And, ere the shades of evening close,
Is scattered on the ground to die!
Yet on that rose's humble bed
The softest dews of night are shed;
As if she wept the waste to see—
But none shall weep a tear for me!

．．．

My life is like the print, which feet
Have left on Tampa's desert strand;
Soon as the rising tide shall beat,
Their track will vanish from the sand;
Yet, as if grieving to efface
All vestige of the human race,
On that lone shore loud moans the sea,
But none shall thus lament for me!

My name is Legion

Source: MARK 5:9
Author: Unknown (traditionally Mark the Apostle)
First transcribed: c.60–75
Type of work: Gospel

Context: Mark, after a brief account of Jesus' baptism and temptation, enters quickly into a narrative recounting the ministry of Christ; in it he tells of Jesus' preaching and of the people He cured of their infirmities. In Chapter 5 Jesus encounters a man possessed by devils—in other words, a madman. The unfortunate creature has become a problem to his community; he has great physical strength, which his insanity has augmented, and all efforts to restrain him have failed. Now he has either fled or been driven out; he lives among the tombs and wanders through the hills, doing violence to himself. At that time cemeteries were thought to be haunted by devils, who always lurked in unclean places or dwelt in unclean beasts such

732

as pigs. It is evident that somewhere in the madman's tortured mind a spark of sanity lingers making him aware that something is very much the matter with him. He approaches Jesus and recognizes Him, and Jesus effects a cure in terms understood by His audience: he calls the devil forth and asks his name. The reply is in accord with a belief of the time, that he who learns the name of a devil has power over him. Jesus is told there are too many of the devils to name. When He replies that they must leave their host, they beg permission to enter a herd of swine. Jesus grants them leave; the pigs immediately stampede over a steep bank and are drowned in the sea. The madman's cure is thus effected, and the people flocking around to observe him find that he is sane once more. Moreover, now that their new hosts are drowned, the devils are somewhere in hell and thus effectively disposed of. This miracle is too much for the people who have witnessed it, and now they ask Jesus to leave the country. The former madman wishes to accompany Him but Jesus tells him to remain as an example of God's mercy and as a testimonial of the things Jesus has done.

And they came over unto the other side of the sea, into the country of the Gadarenes.

And when he was come out of the ship, immediately there met him out of the tombs a man with an unclean spirit,

Who had his dwelling among the tombs; and no man could bind him, no, not with chains:

Because that he had been often bound with fetters and chains, and the chains had been plucked asunder by him, and the fetters broken in pieces: neither could any man tame him.

And always, night and day, he was in the mountains, and in the tombs, crying, and cutting himself with stones.

But when he saw Jesus afar off, he ran and worshipped him,

And cried with a loud voice, and said, What have I to do with thee, Jesus, thou Son of the Most High God? I adjure thee by God, that thou torment me not.

For he said unto him, Come out of the man, thou unclean spirit.

And he asked him, What is thy name? And he answered, saying, **My name is Legion:** for we are many.

And he besought him much that he would not send them away out of the country.

My nearest and dearest enemy

Source: KING HENRY THE FOURTH: PART ONE (Act III, sc. ii, l. 123)
Author: William Shakespeare (1564–1616)
First published: 1598
Type of work: Historical drama

Context: King Henry IV, beset with political problems and rebellion in the north and west of his kingdom, is also plagued by what he assumes to

733

be the dissipation of his son and heir apparent, Prince Hal. At this point, with Worcester, Northumberland, Percy, Glendower, Mortimer, and Douglas actively moving against him, he commands his son to appear before him to face the charges of prodigality. Hal, fresh from his exploits with Falstaff at the Boar's Head Tavern in Eastcheap, is berated by his father for his failure to assume any responsibility in the face of the danger to the throne. Hal has "rudely lost" his "place in the council"; he has become "almost an alien to the hearts/ Of all the court and princes of my blood." Indeed, according to Henry, his son has developed much the same reputation as the base Richard II earlier, when "the skipping king . . . ambled up and down/ With shallow jesters and rash bavin wits." Most galling to the king, however, is the apparent indifference of the heir apparent, who seems to have no regard for the cause to which his father has devoted his very life:

KING HENRY

. . .

. . . Percy, Northumberland,
The Archbishop's grace of York, Douglas, Mortimer,
Capitulate against us, and are up.
But wherefore do I tell these news to thee?
Why, Harry, do I tell thee of my foes,
Which art **my nearest and dearest enemy?**
That thou art like enough, through vassal fear,
Base inclination, and the start of spleen,
To fight against me under Percy's pay,
To dog his heels, and curtsy at his frowns,
To show how much thou art degenerate.

Nae man can tether time or tide

Source: TAM O'SHANTER (Line 67)
Author: Robert Burns (1759–1796)
First published: 1791
Type of work: Narrative poem

Context: Captain Francis Grose (1731?–1791) was an English antiquarian and draftsman, much interested in the old buildings and legends of all parts of Great Britain. In his late years, Robert Burns' father had settled on a farm near Alloway Kirk, close to a dilapidated cemetery which he and neighbors enclosed with a wall, following permission from the Ayr town council. From then on, he had looked upon it as his burial place, as did his son, Robert. When the poet was living at Ellisland, he found the antiquarian visiting nearby, and Robert asked Grose to make a drawing of the church where he intended to have his own bones laid down "when they should no longer be serviceable" to him. The artist agreed

734

on condition that Burns provide him with a legend to be published with his sketch in his book, *Grose's Antiquities of Scotland* (1791). "Tam O'Shanter" was the result, written in one day and proclaimed, with "The Cotter's Saturday Night," the best of Burns' poetry. Indeed one enthusiastic admirer declared that "Tam O'Shanter" of Robert Burns and the Battle of Bannockburn (1314) won by Robert the Bruce, were the two best day's work ever performed by Scotsmen. Tam o' Shanter, husband of Kate, tarries too long at the market, tippling in the tavern with his crony Souter (Shoemaker) Johnny. They exchange stories. The landlord bellows with enjoyment, and his wife shows herself so gracious toward Tam that, remembering his wife's continual nagging about his drinking habits, he has no inclination to go home, though it is midnight. Besides, the weather outside is stormy and blustery. However, as King Canute, the eleventh century King of England, Norway, and Denmark, demonstrated when he ordered his throne set up at the edge of the sea, even a king cannot control tides. As Burns recounts the circumstances:

> But pleasures are like poppies spread,
> You seize the flow'r, its bloom is shed;
> Or like the snow-falls in the river,
> A moment white—then melts forever . . .
>
> . . .
>
> Or like the rainbow's lovely form
> Evanishing amid the storm.—
> **Nae man can tether time or tide;**
> The hour approaches Tam maun ride;
> That hour o' night's black arch the key-stane,
> That dreary hour Tam mounts his beast in;
> And sic a night he taks the road in,
> As ne'er poor sinner was abroad in.

Naked came I out of my mother's womb

Source: JOB 1:21
Author: Unknown
First transcribed: c.900–500 B.C.
Type of work: Religious saga

Context: Job, a good and God-fearing man, lives in the land of Uz. He is a man "perfect and upright." He is blessed by God with much wealth, "so that this man was the greatest of all the men of the east." He is also blessed with seven sons and three daughters. But there comes a time when Satan approaches the throne of God. He tells God that Job is a worshiper of God only in prosperity, that Job will, if plunged into adversity, turn to cursing God. Satan's challenge is met; God grants Satan permission to try Job with evil, saying that Job himself must not be harmed. Soon after a messenger arrives at Job's home to tell him that the Sa-

735

beans have stolen all his oxen and asses and have killed all the servants who guarded them. Hard on the heels of the first messenger comes a second, to tell Job that all his camels have been stolen by three bands of Chaldeans, who slew the servants in charge of the animals. Yet a third messenger arrives, to tell how a great wind came howling out of the wilderness to cave in the roof of the house belonging to Job's eldest son, killing all the sons and daughters of Job, who were gathered together for a feast. Thus, at the hands of Satan, Job is given his trial; but being a just and good man he only groans at the happenings, and does not curse God as Satan predicted he would. Job neither sins against God, nor does he blame God for what has happened:

> Then Job arose, and rent his mantle, and shaved his head, and fell down upon the ground, and worshipped,
> And said, **Naked came I out of my mother's womb,** and naked shall I return thither: the LORD gave, and the LORD hath taken away; blessed be the name of the LORD.
> In all this Job sinned not, nor charged God foolishly.

A nation is not governed, which is perpetually to be conquered

Source: SPEECH ON MOVING HIS RESOLUTIONS FOR RECONCILIATION WITH THE COLONIES
Author: Edmund Burke (1729–1797)
First published: 1775
Type of work: Political speech

Context: The American Colonies had no more articulate and determined friend in the English Parliament than Burke. With his conservative respect for tradition and precedent he pointed to the acts of redress to Ireland and to Wales, and argued that the great profits resulting from those conciliations would be much more than matched by conciliation with America. Moreover, he argued, the stern military suppression which the Parliament was contemplating, was uncertain and if successful would be but temporary:

> . . . Those who wield the thunder of the state, may have more confidence in the efficacy of arms. But I confess, possibly for want of this knowledge, my opinion is much more in favour of prudent management, than of force; considering force not as an odious, but a feeble instrument, for preserving a people so numerous, so active, so growing, so spirited as this, in a profitable and subordinate connexion with us.
> First, Sir, permit me to observe, that the use of force alone is but *temporary*. It may subdue for a moment; but it does not remove the necessity of subduing again: and **a nation is not governed, which is perpetually to be conquered.**

736

Nature in him was almost lost in art

Source: VERSES TO SIR THOMAS HANMER (Line 56)
Author: William Collins (1721–1759)
First published: 1743
Type of work: Commendatory poem

Context: Collins was one of the best of the mid-eighteenth century minor poets. Although his total output was little more than a score of poems, his delicate sense of clarity and structure is notable. These verses addressed to Hanmer on the occasion of his edition of Shakespeare constitute Collins' longest poem. In this work the poet surveys and compares the classical period with the English renaissance and sees in Shakespeare a beginning as splendid as that of any classical figure. He then laments that these beginnings led to no period of comparable development:

> Yet ah! so bright her Morning's op'ning Ray,
> In vain our *Britain* hop'd an equal Day!
> No second Growth the Western Isle could bear,
> At once exhausted with too rich a Year.
> Too nicely *Jonson* knew the Critic's Part;
> **Nature in him was almost lost in Art.**
> Of softer Mold the gentle *Fletcher* came.
> The next in Order, as the next in Name.

. . .

Nature never did betray the heart that loved her

Source: LINES COMPOSED A FEW MILES ABOVE TINTERN ABBEY (Lines 122–123)
Author: William Wordsworth (1770–1850)
First published: 1798
Type of work: Lyric poem

Context: When the French Revolution broke out, Wordsworth, though an Englishman, rejoiced in what was happening and viewed with disfavor the British antagonism to Republican France. As time passed, however, the bloody excesses of the Revolution caused Wordsworth great emotional stress and he changed his mind about it. He came to believe that mankind, whom he had trusted, had betrayed that trust. Only nature, he now thought, would never fail him. In 1798, while on a walking tour, he stopped on a hill overlooking the peaceful valley of the River Wye, to spend an hour musing on the world of men, and how his views had changed in the five years since he had once before stood looking down on the peaceful valley. The poem expresses three consecutive attitudes which Wordsworth believed that he had held toward nature: a simple animal response to it, a response in which the love of mankind had predominated, and a response in which he found the presence of God in nature. The portion of the poem in which this quotation is found is addressed to Dorothy Wordsworth, the poet's sister, who was with him at the time and had helped him in his emotional crises.

> Oh! yet a little while
> May I behold in thee what I was once,
> My dear, dear Sister! and this prayer I make,
> Knowing that **Nature never did betray**
> **The heart that loved her;** 'tis her privilege,
> Through all the years of this our life, to lead
> From joy to joy: for she can so inform
> The mind that is within us, so impress
> With quietness and beauty, and so feed
> With lofty thoughts, that neither evil tongues,
> Rash judgments, nor the sneers of selfish men,
> Nor greetings where no kindness is, nor all
> The dreary intercourse of daily life,
> Shall e'er prevail against us, or disturb
> Our cheerful faith, that all which we behold
> Is full of blessings.

The nature of bad news infects the teller

Source: ANTONY AND CLEOPATRA (Act I, sc. ii, l. 99)
Author: William Shakespeare (1564–1616)
First published: 1623
Type of work: Dramatic tragedy

Context: Antony, one of the triumvirs ruling the Roman Empire after the death of Julius Caesar, has been infatuated with Cleopatra, and, ignoring his imperial duties as well as his wife, Fulvia, has spent his days and nights in Alexandria reveling with and loving the Egyptian Queen. When a messenger arrives from Rome, Antony, to the disgust of his friends, at first dismisses him without a hearing. But then, as Cleopatra puts it, "a Roman thought" possesses him, and he recalls the messenger, who hesitates to speak for fear his bad news may "infect" the messenger, making him seem hateful to the great Antony. But now we see another Antony, one who refuses to turn away from duty or truth. He hears that while he lay idle in Alexandria, the Parthians seized, or "extended," large portions of the Empire. The passage gains in effect by contrast with the way Cleopatra later treats a messenger who brings *her* bad news. Overwrought, she takes her feelings out on the messenger.

ANTONY
Well, what worst?

738

MESSENGER
The nature of bad news infects the teller.

ANTONY
When it concerns the fool or coward. On.
Things that are past, are done. With me, 'tis thus,
Who tells me true, though in his tale lie death,
I hear him as he flattered.

MESSENGER
Labienus—
This is stiff news—hath with his Parthian force
Extended Asia from Euphrates;
His conquering banner shook from Syria
To Lydia and to Ionia,
Whilst—

ANTONY
Antony thou wouldst say—

MESSENGER
O my lord!

ANTONY
Speak to me home, mince not the general tongue,

· · ·

Nature's darling

Source: PROGRESS OF POESY (III, 1, l. 2)
Author: Thomas Gray (1716–1771)
First published: 1757
Type of work: Pindaric ode

Context: Thomas Gray, fifth child of a London broker, and the only one of twelve children to survive, was educated at Eton and Cambridge. Leaving the university without earning a degree, he toured the continent with his friend Horace Walpole (1717–1797). Later at his own press at Strawberry Hill, Walpole published the first collection of Gray's poems. In December, 1754, Gray completed an "Ode in the Greek Manner," which under its other title "The Progress of Poesy," showed his art at its highest. With another ode, now called "The Bard," it was published at the Walpole Press. Not until 1768 did Gray print all the poems he wanted the world to see, a total of ten. Because of these, and despite his small total production, Gray was offered the post of Poet Laureate following the death of Colley Cibber in 1757. He refused it. He wrote only a little more before dying of the gout. While Gray loved to read Spenser, Milton, and Dryden, he considered Shakespeare high above all other poets in all countries and in all times, and naturally included him in the ode describing the history of poetry throughout the ages. Since in comparison with the university-trained poets before and contemporary with him, Shakespeare had little knowledge of Latin and Greek, which were considered in the seventeenth and eighteenth centuries the chief source of learning, Ben Jonson, Milton, and others spoke of him as having been taught by Nature. In his history of poets from Pindar and his Aeolian lyre, through Greece to Italy, Gray comes in the first stanza of Part III to England and Shakespeare. The fact that Shakespeare was born in April, the Springtime, and in Stratford-on-Avon are expressed poetically by Gray.

> Far from the sun and summer gale,
> In thy green lap was **Nature's darling** laid.
> What time, where lucid Avon strayed,
> To him the mighty Mother did unveil
> Her awful face.

Naught venture, naught have

Source: FIVE HUNDRED POINTS OF GOOD HUSBANDRY (Chapter 17, "October's Abstract")
Author: Thomas Tusser (c.1525–1580)
First published: 1557
Type of work: Didactic poem

Context: Thomas Tusser's *Five Hundred Points of Good Husbandry* is an early version of the farmer's almanac; in it various practical instructions, moral observations, and miscellaneous information on weather and climate are given in homely verse. Though much of the poetry is doggerel, it does portray vividly the farm life of early Elizabethan times and has enjoyed considerable popularity during the centuries since it was first published. For all its undoubted usefulness in its own time, however, it did not aid its author to any great extent. Tusser was a gentleman, well born and educated at Eton and Cambridge, who left the city for the farm. He was not a successful farmer, though his knowledge of agriculture was considerable, and he eventually died in a debtor's prison. Part of the charm of his work lies in his use of old familiar sayings, many of them still in use today. We now say "Nothing ventured, nothing gained;" in 1546, when John Heywood (1497–1580) collected the saying in his *Proverbes,* it was "Nought venter, nought have." Tusser, in the selection quoted with this article, uses a variant of the expression. His book begins with short verses (each a chapter) in which general observations are made concerning husbandry and extolling farm life. He then describes the farmer's diet. At this point the main part of the book is begun; after some com-

740

ments on weather and astronomy, he takes up the farmer's year, beginning with September, the best time to assume ownership of a farm. The husbandry of each month is preceded by an abstract, or summary, of what the month's chapter contains. Thus, in chapter seventeen ("October's Abstract") Tusser gives the reader a rapid preview of what will be discussed next.

6. Who soweth in rain,
   Hath weed for his pain;
   But worse shall he speed,
   That soweth ill seed.
7. Now, better than later,
   Draw furrow for water.
   Keep crows, good son;
   See fencing be done.
8. Each soil no vein,
   For every grain.
   Though soil be but bad,
   Some corn may be had.
9. Naught prove, naught crave,
   Naught venture, naught have.
10. One crop, and away,
    Some country may say.
11. All gravel and sand,
    Is not the best land.
    A rottenly mould,
    Is land worth gould.

The nearer the Church the further from God

Source: SERMON ON THE NATIVITY (Number 15)
Author: Launcelot Andrewes (1555–1626)
First published: 1628
Type of work: Sermon

Context: Launcelot Andrewes, himself the son of a school teacher, intended to follow his father's profession, but his professors told him he was too smart for a schoolmaster; he should study for the Church. He quickly proved his capabilities. He became a popular preacher before large audiences until Queen Elizabeth appointed him Dean of Westminster. James I, succeeding her in 1603, made him Bishop of Chichester and head of the committee that assembled the King James version of the Bible. In 1605 Andrewes was made chaplain to James I. One of his duties was to preach a sermon to the court every Christmas morning before they sat down to their boar and venison banquet. Andrewes was a preacher of the old school, quoting Latin and Greek, making detailed analyses of his text, and interjecting jokes. For instance, in one Christmas sermon he quipped that if we have not Immanu-el, which indicates that God is with us, we have Immanu-hell. His sort of preaching went out following the coronation of Charles I in 1625. At Bishop Andrewes' death, Charles ordered two of his fellow clergymen to publish some of the court chaplain's representative sermons, which appeared as *96 Sermons by the Right Honorable and Reverend Father in God Launcelot Andrewes, late Lord Bishop of Winchester, Published by His Majesties Special Command.* By 1641 the work had gone into a fourth edition. The volume contained seventeen Christmas Sermons preached between 1605 and the year before his death (he died in September, 1626), along with other sermons for Ash Wednesday, Easter, and Whitsunday. They are set down in a sort of short hand that he must have expanded while preaching. Number 15, "A Sermon preached before the Kings Majestie at White Hall on Wednesday the 25th of December,

1622, being Christmas Day," took as its text Matthew XI, 1 and 2: "Behold there came Wise Men from the East to Jerusalem; saying Where is the King of the Jews that is born? For we have seen His star in the East and are come to worship Him." It is an excellent example of exegesis. Of the two points, the persons and their errand, Andrewes develops the latter. The Magi were motivated by faith. They believed Him born and wanted to do something about the event. Then the preacher made personal application. The Magi saw a star; we on earth also have a star, St. Peter Lucifer, who summons us. Though we may never see the Magi's star or hear angel voices, we can by the grace of God be moved to seek and worship. But we need to make an effort. Is the "lightly" in parentheses an indication about delivery of the sermon? Is the preacher showing he is preparing to utter a whimsy?

But then for the distance, desolateness, tediousness, and the rest, any of them were enough to mar our *venimus* quite. It must be no great way, first, we must come; we love not that; well fare the Shepherds, yet they come but hard by; rather like them than the Magi. Nay, not like them neither. For with us, the nearer (lightly), the further off. Our Proverb is (you know), **the nearer the Church, the further from God.**

Nor, it must not be through no desert, over no Petrea. If rugged or uneven the way; if the weather be ill disposed; if any never so little danger. it is enough to stay us. To Christ we cannot travel, but weather, and way, and all must be fair. If not, no journey, but sit still and see further.

A nest of singing birds

Source: THE LIFE OF SAMUEL JOHNSON, LL. D. (For 1730)
Author: James Boswell (1740–1795)
First published: 1791
Type.of work: Biography

Context: A friend of Samuel Johnson's, Dr. Adams, told Boswell that when Johnson was at Pembroke College, Oxford, he was much liked by all who knew him, he having been a gay and frolicsome fellow. Boswell mentioned this conversation to Johnson, who said that he was mad and violent, being miserably poor and thus opposed to all power and authority. The Bishop of Dromore told Boswell that Johnson was given to lounging around the college gate with a crowd of his juniors. Boswell could not find that he formed any intimacies with fellow students, but he had a strong love for his college and sent it a complete set of his writings. He was proud of the important men who had been educated at Pembroke. Boswell writes:

. . . He took a pleasure in boasting of the many eminent men who had been educated at Pembroke. In this list are found the names of Mr. Hawkins the Poetry Professor, Mr. Shenstone, Sir William Blackstone, and others, not forgetting the celebrated popular preacher, Mr. George Whitefield, of whom, though Johnson did not think very highly, it must be acknowledged that his eloquence was powerful, his views pious and charitable, his assiduity most incredible, and that since his death, the integrity of his character has been fully vindicated. Being himself a poet, Johnson was peculiarly happy in mentioning how many of the sons of Pembroke were poets; adding, with a smile of sportive triumph, "Sir, we are **a nest of singing birds."**

Never dares the man put off the prophet

Source: ONE WORD MORE (X, Line 99)
Author: Robert Browning (1812–1889)
First published: 1855
Type of work: Dedicatory epilogue

Context: Browning wrote this poem as an epilogue to dedicate a volume of poetry to his wife Elizabeth Browning. In it, he discusses the importance of a private existence for the artist apart from his public personage. "God be thanked, the meanest of his creatures/ Boasts two soul-sides, one to face the world with,/ One to show a woman he loves her!" The poet wishes he could turn to a new medium to express his love for a woman as did Dante, who painted to honor Beatrice, or as did Rafael, who wrote a century of sonnets for his love. These evidences of love are more precious to other lovers than are all the masterpieces that the artists created in their own fields. An artist wishes, at least once, to be only a man and to be judged for the joy of his love and not by the critical standards applicable to his public performance. As an example, Browning cites the parallel of Moses, God's prophet, who must have been ever afraid of desecrating "the deed in doing," proving "perchance, but mortal in the

743

minute." The artist, like the prophet, must appear always perfect in his chosen profession, for each suffers the artist's sorrow:

Thus old memories mar the actual triumph;
Thus the doing savors of disrelish;
Thus achievement lacks a gracious somewhat;

. . .

For he bears an ancient wrong about him,
Sees and knows again the phalanxed faces,

. . .

Oh, the crowd must have emphatic warrant!
Theirs, the Sinai-forehead's cloven brilliance
Right-arm's rod-sweep, tongue's imperial fiat.
Never dares the man put off the prophet.

Never did nature say one thing and wisdom say another

Source: LETTERS ON A REGICIDE PEACE (Number 3)
Author: Edmund Burke (1729–1797)
First published: 1797
Type of work: Political essay

Context: Edmund Burke was consistently a believer in stable government; he was opposed to radicals, as he was opposed to theorists. He believed that the British government was good government because it had evolved slowly through centuries. It is no cause for wonder then that he was opposed to the events of the French Revolution; indeed, he was horrified by them. He detested the theoreticians who toppled the throne, killed the French monarch, and set up a government which was grounded in tyranny. Such a government could never find Burke's favor, and when there were proposals of peace with the French Directory, in 1796, Burke opposed them adamantly. Seeing his country's representatives mistreated by the French officials again and again, Burke thought that they should call for a war against France. Burke is amazed and disheartened by their attitude. It is, he says, like having the British lion amused "in the chase of mice and rats." To declare war in ringing tones, not to continue a dishonorable peace, is what Burke feels is the right reaction "under the smart of patience exhausted and abused." He goes on to elaborate why this course is right:

. . . Such a conduct, as the facts stated in the Declaration gave room to expect, is that which true wisdom would have dictated under the impression of those genuine feelings. Never was there a jar or discord between genuine sentiment and sound policy. **Never, no never, did Nature say one thing and Wisdom say another.** Nor are sentiments of elevation in themselves turgid and unnatural. Nature

744

is never more truly herself than in her grandest forms. The Apollo of Belvedere . . . is as much in nature as any figure from the pencil of Rembrandt, or any clown in the rustic revels of Teniers. Indeed, it is when a great nation is in great difficulties, that minds must exalt themselves to the occasion, or all is lost. Strong passion under the direction of a feeble reason feeds a low fever, which serves only to destroy the body that entertains it. . . .

Never read any book that is not a year old

Source: SOCIETY AND SOLITUDE ("Books")
Author: Ralph Waldo Emerson (1803–1882)
First published: 1870
Type of work: Essay

Context: Early in his career, in *The American Scholar,* Emerson had voiced some of his views on books. There he wrote that he considered books "the best type of the influence of the past." He wrote also in that essay, "Books are the best of things, well used; abused, among the worst." Years later, in the volume entitled *Society and Solitude,* he returned to the subject, to offer the fruits of his thinking over the years. He points out that already in his time there are many, many books—with the number increasing every year. In the face of a vast sea of reading material, he says that we must learn to read what is good and not waste our time on mediocrity, remarking that "'Tis an economy of time to read old and famed books," books which have stood the test of time and testify to the high quality of the minds which produced them. Emerson suggests such great writers as Pindar, Martial, Terence, Galen, Kepler, Galileo, Bacon, Erasmus, and More. He goes on to offer his advice on reading, ending with three rules, of which this quotation is one.

Be sure then to read no mean books. Shun the spawn of the press on the gossip of the hour. Do not read what you shall learn, without asking, in the street and on the train. Dr. Johnson said, "he always went into stately shops;" and good travellers stop at the best hotels; for though they cost more, they do not cost much more, and there is the good company and the best information. In like manner the scholar knows that the famed books contain, first and last, the best thoughts and facts. Now and then, by rarest luck, in some foolish Grub Street is the gem we want. But in the best circles is the best information. If you should transfer the amount of your reading day by day from the newspaper to the standard authors—But who dare speak of such a thing?

The three practical rules, then, which I have to offer, are,— 1. **Never read any book that is not a year old.** 2. Never read any but famed books. 3. Never read any but what you like; . . .

745

Never was patriot yet, but was a fool

Source: ABSALOM AND ACHITOPHEL (Part I, l. 968)
Author: John Dryden (1631–1700)
First published: 1681
Type of work: Satiric poem

Context: The heroic couplet, or rhymed pairs of lines in iambic pentameter containing a complete unit of thought, was Dryden's choice of a substitute for the Elizabethan blank verse. He was influenced by French experiments in metrics that had accompanied the Golden Age experienced by England's rival nation. So Dryden employed the heroic couplets in an allegorical retelling of the Biblical story of Absalom's revolt against his father, King David. In it, the poet satirized the frustrated Whig attempt to make sure that the Duke of Monmouth would succeed Charles II on the throne of England. Achitophel, who counselled the uprising against David in the account in Second Samuel, was intended to stand for the Earl of Shaftesbury (1621–1683).

At the beginning of the poem, Achitophel has united the malcontents of Israel in support of ambitious Absalom (Monmouth). The identities of most of the other figures, masquerading under names in the Bible story, have been established. Absalom has been persuaded and tricked into believing that it is his patriotic duty, and for the good of the nation, to take over his father's throne. Some may not agree with the quoted line, that every patriot is a fool, but it is the opinion of King David (Charles II) that to be a patriot, a person must forget his own personal aspirations, and think only of the people and the politicians who make up the country. Besides, he would be acting against his ruler. And so it is foolish to be a patriot.

. . .

Poor pitied youth, by my paternal care
Rais'd up to all the heights his frame could bear!
Had God ordain'd his fate for empire born
He would have giv'n his soul another turn:
Gull'd with a patriot's name, whose modern sense
Is one that would by law supplant his prince;
The people's brave, the politicians' tool;
Never was patriot yet, but was a fool.

. . .

New presbyter is but old priest writ large

Source: ON THE NEW FORCERS OF CONSCIENCE UNDER THE LONG PARLIAMENT
(Line 20)
Author: John Milton (1608–1674)
First published: 1673
Type of work: Satirical poem

Context: In November of 1640, Charles I of England called the Long Parliament, which was to sit until 1653. This parliament was split into two camps, Royalists and Parliamentarians. The latter began the religious and social revolution that was to plunge England into a terrible civil war and included the beheading of King Charles himself in 1649. The church-reform movement by the Parliamentarians led John Milton to identify himself with their cause, and he wrote a series of pamphlets for it. He was on his way to becoming the great spokesman for the Presbyterian branch of the Parliamentarians when, suddenly, he stopped his publication of the controversial pamphlets, though for a time he had seemed carried away by a vision that the expulsion of bishops would end all of England's theological troubles. In 1642, in the spring of the year, he wrote his last pro-Presbyterian pamphlet; in that same year he contracted his unhappy first marriage with Mary Powell. This marriage was so unhappy for Milton that in 1643 he published his *The Doctrine and Discipline of Divorce,* which was a plea for divorce based upon incompatability. His *Doctrine* was immediately attacked as blasphemous and shameful. The attackers included some of Milton's friends, who were also Presbyterian ministers. Their attacks so embittered Milton, who expressed his bitterness in two sonnets and in *On the New Forcers of Conscience,* that he broke with his former friends and their cause. In this poem he attacks the Presbyterian leaders for becoming forcers of thought and conscience as bad as Archbishop Laud and his fellow-prelates had been. Innocent men, ones to be "held in high esteem with Paul," are now branded, he says, as heretics; he expresses the hope that parliament will take care of them:

> But we do hope to find out all your tricks,
>   Your plots and packing worse than those of Trent,
>   That so the Parliament
> May with their wholesome and preventive shears
> Clip your phylacteries, though balk your ears,
>   And succor our just fears
> When they shall read this clearly in your charge:
> **New presbyter is but old priest writ large.**

A nice derangement of epitaphs

Source: THE RIVALS (Act III, sc. iii)
Author: Richard Brinsley Sheridan (1751–1816)
First published: 1775
Type of work: Dramatic comedy

Context: Mrs. Malaprop, who is the guardian of Lydia Languish, a beautiful young heiress with romantic notions, intercepts a letter to the girl written by "Ensign Beverley," who is really handsome young Captain Absolute. The captain is using the fictitious identity to woo Lydia because she refuses to marry except for pure love; the penniless "ensign" is far more attractive to her than the captain who is wealthy Sir Anthony Absolute's heir! Forced by his father to pay court to Lydia in his own identity, Captain Absolute appears at Mrs. Malaporp's lodgings at Bath, where she tells him about the letter from the "ensign" which she has in her possession, little dreaming that the real author of the letter is the captain who stands before her. Outraged at the comments about her in the letter, Mrs. Malaprop hands it to the captain to read, so that he can know what a scoundrel he has for a rival. As the captain reads the letter aloud, Mrs. Malaprop interrupts occasionally with her comments, illustrating her famous misuse of the language:

MRS. MALAPROP

But go on, sir. You'll see presently.

CAPT. ABSOLUTE

[*Reads.*] *As for the old weather-beaten she-dragon who guards you.*— Who can he mean by that?

MRS. MALAPROP

Me, sir!—me!—he means me!— There—what do you think now?—but go on a little further.

CAPT. ABSOLUTE

Impudent scoundrel!—[*Reads.*] *it shall go hard but I shall elude her vigilance, as I am told that the same ridiculous vanity, which makes her dress up her coarse features, and deck her dull chat with hard words which she don't understand—*

MRS. MALAPROP

There, sir, an attack upon my language! what do you think of that?—an aspersion upon my parts of speech! was ever such a brute! Sure, if I reprehend any thing in this world it is the use of my oracular tongue, and **a nice derangement of epitaphs!**

The night is dark, and I am far from home

Source: THE PILLAR OF THE CLOUD (Line 1)
Author: John Henry Newman (1801–1890)
First published: 1836
Type of work: Lyric poem

Context: Written on shipboard in 1833 when Newman, an Anglican minister, was returning to England from Italy, "The Pillar of the Cloud" is an autobiographical lyric which pictures the poet's perplexities at a time when he was wavering between Anglicanism and Catholicism (he

748

was to become a Catholic in 1845).
The ship is becalmed in a heavy fog,
which symbolizes to the poet his own
situation, and he prays for guidance
from God. Set to music by J. W.
Dykes and universally known as
"Lead, Kindly Light," the lines have
become one of the great Christian
hymns. The frequent use of the hymn
in funeral services involves an interpretation very different from that
originally intended by its author. The
complete poem follows:

Lead, Kindly Light, amid the encircling gloom,
        Lead Thou me on!
The night is dark, and I am far from home—
        Lead Thou me on!
Keep Thou my feet; I do not ask to see
The distant scene,—one step enough for me.

I was not ever thus, nor pray'd that Thou
        Shouldst lead me on.
I loved to choose and see my path, but now
        Lead Thou me on!
I loved the garish day, and, spite of fears,
Pride ruled my will: remember not past years.

So long Thy power hath blest me, sure it still
        Will lead me on,
O'er moor and fen, o'er crag and torrent, till
        The night is gone;
And with the morn those angel faces smile
Which I have loved long since, and lost awhile.

The Niobe of Nations

Source: CHILDE HAROLD'S PILGRIMAGE (Canto IV, stanza 79)
Author: George Gordon, Lord Byron (1788–1824)
First published: 1818 (Canto IV)
Type of work: Narrative poem

Context: Childe Harold, in Byron's
poem, is the poet himself. The poem
is a long one which took seven years
to complete; it depicts a man who is
weary of the world and who wanders
over the face of it, fleeing from himself. The term "childe" is a title of
honor which, in the days of chivalry,
was given to noble youths who were
candidates for knighthood; the candidate so honored bore this title
throughout his probationary period,
which usually involved a pilgrimage
of some sort. The poem recounts Byron's experiences and impressions
during his travels—Portugal and
Spain in Canto I, Turkey in Canto II,
Belgium and Switzerland in Canto
III. In the fourth Canto he visits Venice, Rome, and Florence. In Venice
he stands on the Bridge of Sighs and
contemplates the fading glory of this

great old city. In imagination he sees the history and magnificence that have passed; mentions the fact that he is an expatriate, misses his birthplace but is content to be buried in a foreign land. To Byron, Italy is still "the garden of the world, the home/ Of all Art yields, and Nature can decree;" even the wreckage of her greatness is a glory. He pays tribute to the great Italian poets, and moving on to Rome, speaks of various landmarks along the way. For the Eternal City he reserves his greatest praise. The reference to Niobe likens Rome to the Niobe of Greek legend, who was daughter of Tantalus and wife of Amphion, King of Thebes. She was proud of her twelve children and taunted the goddess Latona, who had only two, Apollo and Diana. Latona commanded her own children to avenge the insult, and they caused all twelve of Niobe's children to die. Niobe was inconsolable and wept herself to death; afterward she was changed into a stone from which water ran like tears. Niobe is thus the personification of maternal sorrow. Two stanzas of Byron's tribute follow:

Oh Rome, my country! city of the soul!
The orphans of the heart must turn to thee,
Lone mother of dead empires! and control
In their shut breasts their petty misery.
What are our woes and sufferance? Come and see
The cypress, hear the owl, and plod your way
O'er steps of broken thrones and temples, Ye!
Whose agonies are evils of a day—
A world is at our feet as fragile as our clay.

The Niobe of Nations! there she stands,
Childless and crownless, in her voiceless woe;
An empty urn within her wither'd hands,
Whose holy dust was scatter'd long ago:
The Scipios' tomb contains no ashes now;
The very sepulchres lie tenantless
Of their heroic dwellers;—dost thou flow,
Old Tiber, through a marble wilderness?
Rise, with thy yellow waves, and mantle her distress!

No better than you should be

Source: THE COXCOMB (Act IV, sc. i)
Authors: Francis Beaumont (1585?–1616) and John Fletcher (1579–1625)
First published: 1647
Type of work: Dramatic comedy

Context: The end of the Elizabethan period of English literature, when James I, the first of the Stuarts, ascended the throne in 1603, found many dramatists still active. To their contemporaries, Beaumont and

750

Fletcher occupied first place in popularity. Between 1616 and 1642, the King's Men, Shakespeare's company, performed 116 plays in London: forty-one by this pair, fifteen by Shakespeare, and seven by Jonson. Fletcher, the older of the collaborators, was the son of an impoverished clergyman and turned to playwriting to earn a living. Probably he met the wealthy law student Beaumont at Inner Temple, and they began writing plays for child actors. When the King's Men took over Blackfriars Theatre, the two were asked to provide the theater with plays. Fletcher was considered the better in plotting ability and in lyric skill; Beaumont was superior in handling tragedy. One of their first collaborations was *The Coxcomb*. Later came the tragicomedy *Philaster or Love Lies A-Bleeding* (c.1609), with its sophisticated emotional appeal, varied plot, and smooth verse. Jacobeans considered it better than anything by Shakespeare. Their best serious play was *The Maid's Tragedy* (1610), with some of the best dramatic writing of the age. *The Knight of the Burning Pestle* (c.1608) is an outstanding comedy. The critic Samuel Pepys (1633–1703) disapproved of *The Coxcomb,* but John Donne (1573–1631) had earlier pointed out that a play should be judged by its effect on the audience, rather than for consistency or probability or dramatic propriety. Trying to summarize its plot, a reader can sympathize with the opinion of the Reverend Alexander Dyce, who edited the eleven-volume edition of Beaumont and Fletcher (London, 1843), that *The Coxcomb* is extravagant in plot, character, and incident. But at least it is the utterance of satirists about men and manners. There are really several interwoven plots. In one, Viola, in love with Ricardo (sometimes written Richardo), runs away from home because of the spying of her father, Andrugio. She is robbed of her dress and jewels by a Tinker and his trull, Dorothy, who leave her tied to a tree. Viola is rescued by a country gentleman, Valerio, but when she will not accept his invitation to replace his "clamorous wife," he sends her on her way. Two milkmaids invite her home with them where she can seek employment from their mistress, the mother of Antonio, the conceited Coxcomb of the other plot. The mother looks with suspicion at her uncalloused hands and thinks the girl must be a designing hussy. (March-pane is a soft confection of egg-whites, sugar, and ground almonds.)

MOTHER
Is this the wench you have brought me? some catch I warrant.
How daringly she looks upon the matter!

MADGE
Yes, forsooth, this is the maiden.

MOTHER
Come hither, wou'd you serve?

751

If it shall please you to accept my service, I hope I shall do
something that shall like you, though it be but truth, and often
praying for you.

MOTHER

You are very curious of your hand methinks,
You preserve it so with gloves; let me see it;
I marry, here's a hand of march-pane, wenches,
This pretty palm never knew sorrow yet;
How soft it is, I warrant you, and supple;
O' my word, this is fitter for a pocket to filch withal
Than to work, I fear me little one,
You are **no better than you should be;** goe to.

VIOLA

My Conscience yet is but one witness to me,
And that heaven knows, is of mine innocence. . . .

MOTHER

You can say well: if you be mine, wench, you must doe well
too, for words are but slow workers, yet so much hope I have of
you, that I'll take you, so you'll be diligent, and do your duty: how
now?

No great man lives in vain

Source: HEROES AND HERO-WORSHIP ("The Hero as Divinity")
Author: Thomas Carlyle (1795–1881)
First published: 1841
Type of work: Moral essay

Context: The various beliefs and theories of Carlyle, appearing in his *Sartor Resartus* and elsewhere, are incorporated into a series of six lectures that he delivered in May, 1840, and published the next year. Previously he had declared that society changes and must do so intelligently, directed by its best men, whom he called its heroes. Now he characterizes these heroes under six headings: Divinity, Prophet, Poet, Priest, Man of Letters, and King. History is a record of their deeds. According to Carlyle's philosophy, Universal History, covering all that man in general has accomplished in the world, is "at bottom the history of the great men who have worked on the earth." This idea contrasts with the theory of the so-called scientific historians like the Frenchman, Taine, that man's surroundings as well as the spirit of his times have had their influence, and it was these which brought the great man or Hero into existence. George Washington did not create the American Revolution; rather, it brought him into being. The undemocratic Carlyle preached that man in masses could not achieve without the strength and wisdom of a few to organize, lead, guide, and even drive the unthinking majority. So in his writing, he runs counter to modern thinking. In the first of his lectures, he says that he was led to consider the subject of great men because we cannot look even imperfectly at one without learning from him. Where did the first Hero come from? He must have been a product of Paganism. Carlyle calls Northland Mythology an impersonation of the visible workings of Nature, by which he probably means "personification," since he developed a kind of German jargon in *Sartor Resartus,* and clung to it in much of his writing. Among the many Norsemen, came one with an original power of thinking. His associates looked up to him, calling him a prophet, a god, and so this man named Odin became the chief Norse god, and worthy of admiration and even adoration. One German philologist derived his name from the Teutonic word meaning "Movement" and "Power." Wednesday is (W)Odin's day.

Thus if the man Odin himself have vanished utterly, there is this huge Shadow of him which still projects itself over the whole History of his People . . . What this Odin saw into, and taught with his runes and his rhymes, the whole Teutonic People laid to heart and carried forward. His way of thought became their way of thought:—such, under new conditions, is the history of every great thinker still . . . Ah, Thought, I say, is always Thought. **No great man lives in vain.** The history of the world is but the Biography of great men.

No light, but rather darkness visible

Source: PARADISE LOST (Book I, l. 63)
Author: John Milton (1608–1674)
First published: 1667
Type of work: Epic poem

Context: Milton tells how the devils were hurled from heaven and lay for the space of nine days on a fiery gulf. He goes on to say that the region in which they are imprisoned is a fiery dungeon like a great furnace, although the flames of hell give forth no light. He is here using the universal symbolism of light and dark to indicate good and evil; when he describes heaven, he does so in terms of brilliant light. He also applies the same symbolism to Satan, who before his fall, as Lucifer, star of the morning, was the brightest of all the angels; as he becomes progressively more evil after his fall, he gradually loses all of his brightness. Milton's hell is often contrasted with Dante's: Milton's is a chaotic, unclear, murky region, but Dante's is highly systematized into a number of divisions and subdivisions. Milton is indicating the lack of order and the confusion inherent in evil; Dante is indicating divine order in the punishment of the sinful:

753

At once as far as angel's ken he views
The dismal situation waste and wild,
A dungeon horrible, on all sides round
As one great furnace flamed, yet from those flames
No light, but rather darkness visible
Served only to discover sights of woe,
Regions of sorrow, doleful shades, where peace
And rest can never dwell, hope never comes
That comes to all; but torture without end
Still urges, and a fiery deluge, fed
With ever-burning sulphur unconsumed:
Such place eternal justice had prepared
For those rebellious, here their prison ordained
In utter darkness, and their portion set
As far removed from God and light of heaven
As from the center thrice to th'utmost pole.

No man can lose what he never had

Source: THE COMPLEAT ANGLER (Part I, chapter 5)
Author: Izaak Walton (1593–1683)
First published: 1653
Type of work: Dialogue on fishing

Context: Having started out to fish early, Piscator and Venator commence their angling at five o'clock in the morning, planning to stop at nine o'clock to eat the breakfast they have brought along with them. While they eat, Piscator promises that he will teach Venator something about the tying of artificial flies and using them in angling. Till then, he advises Venator, angle for trout. Piscator catches a good trout, and then another; each time he is aided by Venator with a net. Venator complains that he is catching no fish, and asks to use Piscator's rod and line. Piscator good-naturedly consents. The fishing and the dialogue continue:

PISCATOR

. . . take mine; and I will fish with yours. Look you, scholar, I have another. Come, do as you did before. And now I have a bite at another. Oh me! he has broke all: there's half a line and a good hook lost.

VENATOR

Ay, and a good Trout, too.

PISCATOR

Nay, the Trout is not lost; for pray take notice, **no man can lose what he never had.**

754

No man is an island

Source: DEVOTIONS (Meditation 17)
Author: John Donne (1572–1631)
First published: 1624
Type of work: Religious meditation

Context: Donne, first a Catholic priest and finally one of the Anglican faith, also a soldier, a wit, and a poet, writes from his bed of grave illness a sermon inspired by the tolling of the church bells. As he hears the death knell sound, Donne says that a person is not to question for whom the bell tolls, for all mankind is one in a transcendent sense—hence "it tolls for thee." By the same token, "no man is an island," but is a small part of the vast continent of humanity.

> . . . **No man is an island,** entire of itself; every man is a piece of the continent, a part of the main. If a clod be washed away by the sea, Europe is the less, as well as if a promontory were, as well as if a manor of thy friend's or of thine own were: any man's death diminishes me, because I am involved in mankind, and therefore never send to know for whom the bell tolls; it tolls for thee.

No man therein doctor but himself

Source: SAMSON AGONISTES (Line 299)
Author: John Milton (1608–1674)
First published: 1671
Type of work: Dramatic tragedy

Context: The work begins with a long soliloquy by Samson, blinded and lying on a sunny bank in Gaza during a great holiday celebration of the Philistines in honor of their god Dagon. The tenor of Samson's reflections is that he had been born for greatness, for the deliverance of his people from the yoke of their hated masters, the Philistines; but he had thrown away his great gift, his physical strength, because he had been weak in his dealings with the treacherous Delilah, who in the drama is his wife, but who in *Judges* 16:4 is merely a woman of the valley of Sorek whom he loves. As he communes with himself he is joined by the Chorus, whom he asks whether or not he is now sung and proverbed as a fool for having told God's secret to a deceitful woman. He says that his great strength of body should have been joined to wisdom. The Chorus tells him that he should not blame God for his situation; many wise men have been deceived by women, and more will be. But why did he have to marry a Philistine? Samson says that as his first marriage to the woman of Timnath had given him occasion to move against the Philistines, so he thought that the second marriage might provide further occasions. Upon the citing of examples of men who had warred against the Philistines, Samson said that God's purposed deliverance of the Jews had not worked out through him. The Chorus says that God's ways are just and are capable of being explained by everyone except those who do not believe in God; such people are fools and belong to no school, and each man must be his own authoritative teacher.

CHORUS

Just are the ways of God
And justifiable to men;
Unless there be who think not God at all:
If any be, they walk obscure;
For of such doctrine never was there school,
But the heart of the fool,
And **no man therein doctor but himself.**
　　Yet more there be who doubt his ways not just,
As to his own edicts, found contradicting,
Then give the reins to wandering thought,
Regardless of his glory's diminution;
Till by their own perplexities involved
They ravel more, still less resolved,
But never find self-satisfying solution.

No mask like open truth to cover lies

Source: THE DOUBLE DEALER (Act V, sc. i)
Author: William Congreve (1670–1729)
First published: 1694
Type of work: Dramatic comedy

Context: Greatest of the comedy writers following the Restoration of the English throne to Charles II in 1660 was William Congreve, son of an army officer. He was brought up in Ireland where his father was a garrison commander, but came to London following the Revolution of 1688 and tried to study law. However, by 1692 he had gained a reputation as a poet and wit. He became a friend of John Dryden (1631–1700), whose plays entertained the "Merry Monarch," Charles. Now to entertain the gay courtiers of William and Mary, Congreve wrote a comedy, *The Old Bachelor* (1693). For it, Jonson, Marston, and Brome are his forerunners, and he shows that Restoration drama had its seeds in the Elizabethan theater. It concerns a bachelor misogynist, Heartwell, and stupid Sir Joseph Wittol. Full of intrigues, it amused London audiences. *The Double Dealer* performed the following year was far less successful, though dedicated to Charles Montague, and launched with a poem of admiration by Dryden, who claimed that Congreve surpassed all preceding

756

wits. It also had a command performance in January, 1694, before Queen Mary, that established Colley Cibber as an actor. However, its sinister, tragic tone, and its attack on real life made it different from the theater to which audiences were accustomed. Its plot, characters, witty dialogue make it one of the best comedies of the period. From it comes the much-quoted line about flattery: "She lays it on with a trowel." In the Dedicatory Epistle, Congreve declares: "It is the business of a comic poet to paint the vices and follies of Human-kind." Restoration dramatists were realistic enough, however, to personify the characteristics held up to ridicule and instill into them the men and women who walked London's streets in the time of William and Mary. They were then given names suggestive of their personalities. So Lady Froth is a co-quette and Lady Plyant encourages lovers. The plot concerns the struggle of Mellefont to win Cynthia (played by the famous actress, Mrs. Bracegirdle), despite the jealousy of wicked Lady Touchwood and the Iago-like villain Maskwell (played by Thomas Betterton). He wants Cynthia for himself, so he plays on the desires of the other characters: Lady Touchwood wants an affair with Mellefont; Careless, his friend, craves Lady Plyant; Lord Plyant wants an heir. Complications reach their height in the final act when they all come together, masked. To keep Mellefont from guessing his purposes, Maskwell decides to follow the precept laid down by Spain's Golden Age dramatist, Lope de Vega (1562–1635) and "deceive with the truth," sure that it will not be believed.

MASKWELL [*alone*]

This is prosp'rous indeed—Why let him find me out a Villain, settled in Possession of a fair Estate, and all Fruition of my Love, I'll bear the Railings of a losing Gamester—But shou'd he find me out before! . . . I must deceive Mellefont once more, and get my Lord to consent to my private Management. He comes opportunely—Now will I, in my old way, discover the whole and real truth of the Matter to him, that he may not suspect one Word on't.

No Mask like open Truth to cover Lies,
As to go Naked is the best Disguise.

No more cakes and ale

Source: TWELFTH NIGHT (Act II, sc. iii, l. 122)
Author: William Shakespeare (1564–1616)
First published: 1623
Type of work: Dramatic comedy

Context: It is after midnight at the home of the wealthy countess Olivia. Sir Toby Belch, her riotous uncle and house guest, and his friend Sir An-drew Aguecheek are joined in their drinking and jesting by Feste, a clownish servant of Olivia. When Feste is prevailed upon to sing, the

757

group becomes so noisy that Maria, Olivia's waiting-woman, warns them that Olivia will surely dispatch her ill-tempered steward, Malvolio, to put an end to the din. Malvolio appears and upbraids the rioters for lack of "wit, manners, and honesty," but Sir Toby and Feste respond by singing contemptuous responses and finally saying to Malvolio:

SIR TOBY

Out o' tune sir, ye lie. Art any more than a steward? Dost thou think because thou art virtuous, there shall be **no more cakes and ale?**

FESTE

Yes by Saint Anne, and ginger shall be hot i' th' mouth too.

SIR TOBY

Th'art i' th' right. Go sir, rub your chain with crumbs. A stoup of wine, Maria.

No praying, it spoils business

Source: VENICE PRESERVED (Act II, sc. ii, l. 22)
Author: Thomas Otway (1652–1685)
First published: 1682
Type of work: Dramatic tragedy

Context: One of the two great tragedies by the best of the Restoration dramatists is *Venice Preserved, or A Plot Discovered,* frequently called "the last of the Elizabethan plays," written in somber blank verse appropriate to its typical Elizabethan theme. Critics see in it the influence of several Shakespearean plays: *The Merchant of Venice, Julius Caesar,* and *Othello.* Because of its emotional appeal, it is probably the most frequently revived of the Restoration tragedies. Part of its popularity lay in its parallel to the many plots of the times of Charles II, when it was introduced. Jaffeir, married to the daughter of a senator of Venice, hates him and is willing to conspire with his friend Pierre against Venice and its governors. In Act II, Pierre enlists the aid of his old love, Aquilina, a courtesan, begging her to extract state secrets from her present love, the Senator Antonio. In Scene II, Pierre and Jaffeir meet on the Rialto. Pierre's mention of the honesty of animals underscores the dishonesty of most of the characters in this play. "Mechanick" (modern Mechanical) implies that he prays automatically or from force of habit, which brings the response that there are more important things to do now, especially since prayer does not bring results.

PIERRE

Speak, who goes there?

758

JAFFEIR

                A dog, that comes to howl
At yonder Moon. What's he that asks the Question?

PIERRE

A friend to dogs, for they are honest Creatures,
And ne'er betray their masters; never fawn
On any that they love not. Well met, friend
Jaffeir!

JAFFEIR

    The same. Oh Pierre! Thou art come in season,
I was just going to pray.

PIERRE

                    Ah, that's mechanick.
Priests make a trade on 't, and yet starve by it too:
No praying, it spoils business, and time's precious.

                 · · ·

No room in the inn

Source: LUKE 2:7
Author: Unknown (traditionally Luke the Apostle)
First transcribed: c. 80–100
Type of work: Gospel

Context: The Gospels of Mark and John begin the story of Jesus with His baptism by John the Baptist. Matthew starts with the search of the Wise men and declares in 2:11: "They came into the house and saw the young child with Mary, his mother." Only in the account by Luke is found mention of the manger on which so much of the Christmas pageantry is based. The third book of the New Testament has been ascribed, since the second century, to a gentile physician, Luke (sometimes called John Luke), a friend of St. Paul and St. Mark. He also supposedly wrote the Acts of the Apostles. The Gospel given his name is, by internal evidence, a literary composition drawing its material from various sources. The unique account of the birth and boyhood of Jesus has long been believed to be based on details supplied by the Virgin Mary. It fits well into Luke's general picture of a Jesus who understood and sympathized with even the most lowly beings, for surely no one could be born in a more humble place than a stable among the mangers or feed troughs from which, according to the Latin derivation of the word, the horses and cattle fed. Now the expression "No room in the inn" is popularly used to describe any crowded conditions. Historically it is known that Quirinus, Governor of Syria, made a population count of Judea in A.D. 6. Scholars believe that he also took an earlier census in 2 B.C., and think

759

this one caused Joseph to journey from Nazareth to Bethlehem along with Mary, who was "great with child." Then according to Luke's account:

> And so it was, that, while they were there, the days were accomplished that she should be delivered.
> And she brought forth her firstborn son, and wrapped him in swaddling clothes, and laid him in a manger; because there was **no room** for them **in the inn.**

No sterner moralist than pleasure

Source: DON JUAN (Canto III, stanza 65)
Author: George Gordon, Lord Byron (1788–1824)
First published: 1821 (Cantos III–V)
Type of work: Satiric poem

Context: The youthful Don Juan, banished from Spain and packed off to sea as discipline for an amorous scrape, ends his voyage as a castaway on an island shore. The beautiful Haidée, daughter of the pirate Lambro who has made her "the greatest heiress of the Eastern Isles," finds the half-drowned youth lying emaciated and unconscious on the sand. She and her maid carry him to a cave and, for fear that her father will return from the sea, find the lad, and sell him into slavery, secretly nurse him back to life and health. Inevitably the two young people fall in love and live together hidden from the world until rumors of Lambro's death send them to claim Haidée's inheritance and install themselves as master and mistress of her father's domains. The lovers, happy in each other, decree that revelry shall be the order of the days and nights and open the doors of the palace to all comers. The poet describes a dinner at which the "lady and her lover [sit] . . . in their beauty and their pride" as they preside over their guests and the feast of a hundred dishes with which they are served. Of the wall coverings in the great dining hall, he says:

> The hangings of the room were tapestry, made
> Of velvet panels, each of different hue,
> And thick with damask flowers of silk inlaid;
> And round them ran a yellow border too;
> The upper border, richly wrought, display'd,
> Embroider'd delicately o'er with blue,
> Soft Persian sentences, in lilac letters,
> From poets, or the moralists their betters.
>
> These Oriental writings on the wall,
> Quite common in those countries, are a kind
> Of monitors adapted to recall,
> Like skulls at Memphian banquets, to the mind

The words which shook Belshazzar in his hall,
  And took his kingdom from him: You will find,
Though sages may pour out their wisdom's treasure,
There is **no sterner moralist than Pleasure.**

No time like the present

Source: THE LOST LOVER (Act IV, sc. i)
Author: Mary de la Rivière Manley (1663–1724)
First published: 1696
Type of work: Dramatic comedy

Context: Mrs. Manley had an unhappy life. Her mother died when Mary was quite young, and her father paid little attention to her beyond leaving her £200 in his will when he died in 1688. At an early age she was drawn into a false marriage with her cousin, John Manley, at a time when his first wife was still alive. But Mary signed the name "Mrs Manley" to the poems, novels, and plays she wrote during the rest of her life. Her first writing took the form of poetry which, with her witty conversation, gave her a better reputation than did her way of living, which was rather dissolute. She was mistress of an alderman at the time of her death, and in feuds with most of the literary figures of her world. Her *Secret Memoirs of Several Persons of Quality of Both Sexes* (1709) was full of slander, especially of the Whigs, and was one reason for her brief term in prison. Swift described her at the age of forty as "very homely and very fat." In the Preface to her *Lost Lover, or The Jealous Husband,* written after the play's unsuccessful initial performance, she says that she wrote the comedy to pass the tedious hours in the country, and acknowledges her little experience in writing plays. "I am convinced that writing for the stage is not very proper for a woman," she confesses, and thanks the critics for "damning her so suddenly," rather than encouraging her by flattery. However, she cannot stop, she says, because she has a tragedy in rehearsal. Indeed her *Royal Mischief,* performed at Lincoln's Inn Field with Betterton in the lead, got a better reception than the *Lost Lover* at the Theatre Royal, in Drury Lane, with the Cibbers in the chief roles. The names of most of the characters are typical of their bearers, except for Smyrna, the jealous Turkey Merchant, and Olivia, forced to marry him by her covetous family. As for the others, Sir Rustick Good-Heart is, according to the prompt book "an ill-bred country gentleman." His son, Wilmore, has a gay young friend, Wildman. Lady Young-Love is "an old conceited lady," with a daughter Marina, in love with Wilmore. Also appearing is an affected poetess, Orinda. There are the usual courtships at cross purposes. Lady Young-Love tries to force young Wilmore to marry her. He is willing to play along as a device to see Marina. Elderly Sir Rustick also has his eyes on Marina. But since this is a comedy, the proper lovers get paired off at the final curtain. In Act IV, at Lady Young-

Love's house, in London, she and Wilmore are talking when in walks Sir Amorous Courtall, always swearing by his life.

LADY YOUNG-LOVE

Where's Sir Rustick, that he has not honoured us with his company?

WILMORE

I left him taking a Grace-Cup with your Ladyship's Chaplain. Mr. Priest-Craft will be too hard for him, they are so used to their Sanctified Wine that they can swallow a large share of our unhallowed juice of the grape. Be pleased to know my friend, Sir Amorous Courtall. (*Exit after Marina.*)

LADY YOUNG-LOVE

As such I must ever value and esteem him.

SIR AMOROUS

Your Ladyship's most Obedient Servant; let me expire if ever I saw anything so taking as your Ladyship's Civility.

LADY YOUNG-LOVE

Lard, Sir Amorous! Do you consider who's in the Company? These young Ladies will have reason to Quarrel at your Judgment, or rather, I shou'd be displeased at your insincerity.

SIR AMOROUS

Let me expire, Madam, if ever I saw anything so engaging as your Air. O that Dress, that Dress, Madam. The Devil take me if the Drawing Room in all its Birth-night finery, can show us any thing equal to it.

LADY YOUNG-LOVE

I wish I had but as good a Title to the rest of your Commendations. But time was, when they might have passed upon me with less injustice.

SIR AMOROUS

Be-gad, Madam, **no time like the present:** The Sun is not in his glory till he is mounted to the Meridian, let me die; if I can imagine yourself cou'd ever exceed yourself.

No worse a husband than the best of men

Source: ANTONY AND CLEOPATRA (Act II, sc. ii, l. 131)
Author: William Shakespeare (1564–1616)
First published: 1623
Type of work: Dramatic tragedy

Context: After the death of Julius Caesar, Antony and Octavius Caesar, together with the ineffectual Lepidus, rule the Roman Empire. Antony, however, whiles away his time in Alexandria with the fascinating Cleopatra but, when he learns that the Empire is threatened by rebellion and invasion, breaks his passionate enthrallment and returns to Rome. Temperamentally and otherwise, Antony and Octavius are at opposite poles and are destined to come to blows. In Rome, Octavius airs a number of grievances against Antony. Finally, it is suggested that, since Antony's wife, Fulvia, has just died, Octavius and Antony might end their quarrels and cement an alliance if Antony were to marry Octavius' sister. Since Antony is scarcely free of his passion for Cleopatra, the marriage ultimately serves as an occasion for further enmity. But for the moment, and only for the moment, the marriage seems a possible source of friendship. A Roman noble, Agrippa, makes the proposal:

AGRIPPA

To hold you in perpetual amity,
To make you brothers, and to knit your hearts
With an unslipping knot, take Antony
Octavia to his wife; whose beauty claims
No worse a husband than the best of men;
Whose virtue and whose general graces speak
That which none else can utter. By this marriage,
All little jealousies which now seem great,
And all great fears, which now import their dangers,
Would then be nothing.

. . .

Nobility is a graceful ornament to the civil order

Source: REFLECTIONS ON THE REVOLUTION IN FRANCE
Author: Edmund Burke (1729–1797)
First published: 1790
Type of work: Political treatise

Context: Though his long tenure in Parliament was the highest political office he ever held, Edmund Burke was one of the greatest political philosophers ever produced by England. His consistent dedication to the support of traditional and established rights led him to support the colonists of America in defense of their rights, but to advance a strong indictment of the French Revolution as a violation of traditionally established orderly government. One aspect of that Revolution which he condemned most severely was its violent and bloody elimination of the nobility:

. . . The strong struggle in every individual to preserve possession of what he has found to belong to him and to distinguish him, is

763

one of the securities against injustice and despotism implanted in
our nature. It operates as an instinct to secure property, and to
preserve communities in a settled state. What is there to shock in
this? **Nobility is a graceful ornament to the civil order.** It is the
Corinthian capital of polished society. . . . He feels no ennobling
principle in his own heart who wishes to level all artificial institutions which have been adopted for giving a body to opinion, and
permanence to fugitive esteem. It is a sour, malignant, envious
disposition, without taste for the reality, or for any image or representation of virtue, that sees with joy the unmerited fall of what
had long flourished in splendour and in honour. I do not like to
see anything destroyed; any void produced in society; any ruin
on the face of the land. . . .

Noble and nude and antique

Source: DOLORES (Stanza 7)
Author: Algernon Charles Swinburne (1837–1909)
First published: 1866
Type of work: Lyric poem

Context: The subtitle of Swinburne's poem is "Notre-Dame des Sept Doleurs," Our Lady of the Seven Sorrows. The Dolores of the poem, called also Our Lady of Pain, is an anti-Madonna; she is a pagan figure, the daughter of Libitina, an ancient Tuscan goddess of death and burial, and Priapus, a Greek deity, the son of Dionysus and Aphrodite, a god of fertility and husbandry. The persona of the poem, who speaks of Dolores, sees her as partly a woman, partly a goddess; she is partly real, partly ideal; she is attractive and she is repellant; she is unchaste, and she is cruel. Swinburne said of her himself, "She is the darker Venus, fed with burnt-offering and blood sacrifice." It is from her ancestry, of course, that Dolores has her two-fold nature: from her father comes the lust and fertility, and from her mother there comes death and pain. The persona of the poem seems to delight in both aspects of Dolores; he is drawn to her love, enjoys it, and yet is pained by it. Dolores, as an idealized figure, lives on, though the individual lovers pass and die:

Who gave thee thy wisdom? what stories
    That stung thee, what visions that smote?
Wert thou pure and a maiden, Dolores,
    When desire took thee first by the throat?
What bud was the shell of a blossom
    That all men may smell to and pluck?
What milk fed thee first at what bosom?
    What sins gave thee suck?

We shift and bedeck and bedrape us,

764

Thou art **noble and nude and antique;**
Libitina thy mother, Priapus
   Thy father, a Tuscan and Greek.
We play with light loves in the portal,
   And wince and relent and refrain;
Lovers die, and we know thee immortal,
   Our Lady of Pain.

The noble savage

Source: THE CONQUEST OF GRANADA, OR ALMANZOR AND ALMAHIDE (Part I,
   Act I, sc. i, l. 207)
Author: John Dryden (1631–1700)
First published: 1670
Type of work: Heroic drama

Context: Written in heroic, or closed, couplets made famous by Neo-Classicist Dryden, *The Conquest of Granada,* concerned with the struggle of the Moors and other rival factions in Spain, includes the plot of Almanzor, a brave soldier and a leader of the Moors against the Spaniards, and Almahide, his beloved who is betrothed to Boabdelin, King of Granada. As the play opens, Boabdelin, conversing with his old friend Abenamar, is interrupted as representatives of the Abencerrago and the Zegry factions rush in, and, scorning attempts at reconciliation, draw their swords. Almanzor, a stranger, enters, steps between the swordsmen, and, before he can be disarmed, kills a man. Boabdelin orders Almanzor killed (a sentence later revoked) and the hero courageously responds in words that anticipate J. J. Rousseau's doctrine of primitivism and of man in a state of nature:

ALMANZOR
No man has more contempt than I of breath
But whence hast thou the right to give me death?
Obeyed as sovereign by thy subjects be,
But know, that I alone am king of me.
I am as free as nature first made man,
Ere the base laws of servitude began,
When wild in woods **the noble savage** ran.

A noisy man is always in the right

Source: CONVERSATION (Line 114)
Author: William Cowper (1731–1800)
First published: 1782
Type of work: Essay in verse

Context: As Cowper can vent his bitter irony and anger on those who deal in slaves or even are uncharitable toward their fellow man, so in *Conversation,* he can show the good and evil of speech, which he calls "a gift and not an Art." In its 906 lines of rhymed couplets, after the style of Alexander Pope (1688–1744), Cowper gives many examples of good and bad uses of talking. In conversations, some take chief delight in contradicting; others, in recounting even the simplest event, swearing often and forcefully as to its truth, "till affirmation breeds a doubt." The poet expresses his abhorrence of "Duels in the form of debate." Then he gives suggestions about arguing, warning against opposition merely for the sake of an argument and pointing out that some people wrongly believe that shouting is more convincing than logic.

> But still remember, if you mean to please,
> To press your point with modesty and ease.
> The mark at which my juster aim I take
> Is contradiction for its own dear sake . . .
> The wrangler, rather than accord with you,
> Will judge himself deceived, and prove it too.
> Vociferated logic kills me quite,
> **A noisy man is always in the right;**
> I twirl my thumbs, fall back into my chair,
> Fix on the wainscot a distressful stare,
> And when I hope his blunders are all out,
> Reply discreetly, "To be sure—no doubt."

None knew thee but to love thee

Source: ON THE DEATH OF JOSEPH RODMAN DRAKE (Line 3)
Author: Fitz-Greene Halleck (1790–1867)
First published: 1821
Type of work: Elegy

Context: In 1819 *The Croaker Papers,* a series of humorous, satirical odes appeared in the New York *Evening Post;* these were the joint effort of Fitz-Greene Halleck and Joseph Rodman Drake. A few months after the popular success of these poems, Drake, who was a medical doctor by profession and a poet by avocation, died. His collaborator, who was a banker by profession and a poet by avocation, wrote this elegy for his friend and fellow-poet. Though Edgar Allen Poe, in his *Literati* sketch, rated Halleck second after Bryant among American poets of the time, Halleck is probably now only known by most readers as the author of this poem on Drake. As an epigraph for his elegy, Halleck used the following well-known lines from Wordsworth, "The good die first,/ And they, whose hearts are dry as summer dust,/ Burn to the sockets." Halleck goes on in his own words:

Green be the turf above thee,
  Friend of my better days!
None knew thee but to love thee,
  Nor named thee but to praise.

Tears fell, when thou wert dying,
  From eyes unused to weep,
And long, where thou art lying,
  Will tears the cold turf steep.

When hearts, whose truth was proven,
  Like thine, are laid in earth,
There should a wreath be woven
  To tell the world their worth.

Nor heaven peep through the blanket of the dark

Source: MACBETH (Act I, sc. v, ll. 54–5)
Author: William Shakespeare (1564–1616)
First published: 1623
Type of work: Dramatic tragedy

Context: Lady Macbeth reads a letter from her husband telling her of the prophetic words delivered to him by three witches: Macbeth, Thane of Glamis, shall become Thane of Cawdor and finally king. The letter adds that already King Duncan has bestowed upon Macbeth the title of Thane of Cawdor as a reward for putting down a rebellion led by Macdonwald and the insurrectionist Thane of Cawdor, who has been executed at the king's command. An attendant interrupts Lady Macbeth to tell her that the king approaches and will spend the night at Inverness, home of Macbeth. Lady Macbeth, fearing her husband lacks the strength to carry out a plot to get Duncan out of the way of his ambition, seizes upon the opportunity of the king's visit to have him murdered and make Macbeth his successor. In a famous soliloquy Lady Macbeth delivers a speech filled with omens of darkness, invoking the spirits to seal off in her the elements of kindness and to allow the dread deed to be done.

LADY MACBETH
  . . . The raven himself is hoarse
That croaks the fatal entrance of Duncan
Under my battlements. . . .
            . . .
        . . . Come thick night,
And pall thee in the dunnest smoke of hell
That my keen knife see not the wound it makes,
Nor heaven peep through the blanket of the dark,
To cry, hold, hold!

767

Not deep the poet sees, but wide

Source: RESIGNATION (Line 214)
Author: Matthew Arnold (1822–1888)
First published: 1849
Type of work: Lyric poem

Context: In this long apologia to "Fausta," Arnold's poetic name for his sister Jane, the poet describes his view of life and explains why he has chosen to write poetry. All men, he says, set goals that they hope to gain before they gain peace; with some men these goals are exciting adventures, but "milder natures, and more free" have resigned themselves to their struggles with passions and time that passes so quickly that they cannot reach their little goals. Ten years have passed since their father used to take them from the noisy town into the quiet countryside, and when they return there, they find that nature has not changed while they have. The unhappiness caused by this change, a separation from nature and from joyful youth, is explained by the gipsies, who wander here and there without purpose but as chance directs; the gipsies' way of life is actually the life of all mankind. The poet is the man who realizes this fact and from it learns that the "secret is not joy, but peace"; however, Fausta disagrees with the poet's idea that nature lasts but man and art perish. The quotation comes from her supposed belief in what the poet should be, an opinion that Arnold later rejects in favor of his central belief that the poet is the completely detached stoic who realizes the pain of life and its lack of solution.

> "Those gipsies," so your thoughts I scan,
> "Are less, the poet more, than man.
> They feel not, though they move and see;
> Deeper the poet feels; but he
> Breathes, when he will, immortal air. . . .
> He leaves his kind, o'er leaps their pen,
> And flees the common life of men.
> He escapes thence, but we abide—
> **Not deep the poet sees, but wide.**"

Not lost, but gone before

Source: AN EXPOSITION OF THE NEW TESTAMENT (Matthew 2:17–18)
Author: Matthew Henry (1662–1714)
First published: 1708–10
Type of work: Biblical commentary

Context: The concept of death as a journey is an ancient one, perhaps as old as man. As a literary expression it seems to have first appeared in the moral epistles of Lucius Annaeus Seneca. (c. 4 B.C.–A.D. 65). Seneca was a Latin philosopher and a Stoic; he was also a dramatist, and composed several rhetorical tragedies for which he is best known today. His *Epistles to Lucilius* are moral essays in the form of letters; in No. LXIII, 16, he speaks of death as follows: *"Et fortasse, si modo vera sapientium fama est recipitque nos locus aliquis, quem putamus perisse, praemissus est* (And perhaps, if only the tale told by the wise men is true and there is a bourne to welcome us, then he whom we think we have lost has only been sent on ahead)." The image of the mystic journey seems to have had a strong appeal for Seneca; in Epistle XCIX, 7, he uses an almost identical expression (*"quem putas perisse, praemissus est"*). This has been rendered, "He whom you say has passed away has only posted on ahead." It is not known who is responsible for a more important translation of this thought: the haunting and unforgettable *"Not lost, but gone before."* It seems to have first appeared in print in the writings of Matthew Henry, whose Biblical commentaries were used almost universally among his Protestant contemporaries and for more than a century after his death. Henry had a gift for the memorable and quotable phrase, and his writings abound with them. It may have originated in one of his sermons, or may have already been popular in the latter part of the seventeenth century; it is said to be inscribed on the tomb of Mary Angell, of Stepney, who died in 1693. Since her day it has been carved on countless other tombstones, featured in sentimental songs and poetry, and quoted in innumerable funeral sermons. Henry used it at least twice: in a biography of his father and in the following passage, wherein he comments upon Herod's massacre of the infants in Bethlehem:

There was a great cry in Egypt when the first-born were slain, and so there was here when the youngest was slain; for whom we naturally have a particular tenderness. Here was a representation of this world we live in. We hear in it *lamentation, and weeping, and mourning,* and see *the tears of the oppressed,* some upon one account, and some upon another. Our way lies through a *vale of tears.* This sorrow was so great, that they *would not be comforted.* They hardened themselves in it, and took a pleasure in their grief. Blessed be God, there is no occasion of grief in this world, no, not that which is supplied by sin itself, that will justify us in refusing to *be comforted! They would not be comforted, because they are not,* that is, *they are not* in the land of the living, *are not* as they were, in their mothers' embraces. If, indeed, *they were not,* there might be some excuse for sorrowing as though we had no hope; but we know they are **not lost, but gone before;** if we forget that *they are,* we lose the best ground of our comfort. . . . Some make this great grief of the Bethlehemites to be a judgment upon them for their contempt of Christ. They that would not rejoice for the birth of the Son of God, are justly made to weep for the death of their own sons; for they only *wondered* at the tidings the shepherds brought them, but did not *welcome* them.

Not poppy, nor mandragora

Source: OTHELLO (Act III, sc. iii, l. 330)
Author: William Shakespeare (1564–1616)
First published: 1622
Type of work: Dramatic tragedy

Context: Iago, ensign to the Moor of Venice, Othello, determines to take revenge against Cassio for gaining the lieutenancy, under Othello, and against the Moor for having made the appointment. He entangles Cassio in a drunken brawl and then sets out to destroy Othello's peace of mind by suggesting that Desdemona, Othello's new bride, and Cassio are more than friends. The seed of jealousy planted, Iago observes the agonizing Othello.

IAGO

. . . The Moor already changes with my poison.
Dangerous conceits are in their natures poisons,
Which at the first are scarce found to distaste,
But with a little, act upon the blood,
Burn like the mines of sulphur. I did say so.

Enter OTHELLO

Look where he comes. **Not poppy, nor mandragora,**
Nor all the drowsy syrups of the world
Shall ever medicine thee to that sweet sleep
Which thou owedst yesterday.

OTHELLO
Ha, ha—false to me?

IAGO
Why how now general? No more of that.

OTHELLO
Avaunt, be gone! Thou hast set me on the rack.
I swear 'tis better to be much abused,
Than but to know't a little.

Not quite the thing

Source: EMMA (Chapter 29)
Author: Jane Austen (1775–1817)
First published: 1816
Type of work: Novel

Context: The most amusing secondary character in this novel is Mr. Woodhouse, father of the heroine. A rich widower living at Hartfield, the great house of the village, with Emma, his younger and unmarried daughter, he is a complete hypochondriac. He is kindly, generous, and hospitable and devoted to his daughter. But life at Hartfield revolves around his health. He has two established daily walks in the grounds, one for the winter and a longer one for the summer. He enjoys entertaining, yet he is torn between his desire to see that his guests are well served and his fear that rich food will give them indigestion. He dislikes parties because he considers late hours unhealthful. Any change in his long-established routine makes him ill. His tranquillity is much disturbed by the visit to the neighborhood of Frank Churchill, a young man who is the stepson of Mrs. Weston, Emma's former governess. Churchill finds social life at the village of Highbury rather dull, and he proposes that a dance be arranged for the younger people in the families that make up local society. But where to have the dance? The Crown Inn at Highbury is decided upon, and then follows much discussion about the size of the rooms. The whole plan is agonizing to Mr. Woodhouse, one of whose obsessions is the extreme danger of draughts. In his usual fashion, he foresees all kinds of dire consequences if the dance should take place.

The doors of the two rooms were just opposite each other. "Might not they use both rooms, and dance across the passage?" It seemed the best scheme; and yet it was not so good but that many of them wanted a better. Emma said it would be awkward; Mrs Weston was in distress about the supper; and Mr Woodhouse opposed it earnestly on the score of health. It made him so very unhappy, indeed, that it could not be persevered in.

"Oh, no," said he, "it would be the extreme of imprudence. I could not bear it for Emma!—Emma is not strong. She would catch a dreadful cold. So would poor little Harriet. So you would all. Mrs Weston, you would be quite laid up; do not let them talk of such a wild thing; pray do not let them talk of it. That young man" (speaking lower) "is very thoughtless. Do not tell his father, but that young man is **not quite the thing.** He has been opening the doors very often this evening, and keeping them open very inconsiderately. He does not think of the draught. I do not mean to set you against him, but indeed he is **not quite the thing.**"

Not to be born is best

Source: OEDIPUS AT COLONUS (Line 1225, as translated by R. C. Jebb)
Author: Sophocles (496–406 B.C.)
First transcribed: 401 B.C.
Type of work: Dramatic tragedy

Context: In this sequel to Sophocles'   better known play, *Oedipus the King,* the aged, cursed Oedipus has now wandered in exile from his native Thebes to Colonus, a sacred wooded area near Athens. Here, the gods have predicted, he will die. The troubles of Oedipus and the entire house of Cadmus, from which he is descended, have been many. Unknowingly, Oedipus had once killed his father, married his own mother, and sired children by that marriage. When he discovers his wrong doings (the subject of *Oedipus the King*), Oedipus blinded himself and declared self-exile. Now twenty years have passed, and, though Oedipus has reached a certain state of ennoblement through suffering, troubles continue to befall his family. His sons have disassociated themselves from their father and, in fact, have been instrumental in urging him out of Thebes. Furthermore, they are warring between themselves over control of that city. Antigone and Ismene, tending to their father in his helpless condition, are kidnaped by Creon of Thebes when Oedipus refuses to return to his home city to save it from a curse. Reflecting on all these misfortunes, the Chorus—in the Greek tragedy the commentator on the action—philosophizes on the inevitable miseries of life, concluding that it would be best if man were never born or, if being born, he could die early in life. Thus man would escape life's calamities.

CHORUS

Not to be born is, past all prizing, **best;** but, when a man hath seen the light, this is next best by far, that with all speed he should go thither, whence he hath come.

For when he hath seen youth go by, with its light follies, what troublous affliction is strange to his lot, what suffering is not therein?—envy, factions, strife, battles and slaughters; and, last of all, age claims him for her own,—age, dispraised, infirm, unsociable, unfriended, with whom all woe of woe abides.

Not to be sneezed at

Source: THE HEIR-AT-LAW (Act II, sc. i)
Author: George Colman the Younger (1762–1836)
First published: 1800
Type of work: Dramatic comedy

Context: Some idea of the kind of humor in this play may be gleaned from the names of the two rustic characters, Zekiel Homespun and his sister Cicely, who came to London as servants for unfortunate Caroline Rormer. Dr. Pangloss, who lards his language with Latin tags and tries to make a cultured man out of Lord Duberly, is a satire on pedantry in general. The death of Caroline's father has ended her comfortable existence of the past, and the disappearance of her sweetheart has deprived her of future hope. At the beginning of Act II, she has sent her faithful retainer Felix Hendrick with a letter requesting help, to her father's old friend, a miserly banker. Now the servant is back to report, with many excuses, that the wealthy friend refuses to help her. He gives Kenrick half a crown which the proud servant flings in his face. Eventually, however, all ends well. Her sweetheart reappears. The servant Cicely Homespun also finds an understanding husband. The miserly banker is thwarted. The great English actor Edmund Kean (1787?–1833) made his debut in this play, with all its melodramatic language that seems so artificial to modern ears. Here is the exchange of dialogue that put the expression "not to be sneezed at," into the English language.

CAROLINE

Pray, pray be silent, Kenrick! Oh nature! spite of the inequalities which birth or education have placed between thy children,— still, nature, with all thy softness, I own thee. The tear of an old and faithful servant, which bedews the ruins of his shelter, is an honest drop that penetrates the heart.

KENRICK

Aye, cry away, my poor dear Miss Caroline; cry away! I shared the sunshine of your family, and it is but fair that I should go halves in the ruin.

CAROLINE

A poor two hundred pounds, Kenrick, are now all that remain to me.

KENRICK

Well, come, two hundred pounds, now-a-days are **not to be sneezed at.**

Not to know me argues yourselves unknown

Source: PARADISE LOST (Book IV, l. 830)
Author: John Milton (1608–1674)
First published: 1667
Type of work: Epic poem

Context: As Adam and Eve sleep in their bower, Gabriel, leader of the night watch, tells Uzziel to take a number of angels to guard the south side of the garden. Next he tells Ithuriel and Zephon to search through the garden, and especially around Adam and Eve's bower, as an infernal spirit escaped from hell has been seen at evening approaching the garden. The two soon find Satan in the likeness of a toad close by the head of Eve, endeavoring to penetrate her fancy with illusions. Ithuriel touches him with his spear and, as no falsehood can endure the celestial touch, he returns to his own likeness. Like a pile of gunpowder into which a spark falls, he

773

starts up in his own shape. The two angels, amazed to see the grisly king, but entirely unmoved by fear, soon accost him: The quoted line means: "You know me as well as you know yourselves."

"Which of those rebel spirits adjudged to hell
Com'st thou, escaped thy prison, and transformed,
Why sat'st thou like an enemy in wait
Here watching at the head of these that sleep?"
　"Know ye not, then," said Satan, filled with scorn,
"Know ye not me? Ye knew me once no mate
For you, there sitting where ye durst not soar;
Not to know me argues yourselves unknown,
The lowest of your throng; or if ye know,
Why aske ye, and superfluous begin
Your message, like to end as much in vain?"
To whom thus Zephon, answering scorn with scorn.
"Think not, revolted spirit, thy shape the same,
Or undiminished brightness, to be known
As when thou stood'st in heaven upright and pure."

. . .

Not without art, but yet to nature true

Source: THE ROSCIAD (Line 699)
Author: Charles Churchill (1731–1764)
First published: 1761
Type of work: Satiric poem

Context: In 1728, Alexander Pope (1688–1744) published a satirical poem in rhymed couplets, called *The Dunciad.* It was an attack on literary charlatanism, originally aimed chiefly at a literary scholar, Lewis Theobald, who had been most uncomplimentary to Pope's edition of Shakespeare. In the 1743 revision, the target as Monarch of Dullness was the Poet Laureate, Colley Cibber (1671–1757), though many other authors, now forgotten, were also pilloried. In imitation of Pope's work, Charles Churchill directed his barbs at theatrical people of London in *The Rosciad,* deriving its title from the great Roman comic actor of the first century B.C., Quin-tus Roscius. With the death of Roscius, says Churchill, many actors sought to occupy his place. He describes a judging of them, one after another, by a tribune of Shakespeare and Dr. Johnson. About the men, the poet has little good to say; however, several of the actresses who appear to be judged, do get his approval. One, Mrs. Vincent (d. 1802), who starred as Polly Peachum in Gay's *The Beggar's Opera* in 1760, gets words of praise, perhaps because during Churchill's riotous youth he was on intimate terms with her. Catherine Clive (1711–1785) is highly praised, as is Jane Pope (1742–1818), who imitated Mrs. Clive and starred in plays by Colman, Garrick, and Farquhar. Finally, David Garrick (1717–1779) presents himself, and though snarling critics bring up objections to him, Churchill pays tribute to him as one who acts naturally. "Hence to thy praises, Garrick, I agree,/ And, pleased with Nature, must be pleased with thee." The judges also decide in his favor, and Shakespeare ends *The Rosciad* with the verdict: If Nature, linked with Art, and powers of acting vast and unconfined deserve the preference, "Garrick, take the chair;/ Nor quit it—'till thou place an Equal there." During the judging of Jane Pope, who, though twenty, acts like a sixteen-year-old, Churchill declares that, like Garrick, she combines art and nature. She will make a good successor to Kitty Clive.

> With all the native vigor of sixteen,
> Among the merry troop conspicuous seen,
> See lively POPE advance in jig and trip,
> Corinna, Cherry, Honeycomb, and Snip.
> **Not without Art, but yet to Nature true,**
> She charms the town with humor just, yet new.
> Chear'd by her promise, we the less deplore
> The fatal time when CLIVE shall be no more.

Nothing can be created out of nothing

Source: DE RERUM NATURA (Book I, line 155)
Author: Lucretius (Titus Lucretius Carus, c. 96–c. 55 B.C.)
First transcribed: c. 60 B.C.
Type of work: Didactic poem

Context: Very little is known of the Roman philosophical poet Lucretius. All that can with certainty be said of his life is that he lived in the earlier part of the last century before Christ and that he died at age forty-five or before. His long didactic poem in six books, *De rerum natura,* remained unfinished at his death. Popular tradition has it that he was rendered insane by a love-potion given him by his wife, and that his masterpiece was written during the lucid intervals of his illness. It is said that he studied Epicurean philosophy in Athens, and that he died by his own hand during a period of madness. *De rerum natura* (*On the Nature of Things*) is a large and ambitious work, addressed by Lucretius to his friend Memmius. In it he sets forth a complete and detailed cosmology based upon the philosophies of Epicurus and Democritus; to their thinking Lucretius adds his own originality and his imagination, presenting a result which is eloquent in its demonstration of his great power as artist and thinker. Natural phenomena, arts and sciences, social origins and history, theories of the human senses and of the basic properties of matter are all explored and discoursed upon. Such difficult materials are not ordinarily considered the stuff of poetry, and that Lucretius was able to make a great and majestic poem of them is testimonial to his stature. He indicates that his purpose in these inquiries is to spare his readers the fear of death, which he blames upon religious superstition. To Lucretius all mysteries have their natural and logical explanation, which can be determined by careful inquiry. In the first part of Book I he takes up the problem of creation and of reproduction:

This terror then of the mind, this darkness must needs be scattered not by the rays of the sun and the gleaming shafts of day, but by the outer view and the inner law of nature; whose first rule shall take its start for us from this, that nothing is ever begotten of nothing by divine will. Fear, forsooth, so contrains all mortal men, because they behold many things come to pass on earth and in the sky, the cause of whose working they can by no means see, and think that a divine power brings them about. Therefore, when we have seen that **nothing can be created out of nothing,** then more rightly after that shall we discern that for which we search, both whence each thing can be created, and in what way all things come to be without the aid of gods.

For if things came to being from nothing, every kind might be born from all things, nought would need a seed. Firstly, men might arise from the sea, and from the land the race of scaly creatures, and birds burst forth from the sky. . . . Nor would the same fruits stay constant to the trees, but all would change: all trees might avail to bear all fruits. . . . But as it is, since all things are produced from fixed seeds, each thing is born and comes forth into the coasts of light out of that which has in it the substance and first-bodies of each; and 'tis for this cause that all things cannot be begotten of all, because in fixed things there dwells a power set apart.

Nothing human is indifferent to me

Source: THE SELF-TORMENTOR (Act I, sc. i)
Author: Terence (Publius Terentius Afer, c. 190–159 B.C.)
First transcribed: c. 163 B.C.
Type of work: Dramatic comedy

Context: Terence's comedy, his third play, is based upon a Greek comedy with the same title by Menander. It is a drama of trickery, action, and recognition, with a double plot involving two love affairs. In the play, Menedemus, the father of Clinia, regrets that he has compelled his son to go abroad to the wars and punishes himself for his action by working hard during Clinia's absence. The reason that Menedemus has sent his son away is that he disapproves of the young man's keeping of a mistress, Antiphilia. One day Menedemus is paid a visit by his farmer-neighbor, Chremes, who tells him that he is working much too hard, though he speaks apologetically to Menedemus, since their acquaintance is but recent. Chremes says that Menedemus, a man of sixty years or more, should let his slaves do the work. He ends by giving Menedemus advice, which ends the opening speech of the play.

His later comment about interest in people and their affairs, translated in many ways, but with one meaning, became famous in Roman times; many Romans referred to it as expressing the common brotherhood of man.

CHREMES

. . . Why, you would do more good if the time which you waste in labouring with your own hands was spent in keeping your slaves hard at work.

MENEDEMUS

Chremes, does your own business afford you so much leisure that you can attend to other people's, with which you have nothing to do?

CHREMES

I am a human being; **I am interested in everything human.** You may take it that I am giving you this advice, or asking you the question: if it is right to do so, then I will do so myself; but if it is wrong, then let me dissuade you from it.

MENEDEMUS

I must do so; you may do what you please.

CHREMES

Must any man torment himself?

MENEDEMUS

I must.

Nothing in his life became him like the leaving it

Source: MACBETH (Act I, sc. iv., ll. 7–8)
Author: William Shakespeare (1564–1616)
First published: 1623
Type of work: Dramatic tragedy

Context: The army of King Duncan of Scotland, led by Macbeth and Banquo, successfully puts down a rebellion of Macdonwald and the Thane of Cawdor. Macdonwald meets death in battle at the hand of Macbeth, and the Thane of Cawdor is condemned to die by the decree of the king. Duncan, awaiting news of the execution, is assured by his son Malcolm that, though the executioners have not returned, reports have come

777

of the death of Thane of Cawdor.

MALCOLM
My liege,
They are not yet come back. But I have spoke
With one that saw him die; who did report,
That very frankly he confessed his treasons,
Implored your Highness' pardon, and set forth
A deep repentance. **Nothing in his life**
Became him like the leaving it. He died,
As one that had been studied in his death,
To throw away the dearest thing he owed,
As 'twere a careless trifle.

DUNCAN
There's no art
To find the mind's construction in the face.
He was a gentleman, on whom I built
An absolute trust. . . .

Nothing is fair or good alone

Source: EACH AND ALL (Line 12)
Author: Ralph Waldo Emerson (1803–1882)
First published: 1839
Type of work: Lyric poem

Context: Emerson's poetry often reflects the same philosophical idealism found in his essays. He sees the universe as a unity, the handiwork of the Deity, which reflects all of the qualities of God: omniscience, omnipotence, and complete benevolence. Since the universe partakes of the qualities of its maker, one will, if he views it wholly, or as wholly as man can in this life, see that it is good. But one must, as Emerson stated in his first great essay, *Nature,* see nature in all its aspects—as commodity, beauty, language, and discipline—not merely as a part of them. If we will look at the wholeness of nature, not just at a part, we shall behold its grandeur; if we can yield ourselves to "the perfect whole," we shall behold the beauty in the parts. Emerson offers examples to show his point. If one brings a songbird home in a cage, the song is not equal to what it was when the bird was part of earth, river, and sky. Seashells, lovely in their usual seashore environment, fetched home and placed upon a shelf, become "poor, unsightly, noisome things" which "left their beauty on the shore." The young girl, seen as one of a throng of young girls, is lovely and fairylike; but when the bridegroom finds her in their new home she is "A gentle wife, but fairy none." The quotation being considered, appearing early in the poem, is actually the author's thesis:

Little thinks, in the field, yon red-cloaked clown
Of thee from the hill-top looking down;
The heifer that lows in the upland farm,
Far-heard, lows not thine ear to charm;
The sexton, tolling his bell at noon,
Deems not that great Napoleon
Stops his horse, and lists with delight,
Whilst his files sweep round yon Alpine height;
Nor knowest thou what argument
Thy life to thy neighbor's creed has lent.
All are needed by each one;
Nothing is fair or good alone.

Nothing is so fatal to religion as indifference

Source: LETTER TO WILLIAM SMITH (January 29, 1795)
Author: Edmund Burke (1729–1797)
First published: 1844
Type of work: Personal letter

Context: Burke was born in Ireland, and although his entire adult life was spent in England he took an active interest in Irish affairs throughout his political career. As a member of Parliament he frequently defended the Irish, and he always felt the Anglican domination of the millions of Irish Catholics constituted a sort of tyranny. William Smith, a member of the Irish Parliament, had spoken in defense of Irish Catholics, and Burke responded with this encouraging letter:

> You need make no apology for your attachment to the religious description you belong to. It proves (as in you it is sincere) your attachment to the great points in which the leading divisions are agreed, when the lesser, in which they differ, are so dear to you. I shall never call any religious opinions, which appear important to serious and pious minds, things of no consideration. **Nothing is so fatal to religion as indifference,** which is, at least, half infidelity. As long as men hold charity and justice to be essential integral parts of religion, there can be little danger from a strong attachment to particular tenets in faith. . . .

Nothing is so good as it seems beforehand

Source: SILAS MARNER (Chapter 18)
Author: George Eliot (1819–1880)
First published: 1861
Type of work: Novel

779

Context: Godfrey Cass comes home one day to impart terrible news to his wife: dishonor has come to the family of Squire Cass, for Godfrey's brother Dunstan's skeleton has been found. Dunstan's disappearance sixteen years before was a mystery; now it is known that he drowned in a nearby stone pit. It is also evident, now that the body has been found, that Dunstan was the person who robbed Silas Marner, the weaver, of his hard-earned gold guineas. This bringing to light of past events moves Godfrey Cass to confess his own sins to his wife. He reveals to her that he is the unknown father of Eppie, a young girl who has been reared by Silas Marner since he took her in as an infant when her mother was found dead in the snow after taking an overdose of laudanum. Nancy Cass tells her husband that he should have revealed this matter to her six years before, when they were about to be married, so that she could have taken Eppie as her daughter, not only giving the young girl love, but also having a child in the house to make it easier to bear the loss of her own infant son. Godfrey replies to this speech, however, that his wife's pride, as well as her father's, would not have let her have anything to do with him had it been known he had been married already to Eppie's mother. Nancy Cass states her opinion on that matter:

"I can's say what I should have done about that, Godfrey. I should never have married anybody else. But I wasn't worth doing wrong for—nothing is in this world. **Nothing is as good as it seems beforehand**—not even our marrying wasn't, you see." There was a faint sad smile on Nancy's face as she said the last words.

Nothing like blood, sir, in hosses, dawgs, and men

Source: VANITY FAIR (Chapter 34)
Author: William Makepeace Thackeray (1811–1863)
First published: 1847–1848
Type of work: Novel

Context: Young James Crawley, a handsome, devil-may-care youth, is sent by his father, an Anglican rector, and his mother to try to make a favorable impression, for himself and his family, on a rich aunt, Miss Crawley. The young man arrives at Brighton with his suitcase, a favorite bulldog, and a basket of produce from the rectory garden. Before reporting to his aunt's residence he spends an evening with a prizefighter and other unsavory company at a local inn of questionable repute. As much as anything to tease James Crawley's over-correct cousin, Pitt Crawley, the aunt takes kindly to her handsome, if somewhat wild, nephew. After dinner on the day of his arrival at the aunt's residence, the elderly woman leaves the two cousins at table to have a bottle or two of wine, and the conversation turns to the pedigree of the family. Pitt Craw-

ley leads his cousin on in both drink and sporting idiom:
and talk, amused at James' conduct

"I think you were speaking of dogs killing rats," Pitt remarked
mildly, handing his cousin the decanter to "buzz."

"Killing rats, was I? Well, Pitt, are you a sporting man? Do you
want to see a dawg as *can* kill a rat? If you do, come down with
me to Tom Corduroy's, in Castle Street Mews, and I'll show you
such a bull-terrier as—Pooh! gammon," cried James, bursting out
laughing at his own absurdity,—"you don't care about a dog or
rat; it's all nonsense. I'm blest if I think you know the difference
between a dog and a duck."

"No; by the way," Pitt continued with increased blandness, "it
was about blood you were talking, and the personal advantages
which people derive from patrician birth. Here's the fresh bottle."

"Blood's the word," said James, gulping the ruby fluid down.
"Nothing like blood, sir, in hosses, dawgs <u>and</u> men. Why, only
last term, just before I was rusticated, that is, I mean just before
I had the measles, ha, ha—there was me and Ringwood of Christ-
church, Bob Ringwood, Lord Cinqbar's son, having our beer at
the 'Bell' at Blenheim, when the Banbury bargeman offered to
fight either of us for a bowl of punch. . . . Bob had his coat off
at once—he stood up to the Banbury man for three minutes, and
polished him off in four rounds easy. Gad, how he did drop, sir,
and what was it? Blood, sir, all blood."

Nothing will come of nothing

Source: KING LEAR (Act I, sc. i, l. 92)
Author: William Shakespeare (1564–1616)
First published: 1608
Type of work: Dramatic tragedy

Context: Full of years, but not of
wisdom, King Lear decides to divide
his kingdom into three parts, the largest of which he will pass to the daughter who declares the greatest love for
him. The young Cordelia, sickened by
the excessive words of her sisters
Goneril and Regan, and loving her father deeply, cannot bring herself to
speak for gain.

LEAR
. . . What can you say, to draw
A third more opulent than your sisters? Speak.

CORDELIA
Nothing my lord.

LEAR
Nothing?

781

CORDELIA

CORDELIA

Nothing.

LEAR

Nothing will come of nothing. Speak again.

CORDELIA

Unhappy that I am, I cannot heave
My heart into my mouth. I love your Majesty
According to my bond, no more nor less.

Now may the good God pardon all good men!

Source: AURORA LEIGH (Book IV, l. 506)
Author: Elizabeth Barrett Browning (1806–1861)
First published: 1857
Type of work: Romance in blank verse

Context: Aurora Leigh, orphaned daughter of an English noble and his Florentine wife, lives in England with an aunt who brings her up very strictly. But in spite of her upbringing, Aurora becomes a poet. She is visited in her aunt's home by her cousin, Romney Leigh, a wealthy young man who intends to dedicate his life to social uplift. Although he has a passion for good works, he is personally rather chilly so far as his emotions are concerned. Romney proposes marriage to Aurora, but as neither one loves the other, she refuses him. At this point in the story the aunt dies, and Aurora moves to London to make her living as a writer; she is markedly successful in her undertaking and gains a modicum of fame. She is visited by the beautiful Lady Waldemar, who is in love with Romney and who wishes to enlist Aurora's aid in breaking off Romney's prospective marriage to Marian Erle, a charming girl of low-class family. Aurora refuses to help Lady Waldemar, but keeps her silence to Romney about Lady Waldemar's project. She hears him call her good and reflects upon all the evil that good people do: good mothers use their children in intrigues, good critics ruin poets, good statesmen pull down states, good patriots ruin their causes. She concludes her reflection with the prayer that God may pardon all good men.

I have known good wives,
As chaste, or nearly so, as Potiphar's;
And good, good mothers, who would use a child
To better an intrigue; good friends, beside
(Very good), who hung succinctly round your neck
And sucked your breath, as cats are fabled to do
By sleeping infants. And we all have known
Good critics who have stamped out poet's hope,

782

Good statesmen who pulled ruin on the state,
Good patriots who for a theory risked a cause,
Good kings who disembowelled for a tax,
Good popes who brought all good to jeopardy,
Good Christians who sate still in easy chairs
And damned the general world for standing up.
Now may the good God pardon all good men!

Nuns fret not at their convent's narrow room

Source: MISCELLANEOUS SONNETS (Part I, sonnet 1)
Author: William Wordsworth (1770–1850)
First published: 1807
Type of work: Sonnet

Context: As a man, Wordsworth was led by the cry for freedom into supporting the French Revolution; he discovered, much to his horror, that too much political or social freedom has turned into a Reign of Terror. As a poet, he was fond of very long, discursive poems like *The Prelude* and *The Excursion*, but he discovered that the freedom of indeterminable length tended to stifle his inspiration and invention. Not until 1801 when his sister was reading to him the sonnets of Milton did he discover that the tight confines of this poetic form, one of the most condensed and strictly organized in English poetry, also had dignity of sentiment and majestic harmony. Trying his hand at the form, he found that he could fully express his conception and still be bound by rules that prevented his tendency to become profuse. As he grew older, he learned that this combination of dignity and tightness was increasingly suited to his talents, and as an elderly poet he produced sonnets that are remarkable for their harmony, simplicity, and serenity. This poem, used by him as an introduction to a collection of sonnets, explains his love for a poetic form which had grown unpopular during the eighteenth century and to which he had given new life.

Nuns fret not at their convent's narrow room;
And hermits are contented with their cells. . . .
In truth the prison, unto which we doom
Ourselves, no prison is: and hence for me,
In sundry moods, 't was pastime to be bound
Within the Sonnet's scanty plot of ground;
Pleased if some Souls (for such there needs must be)
Who have felt the weight of too much liberty,
Should find brief solace there, as I have found.
. . .

783

Nursing her wrath to keep it warm

Source: TAM O'SHANTER (Line 12)
Author: Robert Burns (1759–1796)
First published: 1791
Type of work: Narrative poem

Context: "Tam O'Shanter" is a poem about one poor Scotsman's adventures with Satan's crew, on a night when he is making his way home after an evening of drinking at a tavern. As the epigraph from Gawin Douglas says, it is a tale of "Brownyis and of Bogilis full." The poem describes how Tam O'Shanter, who failed to take the advice offered by his good wife, Kate, always gets drunk when he goes to market-day in the town of Ayr. On one such night the boozing Scotsman canters out of Ayr toward his home, mounted on his faithful horse, Meg. As he approaches Alloway Kirk, he sees it blazing with light, and he stops to watch the unholy crew dance hornpipes, jigs, strathspeys, and reels to the Devil's music. Tam is particularly entranced by the appearance and dancing of a young, pretty, and quite shapely witch in a short skirt. Without thinking of the consequences, Tam calls out his admiration of her dancing, at which the whole devilish crew take out after him. He spurs Meg and barely escapes by racing the horse across the bridge over the River Doon, which, being running water, stops the spirits' and witches' pursuit. The quotation, from the first verse paragraph, tells how men gather on late afternoon, as the market-day ends, to sit and drink together, little thinking of the distance home or the wrath of their wives who are kept waiting:

> When chapman billies leave the street,
> And drouthy neebors, neebors meet,
> As market-days are wearing late,
> An' folk begin to tak' the gate;
> While we sit bousing at the nappy,
> An' getting fou and unco happy,
> We think na on the lang Scots miles,
> The mosses, waters, slaps, and styles,
> That lie between us and our hame,
> Whare sits our sulky, sullen dame,
> Gathering her brows like gathering storm,
> **Nursing her wrath to keep it warm.**

O brother man! fold to thy heart thy brother

Source: WORSHIP (Stanza 13)
Author: John Greenleaf Whittier (1807–1892)
First published: 1848
Type of work: Lyric poem

ligion. But, says Whittier, God does not ask for "taper lights" or "dolorous chant" or "incense clouding up the twilight nave." What He wishes of all men is kindness and love toward one another:

O brother man! fold to thy heart thy brother;
    Where pity dwells, the peace of God is there;
To worship rightly is to love each other,
    Each smile a hymn, each kindly deed a prayer.

Follow with reverent steps the great example
    Of Him whose holy work was "doing good;"
So shall the wide earth seem our Father's temple,
    Each loving life a psalm of gratitude.

Then shall all shackles fall; the stormy clangor
    Of wild war music o'er the earth shall cease;
Love shall tread out the baleful fire of anger,
    And in its ashes plant the tree of peace!

O eloquent, just, and mighty Death!

Source: THE HISTORY OF THE WORLD (Book V, chapter vi, sec. 12)
Author: Sir Walter Raleigh (c. 1552–1618)
First published: 1614
Type of work: History

Context: Sir Walter Raleigh was a true Elizabethan in the sense of his being at one time or another engaged in numerous activities associated with his age. Soldier, sailor, courtier, statesman, colonizer, scholar, patron of poets and scientists, himself a poet and historian, he was a legend in his time and for all time. Influential in his early life in building up the naval power of England, he helped to prepare his nation for the fateful conflict with Spain, the Armada of 1588. Later he turned his attention to the encouragement of English colonization of the New World. His most im- portant prose work was *The History of the World,* written while he was imprisoned at the Tower of London for alleged conspiracy against James I. Sentenced to die in 1603, he was temporarily reprieved and spent his last years in captivity in the Tower until his execution, amply supplied with books by his friends. Although he originally intended to cover the full range of ancient to modern times, the work breaks off at 168 B.C. and appeared as a fragment in 1614. Though incomplete, it remained popular as a universal history well into the eighteenth century. Near the conclusion, he extols Death as the mighty instructor which forces the revelation of truth upon king and commoner alike:

> . . . It is therefore Death alone that can suddenly make man to know himself. He tells the proud and insolent that they are but abjects, and humbles them at the instant; makes them cry, complain, and repent, yea even to hate their forepast happiness. He takes the account of the rich, and proves him a beggar, a naked beggar, which hath interest in nothing but in the gravel that fills his mouth. He holds a glass before the eyes of the most beautiful, and makes them see therein their deformity and rottenness, and they acknowledge it.
> **O eloquent, just, and mighty Death!** whom none could advise, thou hast persuaded; what non hath dared, thou hast done; and whom all the world hath flattered, thou only hast cast out of the world and despised; thou hast drawn together all the far-stretched greatness, all the pride, cruelty, and ambition of man, and covered it all over with these two narrow words, *Hic jacet!*

O, for a blast of that dread horn

Source: MARMION (Canto VI, stanza 33)
Author: Sir Walter Scott (1771–1832)
First published: 1808
Type of work: Narrative poem

Context: Written more hastily than his other metrical romances such as *Lay of the Last Minstrel* and *Lady of the Lake,* Scott's *Marmion,* a tale of the Scottish Border in the early sixteenth century, is flawed by melodrama, yet it maintains the lyric beauty and exciting story of his other dramatic pieces. The title character is Lord Marmion. He had persuaded a nun, Constance de Beverley, to leave her convent and for three years to accompany him, disguised as a page. Then, meeting the heiress Clare Fitz-Clare, he had discarded Constance, and was trying to discredit Clare's sweetheart, Ralph de Wilton, and marry her. He had fought a duel with Wilton and left him for dead on the field. Dispatched by Henry VIII of England to try to persuade James IV of Scotland to stop sending armed raiders across the border into England, Marmion gets as guide a holy palmer, really de Wilton in disguise. Though James refuses to agree, he puts Marmion under the protection of Archibald Douglas, the most powerful of his lords, who is also conveying to his castle an abbess and several nuns, including Constance on her way to execution, and Clare. When the Scotch and English armies meet in battle at Flodden Field, September 9, 1513, the Scotch king is killed, and the English under Thomas Howard, with both Wilton and Marmion fighting in his ranks, are the victors. Mortally wounded, Marmion receives water from Clare and Wilton. He is buried in an unmarked grave, and Clare and Wilton are married. Stanza

786

33 of Canto Six, following the death of Marmion, tells the sad plight of the Scotch. The poet thinks of the episode at the Pyrenees Pass of Roncesvalles when Roland and Oliver made their gallant fight against the Saracens in 778, and Roland too late sounded the trumpet that could have brought Charlemagne with reinforcements.

> By this, though deep the evening fell,
> Still rose the battle's deadly swell,
> For still the Scots, around their King,
> Unbroken, fought in desperate ring.
> Where's now their victor vaward wing,
>   Where Huntly, and where Home?—
> **O, for a blast of that dread horn,**
> On Fontarabian echoes borne.
>   That to King Charles did come,
> When Rowland brave, and Olivier
> And every paladin and peer,
>   On Roncesvalles died!
>   • • •

O how full of briers is this working-day world!

Source: AS YOU LIKE IT (Act I, sc. iii, ll. 11–12)
Author: William Shakespeare (1564–1616)
First published: 1623
Type of work: Dramatic comedy

Context: Rosalind is the daughter of an exiled ruler, Duke Senior, but has remained at court because of her devotion to her cousin Celia, daughter of the usurping ruler, Duke Frederick. Saddened whenever she thinks of her banished father, Rosalind is given new cause for concern. She is in love at first sight with Orlando, tyrannized by his older brother, Oliver. But she has no way of knowing whether her love is returned, though it is. To make matters worse, Orlando has been banished from court by a suspicious Duke Frederick, who, furthermore, is about to banish Rosalind. At this point we find her sighing over her love for the man she would like to marry (whom she calls her "child's father" in anticipation), and being teased by Celia:

CELIA
But is all this for your father?

ROSALIND
No, some of it is for my child's father. **O how full of briers is this working-day world!**

787

CELIA

They are but burs, cousin, thrown upon thee in holiday foolery; if we walk not in the trodden paths our very petticoats will catch them.

ROSALIND

I could shake them off my coat; these burs are in my heart.

O, how quickly doth the glory of the world pass away!

Source: THE IMITATION OF CHRIST (Book I, chapter 3, section VI, as translated by Anthony Hoskins, c.1613)
Author: Thomas à Kempis (1380–1471)
First transcribed: c.1420
Type of work: Spiritual instruction

Context: Sic transit gloria mundi is an old Latin saying usually translated "so passeth away the glory of the world," or "thus passes the glory of this world away." It is used most pointedly and effectively, perhaps, by St. Thomas à Kempis (properly Thomas Hamerken von Kempen) in his religious classic, *Imitatio Christi.* St. Thomas, a German mystic and devotional writer, was educated at Deventer by the Brethren of the Common Life, a religious order committed to a contemplative and scholarly existence. From here he entered the monastery of Mount Saint Agnes, taking his monastic vows a few years later in 1406. He was subsequently ordained priest and eventually became subprior. He was a copyist of considerable excellence and greatly enjoyed such work: but he is remembered today for *The Imitation of Christ,* which some scholars have attributed to another theologian named Gerson. It soon became a permanent religious classic and has since been translated into every language in the Christian world; more than two thousand editions have been published up to the present time. This book instructs, both fervently and humbly, exemplifying the Christian way of life. It begins with the observation that in order to find true illumination and deliverance from all blindness of heart, we must endeavor to conform our lives to that of Christ. It enjoins humility and contempt for the world's vanities; cautions us to avoid inordinate thirst for knowledge, for with knowledge goes great responsibility and we should rather fear the knowledge we have than take advantage of it. Nor should we take pride in it. We should not be forever questioning; to God all things are one, and he is Truth. The individual must strive for unity and simplicity within himself, doing all his many tasks for the honor of God. In this life all perfection is mingled with imperfection, and "a lowly knowledge of thyself is a surer way to God than the deep searchings of man's learning."

Yet learning is not to be blamed, nor the mere knowledge of any thing whatsoever to be disliked, it being good in itself, and ordained by God; but a good conscience and a virtuous life is always to be preferred before it.

But because many endeavour rather to get knowledge than to live well; therefore they are often deceived, and reap either none, or but little fruit.

O, if men bestowed as much labour in the rooting out of vices, and planting of virtues, as they do in moving of questions, neither would there so much hurt be done, nor so great scandal be given in the world, nor so much looseness be practised in Religious Houses.

Truly, at the day of judgment we shall not be examined what we have read, but what we have done; not how well we have spoken, but how religiously we have lived.

Tell me now, where are all those Doctors and Masters, with whom thou wast well acquainted, whilst they lived and flourished in learning?

Now others possess their livings and perhaps do scarce ever think of them. In their lifetime they seemed something, but now they are not spoken of.

O, how quickly doth the glory of the world pass away! O that their life had been answerable to their learning! then had their study and reading been to good purpose.

How many perish by reason of vain learning in this world, who take little care of the serving of God:

And because they rather choose to be great than humble, therefore they become vain in their imaginations.

O Iago, the pity of it

Source: OTHELLO (Act IV, sc. i, l. 207)
Author: William Shakespeare (1564–1616)
First published: 1622
Type of work: Dramatic tragedy

Context: In his plot to destroy Cassio, friend and former lieutenant of Othello, and Othello himself because of Cassio's appointment by Othello to the lieutenancy that he had hoped for, Iago, the Machiavellian villain, discredits Cassio and suggests to Othello that Desdemona, his new bride, is more than a friend to Cassio. Presented with seeming proof of his wife's infidelity, Othello declares his hate and love at the same time.

OTHELLO

Ay, let her rot and perish, and be damned tonight; for she shall not live. No, my heart is turned to stone; I strike it, and it hurts my hand. O the world hath not a sweeter creature; she might lie by an emperor's side, and command him tasks.

. . .

789

will sing the savageness out of a bear—of so high and plenteous wit and invention.

IAGO

She's the worse for all this.

OTHELLO

O a thousand thousand times—and then of so gentle a condition.

IAGO

Ay, too gentle.

OTHELLO

Nay that's certain—but yet the pity of it, Iago. **O Iago, the pity of it, Iago.**

O judgment, thou art fled to brutish beasts

Source: JULIUS CAESAR (Act III, sc. ii, l. 109)
Author: William Shakespeare (1564–1616)
First published: 1623
Type of work: Dramatic tragedy

Context: Before the Capitol of Rome Julius Caesar has been stabbed to death by a group of conspirators, including his friend Brutus, who later explains to the citizens in the Forum that the murder was committed to protect the freedom of the Romans from an ambitious man. The citizens are next addressed by Mark Antony, who, while seeming to agree with Brutus, subtly enrages the mob against the conspirators by recalling Caesar's faithfulness as a friend, his compassion for the poor, and his refusal of the crown. Antony continues:

> ANTONY
> . . . Was this ambition?
> Yet Brutus says, he was ambitious;
> And sure he is an honourable man.
> I speak not to disprove what Brutus spoke,
> But here I am, to speak what I do know;
> You all did love him once, not without cause,
> What cause withholds you then to mourn for him?
> **O judgment, thou art fled to brutish beasts,**
> And men have lost their reason. Bear with me;
> My heart is in the coffin there with Caesar,
> And I must pause, till it come back to me.

O! more than Gothic ignorance

Source: THE HISTORY OF TOM JONES, A FOUNDLING (Book VII, chapter 3)
Author: Henry Fielding (1707–1754)
First published: 1749
Type of work: Novel

Context: Tom Jones, one of Fielding's four novels, represents innovations and advances over preceding works. The author, while accepting human nature as it is, ridicules its faults and foibles, and portrays virtuous living as the most desirable of human achievements. His wife, Charlotte Cradock, was his model for the heroine, Sophia. The country Squire Allworthy, returning from London, finds an infant lying on his bed. He thinks the baby the son of the servant, Jenny Jones, and names him Tom Jones. He brings the child up with master Blifil, son of his widowed sister. Later the boy attracts the attention of Sophia Western by rescuing her from a runaway horse, at the cost of his broken arm. In order to conceal her interest in Tom, Sophia pretends to be in love with Blifil. Sophia's aunt, Mrs. Western, seeing this situation, arranges with her brother to talk to Sophia about a marriage. Their conversation is narrated in Book VII, chapter 3. After painting matrimony as "an institution in which prudent women deposit their funds in order to receive a larger interest than they could have elsewhere," Mrs. Western gets angry when Sophia refuses to consider marriage to Mr. Blifil. When her brother interrupts, she charges him with not having taught Sophia obedience and the duties of a child to her parents. To her, Goths were barbarous and uncivilized, and so she characterizes her brother's ignorance as Gothic. After all, he is not acquainted with philosophy, as she is.

". . . Have I not told you what Plato says on that subject?—a subject on which you was so notoriously ignorant when you came first under my care, that I verily believe you did not know the relation between a daughter and her father."—" 'T is a lie," answered Western. "The girl is no such fool, as to live to eleven years old without knowing that she was her father's relation."—**"O! more than Gothic ignorance,"** answered the lady. "And as for your manners, brother, I must tell you, they deserve a cane." . . .

O Sleep! thou flatterer of happy minds

Source: ELEGY TO SLEEP (Line 1)
Author: William Congreve (1670–1729)
First published: 1710
Type of work: Love lyric

Context: To be a poet of the Restoration period, one had to be elegant, cynical, and witty. He borrowed from the brilliance of the Cavalier poets whose era of gay, clever, but superficial verse was ended by the dour Puritans by the execution of Charles I in 1649. Charles II, regaining the throne in 1660, ushered in a new cycle where a rake could be considered a gentleman if he were sufficiently aloof and elegant, and his mistress was a fine lady if the relationship was secret and the whole affair witty. Congreve was perhaps the culmination of this literary tradition. His plays were satires with a light touch. Their characters were masters of dazzling repartee. The lines were witty, and the action reflected the manners of the aristocracy of the time. With his miscellaneous poetry, however, Congreve was not so successful. Some of the critics maintained that his muse deserted him when called on to perform off-stage, though the author himself was at his wittiest in conversational groups. Yet once or twice he wrote poetry that might have been signed by Sir John Suckling or Richard Lovelace of the Cavalier Poets. An example is one that he classified as "An Elegy," and called "To Sleep." In rhymed couplets, it utters a complaint to Sleep for not living up to Shakespeare's opinion of it in *Macbeth,* as "balm of hurt minds," and that which "knits up the ravell'd sleave of Care." The poet declares that Sleep never comes to him. Does it wait only on the successful lover? Then he decides that perhaps his sleeplessness is his own fault, "For oft I have thy proffer'd aid repell'd/ And my reluctant eyes from rest withheld." At such times as he wrestled with his Muse all night to provide a song for— he breaks off. "Let me not name thee, thou too charming maid." Then he has a comforting thought. Maybe she gets the balm of sleep. Perhaps his lady enjoys the sleep he loses. Once more he addresses Sleep. "For her, O Sleep! thy balmy sweets prepare;/ The peace I lose for her,/ To her transfer." The poem begins with a statement of his disillusionment about the gift of slumber.

O Sleep! thou flatterer of happy minds,
How soon a troubled breast thy falsehood finds?
Thou common friend, officious in thy aid,
Where no distress is shown, nor want betray'd;
But oh, how swift, how sure thou art to shun
The wretch by fortune or by love undone!
Where are thy gentle dews, thy softer powers,
Which us'd to wait upon my midnight hours?

O sovereign mistress of true melancholy

Source: ANTONY AND CLEOPATRA (Act IV, sc. ix, l. 12)
Author: William Shakespeare (1564–1616)
First published: 1623
Type of work: Dramatic tragedy

Context: Domitius Enorbarbus is Mark Antony's trusted friend, as well as one of his most talented and faithful officers. But when Antony decides, after his disastrous defeat at Actium, to risk another battle against Octavius Caesar, Enobarbus, seeing no other way to save his own life and future, abandons Antony to join Caesar's forces near Alexandria. Learning of Enobarbus' desertion, Antony exhibits no ill-will, for he believes that he has lost the right to his friends' and subordinates' loyalty through his own dishonorable actions, which spring from his uncontrollable passion for Cleopatra. So far from being angry, Antony even sends all Enobarbus' treasure after him to Caesar's camp. Antony's charity, and his refusal to become angry, strike Enobarbus with shame. Filled with emotion, he wanders from the Roman camp, berating himself for his disloyalty. He apostrophizes the moon as witness of his repentance just before he falls dead of shame for his revolt.

ENOBARBUS

Be witness to me, O thou blessed moon,
When men revolted shall upon record
Bear hateful memory, poor Enobarbus did
Before thy face repent.

. . .

O sovereign mistress of true melancholy,
The poisonous damp of night disponge upon me,
That life, a very rebel to my will,
May hang no longer on me. Throw my heart
Against the flint and hardness of my fault,
Which being dried with grief will break to powder,
And finish all foul thoughts. O Antony,
Nobler than my revolt is infamous,
Forgive me in thine own particular,
But let the world rank me in register
A master-leaver and fugitive.
O Antony! O Antony!

[*Dies.*]

O tempora! O mores!

Source: IN CATILINAM ("Against Catiline," Book I, division i, l. 1)
Author: Marcus Tullius Cicero (106–43 B.C.)
First spoken: 63 B.C.
Type of work: Oratory of denunciation

Context: Lucius Sergius Catiline (c. 108–62 B.C.) decided to enter public life in Rome, despite his reputation among the gilded youths of the city for excesses and debauchery. He conspired in 63 B.C. to win the office of Consul by murdering some of the competitors. Because the signal was given prematurely, the scheme failed. After having run unsuccessfully against Cicero in 63 B.C., Catiline announced his candidacy for the 62 B.C. elections, which he hoped to win by seizing the government and cancelling debts. Rumor again spread that while Manlius was advancing with his army on Rome, Catiline would murder the leading senators. Amid the terror in the city at the violence of the plans, Cicero called a meeting of the Senate in the Temple of Jupiter Stator, where the members would be safer than in the Senate House. Here in his "First Oration Against Catiline," he denounced the man in a series of dramatic questions, including some known even to those who have never studied Latin: "O tempora! O mores!" That night Catiline left the city. Cicero continued the attack by more oratory that resulted in a vote for the death sentence of the conspirators who had remained in Rome. Few denunciations of any man are more violent than the beginning of this one, called in Latin "In Catilinam." However, it did not result in any Senate action against Catiline, who fled the city and raised an army to control Rome by force. His army was defeated early in 62 B.C. by Antonius, and Catiline perished bravely with his troops.

In heaven's name, Catiline, how long will you abuse our patience? How long will that madness of yours mock us? To what limit will your unbridled audacity vaunt itself? Is it nothing to you that the Palatine has its garrison by night, nothing to you that the city is full of patrols, nothing that the populace is in a panic, nothing that all honest men have joined forces, nothing that the senate is convened in this stronghold, is it nothing to see the look on all these faces? Do you not know that your plans are disclosed? Do you not see that your conspiracy is bound hand and foot by the knowledge of all these men? Who of us do you think is ignorant of what you did last night, what you did the night before, where you were, whom you called together, what plans you took? **O what times! O what customs!** The senate knows these things, the consul sees them. Yet this man lives. Lives, did I say? Nay, more, he walks into the senate, he takes part in the public counsel. He singles out and marks with his glance each one of us for murder.

O thou of little faith

Source: MATTHEW 14:31
Author: Unknown (traditionally Matthew the Apostle)
First transcribed: c. 75–100
Type of work: Gospel

Context: When Herod the Tetrarch married Herodias, former wife of his brother Philip, he was censured heavily by John the Baptist. Philip was still living, and this sort of union was considered adulterous. Herodias, a woman of rare vindictiveness, had John imprisoned and then bided her time until she could arrange his death. When Herod's birthday was celebrated, Salome danced before him. She was Herodias' daughter by her first husband, Herod Boethos, and married Philip the Tetrarch—to whom her mother had also been married. This would appear to be a sordid tangle of human relationships at best, and it is not difficult to understand the feeling of outrage expressed by John and perhaps by the public as well. Herod was pleased with the dancing of Salome and said he would grant her whatever she wished. Salome had been coached by her mother: she asked for John the Baptist's head. Herod regretted his promise, for he liked John the Baptist; but he kept his word. Now, when he hears of the works of Jesus, he thinks John has returned to life again. Clearly his conscience bothers him. Jesus, on the other hand, hears of the Baptist's death and is deeply distressed by it. He and His disciples take ship and go to a secluded spot in the desert; but the multitudes have heard the news and are also distressed. They follow. Jesus heals the sick among them and then feeds the crowd miraculously with five loaves of bread and two fish; these are distributed by His disciples and all five thousand are fed; twelve baskets of food are left over. Jesus then sends His disciples ahead of Him by ship, saying He will follow later, and tells the multitudes to return home. After they are gone He retires to a mountain and prays. By the time He has finished, night has fallen; there is a storm on the sea and the ship is only halfway across. Of the episodes in which Jesus chides His disciples for insufficient faith, the following event is perhaps most memorable.

And straightway Jesus constrained his disciples to get into a ship, and to go before him unto the other side, while he sent the multitudes away.

And when he had sent the multitudes away, he went up into a mountain apart to pray: and when the evening was come, he was there alone.

But the ship was now in the midst of the sea, tossed with waves: for the wind was contrary.

And in the fourth watch of the night Jesus went unto them, walking on the sea.

And when the disciples saw him walking on the sea, they were troubled, saying, It is a spirit; and they cried out for fear.

But straightway Jesus spake unto them, saying, Be of good cheer; it is I; be not afraid.

And Peter answered him and said, Lord, if it be thou, bid me come unto thee on the water.

And he said, Come. And when Peter was come down out of the ship, he walked on the water, to go to Jesus.

But when he saw the wind boisterous, he was afraid; and beginning to sink, he cried, saying, Lord, save me.

And immediately Jesus stretched forth his hand, and caught him, and said unto him, **O thou of little faith,** wherefore didst thou doubt?

And when they were come into the ship, the wind ceased.
Then they that were in the ship came and worshipped him,
saying, Of a truth thou art the Son of God.

O true apothecary! Thy drugs are quick

Source: ROMEO AND JULIET (Act V, sc. iii, ll 119–120)
Author: William Shakespeare (1564–1616)
First published: 1597
Type of work: Dramatic tragedy

Context: In Verona Romeo, of the house of Montague, falls in love with and secretly marries Juliet, of the rival house of Capulet. Determined to end the feud of the families, Romeo accepts the insults of Tybalt, a Capulet, but, when Tybalt kills Mercutio, Romeo's friend and defender, Romeo draws his sword and slays him. Romeo, who has fled to Mantua for safety, hears that Juliet is dead (actually she has taken a potion to make her appear dead to avoid marrying Paris as her parents insist). Romeo goes to the tomb where Juliet lies, apparently in death, takes a fatal poison, and, as he prepares to die says:

ROMEO
. . .
Eyes look your last.
Arms, take your last embrace. And lips, O you
The doors of breath, seal with a righteous kiss
A dateless bargain to engrossing death.
Come bitter conduct, come unsavory guide,
Thou desperate pilot, now at once run on
The dashing rocks thy sea-sick weary bark.
Here's to my love! **O true apothecary!**
Thy drugs are quick. Thus with a kiss I die.

O you chorus of indolent reviewers

Source: EXPERIMENTS. MILTON. HENDECASYLLABICS (Line 1)
Author: Alfred, Lord Tennyson (1809–1892)
First published: 1863
Type of work: Metrical experiment

Context: Although poet laureate and highly acclaimed by his contemporaries, Tennyson was still greatly disturbed by unfavorable reviews; in fact, he often rewrote poems after their publication in order to perfect the meter or to enhance the word order. This almost neurotic fear of censure and an ear for the sounds of his language combined to form some of the most melodious poems of the English tradition. Tennyson strives

796

for the full union of sound, metrics, and meaning; and while he is often criticized for his superfluity, he is recognized as the master of the well structured, musical poem. In this poem he writes in a form alien to English poetry, the eleven-syllable complexly organized line that was mastered by the Latin poet Catullus. By showing his adeptness at such a difficult form, he scorns the very critics who have scorned him.

O you chorus of indolent reviewers,
Irresponsible, indolent reviewers,
Look, I come to the test, a tiny poem
All composed in a metre of Catullus,
All in quantity, careful of my motion,
Like the skater on ice that hardly bears him,
Lest I fall unawares before the people,
Waking laughter in indolent reviewers. . . .

Oaths are but words, and words but wind

Source: HUDIBRAS (Pàrt II, Canto 2, l. 107)
Author: Samuel Butler (1612–1680)
First published: First and second parts, 1663; third part, 1678
Type of work: Burlesque poem

Context: Sir Hudibras, an enthusiastic Presbyterian follower of Cromwell, goes crusading with his squire, the ignorant Ralpho, an Independent in religion, on a campaign against sin. Always unsuccessful, he has a momentary victory over a fiddler, Crowdero, and a bear-tamer, Orsin, but his attempt to punish them inflames the crowd which they are entertaining, and eventually Hudibras is put in the stocks where he had put the peg-legged fiddler. Though a rich Widow had originally spurned him, she comes to him in the stocks and suggests that if he will endure a beating, she will arrange for his release. As an instance of the lengthy discussions and small amount of action in this poem, Hudibras and the Widow talk in detail about incentives to matrimony, and the history of whipping. Some of the aphorisms for which the poem is commended as something at least to dip into, if not to read extensively, appear in their exchange; for instance: "Great wits and valors, like great states,/ Do sometimes sink with their great weights," and "Wedlock without love, some say,/ Is but a lock without a key," and "Though love be all the world's pretence,/ Money's the mythologic sense,/ The real substance of the shadow,/ Which all address and courtship made to." By listing some of the great lovers of the past, whipped for and by their lady loves, including cryptic remarks about contemporaries, the Widow persuades Hudibras to accept a beating. He takes an oath, and so is freed. Because night is coming, the whipping will be delayed until the next day. And with that the first canto of Part Two ends. The attitude of Sir Hudibras toward promises is evi-

797

dently meant by the poet to indicate the hypocrisy of the Puritans toward oaths. He says they commit perjury, readily take oaths, and as readily break them. Sir Hudibras consults with Ralpho about how to escape the whipping. He must wrestle with his conscience. The squire, always ready for an argument, examines the situation with sophistry, and with a sneer at the different ways different religions act. He assures his master that it is heathenish and impious to beat and claw at any human body. Proof is that the heathen scourge themselves. Hudibras must not imitate them.

> This, therefore, may be justly reckon'd
> A heinous sin. Now to the second;
> That saints may claim a dispensation
> To swear and foreswear on occasion,
> I doubt not but it will appear
> With pregnant light; the point is clear.
> **Oaths are but words, and words but wind;**
> Too feeble implements to bind; . . .

Observed of all observers

Source: HAMLET (Act III, sc. i, l. 162)
Author: William Shakespeare (1564–1616)
First published: 1603
Type of work: Dramatic tragedy

Context: Hamlet, Prince of Denmark, charged by the Ghost of his murdered father with the duty of avenging the murder, senses the web of intrigue in the court. When Ophelia, daughter of Polonius, returns his love tokens, he sees her as a part of the conspiracy against him and brutally berates her. She can only believe that madness has overtaken her lover because of her rejection, and laments his condition.

> OPHELIA
> O what a noble mind is here o'erthrown!
> The courtier's, soldier's, scholar's, eye, tongue, sword,
> Th' expectancy and rose of the fair state,
> The glass of fashion, and the mould of form,
> Th' **observed of all observers,** quite, quite down,
> And I of ladies most deject and wretched,
> That sucked the honey of his musicked vows,
> Now see that noble and most sovereign reason,
> Like sweet bells jangled, out of tune and harsh;
> That unmatched form and feature of blown youth
> Blasted with ecstasy. O woe is me
> T' have seen what I save seen, see what I see.

798

Obtruding false rules pranked in reason's garb

Source: COMUS (Line 758)
Author: John Milton (1608–1674)
First published: 1637
Type of work: Masque

Context: John Milton wrote *Comus* as a compliment to the Earl of Bridgewater upon his installation as President of Wales. The earl's daughter and two sons took leading roles in the masque's premiere at Ludlow Castle. The action involves the efforts of the three, known as the Lady, the Elder Brother, and the Second Brother, to make their way at night through a wood haunted by the foul enchanter Comus and his crew of revelers. When the three travelers become lost, the brothers are separated from the Lady, who is soon accosted by Comus. This wicked son of Bacchus and Circe immediately lays plans to undermine the Lady's virtue. Pretending to guide her on her way, Comus leads her to his palace, the scene of his lustful revels. He threatens to rob her of her ability to move by waving his magic wand, but the Lady, unafraid, says that he cannot touch her mind. Thereupon Comus begins to argue that a life of virtue is a waste of youth and beauty. Time lost cannot be regained; beauty, to be of any use, must be displayed in public places. The Lady had not thought to answer Comus's speeches, but she is outraged at the idea that he can charm her reason by advancing falsehoods dressed up as sound reason. She says:

LADY
I had not thought to have unlocked my lips
In this unhallowed air, but that this juggler
Would think to charm my judgment, as mine eyes,
Obtruding false rules pranked in reason's garb.
I hate when vice can bolt her arguments,
And virtue has no tongue to check her pride:
Imposter, do not charge most innocent nature,
As if she would her children should be riotous
With her abundance; she, good cateress,
Means her provision only to the good
That live according to her sober laws,
And holy dictates of spare temperance.

Of its own beauty is the mind diseased

Source: CHILDE HAROLD'S PILGRIMAGE (Canto IV, stanza 122)
Author: George Gordon, Lord Byron (1788–1824)
First published: 1818 (Canto IV)
Type of work: Narrative poem

Context: Canto IV, the last part of *Childe Harold's Pilgrimage,* was written in Venice and published six years after the first two cantos, with Canto III in between, appearing in 1816. Though resembling the other parts in being a narrative in verse, it is a more mature work, carrying its message by indirection and inference, and requiring a greater acquaintance with the history and sights of Italy. While Byron does mention some of the famous places, on many occasions he is led down a poetic bypath to some personal reaction. The mention of ruins along the Appian Way near Rome and the remains of a fountain there, remind Byron of the legend of two lovers Numa and Egeria, who met secretly in the near-by grotto that provides water for it. After six stanzas about the beauties of the surroundings and the delights of the love they shared, Byron is moved to an apostrophe to love in general. He calls it a feeling that in the young runs to waste and only produces "weeds of dark luxuriance," "rank at the core, though tempting to the eye." Here he is probably thinking of his own unfortunate marriage, that ended in a never-explained separation after the birth of a daughter, Ada (to whom he sent a loving greeting at the end of the preceding canto). Then, in development of his theme, Byron discusses love as "an unseen seraph," and declares, "no habitant of the earth art thou." Love is something that has never been looked on by man, but is only a creation of his mind, like the gods and goddesses with whom the Greeks peopled their Olympus, in such shapes and images as their minds needed, and as untrue to life and to Nature as are most creations of poets and painters. The rest of Byron's thoughts on love, beyond the one here quoted, are melancholic and pessimistic. Few find the love they seek, and to most it ends in heart ache. But not for that reason should we abandon the gift of thought; we should try to exert it, even though the divine faculty is from birth "cabin'd, cribb'd, confined," as Shakespeare declares in *Macbeth.*

Of its own beauty is the mind diseased,
And fevers into false creation:—where,
Where are the forms the sculptor's soul hath seized?
In him alone. Can Nature show so fair?
Where are the charms and virtues which we dare
Conceive in boyhood and pursue as men,
The unreach'd Paradise of our despair,
Which o'er-informs the pencil and the pen,
And overpowers the page where it would bloom again?

Of the earth earthy

Source: I CORINTHIANS 15:47
Author: Paul (?–c. 67)
First transcribed: c. 54–57
Type of work: Religious epistle

Context: Paul's stay of eighteen months in Corinth resulted in a well-established church. Rejected by the Jews, he had left the synagogue and preached among the Gentiles, where he gained numerous converts. After he left Corinth and later settled in Ephesus, he received word that the congregation he had built up at Corinth was in the midst of a crisis. An exchange of letters confirmed Paul's worst fears: the church was torn by factions; the congregation was indulging in sexual and other misconduct; and certain rebellious spirits who had assumed leadership were defying Paul's authority. Corinth was a trading center of considerable importance; its population and its religions were alike cosmopolitan, and the city was known throughout the civilized world for its vice. Most of Paul's converts were from the lower classes and retained their pagan moral standards; sexual promiscuity had been encouraged by many of the religions they had abandoned for Christianity. *I Co-rinthians* is a stern rebuke in which Paul censures the Corinthians for their misbehavior. Appealing for unity, he points out the evils of factiousness and competition. He then implies that those persons doing the preaching are misusing their office: the ministry is a holy calling, not a means of self-aggrandizement or a position of power. The man who parades his wisdom does so in the confidence born of ignorance, and is a fool: beside that of God, the wisdom of even a great man is nothing. Paul then reproves the Corinthians for fornication and incest, discusses the nature of spiritual love, and warns them that true wisdom is only to be found in the next world. He then discusses the practice of "speaking with tongues." While this practice is good, it is better to prophesy in words others can understand and thus work for the edification of the church. Paul concludes with a discussion of resurrection.

And so it is written, The first man Adam was made a living soul; the last Adam was made a quickening spirit.

Howbeit that was not first which is spiritual, but that which is natural; and afterward that which is spiritual.

The first man is **of the earth, earthy:** the second man is the Lord from heaven.

As is the earthy, such are they also that are earthy: and as is the heavenly, such are they also that are heavenly.

. . .

Now this I say, brethren, that flesh and blood cannot inherit the kingdom of God; neither doth corruption inherit incorruption.

Behold, I shew you a mystery; We shall not all sleep, but we shall all be changed,

In a moment, in the twinkling of an eye, at the last trump: for the trumpet shall sound, and the dead shall be raised incorruptible, and we shall be changed.

. . .

So when this corruptible shall have put on incorruption, and this mortal shall have put on immortality, then shall be brought to pass

the saying that is written, Death is swallowed up in victory.
O death, where is thy sting? O grave, where is thy victory?

Of whom to be dispraised were no small praise

Source: PARADISE REGAINED (Book III, l. 56)
Author: John Milton (1608–1674)
First published: 1671
Type of work: Epic poem

Context: Following Christ's baptism by John the Baptist, Satan decides to ruin Christ as he once ruined Adam. God announces His intention of letting Christ be tempted, and then Christ goes into the wilderness for forty days. Satan meets Him and asks Him to transform a stone into bread, which act Christ refuses to perform. Next Satan tempts Him with a magnificent banquet, as he had formerly tempted Adam with a fruit. Christ refuses the food, the symbol of luxury. Satan then offers Christ great wealth, but this is refused as a thing a man of virtue does not need. In lowest poverty Gideon, Jephthah, and David did great works. A wise man spurns riches, and likewise the rule of a kingdom is something that no wise man desires, as it brings danger, trouble, care, and sleeplessness. Satan, confounded at Christ's refusals, offers fame from either great wisdom or military glory; he points out that Alexander the Great and Scipio the Younger had both achieved great fame by the time they were of Christ's age. Christ spurns fame on the ground that the common people are undiscriminating and extol vulgar things; fame derived from them is worthless, as they do not have a clear idea of what is admirable. In fact, the wise man takes comfort in the dispraise of the multitude, as it indicates that his course of action is right and just. Christ speaks:

> Thou neither dost persuade me to seek wealth
> For empire's sake, nor empire to affect
> For glory's sake by all thy argument.
> For what is glory but the blaze of fame,
> The people's praise, if always praise unmixed?
> And what the people but a herd confused,
> A miscellaneous rabble, who extol
> Things vulgar, and well weighed, scarce worth the praise?
> They praise and they admire they know not what;
> And know not whom, but as one leads the other;
> And what delight to be by such extolled,
> To live upon their tongues and be their talk,
> **Of whom to be dispraised were no small praise?**
> His lot who dares be singularly good.
> Th' intelligent among them and the wise
> Are few, and glory scarce of few is raised.

This is true glory and renown, when God
Looking on the earth, with approbation marks
The just man, . . .

Off with his head. So much for Buckingham

Source: THE TRAGICAL HISTORY OF KING RICHARD III, ALTER'D FROM SHAKE-
SPEARE (Act IV, sc. 4)
Author: Colley Cibber (1671–1757)
First published: 1699
Type of work: Historical tragedy

Context: Colley Cibber was an unusual man. As an actor, he created a
role for himself, in which he specialized. This part was a new type of fop
—not merely the usual overdressed,
effeminate dandy but a vacuous or
foolish ass as well. He played this
type so well that people thought he
was really the sort of creature he portrayed. He was a popular and successful playwright as well, producing
comedies, ballad operas, and other
works throughout the first half of the
eighteenth century. From 1710 to
1733 he managed Drury Lane Theatre, doing so with shrewdness and in
some cases with courage. He lacked
great facility with words, and his
efforts to write tragedy were unsuccessful; nor was he particularly witty.
His plays were successful because he
devised plots and situations cleverly,
introduced some new comic styles,
kept his action moving effectively and
rapidly. His works were invariably
well staged, and marked by sprightli-
ness and individuality. He was able,
too, to create effective roles for the
actors who worked under him. The
language used by Cibber is that which
was in common use, and it no doubt
contributed to the popularity of his
work. This lack of profundity led to
declarations by his critics that he
murdered English; Pope was especially critical of him, making Cibber
the central character in *The Dunciad,*
a monumental satire celebrating dullness. Cibber was not above rewriting
a play by Shakespeare—transforming
it into common speech, shortening
and rearranging it for the popular
stage of his time. The result is of
course an entirely different play:
there is still a compelling story, but
beauty and poetry are gone; only the
blood and thunder remain. Such practice caused the most violent criticism
of all, but Cibber took it good-
naturedly. He was named Poet Laureate in 1730. An excerpt from his
version of Richard III provides an interesting contrast with the original.
Shakespeare used the expression,
"Off with his head," but it is used by
Gloucester when he consigns the unfortunate Hastings to oblivion. In
Cibber's play, the fiendish Richard
has done to death in the Tower of
London those children who present a
barrier to his ambition but his problems are not over; the Duke of Buckingham has stirred up an insurrection.
Then word comes that the duke is
taken:

803

RATCLIFF

My lord, the Army of Great Buckingham
By sudden Floods, and fall of Waters,
Is half lost and scatter'd,
And he himself wander'd away alone;
No man knows whither.

KING RICHARD

Has any careful officer proclaim'd
Reward to him that brings the traytor in?

RATCLIFF

Such Proclamation has been made, my Lord.

Enter CATESBY

My Liege, the Duke of Buckingham is taken.

KING RICHARD

Off with his head. So much for Buckingham.

CATESBY

My Lord, I am sorry I must tell more News.

KING RICHARD

Out with it.

CATESBY

The Earl of Richmond with a mighty power,
Is landed, Sir, at Milford;
And, to confirm the News, Lord Marquess Dorset,
And Sir Thomas Lovell, are up in Yorkshire.

KING RICHARD

Why ay, this looks Rebellion. Ho! my Horse!

**Oh! God! that bread should be so dear,
and flesh and blood so cheap!**

Source: THE SONG OF THE SHIRT (Stanza 5)
Author: Thomas Hood (1799–1845)
First published: 1843
Type of work: Humanitarian poem

Context: Thomas Hood wrote not only quantities of humorous poetry but he also composed many now-forgotten poems of social protest, like "The Bridge of Sighs," and "The Song of the Shirt." He suffered from tuberculosis and poverty, and perhaps the serious poems were products of that side of his existence, but he was usually cheerful and made his countrymen laugh through the magazines he edited: *Gem* (1829), *Comic Annual* (1830–1842), and *Hood's Magazine and Comic Miscellany* (1844–1845). "The Song of the Shirt" appeared, surprisingly, in the Christmas, 1843, issue of *Punch*. It was based on an actual incident in which a widow with two children was accused in Lambeth Police Court of pawning clothes of her employer from whom she received only seven shillings a week for her work as his seamstress. "Plying her needle and thread" with weary and worn fingers, amid "poverty, hunger, and dirt," the seamstress with "eyelids heavy and red," sings "The Song of the Shirt."

> But why do I talk of Death?
>   That Phantom of grisly bone,
> I hardly fear his terrible shape,
> It seems so like my own—
> It seems so like my own,
>   Because of the fasts I keep;
> **Oh! God! that bread should be so dear,**
> **And flesh and blood so cheap!**

Oh my fur and whiskers!

Source: ALICE'S ADVENTURES IN WONDERLAND (Chapter 4)
Author: Lewis Carroll (Charles Lutwidge Dodgson, 1832–1898)
First published: 1865
Type of work: Imaginative tale for children

Context: Carroll's familiar masterpiece of delightful nonsense begins with Alice sitting beside her sister on the riverbank; the sister is reading a book and Alice is growing drowsy when a white rabbit rushes past her, looking at his watch and exclaiming that he is late. She follows him down a rabbit hole and falls into a magical room which is continually changing and from which she cannot seem to escape. There are various substances lying about which she eats and drinks; each of these either increases or decreases her size. Though either state might help her out of her prison, she is never able to arrive at the proper combination. While she is a giant she weeps, and a large pool of tears gathers on the floor. Then she sees the white rabbit again; her size frightens him. He drops a fan and a pair of gloves he has been carrying and rushes away. Alice finds that she cannot follow him and then discovers that she is growing smaller. She continues to shrink; soon she is the size of a mouse and is swimming about in the pool of tears. A mouse swims past and she seizes his tail. He is nervous, and it seems that no matter what Alice tries to say she manages to touch on the subject of cats, thereby shattering her rescuer's equanimity. Presently they reach shore, accompanied by a crowd of birds and other small creatures

805

which have also fallen in the water. The room that had imprisoned Alice has now disappeared. The group now engages in solemn debate on the question of how they are to dry themselves; here Carroll satirizes a committee meeting. After several lengthy addresses composed of windy nonsense, they find that the problem has solved itself. Then Alice inadvertently mentions cats again and the party breaks up. At this point the white rabbit reappears, hunting desperately for the articles he has lost. He is Carroll's caricature of a fussy, elderly person, officious, nervous and timid; like all cowards he is used to ordering his inferiors about—and in a state of perpetual anxiety over what his superiors may do to him.

It was the White Rabbit, trotting slowly back again, and looking anxiously about as it went, as if it had lost something; and she heard it muttering to itself, "The Duchess! The Duchess! Oh my dear paws! **Oh my fur and whiskers!** She'll get me executed, as sure as ferrets are ferrets! Where *can* I have dropped them, I wonder?" Alice guessed in a moment that it was looking for the fan and the pair of white kid gloves, and she very good-naturedly began hunting about for them, but they were nowhere to be seen—everything seemed to have changed since her swim in the pool; and the great hall, with the glass table and the little door, had vanished completely.

Very soon the Rabbit noticed Alice, as she went hunting about, and called out to her, in an angry tone, "Why, Mary Ann, what *are* you doing out here? Run home this moment, and fetch me a pair of gloves and a fan! Quick, now!" And Alice was so much frightened that she ran off at once in the direction it pointed to, without trying to explain the mistake that it had made.

"He took me for his housemaid," she said to herself as she ran. "How surprised he'll be when he finds out who I am! But I'd better take him his fan and gloves—that is, if I can find them." As she said this, she came upon a neat little house, on the door of which was a bright brass plate with the name "W. RABBIT," engraved upon it. She went in without knocking, and hurried upstairs, in great fear lest she should meet the real Mary Ann, . . .

Oh that those lips had language

Source: ON THE RECEIPT OF MY MOTHER'S PICTURE (Line 1)
Author: William Cowper (1731–1800)
First published: 1798
Type of work: Lyric poem

Context: Though William Cowper's mother died when the poet was only six years old, he remembered her vividly throughout his life. In 1798, his cousin Anne Bodham (1749–1846) found and sent him a portrait of his mother painted by D. Heins and reproduced in the J. C. Bailey, *Poems of William Cowper* (London: Methuen, 1906). So the poet was inspired to write an epistle in which rhymed couplets have rarely been handled so softly and warmly. Of it Tennyson wrote that he hardly dared read it for fear of breaking down. The poem was first printed by itself in 1798 without the author's knowledge or consent, then added to the 1808 edition of his complete works.

> **Oh that those lips had language!** Life has passed
> With me but roughly since I heard thee last.
> Those lips are thine—thy own sweet smiles I see
> That same that oft in childhood solaced me;
> Voice only fails, else how distinct they say,
> "Grieve not, my child, chase all thy fears away!"
> The meek intelligence of those dear eyes
> (Blest be the art that can immortalize,
> The art that baffles time's tyrannic claim
> To quench it) here shines on me still the same.

Oh! that we two were Maying

Source: THE SAINT'S TRAGEDY (Act II, sc. ix)
Author: Charles Kingsley (1819–1875)
First published: 1848
Type of work: Dramatic tragedy

Context: St. Elizabeth of Hungary, daughter of the Hungarian King Andrew II, was born in 1207. She was betrothed at the age of four to Louis (or Lewis), son of the Landgrave of Thuringia, who was about the same age. They were married when she was fourteen. Disliking the splendors and vanities of court, she had already begun to cultivate a pious and charitable way of life; she was widely known for her generosity, particularly during the great famine of 1225. She also built hospitals and engaged in other charitable works, for all of which she was censured by Louis' family. Her husband left on a crusade in 1227 and died en route to the Holy Land; Louis' brother immediately deprived Elizabeth of her regency and exiled her from the court because her charities had wasted state funds. The people she had assisted were afraid to take her in, and her sufferings were great. Eventually she took refuge in the monastery of Kitzingen, where her aunt was abbess. When her husband's companions returned from the crusade with his body, she told them of the wrongs that had been done to her and to her three children; her rights were subsequently restored. She did not accept the regency, but joined the Order of St. Francis instead, devoting her income as Landgravine to charity. She died in 1231 and was canonized four years later. Kingsley's drama is based on the biography by Conrad of Marburg, one of Elizabeth's contemporaries. Kingsley sees her life as an internal struggle between the need for a normal human

807

existence and the demands of a religion which believed that family relationships were depraved. The play opens with Elizabeth sorrowing because people dislike her pious ways, describes her marriage and her conflict between love and doctrine, and introduces Conrad. He is a monk who exercises a great influence over her, taking advantage of her devout nature. He is a cold fanatic devoted to a system rather than to God, and he uses Elizabeth to further his own ambitions and those of the Church. There is a meeting between Louis and his advisers in which the depleted treasury and the seditious preaching of Conrad are discussed; Elizabeth impresses all with her saintly motives. The next scene is an idyllic one, in which Elizabeth sings for her husband:

Oh! that we two were Maying
Down the stream of the soft spring breeze;
Like children with violets playing
In the shade of the whispering trees.

Oh! that we two sat dreaming
On the sward of some sheep-trimmed down,
Watching the white mist steaming
Over river and mead and town.

Oh! that we two lay sleeping
In our nest in the churchyard sod,
With our limbs at rest on the quiet earth's breast,
And our souls at home with God!

Oh! what a tangled web we weave when first we practice to deceive

Source: MARMION (Canto VI, stanza 17)
Author: Sir Walter Scott (1771–1832)
First published: 1808
Type of work: Narrative poem

Context: Marmion is a long romantic poem which tells the story of Lord Marmion of Fontenaye. The second such poem Scott offered to the public, it achieved considerable popularity but was somewhat less successful than its predecessor, *The Lay of the Last Minstrel*. The background of the poem is the battle at Flodden in Northumberland in 1513, in which James IV of Scotland was defeated by the Earl of Surrey. Lord Marmion pays a visit to Castle Norham and learns that his host's wife, the Lady Heron, is across the Scottish border, visiting at the court of King James. He lets it be known that he is going that way and obtains a palmer for companion and guide. Marmion is aware that there are stories about Lady Heron, and women are his weakness. His host jokes about Marmion's former page, who had resembled a girl; Marmion replies angrily that the page is at Lindisfarne. The scene shifts to St. Catherine's abbey, where a novice, the Lady Clare, is being received. In the abbey's dungeon, church officials prepare to execute Marmion's former page, actually Constance de Beverley, who had broken her vows and gone to live with Marmion. Before she is walled up alive, she reveals that Lady Clare, for whom Marmion had thrown her over, has fled to the abbey for protection. Marmion had framed Clare's suitor, Wilton, with forged papers, speared him, and left him for dead. During his journey, Marmion is beset with doubts, fears, and what he considers ill omens; he regrets betraying Constance to the church in order to be rid of her. Arriving at James' court, he is well received; but he and the Lady Heron eye each other, and James is not pleased. She is his mistress, and he has Marmion housed at Tantallon, the castle of Lord Douglas. Meanwhile, Clare and the Abbess have been captured by the Scots and are also being brought to Tantallon. The battle, when it begins, brings Marmion forth to join in the fight. In the midst of battle he sees the palmer, now clad in armor, and recognizes him. He is Wilton, still alive and bent on vengeance.

A sudden light on Marmion broke:—
"Ah! dastard fool, to reason lost!"
He muttered; " 'T was nor fay nor ghost
I met upon the moonlight wold,
But living man of earthly mould.
   O dotage blind and gross!
Had I but fought as wont, one thrust
Had laid De Wilton in the dust,
   My path no more to cross.—
How stand we now?—he told his tale
To Douglas, and with some avail;
   'T was therefore gloomed his rugged brow.—
Will Surrey dare to entertain
'Gainst Marmion, charge disproved and vain?
   Small risk of that, I trow.
Yet Clare's sharp questions must I shun,
Must separate Constance from the nun—
Oh! what a tangled web we weave
When first we practise to deceive!
A Palmer too!—no wonder why
I felt rebuked beneath his eye;
I might have known there was but one
Whose look could quell Lord Marmion."

Oil on troubled waters

Source: ECCLESIASTICAL HISTORY OF THE ENGLISH NATION (Book III, chapter 15)
Author: The Venerable Bede (673–735)
First transcribed: c. 735
Type of work: Church history

Context: Our traditional expressions concerning the use of oil in calming troubled waters, which we use in so many ways, have their origin in a miracle recounted by Bede. He was the first important English scholar and historian, a product of that great though short-lived civilization which flourished in the kingdom of Northumbria during the seventh and eighth centuries. A learned man who wrote in Latin and knew Greek, Bede was the author of a large number of works including Bible commentaries, various treatises, and the *Ecclesiastical History,* for which last he is chiefly remembered. He is also believed to have originated our custom of determining dates from the year of Christ's birth. So highly was his history regarded that it was one of the books which King Alfred translated into Old English for the benefit and instruction of his people. Bede received his education in the Benedictine monastery at Wearmouth and spent his later life at its sister institution in Jarrow, living a holy life and achieving renown as teacher and scholar. He was so deeply and widely respected that during the following century the epithet "Venerable" was attached to his name. His work is of highest importance to students of early England; it is virtually the only comprehensive, contemporary account of its times. Among the many events and personages described in the history is the story of Bishop Aidan, a saintly man who died in 651 and who was said to have performed three miracles. His generosity was proverbial, as was his holiness. Of the miracles attributed to him, the third, which occurred during the last few days of his life, is given below:

. . . A certain priest, whose name was Utta, a man of great gravity and sincerity, and on that account honoured by all men, even the princes of the world, being ordered to Kent, to bring from thence, as wife for King Oswy, Eanfleda, the daughter of King Edwin, who had been carried thither when her father was killed; and intending to go thither by land, but to return with the virgin by sea, repaired to Bishop Aidan, entreating him to offer up his prayers to our Lord for him and his company, who were then to set out on their journey. He, blessing and recommending them to our Lord, at the same time gave them some holy oil, saying, "I know that when you go abroad, you will meet with a storm and contrary wind; but do you remember to **cast this oil I give you into the sea,** and the wind shall cease immediately; you will have pleasant calm weather, and return home safe."

All which fell out as the bishop had predicted. For in the first place, the winds raging, the sailors endeavoured to ride it out at anchor, but all to no purpose; for the sea breaking in on all sides, and the ship beginning to be filled with water, they all concluded that certain death was at hand; the priest at last, remembering the bishop's words, laid hold of the phial and cast some of the oil into the sea, which, as had been foretold, became presently calm. Thus it came to pass that the man of God, by the spirit of prophecy, foretold the storm that was to happen, and by virtue of the same spirit, though absent, appeased the same. Which miracle was not told me by a person of little credit, but by Cynemund, a most faithful priest of our church, who declared that it was related to him by Utta, the priest, on and by whom the same was wrought.

Old families last not three oaks

Source: HYDRIOTAPHIA: URN BURIAL (Chapter 5)
Author: Sir Thomas Browne (1605–1682)
First published: 1658
Type of work: Philosophy

Context: This philosophical physician and scientist set out to write a report concerning some forty or fifty Roman funeral urns which were exhumed near Norwich. His speculative nature led him beyond the bounds of a mere scientific report to a disquisition on burial customs in general, ranging, of course, through his vast knowledge of classical literature. In this final chapter, a speculative dissertation on death, Browne considers the brevity of human life and the impermanence of both human fame and the monuments built to perpetuate it. Ancient heroes, he observes, have already outlasted their monuments; but, since time itself is drawing to an end, it now seems futile to attempt to establish enduring fame.

And therefore restless inquietude for the diuturnity of our memories unto present considerations seems a vanity almost out of date, and superanuated piece of folly. . . . 'Tis too late to be ambitious. The great mutations of the world are acted, our time may be too short for our designes. To extend our memories by monuments, whose death we daily pray for, and whose duration we cannot hope, without injury to our expectations in the advent of the last day, were a contradiction to our beliefs. We whose generations are ordained in this setting part of time, are providentially taken off from such imaginations. And being necessitated to eye the remaining particle of futurity, are naturally constituted unto thoughts of the next world, and cannot excusably decline the consideration of that duration, which maketh pyramids pillars of snow, and all that's past a moment. . . .

There is no antidote against the opium of time, which temporally considereth all things; our fathers find their graves in our short memories, and sadly tell us how we may be buried in our survivors. . . . Generations pass while some trees stand, and

811

old families last not three oaks. To be read by bare inscriptions, . . . to hope for eternity in aenigmaticall epithetes, or first letters of our names, to be studied by antiquaries, who we were, . . . are cold consolations unto the students of perpetuity, even by everlasting languages.

An old man is twice a child

Source: HAMLET (Act II, sc. ii, l. 403)
Author: William Shakespeare (1564–1616)
First published: 1603
Type of work: Dramatic tragedy

Context: Rosencrantz and Guildenstern, former friends of Hamlet, Prince of Denmark, are instructed by King Claudius to cheer up the brooding prince and, if possible, to determine the cause of his melancholy. They fail to learn the real cause of his state of mind, but they are able to inform him of the approach of some traveling actors, whom Hamlet greets with delight. When Polonius, the Lord Chamberlain, who is tedious, naïve, and knowledgeable in the obvious, enters, Hamlet ridicules the old man, and Rosencrantz generalizes on age.

POLONIUS

Well be with you, gentlemen.

HAMLET

Hark you Guildenstern, and you too, at each ear a hearer—that great baby you see there is not yet out of his swaddling-clouts.

ROSENCRANTZ

Happily he is the second time come to them, for they say **an old man is twice a child.**

HAMLET

I will prophesy, he comes to tell me of the players; . . .
. . .

POLONIUS

The actors are come hither my lord.

Old religious factions are volcanoes burnt out

Source: SPEECH ON THE PETITION OF THE UNITARIANS
Author: Edmund Burke (1729–1797)
First published: 1808
Type of work: Parliamentary address

Context: Although Burke spoke with some frequency in Parliament in defense of the Catholics in Ireland, his views generally on religious toleration were not in advance of his age. When Fox, a leader of Parliament, attempted to have repealed several statutes directed against the Unitarians, Burke opposed such action. He argued that government, as representing society, had control over all the "publicly propagated doctrines of men." The Anglican Establishment he considered the agency of that control, and the Unitarians had promoted doctrines hostile to the Church of England. Burke regarded the extension of rights to the Unitarians as a move which would encourage all the evils of religious faction:

Old religious factions are volcanoes burnt out; on the lava and ashes and squalid scoriæ of old eruptions grow the peaceful olive, the cheering vine, and the sustaining corn. Such was the first, such the second condition of Vesuvius. But when a new fire bursts out, a face of desolations comes on, not to be rectified in ages. Therefore, when men come before us, and rise up like an exhalation from the ground, they come in a questionable shape, and we must *exorcise* them, and try whether their intests be wicked or charitable, whether they bring airs from heaven or blasts from hell. This is the first time that our records of Parliament have heard, or our experience or history given us an account of any religious congregation or association known by the name which these petitioners have assumed. . . .

Old Time the clock setter, that bald sexton Time

Source: KING JOHN (Act III, sc. i, l. 324)
Author: William Shakespeare (1564–1616)
First published: 1623
Type of work: Historical drama

Context: England and France have just joined as allies after the marriage of John's niece, Blanch of Spain, to the French dauphin, Lewis, when Cardinal Pandulph comes as a messenger to John from the pope. John refused to allow Stephen Langton to become Archbishop of Canterbury and tells Pandulph that "no Italian priest/ Shall tithe or toll in our dominions." For this disobedience and blasphemy he is immediately excommunicated. Philip, in fear of like excommunication, but baffled over exactly what to do about the newly formed alliance, finally gives up his friendship for England. Blanch is horrified, Elinor, England's queen, is passionately upset, and the Bastard comments that there will be new violence shortly.

PHILIP
. . . England, I will fall from thee.

813

O foul revolt of French inconstancy!

JOHN
France, thou shalt rue this hour within this hour.

BASTARD
Old Time the clock setter, that bald sexton Time,
Is it as he will? Well then, France shall rue.

BLANCH
The sun's o'ercast with blood. Fair day adieu!
Which is the side that I must go withal?
I am with both, . . .
. . .

Older than the rocks among which she sits

Source: THE RENAISSANCE ("Leonardo da Vinci")
Author: Walter Pater (1839–1894)
First published: 1873
Type of work: Aesthetic criticism

Context: English critic, essayist, and novelist, Walter Pater was associated with the Pre-Raphaelite Brotherhood and was one of the most vociferous defenders of the "art for art's sake" aesthetic doctrine. Spending most of his life in scholarly seclusion at Oxford University, he first gained fame with *The Renaissance,* a series of essays on artists whose works best reflect the qualities and beauties of the Renaissance era. Of the works he commented: "To define beauty, not in the most abstract but in the most concrete form possible, to find not its universal formula, but the formula which expresses most adequately this or that special manifestation of it, is the aim of the true student of aesthetics." He was convinced that one's education becomes complete only in proportion to his increased susceptibility to beauty in its various forms. His purpose, then, was to encourage in his readers sympathetic cognizance of the struggle for beauty in an age of intellectual ferment. Pater, in describing the work of Leonardo, asserts the masterpiece to be *La Gioconda,* the Mona Lisa. Seated in a marble chair, in a circle of fantastic rocks, she in her beauty is expressive of "what in the ways of a thousand years men had come to desire." She is the living soul of experience, embodying in her charm all the enigmas of human culture:

. . . All the thoughts and experiences of the world have etched and moulded there, in that which they have of power to refine and make expressive the outward form, the animalism of Greece, the lust of Rome, the mysticism of the middle age with its spiritual ambition and imaginative loves, the return of the Pagan world, the sins of the Borgias. **She is older than the rocks among which she sits;** like the vampire, she has been dead many times, and learned the secrets of the grave; and has been a diver in deep seas, and keeps their fallen day about her; and trafficked for strange webs with Eastern merchants; and, as Leda, was the mother of Helen of Troy, and, as Saint Anne, the mother of Mary; and all this has been to her but as the sound of lyres and flutes, and lives only in the delicacy with which it has moulded the changing lineaments, and tinged the eyelids and the hands. . . .

The oldest man he seemed that ever wore gray hair

Source: RESOLUTION AND INDEPENDENCE (Stanza 8)
Author: William Wordsworth (1770–1850)
First published: 1807
Type of work: Didactic poem

Context: This poem records a meeting Wordsworth actually had with an old man, the one described in the quotation. The old man, survivor of his wife and his ten children, wandered about the English countryside, eking out an existence by gathering leeches, which he sold to doctors to use in drawing blood from their patients. His fortitude impressed the poet greatly. Here was a man who had suffered much and still retained his dignity and his nobility. Wordsworth was at the time more or less despondent, for his poetry had been ridiculed, his income was exceedingly slim, and his inheritance had been withheld, so that to him life seemed empty. The example of the old man gave the poet inspiration to look at life once again with confidence. The poet says he was inspired to faith in his own abilities and that he no longer needed to fear that he might fall victim, like Thomas Chatterton (referred to in Stanza 7), to despondency and suicide. The eighth stanza of the poem tells how Wordsworth, walking along in melancholy fashion and reviewing how life has mistreated him, meets the old leech-gatherer, who seems almost heaven-sent.

> Now, whether it were by peculiar grace,
> A leading from above, a something given,
> Yet it befell that, in this lonely place,
> When I with these untoward thoughts had striven,
> Beside a pool bare to the eye of heaven
> I saw a Man before me unawares:
> **The oldest man he seemed that ever wore grey hairs.**

The Olive Grove of Academe

Source: PARADISE REGAINED (Book IV, l. 244)
Author: John Milton (1608–1674)
First published: 1671
Type of work: Epic poem

Context: As Paradise was lost because man succumbed to the temptation of Satan by eating the forbidden fruit of the Tree of Knowledge in the Garden of Eden, even so, says Milton, Paradise was regained because the man Jesus refused to succumb to the temptation of Satan in his forty days of trial in the wilderness. Satan, observing with alarm the baptism of Christ and the proclamation by God that He is His Son, calls together his council in Hell and determines to attempt to bring about the fall of Christ as he had caused the fall of Eve. Led into the wilderness, Christ, fasting, is tempted by Satan to assume the power of turning stones into bread and of freeing Israel from Roman dominion. Unsuccessful in these temptations, Satan vainly offers Jesus the power of Rome and the wisdom of Athens:

> Look once more e're we leave this specular Mount
> Westward, much nearer by Southwest, behold
> Where on the Aegean shore a City stands
> Built nobly, pure the air, and light the soil,
> Athens the eye of Greece, Mother of Arts
> And Eloquence, native to famous wits
> Or hospitable, in her sweet recess,
> City or Suburban, studious walks and shades;
> See there **the Olive Grove of Academe,**
> Plato's retirement . . .

On a high horse

Source: PRIVATE CORRESPONDENCE OF DAVID GARRICK (Volume I, p. 205)
Author: John Brown (1715–1766)
First published: 1831
Type of work: Personal letter

Context: Several figures important in Georgian literature had a share in the "high horse" expression. The Reverend John Brown phrased it in a letter to the great actor David Garrick (1717–1779), referring to Dr. Samuel Johnson (1709–1784). Someone, probably Garrick with his great vanity, preserved the letter, possibly with a view to writing his autobiography in his declining years. There is no indication of the assembler of this and hundreds of other letters into a huge two-volume folio edition published in London by Colburn and Bentley in 1831, long after the death of all of the writers. The concept of a leader astride a tall horse far above his followers is not new. Mark Antony declared of Julius Caesar that he "sits high on all people's hearts." Oliver Wendell Holmes quotes Elsie Venner: "It makes a man imperious to sit a horse." Even today's scorner tells any would-be important man: "Come off your high horse!" Rivalries were involved in John Brown's eighteenth century use of the phrase. The clergyman was an erratic who shortly afterward committed suicide by cutting his throat when bad health prevented his trip to Russia for work on education. He had been acquainted with the famous actor, David Garrick, for whom he wrote two plays whose Prologues and Epilogues were added by the actor. First came *Barbarossa* (1754), with the popular Mossop in the title role and Garrick as Achmet. Then two years later Brown completed *Athelstan,* in which Garrick played the lead. It was somewhat better theater, though still a turgid tragedy. Following its performance, bickering among various companies of actors, combined with the illness of both Garrick and his beloved wife, decided "Roscius," as Garrick's admirers called him, to spend a year or so on the continent. Brown, who remained in England, completed *The History of the Rise and Progress of Poetry* in 1764, and Samuel Johnson in 1765 finally published his eight-volume edition of Shakespeare. Most scholars greeted its Preface as one of the finest pieces of criticism of the great poet-dramatist's work. But Johnson sometimes criticized Garrick, as when he commented upon one of the actor-playwright's satirical attacks that it lacked the vigor of the bow, but that he dreaded the venom of the shafts. Therefore Brown, friend and collaborator of Garrick, took up the battle, shortly after the Garricks' return to England. He accused Johnson of assuming a high and mighty position from which to comment on Shakespeare. His letter to Garrick, dated Newcastle, October 27, 1765, begins:

MY DEAR SIR:
Visits and engagements have prevented me from sooner answering yours. I am glad to hear of your recovery from your illness, and hope you will have no occasion for your epitaph these fifty years, except to give your friends the pleasure of reading it, which I desire you will do the next time you write to me. I think you were a little quick two or three times in your last letter, which I do not much dislike in a friend, by-the-by, especially when there is not much reason for it, as I look upon it as a proof of his regard—at least it is so with me . . .

I have seen some extracts from Johnson's Preface to his "Shakespeare." In my humble opinion, he is as improper a critic for that great poet as any that have yet appeared. No feeling nor pathos about him! Altogether **upon the high horse,** and blustering about Imperial Tragedy! How is this work relished by the public? . . .

. . . with compliments to Mrs. Garrick, I remain,
Dear SIR, always most truly yours,
J. Brown.

817

Once a gentleman, and always a gentleman

Source: LITTLE DORRITT (Book II, chapter 28)
Author: Charles Dickens (1812–1870)
First published: 1855–1857
Type of work: Novel

Context: Arthur Clennam, bankrupt because of the failure and suicide of the wealthy Mr. Merdle, is in the Marshalsea prison. He resists the urging of his lawyer, Mr. Rugg, to be moved to the more respectable King's Bench prison; his reason for preferring the Marshalsea is that it was the home of the universally beloved Little Dorrit while her father was a prisoner. After Mr. Rugg's departure, John Baptist Cavalletto, Clennam's friend, ushers in the infamous Rigaud Blandois, who had dropped out of sight after being last seen at the home of Clennam's mother, with whom Clennam is not on the best of terms. Clennam tries to get information about what business Rigaud has had with Mrs. Clennam, but Rigaud treats the inquiry with great disdain and refuses to tell what the affair is about. It has always been Rigaud's contention that he is a gentleman born and that it is the part of a gentleman to treat everybody, especially servants and other underlings, with the utmost contempt. He addresses John Baptist, who had once been arrested for smuggling:

"Contrabrand beast," added Rigaud, "bring Port wine! I'll drink nothing but Porto-Porto."

The contrabrand beast, however, assuring all present, with his significant finger, that he peremptorily declined to leave his post at the door, Signor Panco offered his services. He soon returned, with the bottle of wine: which, according to the custom of the place, originating in a scarcity of workscrews among the Collegians (in common with a scarcity of much else), was already opened for use.

"Madman! A large glass," said Rigaud.

Signor Panco put a tumbler before him; not without a visible conflict of feeling on the question of throwing it at his head.

"Haha!" boasted Rigaud. **"Once a gentleman, and always a gentleman.** A gentleman from the beginning, and a gentleman to the end. What the Devil! A gentleman must be waited on, I hope? It's a part of my character to be waited on!"

He half filled the tumbler as he said it, and drank off the contents when he had done saying it.

One among a thousand

Source: JOB 33:23
Author: Unknown
First transcribed: c. 900–500 B.C.
Type of work: Religious saga

Context: Job refuses to blame God, even when he loses his seven sons, his three daughters, and all his wealth. When he remains loyal to God in this adversity, Satan maintains that the test has not been severe enough, whereupon God grants Satan permission to bring physical affliction, short of death, to Job. But even when covered from crown to sole with boils, Job refuses to curse God. He is visited by his three friends: Eliphaz the Temanite, Bildad the Shuhite, and Zophar the Naamathite. The three friends sit with Job in silence for seven days and seven nights before they speak; then they say that Job must be a sinner in order to receive such terrible treatment. But Job maintains his innocence in the face of all their arguments, causing the three friends finally to fall silent. Then Elihu speaks up angrily. He is angry because the three find no way to answer Job, and he is angry because Job justifies himself, rather than God. Elihu seeks in his turn to convict Job of sin which will justify the seeming punishment being visited upon the good man. Elihu maintains that God is greater than man, that He speaks to man, that He saves man, if man will but hear:

> For God speaketh once, yea twice, yet man perceiveth it not.
> In a dream, in a vision of the night, when deep sleep falleth upon men, in slumberings upon the bed;
> Then he openeth the ears of men, and sealeth their instruction,
> That he may withdraw man from his purpose, and hide pride from man.
> He keepeth back his soul from the pit, and his life from perishing by the sword.
> He is chastened also with pain upon his bed, and the multitude of his bones with strong pain:
> So that his life abhorreth bread, and his soul dainty meat.
> His flesh is consumed away, that it cannot be seen; and his bones that were not seen stick out.
> Yea, his soul draweth near unto the grave, and his life to the destroyers.
> If there be a messenger with him, an interpreter, **one among a thousand,** to shew unto man his uprightness:
> Then he is gracious unto him, and saith, Deliver him from going down to the pit: I have found a ransom.

One blast upon his bugle horn were worth a thousand men

Source: THE LADY OF THE LAKE (Canto VI, stanza 18, ll. 481–482)
Author: Sir Walter Scott (1771–1832)
First published: 1810
Type of work: Narrative poem

Context: Ellen Douglas, daughter of a banished lord, appears at Stirling

Castle just after the king has defeated Clan-Alpine, a revolted clan led by the mighty Roderick Dhu. She and her escort, the old minstrel Allan-bane, are conducted into a room filled with rough soldiers. At first the soldiers' attitude towards the girl is one of coarse levity, but when she uncovers her face, her beauty stills them with wonder and admiration. She announces that she has a ring, the gift of the king, the displaying of which to the monarch will gain her admission to her captive father. The officer who appears to conduct her is flippant and forward until he sees the ring; when he examines its design he becomes highly respectful. Ellen is conducted into a room in which there is not her father, but the wounded Roderick Dhu. He demands that Allan-bane sing of the victory of Clan-Alpine over Dermid's race, a song he has heard before. The minstrel obeys and describes the ebbing and flowing fortunes of the battle. At one point the forces of Clan-Alpine are pushed back: and then where was Roderick Dhu, the sound of whose horn was as stimulating as would be the arrival of a thousand fresh soldiers?

· · ·

But Moray wheeled his rearward rank
Of horsemen on Clan-Alpine's flank,—
"My banner-man, advance!
I see," he cried, "their column shake.
Now, gallants! for your ladies' sake,
Upon them with the lance."—
The horsemen dashed among the rout,
As deer break through the broom;
Their steeds are stout, their swords are out,
They soon make lightsome room.
Clan-Alpine's best are backward borne—
Where, where was Roderick then!
One blast upon his bugle horn
Were worth a thousand men.
And refluent through the pass of fear
The battle's tide was poured;
Vanished the Saxon's struggling spear,
Vanished the mountain sword.

· · ·

One-horse town

Source: SKETCHES NEW AND OLD ("The Undertaker's Chat")
Author: Mark Twain (Samuel Langhorne Clemens, 1835–1910)
First published: 1875
Type of work: Anecdote

Context: This brief sketch recounts the tribute paid by an undertaker in a small country village, in a day when the wealth and stature of a community could be measured by its population of horses, to a departed citizen loved by all. It soon becomes evident that the deceased was a plain man, humble and unpretentious, happy by disposition, and blessed with a sense of humor. The language used by the undertaker is that picturesque frontier dialect which Twain employed so effectively, and the recital exhibits his rare ability to describe touching incidents in humorous terms without making them less touching. The departed citizen had known his end was near. His friends had wanted him to have a lavish coffin with a silver plate on the lid; but the dying man refused such ostentation, observing that "wher' he was going to a body would find it considerable better to attract attention by a picturesque moral character." When his relatives planned a big funeral, he "said he was down on flummery—didn't want any procession—fill the hearse full of mourners, and get out a stern line and tow *him* behind." The undertaker, astounded and at the same time filled with admiration for anyone "so down on style," continues his recital:

". . . He was just set on having things the way he wanted them, and he took a solid comfort in laying his little plans. He had me measure him and take a whole raft of directions; then he had the minister stand up behind a long box with a tablecloth over it, to represent the coffin, and read his funeral sermon, saying 'Angcore, angcore!' at the good places, and making him scratch out every bit of brag about him, and all the hifalutin; and then he made them trot out the choir so's he could help them pick out the tunes for the occasion, and he got them to sing 'Pop Goes the Weasel,' because he'd always liked that tune when he was downhearted, and solemn music made him sad; and when they sung that with tears in their eyes (because they all loved him), and his relations grieving around, he just laid there as happy as a bug, and trying to beat time and showing all over how much he enjoyed it; and presently he got worked up and excited, and tried to join in, for, mind you, he was pretty proud of his abilities in the singing line; but the first time he opened his mouth and was just going to spread himself his breath took a walk.

"I never see a man snuffed out so sudden. Ah, it was a great loss—a powerful loss to this poor little **one-horse town.** . . ."

One, if by land, and two, if by sea

Source: PAUL REVERE'S RIDE (Stanza 2)
Author: Henry Wadsworth Longfellow (1807–1882)
First published: 1861
Type of work: Patriotic poem

Context: Paul Revere (1735–1818) was a silversmith by trade; he also worked in gold and was a skilled engraver. Most of his life was spent in Boston. He had some military experience prior to the Revolution, having taken part in the capture of Crown Point in 1756. Afterward he set up shop and produced much fine silverware and a number of prints. Of these, his engraving of the Boston Massacre is probably the best known. He also engraved the plates from which Massachusetts' first paper money was printed. Revere had Revolutionary sympathies and in 1774 became one of a group of men who patrolled Boston at night in order to observe the movements of British troops. On April 14, 1775, it was noted that some sort of military exercise was in preparation; and on the 18th they saw troops marching across the common toward the inner bay. Revere had a prearranged signal set up in one of the Northend churches, either Christ Church or the church in North Square which was later destroyed by the British. He then crossed the river to the Charlestown side, where he had a horse ready, and awaited the signal. When he saw it, he immediately rode to warn the patriots. He was barely in time; by 2:30 A.M. a party of some 800 British troops had landed at Lechmere Point and were marching on Lexington. Revere fought throughout the Revolutionary War and afterward returned to his trade, branching out into bells and cannon; he was the first in America, it is said, to smelt and refine copper. Longfellow's familiar poem has made his name and deeds a household word for many generations. He later incorporated the poem into *Tales of a Wayside Inn;* this is a collection of tales in verse, told by a number of wayfarers staying at an Inn, and *Paul Revere's Ride* is the first tale in the volume. It is a stormy night outside the Red Lion Inn, in Sudbury; but inside all is warmth and good cheer. The characters are introduced, and Longfellow describes the music and laughter. Then silence falls, and everyone begs the Landlord for a story. At length, and after much coaxing, he begins:

Listen, my children, and you shall hear
Of the midnight ride of Paul Revere,
On the eighteenth of April, in Seventy-five;
Hardly a man is now alive
Who remembers that famous day and year.

He said to his friend, "If the British march
By land or sea from the town to-night,
Hang a lantern aloft in the belfry arch
Of the North Church tower as a signal light,—
One, if by land, and two, if by sea;
And I on the opposite shore will be,
Ready to ride and spread the alarm
Through every Middlesex village and farm,
For the country folk to be up and to arm."

Then he said, "Good night!" and with muffled oar
Silently rowed to the Charlestown shore, . . .

One leak will sink a ship, and one sin will destroy a sinner

Source: THE PILGRIM'S PROGRESS (Part II)
Author: John Bunyan (1628–1688)
First published: 1684 (Part II)
Type of work: Religious allegory

Context: As Part I of this work recounted the trials of Christian to avoid temptation and save his soul in reaching the Heavenly Jerusalem, so this part of the work tells of the remorse that struck Christiana, Christian's wife, when she realized that she should have accompanied her husband on his journey. In a mood of contrition she and her children set out to follow Christian to salvation. On the way they pass the same temptations that beset Christian earlier and benefit from the same assistance. Christiana and the children stop at the house of Interpreter, and, as he had done for Christian before them, the good man gives them a store of pious advice to follow on the road ahead:

'Tis easier watching a night or two, than to sit up a whole year together. So 'tis easier for one to begin to profess well, than to hold out as he should to the end.

Every shipmaster, when in a storm, will willingly cast that overboard that is of the smallest value in the vessel; but who will throw the best out first? None but he that feareth not God.

One leak will sink a ship; one sin will destroy a sinner.

He that forgets his friend is ungrateful unto him; but he that forgets his Saviour is unmerciful to himself.

He that lives in sin, and looks for happiness hereafter, is like him that soweth cockle, and thinks to fill his barn with wheat or barley.

One must eat to live, not live to eat

Source: THE MISER (Act III, sc. ii)
Author: Molière (Jean Baptiste Poquelin, 1622–1673)
First published: 1669
Type of work: Dramatic comedy

Context: Miserly Harpagon is giving a party honoring Mariane, the lovely girl he hopes to marry; but he wishes the party to cost no more than necessary. Valère, a rich young Neapolitan who is acting incognito as Harpagon's steward, curries favor with his master by pretending to approve of his stingy ways. When Jacques, the cook, says the banquet should include a great variety of foods, Valère instructs him in the virtue of thrift. (The great man whose name Valère cannot recall was Socrates. "He used to say that other

823

men lived to eat, but that he ate to live."—Diogenes Laertius (c. 200): *Socrates,* 14.)

> VALÈRE
>
> You must learn, maître Jacques, you and your likes, that to invite to a table overladen with food is the act of an assassin; in order to show yourself the friend of those whom you ask, frugality must reign over the repast you give; and, following the old saying, **one must eat to live, and not live to eat** (*il faut manger pour vivre, et non pas vivre pour manger*).
>
> HARPAGON
>
> Ah! that is well said! Come, let me embrace you for that word. It is the finest sentence I have heard in my life. *One must live to eat, and not eat to li* . . . No, that is not it. What was it you said?
>
> VALÈRE
>
> That **one must eat to live, and not live to eat.**
>
> HARPAGON
>
> Yes. Do you hear? Who is the great man who said that?
>
> VALÈRE
>
> I do not now remember his name.

One of love's April-fools

Source: THE OLD BACHELOR (Act I, sc. i)
Author: William Congreve (1670–1729)
First published: 1693
Type of work: Dramatic comedy

Context: Bellmour and Sharper are discussing the fitness of Belinda, Bellmour's love, as a wife. According to Sharper, she is too proud, too inconstant, too affected, and too witty, but Bellmour points out that she is wealthy, a very desirable feature in a wife that makes her undesirable qualities seem of little consequence. The two are joined by old Heartwell, a pretended woman-hater. Bellmour asks him what fine lady he has been putting out of countenance by telling her unpleasant truths about herself. He confesses that he has not been fawning over and flattering any light women. Bellmour remarks that if Heartwell had come a little earlier he could have argued about women with Vainlove. This remark causes Heartwell to say that Vainlove is one of love's April-fools, always on some pointless amatory errand and never accomplishing anything.

824

I confess I have not been sneering fulsome lies and nauseous flattery, fawning upon a little tawdry whore that will fawn upon me again, and entertain any puppy that comes, like a tumbler, with the same tricks over and over. For such I guess may have been your late employment.

BELLMOUR

Would thou hadst come a little sooner! Vainlove would have wrought thy conversion, and been a champion for the cause.

HEARTWELL

What, has he been here? That's **one of love's April-fools,** is always upon some errand that's to no purpose, ever embarking in adventures, yet never comes to harbor.

One of the <u>has beens</u>

Source: THE EVERY-DAY BOOK (June 22)
Author: William Hone (1780–1842)
First published: 1826
Type of work: Day book (miscellany)

Context: The term "has-been," used to indicate one who has outlived his usefulness or fame, is an old one. William Birnie used it in *The Blame of Kirk-Buriall* (1606): "Being now but un-while, and as an hes-beene;" and Robert Burns employs it more amusingly in *The Inventory* (1786). This poem concerns a farmer who must list all his possessions, most of them about worn out, for tax purposes. Referring to the lead horse in his team, the farmer remarks whimsically that "My han' afore's a gude auld has-been." The great popularity of Hone's *Every-Day Book* has probably done most to perpetuate the term. Hone was an unusual man and a tireless collector of unusual information, which he incorporated into a number of books. In *The Every-Day Book* he gives all the days of the year in their chronological order, together with numerous customs, anecdotes, historical passages, and other bits of information relating to them. He saw the work as a combination of history and calendar and a perpetual key to the almanac. The result is a treasury of miscellaneous and curious knowledge. Birthdays of famous persons, holiday customs of the past, unusual traditions, and natural phenomena are all dealt with in one way or another. In addition to these activities, Hone fought for freedom of the press and wrote a few satires and parodies, one of which was entitled *The Apocryphal New Testament.* Another, *The Political House that Jack Built,* was enormously popular. In spite of these successes he was not a practical man and was usually in financial difficulties. Among the information given under June 22 in *The Every-Day Book* is an account of a strange custom formerly held in the village of Garrett. This was a mock election.

Hone visited Garrett and interviewed the only man still living who had once been elected to that whimsical office, "Master of the Horse." His account of the meeting with that dignitary is given below:

> . . . The person so dignified at its latter elections was pointed out as the oldest individual in Wandsworth, who had figured in the "solemn mockery," and as, therefore, most likely to furnish information, from "reminiscences" of his "ancient dignity." He was described as "Old Jack Jones the sawyer;" and it was added, "You'll find him by the water side; turn down by the church; he is lame and walks with a crutch; any body'll tell you of him; he lives in a cottage by the bridge; if you don't find him at home, he is most likely at the Plume of Feathers, or just in the neighborhood; you'll be sure to know him if you meet him—he is a thorough oddity, and can tell all about the Garrett election." The "Plume" was resorted to, and "old Jack Jones" obligingly sought by Mr. Attree the landlord, who for that purpose peregrinated the town; and the "Master of the Horse" made his entry into the parlour with as much alacrity as his wooden assistants helped him to. It was "the accustomed place," wherein he had told his story "many a time and oft;" and having heard, "up town" that there was "somebody quite curious about the Garrett Election," he was dragging his "slow length along," when "mine host of the *Feathers*" met him on the way.
>
> John Jones may be described as **"one of the <u>has</u> beens."** In his day he was tall of stature, stout of body, and had done as much work as any man of his time—when he was at it. But, then, he had overstrained himself, and for some years past had not been able to do a stroke of work; and he had seen a deal of "ran-dan," and a racketty life had racketted his frame. . . .

One prodigious ruin swallow all

Source: THE ILIAD (Book IV, l. 196, as translated by Alexander Pope)
Author: Homer (c. 850 B.C.)
First transcribed: Sixth century, B.C.
Type of work: Epic poem

Context: In the tenth year of the Trojan War a truce prevails for a time between the Greeks and the Trojans; the truce gives an opportunity for the two armies to have a single combat between Paris, who stole Helen from her husband, and Menelaus, the aggrieved spouse. The Trojans and their besiegers agree to let this combat between the two men decide the outcome of the war, caused by the theft of Helen. However, the fight is inconclusive, for Venus, the protector of Paris, rescues him from the fight and spirits him away from the battlefield when it becomes apparent that he will be the loser. After this episode among the mortals, the gods meet in council upon Mount Olympus to discuss the future of the war. They agree to the war's continuation, and Jupiter sends Minerva down to the battlefield to cause a breaking of the truce. Minerva, appearing as the Trojan warrior Laodocus, moves through the throng of Trojans until she finds Pandarus, whom she persuades to shoot an arrow, despite the terms of the truce, at Mene-

laus. The arrow wounds the Greek champion, though not fatally. Agamemnon, the leader of the Greeks, angry at the violation of the truce and the injury to his brother, vows, as the leader of the Greek forces, to open the fighting again. He predicts that total victory will come for the Greeks and that Troy, the kingdom of Priam, will be destroyed:

> Not thus our vows, confirm'd with wine and gore,
> Those hands we plighted, and those oaths we swore,
> Shall all be vain: when Heaven's revenge is slow,
> Jove but prepares to strike the fiercer blow.
> The day shall come, that great avenging day,
> When Troy's proud glories in the dust shall lay,
> When Priam's powers, and Priam's self shall fall,
> And **one prodigious ruin swallow all.**
> I see the god, already from the pole
> Bare his red arm, and bid the thunder roll;
> I see the Eternal all his fury shed,
> And shake his aegis o'er their guilty head.

One religion is as true as another

Source: ANATOMY OF MELANCHOLY (Part III, sec. 4, memb. 2, subs. 1)
Author: Robert Burton (1577–1640)
First published: 1621–1651
Type of work: Essays

Context: Having considered in the first two Partitions of his book the causes and cures of Melancholy, the eccentric bachelor and bookman who wrote it turns in Partition III to "Love-Melancholy." Not only does he parade the world's mad lovers, but his erotic psychology treats with many illustrative anecdotes drawn from his reading the common symptoms of love, from lack of appetite to a frenzy leading to murder or suicide. He gives evidence of the seventeenth century interest in the passionate un-

reasonableness of human nature. Partition III, the final section of *Anatomy of Melancholy*, which its author termed a study of melancholy growing out of love and religion, is chiefly a critique of marriage. Its bachelor compiler quotes twelve reasons in favor of marriage as well as many short synopses of tales of famous lovers of the past. In its final part, Burton proposes that people frightened by a personal Satan and by the Calvinistic doctrines of man's depravity and predestination, cure them-

827

selves by thought of a loving and merciful Christian God, or turn, as the Ancients did, to some other belief. He catalogues practitioners of many different beliefs of the Ancients, who considered Christianity as but one of many possible religions.

> . . . some of all sorts, good, bad, indifferent, true, false, zealous, Ambidexters (or people who would keep in with both parties), Neutralists, lukewarm Libertines, Atheists, etc. They will see these religious Sectaries agree amongst themselves, be reconciled all, before they will participate with, or believe any. They think in the meantime . . . we Christians adore a person put to death, with no more reason than the barbarous Getae worshipped Zamolxis, the Cilicians Mopsus, the Thebans Amphiaraus, and the Lebadeans Trophonius; **one religion is as true as another,** new fangled devices, all for human respects; great witted Aristotle's works are as much authentical to them as Scriptures, subtil Seneca's Epistles as Canonical as Saint Paul's, Pindar's Odes as good as the Prophet David's Psalms, Epictetus's Enchiridion equivalent to wise Solomon's Proverbs. . . .

One sweetly solemn thought

Source: NEARER HOME (Line 1)
Author: Phoebe Cary (1824–1871)
First published: 1854
Type of work: Religious lyric

Context: Phoebe Cary and her sister Alice wrote a considerable volume of verse, much of it with a religious or uplifting tone. "Nearer Home," or as it is sometimes called from its first line, "One sweetly solemn thought," was written by Phoebe after returning home from church one Sunday in 1852. It was published in 1854; and although its author long regarded it with indifference, it was set to music a number of times and became a favorite hymn throughout the entire United States. It is the one piece of work by which Phoebe is still remembered. The basic idea of the poem is that each day brings us closer to "the undiscovered country from whose bourne no traveler returns." But the author of "Nearer Home," unlike Hamlet, does not shrink from the journey. Like William Wordsworth (1770–1850), in "Ode: Intimations of Immortality," she will be returning to her true home, after a brief sojourn on earth. Death will not be something to fear, but a triumph, a reward for having lived in this world. As no one regrets passing from an imperfect condition into a perfect one, the author looks forward to the new life that will begin after the death of the body. The first four stanzas of the seven that comprise the poem are as follows:

One sweetly solemn thought
Comes to me o'er and o'er;
I am nearer home to-day
Than I ever have been before;

Nearer my Father's house,
Where the many mansions be;
Nearer the great white throne,
Nearer the crystal sea;

Nearer the bound of life,
Where we lay our burdens down;
Nearer leaving the cross,
Nearer gaining the crown

But lying darkly between,
Winding down through the night,
Is the silent, unknown stream,
That leads at last to the light.

One that would peep and botanize upon his mother's grave

Source: A POET'S EPITAPH (Stanza 5)
Author: William Wordsworth (1770–1850)
First published: 1800
Type of work: Lyric poem

Context: In his "Essay on Epitaphs" Wordsworth commented that "the writer of an epitaph is not an anatomist, who dissects the internal frame of the mind; he is not even a painter, who executes a portrait at leisure and in entire tranquillity: his delineation . . . is performed by the side of the grave; and, what is more, the grave of one whom he loves and admires." In "A Poet's Epitaph" Wordsworth rejects as epitaphists a Statist, experienced in public conflicts but without love for the individual man; a Lawyer, with "practised eye" and hard face; a fat Gourmand ("This grave no cushion is for thee"); a Soldier—unless he will "lay thy sword aside"; an anatomizing Physician; and a self-worshiping Moralist. But he welcomes the Poet "clad in russet brown," one who sees "In common things that round us lie/ Some random truths he can impart,—/ The harvest of a quiet eye/ That broods and sleeps on his own heart." Such a man may write a proper epitaph. Wordsworth's scornful rejection of the Physician appears in Stanza 5:

Physician art thou?—one, all eyes,
Philosopher!—a fingering slave,
**One that would peep and botanize
Upon his mother's grave?**

829

One thing only has been lent to youth and age in common—discontent

Source: YOUTH'S AGITATIONS (Lines 13–14)
Author: Matthew Arnold (1822–1888)
First published: 1852
Type of work: Sonnet

Context: Thwarted in love and crossed by a father who was too dominating to allow him to develop a sense of harmony with his fellow men, Arnold was the type of person to whom nothing seemed to fulfill its promised hopes; sensitive to his inability to come to terms with himself, he continually faced a deeply rooted sense of frustration. While he was later to form a compromise with life that lifted him above his unhappiness, he underwent several years of attempting to find the contentment that he felt was denied to him; however, even as he looked, he realized that youth, as it passed, had pleasures that he had overlooked. Regardless of how unhappy he had been, he knew that youth was better than death; in this poem, for example, he clearly shows that despite how unhappy he was as a youth, he will probably be equally miserable in age.

. . .

Shall I not joy youth's heats are left behind,
And breathe more happy in an even clime?—
Ah no, for then I shall begin to find
A thousand virtues in this hated time!

Then I shall wish its agitations back,
And all its thwarting currents of desire;
Then I shall praise the heat which then I lack,
And call this hurrying fever, generous fire;

And sigh that **one thing only has been lent
To youth and age in common—discontent.**

The only fault's with time

Source: LURIA (Act V, l. 169)
Author: Robert Browning (1812–1889)
First published: 1846
Type of work: Dramatic tragedy

Context: Browning, early in his literary career, cultivated the friendship of William Charles Macready, the greatest tragic actor of his time. The result of the friendship was a series of dramas encouraged by Macready but not enthusiastically received by the public. There can be no doubt, however, that the work helped to sharpen the talents which would later reach full

830

maturation in the dramatic monologues. In one such drama, Luria, a historical figure of the fifteenth century, is cast as the protagonist of a tragedy. A noble Moor, he is the commander of the Florentine forces against the Pisans. His campaigns on the foreign battlefields are a brilliant success, but so is the scheme of his enemies at home to cover him with suspicion and thus undermine his influence and power in the city. Luria, much like Shakespeare's Coriolanus, is victimized by the fickle populace, but unlike Coriolanus he does not strike back in wrath against his false friends and patrons. Instead, he submits to the ignominy of a public trial and, overwhelmed with grief, later ends his life with poison in a final noble effort just before the falsity and rascality of the charges preferred against him are revealed. Prior to the suicide, Luria converses with Jacopo, the Secretary to the Commissary of the Republic of Florence, who has become convinced of the Moor's innocence:

JACOPO

And if, the trial past, their fame stand clear
To all men's eyes, as yours, my lord, to mine—
Their ghosts may sleep in quiet satisfied. . . .
The heart leads surllier: I must move with you—
As greatest now, who ever were the best.
So, let the last and humblest of your servants
Accept your charge, as Braccio's heretofore,
And tender homage by obeying you! [*Jacopo goes.*]

LURIA

Another! Luria goes not poorly forth.
If we could wait! **The only fault's with time;**
All men become good creatures: but so slow!

The only liberty is a liberty connected with order

Source: SPEECH ON HIS ARRIVAL AT BRISTOL (Oct. 13, 1774)
Author: Edmund Burke (1729–1797)
First published: 1774
Type of work: Political speech

Context: Edmund Burke on this occasion was seeking election to the House of Commons, and he spoke knowingly when he pointed out that Bristol was "a main pillar in the commercial interest of Great Britain, [which] must totter on its base by the slightest mistake with regard to our American measures." He knew that Bristol men could see their advantage in a solution to the problems with the American Colonies which would allow them continued prosperous trade with those Colonies. In this speech Burke tries to show that he supports the British constitutional system and commerce, and that his aim is always to reconcile the liberties of Americans as Britishers with the constitutional system of Great Britain. As he did consistently through his long public career, Burke in this speech clings to a constructively conservative position; his friendliness to the American cause was motivated by his wishes to keep any changes within the structure of the political institutions which had grown up over the centuries:

> When I first devoted myself to the public services, I considered how I should render myself fit for it; and this I did by endeavouring to discover what it was that gave this country the rank it holds in the world. I found that our prosperity and dignity arose principally, if not solely, from two sources; our Constitution and commerce. Both these I have spared no study to understand, and no endeavour to support.
>
> The distinguishing part of our Constitution is its liberty. To preserve that liberty inviolate, seems the particular duty and proper trust of a member of the House of Commons. But the liberty, **the only liberty,** I mean **is a liberty connected with order;** that not only exists along with order and virtue, but which cannot exist at all without them. It inheres in good and steady government, as in its substance and vital principle.

The only wretched are the wise

Source: TO THE HONORABLE CHARLES MONTAGUE, ESQ. (Line 36)
Author: Matthew Prior (1664–1721)
First published: 1707
Type of work: Philosophic poem

Context: Matthew Prior, like so many of his associates in the eighteenth century, was active both as a man of letters and as a public official. His career as a diplomat in Holland and France was crowned by his acting as plenipotentiary in negotiating the peace of Utrecht, known later among his Whig enemies as "Matt's Peace." His initial fame as a poet came in 1687 when he and his friend Charles Montagu (later Earl of Halifax) burlesqued John Dryden's *The Hind and the Panther* in their *Story of the Country-Mouse and the City-Mouse.* Five years later in an epistle to his friend, he enclosed a verse of wry philosophical observation on the vagaries of life, expressing much the same thought that Pope, in *An Essay on Man,* was to articulate in "Man never is, but always to be blest." Man does not perceive the future, and graciously it is so, for his limited perspective allows him the luxury of anticipating a better day and of rationalizing his present woe in terms of its imagined outcome. "Against experience," the "hoary Fool, who many days/ Has struggl'd with continu'd Sorrow,/ Renews his Hope, and blindly lays/ The desp'rate Bett upon to Morrow." Seen from a distance, objects—like life—are subject to the

832

interpretation of imagination; seen from close range, the same objects are desultory and worthless. In this sense, then, ignorance is bliss:

If We see right, We see our Woes:
Then what avails it to have Eyes?
From Ignorance our Comfort flows:
The only Wretched are the Wise.

We waery'd should lie down in Death:
This Cheat of Life would take no more;
If You thought Fame but empty Breath;
I, Phillis but a perjur'd Whore.

Open, Sesame!

Source: THE ARABIAN NIGHTS' ENTERTAINMENTS ("The Tale of Ali Baba and the Forty Thieves")
Author: Unknown
First transcribed: Fifteenth century
Type of work: Tale

Context: One of the best-known tales in *The Book of the Thousand Nights and One Night* (also called *The Arabian Nights' Entertainments*) is "Ali Baba and the Forty Thieves." Hiding from a group of strange horsemen, Ali Baba hears their leader command a rock to open and then to shut after all the horsemen have entered a door in it. Following the later departure of the horsemen, Ali Baba uses the magic command; the rock opens, and he discovers a horde of stolen treasure, some of which he takes. The greed of Ali Baba's brother Kassim later leads to Kassim's murder in the cave and almost results in the killing also of Ali Baba. He is saved, however, by his servant Morgiana, whose ingenuity leads to the deaths of the thieves and the wealth of Ali Baba who prudently uses the fortune Allah has helped him to gain. "Open, Sesame!," one of the most famous magic commands in literature, first appears near the beginning of the tale:

The forty thieves carried their loads to the foot of a large rock which lay at the bottom of the little hill. Then they set down the bags, and the chief cried out in the direction of the rock: **"Open, Sesame!"** [in some translations, Simsim]. At once the surface of the rock gaped; the captain waited until his followers had passed with their burdens through the opening, and then carried his bag in after them. "Shut, Sesame!" he cried from within; and the face of the rock closed upon him. . . .

833

Opinion in good men is but knowledge in the making

Source: AREOPAGITICA
Author: John Milton (1608–1674)
First published: 1644
Type of work: Printed speech

Context: One of the royal prerogatives most offensive to the Puritans was the licensing of the press, a power which in effect permitted the Bishops of the Church of England to control the publications of their theological opposition, the Puritans. When the Puritans gained control of England through the civil wars, however, one of the first proposals considered by Parliament was a law to regulate the press and to require that all books and pamphlets be submitted for examination and licensing prior to publication. Although Milton had long been one of the most effective and articulate spokesmen for the Puritan party, he believed strongly in freedom of speech and conscience. The *Areopagitica,* which takes the form of a classical oration, is his defense of a free press and represents a position he took in defiance of his Puritan compatriots. Milton first points out that none of the great classical civilizations had practised such repressive measures. He then argues that the Catholic Church was the inventor of censorship. To the argument that books promote schism Milton replies that no good man can be corrupted by a bad book and that no bad man can be improved by control of his reading material. Indeed, he continues, difference of opinion is necessary to the discovery of truth:

. . . Where there is much desire to learn, there of necessity will be much arguing, much writing, many opinions; for **opinion in good men is but knowledge in the making.** Under these fantastic terrors of sect and schism, we wrong the earnest and zealous thirst after knowledge and understanding, which God hath stirred up in this city. What some lament of, we rather should rejoice at, should rather praise this pious forwardness among men, to reassume the ill-deputed care of their religion into their own hands again. A little generous prudence, a little forbearance of one another, and some grain of charity might win all these diligences to join and unite into one general and brotherly search after truth; could we but forego this prelatical tradition of crowding free consciences and Christian liberties into canons and precepts of men. . . .

An ornament to her profession

Source: THE PILGRIM'S PROGRESS (Part II)
Author: John Bunyan (1628–1688)
First published: 1684
Type of work: Religious allegory

Context: As Part I of this work described the hazards and temptations faced and overcome by Christian on his journey to spiritual salvation and the heavenly Jerusalem, so in Part II Christiana, Christian's wife, and their children set out for the same goals. Like Christian before them, these travelers came to the town of Vanity, where Vanity Fair was held. There the pilgrims lodged with Mr. Mnason (see Acts 21. 16), who was a very pious man and who introduced them to his friends Mr. Contrite, Mr. Holyman, Mr. Love-saint, Mr. Dare-not-lie, and Mr. Penitent. During the stay in Vanity, Christiana's sons, Samuel and Joseph, were married to their host's daughters, Grace and Martha, and the third daughter, Mercy, joined the group as a fellow pilgrim. Before proceeding on their journey, however, the members of the group spent some time among the people of Vanity doing charitable work:

The time, as I said, that they lay here was long (for it was not now as in former times). Wherefore the pilgrims grew acquainted with many of the good people of the town, and did them what service they could. Mercy, as she was wont, laboured much for the poor; wherefore their bellies and backs blessed her, and she was there **an ornament to her profession.** And to say the truth for Grace, Phebe, and Martha, they were all of a very good nature, and did much good in their place. They were also all of them very fruitful; so that Christian's name, as said before, was like to live in the world.

The 'oss loves the 'ound, and I loves both

Source: HANDLEY CROSS (Chapter 16, 1843 edition; chapter 18, 1854 edition)
Author: Robert Smith Surtees (1803–1864)
First published: 1843
Type of work: Novel

Context: Robert Surtees, as editor of *The New Sporting Magazine,* earned a special place in literature as chronicler and humorist of the sporting field —that is, the fox hunt. In a series of humorous sketches which he contributed regularly to the magazine, he developed the character of John Jorrocks, a London wholesale grocer with a passion for hunting. A volume of these sketches entitled *Jorrocks' Jaunts and Jollities* was published in 1838 and proved quite popular; a second collection, *Handley Cross,* appeared in 1843. A new edition of the latter title, enlarged with additional characters and episodes, was issued in 1854. A sudden burst of prosperity has transformed the little village of Handley Cross, located in the Vale of Sheepwash, from a sleepy hamlet into a flourishing community. There is a need for urban sophistication; social affairs, including the Hunt, must be conducted more formally. Jorrocks has become well known because of his habit of making country excursions, in which he takes orders for groceries while riding with the huntsmen. The Committee of Management therefore sends him an invitation, offering him the post of Master of Foxhounds, Handley Cross Hunt. Thus, Jorrocks' lifelong ambition, to become a Master of Hounds, is realized. Deeply honored and greatly exhilarated, he is almost hysterical when he arrives in Handley Cross. He delivers a spirited address to the townspeople, in which he outlines the attributes of an ideal M.F.H., and promises to live up to that ideal. He also promises to offer a series of lectures on hunting and related matters; and when he speaks of hunting, his emotions nearly give way. The first of these "lectors" is given a few days later. In the introductory remarks Jorrocks again discourses upon the joys of hunting, and again he is nearly betrayed by his emotions. He quickly moves on to his topic of the evening:

"**The 'oss loves the 'ound, and I loves both;** and it is that love wot brings me to these parts, to follow the all-glorious callin' of the chase, and to enlighten all men capable of illumination. To-night I shall instruct you with a lecture on dealin'.

" 'Oh who shall counsel a man in the choice of a wife or an 'oss?' asked that inspired writer, the renowned Johnny Lawrence. 'The buyer has need of a hundred eyes, the seller of but one,' says another equestrian conjuror. Who can take up an 'oss book and read 'bout splints, and spavins, and stringalts, and corns, and cuttin', and farcy, and dropsy, and fever, and thrushes, and grease, and gripes, and mallenders, and sallenders, and ring-bones, and roarin', etcetera, etceterorem, without a shudder lest such a complication of evils should fall to his lot? Who can expect a perfect 'oss, when he sees what an infinity of hills they are heirs to? I hopes I haven't come to 'Andley Cross to inform none on you what an 'oss is, nor to explain that its component parts are four legs, a back-bone, an 'ead, a neck, a tail, and other etceteras, too numerous to insert in an 'and-bill, as old Georgy Robins used to say.

" 'Eavens, wot a lot of rubbish has been written about 'osses!" continued the worthy lecturer, casting up his eyes.

Others abide our question

Source: SHAKESPEARE (Line 1)
Author: Matthew Arnold (1822–1888)
First published: 1849
Type of work: Sonnet

Context: One of the noblest tributes to Shakespeare by a later English poet, Arnold's sonnet celebrates not the writer of comedy who brought to the stage the gaiety and laughter of life, but the poet and dramatist who knew man's weaknesses, his griefs, and the pains of his immortal spirit. Like a great mountain that shows its majestic peak to the heavens and reveals only its mist-shrouded base "To the foiled searching of mortality," Shakespeare knew the "stars and sun-beams" and yet he trod the earth too. The sonnet follows:

Others abide our question. Thou art free.
We ask and ask—Thou smilest and art still,
Out-topping knowledge. For the loftiest hill,
Who to the stars uncrowns his majesty,

Planting his steadfast footsteps in the sea,
Making the heaven of heavens his dwelling-place,
Spares but the cloudy border of his base
To the foiled searching of mortality;

And thou, who didst the stars and sunbeams know,
Self-schooled, self-scanned, self-honoured, self-secure,
Didst tread on earth unguessed at.—Better so!

All pains the immortal spirit must endure,
All weakness which impairs, all griefs which bow,
Find their sole speech in that victorious brow.

Our country, right or wrong

Source: LIFE OF DECATUR (A. S. Mackenzie, Chapter 14)
Author: Stephen Decatur (1779–1820)
First published: 1846
Type of work: Attributed comment

Context: Stephen Decatur was the outstanding naval figure in United States history during the century between John Paul Jones and David Farragut. He refused a clerical life after a good education and went to work for a shipbuilding firm. He was aboard the frigate *United States,* first ship of the U. S. Navy, at the time of her launching. In 1798 he was appointed midshipman and subsequently took part in various minor naval engagements during the French War. Promoted to lieutenant and placed in command of the *Enterprise,* he fought in the war with Tripoli in 1803–1804. Tripoli had captured the American frigate *Philadelphia;* Deca-tur, in a daring exploit, destroyed her in the harbor at Tripoli. In recognition of this act he was promoted to captain and given command of the *Constitution.* During the War of 1812, as captain of the *United States,* he captured the British frigate *Macedonian.* After a year during which the American ports were blockaded, Decatur took command of the frigate *President* and slipped out of New York harbor during a gale. The next morning he fell in with a squadron of five British vessels; in the running fight which ensued he put the British frigate *Endymion* out of action, but was unable to escape and was eventually forced to surrender. After the war he was given command of a squadron and sent to the Barbary States to exact reparation for injuries to American commerce and to enforce peace treaties. He carried out the assignment effectively; the United States was now a power to reckon with and Decatur an able instrument. The Bey of Tunis, the Dey of Algiers, and the Bashaw of Tripoli were forced to comply, and the indemnities were paid. On his return to America Decatur was received with great enthusiasm. Alexander Slidell Mackenzie, popular writer of the era who was also a naval officer, describes the receptions given in Decatur's honor and quotes many of the toasts which were offered:

In the succeeding month of April, professional duties called Decatur to Norfolk, the birthplace of Mrs. Decatur, where they had resided several years, and where they were welcomed by a large circle of attached friends. The gentlemen of the place eagerly took advantage of this opportunity to meet him in a general reunion round the social board. Among the appropriate sentiments, which the occasion called forth, were the following; "The Mediterranean! The sea not more of Greek and Roman, than of American glory." "The crescent! Our stars have dimmed its lustre." "National glory! A gem above all price, and worthy every hazard to sustain its splendor." Decatur responded with a sentiment, which has since become memorable; "Our country! In her intercourse with foreign nations, may she always be in the right; but **our country, right or wrong.**" May it ever remain the rallying cry of patriotism throughout the land; not the least valuable of the legacies left by Decatur to his countrymen.

Not long after, Decatur having occasion to pass through Petersburg in Virginia, the moment his presence there became known, he was waited upon by a committee of the citizens, who presented him with an address, expressive of their admiration and thanks for his public services, and requesting him to partake of an entertainment, on the afternoon of the same day, at Poplar Spring. Decatur accepted the invitation, and three hundred persons assembled, on that short notice, to unite in greeting and honoring him.

Our patience will achieve more than our force

Source: REFLECTIONS ON THE REVOLUTION IN FRANCE
Author: Edmund Burke (1729–1797)
First published: 1790
Type of work: Political treatise

Context: Throughout his long tenure in Parliament, Edmund Burke, one of the greatest political philosophers England has ever produced, steadfastly defended traditional and established rights and the gradual evolution of political process. He regarded the Revolution in France as a vicious and dangerous perversion of the processes of political development, and he objected to the insistence on rapid and radical change just as much as the violence with which these changes were being brought about during the Revolution:

> . . . Political arrangement, as it is a work for social ends, is to be wrought by social means. There mind must conspire with mind. Time is required to produce that union of minds which alone can produce all the good we aim at. **Our patience will achieve more than our force.** If I might venture to appeal to what is so much out of fashion in Paris, I mean to experience, I should tell you that in my course I have known, and, according to my measure, have co-operated with great men; and I have never yet seen any plan which has not been mended by the observations of those who were much inferior in understanding to the person who took the lead in the business. By a slow but well-sustained progress, the effect of each step is watched; the good or ill success of the first, gives light to us in the second; and so, from light to light, we are conducted with safety through the whole series. We see that the parts of the system do not clash.

Our supreme governors, the mob

Source: LETTER TO HORACE MANN (September 7, 1743)
Author: Horace Walpole (1717–1797)
First published: 1833
Type of work: Personal letter

Context: Walpole is generally considered one of the greatest of English letter writers, along with William Cowper and Thomas Gray. He wrote literally thousands of letters, and very few of them fail to be enlivening. In addition to his ability to be generally entertaining, he usually shows in his letters brilliance, charm, wit, humor, and a wide-ranging knowledge including literature, politics, society, and art. Following his years at Cambridge (1735–1739) he made the traditional grand tour of Europe and, while in Florence, met Horace Mann. Although they never met again, they maintained an extensive correspondence. This letter, charming and gossipy, contains an allusion to anti-French sentiment in England and is in response to a query by Mann concerning news of some social events in England:

> You ask me about the marrying Princesses: I know not a tittle. Princess Louisa seems to be going, her cloths are bought; but marrying our daughters makes no conversation. For either of the other two, all thoughts seem to be dropped of it. The Senate of Sweden design themselves to choose a wife for their man of Lubeck.
> The City, and **our supreme governors, the mob,** are very angry

that there is a troop of French players at Cliefden. One of them was lately impertinent to a countryman, who thrashed him. His Royal Highness sent angrily to know the cause. The fellow replied, "he thought to have pleased his Highness in beating one of them, who had tried to kill his father, and had wounded his brother"—This was not easy to answer.

Our sweetest songs are those that tell of saddest thought

Source: TO A SKYLARK (Stanza 18)
Author: Percy Bysshe Shelley (1792–1822)
First published: 1820
Type of work: Lyric poem

Context: The poet hails the skylark not as a bird but as a "blithe Spirit," a symbol of pure joy which springs from earth toward heaven "And singing still dost soar, and soaring ever singest." It is "Like an unbodied joy whose race is just begun." Though the bird is hidden from the poet like a star in the daytime, he still hears its "shrill delight." He seeks comparisons for the voice which fills "All the earth and air. . . ." Drops from a rainbow cloud are less bright than the skylark's "rain of melody." The bird is like a poet "Singing hymns unbidden"; or "Like a high-born maiden" overflowing her bower "With music sweet as love"; or "Like a glow-worm golden" scattering its light "Among the flowers and grass"; or "Like a rose embowered" which with its scent "Makes faint with too much sweet" the winds that deflower it. The music of the skylark surpasses "All that ever was/ Joyous, and clear, and fresh. . . ." "Teach us, Sprite or Bird," pleads the poet, "What sweet thoughts are thine. . . ." He has never heard "a flood of rapture so divine." What are the sources of this joy? The singer in the sky cannot know languor, annoyance, or "love's sad satiety." Of death it "must deem/ Things more true and deep/ Than we mortals dream. . . ." We ever long for what we do not have, pain is mingled with our laughter, our sweetest songs are sad ones. Yet, says the poet, even if we "could scorn/ Hate, and pride, and fear," even if we were free from weeping, he knows not "how thy joy we ever should come near." The heavenly singer, "scorner of the ground," surpasses the sounds of earth, the treasures in books. "Teach me," the poet pleads again, "half the gladness/ That thy brain must know," and then the world will listen to his "harmonious madness" as he listens now. The most famous stanza of the poem is the eighteenth in which Shelley writes of the imperfections in earthly joys and music:

We look before and after,
  And pine for what is not:
Our sincerest laughter
  With some pain is fraught;
Our sweetest songs are those that tell of saddest thought.

840

Our swords shall play the orators for us

Source: TAMBURLAINE THE GREAT (Part I, Act I, ii, 132)
Author: Christopher Marlowe (1564–1593)
First published: 1590
Type of work: Dramatic tragedy

Context: Christopher Marlowe, next greatest Elizabethan dramatist after Shakespeare, was the first to make much use of blank verse on the London stage. Ben Jonson, in his poem to Shakespeare's memory, refers to "Marlowe's mighty line." With his first play, *Tamburlaine,* in two parts, he took the theatrical world by storm. The drama contains romantic figures speaking in passionate language. It is the story of the Scythian shepherd from Samerkand, usually called Tamerlane (1333–1405), or Timur Leng (Timur the Lame), who claimed descent from Jenghiz Khan. By the force of his personality, he inspired his army to fanatical efforts that conquered kingdoms and empires. While still only a shepherd leader, Tamburlaine stops the caravan of lovely Zenocrate, on her way to marry the Sultan. While wooing her by talking of his life and his ambitions, he receives word that a thousand Persian cavalrymen are riding to attack him. He discusses the situation with followers and officers:

TAMBURLANE

A thousand horsemen!—We five hundred foot!—
An odds too great for us to stand against.
But are they rich?—And is their armor good?

SOLDIER

Their pluméd helms are wrought with beaten gold,
Their swords enamelled, and about their necks
Hang massy chains of gold, down to the waist,
In every part exceeding brave and rich.

TAMBURLANE

Then shall we fight courageously with them?
Or look you I should play the orator?

TECHELLES

No; cowards and faint-hearted runaways
Look for orations when the foe is near:
Our swords shall play the orators for us.

USUMCASANE

Come! Let us meet them at the mountain top,
And with a sudden and a hot alarum,
Drive all their horses headlong down the hill.

Out, out, brief candle!

Source: MACBETH (Act V, sc. v, l. 23)
Author: William Shakespeare (1564–1616)
First published: 1623
Type of work: Dramatic tragedy

Context: Macbeth, at Dunsinane in full armor, is ready to fight the advancing enemy when he hears a cry from the women within the castle. He has become so inured to horrors, however, that he hardly fears another lament. Seton, his armor-bearer, is sent to discover the cause of the mourning. He returns with the news of the queen's death. There is no visible breakdown whatsoever on Macbeth's part, although the pace of his speech slows considerably, and he becomes very philosophical. Life signifies nothing, he says; therefore, since she would have died at some time or another, Lady Macbeth's death does not greatly affect him at that moment. At the entrance of a messenger, his tone alters radically, and he again becomes the war-like commander.

SETON
The Queen, my lord, is dead.

MACBETH
She should have died hereafter;
There would have been a time for such a word.
Tomorrow, and tomorrow, and tomorrow,
Creeps in this petty pace from day to day,
To the last syllable of recorded time;
And all our yesterdays have lighted fools
The way to dusty death. **Out, out, brief candle!**
Life's but a walking shadow, a poor player,
That struts and frets his hour upon the stage,
And then is heard no more. It is a tale
Told by an idiot, full of sound and fury
Signifying nothing.

An ower true tale

Source: THE BRIDE OF LAMMERMOOR (Chapter 33)
Author: Sir Walter Scott (1771–1832)
First published: 1819
Type of work: Novel

Context: The engagement between the Master of Ravenswood and Lucy Ashton is broken off by the machinations of Lucy's mother, Lady Ashton, who has a deep and abiding hatred for the Master. Lady Ashton maneuvers Lucy into an engagement with young Hayston of Bucklaw, a wealthy

842

young rake, on the grounds that the Master has deserted her; as a matter of fact, Lady Ashton has been purloining all the letters that pass to and from Lucy and the Master. Just as Lucy has signed a marriage contract with Bucklaw, the Master returns from abroad to hear from her own lips the breaking off of the betrothal; she does not actually repudiate the contract, but is borne out of the room in a dead faint. The marriage between Lucy and Bucklaw takes place four days after the signing of the contract. During the festivities attendant upon the marriage, Lucy leaves the gathering for her room, where she is joined by her new husband. Soon a wild yell rings out from her room, and it is discovered that Lucy has stabbed Bucklaw and has crawled into the chimney. She soon dies in madness; her husband finally recovers his health and spends the rest of his life abroad. This novel is the source of Donizetti's opera *Lucia di Lammermoor*. "Ower true" means "completely true." This is its conclusion:

Bucklaw afterwards went abroad and never returned to Scotland; nor was he known ever to hint at the circumstances attending his fatal marriage. By many readers this may be deemed overstrained, romantic, and composed by the wild imagination of an author, desirous of gratifying the popular appetite for the horrible; but those who are read in the private family history of Scotland during the period in which the scene is laid, will readily discover, through the disguise of borrowed names and added incidents, the leading particulars of **an ower true tale.**

An oyster may be crossed in love

Source: THE CRITIC (Act III, sc. i, l. 302)
Author: Richard Brinsley Sheridan (1751–1816)
First published: 1781
Type of work: Dramatic comedy

Context: A criticism of drama that remains as fresh today as when originally performed is *The Critic, or A Tragedy Rehearsed,* with its playwright, Mr. Puff, the Prince of publicity agents, and Sir Fretful Plagiary (of course suggesting plagiarism). The latter is a caricature of Cumberland, who insulted Sheridan during rehearsals of the latter's *Battle of Hastings* in 1778. *The Critic* is a treatise on dramatic art. Four months after the Spanish Ambassador brought a declaration of war to the Court of St. James, Sheridan put on the stage with its play within a play, this exaggerated historical tragedy, *The Spanish Armada* by Mr. Puff. After introductory matter, the play begins as Act II. The actors utter their lines; those in the audience, especially Sneer, comment on them and criticize both plot and dialogue. This device provided Sheridan with the opportunity to introduce timely comments on contemporary problems of England. In Act III, enter Tilburina "stark mad in white satin," and her

843

confidante "stark mad in white linen," the white because "when a heroine goes mad, she always goes mad in white satin." Another proof of her madness is her speech. Don Wiskerandos is a Spanish sailor whom Tilburina loved. He had been a prisoner in England, and his execution has driven her mad.

TILBURINA

The wind whistles—the moon rises—see
They have kill'd my squirrel in his cage!
Is this a grasshopper!—Ha, no, it is my
Wiskerandos—you shall not keep him—
I know you have him in your pocket—
An oyster may be crossed in love!—Who says
A whale's a bird?—Ha, did you call, my love?
—He's here! He's there!—He's everywhere!
Ah, me! He's nowhere.

Paddle your own canoe

Source: SETTLERS IN CANADA (Chapter VIII)
Author: Frederick Marryat (1792–1848)
First published: 1844
Type of work: Children's adventure novel

Context: Having resigned from the British navy in 1829, Captain Marryat had to write voluminously to try to keep out of debt. Poe charged that the popularity of his sea stories proved him a mediocre writer, but while his conversations sound stilted, his humor and pathos still make him readable, and his pages are filled with an abundance of adventure. In *Settlers in Canada,* his second children's novel, an English doctor with four sons and his sister's two orphan daughters runs into financial difficulty at home chiefly because of his own noble nature. Thinking his small remaining capital will last longer in Canada, he takes the whole family overseas in 1794. In Quebec he gets a deed to land along Lake Ontario for which he sets out, with trapper Martin Super as guide. From him and from an officer, Captain Sinclair, the doctor's family learns about local conditions and about the treachery of Chief Pontiac. In Chapter VIII, they discuss traits of the Indians and their refusal to become Christianized. "Canoe" is a New World (Haitian) word. The local expression about each paddling his own canoe here has a figurative meaning of each person going his own way, a meaning different from that now given to the phrase.

"When the form of worship and creed is simple, it is difficult to make converts, and the Indian is a clear reasoner. I once had a conversation with one of the chiefs on the subject. After we had conversed some time, he said, 'You believe in one God—so do we; you call him one name—we call him another; we don't speak the same language, that is the reason. You say, suppose you do good, you go to land of Good Spirits—we say so too. Then Indians and Yangees (that is, English) both try to gain same object, only try in not the same way. Now I think that it much better that, as we all go along together, that **every man paddle his own canoe.** That my thought.' "

Paper-bullets of the brain

Source: MUCH ADO ABOUT NOTHING (Act II, sc. iii, l. 247)
Author: William Shakespeare (1564–1616)
First published: 1600
Type of work: Dramatic comedy

Context: Don Pedro, Claudio, and Leonato have decided that it would be the height of jests to provoke a romantic liaison between Benedick and Beatrice, two young rebels who delight in mocking love in general and each other in particular. An elaborate intrigue is arranged in which each will overhear a conversation describing the other's love. According to these remarks, the partner who is romantically inclined has been desperate to withhold the truth of his passion lest it be jeered and mocked by the other. Benedick is the first to fall victim to this trap of comic exposure. He eavesdrops as Leonato describes his niece's desperate infatuation with Benedick, the more so since Benedick's mockery of love renders her affection hopeless. And her actions betoken her condition: she writes him love letters, only to tear them up and rail at herself for writing to one who would flout her; she falls upon her knees, ". . . weeps, sobs, beats her heart, tears her hair, prays, curses—O sweet Benedick, God give me patience." When Benedick hears these protestations of her love, he suddenly finds himself sympathetically interested in her, a condition which renders comic the presumptuous hateur of his soliloquy a few lines earlier. In other words, he is now faced with the necessity of denying his former position on grounds which, to him at least, appear rational. His former attitudes, his "paper-bullets of the brain," must now give way to more mature considerations:

BENEDICK
. . .
Love me? Why it must be requited. . . . I did never think to marry. I must not seem proud. Happy are they that hear their detractions, and can put them to mending. . . . I may chance have some odd quirks and remnants of wit broken on me, because I have railed so long against marriage. But doth not the appetite alter? A man loves the meat in his youth that he cannot endure

845

in his age. Shall quips and sentences, and these **paper-bullets of the brain** awe a man from the career of his humour? No, the world must be peopled. When I said I would die a bachelor, I did not think I should live till I were married.

The paradise of fools

Source: PARADISE LOST (Book III, l. 496)
Author: John Milton (1608–1674)
First published: 1667
Type of work: Epic poem

Context: Satan lands upon the earth, bent on destroying by guile God's favorite creation, man. For a time he roams over vast fields of the external sphere of the cosmic system, as yet empty of all life, but later to be filled with the souls of people who on earth engaged in works of vanity. On the moon will be souls of people taken away from the earth without dying, like Enoch, and the mighty men born of the sons of God and the daughters of men (*Genesis* 5: 24) and the original giants (*Genesis* 6: 4). Men will be there like Empedocles, who jumped into the crater of Mt. Etna, on Sicily, so that people would think he had been bodily conveyed to heaven; and there also will be friars and pilgrims, and those who on their deathbeds put on friars' habits in the hope of being passed into heaven in disguise. Just when they will be about to enter heaven, a violent cross-wind will blow them ten thousand leagues away; but since they are fools, they will believe their destination to be Paradise.

. . . Then might ye see
Cowls, hoods, and habits with their wearers tossed
And fluttered into rags, then relics, beads,
Indulgences, dispenses, pardons, bulls,
The sport of winds: all these upwhirled aloft
Fly o'er the backside of the world far off
Into a limbo large and broad, since called
The paradise of fools, to few unknown.
Long after, now unpeopled, and untrod:
All this dark globe the fiend found as he passed,
And long he wandered, till at last a gleam
Of dawning light turned thitherward in haste
His traveled steps. . .

Pardon's the word to all

Source: CYMBELINE (Act V, sc. v, l. 422)
Author: William Shakespeare (1564–1616)
First published: 1623
Type of work: Tragi-comedy

Context: Cymbeline utters these words near the end of the play when the entire complicated plot has been revealed. Imogen is safe in the arms of her husband, Posthumus, who pardons Iachimo for the treacherous, lying acts which almost led to Imogen's death. Arviragus and Guiderius are disclosed by Belarius as the long-lost sons of Cymbeline. Cymbeline pardons Belarius and reinstates him as a courtier. Posthumus also proves that he aided Cymbeline in his fight against the Romans and thereby wins Cymbeline's thanks and love.

IACHIMO
                    I am down again. [*Kneels*.]
But now my heavy conscience sinks my knee,
As then your force did. Take that life, beseech you,
Which I so often owe; . . .

POSTHUMUS
                    Kneel not to me.
The power that I have on you is to spare you;
The malice towards you, to forgive you. Live,
And deal with others better.

CYMBELINE
                    Nobly doomed.
We'll learn our freeness of a son-in-law.
Pardon's the word to all.

The parson knows enough who knows a duke

Source: TIROCINIUM (Line 403)
Author: William Cowper (1731–1800)
First published: 1785
Type of work: Didactic poem

Context: Cowper's work is quiet and meditative, and he is essentially a poet of rural life. A descendant of John Donne, he did not turn seriously to the writing of poetry until he was fifty. He was trained in the law, being called to the bar in 1754; but recurring attacks of insanity forced him to give up his career. The first of these destroyed his hope of marriage and the second led him to attempt suicide. He retired, after his convalescence, to the country and settled at Olney. Turning to poetry as a serious recreation, he published his first volume, *Poems,* in 1782. His greatest work, *The Task,* appeared in 1785. It was written at the suggestion of his friend Lady Austen, who assigned him a topic: the sofa. Using the sofa as a point of departure, Cowper moved into a natural and vivid description of the countryside in winter, the simplicities of daily life, and the world he now saw at a distance. The work exhibits Cowper's abilities at their best;

it is a meditative poem, and in it he discourses freely on man's destiny and moral nature while extolling the virtues of rural life. His Calvinism led him to moralize, and some of his other poems are closely akin to sermons. One such poem is *Tirocinium;* it is one of several poems published with *The Task.* An extended commentary on public education, it decries the lack of moral instruction and encouragement in the schools.

Cowper had been a slight and sensitive child whose mother had died early; he was bullied and harassed unmercifully in school. His memory of those sufferings leads him to denounce such places as a source of depravity. In them, he feels, the young are encouraged to become worldly and are in no way guided toward an honorable life. Sound learning is in a decline; all study is for worldly gain, even for those among the clergy:

"Ah, blind to bright futurity, untaught
The knowledge of the world, and dull of thought!
Church-ladders are not always mounted best
By learned clerks and Latinists profess'd.
Th' exalted prize demands an upward look,
Not to be found by poring on a book.
Small skill in Latin, and still less in Greek,
Is more than adequate to all I seek.
Let erudition grace him, or not grace,
I give the bauble but the second place;
His wealth, fame, honours, at that I intend,
Subsist and centre in one point—a friend.

. . .

His intercourse with peers, and sons of peers—
There dawns the splendour of his future years;
In that bright quarter his propitious skies
Shall blush betimes, and there his glory rise.

. . .

Let rev'rend churls his ignorance rebuke,
Who starve upon a dog's-ear'd Pentateuch,
The parson knows enough who knows a duke."—

A part to tear a cat in, to make all split

Source: A MIDSUMMER NIGHT'S DREAM (Act I, sc. ii, l. 25)
Author: William Shakespeare (1564–1616)
First published: 1600
Type of work: Dramatic comedy

Context: The handicraftsmen Quince, the carpenter; Snug, the joiner; Bottom, the weaver; Flute, the bellows-mender; Snout, the tinker; the Starveling, the tailor, are commanded to prepare a play for possible presentation, at the wedding festivities of Theseus, the Duke of Athens, and his bride Hippolyta, the Queen of the Amazons. These naïve souls have neither dramatic experience nor ability, but they are determined to compensate for any deficiency through sheer effort and flamboyant histrionics. Shakespeare is no doubt having fun at the expense of his profession as he comically depicts the problems of casting and staging. Bottom is the nonpareil of dramatic hams. Convinced he can perform all roles—if need be simultaneously—he is quick to extemporize in order to impress the harassed Quince, who is serving as director. When Quince announces that the play shall be *The Most Lamentable Comedy, and Most Cruel Death of Pyramus and Thisbe,* Bottom immediately voices his approval of the play and calls for casting. Told he is to play the lover Pyramus, he complains that his best talents are being wasted, that his forte is the tyrant's role in which his full range of furious Thespian skills can be exercised:

QUINCE
You, Nick Bottom, are set down for Pyramus.

BOTTOM
What is Pyramus? A lover, or a tyrant?

QUINCE
A lover, that kills himself, most gallant, for love.

BOTTOM
That will ask some tears in the true performing of it. If I do it, let the audience look to their eyes. I will move storms. I will condole in some measure. To the rest. Yet my chief humour is for a tyrant. I could play Ercles rarely, or **a part to tear a cat in, to make all split.**

> *The raging rocks,*
> *And shivering shocks,*
> *Shall break the locks*
> *Of prison gates,*
> *And Phibbus' car*
> *Shall shine from far,*
> *And make and mar*
> *The foolish Fates.*

This was lofty. Now name the rest of the players. This is Ercles' vein, a tyrant's vein. A lover is more condoling.

Parties must ever exist in a free country

Source: SPEECH ON CONCILIATION WITH AMERICA (March 22, 1775)
Author: Edmund Burke (1729–1797)
First published: 1775
Type of work: Parliamentary address

Context: In this speech in the House of Commons, Edmund Burke, believing the time was ripe, on both sides, for conciliation between the American colonists and the British government, spoke up for his government's admitting past wrongs and admitting the colonists into the same status as other Englishmen. He cites the growth of the population in the Colonies and the ever-increasing trade with the home country, trying to show that it is to Britain's advantage to conciliate; he gives historical examples to prove that a free people are easier to govern than a people hounded by tyranny. Not to conciliate the Americans, he says, is to have a perpetual quarrel with them instead of a regular revenue from them. He suggests to his fellow members that it is in the best interest of the government itself to keep the Colonies as vigorous, prosperous portions of Great Britain, in order that revenues from them may benefit the government. He points out, as a member of the opposition, that the party in power should bear in mind the welfare of the people and the country:

Next we know, that **parties must ever exist in a free country.** We know too, that the emulations of such parties, their contradictions, their reciprocal necessities, their hopes, and their fears, must send them all in their turns to him that holds the balance of the state. The parties are the gamesters; but government keeps the table, and is sure to be the winner in the end. When this game is played, I really think it is more to be feared that the people will be exhausted, than that the government will not be supplied.

The patience of Job

Source: JAMES 5:11
Author: James
First transcribed: c. 80–100
Type of work: Religious epistle

Context: Shakespeare was sure that the most illiterate of his audiences would understand the reference when Falstaff declared: "I am as poor as Job, but not so patient" (*Henry IV,* Part II: Act I, sc. ii, l. 145). And the much earlier James, writing to the Jews outside Palestine awaiting the promised coming of the Lord, could urge them to patience by reminding them of the Old Testament story, written between 900 and 500 B.C. Jehovah, boasting of His faithful servant, "the perfect and upright" Job, got the ironical comment from Satan that anyone as wealthy as Job would serve God. So God decided to test him. In a tribal raid, Job lost his five hundred oxen and five hundred she asses; a fire from heaven burned up his seven thousand sheep; the Chaldeans stole his three thousand camels; and his seven sons and three daughters perished when a hurricane blew down their house. But still Job commented: "Jehovah giveth and Jehovah taketh away. Blessed be the name of Jehovah." At Satan's remark

850

that Job had not himself suffered, God covered his body with boils. Still he patiently accepted his lot with the thought that since God gives good, He can also give evil. The rest of the Book of Job consists of three rounds of arguments between Job and his three "Comforters," discussing why the just may suffer and the wicked flourish. Even God, from a cloud, takes part in the argument, pointing out Job's lack of sufficient knowledge to question God's acts. Then God rewards the long-suffering patriarch by giving him ten more children and twice as many possessions as he had lost. The unknown author of this Biblical book never answers the ethical question raised. Many critics believe its present form is imperfect, with some of the original missing, and with additions by later hands, but the poetry of many of Job's speeches is excellent. James must have known that the new Christians were familiar with the story, for he wrote:

> Grudge not one against another, brethren, lest ye be condemned: behold, the judge standeth before the door.
> Take, my brethren, the prophets, who have spoken in the name of the Lord, for an example of suffering affliction, and of patience.
> Behold, we count them happy which endure. Ye have heard of **the patience of Job,** and have seen the end of the Lord; that the Lord is very pitiful, and of tender mercy.

Patience on a monument

Source: TWELFTH NIGHT (Act II, sc. iv, l. 117)
Author: William Shakespeare (1564–1616)
First published: 1623
Type of work: Dramatic comedy

Context: In Illyria, Viola, a shipwrecked gentlewoman, is disguised as a page, "Cesario," in the service of Duke Orsino, whom she secretly loves. Orsino, professing overpowering sentiment for the wealthy Countess Olivia, sends "Cesario" with messages of love to Olivia, who in turn falls in love with "Cesario." Viola, still in disguise, while arguing with Orsino about the ability of a man to love versus the ability of a woman to love, relates the story of her father's daughter, herself of course, who harbored a deep secret passion:

VIOLA
. . .
My father had a daughter loved a man,
As it might be perhaps, were I a woman,
I should your lordship.

DUKE
And what's her history?

851

VIOLA

A blank my lord. She never told her love,
But let concealment like a worm i' th' bud
Feed on her damask cheek. She pined in thought,
And with a green and yellow melancholy
She sat like **Patience on a monument,**
Smiling at grief. Was not this love indeed?
We men may say more, swear more, but indeed
Our shows are more than will; for still we prove
Much in our vows, but little in our love.

Peace at any price

Source: HISTORY OF THE REBELLION (Book VII, para. 233)
Author: Edward Hyde, Earl of Clarendon (1609–1674)
First published: 1702–1704
Type of work: History

Context: Hyde was one of the most distinguished of British statesmen during the mid-seventeenth century. In 1643 he was Chancellor of the Exchequer and in 1645 guardian of the Prince of Wales, the future Charles II. Following the Restoration in 1660 he was made Lord Chancellor, but his austerity brought him into disfavor in the court of the "merry monarch," and he was dismissed and exiled to France in 1674. His *History of the Rebellion* covers the years of strife between Charles I and Parliament, ending with the Restoration. It was intended as a defense of the constitutional royalists who had advised the first Charles, and it frequently deals with what were then highly controversial matters. Lord Falkland was one of Charles's moderate advisers; he defended Anglicanism as the cause of reason against both Rome and Geneva and believed that true liberty consisted in freedom of the mind. Hyde's portrait of Falkland was probably written as early as 1648:

When there was any overture or hope of peace he would be more erect and vigorous, and exceedingly solicitous to press anything which he thought might promote it; and sitting amongst his friends, often after a deep silence and frequent sighs, would, with a shrill and sad accent, ingeminate the word *Peace, Peace,* and would passionately profess that the very agony of the war, and the view of the calamites and desolation the kingdom did and must endure, took his sleep from him, and would shortly break his heart. This made some think, or pretend to think, that he was so much enamoured on **peace** that he would have been glad the King should have bought it **at any price;** which was a most unreasonable calumny; as if a man that was himself the most punctual and precise in every circumstance that might reflect upon conscience or honour could have wished the King to have committed a tresspass against either. . . .

Peace in our time

Source: THE BOOK OF COMMON PRAYER (Page 31)
Author: Traditional; translated and arranged by Archbishop Cranmer (1489–1560)
First published: 1549
Type of work: Litany

Context: The Order for Daily Evening Prayer, from which this quotation is taken, is the second service in the Book of Common Prayer, and like Morning Prayer which precedes it, is a direct descendent of the medieval system of services known as the Canonical Hours or Daily Offices. These offices, in their turn, were developed out of daily practices of instruction, prayer, and praise in use in the early Church from apostolic times. Evening Prayer begins with a series of sentences from the Scriptures which set the theme and the mood for the service to come. The worshipers are then exhorted humbly to confess their "manifold sins and wickedness" to Almighty God in the prayer of *General Confession.* Following the *Declaration of Absolution* come the Lord's Prayer, the Psalms, and the appropriate lessons for the day after which the Daily Offices originally ended. However, during the Middle Ages, it became customary to add brief devotions in the form of versicles and responses (litanies) with prayers suitable for the occasion. The devotions thus appended to Evening Prayer are so arranged that each versicle and response aptly summarizes one of the several prayers that accompany them. The litany containing the quotation and the prayer for peace which immediately follows it are here given.

Minister. O lord, show thy mercy upon us.
Answer. And grant us thy salvation.
Minister. O Lord, save the State.
Answer. And mercifully hear us when we call upon thee.
Minister. Endue thy Ministers with righteousness.
Answer. And make thy chosen people joyful.
Minister. O Lord, save thy people.
Answer. And bless thine inheritance.
Minister. Give **peace in our time,** O Lord.
Answer. For it is thou, Lord, only, that makest us dwell in safety.
Minister. O God, make clean our hearts within us.
Answer. And take not thy Holy Spirit from us.

A COLLECT FOR PEACE

O God, from whom all holy desires, all good counsels, and all just works do proceed; Give unto thy servants that peace which the world cannot give; that our hearts may be set to obey thy commandments, and also that by thee, we, being defended from the fear

of our enemies, may pass our time in rest and quietness; through
the merits of Jesus Christ our Saviour. *Amen.*

Peace with honor

Source: SPEECH AT GREENOCK, SCOTLAND
Author: Lord John Russell (1792–1878)
First published: September 19, 1853
Type of work: Political speech

Context: Lord John Russell, long a prominent Whig and from 1846 to 1852 Britain's Prime Minister, became Foreign Secretary in a new ministry of Whigs and moderate Tories under Lord Aberdeen early in 1853. Within two months he resigned the secretaryship but agreed to remain in the cabinet without office. When Russia, under Tsar Nicholas I, occupied Moldavia and Wallachia, two Balkan provinces of the Ottoman Empire, Britain and France sent fleets into the Aegean. Attempting to avert war, the major European powers drafted a compromise known as the "Vienna Note." The Turks insisted on an amendment designating the Sultan rather than the Tsar as principal protector of the Turkish Christians. Aberdeen's ministry endorsed the amendment, but when it was rejected by the Tsar, the British cabinet, in Russell's absence, decided to press the Turks to accept the original terms. Irate over what seemed to him an abandonment of Britain's earlier commitment to the Turks, Russell wrote Aberdeen on September 17, 1853, of his intention to resign from the ministry. That same evening before a public meeting at Greenock, Scotland, he spoke on the subject of the crisis. The "Vienna Note" failed, and by the end of October, 1853, the Turks' efforts to recover the provinces north of the Danube had marked the beginning of the Crimean War. In his Greenock speech, Russell said:

> While we endeavour to maintain peace, I certainly should be the last to forget that, if **peace** cannot be maintained **with honour** it is no longer peace.

Pelting each other for the public good

Source: CHARITY (Line 623)
Author: William Cowper (1731–1800)
First published: 1782
Type of work: Meditative poem

Context: In this poem Cowper, a very religious man, celebrates the third and greatest of the theological virtues: charity, or love, which he

854

calls "Chief grace below, and all in all above." Early in the poem he praises Captain Cook for the friendliness he bestowed upon the natives of the islands he discovered; the explorer is used as an example of charity in action. As Cowper put it, "While Cook is loved for savage lives he saved,/ See Cortez odious for a world enslaved!" Among his comments about charity, Cowper points out that this virtue does not mean giving alms with a "queazy conscience." Real charity, maintains the poet, intends only another person's good, not one's own.

Cowper suggests that even the satirist, who hopes by his satire to improve mankind, must be careful of his motives; as an example of the satirist gone wrong Cowper cites Jonathan Swift, named in the poem as "St. Patrick's dean," as a satirist who "Too often rails to gratify his spleen." Reform, the object of satire, says the poet, must proceed from love for God or man. Cowper's poem ends with the poet's view of what the world might be if church and state were motivated by charity:

> The statesman, skill'd in projects dark and deep,
> Might burn his useless Machiavel, and sleep;
> His budget, often fill'd yet always poor,
> Might swing at ease behind his study door,
> No longer prey upon our annual rents,
> Nor scare the nation with its big contents:
> Disbanded legions freely might depart,
> And slaying man would cease to be an art.
> No learned disputants would take the field,
> Sure not to conquer, and sure not to yield,
> Both sides deceived if rightly understood,
> **Pelting each other for the public good.**

The people are the masters

Source: SPEECH ON ECONOMICAL REFORM
Author: Edmund Burke (1729–1797)
First published: 1780
Type of work: Political speech

Context: Burke was elated in 1780 when, for once, he and his fellow Whigs were given considerable popular support and were thus able to move from their previous position of ineffective criticism to one of constructive action. Burke immediately introduced a plan for reforming the economic structure of many of the government offices. This plan called for the suppression of useless offices, modification of pension lists, and the abolition of several separate jurisdictional areas. Some of these reforms had been the subject of popular petitions, and Burke cited this support as authority for the changes:

855

. . . Why should we resolve to do nothing, because what I propose to you may not be the exact demand of the petition, when we are far from resolved to comply even with what evidently is so? Does this sort of chicanery become us? **The people are the masters.** They have only to express their wants at large and in gross. We are the expert artists, we are the skilful workmen, to shape their desires into perfect form, and to fit the utensil to the use. They are the sufferers, they tell the symptoms of the complaint; but we know the exact seat of the disease, and how to apply the remedy according to the rules of art. . . .

A perfect democracy is the most shameless thing in the world

Source: REFLECTIONS ON THE REVOLUTION IN FRANCE
Author: Edmund Burke (1729–1797)
First published: 1790
Type of work: Political treatise

Context: Burke was one of the greatest political philosophers England has ever produced. As a member of Parliament he expressed sympathy for the American Colonies both before and during their Revolution, for he considered that they were defending established and traditional rights. The French Revolution, on the other hand, he regarded as a violent, vicious, and dangerous repudiation of all sane and traditional principles of liberty and orderly government; and extensive English sympathy for that Revolution led him to publish his criticisms of it in these *Reflections*. In this section he points out that monarchs are limited by those through whom they must operate and their own concern for fame and reputation; with the rulers of a democracy the case is quite different:

. . . But where popular authority is absolute and unrestrained, the people have an infinitely greater, because a far better founded confidence in their own power. They are themselves, in a great measure, their own instruments. They are nearer to their objects. Besides, they are less under responsibility to one of the greatest controlling powers on earth, the sense of fame and estimation. The share of infamy that is likely to fall to the lot of each individual in public acts, is small indeed; the operation of opinion being in inverse ratio to the number of those who abuse power. Their own approbation of their own acts has to them the appearance of a public judgment in their favour. **A perfect democracy is** therefore **the most shameless thing in the world.** As it is the most shameless, it is also the most fearless. No man apprehends in his person he can be made subject to punishment. . . .

A perfect tragedy is the noblest production of human nature

Source: THE SPECTATOR (No. 39)
Author: Joseph Addison (1672–1719)
First published: April 14, 1711
Type of work: Essay

Context: In the five hundred and fifty-five regular issues of the *Spectator,* Joseph Addison and Richard Steele brought popular essay journalism to a height of perfection never achieved before and seldom since. For a large middle-class reading public they created an interest in public affairs, literary and dramatic criticism, public morality, and manners. In this essay concerned with the development of English drama, Addison summarizes Aristotle's comments on tragedy, discusses several characteristics of classical drama, and reviews the strengths and weaknesses of English dramatists from the time of Shakespeare to his own. The line quoted is from the opening paragraph:

As **a perfect tragedy is the noblest production of human nature,** so it is capable of giving the mind one of the most delightful and most improving entertainments. "A virtuous man," says Seneca, "struggling with misfortunes is such a spectacle as gods might look upon with pleasure." And such a pleasure it is which one meets with in the representation of a well-written tragedy. Diversions of this kind wear out of our thoughts everything that is mean and little. They cherish and cultivate that humanity which is the ornament of our nature. They soften insolence, soothe affliction, and subdue the mind to the dispensations of Providence.

Persuasion hung upon his lips

Source: THE LIFE AND OPINIONS OF TRISTRAM SHANDY, GENT. (Book I, chapter 19)
Author: Laurence Sterne (1713–1768)
First published: 1759–1767
Type of work: Novel

Context: Among the crotchety hypotheses held by Walter Shandy, father of Tristram, was, "That there was a kind of magick bias, which good or bad names, as he called them, irresistibly impressed upon our characters and conduct." Thus, while waiting for his second child to be born he discoursed at length on his notion, expressing "the most unconquerable aversion for TRISTRAM; he had the lowest and most contemptible opinion of it of any thing in the world. . . ." Ironically, when he was told that his wife had presented him with another son, and he informed the maid Susannah that the boy was to be given the noble name of Trismegistus, Susannah misinformed the curate, who then christened the child Tristram, to the endless sorrow of both the father and, later, the son. When writing of the forensic powers of his father, Tristram remarks:

> . . . But, indeed, to speak of my father as he was;—he was certainly irresistible, both in his orations and disputations;—he was born an orator; . . . **Persuasion hung upon his lips,** and the elements of Logick and Rhetorick were so blended up in him,—and, withall, he had so shrewd a guess at the weaknesses and passions of his respondent,—that NATURE might have stood up and said,—"This man is eloquent." . . .

The petty done, the undone vast

Source: THE LAST RIDE TOGETHER (Stanza 5)
Author: Robert Browning (1812–1889)
First published: 1855
Type of work: Dramatic monologue

Context: Rejected by the sweetheart he had hoped to win, a lover recalls how he accepted the rejection, not bitterly but "in pride and thankfulness," blessing her who had, for a while at least, given him hope. He had asked that, before parting, they might take a last ride together, and she had granted his wish. As they rode, he mused on the failure not only of his own hopes but of those of other men as well:

> Fail I alone, in words and deeds?
> Why, all men strive and who succeeds?
> We rode; it seemed my spirit flew,
> Saw other regions, cities new,
>   As the world rushed by on either side.
> I thought,—All labour, yet no less
> Bear up beneath their unsuccess.
> Look at the end of work, contrast
> **The petty done, the undone vast,**
> This present of theirs with the hopeful past!
>   I hoped she would love me; here we ride.

Pharaoh is sold for balsams

Source: HYDRIOTAPHIA: URN BURIAL (Chapter 5)
Author: Sir Thomas Browne (1605–1682)
First published: 1658
Type of work: Philosophy

Context: Browne, in this philosophical work, considers some burial urns of ancient and unknown origin which were dug up in Norfolk. He must have had a bit of the archeologist in him, since he later based another philosophical discourse on some urns found at Brampton. In any case, the urns serve only as a basis for his considerations of death and immortality. In *Urn Burial* he observes that these pathetic relics of men have survived but that all else concerning them is utterly forgotten. He notes that oblivion is the fate of all men—swift for most, postponed for a few. "Had they made as good provision for their names, as they have done for their Reliques," drily comments Browne, "they had not so grosly erred in the art of perpetuation. . . . Vain ashes, which in the oblivion of names, persons, times, and sexes, have found

unto themselves, a fruitless continuation, and only arise unto late posterity, as Emblemes of mortall vanities; Antidotes against pride, vain-glory, and madding vices." Browne pursues the subject further: nothing on earth can survive eternity; even the greatest monument becomes dust at last. We, "being necessitated to eye the remaining particle of futurity, are naturally constituted unto thoughts of the next world, and cannot excusably decline the consideration of that duration, which maketh pyramids pillars of snow, and all that's past a moment." Browne's conclusion is that Christian immortality is the only kind for which we can hope. He describes man's inherent optimism and lists a few of the many ways in which men have tried to achieve some form of self-perpetuation beyond this life:

. . . Afflictions induce callosities; miseries are slippery, or fall like snow upon us, which notwithstanding is no unhappy stupidity. To be ignorant of evils to come, and forgetful of evils past, is a mercifull provision in nature, whereby we digest the mixture of our few and evil dayes, and, our delivered senses not relapsing into cutting remembrances, our sorrows are not kept raw by the edge of repetitions. A great part of Antiquity contented their hopes of subsistency with a transmigration of their souls. A good way to continue their memories, while having the advantage of plurall successions, they could not but act something remarkable in such variety of beings, and enjoying the fame of their passed selves, make accumulation of glory unto their last durations. Others, rather than be lost in the uncomfortable night of nothing, were content to recede into the common being, and make one particle of the public soul of all things, which was no more then to return into their unknown and divine Originall again. Ægyptian ingenuity was more unsatisfied, contriving their bodies in sweet consistencies, to attend the return of their souls. But all was vanity, feeding the winde, and folly. The Ægyptian Mummies, which Cambyses or time hath spared, avarice now consumeth. Mummie is become Merchandise, Mizraim cures wounds, and **Pharaoh is sold for balsams.**

859

Philosophic diner-out

Source: MR. SLUDGE, "THE MEDIUM" (Line 773)
Author: Robert Browning (1812–1889)
First published: 1864
Type of work: Dramatic monologue

Context: Robert Browning sharpened the dramatic monologue to a fine edge in utilizing this poetic genre as a means of exposing the full range of characterization. Characters in love, in hate, in joy, in misery—characters, in short, involved in life itself—parade before us in his poems. In "Mr. Sludge, 'The Medium,'" expressing his distrust of the medium or the spiritualist, he depicts a character involved in cozenage. The poem, possibly occasioned by Browning's severe antagonism against the American spiritualist Daniel D. Home, sets forth Sludge as the protagonist. His deceptions detected, the medium first attempts to win sympathy by confessing the fraud of his trade and his own personal corruption. But as the deceiver is allowed to talk, his confidence begins to reappear, and the defense of his profession takes form; without the gullible people who fall into his snare because they desire to be deluded and to cultivate the thrill of spiritual communication, the practice could not exist. The dramatic monologue, then, in the final analysis becomes a sweeping attack, not merely upon the disreputable practitioner but also upon the individual whose curiosity and lack of common sense render him prey to such blandishments:

> Yet I think
> There's a more hateful form of foolery—
> The social sage's, Solomon of saloons
> And **philosophic diner-out,** the fribble
> Who wants a doctrine for a chopping-block
> To try the edge of his faculty upon,
> Prove how much common sense he'll hack and hew
> I' the critical minute 'twixt the soup and fish!
> These were my patrons: these, and the like of them
> Who, rising in my soul now, sicken it,—
> These I have injured! Gratitude to these? . . .
> So much for my remorse at thanklessness
> Toward a deserving public!

Picker-up of learning's crumbs

Source: AN EPISTLE CONTAINING THE STRANGE MEDICAL EXPERIENCE OF KARSHISH, THE ARAB PHYSICIAN (Line 1)
Author: Robert Browning (1812–1889)
First published: 1855
Type of work: Dramatic monologue

Context: Written as a letter from the humble physician Karshish to his learned friend and teacher Abib, this poem relates what happens when a scientist comes face to face with a miracle. Karshish is openminded and eager in his search for greater knowledge; he closely examines nature for new cures and hopes, during his journey through the Holy Land, to discover herbs and ointments that will be useful in his profession. Though he is willing to go out of his way to study a spider, he cannot accept the story told about Lazarus, who claims that he was raised from the dead by Jesus. With the keen intellect of a scientist, he dismisses this miracle as a tale told by a madman. The irony of the man who humbly seeks ways to heal but discards the Healer is stressed in this quotation; Karshish has such a scientific mind that he cannot accept a miracle, thus leaving the Holy Land with only insignificant knowledge.

Karshish, the **picker-up of learning's crumbs,**
The not-incurious in God's handiwork . . .
The vagrant Scholar to his Sage at home
Sends greeting (health and knowledge, fame with peace)
Three samples of true snake-stone—rarer still,
One of the other sort, the melon-shaped
(But fitter, pounded fine, for charms than drugs)
And writeth now the twenty-second time.

Pig in a poke

Source: FIVE HUNDRED POINTS OF GOOD HUSBANDRY (Chapter 16, "September's Husbandry")
Author: Thomas Tusser (c. 1525–1580)
First published: 1557
Type of work: Didactic poem

Context: Thomas Tusser was a gentleman, from a good family, and was a graduate of Eton and Cambridge; but the urban life for which he had been prepared did not suit him, and he abandoned it for rural simplicity and a farm. He moved from one farm to another and does not appear to have been successful in husbandry, though he had a thorough knowledge of it and wrote books on the subject. As sometimes happens, he was able to tell others how to succeed without being able to do so himself. He died at last in a debtor's prison. His *Five Hundred Points of Good Husbandry,* in which all manner of practical suggestions are given, provides us with an excellent picture of life on an early Elizabethan farm. Included in the book are observations on weather and climate, the planets, and other natural phenomena; there are also moral maxims and various popular sayings. The entire book is done in verse with a rude, homely flavor, some of it mere doggerel but endowed with rustic charm. The first eleven chapters are short verses consisting of general observations on agriculture and farm life, and the twelfth describes the farmer's diet. At this point the main body of Tusser's early "farmer's almanac" actually begins. Chapters thirteen and fourteen discuss the winds and the planets. Chapter fifteen is a summary ("September's Abstract") of the chapter which follows; the latter, "September's Husbandry," begins the farmer's year.

This is the best time, says Tusser, to take over a farm. Change in ownership is not a speedy matter, for the seller is entitled to his harvest; however, the buyer may move in ahead of time on any fallow ground and begin his own work. This is also a good time to drive a bargain, and here Tusser uses one of the familiar sayings of the day; it was already old when John Heywood (1497?–1580?) added it to his collection, *Proverbes* (1546):

1. At Michelmas lightly, new farmer comes in,
   New husbandry forceth him, new to begin;
   Old farmer, still taking, the time to him given,
   Makes August to last, untill Michelmas even.

2. New farmer may enter, (as champions say),
   On all that is fallow, at Lent Lady-day:
   In woodland, old farmer to that will not yield,
   For losing of pasture, and feed of his field.

3. Provide against Michelmas, bargain to make,
   For terme to give over, to keep or to take;
   In doing of either, let wit bear a stroke,
   For buying or selling of **pig in a poke.**

4. Good farm and well stored, good housing and dry,
   Good corn and good dairy, good market and nigh;
   Good shepherd, good tillman, good *Jack* and good *Gill,*
   Make husband and huswife their coffers to fill.

Pigging together in the same truckle-bed

Source: SPEECH ON AMERICAN TAXATION
Author: Edmund Burke (1729–1797)
First published: 1775
Type of work: Political speech

Context: When news of the Boston Tea Party reached London, Lord North, as a Parliamentary leader, proposed strong punitive measures against the offending port. Burke, one of England's greatest political philosophers and stanch defender of the American Colonies, in rebuttal argued vigorously for the expediency of repealing the tea duty. The second portion of the speech is a survey of the whole subject of American taxation since 1766 with several caustically ironic portraits of various politicians concerned with the issue. One of these, Lord Chatham, says Burke, put together such a "checkered and speckled" administration that at times even single offices were shared by "Whigs and Tories, treacherous friends and open enemies":

> . . . I venture to say, it did so happen that persons had a single office divided between them, who had never spoke to each other in their lives, until they found themselves, they knew not how, **pigging together,** heads and points, **in the same truckle-bed.**
> Sir, in consequence of this arrangement, having put so much the larger part of his enemies and opposition into power, the confusion was such, that his own principles could not possibly have any effect or influence in the conduct of affairs. . . .

Pile Pelion on Ossa

Source: THE ODYSSEY (Book XI, l. 388, as translated by Alexander Pope)
Author: Homer (c. 850 B.C.)
First transcribed: Sixth century, B.C.
Type of work: Epic poem

Context: Calypso, commanded by the gods, permits Ulysses to build a small boat and leave her island. Although Neptune sends a terrible storm to torment him, Ulysses, with the help of Leucothea, a sea-goddess, arrives, shipwrecked but alive, on the beach in the land of Phaeacia. There he is found by Nausicaa, the daughter of King Alcinoüs of Phaeacia. The princess clothes the castaway and sends him to her father's court. Asked by Alcinoüs, after a banquet, to tell his story, Ulysses relates his adventures since the fall of Troy, years before. In Book XI of *The Odyssey* he tells of his arrival in Cimmeria and his descent below the surface of the earth to the land of the dead. In Hades he meets Tiresias, the blind seer, who informs him of the future, and he meets Anticlea, his mother, who gives him news of his wife and son. He also sees the shades, or spirits, of many of the ancient heroines of Greek legend: Tyro, beloved of Neptune; Antiope, beloved of Zeus; Alcmena, another woman loved by Zeus; Megara, the mother of Hercules; Jocasta, the mother-wife of Oedipus; and others, including Ephimedia. Homer puts a commentary about each woman into Ulysses' mouth; and Ulysses relates how the sons of Ephimedia, Ephialtes and Otus, grew tall and strong, and challenged the gods themselves. Proud of their strength, they heaved one mountain, Ossa, upon Mount Olympus, and then threw Mount Pelion on top of both. The words of the proverbial version are not quite the same as in Pope's translation:

> The wondrous youths had scarce nine winters told,
> When high in air, tremendous to behold,

863

Nine ells aloft they rear'd their towering head,
And full nine cubits broad their shoulders spread.
Proud of their strength, and more than mortal size,
The gods they challenge, and affect the skies:
Heaved on Olympus tottering Ossa stood;
On Ossa, Pelion nods with all his wood.

The Pilot of the Galilean Lake

Source: LYCIDAS (Line 108)
Author: John Milton (1608–1674)
First published: 1637
Type of work: Elegiac pastoral poem

Context: Milton, after a passage of lamentation for Lycidas, or Edward King, who was drowned in the Irish Sea, wonders why anyone should pursue the poet's calling, as poetry is a neglected art. Why would it not be better to live a life of pleasure than to undergo the pains of writing poetry? But the desire for fame urges him on, to scorn delight and to live in labor to achieve his ends. When, however, the poet, after all of his work, thinks to get the fame that he so eagerly strives for, the fates cut his thread of life and he dies. Milton then reflects that fame in the world of men is not really what he desires; rather, it is the approbation of God, the heavenly reward for work well done: this was one of Milton's basic ideas and is found elsewhere in his poetry. He then turns back to Lycidas and asks what hard fate doomed him to death. Could it have been that the ship he sailed on was built during an eclipse and so was cursed? He next turns his attention to the River Cam, the stream that flows through Cambridge, where the two, King and Milton, were fellow students; and finally St. Peter with his Keys of the Kingdom, who says that there were more than enough unworthy people who might have died instead of the poet.

Next Camus, reverend sire, went footing slow,
His mantle hairy, and his bonnet sedge,
Inwrought with figures dim, and on the edge
Like to that sanguine flower inscribed with woe.
"Ah! Who hath reft," quoth he, "my dearest pledge?"
Last came, and last did go,
The Pilot of the Galilean Lake.
Two massy keys he bore of metals twain,
(The golden opes, the iron shuts amain).
He shook his mitred locks, and stern bespake:
"How well could I have spared for thee, young swain,
Enow of such as for their bellies' sake,
Creep and intrude and climb into the fold?"

The pink of womankind

Source: THE POSIE (Line 7)
Author: Robert Burns (1759–1796)
First published: 1792
Type of work: Lyric poem

Context: "Pink," in the sense of highest point or choicest bit, may be a variant of "pick," as when we say "The pick of the crop." It occurs in many well-known phrases. "The pink of condition" is current. In *Romeo and Juliet,* Shakespeare's character boasted of being "the very pink of courtesy," a phrase later repeated by Steele in *The Tatler,* No. 204. *She Stoops to Conquer,* Act I, speaks of "the very pink of perfection." So Robert Burns in writting a poem to his "ain dear May," calls her "the pink o' womankind," the finest of women, and therefore includes a flower of the variety called Pinks in the Posie, or bouquet, that he gathers for her. Unfortunately, his knowledge of flowers was less than his skill as a poet, because into the bouquet, he manages to put, and tie with the silken band of love, flowers from all seasons of the year: rose, hyacinth, daisy, woodbine, violet, lily, and hawthorn among them. Here are the second and the sixth of the seven stanzas.

> The primrose I will pu', the firstling of the year,
> And I will pu' the pink, the emblem o' my dear,
> For she's **the pink o' womankind,** and blooms without a peer:
>   And a' to be a Posie to my ain dear May . . .
>
> The woodbine I will pu' when the e'ening star is near,
> Amd the diamond drops o' dew shall be her een (eyes) sae
>   clear:
> The violet's for modesty which weel she fa's to wear.
>   And a' to be a Posie to my ain dear May.

A place for everything and everything in its place

Source: THRIFT (Chapter 5)
Author: Samuel Smiles (1812–1904)
First published: 1875
Type of work: Inspirational essay

Context: One of the widely read authors of the late nineteenth century was a Scotch physician and biographer who began his writing career with the life of George Stephenson (1781–1848), who helped introduce the steam locomotive into England when he built the Rocket, that won out over competitors and began pulling trains from Liverpool to Manchester. Encouraged by one success, Smiles employed biographical epi-

865

sodes and moral counsel in a series of inspirational books for young people. *Self-Help* (1859) began the series. Smiles paused long enough to compile a three-volume *Lives of Engineers* (1861–1863), then resumed the didactic series with *Character* (1871), *Thrift* (1875), and *Duty* (1880). The completion of *Thrift* was delayed by an attack of paralysis, but the author rose above his infirmity as he advised his readers to rise above their handicaps. He had written his first book to stress the importance of economizing and the rewards of so doing, but as he comments in the Preface to his third book, thrift is the basis of self-help and the foundation of much that is excellent in character. In its first chapter, he points out the importance of money, and remarks on the need for industry to benefit those who depend on a person. Industry must know how to earn, how to spend, and how to save. So Chapter II considers habits of thrift. It is followed by a contrasting chapter on Improvidence. Chapter IV lists the Means of Saving, and V is filled with Examples of Thrift. It begins with quotations from Lacon (1820) by Charles C. Colton, as well as from Burns, Cicero, and Shakespeare. Then Smiles tells the story of the British dramatist Mrs. Inchbald, who from her small earnings set aside two pounds a week for the benefit of her ailing sister. The author comes to the conclusion that "Benevolence never ruined any one, though thoughtlessness and dissipation have ruined thousands." In the next paragraph he discusses the need for planning and order.

The words "Waste not, want not," carved in stone over Sir Walter Scott's kitchen fireplace at Abbotsford, express in a few words the secret of order in the midst of abundance. Order is most useful in the management of everything—of a household, of a business, of a manufactory, of an army. Its maxim is, **A place for everything and everything in its place.** Order is wealth; for, whoever properly regulates the use of his income, almost doubles his resources. Disorderly people are rarely rich, and orderly people are rarely poor.

A plague of all cowards I say

Source: KING HENRY THE FOURTH: PART ONE (Act II, sc. iv, l. 127)
Author: William Shakespeare (1564–1616)
First published: 1598
Type of work: Historical drama

Context: In one of the chief comic intrigues of the play, Prince Hal and Poins have foiled the robbery of the king's retainers at Gads Hill. Disguised, the two fell upon Falstaff and his cronies—Bardolph, Peto, and Gadshill—and counter-robbed them after they had successfully secured the money from the carriers. Hal and Poins now return to the Boar's Head Tavern where they await Falstaff's return with comic anticipation, anxious to see how the braggadocio will attempt to cover his cowardice. Meanwhile, Falstaff—down but not defeated—has instructed his companions to hack their swords and to tickle their nose with spear-grass so that the bloody shirts and beaten blades will suggest a furious battle. Further, since Hal, to Falstaff's knowledge, did not participate in the robbery as agreed, the "huge bombard of sack" determines that the best defense is a good offense. Consequently, when he and his men stagger into the tavern bloody and beaten, he immediately begins to berate the prince for his cowardice before anyone has an opportunity to question him concerning his Gads Hill activities:

POINS

Welcome Jack, Where hast thou been?

FALSTAFF

A plague of all cowards, I say, and a vengeance too, marry and amen! Give me a cup of sack boy. Ere I lead this life long, I'll sew nether stocks and mend them, and foot them too. A plague of all cowards! Give me a cup of sack rogue. Is there no virtue extant?

PRINCE HENRY

Didst thou never see Titan kiss a dish of butter—pitiful-hearted Titan—that melted at the sweet tale of the sun's? If thou didst, then behold that compound.

FALSTAFF

You rogue, here's lime in this sack too; there is nothing but roguery to be found in villainous man, yet a coward is worse than a cup of sack with lime in it. A villainous coward! . . . There lives not three good men unhanged in England, and one of them is fat, and grows old, . . .

. . .

Play out the play

Source: KING HENRY THE FOURTH: PART ONE (Act II, sc. iv, l. 531)
Author: William Shakespeare (1564–1616)
First published: 1598
Type of work: Historical drama

Context: Falstaff and his companions, having been ignominiously foiled in their efforts to rob the king's retainers at Gads Hill, attempt to conceal their failure behind a fantastic lie. They hack their swords and tickle their noses with spear-grass so that, bloody and beaten, they will give the appearance of having engaged in a furious battle. Their attempts are to no avail, however, for Prince Hal and Poins expose their lie and reveal that the two of them robbed Falstaff's group without so much as one sword's blow. When news from court interrupts this merry scene and Hal is commanded to appear before his father the next morning, Falstaff and Hal exchange the roles of father and son in comic anticipation of the father's anger at his son's prodigality. With Falstaff in the role of the son, he implores the father not to banish "sweet," "kind," "true," "valiant Jack Falstaff, and therefore more valiant, being, as he is, old Jack Falstaff." When the sheriff suddenly arrives at the tavern to arrest Falstaff, the "tun of man"—desirous both of adding further self praise in his "role" and of diverting Hal's attention from admitting the sheriff—calls for the action to continue:

BARDOLPH

O, my lord, my lord, the sheriff with a most monstrous watch is at the door.

FALSTAFF

Out ye rouge, **play out the play.** I have much to say in behalf of that Falstaff.

Enter HOSTESS
HOSTESS

O Jesu, my lord, my lord—

PRINCE HENRY

Heigh, heigh, the devil rides upon a fiddlestick. What's the matter?

HOSTESS

The sheriff and all the watch at the door; they are come to search the house, shall I let them in?

FALSTAFF

Dost thou hear, Hal, never call a true piece of gold a counterfeit. Thou art essentially made without seeming so.

PRINCE HENRY

And thou a natural coward, without instinct.

FALSTAFF

I deny your major; if you will deny the sheriff, so; if not, let him enter.
. . .

Play the fool, but at a cheaper rate

Source: RETIREMENT (Line 562)
Author: William Cowper (1731–1800)
First published: 1782
Type of work: Meditative poem

Context: Cowper, a descendant of John Donne, did not turn to the writing of poetry as a serious occupation until he was fifty. He entered upon the legal profession as a career and was called to the bar in 1754, but was forced into retirement by attacks of insanity. The first cost him the girl he had hoped to marry; the second drove him to attempted suicide. After a long convalescence he retired to the country, moving first to Huntingdon and later to Olney, where he lived with friends in quiet seclusion. His Calvinism, a source of both grief and hope to him, was undoubtedly a factor in his recurrent melancholia; it also led him to moralize in his writings. His first volume, *Poems,* appeared in 1782. Cowper is primarily a poet of rural life; he surveys the pleasant countryside and deals with the simple routines and pleasures of his days. He reflects on the nature of human existence, meditates on man's higher destiny, and considers the outside world. His love of nature is revealed in his vivid, if tranquil, descriptions of its beauty. His greatest work, *The Task,* exhibits these qualities at their best. Comparatively little of Cowper's emotional and spiritual stress appears in his poetry; he had a sweet disposition and a few of his works are humorous, whimsical, or quietly satirical. He translated Homer and a number of lesser writings, edited Milton, and wrote a number of lasting hymns. His religious convictions are always more or less apparent in his work, and some of his poems are akin to sermons. *Retirement* meditates on the stresses and moral dangers of competitive activity in the world, notes that some form of escape is the dream of all, and prescribes God's handiwork—nature and rural simplicity—as the best refuge. He then describes many walks of life and their problems, indicating the benefits a vacation might provide. Among them is the example of a young heir and his encumbered estate: his debts force him into retirement which he heartily dislikes:

> Anticipated rents and bills unpaid
> Force many a shining youth into the shade
> Not to redeem his time, but his estate,
> And **play the fool, but at a cheaper rate.**
> There, hid in loathed obscurity, removed
> From pleasures left, but never more beloved,
> He just endures, and with a sickly spleen
> Sighs o'er the beauties of the charming scene.
> Nature indeed looks prettily in rhyme,
> Streams tinkle sweetly in poetic chime,
> The warblings of the blackbird, clear and strong,

Are musical enough in Thomson's song,
And Cobham's groves and Windsor's green retreats
When Pope describes them, have a thousand sweets.
He likes the country, but in truth must own,
Most likes it, when he studies it in town.

Please, sir, I want some more

Source: OLIVER TWIST (Chapter 2)
Author: Charles Dickens (1812–1870)
First published: 1837–1839
Type of work: Novel

Context: Oliver Twist is a foundling whose mother died without revealing her identity after she was found in the street. As an infant Oliver is farmed out to the branch-workhouse operated by elderly Mrs. Mann, who receives seven-and-a-half pence each week for his keep, most of which she pockets for herself, so that Oliver, like the other small boys in Mrs. Mann's care, grows up hungry. Oliver is luckier than some of her charges, for he is not smothered by accident, does not die by falling into the fireplace while unwatched, nor sickens and dies without any medical care. On Oliver's ninth birthday Mr. Bumble, the parish beadle, who gave Oliver Twist his name, arrives to take the boy to the workhouse itself. He removes him from Mrs. Mann's house and takes him for an appearance before the parish board, made up of fat, well-fed gentlemen, who examine the boy briefly and then consign him to the workhouse as an oakum picker. In the workhouse Oliver is the victim of slow starvation, his diet consisting of three small bowlfuls of oatmeal gruel per day, with an onion twice a week and a roll on Sunday. Under this regimen which reduces the boys to living skeletons, Oliver and his companions become voraciously hungry. At last they hold a council among themselves and resolve to choose by lot one of their number to ask the overseer for more gruel. The victim of the lottery is Oliver Twist:

The evening arrived; the boys took their places. The master, in his cook's uniform, stationed himself at the copper; his pauper assistants ranged themselves behind him; the gruel was served out; and a long grace was said over the short commons. The gruel disappeared; the boys whispered each other, and winked at Oliver, while his next neighbors nudged him. Child as he was, he was desperate with hunger, and reckless with misery. He rose from the table; and advancing to the master, basin and spoon in hand, said: somewhat alarmed at his own temerity:
"Please, sir, I want some more."
The master was a fat, healthy man; but he turned very pale. He gazed in stupefied astonishment on the small rebel for some sec-

870

onds, and then clung for support to the copper. The assistants were paralysed with wonder; the boys with fear.

"What!" said the master at length, in a faint voice.

"Please, sir," replied Oliver, **"I want some more."**

The master aimed a blow at Oliver's head with the ladle; pinioned him in his arms; and shrieked aloud for the beadle.

Pleasure is labor too, and tires as much

Source: HOPE (Line 20)
Author: William Cowper (1731–1800)
First published: 1782
Type of work: Meditative poem

Context: Cowper, the last English poet to belong to what has been called the cult of simplicity, was late in blooming; though he wrote a few verses in his youth, he did not turn seriously to the writing of poetry until he was fifty. His education was in the legal profession and he was called to the bar in 1754. He fell in love with his cousin, but emotional stress brought on an attack of insanity and he was forbidden to see or marry her. Another attack occurred while he was preparing for an examination in 1763, and he attempted suicide. There was a lengthy convalescence, after which he retired to the country, living first at Huntingdon and later at Olney. He never married. Cowper was a Calvinist and a deeply religious man; though his faith brought him comfort, it also brought despair and was undoubtedly a major factor in the recurring periods of depression from which he suffered. During one of these, he was convinced, God had told him he could have no hope of salvation. At another time he believed God had told him to kill himself, but that the Deity had subsequently retracted this command. Comparatively little of this intense spiritual suffering appears in Cowper's work; his poetry deals with simple rural life, with the quiet countryside, and the unassuming pleasures and routines of the day. His descriptions of the landscape are vivid but tranquil; he meditates and reflects, and his religious convictions encourage him to moralize. His first volume, *Poems,* appeared in 1782 and was followed three years later by his greatest work, *The Task. Hope,* a poem of moderate length in the first volume, is typical of his more consistently meditative poems. In it he considers the nature of man's earthly life and reflects upon human attitudes toward it. The world is neither the place of despair we sometimes believe it to be, nor is it one of unthinking joy: what really sustains man is hope. Cowper's poem begins with the negative attitude of the disillusioned:

Ask what is human life—the sage replies,
With disappointment low'ring in his eyes,
A painful passage o'er a restless flood,
A vain pursuit of fugitive false good,

A scene of fancied bliss and heartfelt care,
Closing at last in darkness and despair.—
The poor, inured to drudgery and distress,
Act without aim, think little, and feel less,
And nowhere, but in feign'd Arcadian scenes,
Taste happiness, or know what pleasure means.
Riches are pass'd away from hand to hand,
As fortune, vice, or folly may command;
As in a dance the pair that take the lead
Turn downward, and the lowest pair succeed,
So shifting and so various is the plan
By which Heav'n rules the mix'd affairs of man;
Vicissitude wheels round the motley crowd,
The rich grow poor, the poor become purse-proud,
Bus'ness is labour, and man's weakness such,
Pleasure is labour too, and tires as much,
The very sense of it foregoes its use,
By repetition pall'd, by age obtuse.
Youth lost in dissipation, we deplore
Through life's sad remnant, what no sighs restore;
Our years, a fruitless race without a prize,
Too many, yet too few to make us wise.

The plot thickens

Source: THE REHEARSAL (Act III, sc. ii)
Author: George Villiers, Duke of Buckingham (1628–1687)
First published: 1672
Type of work: Dramatic comedy

Context: Buckingham's play *The Rehearsal* was written to ridicule the extravagances of the heroic drama being written and staged during the reign of Charles II. In these plays, quite popular with the London audiences of the time, one finds characters dominated by love and honor to the point of absurdity. The dialogue is bombastic and unreal; the action is noisy and confused. The scenery is fanciful; and songs and dances are introduced at ridiculous points in the plays. The specific butt of the satire in *The Rehearsal* is John Dryden, as the playwright named Bayes, who was highly successful at penning heroic dramas and whose extravagant *The Conquest of Granada* had been produced in 1670. In *The Rehearsal* Bayes the playwright is commenting about his new play to Smith and Johnson, two men who have come to observe the rehearsal of Bayes' drama. The play-within-the-play has a ludicrously involved plot about the usurpation of two thrones. The hero of it is Prince Pretty-Man, who was taken from his cradle by a fisherman and brought up as the commoner's son. The foster father is suspected of a murder and arrested:

872

JOHNSON

But, Mr. Bayes, is not this some disparagement to a prince to pass for a fisherman's son? Have a care of that, I pray.

BAYES

No, no, not at all; for 'tis but for a while: I shall fetch him off again presently, you shall see.

[*Enter* PRETTY-MAN AND THIMBLE]
PRETTY-MAN

By all the gods, I'll set the world on fire
Rather than let 'em ravish hence my sire.

THIMBLE

Brave Pretty-Man, it is at length reveal'd
That he is not thy sire who thee conceal'd.

BAYES

Lo, you now; there he's off again.

JOHNSON

Admirably don, i' faith.

BAYES

Aye, now **the plot thickens** very much upon us.

Pluck bright honor from the pale-faced moon

Source: KING HENRY THE FOURTH: PART ONE (Act I, sc. iii, l. 202)
Author: William Shakespeare (1564–1616)
First published: 1598
Type of work: Historical drama

Context: When young Henry Percy, called Hotspur, is reprimanded by King Henry for refusing to release to him prisoners of war captured by Percy, the valiant youth declares to his father and uncle his opposition to the king. Recalling that they have helped to crown this man when the throne belonged to Mortimer only to find themselves dismissed by the king, Hotspur rages and thinks only of recapturing the family honor.

HOTSPUR

By heaven methinks it were an easy leap,
To **pluck bright honour from the pale-faced moon,**
Or dive into the bottom of the deep,
Where fathom-line could never touch the ground,
And pluck up drowned honour by the locks,

873

So he that doth redeem her thence might wear
Without corrival all her dignities. . . .

Poetry is the record of the best and happiest moments
of the happiest and best minds

Source: A DEFENCE OF POETRY
Author: Percy Bysshe Shelley (1792–1822)
First published: 1840
Type of work: Essay

Context: One of the greatest British poets of the Platonic tradition, Shelley wrote this long, lyrical statement of the nature of poetry and the role of the poet in modern society as a reply to Thomas Love Peacock's humorous satire of Romantic poetry, *The Four Ages of Poetry* (1820). Unlike the mundane Peacock, who thought that poetry was merely a toy for adults, Shelley believes that the poetic experience is one that comes to a man from the gods and tears the veils from ordinary nature so that the poet can see the hidden truths of the universe. Since such vision is denied to the average man, the poet also is the true seer and legislator of the world to whom all men must look if they seek truth or order. Well aware of the implications of this assumption, Shelley claims that poetry is divine in origin and comes only through the gift of inspiration; he also adds that, since the poet is the instrument of the divine, the most moral and best men alone have been raised to the role of poet, as the result of divine grace.

Poetry is the record of the best and happiest moments of the happiest and best minds. . . . It is, as it were, the interpenetration of a diviner nature through our own; but its footsteps are like those of a wind over the sea, which the coming calm erases, and whose traces remain only, as on the wrinkled sand which paves it. These and corresponding conditions of being are experienced principally by those of the most delicate sensibility and the most enlarged imagination; and the state of mind produced by them is at war with every base desire. . . .

Poetry, therefore, is a more philosophical and
a higher thing than history

Source: POETICS (Section IX)
Author: Aristotle (384–322 B.C.)
First transcribed: c. 334–232 B.C.
Type of work: Critical treatise

Context: Aristotle is, of course, the universal critic. In the fields of science, philosophy, morals, and literature he records the wisdom of the Grecian era. In the *Poetics* he describes tragic drama, the particular type of literature which was most admired in Greece and in the production of which Athenians excelled. Aristotle draws initial distinctions between tragedy and comedy and, in turn, between tragedy and epic poetry in such matters as origin and style. More specifically, he addresses himself to the particular components of the tragic form—plot, character, diction, music, scenic design. The plot, "an imitation of an action that is complete and whole and of a certain magnitude" and the most significant of these components, depicts a noble character involved in a disastrous reversal of fortune resulting from the fatal effects of pride upon his character. Theoretically, the spectators—involved vicariously in the emotion of the scene—are cleansed of pity and fear and thus undergo a spiritually cathartic experience. At one point, Aristotle compares the tragic poet to the historian. Since the dramatist conventionally deals with legendary heroes, both he and the historian are concerned with the re-creation of action from the past; but the object of the historian is the exact reporting of fact, that of the poet the rearrangement of detail for emotional potential:

. . . It is, moreover, evident from what has been said that it is not the function of the poet to relate what has happened but what may happen—what is possible according to the law of probability and necessity. The poet and the historian differ not by writing in verse and in prose. The work of Herodotus might be put into verse, and it would still be a species of history, with meter no less than without it. The true difference is that one relates what has happened, the other what may happen. **Poetry, therefore, is a more philosophical and a higher thing than history;** for poetry tends to express the universal, history the particular. . . .

The poet's eye, in a fine frenzy rolling

Source: A MIDSUMMER NIGHT'S DREAM (Act V, sc. i, l. 12)
Author: William Shakespeare (1564–1616)
First published: 1600
Type of work: Dramatic comedy

Context: The marriage of Theseus, Duke of Athens, to Hippolyta, captive Queen of the Amazons, is an occasion of general merriment. The legendary story of Pyramus and Thisbe is enacted by a group of craftsmen as part of the nuptial festivities. Hippolyta comments on the strangeness of the fantasy they have witnessed, and Theseus agrees that all poets exaggerate past credence.

875

. . . I never may believe
These antique fables, nor these fairy toys.
Lovers and madmen have such seething brains,
Such shaping fantasies, that apprehend
More than cool reason ever comprehends.
The lunatic, the lover, and the poet
Are of imagination all compact.
One sees more devils than vast hell can hold;
That is the madman. The lover, all as frantic,
Sees Helen's beauty in a brow of Egypt.
The poet's eye, in a fine frenzy rolling,
Doth glance from heaven to earth, from earth to heaven.
And as imagination bodies forth
The forms of things unknown, the poet's pen
Turns them to shapes, and gives to airy nothing
A local habitation, and a name.
Such tricks hath strong imagination,
That if it would but apprehend some joy,
It comprehends some bringer of that joy.
Or in the night imagining some fear,
How easy is a bush supposed a bear!

Politics and the pulpit are terms that have little agreement

Source: REFLECTIONS ON THE REVOLUTION IN FRANCE
Author: Edmund Burke (1729–1797)
First published: 1790
Type of work: Political treatise

Context: Burke was certainly one of the greatest political philosophers England has ever produced. Though he was for some time a member of the English Parliament and influenced extensively the political thinking of an entire era, he never rose to high political office. The American Revolution he lamented, but he considered it to be a justifiable defense of traditional liberties; the French Revolution, on the other hand, he regarded as a dangerous and vicious repudiation of all sane principles of liberty and just government. When a non-conforming minister preached a sermon in which he expressed sympathy for the revolution, he violated a principle of separation of function which Burke considered essential. In the opening pages of his *Reflections on the Revolution in France* he devotes himself to a repudiation of the various expressions of sympathy for the French Revolution which had been heard in England, this sermon among them:

For my part, I looked on that sermon as the public declaration
of a man much connected with literary caballers, and intriguing

philosophers; with political theologians, and theological politicians, both at home and abroad. I know they set him up as a sort of oracle; because, with the best intentions in the world, he naturally *philippizes,* and chaunts his prophetic song in exact unison with their designs. . . . Supposing, however, that something like moderation were visible in this political sermon; yet **politics and the pulpit are terms that have little agreement.** No sound ought to be heard in the church but the healing voice of Christian charity. The cause of civil liberty and civil government gains as little as that of religion by this confusion of duties. Those who quit their proper character, to assume what does not belong to them, are, for the greater part, ignorant both of the character they leave, and of the character they assume. . . .

Politics go by the weather

Source: THE SPLEEN (Line 171)
Author: Matthew Green (1696–1737)
First published: 1737
Type of work: Didactic poem

Context: The most common, or at least most fashionable, disease of the eighteenth century in England was a form of malancholia called at that time the "spleen," inasmuch as the popular belief was that that organ of the body was the seat of the complaint. So many people suffered, or thought they did, from "the English malady," as it was also called, that any and all advice was taken seriously in some quarter or another. Earlier, Lady Winchelsea had written a Pindaric ode on the same topic; her poem was popular, but its popularity was usurped by Green's work, even though Doctor Samuel Johnson, England's literary arbiter, declared Green's poem to have no poetry in it. The poet recites a number of conditions which seem to cause the onset or intensification of the malady, including rainy weather; it is in this portion of the poem that the comment upon politics occurs:

> In such dull weather, so unfit
> To enterprize a work of wit,
> When clouds one yard of azure sky,
> That's fit for simile, deny,
> I dress my face with studious looks,
> And shorten tedious hours with books.
> But if dull fogs invade the head,
> That mem'ry minds not what is read,
> I sit in window dark as ark,
> And on the drowning world remark:
> Or to some coffee-house I stray
> For news, the manna of the day,
> And from the hipp'd discourses gather,

877

That **politics go by the weather:**
Then seek good-humour'd tavern chums,
And play at cards, but for small sums.

The poor, and the maimed, and the halt, and the blind

Source: LUKE 14:21
Author: Unknown (Traditionally Luke the Apostle)
First transcribed: c. 80–100
Type of work: Gospel

Context: The fourteenth chapter of the Gospel of St. Luke tells of a sabbath day on which Jesus stopped to eat in the house of an important Pharisee. The Pharisees, as usual, are watching Jesus in the hope that He may be caught in the act of breaking some law. Among those present is a man who suffers from dropsy; Jesus heals him, pointing out to the Pharisees that none of them would hesitate to rescue a domestic animal on the Sabbath. His detractors have no reply to this; the Pharisees have already learned that Jesus has a logical answer to any objections they may raise and that He usually leaves them with nothing to say. The effect these exchanges produce is a growing determination on their part to see that He is destroyed. Jesus now offers two parables for His listeners to consider. In the first He points out that if a person chooses the best accommodations available, he will in all probability be asked to vacate them in favor of someone more important than he; while, if he takes the poorest room to be had, he is likely to be treated with greater consideration. This is a contrast between the person who inflates his own importance in order to impress others and the humble person, who, because he does not claim importance, sometimes finds it thrust upon him. The first of these is often humiliated, while the second receives recognition. Furthermore, Jesus adds, we should not bestow our feasts upon those who are as well off as we and who are well able to repay us; rather we should share such bounties with those who cannot recompense us in any way. In a second parable which elaborates this admonition, He also points out the fact that those who are able to repay do not always appreciate our generosity.

And when one of them sat at meat with him heard these things, he said unto him, Blessed is he that shall eat bread in the kingdom of God.

Then said he unto him, A certain man made a great supper, and bad many:

And sent his servant at supper time to say to them that were bidden, Come; for all things are now ready.

And they all with one consent began to make excuse. The first said unto him, I have bought a piece of ground, and I must needs go and see it: I pray thee have me excused.

878

And another said, I have bought five yoke of oxen, and I go to prove them: I pray thee have me excused.

And another said, I have married a wife, and therefore I cannot come.

So that servant came, and shewed his lord these things. Then the master of the house being angry said to his servant, Go out quickly into the streets and lanes of the city, and bring in hither **the poor, and the maimed, and the halt, and the blind.**

And the servant said, Lord, it is done as thou hast commanded, and yet there is room.

And the lord said unto the servant, Go out into the highways and hedges, and compel them to come in, that my house may be filled.

For I say unto you, That none of those men which were bidden shall taste of my supper.

Poor is the triumph o'er the timid hare!

Source: THE SEASONS: AUTUMN (Line 401)
Author: James Thomson (1700–1748)
First published: 1730
Type of work: Nature poem

Context: Following Thomson's death, in early autumn, 1748, the poet William Shenstone (1714–1763) wrote: "Though Thomson, sweet descriptive bard,/ Inspiring Autumn sung,/ Yet how should we the months regard/ That stopp'd his flowing tongue?" Though Thomson's style is at times monotonous, and his poems contain frequent digressions, this friend of Samuel Johnson, Boswell, Pope, Lord Buchan, Sir Robert Walpole, and many other important figures of the early eighteenth century, was a master at picturing scenery and rural life. Nature was, to him, an object of profound reverence, and even the digressions in his poems about it, such as the History of Celadon and Amelia, are like figures in a landscape. Thomson's patriotic poetry was also highly regarded and his "Rule, Britannia" has become a national song. He hated hunting practiced in autumn. He wrote of "the rude clamor of the Sportsman's joy," and protested "the falsely cheerful, barbarous game of death." He pitied the victims of the "cruel chase," the birds, the stag, the fox, the brindled boar, and the rabbit, fleeing the hounds.

Poor is the triumph o'er the timid hare,
Scar'd from the corn, and now to some lone seat
Retired,—the rushy fen; the ragged furze;
. . .
Of the same friendly hue, the withered fern;
. . .
Vain is her best precaution; though she sits

879

Conceal'd, with folded ears, unsleeping eyes,
By Nature raised to take the horizon in,
And head couch'd close betwixt her hairy feet,
In act to spring away. The scented dew
Betrays her early labyrinth; and deep
In scatter'd sullen openings, far behind,
With every breeze she hears the coming storm.

Poor splendid wings

Source: A BALLAD OF FRANÇOIS VILLON (Line 21)
Author: Algernon Charles Swinburne (1837–1909)
First published: 1878
Type of work: Lyric poem

Context: One of the earliest and greatest lyric poets of France, François Villon (1431–?), was very influential upon the development of modern lyric poetry; however, while his verse is noted for its polish and raciness, he is remembered as the leader of a band of thieves and for his imprisonment for robbery. Seeing a kinship between himself and Villon, Swinburne calls the Frenchman the "Prince of all Ballad-Makers" and his own "sad bad glad mad brother." Like Swinburne, Villon created his best verse when in his deepest dejection; thus, in this poem the contrast of the French poet's miserable life and birdlike song becomes a lament for the man and a paean for the remarkable verse that transcends his personal misfortunes.

Poor splendid wings so frayed and soiled and torn!
  Poor kind wild eyes so dashed with light quick tears!
Poor perfect voice, most blithe when most forlorn,
    That rings athwart the sea whence no man steers
    Like joy-bells crossed with death-bells in our ears! . . .

Prince of sweet songs made out of tears and fire,
A harlot was thy nurse, a God thy sire;
    Shame soiled thy song, and song assoiled thy shame.
But from thy feet now death has washed the mire, . . .

The post of honor is a private station

Source: CATO (Act IV, sc. iv, l. 142)
Author: Joseph Addison (1672–1719)
First published: 1713
Type of work: Dramatic tragedy

This tragedy of a banished leader of unimpeachable integrity held great attraction to both Whigs and Tories in the complex political situation of the early eighteenth century. Cato, the great and austere champion of constitutional government, stands for Roman virtue against the popular military dictator, Caesar. By the fourth act Cato's efforts to save Rome from herself and Caesar have failed, and it has become obvious that Cato must die. His son, Portius, brings to him the corpse of his other son, who has fallen in battle. Cato tells his friends that he intends to take all the blame and all of Caesar's punishment, then tells his remaining son to live a virtuous life but not to seek public office and power:

> Portius, draw near! My son, thou oft hast seen
> Thy sire engaged in a corrupted state,
> Wrestling with vice and faction. Now thou see'st me
> Spent, overpowered, despairing of success;
> Let me advise the to retreat betimes
> To thy paternal seat, the Sabine field,
> Where the great Censor toiled with his own hands,
> And all our frugal ancestors were blessed
> In humble virtues and a rural life.
> There live retired, pray for the peace of Rome;
> Content thyself to be obscurely good.
> When vice prevails, and impious men bear sway,
> **The post of honor is a private station.**

Poured forth his unpremeditated strain

Source: THE CASTLE OF INDOLENCE (Canto I, stanza 68)
Author: James Thomson (1700–1748)
First published: 1748
Type of work: Descriptive poem

Context: A poem originally intended to be a few stanzas ridiculing the lack of energy of the author and some of his friends, occupied Thomson for fifteen years before finally appearing in two cantos and 156 stanzas. It was the last product of his pen that he lived to print. The poem contains more poetic invention than any of his other works. To suit contemporary taste, it included allegory, now scorned. However, that device, like obsolete words of the poem, appears because the poet was imitating Edmund Spenser (1528?–1599). To a castle belonging to the wizard Indolence come pilgrims seeking an easy life. Here they can woo the Muse, while watching the world in a magic crystal globe. In Canto II, the Knight of Art and Industry arrives to show them the evils of this sort of life. Many of the poetic portraits of the guests have never been identified. The stanza containing the lines quoted describes Thomson himself as a writer of simple and unstudied verse. A footnote declares that all except the first line of the stanza was written by Thomson's friend, the celebrated George, Lord Lyttelton (1709–1773). The quoted line may have been suggested by the "unpremeditated verse" of Milton's *Paradise Lost* (IX, 24).

A bard here dwelt, more fat than bard beseems;
Who, void of envy, guile, and lust of gain,
On virtue still, and nature's pleasing themes,
Pour'd forth his unpremeditated strain;
The world forsaking with a calm disdain,
Here laugh'd he careless in his easy seat;
Here quaff'd, encircled with the joyous train,
Oft moralizing age; his ditty sweet
He loathèd much to write, ne carèd to repeat.

Poverty has strange bedfellows

Source: THE CAXTONS (Part IV, chapter 4)
Author: Edward Bulwer-Lytton (1803–1873)
First published: 1849
Type of work: Novel

Context: The Caxtons is first in a series of three novels which narrate the history and fortunes of an upper middle-class family in England. The writing of these was in the nature of an experiment for Bulwer-Lytton, who had earned his fame as an author through a number of historical romances and several novels of crime and social injustice. He experimented with many literary forms during his lifetime: the drama, poetry, the novel, and some tales of fantasy, terror, and the supernatural. His historical novels are in the tradition of Scott —well researched and carefully prepared, rather scholarly, smoothly constructed, and with heavy emphasis on history. This last is made palatable by an overlay of romance. The group of novels which he called "Varieties of English Life," on the other hand, is characterized by realism and humor. *The Caxtons* is one of the best of these; the humorous passages, according to the author, are not put in for satirical purposes but instead are intended to delineate amiable characters. As a result, the people in the novel are both likeable and memorable. The story is told by Pisistratus Caxton and begins with several anecdotes relating to his own birth; these are amusing sidelights on his father, who is totally and absent-mindedly immersed in a monumental work he is writing on the history of human error. The story traces young Caxton's childhood and his days at a boarding school. He becomes acquainted with his two uncles. Uncle Jack is a versatile and colorful genius who continually victimizes himself with get-rich-quick schemes. The other uncle, Roland, is preoccupied with chivalry, honor, heroism, and heraldry. Uncle Jack persuades Mr. Caxton to move to London, where he can finish his book and meet publishers. Young Caxton, however, goes on foot. On the journey he encounters two picturesque vagrants, Mr. Peacock, and a younger man. Caxton buys them a meal; during the ensuing conversation Mr. Peacock asks young Caxton whether he likes plays and is astounded when he learns that this rural youth has never seen one. His astonishment is expressed in a flight of melodramatic oratory which Caxton finds amusing:

I laughed outright—may I be forgiven for the boast, but I had the reputation at school of a pleasant laugh. The young man's face grew dark at the sound: he pushed back his plate and sighed.

"Why," continued his friend, "my companion here, who, I suppose, is about your own age, he could tell you what a play is! he could tell you what life is. He has viewed the manners of the town: 'perused the traders,' as the swan poetically remarks. Have you not, my lad, eh?"

Thus directly appealed to, the boy looked up with a smile of scorn on his lips—

"Yes, I know what life is, and I say that life, like **poverty, has strange bedfellows.** Ask me what life is now, and I say a melodrama; ask me what it is twenty years hence, and I shall say—"

"A farce?" put in his comrade.

" No, a tragedy—or comedy as Molière wrote it."

"And how is that?" I asked, interested and somewhat surprised at the tone of my contemporary.

"Where the play ends in the triumph of the wittiest rogue. My friend here has no chance!"

Poverty's catching

Source: THE ROVER; OR, THE BANISH'D CAVALIERS, PART II (Act I, sc. i)
Author: Aphra Behn (1640–1689)
First published: 1681
Type of work: Dramatic comedy

Context: Willmore, the Rover, is an English Cavalier banished from his native land because of his loyalty to the crown during the civil wars. He has become a professional soldier who travels about Europe seeking employment and pleasure. Arriving in Madrid, he meets two women who fall in love with him. One is La Nuche, a Spanish courtesan; the other is Ariadne, stepdaughter to the English ambassador. The latter is engaged to marry Beaumond, the ambassador's nephew and Willmore's friend. Beaumond, too, is fascinated by La Nuche. One day while Willmore is talking with La Nuche they are interrupted by Don Carlo, an aged admirer of the courtesan. Later, after a scuffle, Willmore rejoins La Nuche in a nearby church, where he accuses the girl of having loved him for his appearance and supposed wealth; she accuses him of being too eager to know every woman he can. Because La Nuche's bawd, Petronella Elenora, has made advances to Nicholas Fetherfool, Willmore accuses La Nuche of being interested only in plying her trade. La Nuche angrily replies that Willmore ought to try the trade before he treats her so harshly.

As they argue with each other, Petronella, accompanied by Sancho, La Nuche's bodyguard, comes up. Observing La Nuche wasting her time, as the bawd sees it, with a penniless man, Petronella makes a caustic comment to her and then speaks to Sancho, bidding him go with her:

LA NUCHE [*to Willmore*]
There's your eternal Quarrel to our Sex, 'twere a fine Trade indeed to keep a Shop and give your Ware for Love: would it turn to account think ye, Captain, to trick and dress, to receive all wou'd enter? faith, Captain, try the Trade.

PETRONELLA ELENORA
What in discourse with this Railer!—come away; **Poverty's catching.** [*Speaking to Sancho.*]

Praise is the best diet

Source: A MEMOIR OF THE REVEREND SYDNEY SMITH BY HIS DAUGHTER LADY HOLLAND (Chapter 9)
Author: Sydney Smith (1771–1845)
First published: 1855
Type of work: Biographical memoir

Context: Part of Chapter IX of the biography of the Reverend Sydney Smith, written by his daughter Saba, Lady Holland (1802–1866), sets down in unconnected paragraphs bits of Smith's conversations. They show the basis for his general reputation as a great wit and master of repartee. Here are a few of them:

"Ah, you flavor everything; you are the vanille of society!"

. . .

"To take Macaulay out of literature and society, and put him in the House of Commons, is like taking the chief physician out of London during a pestilence."

. . .

Some one, observing the wonderful improvement in —— since his success, "Ah!" he said, **"praise is the best diet** for us, after all."

. . .

An American said to me: "You are so funny, Mr. Smith! do you know you remind me of our great joker, Dr. Chamberlaque." "I am much honored," I replied, "but I was not aware you had such a functionary in the United States."

Praise the bridge that carried you over

Source: THE HEIR-AT-LAW (Act I, sc. i)
Author: George Colman the Younger (1762–1836)
First published: 1800
Type of work: Dramatic comedy

Context: An actress, Elizabeth Inchbald (1753–1821), was responsible for the preservation of fifty eighteenth and nineteenth century English dramas, by retiring from the stage to compile two series of plays, using the original prompt copies, and preceding each play by a brief critical comment. One of the popular playwrights was George Colman (or Coleman), Junior, son of a dramatist who directed the famous Haymarket Theatre of London. The son took over his father's duties in 1789 when the older Colman became insane. He also wrote slapstick comedies and a few serious plays such as *Inkle and Yarico* and *Surrender at Calais,* whose original thought, elevated sentiments, and natural action were highly commended by his contemporaries. However, the farcical humor of the comedies that acted well and had funny lines and situations, was also well received. One such was *Heir-at-Law.* At the opening of the comedy, the former "plain Daniel Dowlas of Gosport," who a week previously had inherited the title of old Baron Duberly, is having breakfast with his wife, the new "Lady Duberly." She is trying to teach him manners befitting his new position. He wants her to remember that he was a respectable merchant before he became a baron. She agrees that he has no cause to disparage what brought him to his present position as a peer of the realm, but now all this should be forgotten. They discuss the strange circumstances that achieved his elevation: the nearest heir, Henry Morland's being lost at sea, and the lawyer's advertising for any heir-at-law of the late Baron Duberly. One other character in the comedy is Dr. Pangloss, reminiscent of the Professor of Abstract Nonsense of the same name who sought to bring culture to Voltaire's Candide (1759). He comes to try to improve the English of the new lord and his son, Dick Dowlas, and by his caricature satirizes pedantry. (Mrs. Inchbald declared that the comedy contains so much dialect that any literary pleasure or entertainment is impossible.) As could be guessed, eventually the lost heir turns up, and Daniel Dowlas and Deborah his wife are happy to return to their more fitting life in Gosport. Here is part of the breakfast conversation in Act I:

LORD DUBERLY
. . . You hold a merchant as cheap as if he trotted about with all his property in a pack, like a pedlar.

LADY DUBERLY
A merchant, indeed! Curious merchandise you dealt in, truly!

LORD DUBERLY

A large assortment of articles:—coals, cloth, herrings, linen, candles, eggs, sugar, treacle, tea, bacon, and brick-dust;—with many more, too tedious to mention, in this here advertisement.

LADY DUBERLY

Well, **praise the bridge that carried you over;** but you must now drop the tradesman, and learn life. Consider, that by the strangest accident you have been raised to neither more nor less than a peer of the realm.

A pretty flim-flam

Source: THE LITTLE FRENCH LAWYER (Act II, sc. iii)
Authors: Francis Beaumont (1585–1616) and John Fletcher (1579–1625)
First published: 1647
Type of work: Tragi-comedy

Context: The Little French Lawyer takes its title from one of the characters of the play, a lawyer who is a coward till he is forced to fight a duel; his success in his first engagement of honor turns him into a swashbuckling and ready duellist. The action of the play really turns, however, on Dinant, who still loves the beautiful Lamira, even though she marries a lame old gentleman named Champernel. Dinant and his friend Cleremont intercept the wedding party on the way to the church to insult both the bridegroom and the bride. As a result of their rudeness, the two men are challenged to a duel by Beaupré, Lamira's brother, and Verdone, the bridegroom's nephew. Lamira, learning of the duel, sends Dinant off on a false errand, supposed to protect her honor, thus keeping him from the duel. In Dinant's absence Cleremont has to seek help from a passerby, the cowardly lawyer named La-Writ, who, through his success in disarming the two men who oppose him and Cleremont, finds courage. La-Writ a while later meets Dinant, who believes La-Writ to be the man Lamira sent him to fight. They are about to cross swords when they are interrupted by Cleremont. Cleremont upbraids Dinant for failing to appear for the earlier duel with Beaupré and Verdone. When Dinant tells his excuse for not being there, Cleremont calls the story "a pretty flim-flam," meaning that it is a contemptible trick that has been played on him.

CLEREMONT

Why were you absent?

DINANT

You know I am no coward, you have seen that,
And therefore out of fear forsook you not;
You know I am not false, of a treacherous nature,

Apt to betray my friend; I have fought for you too:
You know no business that concern'd my state,
My kindred, or my life—

CLEREMONT
Where was the fault then?

DINANT
The honour of that lady I adore,
Her credit, and her name: ye know she sent for me,
And with what haste.

CLEREMONT
What was he that traduc'd?

DINANT
The man i' th' moon, I think; hither was I sent,
But to what end—

CLEREMONT
This is **a pretty flim-flam!**

Pride, the never-failing vice of fools

Source: ESSAY ON CRITICISM (Part II, l. 204)
Author: Alexander Pope (1688–1744)
First published: 1711
Type of work: Satire

Context: In his poetic *Essay on Criticism,* Alexander Pope notes the difficulties of the critic. Though a man may make a fool of himself by writing a bad poem, it is infinitely worse, says Pope, for a man to express an unjust judgment on the work of another. Contending that critical genius is indeed rare, he points out that pride, which fills in the void left by lack of sense, is a prime cause of bad judgment:

Of all the causes which conspire to blind
Man's erring judgment, and misguide the mind,
What the weak head with strongest bias rules,
Is **pride, the never-failing vice of fools.**
Whatever nature has in worth denied,
She gives in large recruits of needless pride!
For as in bodies, thus in souls, we find
What wants in blood and spirits, swell'd with wind:
Pride, where wit fails, steps in to our defence,
And fills up all the mighty void of sense.
If once right reason drives that cloud away,

887

Truth breaks upon us with resistless day.
Trust not yourself; but, your defects to know,
Make use of every friend—and every foe.
A little learning is a dangerous thing; . . .

The priest who slew the slayer, and shall himself be slain

Source: LAYS OF ANCIENT ROME ("The Battle of Lake Regillus," Stanza 10)
Author: Thomas Babington Macaulay (1800–1859)
First published: 1842
Type of work: Narrative poem

Context: Macaulay early became interested in poetry. By the age of eight, he had written a three-canto romance using Scott as his model. While studying at Trinity College, Cambridge, he won the 1819 and 1821 poetry prizes. With his classical background, he composed a volume of four *Lays of Ancient Rome,* for which he provided a scholarly Preface. Best known of the Lays is the first, "Horatius." The second Lay is "The Battle of Lake Regillus," dealing with the 499 B.C. struggle in which Rome won control of Latium, defeating the Thirty Cities, supposedly with the assistance of the equestrian Twin Gods, Castor and Pollux. This ballad is imagined to have been composed in 451 for a celebration before their temple in the Forum. It shows Macaulay's indebtedness to the Iliad, for this is a Homeric battle with cavalry replacing chariots. In the first two of its 40 stanzas, the celebration in the Forum is described. Then the poet talks of the present peaceful aspect of what was once a bloody field of battle. Aricia is an ancient town 16 miles from Rome, the site of a grove dedicated to the worship of Diana Aricina. Her priest was always a runaway slave who won his office by killing his predecessor in single combat. The poet describes the dawn, and the date. The Ides of Quintilis was July 15. Having mentioned the standards of the Thirty Cities, Macaulay reports that the warriors came from all parts of Latium, hoping to defeat Rome.

Up rose the golden morning
  Over the Porcian height,
The proud Ides of Quintilis
  Marked evermore with white.
Not without secret trouble
  Our bravest saw the foes;
For girt by threescore thousand spears
  The thirty standards rose.
    •   •   •

From the still glassy lake that sleeps
  Beneath Aricia's trees,—
Those trees in whose dim shadow
  The ghastly priest doth reign,

888

The priest who slew the slayer,
And shall himself be slain;
. . .

Princes hate the traitor though they love the treason

Source: CLEOPATRA (Act IV, sc. i)
Author: Samuel Daniel (1562–1619)
First published: 1594
Type of work: Dramatic tragedy

Context: In 1594 the Countess of Pembroke started a campaign for "imaginative literature," following the precepts laid down in *Apologie for Poetry* (1580) by Sir Philip Sidney. She settled on the poet Samuel Daniel to provide an original English play as the model of all tragedies. It would have to be written within the neoclassical formula and have unity, with outward action pared to a minimum. With misgivings, the "sweete honey-dropping Daniel" undertook the task. He realized the need to concentrate on the character of Cleopatra, making the struggle that of the instincts of a queen against those of a mother. Scholars who have analyzed earlier versions realize how masterly were Daniel's efforts, and how well he manipulated the episodes. But the difficult task turned him into the "sober-minded Daniel" praised by Coleridge. Everyone knows the story of Julius Caesar and Cleopatra and of Caesario, their son whom she tries to dismiss both for Egypt's sake and her own. The dramatist makes the repentance of her secretary Seleucus for his betrayal of her secrets to Caesar one of the high points of the action. Scholars believe that Daniel's closet drama furnishes an explanation of Shakespeare's unusual use of two climaxes when he wrote his version later: the death of Antony, followed by a long act devoted to Cleopatra. From Daniel, Shakespeare learned how much more could be made of Cleopatra than a mere "bad woman." From Daniel he got his conception of the queen as the embodiment of a love that transcended worldly obligations. At the beginning of Act IV of Daniel's play, Seleucus comes upon Rodon, tutor to Caesario, and eagerly greets him because "Never friend Rodon in a better hour/ Could I have met thee than e'en now I do,/ Having affliction in the greatest power/ Upon my soul and none to tell it to." Rodon begs him to explain what is bothering him, and Seleucus embarks upon a confession of his regret for his treachery.

SELEUCUS
Well, then thou know'st how I have liv'd in grace
With Cleopatra and esteem'd in court
As one of counsel, and of chiefest place
As ever held my credit in that fort.
Till now in this confusion of our state

889

When thinking to have us'd a means to climb
And fled the wretched, flown unto the great
   (Following the fortunes of the present time)
Am come to be cast down and ruin'd clean:
   And in this course of mine own plot undone,
For having all the secrets of the Queen
   Reveal'd to Caesar, to have favor won,
My treachery is quited with disgrace,
   My falsehood loath'd, and not without great reason
Though good for him, yet **Princes** in this case
   Do **hate the Traitor, though they love the treason.**

Probability is the very guide of life

Source: THE ANALOGY OF RELIGION (Introduction)
Author: Bishop Joseph Butler (1692–1752)
First published: 1736
Type of work: Religious treatise

Context: In May, 1736, the Reverend Joseph Butler, LL.D., signed his name to the Advertisement of his *Analogy of Religion, Natural and Revealed, to the Constitution and Course of Nature.* It is directed to those who consider Christianity fictitious and "a principle Subject of Mirth and Ridicule as it were by Way of Reprisals, for its having so long interrupted the Pleasures of the World." Its author was an English theologian whose preaching at the Rolls Chapel, London, had resulted in the influential book, *Fifteen Sermons* (1726). Then Butler became Rector of Stanhope, where he wrote the *Analogy of Religion,* to combat the influence in England of the Deists, which was a sect of the seventeenth and eighteenth centuries that held that the Natural world was sufficient proof of the existence of God, and therefore that any formal religion was unnecessary. Neither need there be any supernatural revelation. Nature was enough. Voltaire and Jean Jacques Rousseau in France, and Jefferson and Franklin in America, were among these Freethinkers. Their belief grew out of the rationalism of the period, so Butler attacked their thinking by logic. By the time the second edition appeared, in 1738, he had been advanced to Bishop of Bristol, and the third edition, in 1740, found him Dean of St. Paul's, and influential in the court of George II and Queen Charlotte. Two years later he was appointed head of the See of Durham, one of the richest in England, a position he enjoyed only two years until his death. As he argued, obviously there could be no demonstrated evidence of the beliefs of Religion. All that can be adduced is probable evidence which, he says, differs from demonstrative evidence in that it admits of degrees, from the highest moral certainty to the lowest presumption. Nothing can be called true by one presumption, since probabilities may exist on both sides. A man may observe the ebb and flow of the

890

tide for one day and draw some presumption, though to a low degree, that it will happen again tomorrow; only observation of the event for months and ages provides full assurance. Probability is expressed by the word "likely"; that is, like some truth or true event. If we consider that something will probably happen, it is because the mind has found in it a likeness to some other event. So Bishop Butler compares the known course of things with what is said to be the Moral System of Nature; the acknowledged Dispensations of Providence or that government under which people live, with what Religion teaches them to believe and expect. Both can be traced to the same general laws and resolved with the same principles of divine conduct. While not completely assured, they are probable. As he explains it:

> Probable Evidence, in its very Nature, affords but an imperfect kind of Information; and it is to be considered as relative only to Beings of limited Capacities. For Nothing which is the possible object of Knowledge, whether past, present, or future, can be probable to an infinite Intelligence; since it cannot but be discerned absolutely as to itself, certainly true, or certainly false. But to Us, **Probability is the very Guide of Life.**

Progress is not an accident, but a necessity

Source: SOCIAL STATICS (Part I, chapter 2, section 4)
Author: Herbert Spencer (1820–1903)
First published: 1850
Type of work: Scientific treatise

Context: English philosopher and social scientist, Herbert Spencer is known for his application of the scientific doctrines of evolution to philosophy and ethics. His central principle is that Force is the agent of all change and organization in the universe. His ethics, which emphasize the role and function of the individual, was derived from Bentham's Utilitarianism. Inasmuch as a thorough knowledge of science would provide the key to the progress of today and the evolution of tomorrow, he saw little value in a liberal arts education. Beginning with such fundamental premises as the persistence of force, the conservation of energy, and the indestructability of matter, Spencer devised his definition of evolution: "The integration of matter and the concomitant dissipation of motion during which the matter passes from an indefinite incoherent homogeneity to a definite heterogeneity, and during which the retained motion undergoes a parallel transformation." Spencer, like many of his associates, believed that evolution was the means to man's perfectibility. The evolutionary process has currently reached a critical state of imbalance; man is not yet adapted to his social state because he retains his primitive instincts to survive at the expense of his fellowmen.

891

"His primitive circumstances required that he should sacrifice the welfare of others to his own; his present circumstances require that he shall not do so." The continued process of adaptation is vital to the eventual evolution of the complete being:

> **Progress,** therefore, **is not an accident, but a necessity.** Instead of civilization being artificial it is a part of nature; all of a piece with the development of an embryo or the unfolding of a flower. The modifications mankind have undergone, and are still undergoing, result from a law underlying the whole organic creation; and provided the human race continues, and the constitution of things remains the same, these modifications must end in completeness. . . . So surely must evil and immorality disappear; so surely must man become perfect.

A proper man as one shall see in a summer's day

Source: A MIDSUMMER NIGHT'S DREAM (Act I, sc. ii, ll. 89–90)
Author: William Shakespeare (1564–1616)
First published: 1600
Type of work: Dramatic comedy

Context: The marriage of Theseus, Duke of Athens, and Hippolyta, the fair captive Queen of the Amazons, is to be celebrated when the new moon shall appear. Among the revelries planned is the production of a homely version of the Pyramus and Thisbe legend put on by a group of craftsmen. The weaver, Bottom, vies for every part until finally Quince, a carpenter who has written the play, tells Bottom that the role of Pyramus is clearly his:

QUINCE
You can play no part but Pyramus, for Pyramus is a sweet-faced man, **a proper man as one shall see in a summer's day;** a most lovely, gentleman-like man. Therefore you must needs play Pyramus.

BOTTOM
Well, I will undertake it. What beard were I best to play it in?

QUINCE
Why, what you will.

The proverb is something musty

Source: HAMLET (Act III, sc. ii, ll. 358–359)
Author: William Shakespeare (1564–1616)
First published: 1603
Type of work: Dramatic tragedy

Context: Rosencrantz and Guildenstern, friends of Hamlet's youth, have, at the request of the king and queen, made one unsuccessful attempt to discover the cause of Hamlet's "distemper." Now that Hamlet has, by watching King Claudius' reaction to a play within the play, satisfied himself that Claudius did indeed kill his father (though only Hamlet and his friend, Horatio, know of the king's guilt), Rosencrantz and Guildenstern make another attempt, which is again fended off by Hamlet's turning the conversation to the fact that his uncle was given the throne rather than he. Rosencrantz reminds him that Claudius has already suggested Hamlet as his heir, whereupon Hamlet, playing with fire, but scarcely caring at this point, recalls an old proverb, "While the grass is growing, the horse starves," implying that he is hungry for the throne:

ROSENCRANTZ

Good my lord, what is the cause of your distemper? You do surely bar the door upon your own liberty, if you deny your griefs to your friend.

HAMLET

Sir, I lack advancement.

ROSENCRANTZ

How can that be, when you have the voice of the King himself for your succession in Denmark?

HAMLET

Ay, sir, but while the grass grows—**the proverb is something musty.**

Public schools 'tis public folly feeds

Source: TIROCINIUM (Line 250)
Author: William Cowper (1731–1800)
First published: 1785
Type of work: Didactic poem

Context: Cowper, a descendant of John Donne, was primarily a poet of rural life; he was the last English poet who belonged to the "cult of simplicity." Trained for the law and called to the bar in 1754, he was forced to

893

abandon this career by attacks of insanity; the first of these made it impossible for him to marry the cousin with whom he had fallen in love, and another drove him to attempt suicide. Following his convalescence, he retired to the country and eventually settled at Olney, where he lived with friends in quiet seclusion. He did not begin to write poetry as a serious recreation until he was fifty. His first volume, *Poems* (1782) was followed in 1785 by his greatest work, *The Task*. The latter work was written at the suggestion of his friend Lady Austen, who had also given him the topic—a sofa. Beginning with this unlikely subject, Cowper allowed the poem to grow into a lengthy description of the countryside in winter, the simple routines and pleasures of the day, and his thoughts and meditations on life and the distant outside world. When *The Task* was published a few other poems were added to round out the volume, among them his famous humorous poem, *John Gilpin's Ride*. Another such inclusion was his commentary on the education of boys, *Tirocinium*. Cowper was deeply religious; his Calvinism both comforted him and entered into his fits of melancholia. It also encouraged him to moralize, and some of his poems are akin to sermons. In *Tirocinium* he considers the divine origin of man's intellect and the need of spiritual uplift in contemporary schools, where a harmful and worldly training is received instead. Cowper had been a slight and sensitive child who had lost his mother at an early age, and he had been bullied unmercifully in school; now he condemns conditions that lead young men to sneer at simple spiritual truths they have learned as children, and he attacks educational systems which, he feels, breed depravity. He is arguing for private education by a tutor and against education in the great public schools of his day.

> Would you your son should be a sot or dunce,
> Lascivious, headstrong, or all these at once,
> That, in good time, the stripling's finish'd taste
> For loose expense and fashionable waste,
> Should prove your ruin and his own at last;—
> Train him in public with a mob of boys,
> Childish in mischief only and in noise,
> Else of a mannish growth, and five in ten
> In infidelity and lewdness, men.
> There shall he learn, ere sixteen winters old,
> That authors are most useful, pawn'd or sold;
> That pedantry is all that schools impart,
> But taverns teach the knowledge of the heart;
> There waiter Dick with Bacchanalian lays
> Shall win his heart, and have his drunken praise,
> His counsellor and bosom-friend shall prove,
> And some street-pacing harlot his first love.
>   . . .
> Such youths of spirit, and that spirit too,
> Ye nurs'ries of our boys, we owe to you!

894

Though from ourselves the mischief more proceeds,
For **public schools 'tis public folly feeds.** . . .

Publicans and sinners

Source: MATTHEW 11:19
Author: Unknown (traditionally Matthew the Apostle)
First transcribed: c. 75–100
Type of work: Gospel

Context: In the Sermon on the Mount, Jesus has instructed His disciples in the basic principles of His religion and His work. It is already apparent from the size of the multitudes which follow Him about that Jesus must train others who can assist Him. He does not send them forth immediately, however; the number of His apostles is not yet complete and those He has instructed are not ready. He continues to heal and to set an example of faith and of conduct for them; and once, when they have embarked on a ship and a storm arises, the example is strongly reinforced. Waves break over the craft and the disciples, terrified, awaken Jesus. Reproving them for their lack of faith, He quiets the storm. After He has called Matthew, and His disciples number twelve, He empowers them to perform miracles and sends them forth to preach among the children of Israel. Then He returns to His own work in the cities. John the Baptist, imprisoned but in no way daunted, sends two of his own disciples to ask Jesus if He is truly the Messiah who has been foretold. John is not entirely satisfied with Christ's claims. Jesus asks John's disciples to carry a report of His activities back to their master, then speaks of John to the multitudes. John, He tells them, is the messenger —Elias reborn—who has been sent to herald the coming of the Messiah. He follows this statement with a parable in which He likens His generation to willful children who refuse to play merely for the sake of refusal. John has led a solitary life and people have criticized him; Jesus has led a public life and has been criticized by the same people. He has been asked (see Chapter 9) by the Pharisees why He spends his time with publicans and sinners; a number of these persons had come to hear him speak. Jesus' reply was that people who are well do not require the services of a physician. The incident has formed the basis for His parable.

Verily I say unto you, Among them that are born of women there hath not risen a greater than John the Baptist: notwithstanding he that is least in the kingdom of heaven, is greater than he.
And from the days of John the Baptist, until now, the kingdom of heaven suffereth violence, and the violent take it by force.
For all the prophets and the law prophesied until John.
And if ye will receive it, this is Elias which was for to come.

He that hath ears to hear, let him hear.

But whereunto shall I liken this generation? It is like unto children sitting in the markets, and calling unto their fellows,

And saying, We have piped unto you, and ye have not danced; we have mourned unto you, and ye have not lamented.

For John came neither eating nor drinking, and they say, He hath a devil.

The Son of man came eating and drinking, and they say, Behold, a man gluttonous, and a winebibber, a friend of **publicans and sinners.** But wisdom is justified of her children.

Then began he to upbraid the cities wherein most of his mighty works were done, because they repented not.

Pull for the shore, sailor, pull for the shore

Source: PULL FOR THE SHORE (Line 1 of chorus)
Author: Philip P. Bliss (1838–1876)
First published: 1874
Type of work: Hymn

Context: Philip P. Bliss, a singing evangelist, was the author of *Gospel Songs* (1874) which, combined with Ira David Sankey's *Sacred Songs and Solos* (1873), became the foundation for six volumes of *Gospel Hymns* (1875–1891), containing many of America's most popular Protestant hymns in the late nineteenth and the first half of the twentieth centuries. Among these was "Pull for the Shore" (words and music by Philip P. Bliss), of which the first stanza and the chorus follow:

Light in the darkness, sailor, day is at hand!
See o'er the foaming billows fair Haven's land,
Drear was the voyage, sailor, now almost o'er,
Safe with-in the life-boat, sailor, pull for the shore.

Pull for the shore, sailor, pull for the shore!
Heed not the rolling waves, but bend to the oar,
Safe in the life-boat, sailor, cling to self no more!
Leave the poor old stranded wreck, and pull for the shore.

Punic faith

Source: JUGURTHA (CVIII, 3)
Author: Sallust (Gaius Sallustius Crispus, 86–34 B.C.)
First transcribed: 41 B.C.
Type of work: Historical narrative

Context: Sallust, after service under Caesar in the Civil War and after holding the governorship of Numidia, returned to Rome to devote himself to writing. Two of his works are extant—*De Coniuratione Catilinae*, an account of the Catiline conspiracy, and *Bellum Jugurthinum*, a record of Rome's war with Jugurtha. His most significant work, *Historiae*, a description of Rome from 78–67 B.C., is almost entirely lost. *Bellum Jugurthinum* relates the empire's struggles with the Numidian prince, an event chosen, as the author tells us, "because of its perfidious nature and shifting fortunes, and because it marked the beginning of successful resistance to the dominant power of the nobles." Sallust in his approach to history professes complete objectivity, and his fairness in the delineation of Metellus and Marius in *Jugurtha* supports his claim. Even so, by modern standards, the account reads more like Sir Walter Scott's historical novels than pure history. Chronology, locations, even the sequence of events the author does not hesitate to alter for the sake of a more effective narrative. As a result, if *Jugurtha* is second-rate history, it is first-rate narrative. The author's style, quite unlike that of Caesar of Cicero, is modeled after Thucydides; the chief features are highly rhetorical language, archaisms, and brevity of expression. At one point in the account, Jugurtha and his forces are encamped within two miles of the Roman forces. Bocchus, a Numidian who claims fidelity to Rome, acts as a mediator between Jugurtha and Sulla, the Roman leader, in establishing a conference between the chiefs. Bocchus reported that he "was ready to do what the Roman people wished," but actually he was carefully weighing which side to betray. Hence, the phrase "Punic faith,"—which to the Romans, with their memory of the Punic Wars, had come to mean "perfidy"—is used.

I believe it was rather with **Punic faith** than for the reasons which he made public that Bocchus beguiled both the Roman and the Numidian with the hope of peace, and that he pondered for a long time whether to betray Jugurtha to the Romans or Sulla to Jugurtha; that his inclination counselled against us, but his fears in our favour.

The questing beast

Source: LE MORTE D'ARTHUR (Book IX, chapter 12)
Author: Sir Thomas Malory (? –1471)
First published: 1485
Type of work: Medieval romance

Context: After Malory had been sentenced to life imprisonment for various escapades, he whiled away the months and years by gathering together for the first time all the legends of King Arthur and his Knights of the Round Table. Editing and reshaping this great cycle of tales, he gave them permanent and coherent form of epic proportions. Among the stories he collected were those of the Holy Grail and of Tristram; neither of them had originally been a part of the Arthurian cycle, but they had nonetheless become incorporated into it long before Malory's time. The tale of Sir Tristram of Lyonesse is one of the great love stories of the ages, and has been the subject of numerous works including poetry by Tennyson, Arnold, and Swinburne, and the opera *Tristan und Isolde* by Richard Wagner. Cured of a wound by Isoud (Ysolde, Iseult), daughter of the King of Ireland, Tristram negotiates her marriage to his uncle, King Mark of Cornwall, as the latter has instructed him to do. His task is made more difficult because he has fallen in love with her and she with him. His affections discovered by his uncle, Tristram is banished to Brittany, where he marries another woman who is also named Isoud. Learning of his marriage, the first Isoud begs him to return with his wife for an extended visit. Tristram accepts her invitation, but his vessel is wrecked on the coast of North Wales. Directing his party to proceed into Cornwall if he does not return in ten days, he goes into the forest in search of adventure. His first encounter is with another knight, Sir Lamorak de Galis, with whom he has an old score to settle; but they are evenly matched, and after a long hard fight they swear mutual friendship and agree not to fight each other again. While they are resting, another knight appears on the scene, bound on a quest of his own. The usual challenge is given; much to their chagrin, the two stalwarts are quickly defeated by the newcomer, who then continues on his way:

And this meanwhile there came Sir Palomides, the good knight, following **the questing beast** that had in shape a head like a serpent's head, and a body like a leopard, buttocks like a lion, and footed like an hart; and in his body there was such a noise as it had been the noise of thirty couple of hounds questing, and such a noise that beast made wheresomever he went; and this beast evermore Sir Palomides followed, for it was called his quest. And right so as he followed this beast it came by Sir Tristram, and soon after came Palomides. And to brief this matter he smote down Sir Tristram and Sir Lamorak both with one spear; and so he departed after the beast Galtisant, that was called **the questing beast;** . . .

Quiet to quick bosoms is a hell

Source: CHILDE HAROLD'S PILGRIMAGE (Canto III, stanza 42)
Author: George Gordon, Lord Byron (1788–1824)
First published: 1816 (Canto III)
Type of work: Narrative poem

Context: The first two cantos of *Childe Harold's Pilgrimage,* which appeared in 1812, offered a kind of facile versifying that so caught the popular fancy that, as Byron said, he became famous overnight. The book was a romanticized travelogue based on his own trip to Greece and Turkey after graduation. After its publication, he made a marriage that he soon considered incompatible, and he left his wife five weeks after the birth of their child, to spend the summer in Switzerland with Shelley. Here he wrote the third canto of *Childe Harold's Pilgrimage,* a much improved example of his poetry that contained a famous description of the Battle of Waterloo, of 1815. Standing on that battlefield, the poem's romantic hero thinks of what happened there. A rebel against conventions himself, unhappy among people, and at peace only with nature, Harold recreates that revelry in Brussels on the eve of the battle, the sound of the first cannon shot, the figures in the fight: the Duke of Brunswick who hurried to the battlefield and died in the fighting, and the many others who, after the night of dancing and gaiety, marched away at dawn to destruction. He declares Napoleon "greatest nor the worst of man," who might still be in power except that his lack of balance, while it brought him power, made impossible any hope of maintaining it. He might have endured if he had stood like a tower on a rock. But there are people, Byron mused, perhaps thinking of himself, who crave high adventure and are exhausted by doing nothing. Such a love of action is fatal to anyone who possesses it. In Napoleon's case, he became "conqueror and captive of the world," still feared even though in exile, an example of how a favorite of Fortune can stand unbowed under misfortune. Harold goes on to think what might have happened if Napoleon had shown more regard for human beings whom he had scorned but employed. He had used man's admiration only for his pleasure and advancement, and had failed to follow "stern Diogenes," who disregarded and mocked men and their opinions. Stanza 42 expresses the belief of the author, through the lips of Harold, that this feeling of adventure was very deep in the conquered French leader of Waterloo.

But **quiet to quick bosoms is a hell,**
And *there* hath been thy bane; there is a fire
And motion of the soul which will not dwell
In its own narrow being, but aspire
Beyond the fitting medium of desire;
And, but once kindled, quenchless evermore,
Preys upon high adventure, nor can tire
Of aught but rest; a fever at the core
Fatal to him who bears, to all who ever bore.

The quiet-colored end of evening

Source: LOVE AMONG THE RUINS (Line 1)
Author: Robert Browning (1812–1889)
First published: 1855
Type of work: Dramatic monologue

Context: In this poem a lover is speaking of his conviction that love, itself, is the highest value in life. In a mood of impassioned reflection, he describes the ruins which he and his love have used as a rendezvous. The ruins, themselves, are all that remains of the capital of a vanished civilization. This civilization was once so powerful that it sent millions of warriors to fight abroad while holding in reserve a thousand gold chariots at home. Of all this might and glory there is only a "single turret that remains." Displaying a quality of restrained passion, warmth, and serenity, the lover places greater value on his present love affair than on all the past grandeur of dead civilizations. These ruins assume worth only because "a girl with eager eyes and yellow hair/ Awaits me there." The poem opens with a balanced description of the setting:

> Where **the quiet-coloured end of evening** smiles,
>   Miles and miles
> On the solitary pastures where our sheep
>   Half-asleep
> Tinkle homeward through the twilight, stray or stop
>   As they crop—
> Was the site once of a city great and gay
>   (So they say),
> Of our country's very capital, its prince
>   Ages since
> Held his court in, gathered councils, wielding far
>   Peace or War.

Quiring to the young-eyed cherubins

Source: THE MERCHANT OF VENICE (Act V, sc. i, l. 62)
Author: William Shakespeare (1564–1616)
First published: 1600
Type of work: Dramatic comedy

Context: As Lorenzo, friend of Bassanio, and his bride Jessica, daughter of the Jew Shylock, speak tenderly on a moonlit night along the avenue to Belmont, home of Portia and her husband Bassanio, they are interrupted by messengers telling of the arrival of the master and mistress of the house. Lorenzo and Jessica, who feel duty-bound to oversee the preparations for the return of Bassanio and Portia, nevertheless put off going inside. Lorenzo orders the servants to call for music, reminding Jessica that the soul, if it were not hindered by the lowly flesh, could, on such a night, hear the choirs of cherubim produced by the harmony of the universe.

LORENZO
Sit Jessica. Look how the floor of heaven

900

Is thick inlaid with patens of bright gold.
There's not the smallest orb which thou behold'st
But in his motion like an angel sings,
Still **quiring to the young-eyed cherubins;**
Such harmony is in immortal souls,
But whilst this muddy vesture of decay
Doth grossly close it in, we cannot hear it.

Railing at life, and yet afraid of death

Source: GOTHAM (Book I, l. 218)
Author: Charles Churchill (1731–1764)
First published: 1764
Type of work: Philosophical poem

Context: Churchill was a dissipated clergyman who won for himself both fame and notoriety as a satiric poet during the last four years of his life. Much of the harsh and vitriolic nature of his verse seems to have been determined by his association with the unscrupulous editor of the *North-Briton,* John Wilkes. He surprised his readers, however, in the long and rambling *Gotham* by turning away from satire to discuss political and social freedom. He included such humanitarian reflections as won the approval of his former schoolmate, the gentle William Cowper. In the introduction to this poem, named for a village whose inhabitants were proverbial for their foolish actions, Churchill surveyed the various stages of human life beginning with infancy and proceeding through childhood to youth, manhood, and finally old-age:

OLD-AGE, a *second Child,* by Nature curs'd
With more and greater evils than the first,
Weak, sickly, full of pains; in ev'ry breath
Railing at life, and yet afraid of death;
Putting things off, with sage and solemn air,
From day to day, without one day to spare;
Without enjoyment, covetous of pelf,
Tiresome to friends, and tiresome to himself,
His faculties impair'd, his temper sour'd,
His memory of recent things devour'd
E'en with the acting, on his shatter'd brain
Tho' the stale Registers of Youth remain;
From morn to evening babbling forth vain praise
Of those rare men, who liv'd in those rare days
When He, the Hero of his tale, was Young,
Dull Repetitions falt'ring on his tongue, . . .

901

The rainbow comes and goes

Source: ODE. INTIMATIONS OF IMMORTALITY FROM RECOLLECTIONS OF EARLY
        CHILDHOOD (Stanza 2)
Author: William Wordsworth (1770–1850)
First published: 1807
Type of work: Ode

Context: In his most famous ode Wordsworth consciously used what he termed "the notion of pre-existence of the human soul" in order to develop poetically the idea that as we grow from infancy into childhood and youth and finally into maturity we lose our sense of the freshness and radiance in our existence. The poet himself was briefly grieved when he discovered his own sense of loss, but the grief was banished by "a timely utterance," and again it seems that "all the earth is gay." He feels the fullness of earth's bliss as he looks about him and listens. Yet he is aware of "something that is gone." Where has it fled? At physical birth our soul trails "clouds of glory" brought from its home with God, but this glory is soon forgotten. The earth even encourages this forgetting "with pleasures of her own." But we do not forget entirely. Even when we have traveled far beyond our infancy, we have momentary glimpses of "that immortal sea" on whose shore we "see the Children sport." Thus we will rejoice that, "Though nothing can bring back the hour/ Of splendour in the grass, of glory in the flower," we will be strengthened by our bond with eternity, our love for suffering man, our "faith that looks through death," and the growth of our philosophic minds. The poet's present love of Nature surpasses that of his youth because, through his sympathy with other men, even the sight of a simple flower can bring "Thoughts that do often lie too deep for tears." In the second stanza of his ode, Wordsworth lists the beauties of the earth and then sadly speaks of the glory that has gone:

> **The Rainbow comes and goes,**
> And lovely is the Rose,
> The Moon doth with delight
> Look round her when the heavens are bare;
> Waters on a starry night
> Are beautiful and fair;
> The sunshine is a glorious birth;
> But yet I know, where'er I go,
> That there hath passed away a glory from the earth.

902

A rare bird

Source: SATIRES (Number VI, l. 165, as translated by the Reverend Lewis Evans)
Author: Juvenal (c. 55–c. 135)
First transcribed: First century or early second century
Type of work: Satire

Context: Juvenal, who satirizes almost every phase of Roman life, ruthlessly attacks the female sex in Satire VI. If a worthy wife exists, the poet says, she is indeed *a rare bird.* In the translation of Evans the passage reads:

"Is there not one, then, out of such large herds of women, that seems to you a worthy match?" Let her be beautiful, graceful, rich, fruitful; marshal along her porticoes her rows of ancestral statues; let her be more chaste than any single Sabine that, with hair dishevelled, brought the war to a close; be a very phenix upon earth, **rare as a black swan;** who could tolerate a wife in whom all excellencies are concentrated! I would rather, far rather, have a country maiden from Venusia, than you, O Cornelia, mother of the Gracchi, if along with your exalted virtues you bring as portion of your dower a haughty and disdainful brow, and reckon as part of your fortune the triumphs of your house! Away, I beg, with your Hannibal and Syphax conquered in his camp, and tramp with all your Carthage!

A rascally yea-forsooth knave

Source: KING HENRY THE FOURTH: PART TWO (Act I, sc. ii, l. 41)
Author: William Shakespeare (1564–1616)
First published: 1600
Type of work: Historical drama

Context: Falstaff, having covered his base cowardice on the battlefield of Shrewsbury with an elaborate scheme, has emerged from the wars with a reputation of sorts. By taking up the body of Hotspur, whom Hal had slain in single combat, and announcing that the adversary had come to life again, Falstaff was able to claim the victory in combat over the leader of the rebellious party. Consequently, when we first meet him in this continuation of the play, he has been lauded for his exploits and is attended by a page. But honors, of course, do not change the man. As might have been expected, his ego has been fed by his ill-won honor, and his customary hauteur has been inflated by the feeling of self-importance. And, as also might have been expected, the buffoon is concerned primarily with the means by which he can gratify his sensuality at another's

903

expense. To this end he has sent his page to purchase for him on credit some satin material from which he intends to design an outfit suitable for his exalted position. When he learns that the tailor is impressed neither by his title nor his security, he bursts forth with his wonted arrogance:

FALSTAFF

. . .

What said Master Dommelton about the satin for my short cloak and my slops?

PAGE

He said sir, you should procure him better assurance than Bardolph, he would not take his bond and yours, he liked not the security.

FALSTAFF

Let him be damned like the glutton, pray God his tongue be hotter. A whoreson Achitophel! **A rascally yea-forsooth knave,** to bear a gentleman in hand, and then stand upon security! The whoreson smooth-pates do now wear nothing but high shoes, and bunches of keys at their girdles, and if a man is through with them in honest taking-up, then they must stand upon security.

. . .

I looked 'a should have sent me two and twenty yards of satin, as I am a true knight, and he send me security.

. . .

Reading is to the mind what exercise is to the body

Source: THE TATLER (Number 147)
Author: Sir Richard Steele (1672–1729)
First published: March 17, 1710
Kind of work: Essay

Context: Between April, 1709, and January, 1711, Joseph Addison and Richard Steele published 271 issues of a news and essay sheet called *The Tatler*. Steele originated the idea and was sole author of 188 numbers. Addison contributed some, and together they were responsible for 36 more. One of their collaborations was No. 147, dated March 17, 1709/1710. The double date is due to the change in calendars in England, from the Old Style Julian to the New Style Gregorian, that went into effect in 1752. Before then, the new year began on March 25. So, to reckon by present chronology, both figures are given. This issue appeared in 1710. The original purpose of *The Tatler* was to entertain and instruct. News items, gossip for the women, and essays on literary subjects made up the various issues that appeared three times a week. Under a motto from Ovid, is-

Reading is to the mind what exercise is to the body. As by the one, health is preserved, strengthened, and invigorated; by the other, virtue (which is the health of the mind) is kept alive, cherished and confirmed. But as exercise becomes tedious and painful when we make use of it only as the means of health, so reading is apt to grow uneasy and burdensome, when we apply ourselves to it only for our improvement in virtue. For this reason, the virtue which we gather from a fable or an allegory, is like the health we get by hunting, as we are engaged in an agreeable pursuit that draws us on with pleasure, and makes us insensible of the fatigues that accompany it.

Reason is the life of the Law

Source: INSTITUTES: COMMENTARY UPON LITTLETON. FIRST INSTITUTE (Book II, chapter 6, section 138)
Author: Sir Edward Coke (1552–1634)
First published: 1628
Type of work: Legal commentary

Context: The relationship of law and reason has always been taken for granted. Sir John Powell, in the case of Coggs vs. Bernard, said: "Consider the reason of the case, for nothing is law that is not reason." He was merely repeating a tenet of English Common Law stated nearly five centuries earlier by one who had been Judge of Assize and Judge of Common Pleas in fifteenth century England. Sir Thomas Littleton (1422–1481) was a jurist who decided to put into writing, principles about dealing with estates in land in England. He wrote in French and called the work *Tenures.* According to the earliest manuscript, it was "complete in the 14th year of the Reign of Edward IV," that is, 1475, but was not published until after the author's death, to become one of the first books printed in London. For a long time, it was admired for its concise and simple qualities, and was fundamental in British legal education. However in the course of 150 years, conditions changed, new problems arose, and in 1628, the man called "the greatest of all English common lawyers," Edward Coke (or Cooke), republished it in French and English in parallel columns along with his commentary in a third column, in Latin and English. This "Coke upon Littleton" remained the standard text until the nineteenth century. For instance, Book II, chapter 6, section 138, discussed the obligations of a tenant to his master. The lawyer distinguished between the kinds of tenants, whether frankmarriage or frankal-moigne. He declared: "a tenant in frankalmoign by reason of his tenure shall doe divide service for his Lord, as is said before; and this he is charged to do by the Law of the holy Church and therefore he is excused and discharged of fealty; but tenant in frankmarriage shall not doe for his tenure such service; and if he doth not fealty, he shall not doe any manner of service to his Lord, neither spiritual not temporall, which would be inconvenient, and against reason. . . ." Coke, commenting on this declaration, says in a parallel column:

And this is another strong argument in Law, *Nihil quod est contra rationem est licitum* [Nothing contrary to reason is permitted]; For **Reason is the life of the Law.** Nay the Common Law itselfe is nothing else but reason; which is to be understood of an artificiall perfection of reason, gotten by long study, observation, and experience, and not of every man's naturall reason. . . .

The Recording Angel dropped a tear upon the word, and blotted it out forever

Source: THE LIFE AND OPINIONS OF TRISTRAM SHANDY, GENT. (Book VI, chapter 8)
Author: Laurence Sterne (1713–1768)
First published: 1759–1767
Type of work: Novel

Context: Tristram Shandy's Uncle Toby is a man devoted to the study of military history, strategy, and tactics. With him lives his servant, Corporal Trim. The corporal discovers, at a local inn, an army lieutenant and his child, a son, in great distress; the father is very ill and suffering, as well, from lack of funds. Discovering that Lieutenant Le Fever is known to Captain Shandy, Corporal Trim promises to get help for him. Uncle Toby is quite stricken for the lieutenant, whose wife was killed in his arms by an enemy bullet at Breda. So moved is the amateur strategist that he utterly gives up for the moment his reënactment of the siege of Dendermond, in order to help Le Fever, vowing to do all he can with his hospitality, purse, and nursing to put the sick man back on his feet. An argument ensues between Uncle Toby and Corporal Trim over whether the man can be cured; during the argument Uncle Toby lets fly an oath which, says the author, was forgiven on high:

. . . He shall march, cried my uncle Toby, marching the foot which had a shoe on, though without advancing an inch,—he shall march to his regiment.—He cannot stand it, said the corporal;—He shall be supported, said my uncle Toby;—He'll drop at last, said the corporal, and what will become of his boy?—He shall not drop, said my uncle Toby firmly.—A-well-a-o'day,—do what we can for him, said Trim, maintaining his point,—the poor soul will die:—He shall not die, by G—, cried my uncle Toby.

—The Accusing Spirit, which flew up to heaven's chancery with the oath, blushed as he gave it in;—and **the Recording Angel, as he wrote it down, dropped a tear upon the word, and blotted it out for ever.**

The red fool fury of the Seine

Source: IN MEMORIAM (Part CXXVII, stanza 2)
Author: Alfred, Lord Tennyson (1809–1892)
First published: 1850
Type of work: Elegy

Context: This elegy was written as a monument to Arthur Henry Hallam, a young man of extraordinary promise and an intimate friend of Tennyson, who died suddenly in Vienna at the age of twenty-two. The poem records the slow, spiritual progress of Tennyson from his initial depth of personal sorrow to the gradual healing of grief through a sense of spiritual contact with Hallam in a wider love of God and humanity. This portion of the elegy confirms the survival of the spirit after death. The opening words of CXXVII—"And all is well" —link it with the preceding section which affirmed the reality of love. Love is the Lord whom Tennyson serves on earth and Hallam serves in the spiritual realm. The rule of love means "all is well" even though the forms in which faith has formerly embodied herself have been deserted by her and even though the present social order may perish in the convulsions which mark the end of one age and the beginning of a better one. This section thus unites the two main themes of the elegy: love and universal law, which assure immortality of spirit. All the upheavals are signs of human progress toward a great race of men of which Hallam is the archetype. In the poem Tennyson refers to a relatively recent social upheaval in France. In July of 1830, the republican elements in Paris staged a popular revolt against the anachronistic reforms of King Charles X. Charles, the last of the older Bourbon line, fled Paris and the kingship; and there was the second revolution of 1848, which deposed Louis Philippe.

And all is well, tho' faith and form
  Be sunder'd in the night of fear;
Well roars the storm to those that hear
A deeper voice across the storm,

Proclaiming social truth shall spread,
  And justice, even tho' thrice again
  The red fool fury of the Seine
Should pile her barricades with dead.

Regions Caesar never knew

Source: BOADICEA (Line 29)
Author: William Cowper (1731–1800)
First published: 1782
Type of work: Ode

Context: An ode to Boadicea, the British Queen who led the last uprising against the Romans, about A.D. 60, was included in a first volume of poetry published by a fifty-year-old man. History records that the queen poisoned herself rather than die in battle, but the poet's version makes a better climax in this patriotic vision about the descendants of Boadicea, whose global empire occupies lands unknown in Caesar's times.

"Then the progeny that springs
From the forests of our land,
Armed with thunder, clad with wings,
Shall a wider world command.

"Regions Caesar never knew
Thy posterity shall sway
Where his eagles never flew,
None invincible as they."

Such the bard's prophetic words,
Pregnant with celestial fire,
Blending as he swept the chords
Of his sweet but awful lyre.

She with all a monarch's pride,
Felt them in her bosom glow;
Rushed to battle, fought and died,
Dying, hurled them at the foe.

"Ruffians, pitiless as proud,
Heaven awards the vengeance due;
Empire is on us bestowed,
Shame and ruin wait for you."

Religion is by no means a proper subject for conversation in a mixed company

Source: LETTER TO HIS GODSON (Undated; Carnarvon number CXLII; Dobrée number 2415)
Author: Philip Dormer Stanhope, Lord Chesterfield (1694–1773)
First published: 1800
Type of work: Personal letter

Context: In writing a letter of advice to his godson, Philip Stanhope (1755–1815), later the Fifth Earl of Chesterfield, Lord Chesterfield tells the boy never to affect nor assume a particular character not his own, as it will only make him ridiculous in the eyes of the discerning. He should always observe decorum, which, he says, encompasses morals and a general decency. He is to study English more carefully than most people do and get the habit of speaking it well. There are few things more disagreeable than to hear a man use barbarisms, solecisms, and vulgarity. On the other hand, avoid using long and learned words when simpler ones will serve the purpose. Having briefly attempted to define a word, he goes on to say:

The three commonest topics of conversation are religion, politics and news. All people think that they understand the two first perfectly, though they never studied either, and are therefore very apt to talk of them both, dogmatically and ignorantly, consequently with warmth. But **religion is by no means a proper subject for conversation in a mixed company.** It should only be treated among a very few people of learning, for mutual instruction.

Religion is the opium of the people

Source: TOWARD THE CRITIQUE OF THE HEGELIAN PHILOSOPHY OF RIGHT
Author: Karl Marx (1818–1883)
First published: 1844
Type of work: Philosophical essay

Context: Marx is best known today, of course, as the creator of the philosophical basis of modern communism. He is generally regarded as supremely materialistic and as a vigorous exponent of atheism. Many philosophical attacks against religious institutions were made by German thinkers of the nineteenth century, not the least of which was that of Hegel. According to his more sympathetic Western critics, Marx does not set himself against the "spiritual" in his reply to Hegel, but instead he calls for the abandonment of the illusions enforced by conventional orthodoxy and the overthrow of "a condition which requires illusions," namely, the exploitation of workers by capitalism. In the opening paragraphs he gives his assessment of the role of religion in his world:

. . . Religion is the general theory of this world, its encyclopedic compendium, its logic in popular form, its spiritual *point d'honneur*, its enthusiasm, its moral sanction, its solemn complement, its general basis of consolation and justification. It is *the fantastic realization* of the human being inasmuch as the *human being* possesses no true reality. The struggle against religion is,

909

therefore, indirectly a struggle against *that world* whose spiritual *aroma* is religion.

Religious suffering is at the same time an *expression* of real suffering and a *protest* against real suffering. **Religion** is the sigh of the oppressed creature, the sentiment of a heartless world, and the soul of soulless conditions. It **is the opium of the people.**

The abolition of religion as the *illusory* happiness of men, is a demand for their *real* happiness. The call to abandon their illusions about their conditions is a *call to abandon a condition which requires illusions.*

The religion of gold

Source: THE ENGLISH CONSTITUTION (Chapter 4)
Author: Walter Bagehot (1826–1877)
First published: 1867
Type of work: Political study

Context: Bagehot's *The English Constitution* has a somewhat misleading title to most Americans. To us a constitution is a written document which outlines a form of government, delegating certain responsibilities to that government and imposing certain limitations upon it; at the same time, it usually guarantees a number of rights and privileges to those who are subject to it. Thus, to Americans, a book about any constitution either traces its origins and evolution or interprets it. The British, however, have no such historic document. By their constitution they mean the actual social and political order, in its entirety, of their nation; this term includes all laws, customs, traditions, and precedents through which their system of government operates. Thus Bagehot's book is a consideration of those forces and institutions which regulate English social and political life. In it he considers the various branches of government; the system of checks and balances which operates within the structure is discussed, and the forms of cabinet government are compared. As Bagehot observes, it is difficult to attempt any descriptive analysis of "a living Constitution:" the thing being studied is constantly changing, and the governments it is compared with are changing simultaneously. The structure analyzed in this volume applies to 1865–1866; when a second edition was published in 1872, Bagehot found it necessary to write a lengthy preface in order to bring his material up to date, and in it he implies that he is startled to find that so many changes have occurred in the interim. The volume begins with a study of the Cabinet and of the concept and function of monarchy; it then takes up the House of Lords:

The use of the House of Lords—or, rather, of the Lords, in its dignified capacity—is very great. It does not attract so much reverence as the Queen, but it attracts very much. The office of an

910

order of nobility is to impose on the common people—not necessarily to impose on them what is untrue, yet less what is hurtful; but still to impose on their quiescent imaginations what would not otherwise be there. The fancy of the mass of men is incredibly weak; it can see nothing without a visible symbol, and there is much that it can scarcely make out with a symbol. Nobility is the symbol of mind. It has the marks from which the mass of men always used to infer mind, and often still infer it. A common clever man who goes into a country place will get no reverence; but the "old squire" will get reverence. Even after he is insolvent, when everyone knows that his ruin is but a question of time, he will get five times as much respect from the common peasantry as the newly-made rich man who sits beside him. The common peasantry will listen to his nonsense more submissively than to the new man's sense. An old lord will get infinite respect. His very existence is so far useful that it awakens the sensation of obedience to a *sort* of mind in the coarse, dull, contracted multitude, who could neither appreciate or perceive any other.

The order of nobility is of great use, too, not only in what it creates, but in what it prevents. It prevents the rule of wealth— **the religion of gold.** . . . In reverencing wealth we reverence not a man, but an appendix to a man; in reverencing inherited nobility, we reverence the probable possession of a great faculty —the faculty of bringing out what is in one. . . .

A remnant of our Spartan dead

Source: DON JUAN (Canto III, stanza 86)
Author: George Gordon, Lord Byron (1788–1824)
First published: 1821 (Cantos III–V)
Type of work: Satiric poem

Context: In Venice, in the summer of 1818, Byron started what he intended to be an epic poem. Instead of the Spenserian stanzas of his earlier *Childe Harold's Pilgrimage,* he chose the Italian meter called ottava rima, the meter in which Ludovico Ariosto (1474–1533) wrote the highest literary achievement of the Italian Renaissance, *Orlando Furioso.* Perhaps its reputation as the greatest of poetic romances influenced the British poet to select its eight-line, ten-syllable stanza for what turned out to be his own masterpiece. The Italian ro-

mance, however, is a serious work, while *Don Juan* sounds at times like a jest, often rising to great heights of poetic inspiration, only to poke fun at the reader for taking it seriously. There is as much satire in it as romance, beginning with the dedication that insults Southey, the Poet Laureate of the time, and criticizes Wordsworth and Coleridge, along with other contemporary writers, as the work progresses. Don Juan Tenorio was a famous character of Spanish romanticism, based on a Golden Age original, but he has little relationship

911

to the title character of this poem, except as both were persistent pursuers of women. The English poem begins with the childhood of the hero, brought up by his mother, an intellectual, and getting his first knowledge of love-making through an affair with his mother's friend Donna Julia, the twenty-three-year-old wife of elderly Don Alfonso. From June until November they carry on their affair undiscovered; then Don Alfonso learns of the intrigue. Juan's mother decides to send the young man on a tour of Europe to improve his morals, and the first canto ends with the statement by the poet that whether he continues with Don Juan's adventures depends on how well the public buys the first sample. Despite the storm of protests rising because of Byron's voluptuousness that came when an anonymous publisher issued the anonymous first and second cantos published together, in July, 1819, Byron was encouraged to continue with Canto III which, like Canto III of *Childe Harold's Pilgrimage,* is the most admired of them all. It expresses his devotion to Greece. In it, asked to sing at a party, Don Juan obliges. Having traveled much, he is able to fit his theme to the nationality of his audience, and so, following the 86th stanza, are inserted sixteen stanzas of his song, beginning with one of Byron's most quoted lines: "The isles of Greece, the Isles of Greece,/ Where burning Sappho loved and sung." The lover of liberty wonders, as he sings of the greatness of Greece, whether the present generation is content merely to blush when earlier Greeks bled for their land. The reference is to the 300 Spartans under Leonidas who held back the Persians under Xerxes in 480 B.C. at the Pass of Thermopylae for three days until the forces of Greece could gather to oppose him.

> Must *we* but weep o'er days more blest?
> Must *we* but blush?—Our fathers bled.
> Earth! render back from out thy breast
> **A remnant of our Spartan dead!**
> Of the three hundred grant but three,
> To make a new Thermopylae.

Remorse, the fatal egg by pleasure laid

Source: THE PROGRESS OF ERROR (Line 239)
Author: William Cowper (1731–1800)
First published: 1782
Type of work: Didactic poem

Context: Cowper, the last English poet who belonged to what has been called the cult of simplicity, was a descendant of John Donne. He was trained for the law and called to the bar in 1754. He fell in love with his cousin but suffered an attack of insanity and was forbidden to see or marry her. A later emotional crisis, the strain of preparing for an examination, brought on a subsequent attack. On this occasion, in 1763, he attempted suicide. After a long convalescence, Cowper retired to the country and spent the rest of his life in rural seclusion with friends, first at Huntingdon and later at Olney. He never married. His Calvinism brought him both comfort and despair, and was an important factor in his recurrent fits of depression. He believed that on one occasion, God had told him he was irrevocably damned; that on another, God had ordered him to kill himself—but that the command had been retracted. Little of this melancholia appears in his poetry, which is primarily a quiet view of rural life; Cowper reflects and meditates, describes the pleasant countryside, and extols domestic simplicity. The deeper feelings he expresses come from his religious convictions, and he frequently injects moral lessons into his work. He had written a few verses in his youth, but it was not until he was fifty that he turned to the writing of poetry as a serious form of recreation. The first volume, *Poems,* was published in 1782; his greatest work, *The Task,* appeared three years later. The latter was written at the suggestion of his friend Lady Austen; he began with the subject she had assigned him, a sofa, but soon expanded the topic into a meditative description of the rural world about him. He also produced a number of hymns. Of his more consistently moralistic poems, *The Progress of Error* is a good example. In it Cowper attacks the dangers of high living, with its innumerable daily temptations; such pleasures are harmful, and endanger the soul even when enjoyed in moderation:

> Is man then only for his torment placed,
> The centre of delights he may not taste?
> Like fabled Tantalus, condemn'd to hear
> The precious stream still purling in his ear,
> Lip-deep in what he longs for, and yet curst
> With prohibition and perpetual thirst?
> No, wrangler—destitute of shame and sense,
> The precept, that enjoins him abstinence,
> Forbids him none but the licentious joy,
> Whose fruit, though fair, tempts only to destroy.
> **Remorse, the fatal egg by pleasure laid**
> In every bosom where her nest is made,
> Hatch'd by the beams of truth, denies him rest,
> And proves a raging scorpion in his breast.
> No pleasure? Are domestic comforts dead?
> Are all the nameless sweets of friendship fled?
> Has time worn out, or fashion put to shame,
> Good sense, good health, good conscience, and good fame?
> All these belong to virtue, and all prove
> That virtue has a title to your love.

Repentance is but want of power to sin

Source: PALAMON AND ARCITE (Book III, l. 813)
Author: John Dryden (1631–1700)
First published: 1700
Type of work: Chivalric romance

Context: Having on hand translations of bits of Homer and Virgil, Dryden decided that in order to have enough material to publish a volume, he would modernize part of the *Canterbury Tales* by the "Father of English poetry," Geoffrey Chaucer (c. 1340–1400). Dryden selected the Knight's tale of "Palamon and Arcite," Chaucer's longest and one of his best, which he adapted from a chivalric romance by the Italian Boccaccio (1313–1375). Shakespeare and Fletcher dramatized it as *The Two Noble Kinsmen* (1613). Theseus, returning to Athens with his Queen Hippolyta and her sister Emilia, meets a group of wives in mourning who beg him to force King Creon of Thebes to allow decent burial for their dead husbands. In the course of the ensuing battle, Theseus captures two Theban knights, Palamon and Arcite, whom he imprisons. From their prison window they see and fall in love with Emilia. Arcite is released and later returns to Athens. Palamon escapes to meet and challenge his rival. Learning of the proposed battle between the two knights of Thebes, Theseus arranges for a joust between them, the winner to marry Emilia, who loves neither of them. Both the warriors pray to the gods, and each is promised victory by a god. To settle this strife in Olympus, Saturn arranges a compromise. Arcite wins the joust, but he is hurt when his horse is frightened by fire bursting from the ground. He confesses that he had plotted unchivalrously against his rival. He begs Emilia to wed Palamon. He adds cynically that he is now repentant only because he is no longer able to continue with his evil scheme. In this way Dryden has modernized Chaucer's version of Arcite's plea. Emilia is, in the language of chivalry, his "friendly enemy," since knights looked upon courtship as a sort of battle with their sweethearts.

*   *   *

Ah, my sweet foe, for you, and you alone,
I broke my faith with injur'd Palamon.
But love the sense of right and wrong confounds,
Strong love and proud ambition have no bounds.
And much I doubt, should Heav'n my life prolong,
I should return to justify my wrong:
For while my former flames remain within,
Repentance is but want of pow'r to sin.
With mortal hatred I pursued his life;
Nor he, nor you, were guilty of the strife;

*   *   *

The Republic of Letters

Source: THE CITIZEN OF THE WORLD (Letter 20)
Author: Oliver Goldsmith (1728–1774)
First published: 1762
Type of work: Essay

Context: Oliver Goldsmith wrote these satires in a way that was both acceptable and somewhat the fashion in the eighteenth century: he created a persona who came from another culture, who could speak candidly, if with some pleasant naïveté, about the country and the culture in which he found himself; in this case a Chinese comments about Great Britain. Goldsmith creates a fictional Chinese mandarin named Lien Chi Altangi, from Canton, who writes a series of letters to his former teacher, Fum Hoam, "first president of the Ceremonial Academy, at Pekin, China." Some of the letters are about European culture generally, others are about England and its culture, more specifically. Letter 20 is one of the former; it describes the European literary scene as Goldsmith knew it. Goldsmith characterizes his fellow men-of-letters as persons who regard other authors as rivals, rather than as men engaged in a common pursuit of a single goal. He says of them, through his Chinese writer, "They calumniate, they injure, they despise, they ridicule each other: if one man writes a book that pleases, others shall write books to shew that he might have given still greater pleasure, or should not have pleased." Goldsmith has his fictional Chinese begin by noting that to call the literary world of the time a republic is only ironic:

The Republic of Letters is a very common expression among the Europeans; and yet when applied to the learned of Europe, is the most absurd that can be imagined, since nothing is more unlike a republic than the society which goes by that name. From this expression, one would be apt to imagine that the learned were united into a single body, joining their interests, and concurring in the same design. From this one might be apt to compare them to our literary societies in China, where each acknowledges a just subordination; and all contribute to build the temple of science, without attempting, from ignorance or envy, to obstruct each other.

But very different is the state of learning here: . . .

The rest is silence

Source: HAMLET (Act V, sc. ii, l. 369)
Author: William Shakespeare (1564–1616)
First published: 1603
Type of work: Dramatic tragedy

Context: With Queen Gertrude, King Claudius, and Laertes victims of violent deaths in the last scene of the play, Hamlet, Prince of Denmark, fatally wounded, passes the rights of the throne of Denmark to Fortinbras, Prince of Norway, who has a claim to the throne. All matters being settled, Hamlet speaks his last line and dies. Horatio bids him farewell.

HAMLET

O I die Horatio,
The potent poison quite o'er-crows my spirit.
I cannot live to hear the news from England,
But I do prophesy th' election lights
On Fortinbras, he has my dying voice;
So tell him, with th' occurrents more and less
Which have solicited—**the rest is silence.** [*Dies.*]

HORATIO

Now cracks a noble heart. Good night sweet Prince,
And flights of angels sing thee to thy rest. . . .

Rich beyond the dreams of avarice

Source: THE GAMESTER (Act II, sc. ii)
Author: Edward Moore (1712–1757)
First published: 1753
Type of work: Dramatic tragedy

Context: After a volume of fables for females and a simple comedy, *The Foundling*, in 1753 Moore became editor of *The World*, a weekly periodical that attacked the foibles and vices of the fashionable. He carried his campaign into the theater with *The Gamester*, whose opening was ruined by a campaign by gambling-house owners to stop its performance and weaken its message. Finally Moore declared that his purpose was rather to rouse pity for the victims than hatred for the vice. The preachment is stated at the final curtain: "Let frailer minds take warning; and from example learn, that want of prudence is want of virtue." Actually, as one character declares, how can a cure be found for the excitement involving the anxious hope of winning money and the agonizing fear of losing it? Moore tries by picturing Beverley as a person who prefers the delight of dice and bad company to the charms of his wife. By his gambling he has dissipated not only his own fortune and that of his wife, but that entrusted to him by a loving sister. However, more than gambling brings about Beverley's downfall. The villainous Stukely plots his ruin as an approach to his wife. He reveals his scheming in a soliloquy at the end of the first act. The message of the play starts with the rising curtain. Mrs. Beverley acknowledges the low state of their fortune while her sister-in-law Charlotte curses her brother and his "pernicious vice of gambling." Her

916

hope is that his little son may be taught prudence by his father's example. Both women express suspicion of the supposed friend Stukely. In comes Lewson, in love with Charlotte. They are the only normal people in the play. He announces that at the previous day's sale of Beverley's house and furniture, a friend bought much of it which he wants Mrs. Beverley to use. Stukely plots a rigged gambling session further to ruin Beverley, though he claims to have sold most of his possessions to pay off the creditors of his great friend. As a final villainy, he plans to get Lewson murdered with suspicion pointing to Beverley, who will be jailed as a debtor, so opening Stukely's path to Mrs. Beverley. In the final act, Stukely's servant Bates announces he has stabbed Lewson according to orders. Beverley is also jailed. The news that his uncle has suddenly died naming him the heir, will not help his desperate situation because he has already sold his expectations to repay Stukely. So he takes poison. Too late to save the gamester's life, Stukely is unmasked by Bates, and Lewson reappears alive. The acting of the Popes in the initial performance and of Kemble and Mrs. Siddon in revivals helped make audiences overlook the silliness of Beverley and the imprudence of his wife. Garrick, director at the Drury Lane Theatre where the play opened, is supposed to have rewritten and tightened several scenes, especially the fourth-act clash between Lewson and Stukely. With all its flaws, according to modern standards, the tragedy was translated into French, German, and Dutch. In Act II, scene ii, begins what seems like a reconciliation.

BEVERLEY

They hurt me beyond bearing.—Is Stukely false! Then honesty has left us! 'T were sinning against Heaven to think so.

MRS. BEVERLEY

I never doubted him.

BEVERLEY

No; you are charity. Meakness and ever-during patience live in that heart, and love that knows no change.—Why did I ruin you?

MRS. BEVERLEY

You have not ruined me. I have no wants, when you are present, nor wishes in your absence, but to be blest with your return. Be but resigned to what has happened, and I am **rich beyond the dreams of avarice.**

BEVERLEY

My generous girl!

917

Riddles of death Thebes never knew

Source: HELLAS (Line 1083)
Author: Percy Bysshe Shelley (1792–1822)
First published: 1822
Type of work: Poetic drama

Context: The composition of *Hellas* was occasioned by the beginning of the revolt of the Greeks against Turkey. In country after country in southern Europe the native populations had shaken off the tyranny of foreign overlords. These revolutions had been a matter of intense interest to Shelley, and when in 1821 Greece also arose in a bid for freedom, he was so powerfully moved that he cast the events of the struggle into a drama. He worked, however, under the great disadvantage of not knowing how the conflict would come out. Like a Greek drama, Shelley's play has no on-stage action. The progress of the war up to the date of writing is given: although the Greeks had had scattered victories, the Turks had for the most part won the battles. In the play Mahmud, Sultan of Turkey, summons the ancient Jewish sage Ahasuerus; Mahmud wishes to learn the future, but Ahasuerus contends that the only reality is thought and that he cannot prophesy. He advises Mahmud to stop the war. The phantom of Mahomet II appears and prophesies ruin for Mahmud and his empire but will not tell when the ruin will be accomplished. As cries of "Victory" ring out, the chorus of Greek captive women chants of a rebirth of Greece, which will be great even though a subtler Sphinx whose riddle Oedipus solved on the outskirts of Thebes propounds new riddles for a modern world.

> Oh, write no more the tale of Troy,
>   If earth Death's scroll must be!
> Nor mix with Laian rage the joy
>   Which dawns upon the free:
> Although a subtler Sphinx renew
> **Riddles of death Thebes never knew.**
>
> Another Athens shall arise,
>   And to remoter time
> Bequeath, like sunset to the skies,
>   The splendour of its prime;
> And leave, if nought so bright may live,
> All earth can take or Heaven can give.

Ride in triumph through Persepolis

Source: TAMBURLÀINE THE GREAT (Part I, Act II, sc. v, l. 49)
Author: Christopher Marlowe (1564–1593)
First published: 1590
Type of work: Dramatic tragedy

Context: Marlowe, with Thomas Kyd (1558–1594), author of *The Spanish Tragedy,* discovered the possibilities of dramatic blank verse and made it available for the English Romantic drama. They ended the authority of Seneca and pseudo-classicism. What has been considered Marlowe's first play deals in ten acts with Tamburlaine or Tamerlane, the fourteenth century "Scourge of God," whose empire eventually extended from the Wall of China to the Mediterranean and from Siberia to the Ganges. In the beginning of Part I, he has captured the Egyptian Zenocrate, on her way to marry the sultan, and has won over by his personality the Persian cavalry sent to capture him. He persuades Cosroe, brother of the Persian King Mycetes, to join with him in dethroning the monarch, now marching to attack him. Cosroe departs to occupy the Persian capital Persepolis, while his brother and the army are busy fighting Tamburlaine.

COSROE

And till thou overtake me, Tamburlaine,
(Staying to order all the scattered troops,)
Farewell, lord regent and his happy friends!
I long to sit upon my brother's throne.

MEANDER

Your Majesty shall shortly have your wish,
And **ride in triumph through Persepolis.**
                    [Exeunt the Persians.]

TAMBURLAINE

"And **ride in triumph through Persepolis!**"
Is it not brave to be a king, Techelles?
Usumcasane and Theridamas,
Is it not passing brave to be a king,
"And **ride in triumph through Persepolis**"?

TECHELLES

Oh, My Lord, 'tis sweet and full of pomp.

USUMCASANE

To be a king is half to be a god.

THERIDAMAS

A god is not so glorious as a king.
I think the pleasures they enjoy in Heaven,
Cannot compare with kingly joy on earth; . . .

919

The right of election is the very essence of the constitution

Source: LETTERS (To His Grace the Duke of Grafton, Letter XI, April 24, 1769)

Author: Junius, pseud.

First published: 1769

Type of work: Political letter

Context: Junius was a mystery in his own time and so remains. No one knows who he really was. He wrote what we would consider "letters to the editor," though they were open letters addressed to various public figures active in British government; they appeared in the *Public Advertiser* from 1767 to 1772. In them Junius skillfully chastised the administration for its abuses, castigating various individuals as he did so. The purpose these philippics served was an admirable one. They gave the public an awareness of its constitutional rights; they were well written and carried the ring of authority; their arguments were sound and logical; and they held strictly to basic constitutional principles. The immediate popularity they achieved was greater than that of any such series of letters before or since. Junius, cloaked by his pseudonym, was able to see the great influence of his work and to enjoy the efforts, some of them frantic, to uncover him. "He beheld," says one scholar, "the people extolling him,

the court execrating him, and ministers and more than ministers trembling beneath the lash of his invisible hand." Parliament smarted under his biting attacks, and even the king was not safe from him. Whoever Junius was, he led from a sound footing: he held some position within the government that made him privy to what transpired there. A Whig, he detested the Duke of Grafton, an unscrupulous politician; to Junius, he was a man utterly without principle. In the letter quoted here Junius takes Grafton to task for rigging an election in Middlesex by running a man of his own choosing against Wilkes, the people's choice; Grafton has expelled Wilkes from the House of Commons repeatedly; now he has declared Wilkes ineligible because of the expulsions and declared his own man representative instead. Junius has already noted that Grafton balances nonexecution of laws with breaches of the constitution; now he turns to the matter of the election:

. . . With this precedent before you, with the principles on which it was established, and with a future House of Commons, perhaps less virtuous than the present, every county in England, under the auspices of the Treasury, may be represented as completely as the county of Middlesex. Posterity will be indebted to your Grace for not contenting yourself with a temporary expedient, but entailing upon them the immediate blessings of your administration. Boroughs were already too much at the mercy of government. Counties could neither be purchased nor intimidated. But their solemn determined election may be rejected, and the man they detest may be appointed, by another choice, to represent them in Parliament. . . . With every good-natured allowance for your Grace's youth and inexperience, there are some things which you cannot but know. You cannot but know that the right of the freeholders to adhere to their choice (even supposing it improperly exerted) was as clear and indisputable as that of the House of Commons to exclude one of their own members:—nor is it possible for you not to see the wide distance there is between the negative power of rejecting one man, and the positive power of appointing another. The right of expulsion, in the most favourable sense, is no more than the custom of parliament. **The right of election is the very essence of the constitution.** To violate that right, and much more to transfer it to any other set of men, is a step leading immediately to the dissolution of all government. . . .

Ring in the Christ that is to be

Source: IN MEMORIAM (Part CVI, stanza 8)
Author: Alfred, Lord Tennyson (1809–1892)
First published: 1850
Type of work: Elegy

Context: This elegy was written as a monument to Arthur Henry Hallam, a young man of extraordinary promise and an intimate friend of Tennyson who died suddenly in Vienna at the age of twenty-two. The poem records the slow, spiritual progress of Tennyson from his initial depth of personal sorrow to the gradual healing of grief through a sense of spiritual contact with Hallam in a wider love of God and humanity. This section and the two preceding sections mark the fourth part of the poem; they describe Christmastide and New Year in Tennyson's new home—the third such season since the death of his friend. Happy, jubilant bells mark the arrival of the New Year; Tennyson's emotional state is equally jubilant. The poet hopes that the bells will ring out the old emotions and old ideas which have isolated man from humanity and stunted his spiritual well-being. He hopes the bells will ring in powers which will unite mankind. He leaves behind "the griefs that sap the mind" and looks forward to an earthly paradise. In the last stanzas, Tennyson calls for a new man typified by Hallam. In the same way that Hallam has been elevated, apotheosized, and finally merged with Christ in the elegy, all mankind will move toward this elevated character as the Spirit of Christ grows to include all men and all religions:

> Ring out old shapes of foul disease;
>   Ring out the narrowing lust of gold
>   Ring out the thousand wars of old,
> Ring in the thousand years of peace.

921

Ring in the valiant man and free,
   The larger heart, the kindlier hand;
Ring out the darkness of the land,
Ring in the Christ that is to be.

The ringing grooves of change

Source: LOCKSLEY HALL (Line 182)
Author: Alfred, Lord Tennyson (1809–1892)
First published: 1842
Type of work: Dramatic monologue

Context: Locksley Hall is, among other things, a striking forecast—especially so for 1842—of the world to come, in which Tennyson glimpses the wonders that will be wrought by man's ingenuity. This vision of the future is central to the theme of the poem, which begins with the speaker's own despair. The woman he loves has, in obedience to the customs of the day, married a gross and stupid country landowner chosen by her parents. The speaker tortures himself with a vivid forecast of the life of disappointment and heartbreak she must now lead; he condemns her weakness bitterly and for a moment considers renouncing civilization, exiling himself to some tropic isle, and ending there. But he has been born into an age of exciting change, a world of promise: once, before his disastrous love affair, he had seen into the future. In spite of personal grief, he must remain a part of civilization and see his vision of it become reality. What he had seen forms an interesting source of speculation for the reader, who is left with the uncanny impression that Tennyson really did see a hundred years ahead:

"For I dipt into the future, far as human eye could see,/ Saw the Vision of the world, and all the wonder that would be;/ Saw the heavens fill with commerce, argosies of magic sails,/ Pilots of the purple twilight, dropping down with costly bales;/ Heard the heavens fill with shouting, and there rain'd a ghastly dew/ From the nations' airy navies grappling in the central blue;/ Far along the world-wide whisper of the south-wind rushing warm,/ With the standards of the peoples plunging thro' the thunderstorm;/ Till the war-drum throbb'd no longer, and the battle-flags were furl'd/ In the Parliament of man, the Federation of the world./ There the common sense of most shall hold a fretful realm in awe,/ And the kindly earth shall slumber, lapt in universal law." The vision does not blind him to social ills; he is aware of starving multitudes: "Slowly comes a hungry people, as a lion, creeping nigher,/ Glares at one that nods and winks behind a slowly-dying fire." But he must take the future as it comes and be a part of it; the island paradise, to which, for a moment, he considers escaping, is only a foolish dream.

Mated with a squalid savage—what to me were sun or
  clime?
I the heir of all the ages, in the foremost files of time—

I that rather held it better men should perish one by one,
Than that earth should stand at gaze like Joshua's moon
  in Ajalon!

Not in vain the distance beacons. Forward, forward let
  us range,
Let the great world spin forever down **the ringing
grooves of change.**

Thro' the shadow of the globe we sweep into the younger
  day:
Better fifty years of Europe than a cycle of Cathay.

Mother-Age (for mine I knew not) help me as when life
  begun:
Rift the hills, and roll the waters, flash the lightnings,
  weigh the sun.
                     .   .   .
Howsoever these things be, a long farewell to Locksley
  Hall!
Now for me the woods may wither, now for me the
  roof-tree fall.

The ripest fruit first falls

Source: KING RICHARD THE SECOND (Act II, sc. i, l. 153)
Author: William Shakespeare (1564–1616)
First published: 1597
Type of work: Historical drama

Context: John of Gaunt, revered
elder statesman, lies dying at Ely
House in London, surrounded by his
close kinsmen and associates, who
hear his final words of concern for
England under the misguided and er-
roneous rule of his nephew, King
Richard II. Richard, instead of accepting the advice of Gaunt for reform, indicates that he will continue
in his ruthless manner as he accepts
the death of his uncle simply as
timely and announces that he will
confiscate Gaunt's estate as revenue
for the Irish wars, since Bolingbroke,
son and heir of Gaunt, is in exile at
the king's decree.

RICHARD
The ripest fruit first falls, and so doth he;
His time is spent, our pilgrimage must be;

923

So much for that. Now for our Irish wars—
We must supplant these rough rug-headed kerns,
Which live like venom, where no venom else
But only they have privilege to live.
And for these great affairs do ask some charge,
Towards our assistance we do seize to us
The plate, coin, revenues, and moveables,
Whereof our uncle Gaunt did stand possessed.

Roar you as gently as any sucking dove

Source: A MIDSUMMER NIGHT'S DREAM (Act I, sc. ii, ll. 84–85)
Author: William Shakespeare (1564–1616)
First published: 1600
Type of work: Dramatic comedy

Context: The festivities have begun in Athens to celebrate the approaching marriage of Duke Theseus and Hippolyta, fair captive Queen of the Amazons. At the house of Quince, a carpenter, rehearsals are beginning for the enactment of a play based upon the Pyramus and Thisbe legend. The weaver, Bottom, who monopolizes the conversation, is not satisfied with having the leading role of Pyramus, but also demands the parts of Thisbe and of the lion. Chided by his friends that he would roar too loudly and frighten the ladies so badly that the whole company would be hanged, Bottom responds:

BOTTOM
I grant you, friends, if you should fright the ladies out of their wits, they would have no more discretion but to hang us; but I will aggravate my voice so, that I will **roar you as gently as any sucking dove;** I will roar you an 'twere any nightingale.

A Roman by a Roman valiantly vanquished

Source: ANTONY AND CLEOPATRA (Act IV, sc. xv, ll. 56–57)
Author: William Shakespeare (1564–1616)
First published: 1623
Type of work: Dramatic tragedy

Context: Twice defeated by Octavius Caesar in their struggle to gain control of the Roman Empire, Mark Antony falls on his own sword, fatally wounding himself. Before he dies, however, he is carried by his guard to the monument where Cleopatra, the Queen of Egypt and his lover, has taken refuge from Caesar's forces. Although he has twice seen victory against Octavius Caesar slip from his grasp because of Cleopatra's desertion of his forces, the dying Antony still loves the Egyptian queen, as she loves him. Her attendants lift Antony to her place of refuge, that he may kiss her once more before he dies. Held in his beloved's arms, Antony bids Cleopatra neither lament nor feel sorrow at his defeat and death. He tells her to remember him as he once was, the noblest Roman and the strongest. He reminds her that he dies by his own hand, by his own choice, and not conquered by a fellow Roman.

ANTONY

The miserable change now at my end
Lament nor sorrow at; but please your thoughts
In feeding them with those my former fortunes
Wherein I lived, the greatest prince o' th' world,
The noblest; and do now not basely die,
Not cowardly put off my helmet to
My countryman—**a Roman by a Roman
Valiantly vanquished.** Now my spirit is going,
I can no more.

A Roman holiday

Source: CHILDE HAROLD'S PILGRIMAGE (Canto IV, stanza 141)
Author: George Gordon, Lord Byron (1788–1824)
First published: 1818 (Canto IV)
Type of work: Narrative poem

Context: Reaching Rome in the Fourth Canto of *Childe Harold's Pilgrimage,* Byron lists and describes some of its most notable sights, and mention of them leads him into bypaths of his own personal philosophy. His description of the ruins along the Appian Way near Rome and the fountain where the lovers Numa and Egeria traditionally met in secret, turns his thoughts to love in general and to the part that the mind plays in creating its physical representation. He then looks on the Coliseum and is led to ponder on the power of Time to cast a spell of beauty over things of the past. Perhaps Time will bestow a gift on him. After his death, it may reveal the truth of the calumny spread about him and act as a balance to give him someday his just position in the literary world. Back to the Coliseum, he thinks of the many people slain in its arena. He is reminded of the famous statue, then called "The Dying Gladiator," now believed to represent a dying Gaul. How unjust that man's death was, killed to provide excitement for a crowd of blood-thirsty spectators enjoying a holiday! In his anger Byron calls on the Goths to take revenge on Rome. Then looking around, he sees that Time has already had its revenge. Now the city lies in ruins, plundered to provide building material for many walls and palaces. Beginning in Stanza 140, the poet declares that in his imagination:

I see before me the gladiator lie:
He leans upon his hand—his manly brow
Consents to death, but conquers agony . . .
The arena swims around him—he is gone,
Ere ceased the inhuman shout which hail'd the wretch
    who won.

He heard it, but he heeded not—his eyes
Were with his heart, and that was far away;
He reck'd not of the life he lost nor prize,
But where his rude hut by the Danube lay,
There were his young barbarians all at play,
There was their Dacian mother—he, their sire,
Butcher'd to make **a Roman holiday**—
All this rush'd with his blood.—Shall he expire
And unavenged?—Arise! ye Goths, and glut your ire!

The rosebud garden of girls

Source: MAUD (Part I, sec. xxii, l. 902)
Author: Alfred, Lord Tennyson (1809–1892)
First published: 1855
Type of work: Narrative poem

Context: When the narrator of this poem is a small boy and Maud is yet unborn, her father-to-be proposes that if his child is a girl she shall eventually marry the narrator. This agreement, however, is broken in later years when the narrator's father loses his wealth, for Maud's family want her to marry a rich man. The situation gives Tennyson the opportunity to attack the lack of ethics in the business world of the time and the materialistic attitude that made the possession of wealth the all-important factor in a marriage. Maud's brother has found what he considers to be an excellent match for her in the person of a newly-rich, newly-enobled young man. The brother has political ambitions; and to further them, he gives a large dinner and ball to which the narrator is not invited. Maud and her lover, however, plan to meet for a few moments in the garden of her home after the ball is over. While waiting for her to appear, the narrator compares her to the flowers blooming around him:

Queen rose of **the rosebud garden of girls,**
    Come hither, the dances are done,
In gloss of satin and glimmer of pearls,
    Queen lily and rose in one;
Shine out, little head, sunning over with curls,
    To the flowers, and be their sun.

926

A rose-red city half as old as Time

Source: PETRA (or PEDRA) (Line 132)
Author: John William Burgon (1813–1888)
First published: 1845
Type of work: Descriptive poetry

Context: The English poet and minister, the Reverend John W. Burgon, born in Smyrna, the son of a Turkish merchant, portrayed the ruins of Petra in a long descriptive poem in rhymed couplets, of which only one line is remembered today. There is very little left of a city that dates back at least to the fourth century B.C. Since then it has been captured and recaptured by Arab, Greek, Roman, and Frank. It lies in Jordan, in a valley near the Gulf of Aqaba, and once was the center of a great trade route. It was the capital of the ancient Natateans who inhabited Arabia from Syria to Arabia and from the Euphrates to the Red Sea. Their history can be carried back at least to 312 B.C., when Antigonus I vainly laid siege to Petra. Tombs nearby date all the way from pre-Hellenic times through the period of the Ptolomies. In 106, the region was absorbed into the Roman Empire as Arabia Petraea. Strabo (63? B.C.–A.D. 24) described it in his *Geography* (XVI, 779) as did Pliny (23–79) in his *Natural History* (VI, 32). It was also mentioned during the First Crusades, when the Franks held it briefly. Its appearance offers a fantastic and romantic sight, the work of some enchanter. Unlike the white ruins in Greece or the gray cathedrals (a "minster fane" is a large cathedral) on the hills or plains of Europe, the ruins of Petra have the pink hue of sunrise, reminding the onlooker that they date from the dawn of time. A realist trying to calculate the age imputed to it by the poet might ask: "How old is Time?" but the figure is at least striking and poetic. The poem won the Newdigate Prize at Oxford in 1845 and was printed there in that year; the section containing the one famous line has often been reprinted separately. Wrote Dr. Burgon:

> It seems no work of man's creative hand
> By labor wrought as wavering fancy plann'd,
> But from the rock as if by magic grown,
> Eternal, silent, beautiful, alone!
> Not virgin-white like the old Doric shrine
> Where erst Athene held her rites divine;
> Nor saintly-grey, like many a minster fane,
> That crowns the hill, and consecrates the plain;
> But rosy-red as if the blush of dawn
> That first beheld them were not yet withdrawn;
> The hues of youth upon a brow of woe,
> Which men deemed old two thousand years ago.
> Match me such marvel save in Eastern clime,
> **A rose-red city half as old as Time.**

927

The rude forefathers of the hamlet sleep

Source: ELEGY WRITTEN IN A COUNTRY CHURCHYARD (Line 16)
Author: Thomas Gray (1716–1771)
First published: 1751
Type of work: Didactic elegy

Context: At the opening of his poem Gray depicts the quiet twilight atmosphere of a rural churchyard in England. He notes the tolling of the curfew bell, the herd of cattle going to be milked, the ploughman weary with having marched behind his team and plow all day, the fading light in the west, the buzz of a beetle close by, and the tinkling of sheep-bells in the distance. He then turns his attention to the graves about him, in which lie the previous generations of the neighboring population, each like a monk in "his narrow cell." The poet notes that no historian or biographer has given an account of these humble people, even though they lived as useful lives as more famous persons. He asks the reader to remember that these unknown men had wives and children they loved, had hearths which gave them contentment after a hard day's work, and that these men struggled to make a living from the surrounding fields, meadows, and woods. We should not, he comments, "hear with a disdainful smile,/ The short and simple annals of the poor." He writes of the lowly but honest dead with affection:

> Beneath those rugged elms, that yew-tree's shade,
>> Where heaves the turf in many a mold'ring heap,
> Each in his narrow cell forever laid,
>> **The rude forefathers of the hamlet sleep.**
>
> The breezy call of incense-breathing Morn,
>> The swallow twitt'ring from the straw-built shed,
> The cock's shrill clarion, or the echoing horn,
>> No more shall rouse them from their lowly bed.
>
> For them no more the blazing hearth shall burn,
>> Or busy housewife ply her evening care:
> No children run to lisp their sire's return,
>> Or climb his knees the envied kiss to share.
>
> Oft did the harvest to their sickle yield,
>> Their furrow oft the stubborn glebe has broke;
> How jocund did they drive their team afield!
>> How bow'd the woods beneath their sturdy stroke!

Rugged the breast that beauty cannot tame

Source: SONNET IN PRAISE OF DELIA
Author: John Codrington Bampfylde (1754–1796)
First published: 1778
Type of work: Sonnet

Context: Many names have been rescued from oblivion because of one small act. Probably more people remember Sir Walter Raleigh for his courtly gesture of spreading his cloak over a mudhole so that his queen might walk without dirtying her shoes than for any of his more adventurous deeds. The name of the sixteenth century Spaniard Gutierre de Cetina has for four centuries occupied a place in literary history for one short madrigal of ten lines, "Ojos claros, serenos" (Clear, calm eyes), sometimes called the most perfect poem in Spanish. Of the hundreds of poets writing in the eighteenth century whose names are forgotten, John Codrington Bampfylde remains in memory because of a sheaf of poetry that he published in 1778 under the title *Sixteen Sonnets*. For everything else connected with his life, he deserves to be forgotten. But half a dozen anthologies reprint some or all of these sonnets. Robert Southey (1774–1843) reprinted all sixteen of them in his *Specimens of Later English Poets* (1807) along with two other poems that he had discovered, noting that Bampfylde had written fresh, natural descriptions that were "some of the most original in our tongue." Bampfylde, whose family was originally Bampfield, was the younger son of Sir Richard Warwick Bampfylde of Poltimore, Devonshire. He was educated at Cambridge, where he fell in love with Delia Palmer, niece of the English painter Sir Joshua Reynolds. She was the inspiration for most of his poetry. When Reynolds rightly objected to her marriage to a dissolute and penniless poet, Bampfylde broke windows in the Reynolds mansion. He was arrested and sent to Newgate Jail. Delia took her uncle's advice and became the Marchioness Thomond; perhaps as a result of this marriage, Bampfylde removed the sonnet quoted from the sixteen he printed. Released from jail, he continued his dissipated life, ending in confinement in a madhouse and dying from consumption. Samuel Daniel (1562–1619) had previously written a number of "Sonnets to Delia," which Bampfylde may have had in mind, especially since the earlier poet wrote of going to America if his Delia scorned him. The "youthful graces" in the sonnet refer to a young man who completed and published his love poems before he was twenty-four. Let others sail westward to plunder America. Taught by Delia to love nature, this poet is content to "waste" his time loving his mentor and writing poetry to her. Though the word "enslave" seems highly emotional, it is only part of the period's conventional language. The object of a man's affection was his queen. He was her slave, subject to her whims. The rest of the language, including his "mild tumult," testifies to the low emotional key of the whole sonnet.

Cold is the senseless heart that never strove
With the mild tumult of a real flame;
Rugged the breast that beauty cannot tame,
    Nor youth's enlivening graces teach to love
    The pathless vale, the long-forsaken grove,
The rocky cave that bears the fair one's name,
With ivy mantled o'er—For empty fame,
    Let him amidst the rabble toil, or rove
In search of plunder far to western clime.
    Give me to waste the hours in amorous play
With Delia, beauteous maid, and build the rhyme
Praising her flowing hair, her snowy arms,
And all that prodigality of charms
    Formed to enslave my heart and grace my lay.

Rule with a rod of iron

Source: REVELATION 2:27
Author: St. John the Divine
First transcribed: c. 90–96
Type of work: Apocalyptic epistle

Context: It is uncertain who wrote the almost overwhelming vision presented in Revelation. The writer has been variously identified as John the Apostle, John the Presbyter, and John of Patmos, and it is even possible that he wrote under a pseudonym. Scholarship indicates that he did not write the fourth gospel or the epistles; his literary style is quite different. Evidently he was Jewish in origin and a native of Palestine, who had been with the Christians at Ephesus, and was exiled with many other Christians to the penal colony on the island of Patmos. He was a student of the Old Testament and refers frequently to the apocalyptic visions recorded therein. His principal purpose in Revelation is to reassure other Christians and bolster their faith through the visions he has seen of heaven and of the salvation to come. Certainly, the Christians at that time were in need of reassurance; John wrote during the reign of the Roman Emperor Domitian, who hated Christians and rigidly enforced the practice of Caesar-worship. The reign of terror lasted until his death in A.D. 96, and his persecution of Christianity was extreme. John's visions were such that he found them difficult to communicate; some were evidently not expressible in words. Symbolism and allegory form a large part of them. His principal point is that suffering is transitory for the faithful, and that spiritual and not material forces will triumph in the end. The devout must be prepared for the end and for the coming of Christ. He begins by stating that his vision has been sent him by God, through Christ, and delivered by an angel. In a prologue he tells the nature of what he has seen. In Chapter 2 he quotes the letters Christ has commanded him to write to the seven churches in Asia. One of the letters, to the church at Thyatira, indicates the urgency of these messages:

> And unto the angel of the church in Thyatira write; These things saith the Son of God, who hath his eyes like unto a flame of fire, and his feet are like fine brass;
> I know thy works, and charity, and service, and faith, and thy patience, and thy works; and the last to be more than the first.
> Notwithstanding I have a few things against thee, because thou sufferest that woman Jezebel, which calleth herself a prophetess, to teach and to seduce my servants to commit fornication, and to eat things sacrificed unto idols.
> And I gave her space to repent of her fornication; and she repented not.
> Behold, I will cast her into a bed, and them that commit adultery with her into great tribulation, except they repent of their deeds.
> And I will kill her children with death; and all the churches shall know that I am he which searcheth the reins and hearts: and I will give unto every one of you according to your works.
> But unto you I say, and unto the rest in Thyatira, as many as have not this doctrine, and which have not known the depths of Satan, as they speak; I will put upon you none other burden.
> But that which ye have already hold fast till I come.
> And he that overcometh, and keepeth my works unto the end, to him will I give power over the nations:
> And he shall **rule** them **with a rod of iron;** as the vessels of a potter shall be broken to shivers: even as I received of my Father.

Rum, Romanism, and Rebellion

Source: SPEECH, NEW YORK CITY (October 29, 1884)
Author: Dr. Samuel D. Burchard (1812–1891)
First published: 1884
Type of work: Political speech

Context: At a reception in New York honoring James G. Blaine, the Republican candidate for President, the principal speaker, the Reverend Dr. Samuel D. Burchard, made a tactless remark that turned into a political blunder which has given him a somewhat dubious immortality. He conducted a group of clergymen to Blaine's hotel, and there uttered a slurring comment on the Democratic party which was widely circulated. Blaine perhaps failed to hear what Burchard said; at any rate, he did not repudiate the minister's words. The Democrats were quick to seize on the words as an insult to the Catholic Church. The election was very close; and it is believed that the victorious Democratic candidate, Grover Cleveland, gained thousands of votes in the crucial State of New York as a result of Burchard's tactless phrase. The unfortunate clergyman said, in part:

931

. . . We are Republicans, and don't propose to leave our party and identify ourselves with the party whose antecedents are **Rum, Romanism, and Rebellion**. . . .

Running a man down

Source: LETTER TO A VERY YOUNG LADY ON HER MARRIAGE
Author: Jonathan Swift (1667–1745)
First published: 1727
Type of work: Letter

Context: Several recipients have been suggested for this letter, one being Lady Betty Moore, daughter of the Earl of Drogheda; upon its publication in *Miscellanies,* Vol. II (1727), the name of Miss Staunton was associated with it, before she became Mrs. John Rochfort. At any rate, the recipient could hardly have taken it as a compliment either to her or to her sex. Its purpose was to exhort her to avoid "the many errors, fopperies, and follies, to which your sex is subject." Swift urges that the young lady avoid show of fondness for her husband in front of witnesses, that she become uneasy and worry when he is away, that she "abate a little that violent passion for clothes, so prominent in your sex," and that she listen instead of taking part in conversations in the company of men of learning. His confession that he has "little respect for the generality of her sex" cannot have endeared him to her. No wonder biographers doubt that, despite Swift's pondering whether Stella would fit well into the country church where he was preaching, this clergyman of keen wit and sharp tongue ever married. Close to the end of the letter, Swift warns the bride-to-be against gossiping:

> There is never wanting in this town, a tribe of bold, swaggering, rattling ladies, whose talents pass among coxcombs for wit and humour; their excellency lies in rude, shocking expressions, and what they call **"running a man down."** If any gentleman in their company happens to have any blemish in his birth or person, if any misfortune hath befallen his family or himself, for which he is ashamed, they will be sure to give him broad hints of it without any provocation. . . .

Sable-vested night, eldest of things

Source: PARADISE LOST (Book II, l. 962)
Author: John Milton (1608–1674)
First published: 1667
Type of work: Epic poem

Context: At the great council of the devils in their newly built hall, Pandemonium, ways of evening scores with God are considered. Finally the devils agree that the fittest revenge would not be the physical destruction of man, but the moral destruction of God's newest and dearest creation. Satan, wanting all the credit for the enterprise, points out the dangers, volunteers to go on the mission, and then immediately adjourns the meeting. He makes his way towards the gates of hell, where he meets the two monsters, Sin and Death. Sin is his daughter, having issued from his head while he was plotting against God; Death is their son, the result of their incestuous intercourse. Satan flatters Sin into opening the gates of hell, which she had been commanded to keep closed. She unlocks the gates, and she and Satan look out into the wild wilderness of chaos. Finally Satan plunges into it and begins to fight his way upward towards the earth; sometimes he rises and sometimes he falls, but he continues to struggle upward. "Black Night" is the oldest of things because created first.

At length a universal hubbub wild
Of stunning sounds and voices all confused
Borne through the hollow dark assaults his ear
With loudest vehemence: thither he plies,
Undaunted to meet there whatever power
Or spirit of the nethermost abyss
Might in that noise reside, of whom to ask
Which way the nearest coast of darkness lies
Bordering on light; when straight behold the throne
Of Chaos, and his dark pavilion spread
Wide on the wasteful deep; with him enthroned
Sat **sable-vested Night, eldest of things,**
The consort of his reign; and by them stood
Orcus and Ades, and the dreadful name
Of Demogorgon; Rumor next and Chance,
And Tumult and Confusion all imbroiled,
And Discord with a thousand various mouths.

Sacrifice to the Graces

Source: LETTERS TO HIS SON (Letter 32)
Author: Philip Dormer Stanhope, Lord Chesterfield (1694–1773)
First published: 1774
Type of work: Personal letter

Context: The Earl of Chesterfield had high hopes for his illegitimate son's rising above his birth and becoming an eminent man whose talents would be so great that his base birth would be overlooked. Motivated by the desire to see his son get ahead in the world, the earl wrote a long series of letters to him. These letters constitute both a book of manners

933

and a manual on how to succeed in life. One element of the man of affairs lacking in the son's make-up was grace, and this element the earl tirelessly emphasized. And so he begins the letter of March 9, 1746, by conjuring him to sacrifice to the Graces, as grace leads to women's hearts. The earl constantly counselled his son to cultivate the wives of prominent men, as they are usually extremely helpful, when well disposed, in aiding the rise of an aspiring young man.

> Dear Boy: I must from time to time, remind you of what I have often recommended to you, and of what you cannot attend to too much; **SACRIFICE TO THE GRACES.** The different effects of the same things, said or done, when accompanied or abandoned by them, is almost inconceivable. They prepare the way to the heart; and the heart has such an influence over the understanding, that it is worth while to engage it in our interest. It is the whole of women, who are guided by nothing else: and it has much to say, even with men, and the ablest men too, that it commonly triumphs in every struggle with the understanding. . . .

A sadness sweeter than a smile

Source: DON JUAN (Canto I, stanza 72)
Author: George Gordon, Lord Byron (1788–1824)
First published: 1819 (Cantos I and II)
Type of work: Satiric poem

Context: Don Jóse has died leaving his son and heir, Don Juan, in the hands of the child's mother, "Sagest of women, even of widows, . . ." This learned and virtuous lady has long since decided that her son shall be molded by her into a paragon worthy of the noble line from which he springs. All the accomplishments of chivalry plus the erudition for which she is so justly famous shall be his, but beyond these, Donna Inez (remembering her late lord's frailties) desires for him an education strictly moral with ". . . not a page of anything that's loose,/ Or hints continuation of the species, . . ." With his tutors, his confessor, and his mother his every-day companions, the child grows in beauty, charm, and grace. The only other female he ever sees except the household's ancient maids is the lovely young Donna Julia, his mother's friend, who ". . . saw, and, as a pretty child,/ Caress'd him often— . . .", a thing quite innocent when she was twenty and he thirteen. But now she is twenty-three and he sixteen, and suddenly there is a subtle change, the reason for which is all too apparent to the married Donna Julia though lost on the long-sequestered Juan.

Whate'er the cause might be, they had become
   Changed; for the dame grew distant, the youth shy,
Their looks cast down, their greetings almost dumb,
   And much embarrassment in either eye;
There surely will be little doubt with some
   That Donna Julia knew the reason why,
But as for Juan, he had no more notion
Than he who never saw the sea of ocean.

      . . .

And if she met him, though she smiled no more,
   She look'd **a sadness sweeter than her smile,**
As if her heart had deeper thoughts in store
   She must not own, but cherish'd more the while
For that compression in its burning core;
   Even innocence itself has many a wile,
And will not dare to trust itself with truth,
And love is taught hypocrisy from youth.

The safety of the people shall be their highest law

Source: DE LEGIBUS (On Laws, III, iii, 8)
Author: Marcus Tullius Cicero (106–43 B.C.)
First transcribed: 51–46 B.C.
Type of work: Codification of laws

Context: Cicero was a public figure of Rome. Several times he ran for the office of Consul. He decided to follow in the footsteps of his esteemed Plato, who wrote a treatise on the Republic and its functions. Cicero's original plan was for an imaginary conversation between early Roman statesmen; however, upon the advice of those who saw his draft of the first books, he turned them first into essays, and finally into a series of conversations between his brother and himself, two books a day over three days. Having completed his task about 46 B.C., he started another series of conversations, this time about laws; beginning with an introduction concerning Law and Justice in general. This was followed by a section stating what religious laws his ideal state required, and finally, laws governing officials of the state. Whatever additional books he completed have not survived. The chief importance of the work is its statement of Cicero's political ideals. The earliest manuscript, at Leyden, dates from 800–1100. A variation of this quotation, instead of "Salus populi" (The health [or safety] of the people) is "Vox populi, vox dei," "The voice of the people is the voice of god." Alcuin (735–844) used this version in a letter to Charlemagne, about 800, and the Archbishop Walter Reynolds repeated it in an admonition during the coronation sermon when Edward III ascended the English throne in 1327. Cicero's phrasing of this democratic idea is:

935

Let two magistrates be invested with sovereign authority. Since they lead, judge, and confer, from their functions they shall be called praetors, judges, and consuls. In the field they shall hold the supreme military power; they shall be subject to no one; **the safety of the people shall be their highest law.** . . . .

Saint Praxed's ever was the church for peace

Source: THE BISHOP ORDERS HIS TOMB AT SAINT PRAXED'S CHURCH (Line 14)
Author: Robert Browning (1812–1889)
First published: 1845
Type of work: Dramatic monologue

Context: The setting of this poem —which Ruskin maintained had summed up in a few lines all that he had said about the Italian Renaissance in thirty pages of *The Stones of Venice*—is at the bedside of the dying Bishop surrounded by his illegitimate sons. As the Bishop draws closer to death, his delirious mind wanders back into his past, especially to his life-long enmity for a fellow churchman, one Gandolf. The two have always been bitter rivals: the Bishop won the first victory by gaining the love of the woman who was the mother of the sons to whom he is speaking. To Gandolf, however, went the second round in the contest, for that priest, dying first, had secured a better place for his tomb in the Church of St. Praxed. The speaker, therefore, deprived of a conspicuous position for his burial-niche, must compensate by an especially splendid tomb; and it is for this purpose that he has summoned his sons, whom he euphemistically calls "nephews." There is a double irony in the poem: the reader knows that the sons, as greedy as is their father, will not give him the magnificent tomb he craves; and that Saint Praxed's, because of the strife between the Bishop and his rival, has hardly merited the title of "the church for peace." Part of the Bishop's monologue follows:

> Life, how and what is it? As here I lie
> In this state-chamber, dying by degrees,
> Hours and long hours in the dead night, I ask
> 'Do I live, am I dead?' Peace, peace seems all.
> **Saint Praxed's ever was the church for peace;**
> And so, about this tomb of mine. I fought
> With tooth and nail to save my niche, ye know:
> —Old Gandolf cozened me, despite my care;
> Shrewd was that snatch from out the corner South
> He graced his carrion with, God curse the same!
> Yet still my niche is not so cramped but thence
> One sees the pulpit o' the epistle-side,
> And somewhat of the choir, those silent seats,
> And up into the aery dome where live
> The angels, and a sunbeam's sure to lurk; . . .

The same bright, patient stars

Source: HYPERION (Book I, l. 352)
Author: John Keats (1795–1821)
First published: 1820
Type of work: Narrative poem

Context: Hyperion is an account of the overthrow of the old gods, the Titans, by Zeus, or Jupiter, and his brothers and sisters, the younger gods. The king among the Titans was Cronus, here called by his Roman name, Saturn. The opening scene is one of absolute stillness; beside a river lies the giant body of the monarch Saturn, deposed from his throne as ruler of the world by his own children. There has been bitter war, and the fallen king is stunned by his defeat. He is visited by Thea, wife of the sun-god Hyperion; she tries to comfort him in his misery. He wonders why he cannot create a new world to rule, and Thea leads him away to where the other gods lie. Meanwhile, one Titan who had not been deposed, Hyperion, has been busy conducting the sun across the heavens. He finishes his journey and enters his great golden palace in the sky. He is in a rage at what has happened to his fellow Titans and wonders if he too will be removed from his office and driven from his home. His mother, Coelus, attempts to comfort him and tells him to consult with Saturn down on earth. Hyperion, heeding her words, arises and looks at the stars—the same bright patient stars—and plunges into the night.

> Ere half this region-whisper had come down,
> Hyperion arose, and on the stars
> Lifted his curved lids, and kept them wide
> Until it ceased; and still he kept them wide:
> And still they were **the same bright, patient stars.**
> Then with a slow incline of his broad breast,
> Like to a diver in the pearly seas,
> Forward he stooped over the airy shore,
> And plunged all noiseless into the deep night.

The same heart beats in every human breast

Source: THE BURIED LIFE (Line 23)
Author: Matthew Arnold (1822–1888)
First published: 1852
Type of work: Lyric poem

Context: Two series of Arnold's love poems, "Switzerland" and "Faded Leaves," were apparently inspired by a girl whom he met in Switzerland in the 1840's. Sometimes called Marguerite, she is unnamed in "The Buried Life" (a poem related to the two series), in which the poet con-

937

trasts the self revealed to the world with that buried deep within. In the opening lines Arnold pleads for an end to "light words" and "gay smiles." "Give me thy hand," he says, "and hush awhile." Let me read in "those limpid eyes . . . thy inmost soul." Though most men hide their true selves from the world, surely lovers need not do so from each other.

Alas! is even love too weak
To unlock the heart, and let it speak?
Are even lovers powerless to reveal
To one another what indeed they feel?
I knew the mass of men concealed
Their thoughts, for fear that if revealed
They would by other men be met
With blank indifference, or with blame reproved;
I knew they lived and moved
Tricked in disguises, alien to the rest
Of men, and alien to themselves—and yet
The same heart beats in every human breast!

But we, my love!—doth a like spell benumb
Our hearts, our voices?—must we too be dumb?

Samson hath quit himself like Samson

Source: SAMSON AGONISTES (Lines 1709–1710)
Author: John Milton (1608–1674)
First published: 1671
Type of work: Dramatic tragedy

Context: The play opens with the last phase of the life of Samson, the Old Testament hero. The Philistines have blinded him and hold him prisoner in Gaza. The play, modeled after a Greek tragedy, depicts the restoration of the fallen Samson to the grace of God. Samson has already been tested by God and failed the test. Having been punished and having repented his sin, he now undergoes trials of his will and integrity to prove that he is worthy to be tested a second time. Surmounting these tests, he is summoned to entertain the Philistine nobles at the feast of the pagan god Dagon. At first he refuses. However, he is prompted by God's Providence to change his mind. He leaves for the feast and is not seen again. His final triumph over the Philistines is described by a messenger, who reports the spectacular catastrophe that Samson creates by pulling down the temple of Dagon on the priests, the nobility, and himself. The Chorus praises Samson's dearly bought revenge and the rebirth of his fame. Manoa, his father, sadly glorifies the regained identity of his dead son in an exultant epitaph:

Come, come, no time for lamentations now,
Nor much more cause, **Samson hath quit himself
Like Samson,** and heroicly hath finish'd
A life Heroic, on his enemies
Fully reveng'd, hath left them years of mourning,
And lamentation to the Sons of Caphtor
Through all Philistian bounds. To Israel
Honour hath left, and freedom, let but them
Find courage to lay hold on this occasion,
To himself and Father's house eternal fame;
And which is best and happiest yet, all this
With God not parted from him, as was feard,
But favouring and assisting to the end.

Sans teeth, sans eyes, sans taste, sans everything

Source: AS YOU LIKE IT (Act II, sc. vii, l. 166)
Author: William Shakespeare (1564–1616)
First published: 1623
Type of work: Dramatic comedy

Context: Driven from home by his wicked brother, Orlando and his faithful old servant, Adam, arrive in the Forest of Arden, tired and hungry. Leaving the weary Adam, Orlando rudely demands food of the exiled ruler, Duke Senior, only to find it offered to him courteously and instantly. While Orlando leaves to find Adam, Duke Senior and his follower, the "melancholy Jaques," comment on the unhappiness to be discerned in the world—"This wide and universal theatre." Jaques now delivers his famous speech on the "seven ages" of man, ages that begin in toothless infancy and end in toothless second childhood. Just as Jaques concludes, as though in ironic comment on the speech, Adam totters in, almost carried by Orlando:

JAQUES
        All the world's a stage,
And all the men and women merely players.
They have their exits and their entrances.
And one man in his time plays many parts,
He acts being seven ages. At first the infant,
Mewling, and puking in the nurse's arms.
Then the whining schoolboy with his satchel
           • • •
        Last scene of all,
That ends this strange eventful history,
Sans teeth, sans eyes, sans taste, sans everything.
Is second childishness and mere oblivion,

939

Sapping a solemn creed with solemn sneer

Source: CHILDE HAROLD'S PILGRIMAGE (Canto III, stanza 107)
Author: George Gordon, Lord Byron (1788–1824)
First published: 1816 (Canto III)
Type of work: Narrative poem

Context: Four years after writing the first two cantos of a travel book based on Byron's own postgraduate Grand Tour to Europe and the Orient, the poet began a sequel that turned out to be greatly superior to his first effort. Canto III, written while he was spending a summer in Switzerland with the Shelley family, presents the Byronic hero Childe (that is, Young Lord) Harold, standing on the spot where Wellington crushed Napoleon the year before. Byron contrasts the revelry by night before Waterloo with the massacre of friends and foes in one red burial afterward. He ponders on the personality of Napoleon whose downfall, like his rise, came because he did not seek a golden mean. Harold is full of melancholic thoughts. He who ascends the mountains will find "the loftiest peaks most wrapped in clouds." He who subdues his fellow men will be the target of their hatred. Then the traveler turns from men to ponder on nature. Going down the Rhine, he is led by sight of the castles to think of the bloodshed there, washed away by time. Lake Leman (Geneva) makes him think that "there is too much of man here," though he is reminded of Rousseau, who lived there and there had his loves. Passing through Lausanne and Ferney, Harold recalls Voltaire and the English historian of the Roman Empire, Edward Gibbon (1737–1794). Finally he reaches Italy where he decides: "I have not loved the world nor the world me." However, Byron concludes the canto with the 118th stanza, remembering his "child of love," Ada, and sending his blessings back to her. Having been reminded in Stanza 105 of Voltaire and Gibbon, he devotes Stanza 106 to Voltaire and 107 to Gibbon. In 107, he declares that the historian gathered material exhaustively, then cuttingly attacked what Gibbon regarded as the outworn creed of Christianity, undermining it by his irony. Perhaps the series of "s's" in the line was to imitate the hiss of scorn. The defenders of Christianity retaliated by damning Gibbon as an atheist.

> The other, deep and slow, exhausting thought,
> And hiving wisdom with each studious year,
> In meditation dwelt, with learning wrought,
> And shaped his weapon with an edge severe,
> **Sapping a solemn creed with solemn sneer;**
> The lord of irony,—that master-spell,
> Which stung his foes to wrath which grew from fear,
> And doom'd him to the zealot's ready Hell,
> Which answers to all doubts so eloquently well.

940

Save, oh, save me, from the candid friend

Source: NEW MORALITY (Line 210)
Author: George Canning (1770–1827)
First published: 1798
Type of work: Political poem

Context: In attacking the political leaders of Great Britain, the only one for whom Byron had a word of praise in his *Don Juan* was the statesman George Canning. Canning was converted to Toryism by the French Revolution and threw in his lot with William Pitt, serving as his undersecretary for foreign affairs. To bring ridicule on the English radicals and liberals, he founded The *Anti-Jacobin Examiner* (1797–1798). His opinions of England's problems are contained in a six-volume collection of speeches in which he came out for free trade, the end of slavery, and Greek independence. He died after serving only five months as England's Prime Minister. Besides his speeches, Mr. Canning occasionally expressed himself in verse, as in "The Slavery of Greece," and in a poem in the *Examiner* entitled "New Morality" which begins with the statement that much still remains to be done before England's eyes can be purged of their mental mist and all the current lies denied. Only fools would believe the times are barren of folly and devoid of crimes, such crimes as Pope thundered against in his poetry. Some writers since Pope have attacked conditions, in works like *The Baviad* by W. Gifford, "the hand that brush'd a swarm of fools away." But it is time to do so again, and someone should awaken and pour out "indignant strains" against "learning's, virtue's, truth's, and religion's foes." Never listen to "Candor," that insists: "Much may be said on both sides," or "finds with keen discriminating sight/ Black's not so black; nor white so very white." But Canning longs for the "bold, discriminating mind," even though it may make mistakes. If your enemy is outspoken, at least you will know where he stands. "Fox, to be sure, was vehement and wrong;/ But then, Pitt's words, you'll own, were rather strong./ Both must be blamed, but pardoned." The poet cries out for someone to face a situation:

> Give me th'avow'd, the erect, the manly foe,
> Bold I can meet,—perhaps may turn his blow;
> But of all plagues, good Heaven, thy wrath can send,
> **Save, save, oh! save me from the candid friend!**

Science is organized knowledge

Source: EDUCATION (chapter 2)
Author: Herbert Spencer (1820–1903)
First published: 1860
Type of work: Educational philosophy

941

Context: Herbert Spencer's *Education* is a group of magazine articles written in the 1850's and first published in book form in 1860—well over a century ago. Yet is has a striking immediacy; many of the ideas that were new at that time are today considered either new or quite recent by many. In his discussion of intellectual education Spencer discusses the progress being made in regard to educational philosophies. He notes that "the increase of political liberty, the abolition of law restricting individual action, and the amelioration of the criminal code, have been accompanied by a kindred progress toward non-coercive education: the pupil is hampered by fewer restraints, and other means than punishments are used to govern him." He feels that the many new and experimental methods of education are healthy and must be tried, because the best is yet to be discovered. "However impatiently, therefore, we may witness the present conflict of educational systems, and however much we may regret its accompanying evils, we must recognize it as a transition stage needful to be passed through, and beneficent in its ultimate effects." Among the newer trends is the "conviction that body and mind must both be cared for, and the whole being unfolded." Rote learning is now largely discredited; arithmetic is being taught experimentally; teaching by principles which can be applied generally has taken the place of teaching by rules. Most important, Spencer feels, is the systematic culture of observation; "what was once thought mere purposeless action, or play, . . . is now recognized as the process of acquiring a knowledge . . ." Science is now taught by allowing children to perform experiments; real objects and materials are used. Of great significance to Spencer is "the growing desire to make the acquirement of knowledge pleasurable rather than painful. . . . Hence the efforts to make early education amusing, and all education interesting. Hence the lectures on the value of play. Hence the defence of nursery rhymes, and fairy tales. . . . And so with later education. Short breaks during school-hours, excursions into the country, amusing lectures, choral songs. . . ." Spencer advances certain principles of education: that it should proceed from the simple to the complex and from the concrete to the abstract; that the individual's education should evolve gradually as has that of his race; that it should proceed from the empirical to the rational and that self-development should be encouraged to the fullest possible extent.

. . . A leading fact in human progress is, that every science is evolved out of its corresponding art. It results from the necessity we are under, both individually and as a race, of reaching the abstract by way of the concrete, that there must be practice and an accruing experience with its empirical generalizations, before there can be science. **Science is organized knowledge;** and before knowledge can be organized, some of it must be possessed. Every study, therefore, should have a purely experimental introduction; and only after an ample fund of observations has been accumulated, should reasoning begin . . .

942

A scientific faith's absurd

Source: EASTER-DAY (Stanza vi)
Author: Robert Browning (1812–1889)
First published: 1850
Type of work: Dramatic monologue

Context: The concept of evolution was one of the burning issues on the Victorian mind. From those like Thomas Huxley to those like William Wilberforce, the factions took solid positions from which neither scientific evidence nor mystic revelation would shake them. And it was a time when compromise was a virtual impossibility—the world resulted either from God or from accident. Browning frequently touches upon this theme in his poetry. In "Caliban Upon Setebos," for instance, he depicts the kind of man who can and must accept the naturalist's position. Also, in "Easter-Day" he sets forth a spokesman who is being assailed for his position in faith. The speaker, who embodies Browning's philosophy that the efficacy of life is gained through the effort one expends in the inevitable struggles and conflicts, concludes that it is blessed to be "crossed and thwarted as a man,/ Not left in God's contempt apart,/ With ghastly smooth life, dead at heart,/ Tame in earth's paddock as her prize." He thanks God that he finds it "hard to be a Christian," for the activity of struggle is the essence of life itself. In the opening sections of the poem, the speaker confronts the conventional issue concerning the scientific proof of Christ and his teachings:

> So, the old process, I conclude,
> Goes on, the reasoning's pursued
> Further, You own, " 'Tis well averred,"
> **A scientific faith's absurd,**
> —Frustrates the very end 'twas meant
> To serve. So, I would rest content
> With a mere probability,
> But, probable; the chance must lie,
> Clear on one side,—lie all in rough,
> So long as there be just enough
> To pin my faith to, though it hap
> Only at points: from gap to gap
> One hangs up a huge curtain so,
> Grandly, nor seeks to have it go
> Foldless and flat along the wall.

The Scripture moveth us in sundry places

Source: THE BOOK OF COMMON PRAYER (Page 5)
Author: Traditional; translated and arranged by Archbishop Cranmer (1489–1560)
First published: 1549
Type of work: Exhortation

Context: The Order for Daily Morning Prayer, the first service in The Book of Common Prayer, derives directly from the system of daily services sung during the Middle Ages and known then as the Canonical Hours. The Order, as it is now set forth, begins with a series of opening sentences setting the theme and the mood of the service to follow. Since all of the sentences dwell on repentence or forgiveness and suggest the "sundry places" in which "the Scripture moveth us" to confession and reconciliation, they lead quite naturally into the Exhortation which comes after them. The Exhortation reminds the worshiper that no converse with God can be profitable, much less fitting, until he has laid bare his sin and asked God's forgiveness for his transgressions. It then outlines the elements that go to make up any complete act of corporate worship: 1. Penitence, 2. Praise and Thanksgiving, 3. Instruction in God's Holy Word, and 4. Prayer, for what is desired and what is needful, both for the body and for the soul.

Dearly beloved brethren, **the Scripture moveth us, in sundry places,** to acknowledge and confess our manifold sins and wickedness; and that we should not dissemble nor cloak them before the face of Almighty God our heavenly Father; but confess them with an humble, lowly, penitent, and obedient heart; to the end that we may obtain forgiveness of the same, by his infinite goodness and mercy. And although we ought, at all times, humbly to acknowledge our sins before God; yet ought we chiefly so to do, when we assemble and meet together to render thanks for the great benefits that we have received at his hands, to set forth his most worthy praise, to hear his most holy Word, and to ask those things which are requisite and necessary, as well for the body as the soul. . . .

See the conquering hero comes

Source: JUDAS MACCABAEUS (Part III, number 58)
Author: Thomas Morell (1703–1784)
First published: 1746
Type of work: Sacred oratorio

Context: Just as an overture by Gioacchino Rossini (1792–1869) had a tryout with two previous operas before ending up permanently attached to the *Barber of Seville* (1816), so a poem by an English classical scholar was used in two oratories and a play. Rossini's two earlier operas are forgotten today but *Joshua, Judas Maccabaeus,* and even *The Rival Queen* are still performed. George Frederick Handel (1689–1739) was a German composer of operas who went to England in 1712. He found the atmosphere so congenial to his music that in 1726 he became a British citizen. He directed the Royal Academy of Music and the King's Theatre in Covent Garden, and still had time to turn out forty operas, twenty-three oratorios, and a great quantity of church and chamber music. He is best remembered today for his *Messiah* (1742). One of Handel's neighbors, in Middlesex, was a classical scholar, Thomas Morell, friend of the poet Thomson, the actor Garrick, and the artist Hogarth. He was a product of King's College, Cambridge, from which he received a B.A. (1726), an M.A. (1730), and a D.D. (1743). Trained in Greek, he translated two volumes of Euripides' plays and other classical works. He also published several volumes of verse, chiefly sacred, but including *Congratulary Verses on the Marriage of the Prince of Orange with the Princess Ann* (1737). Morell's skill as an organist led to an acquaintance with Handel, who suggested he provide a libretto for an oratorio about Judas Maccabaeus, in 1746. This was the first of eight oratorios in which they collaborated. *Joshua* came two years later. The same poem appears in both oratorios. Later it also was inserted into a tragedy, *The Rival Queens* by Nathaniel Lee. It became so well known as part of that much-produced drama that its composition has more than once been attributed to Lee. In Part I of *Judas Maccabaeus,* Judas and his brother Simon lament the death of their father Mattathias, who had died leading the Jewish people against the cruel Syrian King Antiochus Epiphanes. The people determine to continue to seek liberty, counting on the help of God and choosing Judas to guide them. In Part II, after a partial victory, the Jews turn to the restoration of the Sanctuary in Jerusalem, desecrated by heathen idolatry. In the final part, having dedicated Jerusalem, they welcome Judas, returning victorious. It is in this third part that the poem occurs, sung by the Israelite youths and maidens.

CHORUS OF YOUTHS:
See the conquering hero comes,
Sound the trumpet, beat the drums;
Sports prepare, the laurel bring,
Songs of triumph to him sing.

CHORUS OF VIRGINS:
See the godlike youth advance,
Breathe the flutes and lead the dance;
Myrtle wreaths and roses twine,
To deck the hero's brows divine.

945

See through a glass darkly

Source: I CORINTHIANS 13:12
Author: Paul
First transcribed: c. 54–57
Type of work: Religious epistle

Context: Paul visited Corinth during his second missionary journey and was there for eighteen months. He began by going to the synagogue, as was customary with him, and spent some time preaching and discussing Scripture. The Jews rejected him, however; he abandoned this approach, and directed his efforts toward the conversion of Gentiles. The house of a man named Justus became his headquarters. His preaching won him numerous converts, and when he left Corinth the church was well established. After he had settled in Ephesus, Paul received the disturbing news that there was a crisis in the church he had founded at Corinth. The latter city was an important trading center and had a cosmopolitan population, with a corresponding variety of religions. Many of these encouraged various forms of excess, and Corinth was famed for the vice that flourished in it. Some of Paul's converts were men of standing, but most were from the lower classes and still adhered to pagan moral standards. An exchange of letters confirmed Paul's worst fears: the Corinthian congregation was torn by factions, indulging itself with fornication and incest, and defying his authority. It was at this time that he wrote I Corinthians, a stinging rebuke which censures the Corinthians for their moral lapses. Paul begins with an appeal for unity and an end of factions; those doing the preaching, he implies, are inflated with the false wisdom that is often born of ignorance. Such men are fools; even great human wisdom is nothing beside that of God. The minister's calling is a holy one and not a position of self-importance. After reproving the Corinthians for their unsavory sexual behavior and other misconduct, Paul discusses the nature of spiritual love. He urges his readers to strive for spiritual maturity and gives them some memorable comments on the nature of charity and the imperfection of any wisdom acquired in this life.

Charity suffereth long, and is kind; charity envieth not; charity vaunteth not itself, is not puffed up,

Doth not behave itself unseemly, seeketh not her own, is not easily provoked, thinketh no evil;

Rejoiceth not in iniquity, but rejoiceth in the truth;

Beareth all things, believeth all things, hopeth all things, endureth all things.

Charity never faileth: but whether there be prophecies, they shall fail; whether there be tongues, they shall cease; whether there be knowledge, it shall vanish away.

For we know in part, and we prophesy in part.

But when that which is perfect is come, then that which is in

946

part shall be done away.

When I was a child, I spake as a child, I understood as a child, I thought as a child: but when I became a man, I put away childish things.

For now we **see through a glass, darkly;** but then face to face: now I know in part; but then shall I know even as also I am known.

And now abideth faith, hope, charity, these three; but the greatest of these is charity.

Seeking the bubble reputation even in the cannon's mouth

Source: AS YOU LIKE IT (Act II, sc. vii, ll. 152–153)
Author: William Shakespeare (1564–1616)
First published: 1623
Type of work: Dramatic comedy

Context: Duke Senior, a deposed ruler, has already spent a number of pleasant years in the paradisal Forest of Arden. To the forest now come other sanctuary-seekers, among them Orlando, a young gentleman who, together with his faithful old servant, Adam, left home when he discovered that his evil brother, Oliver, intended to murder him. In need of food, Orlando rudely interrupts Duke Senior's dinner but, to his shame, finds himself and Adam courteously invited to partake. While Orlando leaves to find Adam, Duke Senior points out to the "melancholy Jaques" that others have reason to be melancholy too: "Thou seest, we are not all alone unhappy./ This wide and universal theatre/ Presents more woeful pageants than the scene/ Wherein we play in." Not to be outdone, Jaques responds with his famous speech: "All the world's a stage,/ And all the men and women merely players./ They have their exits and their entrances,/ And one man in his time plays many parts,/ His acts being seven ages." Both ideas—the world as a stage and the seven ages of man—are Classical and Renaissance commonplaces. The seven ages include those of the infant, the schoolboy, the lover, the soldier, the justice, the old man, and finally, man in his second childhood. Jaques has something cynical to say about each. The soldier he describes as:

JAQUES
Full of strange oaths, and bearded like the pard,
Jealous in honor, sudden and quick in quarrel,
Seeking the bubble reputation
Even in the cannon's mouth.
. . .

947

Self is hateful

Source: PENSÉES (Section VII, number 455)
Author: Blaise Pascal (1623–1662)
First published: 1670
Type of work: Philosophic commentary

Context: French philosopher and mathematician, Pascal was born in Clermont Ferrand, Auvergne. Until 1656 he led the life of a young man of ample means. At that date he experienced a religious conversion, withdrawing from society to a simple and austere existence. He accepted in 1656 the invitation to write a defense of Antoine Arnauld, a Jansenist accused of heresy by the Sorbonne, and the first of his *Lettres Provinciales* appeared. The letter was widely read, and his fame continued to grow through seventeen additional letters. *Pensées,* found among the author's effects after his death, probably represents Pascal's notes for a projected defense of Christianity. These reflections, as T. S. Eliot has observed, constitute his spiritual autobiography.

"Above all, he was a man of strong passions; and his intellectual passion for truth was reinforced by his passionate disaffection with human life unless a spiritual explanation could be found." Concerning religious belief, all men, according to Pascal, are either dogmatists or skeptics, believing either by faith or rejecting by logic. "What a chimera then is man' What a novelty! What a monster, what a chaos, what a contradiction, what a prodigy! Judge of all things, imbecile worm of the earth; depositary of truth, a sink of uncertainty and error; the pride and refuse of the universe!" Man, in short, is his own worst enemy; his reason would aspire on the one hand to godliness and on the other to a certainty never possible in spiritual matters:

Self is hateful. You, Milton, conceal it; you do not for that reason destroy it; you are, then, always hateful. . . . In a word, the Self has two qualities; it is unjust in itself since it makes itself the centre of everything; it is inconvenient to others since it would enslave them; for each Self is the enemy, and would like to be the tyrant of all others. You take away its inconvenience, but not its injustice, and so you do not render it lovable to those who hate injustice; you render it lovable only to the unjust, who do not any longer find in it an enemy. And thus you remain unjust, and can please only the unjust.

Sentence first—verdict afterward

Source: ALICE'S ADVENTURES IN WONDERLAND (Chapter 12)
Author: Lewis Carroll (Charles Lutwidge Dodgson, 1832–1898)
First published: 1865
Type of work: Imaginative tale for children

Context: The Reverend Charles Dodgson, a lecturer on mathematics at Oxford University, cared little for most people. Only with children did he unbend. On one occasion, during a boating trip with three of them, he started telling a nonsense story whose chief character was called Alice, after one of the picnickers, the daughter of Dean Liddell. Supplied with 42 illustrations by Sir John Tenniel (1820–1914), it became a favorite children's book, and some of its characters, like the March Hare, White Rabbit, and Red Queen, have passed into folklore and popular speech. More serious adults can read *Alice's Adventures in Wonderland* as a satirical commentary on life. This is true of Chapters 11 and 12, narrating the trial of the Knave of Hearts for stealing tarts baked by the Queen. Man's tendency to want to punish even before making sure of guilt is satirized by the quotation under consideration. The stupid birds and animals in the jury box are called upon by the Royal Judge to consider their verdict as soon as the White Rabbit reads the accusation. But he is persuaded to wait until the witnesses are called: the Mad Hatter, still clutching a cup of tea and a sandwich, the Duchess' cook, and finally small Alice, who has been regaining her original size as the trial progresses. After the introduction of a particularly incomprehensible poem supposedly written by the prisoner, the chapter continues:

. . . "Let the jury consider their verdict," the King said, for about the twentieth time that day.

"No, no!" said the Queen. **"Sentence first—verdict afterward."**

"Stuff and nonsense!" said Alice loudly. "The idea of having the sentence first!"

"Hold your tongue!" said the Queen, turning purple.

"I won't!" said Alice.

"Off with her head!" the Queen shouted at the top of her voice. Nobody moved.

"Who cares for *you?*" said Alice. (She had grown to her full size by this time.) "You're nothing but a pack of cards!"

Sermons and soda-water

Source: DON JUAN (Canto II, stanza 178)
Author: George Gordon, Lord Byron (1788–1824)
First published: 1819 (Cantos I and II)
Type of work: Satiric poem

Context: Lord Byron's precocious hero, Don Juan, has already, at sixteen, succeeded in causing a divorce and one of the most notorious scandals in all Spain. For his waywardness he has been banished from his homeland and packed off to sea accompanied by his mother's expectations that the salt air will wean him from the ways—especially amorous —of the world and restore his lost innocence. Alas! for this moral lady's

949

hopes, a great storm comes up and dashes to destruction the ship and its company, all except for Juan, whom it deposits half-drowned on an island shore. Along the beach, with her maid, comes the beautiful Haidée, "The greatest heiress of the Eastern Isles." The two ladies find the battered castaway unconscious on the sand, place him in a cave, and nurse him back to health. Inevitably the handsome youth and his lovely rescuer fall in love. The poet describes the "wild and breaker-beaten coast" along which the lovers walk, and then pauses to digress a bit. (*Sermons and Soda-water* has been used as the title for a volume of short stories by the contemporary John O'Hara.)

> It was a wild and breaker-beaten coast,
>   With cliffs above, and a broad sandy shore
> Guarded by shoals and rocks as by an host,
>   With here and there a creek, whose aspect wore
> A better welcome to the tempest-tost;
>   And rarely ceased the haughty billow's roar,
> Save on the dead long summer days, which make
> The outstretch'd ocean glitter like a lake.
>
> And the small ripple spilt upon the beach
>   Scarcely o'erpassed the cream of your champagne,
> When o'er the brim the sparkling bumpers reach,
>   That spring-dew of the spirit! the heart's rain!
> Few things surpass old wine; and they may preach
>   Who please,—the more because they preach in vain,—
> Let us have wine and women, mirth and laughter,
> **Sermons and soda-water** the day after.

Sermons in stones

Source: AS YOU LIKE IT (Act II, sc. i, l. 17)
Author: William Shakespeare (1564–1616)
First published: 1623
Type of work: Dramatic comedy

Context: A Duke, known only as Duke Senior, his throne usurped by his brother, Duke Frederick, lives in exile in the Forest of Arden with a company of followers to whom he expounds his ideas of the superiority of a simple rustic life to that of the court:

DUKE SENIOR
> Now my co-mates and brothers in exile,
> Hath not old custom made this life more sweet
> Than that of painted pomp? Are not these woods
> More free from peril than the envious court?
> Here feel we not the penalty of Adam,

950

The seasons' difference, as the icy fang
And churlish chiding of the winter's wind,
Which when it bites and blows upon my body
Even till I shrink with cold, I smile, and say
This is no flattery; these are counsellors
That feelingly persuade me what I am.
Sweet are the uses of adversity,
Which, like the toad ugly and venomous,
Wears yet a precious jewel in his head.
And this our life, exempt from public haunt,
Finds tongues in trees, books in the running brooks,
Sermons in stones, and good in every thing.

Serve it right for being so dear

Source: NICHOLAS NICKLEBY (Chapter 5)
Author: Charles Dickens (1812–1870)
First published: 1838–1839
Type of work: Novel

Context: Nicholas Nickleby, the young son of a man who has but recently died penniless and faced with the necessity of earning his living, is prevailed upon by his cold-hearted but wealthy uncle, Ralph Nickleby, to accept a position as a teacher at a school at Dotheboys, Yorkshire. His employer is the one-eyed sadist, Wackford Squeers, whose school is in reality an institution to which people commit unwanted boys, who either die of mistreatment or in desperation run away. In any event, they are taught little or nothing. Nicholas, who is a fine young fellow, innocently accepts the position and immediately makes preparations to leave his mother and sister and go to Yorkshire. When he arrives at the Saracen's Head Inn, from which place the coach is to depart, he finds Squeers having a luxurious breakfast in the sight of five of his new boys, for whom he orders two pennysworth of milk. This proves to be an extremely small amount, but he knows a remedy for this situation:

"This is twopenn'orth of milk, is it, waiter?" said Mr. Squeers, looking down into a large blue mug, and slanting it gently, so as to get an accurate view of the quantity of liquid contained in it.

"That's twopenn'orth, sir," replied the waiter.

"What a rare article milk is, to be sure, in London!" said Mr. Squeers with a sigh. "Just fill that mug up with lukewarm water, William, will you?"

"To the wery top, sir?" inquired the waiter. "Why, the milk will be drownded."

"Never you mind that," replied Mr. Squeers. **"Serve it right for being so dear.** You ordered that bread and butter for three, did you?"

951

"Coming directly, sir."

"You needn't hurry yourself," said Squeers, "there's plenty of time. Conquer your passions, boys, and don't be eager after vittles." As he uttered this moral precept, Mr. Squeers took a large bite out of the cold beef, and recognized Nicholas.

"Sit down, Mr. Nickleby," said Squeers. "Here we are, a breakfasting you see!"

Nicholas did *not* see that anybody was breakfasting, except Mr. Squeers; but he bowed with all becoming reverence, and looked as cheerful as he could.

Set your faces like a flint

Source: THE PILGRIM'S PROGRESS (Part I)
Author: John Bunyan (1628–1688)
First published: 1678
Type of work: Religious Allegory

Context: In this great religious allegory Bunyan pictures the struggles of the pious soul to achieve redemption as a journey taken by the protagonist, Christian, along a way beset with many deluding snares and temptations. Not all of Christian's encounters, however, are with those who would lead him away from the true road; he also meets those who assist him with good advice. After he has successfully passed through the Valley of the Shadow of Death, Christian is joined by Faithful. As they proceed together, they meet Evangelist, to whom they recount their difficulties in arriving thus far. Evangelist congratulates them upon their victories over temptation up to this moment, but also advises them that there are many more to come:

. . . The crown is before you, and it is an incorruptible one; so run that you may obtain it. Some there be that set out for this crown, and after they have gone far for it, another comes in and takes it from them: hold fast therefore that you have; let no man take your crown. You are not yet out of the gun-shot of the devil; you have not resisted unto blood, striving against sin; let the kingdom be always before you, and believe steadfastly concerning things that are invisible. Let nothing that is on this side the other world get within you; and above all, look well to your own hearts and to the lusts thereof, for they are deceitful above all things and desperately wicked; **set your faces like a flint;** you have all the power in heaven and earth on your side.

The sex whose presence civilizes ours

Source: CONVERSATION (Line 254)
Author: William Cowper (1731–1800)
First published: 1782
Type of work: Verse essay

Context: In his didactic essay on the gift of conversation—for the poet Cowper denies that it is an art—he lists and describes many talkers: those who underscore each assertion by an oath; those who love to contradict; and those who believe a shout convinces better than logic. Others who fall under the poet's displeasure are Mr. Dubius, who avoids definite assertions, and his opposite, who asserts everything, regardless of its obvious nonsense. Cowper points out the sometimes fatal consequences of angry arguments. One object of his scorn is the storyteller whose pipe puffing interrupts his tale. Not only does it interrupt the telling, but the stench of the smoke offends the ladies who listen.

> The dozing sages drop the drowsy strain,
> Then pause, and puff—and speak, and pause again.
> Such often, like the tube they so admire,
> Important triflers! have more smoke than fire.
> Pernicious weed! whose scent the fair annoys,
> Unfriendly to society's chief joys,
> Thy worst effect is banishing for hours
> **The sex whose presence civilizes ours.** . . .

The shadow cloaked from head to foot

Source: IN MEMORIAM (Part XXIII, stanza 1)
Author: Alfred, Lord Tennyson (1809–1892)
First published: 1850
Type of work: Elegy

Context: This elegy was written as a monument to Arthur Henry Hallam, a young man of extraordinary promise and an intimate friend of Tennyson, who died suddenly in Vienna at the age of twenty-two. The poem records the slow, wavering spiritual progress of Tennyson from his initial depth of personal sorrow to the gradual healing of grief through a sense of spiritual contact with Hallam in a wider love of God and humanity. The opening sections of the poem express Tennyson's deep sense of personal loss. Sections XXII–XXV are a retreat to the past, comparing the happy five years Tennyson and Hallam spent together with the sad isolation of the present. Hallam's death occurred in the autumn of their friendship's fifth year. Death is depicted as "the Shadow fear'd of man" who spreads his dark, cold mantle over his victim and bears him away to

953

a place where no living man may follow. In the poem's only allusion to his own death wish, Tennyson states that as he walks hastily, he thinks:

> . . . that somewhere in the waste
> The Shadow sits and waits for me.
>
> Now, sometimes in my sorrow shut
>   Or breaking into song by fits,
>   Alone, alone, to where he sits,
> **The Shadow cloak'd from head to foot,**
>
> Who keeps the keys of all the creeds,
>   I wander, often falling lame,
>   And looking back to whence I came,
> Or on to where the pathway leads; . . .

Shake well before using

Source: BROAD GRINS
Author: George Colman the Younger (1762–1836)
First published: 1797
Type of work: Humorous verse

Context: George Colman, Senior, was manager of the Haymarket Theatre when his son was born. Colman the Younger, brought up in the theatrical world, escaped a career in law by writing plays. *Turk or No Turk* (1785) was followed by musical comedies. Then came a volume of humorous poetry, and his *My Nightgown and Slippers* (1797) was quickly sold out. A second edition, enlarged, appeared in 1802. One of its tales in verse concerns "The Newcastle Apothecary" Benjamin Bolus, who both brought children into the world as a midwife and ushered them out with his pills. Esteeming himself a literary man, the druggist wrote poetic directions for his medicine. The six stanzas of the poem tell how, taken too literally, the prescription accompanying one bottle caused the death of the invalid because, as the druggist is finally told, the servants administered one dose, then shook their master. When that treatment did not cure him, they repeated the dosage, then "A third we tried."/ "Well, and what then?" "Then, sir, my master died." The modern version of the phrase is, of course, "Shake well before using." At the beginning of the poem, Colman sets the stage.

> He had a patient lying at death's door,
> Some three miles from the town—it might be four;
> To whom, one evening, Bolus sent an article,
> In Pharmacy, that's call'd cathartical.
>   And on the label of the stuff,

He wrote this verse,
Which, one would think, was clear enough,
And terse:—
**"When taken,
To be well shaken."**

Shall I not take mine ease in mine inn?

Source: KING HENRY THE FOURTH: PART ONE (Act III, sc. iii, ll. 89–90)
Author: William Shakespeare (1564–1616)
First published: 1598
Type of work: Historical drama

Context: Falstaff, boon companion in fun to Prince Hal, faced the threat of arrest when the sheriff suddenly appeared at the Boar's Head Tavern in Eastcheap while Hal and the "huge bombard of sack" were comically exchanging roles of father and son in anticipation of Hal's confrontation with his father the next morning. The sheriff was pursuing a report that an old fat man had been involved in the Gads Hill robbery of the king's retainers. Just as so frequently before, Hal had protected his crony by bidding him to hide behind the arras while he told the sheriff that Falstaff was engaged on a royal errand. The "tun of man" was so assured of the safety of the royal protection that he fell asleep and snored loudly. After the sheriff departed, the disgusted Hal picked his pockets, finding only bill upon bill for sack and bread. Now, in a later scene, Falstaff uses this action for his own purposes. With the hostess berating him for nonpayment of his tavern bills, he haughtily claims that he has been robbed and slanders her for operating an establishment in which a guest is not safe from a pickpocket. He also slanders Prince Hal, who—unknown to him—has walked on stage behind him. Thus the scene is set for another moment of comic exposure in which Falstaff will be forced to use his wits to free himself from an awkward situation:

HOSTESS
. . . You owe money here besides, Sir John, for your diet, and by-drinkings, and money lent you, four and twenty pound.

FALSTAFF
He [Bardolph] had his part of it, let him pay.

HOSTESS
He? Alas he is poor, he hath nothing.

FALSTAFF
How? Poor? Look upon his face. What call you rich? Let them coin his nose, let them coin his cheeks, I'll not pay a denier. What,

955

will you make a younker of me? **Shall I not take mine ease in mine inn,** but I shall have my pocket picked? I have lost a seal-ring of my grandfather's worth forty mark.

. . .

. . . The Prince is a Jack, a sneak-up. 'Sblood an he were here, I would cudgel him like a dog if he would say so. . . .

Shall we gather at the river?

Source: SHALL WE GATHER AT THE RIVER? (Line 1)
Author: Robert Lowry (1826–1899)
First published: 1865
Type of work: Hymn

Context: Robert Lowry's most famous hymn is "Shall We Gather at the River?" It was written in July, 1864, when an epidemic was raging in Brooklyn, New York, where Lowry was pastor of a Baptist church. Brooding on the passage of so many souls across the river of death, Lowry is said to have questioned inwardly whether those who die shall meet again at the heavenly river of life. Sitting at his parlor organ, the pastor composed both the words and music for his hymn, which was published the following year. The first stanza and the chorus read:

Shall we gather at the river,
    Where bright angel-feet have trod,
With its crystal tide forever
    Flowing by the throne of God?

Yes, we'll gather at the river,
    The beautiful, the beautiful river;
Gather with the saints at the river
    That flows by the throne of God.

She could not think, but would not cease to speak

Source: TALES: THE STRUGGLES OF CONSCIENCE (No. 14, l. 343)
Author: George Crabbe (1754–1832)
First published: 1812
Type of work: Narrative poem

Context: A serious-minded dealer in toys became a convert to one of the small, strict, dissenting religious sects. His nephew Fulham, to humor his uncle, also joined the church, but the preacher made such an impression on him that he decided always to live in the light of his conscience. At this point, his uncle died and left him the toy store and a sum of money. At first Fulham heeded what his conscience told him, but soon he embarked on dubious courses. He and his conscience had stiff battles, but usually he overrode her. When he observed how profitable the state lottery was, he tied in sales of his toys with counterfeit lottery tickets. When conscience reproached him, he said that the odds against his selling a winning ticket were a hundred thousand to one, and if a winner turned up, he could run away. He overcharged excessively for his goods, much to the distress of his conscience. He changed his religion and got himself elected a trustee of large sums of money held for the benefit of the poor, although he did not immediately make any profit from this activity. One of his fellow trustees was the guardian of a rich young girl who was not mentally much above an idiot. Fulham insinuated himself into the guardian's good graces and married the girl over the strenuous objections of his conscience. He explained that he intended to treat the wife very well, but conscience insisted that the marriage was purely a deal for the sake of the money involved. The wife, however, by no means silently retreated into the background; she asserted herself at every opportunity, and he found himself utterly unable to control her:

> The Wife was pretty, trifling, childish, weak;
> **She could not think, but would not cease to speak:**
> This he forbad—she took the caution ill,
> And boldly rose against his sovereign will;
> With idiot-cunning she would watch the hour,
> When friends were present, to dispute his power:
> With tyrant-craft, he then was still and calm,
> But raised in private terror and alarm:
> By many trials, she perceived how far
> To vex and tease, without an open war;
> And he discover'd that so weak a mind
> No art could lead, and no compulsion bind; . . .

She is the thing that she despises

Source: AMORET (Last line)
Author: William Congreve (1670–1729)
First published: 1698
Type of work: Song

Context: Congreve, called the greatest of Restoration writers of comedy, was probably born in England and educated in Ireland, though Samuel Johnson, one of the first to publish his poetry, gave his birthplace as Ireland and the date, according to the inscription on his monument, 1672. However, Johnson added that to doubt his claim of birth in Leeds in 1670 is to be "very deficient in candor." The Revolution drove him from Ireland to study law in London. There he wrote a number of comedies that established his reputation as the greatest comic dramatist since the theater was opened in 1660 after being closed by the Puritans in 1642. To these Restoration writers, wit and elegance were essential. Judged by the customs of the time, the comedies were not especially immoral, but a literary quarrel with the Reverend Jeremy Collier about immorality and profanity on the English stage caused Congreve's best play, *The Way of the World* (1700), to be badly received. In anger, Congreve severed his connections with the theater and enjoyed witty conversations with his friends until his death. The literary life no longer appealed to him. He did write some light verse, but though acquainted with Steele and Addison, he contributed only once to the *Tatler* and never to the *Spectator*. Apparently he preferred being a gentleman of fashion to being a literary light.

However, when he said as much to Voltaire, who came to visit him, the Frenchman replied in disgust: "If you had been only a gentleman, I would not have come to see you." The same Restoration fashion of gaiety attacked the women, too. As the truly fine gentleman was a rake, but an elegant and charming rake, so the truly fine lady was often the mistress of a rake, but in an elegant, aloof, and secret way. It was to some such unknown "fine lady" that Congreve wrote "Amoret," one of his best lyrics. It was first published in a single-sheet on March 19, 1698, with music by John Eccles. It seems symbolic of the life of idleness the poet was living at the time. But its sixteen lines analyze for all time the mind of a coquette, its tricks, deceptions, contradictions, and the final tragic perception of its own emptiness.

Fair Amoret is gone astray;
  Pursue and seek her, every lover;
I'll tell the signs by which you may
  The wandering shepherdess discover.

Coquet and coy at once her air,
  Both study'd, though both seem neglected;
Careless is she with artless care,
  Affecting to seem unaffected.

With skill her eyes dart every glance,
  Yet change so soon you'd ne'er suspect them;
For she'd persuade they wound by chance,
  Though certain aim and art direct them.

She likes herself, yet others hates
  For that which in herself she prizes;
And while she laughs at them, forgets
  She is the thing that she despises.

She just wore enough for modesty—no more

Source: WHITE ROSE AND RED (Part I, poem 5, l. 60)
Author: Robert Williams Buchanan (1841–1901)
First published: 1870
Type of work: Narrative poem

Context: In this long, monotonous poem written in several different metrical patterns like Tennyson's *Maud* and dedicated to Walt Whitman, who would hardly have appreciated it, Buchanan joins sentimentality and bathos to relate an impossible love story. Carrying the concept of the Noble Savage to an extreme, the love story opens with the capture of Eureka Hart by the Indians, who prove to be so kind and gentle that the poet confuses the American frontier with the Garden of Eden. Although he frequently interrupts the flow of his meager story to tell the reader that he knows better, Buchanan cannot conceal his aversion to genteel manners and, like many primitivists, is bitter in his unreasonable criticism of modern life. Still, the poem is significant, for, as nineteenth century England became more and more torn by controversy, men turned to their imaginations for the freedom of idyllic youth. This poem represents the excess to which such longing could lead. For example, the clothing of the Indian princess was

> Nimbus enough of drapery
> And ornament, just to suggest
> The costume that became her best—
> Her own brave beauty. **She just wore**
> **Enough for modesty—no more.**
> She was not, as white beauties seem,
> Smother'd, like strawberries in cream,
> With folds of silk and linen! No!

She lays it on with a trowel

Source: THE DOUBLE-DEALER (Act III, sc. iii)
Author: William Congreve (1670–1729)
First published: 1694
Type of work: Dramatic comedy

Context: In Lord Touchwood's house, a group of fashionable people —Cynthia, Lord Froth, Lady Froth, and Brisk—discuss a set of verses that Lady Froth is writing on her coachman. Although the verses are empty of meaning, everyone applauds them. The people turn from this activity to the criticism of some of their acquaintances, Lady Whifler and Mr. Sneer. The latter, nephew of Lady Toothless, is held to be a nauseating creature, and his aunt has horrible manners: she grins toothlessly, like an oyster at low tide. And then there is the fat female fool whose name no one at the moment remembers, who paints her face to excess: she lays color on with a trowel. Lady Froth suggests that Brisk write a song on her, but he has already done so. The gist of it is that the lady makes her own faces, and every day has a new one.

LADY FROTH

Then that t'other great strapping lady—I can't hit of her name —the old fat fool that paints so exorbitantly.

BRISK

I know whom you mean—but, deuce take me! I can't hit of her name neither.—Paints, d'ye say? why she lays it on with a trowel. —Then she has a great beard that bristles through it, and makes her look as if she were plastered with lime and hair, let me perish!

LADY FROTH

Oh, you made a song upon her, Mr. Brisk.

BRISK

He! egad, so I did:—my lord can sing it.

She looked a lecture

Source: DON JUAN (Canto I, stanza 15)
Author: George Gordon, Lord Byron (1788–1824)
First published: 1819 (Cantos I and II)
Type of work: Satiric poem

Context: Byron, preparing to write a satiric epic, looks about for an appropriate hero for his poem. Failing to find "in the present age" a fitting protagonist, he looks to the heroes of the past and chooses from among them "our ancient friend Don Juan." Most epic poets, says Byron, start their poems in the middle of things from which point the reader is brought up to date by a series of recollections delivered by the hero to a circle of friends after dinner or to his mistress in a tavern or a bower. But with *Don Juan,* "My way is to begin with the beginning; . . . / Narrating somewhat of Don Juan's father,/ And also of his mother, if you'd rather." If the father, Don Jóse, was a true aristocrat of Spain, his wife, Donna Inez, was all of this and much more. She was, indeed, a lady learned in the sciences and in mathematics, with virtues equalled only by her wit, before whom even the cleverest people quailed, and the best of them were put into the shade. In short, she was perfection beyond parallel. Of this formidable lady, a satiric portrait of Lady Byron, who had left her husband three years before the publication of the first canto of *Don Juan,* the poet writes that while

960

Some women use their tongues—she **look'd a lecture,**
   Each eye a sermon, and her brow a homily,
An all-in-all sufficient self-director,
   Like the lamented late Sir Samuel Romilly,
The Law's expounder, and the State's corrector,
   Whose suicide was almost an anomaly—
One sad example more, that "All is vanity,"—
(The jury brought their verdict in "Insanity.")

In short, she was a walking calculation,
   Miss Edgeworth's novels stepping from their covers,
Or Mrs. Trimmer's books on education,
   Or "Coelebs' Wife" set out in quest of lovers,
Morality's grim personification,
   In which not Envy's self a flaw discovers;
To others' share let "female errors fall,"
For she had not even one—the worst of all.

She speaks poniards

Source: MUCH ADO ABOUT NOTHING (Act II, sc. i, l. 254)
Author: William Shakespeare (1564–1616)
First published: 1600
Type of work: Dramatic comedy

Context: Beatrice, the merry and quick-tongued niece of Leonato, Governor of Messina, stoutly claims that marriage is not for her. However, she especially directs her gay and often chiding repartee at a particular young gentleman, Benedick. At a masked ball Beatrice, who covertly recognizes Benedick, rails at him, saying he is just a jester for the prince, Don Pedro, first laughed at for his slanderous jokes and then beaten for them. After the ball, Benedick tells the prince of his humiliation at the tongue of the quick-witted Beatrice:

BENEDICK

O she misused me past the endurance of a block. An oak but with one green leaf on it would have answered her; my very visor began to assume life, and scold with her. She told me, not thinking I had been myself, that I was the Prince's jester, that I was duller than a great thaw; huddling jest upon jest, with such impossible conveyance upon me, that I stood like a man at a mark, with a whole army shooting at me. **She speaks poniards,** and every word stabs. If her breath were as terrible as her terminations, there were no living near her, she would infect to the north star. I would not marry her, though she were endowed with all that Adam had left him before he transgressed.

Ships that pass in the night

Source: TALES OF A WAYSIDE INN ("The Theologian's Tale: Elizabeth," Part IV)
Author: Henry Wadsworth Longfellow (1807–1882)
First published: 1873 (Part III)
Type of work: Narrative poem

Context: Tales of a Wayside Inn is a collection of stories, in verse, related by a group of travelers staying at the Red Lion Inn in Sudbury, Massachusetts. The storytellers include the Landlord, the Musician, the Spanish Jew, the Poet, the Sicilian, the Theologian, and the Student. These characters were all close friends of Longfellow, so thinly disguised that they were easily recognizable from his descriptions of them. The Musician, for example, is Ole Bull, famous violinist, who plays his Stradivarius for the assembled company. The stories these people tell are Longfellow's creations; some were published previously; most composed for this work. Part I occurs on a stormy evening in autumn; the storytelling continues to a late hour. In Part II the following day dawns rainy and miserable; so the stories are resumed until late afternoon, when the storm clears. The third and last part of the volume takes place that evening. Stories are told by the Spanish Jew, the Poet, and the Student. The fire is replenished; the clock strikes eight; and the Theologian embarks on his tale of Elizabeth Haddon, a Quaker farm girl. She is chatting with her housemaid, Hannah, remarking that she likes the snow but wonders how they will get to Meeting on First-Day. Joseph, the servant boy, is late returning from town. It would be lonely here, adds Elizabeth, if friends did not stop in often. Hannah chides her for her generosity—these people will eat them out of house and home. Elizabeth replies that she obeys the Lord. She then mentions John Estaugh, a man she saw long ago in London; she has a premonition she will see him again. Joseph now arrives, bringing a stranger who proves to be John Estaugh. After a brief visit during which he and Elizabeth remember each other, he leaves, to return the following May. When he does, Elizabeth tells him that she loves him. He thanks her but replies that the Lord has not yet given him a sign. Confident that he will return to her, she replies that she is content to wait.

> Ships that pass in the night, and speak each other in
>   passing,
> Only a signal shown and a distant voice in the darkness;
> So on the ocean of life, we pass and speak one another,
> Only a look and a voice, then darkness again and a si-
>   lence.

> Now went on as of old the quiet life of the homestead.
> Patient and unrepining Elizabeth labored, in all things
> Mindful not of herself, but bearing the burdens of

962

others,
Always thoughtful and kind and untroubled . . .

Meanwhile, John Estaugh departed across the sea,
and departing
Carried hid in his heart a secret sacred and precious . . .
O lost days of delight, that are wasted in doubting and
waiting!
O lost hours and days in which we might have been
happy!
But the light shone at last, and guided his wavering
footsteps,
And at last came the voice, imperative, questionless,
certain.

Then John Estaugh came back o'er the sea for the
gift that was offered,
Better than houses and lands, the gift of a woman's
affection.
And on the First-Day that followed, he rose in the
Silent Assembly,
Holding in his strong hand a hand that trembled a
little,
Promising to be kind and true and faithful in all things.
Such were the marriage rites of John and Elizabeth
Estaugh.

The short and simple annals of the poor

Source: ELEGY WRITTEN IN A COUNTRY CHURCHYARD (Line 32)
Author: Thomas Gray (1716–1771)
First published: 1751
Type of work: Didactic elegy

Context: Gray's poem teaches that death comes to all men, the poor as well as the rich, the unknown as well as the famous. The poem begins by noting the twilight environment of a country churchyard, especially the sounds of evening. Then the attention of the poet and, of course, the reader turns to the graves of the simple people, the preceding generations of the peasants of the countryside, who are buried there. The poet notes how the unknown dead worked and lived, spending their days in toil and their evenings in simple pleasure. But, he adds, we should not pass them by, mocking their simple lives or disdaining their records, those "short and simple annals." The poet says that famous persons, whose lives are recorded in history at greater length, come alike and inevitably to death; that "The paths of glory lead but to the grave." Later in the poem Gray says that, if but given the chance, these almost unknown dead might have been heroes of their times:

963

Let not Ambition mock their useful toil,
  Their homely joys, and destiny obscure;
Nor Grandeur hear, with a disdainful smile,
  The short and simple annals of the poor.

The boast of heraldry, the pomp of pow'r,
  And all that beauty, all that wealth e'er gave,
Awaits alike th' inevitable hour.
  The paths of glory lead but to the grave.

Nor you, ye proud, impute to these the fault,
  If Mem'ry o'er their tomb no trophies raise,
Where through the long-drawn aisle and fretted vault
  The pealing anthem swells the note of praise.

Show it a fair pair of heels

Source: KING HENRY THE FOURTH: PART ONE (Act II, sc. iv, l. 52)
Author: William Shakespeare (1564–1616)
First published: 1598
Type of work: Historical drama

Context: Prince Hal and Poins, having conceived an elaborate scheme for exposing Falstaff's true colors as a braggadocio, await his return at the Boar's Head Tavern in Eastcheap. They have foiled his plan to rob the king's retainers at Gads Hill by counter-robbing the four in his party. Now, convinced that "the huge bombard of sack," Falstaff, will manufacture some excuse that will be worth a "month's laughter," they bide their time in comic badinage with Francis, a drawer at the tavern. In effect, Shakespeare is providing yet another glimpse of Hal's good-natured wit which is to serve him so well later as "the mirror of Christian kings." Also, of course, the action provides a credible delay for Falstaff and his cronies to hack their swords and tickle their noses with spear-grass so that, bloody and beaten, they will give the appearance of having engaged in a furious battle. In the fun at Francis' expense, Poins and Hal place themselves at opposite ends of the tavern and, by alternately calling for the drawer's attention, succeed in utterly confusing and frustrating him. At one point Hal comically tests Francis' fidelity as an apprentice to his master:

PRINCE HENRY
Come hither Francis.

FRANCIS
My lord?

PRINCE HENRY
How long hast thou to serve, Francis?

964

Forsooth, five years, and as much as to—

POINS [*within.*]
Francis!

FRANCIS
Anon, anon, sir.

PRINCE HENRY
Five year, by'r lady a long lease for the clinking of pewter. But Francis, darest thou be so valiant as to play the coward with thy indenture, and **show it a fair pair of heels,** and run from it?

FRANCIS
O lord sir, I'll be sworn upon all the books in England, I could find it in my heart—

Shuffled off this mortal coil

Source: HAMLET (Act III, sc. i, l. 67)
Author: William Shakespeare (1564–1616)
First published: 1603
Type of work: Dramatic tragedy

Context: Hamlet, Prince of Denmark, urged by the Ghost of his murdered father to take revenge against the murderer, his uncle and father's brother, considers his course of action. A meditative rather than an active man, he weighs the delight of suicide against the consequences of the act after the earthly body has been uncoiled from about the immortal part of man. The word "coil" also meant "bustle" or "turmoil" in Shakespeare's day.

HAMLET
To be, or not to be, that is the question—
Whether 'tis nobler in the mind to suffer
The slings and arrows of outrageous fortune,
Or to take arms against a sea of troubles,
And by opposing end them. To die, to sleep—
No more; and by a sleep to say we end
The heart-ache, and the thousand natural shocks
That flesh is heir to; 'tis a consummation
Devoutly to be wished. To die, to sleep—
To sleep, perchance to dream, ay there's the rub,
For in that sleep of death what dreams may come
When we have **shuffled off this mortal coil,**
Must give us pause; there's the respect
That makes calamity of so long life. . . .

Sighing through all her Works gave signs of woe, that all was lost

Source: PARADISE LOST (Book IX, ll. 783–784)
Author: John Milton (1608–1674)
First published: 1667
Type of work: Epic poem

Context: Evicted from Heaven for revolting against God, Satan and the other fallen angels meet in council in Hell to determine a course of revenge. Satan decides to go to the newly created Earth; there, assuming the form of a serpent, he gains audience with Eve. Eve, astonished that a serpent can speak, is told that he has gained this ability by eating the fruit of the Tree of Knowledge. Though forbidden by God on penalty of death to eat the fruit, and forewarned by the angel Raphael that Satan will attempt to cause her fall, Eve, seeing that the serpent has not been harmed by eating the forbidden fruit, decides to eat of the Tree of Knowledge:

> So saying, her rash hand in evil hour
> Forth reaching to the Fruit, she pluck'd, she eat:
> Earth felt the wound, and Nature from her seat
> **Sighing through all her Works gave signs of woe,**
> **That all was lost.** Back to the Thicket slunk
> The guiltie Serpent, and well might, for Eve
> Intent now wholly on her taste, naught else
> Regarded, such delight till then, as seemd,
> In fruit she never tasted, whether true
> Or fansied so, through expectation high
> Of knowledg, nor was God-head from her thought.

A sight to dream of, not to tell

Source: CHRISTABEL (Part I, l. 253)
Author: Samuel Taylor Coleridge (1772–1834)
First published: 1816
Type of work: Narrative poem

Context: On a chilly, but dark, midnight in April, Christabel, beloved daughter of the baron, Sir Leoline, retires to the woods outside the castle to pray for her absent lover. She kneels at the base of a huge oak, from the other side of which comes a moan. She discovers a beautiful damsel in a white silken robe, with bare feet, lying on the ground. She is Geraldine, and later she says that she is the daughter of Sir Roland de Vaux of Tryermaine, a former friend of the baron, although the friendship has been broken up by a quarrel. Geraldine tells of being abducted by five men on white horses who will soon return to her. Christabel conducts her into the castle; the old mastiff growls in her sleep as they pass, a sound Christabel had never heard her make. In her own chamber Christabel mentions her mother and says that she wishes she were present, a sentiment echoed by Geraldine. In a moment Geraldine, apparently addressing the empty air, commands the wandering mother to be off and says that this hour is hers. Christabel disrobes for bed, as does Geraldine. As Geraldine's clothing drops from her, Christabel sees her breast and half her side, a sight to cause nightmares but impossible to put into words:

> Beneath the lamp the lady bowed,
> And slowly rolled her eyes around;
> Then drawing in her breath aloud,
> Like one that shuddered, she unbound
> The cincture from beneath her breast:
> Her silken robe, and inner vest,
> Dropt to her feet, and full in view,
> Behold! her bosom and half her side—
> **A sight to dream of, not to tell!**
> O shield her! shield sweet Christabel!

Silence is deep as Eternity; speech is shallow as Time

Source: CRITICAL AND MISCELLANEOUS ESSAYS (Vol. IV, "Sir Walter Scott")
Author: Thomas Carlyle (1795–1881)
First published: 1838
Type of work: Book review

Context: One of the means Carlyle had to earn a living was as a book reviewer for a number of periodicals. Using a recently published book as a peg, he would hang onto it a biography of the subject, incorporating many of his own theories and ideas. In 1837 appeared a six-volume *Memoirs of the Life of Sir Walter Scott, Baronet* by John G. Lockhart. On the theory of "Set a Scot to appreciate a Scott," Carlyle was asked to review it. His long essay appeared in the *London and Westminster Review,* in 1838, and was collected in book form the following year. Commenting on the instinctive tendency of people to want to look upon any man who has become distinguished, Carlyle is not willing to state that Scott was a great man, but at least he was noteworthy. Despite that fact, should someone, even Scott's son-in-law, devote six volumes, with a spill-over into a seventh not yet published, about a man who had already delineated himself in two hundred volumes of his own, and has "lived for thirty years amid the universal speech of friends?" Surely by now "he must have left some likeness of himself." In passing, Carlyle comments that the biographer has told too much. He has "been too communicative, indiscreet, and has recorded much that ought to have been suppressed." Still, the reviewer declares that it is an interesting work that can be purchased, or borrowed from a lending library, "with more than the usual assurance that even at the cost of so many volumes, he has ware for his money." In the case of the subject of the biography, Carlyle comments that he, too, wrote too much. "Our dear Fenimore Cooper" might likewise "have given us one Natty Leatherstocking." Then the reviewer reverts to an idea expressed several times before in his writing: that silence is golden. In his *Journal,* he declared: "Speech is human, silence is divine." In *Sartor Resartus,* Book III, chapter 3, he says: "Speech is Time, Silence is Eternity," and on his essay on Scott, he rephrases the idea:

> There is a great discovery still to be made in literature, that of paying literary men by the quantity they *do not* write. Nay, in sober truth, is not this actually the rule in all writing; and moreover in all conduct and acting? Not what stands aboveground, but what lies unseen *under* it, at the root and subterrene element it sprang from and emblemed forth, determines the value. Under all speech that is good for anything there lies a silence that is better. **Silence is deep as Eternity; speech is shallow as Time.**

Silence is the virtue of a fool

Source: THE ADVANCEMENT OF LEARNING (Book VI, chapter 3, Antitheses, 31, as translated by Francis Headlam)
Author: Sir Francis Bacon (1561–1626)
First published: 1605
Type of work: Philosophy

Context: Sir Francis Bacon, remembered today as a philosopher, spent most of his life in politics. His list of titles is impressive: Baron of Verulam, Viscount St. Albans, and Lord High Chancellor of England. A member of Parliament for many years, he was trained in the legal profession and was a magistrate, though not one immune to temptation. He took care to associate himself with royal favorites; one was the ill-starred Essex, whose final conviction he assisted, and another was George Villiers, Duke of Buckingham. Bacon received a number of royal favors before Buckingham's popularity failed; afterward he was charged with accepting bribes from persons who had appeared in his court. He admitted the truth of these charges and was fined, imprisoned briefly, and pardoned. Forbidden to enter politics again, he was allowed to retire and spent his remaining years engaged in the voluminous writings which have insured his lasting fame. Most of these were devoted to the promotion of his intellectual ideals and were intended to form parts of a vast work entitled *The Great Instauration.* His purpose was to reorganize all systems of knowledge on a sound and comparatively scientific basis, using inductive reasoning and an experimental approach. The introductory essay, *De Dignitate et Augmentis Scientiarium* (*Of the Dignity and Advancement of*

968

Learning, a title usually shortened), is a full-length work in itself. In it Bacon surveys and summarizes the knowledge of his time and sets forth his ideals of scientific observation, critical examination and objectivity. He exerted an enormous influence on later thought. In Book VI of *The Ad-* *vancement of Learning,* Bacon takes up rhetoric, discourse, and argument. Following a discussion of sophistry, he presents a list of antitheses—aphoristic and epigrammatic arguments for and against particular things. An example follows:

XXXI. LOQUACITY

FOR

He that is silent betrays want of confidence either in others or in himself.

All kinds of constraint are unhappy, that of silence the most miserable of all.

Silence is the virtue of a fool. And therefore it was well said to a man that would not speak, "If you are wise you are a fool; if you are a fool, you are wise."

Silence, like night, is convenient for treacheries.

Thoughts are wholesomest when they are like running waters.

Silence is a kind of solitude.

He that is silent lays himself out for opinion.

Silence neither casts off bad thoughts nor distributes good.

AGAINST

Silence gives to words both grace and authority.

Silence is the sleep which nourishes wisdom.

Silence is the fermentation of thought.

Silence is the style of wisdom.

Silence aspires after truth.

Silence more musical than any song

Source: REST (Line 10)
Author: Christina Georgina Rossetti (1830–1894)
First published: 1849
Type of work: Sonnet

Context: The poetess, sister of Dante Gabriel and William Rossetti, was a deeply religious person. Her failure to marry either of the two young men who loved her deeply—and whom she loved—was due to religious sentiments. In an age marked by skepticism, Miss Rossetti was a person of faith in the Anglican Church and the Deity. Her poetry reflects her faith in her religion. In many of her poems she discusses death, not as a fearful end to a life which men should not wish to leave, but rather as God's

969

peace granted to mankind after the troubles of the earthly life. Such a poem is this sonnet, which shows death as a rest after the labor of living. The stillness of the grave, the music of silence, is "almost Paradise." And from death to the Resurrection, says this Christian poet, is not long:

O earth, lie heavily upon her eyes;
   Seal her sweet eyes weary of watching Earth;
   Lie close around her; leave no room for mirth
With its harsh laughter, nor for sound of sighs.
She hath no questions, she hath no replies,
   Hushed in and curtained with a blessed dearth
   Of all that irked her from the hour of birth;
With stillness that is almost Paradise.
Darkness more clear than noonday holdeth her,
   Silence more musical than any song;
Even her very heart has ceased to stir;
   Until the morning of Eternity
Her rest shall not begin nor end, but be;
   And when she wakes she will not think it long.

The silent cities of the dead

Source: ON THE STAR OF "THE LEGION OF HONOUR" (Line 38)
Author: George Gordon, Lord Byron (1788–1824)
First published: 1815
Type of work: Patriotic poem

Context: The printed copy of this poem contains as explanatory title "From the French." There is no indication whether or not it is a translation, but certainly the rhymed couplets seem like the original work of Byron, with their combination of admiration and irony, and the fervent praise of the search for Freedom. The Legion of Honour was created by Napoleon Bonaparte in 1802, with the Consul of France as the Grand Master of the order. Below him came holders of the Grand Cross, Grand Officers, Commanders, a limited number of officers, and an unlimited number of knights decorated for bravery and service to France. Its purpose was to encourage and reward bravery in battle and sacrifices for the country. For that reason, Byron refers to the decoration as "adored deceit." Many of Napoleon's soldiers died trying to win the decoration. Now they are in the cemeteries, the silent cities of the dead. Napoleon designed the decoration, a cross hanging from a red ribbon of watered silk, and a rosette. However, instead of the usual cross with four arms, it has five, resembling somewhat the Christmas star whose five points are supposed to symbolize the five wounds of Christ on the cross. But there is a difference. Each of the bars is notched, making a total of ten points. This most unusual

970

form does not seem to appear elsewhere, though the heraldry books illustrate nearly 500 variants of crosses and stars. In describing the badge as a symbol of France, Byron thinks of the tricolors, which he refers to as a rainbow of the free. He was always full of admiration for France and Napoleon. Unfortunately for the dream of the world, in 1815, following the Battle of Waterloo, Napoleon abdicated and went into exile. And those who had died for his glory had wasted their lives. The poet longs for liberty or death. The poem begins:

Star of the brave! whose beam hath shed
Such glories o 'er the quick and dead—
Thou radiant and adored deceit!
Which millions rush'd in arms to greet!
Wild meteor of immortal birth!
Why rise in Heaven to set on Earth?

. . .

Star of the brave! thy ray is pale,
And darkness must again prevail!
But, oh thou Rainbow of the free!
Our tears and blood must flow for thee.
When thy bright promise fades away,
Our life is but a load of clay.

And Freedom hallows with her tread
The silent cities of the dead;
For beautiful in death are they
Who proudly fall in her array;
And soon, Oh Goddess! may we be
For evermore with them or thee!

A simple child, what should it know of death?

Source: WE ARE SEVEN (Stanza 1)
Author: William Wordsworth (1770–1850)
First published: 1798
Type of work: Lyric poem

Context: The poet meets a curly-haired eight-year-old girl and asks how many children are in her family. "Seven are we," she answers; "And two of us at Conway dwell,/ And two are gone to sea./ Two of us in the church-yard lie,/ My sister and my brother,/ And, in the church-yard cottage, I/ Dwell near them with my mother." Trying to correct the child, the poet remarks, "If two are in the church-yard laid,/ Then ye are only five." But the maid explains, "Their graves are green, they may be seen." She knits or sews by the graves, she sings to her sister and brother, and sometimes eats her supper there. Jane died first and John was soon laid by her side. The poet repeats his question: "How many are you then

971

. . . / If they two are in heaven?"
When she answers, "O master! we are
seven," he insists, "But they are dead;
those two are dead!/ Their spirits are
in heaven!" The child's mind, though,
cannot conceive of death as the poet's
does, and her final reply is "Nay, we
are seven." The unreality of death to
a healthy young child is suggested by
the poem's opening stanza, which was
written, Wordsworth said, not by
himself but by his friend and collaborator, Samuel Taylor Coleridge:

—**A simple Child,**
That lightly draws its breath,
And feels its life in every limb,
What should it know of death?

Simplify, simplify

Source: WALDEN (Chapter 2, "Where I Lived, and What I Lived for)
Author: Henry David Thoreau (1817–1862)
First published: 1854
Type of work: Literary journal

Context: Thoreau went to live in a
small hut he built for himself on the
shores of Walden Pond; there he
stayed during 1845–1847, reflecting
upon life and its meaning for man,
and living while he was thinking
about life. He says of the experience:
"I wanted to live deep and suck out
all the marrow of life, to live so stur-
dily and Spartan-like as to put to rout
all that was not life, to cut a broad
swath and shave close, to drive life
into a corner, and reduce it to its lowest terms, and, if it proved to be
mean, why then to get the whole and
genuine meanness of it, and publish
its meanness to the world; or if it
were sublime, to know it by experience, and be able to give a true account of it in my next excursion."
Before he went to live at Walden
Pond, Thoreau tells the reader, he
barely escaped buying a farm and
thus becoming saddled with too much
of the world and its goods. He felt
that men "live meanly, like ants,"
frittering away their lives upon details. His answer, in his life and in his
writings, is to avoid the pettiness of
life brought on by making life complicated, by accumulating the burdens
of possession that most men strive
for. Simplicity is the text for his homily:

. . . Our life is frittered away by detail. An honest man has
hardly need to count more than his ten fingers, or in extreme cases
he may add his ten toes, and lump the rest. Simplicity, simplicity,
simplicity! I say, let your affairs be as two or three, and not a
hundred or a thousand; instead of a million, count half a dozen,
and keep your accounts on your thumb nail. In the midst of this
chopping sea of civilized life, such are the clouds and storms and
quicksands and thousand-and-one items to be allowed for, that a

972

man has to live, if he would not founder and go to the bottom and not make his port at all, by dead reckoning, and he must be a great calculator indeed who succeeds. **Simplify, simplify.** Instead of three meals a day, if it be necessary eat but one; instead of a hundred dishes, five; and reduce other things in proportion. . . .

Sit attentive to his own applause

Source: EPISTLE TO DR. ARBUTHNOT (Line 210)
Author: Alexander Pope (1688–1744)
First published: 1735
Type of work: Satire

Context: Pope's poem, written in the form of a dialogue between himself and Dr. John Arbuthnot, his friend and a fellow literary man, became a vehicle for satirizing many persons, among them Charles Gildon, Lewis Theobald, Ambrose Philips, and Edmund Curll. Some of the persons perhaps deserved the acid comments made about them; but in other cases no reason is known, at least, for the poet's attacks. For example, Pope thought he had real reason for attacking Joseph Addison. He believed that Addison had been the rival translator of an English version of Homer's *Iliad*. He also believed that Addison had paid Charles Gildon ten pounds to abuse him in a biography of William Wycherley that Gildon wrote. About 1720 Pope wrote a satirical portrait of Addison, using the name Atticus for him; this portrait, first published in 1722, three years after Addison's death, was later incorporated into the *Epistle to Dr. Arbuthnot*. The quotation about sitting attentive to his own applause appears in the portrait, given in part below:

> Willing to wound, and yet afraid to strike,
> Just hint a fault, and hesitate dislike;
> Alike reserv'd to blame, or to commend,
> A tim'rous foe, and a suspicious friend;
> Dreading ev'n fools, by flatterers besieg'd,
> And so obliging, that he ne'er oblig'd;
> Like Cato, give his little senate laws,
> And **sit attentive to his own applause;**
> While wits and Templars ev'ry sentence raise,
> And wonder with a foolish face of praise—
> Who but must laugh, if such a man there be?
> Who would not weep, if Atticus were he?

Sits the wind in that corner?

Source: MUCH ADO ABOUT NOTHING (Act II, sc. iii, l. 103)
Author: William Shakespeare (1564–1616)
First published: 1600
Type of work: Dramatic comedy

Context: Don Pedro, Leonato, and Claudio have undertaken the Herculean task of provoking a romantic affair between the comic anti-lovers Benedick and Beatrice. To that end, they scheme to allow each to overhear a conversation in which the other's love is described. In both cases the refusal to admit romantic interest openly is said to be a result of the fear of mockery and disdain by the other. In what would appear to the spectator as one continuous scene, first Benedick, then Beatrice, is —by careful arrangement on the part of the intriguers—an eavesdropper on the conversation. And in both cases the bait takes; the ultimate marriage of these mockers of love is one of the major resolutions of the action. As Benedick prepares for his moment of comic exposure, he delivers a lengthy soliloquy denouncing as foolish and stupid any man who falls in love; ". . . till all graces be in one woman, one woman shall not come in my grace." When he is led to believe that Beatrice is romantically inclined, however, his mockery turns to sympathetic interest and eventually to love:

DON PEDRO
. . . Come hither Leonato. What was it you told me of to-day, that your niece Beatrice was in love with Signior Benedick?

CLAUDIO
[*Aside to* DON PEDRO] O ay, stalk on, stalk on; the fowl sits.— I did never think that lady would have loved any man.

LEONATO
No nor I neither, but most wonderful, that she should so dote on Signior Benedick, whom she hath in all outward behaviours seemed ever to abhor.

BENEDICK [*aside.*]
Is't possible? **Sits the wind in that corner?**

LEONATO
By my troth my lord, I cannot tell what to think of it, but that she loves him with an enraged affection—it is past the infinite of thought.

. . .

974

BENEDICK [*comes forward.*]

This can be no trick. The conference was sadly borne. They have the truth of this from Hero. They seem to pity the lady. It seems her affections have their full bent. Love me? Why it must be requited. . . .

Six of one and half-a-dozen of the other

Source: THE PIRATE (Chapter 4)
Author: Frederick Marryat (1792–1848)
First published: 1836
Type of work: Adventure novel

Context: Captain Marryat of the British navy served afloat for twenty-three years, beginning in 1806 as a midshipman aboard the frigate *Impérieuse* under Lord Cochrane, and ending as a Commander. Then he fell from favor through his articles against the impressment of sailors, and he retired to write exciting sea stories about young men corrupted by the navy where advance came only through cruelty and where the most responsible had the least ability. As editor of the *Metropolitan Magazine* from 1832 to 1835, he wrote some of his best novels, with delightful humor and genuine pathos. That he is not entirely out of date a century later is proved by a twenty-six-volume set of his works that appeared in 1930. *The Pirate* is one of four novels that he published in 1836. In the publication of his complete works it appears in Volume X, with *Olla Podrida*. The story begins in the Bay of Biscay in 179-, where the schooner *Circassian,* with cotton out of New Orleans for Liverpool, has been driven by a storm, following the crash of its mast. Aboard are a Negress, her companion, and "Massa Edward," one of the twin grandsons of an English trader. The baby's mother and other twin were rescued, but waves prevented the return of the boat for the rest. Now a pirate ship is bearing down on the wreck. Then comes a flashback; not until much later is the thread resumed. The baby has been saved and brought up as Francisco, a pirate. Years later, when he is captured and is about to be hanged, his identity is discovered, and he and his twin brother are reunited. In Chapter IV, part of the flashback, details of the trip from America are described. Oswald, the chief mate, overhears the sailors discussing their hope of a long layover and shore leave at Liverpool. One of them, Bill, says he will make use of the time to get married. The expression "six of one and half-a-dozen of the other" indicating a supposed difference where none really exists, is now very common.

"Why, how often do you mean to get spliced, Bill? You've a wife in every State, to my sartain knowledge."
"I arn't got one at Liverpool, Jack."

"Well, you may take one there, Bill; for you've been sweet upon that nigger girl for these last three weeks."

"Any port in a storm, but she won't do for harbour duty. But the fact is, you're all wrong there, Jack: it's the babies I likes— I likes to see them both together, hanging at the nigger's breasts. I always think of two spider-monkeys nursing two kittens."

"I knows the women, but I never knows the children. It's just **six of one and half-a-dozen of the other;** an't it, Bill?"

"Yes, like two bright bullets out of the same mould. I say, Bill, did any of your wives ever have twins?"

"No; nor I don't intend, until the owners give us double pay."

Slavery is a weed that grows in every soil

Source: SPEECH ON MOVING HIS RESOLUTIONS FOR RECONCILIATION WITH THE COLONIES
Author: Edmund Burke (1729–1797)
First published: 1775
Type of work: Political speech

Context: Burke was the firm and articulate friend of the American Colonies during the years before the Revolution. As a member of the English Parliament he strongly opposed the harsh measures of taxation and military suppression which were being considered as a response to unrest in the Colonies. The colonists were Englishmen and love liberty as Englishmen do, he argued; if they were granted liberty, they would remain loyal subjects; but if they were denied freedom, they would demand independence:

. . . Let the colonies always keep the idea of their civil rights associated with your government;—they will cling and grapple to you; and no force under heaven will be of power to tear them from their allegiance. But let it be once understood, that your government may be one thing, and their privileges another; that these two things may exist without any mutual relation; the cement is gone; the cohesion is loosened; and everything hastens to decay and dissolution. As long as you have the wisdom to keep the soverign authority of this country as the sanctuary of liberty, the sacred temple consecrated to our common faith, wherever the chosen race and sons of England worship freedom, they will turn their faces towards you. The more they multiply, the more friends you will have; the more ardently they love liberty, the more perfect will be their obedience. **Slavery** they can have anywhere. It **is a weed that grows in every soil.** They may have it from Spain, they may have it from Prussia. But, until you become lost to all feeling of your true interest and your natural dignity, freedom they can have from none but you. . . .

976

Sleep in spite of thunder

Source: MACBETH (Act IV, sc. i, l. 86)
Author: William Shakespeare (1564–1616)
First published: 1623
Type of work: Dramatic tragedy

Context: The greatly troubled Macbeth is insecure as king. He revisits the old witches to ask for more prophesy, so that he might know what to expect. The witches perform their incantations. The first apparition, an armed Head, tells Macbeth to beware of Macduff, whom he had already suspected and feared. An apparition of a bloody child tells Macbeth not to fear, for no man of woman born can harm him. Somewhat pacified for the moment, Macbeth almost decides to let Macduff live. However, his usual fear and suspicion overcome him; he quickly changes his mind and plans for Macduff's death so that he may sleep in peace once again—as he had slept before he murdered Duncan.

> SECOND APPARITION
> Be bloody, bold, and resolute; laugh to scorn
> The power of man. For none of woman born
> Shall harm Macbeth.
>
> [*Descends.*]
>
> MACBETH
> Then live Macduff, what need I fear of thee?
> But yet I'll make assurance double sure,
> And take a bond of fate. Thou shalt not live;
> That I may tell pale-hearted fear it lies;
> And **sleep in spite of thunder.**

Sleep is sweet to the laboring man

Source: THE PILGRIM'S PROGRESS (Part I)
Author: John Bunyan (1628–1688)
First published: 1678
Type of work: Religious allegory

Context: As the protagonist, Christian, pursues his way through this allegory of spiritual salvation, he meets and overcomes many perilous temptations, some terrifying and others quite innocent in appearance but equally deadly to the soul. Christian also has numerous companions at various times along the way. Some of these are evil counsellors who would lead him from the straight and arduous road to salvation; others, like Faithful and Evangelist, give him true and valuable advice and help him to overcome temptations; still others are pious and well-intentioned but weak

977

persons who require assistance themselves. Such a feeble companion is Hopeful. The narrator describes one portion of this dream allegory as follows:

I saw then in my dream that they went till they came into a certain country whose air naturally tended to make one drowsy, if he came a stranger into it. And here Hopeful began to be very dull and heavy of sleep: wherefore he said unto Christian, I do now begin to grow so drowsy that I can scarcely hold up mine eyes; let us lie down here and take one nap. By no means, said the other; lest sleeping, we never awake more.

HOPE
Why, my brother? **Sleep is sweet to the labouring man;** we may be refreshed if we take a nap.

CHRISTIAN
Do you not remember that one of the Shepherds bid us beware of the Enchanted Ground? He meant by that, that we should beware of sleeping; wherefore "let us not sleep as do others, but let us watch and be sober."

HOPE
I acknowledge myself in a fault; and had I been here alone, I had by sleeping run the danger of death. . . .

Slow and steady wins the race

Source: THE HARE AND THE TORTOISE (Last line)
Author: Robert Lloyd (1733–1764)
First published: 1757
Type of work: Verse fable

Context: In this poem based on an ancient, familiar fable, Robert Lloyd asserts that genius alone is not enough for success; it must be joined to hard and continuous work. Lloyd himself had neither genius nor perseverance, but he says that application may prevail, even in the absence of genius. He then goes on to his fable, which deals with a hare that is extremely boastful about his speed in running: he could, in fact, outrun dog and horse, and even his own brethren. A tortoise nearby, becoming angered at the hare's boasting, challenges him to a footrace. The hare eagerly accepts the challenge, bets are laid, judges secured, the distance agreed upon, and off go the contestants. The hare covers almost the whole course before the lumbering tortoise is well started. The hare then scornfully announces that he will take a nap; after he wakes up he will easily win the race. While he sleeps, the tortoise plods along and finally crosses

978

the finish line. The tortoise then reads the defeated hare a lesson to the effect that not fits and starts, but per-severance, is what wins contests. The poem concludes thus:

> The tortoise heard his taunting jeer,
> But still resolved to persevere,
> Still drawed along, as who should say,
> "I'll win, like Fabius, by delay";
> On to the goal securely crept,
> While Puss unknowing soundly slept.
>   The bets were won, the hare awake,
> When thus the victor tortoise spake:
> "Puss, though I own thy quicker parts,
> Things are not always done by starts,
> You may deride my awkward pace,
> But **slow and steady wins the race.**"

Slow rises worth, by poverty depressed

Source: LONDON (Line 176)
Author: Samuel Johnson (1709–1784)
First published: 1738
Type of work: Didactic poem in imitation of the third satire of Juvenal

Context: This poem, first published anonymously in the *Gentleman's Magazine* for May, 1738, earned for its author the sum of ten guineas; Johnson once remarked that he had insisted upon that amount because of the price paid by the same editor, Edward Cave, to one of his rivals for a poem. The poem was written in imitation of Juvenal, using the latter's "Third Satire" as a model. It was so popular that a second publication of it appeared within a week. The first lines say that it is prompted by the departure of Thales, perhaps Johnson's friend, Richard Savage, for a pleasanter place to live than the city. Then follows a satirical portrait of the city, showing some of the faults of London and its people, faults the poet knew all too well from his own experiences there. He had come to London, as a young man, to make his way up from poverty and anonymity to some wealth and a great deal of fame, but the way up had not been easy, nor had it been easy for many of his meritorious friends. The verse paragraph in which the quotation appears shows both Johnson's thoughts and feelings born of his experience:

> Has Heav'n reserv'd, in pity to the poor,
> No pathless waste, or undiscover'd shore?
> No secret island in the boundless main?
> No peaceful desert yet unclaim'd by Spain?
> Quick let us rise, the happy seats explore,
> And bear Oppression's insolence no more.

This mournful truth is ev'rywhere confess'd,
Slow rises worth, by poverty depress'd:
But here more slow, where all are slaves to gold,
Where looks are merchandise, and smiles are sold;
Where won by bribes, by flatteries implor'd,
The groom retails the favours of his lord.

Smiling through tears

Source: THE ILIAD (Book VI, l. 484, as translated by Alexander Pope)
Author: Homer (c. 850 B.C.)
First transcribed: Sixth century B.C.
Type of work: Epic poem

Context: The seventeenth century Thomas Heywood followed the *Greek Anthology* in declaring: "Seven cities warred for Homer being dead." Many more than that number of translators have tried to keep him alive with their versions in English of his *Iliad* and *Odyssey*. Chapman provided a translation for Shakespeare's generation. Alexander Pope's 1715 translation was long the most admired, but several more modern ones provide easier reading today, such as the one by E. V. Rieu or one in 1898 by Samuel Butler, author of *The Way of All Flesh.* Whether the author was one man, blind, elderly, and wandering with his harp from one Greek city to another, or some one who later collected the various legends that sprang up after the Trojan War, will probably never be settled, though the majority of scholars today lean toward the single poet theory. *The Iliad* covers a brief period in the ten-year-long Siege of Troy, about 1200 B.C. Agamemnon covets Briseis, a captive of Achilles, son of Zeus, and being King of the Achaians, he gets the maiden. Achilles withdraws from the siege and sulks in his tent. Then Zeus, to avenge the injustice to his son, urges Agamemnon in a dream to risk defeat and attack the city. The Trojans come out to defend it. Paris, whose love for Helen had motivated the war, suggests a single combat between the Greek Menelaus, Helen's wronged husband, and himself to settle the matter. As Paris is being beaten, a goddess snatches him away, so Menelaus is declared victor. But Athena interferes and causes a Trojan archer to shoot an arrow at the victor. That treachery starts a general conflict. In Book VI, the Trojan warrior Hector, seeing the battle going against his side, retires to Ilium (Troy) to sacrifice to Athena. Foreseeing that he will die, he seeks his wife Andromache, to bid her farewell. She has gone to the walls with their small son, but hurries to meet Hector. In a sentimental scene, the sight of the warrior in shining armor with the horsehair plume nodding fiercely from his helmet frightens the baby, so Hector takes the helmet off and lays it gleaming on the ground. Then as Pope translated the scene:

980

He spoke, and fondly gazing on her charms,
Restored the pleasing burden to her arms;
Soft on her fragrant breast the babe she laid,
Hush'd to repose, and with a smile survey'd.
The troubled pleasure soon chastised by fear,
She mingled with a smile a tender tear.
The soften'd chief with kind compassion view'd,
And dried the falling drops, and thus pursued: . . .

Smoked like a chimney

Source: THE INGOLDSBY LEGENDS ("The Lay of St. Odille," l. 19)
Author: Richard Harris Barham (1788–1845)
First published: 1840
Type of work: Humorous narrative poem

Context: The Ingoldsby Legends is a collection of tales in verse and prose, purporting to be relics and records of the Ingoldsby family as compiled by Thomas Ingoldsby. However, they are in reality the light-hearted compositions of the Reverend Richard Barham. Much of the humor is derived through the use of informal and colloquial expressions. "The Lay of St. Odille" is the story of a beautiful girl, Odille; she is the daughter of Count Otto, Lord of Alsace. She has many suitors but will take no interest in any of them: she intends to take the veil at St. Ermengarde's convent instead. Finally one Count Herman appears on the scene and plies her father with good strong beer, whereupon the old man waxes mellow and wishes him luck in his efforts to win Odille. Odille, feeling her position untenable, runs away in the direction of the convent. "When he found she'd levanted, the Count of Alsace/ At first turn'd remarkably red in the face;/ He anathematized, with much unction and grace,/ Every soul who came near, and consign'd the whole race/ Of runaway girls to a very warm place. . . ." Of course everyone rushes off in pursuit, and Odille is presently trapped on top of a hill. She prays to St. Ermengarde, who claps her into a cave and then reveals herself to Count Otto and his companions. "All at the sight, From the knave to the knight,/ Felt a very unpleasant sensation, call'd fright;/ While the Saint, looking down, With a terrible frown,/ Said, 'My Lords, you are done most remarkably brown!—' " Otto's choice is clear: he must let Odille have her way and be a nun or else lose her forever. He sensibly says to himself, "I can't do as I would,—I must do as I can;" and surrenders handsomely: " 'They shall build a new convent,—I'll pay the whole bill/ (Taking discount),—its Abbess shall be my Odille.' " The poem concludes with the description of a hill near Friberg, split from top to bottom, from which Odille was presumably released. The moral, according to Barham, is that a woman is bound to get her own way—but that fortunately there are not enough saints to save them all. On the other hand, one can scarcely blame Odille for trying to get away:

981

Lords, Dukes, and Electors, and Counts Palatine
Came to seek her in marriage from both sides the Rhine;
   But vain their design, They are all left to pine,
Their oglings and smiles are all useless; in fine
Not one of these gentlefolks, try as they will,
Can draw, "Ask my papa" from the cruel Odille.

At length one of her suitors, a certain Count Herman,
A highly respectable man as a German,
Who **smoked like a chimney,** and drank like a Merman,
Paid his court to her father, . . .

A snake in the grass

Source: ECLOGUES (III, l. 93)
Author: Virgil (Publius Vergilius Maro, 70–19 B.C.)
First transcribed: c. 40–37 B.C.
Type of work: Pastoral poem

Context: The greatest poet of ancient Rome, Virgil, was born near Mantua and hence became known as the Mantuan Swan. A master of epic, didactic, and idyllic verse, he is most famous for the *Aeneid,* the *Eclogues* or *Bucolics,* and the *Georgics.* Tennyson called him a "lord of language" who achieved the ultimate in lyric beauty, melody, and significance. The *Bucolics,* ten in number, are pastoral poems in the spirit of the Idylls of the Sicilian poet Theocritus. The songs and dialogues of rustic swans are aptly named "bucolic" (pastoral); the term eclogue (selection) appears in the manuscripts for the individual poems, and the name is frequently used to designate the group as a whole. In the third Eclogue, Menalcas and Damoetas engage in a sparkling wit combat; each, convinced he can best the other in ingenuity of phrasing, has staked a precious possession, Damoetas a heifer, Menalcas a finely wrought cup. The contest flourishes apace for some time with neither participant revealing the slightest weakness in mental dexterity or physical stamina. Finally, Palaemon admits his inability to judge the better in such a fray. "Us it skills not to determine this strife between you: both thou and he are worthy of the heifer, and whosoever shrinks not from Love's sweetness shall not taste his bitterness. Shut off the rivulets now, my children: the meadows have drunk their fill":

DAMOETAS
—Let him who loves thee, Pollio, come where thou too takest delight: let honey flow for him, and the rough briar yield him spice.

982

MENALCAS

—Who hates not Bavius, let him love thy songs, O Maevius, and withal yoke foxes and milk he-goats.

DAMOETAS

—Gatherers of flowers and ground-strawberries, fly hence, O children, **a cold snake lurks in the grass.**

MENALCAS

—Stay, my sheep, from too far advance: ill is it to trust the bank: the lordly ram even now dries his fleece.

DAMOETAS

—Tityrus, put back the grazing kids from the river: myself, when the time comes, will wash them all in the spring.

A snapper-up of unconsidered trifles

Source: THE WINTER'S TALE (Act IV, sc. iii, l. 23)
Author: William Shakespeare (1564–1616)
First published: 1623
Type of work: Tragi-comedy

Context: When all appears gloomy— King Leontes, it seems, has caused the deaths of his wife, his son, and his daughter, and is estranged from his dearest friend, the King of Bohemia —suddenly Autolycus, a vender and ballad-monger, appears, singing a light-hearted ballad about daffodils and spring. Autolycus ends his song and delivers a short soliloquy about himself:

AUTOLYCUS
. . .

My traffic is sheets; when the kite builds, look to lesser linen. My father named me Autolycus, who being, as I am, littered under Mercury, was likewise **a snapper-up of unconsidered trifles.** With die and drab I purchased this caparison and my revenue is the silly cheat. Gallows and knock are too powerful on the highway. Beating and hanging are terrors to me. For the life to come, I sleep out the thought of it. . . .

So much of earth—so much of heaven

Source: RUTH (Stanza 21)
Author: William Wordsworth (1770–1850)
First published: 1800
Type of work: Narrative poem

Context: This poem, first appearing in the second edition of *Lyrical Ballads,* relates the tale of an English girl whose entire life was filled with misery and woe. Ruth, her mother dying shortly after the birth and her father remarrying, was neglected as a child and grew to maturity in melancholy isolation. Wooed by a handsome youth from Georgia who stirred her imagination with his tales of the strawberries, magnolias, cypress trees, and lakes in his native land, she took him as mate and "did agree/ With him to sail across the sea,/ And drive the flying deer." Before they could sail, however, her mate fell in with a disreputable group and gave himself to dissolute living. He promised reform, however, and again they laid plans to go to America. But again his base desires were master of his good intentions, and he deserted her at the shore. The distraught Ruth, who had vainly sought for happiness in life, was driven mad by the abandonment. Placed in an asylum, she escaped after three years and spent the remainder of her life roaming aimlessly throughout the countryside. Wordsworth directly relates her husband's lack of self-control to the nature of his experiences before he met Ruth:

> But, as you have before been told,
> This Stripling, sportive, gay, and bold, . . .
> Had roamed about, with vagrant bands
> Of Indians in the West.
> The wind, the tempest roaring high,
> The tumult of a tropic sky,
> Might well be dangerous food
> For him, a youth to whom was given
> **So much of earth—so much of heaven,**
> And such impetuous blood.
>
> His genius and his moral frame
> Were thus impaired, and he became
> The slave of low desires: . . .

So near and yet so far

Source: IN MEMORIAM (Part XCVII, stanza 6)
Author: Alfred, Lord Tennyson (1809–1892)
First published: 1850
Type of work: Elegy

Context: In Memoriam, which has been called the crucial poem of the nineteenth century, was written over a period of seventeen years. While a student at Trinity College, Cambridge, Tennyson had formed a deep friendship with another undergraduate, Arthur Henry Hallam, who was a leading member of the "Apostles," a group of young men who met frequently for discussions of current political, moral, and artistic questions.

Hallam made a remarkable impression upon his contemporaries, all of whom predicted for him a future of exceptional brilliance. Not only was Hallam the most intimate friend of Tennyson's undergraduate years; he became the betrothed of the poet's sister Emily. The great tragedy occurred in the autumn of 1833, when Hallam died suddenly in Vienna. His death plunged Tennyson into a profound gloom from which he did not recover for years. He considered Hallam "as near perfection as mortal man could be," an opinion in which all of the dead man's friends concurred. The long poem of *In Memoriam* was the result of Tennyson's brooding over the death of his friend and future brother-in-law. In it he considers not only the eternal questions of death and loss but also the problems raised by the new science of geology and by the pre-Darwinian theories of evolution, which had seriously weakened religious faith. Throughout the poem, Tennyson finds many metaphors by which to express his admiration for Hallam and his belief in his friend's intellectual superiority, both to himself and to their contemporaries at Cambridge. In Part XCVII he uses the comparison of a married couple who were happy and equal companions in their youth. But the husband has intellectually outstripped the wife, so that she can no longer understand his ideas. Yet though she cannot be his mental companion, she still loves him and knows that he loves her "whate'er the faithless people say." So Tennyson, in his humility, felt that his relationship with the superbly gifted Hallam had been. Part of the elaborate metaphor is as follows:

These two—they dwelt with eye on eye,
   Their hearts of old have beat in tune,
   Their meetings made December June,
Their every parting was to die.

Their love has never past away;
   The days she never can forget
   Are earnest that he loves her yet,
Whate'er the faithless people say.

Her life is lone, he sits apart;
   He loves her yet, she will not weep,
   Tho' rapt in matters dark and deep
He seems to slight her simple heart.

He thrids the labyrinth of the mind,
   He reads the secret of the star,
   He seems **so near and yet so far,**
He looks so cold: she thinks him kind.

She keeps the gift of years before,
   A wither'd violet is her bliss:
   She knows not what his greatness is,
For that, for all, she loves him more.

Soar not too high to fall; but stoop to rise

Source: THE DUKE OF MILAN (Act I, sc. ii, l. 46)
Author: Philip Massinger (1583–1640)
First published: 1623
Type of work: Dramatic tragedy

Context: In the opening scene of the play, Tiberio, a courtier, explains the present situation in the court of the city state of Milan to Stephano, another courtier. The duke, Ludovico Sforza, had always lived in the midst of danger, but his bravery and judgment had always brought the state safely through its hazards. Now, however, Charles V, the Holy Roman Emperor, and Francis I, King of France, are fighting for possession of Italy, and into the conflict they have drawn most of the city states on one side or the other. Sforza had cast his lot on the French side. If the Emperor wins, Sforza will be completely ruined. Tiberio adds that it is also the duchess's birthday and explains that the duchess, although the soul of honor, bears herself so proudly that she has offended Isabella, the duke's mother, and Mariana, his sister, both of whom resent the duchess's overbearing manner. In the second scene Mariana states to her mother that she will not attend the birthday celebration, and Isabella is of the opinion that she will not, either. Francisco, the duke's special favorite and Mariana's husband, urges them both to reconsider so as not to offend the duke, as he will be most ill disposed towards them if they slight his celebration. Isabella and Mariana both agree to do their duty, and Francisco tells them that they would be wise not to exalt themselves too high because doing so might bring about a fall; if they want to rise in the future, they would do well to bear themselves lowly at the present moment.

ISABELLA
     You are ever forward
To sing her praises.

MARIANA
     Others are as fair;
I am sure, as noble.

FRANCISCO
     I detract from none,
In giving her what's due. Were she deformed,
Yet being the duchess, I stand bound to serve her;
But, as she is, to admire her. Never wife
Met with a purer heat her husband's fervor;
A happy pair, one in the other blest!
She confident in herself he's wholly hers,
And cannot seek for change; and he secure,
That 'tis not in the power of man to tempt her. . . .

986

MARIANA
I shall do
What may become the sister of a prince;
But will not stoop beneath it.

FRANCISCO
Yet, be wise;
Soar not too high, to fall; but stoop to rise.

Soldier, rest! thy warfare o'er

Source: THE LADY OF THE LAKE (Canto I, stanza 31, l. 624)
Author: Sir Walter Scott (1771–1832)
First published: 1810
Type of work: Narrative poem

Context: Beside Loch Katrine a lost huntsman, from whom his prey, a stag, had escaped, blows his hunting horn to summon help, and succeeds in calling up a wondrously beautiful young woman, the Lady of the Lake. She had thought that her father had blown the horn, but she invites the stranger to come to her island home for entertainment for the night. She explains that all was prepared for him: his bed was made and ample game had been shot and fish netted for his food. When he explains that he is a total stranger to this part of the country, the lady, Ellen by name, replies that she is aware of that fact, for old Allan-bane had last night foretold his coming and perfectly described him. The two row to an island and follow a hidden road to a dwelling made from a wide variety of local materials. As they enter the house, a great sword falls to the floor from its place on a deer's antlers on the wall. The guest remarks that he has known only one man strong enough to wield it, but no explanation is given as to its ownership. The walls inside the building are covered with trophies of the battle and the hunt. The hostess of the house, the Lady Margaret, a relative, acts in place of a mother to Ellen. After dinner, to the sounds of an unseen harp, Ellen sings a song which begins with the statement that the soldier's fighting is over.

> **Soldier, rest! thy warfare o'er,**
>   Sleep the sleep that knows not breaking;
> Dream of battled fields no more,
>   Days of danger, nights of waking.
> In our isle's enchanted hall,
>   Hands unseen thy couch are strewing,
> Fairy strains of music fall,
>   Every sense in slumber dewing.
> Soldier, rest! thy warfare o'er,
> Dream of fighting fields no more;

987

Sleep the sleep that knows not breaking,
Morn of toil, nor night of waking.

Soldiers of the ploughshare as well as soldiers of the sword

Source: UNTO THIS LAST (Essay III, section 54)
Author: John Ruskin (1819–1900)
First published: 1860
Type of work: Essay on political economy

Context: John Ruskin always considered himself to be a kind of prophet. During the first part of his life he saw his primary task as bringing to the human race enlightenment and education in the perception of beauty and the religion of art. Regarding his society as faithless, perverse, and dislocated, he was convinced that he must deliver his message to the world at any cost. This intensity concerning art and architecture he carried to the arena of social philosophy in his later life. His concern had now expanded beyond the spiritual meaning of work to the conditions under which objects were produced or manufactured. He became convinced that the ultimate test of work and whatever it produced was its effect upon the human soul and the dignity of the individual. In the four essays which comprise *Unto This Last,* first published in the *Cornhill Magazine,* he attacks the orthodox principles of the existing political philosophy—not with a cry that it be abolished but with the demand for legislation to protect the interests of the worker from exploitation. Above all, he maintains the necessity of Captains of Industry, men of superior talent with a humanitarian perspective who will respect the freedom and creativity of all whom they direct. This principle he reiterates near the conclusion of the third essay:

. . . My continual aim has been to show the eternal superiority of some men to others, sometimes even of one man to all others; and to show also the advisability of appointing such persons or person to guide, to lead, or on occasion even to compel and subdue, their inferiors, according to their own better knowledge and wiser will. My principles of Political Economy were all involved in a single phrase spoken three years ago at Manchester: **"Soldiers of the ploughshare as well as soldiers of the sword:"** and they were all summed in a single sentence in the last volume of *Modern Painters*—"Government and co-operation are in all things the Laws of Life; anarchy and competition the Laws of Death."

988

The solitary monk who shook the world

Source: LUTHER, OR ROME AND THE REFORMATION (Canto 7, "The Solitary Monk," l. 1)
Author: Robert Montgomery (1807–1855)
First published: 1842
Type of work: Religious verse

Context: The illegitimate son of a comedian, Robert Gomery, born at Bath, England, tried to give himself status by prefixing to his name the aristocratic "Mont." Inspired by the spirit of Byron, at the age of twenty he wrote a long poem, "The Stage Coach," full of his feelings while making a trip through England by coach, and ending with moralizing conclusions. In the frontispiece portrait he is dressed like Byron. "The Stage Coach" was followed by a two-part poetic satire on contemporary mankind, "The Age Reviewed." Both were several times reprinted, and they won commendations by such contemporaries as Wordsworth and Southey. Montgomery's friends compared him to Milton, especially after the publication of his *Satan or Intellect Without God* that, because of its appeal to the evangelistic party, ran through more editions than anything since the time of Byron. Macaulay, provoked by such success, tried to destroy Montgomery's reputation in an unfair review in poor taste that appeared in the April, 1830, number of *Edinburgh Review.* It called him "a poetaster whose work has gone into a dozen volumes and needs to be taken down." Instead, the review helped sell eight more editions of *Satan* in twelve years. Collected editions of his poems in six volumes appeared in 1840 and again in 1841, and in 1854, just before his death, the poet issued a volume of poetry "collected and revised by their author." Another poem, *Omnipresence of God,* had its twenty-eighth edition in 1858. Montgomery's most ambitious work was *Luther,* a poem in thirty-one cantos, first published in 1842. He declared it "An attempt to reflect in poetical form (blank verse), some permanent features and prevailing expressions in the life, character, and work of Martin Luther, viewed in historical connection with the Reformation of the sixteenth century." His Preface contains an apology for its imperfections, but none for the Christian Principles that it attempts to embody. A sixth edition, in 1851, contains some changes, but the 1854 edition, as its author declared, was "elaborately revised, extensively corrected, and in many places rewritten and newly arranged." Canto 7, "The Solitary Monk," maintains its position in all editions. Its first line, here quoted, was used on the titlepage of all subsequent printings. The section declares that the appearance of Martin Luther shook the Roman Catholic Church, forcing it to reappraise its doctrines, many of which were found faulty. An appendix, at the end of this hundred-page poem, lists and studies some of the teachings with which Protestants disagreed. This is the way the canto begins, in the seventh edition:

The solitary monk, who shook the World
From pagan slumber, when the gospel-trump
Thunder'd its challenge from his dauntless lips,
In peals of truth, round hierarchal Rome,
Till mitred Pomp, and cowl'd Imposture quail'd,
And each false priesthood, like a fiend unmask'd
And stripp'd of light fictitiously assumed,
By some detecting Angel, shrunk dismay'd
And shiver'd, in thy vast exposure seen,—
Thee would I image, thou colossal Mind.

Some credit in being jolly

Source: MARTIN CHUZZLEWIT (Chapter 5)
Author: Charles Dickens (1812–1870)
First published: 1843–1844
Type of work: Novel

Context: Tom Pinch, the poor, honest, cheerful, and underpaid assistant to Mr. Pecksniff, a hypocrite who takes money for keeping pupils in his house to be instructed in architecture, although the instruction amounts to practically nothing, is driving Mr. Pecksniff's rawboned horse towards Salisbury to bring home a new student. He comes up with Mark Tapley, who is walking with a quick, light step and singing loudly and musically; he is also well dressed. When Tom refers to Mark's spruceness of attire, Mark replies that there is little credit in being cheerful when one is well dressed but there is credit to be gained if one is ragged. Mark's object in life is to be cheerful under the most adverse circumstances. The conversation is as follows:

". . . If I was very ragged and very jolly, then I should begin to feel that I had gained a point, Mr. Pinch."

"So you were singing just now, to bear up, as it were, against being well dressed, eh, Mark?" said Pinch.

"Your conversation's always equal to print, sir," rejoined Mark, with a broad grin. "That was it."

"Well!" cried Pinch, "you are the strangest young man, Mark, I ever knew in my life. I always thought so; but now I am quite certain of it. I am going to Salisbury, too. Will you get in? I shall be very glad of your company."

The young fellow made his acknowledgements and accepted the offer; stepping into the carriage directly, and seating himself on the very edge of the seat with his body half out of it, to express his being there on sufferance, and by the politeness of Mr. Pinch. As they went along, the conversation proceeded after this manner.

"I more than half believed, just now, seeing you so very smart," said Pinch, "that you must be going to be married, Mark."

"Well, sir, I've thought of that, too," he replied. "There might be **some credit in being jolly** with a wife, 'specially if the children had the measles and that, and was very fractious indeed. But I'm a'most afraid to try it. I don't see my way clear."

Some eastward, and some westward, and all wrong

Source: HOPE (Line 281)
Author: William Cowper (1731–1800)
First published: 1782
Type of work: Essay in verse

Context: The wise man, says the poet Cowper, sees human life as "a vain pursuit of fugitive false good." Man deals with Life as children do with a toy, misusing it and then throwing it away. Only when, under the influence of the Scriptures, man is filled with a scorn of sensual evils and of everything "deemed substantial since the Fall," can he know Hope. Next the poet describes Man throughout his life, persistently following self-interest in every field. Man seeks pleasure "as if Paul of Tarsus had lived and died a Jew" and had never revealed God's guidance and purposes. Therefore, man ends hopeless and in despair.

> As, when two pilgrims in a forest stray,
> Both may be lost, yet each in his own way;
> So fares it with the multitudes beguiled
> In vain opinion's waste and dangerous wild;
> Ten thousand rove the brakes and thorns among,
> **Some eastward, and some westward, and all wrong.**
> But here, alas! the fatal difference lies,
> Each man's belief is right in his own eyes.

Some lost lady of old years

Source: WARING (Section IV)
Author: Robert Browning (1812–1889)
First published: 1842
Type of work: Dramatic monologue

Context: Alfred Domett (1811–1887) was a remarkable man, with diverse talents and a many-faceted personality. His father had been a sailor under Nelson, but Domett did not follow the sea. He attended Cambridge three years and left without graduating; already interested in literature, he was publishing verse and receiving some notice as a rising poet. He was called to the bar in 1841 and went to New Zealand in 1842, where

991

he settled and became a magistrate. In succeeding years he held numerous government posts of importance, becoming Prime Minister of the colony in 1862. He and Browning had always been friends; on his return to England in 1871, they saw much of each other, and Domett published a few more volumes of poetry. Browning's poem "Waring," written upon the occasion of Domett's departure in 1842, is one of his customary studies of character; but it is clear that Domett's is a character which baffles Browning, and his mixed emotions are evident. This is a poem of warmth and good humor, and it bespeaks affectionate exasperation. He cannot quite understand why Domett (Waring) should break all ties and charge off into the wilderness; the act is harebrained but somehow admirable. There is something of the cavalier in Domett, a lusty enjoyment of life; he is a man of action and adventure. Browning has none of these qualities, but as he describes them there is a hint of envy in his words. He covers his sense of loss with the conviction that no matter what his friend does, it will be something unusual and perhaps remarkable. The exasperation, affectionate though it may be, is nonetheless genuine: Browning wants the fellow to settle down and put his talents to work, and so far there has been little more than an indication of promise. Throughout the poem there shines Domett's warm and magnetic personality:

Meantime, how much I loved him,
I find out now I've lost him.
I who cared not if I moved him,
Who could so carelessly accost him,
Henceforth never shall get free
Of his ghostly company.
His eyes that just a little wink
As deep I go into the merit
Of this and that distinguished spirit—
His cheeks' raised color, soon to sink,
As long I dwell on some stupendous
And tremendous (Heaven defend us!)
Monstr'-inform'-ingens-horrend-ous
Demoniaco-seraphic
Penman's latest piece of graphic.
Nay, my very wrist grows warm
With his dragging weight of arm.
E'en so, swimmingly appears,
Through one's after-supper musings,
Some lost lady of old years
With her beauteous vain endeavor
And goodness unrepaid as ever. . . .
· · ·

Some men must love my lady, and some Joan

Source: LOVE'S LABOUR'S LOST (Act III, sc. i, l. 207)
Author: William Shakespeare (1564–1616)
First published: 1598
Type of work: Dramatic comedy

Context: Act III of *Love's Labour's Lost* reveals love affairs beginning to spring up between the men close to Ferdinand, King of Navarre, and the ladies attending the Princess of France. Berowne, one of the men, employs Costard, a clown, to deliver a love letter for him to the lady he admires. After Costard leaves, Berowne begins a soliloquy on love and the fact that he is now involved in it. Then he sketches the negative qualities of the lady he loves and somewhat laments the fact that he has been attracted by the headstrong one in the group. Still, he plans to woo her in an earnest and ardent manner because this is the lady he is in love with. He thus philosophizes that some men just have to fall in love with the sort of woman who has aristocratic inclinations and ideas of courtly love. In a footnote to his edition of the play, G. B. Harrison tells us that the name "Joan" is a general term referring to "a country wench." Thus Berowne must also be lamenting that he did not fall in love with a country wench who would not require such wooing and attention. Love would be far simpler with "Joan."

BEROWNE

. . .

A whitely wanton, with a velvet brow,
With two pitch-balls stuck in her face for eyes,
Ay, and by heaven one that will do the deed,
Though Argus were her eunuch and her guard.
And I to sigh for her, to watch for her,
To pray for her, go to! It is a plague
That Cupid will impose for my neglect
Of his almighty dreadful little might.
Well, I will love, write, sigh, pray, sue, and groan.
Some men must love my lady, and some Joan.

Some mute inglorious Milton

Source: ELEGY WRITTEN IN A COUNTRY CHURCHYARD (Line 59)
Author: Thomas Gray (1716–1771)
First published: 1751
Type of work: Didactic elegy

Context: Gray's poem is about the little-known people of the English countryside, as opposed to the famous figures of English history, the

993

men and women who are buried in such places as Westminster Abbey. Had the fortunes of the humbler people been different, says the poet, these poor, simple, but honest persons buried in the obscure country churchyard might have done great deeds, found fame during life, and a place in the nation's history books. Here in a humble churchyard lie those who were kept from being great only by poverty and a lack of education. Here, says the poet, may lie some man who fought against a petty tyrant of the countryside in much the same way and with the same courage as John Hampden opposed King Charles I himself. Here may lie some man who, given the education, might have written as great poetry as John Milton. Or, adds Gray, here may lie a man who, given the chance, might have led his countrymen in a civil war, as did Oliver Cromwell in the 1640's, spilling the blood of commoner, aristocrat, and king. But, Gray comments, if the chance for fame of these people was circumscribed narrowly, so was their opportunity to commit crimes:

> Some village-Hampden, that with dauntless breast
> The little tyrant of his fields withstood;
> **Some mute inglorious Milton** here may rest,
> Some Cromwell guiltless of his country's blood.

> Th' applause of list'ning senates to command,
> The threats of pain and ruin to despise,
> To scatter plenty o'er a smiling land,
> And read their hist'ry in a nation's eyes,

> Their lot forbade: nor circumscrib'd alone
> Their growing virtues, but their crimes confin'd;
> Forbade to wade through slaughter to a throne,
> And shut the gates of mercy on mankind,

> The struggling pangs of conscious truth to hide,
> To quench the blushes of ingenuous shame,
> Or heap the shrine of Luxury and Pride
> With incense kindled at the Muse's flame.

Some people are more nice than wise

Source: MUTUAL FORBEARANCE NECESSARY TO THE HAPPINESS OF THE MARRIED STATE (Line 20)
Author: William Cowper (1731–1800)
First published: 1782
Type of work: Humorous didactic poem

Context: Although he produced a few verses in his youth, Cowper did not turn to the writing of poetry as a serious form of recreation until he

994

was fifty. He was a descendant of John Donne, and the last English poet who belonged to what has been called the cult of simplicity. His education was for a career in the legal profession; he was called to the bar in 1754. He never married; he fell in love with his cousin but suffered an attack of insanity and was forbidden to see or marry her. The strain of preparing for an examination in 1763 brought on another breakdown, during which he attempted suicide. His convalescence was lengthy; he then retired to the country, first living at Huntingdon and later, in 1767, moving to Olney. Though his Calvinism brought him comfort, it also brought despair; it was a major factor in the recurring periods of depression from which he suffered. He began to write poetry in 1781 and the first volume, *Poems,* appeared in 1782. His poetry is primarily a view of rural life, of country pleasures and domestic simplicity; its mood is meditative, reflective, and quiet. The deeper feelings he expresses arise from his equally deep religious convictions. The resulting tendency to moralize, and his lack of fire, have earned him a certain amount of criticism. His greatest work, *The Task,* was written at the suggestion of his friend Lady Austen, who also provided him with the subject: a sofa. Though he began with the sofa, the poem soon became a pleasant description of the countryside in winter, the simple rural life he led, and a distant view of the outside world. He also wrote a number of lasting hymns. In addition, he occasionally wrote humorous verse. One such poem, *John Gilpin's Ride,* enjoyed great popularity and became one of his best-known works. Another, perhaps more typical of him, is *Mutual Forbearance.* The latter half of this brief poem is a moral lesson in the values of human tolerance; the first half is an amusing dialogue between a bored, dissatisfied wife and her deaf husband. (The word "nice" is here used in its older sense of "finical" or "punctilious.")

The lady thus address'd her spouse—
What a mere dungeon is this house!
By no means large enough; and, was it,
Yet this dull room and that dark closet,
Those hangings with their worn-out graces,
Long beards, long noses, and pale faces,
Are such an antiquated scene,
They overwhelm me with the spleen.
—Sir Humphry, shooting in the dark,
Makes answer quite beside the mark:
No doubt, my dear, I bade him come,
Engaged myself to be at home,
And shall expect him at the door
Precisely when the clock strikes four.
　　You are so deaf, the lady cried,
(And raised her voice, and frown'd beside,)
You are so sadly deaf, my dear,
What shall I do to make you hear?

Dismiss poor Harry! he replies,
Some people are more nice than wise,—
For one slight trespass all this stir?
What if he did ride, whip and spur,
'Twas but a mile—your fav'rite horse
Will never look one hair the worse.

Some rise by sin, and some by virtue fall

Source: MEASURE FOR MEASURE (Act II, sc. i, l. 39)
Author: William Shakespeare (1564–1616)
First published: 1623
Type of work: Tragi-comedy

Context: Angelo, having assumed command of Vienna upon Vincentio's supposed absence, has ordered strict compliance with laws which for many years have not been enforced. One such law requires capital punishment for getting a woman with child out of wedlock, and Claudio, a young gentleman of the city, is arrested for this violation even though he stanchly asserts that Julietta "is fast my wife,/ Save that we do the denunciation lack/ Of outward order." In his new position of authority, Angelo refuses to exercise mercy, claiming that only a rigid application of the letter of the law will redeem the city from its dissolute behavior. When the new ruler is warned by Escalus, an old counselor who is second-in-command, that he himself is subject to certain vices he so peremptorily condemns, Angelo pompously replies " 'Tis one thing to be tempted, Escalus,/ Another thing to fall." In the course of the action of the play, however, this deputy is to become a prime illustration of the fact that absolute power corrupts absolutely. When confronted by Isabella, Claudio's sister, who pleads for her brother's life, Angelo lusts for her and treacherously offers her brother's life for her own honor, a pledge he does not intend to fulfill once he has satisfied his pleasure. Escalus' reaction to Angelo's decree early in the play serves two primary purposes: it heightens the tension by foreshadowing the major conflict between Angelo and Isabella, and it suggests ironically that the extremes of indiscriminate virtue and vice are equally heinous in that each is motivated by self-gratification which disregards the welfare of others:

ANGELO
See that Claudio
Be executed by nine to-morrow morning.
Bring him his confessor, let him be prepared,
For that's the utmost of his pilgrimage.

ESCALUS [*Aside.*]
Well, Heaven forgive him, and forgive us all.

996

Some rise by sin, and some by virtue fall.
Some run from breaks of ice, and answer none,
And some condemned for one fault alone.

Something between a hindrance and a help

Source: MICHAEL (Line 189)
Author: William Wordsworth (1770–1850)
First published: 1800
Type of work: Pastoral poem

Context: The poem "Michael" is the narrative of a shepherd whose only child, a son, arrived late in the father's life. The poem tells of the father's patience with the tiny infant and the shepherd's continued interest and time spent with the boy. And when the boy reached five years of age, Michael made his son a shepherd's staff from a sapling so that the boy could be with him more and begin to help him. Since the boy was so young for shepherding or since "to his office prematurely called," he was "something between a hindrance and a help" to his father.

And when by Heaven's good grace the boy grew up
A healthy Lad, and carried in his cheek
Two steady roses that were five years old;
Then Michael from a winter coppice cut
With his own hand a sapling, which he hooped
With iron, making it throughout in all
Due requisites a perfect shepherd's staff,
And gave it to the Boy; wherewith equipped
He as a watchman oftentimes was placed
At gate or gap, to stem or turn the flock;
And, to his office prematurely called,
There stood the urchin, as you will divine,
Something between a hindrance and a help;
And for this cause not always, I believe,
Receiving from his Father hire of praise;
Though nought was left undone which staff, or voice,
Or looks, or threatening gestures, could perform.

The soul is not more than the body

Source: SONG OF MYSELF (Canto 48)
Author: Walt Whitman (1819–1892)
First published: 1855
Type of work: Lyric poem

997

Context: *Leaves of Grass,* an extraordinary publication of twelve poems and ninety-four pages, financed by its author, that appeared in 1855, first introduced Walt Whitman and his free verse. Nine later editions added to and rearranged the contents, which embodied such themes as love, death, democracy, religion, and the beauty and importance of the human body. The beginning of Canto 48 voices several of Whitman's themes.

I have said that **the soul is not more than the body,**
And I have said that the body is not more than the soul,
And nothing, not God, is greater to one than one's soul is,
And whoever walks a furlong without sympathy walks to
     his own funeral drest in his shroud,
And I or you pocketless of a dime may purchase the pick
     of the earth,
         .   .   .

And I say to any man or woman, Let your soul stand cool
     and composed before a million universes.

And I say to Mankind, Be not curious about God,
For I who am curious about each am not curious about
     God,
(No array of terms can say how much I am at peace about
     God and about death.)

A sound mind in a sound body

Source: SATIRES (Number X)
Author: Juvenal (c. 55–c. 135)
First transcribed: 112–128
Type of work: Satire

Context: In his satires Juvenal notes the faults of almost every phase of life—the hypocrisy of scholars, the subjugation of the poor by the wealthy and the extravagance of the poor, the tyranny of rulers, the fickleness and baseness of women, the difficulty faced by those producing works of literature and art, the degeneration of the nobility and the retention of pride, the condition of servitude of one who sins, the vanity of worldly desires, the extravagance and luxury of the times, the poor examples set by parents for their children, and the unjust control of civil affairs by military forces. In the tenth satire, directed at the vanity of human wishes, Juvenal points out the difficulties incurred by those who desire and receive power, beauty, longevity, or any of the most coveted human wishes. Since it is the nature of man to pray for things desired, the writer suggests that:

998

. . . your prayer must be that you may have **a sound mind in a sound body.** Pray for a bold spirit, free of all dread of death; that reckons the closing scene of life among Nature's kindly boons; that can endure labour, whatever it be; that knows not the passion of anger; that covets nothing; that deems the gnawing cares of Hercules, and all his cruel toils, far preferable to the joys of Venus, rich banquets, and the downy couch of Sardanapalus. I show thee what thou canst confer upon thyself. . . .

The sound must seem an echo to the sense

Source: ESSAY ON CRITICISM (Part II, l. 365)
Author: Alexander Pope (1688–1744)
First published: 1711
Type of work: Satire

Context: Warning that to be a bad critic is far worse than to be a bad poet, Pope notes that many critics lack genius and more a proper education. Among the causes of poor critical judgment are false pride, the tendency to consider a work of art as segments rather than a whole, and the habit of delighting in a single aspect of poetry, such as wit, flowery language, or smooth versification. The versification, says Pope, is good only if it is appropriate to the sense of the poem:

Tis not enough no harshness gives offence,
The sound must seem an echo to the sense:
Soft is the strain when Zephyr gently blows,
And the smooth stream in smoother numbers flows;
But when loud surges lash the sounding shore,
The hoarse, rough verse should like the torrent roar.
When Ajax strives some rock's vast weight to throw,
The line too labours, and the words move slow:
Not so, when swift Camilla scours the plain,
Flies o'er the unbending corn, and skims along the main.
Hear how Timotheus' varied lays surprise,
And bid alternate passions fall and rise!
While, at each change, the son of Libyan Jove
Now burns with glory, and then melts with love:
Now his fierce eyes with sparking fury glow,
Now sighs steal out, and tears begin to flow:
Persians and Greeks like turns of nature found
And the world's victor stood subdued by sound!

Spare the rod, and spoil the child

Source: HUDIBRAS (Part II, Canto 1, l. 844)
Author: Samuel Butler (1612–1680)
First published: First and second parts, 1663; third part, 1678
Type of work: Burlesque poem

Context: In imitation of Cervantes' account in prose of the exploits of the knight-errant Don Quixote and his squire Sancho Panza, to right the wrongs of Spain, the English poet Samuel Butler sent the Presbyterian Sir Hudibras and his squire Ralpho out to fight sin and superstition in England. And as Cervantes was speeded into completing his sequel by the appearance of a spurious second part by a smart lawyer calling himself Avellaneda, so, to hasten Butler, the first part of Sir Hudibras' adventures brought a sequel by another hand the same year, the first of fifteen imitations to appear within a century. One great difference between the Spanish and the English books is that Cervantes showed tenderness for his chief character, and so made readers admire and sympathize with him, despite his misfortunes and lack of success. Butler had neither pity nor respect for the product of his pen. To make fun of the Puritans, he portrayed them as obnoxious nuisances. In 1663, Butler published the First Part, of three cantos and 3,488 lines followed by the publication of Part Two, also in three cantos. Growing out of the author's classical interest, it begins with an imitation of the Fourth Book of Virgil's *Aeneid*. The poet had left Hudibras and his squire prisoners in the stocks. When a Widow whom he had been wooing hears of his plight, she visits him in one of the poem's amusing moments. He had intended to impress her. She pretends not to recognize the sorry specimen. After a long discussion of the possibility of matrimony between them, she offers to try to get him freed if he will consent to a whipping such as lovers endure for their ladies, and which serves Virtue and corrects the mistakes of Nature. She explains her belief:

And I'll admit you to the place
You claim as due in my good grace.
If matrimony and hanging go
By dest'ny, why not whipping too?
What med'cine else can cure the fits
Of lovers when they lose their wits?
Love is a boy by poets styl'd,
Then **spare the rod, and spoil the child.**

1000

Speak of the moderns without contempt, and of the ancients without idolatry

Source: LETTERS TO HIS SON (Letter 30)
Author: Philip Dormer Stanhope, Lord Chesterfield (1694–1773)
First published: 1774
Type of work: Personal letter

Context: During thirty years the Earl of Chesterfield wrote letters to his illegitimate son, Philip, in hope of turning him into a polished, ambitious person like his father. They were personal letters, never meant for other eyes, but immediately upon the death of Lord Chesterfield, his wife hurried to find a publisher willing to pay 1,575 pounds for them, and they came out in two volumes in 1774, and in two more reprintings the same year in four volumes. Unfortunately, young Philip Stanhope had neither the talent nor the persistence to take advantage of the stream of counsel from the letters; so he died in 1768 at the age of 36 without having achieved the success for which his father had hoped. Lord Chesterfield's chief aim was to help his son cultivate "The Graces," and become a polished gentleman. Some critics accuse the earl of advocating questionable action. He did say that dissimulation such as demanded by politeness and good manners should be employed, for it means no more than "your humble servant" at the end of a letter. He recommended flattery, too, as a royal road to success, though not flattery of a person's vices and crimes. Because of a low regard for women, he suggested flattery of their beauty "upon which scarce any flattery is too gross for them to swallow." Chief criticism against him is his recommendation of irregular attachment, which used to be called "gallantry," with married women, as part of the education of a young gentleman. Actually such flagrant advice by a father to his son occurs in only a half dozen letters out of a total of 421, and those were written when his son was in Paris, where even Montesquieu agreed that "honor" permitted such behavior. Samuel Johnson, though no admirer of Lord Chesterfield, commented that after some excisions, this collection of letters "should be put into the hands of every young gentleman." Letter Number 30, dated at Bath (where Chesterfield had gone for his gout), February 22, 1748, is a good example. It deals with learning. The father tells his son that "learning (I mean Greek and Roman learning) is a most useful and necessary ornament," but there are cautions to be observed. Some learned men are so much at home with the classics that they refer naturally to "Old Homer," "that sly rogue Horace," and "Naso" instead of Ovid. This practice is good if you are really that familiar with them, but too many pedants only pretend to be. When you are making a speech, says this man who was one of the best orators of his time, do not drag in imaginary parallels with the ancients. Be modest about your knowledge; do not go around pulling a volume of some classic author out of your pocket. "Elzevir" refers to Louis Elzevir (1540–1617) who, with his descendants, published a series of sturdy, inexpensive editions of the classics, very popular with impoverished students who could not find them elsewhere. Then Lord Chesterfield sums up his position:

> . . . I would by no means have you disown your acquaintance with the ancients; but still less would I have you brag of an exclusive intimacy with them. **Speak of the moderns without contempt, and of the ancients without idolatry;** judge them all by their merits, but not by their ages; and if you happen to have an Elzevir classic in your pocket, neither show it nor mention it.

Speech is the small change of silence

Source: THE ORDEAL OF RICHARD FEVEREL (Chapter 34)
Author: George Meredith (1828–1909)
First published: 1859
Type of work: Novel

Context: How far can education go and what are its results? This is the question posed and answered in this novel, the most autobiographical of Meredith's prose works. Sir Austen, the dogmatic father, attempts to educate his son by making the boy into a tool of reason controlled from without, but in his zeal for rationality he neglects his son's emotions. Thus when young Richard falls in love with the charming Lucy, he loses control and marries against his father's wishes. Sir Austen, however, is unwilling to let his son find happiness in marriage: he gets his nephew Adrian to help him separate the lovers. The quotation comes from the section in which Richard first brings Adrian into his home, unaware of the schemes of his father. As he tries to learn of his father's reaction to his marriage, Adrian cleverly plays with his emotions, the most vulnerable part of his character:

> Richard fretted restlessly opposite his cool relative.
> "Adrian! what did he say when he heard of it? I want to know exactly what words he said."
> "Well says the sage, my son! **'Speech is the small change of Silence.'** He said less than I do."
> "That's how he took it!" cried Richard, and plunged in meditation.

Spring comes slowly up this way

Source: CHRISTABEL (Part I, l. 22)
Author: Samuel Taylor Coleridge (1772–1834)
First published: 1816
Type of work: Narrative poem

Context: This tale of the supernatural begins with the midnight owls awakening the crowing cock—and both hooting owls and cocks crowing at midnight have connotations of the world of spirits. Sir Leoline, the baron, has an aged, toothless mastiff bitch that howls at midnight, four for the quarter-hours and twelve for the hour; some say that the old dog sees the shroud of the baron's dead wife. The night upon which the poem opens is chilly, but not dark, as a thin layer of clouds but partially veils the full moon, which looks small and dull. It is April, but spring is late in arriving in this region.

'Tis the middle of night by the castle clock,
And the owls have awakened the crowing cock;
Tu—whit!—Tu—whoo!
And hark, again! the crowing cock,
How drowsily it crew.

Sir Leoline, the Baron rich,
Hath a toothless mastiff bitch;
From her kennel beneath the rock
She maketh answer to the clock,
Four for the quarters, and twelve for the hour;
Ever and aye, by shine and shower,
Sixteen short howls, not over loud;
Some say, she sees my lady's shroud.

Is the night chilly and dark?
The night is chilly, but not dark.
The thin gray cloud is spread on high,
It covers but not hides the sky.
The moon is behind, and at the full;
And yet she looks both small and dull.
The night is chill, the cloud is gray:
'Tis a month before the month of May,
And the **Spring comes slowly up this way.**

Springes to catch woodcocks!

Source: HAMLET (Act I, sc. iii, l. 115)
Author: William Shakespeare (1564–1616)
First published: 1603
Type of work: Dramatic tragedy

OPHELIA

My lord, he hath importun'd me with love
In honourable fashion.

POLONIUS

Ay, fashion you may call it; go to, go to.

OPHELIA

And hath given countenance to his speech, my lord,
With almost all the holy vows of heaven.

POLONIUS

Ay, **springes to catch woodcocks.** I do know,
When the blood burns, how prodigal the soul
Lends the tongue vows. These blazes daughter,
Giving more light than heat, extinct in both,
Even in their promise, as it is a-making,
You must not take for fire. From this time
Be something scanter of your maiden presence.

. . .

OPHELIA

I shall obey, my lord.

Squandered a whole summer while 'twas May

Source: DON JUAN (Canto I, stanza 213)
Author: George Gordon, Lord Byron (1788–1824)
First published: 1819 (Cantos I and II)
Type of work: Satiric poem

Context: Lord Byron, after bringing to its tempestuous and unseemly end the young Don Juan's first amorous scrape, sets to musing. The future of his projected poem, he says, will depend on the public's reaction to its hero's first adventure. The work is to be an epic, he assures his readers, with the epic's requisite number of books, loves, wars, gales, lists, and episodes, after the style of Virgil and Homer but with—at least—one advantage over his great forebears who ". . . so embellish, that 'tis quite a bore/ Their labyrinth of fables to thread through,/ Whereas this story's actually true." And should any reader assume that this tale will not be moral, he begs that he not cry out be-fore he's hurt. After all, in Canto XII, doesn't he intend to "show the very place where wicked people go?" Nor should the public fail to take *his* word about the matter rather than listen to the opinions of the hostile *Edinburgh Review* and *The Quarterly*, both of which had attacked his early poetry, and both of which, he in turn, had attacked in *English Bards and Scotch Reviewers* (1809).

But now at thirty years my hair is grey—
   (I wonder what it will be like at forty?
I thought of a peruke the other day—)
   My heart is not much greener; and, in short, I
Have **squander'd my whole summer while 'twas May,**
   And feel no more spirit to retort; I
Have spent my life, both interest and principal,
And deem not, what I deem'd, my soul invincible.

No more—no more—Oh! never more on me
   The freshness of the heart can fall like dew,
Which out of all the lovely things we see
   Extracts emotions beautiful and new;
Hived in our bosoms like the bag o' the bee.
   Think'st thou the honey with those objects grew?
Alas! 'twas not in them, but in thy power
To double even the sweetness of a flower.

Square and above board

Source: CHARACTERS OF VIRTUES AND VICES ("Of an Honest Man")
Author: Bishop Joseph Hall (1574–1656)
First published: 1608
Type of work: Character writing

Context: A seventeenth century literary fad was the writing of "characters," the originals of this type having been invented by Theophrastus (322? B.C.–288 B.C.), a Greek. The object was to write a short essay upon a human characteristic, profession, trade, calling, or something of the sort; the pieces were always couched in general terms. In "Of the Honest Man," Bishop Hall says that the honest man does not consider what he might do, but what he should do; justice is his first guide, expedience his second. His simple uprightness allows him to be victimized by the crafty, but he laments their faithlessness more than his own credulity. His word is his oath, and he is honest and upright, even in acting as an executor of a dead man's estate, scorning to swindle a dead friend. All his dealings are square and above board: here Hall employs a figure of speech derived from card playing. The person who deals above the board acts in the sight of everyone, and everyone can have visual evidence of his honesty. The author says:

When he is made his friend's executor, he defrays debts, pays legacies; and scorneth to gain by orphans, or to ransack graves: and therefore will be true to a dead friend, because he sees him not. All his dealings are **square, and above the board:** he bewrays the fault of what he sells, and restores the overseen gain of a false reckoning. He esteems a bribe venomous, though it come gilded over with the color of gratuity. His cheeks are never stained with the blushes of recantation; neither doth his tongue falter to make good a lie, with the secret glosses of double or reserved senses: and when his name is traduced his innocency bears him out with courage: then, lo, he goes on in the plain way of truth, and will either triumph in his integrity, or suffer with it.

Squire of Dames

Source: THE FAERIE QUEENE (Book III, Canto 8, stanza 44)
Author: Edmund Spenser (c. 1552–1599)
First published: 1590
Type of work: Allegorical poem

Context: In *The Faerie Queene,* a long allegorical poem made up of a series of knightly adventures, a knight known as "the Squire of Dames," assigned by his ladylove the task of seeking pledges of love from as many ladies as possible in a year's time, has received pledges from three hundred, but, when his lady sends him forth to seek an equal number of examples of chastity, he finds only three ladies in three years willing to reject his advances. The Squire of Dames, who happens upon a giantess carrying off the lady Florimell, allows Florimell to escape but is himself snatched up by the giantess. Sir Satyrane rescues the squire, and together they search for a monster like a hyena that the witch has sent after Florimell. Then Sir Satyrane:

Who having ended with that **Squire of Dames**
A long discourse of his adventures vaine,
The which himselfe, then Ladies, more defames,
And finding not th' Hyena to be slaine,
With that same Squire, returned backe againe
To his first way.

A stage where every man must play a part, and mine a sad one

Source: THE MERCHANT OF VENICE (Act I, sc. i, ll. 78–79)
Author: William Shakespeare (1564–1616)
First published: 1600
Type of work: Dramatic comedy

Context: This play seems to have been occasioned by an outbreak of anti-Semitism in London about 1594. In the play Antonio, the merchant, borrows money from the rich Jew, Shylock, in order to assist a friend, pledging, according to Shylock's diabolical demand, that pound of flesh nearest his heart as surety for the loan. When the play opens, however, no difficulties have arisen; yet Antonio is sad. His friend, Solanio, insists that if business reverses have not occasioned the sadness, then Antonio must be in love. They encounter three friends, and after some conversation Antonio; Bassanio, the friend Antonio will assist later in the play; Gratiano; and Lorenzo are left on stage. Gratiano in his turn tries to cheer up Antonio:

GRATIANO
You look not well Signior Antonio,
You have too much respect upon the world.
They lose it that do buy it with much care;
Believe me you are marvellously changed.

ANTONIO
I hold the world but as the world, Gratiano,
A stage where every man must play a part,
And mine a sad one.

GRATIANO
          Let me play the fool;
With mirth and laughter let old wrinkles come,
And let my liver rather heat with wine
Than my heart cool with mortifying groans.
Why should a man whose blood is warm within,
Sit like his grandsire cut in alabaster?
          • • •

The star-led wizards haste with odors sweet

Source: ON THE MORNING OF CHRIST'S NATIVITY (Stanza 4)
Author: John Milton (1608–1674)
First published: 1645
Type of work: Religious poem

1007

Context: Milton begins by saying that this is the morning when the Son of heaven's King was born to the Virgin; He brought our great redemption from above; He paid the forfeit for our sins. He had laid aside the tremendous brilliance of His heavenly form, in which He was clothed when He counselled with the Father and the Holy Spirit in heaven; He forsook the everlasting day to inhabit a dark house of mortal clay. Milton then asks the heavenly Muse if there is no verse or hymn to welcome Christ to His new home. The star-led wizards, the Magi, are coming to present their frankincense; the poet therefore conjures the Muse to hurry before them to offer a song to Him and thus have the first honor, and to join her voice with the angelic choir that hymned Him in heaven. "Prevent" has its archaic meaning of "come ahead of some one."

See how from far upon the Eastern road
The star-led wizards haste with odors sweet:
O run, prevent them with thy humble ode,
And lay it lowly at his blessed feet;
Have thou the honor first, thy Lord to greet,
    And join thy voice unto the angel choir,
From out his secret altar touched with hallowed fire.

The stars move still, time runs, the clock will strike

Source: THE TRAGICAL HISTORY OF DOCTOR FAUSTUS (Scene xix, l. 144)
Author: Christopher Marlowe (1564–1593)
First published: 1604
Type of work: Dramatic tragedy

Context: Dr. Faustus, a great and learned scholar, tired of various mundane studies, sells his soul to the Devil for the power to have the evil spirits of the other world at his command. Though his friends, and even a Good Angel, call upon him to repent and return to God's grace, Faustus refuses. For twenty-four years, the length of his compact with the Devil, Faustus deals grandiosely with the world, helped by Mephistopheles, the fiend given him as a servant by Satan. On his last night on earth Faustus is persuaded that for a few years of earthly vanities he has given up his soul and eternal felicity. Some of his scholar-friends visit him to help him pray, but he bids them depart, for their safety's sake. They retire to another room to pray for him, after he tells them that if he lives until morning he will join them, but that if he fails to join them his soul has gone to Hell. When his friends have left him, the clock strikes eleven, and Faustus, knowing he has but one hour left before Satan demands his due, cries out in terror:

1008

Ah Faustus,
Now hast thou but one bare hower to live,
And then thou must be damnd perpetually:
Stand stil, you ever mooving spheres of heaven,
That time may cease, and midnight never come:
Faire Nature's eye, rise, rise againe, and make
Perpetuall day, or let this houre be but
A year, a month, a week, a natural day,
That Faustus may repent, and save his soul,
O lente, lente curite noctis equi:
The stars moove stil, time runs, the clocke wil strike,
The devil wil come, and Faustus must be damnd.
O I'll leap up to my God: who pulles me down?
See, see where Christ's blood streames in the firmament.
One drop would save my soul, half a drop, ah my Christ.
Ah rend not my heart for naming of my Christ,
Yet will I call on him: O, spare me *Lucifer!*

Stern daughter of the voice of God

Source: ODE TO DUTY (Line 1)
Author: William Wordsworth (1770–1850)
First published: 1807
Type of work: Philosophic poem

Context: In this work Wordsworth makes his most notable departure from his resolution not to use abstractions as the material for poetry. Under the name of "stern daughter of the voice of God" he addresses Duty, which he says is a light to guide human beings and a rod to correct and reprove them when they err; it is a calming force. There are some people who customarily do what they should do without the need for any form of compulsion, but there are others who need the discipline of duty. Our days will be serene and bright when we all do what we should, but now we need a firm support. The poet himself has not been overly addicted to performing his duty; he has lived at liberty and has been his own guide, but he feels that too much liberty is oppressive and so feels that he will be happier if he lives a more strictly regimented life than in the past. Toward the end of the poem he equates duty with natural law: "Thou dost preserve the stars from wrong; /And the most ancient heavens, through Thee, are fresh and strong." But he calls Duty to a humbler function, that is, regulating his own private life.

Stern Daughter of the Voice of God!
O Duty! if that name thou love
Who art a light to guide, a rod
To check the erring, and reprove;

1009

Thou, who art victory and law
When empty terrors overawe;
From vain temptations dost set free;
And calm'st the weary strife of frail humanity!

There are who ask not if thine eye
Be on them; who, in love and truth,
Where no misgiving is, rely
Upon the genial sense of youth;
Glad Hearts! without reproach or blot;
Who do thy work, and know it not:
Oh! if through confidence misplaced
They fail, thy saving arms, dread Power! around them cast.

A stiffnecked people

Source: EXODUS 33:3
Author: Unknown
First transcribed: c. 1000–300 B.C.
Type of work: Religious history and law

Context: When Jacob's migration settled in Egypt, that land was ruled by the Hyksos Kings; being of Asiatic origin themselves they were not unfriendly to the Israelites. At the end of about four centuries, however, a new dynasty of native Egyptians arose who feared the rapidly multiplying group; the Israelites were accordingly enslaved and set to hard labor in the building of cities, and it was decreed that all their male children be destroyed at birth. One who escaped the edict was Moses; his mother caused him to be found by Pharaoh's daughter, who reared him as an Egyptian. His sympathies lay with his own people, however, and in interceding for one of them he killed an Egyptian taskmaster. For this act of temper he was forced to exile himself to Midian, where he married and lived for some time. When an angel of the Lord appeared before him and bade him deliver his people from bondage, Moses returned to Egypt and endeavored to gain concessions from Pharaoh. He was unsuccessful until a series of plagues convinced the monarch that it was unwise to hold the Israelites any longer. Moses accordingly led his people from Egypt into the Sinai peninsula; Pharaoh, pursuing this multitude with the intention of wiping it out, was overtaken by the sea. Arrived at Sinai, Moses ascends the mountain and converses with God, receiving and carrying out instructions for proper worship of the Lord; returning from an unusually long absence he finds that many of his people have turned away from him and are worshiping a golden calf and indulging in an orgy, in the Egyptian manner. In a fit of temper he destroys the sacred tablets God has given him and orders those still faithful to him to kill the dissenters. Then he returns to the mountain, to beg that the Lord forgive his people. But the Lord is angered by their stubbornness and is not easily appeased:

> And Moses returned unto the LORD, and said, Oh, this people have sinned a great sin, and have made them gods of gold.
>
> Yet now, if thou wilt forgive their sin—; and if not, blot me, I pray thee, out of thy book which thou hast written.
>
> And the LORD said unto Moses, Whosoever hath sinned against me, him will I blot out of my book.
>
> Therefore now go, lead the people unto the place of which I have spoken unto thee: behold, mine Angel shall go before thee: nevertheless in the day when I visit I will visit their sin upon them.
>
> And the LORD plagued the people, because they made the calf, which Aaron made.
>
> And the LORD said unto Moses, Depart, and go up hence, thou and the people which thou hast brought up out of the land of Egypt, unto the land which I sware unto Abraham, to Isaac, and to Jacob, saying, Unto thy seed will I give it:
>
> And I will send an angel before thee; and I will drive out the Canaanite, the Amorite, and the Hittite, and the Perizzite, the Hivite, and the Jebusite:
>
> Unto a land flowing with milk and honey: for I will not go up in the midst of thee; for thou art **a stiffnecked people:** lest I consume thee in the way.
>
> And when the people heard these evil tidings, they mourned: and no man did put on him his ornaments.

A still small voice

Source: I KINGS 19:12
Author: Unknown
First transcribed: c. 600 B.C.
Type of work: Religious history

Context: During the reign of Solomon (977–937 B.C.) the Israelites became an actual nation; the times were marked by success in international politics, great organization of the country's natural and human resources, and a court famous for its splendor. After Solomon's death, however, the nation was divided into two kingdoms: Israel, in the north, and Judah, in the south. The former drew away because its people had been exploited by Solomon. The people of Judah rebelled against his successors because of the system of indentured labor, and the revolt was put down. Judah subsequently became a pawn of Syria. Israel passed through several dynasties and achieved considerable material progress. Its seventh king, Ahab, married the Tyrian princess Jezebel, thus contracting an alliance with Tyre. Another marriage within the dynasty cemented relations with Judah; and a defensive alliance with Syria, against the Assyrians, was established. These alliances weakened the religious life of the nation; Jezebel was a worshiper of Melkart and Astarte, and other cults were encouraged by royal favor. At this time Elijah appears on the scene to remind Israel that Jehovah is the only true God. He prophesies a severe drought, retires to the wilderness, and is fed by ravens. After the drought has continued for a time he returns and tells Ahab he will send rain again, then causes the prophets of Baal to assemble. They build an altar to Baal, and Elijah builds one for Jehovah; then each calls on his own god to burn the sacrifice. Baal does not respond, but a lightning bolt strikes the altar of Jehovah and ignites the fire. At Elijah's suggestion, Ahab orders that the priests of Baal be slain. Soon after they are despatched, a rain squall is seen approaching, and in a few moments there is a torrential downpour. Elijah has already performed other miracles, but these are particularly impressive. Jezebel is not impressed favorably, however: she sends word to Elijah that she has marked him for death. He flees into the wilderness, is fed by an angel, and takes refuge on Mount Horeb.

And he came thither unto a cave, and lodged there; and, behold, the word of the LORD came to him, and he said unto him, What doest thou here, Elijah?

And he said, I have been very jealous for the LORD God of hosts: for the children of Israel have forsaken thy covenant, thrown down thine altars, and slain thy prophets with the sword; and I, even I only, am left; and they seek my life, to take it away.

And he said, Go forth, and stand upon the mount before the LORD. And behold, the LORD passed by, and a great and strong wind rent the mountains, and brake in pieces the rocks before the LORD; but the LORD was not in the wind: and after the wind an earthquake; but the LORD was not in the earthquake:

And after the earthquake a fire; but the LORD was not in the fire: and after the fire **a still small voice.**

And it was so, when Elijah heard it, that he wrapped his face in his mantle, and went out, and stood in the entering in of the cave. And behold, there came a voice unto him, and said, What doest thou here, Elijah?

And he said, I have been very jealous for the LORD God of hosts: because the children of Israel have forsaken thy covenant thrown down thine altars, and slain thy prophets with the sword; and I, even I only, am left; and they seek my life, to take it away.

The still-vexed Bermoothes

Source: THE TEMPEST (Act I, sc. ii, l. 229)
Author: William Shakespeare (1564–1616)
First published: 1623
Type of work: Tragi-comedy

Prospero that his will has been obeyed—the passengers, all safe, are scattered about the island, and the ship is anchored safely in a harbor that Prospero will remember, because he once summoned Ariel to that place, ordering him to bring him some dew from the ever-stormy Bermudas (*the still-vexed Bermoothes*):

ARIEL
Safely in harbour
Is the King's ship, in the deep nook, where once
Thou call'dst me up at midnight to fetch dew
From **the still-vexed Bermoothes,** there she's hid;
The mariners all under hatches stowed,
Who, with a charm joined to their suffered labour,
I have left asleep. And for the rest o' the fleet,
Which I dispersed, they all have met again,
And are upon the Mediterranean float,
Bound sadly home for Naples,
Supposing that they saw the King's ship wrecked,
And his great person perish.

The story always old and always new

Source: THE RING AND THE BOOK (Book II, "Half-Rome," l. 214)
Author: Robert Browning (1812–1889)
First published: 1868–1869
Type of work: Dramatic monologue

Context: Consisting of twelve long books, this poem presents the story of a famous murder trial that occurred in Italy; told from different points of view, the chronology of the story becomes clear only when all of the speakers have been heard. The speaker of this monologue, a man who takes Guido's side on the grounds that he was deceived from the beginning, argues that Guido should be released for doing what any self-respecting husband would do. He tells of the marriage of the destitute nobleman Guido Franceschini to Pompilia Comparini, who was thought to be heiress to a considerable fortune. After Guido had mistreated Pietro and Violante Comparini, however, they claimed that Pompilia was not actually their child but had been purchased from a prostitute. The speaker, blaming the Comparinis for deceiving the poor Guido, says that Pietro's rearing Pompilia as his own child and legal heir was the original act that led to the murder, and consequently the husband had the right to defend his honor when he dis-   covered the fraud.

> Moreover,—here's the worm i' the core, the germ
> O' the rottenness and ruin which arrived,—
> He owned some usufruct, had moneys' use
> Lifelong, but to determine with his life
> In heirs' default: so, Pietro craved an heir,
> **(The story always old and always new)**
> Shut his fool's-eyes fast on the visible good
> And wealth for certain, opened them owl-wide
> On fortune's sole piece of forgetfulness,
> The child that should have been and would not be.

Struck all on a heap

Source: THE DUENNA (Act II, sc. ii)
Author: Richard Brinsley Sheridan (1751–1816)
First published: 1777 (as *The Governess,* Dublin)
Type of work: Comic opera

Context: Louisa loves Antonio. Her brother Ferdinand loves Clara. But Don Pedro and his second wife plan to place Clara in a convent, and Don Jerome, father of Ferdinand and Louisa, intends to force Louisa to marry odious Isaac Mendoza. Jerome has sworn not to see or speak to Louisa until she consents to the marriage. Margaret, the homely old duenna, agrees to help Louisa elope if Louisa will resign Isaac to her, which plan Louisa is happy to consent to. To Ferdinand, Jerome confesses he married Ferdinand's mother for her money; thus he sees no reason why Louisa should not marry Isaac for his. Caught (as she intended) with an incriminating letter, Margaret confesses plotting to aid Louisa's elopement with Antonio, and Jerome dismisses her. This act enables Louisa to leave dressed as Margaret and undetected by Jerome. Meeting Clara, who has just run away from *her* father, Louisa asks and is granted permission to pretend to be Clara when she meets Isaac, who has never seen her. Happy to take the supposed Clara to meet Antonio, who once loved Clara and may fall again, Isaac leaves Louisa at his lodgings until he can visit Don Jerome and meet the beauteous Louisa. She warns him that he may find Louisa rather matronly. In Jerome's library he lists for Isaac his daughter's beauties—her sparkling eyes, her dimple, her lovely skin and voice of a nightingale—and sends him to woo her in her dressing room. Meeting the duenna, Isaac mutters, ". . . zounds this can never be Louisa—she's as old as my mother"; but when she mentions her father he concludes. ". . . 'tis well my affections are fixed on her fortune and not her person."

1014

Signor, wont you sit?   [*She sits.*]

ISAAC

Pardon me, madam, I have scarce recover'd my astonishment
at—your condescension, madam—she has the devil's own dimples
to be sure.   [*Aside.*]

DUENNA

Nay, you shall not stand [*he sits*]. I do not wonder, Sir, that you
are surpriz'd at my affability—I own Signor, that I was vastly pre-
posessed against you, and being teiz'd by my father, I did give
some encouragement to Antonio. But then, Sir, you were described to me as a quite different person.

ISAAC

Aye, and so you was to me upon my soul, madam.

DUENNA

But when I saw you, I was never more struck in my life.

ISAAC

That was just my case too, madam; I was **struck all on a heap**
for my part.

Studious of laborious ease

Source: THE TASK (Book III, l. 361)
Author: William Cowper (1731–1800)
First published: 1785
Type of work: Meditative poem in blank verse

Context: Cowper, although he wrote
a few verses in his youth, did not turn
seriously to the writing of poetry until
he was fifty. He was trained in the
law and was called to the bar in
1754. Attacks of insanity forced him
into an early retirement; the first of
these made it impossible for him to
marry the cousin he had fallen in love
with and the second, occurring while
he was preparing for an examination
in 1763, drove him to attempted suicide. After a long convalescence he
moved to the country and finally settled at Olney, where he lived with his
friends the Unwins. Here he began to
write poetry and the first volume,
Poems, was published in 1782. A humorous poem, *John Gilpin's Ride,*
was sent to a newspaper the same
year and enjoyed great popularity.
His greatest work, *The Task,* appeared in 1785 and ensured his lasting fame. Cowper was the last English poet who belonged to what has
been called the cult of simplicity; he
was primarily a poet of rural life. *The
Task* was written at the suggestion of
his friend Lady Austen, who also
provided him with the subject: a sofa.

Cowper dutifully began with the sofa but soon enlarged the topic with a pleasant and natural description of the countryside and of the simple tasks and pleasures of his days. His reflections upon human nature and moral problems, together with his thoughts regarding the troubles of the distant outside world, form a considerable portion of the work. Cowper's strong Calvinism, a factor in his recurrent periods of severe depression, was also a source of comfort to him; he moralizes frequently and some of his poems are akin to sermons. After describing the beauty of the countryside in winter, he discusses the troubled world and thus completes Book II of *The Task*. He continues these thoughts in Book III, and remarks sadly on those people who come to the country only to raise holiday havoc, without any true appreciation of its beauty. Then he turns to a description of his garden, and of the simple and wholesome pleasure it gives him:

How various his employments, whom the world
Calls idle, and who justly in return
Esteems that busy world an idler, too!
Friends, books, a garden, and perhaps his pen,
Delightful industry enjoy'd at home,
And nature in her cultivated trim
Dress'd to his taste, inviting him abroad—
Can he want occupation who has these?
Will he be idle who has much t' enjoy?
Me, therefore, **studious of laborious ease,**
Not slothful; happy to deceive the time,
Not waste it; and aware that human life
Is but a loan to be repaid with use,
When He shall call his debtors to account,
From Whom are all our blessings; bus'ness finds
Ev'n here: while sedulous I seek t' improve,
At least neglect not, nor leave unemploy'd
The mind He gave me; driving it, though slack,
Too oft, and much impeded in its work
By causes not to be divulged in vain,
To its just point—the service of mankind.

Such ever was love's way: to rise, it stoops

Source: A DEATH IN THE DESERT (Line 134)
Author: Robert Browning (1812–1889)
First published: 1864
Type of work: Narrative poem

Context: Supposedly written by Pamphylax, a first century Christian, this poem presents an eyewitness account of the death of St. John, author of the fourth Gospel and Revelation. As he is dying, the Apostle recollects his life, especially his experience on Patmos, where he saw the vision of the Apocalypse. Ironically, this man —the last living man who had personally seen Jesus—fights the skepticism that the persecutions have brought into Christianity; foreshadowing the religious doubts of the nineteenth century, St. John is afraid that people will not believe a vision that they are just told about and fears that the new religion will die when there are no more survivors who actually knew Jesus. But he is partly assured that the love that he experienced at firsthand will not perish, because in writing both the Gospel and Revelation he has found a way, however humble, of preserving his witness for the generations that will follow. This hope is his means of finally reconciling himself to a death that might otherwise mean the end of Christianity.

Such ever was love's way: to rise, it stoops.
Since I, whom Christ's mouth taught, was bidden teach,
I went, for many years, about the world,
Saying "It was so; so I heard and saw,"
Speaking as the case asked: and men believed.
Afterward came the message to myself
In Patmos isle; I was not bidden teach,
But simply listen, take a book and write,
Nor set down other than the given word,
With nothing left to my arbitrament
To choose or change: I wrote, and men believed. . . .

Such is the custom of Branksome Hall

Source: THE LAY OF THE LAST MINSTREL (Canto I, stanza 7, l. 52)
Author: Sir Walter Scott (1771–1832)
First published: 1805
Type of work: Narrative poem

Context: The last minstrel begins his song by telling that when the feast was over in Branksome Hall the Ladye had gone to her secret bower, a room that was so securely guarded by magic that no one else dared enter it. The weary stag-hounds lay on the floor of the hall and dreamed of the chase, while round about loitered twenty-nine knights, each of whom was served by a squire and a yeoman. Ten of them were always clad in complete armor, both by day and by night. They lay down to sleep with their corslets laced, their pillows being their shields. They carved at table with their mail-gloved hands and drank their wine through the bars of their helmets. Ten squires and ten yeomen, also dressed in mail, were always ready, and in the stables thirty fast horses were always bridled and saddled; a hundred more moved freely in their stalls. Always men were on the alert to hear the baying of the bloodhounds and the braying of the war-horns. They watched to see the red cross of St. George of

England sweep across the English-Scottish border. They stood guard lest the Scroops, the Howards, or the Percies might threaten the castle with forces from Warkworth, Naworth, or Carlisle. They do all these warlike acts because such is the custom of Branksome Hall.

> Why do these steeds stand ready dight?
> Why watch these warriors armed by night?
> They watch to hear the bloodhound baying;
> They watch to hear the war-horn braying;
> To see Saint George's red cross streaming,
> To see the midnight beacons gleaming;
> They watch against Southern force and guile,
>   Lest Scroop or Howard or Percy's powers
>   Threaten Branksome's lordly towers,
> From Warkworth or Naworth or merry Carlisle.

Such is the custom of Branksome Hall.

Such sweet compulsion doth in music lie

Source: ARCADES (Line 68)
Author: John Milton (1608–1674)
First published: 1645
Type of work: Masque

Context: Arcades was presented as part of an entertainment in honor of the Countess Dowager of Derby at Harefield, the roles being taken by members of her family and other scions of nobility. The "Arcades" are natives of Arcady, or Arcadia, beloved of poets. After some opening stanzas in praise of the countess, the Genius of the Wood, acted by the musician Henry Lawes, appears to tell how he cares for the trees and plants in his domain. At dawn he visits every sprout to see that it is safe and well, but during the night he gives his attention to the music of the spheres. He explains that upon each of the crystalline spheres of the eight planets and the fixed stars there sits a celestial siren who sings to the three Fates, who determine men's destinies and turn the adamant spindle, or axle, that runs through all of the crystalline spheres. The siren on each sphere sings only one note, but the combination of their notes makes the music of the spheres, heavenly music that is inaudible to mortal ears. Such music, however, is fittest to celebrate the manifold virtues of the countess. The passage derives from Plato's Vision of Er and is an explanation of the divine harmony that organizes and governs the universe. It is interesting to notice that it is Ptolemaic rather than Copernican cosmology.

> . . . when drowsiness
> Hath locked up mortal sense, then listen I

1018

To the celestial Sirens' harmony,
That sit upon the nine enfolded spheres
And sing to those that hold the vital shears
And turn the adamantine spindle round,
On which the fate of gods and men is wound.
Such sweet compulsion doth in music lie,
To lull the daughters of necessity,
And keep unsteady nature to her law,
And the low world in measured motion draw
After the heavenly tune, which none can hear
Of human mold with gross unpurgèd ear.

Suffrance is the badge of all our tribe

Source: THE MERCHANT OF VENICE (Act I, sc. iii, l. 111)
Author: William Shakespeare (1564–1616)
First published: 1600
Type of work: Dramatic comedy

Context: To further his quest for the hand of the fair Portia, Bassanio, a young gentleman of Venice, seeks a loan from his friend Antonio, a merchant in Venice. Since Antonio cannot advance the money to Bassanio until his ships come to port, Shylock, a rich Jew, is approached for a temporary loan. Though Shylock hates and is hated by the Gentiles, he agrees to lend Bassanio three thousand ducats with Antonio standing bond. Pointing out the irony of the request for a loan by one who has badly mistreated him at the Rialto, the Venetian exchange, Shylock says:

Signior Antonio, many a time and oft
In the Rialto you have rated me
About my moneys and my usances.
Still have I borne it with a patient shrug,
For **sufferance is the badge of all our tribe.**
You call me misbeliever, cut-throat dog,
And spit upon my Jewish gaberdine,
And all for use of that which is mine own.

The sum of earthly bliss

Source: PARADISE LOST (Book VIII, l. 522)
Author: John Milton (1608–1674)
First published: 1667
Type of work: Epic poem

Context: After Raphael had described the creation of the world and had explained the workings of the cosmos, Adam tells of his own discovery of himself as a living being. God gives everything to him but the one tree of the knowledge of good and evil, which he is to avoid at all hazards. Adam indicates his gratitude to God for His manifold gifts but says that he, being alone, cannot fully appreciate everything; what he needs is an equal with whom to share his bliss. God, pleased with him for his desire and his recognition that he cannot find equality among the lower animals, puts him to sleep and removes a rib, which he transforms into a woman. It is noteworthy that here Milton totally disregards the creation of man and woman by fiat, as given in Genesis 1: 27, since it was Milton's purpose to have Eve a second-ary creation not equal in all respects to Adam. The woman created from Adam's rib was so lovely and fair that all the rest of creation seemed mean in comparison with her: Milton is here preparing for the surge of Adam's passion that will overrule his intelligence and lead to his fall. Adam recognizes that the woman is bone of his bone and flesh of his flesh: this conception that two married people were physically one was to have profound and far-reaching influence—on Henry VIII, for instance. Adam led this new creation to the nuptial bower, and all heaven and the happy constellations shed their selectest influences.

> The earth
> Gave sign of gratulation, and each hill;
> Joyous the birds; fresh gales and gentle airs
> Whispered it to the woods, and from their wings
> Flung rose, flung odors from the spicy shrub,
> Disporting, till the amorous bird of night
> Sung spousal, and bid haste the evening star
> On his hill top, to light the bridal lamp.
> Thus have I told thee all my state, and brought
> My story to **the sum of earthly bliss**
> Which I enjoy, and must confess to find
> In all things else delight indeed, but such
> As used or not, works in the mind no change,
> Nor vehement desire, these delicacies
> I mean of taste, sight, smell, herbs, fruits, and flowers,
> Walks, and the melody of birds; . . .

Superstition is the religion of feeble minds

Source: REFLECTIONS ON THE REVOLUTION IN FRANCE
Author: Edmund Burke (1729–1797)
First published: 1790
Type of work: Political treatise

Context: Edmund Burke detested what he saw happening in France during the French Revolution, as his essay amply shows. He was not, however conservative his position, a man to forego improvement in society just because improvement involves change, but what he saw as the appropriate way to effect betterment was to work through existing cultural institutions, not to destroy them. One reason he gives for using existing institutions is that they afford the great leader additional power for improvement, that he can use them as a mechanism, a pry, which will help him accomplish good. Burke comments, ". . . institutions are the products of enthusiasm; they are the instruments of wisdom." But he recognizes that institutions have some dangers, too. He believes they "savour of superstition in their very principle." And Burke, as he does consistently in his writings, expresses a fear of superstition; he wants to make a sharp distinction between it and religion. He says that in its excesses superstition becomes a very great evil, and then he goes on to explain how superstition differs from true religion:

. . . **Superstition is the religion of feeble minds;** and they must be tolerated in an intermixture of it, in some trifling or some enthusiastic shape or other, else you will deprive weak minds of a resource found necessary to the strongest. The body of all true religion consists, to be sure, in obedience to the will of the Sovereign of the world; in a confidence in his declarations; and in imitation of his perfections. The rest is our own. It may be prejudicial to the great end; it may be auxiliary. Wise men, who as such are not *admirers* (not admirers at least of the *Munera Terrae*), are not violently attached to those things, nor do they violently hate them. Wisdom is not the most severe corrector of folly. They are the rival follies, which mutually wage so unrelenting a war; . . .

The supreme good

Source: DE OFFICIIS ("Concerning Duty," Book I, division ii, l. 5)
Author: Marcus Tullius Cicero (106–43 B.C.)
First transcribed: c. 43 B.C.
Type of work: Moral treatise

Context: After a career as a defense lawyer for the victims of political injustice, with his defense of the poet Archias as a high point, and his few appearances as prosecutor, especially against Cataline for conspiracy, Cicero ended his life in writing treatises on philosophy, government, old age, friendship, and the like. "De Officiis," a manual of ethics, remains the most readable and most popular. It was written close to the end of his life, probably for his son studying in Athens. Cicero also wrote letters which, edited and published after his death by his secretary Tiro, mark him for brilliance of style as one of the world's great letter writers. In his philosophical thought, Cicero tried to reconcile imperialism with liberty, progress with prosperity, intellectual culture with morality, and social and political discipline with wealth and luxury. Following the assassination of

Julius Caesar and the bitterness of civil war, he saw certain disaster for Rome ahead. Thus he penned this manual of ethics, avowedly based on the work of Panaetius, a Greek Stoic philosopher of the second century B.C., and on the memorandum of another Stoic of a century later, Athenodorus. The Stoics, so-called because they originally gathered at the Painted Porch (Stoa) in Athens to listen to lectures by the philosopher Zeno, believed in living "consistently with Nature." As a Stoic, Cicero's avowal of a universal force that pervades all things and becomes the reason and the soul in the animate creation, gave him a basic identity with Christianity. The ethical creed of the Stoics accepted virtue as life's "summum bonum," which can be translated as "supreme good," or "highest good."

". . . who would presume to call himself a philosopher, if he did not inculcate any lessons of duty? But there are some schools that distort all notions of duty by the theories they propose touching **the supreme good** and the supreme evil. For he who posits the supreme good as having no connection with virtue and measures it not by a moral standard but by his own interests—if he should be consistent and not rather at times over-ruled by his better nature, he could value neither friendship nor justice nor generosity; and brave he surely cannot possibly be that counts pain the supreme evil, nor temperate he that holds pleasure to be the supreme good."

Suspend your mad career

Source: TABLE TALK (Line 435)
Author: William Cowper (1731–1800)
First published: 1782
Type of work: Essay in verse

Context: After discussing kings, good and bad, with special reference to George III of England, the two who are conversing over the breakfast table, indicated only as A. and B., talk about the liberty-loving qualities of an Englishman, whom they name Nature's "favorite man of all mankind." A typical Frenchman cannot compare with him. But those who love liberty can sometimes carry this love to excess through the violence of their attempts to achieve it. This idea brings a discussion of the need for a magistrate who can keep this love of liberty under control, and so, naturally, they pause for a panegyric of the late William Pitt, Earl of Chatham, who had died in 1778. They wonder who will take his place in controlling England. When A. mentions an essay by the Reverend John Brown (1715–1766) on *An Estimate of the Manners and Principles of the Times* (1757), B. brings into the conversation a country, "One that I could name" (prob-

1022

ably France on the eve of its revolution), and goes on to describe its present godless condition and warn of what will follow.

B. When profanation of the sacred cause
In all its parts, times, ministry, and laws,
Bespeaks a land, once Christian, fallen and lost
In all that wars against that title most;
What follows next let cities of great name
And regions long since desolate proclaim:
Nineveh, Babylon, and ancient Rome
Speak to the present times and times to come;
They cry aloud in every careless ear,
"Stop, while ye may, **suspend your mad career!**
O learn from our example and our fate,
Learn wisdom and repentance ere too late!"

Sweep on you fat and greasy citizens

Source: AS YOU LIKE IT (Act II, sc. i, l. 55)
Author: William Shakespeare (1564–1616)
First published: 1623
Type of work: Dramatic comedy

Context: An exiled ruler, Duke Senior, lives out his banishment in the pleasant Forest of Arden, an existence he and his followers delight in as simple, natural, and wholesome. "Hath not old custom made this life more sweet/ Than that of painted pomp?" asks the Duke. There is, however, one dissenter among his followers—the melancholy Jaques, who bemoans the slaying of deer for food and is otherwise unhappy. Another of the Duke's followers describes Jaques' reaction to the sight of a wounded stag weeping into a stream and being ignored by a passing herd, a sight that permits Jaques to moralize on human complacency:

FIRST LORD

. . .

                    Anon a careless herd,
Full of the pasture, jumps along by him, [the wounded deer]
And never stays to greet him. Ay, quoth Jaques,
Sweep on you fat and greasy citizens,
'Tis just the fashion; wherefore do you look
Upon that poor and broken bankrupt there?
Thus most invectively he pierceth through
The body of the country, city, court,
Yea, and of this our life, swearing that we
Are mere usurpers, tyrants, and what's worse,
To fright the animals, and to kill them up
In their assigned and native dwelling-place.

1023

Sweet are the slumbers of the virtuous man!

Source: CATO (Act V, sc. iv, 1. 27)
Author: Joseph Addison (1672–1719)
First published: 1713
Type of work: Dramatic tragedy

Context: Addison's *Cato,* produced during a period of political anxiety in Britain, ironically received the applause of both Whig and Tory, each party assuming that the playwright identified his party with the party led by the blameless Cato, heroic defender of liberty during the Roman civil war. As the play ends, the defeated Cato arranges for the evacu- ation of the survivors of his party from the sword of Caesar, then falls upon his own sword and dies. In the last moments before his suicide, Cato rests in his bedchamber, watched over by Lucius, a senator and friend. Lucius, going from the bedside to the next room where Cato's son and daughter wait, says to Marcia, the daughter:

LUCIUS

Sweet are the slumbers of the virtuous man!
O Marcia, I have seen thy godlike father:
Some pow'r invisible supports his soul,
And bears it up in all its wonted greatness.
A kind refreshing sleep is fall'n upon him.
I saw him stretched at ease, his fancy lost
In pleasing dreams; as I drew near his couch,
He smiled, and cried, "Caesar, thou can'st not hurt me."

Sweet bells jangled out of tune

Source: HAMLET (Act III, sc. i, 1. 166)
Author: William Shakespeare (1564–1616)
First published: 1603
Type of work: Dramatic tragedy

Context: Hamlet, Prince of Denmark, is in profound melancholia over the sudden death of his father, King Hamlet, and the hasty marriage of his mother to Claudius, brother of the late king and usurper of the crown. In an interview with his father's ghost, the prince learns that the king's death was not a natural one, but that he was murdered by Claudius. The ghost makes Hamlet swear to avenge this "foul and most unnatural murder." In order to protect himself against suspicion while planning his revenge, Hamlet feigns madness. Claudius suspects that the madness is not genuine but has no proof. Polonius, Lord Chamberlain, is convinced that the prince's insanity is real and is caused by unrequited love for his daughter, Ophelia, to whom Hamlet has paid court. In order to prove his

1024

point, he suggests that he and Claudius, hidden behind a tapestry, spy on an interview between the two lovers. Hamlet, knowing that he and Ophelia are being overheard and furious with her for lying to him by saying that her father is at home, treats her brutally; so that when he has left the stage, the bewildered young girl, who believes that he is really mad, gives in a soliloquy a description of the prince as he was before the death of his father.

OPHELIA

O what a noble mind is here o'erthrown!
The courtier's, soldier's, scholar's, eye, tongue, sword,
Th' expectancy and rose of the fair state,
The glass of fashion, and the mould of form,
Th' observed of all observers, quite, quite down,
And I of ladies most deject and wretched,
That sucked the honey of his musicked vows,
Now see that noble and most sovereign reason,
Like **sweet bells jangled, out of tune** and harsh;
That unmatched form and feature of blown youth
Blasted with ecstasy. O woe is me
T' have seen what I have seen, see what I see.

Sweet childish days

Source: TO A BUTTERFLY: I'VE WATCHED YOU NOW (Line 18)
Author: William Wordsworth (1770–1850)
First published: 1807
Type of work: Lyric poem

Context: The poet addresses a butterfly which has sat for half an hour on a yellow flower. He does not know whether it sleeps or feeds, but it has been as motionless as a frozen sea. But joy awaits it when the breeze finds it, and it returns to its usual activity. He says that the garden is theirs; the trees are his and the flowers are his sister's, but the butterfly is always welcome to use the place as a sanctuary and rest its wings. It should come often, as no wrong will be done to it. The poet and his sister will converse of sunshine and song, and of summer days when they were young, the sweet childish days that were as long as twenty days now are.

This plot of orchard-ground is ours;
My trees they are, my Sister's flowers;
Here rest your wings when they are weary;
Here lodge as in a sanctuary!
Come often to us, fear no wrong;
Sit near us on the bough!
We'll talk of sunshine and of song,
And summer days, when we were young;

1025

Sweet childish days, that were as long
As twenty days are now.

The sweet post-prandial cigar

Source: DE BERNY
Author: Robert Williams Buchanan (1841–1901)
First published: 1866
Type of work: Poem

Context: Robert Buchanan is more often mentioned as the man whose slanders killed D. G. Rossetti than as a minor poet of little talent. While his poems are frequently monotonous, weak in meters and rhymes, and shallow in conception, he occasionally strikes a good note. "De Berny" is one such high spot. The poem is a character study, obviously influenced by Robert Browning's dramatic monologues, of one who to all outward appearances is a failure; however, Buchanan develops the character to show that even this penniless *émigré* had redeeming traits that set him apart and earned for him respect as a man, for De Berny was intensely interested in the welfare of others. His last act was to give a crumpled five-pound note to the Italian Garibaldi as a contribution to the liberty of man.

Did he not walk as if he walk'd on thrones,
With smiles of vacant patronage for all?
And who could guess he had not breakfasted,
Had little chance of dining, since his purse
Held just the wherewithal to buy a loaf—
Change from the shilling spent in purchasing
The sweet post-prandial cigar!

Sweet reasonableness

Source: LITERATURE AND DOGMA (Chapter XII, section 2)
Author: Matthew Arnold (1822–1888)
First published: 1873
Type of work: Religious and literary essay

Context: In the poetry of the early part of his life, Arnold gave expression to the various forces of the Victorian era which tended to frustrate him and dislocate him spiritually. Turning to prose in the latter half of his life, he produced a series of essays with a remarkably consistent and persistent perspective. If, he said, the old religion based on faith and in its forms and conventions restrictive to a world which man had outgrown was no longer operative as the foundation for human civilization, then something must replace it. This substitute was culture—"the best that has been said and thought in the world." Through education which would inculcate into the new generations the inherent human values as they have been articulated in the great aesthetic creations of the past, man could be taught to respect and to sanctify the traditions of his civilization which have been inspired and crystallized under the impetus of religious worship. More precisely, such an education would provide the power, through reading, to estimate the proportion and relation in what is read. The result would be neither a destruction of the Jewish Messiah or the Christian Jesus, but an abstraction of the inherent values which such deities possess apart from the dogma and institutions which through the centuries have encrusted them in human error:

> But there remains the question: what righteousness really is. The method and secret and **sweet reasonableness** of Jesus. But the world does not see this; for it puts, as righteousness, something else first and this second. So that here, too, as to seeing what righteousness really is, the world now is much in the same position in which the Jews, when Jesus Christ came, were. It is often said: if Jesus Christ came now, his religion would be rejected. And this is only another way of saying that the world now, as the Jewish people formerly, has something which thwarts and confuses its perception of what righteousness really is. It is so; and the thwarting cause is the same now as then:—the dogmatic system current, the so-called orthodox theology. . . .

Sweet seventeen

Source: THE BROOK (Line 112)
Author: Alfred, Lord Tennyson (1809–1892)
First published: 1855
Type of work: Lyric poem

Context: Lawrence Aylmer, after a twenty-year absence, revisits a farm he once knew, and remembers a poem that his beloved but now-dead brother Edmund wrote about the brook which flows by the farm. Four times Lawrence interrupts his musing on the past to recall the progressive stanzas of the poem in which Edmund followed the course of the brook from its source to where it joined "the brimming river." Each group of stanzas ends with the refrain "For men may come and men may go,/ But I go on forever." Looking at the farm "where brook and river meet," Lawrence hears in memory the endless talk of Old Philip, the farmer, who "chatter'd more than brook or bird." Philip's only child, "darling Katie Willows," had asked a favor of Lawrence the week before he "parted with poor Edmund," Lawrence to go to service in India and Edmund to death in Florence. A difference had arisen between Katie and James Willows, "her far-off cousin and betrothed," whose "flickering jealousies" had angered her. But each time James had returned so that he and Katie could patch up their quarrel, garrulous Philip talked so much that James left, angry with both Katie and her father. Would Lawrence be a listener to the old man's chatter while Katie and James talked things over? Now, twenty years later, remembering in detail the flood of Philip's words, Lawrence humorously sighs, "O Katie, what I suffered for your sake!" But Katie's ruse succeeded. While Lawrence walked about the farm and listened until "the falling sun," Katie and James were reconciled. They married and moved to Australia but, unknown to Lawrence, they returned to England and now live on Philip's farm. As the poem ends Lawrence sees a young Katie, the image of her mother at "sweet seventeen," who invites him to talk over the old days with the Katie he once knew. The passage containing the famous phrase appears in the poem when Lawrence recalls his asking if James ever came to try to settle his quarrel with Katie, and she answered that he came every day:

". . . ever longing to explain,
But evermore her father came across
With some long-winded tale, and broke him short;
And James departed vext with him and her."
How could I help her? "Would I—was it wrong?"
(Claspt hands and that petitionary grace
Of **sweet seventeen** subdued me ere she spoke)
"O would I take her father for one hour,
For one half-hour, and let him talk to me!"

Sweetest melodies are those that are by distance made more sweet

Source: PERSONAL TALK (Sonnet 2)
Author: William Wordsworth (1770–1850)
First published: 1807
Type of work: Sonnet

Context: Wordsworth was, as he openly admitted, a recluse; after he had thrown himself into human affairs at the beginning of the French Revolution and had learned from bitter experience that men use high-sounding words to conceal their selfishness and cruelty, he regained his mental health by returning to the scenes of his childhood. This return to nature reinforced the memories he had of a time before he became a passionate liberal, eager to advance the goals of rational enlightenment; it re-established the inner peace such as a child surrounded by a pleasant environment might possess. Unwilling to face again the misery that had tormented him during the time that he wandered about in complete disillusionment, he retired to Grasmere with his sister and seldom entertained anyone except his closest friends. In this series of four sonnets, he defends his voluntary retirement by saying that as a recluse he is not touched by the pretense of society and that in such solitude he is able to develop his powers of imagination. Believing that "poetry is the spontaneous overflow of powerful feelings," he had little patience with people who insisted that poetry arose from immediate sensations; in fact, he thought, as he states in this quotation, that the imagination and memory alone can bring happiness, and release a man from present conflicts in order that he may write great poetry.

Children are blest, and powerful; their world lies
More justly balanced, partly at their feet,
And part far from them: **sweetest melodies**
Are those that are by distance made more sweet;
Whose mind is but the mind of his own eyes,
He is a Slave; the meanest we can meet!

Sweetest Shakespeare, Fancy's child

Source: L'ALLEGRO (Lines 134–135)
Author: John Milton (1698–1674)
First published: 1645
Type of work: Lyric poem

Context: Masterful English poet John Milton is noted for his impressive *Paradise Lost,* his sonnets, as well as many other poems, including the companion poems, *L'Allegro* and *Il Penseroso.* In *L'Allegro,* the poet dismisses Melancholy and calls upon Mirth to accompany him through the day. Noting the sights and sounds of dawn, the activities of the day, and observing the panorama of the landscape, the poet calls to mind the pleasures of evening next—the drinking of brown ale, the recounting of shepherds' tales with fairies and elves, the sweet sounds of music, and the merriment of the stage with plays of scholarly Ben Jonson and fanciful William Shakespeare:

Then to the well-trod stage anon,
If Jonson's learn'd sock be on,
Or **sweetest Shakespeare, Fancy's child,**
Warble his native wood-notes wild.

Sword of common sense

Source: ODE TO THE COMIC SPIRIT (Line 1)
Author: George Meredith (1828–1909)
First published: 1892
Type of work: Philosophic poem

1029

Context: Because of the turmoil in nineteenth century thought—the conflict of science and religion, the clash of contrasting values, the general crisis of rapid industrialization—men often found themselves in the situation of having no arguments against the critics who threatened their very existences. One of the remarkable features of Victorian England was its ability to maintain political and social stability while the rest of Europe was torn by revolutions and civil wars. Asking himself why his country should have such stability, George Meredith came to understand the strong roles that ridicule and common sense played in England. As he describes it in this poem, common sense—the consensus of middle-class opinion—overcomes the outlandish by laughing at the false pretenses of change; in fact, the comic spirit, so important in England at that time, was the strength that made the good and just prevail.

> Sword of Common Sense!—
> Our surest gift: the sacred chain
> Of man to man: firm earth for trust
> In structures vowed to permanence:—
> Thou guardian issue of the harvest brain!

Syllables govern the world

Source: TABLE-TALK ("Power, State")
Author: John Selden (1584–1654)
First published: 1689
Type of work: Recorded conversation

Context: Selden was a very learned scholar and jurist of the first half of the seventeenth century. Among his friends he numbered such literary lights as Ben Jonson and William Shakespeare, although that poetry of his which has come down to us is not first class. By far the largest part of his literary remains is concerned with the law; in fact, his treatise on tithing earned him the enmity of the narrow-minded and captious James I. He was arrested and imprisoned briefly for having the courage to stand by his convictions. Selden's *Table-Talk* consists of bits of his conversation taken down by his secretary, the Reverend Richard Milward, and arranged by subject matter. In this particular section are collected a number of Selden's comments concerning the power of the state and its officials:

1. There is no streching of Power. 'Tis a good rule, Eat within your Stomach, act within your Commission.
2. They that govern most make least noise. You see when they row in a Barge, they that do drudgery-work, slash, and puff, and sweat; but he that governs, sits quietly at the Stern, and scarce is seen to stir.

1030

3. **Syllables govern the world.**

4. *All power is of God,* means no more than *Fides est servanda.* When St. *Paul* said this, the People had made *Nero* Emperor. They agree, he to command, they to obey. . . .

5. Christ himself was a great observer of the Civil power, and did many things only justifiable, because the State required it, which were things merely Temporary, for the time that State stood. . . .

Take care of the minutes; for hours will take care of themselves

Source: LETTERS TO HIS SON (Letter 19)
Author: Philip Dormer Stanhope, Lord Chesterfield (1694–1773)
First published: 1774
Type of work: Personal letter

Context: The letters of Lord Chesterfield to his son were never meant for publication. As he told the boy, "My father was neither desirous nor able to advise me." So he wrote many letters of counsel in order that his son should never make that reproach against him. He was well fitted to give advice. He made the tour of Europe after graduation without the insular viewpoint that prevented so many of his countrymen from gaining its advantages. He could preach tolerance and understanding. He could warn against gambling from bitter personal experience, and as one who learned manners in Paris and courtly behaviour at the court of George II, he could write about "The Graces." In 1733, Philip Stanhope had married a charming woman generally believed to be an illegitimate daughter of George I. But it was to an illegitimate son Philip, son of Madame de Bouchet, whom Chesterfield knew while serving as British Ambassador at the Hague, that these letters were written. Born in 1732, young Philip was educated at Westminster School.

The first twenty-six letters were written in French. Not until the twenty-seventh, dated July 8, 1739, did Lord Chesterfield begin writing in English the letters that he would continue to write for thirty years. Unfortunately they accomplished little in making his son a success. Young Philip was not especially attractive, and his birth was against him. Because of these factors, and because his father was usually at odds with the government in power, the young man found it hard to get diplomatic appointments. He died a failure in 1768, five years before his disappointed father. Letter 19, dated London, November 6, 1747, following a period during which he had not heard from his son, begins with wonder whether the boy is so involved in abstract speculations as to have forgotten the common and necessary duties of life, or is he perhaps sitting by the fire doing nothing, or wasting his time looking out the window. Speaking of wasting time, Chesterfield quotes "a very covetuous, sordid fellow," actually William Lowndes (1652–1724), British Secretary of the Treasury, about the value of saving money. He writes:

> . . . I knew once, a very covetuous, sordid fellow, who used frequently to say, "Take care of the pence; for the pounds will take care of themselves." This was a just and sensible reflection in a miser. I recommend to you to **take care of the minutes; for hours will take care of themselves.** I am very sure, that many people lose two or three hours every day, by not taking care of the minutes. Never think any portion of time whatsoever too short to be employed; something or other may always be done in it.

Take, O take, those lips away

Source: MEASURE FOR MEASURE (Act IV, sc. i, l. 1)
Author: William Shakespeare (1564–1616)
First published: 1623
Type of work: Tragi-comedy

Context: When the Duke of Vienna wishes to enforce the laws of his city, he appoints the stern Angelo and then removes himself from the place of responsibility. The first to fall to the new government is Claudio, who has got a child on his betrothed. Condemned to death, he pleads with his sister, Isabella, for help. The seemingly cold Angelo, on seeing the beautiful Isabella, is so taken with her that he promises Claudio's life for her virtue. When the duke, disguised as Friar Lodowick, learns of the situation, he sets about to free Claudio by involving Angelo, who had once refused to marry his betrothed, Mariana, which betrothal amounted to marriage. Planning to substitute Mariana for Isabella in a tryst with Angelo, the duke approaches the unhappy Mariana with the plot. He finds her listening to a page singing of blighted love.

PAGE [*sings.*]
Take, o take those lips away,
> *That so sweetly were forsworn,*
> *And those eyes, the break of day,*
> *Lights that do mislead the morn;*
> *But my kisses bring again, bring again;*
> *Seals of love, but sealed in vain, sealed in vain.*

Take up thy bed, and walk

Source: JOHN 5:8
Author: Unknown (traditionally John the Apostle)
First transcribed: By 130
Type of work: Gospel

1032

Context: John's Gospel does not conform to the other three Gospels in many respects and for this reason some have doubted its historical accuracy, believing it to be a symbolic work for doctrinal and devotional purposes rather than a record of events. Others believe, however, that one of John's purposes was to record episodes in the ministry of Christ which are not included in the first three Gospels. It is true that he provides more commentary and interpretation than the others do. The authorship of this Gospel is uncertain; but scholarly opinion is that the writer, if not John the Apostle, is one John the Elder—who had apparently some close personal connection with him. If John's testimony is added to that of the other Gospels, it becomes likely that Jesus made numerous trips to Jerusalem during the period of His ministry, which may have lasted three years. These trips were made at times of festival, when the city was crowded and He could preach to large audiences; and His arguments with the Pharisees in the Temple were frequent enough for them to consider Him a real threat to the religio-political establishment of the time. This fear would have been reinforced by the ease with which He confounded their arguments and turned their accusations of lawbreaking against them, the unanswerable refutations of their arguments, and the large crowds which gathered to hear Him. If it is accepted that John's testimony is largely supplementary, then the Pharisees' fanatical determination to kill Jesus becomes more plausible. John describes one of these episodes in Chapter 5; Jesus heals a helpless invalid, infuriating the Pharisees. He later delivers an inspired sermon which effectively confounds all their accusations. John's description of the invalid and his cure carries an unusually strong effect of realism and immediacy, as though he had seen it occur:

> After this there was a feast of the Jews; and Jesus went up to Jerusalem.
>
> Now there is at Jerusalem by the sheep market a pool, which is called in the Hebrew tongue Bethesda, having five porches.
>
> In these lay a great multitude of impotent folk, of blind, halt, withered, waiting for the moving of the water.
>
> For an angel went down at a certain season into the pool, and troubled the water: whosoever then first after the troubling of the water stepped in was made whole of whatsoever disease he had.
>
> And a certain man was there, which had an infirmity thirty and eight years.
>
> When Jesus saw him lie, and knew that he had been now a long time in that case, he saith unto him, Wilt thou be made whole?
>
> The impotent man answered him, Sir, I have no man, when the water is troubled, to put me into the pool: but while I am coming, another steppeth down before me.
>
> Jesus saith unto him, Rise, **take up thy bed, and walk.**
>
> And immediately the man was made whole, and took up his bed, and walked: and on the same day was the sabbath.

The Jews therefore said unto him that was cured, It is the sabbath day: it is not lawful for thee to carry thy bed.

He answered them, He that made me whole, the same said unto me, **Take up thy bed, and walk.**

Tale of a tub

Source: THE WHITE DEVIL (Act II, sc. i, l. 92)
Author: John Webster (1580?–1625?)
First published: 1612
Type of work: Dramatic tragedy

Context: Paulo Giordano Ursini, Duke of Brachiano, becomes infatuated with Vittoria Corombona, wife of Camillo, a poor stick of a man. Aided by Flamineo, his secretary and Vittoria's brother, the duke pursues Vittoria with success. The duchess, incensed at her husband's conduct in pursuing other women in a public manner, appeals to her brother, Francisco de Medicis, the Duke of Florence. Accompanied by Cardinal Monticelso, Francisco de Medicis calls on Duke Brachiano to upbraid him for his scandalous conduct. At the interview Monticelso speaks first to Brachiano about his public pursuit of Vittoria, but to no avail. Then Francisco de Medicis argues for his sister. He also points out that Brachiano is neglecting his political duties, as well as his marital responsibilities. He complains that he sent to Brachiano for a conference about dealing with the depredations of pirates and received no answer, that he had to come in person, and even then had difficulty in meeting with Brachiano, who claimed to be too busy:

FRANCISCO DE MEDICIS
We send unto the duke for conference
'Bout levies 'gainst the pirates; my lord duke
Is not at home: we come ourself in person;
Still my lord duke is busied. But we fear,
When Tiber to each prowling passenger
Discovers flocks of wild ducks; then, my lord,
'Bout moulting time I mean, we shall be certain
To find you sure enough, and speak with you.

BRACHIANO
Ha!

FRANCISCO DE MEDICIS
A mere **tale of a tub,** my words are idle;
But to express the sonnet by natural reason,—
When stags grow melancholic, you'll find the season.

1034

A tale which holdeth children from play

Source: DEFENCE OF POESIE
Author: Sir Philip Sidney (1554–1586)
First published: 1595
Type of work: Essay

Context: Stephen Gosson came to London to be a playwright, but failing at his chosen profession, he turned critic and attacked the popular drama with great vehemence and bombast in *The School of Abuse* (1579), dedicated with audacity but without permission to Sir Philip Sidney. Poetry and drama had their defenders, and the debate over their merits continued for years; however, Sidney responded with this essay published after his death. He begins by pointing to the antiquity of poetry, the prestige it has been accorded in every age, and its neoclassical types, or genres. His most important discussion is his analysis of the creative imagination. The poet, he says, is a finer influence than the historian, the philosopher, or the mathematician because he is more creative; he can transcend nature, rather than merely analyze her, and present an ideal world:

Now therin of all sciences (I speak still of humane, and according to the humane conceit) is our poet the monarch. For he doth not only shew the way, but giveth so sweet a prospect into the way as will entice any man to enter into it. Nay, he doth, as if your journey should lie through a fair vineyard, at the very first give you a cluster of grapes, that, full of that taste, you may long to pass further. He beginneth not with obscure definitions, which must blur the margent with interpretations, and load the memory with doubtfulness; but he cometh to you with words set in delightful proportion; . . . and with a tale forsooth he cometh unto you, with **a tale which holdeth children from play** and old men from the chimney corner. And, pretending no more, doth intend the winning of the mind from wickedness to virtue: even as the child is often brought to take most wholesome things by hiding them in such other as have a pleasant taste. . . . So is it in men (most of which are childish in the best things, till they be cradled in their graves): glad they will be to hear the tales of Hercules, Achilles, Cyrus, Aeneas; and, hearing them, must needs hear the right description of wisdom, valor, and justice; which, if they had been barely, that is to say philosophically, set out, they would swear they be brought to school again. . . .

Talk of graves, of worms, and epitaphs

Source: KING RICHARD THE SECOND (Act III, sc. ii, l. 145)
Author: William Shakespeare (1564–1616)
First published: 1597
Type of work: Historical drama

Context: King Richard, who has been engaged in the Irish wars, returns to England to find that his Welsh army has been dispersed on a rumor of his death, that his exiled cousin Bolingbroke has returned to claim his inheritance seized by Richard upon the death of John of Gaunt, uncle of the king and father of Bolingbroke, and that the companions of Richard, Bushy, Green, and the Earl of Wiltshire, in whose charge he left the Castle of Bristol, have been executed. Aumerle, cousin of Richard and his companion on the Irish mission, asks the messenger about the forces led by the Duke of York (father of Aumerle and uncle of the king), who has been left in charge of the affairs of state in Richard's absence, but the downcast monarch asserts:

> RICHARD
> No matter where, of comfort no man speak.
> Let's **talk of graves, of worms, and epitaphs,**
> Make dust our paper, and with rainy eyes,
> Write sorrow on the bosom of the earth.
> Let's choose executors and talk of wills.
> And yet not so, for what can we bequeath,
> Save our deposed bodies to the ground?
> Our lands, our lives, and all are Bolingbroke's,
> And nothing can we call our own, but death;
> And that small model of the barren earth,
> Which serves as paste, and cover to our bones.
> . . .

Tall oaks from little acorns grow

Source: LINES WRITTEN FOR A SCHOOL DECLAMATION
Author: David Everett (1770–1813)
First published: c. 1790
Type of work: Didactic poem

Context: Everett was at various times a lawyer, a journalist, and a school teacher. Following his undergraduate education at Dartmouth he taught grammar school for several years at New Ipswich, N. H. Leaving the teaching profession he began the study of law, which he practised for some time. He also was a reporter for the Boston *Gazette* and, later, for the *Farmer's Museum,* to which he contributed a number of *Poor Richard*

1036

type of articles. His literary output included a five-act drama in blank verse and a two-act play concerned with slavery. These *Lines,* also known as "The Boy Reciter," were written during his teaching years for a seven-year-old pupil to deliver at a recitation period:

> You'd scarce expect one of my age
> To speak in public on the stage,
> And if I chance to fall below
> Demosthenes or Cicero,
> Don't view me with a critic's eye,
> But pass my imperfections by.
> Large streams from little fountains flow,
> **Tall oaks from little acorns grow;**
> And though now I am small and young,
> Of judgment weak and feeble tongue,
> Yet all great, learned men, like me
> Once learned to read their ABC.
> But why may not Columbia's soil
> Rear men as great as Britain's Isle,
> Exceed what Greece and Rome have done
> Or any land beneath the sun?
>
> . . .

Tamburlaine, the Scourge of God, must die

Source: TAMBURLAINE THE GREAT (Part II, Act V, sc. iii, l. 4641)
Author: Christopher Marlowe (1564–1593)
First published: 1590
Type of work: Dramatic tragedy

Context: Tamburlaine rose from being an unknown Scythian shepherd, by devastating war and unbridled cruelty, to become ruler of the East. His good fortune seems boundless for many years, as victory follows victory. But every life has its sorrows and its end. Zenocrate, daughter of the Sultan of Egypt, who is Tamburlaine's deeply beloved queen, dies, leaving the conqueror so unconsolable in his grief that he causes her body to be placed in a golden coffin, to remain unburied, vowing she should not receive burial before him. Then one of his three sons by Zeno-crate, Calyphas, refuses to go into a battle. In vengeance the father stabs him. Victorious over the Turks, Tamburlaine seems irresistible in his power. But illness strikes the great conqueror. He calls his remaining two sons to his bedside and traces his conquests on a map for them. Knowing he must die, Tamburlaine places his crown on the head of Amyras, as his heir. Then he causes the hearse laden with Zenocrate's body to be brought, to be by him in his dying hour. He bids Amyras rule strongly and well, lest the lands and peoples subdued by the father slip from the son's grasp. Tamburlaine then bids farewell to Amyras, Celebinus, and the courtiers standing about:

TAMBURLAINE

Farewell my boys, my dearest friends, farewell,
My body feels, my soul doth weep to see
Your sweet desires depriv'd my company,
For **Tamburlaine, the Scourge of God, must die.**

Taught the doubtful battle where to rage

Source: THE CAMPAIGN (Line 286)
Author: Joseph Addison (1672–1719)
First published: 1705
Type of work: Patriotic poem

Context: The occasion of this poem was the great victory won for the British and their allies at the Battle of Blenheim. In 1699 Addison was awarded a traveling fellowship from Oxford, during which he was expected to be a partisan writer for the Whigs, the party then in power. But he lost his fellowship when the Tories obtained control of the government. Ironically, however, the Tories, desperately in need of a poet to celebrate Marlborough's victory, chose Addison as the man to be their laureate. The poem, which has been called "a gazette in rhyme," established Addison's fame as a poet in his own time, although he had previously published other poetry. The tenor of this poem is praise for England generally, and John Churchill, Duke of Marlborough, specifically, whose campaign on the Continent is compared by Addison to the Trojan War. The quotation is from a passage describing Marlborough during the famous battle:

'Twas then great Malbro's mighty soul was prov'd,
That, in the shock of charging hosts unmov'd,
Amidst confusion, horror, and despair,
Examin'd all the dreadful scenes of war;
In peaceful thought the field of death survey'd,
To fainting squadrons sent the timely aid,
Inspir'd repuls'd battalions to engage,
And **taught the battle where to rage.**
So when an angel by divine command
With rising tempests shakes a guilty land,
Such as of late o'er pale Britannia past,
Calm and serene he drives the furious blast;
And, pleas'd the Almighty's orders to perform,
Rides in the whirlwind and directs the storm.

Teach the unforgetful to forget

Source: THE HOUSE OF LIFE (Part I, sonnet ci, "The One Hope")
Author: Dante Gabriel Rossetti (1828–1882)
First published: 1870
Type of work: Sonnet

Context: Rossetti had a great feeling for the sonnet as an art form; he called it, in a sonnet prefixed to *The House of Life* and entitled simply "The Sonnet," a "moment's monument—/ Memorial from the Soul's eternity/ To one dead deathless hour." The poems in this sequence were written for Elizabeth Siddall who became his wife and, just as important, became a symbol in her beauty for Rossetti and the other members of the famous Victorian group of artists, defended by Ruskin, who called themselves the Pre-Raphaelite Brotherhood. Indeed, at her death Rossetti buried with his wife a bundle of his manuscripts, including a portion of *The House of Life,* which years later was exhumed from its resting place with the corpse. In this particular sonnet, in which the quotation occurs, the reader finds two qualities typical of the entire sequence: one is the difficulty of being sure of the poet's precise meaning, and the other is the sense of conflict in life which the poet achieves:

> When vain desire at last and vain regret
>   Go hand in hand to death, and all is vain,
>   What shall assuage the unforgotten pain
> And **teach the unforgetful to forget?**
> Shall Peace be still a sunk stream long unmet,—
>   Or may the soul at once in a green plain
>   Stoop through the spray of some sweet life-fountain
> And cull the dew-drenched flowering amulet?
>
> Ah! when the wan soul in that golden air
>   Between the sculptured petals softly blown
>   Peers breathless for the gift of grace unknown,—
> Ah! let none other written spell soe'er
> But only the one Hope's one name be there,—
>   Not less nor more, but even that word alone.

Tell me a man's a fox-hunter, and I loves him at once

Source: HANDLEY CROSS (Chapter 11)
Author: Robert Smith Surtees (1803–1864)
First published: 1843
Type of work: Novel

Context: Robert Smith Surtees, as editor of *The New Sporting Magazine,* quickly found his place in literature as the humorist and chronicler of the hunting field. In humorous sketches written regularly for the magazine, he developed the character of John Jorrocks, a cockney grocer of London, whose great ambition is to become a Master of Foxhounds. These sketches first appeared in book form in a volume entitled *Jorrocks Jaunts and Jollities* (1838); it was well received and others followed. A second collection, *Handley Cross,* was published in 1843; a further edition, greatly enlarged with additional characters and episodes, appeared in 1854. The little village of Handley Cross, located in the Vale of Sheepwash, has just experienced a burst of prosperity. Now a flourishing community, it must arrange its social affairs—among them the fox hunt—more formally. Jorrocks has become known far and wide because he has combined business with pleasure, making excursions to the countryside and taking orders for groceries while riding with the huntsmen. The Handley Cross Committee of Management, wishing to employ a Master of Foxhounds, forwards a letter of invitation to Jorrocks—and his dreams are realized. Upon his arrival he is asked to speak to the townspeople, and delivers a spirited address. In it he outlines his concept of what the ideal Master of Foxhounds should be, and assures his listeners that he intends to fit the outline. When he states that this post is a greater honor than could be achieved by a Member of Parliament, he is overcome with emotion and nearly breaks down. After a pause in which he manages to regain his self-control, he extols the joys of hunting —"the image of war without its guilt, and only five-and-twenty per cent. of its danger." Once again he is nearly overcome by enthusiasm:

". . . Oh, my frinds! if I could but go to the kennel now, get out the 'ounds, find my fox, have a good chivey, and kill him, for no day is good to me without blood, I'd—I'd—I'd—drink three pints of port after dinner 'stead of two! (loud cheers). That's the way to show Diana your gratitude for favours past, and secure a continuance of her custom in future (cheers). But that we will soon do, for if you've—' 'Osses sound, and dogs 'ealthy, / Earths well-stopped, and foxes plenty,' no longer shall a master be wantin' to lead you to glory (loud cheers). I'll not only show you how to do the trick in the field, but a scientific course o' lectors shall train the young idea in the art at 'ome. I've no doubt we shall all get on capitally—fox 'unters are famous fellows—**tell me a man's a fox-hunter, and I loves him at once.** We'll soon get 'quainted, and then you'll say that John Jorrocks is the man for your money. At present I've done—hoping werry soon to meet you all in the field—I now says adieu."

Hereupon Mr. Jorrocks bowed, and kissing his hand, backed out of the balcony, leaving his auditory to talk him over at their leisure.

Tell me where is fancy bred

Source: THE MERCHANT OF VENICE (Act III, sc. ii, l. 63)
Author: William Shakespeare (1564–1616)
First published: 1600
Type of work: Dramatic comedy

Context: According to the will of her father, the lovely heiress Portia must marry whichever suitor who, selecting among three caskets, golden, silver, and lead, selects the casket of lead which contains the portrait of Portia. Of all her suitors Portia loves only Bassanio, but she cannot, even for love, break her father's dying wish by revealing to Bassanio which casket to choose. She devises the scheme, however, of having music to aid Bassanio in his choice, and to provide a fitting flourish if he should fail. This song is sung:

SONG

Tell me where is fancy bred,
Or in the heart, or in the head,
How begot, how nourished?
All. *Reply, reply.*
It is engendered in the eyes,
With gazing fed, and fancy dies
In the cradle where it lies.
Let us all ring fancy's knell;
I'll begin it, ding, dong, bell.
All. *Ding, dong, bell.*

Ten thousand difficulties do not make one doubt

Source: APOLOGIA PRO VITA SUA (Chapter V)
Author: John Henry Newman (1801–1890)
First published: 1864
Type of work: Autobiography

Context: English churchman and author, John Henry Newman is famous as a leader of the Oxford Movement in the nineteenth century. Torn by dissension largely as a result of the onslaught of scientific hypothesis and discovery, the Anglican Church experienced internal turmoil—the Low Church Party advocating an evangelical return to an emotional religion, the Broad Church Party a liberalizing and uniting of Christians in the face of a common enemy, and the High Church Party a return to the security of unquestionable religious dogma. Newman, as author of many of the *Tracts* which supported an Anglo-Catholic position for the Church, eventually was to find his personal spiritual peace in Roman Catholicism. Following his alteration of religious coats, he was peremptorily challenged concerning the sincerity of his convictions by the writer Charles Kingsley. Newman's response, the *Apologia,* is one of the classic statements of faith. At one point he candidly admits the difficulty of accepting the revelation of truth by faith, affirming that this difficulty in no way mitigates the efficacy of the doctrine:

> . . . I am far of course from denying that every article of the Christian Creed, whether as held by Catholics or by Protestants, is beset with intellectual difficulties; and it is simple fact, that, for myself, I cannot answer those difficulties. Many persons are very sensitive of the difficulties of Religion; I am as sensitive of them as any one; but I have never been able to see a connexion between apprehending those difficulties, however keenly, and multiplying them to any extent, and on the other hand doubting the doctrines to which they are attached. **Ten thousand difficulties do not make one doubt,** as I understand the subject; difficulty and doubt are incommensurate. There of course may be difficulties in the evidence; but I am speaking of difficulties intrinsic to the doctrines themselves, or their relations with each other. . . . Of all points of faith, the being of a God is, to my own apprehension, encompassed with most difficulty, and yet borne in upon our minds with most power.

That dark inn, the grave

Source: THE LORD OF THE ISLES (Canto VI, stanza 26)
Author: Sir Walter Scott (1771–1832)
First published: 1815
Type of work: Narrative poem

Context: The Lord of the Isles, King Robert Bruce (1274–1329), the Liberator of Scotland, fights against great odds to free his native land from English domination. Large armies of the two powers are ranged to meet each other in battle before Stirling. On the day before the battle begins, Bruce rides out in front of his army and is immediately charged by Sir Henry Boune, of Hereford. Bruce avoids Boune's lance and kills him with an axe. Next, Earl Randolph of Moray leads his troop against an English force and puts it to flight. The next day the great battle begins with the advance of ten thousand English archers, who shoot clouds of arrows into the Scottish host. Edward Bruce leads a force of armed knights against them, cuts them down, and puts the survivors to flight. King Edward I (1272–1307) of England, known as Longshanks, scornfully witnesses the defeat of his commoners and orders the chivalry into action. The English knights charge, but Bruce had had the territory they must cross provided with pits covered with sods and bushes. As the horses fall into the pits, the battle is joined, and slaughter is general on both sides. The English and the Scots fight fiercely, but knights and common soldiers alike take their way to that dark inn, the grave.

> Yet fast they fell, unheard, forgot,
> Both Southern fierce and hardy Scot;
> And O, amid that waste of life
> What various motives fired the strife!
> The aspiring noble bled for fame,
> The patriot for his country's claim;
> This knight his youthful strength to prove,
> And that to win his lady's love:
> Some fought from ruffian thirst of blood,
> From habit some or hardihood.
> But ruffian stern and soldier good,
>   The noble and the slave,
> From various cause the same wild road,
> On the same bloody morning, trode
>   To **that dark inn, the grave!**

That men should put an enemy in their mouths, to steal away their brains

Source: OTHELLO (Act II, sc. iii, ll. 291–292)
Author: William Shakespeare (1564–1616)
First published: 1622
Type of work: Dramatic tragedy

Context: Cassio, lieutenant to Othello, the noble Moor of Venice, has gained the position that Iago, ensign to Othello, had hoped for. The jealous Iago plans for the removal of Cassio by involving him in some deed which will turn his just lord against him. In the merriment over the destroyed Turkish fleet, Iago succeeds in getting Cassio, who does not hold his liquor well, to drink more than he should and then to create a scandal by beating, as planned, Roderigo, and stabbing Montano. Removed from office by Othello, Cassio laments his experience with liquor:

CASSIO

I remember a mass of things, but nothing distinctly; a quarrel, but nothing wherefore. O God, **that men should put an enemy in their mouths, to steal away their brains;** that we should, with joy, pleasance, revel, and applause, transform ourselves into beasts.

IAGO

Why, but you are now well enough. How come you thus recovered?

It hath pleased the devil drunkeness to give peace to the devil wrath; one unperfectness shows me another, to make me frankly despise myself.

That sweet city with her dreaming spires

Source: THYRSIS (Line 19)
Author: Matthew Arnold (1822–1888)
First published: 1866
Type of work: Elegy

Context: "Thyrsis" is an elegy written in traditional pastoral form. The poem expresses Arnold's love for his friend Arthur Hugh Clough as well as the love both the young poets felt for the countryside around Oxford. As the poet retraces in verse the countryside often visited by the two, Arnold gives the pastoral name "Thyrsis" to Clough who had died in Florence in 1861. Treading a particular path the two must have walked many times, the poet comes upon a view of Oxford that can be seen from a hill. This lovely sight the two young men probably enjoyed on numerous walks because Arnold tells us that "Lovely all times she lies. . . ." Oxford is the "sweet city" to which the poet fondly refers.

> The signal-elm, that looks on Ilsley Downs,
>   The Vale, the three lone weirs, the youthful
>   Thames?—
>   This winter-eve is warm,
> Humid the air! leafless, yet soft as spring,
>   The tender purple spray on copse and briers!
> And **that sweet city with her dreaming spires**,
> She needs not June for beauty's heightening.

That sweet enemy, France

Source: ASTROPHEL AND STELLA (Sonnet XLI)
Author: Sir Philip Sidney (1554–1586)
First published: 1591
Type of work: Sonnet

Context: In this series of sonnets interspersed with songs Sidney looks into his own heart and writes of his late-awakened and frustrated love for Penelope Devereux. The sequence was probably written between the marriage of Penelope (Stella) to Lord Rich and that of Sidney (Astrophel) to Frances Walsingham two years later. These sonnets and songs do not tell a story with a "plot," but are individual flashes of crystallized introspection; they are generally considered to be among the greatest love poems in the English language. In Sonnet XLI the poet alludes to his excellent performance in a tournament but insists that the cause of his excellence was not what the spectators thought it to be:

> Having this day my horse, my hand, my lance
> Guided so well that I obtain'd the prize,
> Both by the judgment of the English eyes
> And of some sent from **that sweet enemy, France;**
> Horsemen my skill in horsemanship advance,
> Townfolks my strength; a daintier judge applies
> His praise to sleight which from good use doth rise;
> Some lucky wits impute it but to chance;
> Others, because of both sides I do take
> My blood from them who did excel in this,
> Think nature me a man-at-arms did make.
> How far they shot awry! The true cause is,
> Stella look'd on, and from her heav'nly face
> Sent forth the beams which made so fair my race.

That unextinguishable laugh in heaven

Source: THE GARDEN OF CYRUS (Chapter II)
Author: Sir Thomas Browne (1605–1682)
First published: 1658
Type of work: Philosophy

Context: Thomas Browne was a very devout but curious physician and scientist of the seventeenth century. In this essay he collects for question and speculation from books and from observation all of the examples in nature or in human arts of objects arranged in the quincunx, or five-spot, relationship. His purpose is to determine if perhaps this figure does not represent some fundamental structural principle in nature or, indeed, in the universe. The second chapter is much concerned with classical antiquity, and at one point he digresses from a comparison of nets used by Roman gladiators and nets currently in use in England to speculate on a net associated with a famous anecdote from Greek mythology:

> That the networks and nets of antiquity were little different in the form from ours at present, is confirmable from the nets in the hands of the retiarie gladiators, the proper combatants with the secutores. To omit the ancient conopeion or gnatnet of the Aegyptians, the inventors of that artifice: the rushey labyrinths of Theocritus; the nosegaynets, which hung from the head under the nostrils of Princes; and that uneasy metaphor of *Reticulum Jecoris,* which some expound the lobe, we the caule

1045

(above) the liver. As for that famous network of Vulcan, which inclosed Mars and Venus, and caused **that unextinguishable laugh in heaven;** since the gods themselves could not discern it, we shall not pry into it; Although why vulcan bound them, Neptune loosed them, and Apollo should first discover them, might afford no vulgar mythology. Heralds have not omitted this order or imitation thereof, whiles they symbollically adorn their scuchions with mascles fusils and saltyrs, and while they disposed the figures of ermines and varied coats in this quincuncial method.

That which is everybody's business is nobody's business

Source: THE COMPLEAT ANGLER (Part I, chapter 2)
Author: Izaak Walton (1593–1683)
First published: 1653
Type of work: Dialogue on fishing

Context: Piscator and Venator discuss the dangers to rivers and fishing, beginning with the necessity of killing otters which catch and eat so many fish, the topic being on their minds from their having killed a female otter and her young the previous day. Piscator mentions that it is necessary, too, to keep the fence-months, lest fishing be so destroyed that there be few fish to eat on days of abstinence from flesh. When Venator asks the nature of the fence-months, Piscator explains that they are usually March, April, and May—the months when the salmon return from the sea to spawn in the fresh water of the rivers. Piscator complains that greedy people take fish at spawning time and, also, make weirs and other apparatus for trapping both the salmon going out to sea and the older fish returning to spawn. He notes that laws against such greediness were on the statute books from the reigns of Edward I and Richard II, but that they are not enforced:

PISCATOR

. . . He that shall view the wise Statutes made in the 13th of Edward the First, and the like in Richard the Second, may see several provisions made against the destruction of fish: and though I profess no knowledge of the law, yet I am sure the regulation of these defects might be easily mended. But I remember that a wise friend of mine did usually say, **"that which is everybody's business is nobody's business":** if it were otherwise, there could not be so many nets and fish, that are under the statute size, sold daily amongst us; and of which the conservators of the waters should be ashamed.

But, above all, the taking fish in spawning-time may be said to be against nature: it is like taking the dam on the nest when she hatches her young, a sin so against nature, that Almighty God hath in the Levitical law made a law against it.

1046

That world-earthquake, Waterloo!

Source: ODE ON THE DEATH OF THE DUKE OF WELLINGTON (Line 133)
Author: Alfred, Lord Tennyson (1809–1892)
First published: 1852
Type of work: Elegiac ode

Context: Arthur Wellesley, Duke of Wellington (1769–1852) was one of England's most loudly acclaimed heroes, especially after his defeat of Napoleon at Waterloo on a Sunday in 1815. When he died, the English mourned his passing as the death of a great man who represented the epitome of what his nation expected from a leader—a valiant warrior, great statesmen, and loyal citizen. Having been appointed poet laureate in 1850, Tennyson was called upon to write a commemorative poem in honor of this hero; this poem was thus his first occasional piece and is usually regarded as the best of the poems that he wrote in his official role. With the enthusiasm of his grieving contemporaries, Tennyson compares Wellington to the naval hero Lord Nelson, also buried in St. Paul's Cathedral, and describes with growing excitement how Wellington saved the land from the French Eagle while Nelson defeated the French at sea. These two British heroes ended the threat to the freedom of Europe and are eulogized as representing the two sources of the peace and prosperity of the 1850's.

> Again their ravening eagle rose
> In anger, wheel'd on Europe-shadowing wings,
> And barking for the thrones of kings;
> Till one that sought but Duty's iron crown
> On that loud Sabbath shook the spoiler down;
> A day of onsets of despair! . . .
> So great a soldier taught us there
> What long-enduring hearts could do
> **In that world-earthquake, Waterloo!**

That's my last duchess painted on the wall

Source: MY LAST DUCHESS (Line 1)
Author: Robert Browning (1812–1889)
First published: 1842
Type of work: Dramatic monologue

Context: In "My Last Duchess" the Duke of Ferrara, having lost his first wife, is negotiating with an agent of a neighboring count his marriage to the count's daughter. Showing the ambassador a portrait of the dead duchess, the duke comments on both the portrait and the woman who posed for it. She did not sufficiently appreciate being honored by the "gift of a nine-hundred-years-old name. . . ." The "spot of joy" that shows in her cheek was too easily brought there by a slight courtesy or a trivial gift from anybody. One would not stoop to complain about "This sort of trifling" or even to instruct her in her wifely duties "and I choose/ Never to stoop." She smiled at her husband but she smiled as readily at others. "This grew; I gave commands,/ Then all smiles stopped. . . ." The duke may have had her killed or simply put her away in a convent. As his little speech ends, the duke indicates his expectation of a munificent dowry with his new wife and then casually comments on another of his works of art, a bronze statue. The monologue begins:

> That's my last Duchess painted on the wall,
> Looking as if she were alive. I call
> That piece a wonder, now: Fra Pandolf's hands
> Worked busily a day, and there she stands.
> Will't please you sit and look at her? . . .

Them's my sentiments!

Source: VANITY FAIR (Chapter 21)
Author: William Makepeace Thackeray (1811–1863)
First published: 1847–1848
Type of work: Novel

Context: Thackeray believed people all have a strong tendency toward snobbery and often made a point of showing how absurd persons can become when they indulge themselves in this weakness. In this chapter of *Vanity Fair* he shows how money makes its claims and induces snobbishness in people who are not ordinarily malicious. Miss Rhoda Swartz, an heiress, is introduced to the Osborne family, who quickly make much of her. Father and daughters find many kind sentiments for their new friend, just because she has money. The Osborne girls immediately decide that Rhoda Swartz would be a fine wife for their brother, George Osborne, who with a wealthy wife could leave the British Army, and go into Parliament for a political career. Their father, ordinarily a quiet, conservative British merchant, agrees with his daughters, even going further, to dream that as an heiress' husband George might acquire a title. Young Fred Bullock, engaged to Maria Osborne, looks at the matter in the same way as his fiancée's family:

> . . . "Let George cut in directly and win her," was his advice. "Strike while the iron's hot, you know—while she's fresh to the town: in a few weeks some d—— fellow from the West End will come in with a title and a rotten rent-roll and cut all us City men out, as Lord Fitzrufus did last year with Miss Grogram, who

was actually engaged to Podder, of Podder & Brown's. The sooner it is done, the better, Mr. Osborne; **them's my sentiments,"** the wag said; . . .

There are a thousand doors to let out life

Source: THE PARLIAMENT OF LOVE (Act IV, sc. ii)
Author: Philip Massinger (1583–1640)
First published: 1805
Type of work: Tragi-comedy

Context: Extant in only fragmentary form, *The Parliament of Love* has a complex plot involving various matters of love and lovers. Among the latter is Cleremond, whom Leonora berates after he has bribed a servant to let him in her home so that he may apologize for having earlier asked her ultimate favors before marriage. To test him when he swears he will do anything for her if she will marry him, she asks him to kill his best friend. Believing that Montrose is possibly his truest friend, Cleremond pretends that he is to fight a duel and that he needs a second. Montrose volunteers to aid him regardless of any danger to himself. Cleremond, now feeling sure that Montrose is his best friend—a man of action, not of mere words—, determines that he must die. Reaching the site of the supposed duel, Cleremond reveals his villainous intent. But in the fight it is Cleremond who falls wounded. When he begs Montrose to kill him, Montrose refuses, pitying him in his seeming madness. Montrose pleads:

MONTROSE
. . .
Live, O live, Cleremond, and, like a man,
Make use of reason, as an exorcist
To cast this devil out, that does abuse you;
This fiend of false affection.

CLEREMOND
Will you not kill me?
You are then more tyrannous than Leonora.
An easy thrust will do it: you had ever
A charitable hand; do not deny me,
For our old friendship's sake: no! will't not be?
There are a thousand doors to let out life;
You keep not guard of all: and I shall find,
By falling headlong from some rocky cliff,
Poison, or fire, that long rest which your sword
Discourteously denies me.

[*Exit.*]

1049

I will follow:
And something I must fancy, to dissuade him
From doing sudden violence to himself:
That's now my only aim; and that to me,
Succeeding well, is a true victory.

[*Exit.*]

There are more things in heaven and earth, Horatio, than are dreamt of in your philosophy

Source: HAMLET (Act I, sc. v, ll. 166–167)
Author: William Shakespeare (1564–1616)
First published: 1603
Type of work: Dramatic tragedy

Context: Hamlet, Prince of Denmark, is led by Horatio and the guards to the part of Elsinore Castle where the prince confronts the Ghost of his father, murdered by Claudius, brother to the former king and now king himself. The Ghost explains the murder and demands vengeance through Hamlet. Shocked but determined not to reveal what he knows, Hamlet jests with Horatio and the guards and calls on them to swear that they will not tell of the happenings of the night.

HAMLET
. . .

Come hither gentlemen,
And lay your hands again upon my sword.
Swear by my sword,
Never to speak of this that you have heard.

GHOST [*beneath.*]
Swear by his sword.

HAMLET
Well said old mole, canst work i' th' earth so fast?
A worthy pioneer. Once more remove, good friends.

HORATIO
O day and night, but this is wondrous strange.

HAMLET
And therefore as a stranger give it welcome.

**There are more things in heaven and earth, Horatio,
Than are dreamt of in your philosophy.**

There are no fields of amaranth on this side of the grave

Source: IMAGINARY CONVERSATIONS (First Series, Number II, "Aesop and
  Rhodopè")
Author: Walter Savage Landor (1775–1864)
First published: 1824
Type of work: Literary colloquy

Context: The ninety years of Landor's life span three eras of English
literature. He was born in Wordsworth's period and was still young in
the age of Romanticism. In his later
years he saw the Victorians come into
greatness. Though he experimented
along all these lines, at heart he was a
classicist, but with the violent emotions of romanticism. His fierce temper got him expelled from Cambridge
University and caused a break with
his father, on which account he retired to Wales, where he remained
until his father's death in 1805. While
there, Landor published poetry in
Latin and English and wrote *Gebir*, a
tale of the Moorish invasion of Spain
which explains why he volunteered in
the Spanish uprising of 1808 against
Napoleon. Back in England afterward, he made an unhappy marriage
from which he fled to Italy for a sojourn of twenty years. A return visit
to England involved this man, so
fond of law suits against others, in a
libel suit against himself, so back he
went to the peace of Italy, this time
for the rest of his life. Landor's fascination with the ancient classical
world and his wide reading combined
in his most unusual composition, five
volumes of *Imaginary Conversations
of Literary Men and Statesmen* and
*Imaginary Conversations of Greeks
and Latins,* some 150 prose dialogues
between such people as Achilles
and Helen, Boccaccio and Petrarch,
Henry VIII and Anne Boleyn, and
Aesop and Rhodopè. The speakers
serve more as spokesmen for the author than as individuals of the past,
though in a sense they anticipate the
dramatic monologues in verse by
Landor's Italian neighbor, Browning.
Aesop and Rhodopè are both slaves
of Xanthus, a Samanian. Aesop wonders why the girl is friendly to one as
ugly as he, when she is the loveliest of
the slaves. He predicts that she will
become famous in Egypt for her
wealth and beauty. They discuss his
fables, and he tells her one about the
earth that called on Jupiter to make
rain. Then they speak of truth. Aesop
comments that man does not utter
truth until he is ready to die. She declares that she must die early, and he
discourses upon death. "Amaranth"
is a flower which, according to mythology, never fades.

AESOP

Laodameia died; Helen died; Leda, the beloved of Jupiter,

1051

went before. It is better to repose in the earth betimes than to sit up late; better than to cling pertinaciously to what we feel crumbling under us, and to protract an inevitable fall. We may enjoy the present while we are insensible of infirmity and decay; but the present, like a note in music, is nothing but as it appertains to what is past and what is to come. **There are no fields of amaranth on this side of the grave;** there are no voices, O Rhodopè, that are not soon mute, however tuneful; there is no name, with whatever emphasis of passionate love repeated, of which the echo is not faint at last.

There are tears for misfortune

Source: THE AENEID (Book I, as translated by John Jackson)
Author: Virgil (Publius Vergilius Maro, 70–19 B.C.)
First transcribed: (29–19 B.C.)
Type of work: Epic poem

Context: Virgil, fired with patriotism, wrote the epic *The Aeneid,* reminiscent of *The Iliad* and *The Odyssey* of Homer, in an effort to give to Rome a fitting background and destiny. Aeneas, son of Venus and a hero of the Trojan War, in attempting to reach Italy, is driven by stormy seas to Carthage. He is deeply moved when he sees engraved upon the walls in the city the battles of Ilium, in which he fought, and exclaims to his faithful friend, Achates, the line above, "There are tears for misfortune." In the translation of Jackson, the passage reads:

. . . He stayed his foot, and, "Achates," he cried, "is there any place, is there any land of all the lands, that is not yet rife with our tale of sorrow? Lo, here is Priam! Even here, virtue hath her rewards, and **mortality her tears:** even here, the woes of man touch the heart of man! Dispel thy fears; this fame of ours is herald to some salvation!" He said, and sated his soul with the barren portraiture; and oft he sighed, and his cheeks were wet with the welling flood. . . .

There are three sexes—men, women, and clergymen

Source: A MEMOIR OF THE REVEREND SYDNEY SMITH BY HIS DAUGHTER LADY HOLLAND (Chapter 9)
Author: Sydney Smith (1771–1845)
First published: 1855
Type of work: Biographical memoir

Context: Most of what is known   about the personal life and thoughts of the Reverend Sydney Smith comes from the biography of him by his daughter Saba, Lady Holland (1802–1866), so retiring that her name appears only twice in the account of her father. The biography is listed and catalogued under her father's name. Chapter IX contains a collection of his opinions on a variety of topics, extracted from the minister's conversations in London. They are set down with no attempt at unity or continuity. Indeed, few of them carry any indication of the occasion on which they were uttered or the person to whom they refer. Bons mots offered in this way frequently lose their glitter, as do jewels out of their setting. It would be interesting to know why this minister quoted a disparaging French remark about men of his calling, but Lady Holland does not tell the reader. She only relates the words, without context and in the midst of other clever remarks:

The charm of London is that you are never glad or sorry for ten minutes together; in the country you are one and the other for weeks.

. . .

Yes, he has spent all his life in letting down empty buckets into empty wells; and he is frittering away his age in trying to draw them up again.

. . .

Don't you know, as the French say, **there are three sexes— men, women, and clergymen?**

There is a limit at which forbearance ceases to be a virtue

Source: OBSERVATIONS ON A LATE PUBLICATION INTITULED "THE PRESENT STATE OF THE NATION"
Author: Edmund Burke (1729–1797)
First published: 1769
Type of work: Political treatise

Context: At this time in England there was considerable popular discontent with the government: the king's policy was unpopular, there were riots in London, the Colonies in America were restive, and there were grave public doubts concerning foreign policy. One pamphlet in particular, indicative of this unrest, attacked with general charges irresponsibility and corruption in matters of government finance. Burke, as an important Whig member of Parliament, responded in this essay, in which he shows most clearly his complete mastery of the details of finance. Early in the tract Burke argues that the party in power has borne criticism in silence rather than create new division, but, he continues, such a policy must have a limit:

. . . These virtuous men, such I am warranted by public opinion to call them, were resolved rather to endure everything . . . A diversity of opinion upon almost every principle of politics had indeed drawn a strong line of separation between them and some others. However, they were desirous not to extend the misfortune by unnecessary bitterness; they wished to prevent a difference of opinion on the commonwealth from festering into rancorous and incurable hostility. Accordingly they endeavored that all past controversies should be forgotten; and that enough for the day should be the evil thereof. **There is** however **a limit at which forbearance ceases to be a virtue.** Men may tolerate injuries whilst they are only personal to themselves. But it is not the first of virtues to bear with moderation the indignities that are offered to our country.

There is all Africa and her prodigies in us

Source: RELIGIO MEDICI (Part I, section 15)
Author: Sir Thomas Browne (1605–1682)
First published: 1642
Type of work: Philosophy

Context: This introspective examination of a doctor's religious convictions is a significant contribution to the Christian humanism of a period in which the "new science" seemed to cast doubt on all received doctrines. This section appears toward the end of a long discussion (Sections 6–16) of the relationship between reason and religion. There are many wonders in nature, Browne says, which give evidence of the wisdom and power of God. In all of nature, however, he continues, the most wondrous creation is man:

. . . I could never content my contemplation with those general pieces of wonder, the flux and reflux of the sea, the increase of Nile, the conversion of the needle to the North; and therefore have studied to match and parallel those in the more obvious and neglected pieces of Nature, which without further travel I can do in the cosmography of my self; we carry with us the wonders, we seek without us: **There is all Africa, and her prodigies in us;** we are that bold and adventurous piece of nature, which he that studies wisely learns in a compendium, what others labour at in a divided piece and endlesse volume.

There is no drinking after death

Source: THE BLOODY BROTHER (Act II, sc. ii)
Author: John Fletcher (1579–1625)
First published: 1639
Type of work: Dramatic tragedy

Context: Rollo, Duke of Normandy, and his younger brother, Otto, sworn enemies to each other, meet for a parley, and are reconciled by their mother, Sophia. Latorch, Rollo's toady, however, urges a breaking of the truce and the murder of Otto. Rollo agrees to do as Latorch advises, and Latorch leaves to see how the preparations for the banquet of reconciliation are progressing. The next scene involves the servants concerned with the preparation of the food; the cook explains what splendid viands he will prepare. All the servants then sing:

THE DRINKING SONG

Drink to-day and drown all sorrow;
You shall perhaps not do it to-morrow;
Best while you have it, use your breath:
There is no drinking after death.

Wine works the heart up, wakes the wit;
There is no cure 'gainst age but it.
It helps the headache, cough, and tissick,
And is for all diseases physic.

Then let us swill, boys, for our health;
Who drinks well loves the commonwealth.
And he that will to bed go sober,
Falls with the leaf still in October.

There is no finding anything truer than the true

Source: THE FIFTH ENNEAD (Book V, section 2)
Author: Plotinus (205-270)
First transcribed: c. 260
Type of work: Philosophical treatise

Context: This Roman philosopher of the third century was the founder of an important school of Neoplatonism. As a youth he studied in Rome and then joined an expedition to the East with the Emperor Gordian about the year 243. The emperor died of sickness while the expedition was yet far from its destination, and Plotinus returned to Rome to begin his teaching the following year. He did not begin to write until some time after 254. His teaching and writings were based upon a rather mystical interpretation of the then extant works of Plato, Aristotle, and their early followers, with some elements of Stoicism mixed in. The true end of the soul, asserted Plotinus, is reassimilation with the One or the Good. This union, the first principle of reality, is beyond thought or description and must be prepared for by the attainment of moral and intellectual perfection. In the fifth book of the *Fifth Ennead* he discusses the nature of knowledge and of the Good. The evidence of the senses is not to be trusted, and true reality must be sought mystically within the soul:

1055

Thus veritable truth is not accordance with an external; it is self-accordance; it affirms and is nothing than itself and is nothing other; it is at once existence and self-affirmation. What external, then, can call it to the question and from what source of truth could the refutation be brought? Any counter affirmation [of truth] must fall into identity with the truth which first uttered itself; brought forward as new it has to appear before the Principle which made the earlier statement and to show itself identical with that: for **there is no finding anything truer than the true.**

There is no great genius without some touch of madness

Source: ON TRANQUILLITY OF THE MIND (XVII, 10)
Author: Seneca (c. 4 B.C.–A.D. 65)
First transcribed: c. 60
Type of work: Moral dialogue

Context: De Tranquillitate Animi is one of a number of Seneca's works addressed to Annaeus Serenus, a young prefect of Nero and a good friend of the author. The *De Constantia Sapientis* and *De Otio* were also addressed to this young man. In *On Tranquillity of the Mind* Seneca gives wise advice to his friend, who is troubled by irresolution in facing life as he finds it in first century Rome. Serenus sees an appeal in various aspects of life: in luxury, in literature, and in fame as a writer, as well as in participation in public affairs. The dialogue takes up the causes of man's restlessness and boredom, and then moves on to present Seneca's practical rules for happiness and peace of mind, rules based upon reason and virtue. While Seneca credits Aristotle with the comment on genius, it is found in the writings of many authors of the ancient world, in Plato's *Phaedrus,* for example, as well as in Aristotle's *Problemata.* The mind, says Seneca, must sometimes be "drawn into rejoicing and freedom," and he suggests that the use of wine, granted judiciousness on the part of the user, leads to a release of the human spirit.

But, as in freedom, so in wine there is a wholesome moderation. It is believed that Solon and Arcesilaus were fond of wine, and Cato has been reproached for drunkenness; but whoever reproaches that man will more easily make reproach honorable than Cato base. Yet we ought not to do this often, for fear that the mind may contract an evil habit, nevertheless there are times when it must be drawn into rejoicing and freedom, and gloomy sobriety must be banished for a while. For whether we believe with the Greek poet that "sometimes it is a pleasure also to rave," or with Plato that "the sane mind knocks in vain at the door of poetry," or with Aristotle that **"no great genius has ever existed without some touch of madness"**— be that as it may, the lofty utterance that rises above the attempts of others is impossible unless the mind is excited.

1056

There is no sin except stupidity

Source: THE CRITIC AS ARTIST (Part II)
Author: Oscar Wilde (1856–1900)
First published: 1890
Type of work: Literary criticism

Context: Oscar Fingal O'Flahertie Wills Wilde, born in Dublin, received his advanced education at Oxford University. Here he was especially fascinated by the aesthetic teachings of Walter Pater (1839–1894) and John Ruskin (1819–1900). Later Wilde, with a wife to support and unable to make a living by poetry or lecturing, turned to book reviews and articles. For one of them, ordered by the editor of *Nineteenth Century,* he expounded the idea that criticism exists to aid people in understanding art. He employed a Platonic dialogue to provide a light tone to serious argument. The conversation takes place between Gilbert and Ernest in the library of a house in Piccadilly. Part I stresses the importance of discussing everything. The second part contains "Remarks upon the Importance of Doing Nothing." Gilbert provides the ideas. Ernest merely asks questions. Criticism, says Gilbert, makes the mind a fine instrument and makes culture possible. But one should not take a final position. Second-rate politicians and third-rate theologians, lacking "sweet reasonableness," do so and then quarrel with those who oppose them. Then Gilbert goes on to say:

. . . We are dominated by the fanatic, whose worst vice is his sincerity. Anything approaching to the free play of the mind is practically unknown amongst us. People cry out against the sinner, yet it is not the sinful, but the stupid, who are our shame. **There is no sin except stupidity.**

There is no wealth but life

Source: UNTO THIS LAST (Essay IV, section 77)
Author: John Ruskin (1819–1900)
First published: 1860
Type of work: Essay on political economy

Context: Ruskin was an erratic but brilliant personality and a gifted writer whose genius had many facets. He was a notable painter, an art critic, and an essayist of great ability whose writing often has the rhythmic grace of blank verse. He and William Morris attempted to reform the artistic tastes of Victorian England and were associated with the Pre-Raphaelite movement. This was a group of artists and poets formed in 1848 and led by Dante Gabriel Rossetti; its purpose was to cultivate the methods and spirit of early Italian painters and to promote, in literature and art, a craftsmanship equal to that in works produced prior to Raphael's time. One of the first "Little Magazines" was published by this group. Ruskin exerted himself on behalf of this drive for a return to craftsmanship, attempting to reëstablish the craftsmen's guilds of the Middle Ages. A lover of nature, he also led a movement to prevent railroads from wrecking the natural beauty of the countryside, advocating governmental control of railways. He lectured frequently. In addition to his other activities, he was deeply interested in economics and in social problems; he fought against the materialism of his day and expressed himself with eloquence both on the lecture platform and in his writings. *Unto This Last* is a series of articles dealing with wealth. Here he attempts to give wealth a logical definition and to show that its acquisition is possible only under certain moral conditions of society—the first of these being a belief in honesty. As in all his writings, the ethical tone is basic. What Ruskin desires most is a happy and noble society in which material possessions are used only for high ends. "The real science of political economy, which has yet to be distinguished from the bastard science, as medicine from witchcraft, and astronomy from astrology, is that which teaches nations to desire and labor for the things that lead to life; and which teaches them to scorn and destroy the things that lead to destruction." He does not believe, however, that a moral problem can be solved by legislation: "Note finally that all effectual advancement towards this true felicity of the human race must be by individual, not public effort." Ruskin's definition of wealth follows:

It is, therefore, the manner and issue of consumption which are the real tests of production. Production does not consist in things laboriously made, but in things serviceably consumable; and the question for the nation is not how much labor it employs, but how much life it produces. For as consumption is the end and aim of production, so life is the end and aim of consumption. . . . I desire, in closing the series of introductory papers, to leave this one great fact clearly stated. **THERE IS NO WEALTH BUT LIFE.** That country is the richest which nourishes the greatest number of noble and happy human beings; that man is richest who, having perfected the functions of his own life to the utmost, has also the widest helpful influence, both personal, and by means of his possessions, over the lives of others.

A strange political economy; the only one, nevertheless, that ever was or can be; all political economy founded on self-interest being but the fulfilment of that which once brought schism into the Policy of angels, and ruin into the Economy of Heaven.

There may be heaven; there must be hell

Source: TIME'S REVENGE (Line 65)
Author: Robert Browning (1812–1889)
First published: 1845
Type of work: Dramatic monologue

Context: "Time's Revenge" treats the humiliation of love, a theme seldom found in Browning. The opening portions of the poem describe the poet-narrator's close friend—a person of clumsy ways and heavy boots but one who is completely devoted to the speaker. On this night in the poet's freezing garret, his friend, who so fiercely slaughtered the poet's unappreciative critics, would be sorely welcome. It is two in the morning, and the narrator says he cannot think, read, nor write. Ironically, the love for the devoted friend no longer has a place in the poet's heart, for it has been replaced by the love for a lady who treats the poet cruelly. He describes what loving her has done to him in violent terms: "To think I kill for her, at least,/ Body and soul and peace and fame,/ Alike youth's end and manhood's aim—." He then describes his new love's attitude toward him:

> . . . and she
> (I'll tell you) calmly would decree
> That I should roast at a slow fire,
> If that would compass her desire
> And make her one whom they invite
> To the famous ball tomorrow night.
> **There may be heaven; there must be hell;**
> Meantime, there is our earth here—well!

There shall be no love lost

Source: EVERY MAN OUT OF HIS HUMOUR (Act II, sc. i, l. 103)
Author: Ben Jonson (1573?–1637)
First published: 1600
Type of work: Dramatic comedy

Context: Fastidious Brisk, a pretentious, foppish courtier, arrives on the scene and delivers a series of affected remarks which causes Carlo Buffone to say that he leaps from one thing to another, like the wild Irish running over a bog. The reference to the Irish makes Brisk announce that he was riding to the court. This statement allows him to bring up the subject of his hobby, which is a breed of small horse of Irish origin. He boasts that a courtier offered him £100 (a colossal sum) for it. Buffone remarks that Brisk will turn morris-dancer and caper in a hobby-horse, a small figure of a horse that a man wore as though he were riding it. Sogliardo, a newly-rich fool, taking the reference to the hobby-horse literally, says that he has one on his wall at home that his father danced in. He adds that he has also danced in it. Buffone asserts that Brisk loves Sogliardo very much, and in reply Sogliardo says that there will be no love lost. The expression here implies that Sogliardo will return Brisk's love in full measure; this sense is contrary to the modern meaning that there will be no love at all between the two.

CARLO BUFFONE

Who, he? a gull, a fool, no salt in him i' the earth, man: he looks like a fresh salmon kept in a tub; he'll be spent shortly. His brain's lighter than his feather already, and his tongue more subject to lie than that's to wag: he sleeps with a musk-cat every night, and walks all day hanged in pomander chains for penance; he has his skin tanned in civet, to make his complexion strong, and the sweetness of his youth lasting in the sense of his sweet lady. A good empty puff; he loves you well, signior.

SOGLIARDO

There shall be no love lost, sir, I'll assure you.

There was a laughing Devil in his sneer

Source: THE CORSAIR (Canto I, stanza 9)
Author: George Gordon, Lord Byron (1788–1824)
First published: 1814
Type of work: Narrative poem

Context: Because of the popularity of Byron's poetry and the romanticism of the author, then at the peak of his popularity, ten thousand copies of *The Corsair* were sold on the day of its publication. It was dedicated to the Irish poet Thomas Moore (1779–1852), who had planned a series of oriental tales in verse, but was forestalled by Byron's writings. Moore did produce one of this sort, *Lalla Rookh* (1817), that earned him a European reputation. Byron entrusted to Moore the manuscript of his Memoirs, but with the explanation that its publication might do injustice to Byron, Moore let it be destroyed and himself wrote a life of the poet in 1830. In the Dedicatory Letter accompanying *The Corsair,* Byron declared it "the last production with which I shall trespass on noble patience for some years." He would not tempt any further the awards "of gods, men, nor columns." Actually *Lara* was published that same year; *Hebrew Melodies* appeared in 1815; and four important poems, including Canto III of *Childe Harold's Pilgrimage* were published in 1816. Obviously, he did not entirely cease writing. Concerning its poetic form, Byron wrote that while the Spenserian stanza, which he used for *Childe Harold,* is the one he liked best, it

1060

may be too slow and dignified for narration. Blank verse is a difficult form better used by dramatists, so he decided on heroic couplets. To the romanticists, the corsair or pirate was a popular figure. Romanticism has as its dominant tone a despair of the world. Sometimes the romantic hero is a highly sensitive person crushed by the cruelties of life, like Byron's Childe Harold. Sometimes he has stronger and more rebellious traits and reacts by a refusal to succumb to those cruelties and by a determination to wage unending war against life. As Goethe's *The Sorrows of Young Werther* is the archetype of the first, so *The Robbers* by Schiller represents the second type, often called "The Titan." And where can his personality be better displayed than in a pirate? Byron deals with a pirate in both *The Bride of Abydos* and *The Corsair*. The latter opens with a description of life on the Pirate's Isle, where the inhabitants carouse or prepare for a raid under the command of their chief, Lord Conrad, whose name is feared on every sea and shore. Stanza 9 of the first canto describes him. Unlike the handsome heroes of fiction, he is rather common in appearance, of average height, with sunburned cheeks, high forehead, and black, curly hair. His lips have a haughty curve, and his glance is the kind that strikes fear to anyone on whom his searching eyes fall.

> He had the skill, when Cunning's gaze would seek
> To probe his heart and watch his changing cheek,
> At once the observer's purpose to espy,
> And on himself roll back his scrutiny,
> Lest he to Conrad rather should betray
> Some secret thought, than drag that chief's to day.
> **There was a laughing Devil in his sneer,**
> That raised emotions both of rage and fear;
> And where his frown of hatred darkly fell,
> Hope withering fled, and Mercy sigh'd farewell!

There was lack of woman's nursing, there was dearth of woman's tears

Source: BINGEN ON THE RHINE
Author: Caroline Norton (1808–1877)
First published: 1833
Type of work: Narrative poem

Context: Caroline Elizabeth Sarah Sheridan was one of three famous granddaughters of Richard Brinsley Sheridan (1751–1816). Two of them were especially noted for their beauty and wit. Caroline was described as "a brunette with dark, burning eyes, a pure Greek profile, and a clear olive complexion." Brought up by her novelist mother from the age of nine, she married the Honorable George Chapple Norton in 1827. She wrote a mel-

1061

ancholy tale, *The Sorrows of Rosalie* (1829), and many poems with a Byronic touch, for the magazines. A collected volume was published in Boston in 1833. One year she earned £1400 by her pen. Accusations of misconduct with Lord Melbourne brought her into the divorce courts. She won, but her husband was awarded custody of the children, for whose care she had to pay with the money she was earning. Her indignation took the form of a pamphlet, *English Laws for Women in the Nineteenth Century* (1854) and a *Letter to the Queen* (1855), that were very helpful in getting a revision of laws about divorce, custody of children, and the wife's property. There is no evidence that the poem "Bingen on the Rhine" refers to any particular battle. It is only part of Byron's Romantic movement that Mrs. Norton imitated so well that she, too, had imitators. One of the most popular of her poems it describes the aftermath of a battle, as the wounded and dying are being looked after by their friends. War nursing by women got its start in the Crimean War with Florence Nightingale (1820–1910). A nameless soldier, whose life-blood is ebbing, begs his friend to return to his home with the story of his death and the sword that he and his father before him had bravely carried in their fights. Let it be put back on the wall. He wants his brothers to be exhorted to look after their mother and insure her comfort in her old age, and especially does he want his loving farewell carried to his sweetheart with whom he used to go strolling to look down on the blue Rhine. The poem begins:

A soldier of the Legion lay dying in Algiers,
There was lack of woman's nursing, there was dearth of woman's tears;
But a comrade stood beside him, while his life-blood ebbed away,
And bent with pitying glances, to hear what he might say.
The dying soldier faltered, as he took his comrade's hand,
And he said, "I nevermore shall see my own, my native land.
Take a message, and a token, to some distant friends of mine,
For I was born at Bingen—at Bingen on the Rhine."

There's daggers in men's smiles

Source: MACBETH (Act II, sc. iii, l. 146)
Author: William Shakespeare (1564–1616)
First published: 1623
Type of work: Dramatic tragedy

Context: The household of Macbeth is awakened by the knocking of Macduff and Lennox, who have come to call on the king. Macduff goes to seek him and finds him dead. Aghast, he reports to Macbeth and Lennox who go to see for themselves. Lady Macbeth, Malcolm, and Donalbain are roused and the king's sons informed of his murder, done supposedly by his chamber-men, who were found covered with blood and in possession of bloody daggers. Macbeth, however, when he goes to see the body, kills them, supposedly in a rage of violent feeling, but actually to keep them from talking. Malcolm, Duncan's heir, and Donalbain, the younger son, fear for their lives and decide to leave in the confusion. They are suspicious of all, and because of their position, they feel they will be safer elsewhere.

MALCOLM
. . . Let's not consort with them.
To show an unfelt sorrow is an office
Which the false man does easy. I'll to England.

DONALBAIN
To Ireland, I. Our separated fortune
Shall keep us both the safer. Where we are,
There's daggers in men's smiles; the near in blood,
The nearer bloody.

MALCOLM
This murderous shaft that's shot
Hath not yet lighted, and our safest way
Is to avoid the aim. Therefore to horse,
And let us not be dainty of leave-taking,
But shift away. . . .

There's death in the cup—so beware!

Source: INSCRIPTION ON A GOBLET (Line 1)
Author: Robert Burns (1759–1796)
First published: 1797
Type of work: Occasional poem

Context: In January of 1796 the poet, on his way home after an evening spent in the conviviality of a tavern, was overpowered by drowsiness and drink; falling asleep on the way, he spent several hours in the cold of a winter night. As a result of his experience he fell ill and never completely recovered. The lines inscribed upon a goblet, written after this illness afflicted him, reflect the knowledge he had gained about drink in large quantity. The verse was written at the home of Mr. Syme, the "man" of the last line of the quatrain. One tradition, perhaps apocryphal, has it that

1063

Burns inscribed the lines on a goblet which he presented to Jessy Lewars, a young woman who nursed him when he was ill. According to tradition, Burns made the gift when the young woman herself fell ill, the poet telling her that the "Inscription on a Goblet" should be a companion piece to a toast he had written in her honor. The line quoted is the first line of the quatrain:

> There's death in the cup—sae beware!
> Nay, more—there is danger in touching;
> But wha can avoid the fell snare?
> The man and his wine's sae bewitching?

There's no getting blood out of a turnip

Source: JAPHET IN SEARCH OF A FATHER (Chapter 4)
Author: Frederick Marryat (1792–1848)
First published: 1836
Type of work: Picaresque novel

Context: Years of service in the British navy, during which he progressed from midshipman to captain, provided background for many thrilling tales of adventure by the British novelist Frederick Marryat. He is perhaps best known for his *Mr. Midshipman Easy* (1836). He also wrote stories for children, and some poetry. *Japhet in Search of a Father* is one of Marryat's quartet of publications in 1836. It follows the pattern of Spain's picaresque novels, sometimes called "romances of roguery." Japhet and his faithful Timothy have qualities in common with Don Quixote and Sancho Panza, or with the *galán* hero and the *gracioso* servant of the Spanish Golden Age dramas of Cape and Sword. The rest of the figures in the book are stock characters: Mr. Phin-eas Cophagus and his catchwords, and the melodramatic Melchior and Netta. Only Aramathea Judd, the young girl who masquerades as her aunt, is something new. It is a pity that her creator discarded her so soon. The novel starts in true picaresque style in the first person with the arrival of the hero, Japhet, in a basket at a foundling home. Because he is quick to learn spelling and reading, and can write with a good round hand, he is prepared for a career in medicine, and apprenticed, along with Timothy, another boy, to an apothecary, Mr. Cophagus. The expression "getting blood out of a turnip" (or from a stone) as a description of an unrewarding task, is given a literal interpretation in Chapter 4.

. . . every evening I read surgical and medical books, put into my hands by Mr. Cophagus, who explained whenever I applied to him, and I soon obtained a very fair smattering of my profession. He also taught me how to bleed, by making me, in the

1064

first instance, puncture very scientifically all the larger veins of a cabbage-leaf, until well satisfied with the delicacy of my hand and the precision of my eye, he wound up his instructions by permitting me to breathe a vein in his own arm.

"Well," said Timothy, when he first saw me practicing, "I have often heard it said, **'there's no getting blood out of a turnip;'** but it seems there is more chance with a cabbage. I tell you what, Japhet, you may try your hand upon me as much as you please for two-pence a go."

There's no repentance in the grave

Source: DIVINE SONGS ("Solemn Thoughts of God and Death")
Author: Isaac Watts (1674–1748)
First published: 1715
Type of work: Hymn

Context: Like Charles Wesley, Isaac Watts was a writer who joined his position in the clergy to his ability to write poetry. Although his textbooks on philosophy have long since been forgotten, his hymns can still be found in many Protestant hymnals. Limited by his subject matter, he sought originality in the well-turned phrase and the easily-remembered beauty of choice word selection, and thus made himself one of the foremost poets of his kind. In *Divine Songs for Children* he attempted to fill a vacuum in religious literature: devotional poetry for minors that incorporated the major tenets of Christian belief. Although the morbid tone of many of the songs makes them questionable today, at least he pioneered in a field that has since grown closer to the child and less ponderous with theology.

There is an hour when I must die,
Nor do I know how soon 'twill come:
A thousand children young as I,
Are call'd by Death to hear their doom.

Let me improve the hours I have,
Before the day of grace is fled;
There's no repentance in the grave,
Nor pardons offer'd to the dead.

There's nothing like eating hay when you're faint

Source: THROUGH THE LOOKING-GLASS (Chapter 7)
Author: Lewis Carroll (Charles Lutwidge Dodgson, 1832–1898)
First published: 1871
Type of work: Imaginative tale for children

Context: The Looking-Glass House, which Alice enters when the mirror above her fireplace turns into mist, is a reversed world that serves as the setting for the sequel to *Alice's Adventures in Wonderland,* published in 1865, by the Reverend Charles L. Dodgson, under the pen name of Lewis Carroll. It is a place where everything is illogically logical in a backhanded way. It is peopled by dream-world figures from Mother Goose verses, by talking flowers, and by chess men. Well-known poems are parodied in "Tweedledum and Tweedledee," "I give thee all," and even "Hushabye Baby." The author introduces one poem, "Jabberwocky," that he had written as a scholarly joke fifteen years earlier, in parody of an Anglo-Saxon poem, while he was studying at Christ Church College, Oxford. Now, when Alice meets Humpty Dumpty, he explains its meaning and gives her a lecture on portmanteau or suitcase words, that pack two meanings into one. In the line: " 'Twas brillig, and the slithy toves," he explains that "slithy" combines "slimy" and "lithe," and "toves" are "something like badgers —they're something like lizards, and they are something like corkscrews." While children are being amused by the funny situations, the author's virtuosity with words and his vast store of whimsy cannot help impressing adults. As Alice and Humpty Dumpty talk, a crash shakes the forest. Soldiers come running from all directions, followed by horsemen, and finally by the White King, along with his two messengers. He explains to Alice that he must have two,—to fetch and carry: one to fetch and one to carry. The exhaustion of one messenger causes the king to become alarmed and hungry.

". . . I feel faint—give me a ham-sandwich!"

On which the Messenger, to Alice's great amusement, opened a bag that hung round his neck, and handed a sandwich to the King, who devoured it greedily.

"Another sandwich!" said the King.

"There's nothing but hay left now," the Messenger said, peeping into the bag.

"Hay, then," the King murmured in a faint whisper.

Alice was glad to see that it revived him a good deal. **"There's nothing like eating hay when you're faint,"** he remarked to her as he munched away.

"I should think throwing cold water over you would be better," Alice suggested: "—or some sal-volatile."

"I didn't say there was nothing *better*," the King replied. "I said there was nothing *like* it." . . .

There's place and means for every man alive

Source: ALL'S WELL THAT ENDS WELL (Act IV, sc. iii, l. 375)
Author: William Shakespeare (1564–1616)
First published: 1623
Type of work: Dramatic comedy

Context: Bertram, Count of Rousillon, has been forced by the King of France to marry Helena. She has miraculously cured the king of a fistula and been granted the boon of selecting a husband from among the bachelors at court. Actually, Helena has traveled to the court and cured the king primarily to win Bertram, with whom she has long been secretly in love. Bertram, however, forced to wed at the king's pleasure, has nothing but scorn for his new bride, and, without so much as a kiss, he orders her home while he leaves the country to fight under the banner of the Duke of Florence. Parolles, a follower of Bertram, accompanies the count in his military adventures. And while Bertram distinguishes himself in battle, Parolles—whose name signifies mere empty words—reveals his true colors as an arrant coward and braggadocio. In one scene the bully is taken blindfold among his old acquaintances, and he vilifies their characters to their faces in the belief that he is talking to their enemies. The Count of Rousillon observes the truth indeed of Helena's previous comment that Parolles is "a notorious liar," "a great fool," "solely a coward." Exposed and shamed, the braggart is nonetheless determined to find another position in which to exercise his talents:

PAROLLES

Yet I am thankful. If my heart were great
'Twould burst at this. Captain I'll be no more;
But I will eat and drink, and sleep as soft
As captain shall. Simply the thing I am
Shall make me live. Who knows himself a braggart,
Let him fear this; for it shall come to pass,
That every braggart shall be found an ass.
Rust sword, cool blushes, and Parolles, live
Safest in shame. Being fooled, by foolery thrive.
There's place and means for every man alive.

· · ·

There's such divinity doth hedge a king

Source: HAMLET (Act IV, sc. v, l. 123)
Author: William Shakespeare (1564–1616)
First published: 1603
Type of work: Dramatic tragedy

Context: Hamlet has mistakenly killed the Lord Chamberlain, Polonius. Polonius' son, Laertes, knowing little of the circumstances of his father's death, but lusting for revenge, comes roaring back from France to Denmark, and leads a mob to the castle. There he is faced down by King Claudius, who asserts that "divine right" will throw a hedge of safety around him. The idea, of course, is a commonplace. In the play it serves to show Claudius as the shrewd and brave man he is, a worthy opponent

1067

to Hamlet. It also is ironic, for "divine right" has, in this case, descended to a murderer and an adulterer, who seeks Hamlet's death and who shortly makes Laertes an accomplice to his plan for the slaying of Hamlet:

KING

What is the cause, Laertes,
That thy rebellion looks so giant-like?
Let him go Gertrude, do not fear our person.
There's such divinity doth hedge a king
That treason can but peep to what it would,
Act little of his will. Tell me Laertes,
Why thou art thus incensed—let him go, Gertrude—
Speak man.

They make a desert and call it peace

Source: AGRICOLA (Section 30)
Author: Cornelius Tacitus (c. 55–c. 120)
First transcribed: c. 98
Type of work: Biography

Context: One of the most famous passages in Tacitus' life of his father-in-law, Cnaeus Julius Agricola, is that in which, before the decisive battle of Mount Graupius—which the Romans were to win—, one of the "Barbarian" chieftains named Galgacus addresses the army of defenders. In his moving speech he speaks of the love of freedom and the willingness to fight for it on the part of those who will defend their homeland against the Romans. Then he pictures the rapacity and the destructiveness of the would-be conquerors. In Bryon's *The Bride of Abydos* (1813) the chieftain (called Calgacus) says, referring to the Romans: "Mark! where his carnage and his conquests cease!/ He makes a solitude, and calls it—peace!" (Canto II, l. 428).

Whenever I consider the origin of this war and the necessities of our position, I have a sure confidence that this day . . . will be the beginning of freedom to the whole of Britain. To all of us slavery is a thing unknown; there are no lands behind us, and even the sea is not safe, menaced as we are by a Roman fleet. . . . To us who dwell on the uttermost confines of the earth and of freedom, this remote sanctuary of Britain's glory has up to this time been a defence. Now, however, the furthest limits of Britain are thrown open, and the unknown always passes for the marvellous. But there are no tribes beyond us, nothing indeed but waves and rocks, and the yet more terrible Romans, from whose oppression escape is vainly sought by obedience and submission. Robbers of the world, having by their universal plunder exhausted the land, they rifle the deep. If the enemy be rich, they are rapacious; if he be poor, they lust for dominion; neither the east nor the west has been able to satisfy them. Alone among men they covet with equal eagerness poverty and riches. To robbery, slaughter, plunder, they give the lying name of empire; **they make a desert and call it peace.**

They make truth serve as a stalking-horse to error

Source: LETTERS ON THE STUDY AND USE OF HISTORY (Letter IV)
Author: Henry St. John, Viscount Bolingbroke (1678–1751)
First published: 1752
Type of work: Philosophical essay

Context: At various times Bolingbroke was politician, statesman, philosopher, man of letters, and historian. As a member of Queen Anne's Tory ministry he was important in the negotiations leading to peace with France; at other times he turned Grub Street journalist to edit successively the *Examiner* and the *Craftsman.* As a philosopher he strongly opposed religious orthodoxy and was important in the eighteenth century development of Deism, contributing much to the *Essay on Man* of the otherwise Catholic Alexander Pope. His *Letters on the Study and Use of History* concerns the importance of history as a branch of humanistic study, but his distaste for orthodox religion permeates the work. In the fourth letter he discusses the authenticity of the historical record, defending it against French philosophers who alleged it to be all fable but insisting that religious historians have deliberately distorted and misrepresented the testimony of history:

Baillet . . . and other learned men of the Roman church have thought it of service to their cause, since the resurrection of letters, to detect some impostures, and to depose, or to unniche, according to the French expression, now and then a reputed saint: but they seem in doing this to mean no more than a sort of composition: they give up some fables, that they may defend others with greater advantage, and **they make truth serve as a stalking-horse to error.** The same spirit that prevailed in the Eastern church, prevailed in the Western, and prevails still.

1069

They must upward still, and onward, who would keep abreast of Truth

Source: THE PRESENT CRISIS (Last stanza)
Author: James Russell Lowell (1819–1891)
First published: 1845
Type of work: Lyric poem

Context: In the 1840's the question of slavery was already a burning issue in the United States; many, in both North and South, had come to the conclusion that slavery of other human beings was wrong, regardless of the question of race. As the war with Mexico seemed a probability, men of perspective in the North, especially in New England, foresaw that it could be interpreted as an opportunity to bring additional slave-owning territory into the Union. Such far-sighted men spoke out, as Lowell does in this poem. Lowell proclaims that mankind must continue to seek good, must not be impressed or imprisoned by the past; he calls the people of the "Mayflower" iconoclasts, and bids their descendants be not cowardly in looking at the evils of slavery; he challenges New Englanders to break with slavery as their forefathers had broken with ecclesiastical institutions. He calls slavery one of the "Sons of Force and Darkness, who have drenched the earth with blood," and he asks, "Shall we guide his gory fingers where our helpless children play?" He ends the poem with the following stanzas:

They have rights who dare maintain them; we are traitors to our sires,
Smothering in their holy ashes Freedom's new-lit altar-fires;
Shall we make their creed our jailer? Shall we, in our haste to slay,
From the tombs of the old prophets steal the funeral lamps away
To light up the martyr-fagots round the prophets of today?

New occasions teach new duties; Time makes ancient good uncouth;
They must upward still and onward, who would keep abreast of Truth;
Lo, before us gleam her camp-fires! we ourselves must Pilgrims be,
Launch our Mayflower, and steer boldly through the desperate winter sea,
Nor attempt the Future's portal with the Past's blood-rusted key.

1070

They never sought in vain that sought the Lord aright!

Source: THE COTTER'S SATURDAY NIGHT (Line 54)
Author: Robert Burns (1759–1796)
First published: 1786
Type of work: Narrative poem

Context: One of Burns' most ambitious poems was "The Cotter's Saturday Night." Much of his verse was written in what has been called the "Burns Stanza," four lines of which have eight syllables, and lines four and six have only four. However, Burns was frequently self-conscious about his lack of elegance in style. To give this poem a neoclassic polish, he used the Spenserian stanza, made famous by the first of the Elizabethan poets, Edmund Spenser (1522–1599). However it is in dialect, and as one critic remarked, Burns' attempts at neoclassic rhetoric in English usually failed. His immortal works were written chiefly in the Scottish dialect. Burns needed no research for the background of "The Cotter's Saturday Night." His father, William Burnes, as he spelled his name, had lived in a clay cottage on a farm where poor soil and high rent kept him continually in debt. He served as model for the chief figure in the poem. Fortunately, though always hard-pressed financially, the elder Burnes was insistent that his sons get the best possible education. Those who scorn Robert Burns as a simple poet, illiterate and ignorant, do not realize that he was brought up on Shakespeare, Pope, and Locke, and was able to read French poetry and novels. But he also knew hard work. He began toiling at the age of twelve, and by fifteen was employed at $35 a year in labor so arduous that it brought about the heart damage that killed him prematurely at the age of thirty-seven. Burns' use of the Scotch dialect lent freshness to the literary scene, and his accurate pictures of his fellow rural Scots brought him popularity. Like Thomas Gray, from whom a stanza is quoted at the beginning of "The Cotter's Saturday Night," he was narrator of "the short and simple annals of the poor." This narrative poem is dedicated to his friend Robert Aiken of Ayr, a product of more aristocratic surroundings. The time is the weekend. The toil-worn cotter collects his tools for storage because Sunday will bring "a morn in ease and rest to spend." By the time he gets home, the children who have been working on nearby farms are also gathering, excited about seeing the family again. The mother has an eye out for clothes to mend, and the father gives them admonitions.

> Their master's an' their mistress's command,
>   The younkers a' are warnèd to obey;
> An' mind their labours wi' an eyedent hand,
>   An' ne'er, tho' out o' sight, to jauk or play;
> "And O! be sure to fear the Lord alway,
>   An' mind your duty, duly, morn an' night!
> Lest in temptation's path ye gang astray,

Implore His counsel and assisting might;
They never sought in vain that sought the Lord aright."

They say miracles are past

Source: ALL'S WELL THAT ENDS WELL (Act II, sc. iii, l. 1)
Author: William Shakespeare (1564–1616)
First published: 1623
Type of work: Dramatic comedy

Context: Helena, the young and beautiful ward of the Countess of Rousillon, is hopelessly in love with the Countess' son Bertram. Consequently, when he is commanded to attend the king at court, she seizes the opportunity to travel there to attempt to cure the king of a fistula. The leading physicians of the country have attempted to treat the ruler but, unable to do so successfully, have pronounced him incurable. Nevertheless, Helena believes that cure is possible; her late father, the famous physician Gerard de Narbon, has left her certain "prescriptions/ Of rare and proved effects," among which ". . . is a remedy, approved, set down,/ To cure the desperate languishings whereof/ The King is rendered lost." She offers the forfeit of her life as a pledge for the efficacy of the treatment and, in turn, requests that the king—if she succeed —allow her to choose a husband from among the bachelors of the court. Thus the stage is set for her selection of Bertram and her declaration of love which she for so long has kept secret. When the king responds to Helena's medicine, Lafeu, an old lord of the court, announces the fantastic news with breathless excitement:

> **They say miracles are past,** and we have our philosophical persons, to make modern and familiar, things supernatural and causeless. Hence is it, that we make trifles of terrors, ensconcing ourselves into seeming knowledge, when we should submit ourselves to an unknown fear. . . . To be relinquish'd of the artists— . . . of all the learned and authentic fellows— . . . that gave him out incurable— . . . not to be helped— . . . Uncertain life, and sure death. . . . I may truly say it is a novelty to the world. . . . A showing of a heavenly effect in an earthly actor.

They seemed like old companions in adversity

Source: A WINTER PIECE (Lines 26–27)
Author: William Cullen Bryant (1794–1878)
First published: 1821
Type of work: Lyric poem

Context: In "A Winter Piece" Bryant
paints poetically a lovely winter landscape and contrasts it briefly with the same scene in other seasons of the year. The poem opens, like Wordsworth's "Tintern Abbey," with the poet's memories of past pleasures inspired by beautiful natural scenes, and his early feeling of closeness to Nature in both happy and despondent moods:

> While I stood
> In Nature's loneliness, I was with one
> With whom I early grew familiar, one
> Who never had a frown for me, whose voice
> Never rebuked me for the hours I stole
> From cares I loved not, but of which the world
> Deems highest, to converse with her. When shrieked
> The bleak November winds, and smote the woods,
> And the brown fields were herbless, and the shades,
> That met above the merry rivulet,
> Were spoiled, I sought, I loved them still; **they seemed**
> **Like old companions in adversity.**

They told me, Heraclitus, they told me you were dead

Source: HERACLITUS (Line 1)
Author: William Cory (1823–1892)
First published: 1858
Type of work: Lyric poem

Context: William Cory, a classical scholar, was headmaster of the famous English school, Eton; besides performing his duties as head of the institution, he also taught a class in Greek. To stimulate his charges into an appreciation of what they were studying, he wrote "Heraclitus." His note to the poem is, "Written for the boys doing Farnaby (School book of easy Greek pieces). Autumn 1845"; it was published in a collection of his verse entitled *Ionica,* in 1858. The poem, however, is not an original composition; it is, rather, a loose paraphrase of a work in the Greek Anthology (Book VII, Epigram 80) by Callimachus. Heraclitus (c. 500 B.C.) had written a poem entitled "The Nightingales." Callimachus, who lived two and a half centuries later, was so moved by the poem that he felt that its author had been his friend and that they had actually talked together. But though Heraclitus is dead, the nightingales of which he wrote still live on and are still singing. Nature, therefore, endures, while man passes away. The little poem has been translated, somewhat less sentimentally, by Lilla Cabot Perry. (1848–1931). Cory's version follows:

> **They told me, Heraclitus, they told me you were dead,**
> They brought me bitter news and bitter tears to shed.

I wept, as I remembered, how often you and I
Had tired the sun with talking and sent him down the
   sky.

And now that thou art lying, my dear old Carian guest,
A handful of grey ashes, long, long ago at rest,
Still are thy pleasant voices, thy nightingales, awake;
For Death, he taketh all away, but them he cannot take.

They went and told the sexton, and the sexton tolled the bell

Source: FAITHLESS SALLY BROWN (Last stanza)
Author: Thomas Hood (1799–1845)
First published: 1826
Type of work: Comic ballad

Context: Thomas Hood, a very minor figure in the Romantic Movement and in the transition to the Victorian era, was a prolific writer. He is remembered today, if at all, for his humanitarian poems, the best known of which are "The Song of the Shirt" (1843) and "The Bridge of Sighs" (1844). These rather sentimental effusions have been termed by critics social documents rather than poems. Yet Hunt was genuinely sincere in his concern for the terrible conditions of the London poor during the first half of the nineteenth century. "Faithless Sally Brown" represents another side of his work. Hunt was the author of a large amount of comic verse, almost all of which has long since been forgotten. His humor is, to modern readers, extremely heavy-handed; it depends for its effect entirely on elaborate plays upon words. Since the pun is no longer favored as a comic device, such poems as those of Hunt are not likely to amuse. However, Hunt must be given credit for his ability to extend the punning through stanza after stanza. "Faithless Sally Brown" is also a parody of the traditional ballad of the cruel sweetheart type as well as of the sentimental popular ballads of the late eighteenth century. The ballad tells of the love of Ben, a carpenter, for Sally, a lady's maid. Ben becomes the victim of a press gang and is taken to a naval tender ship which Sally decides is a hardship. He serves in the Royal Navy for two years and returns to find his Sally married to another. Says Ben:

"O Sally Brown, O sally Brown,
   How could you serve me so?
I've met with many a breeze before,
   But never such a blow!"

. . .

And then he tried to sing "All's Well,"
   But could not though he tried;

1074

His head was turned, and so he chew'd
　　His pigtail till he died.

His death, which happen'd in his berth,
　　At forty-odd befell;
They went and told the sexton, and
The sexton toll'd the bell.

They who drink beer will think beer

Source: THE SKETCH-BOOK OF GEOFFREY CRAYON, GENT. (Stratford-on-Avon, f.n.)
Author: Washington Irving (1783–1859)
First published: 1819–1820
Type of work: Miscellany

Context: Like many tens of thousands of admirers of Shakespeare's plays, Washington Irving made a sentimental journey to Stratford-on-Avon to visit the town where Shakespeare was born and reared, making what he has his persona, Geoffrey Crayon, call "a poetical pilgrimage." Irving describes his experience in visiting the house which was Shakespeare's birthplace and being shown around by a garrulous old lady who displayed all the relics, or alleged relics, of the dramatist's life. He also describes a visit with the sexton who presides over the churchyard and the church where Shakespeare is buried, and tells of a visit to the scene where, allegedly, the young bard was apprehended poaching deer belonging to Sir Thomas Lucy. Of that episode in the dramatist's life, Irving comments that it must have struck the young man as "something delightfully adventurous." In a footnote to this comment, Irving notes that the towns of Bedford and Stratford at one time held beer-drinking contests, and that Shakespeare is alleged by some to have been a one-time champion in such a match; he notes that this episode was earlier mentioned in Ireland's *Picturesque Views on the Avon.* Irving comments:

. . . Two societies of the village yeomanry used to meet, under the appellation of the Bedford Topers, and to challenge the lovers of good ale of the neighbouring villages to a contest of drinking. Among others, the people of Stratford were called out to prove the strength of their heads; and in the number of champions was Shakespeare, who, in spite of the proverb that **"They who drink beer will think beer,"** was as true to his ale as Falstaff to his sack. The chivalry of Stratford was staggered at the first onset, and sounded a retreat while they had legs to carry them off the field. . . .

1075

They will pay on the Greek Kalends

Source: LIVES OF THE CAESARS (Book II, "Octavius Augustus")
Author: Suetonius (Gaius Suetonius Tranquillus, c. 70–c. 140)
First transcribed: c. 120
Type of work: Biography

Context: Little is known of Suetonius, Roman scholar, biographer, and historian. His life spanned the end of the first century A.D. and the beginning of the second, and he was for a time private secretary to Hadrian. Augustus Caesar (63 B.C.–A.D. 14) was removed from the time of Suetonius by not much over half a century; thus the latter had access to all manner of personal information about the man. The picture he draws of Augustus is well-rounded and convincing. The emperor's personal habits are perhaps the most interesting part of Suetonius' account; and they may well have been most interesting to Suetonius, for he covers them in great detail. We learn among other information that Augustus was simple in his tastes and not fond of display; the dinners he gave were excellent without being extravagant. Expense was not spared, but there was a simple elegance, and those who attended invariably had a good time. He was a light eater and nibbled between meals; he drank very little because wine upset his stomach.

He hated to rise early; he required little sleep and generally worked until late at night. He was a handsome man, according to Suetonius, but cared nothing for personal adornment. One of the qualities of this biography that make it vivid is the care with which Suetonius presents less complimentary facts. For example, Augustus' teeth were unsightly. He also suffered from bladder stones, sinus infections, and other ailments. Sensitive to temperatures, he dressed heavily in winter and suffered from heat in summer; unable to bear the direct sun at any time, he wore a broadbrimmed hat outdoors and traveled in a litter, usually at night. Augustus was an accomplished scholar who strove to speak and write as clearly as possible; he cultivated the use of slang and colloquial expressions whenever he felt they would help to accomplish this purpose. Finally, he was not without an ironic sense of humor (in fact, this quotation means "never," for the Greeks had nothing corresponding to the Roman Kalends):

. . . He looked on innovators and archaizers with equal contempt, as faulty in opposite directions, and he sometimes had a fling at them, in particular his friend Maecenas, whose "unguent-dripping curls," as he calls them, he loses no opportunity of belaboring and pokes fun at them by parody. He did not spare even Tiberius, who sometimes hunted up obsolete and pedantic expressions; and as for Mark Antony, he calls him a madman, for writing rather to be admired than to be understood. Then going on to ridicule his perverse and inconsistent taste in choosing an oratorical style, he adds the following: "Can you doubt whether you ought to imitate Annius Cimber or Verianus Flaccus, that you use the words which Sallustis Crispus gleaned from Cato's *Origines?* Or would you rather introduce into our tongue the verbose and unmeaning fluency of the Asiatic orators . . . ?"

That in his everyday conversation he used certain favorite and peculiar expressions appears from letters in his own hand, in which he says every now and then, when he wishes to indicate that certain men will never pay, that **"they will pay on the Greek Kalends."**

They'll take suggestion as a cat laps milk

Source: THE TEMPEST (Act II, sc. i, l. 288)
Author: William Shakespeare (1564–1616)
First published: 1623
Type of work: Tragi-comedy

Context: On an island are a number of survivors of a shipwreck. Among them are Antonio, the usurping Duke of Milan; Alonso, King of Naples; and Sebastian, his brother. Believing Alonso's son Ferdinand to be dead, Antonio privately tells Sebastian that if Alonso were dead Sebastian could become King of Naples. Because of Ferdinand's supposed death, the rightful heir to the throne of Naples would be Alonso's daughter Claribel, Queen of Tunis. But Antonio hints that Sebastian can usurp the throne of Naples as Antonio once usurped his brother Prospero's dukedom of Milan. Let not Sebastian's prudence or conscience hold him back, counsels Antonio. If Antonio murders Alonso (who is sleeping nearby), Sebastian's usurpation will be accepted just as Antonio's was:

ANTONIO
. . .
                          Here lies your brother,
No better than the earth he lies upon,
If he were that which now he's like—that's dead—
Whom I with this obedient steel, three inches of it,
Can lay to bed forever; whiles you doing thus,
To the perpetual wink for aye might put
This ancient morsel, this Sir Prudence, who
Should not upbraid our course. For all the rest,
They'll take suggestion as a cat laps milk;
They'll tell the clock to any business that
We say befits the hour.

1077

They're only truly great who are truly good

Source: REVENGE FOR HONOR (Act V, sc. ii, l. 341)
Author: George Chapman (1559–1634)
First published: 1654
Type of work: Dramatic tragedy

Context: Almanazor, Caliph of Arabia, enraged at his son's supposed rape of Caropia, wife of the soldier Mura, condemns the son, Abilqualit, to be blinded. When later Almanazor learns that the soldiers have invaded his castle to rescue Abilqualit, he, suspecting a plot to overthrow him, has his son strangled by mutes. Almanazor then drops dead as a result of inhaling poison from a handkerchief given him by his ambitious and villainous younger son, Abrahen. Upon Abrahen's leaving the scene, Abilqualit, who had not really been strangled by the faithful mutes, escapes from the city. Abrahen is proclaimed caliph and easily gains the love of the fickle and ambitious Caropia. The next day, when confronted by Abilqualit, Abrahen stabs Caropia to keep Abilqualit from enjoying her love; he then inhales from the poisoned handkerchief and dies. The dying Caropia, in jealousy, stabs Abilqualit, who, as he dies bequeathes the title of caliph upon Tarisa, his faithful old tutor. The play ends thus:

ABILQUALIT

And for those soldiers and those our most faithful
Mutes, that my life saved once, let them be well
   Rewarded. Death and I are almost now
At unity. Farewell!

TARISA

              Sure I shall not
Survive these sorrows long. Mutes, take those traitors
To prison; we will shortly pass their sentence,
Which shall be death inevitable. Take up
That fatal instrument of poisonous mischief,
And see it burned, Gaselles. Gentlemen,
Fate has made us your king against our wishes.

SELINTHES

Long live Tarisa, Caliph of Arabia!

TARISA

We have no time now for your acclamations;
These are black sorrow's festival. Bear off
In state that royal body; for the other,
Since 'twas his will, let them have burial,
But in obscurity. By this it may,

1078

As an evident rule, be understood,
They're only truly great vho are truly good.

Things that love night love not such nights as these

Source: KING LEAR (Act III, sc. ii, ll. 42–43)
Author: William Shakespeare (1564–1616)
First published: 1608
Type of work: Dramatic tragedy

Context: King Lear of Britain has made a foolish mistake: he has divided his kingdom between two daughters, Goneril and Regan, who boast of their boundless love for him; disowned his youngest daughter, Cordelia, who tells him frankly that her love for him cannot be boundless, for she must have some for her husband when she marries; and banished the Earl of Kent, who seeks to stem Lear's "hideous rashness." Too late, Lear discovers the nature of Goneril and Regan, who deliberately abuse and slight him. Maddened by the sense of his daughters' ingratitude and his own helplessness, the king, together with his court jester, wanders on the open heath during a great storm. There he is discovered by the faithful Kent, who has followed him in disguise despite Lear's harsh and rash banishment of him. To Lear, the storm is an echo of his own feelings: "Blow winds, and crack your cheeks. Rage, blow,/ You cataracts, and hurricanoes, spout/ Till you have drenched our steeples, drowned the cocks." To Kent, of course, the storm is enough to terrify—"gallow"—the wild creatures that live and hunt at night:

> KENT
> Alas Sir are you here? **Things that love night**
> **Love not such nights as these.** The wrathful skies
> Gallow the very wanderers of the dark,
> And make them keep their caves. Since I was man,
> Such sheets of fire, such bursts of horrid thunder,
> Such groans of roaring wind, and rain, I never
> Remember to have heard. Man's nature cannot carry
> Th' affliction, nor the fear.

Think of your forefathers and of your posterity!

Source: ORATION DELIVERED AT PLYMOUTH, MASS. (Dec. 22, 1802)
Author: John Quincy Adams (1767–1848)
First published: 1802
Type of work: Patriotic oration

Context: The founders of Plymouth Colony sailed from the Netherlands

1079

in search of religious freedom. In December, 1620, aboard the *Mayflower,* they entered Plymouth Harbor, Massachusetts, and founded their settlement. After a cruel winter, in which a large proportion of them died, the survivors established friendship with the Indians and built houses. Besides setting up a commemorative monument, their descendants in later years observed the anniversary with meetings and speeches. It was no wonder, then, that the Plymouth Town Committee should invite their neighbor, John Quincy Adams, the thirty-five-year-old son of the recent President of the United States, to make a speech on one such occasion. After graduating from Harvard with a degree in law, John Quincy Adams had been sent by President Washington as Minister to the Netherlands from where the Pilgrims sailed. He had returned to Massachusetts the previous summer after representing his country in Prussia, and was now talking of running for the Senate from Massachusetts. He was an excellent choice for the Plymouth orator. His words made so deep an impression that the Council decided to pay the printing firm of Russell and Cutler in Boston for publishing them as a thirty-one-

page pamphlet with the long title: "Oration Delivered at Plymouth, December 22, 1802, at the Anniversary Commemorative of the First Landing of our Ancestors at that Place." Adams struck the "commemoration" key in his first sentence. "Among the sentiments of most powerful operation upon the human heart and most highly honorable to the human character, are those of veneration for our ancestors, and of love for our posterity." Then he went on expanding and adding patriotic and religious notes. "Man was not made for himself alone. No, he was made for his country, for his species, for all ages past and for all future times. He is not a puny insect shivering at a breeze, but the glory of creation." Adams had studied the classics in Harvard. He had read widely in Latin literature, and so, to underscore the relation of man to other generations, he referred, without quoting it, to a saying attributed to a Caledonian defender of his country against the Roman legions under Agricola. At the Battle of Mt. Graupius, in A.D. 84, Galgacus was reported to have exclaimed: "Proinde ituri in aciem, et majores vestros et preteros cogitate," which the orator translated in his speech.

The voice of history has not in all its compass a note but answers in unison with these sentiments. The barbarian chieftain who defended his country against Roman invasion, driven to the remotest extremity of Britain, and stimulating his followers to battle by all that has power of persuasion upon the human heart, concluded his persuasion by an appeal to those irresistible feelings: **"Think of your forefathers and of your posterity!"** . . .

Think only what concerns thee and thy being

Source: PARADISE LOST (Book VIII, l. 174)
Author: John Milton (1608–1674)
First published: 1667
Type of work: Epic poem

Context: When Raphael has finished his story of the creation of the world, Adam asks him why the earth, which is such a tiny sphere in comparison with the rest of the universe, is served by so many planets and stars that revolve about it at such an incomprehensible speed. Adam is, of course, referring to the Ptolemaic system of astronomy: according to it, the earth is motionless and the rest of the cosmos revolves around it. He says that it would be more economical to have the earth revolve and the rest of the astral bodies remain still. At this point Eve, who has listened to the angel's story, removes herself from the scene to go about her work, not that she cannot comprehend Raphael, but because it will be pleasanter to have Adam explain matters when the two of them are alone. Raphael says that Adam does well to question these things, but the great Architect made things as he wanted them, and he will be amused at men's explanations of them. He says that the earth, though perhaps small and dark, is more important than larger and brighter bodies, as large size and brightness are not necessarily signs of great value. He asks a number of rhetorical questions about the constitution of the cosmos, the answers to which would indicate that the cosmos would work as well if the earth moved as it does with the astral bodies moving. Milton is here giving at least a nod of recognition to the Copernican system of astronomy, which was still a matter of debate in his time, more than a century after it had been published. Milton also hints his belief that the moon and innumerable other planets are inhabited.

> But whether thus these things, or whether not,
> Whether the sun predominant in heaven
> Rise on the earth, or earth rise on the sun,
> He from the east his flaming road begin,
> Or she from west her silent course advance
> With inoffensive pace that spinning sleeps
> On her soft axle, while she so paces even,
> And bears thee soft with the smooth air along,
> Solicit not thy thoughts with matters hid,
> Leave them to God above, Him serve and fear;
> Of other creatures, as Him pleases best,
> Wherever placed, let Him dispose; joy thou
> In what He gives to thee, this paradise
> And thy fair Eve: heaven is for thee too high
> To know what passes there; be lowly wise:
> **Think only what concerns thee and thy being;**
> Dream not of other worlds, what creatures there

Live, in what state, condition or degree,
Contented that thus far hath been revealed
Not of earth only but of highest heaven.

Thinking is the greatest fatigue in the world

Source: THE RELAPSE; OR, VIRTUE IN DANGER (Act II, sc. i)
Author: Sir John Vanbrugh (1664–1726)
First published: 1697
Type of work: Dramatic comedy

Context: Vanbrugh's *The Relapse* is a comedy of manners reflecting an age in which the realistic comedy held up to their own gaze the foibles of a group of courtiers who concerned themselves most with love, preferably outside of marriage. The chief characters of the play are Loveless, a handsome young man who has acquired a place again in the world of fashion by marrying Amanda, a rich and virtuous young widow. Loveless brings his pretty bride from the country to London, where they are visited by other persons of their class. Among the visitors is Lord Foppington, who is the kind of man his name implies. He pays great attention to himself and to his dress; he has a gallery which is furnished, as he says, with nothing but books—and mirrors. He loves to go to the chocolate houses where, he says, one has the prettiest prospect in the world, as there are mirrors all about the rooms. He spends his time in the pursuit of pleasure, including four hours a day during which he toasts himself drunk. Upon meeting Amanda, Loveless' new bride, he immediately states his intent to seduce her. When he learns that Amanda has been living in the countryside he sympathizes with her and asks, in his affected way:

LORD FOPPINGTON
. . . Far Gad's sake, Madam, haw has your Ladyship been able to subsist thus long under the fatigue of a country life?

AMANDA
My life has been very far from that, my Lord; it has been a very quiet one.

LORD FOPPINGTON
Why, that's the fatigue I speak of, Madam, for 'tis impossible to be quiet without thinking: now **thinking is** to me **the greatest fatigue in the world.**

AMANDA
Does not your Lordship love reading then?

1082

Third among the sons of light

Source: ADONAIS (Stanza 4)
Author: Percy Bysshe Shelley (1792–1822)
First published: 1821
Type of work: Elegy

Context: Adonais is an elegy upon the death of John Keats, who died in Rome in 1821 of tuberculosis. Shelley keenly felt the loss of his fellow poet, whose work he greatly admired. He begins by saying that Adonais, or Keats, will be remembered as long as the future remembers the past. He invokes Urania, the heavenly Muse, or the Muse of astronomy, to weep for the death of Adonais. By way of indicating that death is inevitable, he mentions in stanza 4 the decease of John Milton, blind, old, and lonely, who passed away when the freedom of the Commonwealth was being stamped out by the liberticides of the Restoration. He was not terrified at the thought of death, and his clear spirit still reigns on earth. Here Shelley regards Milton much as Wordsworth did in the sonnet "Milton, thou should'st be living at this hour." Shelley considers Milton to be the third of the sons of light, that is, great epic poets; the first two are Homer and Dante. Shelley continues with the idea that others have been struck down, and some now living will have a hard journey on the road to fame. But Urania's youngest, dearest child, the twenty-six-year-old Keats, has died.

> Most musical of mourners, weep again!
> Lament anew, Urania!—He died,
> Who was the Sire of an immortal strain,
> Blind, old, and lonely, when his country's pride,
> The priest, the slave, and the liberticide,
> Trampled and mocked with many a loathed rite
> Of lust and blood; he went, unterrified,
> Into the gulf of death; but his clear Sprite
> Yet reigns o'er earth; the **third among the sons of light.**

This and that way swings the flux of mortal things

Source: WESTMINSTER ABBEY (Lines 151–152)
Author: Matthew Arnold (1822–1888)
First published: 1882
Type of work: Elegy

Context: This long poem, written in honor of the poet's dear friend the Dean of Westminster, Arthur Penrhyn Stanley, recounts the promises of the past and the despair of the religious world of the nineteenth century. According to legend, the famous church, built early in the seventh century, was consecrated by St. Peter: a fisherman was asked to row a stranger across the river and later discovered that his passenger was the Apostle who came from heaven to consecrate the church built in his honor. Dean Stanley seemed in life to fulfill the promise of this consecration, but however pure he seemed, his life was short, and before he could reach the peak to which he seemed destined, he died. In this way, he was like the Eleusinian prince Demopheön, whom the goddess wanted to make immortal but who lived and died as a man because his parents disturbed the miracle. Still, Arnold says, the promise may be eventually fulfilled because the course of history leads through its alternating terms toward greater and greater light; in fact, if Dean Stanley had lived longer, he would probably have seen his own work thwarted as history continued on its relentless course:

> For **this and that way swings**
> **The flux of mortal things,**
> Though moving only to one far-set goal.
> What had our Arthur gain'd, to stop and see,
> After light's term of cecity,
> A church once large and then grown strait in soul? . . .

This is hell, nor am I out of it

Source: THE TRAGICAL HISTORY OF DOCTOR FAUSTUS (Scene iii, l. 79)
Author: Christopher Marlowe (1564–1593)
First published: 1604
Type of work: Dramatic tragedy

Context: Much mystery surrounds the source of this pageant. There was actually a Dr. John Faust, a medical quack who flourished about 1530. A *Faustbuch* about him was published in Germany in 1587, and either Marlowe knew German or an English translation quickly appeared, which is now lost. It is not fair to compare this hastily composed *Doctor Faustus* by a young man with little literary background to the *Faust* of the mature Goethe (1749–1832), who had two centuries of culture behind him. But the earlier version does reach wonderful heights of pure poetry and achieves a climax of thrilling intensity. It opens showing the learned Dr. Faustus in his study, thinking of his achievements and extensive knowledge, yet realizing the futility of such accomplishments. He decides to explore the field of magic. A good angel attempts to dissuade him and an evil angel to encourage him. He summons Mephistopheles to appear in the guise

1084

of a Franciscan Friar, and orders him to obey every wish. They discuss Lucifer, with whom Mephistopheles was exiled from Heaven and damned forever.

FAUSTUS
Where are you damned?

MEPHISTOPHELES
In hell.

FAUSTUS
How comes it then that thou art out of hell?

MEPHISTOPHELES
Why **this is hell, nor am I out of it:**
Think'st thou that I, who saw the face of God
And tasted the eternal joys of Heaven,
Am not tormented with ten thousand hells
In being deprived of everlasting bliss?
Oh, Faustus! leave these frivolous demands,
Which strike a terror to my fainting soul.

This is war

Source: CHARLES FRANCIS ADAMS (Page 342)
Author: Charles Francis Adams (1835–1915)
First published: 1900
Type of work: Biography

Context: As United States minister to England during the Civil War, Charles Francis Adams exerted strenuous diplomatic efforts to keep England neutral. Having learned that two ironclad rams were being constructed by the British firm of Laird Brothers for use by the Confederacy in breaking the Federal blockade of Confederate ports, Adams determined to do what he could to prevent the rams from leaving England. Upon reception of a notice that one of the rams was preparing to depart, he sent Lord Russell, the foreign secretary, a strong note on September 4, 1863, warning of the danger involved. An answering note informed him that "the government could find no evidence to proceed in stopping the vessel." As Adams' son writes in the biography of his father, he then sent an even stronger note. Three days later Adams learned that he had succeeded. A note from Lord Russell informed him that the government would prevent the departure of the rams. They were detained on September 9 and were seized by the British government on October 9, 1863. The biographer describes the writing of the note as follows:

1085

The following day it was that, after a night of anxious reflection over what yet might by possibility be done, he wrote and forwarded to Earl Russell, then in Scotland, the dispatch of September 5th, which contains his single utterance since borne in memory. It was the dispatch in which he used the expression afterwards famous: "It would be superfluous in me to point out to your lordship that **this is war.**"

This music crept by me upon the waters

Source: THE TEMPEST (Act I, sc. ii, l. 391)
Author: William Shakespeare (1564–1616)
First published: 1623
Type of work: Tragi-comedy

Context: The learned Duke Prospero of Milan, his throne usurped by his wicked brother Antonio, lives on an island with his daughter Miranda, a spirit, Ariel, and a savage creature, Caliban. Using sorcery and the assistance of Ariel, Prospero causes the ship of Antonio and other noblemen of Milan and Naples to wreck near his island, though the men aboard all reach shore safely. Ariel, in the form of a water nymph, employs bewitching music to entice Prince Ferdinand of Naples to Prospero and Miranda. In wonder at his experience, Ferdinand exclaims:

FERDINAND
Where should this music be? I' the air, or the earth?
It sounds no more. And sure it waits upon
Some god o' the island. Sitting on a bank,
Weeping again the King my father's wreck,
This music crept by me upon the waters,
Allaying both their fury and my passion
With its sweet air. Thence I have followed it,
Or it hath drawn me rather—but 'tis gone.
No, it begins again.

This night thy soul shall be required of thee

Source: LUKE 12:20
Author: Unknown
First transcribed: c. 80–100
Type of work: Gospel

Context: In Chapter 12 of the Gospel of St. Luke, Jesus warns His disciples of the dangers that lie in hypocrisy and impresses upon them that no man can have secrets from God. Nothing can be hidden from Him;

therefore, what they do must be done openly and without fear. For, as He tells them, they have no need to fear those who have power only to kill the body, "and after that have no more that they can do." The only one they must fear is one who can punish after death, who knows the most minute and trifling things, let alone the things that are important. Man is not to be feared, but God is. Jesus then gives examples of the various ways, based on hypocrisy, in which men can earn their own damnation. If a man confesses his acceptance of Jesus before men, then Jesus will transmit that acceptance to God; but the man who denies Jesus publicly is automatically denied before God. Those who speak against Jesus as a man may be for-

given, but there is no forgiveness for those who speak against the Holy Ghost. To speak against the man is one thing, to speak against the Faith is another. In this way Jesus impresses upon His disciples that they are not to give way to physical fear when under pressure, or to quibble or be evasive when their mission leads them into personal danger; God will know what is in their minds. He then tells His disciples that they will be upheld in time of trial, for the Holy Ghost will tell them in their hour of need what it is that they should say. He then warns against covetousness and presents a parable. This concerns a wealthy man who has spent his whole life piling up material things so that he can retire and enjoy them.

And he spake a parable unto them, saying, The ground of a certain rich man brought forth plentifully:

And he thought within himself, saying, What shall I do, because I have no room where to bestow my fruits?

And he said, This will I do: I will pull down all my barns, and build greater; and there will I bestow all my fruits and my goods.

And I will say to my soul, Soul, thou hast much goods laid up for many years; take thine ease, eat, drink, and be merry.

But God said unto him, Thou fool, **this night thy soul shall be required of thee:** then whose shall those things be, which thou hast provided?

So is he that layeth up treasure for himself, and is not rich toward God.

And he said unto his disciples, Therefore I say unto you, Take no thought for your life, what ye shall eat; neither for the body, what ye shall put on.

The life is more than meat, and the body is more than raiment.

Consider the ravens: for they neither sow nor reap; which neither have storehouse nor barn; and God feedeth them: how much more are ye better than the fowls?

And which of you with taking thought can add to his stature one cubit?

If ye then be not able to do that thing which is least, why take ye thought for the rest?

This submerged tenth

Source: IN DARKEST ENGLAND: AND THE WAY OUT (Chapter 2)
Author: William Booth (1829–1912)
First published: 1890
Type of work: Sociological treatise

Context: William Booth, founder of one of the world's great charitable organizations, spent his working life in an effort to aid those unfortunates who were buried in poverty and crime. Born and educated in Nottingham, England, he was a minister of the Methodist New Connection from 1852 to 1861. He was a zealous evangelist, but his methods were unconventional and shocked the old-fashioned. Nonetheless, he was successful in reaching a class of people who were without church connections, and was presently able to work with the assistance of a group of reformed criminals he had converted. He subsequently devoted himself to missionary work among the lower classes in London's East End; and at the same time he began to organize his work and his assistants along military lines. Since 1877 the product of his industry and enthusiasm has been known as the Salvation Army—a name synonymous with mercy and assistance both at home and abroad. The Army's primary objective was the evangelization and social uplift of the unfortunate. King Edward VII supported and encouraged it. In his book, *In Darkest England: and the Way Out,* "General" Booth undertakes a description of the people he and his soldiers are working with and estimates that they amount to a tenth of the population. He gives sample case histories; some are people for whom the Army was successful in finding employment, more are those who seem unemployable. Booth's proposal is to set up farm colonies away from the squalor of the city slums for these people, so that their environment will no longer be unendurable. Beginning with a description of slum conditions and the destitute population existing therein, Booth compares statistics and finds that of the thirty-one million persons in Great Britain (exclusive of Ireland) in 1889, some three million are destitute. He then proceeds with moving eloquence to state the extent of that task which must be undertaken:

Darkest England, then, may be said to have a population about equal to that of Scotland. Three million men, women, and children, a vast despairing multitude in a condition nominally free, but really enslaved—these it is whom we have to save.

It is a large order. England emancipated her negroes sixty years ago, at a cost of £40,000,000, and has never ceased boasting about it since. But at our own doors, from "Plymouth to Peterhead," stretches this waste Continent of humanity—three million human beings who are enslaved—some of them to taskmasters as merciless as any West Indian overseer, all of them to destitution and despair.

Is anything to be done with them? Can anything be done for them? Or is this million-headed mass to be regarded as offering a problem as insoluble as that of the London sewage, which, feculent and festering, swings heavily up and down the basin of the Thames with the ebb and flow of the tide?

This Submerged Tenth—is it, then, beyond the reach of the nine-tenths in the midst of whom they live, and around whose homes they rot and die? No doubt, in every large mass of human beings there will be some incurably diseased in morals and in body, some for whom nothing can be done, some of whom even the optimist must despair, and for whom he can prescribe nothing but the beneficently stern restraints of an asylum or a jail.

But is not one in ten a proportion scandalously high? . . .

This weak piping time of peace

Source: KING RICHARD THE THIRD (Act I, sc. i, l. 24)
Author: William Shakespeare (1564–1616)
First published: 1597
Type of work: Historical drama

Context: Shakespeare's depiction of the character of Richard III, similar to those of the leading Tudor historians, is that of an arrant Machiavellian who sets his crooked sights on the throne of England and determines to wade through murder, if need be, to achieve it. As the play opens, Edward IV rules, and there is a temporary lull in the struggle between the Yorkists and the Lancastrians for the throne. With Henry VI dead, the Yorkists for the moment are firmly entrenched. But for Richard this situation is small comfort indeed; between him and control of England stand the ruling Edward and his two royal Princes as well as his own older brother George, Duke of Clarence. In the soliloquy with which the play begins, Richard sets forth his plan with cold-blooded ruthlessness. Deformed of body, he can take no pleasure in women; twisted of mind, he can delight only in the destruction of those who stand in power around him. To this end, he has laid plots to "set my brother Clarence and the King/ In deadly hate the one against the other." And, like Iago, he will manipulate every opportunity that arises from the dissension:

. . .
I, that am curtailed of this fair proportion,
Cheated of feature by dissembling nature,
Deformed, unfinished, sent before my time
Into this breathing world, scarce half made up,
And that so lamely and unfashionable
That dogs bark at me as I halt by them—
Why I, in **this weak piping time of peace,**
Have no delight to pass away the time,

Unless to see my shadow in the sun,
And descant on mine own deformity.
And therefore, since I cannot prove a lover,
To entertain these fair well-spoken days,
I am determined to prove a villain,
And hate the idle pleasures of these days.

. . .

This will never do!

Source: EDINBURGH REVIEW (November, 1814, page 1)
Author: Francis, Lord Jeffrey (1773–1850)
First published: 1814
Type of work: Critical review

Context: When William Wordsworth (1770–1850) began, with *Lyrical Ballads* (1798), to write poetry in a new vein, he pleased some of the public and exasperated a larger part of it, by not writing in a "poetical" manner. Because of his stated intention to write about everyday matters, which he was to render poetical by his treatment of them, he undeniably wrote a fairly large amount of dull verse—although it must be admitted that he also wrote some of the finest of English poetry. Francis Jeffrey, the critic who had the least patience with the dull works, wrote a number of reviews castigating the poet for foisting such productions on the public. The present review is of *The Excursion,* a work of 447 pages detailing three days of the poet's wanderings in the English Lake Country. Wordsworth's statement that this large mass of verse was but a portion of a longer work, *The Recluse,* was too much for Jeffrey's patience. He begins his review thus:

This will never do! It bears no doubt the stamp of the author's heart and fancy: but unfortunately not half so visibly as that of his peculiar system. His former poems were intended to recommend that system, and to bespeak favor for it by their individual merit;—but this, we suspect, must be recommended by the system —and can only expect to succeed where it has been previously established. It is longer, weaker, and tamer, than any of Mr. Wordsworth's other productions; with less boldness of originality, and less even of that extreme simplicity and lowliness of tone which wavered so prettily in the *Lyrical Ballads,* between silliness and pathos. We have imitations of Cowper, and even of Milton here; engrafted on the natural drawl of the Lakers—and all diluted into harmony by that profuse and irrepressible wordiness which deluges all the blank verse of this school of poetry, and lubricates and weakens the whole structure of their style.

This world is a comedy to those that think, a tragedy to those that feel

Source: LETTER TO THE COUNTESS OF OSSORY (August 16, 1776)
Author: Horace Walpole (1717–1797)
First published: 1857–1859
Type of work: Personal letter

Context: The occasion of this letter was the suicide of a wealthy acquaintance of Walpole, a Mr. Damer, who shot himself with a pistol at a tavern in Covent Garden the day before Walpole's letter to the countess was written. Walpole tells the countess of their friend's death and then comments, "It is almost impossible to refrain from bursting out into common-place reflections on this occasion." He goes on to say that the deceased had five thousands pounds income a year, with 22,000 pounds in reversion. And these, he notes, "are insufficient for happiness, and cannot check a pistol." He says that in the present state of the nation he cannot wish Lord Ossory a son or Lady Anne greatly married. He comments that it is no wonder, with everyone so upset in England, that the doctors die rich men. He tells the countess that there was a time when, if he heard a noise at night, he thought it was some degenerate gambler trying to break into his house; now, "every flap of a door is a pistol." Walpole goes on to make his famous comment, perhaps the best-known of his aphorisms:

I have often said, **this world is a comedy to those that think, a tragedy to those that feel:** but when I thought so first, I was more disposed to smile than to feel; and besides, England was not arrived at its present pitch of frenzy. I begin to doubt whether I have not lived in a system of errors. All my ideas are turned topsy-turvy. One must go to some other country and ask whether one has a just notion of anything. To me, everybody round me seems lunatic; yet I think they were sober and wise folks from whom I received all my notions on money, politics, and what not.

Those who have much to hope and nothing to lose, will always be dangerous

Source: LETTER TO THE HONORABLE C. J. FOX (Oct. 8, 1777)
Author: Edmund Burke (1729–1797)
First published: 1844
Type of work: Personal letter

Context: Burke and Fox were members of Parliament for a considerable time. They were also close friends and worked together on many political issues. Burke, with assistance from Fox, defended the American

1091

Colonies both before and during the Revolutionary War. Although the present letter is primarily concerned with plans to take advantage of every opportunity to support the cause of the Colonies, near the end Burke disgresses to talk of Ireland, the country of his birth. The people of Ireland, he asserts, are restive because they have no political power; Ireland is governed by a small clique of vested interests:

> . . . The Protestants of Ireland will be, I think, in general, backward. They are, for the infinitely greater part, the landed, and the moneyed interests, and they will not like to pay. The Papists are reduced to beasts of Burthen: they will give all they have, their Shoulders, readily enough, if they are flattered. Surely the state of Ireland ought forever to teach parties moderation in their victories. People crushed by law have no hopes but from power. If laws are their enemies, they will be enemies to laws; **and those who have much to hope and nothing to lose will always be dangerous,** more or less. But this is not our present business.

Thou art in a parlous state

Source: AS YOU LIKE IT (Act III, sc. ii, ll 44–45)
Author: William Shakespeare (1564–1616)
First published: 1623
Type of work: Dramatic comedy

Context: Into the pleasant exile of the Forest of Arden comes Touchstone, the court jester, following Rosalind, daughter of the banished Duke Senior, and Celia, daughter of the usurper, Duke Frederick. Duke Senior has spent a good many years in the Forest of Arden, and earlier in the play he compared his life in the woods quite favorably with his life at court: "Are not these woods/ More free from peril than the envious court?" Now the theme of court versus country is developed by Touchstone, in a conversation with the shepherd Corin. Touchstone gravely tells Corin that, since the rustic has never been at court, he is damned. Corin protests:

CORIN
For not being at court? Your reason?

TOUCHSTONE
Why, if thou never wast at court, thou never saw'st good manners; if thou never saw'st good manners, then thy manners must be wicked, and wickedness is sin, and sin is damnation. **Thou art in a parlous state** shepherd.

Not a whit Touchstone; those that are good manners at the court, are as ridiculous in the country as the behavior of the country is most mockable at the court.

. . .

Thou didst eat strange flesh

Source: ANTONY AND CLEOPATRA (Act I, sc. iv, l. 67)
Author: William Shakespeare (1564–1616)
First published: 1623
Type of work: Dramatic tragedy

Context: At the opening of the play, Antony and Cleopatra are immersed in love and pleasure. But as messengers bring news of rebellion, invasion, and the death of his wife, Fulvia, Antony is transformed until he becomes again the great general, one of the three rulers of the Roman Empire. He leaves for Rome, where he is awaited impatiently by the other triumvirs, Lepidus and Octavius Caesar. Fearing rebellion and piracy, even Caesar, who loathes Antony, pays tribute to Antony's qualities as a soldier:

CAESAR
                 Antony,
Leave thy lascivious wassails. When thou once
Was beaten from Modena, where thou slew'st
Hirtius and Pansa, consuls, at thy heel
Did famine follow, whom thou fought'st against
Though daintily brought up, with patience more
Than savages could suffer. Thou didst drink
The stale of horses, and the gilded puddle
Which beasts would cough at. Thy palate then did deign
The roughest berry on the rudest hedge;
Yea, like the stag, when snow the pasture sheets,
The barks of trees thou browsed. On the Alps,
It is reported **thou didst eat strange flesh,**
Which some did die to look on. And all this—
It wounds thine honour that I speak it now—
Was borne so like a soldier, that thy cheek
So much as lanked not.

Thou god of our idolatry, the press

Source: THE PROGRESS OF ERROR (Line 461)
Author: William Cowper (1731–1800)
First published: 1782
Type of work: Essay in verse

Context: Man, says Cowper, is prone to fall into error and pursue vice, rather than virtue. The poet pictures the hunter, and the churchman who slights his holy calling to seek flattery, or overeats, or plays the fiddle for irreligious dancing. Even a slight lapse from virtue, says Cowper, leaves the way open to greater lapses. Education, instead of stressing self-control, merely provides sophistry that helps gloss over lapses. The "Grand Tour" of Europe after graduation brings a young man face to face with endless temptations. Novelists glamorize the pleasures of lust. But especially culpable is the newspaper, which has such possibilities to work for good. However, its columns too often, by their mention of all sorts of sin, suggest to the reader other possible vices.

How shall I speak thee, or thy power address,
Thou god of our idolatry, the press?
By thee religion, liberty, and laws,
Exert their influence, and advance their cause;
By thee worse plagues than Pharaoh's land befell
Diffused, make earth the vestibule of hell;
Thou fountain, at which drink the good and wise,
Thou ever-bubbling spring of endless lies,
Like Eden's dread probationary tree,
Knowledge of good and evil is from thee.

Thou hast conquered, O pale Galilean

Source: HYMN TO PROSERPINE (After the Proclamation in Rome of the Christian Faith, Line 35)
Author: Algernon Charles Swinburne (1837–1909)
First published: 1866
Type of work: Lyric poem

Context: "Hymn to Proserpine" is sung by a pagan after the proclamation in Rome of the Christian faith. The poem is also an expression of Swinburne's philosophy that all things will pass, including love: "I have lived long enough, having seen one thing, that love hath an end." The speaker in the poem advances the thought that much is taken out of life by the new Christian God. This new God does not recognize that gaiety and sensuous pleasure and beauty, as well as cruelty, are a part of the pleasure and pain of life. In this time of crisis, the speaker asks his favorite goddess, Proserpine, who is Queen of the Underworld and the personification of death, to remain near him. Whereas many have accepted and embraced the new emphasis on compassion, pity, and mercy, he cannot see that these values will endure. He looks upon them as being transient and a definite barrier to living life to its fullest—"And all the wings of the Loves, and all the joy before death." With Christ being the leader of this new religion with its milder values, he is spoken of as the

1094

"pale Galilean." And since Christianity has become the proclaimed religion, the "pale Galilean" has conquered.

> For no man under the sky lives twice, outliving his day.
> And grief is a grievous thing, and a man hath enough
>   of his tears:
> Why should he labour, and bring fresh grief to blacken
>   his years?
> **Thou hast conquered, O pale Galilean;** the world has
>   grown grey from thy breath;
> We have drunken of things Lethean, and fed on the
>   fullness of death.
> Laurel is green for a season, and love is sweet for a
>   day; . . .

Thou hast nor youth, nor age

Source: MEASURE FOR MEASURE (Act III, sc. i, l. 31)
Author: William Shakespeare (1564–1616)
First published: 1623
Type of work: Tragi-comedy

Context: When Vincentio, the Duke of Vienna, to tighten the laws of his loose city, turns the reins of the government over to the stern Angelo and the wise Escalus, the first victim of the new stringency is Claudio, who has begot a child upon his fiancée, Juliet. Condemned to death although he would have married his betrothed except for a difficulty of form, Claudio sends for help from his sister Isabella, who, in her pleading before Angelo, catches the eye of the stern judge. Meanwhile, Vincentio, disguised as Friar Lodowick, to observe the implementation of his orders, learns of Claudio's plight and seeks to prepare the young man for whatever may come. In an indirect apostrophe, he comments to Claudio on the burden of life.

> DUKE
> . . . Reason thus with life:
> If I do lose thee, I do lose a thing
> That none but fools would keep;
>   . . .
> **Thou hast nor youth, nor age,**
> But as it were an after-dinner's sleep,
> Dreaming on both, for all thy blessed youth
> Becomes as aged, and doth beg the alms
> Of palsied eld; and when thou art old, and rich,
> Thou hast neither heat, affection, limb, nor beauty,
> To make thy riches pleasant. . . .

1095

Thou speakest wiser than thou art aware of

Source: AS YOU LIKE IT (Act II, sc. iv, l. 57)
Author: William Shakespeare (1564–1616)
First published: 1623
Type of work: Dramatic comedy

Context: Two aspects of love—the pain of passion and the silly behavior that passion can lead to—are suggested at this point in the play. Hearing the shepherd Silvius describe his love for the shepherdess Phebe, Rosalind is reminded of her own passion for Orlando. But the clown Touchstone reminds her also that lovers can behave quite foolishly. Indeed, says he, everyone who falls in love proves his humanity by his folly:

TOUCHSTONE
. . .
We that are true lovers run into strange capers; but as all is mortal in nature, so is all nature in love mortal in folly.

ROSALIND
Thou speak'st wiser than thou art ware of.

TOUCHSTONE
Nay, I shall ne'er be ware of mine own wit, till I break my shins against it.

ROSALIND
Jove, Jove, this shepherd's passion
Is much upon my fashion.

TOUCHSTONE
And mine, but it grows something stale with me.

Though her body die, her fame survives

Source: SAMSON AGONISTES (Line 1706)
Author: John Milton (1608–1674)
First published: 1671
Type of work: Dramatic tragedy

Context: The play opens with the last phase of the life of Samson, the Old Testament hero. The Philistines have blinded him and hold him prisoner in Gaza. The play, structured as a Greek tragedy, depicts the restoration of the fallen Samson to the grace of God. Samson has already been tested by God and failed. Having been punished and having repented his sin, he now undergoes trials of his will and integrity to prove that he is worthy to be tested a second time. Surmounting these trials, he is summoned to entertain the Philistine nobles at the feast of the pagan god Dagon. He at first refuses. However, he is prompted by God's Providence to change his mind. He leaves for the feast and is not seen again. His final triumph over the Philistines is described by a messenger, who reports the spectacular catastrophe that Samson creates by pulling down the temple of Dagon on the priests, the nobility, and himself. Manoa, his father, in despair has asked for all the details of the bloody end. After the details are related, the Chorus judges Samson's action as "dearly-bought revenge, but glorious." In an extended simile, Samson's divinely restored strength and earthly fame are compared to the phoenix, the age-old symbol of death and rebirth:

> So vertue giv'n for lost
> Deprest, and overthrown, as seem'd,
> Like that self-begotten bird
> In the Arabian woods embost,
> That no second knows nor third,
> And lay e're while a Holocaust
> From out her ashie womb now teem'd
> Revives, reflourishes, then vigorous most
> When most inactive deem'd
> **And though her body die, her fame survives**
> A secular bird ages of lives.

Though I be poor, I'm honest

Source: THE WITCH (Act III, sc. ii, l. 231)
Author: Thomas Middleton (1570?–1627)
First published: 1778
Type of work: Tragi-comedy

Context: Sebastian comes home to Ravenna after three years spent in a war. Upon the day of his arrival he finds that Isabella, to whom he was betrothed when he left, is being married to Antonio. Her uncle, the governor of Ravenna, favoring Antonio, has given his niece to the new suitor. Sebastian vows that he can never have any peace without his beloved and goes to the witch Hecate for spells which will cause the newlyweds to have no joy in their marriage, but the witch tells him that the marriage has been made by God and so is beyond the power of any evil spirit. Sebastian then goes, in disguise, to become a servant in Antonio's household. There he soon learns that Antonio has had a mistress, Florida, for five years, and that the woman is still entertained in Antonio's home. The disguised Sebastian tells the newly-married Isabella of her husband's infidelity, but Isabella refuses to believe him. Sebastian defends himself to her as an honest man:

1097

ISABELLA

ISABELLA
Thou'st found out thine own ruin; for to my knowledge
Thou dost belie him basely: I dare swear
He's a gentleman as free from that folly
As ever took religious life upon him.

SEBASTIAN
Be not too confident to your own abuse, madam.
Since I've begun the truth, neither your frowns—
The only curses that I have on earth,
Because my means depends upon your service—
Nor all the execrations of man's fury,
Shall put me off: **though I be poor, I'm honest,**
And too just in this business. I perceive now
Too much respect and faithfulness to ladies
May be a wrong to servants.

Though it be a foul great lie: set upon it a good face

Source: KING JOHN (Line 1991)
Author: John Bale (1495–1563)
First published: c.1548
Type of work: Morality play

Context: In the time of the Tudors, John Bale, Bishop of Ossory, was such a vitriolic defender of Protestantism that he was ejected from his pulpit for excessive vehemence. Thereafter, using the stage as a vehicle for propaganda, he turned sections of the Bible story into pious drama in such productions as *The Chief Promises of God, John Baptistes Preaching in the Wilderness,* and *The Temptation of our Lord by Satan.* His best known work is *King John,* evidently first composed during the reign of Edward VI and later recast during the reign of Elizabeth. The drama was not printed and, hence, was unknown until a century ago when a manuscript was discovered at Ipswich, where the author had spent his final years. The plot, which illustrates the transition from the morality play to Elizabethan drama as we know it, sets forth Widow England and her blind son Commonalty whom King John courageously attempts to save but whose efforts are foiled by agents of Rome. Declaring that his purpose is to vindicate a patriot king from the Rome-inspired slanders of Polydore Vergil—historian of the time of Henry VIII—Bale parades before his audience an admixture of allegorical personifications and characters from history. England's salvation, he counsels, is to be found in the new learning, and, in an obvious move to curry royal favor, he concludes the play with Verity pronouncing a benediction upon Elizabeth's labors for the true religion. After John's attempts to defy the Roman Church have failed, Cardinal Pandulph, Sedition, and Dissimulation consider how the king might be dispatched:

DISSIMULATION

Sir, this is my mind: I will give King John this poison,
So making him sure that he shall never have foison.
And this must thou say to color with the thing,
That a penny loaf he would have brought to a shilling.

SEDITION

Nay, that is such a lie as easily will be felt.

DISSIMULATION

Tush, man, among fools it never will be outsmelt!
Though it be a foul great lie: set upon it a good face,
And that will cause men believe it in every place.

SEDITION

I am sure, then, thou wilt give it him in a drink.

DISSIMULATION

Marry, that I will and the one half with him swynk,
To encourage him to drink the bottom off.

Though poor in gear, we're rich in love

Source: THE SODGER'S RETURN (Stanza 7)
Author: Robert Burns (1759–1796)
First published: 1793
Type of work: Ballad

Context: A soldier's return from the wars has been a theme for poets since wars began. Some poems are sad, because the girl left behind grew tired of waiting. Some are happy. Burns chose to write a happy story about Willie's arrival in "The Sodger's Return" (sometimes reprinted as "The Soldier's Return"). It contains no local color, no clue to what war he has been fighting, and only one geographical identification as the "sodger" (twice rhymed with "lodger") comes back to Scotia, thinking about his Nancy on the banks of the Coil. So it is set in Kyle, a district of Ayrshire named from an ancient Pictish monarch. There are eight stanzas to be sung to the tune of "The Mill Mill O." It takes place "When wild war's deadly blast was blawn,/ And gentle peace returning," and reports the thoughts of a "poor and honest sodger," bringing back nothing but his knapsack because his hands are "unstain'd wi' plunder." Suddenly he sees Nancy down by her mother's dwelling, and has to turn away to conceal the flood of tears welling from his eyes. But he greets her with a joke. "I've serv'd my King and Country lang," he tells her. "Won't you give me shelter?" For a moment, she does not recognize him, but nevertheless welcomes him. "A sodger ance (once) I lo'ed," she replies. "For the sake of that gallant badge, The dear cockade in your hat,

I'll gladly give you lodging." Then suddenly recognizing him, she rushes into his arms, with a cry: "Art thou my ain (own) dear Willie?" There is still a moment of suspense. He has to confess that all he can offer her is the richness of his love because his possessions are few. All that a soldier receives for his sacrifices is honor. However, she has good news for him. She is rich. Her grandfather left her gold and a fairly well provided farm. And she'll be glad to share it with a man who was his country's defense in time of danger. The last two stanzas narrate the happy ending.

> The wars are o'er, and I'm come hame,
> And find thee still true-hearted:
> **Tho' poor in gear, we're rich in love,**
> And mair we'se ne'er be parted.
> Quo' she, My grandsire left me gowd,
> A mailen plenish'd fairly;
> And come, my faithful sodger lad,
> Thou'rt welcome to it dearly!
>
> For gold the merchant ploughs the main,
> The farmer ploughs the manor;
> But glory is the sodger's prize;
> The sodger's wealth is honor;
> The brave poor sodger ne'er despise,
> Nor count him as a stranger,
> Remember he's his Country's stay
> In day and hour of danger.

Thought which saddens while it soothes!

Source: PICTOR IGNOTUS (Line 3)
Author: Robert Browning (1812–1889)
First published: 1845
Type of work: Dramatic monologue

Context: The painter in this poem is one of those early artists, now nameless and unknown, who painted formalized idealizations of the Virgin, Infant, and Saints. In the course of the poem the unknown painter defends his attitude toward art in the face of the current vogue for worldly painters who depict the ordinary faces of contemporary men. The unknown artist claims that he, too, has had dreams of earthly fame: "Oh thus to live, I and my picture, linked/ With love about, and praise, till life should end,/ And then not go to heaven, but linger here." But the cold, business-like attitude that was necessary to sell his paintings to those who considered them "household stuff" turned him from the possibility of earthly fame. He admits that: "My heart sinks, as monotonous I paint/ . . . the same series, Virgin, Babe, and Saint/ With the same cold calm

1100

beautiful regard—/ At least no merchant traffics in my heart." The painter opens his self-defense by remarking:

> I could have painted pictures like that youth's
> Ye praise so. How my soul springs up. No bar
> Stayed me—ah, **thought which saddens while it soothes!**
> —Never did fate forbid me, star by star,
> To outburst on your night with all my gift
> Of fires from God; nor would my flesh have shrunk
> From seconding my soul. . . .

Three things I never lends—my 'oss, my wife, and my name

Source: HILLINGDON HALL (Chapter 33)
Author: Robert Smith Surtees (1803–1864)
First published: 1845
Type of work: Novel

Context: Robert Surtees, scion of an old family in Durham, took up sporting journalism after a brief and unsuccessful career as a solicitor in London. He soon became editor of *The New Sporting Magazine,* and found his proper niche in literature as chronicler and humorist of the hunting field. A number of humorous sketches were written for the magazine, in which Surtees developed a character named John Jorrocks. Jorrocks, a London grocer, dreams of becoming a Master of Foxhounds. These sketches appeared in a book entitled *Jorrocks's Jaunts and Jollities* (1838), which was well received; Dickens had used the same arrangement of material in *Pickwick Papers* (1836–1837), and John Gibson Lockhart suggested that Surtees attempt a novel. By this time the latter had succeeded to his family estate and could devote his time to such activity. A number of novels and other works appeared, all dealing with fox hunting and country life. These are rollicking, exuberant books, best appreciated by a genuine lover of the sport. Jorrocks reappears in several of them. *Handley Cross* recounts his adventures as a Master of Hounds; in *Hillingdon Hall* he becomes a country squire. The Duke of Donkeyton has made him a justice of the peace, and Jorrocks' appearances on the bench are remarkable, to say the least. The book contains many amusing episodes; that in Chapter 33 is a good example. Mrs. Flather is determined to capture the Marquis of Bray for her daughter, who would rather capture him unaided. Mrs. Flather decides to visit Donkeyton Castle and speak to the marquis, but has no carriage; Jorrocks would drive her over, but will monopolize the marquis if he does so. If she can borrow a horse from Jorrocks she can borrow the carriage elsewhere. She writes him a note, asking for the loan of a horse so that her man can go to the druggist for a prescription. Jorrocks favors her with the following characteristic reply:

"DEAR MRS. F.,—**Three things I never lends—my 'oss, my wife, and my name.** Howsomever, to-morrow being our beakday, when us Jestices of our Sovereign Lady the Queen assemble to hear all manner of treasons, sorceries, burnins, witchcrafts, felonies, puzzonins, trespasses, and naughty be'aviour generally, if you'll send me the prescription, I'll be 'appy to bring the physic 'ome in my pocket. Meanwhile I sends you a couple of Seidlitz, and if you want anythings else, Mrs. J. will be 'appy to lend you a few 'Cockle's Antibilious'—werry extensively patronised. A leash o' Dukes, five brace o' Markisses, sixteen Earls, one-and-twenty Wiscounts, Barons, Lords, Bishops, and Baronets without end.—Yours to serve,

"JOHN JORROCKS,
"J. P., and one of the quorum.

"*P.S.*—Dissolve the powder in the blue paper first, then add the white—stir 'em up, and drink while fizzin'."

Three-o'-clock-in-the-morning courage

Source: WALDEN (Chapter 4, "Sounds")
Author: Henry David Thoreau (1817–1862)
First published: 1854
Type of work: Literary journal

Context: Walden was the result of Thoreau's voluntary semi-isolation between 1845 and 1847, when he lived in a small hut of his own construction at Walden Pond, near the village of Concord, Massachusetts. Thoreau undertook this life so he could live in nature, with an uncluttered existence that would give him the time and opportunity to think clearly, deeply, and long about man and his condition. In this chapter of *Walden,* Thoreau writes of his surroundings, devoting a fairly long passage to the Fitchburg Railroad and its trains, which he heard pass at a distance from his hermitage at Walden Pond. He sees that the advent of the railroad has almost made new men of some, even to making them courageous, or prompt. Though he was a transcendentalist, Thoreau was also a man interested in the world as at least foreshadowing a better existence, so he can write with appreciation, as well as criticism, for the things of this life. In writing about the railroad, he comments on the men who man the railroad's snowplows in the wintertime:

. . . I am less affected by their heroism who stood up for half an hour in the front line at Buena Vista, than by the steady and cheerful valor of the men, who inhabit the snow-plow for their winter quarters; who have not merely the **three-o'-clock-in-**

1102

the-morning courage, which Bonaparte thought was the rarest, but whose courage does not go to rest so early, who go to sleep only when the storm sleeps or the sinews of their iron steed are frozen. On this morning of the Great Snow, perchance, which is still raging and chilling men's blood, I hear the muffled tone of their engine bell from out of the fog bank of their chilled breath, which announces that the cars *are coming,* without long delay, notwithstanding the veto of a New England northeast snowstorm, and I behold the plowmen covered with snow and rime, their heads peering above the mould-board which is turning down other than daisies and the nests of field-mice, like bowlders of the Sierra Nevada, that occupy an outside place in the universe.

Thrice he routed all his foes; and thrice he slew the slain

Source: ALEXANDER'S FEAST: OR, THE POWER OF MUSIC (Stanza 4)
Author: John Dryden (1631–1700)
First published: 1697
Type of work: Lyric poem

Context: Saint Cecilia, a third or fourth century Christian martyr, who sang Christian songs during her wedding and refused to consummate the marriage, became the patron saint of musicians and was supposed to have invented the organ. For the celebration of her feast on November 22, 1697, Dryden wrote the greatest of his lyric poems. It was later set to music, in 1711 by Thomas Clayton, and in 1736 by George Frederick Handel (1685–1759). In the poem, the poet describes a feast in honor of Alexander the Great of the fourth century, B.C. Timotheus, his minstrel, has sung a love song with the refrain, "None but the brave deserve the fair." It causes the king to remember and boast over and over to Thais beside him, of his prowess in battle. He tells several times of each victory and by memories of his own vengeance works himself up into a near rage. Timotheus, seeing his condition, calms him with a melancholic song. The Lydian measure is a minor key often used for laments. Later Timotheus uses his musical ability to rouse Alexander to enthusiasm for battle. The ode ends with praise of St. Cecilia, who by her music could achieve results that surpassed even those of Alexander the Great's famous court singer.

> Sooth'd with the sound, the King grew vain;
>   Fought all his battles o'er again;
>   And **thrice he routed all his foes; and thrice he slew
>   the slain.**
> The master saw the madness rise;
> His glowing cheeks, his ardent eyes;
> And while he heav'n and earth defied,
> Chang'd his hand and check'd his pride.

1103

He chose a mournful muse
Soft pity to infuse; . . .

Thy eternal summer shall not fade

Source: SONNET 18 (Line 9)
Author: William Shakespeare (1564–1616)
First published: 1609
Type of work: Sonnet

Context: The poet, seeking an image to describe the fair one to whom the sonnet is addressed, declines to equate the person with the image of a summer day which can be marred by wind, cloud, or change of season, because the loveliness of the one addressed has captured eternal beauty through the verse which will exist as long as man exists. The poet's comparison follows:

Shall I compare thee to a summer's day?
Thou art more lovely and more temperate,
Rough winds do shake the darling buds of May,
And summer's lease hath all too short a date.
Sometime too hot the eye of heaven shines,
And often is his gold complexion dimm'd;
And every fair from fair sometime declines,
By chance, or nature's changing course, untrimm'd;
But **thy eternal summer shall not fade,**
Nor lose possession of that fair thou ow'st,
Nor shall Death brag thou wander'st in his shade,
When in eternal lines to time thou grow'st.
    So long as men can breathe or eyes can see,
    So long lives this, and this gives life to thee.

Thy necessity is yet greater than mine

Source: THE LIFE OF SIR PHILIP SIDNEY (Chapter 12)
Author: Sir Philip Sidney (1554–1586), as quoted in the biography by Sir
    Fulke Greville, Lord Brooke (1554–1628)
First published: 1652
Type of work: Biography

Context: Sir Philip Sidney, commander of an English force riding towards Zutphen to engage a Spanish army in battle, came up, while on his way to the scene of the action, with the marshal of the English army. Sidney, observing that the marshal wore only light armor, and not wishing to enter the battle except on equal terms with him, discarded his cuisses, or leg armor, as he rode along. (Although this is the most widely known reason for Sidney's engaging in action without his complete armor, there are several other contradictory explanations, and all apparently on as good authority as that of Fulke Greville.) The troop led by Sidney came upon the Spaniards in a mist at very close range, and very quickly Sidney's thigh bone was broken by a musket ball. His horse, which became unmanageable, carried him to the station of his uncle, Robert Dudley, Earl of Leicester. As he lay on the field he became exceedingly thirsty from excess of bleeding and called for water. Thereupon there followed the famous event in which Sidney gave his water bottle to a poor common soldier. The word "necessity" is usually misquoted as "need." In the words of Fulke Greville the event happened thus:

. . . as he was putting the bottle to his mouth, he saw a poor soldier carried along who had eaten his last at the same feast, ghastly casting up his eyes at the bottle. Which Sir Philip Sidney perceiving, took it from his head before he drank, and delivered it to the poor man with these words, **"Thy necessity is yet greater than mine."** And when he had pledged this poor soldier, he was presently carried to Arnheim.

Thy soul was like a star, and dwelt apart

Source: LONDON, 1802 (Line 9)
Author: William Wordsworth (1770–1850)
First published: 1807
Type of work: Sonnet

Context: This poem, also known as "National Independence and Liberty," is one of Wordsworth's best sonnets, a full union of harmonious sound and dignified meaning. Addressed to Milton, who was not only a master of the sounds of poetry but also a stanch defender of personal freedom, the sonnet laments the changes that threatened to end the happiness and liberty of the English people. During the French Revolution, the British government became highly repressive from fear that the radical ideas would cross the Channel and explode into a revolution at home; thus the ministry started censorship and abandoned some of the basic rights of Englishmen. In the seventeenth century there was a similar repression, and the calm and humble voice of Milton had cried out for the restoration of rights. In the early nineteenth century there seemed to Wordsworth to be no leader who could assume such responsibility. In this quotation Wordsworth both praises Milton and hopes to raise another great spokesman to put an end to the stagnation that seems to be choking English life.

We are selfish men;
Oh! raise us up, return to us again;

1105

And give us manners, virtue, freedom, power.
Thy soul was like a star, and dwelt apart:
Thou hadst a voice whose sound was like the sea:
Pure as the naked heavens, majestic, free,
So didst thou travel on life's common way,
In cheerful godliness; and yet thy heart
The lowliest duties on herself did lay.

Time hath an art to make dust of all things

Source: HYDRIOTAPHIA: URN BURIAL (Chapter 5)
Author: Sir Thomas Browne (1605–1682)
First published: 1658
Type of work: Philosophy

Context: This philosophical physician and scientist set out to write a report concerning some forty or fifty Roman funeral urns which were exhumed near Norwich. His speculative nature led him beyond the bounds of a mere scientific report to a disquisition on burial customs in general, ranging, of course, through his vast knowledge of classical literature. In this final chapter, which has been described as "a prose poem on death of perhaps unequaled verbal harmony," Browne discusses the impermanence of human fame and monuments. These bones removed from the funeral urns, he says, because of their anonymity have already outlasted all the buildings built over them:

Now since these dead bones have already out-lasted the living ones of Methuselah, and in a yard under ground, and thin walls of clay, out-worn all the strong and specious buildings above it; and quietly rested under the drums and tramplings of three conquests; What Prince can promise such diuturnity unto his Reliques, . . . **Time** which antiquates antiquities, and **hath an art to make dust of all things,** hath yet spared these minor monuments. In vain we hope to be known by open and visible conservatories, when to be unknown was the means of their continuation and obscurity their protection: If they died by violent hands, and were thrust into their urns, these bones become considerable, and some old philosophers would honour them, whose souls they conceived most pure, which were thus snatched from their bodies; and to retain a stronger propension unto them: whereas they weariedly left a languishing corpse, and with faint desires of re-union. . . .

Time hath, my lord, a wallet at his back

Source: TROILUS AND CRESSIDA (Act III, sc. iii, l. 145)
Author: William Shakespeare (1564–1616)
First published: 1609
Type of work: Dramatic tragedy

Context: In the eighth year of the Trojan War, the Greeks find their military power lacking chiefly because of the pride and, consequently, the insubordination of their greatest fighter, Achilles. When a challenge to single combat comes from Hector, the Trojan champion, the Greek generals, knowing well that the challenge is directed at Achilles, plan to send the dull Ajax to accept the challenge as a slight to Achilles, their most noted warrior. When Achilles, aware of the snub, asks whether his own deeds are forgotten, Ulysses replies:

ULYSSES

Time hath, my lord, a wallet at his back,
Wherein he puts alms for oblivion,
A great-sized monster of ingratitudes.
Those scraps are good deeds past, which are devoured
As fast as they are made, forgot as soon
As done. Perseverance, dear my lord,
Keeps honour bright; to have done, is to hang
Quite out of fashion, like a rusty mail,
In monumental mockery. Take the instant way
For honour travels in a strait so narrow,
Where one but goes abreast; keep then the path.
For emulation hath a thousand sons,
That one by one pursue. If you give way,
Or hedge aside from the direct forthright,
Like to an entered tide they all rush by,
And leave you hindmost; . . .

Time, not Corydon, hath conquered thee

Source: THYRSIS (Line 80)
Author: Matthew Arnold (1822–1888)
First published: 1866
Type of work: Elegy

Context: The elegy "Thyrsis" was written to commemorate Arthur Hugh Clough, to whom the title of the poem applies and who had died in 1861. Arnold takes on another pastoral name for himself, Corydon, in keeping with the traditional form for classical elegies. One of the reasons that the two men were close was that both were poets, and, though the best of friends, enjoyed engaging in competition in their writing. Also each

1107

helped intensify the other's appreciation of the beauty of the countryside. In the poem Arnold feels acutely the absence of his "mate" in singing of sylvan beauty. And sadly, neither poet won the competitive prize because death rather than Corydon (Arnold) "conquer'd" Thyrsis (Clough). Gone forever, Thyrsis will never again be able to roam the beautiful countryside. The "he" of the first line refers to the cuckoo which, so Arnold thought, migrates in June.

> He hearkens not! light comer, he is flown!
>   What matters it? next year he will return,
>   And we shall have him in the sweet spring-days,
>   With whitening hedges, and uncrumpling fern,
>   And blue-bells trembling by the forest-ways,
>   And scent of hay new-mown.
> But Thyrsis never more we swains shall see;
>   See him come back, and cut a smoother reed,
>   And blow a strain the world at last shall heed—
> For **Time, not Corydon, hath conquer'd thee!**

Time, the avenger

Source: CHILDE HAROLD'S PILGRIMAGE (Canto IV, stanza 130)
Author: George Gordon, Lord Byron (1788–1824)
First published: 1818 (Canto IV)
Type of work: Narrative poem

Context: Between the composition of the beginning and the end of *Childe Harold's Pilgrimage* stretches a space of six years. In the first two cantos, published in 1812, is seen the spontaneity of a young man of the Romantic Movement, enjoying adventurous experiences in oriental lands and writing about them in facile verse. The publication brought immediate fame to Byron. Canto III, after a four-year interval, shows a great advance in technique, and its description of the Battle of Waterloo helps to make it the best part of the poem. With Canto IV came another change. The poet dispensed with Childe (Young Lord) Harold as a spokesman, and made himself and his opinions the subject of the poem. But the travelogue, which provides the continuity for the entire work, is combined with a review of Italian history and literature, full of indirect references. Some are recognizable to the general reader, such as "The Bard of Hell," for Dante, but many readers will be doubtful about "The Bard of Chivalry," or the reference to "he who lies in a tomb in Arqua," or "the Roman

1108

friend of Rome's least-mortal mind" (Aervius Sulpicius), the "Goddess loves in stone," or "the hyaena bigots." However, Byron does include many memorable bits in this canto in unforgettable poetic descriptions of Nature, notably the six magnificent stanzas near the end, beginning: "Roll on, thou deep and dark blue Ocean, roll." Harold and his human prototype frequently voice their dislike of humanity and their joys of solitary communion with Nature. Byron's search for Liberty and his ha-

tred of despots and tyrants who deprive men of their freedom are the occasions for highly colored lines, as are his feelings of a Romanticist who has lived too long and seen everything, and his belief that all is temporary and doomed to destruction. However, the passing years, even while destroying, give a patina of beauty to what they destroy. And in the case of people and their productions, Time, while avenging, acts as a balance to establish true values.

> Oh, Time! the beautifier of the dead,
> Adorner of the ruin, comforter
> And only healer when the heart hath bled—
> Time! the corrector where our judgments err,
> The test of truth, love—sole philosopher,
> For all besides are sophists—from thy thrift,
> Which never loses though it doth defer—
> **Time, the avenger,** unto thee I lift
> My hands, and eyes, and heart, and crave of thee a gift.

Time, thou devourer of all things

Source: THE METAMORPHOSES (Book XV, 234)
Author: Ovid (43 B.C.– A.D. 18)
First transcribed: Before A.D. 8
Type of work: Mythological tales in verse

Context: Publius Ovidius Naso caused a scandal with his *Art of Love.* For it he was banished in 8 B.C. by Emperor Augustus to a half-barbaric Rumanian town at the mouth of the Danube. There he died. More admirable was his fifteen-book *Metamorphoses,* written in hexameters. It is an account of miraculous transformations, from classical mythology to the story of Julius Caesar's metamorphosis into a star. In the final book, Ovid tells of the founding of Crotona, through the trickery

of Hercules. It was here, says Ovid, that Pythagoras, a fugitive from Samos, tried to persuade men to be vegetarians, decrying the practice of eating the flesh of animals. He also preached the transmigration of the soul. Using the analogy of changes in nature during the annual cycle, Pythagoras brought up the birth and aging of man, using as examples powerful Milo, the Crotona athlete who could kill a bull with one blow of his fist, and lovely Helen of Troy, both later victims of "Tempus edax rerum

1109

(Time, the devourer of things)."

Milo, now grown old, weeps when he sees his arms, which once equalled those of Hercules in the massiveness of solid muscle, hang weak and exhausted. The daughter of Tyndarus (Helen) weeps, too, as she beholds in her mirror the wrinkles of old age, and enquires of herself why it is that she was twice ravished. **Time, thou devourer of all things,** and thou, hateful Old Age, together destroy all things; and by degrees ye consume each thing, decayed by the teeth of age, with a slow death.

Time will run back, and fetch the age of gold

Source: ON THE MORNING OF CHRIST'S NATIVITY: THE HYMN (Stanza 14)
Author: John Milton (1608–1674)
First published: 1645
Type of work: Religious poem

Context: When Christ was born, Peace came down to earth (Christ was born during the *Pax Romana*); the ocean was smooth; and the halcyons, the birds of calm, sat on their nests on the water. The stars stood fixed; and the sun hid his face, as he saw a greater Sun come to enlighten the world. The shepherds little thought, as they sat in the fields, that the mighty Pan, the Good Shepherd, was come to earth. There was music like that of the spheres that would hold heaven and earth in union. The cherubim and the seraphim appeared in the sky, harping the birth of the heir of heaven. The poet asks that the music of the spheres may be heard by mortals, because, if such holy harmony becomes audible, time will turn backward and produce the golden age again. The first golden age was that time before the fall of Adam when there was no war, no money, no commerce, no crime, no sin. Instead, all lived in peace and harmony in a perfect world:

> Ring out ye crystal spheres,
> Once bless our human ears,
>   (If ye have power to touch our senses so)
> And let your silver chime
> Move in melodious time;
>   And let the bass of heaven's deep organ blow;
> And with your ninefold harmony
> Make up full consort of th'angelic symphony.
>
> For if such holy song
> Enwrap our fancy long,
>   **Time will run back, and fetch the age of gold,**
> And speckled vanity
> Will sicken soon and die,

1110

And leprous sin will melt from earthly mould,
And hell itself will pass away,
And leave her dolorous mansions to the peering day.

Tip me the black spot

Source: TREASURE ISLAND (Part I, chapter 3)
Author: Robert Louis Stevenson (1850–1894)
First published: 1883
Type of work: Novel

Context: Bill Bones, a pirate, hides out at a little inn, the Admiral Benbow, on a cove along the English coast. Bones was first mate with Captain Flint, the notorious buccaneer, and has in his possession the map showing where Flint's treasure has been hidden. Bones fears the other men still alive from the captain's crew will come looking for him, guessing that Flint, before he died at Savannah, told his first mate about the treasure's hiding place. The old pirate suffers a stroke himself, although warned by Dr. Livesey not to drink so much rum. In his weakness Bones takes Jim, the innkeeper's son, into his confidence and tells the boy of his fears. He tells Jim that the black spot is a summons among the pirates; it turns out to be a paper with a black spot that, even among illiterates, carries its message clearly. The old pirate says to Jim that a previous visitor, Black Dog, may return:

. . . *"He's* a bad'un; but there's worse that put him on. Now, if I can't get away nohow, and they **tip me the black spot,** mind you, it's my old sea-chest they're after; you get on a horse— you can, can't you? Well, then, you get on a horse, and go to—well, yes, I will!—to that eternal Doctor swab, and tell him to pipe all hands—magistrates and sich—and he'll lay 'em aboard at the 'Admiral Benbow'—all old Flint's crew, man and boy, all on 'em that's left. I was first mate, I was, old Flint's first mate, and I'm the on'y one as knows the place. He gave it me to Savannah, when he lay a-dying, like as if I was to now, you see. But you won't peach unless they get the black spot on me, or unless you see that Black Dog again, or a seafaring man with one leg, Jim—him above all."

'Tis an awkward thing to play with souls

Source: A LIGHT WOMAN (Stanza 12)
Author: Robert Browning (1812–1889)
First published: 1855
Type of work: Dramatic monologue

Context: "A Light Woman" is a monologue by a worldly yet essentially good-hearted man who briefly recounts a triangular story of love. Seeing his friend caught by the "hunting-noose" of a light woman and wishing to save him, the speaker chose to prove that the woman preferred an eagle like himself to a wren like his friend. The friend eyed him with hatred for having turned "his day to night." But now that she has been taken as easily as a pear from a tree, the speaker has no taste for her. She will soon hate him as his friend already does, and he finds himself no hero. As he breaks off his unfinished story he offers it to Browning with the invitation to see what he can do with it.

> 'Tis an awkward thing to play with souls,
>   And matter enough to save one's own:
> Yet think of my friend, and the burning coals
>   He played with for bits of stone!
>
> One likes to show the truth for the truth;
>   That the woman was light is very true:
> But suppose she says,—Never mind that youth!
>   What wrong have I done to you?
>
> Well, any how, here the story stays,
>   So far at least as I understand:
> And, Robert Browning, you writer of plays,
>   Here's a subject made to your hand!

'Tis beauty calls, and glory shows the way

Source: THE RIVAL QUEENS; OR, THE DEATH OF ALEXANDER THE GREAT (Act IV, sc. ii, last line)
Author: Nathaniel Lee (1655–1692)
First published: 1677
Type of work: Dramatic tragedy

Context: Lee's play, based largely on La Calprenède's heroic romance entitled *Cassandre,* follows the traditions of the French romances. The love interest involves three persons, one of whom destroys the happiness of the others and leads to their deaths. The three lovers are Alexander, Roxana, and Statira. Roxana is the first wife of Alexander, and she is carrying his unborn child. But she has been for a time set aside in favor of Statira, daughter of Darius, whom Alexander married. Given a chance, Roxana has tried to win her husband back, much to Statira's chagrin. Statira has made Alexander promise not to see Roxana. The two are brought together at Alexander's court at Babylon, where they play the rivals for the king's love. Statira's pride causes her to vow not to remain with Alexander, but he and his court beg her to stay, and she complies with their entreaties. Roxana, seeing herself rejected, plots with members of the court for revenge. With her fellow-conspirators and a guard of Zogdian slaves, she breaks into the bower of Semiramis, where Statira is sleeping, intending to kill her rival. Perdiccas, who by chance discovers the happenings, runs to warn Alexander, interrupting a banquet at which the king has just slain a faithful follower. The king's sorrow over the death of Clytus is broken by the news of Roxana's attack:

ALEXANDER
What says Perdiccas? Is the queen in danger?

PERDICCAS
She dies unless you turn her fate, and quickly.
Your distance from the palace asks more speed,
And the ascent to th' flying grove is high.

ALEXANDER
Thus from the grave I rise to save my love;
All draw your swords, with wings of lightning move;
When I rush on, sure none will dare to stay,
'Tis beauty calls, and glory shows the way.

'Tis Death is dead, not he

Source: ADONAIS (Stanza 41)
Author: Percy Bysshe Shelley (1792–1822)
First published: 1821
Type of work: Elegy

Context: In *Adonais,* Shelley's lament for John Keats (1795–1821), who died in Rome at the age of twenty-six years of tuberculosis—brought on, according to Shelley, by a savage review of Keats' *Endymion* in *The Quarterly Review*—the poet depicts himself visiting the bier of the dead Adonais, or Keats. The poet is a frail form, a phantom among men, companionless, an outcast, neglected and apart; he bares his brow, which is branded like Cain's or Christ's. He next depicts Joseph Severn (1793–1879), the young artist who was Keats' devoted nurse in the last illness. The poet then castigates the reviewer who struck Keats' death blow; this person, says the poet, will always be free to spill his venom, but remorse and self-contempt should cling to him and shame should burn his brow for the crime he has committed. The poet says that Keats is not dead, nor does he sleep; instead, he has awakened from the dream of life—a sentiment much like that of William Wordsworth's *Ode: Intimations of Immortality*—and has become a part of the infinite. It is we, the living, who decay like corpses. He has outsoared envy, calumny, hate, and pain, and is secure from the world's slow stain. He is alive and

1113

awake; death is dead, not he, and so   we do wrong to mourn for him.

> He lives, he wakes—'tis Death is dead, not he,
> Mourn not for Adonais.—Thou young Dawn,
> Turn all thy dew to splendor, for from thee
> The spirit thou lamentest is not gone;
> Ye caverns and ye forests, cease to moan!
> Cease, ye faint flowers and fountains, and thou Air,
> Which like a mourning veil thy scarf hadst thrown
> O'er the abandoned Earth, now leave it bare
> Even to the joyous stars which smile on its despair!

'Tis death that makes life live

Source: THE RING AND THE BOOK (Book XI, "Guido," Line 2375)
Author: Robert Browning (1812–1889)
First published: 1868–1869
Type of work: Dramatic monologue

Context: This poem is the most long sustained of Browning's works and is considered his masterpiece. It is based on an old book he found in Florence, which contains the transcript of a sensational murder trial that occurred there in 1698. The title of Browning's poem comes from the circle of evidence which is sifted in it and from the old manuscript book on which it is based. In the poem Browning restates the evidence from twelve different viewpoints and weighs it, revealing the character of each major figure through testimony. The central person is Guido Franceschini, a nobleman of fifty from Arezzo, who married a young heiress named Pompilia in order to rebuild his crumbling fortunes. She is not really the child of her supposed parents, Pietro and Violante; she has been supplied by them in order that certain property may not be transmitted to another branch of the family. When she learns from Guido why he has married her, Pompilia tells him the truth. A trial is then held to settle the property. Guido is a cruel, fiercely proud man incapable of love; his brutality now asserts itself and is such that his bride leaves him, fleeing under the protection of a young priest named Caponsacchi. Guido pursues and has them arrested, charging them with adultery; this trial ends in a separation, Pompilia going to a convent and Caponsacchi to temporary exile. She is expecting a child, however, and is allowed to go to live with her parents, where she begins a suit for divorce. Guido, in an uncontrollable fury, butchers all three; but Pompilia lives long enough to testify against him. He claims justifiable homicide at his trial but loses, and an appeal is denied by the pope. Guido's first testimony gives the impression that he is a noble man who has been unbearably humiliated and denied his rights, but his true nature is gradually revealed. In prison, awaiting execution, he talks at length to the cardinal and the abate, who have come to offer him the consolation of the

1114

Church. Here he reveals himself in all his repellent nature. He rails at the Church and its politics, attempts various deals, tries to turn back the clock to perform his murders more effectively. He reveals many of the abuses he heaped upon Pompilia, who now haunts him; he wants custody of the child to bring it up sternly. In the end he begs abjectly for mercy; this act is all the more shocking for its contrast with the bravado immediately preceding it:

> What if I be o'ertaken, pushed to the front
> By all you crowding smoother souls behind,
> And reach, a minute sooner than was meant,
> The boundary whereon I break to mist?
> Go to! the smoothest safest of you all,
> . . . .
> Will rock vertiginously in turn, and reel,
> And, emulative, rush to death like me.
> Later or sooner by a minute then,
> So much for the untimeliness of death!
> And, as regards the manner that offends,
> The rude and rough, I count the same for gain.
> Be the act harsh and quick! Undoubtedly
> The soul's condensed and, twice itself, expands
> To burst through life, by alternation due,
> Into the other state whate'er it prove.
> You never know what death means till you die:
> Even throughout life, 't is death that makes life live,
> Gives it whatever the significance.

'Tis not in mortals to command success, but we'll do more, Sempronius; we'll deserve it

Source: CATO (Act I, sc. ii, ll. 44–45)
Author: Joseph Addison (1672–1719)
First published: 1713
Type of work: Dramatic tragedy

Context: The battle of Pharsalia over, clearly Caesar has triumphed in the Roman civil war over the party of Pompey, led by Cato. While Cato meets with the remnant of his followers in the senate at Utica, his son Portius speaks with Sempronius, a senator who, though he covertly dislikes Portius, vainly seeks the hand of Marcia, sister of Portius. Portius, departing, tells Sempronius that he is going to attempt to revive the spirits of the soldiers, making them at least deserve success, though mortals cannot command it:

1115

PORTIUS

I'll straight away,
And while the fathers of the senate meet
In close debate to weigh th' events of war,
I'll animate the soldier's drooping courage,
With love of freedom and contempt of life:
I'll thunder in their ears their country's cause,
And try to rouse up all that's Roman in 'em.
'Tis not in mortals to command success,
Be we'll do more, Sempronius; we'll deserve it.

'Tis not too late to-morrow to be brave

Source: THE ART OF PRESERVING HEALTH (Book IV, l. 460)
Author: John Armstrong (1709–1779)
First published: 1744
Type of work: Didactic poem

Context: Dr. John Armstrong was a physician of the mid-eighteenth century who cultivated a wide number of friendships among the literary figures of his day, including Samuel Johnson and the poet James Thomson. These associations presumably led him to the composition of a substantial amount of poetry. Among his works are included a tragic drama, a long poem of medical advice in four books called *The Art of Preserving Health,* two verse epistles on Benevolence and Taste, and some imitations of Shakespeare and Spenser. Of prose he composed an almanac and a large number of short essays. Toward the end of *Preserving Health* he discusses the effects of the various passions on the health and warns against being led into duels by intemperate anger:

While Choler works, good Friend, you may be wrong;
Distrust yourself, and sleep before you fight.
'Tis not too late to-morrow to be brave;
If honour bids, to-morrow kill or die.
But calm advice against a raging fit
Avails too little; and it braves the power
Of all that ever taught in Prose or Song,
To tame the Fiend that sleeps a gentle Lamb,
And wakes a Lion. Unprovok'd and calm,
You reason well; see as you ought to see
And wonder at the madness of mankind:
Seiz'd with the common rage, you soon forget
The speculations of your wiser hours.

1116

'Tis not what man does which exalts him, but what man would do!

Source: SAUL (Line 295)
Author: Robert Browning (1812–1889)
First published: 1855
Type of work: Dramatic monologue

Context: David, the shepherd boy, recounts how he cured King Saul of his melancholic despair of pleasure in all things. David tells of his meeting with Abner, his entry into Saul's darkened tent, and his first glimpse of the king. David catalogues all of the good things of the earth for which Saul should thank heaven. On his harp, he tells of the God-given signs of order in all creatures and of men working together as a society. David sings of the joys of living and of Saul's great worth. Slowly, Saul regains his kingly habits and bearing. It is through David's deep love and desire to help that the boy suddenly attains a mystical glimpse of Truth. He breaks off singing and speaks aloud of the perfection of God's plan: "All's love, yet all's law." David realizes that he has been wrong in attempting to cure Saul without honestly seeking God's help. He wishes to save, redeem, and restore the king, but God alone can grant him success, for it is God's will that is the basis for all creation. David compares his own human abilities with those of the Divine:

> *I* will?—the mere atoms despise me! Why am I not loth
> To look that, even that in the face too? Why is it I dare
> Think but lightly of such impuissance? What stops my
> despair?
> This—*'tis not what man Does which exalts him, but
> what man Would do!*
> See the King—I would help him but cannot—the wishes
> fall through.
> Could I wrestle to raise him from sorrow, grow poor
> to enrich,
> To fill up his life, starve my own out, I would—know-
> ing which,
> I know that my service is perfect. . . .

'Tis pride that pulls the country down

Source: OTHELLO (Act II, sc. iii, l. 98)
Author: William Shakespeare (1564–1616)
First published: 1622
Type of work: Dramatic tragedy

Context: Enraged over the appoint- ment of Cassio as lieutenant to

Othello, Iago jealously sets out to blacken the name of Cassio and thus cause his removal from his preferred place. Knowing that Cassio does not hold his liquor well, Iago, under the pretense of celebrating the destruction of the Turkish fleet and with high good humor, prevails on Cassio to drink. There follows a planned brawl in which Cassio degrades himself and is removed from office. In the course of Cassio's temptation to drink, Iago sings a jolly song for the purpose of establishing the merriment of the moment:

IAGO

[*Sings.*]

King Stephen was and a worthy peer,
His breeches cost him but a crown,
He held them sixpence all too dear,
With that he called the tailor lown.
He was a wight of high renown,
And thou art but of low degree.
'Tis pride that pulls the country down,
Then take thine auld cloak about thee.

'Tis safest in matrimony to begin with a little aversion

Source: THE RIVALS (Act I, sc. ii)
Author: Richard Brinsley Sheridan (1751–1816)
First published: 1775
Type of work: Dramatic comedy

Context: This play and *The School for Scandal* are the two masterpieces of Sheridan's brief but brilliant career as a dramatist; in them he attempted to rescue comedy from the bathos of sentimentality into which it had fallen. In this play Miss Lydia Languish is a sentimental heiress who romantically wishes to marry a poor man. Captain Absolute, son of wealthy Sir Anthony Absolute, has come to town disguised as the impoverished Ensign Beverley in order to attract Lydia. Mrs. Malaprop, the aunt with whom Lydia resides, has been trying to promote Lydia's interest in Captain Absolute and is distressed when she realizes her plans may be foiled by Lydia's interest in Beverley. Neither of them realizes that Absolute and Beverley are the same. When her aunt charges her with her interest in Beverley, Lydia protests she has none, but her aunt persists:

MRS. MALAPROP

Now don't attempt to extirpate yourself from the matter; you know I have proof controvertible of it.—But tell me, will you promise to do as you're bid?—Will you take a husband of your friend's choosing?

1118

LYDIA

Madam, I must tell you plainly, that had I no preference for any one else, the choice you have made would be my aversion.

MRS. MALAPROP

What business have you, Miss, with *preference* and *aversion?* They don't become a young woman; and you ought to know, that as both always wear off, **'tis safest in matrimony to begin with a little aversion.** I am sure I hated your poor dear uncle before marriage as if he'd been a black-a-moor—and yet, Miss, you are sensible what a wife I made!—and when it pleas'd heaven to release me from him, 'tis unknown what tears I shed! . . .

To be constant, in nature were inconstancy

Source: INCONSTANCY (Lines 19–20)
Author: Abraham Cowley (1618–1667)
First published: 1647
Type of work: Lyric poem

Context: "Inconstancy" is a defense of fickle love, and it is a poem which, in both its abruptness and extended figure of speech, is reminiscent of the earlier "metaphysical" poems of John Donne. To the woman who accuses the man of inconstancy because he loved her five years before, the "I" of the poem replies that he must not be labeled inconstant. He points out that he simply is not the same man he was, that the body, as well as the mind, has changed. He further construes that, since the old members of his body were father to the present members, to be constant were to commit incest, forbidden by nature. He also states that all nature is a state of flux; change is the rule of existence: no one, nor anything, can be blamed for following its nature. The days, the seasons, all in nature must move on blamelessly. He ends by saying that it is as senseless to expect deathless love as to expect beauty and color found in the living person to remain with the corpse.

> You might as well this day inconstant name,
> Because the weather is not still the same
> That it was yesterday; or blame the year,
> 'Cause the spring, flowers, and autumn, fruit does bear.
> The world's a scene of changes, and **to be
> Constant, in nature were inconstancy;**
> For 'twere to break the laws herself has made:
> Our substances themselves do fleet and fade;
> The most fixed being still does move and fly,
> Swift as the wings of time 'tis measured by.

To Carthage I came

Source: CONFESSIONS (Book III, Chapter 1)
Author: St. Augustine (354–430)
First transcribed: 397–401
Type of work: Autobiography

Context: This autobiography, one of the earliest, was written as a testimonial to the infinite mercies of God. Its author, one of the most renowned fathers of Christianity, did not in youth and early manhood give any indication that he would become one of the great religious figures of the ages. His father, Patricius, was a pagan; his mother, Monica, was a Christian. She instructed him carefully in her faith, but it was many years before he allowed her teachings to influence him to any great extent. Instead, he pursued a life of sensuality, which continued after he was sent to Carthage to study for the profession of rhetorician. Here he became interested in theology and was a Manichaean for nine years; then, in 386, he was converted to the orthodox church by the study of Scripture and the discourses of St. Ambrose. In time he became bishop of Hippo, in which office he was distinguished by his greatness of heart, his wisdom as displayed in various theological controversies, and his belief in individual merit and divine grace as applied to the doctrine of predestination. His authority has always been high in Roman Catholicism, and is still cited in regard to doctrinal questions. His autobiography, *Confessions,* was written to exhibit the manner in which a flagrant sinner can be reformed and uplifted through divine grace; it has enjoyed a wide influence since his time. In it he describes his childhood and youth with deep regret over the lost opportunities for better use of his time. He recounts manfully the things he would rather forget—idleness, inattention to his studies, an addiction to sexual pleasures, and the cultivation of bad companions who led him to thievery. Augustine then describes, in the light of later wisdom, that Carthage to which he was sent in pursuit of his studies, seeing it now as a place of vice and corruption and not as the glamorous and exciting place he had found it then:

To Carthage I came, where there sang all around me in my ears a cauldron of unholy loves. I loved not yet, yet I loved to love, and out of a deepseated want, I hated myself for wanting not. I sought what I might love, in love with loving, and safety I hated, and a way without snares. For within me was a famine of that inward food, Thyself, my God; yet, through that famine I was not hungered; but was without all longing for incorruptible sustenance, not because filled therewith, but the more empty, the more I loathed it. For this cause my soul was sickly and full of sores, it miserably cast itself forth, desiring to be scraped by the touch of objects of sense. Yet if these had not a soul, they would not be objects of love. To love them, and to be beloved, was sweet to me; but more, when I obtained to enjoy the person I loved. I defiled, therefore, the spring of friendship with the filth of concupiscence, and I beclouded its brightness with the hell of lustfulness; and thus foul and unseemly, I would fain, through exceeding vanity, be fine and courtly. I fell headlong then into the love wherein I longed to be ensnared. My God, my Mercy, with how much gall didst Thou out of Thy great goodness besprinkle for me that sweetness? For I was both beloved, and secretly arrived at the bond of enjoying; and was with joy fettered with sorrow-bringing bonds, that I might be scourged with the iron-burning rods of jealousy, and suspicion, and fears, and angers, and quarrels.

To compare great things with small

Source: PARADISE LOST (Book II, ll. 921–922)
Author: John Milton (1608–1674)
First published: 1667
Type of work: Epic poem

Context: It having been decided in the great council of the devils that Satan should seduce mankind so as to destroy God's favorite creation, Satan makes his way towards the gates of hell. He meets a creature that is a woman above and a serpent below; this monster announces that she is Sin, who issued from Satan's head, as Athena had issued from the head of Zeus. There is a specter with her who is the product of Satan's incestuous dalliance with Sin; he is Death, and is inseparable from Sin. Satan cajoles Sin into opening the gates of hell so that he can go up to earth on his wicked errand. She opens the gates, but for ever cannot close them again. Satan and Sin look out on the hoary deep where Chaos and Night, the ancestors of nature, rule. Here the four elements war for mastery, and Chance governs all. Satan stands on the brink of hell and contemplates the wild abyss, pondering his trip. To compare the noises of hell with the sounds caused by the Roman Goddess of War is to compare objects on two levels. "Frith" is a clearing in the woods.

> Into this wild abyss the wary fiend
> Stood on the brink of hell and looked a while,
> Pondering his voyage: for no narrow frith
> He had to cross. Nor was his ear less pealed
> With noises loud and ruinous (**to compare
> Great things with small**) than when Bellona storms,
> With all her battering engines set to raze
> Some capital city, or less than if this frame
> Of heaven were falling, and these elements
> In mutiny had from her axle torn
> The steadfast earth.

1121

To die in the last ditch

Source: HISTORY OF HIS OWN TIMES (Under date 1672)
Author: Bishop Gilbert Burnet (1643–1715)
First published: 1724
Type of work: History

Context: Gilbert Burnet, born and educated in Scotland, was a strongly anti-Catholic professor of divinity in Glasgow; a man of learning, orthodox in his faith, but honest and bold. He got into difficulties by reprimanding Charles II for his dissolute living, and was outlawed to Holland during the reign of James II. He returned to England for the coronation of William III and Mary, for whom he preached the coronation sermon. They made him Bishop of Salisbury. He was also influential in court during the life of Queen Mary and Queen Anne, who followed her. His son William (1688–1724) served as governor of the colonies of New York, New Jersey, and Massachusetts. As a writer, Bishop Burnet had a casual and inelegant style, but his work was interesting because he knew most of the important political people of his time. So his *History of His Own Times*, published after his death, is a gossipy account of goings-on, written by an incurable name-dropper: "As the Duke of Buckingham said to me," "Mr. May of the privy purse told me," "Lord Lauderdale and Sir Robert Murray asked my opinion." One criticism leveled at him as a historian is that he was too uncritical of his sources. On one occasion, mentioning a scandal about the Duchess of Orléans, he writes, "It was told me by a person of distinction who had it from some who were well informed about the matter." In his personal copy, Swift scribbled alongside this sentence: "Poor authority." However, there were many matters included on good authority published in the first folio volume that was printed in 1724. It covers the reigns of Charles II and James II. The second volume, appearing in 1734, edited by the bishop's youngest son, Sir Thomas Burnet, included a note that manuscripts of both the volumes had been deposited in the Cotton Library (associated with the British Museum). However, researchers have never found them. For later editions, like the four-volume 1753 edition and the six-volume Oxford University edition of 1833, notes and corrections by Dean Swift, the Earl of Dartmouth, and the Earl of Hardwicke, have been incorporated to insure accuracy. The historian begins by a survey of conditions in Scotland before the restoration of Charles II in 1660. Book II covers the first twelve years of Charles' reign. The chatty style makes pleasant reading, with the additional satisfaction of knowing it is a firsthand account. There is no chapter division, but the year covered appears at the head of the page. Under the date 1672, Bishop Burnet is describing difficulties encountered by the Prince of Orange whose territory had been seized by the King of France. Burnet pictures the extremities of the Dutch and the partiality of the British Embassy toward the French in negotiations. Its head, the Duke of Buckingham, is trying to get the Prince of Orange to put himself into his hands, but the prince objects because his country trusts him and he will not betray it.

> . . . The duke answered, he was not to think any more of his country, for it was lost: if it should weather out the summer, by reason of the waters that had drowned a great part of it, the winter's frost would lay them open: and he repeated the words often, "Do not you see it is lost?" The prince's answer deserves to be remembered: he said, he saw it was indeed in great danger; but there was a sure way never to see it lost, and that was **to die in the last ditch.**

To enjoy one's past life is to live twice

Source: EPIGRAMS (Book X, 23)
Author: Martial (Marcus Valerius Martialis, c. 40–c. 104)
First transcribed: c. 84
Type of work: Epigram

Context: Marcus Valerius Martialis, born in Bilbilis, Spain, went to Rome and attached himself to influential patrons, including Emperors Titus and Domitian. His brief satirical epigrams are revealing of Roman life of the first century. In *Epigram* *XXIII, on M. Antonius Primus,* Martial writes of a man, who at the age of seventy-five looks back on all of his days with pleasure, and hence, by the joy of reflection on his previous happiness, in effect doubles the time of his existence:

> The happy Antonius Primus now numbers fifteen Olympiads (75 years) passed in tranquility; he looks back upon the days that are gone, and the whole of his past years, without fearing the waters of Lethe to which he daily draws nearer. Not one day of his brings remorse or an unpleasant reflection; there is none which he would be unwilling to recall. A good man lengthens his term of existence; to be able **to enjoy our past life is to live twice.**

To have great poets, there must be great audiences, too

Source: NOTES LEFT OVER ("Ventures, on an Old Theme")
Author: Walt Whitman (1819–1892)
First published: 1882
Type of work: Essay

Context: Walt Whitman is known today for his poetry depicting the America of his time in all its facets, sordid as well as sublime. That he wrote a sizeable quantity of prose is not as well known. Much of the latter was editorial writing. At the age of thirteen he worked on the press of the *Long Island Star*; at sixteen he was a compositor in New York. Following a brief interlude as teacher, he bought a press and founded the *Long Islander*, in Huntington. Here he continued for a year, then returned to New York and became managing editor of the *Daily Aurora*. During the next few years he worked for several newspapers, one of them in New Orleans. When *Leaves of Grass* was published, Whitman had high hopes for it; but his poetry was greeted with widespread condemnation. He returned to journalism in order to earn a living, becoming editor of the Brooklyn *Daily Times*. After his service nursing the wounded during the Civil War, he held some minor jobs in Washington, and during this time he wrote more or less steadily. His poetry was still a victim of censorship and prejudice; he did not live to see it widely accepted. Although much of his prose is editorial writing in condemnation of social and political ills, crusading for reforms, there are a number of pieces which pertain to the craft of writing. "Ventures, on an Old Theme," from one of the collections of his miscellaneous writings, is such a work. It begins with a dialogue in which one person observes that we do certain things in privacy that society would not allow us to do in public: the same should be true of poetry. The poet replies that poetry is true freedom, and that in the deepest sense it cannot offend. He believes it is time to break down the barriers of false morality and the strict conventions of poetic composition. The new poetry should disregard that artificial distinction between prose and verse, and its inspiration should come from that part of America which is bursting with energy and growth.

Of poems of the third or fourth class, (perhaps even some of the second,) it makes little or no difference who writes them—they are good enough for what they are; nor is it necessary that they should be actual emanations from the personality and life of the writers. The very reverse sometimes gives piquancy. But poems of the first class, (poems of the depth, as distinguished from those of the surface,) are to be sternly tallied with the poets themselves, and tried by them and their lives. . . .

In these States, beyond all precedent, poetry will have to do with actual facts, with the concrete States, and—for we have not much more than begun—with the definitive getting into shape of the Union. Indeed I sometimes think *it* alone is to define the Union, (namely, to give it artistic character, spirituality, dignity.) What American humanity is most in danger of is an overwhelming prosperity, "business" worldliness, materialism: what is most lacking, east, west, north, south, is a fervid and glowing Nationality and patriotism, cohering all the parts into one. Who may fend that danger, and fill that lack in the future, but a class of loftiest poets?

If the United States haven't grown poets, on any scale of grandeur, it is certain they import, print, and read more poetry than any equal number of people elsewhere—probably more than all the rest of the world combined.

Poetry (like a grand personality) is a growth of many generations—many rare combinations.

To have great poets, there must be great audiences, too.

To hold the mirror up to nature

Source: HAMLET (Act III, sc. ii, l. 23)
Author: William Shakespeare (1564–1616)
First published: 1603
Type of work: Dramatic tragedy

Context: Hamlet, Prince of Denmark, urged by the Ghost of his dead father to avenge his murder, is uncertain of the nature of the Ghost. To determine whether the Ghost is good or evil and whether it tells the truth of his father's death at the hands of King Claudius, he plans to insert into a play a few lines which will indicate, by the reaction of Claudius, the guilt or innocence of the accused. In his famous speech to the actors, Hamlet (and Shakespeare) directs them in the method of acting:

Be not too tame neither, but let your own discretion be your tutor. Suit the action to the word, the word to the action, with this special observance, that you o'erstep not the modesty of nature. For anything so o'erdone is from the purpose of playing, whose end both at the first, and now, was and is, **to hold** as 'twere **the mirror up to nature;** to show virtue her own feature, scorn her own image, and the very age and body of the time his form and pressure. . . .

To innovate is not to reform

Source: A LETTER TO A NOBLE LORD
Author: Edmund Burke (1729–1797)
First published: 1796
Type of work: Open Letter

Context: Burke's retirement from Parliament in 1794 was soon followed by the very tragic death of the son in whom he had taken great pride. After a lifetime spent in dedicated service to the public welfare, Burke hoped at last to spend his final years in tranquillity. He should have been able to do so, for the king had granted him a generous, but not excessive, pension. He was not to find peace, however, for in 1795, in the House of Lords, the Duke of Bedford and the Earl of Lauderdale attacked both Burke and his pension. Thus, in his last months, he was constrained to take up his pen once more in his own defense. In this public letter, which is that defense, Burke begins by surveying his services to his country, especially in the area of reform:

> . . . Change is novelty; and whether it is to operate any one of the effects of reformation at all, or whether it may not contradict the very principle upon which reformation is desired cannot be certainly known beforehand. Reform is not a change in the substance or in the primary modification of the object, but a direct application of a remedy to the grievance complained of. . . .
> All this, in effect, I think, but am not sure, I have said elsewhere. It cannot at this time be too often repeated, line upon line, precept upon precept, until it comes into the currency of a proverb,—**To innovate is not to reform.** The French revolutionists complained of everything; they refused to reform anything; and they left nothing, no, nothing at all, *unchanged.* The consequences are *before* us,—not in remote history, not in future prognostication: they are about us, they are upon us. They shake the public security; they menace private enjoyment. . . .

To live in hearts we leave behind is not to die

Source: HALLOWED GROUND (Stanza 6)
Author: Thomas Campbell (1777–1844)
First published: 1824
Type of work: Patriotic poem

Context: Thomas Campbell was a Scotch poet, once highly regarded but now largely forgotten, except for his didactic *Pleasures of Hope* (1799), that contributed such phrases as: " 'Tis distance lends enchantment to the view," and "Like angel-visits, few and far between." He also made patriotic hearts throb with a dozen bold poems like "Ye Mariners of England." (1801). After considering emigrating to America where his brothers were already settled, he gave up the idea when a publisher paid him sixty pounds for *Pleasures of Hope.* He then started working on a long poem called *Gertrude of Wyoming or the Pennsylvania Cottage,* his closest contact with the New World. It deals with an Indian massacre and was published in 1809. Among other of his hack work were a three-volume *Annals of Great Britain* (1802), and a seven-volume *Specimens of British Poets* (1819). Of himself, he said, "the only important event of his life's little history" was his proposal to establish the University of London, which was accomplished with the aid of Henry Peter Brougham (1778–1868) and Joseph Hume (1777–1855). For his contribution to literature, as well as to education, he was given burial in the Poets' Corner of Westminster Abbey. Because of his stirring patriotic *Lines on Poland* and *The Power of Russia,* both of 1831, as well as his interest in 1832 in the Polish Literary Association, a guard of Polish nobles sprinkled on his grave earth from the grave of Kosciusko. The poem "Hallowed Ground" begins with a demand to know the meaning of the phrase. Did God set apart some section of the earth not to be sullied by the foot of man, made in the image of God? Does the expression refer to the grave where "lips repose our love has kissed?" No, because that soul still lives on, a part of oneself. Everything except true love fades, and that will not cool "until the heart itself be cold in Lethe's pool." Campbell then answers his question in stanzas five and six, and in a stirring final stanza.

What hallows ground where heroes sleep?
'T is not the scuptured piles you heap!
In dews that heavens far distant weep
    Their turf may bloom;
Or Genii twine beneath the deep
    Their coral tomb.

But strew his ashes to the wind
Whose sword or voice has served mankind—
And is he dead whose glorious mind
    Lifts thine on high?—
To live in hearts we leave behind
    Is not to die.

                    . . .

What's hallowed ground? 'Tis what gives birth
To sacred thoughts in souls of worth!—
Peace! Independence! Truth! go forth
    Earth's compass round,
And your high priesthood shall make earth
    All hallowed ground.

To lose thee were to lose myself

Source: PARADISE LOST (Book IX, l. 959)
Author: John Milton (1608–1674)
First published: 1667
Type of work: Epic poem

Context: When Eve has been deceived by Satan disguised as a serpent into eating the forbidden fruit of the tree of the knowledge of good and evil, she is stimulated and intoxicated by what she has done. She wonders whether she should tell Adam of her act, as sharing the fruit with him will elevate him and remove her newly acquired superiority, and she feels great pleasure in feeling superior. She then thinks that if death actually does come upon her, as had been threatened by God and reiterated by his angels, Adam will live on in the garden in his innocence and will take to himself another Eve. She cannot stand this idea and decides that he must eat

1127

the fruit and so share her fate, whatever it will be. She approaches him and confesses what she has done; she extols the fruit highly, as it has made her feel like a god. Adam is horrorstriken at her disclosure, but his uncontrolled passion will not tolerate the idea of his living alone after her death, and therefore he will eat the fruit and share her fate. He then begins to think that God will not actually kill them, as killing them would be to uncreate what he has created. Killing Adam and Eve would be a triumph for the enemy of mankind, who would, according to Adam, say:

> "Me first
> He ruined, now mankind; whom will He next?"
> Matter of scorn, not to be given the foe.
> However, I with thee have fixed my lot,
> Certain to undergo like doom, if death
> Consort with thee, Death is to me as life;
> So forcible within my heart I feel
> The bond of nature draw me to my own,
> My own in thee, for what thou art is mine;
> Our state cannot be severed, we are one,
> One flesh; **to lose thee were to lose myself.**

To make your children capable of honesty is the beginning of education

Source: TIME AND TIDE (Letter viii)
Author: John Ruskin (1819–1900)
First published: 1867
Type of work: Letters

Context: English painter, art critic, and essayist, John Ruskin devoted his long life and his boundless energies to a denunciation of the materialistic standards of Victorian life. In his early writings he proclaimed the means of perceiving beauty in art to a society which he believed to be faithless and dislocated. In his later life his interests turned to the social conditions which forced workers to slave for long hours in production lines that brought no satisfaction or sense of creativity with a finished product. He became convinced that the ultimate test of the value of work and whatever it produces was its effect upon the human soul and the dignity of the individual. *Time and Tide* was originally a series of letters written in the early spring of 1867 to Thomas Dixon, a working cork-cutter of Sunderland, in support of the local agitation for reform. His central thesis is that reform will come not merely from parliamentary influence but from a knowledgeable determination on the part of the people themselves to seek a higher standard of life. Until the people are able to articulate or to visualize such a life, no decrees of parliament will create it. In the eighth letter, he stresses the absolute necessity of a strong moral foundation, of good character, for the realization of a meaningful life:

> . . . your honesty is not to be based either on religion or policy. Both your religion and policy must be based on it. Your honesty must be based, as the sun is, in vacant heaven; poised, as the lights in the firmament, which have rule over the day and over the night. If you ask why you are to be honest—you are, in the question itself, dishonored. "Because you are a man," is the only answer; and therefore I said in a former letter that **to make your children "capable of honesty" is the beginning of education.** Make them men first, and religious men afterwards, and all will be sound; but a knave's religion is always the rottenest thing about him.

To play billiards well was a sign of an ill-spent youth

Source: LIFE AND LETTERS OF HERBERT SPENCER (Chapter 20)
Author: David Duncan (1839–1923)
First published: 1908
Type of work: Attributed comment

Context: Most of Spencer's working life was spent in promoting and elaborating Darwinian theories of evolution. The philosophy which he developed from these theories he applied to every phase of man's development, applying the same principles he had already elaborated in biology to other aspects of human growth and society. In working out these systems of evolutionary development he gave his attention to psychology, sociology, ethics, education, and other matters. In education he scorned any study of the liberal arts, believing that all things must have a scientific basis and that science should itself be the basis of all education. His work gained him numerous honors and academic degrees, all of which he politely refused. His later years were spent in preparing his autobiography and in gathering his letters and miscellaneous writings together for publication, work in which David Duncan assisted him. At the same time he spoke up for numerous causes in which liberty played a part. During the last decade of his life an anecdote became current in which Spencer was said to have condemned billiards, a genteel indoor sport highly esteemed and long popular. The story was published repeatedly in various papers, with many variations on the basic theme; though a minor and even petty matter, it was a source of irritation to Spencer. Shortly before Spencer's death, Duncan asked him to dictate a statement that would give the truth of the story and settle it permanently. Spencer obliged with the following account of the anecdote's origin and original form. It is evident that he bitterly regrets having repeated the expression, which has now haunted him for so long:

1129

One afternoon some ten years ago, when seated in the billiard room of the Athenaeum Club, it was remarked to me by the late Mr. Charles Roupell (an Official Referee of the High Court of Justice) that **to play billiards well was a sign of an ill-spent youth.** Whether there was or was not any game going on at the time I cannot remember, but I am sure he would not have made a remark any way offensive to any one in the room.

In the course of that autumn or a subsequent autumn, when we had our interchange of visits with the United Service Club opposite, I repeated this saying of Roupell's—*repeated,* I say, not giving any implication that it was an idea of my own, and most positively not making it in reference to any game I was playing or had played, or in reference to games played by any one else: it was absolutely dissociated from anybody, and was simply uttered by me as an abstract proposition. This abstract proposition presently made its appearance in. I presume, one or other evening paper. In the first version, I think a young Major was the other party to the story. Then from time to time it went the round of the papers, and having dropped for a while, reappeared in other papers (provincial included), always with variations and additions: the result being a cock-and-bull story, having no basis whatever further than the fact that I once repeated this saying of Roupell's apropos of nobody.

To produce a mighty book, you must choose a mighty theme

Source: MOBY DICK (Chapter 104)
Author: Herman Melville (1819–1891)
First published: 1851
Type of work: Novel

Context: At the beginning of this chapter Melville begins to write in an almost florid style, in keeping with the subject matter of the chapter; as he says, "From his mighty bulk the whale affords a most congenial theme whereon to enlarge, amplify, and generally expatiate." Using the old-fashioned terminology of the printers and bookbinders in the seventeenth century, he says that the only appropriate treatment of the whale should be done in an "imperial folio." Saying that he will now treat of the whale "in an archaeological, fossiliferous, and antediluvian point of view," in portly terms "unwarrantably grandiloquent" for any creature but the Leviathan, Melville comments that for his present purpose he uses only a huge quarto edition of Dr. Samuel Johnson's *Dictionary,* it being the only lexicon, and its author the only lexicographer, appropriate to the subject. Melville says how he feels about writing on the subject of whales, and one senses that the passage is only partly humorous in tone:

One often hears of writers that rise and swell with their subject,

1130

though it may seem but an ordinary one. How, then, with me, writing of this Leviathan? Unconsciously my chirography expands into placard capitals. Give me a condor's quill! Give me Vesuvius' crater for an inkstand! Friends, hold my arms! For in the mere act of penning my thoughts of this Leviathan, they weary me, and make me faint with their outreaching comprehensiveness of sweep, as if to include the whole circle of the sciences, and all the generations of whales, and men, and mastodons, past, present, and to come, with all the revolving panoramas of empire on earth, and throughout the whole universe, not excluding its suburbs. Such, and so magnifying, is the virtue of a large and liberal theme! We expand to its bulk. **To produce a mighty book, you must choose a mighty theme.** No great and enduring volume can ever be written on the flea, though many there be who have tried it.

To see her is to love her

Source: BONIE LESLEY (Stanza 2)
Author: Robert Burns (1759–1796)
First published: 1787
Type of work: Lyric poem

Context: Because of the demands on Burns to provide lyrics for songs, he turned every occurrence into an inspiration for a song that went either to James Johnson for his five-volume *Scots Musical Museum* (1787–1803) or to George Thomson for his six-volume *Select Collection of Original Scottish Airs for the Voice* (1793–1811). In these two publications can be found 268 such beautiful songs as "Flow Gently Sweet Afton," "John Anderson, My Jo," and "My Heart's in the Highland." One day a friend, Mr. Bailie of Ayrshire, stopped to visit Burns at Dumfries, on his way to England. Two of his daughters came with him. Burns was always a man moved by feminine beauty, and Miss Lesley Bailie especially attracted him. When they left, he saddled his horse and accompanied them a dozen miles along their journey. Then he told them goodbye and rode slowly homeward, composing a song to the clack of his horse's hoofs. He called it "Bonie Leslie," with "Bonie" rhyming with "Caledonie." He always spelled the word that way in the titles for a dozen other songs, and left it for other Scots to write of Bonnie Annie Laurie or Bonnie Prince Charlie. Its tune is "The Collier's bonie Dochter." At first, Burns compares her to Alexander the Great, seeking new worlds to conquer. "Sic anither" is "such another." "Deil" is "devil." In "belang" and "wrang," the Scotch dialect substitutes "a" for "o." Some one has commented that Burns' waning popularity is due to the fact that to understand and appreciate him, a reader has to learn the Scotch dialect. However, only a little imagination is necessary to read most of his poetry. Here are stanzas one, two, four, and six of "Bonie Lesley"

O saw ye bonie Lesley
    As she gaed o'er the border?
She's gane, like Alexander,
    To spread her conquests farther.

To see her is to love her,
    And love but her for ever;
For Nature made her what she is,
    And ne'er made sic anither!
       • • •

The Deil he could na scaith thee,
    Or aught that wad belang thee;
He'd look into thy bonie face,
    And say, "I canna wrang thee."
       • • •

Return again, Fair Lesley,
    Return to Caledonie!
That we may brag, we hae a lass
    There's nane again sae bonie.

To set a candle in the sun

Source: ANATOMY OF MELANCHOLY (Partition III, sec. 2, memb. I, subsec. 2)
Author: Robert Burton (1577–1640)
First published: 1621–1651
Type of work: Essays

Context: So vast an outpouring of learning, whimsy, wit, sentiment, and noble ideas has rarely been expressed with satire and irony in one book as the Reverend Robert Burton, clergyman and instructor at Christ Church College, Oxford, crowded into his *Anatomy of Melancholy.* It is further adorned with quotations from the Bible and from French, Latin, and Greek authors. It first appeared in 1621, followed by corrected and enlarged editions in 1624, 1628, 1632, 1636, and finally the one that the author promised would be the last version he would ever prepare, the edition that appeared posthumously, in 1651. It has been consulted ever since by poets such as Milton and Keats, dramatists such as John Ford, and novelists such as Sterne and Thackeray. Poetry, philosophy, unnatural Natural History, medicine, history, theology, and many other subjects occupied Burton's attention, the statements being attested by reference to at least two hundred authors. Perhaps the title should have been "An Analysis of Morbid Psychology." In that field Burton anticipated Freud. The first two Partitions deal respectively with the causes and the cures of melancholy. In the third part, the author discusses Love-Melancholy. It is divided into Sections, then into Members and Subsections. Its bachelor-author begins with a discussion of the development of love, a subject subdivided into the objects of a man's love, and a treatise on charity. The second section deals with "Heroical love," as a cause of melancholy; and its second subsection: How Love tyranizes over man. In this part, Burton discusses passions created in men. Remarking that Helen was not the first female that caused a war, he names three or four other guilty women. He then considers unnatural love, of many varieties, and finally comes to "that Heroical love" that is a frequent cause of melancholy. Chaucer and the Bible are cited to testify that all men have at least once known this sentiment. Many have discovered how easily it can burst its bounds. In developing this topic, the author first talks of the insatiable lust for women, but after pursuing the subject over several pages, he calls a halt. He can never exhaust this topic. It is foolish to cast the little light he can, in comparison with the blazing magnitude of the subject. As he puts it:

> But to enlarge or illustrate this power and effect of love is **to set a candle in the sun.** It rageth with all sorts and conditions of men, yet is most evident among such as are young and lusty, in the flower of their years, nobly descended, high fed, such as live idly, and at ease; and for that cause (which our Divines call burning lust) this mad and beastly passion, as I have said, is named by our Physicians Heroical Love, and a more honorable title put upon it, Noble Love, as Savanarola styles it, because Noble men and women make common practice of it, . . .

To suckle fools, and chronicle small beer

Source: OTHELLO (Act II, sc. i, l. 161)
Author: William Shakespeare (1564–1616)
First published: 1622
Type of work: Dramatic tragedy

Context: Desdemona, fair bride to Othello, the Moor of Venice, awaits the arrival of her husband on Cyprus. Iago, ensign to Othello, entertains Desdemona and Emilia, his wife, by displaying his wit in the form of couplet praise for various types of women. Desdemona asks how he would praise the woman whose virtue would disprove the proof of evil itself. He describes the lady and then concludes by saying that her role in life will be that of the mother of fools and the keeper of small household accounts (small beer).

DESDEMONA
. . . But what praise couldst thou bestow on a deserving woman indeed, one that in the authority of her merit, did justly put on the vouch of very malice itself?

1133

She that was ever fair, and never proud,
Had tongue at will, and yet was never loud;
Never lacked gold, and yet went never gay,
Fled from her wish, and yet said, now I may;

. . .

She that could think, and ne'er disclose her mind,
See suitors following, and not look behind;
She was a wight, if ever such wight were—

DESDEMONA

To do what?

IAGO

To suckle fools, and chronicle small beer.

To tax and to please is not given to men

Source: SPEECH ON AMERICAN TAXATION
Author: Edmund Burke (1729–1797)
First published: 1775
Type of work: Political speech

Context: Lord North, an important leader in Parliament, was determined to take strong punitive measures when news of the Boston Tea Party reached London. Burke, perhaps the greatest political philosopher England has ever produced, spoke in defense of the American Colonies, as he was to do on numerous occasions. The first part of his speech is a close and vigorous argument concerning the expediency of repealing the tax on tea; the second part consists of a history of the whole subject of the American taxation issue with several caustically ironic portraits of the various politicians who had concerned themselves with the matter. One of these politicians, Charles Townshend, attempted to exercise his fiscal powers so as to provide revenue and to offend no one; he was singularly unsuccessful:

Here this extraordinary man, then Chancellor of the Exchequer, found himself in great straits. To please universally was the object of his life; but **to tax and to please,** no more than to love and to be wise, **is not given to men.** However, he attempted it. To render the tax palatable to the partisans of American revenue, he made a preamble stating the necessity of such a revenue. To close with the American distinction, this revenue was *external* or port-duty; but again, to soften it to the other party, it was a duty of *supply.* To gratify the *colonists,* it was laid on British manufacturers; to satisfy the *merchants of Britain,* the duty was trivial, and (except that on tea, which touched only the devoted East India Company) on none of the grand objects of commerce. . . .

To teach the young idea how to shoot

Source: THE SEASONS: SPRING (Line 1149)
Author: James Thomson (1700–1748)
First published: 1728 ("Spring")
Type of work: Pastoral poem

Context: Thomson, an English poet, was a forerunner of romanticism. At the time when he wrote his long work, *The Seasons,* neoclassicism was the current style in literature. Thomson introduced a number of romantic qualities into his poetry which were then unique; among these were a love of nature, sensuous imagery, a humanitarian impulse, and touches of fantasy. He is one of the founders of nature poetry as a literary form. In *The Seasons* he also reintroduced blank verse as an acceptable medium of poetic expression and helped to establish the tradition of Milton as a strong influence in the development of poetry in England. *The Seasons* is the first nature poem of any length in the English language; it was published over a period of time, from 1726 to 1730. The four sections, though not devoted to nature exclusively, never diverge from it altogether. "Spring" begins with an invocation; Thomson sings of the new grass, the flowers, and the soft rain. Winter is gone at last, though the change is not yet complete. Presently the sun and air grow warmer; the streams become torrents and the grip of the frost is finally broken. Crops are sown. "Ye generous Britons, venerate the plough!" is Thomson's exhortation, as he considers the blessings with which nature has endowed the land. Leaves appear on the trees, and the hills turn green. It is a precarious season, and the dangers of gale, frost, insect plagues, and wet summers are yet to be passed. But in the year of the poet's description none of these tragedies occurs; all things grow and flourish. After a brief digression concerning man's disastrous abandonment of his happy pastoral estate, Thomson returns to the progress of the season, and we have a glimpse of the poet himself. The spring runoff has ended, and the streams are clear: "now is the time,/ While yet the dark-brown water aids the guile,/ To tempt the trout. The well-dissembled fly,/ The rod fine-tapering with elastic spring,/ Snatch'd from the hoary steed the floating line,/ And all thy slender watry stores prepare./ But let not on thy hook the tortur'd worm,/ Convulsive, twist in agonizing folds;/ Which, by rapacious hunger swallow'd deep,/ Gives, as you tear it from the bleeding breast/ Of the weak helpless uncomplaining wretch,/ Harsh pain and horror to the tender hand." Thomson now abandons the joys of fishing and takes up the profusion of spring flowers and of birds; he discourses on the joys of love and notes the mating of all living things. He ends with what is essentially a benediction:

> . . . those whom love cements in holy faith,
> And equal transport, free as Nature live,
> Disdaining fear. What is the world to them,

Its pomp, its pleasure, and its nonsense all!
Who in each other clasp whatever fair
High fancy forms, and lavish hearts can wish;
Something than beauty dearer, should they look
Or on the mind, or mind-illumin'd face;
Truth, goodness, honour, harmony, and love,
The richest bounty of indulgent heav'n.
Meantime a smiling offspring rises round,
And mingles both their graces. . . .
Then infant reason grows apace, and calls
For the kind hand of an assiduous care.
Delightful task! to rear the tender thought,
To teach the young idea how to shoot,
To pour the fresh instruction o'er the mind. . . .

To the public good private respects must yield

Source: SAMSON AGONISTES (Lines 867–868)
Author: John Milton (1608–1674)
First published: 1671
Type of work: Dramatic tragedy

Context: Samson, blinded, betrayed to the Philistines by Delilah, who, in Milton's drama is his wife but who in *Judges* 16:4 is merely a woman from the valley of Sorek whom he loved, laments his great fall from the position of God's elect to that of a slave to the enemy. Delilah appears on the scene and is scorned by Samson as a traitoress, but she says that she comes in conjugal affection and hopes to lighten his sufferings. She tries to justify her betrayal of him to his enemies and says that it was her womanly weakness of natural curiosity, a product of her love for him, that made her pry into the secret of his strength; and if she should not have tried to learn his secret, he, on the other hand, should not have told it to her. She says that she did not want to be deserted like Samson's former wife at Timnath and thought that she could bind him to her if she knew his secret. And furthermore, the Philistines who bribed her to tell the secret assured her that all that was intended against Samson was to place him in safe custody, where she could enjoy his company and his love the while he remained safely out of danger. Samson belittles her reasons by saying that any criminal could excuse his wrongful acts by pleading his own weakness, and how could she expect his love to be a product of her betrayal? Delilah then says that the proposal to betray him was presented to her as her duty to entrap a common enemy; that is, it was her public duty:

Only my love of thee held long debate,
And combated in silence all these reasons
With hard contest: at length that grounded maxim

1136

So rife and celebrated in the mouths
Of wisest men, that **to the public good
Private respects must yield,** with grave authority
Took full possession of me and prevailed;
Virtue, as I thought, truth, duty so enjoining.

To the windward of the law

Source: THE GHOST (Book III, l. 56)
Author: Charles Churchill (1731–1764)
First published: 1762–63
Type of work: Satiric poem

Context: Churchill was a dissipated clergyman who won for himself both fame and notoriety as a satiric poet during the last few years of his life. Much of the character of his verse seems to have been determined by his association with the unscrupulous editor of the *North-Briton,* John Wilkes. The story of the Cock Lane Ghost broke in 1762 when William Kent was accused of having committed adultery with and subsequently murdered his sister-in-law, Fanny Lynes. The accusation was made by Richard Parsons, whom Kent had sued for debt, and the evidence was the testimony of Fanny's ghost given through Parsons' daughter as a medium. Kent appealed to the courts to vindicate his character, and a commission including Dr. Samuel Johnson investigated the affair and pronounced it all a fraud. The affair was a very popular butt for satirists, including the dramatists, and Churchill's somewhat rambling comic treatment extends to four books. Book III, which is concerned with the doings of the commission of inquiry, is prefaced by a long introductory passage giving in mock-epic fashion the setting:

It was the Hour, when Devotees
Breathe *pious curses* on their knees,
When they with pray'rs the day begin
To sanctify a Night of Sin;
When Rogues of Modesty, who roam
Under the veil of Night, sneak home,
That free from all restraint and awe,
Just **to the windward of the Law,**
Less modest Rogues their tricks may play,
And plunder in the face of day.
    But hold—whilst thus we play the fool,
In bold contempt of ev'ry rule,
Things of no consequence expressing,
Describing now, and now *digressing,*
To the discredit of our skill,
The main concern is standing still.

1137

To whose profit?

Source: PRO MILONE (For Milo, XII)
Author: Marcus Tullius Cicero (106–43 B.C.)
First transcribed: 52 B.C.
Type of work: Oration

Context: On very few occasions was Cicero a prosecutor. Usually he was a defense lawyer, which role he declared the more honorable. The gangster Titus Annius Papinianus (95–47 B.C.) got the nickname "Milo" from the athlete Milo of Crotona. He entered politics and by tough tactics won his offices. While tribune of the people, in 57 B.C., Milo obtained the recall of Cicero from an exile that had grown out of his prosecution of Catiline's group of conspirators. In the anarchy in Rome that followed the clash between Pompey and Caesar, Milo's political gang fought with that of a political rival, Clodius, on the Appian Way, and Milo killed his enemy. Brought to trial, he asked Cicero, in return for previous favors, to defend him. According to Roman criminal practices, five days were devoted to the trial. One day was given to the torture of the slave witnesses, and three more to hear their testimony. On the final day, the prosecutor had two hours to present his case, followed by three hours for the speech of the defense. At the begin-ning of the trial, eighty-one judges of peers were selected, reduced on the final day to the jury of fifty-one, who voted on the verdict. There is one account that Pompey, who had been appointed sole consul of Rome, so intimidated Cicero that he did not appear in person to make his speech. At any rate, Milo was found guilty by a vote of thirty-eight to thirteen, and was sent into exile. Cicero's speech of defense, later published, is a skillful blending of proof, paradox, and pathos. At the beginning, he asserts that Clodius plotted against Milo. The test question is attributed to Cassius. (Not the "lean and hungry" conspirator against Caesar, but a much earlier consul who asked *Cui bono fuerit,* variously translated as, "Who stood to gain?" "For whose gain," or "To whose profit?" when seeking the perpetrator of a crime.) Today the expression is frequently misapplied. Having previously asserted that Clodius plotted against Milo, who was a candidate for the consulship, Cicero questions how the removal of a rival would profit him.

How then can I prove to your satisfaction that it was Clodius who laid a plot against Milo? Dealing as we are with a monster of such reckless impiety, it is enough to demonstrate that he had a great inducement to kill Milo, and great expectations and great advantages held out to him in the event of his death. Accordingly let Cassius' famous test, **"To whose profit,"** be applied to the characters before us; only let us remember that no self interest will ever drive a good man to crime, while the bad man is often impelled thereto by one that is but trivial. . . .

Toes turned up to the daisies!

Source: THE INGOLDSBY LEGENDS (*The Babes in the Wood; or, The Norfolk Tragedy,* Stanza 3)
Author: Richard Harris Barham (1788–1845)
First published: 1840
Type of work: Humorous narrative poem

Context: The tragic old story of the Babes in the Woods is of course well known to nearly everyone. Barham's version of this tale about the two children abandoned to their death in the forest is a light and cheerful burlesque of the original. Here the parents die of a familiar malady caused by eating too many fresh plums and leave a modest fortune to their two children, naming a wicked uncle the guardian. No sooner are the parents "put to bed with a spade by the sexton" than the uncle leaves town with Jane and Johnny, ostensibly to educate them. Instead, he hires two ruffians to take them into the forest and dispose of them. The children, de- lighted with a ride on horseback, "prattle so nice on the journey/ That the rogues themselves wish to the heart/ They could finish the job by attorney." One vows he cannot do the foul deed, but the other points out that they have already been paid for it—"So out with your whinger at once,/ And scrag Jane, while I spifli- cate Johnny." A duel ensues, in which the kindlier ruffian gives "the truculent rascal his gruel." Then he reassures the children and abandons them to their death. The wicked uncle, though he inherits all, does not prosper. He suffers from bad dreams, gout, indigestion, and worry; his crops fail and worse things follow:

> There was hardly a day but some fox
>   Ran away with his geese and his ganders:
> His wheat had the mildew, his flocks
>   Took the rot, and his horses the glanders;
> His daughters drank rum in their tea,
>   His son, who had gone for a sailor,
> Went down in a steamer at sea,
>   And his wife ran away with a tailor!

Obviously under a curse, the wicked uncle is shunned by everyone and eventually lands in the work- house; finally his man confesses all to the authorities, and the uncle com- mits suicide. Barham provides a moral to the story:

> Ponder well now, dear Parents, each word
>   That I've wrote, and when Sirius rages
> In the dog-days, don't be so absurd
>   As to blow yourselves out with Green-gages!
> Of stone-fruits in general be shy,
>   And reflect it's a fact beyond question

That Grapes, when they're spelt with an *i*,
Promote anything else but digestion.

And the reader is left to ponder the children's sad fate and the utter fu-tility of their mother's last request:

"Now, think, 'tis your sister invokes
Your aid, and the last word she says is,
Be kind to those dear little folks
When our **toes** are **turned up to the daisies!—**"

. . .

Toil, envy, want, the patron, and the jail

Source: THE VANITY OF HUMAN WISHES (Line 160)
Author: Samuel Johnson (1709–1784)
First published: 1749
Type of work: Didactic poem in imitation of the tenth satire of Juvenal

Context: The poet assails the love of wealth and tells how those who possess it live in fear of losing it, whereas the poor have little dread from confiscation and robbery. Those who strive for political power lead equally insecure and anxious lives. The rising politician is courted by suppliants, but when he begins to decline he is scorned by those who courted his favors. Cardinal Wolsey is the type of statesman who rises to supreme power, only to see it evaporate. He acquired so much power that there was none left to seize, but at that point his king began to frown, and he was ruined. The course of the young soldier is no better; he studies to make himself famous, but he should pause to contemplate the scholar's rewards, which are nothing but hardship. Johnson himself toiled mightily at his literary projects and lived in abject want during most of his life. The support of his supposed patron, Philip Dormer Stanhope, fourth Earl of Chesterfield, was so small during the time of the composition of the *Dictionary* that Johnson came to loathe the very name of patron. Johnson at one time was in debtors' prison. Some of his general bitterness is expressed as follows:

Yet should thy soul indulge the generous heat
Till captive science yields her last retreat;
Should reason guide thee with her brightest ray,
And pour on misty doubt resistless day;
Should no false kindness lure to loose delight,
Nor praise relax, nor difficulty fright;
Should tempting novelty thy cell refrain,
And sloth effuse her opiate fumes in vain;
Should beauty blunt on fops her fatal dart,
Nor claim the triumph of a lettered heart;

Should no disease thy torpid veins invade,
Nor melancholy's phantoms haunt thy shade;
Yet hope not life from grief or danger free,
Nor think the doom of man reversed for thee.
Deign on the passing world to turn thine eyes,
And pause awhile from letters to be wise;
There mark what ills the scholar's life assail,
Toil, envy, want, the patron, and the jail.

Tomorrow let us do or die!

Source: GERTRUDE OF WYOMING (Part III, stanza 37)
Author: Thomas Campbell (1777–1844)
First published: 1809
Type of work: Narrative poem

Context: Gertrude of Wyoming was the most popular of those literary ballads for which the Scottish poet Thomas Campbell is known. The Wyoming here referred to is not the State but a colonial settlement in Pennsylvania, located in a valley of the same name. During the American Revolution most of the men who lived there joined the Continental Army; those who remained were attacked by British troops and Indians, and Forty Fort near Wilkes-Barre, in which they had taken refuge, was captured by the enemy after a desperate battle fought on July 3, 1778. The defenders were outnumbered 1100 to 400, were mostly old men and boys, and about two-thirds were killed; many of those captured were tortured by the Indians. The valley was devastated. Most of its inhabitants had to flee the region, and they endured severe hardships. Using this historical background as a framework, Campbell builds the romantic story of an earthly paradise and of a beautiful girl who lives there with her widowed father, Albert. They are visited by Outalissi, chief of the Oneidas, who brings them young Henry Waldegrave, orphaned son of an old friend. Outalissi had saved Henry from the Hurons. The boy, about Gertrude's age, remains with them three years; relatives then call him home to England and he and the girl are grown when he returns. They fall in love and are married. After three idyllic months, war breaks out; Henry must leave to serve in the Revolutionary Army. Before he can depart, the now aged Outalissi arrives to tell them that Brandt and his Mohawks have wiped out the Oneidas and are coming to destroy the valley. They retire to the fort, but both Albert and Gertrude are killed by enemy bullets before they can enter. After their burial, Henry lies weeping on his wife's grave; and old Outalissi, knowing none are likely to survive the next day's battle, sings his own death song:

"And I could weep;"—th' Oneyda chief
His descant wildly thus begun;

1141

"But that I may not stain with grief
The death-song of my father's son!
.   .   .
But thee, my flow'r, whose breath was giv'n
By milder genii o'er the deep,
The spirits of the white man's heav'n
Forbid not thee to weep:
Nor will the Christian host,
Nor will thy father's spirit grieve,
To see thee, on the battle's eve,
Lamenting, take a mournful leave
Of her who lov'd thee most:
She was the rainbow to thy sight!
Thy sun—thy heav'n—of lost delight!
.   .   .

Tomorrow let us do or die!"

Tom's a-cold

Source: KING LEAR (Act III, sc. iv, l. 58)
Author: William Shakespeare (1564–1616)
First published: 1608
Type of work: Dramatic tragedy

Context: Edgar, son of the Earl of Gloucester, is the innocent victim of a plot by his father's bastard son, Edmund. Edmund has convinced the earl that Edgar wishes to murder the old man for the sake of the inheritance, and Edgar is forced to flee for his life. He disguises himself as a "bedlam beggar," one who is mad or pretends madness: ". . . my face I'll grime with filth,/ Blanket my loins, elf all my hairs in knots,/ And with presented nakedness outface/ The winds and persecutions of the sky."

Such beggars were common enough in Shakespeare's time. "Tom" was the name generally assumed by them. During a great storm Edgar takes shelter in a hovel, which is entered by King Lear, also a victim, one genuinely maddened by the ingratitude of his daughters, Goneril and Regan. Lear, in fact, can think of little else. Edgar uses the phrase "Tom's a-cold" a number of times in the course of the scene, at first in a famous speech concerning the "foul fiend":

LEAR

Didst thou give all to thy daughters?
And art thou come to this?

EDGAR

Who gives anything to poor Tom, whom the foul fiend hath led through fire, and through flame, through ford and whirlpool, o'er bog and quagmire, that hath laid knives under his pillow, and hal-

1142

ters in his pew, set ratsbane by his porridge, . . . Bless thy five wits, **Tom's a-cold.** O do, de, do, de, do, de. . . . .

Tonight the American flag floats from yonder hill or Molly Stark sleeps a widow!

Source: SPEECH BEFORE THE BATTLE OF BENNINGTON
Author: John Stark (1728–1822)
First spoken: August 14, 1777
Type of work: Battlefield address

Context: Born in Londonderry, New Hampshire, John Stark gained fame as an American Revolutionary soldier. Having achieved the rank of colonel in 1775, he led the American forces against the British at Breed's Hill and aided in the fortification of New York. In the following year he commanded brilliantly both at Princeton and Trenton. In the spring of 1777, when a new promotion list failed to include his name, Stark resigned his commission and returned to his farm. Meanwhile, General Burgoyne was effecting a successful march, and New Hampshire was called upon to raise forces in her defense. Stark was requested to take command of the troops, but he refused to do so unless his command be decreed independent of all save the state. His conditions accepted, he encamped at Bennington with his independent troop. Burgoyne, having heard of the dissension in the American ranks, determined to send Colonel Baum to cut off Stark's detachment and thus crush the New England resistance. These events precipitated the Battle of Bennington, fought, not at Bennington, not even in Vermont, but about seven miles from the former place and two miles inside the New York state line. Under Baum were one thousand Tories, Canadian rangers, marksmen, chasseurs, Hessians, and Indians. Stark's force totaled more; but, whereas Baum's men were seasoned fighters, Stark's militia had seen no action of any sort. On the morning of August 14 Stark formed his troops for attack and delivered his now-famous address. The result was an overwhelming American victory, including the capture of substantial materials and over seven hundred troops. More important, the success breathed new spirit into the American cause, and, with greater confidence, the Colonies defeated Burgoyne at Saratoga. In his speech Stark struck sharply at the difference between the professional fighters of the enemy and the home guard of his own command:

. . . My men, yonder are the Hessians. They were bought for seven pounds and ten pence a man. Are you worth more? Prove it. **To-night the American flag floats from yonder hill or Molly Stark sleeps a widow!**

1143

Too much of water hast thou, poor Ophelia

Source: HAMLET (Act IV, sc. vii, l. 187)
Author: William Shakespeare (1564–1616)
First published: 1603
Type of work: Dramatic tragedy

Context: Ophelia has gone mad—in contrast to Hamlet's feigning madness—upon learning that her former lover, Hamlet, has mistakenly slain her father, Polonius. Her brother, Laertes, and Hamlet's uncle, King Claudius, have just plotted the death of Hamlet (Laertes, because he wishes to revenge the death of his father; Claudius, because, with the death of Hamlet's father on his conscience, he fears the son) when news is brought of the drowning of Ophelia. According to the queen, Ophelia fell into a stream while hanging gar-lands on a willow tree: "Her clothes spread wide,/ And mermaid-like awhile they bore her up,/ Which time she chaunted snatches of old tunes,/ as one incapable of her own distress,/ . . . but long it could not be. . . ." Momentarily, the news of Ophelia's death by water puts out—drowns—the fires of Laertes' fierce resolution, and he rushes from the stage in tears, although, he promises, afterward the tearful woman in him will be gone and he will be ready to take his revenge:

LAERTES
Too much of water hast thou poor Ophelia,
And therefore I forbid my tears; but yet
It is our trick, nature her custom holds,
Let shame say what it will; when these are gone,
The woman will be out. Adieu my lord.
I have a speech of fire that fain would blaze
But that this folly drowns it.

Too quick a sense of a constant infelicity

Source: THE RULE AND EXERCISES OF HOLY DYING (Chapter I, section v)
Author: Jeremy Taylor (1613–1667)
First published: 1651
Type of work: Devotional treatise

Context: This book and its companion volume, *The Rule and Exercises of Holy Living,* are the first manuals of private devotion in English following the Reformation. In them this Anglican bishop explains to his readers the proper way for a pious Chris-tian to live his life and to leave it. In Chapter I of *The Rule and Exercises of Holy Dying* Taylor instructs his readers concerning "A General Preparation Towards a Holy and Blessed Death." He first contemplates the "vanity and shortness of man's life" and the practical consideration which should result from an understanding of them. Following a section devoted to the "rules and spiritual arts . . . to take off the objection of a short life," he contemplates at length "the miseries of man's life." Section five is a practical consideration of the preceding discussion of man's miseries. The "careless merry sinner," Taylor says, has no awareness of the world's miseries; but

> . . . if we could from one of the battlements of heaven espy how many men and women at this time lie fainting and dying for want of bread, how many young men are hewn down by the sword of war, how many poor orphans are now weeping over the graves of their father by whose life they were enabled to eat: if we could but hear how many mariners and passengers are at this present in a storm, and shriek out because their keel dashes against a rock, or bulges under them, how many people there are that weep with want, and are mad with oppression, or are desperate by **too quick a sense of constant infelicity;** in all reason we should be glad to be out of the noise and participation of so many evils. This is a place of sorrows and tears, of great evils and a constant calamity: let us remove from hence, at least in affections and preparation of mind.

Trade is the golden girdle of the globe

Source: CHARITY (Line 86)
Author: William Cowper (1731–1800)
First published: 1782
Type of work: Verse essay

Context: Because of Cowper's morbidity and frequent periods of mental disorganization, his poetic output is of unequal quality. During his periods of belief in religious persecution, he wrote a number of hymns in collaboration with the Reverend John Newton. Following one sojourn in an insane asylum, Cowper spent a period of recuperation at the Newton home, subsidized by a wealthy merchant, John Thornton (1720–1790). The poet dedicated this poem, "Charity," to him and to John Howard, a prison reformer who died the year of its publication. Charity, in the sense of love of one's fellow men, is its theme. Cowper contrasts Capt. James Cook (1728–1779) and his humane treatment of savages in the South Seas, with the cruel treatment by Hernán Cortez (1485–1547) of the Indians of Mexico. Cowper's philosophy is better than his knowledge of history, because Montezuma met his death, not from the Spaniards, but by a stone thrown by one of his own Aztec courtiers. In his discussion of charity in business dealings, he believes that trade links people and lands around the world.

Again—the band of commerce was designed
T' associate all the branches of mankind;
And, if a boundless plenty be the robe,
Trade is the golden girdle of the globe.
Wise to promote whatever end he means,
God opens fruitful Nature's various scenes:
Each climate needs what other climes produce;
And offers something to the general use:
No land but listens to the common call,
And in return receives supply from all.

Tramp! tramp! along the land they rode

Source: WILLIAM AND HELEN (Stanza LVII)
Author: Sir Walter Scott (1771–1832)
First published: 1796
Type of work: Ballad

Context: This poem, the first published by Scott, was a translation or imitation of a German ballad by Gottfried Augustus Bürger. The story is that an army returns and all the girls are reunited with their lovers except Helen, whose William is absent. Helen falls into despondency, from which her mother unsuccessfully tries to rouse her. She advises her to turn to prayer, which Helen contends is unavailing. At midnight there is a sound of a horse's approach, the dismounting of a mail-clad rider, and heavy footsteps on the stairs. There is a knock at the door, and William enters; he bids Helen prepare to ride behind him on his horse a hundred miles, so that they can, before break of day, reach their bridal bed. She, filled with wonder, does as commanded, and they set off at a furious pace. Over mountains, meadows, and plains they go, over the land and through the sea they rush. Finally they ride into a church and stop beside an open grave, where William turns into a skeleton in Helen's arms. The horse gives a wild bound and disappears, leaving Helen on the ground amid ghosts and pale spectres. Three times within the poem the "tramp! tramp! splash! splash!" chorus occurs.

"Dost fear? dost fear? the moon shines clear,
    And well the dead can ride;
Dost faithful Helen fear for them?"—
    "O leave in peace the dead!"—

"Barb! Barb! methinks I hear the cock;
    The sand will soon be run:
Barb! Barb! I smell the morning air;
    The race is well-nigh done."

Tramp! tramp! along the land they rode,
Splash! splash! along the sea:
The scourge is red, the spur drops blood,
The flashing pebbles flee.

"Hurrah! hurrah! well ride the dead;
The bride, the bride is come;
And soon we reach the bridal bed,
For, Helen, here's my home."

Traveling is the ruin of all happiness

Source: CECILIA (Book IV, chapter 2)
Author: Fanny Burney (Mme. d'Arblay, 1752–1840)
First published: 1782
Type of work: Sentimental novel

Context: Though unable to read or write until she was eight, Fanny, the daughter of the organist Dr. Burney, made up for her late start. At the age of fifteen, she had such an accumulation of poems, stories, and essays that in an attack of conscience over the waste of time it represented, she burned everything. Then struck by the ridiculousness of her act, she used the episode as the basis for a novel, *Evelina* (1778), published anonymously. It became popular at once. Dr. Johnson and Sir Joshua Reynolds enjoyed it. Sheridan suggested she write a play for him. Under pressure from her father, she started another novel, *Cecilia,* in five volumes, that appeared in June, 1782, and sold as fast as copies could be rushed from the press. Edmund Burke (1729–1796) wrote to praise her natural vein of humor, her "tender pathetic," and the comprehensive and noble moral. Later, in 1793, Fanny married a French refugee from the Revolution, Alexander Gabriel Jean Baptist Pieuchard d'Arblay (1752–1818) a friend of Lafayette and commander of the prison guard that once allowed King Louis to escape. The couple lived in France until after the Battle of Waterloo, then returned permanently to England. *Cecilia, or Memoirs of an Heiress* follows the fortunes of Cecilia Beverley for two years, from the time she leaves the country estate of her family at the age of twenty-two for a life in London, until she marries young Delvile. It is a lachrymose novel, with men and women quick to weep and readers also moved to tears over her misfortunes. Cecilia faces an obstacle to her marriage. Her uncle, wanting to carry on his name, offers her an income of £3,000 a year, if her husband will take his name. The prospective husband has a father who values the Delvile name more than riches, and will not consent to the union on such conditions. Other obstructions are an unreal villain, Monckton, and Mrs. Belfield, "that grossly natural woman who resembles half the *decent* women of the Burough." Near the close of the novel, Cecilia, an Ophelia-like creature of innocence and beauty gone mad under pain and rough usage, lies dying while her lover, young Delvile, the source of her miseries, looks down at her figure, "sweet even in the arms of death and insanity," and mutters: "Well, then—I may grieve, perhaps, hereafter!" However, before Cecilia dies, or floats on the water, or even goes completely mad, and while the gentle reader continues on, with tear-filled eyes, the elder Mr. Delvile is persuaded to reconsider his son's marriage, and Cecilia's woes come to an end. Besides its sadness, the book contains much humor. Mrs. Belfield is a satirized character, as is her son, who escapes a career "in trade," like his father's, and becomes a gentleman of fashion. The retired London man of business, Mr. Hobson (formerly a bricklayer and landlord) and his cringing friend, Mr. Simkins, and the loquacious Miss Larolles, provide smiles, as does the languid fop, Mr. Meadows, who scorns England and adores Europe. The second chapter of Book IV takes place at the Pantheon, and is entitled "A Man of the Ton." Mr. and Mrs. Harrel have invited Cecilia to accompany them there. Several others join them. Mr. Meadows saunters up, demanding to be introduced. Then he lolls in the vacant place next to Cecilia, hoping to devastate her with his conversation.

"Have you been long in town, ma'am?"
"No, sir."
"This is not your first winter?"
"Of being in town, it is."
"Then you have something new to see: O charming! how I envy you!—Are you pleased with the Pantheon?"
"Very much; I have seen no building at all equal to it."
"You have not been abroad. **Traveling is the ruin of all happiness!** There's no looking at a building here after seeing Italy."

The tree of life

Source: GENESIS 2:9
Author: Unknown
First transcribed: c.1000–300 B.C.
Type of work: Religious history and law

Context: The first chapter of Genesis relates how God created the heavens and the earth, how He made light, and how He caused the dry land to appear. It relates also how on the fifth day of creation, having already made the vegetation and the sun and the moon, God created the creatures of the water and the air, including the great whales. He bade the creatures of the waters and the air to "Be fruitful and multiply." On the sixth day of creation, as it is told in Genesis, God fashioned the animals who inhabit the dry land, including man. In Chapter Two of the account, we learn how God rested from His labors on the seventh day. This chapter relates, too, how a mist rose from the ground, in lieu of rainfall, to water the ground and make the vegetation grow. It tells, also, how man was created, as a living soul, and placed in an earthly paradise, in which grew both the tree of life and the tree of knowledge of good and evil, the latter of which figures in Adam's and Eve's disobedience and their subsequent expulsion from the garden; for God says, after Adam and Eve have eaten of the fruit of the tree of knowledge of good and evil, that they must be expelled from Eden, lest they "take also of the tree of life, and eat, and live forever":

> And the LORD God planted a garden eastward in Eden; and there he put the man he had formed.
> And out of the ground made the LORD God to grow every tree that is pleasant to the sight, and good for food; **the tree of life** also in the midst of the garden, and the tree of knowledge of good and evil.
> And a river went out of Eden to water the garden; and from thence it was parted, and became into four heads.

Triton blowing loud his wreathed horne

Source: COLIN CLOUT'S COME HOME AGAIN (Line 245)
Author: Edmund Spenser (c. 1552–1599)
First published: 1595
Type of work: Allegorical pastoral poem

Context: Spenser creates the persona Colin Clout to achieve his purposes in this poem, which does two things: it praises Sir Walter Raleigh (Shepherd of the Ocean), who was Spenser's sponsor at court, and it praises Queen Elizabeth I for her favors. Colin, safe back home in Ireland, describes for his shepherd friends the fabulous trip he has taken, the places he has seen, and the great persons he has met. He tells of his first ocean voyage, surrounded by sea and sky as far as the eye could see. He asks the Shepherd of the Ocean to explain this fearful, strange, new world he sees around him. In an extended metaphor which skillfully praises Elizabeth as Cynthia, the chief Shepherdess of the Queen, the Shepherd tells Colin that the oceans are the hills and pastures of Cynthia's realm. Here Cynthia is served by multitudes: hundreds of nymphs, Triton, Proteus, and the Shepherd himself. The phrase is later echoed by Wordsworth in his sonnet "The World Is Too Much with Us" (1807).

> These be the hills (quoth he) the surges hie,
> On which fair Cynthia her heards doth feed:
> Her heards be thousand fishes with their frie
> Which in the bosome of the billowes breed.
> Of them the shepherd which hath charge in chief,
> Is **Triton blowing loud his wreathed horne:**
> At sound whereof, they all for their relief
> Wend too and fro at evening and at morne.

Trodden the winepress alone

Source: ISAIAH 63:3
Author: Isaiah
First transcribed: c. 800–200 B.C.
Type of work: Religious prophecy and exhortation

Context: Chapter 63 of Isaiah describes a vision seen by this eloquent poet and prophet, probably from a mountaintop. It may have been inspired by an approaching thunderstorm, reddened by the setting sun. At one time scholars thought this passage a prophecy relating to Christ, but it has since been observed with some justification that the awesome being described is far more consistent with the Old Testament Jehovah than it is with the character of Jesus. Isaiah's vision is of a mighty figure approaching out of Edom, glorious in scarlet and purple robes; the impression created by his words is one of vastness and of something inexorable in purpose; and when the figure speaks it is in a voice of thunder. The impression of an approaching storm is very strong. Whatever the phenomenon that inspired Isaiah's mind and pen, its aspect was majestic and awe-inspiring. For centuries the people of Israel have suffered under the oppressor's heel; their land has been conquered and plundered; they have been enslaved, abused, exiled, or killed. Now Isaiah sees the Lord sweeping across the earth in garments the color of blood, to avenge the tribulations of His people and to stamp out their enemies. He will trample them as wine is trampled out of the grapes, and His robes will be stained by the fury of His labor. But this terrifying vision is of the future, and Isaiah begs the Lord to remember His people in their present adversity, to renew His love for them and to raise their afflictions. In the prayer with which he ends this chapter are combined humility, simple devotion, and a deep sorrow; there is genuine pathos in it and the suffering it mirrors is unmistakeable.

Who is this that cometh from Edom, with dyed garments from Bozrah? this that is glorious in his apparel, travelling in the greatness of his strength? I that speak in righteousness, mighty to save.

Wherefore art thou red in thine apparel, and thy garments like him that treadeth in the winefat?

I have **trodden the winepress alone;** and of the people there was none with me: for I will tread them in mine anger, and trample them in my fury; and their blood shall be sprinkled upon my garments, and I will stain all my raiment.

For the day of vengeance is in mine heart, and the year of my redeemed is come.

And I looked, and there was none to help; and I wondered that there was none to uphold: therefore mine own arm brought salvation unto me; and my fury, it upheld me.

And I will tread down the people in mine anger, and make them drunk in my fury, and I will bring down their strength to the earth.

I will mention the lovingkindnesses of the LORD, and the praises of the LORD, according to all that the LORD hath bestowed on us, . . .

For he said, Surely they are my people, children that will not lie: so he was their Saviour.

In all their affliction he was afflicted, and the angel of his presence saved them: in his love and in his pity he redeemed them; and he bare them, and carried them all the days of old.

      •   •   •

O LORD, why hast thou made us to err from thy ways, and hardened our heart from thy fear? Return for thy servants' sake, the tribes of thine inheritance.

The people of thy holiness have possessed it but a little while: our adversaries have trodden down thy sanctuary.

Troilus mounted the Trojan walls

Source: THE MERCHANT OF VENICE (Act V, sc. i, l. 4)
Author: William Shakespeare (1564–1616)
First published: 1600
Type of work: Dramatic comedy

Context: Along the moonlit avenue to Belmont, home of the fair heiress Portia, bride of Bassanio, Bassanio's friend, Lorenzo, and his bride Jessica, daughter of Shylock, talk poetically. They are reminded that on such a night the legendary Troilus, hero of *Troilus and Criseyde* by Geoffrey Chaucer and of *Troilus and Cressida* by William Shakespeare, looked longingly from the height of the Trojan wall toward the Greek camp where his beloved Cressida lay:

LORENZO
The moon shines bright. In such a night as this,
When the sweet wind did gently kiss the trees,
And they did make no noise, in such a night
Troilus methinks **mounted the Trojan walls,**
And sighed his soul toward the Grecian tents
Where Cressid lay that night.

JESSICA
      In such a night
Did Thisbe fearfully o'ertrip the dew,
And saw the lion's shadow ere himself,
And ran dismayed away.

      •   •   •

LORENZO
      In such a night

1151

Did Jessica steal from the wealthy Jew,
And with an unthrift love did run from Venice,
As far as Belmont.

Trouts are tickled best in muddy water

Source: ON A HYPOCRITICAL NONCONFORMIST (Stanza IV)
Author: Samuel Butler (1612–1680)
First published: 1759
Type of work: Satirical poem

Context: Samuel Butler was best known as the author of a spirited burlesque in verse, *Hudibras,* full of quotable lines, about Oliver Cromwell and his followers. It was circulated in manuscript until after the Restoration in 1660. Then Charles II was so delighted with it that there are stories of an annual pension for the poet. Butler went on to write many poems and character studies but, with no royal backers, he could find no publisher. Not until 1759 did *The Genuine Remains in Verse and Prose of Samuel Butler* get into print. Then a Mr. Thyer, obtaining the manuscript from the estate of Mr. Longueville who had paid for burying the poet, issued it in a subscription edition. It did not reach the artistic level of *Hudibras.* One of the poems is entitled "On a Hypocritical Nonconformist (A Pindaric Ode)." Pindar was a Theban poet of the fifth century B.C. who wrote a long series of odes to celebrate great victories in the Grecian national games. However, as employed by Butler, the expression "Pindaric Ode" was originated by Abraham Cowley (1618–1667) through a volume of poems characterized by looseness, irregularity, metrical license, and grandiose diction. The form was later taken up by John Dryden, Alexander Pope, Jonathan Swift, and Butler, who also penned a Pindaric Ode on "Modern Critics." In twelve stanzas, Butler attacks his victim. A Turk, says the poet, about to commit some crime against religion, can send his soul on a pilgrimage so that it will be absent from his body. He holds that the end justifies the means when the end is the advance of religion. His brother Christian is no less hypocritical, the reason that holy wars are so cruel and evil. "For when Religion does recede/ From her own Nature, nothing but a breed/ Of prodigies and hideous Monsters can succeed." In lesser crimes, anyone with a pretense to piety and godliness can get off unpunished. Of course, the poet was talking about "Pagans," but Christians can also manage to make "their Godly interests" produce great gains. The best way to "get by" is to use dull nonsense and proceed against stupid people. Fishermen can sometimes capture a fish by sliding their hand under its body, and tickling it until the hand is in a position to heave the fish out of water onto dry land. But the trick works best when the water is too muddy to let the fish see its pursuer. Concerning the significance of a spider spinning its "gin" or

1152

snare, folklore provides a difference   a sunny day.
of opinion. Some hold it as the sign of

> The subtle spider never spins,
> But on dark days, his slimy gins;
> Nor does our engineer, much care to plant
> His spiritual machines
> Unless among the weak and ignorant,
> Th' inconstant, credulous, and light,
> The vain, the factious, and the slight,
> That in their zeal are most extravagant;
> For **trouts are tickled best in muddy water;**
> And still, the muddier he finds their brains,
> The more he's sought and followed after,
> And greater ministrations gains; . . .

Truth is rarely pure and never simple

Source: THE IMPORTANCE OF BEING EARNEST (Act I)
Author: Oscar Wilde (1856–1900)
First published: 1895
Type of work: Dramatic comedy

Context: Writing witty and paradoxical, though rarely profound, came from the pen of the Dublin-born author, Oscar Fingal O'Flahertie Wills Wilde, and provided a model for Gilbert Keith Chesterton (1874–1936) and Bernard Shaw (1856–1950). Much of his humor consists of puns and twisted clichés. *The Importance of Being Earnest,* Wilde's best comedy, is a reworking of French originals with stock characters and situations, but saved from oblivion by its dialogue of affectation and nonsense, relieved by flashes of shrewd wisdom. The title involves a pun. The important characters, Algernon Moncrieff and his friend Jack Worthing, live double lives. Algy has invented a friend, Bunbury, whose failing health requires Algy's absence from London whenever one of Aunt Augusta Bracknell's dull dinners is in the offing. Jack, the guardian of Miss Cecily Cardew, has invented a brother, Ernest, whose name satirizes Victorian earnestness and priggishness, but whose reputation as a reprobate has aroused the interest of Lady Bracknell's daughter, Gwendolen, with whom Jack is in love. In the first act, Jack explains his scheme to Algy:

JACK

My dear Algy, I don't know whether you will be able to understand my real motives . . . When one is placed in the position of guardian, one has to adopt a very high moral tone on all subjects. . . . And as a high moral tone can hardly be said to con-

1153

duce very much to either one's health or one's happiness, in order to get up to town I have always pretended to have a younger brother by the name of Ernest, who lives in the Albany, and gets into the most dreadful scrapes. That, my dear Algy, is the whole truth pure and simple.

ALGERNON

The truth is rarely pure and never simple. Modern life would be very tedious if it were either, and modern literature a complete impossibility!

Truth lies somewhere, if we knew but where

Source: HOPE (Line 424)
Author: William Cowper (1731–1800)
First published: 1782
Type of work: Meditative poem

Context: Cowper was primarily a poet of rural life; his writings deal with the quiet countryside and with domestic simplicity. His mood is one of meditation or of reflection with religious overtones. A descendant of John Donne, he wrote a few verses in his youth but did not turn seriously to the writing of poetry until much later. Trained for the law, he was called to the bar in 1754. He fell in love with his cousin but was forbidden to see or marry her after he suffered an attack of insanity. He was preparing for an examination in 1763 when he suffered a second attack and attempted suicide. After a lengthy convalescence, he moved first to Huntingdon and later, in 1767, to Olney, where he lived in rural seclusion. He did not begin to write poetry as a serious recreation until he was fifty. The first volume, *Poems,* was published in 1782. The same year he sent his humorous poem, "John Gilpin's Ride," to a newspaper; the poem enjoyed great popularity and remains one of Cowper's best-known works.

The following year he began his greatest work, *The Task.* His friend Lady Austen had suggested he produce a major work, and had given him the subject: a sofa. Cowper dutifully started with the sofa but soon expanded the topic into an easy and natural description of the local countryside in winter, the simple routines and pleasures of the day, and of an outside world that was comfortably remote. In it as in his other poems, his deeper feelings arise from his religious convictions and carry with them a tendency to moralize. His Calvinism brought him both comfort and despair, and was a major factor in the recurring fits of melancholia from which he suffered. He wrote a number of important hymns. "Hope," one of the long poems in his first volume, is in many ways typical of his work. In it he reflects that the world is neither a place of despair nor one of unthinking joy, and that most of man's unhappiness comes from his own careless attitudes; what sustains us is hope. An imaginary conversation fol-

1154

lows, in which several revelers discuss   the nature of salvation:

> Right, says an ensign, and for aught I see,
> Your faith and mine substantially agree:
> The best of ev'ry man's performance here,
> Is to discharge the duties of his sphere.
> A lawyer's dealing should be just and fair,
> Honesty shines with great advantage there;
> Fasting and pray'r sit well upon a priest,
> A decent caution and reserve at least.
> A soldier's best is courage in the field. . . .
>
> . . .
>
> Sir Smug! he cries (for lowest at the board,
> Just made fifth chaplain of his patron lord,
> His shoulders witnessing by many a shrug,
> How much his feelings suffered, sat Sir Smug)
> Your office is to winnow false from true,
> Come, prophet, drink, and tell us what think you?
> Sighing and smiling as he takes his glass,
> Which they that woo preferment rarely pass,
> Fallible man, the church-bred youth replies,
> Is still found fallible, however wise,
> And differing judgments serve but to declare
> That **truth lies somewhere, if we knew but where.**

Truth never hurts the teller

Source: FIFINE AT THE FAIR (Stanza xxxii)
Author: Robert Browning (1812–1889)
First published: 1872
Type of work: Dramatic monologue

Context: Among Browning's greatest achievements in poetry was his refinement of the dramatic monologue. In his hands it became an instrument of penetrating and incisive revelation of the psychology of human action. Frequently, he dealt with subjects and characters that offended the propriety of his age. In Fifine, for example, he describes—by the contrasts of her admitted standards and values—the falsity and hypocrisy of those who come to observe her at the fair. In the introduction, drawn from Molière's *Don Juan ou le Festin de Pierre,* Donna Elvira berates Don Juan—who needs "must declare the truth" —for his inability to maintain his wonted social façade. The poem itself, as Juan and Elvira decide to trip arm in arm and observe the "tumbling-troop" of the fair, contrasts the hypocrisy of the socially élite with the unabashed frankness of those who form the entourage of the carnival; the one lives in a world which hides the truth from his companions; the other lives in a world which exploits the truth for the profit possible because of human curiosity. In the monologue Juan quips that those of the fair traffic in "just the things/ We, —the proud ones who do scorn dwellers without the pale" hold so private. "I say, they sell what we most pique us that we keep:/ How comes it, all we hold so dear they count so cheap?" And yet, he admits, there is a freshness, if not about Fifine's life, about her attitude toward it—an attitude so antithetical to the civilized mores of social pride:

> Well, then, thus much confessed, what wonder if there steal
> Unchallenged to my heart the force of one appeal
> She makes, and justice stamp the sole claim she asserts?
> So absolutely good is truth, **truth never hurts**
> **The teller,** whose worst crime gets somehow grace, avowed.
> To me, that silent pose and prayer proclaimed aloud
> "Know all of me outside, the rest be emptiness
> For such as you!" . . .

'Twas strange, 'twas passing strange

Source: OTHELLO (Act I, sc. iii, l. 160)
Author: William Shakespeare (1564–1616)
First published: 1622
Type of work: Dramatic tragedy

Context: Othello, the Moor of Venice, having taken the fair Desdemona to wife, is accused by her father, Brabantio, of having won her love through spells or potions. Othello declares that he has gained Desdemona's love only by relating the whole of his adventuresome life to the fascinated girl.

OTHELLO
> . . . My story being done,
> She gave me for my pains a world of sighs.
> She swore, in faith **'twas strange, 'twas passing strange,**
> 'Twas pitiful, 'twas wondrous pitiful.
> She wished she had not heard it, yet she wished
> That heaven had made her such a man. She thanked me,
> And bade me, if I had a friend that loved her,
> I should but teach him how to tell my story,
> And that would woo her. Upon this hint I spake.
> She loved me for the dangers I had passed,
> And I loved her that she did pity them.
> This only is the witchcraft I have used. . . .

'Twixt you, me, and the gatepost

Source: THE INN ALBUM (Section II, l. 103)
Author: Robert Browning (1812–1889)
First published: 1875
Type of work: Poetic dialogue

Context: The Inn Album is one of numerous psychological studies of villainy which Browning produced; this one is based to some extent on a card-sharper case involving one Lord De Ros, a friend of Wellington, and recounted in Greville's memoirs. Browning adapted this material and added some other ideas which he took from the famous case of the Tichborne Claimant. The poem begins at an inn, where a young man and an older one have spent the night playing cards. The older man reckons up their winnings and losses on blank pages and margins in the inn's album. The two are friends but their friendship is one of convenience. The young man, relatively uncouth, is the son of a successful tradesman and has just inherited a million pounds. The older man is a person of refinement whose brother is a duke; however, he is relatively poor. Each cultivates the other for something he wants—the young man wishes to be instructed in the ways of that society in which his wealth may enable him to move; his companion sees in this unsophisticated youth a source of funds. When the game breaks up at dawn, the older man has lost and owes his companion ten thousand pounds, which he will have difficulty raising. The younger generously offers to forget the whole thing, but the older man is indignant—word might get around the clubs and ruin his reputation. They walk toward the station, where the older man will take a train to the city. His young companion suggests they have time for conversation, and they accordingly seat themselves on a convenient gate. The youth is curious: why should a man of the world, clever and urbane, be destitute? Why has he not found himself a sinecure? He begins prying into the older man's past, never guessing what sort of misfortune this may involve him in:

". . . The puzzle's past my power,
How you have managed—with such stuff, such means—
Not to be rich nor great nor happy man:
Of which three good things where's a sign at all?
        • • •
"Old man, no nonsense!—even to a boy
That's ripe at least for rationality
Rapped into him, as maybe mine was, once!
I've had my own small adventure lesson me
Over the knuckles!—likely, I forget
The sort of figure youth cuts now and then,
Competing with old shoulders but young head
Despite the fifty grizzling years!"
                "Aha?

1157

Then that means—just the bullet in the blade
Which brought Dalmatia on the brain,—that, too,
Came of a fatal creature? Can't pretend
Now for the first time to surmise as much!
Make a clean breast! Recount! a secret's safe
'Twixt you, me, and the gate-post!"

Two of a trade, lass, never agree!

Source: JUGGLING JERRY (Stanza 9)
Author: George Meredith (1828–1909)
First published: 1859
Type of work: Dramatic monologue

Context: On a day in England in the month of May, when the smell of gorse is in the air, an elderly juggler and his wife stop their travels, and the wife pitches their tent as a place for her husband to die, on a piece of common ground near where Jerry, the juggler, grew up, and where the couple had often camped before. The juggler speaks his last words to his wife, thinking of his trade and his past. He tells her that he has always been honest and a good juggler, so that he is not ashamed of his trade, though some persons may sneer at it. He speaks also of his boyhood and young manhood, when he played at cricket, visited the thatch-roofed alehouse in his village, and courted his faithful spouse. He says he has studied men closely from his "topsy-turvy" world, that some are good, some are bad, and many a mixture of the two. He tells his wife he has saved enough so that she will not be in want as a widow, and he recalls how one night by the shore, as the moon rose, they saw two seagulls fly, and one fall with the crack of a gun, while the other flew away; the gull that fell is like himself, says Jerry; he has his creature comforts in his last hours, as well as his talk: a cup of ale, and the nutlike smell of the gorse carried to him by the wind. In the ninth stanza, the juggler says he is past the need of either parson or doctor in his dying:

It's past parsons to console us:
　　No, nor no doctor fetch for me:
I can die without my bolus;
　　Two of a trade, lass, never agree!
Parson and Doctor!—don't they love rarely,
　　Fighting the devil in other men's fields!
Stand up yourself and match him fairly:
　　Then see how the rascal yields.

1158

Two souls with but a single thought, two hearts that beat as one

Source: INGOMAR THE BARBARIAN (Act II)
Author: Friederich Halm (Eligius Franz Joseph von Münch-Bellinghausen, 1806–1871), translated by Maria Anne Lovell
First published: Der Sohn, 1842; *Ingomar,* 1851
Type of work: Tragi-comedy

Context: In Act II of the play *Der Sohn der Wildnis,* translated as *Ingomar the Barbarian,* Myron, an armorer and a citizen of Massilia, captured by raiding Alemanni under Ingomar and enslaved, is forced to serve his new masters, especially Ingomar, captain of the brigand band. Ingomar decries the settled life with wife and children in cities and praises the wild, free existence in the wilderness; but Myron continues to lament his lost liberty and his beloved family. Alastor enters the scene, having on a pillaging raid captured a girl, who gave herself up rather easily, requesting to be conducted to the chief of the band. She, Parthenia by name, has come to try to free Myron, her father. She asserts that Myron should be able to earn his ransom if allowed to work where there are people, but in the wilderness he will die and be a total loss to the robber band. She offers herself as a pledge for his return; she will work diligently so as not to be a burden to the bandits. The bandits accept her offer, and Myron departs. Parthenia, weaving garlands to bedeck the cups and goblets used by the members of the band, falls into a discussion of love with Ingomar, who is completely ignorant of the matter. He is so taken by her manner and her resemblance to his brother, who had died in childhood, that he fetches flowers for her to use in her garland-making. To illustrate what love is she sings him a song:

> What love is, if thou wouldst be taught,
>   Thy heart must teach alone,—
> **Two souls with but a single thought,**
>   **Two hearts that beat as one.**
>
> And whence comes love? like morning's light,
>   It comes without thy call;
> And how dies love?—A spirit bright,
>   Love never dies at all!

Tyranny arises out of democracy

Source: THE REPUBLIC (Book VIII, 564, as translated by Benjamin Jowett)
Author: Plato (427–347 B.C.)
First transcribed: Fourth century B.C.
Type of work: Political philosophy

Context: In dealing with the question of what constitutes the ideal State, Socrates, the principal speaker in *The Republic,* describes and analyzes the possible types of government: aristocratic, timocratic, oligarchic, democratic, tyrannical. Following the Greek conception of history as an ever-turning wheel, he explains how each system eventually changes into another and lower one because of the principle that "the excessive increase of anything often causes a reaction in the opposite direction." Thus oligarchy (rule based on the ownership of property) results in the insatiable demand for wealth on the part of the rulers and, by reaction, brings about a greater demand for liberty on the part of the populace. So the system of government changes to democracy, the rule of the "people." But this form of government in turn engenders its own reaction: the more liberty men have, the more they demand, until a situation arises that is strikingly similar to that found today. And we have, says Socrates, "subjects who are like rulers, and rulers who are like subjects"; "the master fears and flatters his scholars, and the scholars despise their master"; "the father grows accustomed to descend to the level of his sons and to fear them, and the son is on a level with his father." Hence, law and authority cease to function, and there appears a class of "idle spendthrifts" who destroy the State. Society divides into three classes: the drones who live upon others; the orderly and wealthy class who are fed upon by the drones; and the workers whose leaders "deprive the rich of their estates and distribute them among the people, at the same time taking care to reserve the larger part for themselves." The rich naturally try to defend their property as best they can; hence, the people, the "demos," find a champion for their cause; and this champion, with the mob at his back, turns into a tyrant. Thus the wheel has turned: oligarchy has become democracy, and democracy has become tyranny. As Socrates sums it up in his dialogue with Adeimantus:

The ruin of oligarchy is the ruin of democracy; the same disease magnified and intensified by liberty overmasters democracy—the truth being that the excessive increase of anything often causes a reaction in the opposite direction; and this is the case not only in the seasons and in vegetable and animal life, but above all in forms of government.

True.

The excess of liberty, whether in States or individuals, seems only to pass into excess of slavery.

Yes, the natural order.

And so **tyranny** naturally **arises out of democracy,** and the most aggravated form of tyranny and slavery out of the most extreme form of liberty?

As we might expect.

Tyrants seldom want pretexts

Source: LETTER TO A MEMBER OF THE NATIONAL ASSEMBLY
Author: Edmund Burke (1729–1797)
First published: 1791
Type of work: Political essay

Context: This letter was written as an answer to some objections to Burke's *Reflections on the French Revolution.* In this epistolary essay Burke once again takes his stand against government which is founded in revolution, and which appeals for its existence to theory. Burke maintains always that government must evolve slowly, as the British government has, and must be grounded in real situations, as well as in theory, lest it become tyrannous to the very people that it is supposed to benefit and protect. Of revolutionists, Burke has this to say, "Those who have been once intoxicated with power, and have derived any kind of emolument from it, even though but for one year, never can willingly abandon it." Government by revolutionists, he says, can only become the accomplice of robbers. He goes on to state his view that the present French government is using the French king as a passive tool, exploiting the veneration which many Frenchmen have for their monarch. Burke says he may be accused of fostering regicide by his statements, but that in reality the revolutionists will need no excuse for ridding themselves of the king when he is no longer useful to them; that is, when public sentiment for him is gone:

> . . . They calculate the duration of that sentiment; and when they find it nearly expiring, they will not trouble themselves with excuses for extinguishing the name, as they have the thing. . . . **Tyrants seldom want pretexts.** Fraud is the ready minister of injustice; and whilst the currency of false pretence and sophistic reasoning was expedient to their designs, they were under no necessity of drawing upon me to furnish them with that coin. But pretexts and sophisms have had their day, and have done their work. The usurpation no longer seeks plausibility. It trusts to power.

Ultima Thule

Source: GEORGICS (Book I, l. 30)
Author: Virgil (Publius Vergilius Maro, 70–19 B.C.)
First transcribed: c. 37–30 B.C.
Type of work: Didactic poem

Context: As Virgil commences his poetic treatise on agriculture, he calls upon the appropriate gods. Then addressing Caesar, he suggests that if the emperor should prefer to rule the sea instead of the land, mariners, even to *Ultima Thule,* would pray to him and that Neptune would declare his resignation as God of the Sea. In the translation of Dryden, the passage appears:

> Or wilt thou, Caesar, choose the watery reign,
> To smooth the surges, and correct the main?
> Then mariners, in storms, to thee shall pray;
> E'en **utmost Thule** shall thy power obey;
> And Neptune shall resign the fasces of the sea.

Under which king, Besonian? Speak, or die

Source: KING HENRY THE FOURTH: PART TWO (Act V, sc. iii, l. 119)
Author: William Shakespeare (1564–1616)
First published: 1600
Type of work: Historical drama

Context: Falstaff, having survived both the Battle of Shrewsbury against Hotspur and the Battle of Gaultree Forest against the Archbishop of York, has returned to Gloucestershire to renew his acquaintance with his old friend Justice Shallow. Actually, as a soldier this braggadocio has been more of a hindrance than an asset to the forces of King Henry. Before each battle he was granted a sum of money to be used for the impressment of his force; and in both cases he spent the funds on sack rather than on able-bodied men. Consequently, he led into battle the motliest bunch of raga-muffins and released prisoners who ever bore arms in the name of England. Nor are Falstaff's intentions honorable concerning his visit to Shallow. He sees in the old justice, living in his senility on his memories of the past when he attended the Inns of Court in London, yet another opportunity to increase his fortune. Certainly Falstaff's crass willingness to fleece his old companion tends to darken his character and to prepare the audience for the moment when Hal, as Henry V, will banish his erstwhile crony. But, when Henry IV dies, the "bombard of sack" assumes that his rise to power is complete. Pistol, his rowdy associate, brings him news of the old king's death and gives a sharp retort to Justice Shallow's remonstrances to speak more directly to the point:

SHALLOW
Give me pardon sir; if sir you come with news from the Court, I take it there's but two ways, either to utter them, or to conceal them. I am sir under the King in some authority.

PISTOL
Under which king, Besonian? Speak or die.

1162

SHALLOW

Under King Harry.

PISTOL

Harry the Fourth or, Fifth?

SHALLOW

Harry the Fourth.

PISTOL

A foutra for thine office!
Sir John, thy tender lambkin now is King.
Harry the Fifth's the man. I speak the truth.
When Pistol lies, do this, and fig me, like
The bragging Spaniard.

The undiscovered count·y, from whose bourn no traveller returns

Source: HAMLET (Act III, sc. i, ll. 79–80)
Author: William Shakespeare (1564–1616)
First published: 1603
Type of work: Dramatic tragedy

Context: In a mistaken attempt to prove that Hamlet's assumed madness is the result of love for his daughter, Ophelia, Polonius has placed her in Hamlet's path while Polonius and King Claudius hide themselves and listen. Hamlet enters and delivers the most famous speech in the entire Shakespearian canon, a discourse on the merits of life and death, life seen as a "sea of troubles," man as groaning under burdens—"fardels." Death would be preferable if only one could be certain that it involved nothing more than sleep, but death is for the living an unexplored country, and fear of it forces one to put up with the calamity of life:

HAMLET

To be, or not to be, that is the question—
Whether 'tis nobler in the mind to suffer
The slings and arrows of outrageous fortune,
Or to take arms against a sea of troubles,
And by opposing end them. To die, to sleep—
No more; and by a sleep to say we end
The heart-ache, and the thousand natural shocks
That flesh is heir to; 'tis a consummation
Devoutly to be wish'd. To die, to sleep—
To sleep, perchance to dream, ay there's the rub,
For in that sleep of death what dreams may come
When we have shuffled off this mortal coil,

1163

Must give us pause; there's the respect
That makes calamity of so long life.
For who would bear the whips and scorns of time,
Th' oppressor's wrong, the proud man's contumely,
The pangs of despised love, the law's delay,
The insolence of office, and the spurns
That patient merit of th' unworthy takes,
When he himself might his quietus make
With a bare bodkin? Who would fardels bear,
To grunt and sweat under a weary life,
But that the dread of something after death,
**The undiscovered country, from whose bourn
No traveller returns,** puzzles the will,
And makes us rather bear those ills we have,
Than fly to others that we know not of?

· · ·

Unearned increment

Source: DISSERTATIONS AND DISCUSSIONS (1859 Edition, Volume IV, p. 299)
Author: John Stuart Mill (1806–1873)
First published: 1859
Type of work: Essay in Political Economy

Context: John Stuart Mill was a precocious child, educated by his father; he became an astonishing philosopher and economist whose works in Philosophy, Logic, and Political Science have long outlived him. His *Autobiography* has become a classic, and nearly a century after its publication is required reading in English classes for its style and logical development. His essay on "Liberty" is read by university classes in English and Government, and even his text on logic can still be read with profit. However, it is his work on economics that remains Mill's greatest contribution to modern thought. His *Principles of Political Economy* that came out in 1848 in an edition of 1,000 copies, had an equal edition the next year, and an increase to 1,200 copies in 1852, with continually larger editions following. Mill followed the abstract theories of rent of David Ricardo (1772–1823), but applied economic doctrines to social conditions. His thinking was sharpened by an important event in his life. In 1831 he met and fell in love with Helen Taylor, but not until her husband's death in 1851 did he marry her. They enjoyed seven happy years together while he was developing many of his theories. He acknowledges in his *Autobiography* that his conviction of the complete equality of the sexes in legal, political, social, and domestic relations probably came from Helen Taylor. The first printing of his *Political Economy* carried a dedicatory acknowledgment of her help, but her dislike of publicity prevented its insertion in later copies. The author also made other changes in the book in its subsequent publications, up to the seventh edition, in

1870, the last during his lifetime. Some of Mill's ideas were published in *Westminster Review,* and in the *London Review,* as well as in *The Review,* when they were combined. At the suggestion of his wife, he started collecting and re-editing, and published the articles in two volumes of *Dissertations and Discussions* in 1859. Their reception was so friendly that he issued a third volume with an "Essay on Plato," originally appearing in the *Edinburgh Review* as its most important entry. In the fourth volume appeared an essay restating and rephrasing one of his most important contributions to economic thought and taxation, that put the phrase "unearned increment" into the vocabulary of Economics. The term was new, though the idea was not. Adam Smith (1723–1790), in his *In-quiry into the Nature and Causes of the Wealth of Nations* (1775), had written that "Landlords, like other men, love to reap where they never sowed." The belief grew that wealth which comes to a man without any effort of his own should not belong to him, and ought to be taken, all or in part, for the good of everybody, through taxation. Mill explains the theory and calls this windfall "unearned increment," in the fourth volume of his *Dissertations and Discussions,* and "unearned appendage" in his *Principles of Economic Theory.* A man who owns farm land, for instance, may suddenly find its value greatly increased because the city grows in his direction or a railroad extension makes the land attractive to factory builders. This is Mill's belief:

Before leaving the subject of Equality of Taxation, I must remark that there are cases in which exceptions may be made to it, consistently with that equal justice which is the groundwork of the rule. Suppose that there is a kind of income which consistently tends to increase, without any exertion or sacrifice on the part of the owner, those owners constituting a class in the community whom the natural course of things progressively enriches, consistently with complete passiveness on their own part. In such a case it would be no violation of the principles on which private property is grounded if the state should appropriate this increase of wealth, or part of it, as it arises. This would not properly be taking anything from anybody, it would be merely applying an accession of wealth, created by circumstances, to the benefit of society, instead of allowing it to become the Unearned appendage **(unearned increment)** to the riches of a particular class.

Unfaith in aught is want of faith in all

Source: IDYLLS OF THE KING ("Merlin and Vivien," Line 387)
Author: Alfred, Lord Tennyson (1809–1892)
First published: 1859
Type of work: Narrative poem

1165

Context: King Mark of Cornwall, who greatly dislikes Arthur and his court for their supposed slights upon him, hears a visitor at his table say that Lancelot and Queen Guinevere have a pure and perfect friendship and that some of the young knights of the court imitate him in living lives of virginity. Mark, in envy, enlists the aid of the wily Vivien, whose father had been killed fighting against Arthur's forces, to corrupt the court. Vivien goes to Camelot and, saying that she is being persecuted by King Mark, requests Guinevere's protection, which the queen promises her. Guinevere and Lancelot ride into the field to try out a falcon that Lancelot had trained for the queen. Vivien watches them depart, but Lancelot and Guinevere, once in the field, talk only of falconry. Vivien becomes established at court; she bears herself humbly, but gives out whispers and hints that all is not morally right among the highly placed ones. She even tries to tempt Merlin, who thinks longingly of her; he departs from the court in a boat, accompanied by Vivien, and in the wilderness to which they go she tries to seduce him into teaching her a magic spell that will give her power in the court. When Merlin refuses her request, she says that he is ignorant of the verses that indicate there must be equal faith in love.

I think ye hardly know the tender rhyme
Of "trust me not at all or all in all."
I heard the great Sir Lancelot sing it once,
And it shall answer for me. Listen to it.

"In Love, if Love be Love, if Love be ours,
Faith and unfaith can ne'er be equal powers:
Unfaith in aught is want of faith in all.

It is the little rift within the lute,
That by and by will make the music mute,
And ever widening slowly silence all.

The little rift within the lover's lute
Or little pitted speck in garnered fruit,
That rotting inward slowly moulders all.

It is not worth the keeping: let it go:
But shall it? answer, darling, answer, no.
And trust me not at all or all in all."

The union of hands and hearts

Source: THE MARRIAGE RING (Part I)
Author: Jeremy Taylor (1613–1667)
First published: 1653
Type of work: Sermon

Context: Taylor was a well-educated and popular preacher at St. Paul's Cathedral in London for some time. He was some time later a chaplain to the king, and, still later, preacher to the University of Oxford. As a prominent Anglican he was twice imprisoned by the Puritans, although he seems to have been friendly and tolerant himself. In an age when sermons of popular preachers were frequently published subsequent to delivery, he produced a volume of twenty-seven sermons for the summer half-year in 1651 and a similar group for the winter weeks in 1653. In this discourse on marriage, Taylor examines in very learned fashion the traditional reverence of the church for celibacy, but concludes that the married state is also a state of spiritual beauty:

> Here is the proper scene of piety and patience, of the duty of parents and the charity of relatives; here kindness is spread abroad, and love is united and made firm as a centre: marriage is the nursery of heaven; the virgin sends prayers to God, but she carries but one soul to Him; but the state of marriage fills up the numbers of the elect, and hath in it the labour of love, and the delicacies of friendship, the blessing of society, and **the union of hands and hearts;** it hath in it less of beauty, but more of safety, than the single life; it hath more care, but less danger; it is more merry, and more sad; is fuller of sorrows, and fuller of joys; it lies under more burdens, but it is supported by all the strengths of love and charity, and those burdens are delightful. Marriage is the mother of the world, and preserves kingdoms, and fills cities, and churches, and heaven itself.

Unmissed but by his dogs and by his groom

Source: THE PROGRESS OF ERROR (Line 95)
Author: William Cowper (1731–1800)
First published: 1782
Type of work: Essay in verse

Context: In the opening lines of this moral essay in rhymed couplets, Cowper calls on his Muse to sing the way by which "the serpent, error, twists round human hearts." Then he follows the course of human weaknesses from their start in the search for pleasure to their end in ruin and vanity. To him, vanity was one of man's great sins. Writing out of a deeply religious background and intent on improving man, he characterizes some of his own writing in one couplet of this poem: "The clear harangue, and cold as it is clear/ Falls soporific on the listless ear." But, though sometimes dull, his descriptions of the life of the common people and of the pleasures offered by Nature were practice for the later and greater Nature poetry of *The Task.* In one section of this poem, he portrays the hunter who carries to excess his pleasures that in moderation are in-

1167

nocent. The man's too-frequent hunts in pursuit of his prey leave him no time for the pursuit of virtue. But the hunter is bound to resent criticism of what he considers his healthy way of life. Yet, when it brings him to his death, he will be missed by none except his animals and the groom who gets him ready for the hunt.

> Grey dawn appears; the sportsman and his train
> Speckle the bosom of the distant plain;
>
> . . .
>
> For persevering chase and headlong leaps
> True beagle as the staunchest hound he keeps.
> Charged with the folly of his life's mad scene,
> He takes offence, and wonders what you mean;
> The joy, the danger, and the toil o'erpays;
> 'T is exercise, and health, and length of days.
> Again impetuous to the field he flies;
> Leaps every fence but one, there falls and dies;
> Like a slain deer, the tumbrel brings him home,
> **Unmissed but by his dogs and by his groom.**

The unplumbed, salt, estranging sea

Source: TO MARGUERITE—CONTINUED (Line 24)
Author: Matthew Arnold (1822–1888)
First published: 1852
Type of work: Love poem

Context: This poem is the fifth of a group of six love poems grouped under the title "Switzerland." The group is a chronicle of a love affair between the speaker and Marguerite: the beginning, development, conclusion, and aftermath. In "Isolation. To Marguerite" the speaker describes how the affair closed. Although they had been apart, the speaker had remained faithful, believing that her love, too, grew each day. He sadly learns, however, that "The heart can bind itself alone,/ And faith may oft be unreturned." He envies other men whose faith in the power of love releases them from their isolation. He develops this idea in an extended metaphor in "To Marguerite—Continued." Here he describes mankind as solitary islands dotting the sea of life. Only on spring-like, song-filled, starry nights do they long for union: "For surely once, they feel, we were/ Parts of a single continent!" The speaker asks why this state cannot be:

> Who ordered, that their longing's fire
> Should be, as soon as kindled, cooled?
> Who renders vain their deep desire?—
> A God, a God their severance ruled!

1168

And bade betwixt their shores to be
The unplumbed, salt, estranging sea.

The unpremeditated lay

Source: THE LAY OF THE LAST MINSTREL (Introduction, l. 18)
Author: Sir Walter Scott (1771–1832)
First published: 1805
Type of work: Narrative poem

Context: The Lay of the Last Minstrel was Sir Walter Scott's first literary venture of any importance. The story, which takes place about the middle of the sixteenth century, is told by the last surviving wandering Scottish minstrel; just when he lived is not made clear, but as the revolution under the Young Pretender was a thing of the past, he probably lived after the middle of the eighteenth century. In the Middle Ages the wandering minstrel was a welcomed guest at every castle and manor house; he was eagerly listened to, sumptuously entertained, and sent on his way with a rich reward of gold pieces. According to the words of the poem, he sang unpremeditated lays to lords and ladies. This statement means that he could sing extemporaneously; the ability to do so is frequently mentioned in literature. The Norwegians were much given to flytings, or poetical scolding matches, made up on the spur of the moment; and the genuine calypso singer of the West Indies also has the ability to compose as he sings. The practice was made possible in the Middle Ages by the fact that the meter employed was not in the regular feet of later poetry. In *The Lay of the Last Minstrel,* Scott uses a variety of the irregular medieval meters; he said that the poem was "in a light-horseman sort of stanza," which he contended was a combination of the old minstrel meters colored by modern versification.

> The way was long, the wind was cold,
> The Minstrel was infirm and old:
> His withered cheek, and tresses gray
> Seemed to have known a better day;
> The harp, his sole remaining joy,
> Was carried by an orphan boy.
> The last of all the Bards was he,
> Who sung of Border chivalry;
> For, well-a-day! their date was fled,
> His tuneful brethren all were dead;
> And he, neglected and oppressed,
> Wished to be with them and at rest.
> No more on prancing palfrey borne,
> He carolled, light as lark at morn;
> No longer courted and caressed,
> High placed in hall, a welcome guest,

1169

He poured, to lord and lady gay,
The unpremeditated lay:
Old times were changed, old manners gone. . . .

The unreturning brave

Source: CHILDE HAROLD'S PILGRIMAGE (Canto III, stanza 27)
Author: George Gordon, Lord Byron (1788–1824)
First published: 1816 (Canto III)
Type of work: Narrative poem

Context: Not since the *Faerie Queene* of 1590–1596, by Edmund Spenser (1552–1599), the first important epic in English by a major poet, had the Spenserian stanza he devised been put to such good use as in Byron's *Childe Harold's Pilgrimage.* The stanza consists of nine lines, the first eight in iambic pentameter, and the last line with an additional foot. The rhyme is ababbcbcc. Byron uses it to record the wanderings of Harold, a Romantic figure, disillusioned and unable to live with his fellow men. Only in Nature can he find relief from his bitter thoughts. In Cantos I and II, published in 1812, the young lord follows the pilgrimage made by Byron himself, through the Mediterranean to Greece, beloved because of its struggle for liberty. In Canto III, not published until 1816, Childe Harold has reached the battlefield of Waterloo where the previous year Wellington had ended forever Napoleon's aspirations to power, and made it, as Byron declares, "the grave of France." The poet describes social activities in "Belgium's capital" when "fair women" and "brave men" in the ballroom are more interested in their

dancing than in the struggle of Napoleon and Ney against Wellington and Blücher. However, the cannon roar tells the Duke of Brunswick that death is near. He rushes to the conflict and is one of the first to fall. After sudden partings amid tears, with the mustering of squadrons and the clattering of cars, the suddenly-awakened soldiers are drummed into ranks. Bagpipes shrill; the sound of "Cameron's gathering" inspires the soldiers to extra bravery. On to the battlefield they march, under the trees of what Shakespeare had called "The forest of Arden," but known as "the Ardennes Woods" to American soldiers of the First World War. In the early morning they are dripping dew as if mourning for those who will never come back. Battle figures for that day in June assign 32,000 casualties to the French and 23,000 to the allied British and Prussians. They were the brave who never returned. Describing the march to the battlefield at the beginning of the struggle —how next year some will be beneath the grass over which they now walk—Byron writes in Stanza 27

And Ardennes waves above them her green leaves,
Dewy with nature's tear-drops, as they pass,
Grieving, if aught inanimate e'er grieves,

1170

Over **the unreturning brave**—alas!
Ere evening to be trodden like the grass
Which now beneath them, but above shall grow
In its next verdure, when this fiery mass
Of living valour, rolling on the foe
And burning with high hope shall moulder cold and low.

Unwept, unhonored, and unsung

Source: THE LAY OF THE LAST MINSTREL (Canto VI, stanza 1, l. 16)
Author: Sir Walter Scott (1771–1832)
First published: 1805
Type of work: Narrative poem

Context: When the old minstrel pauses during the telling of his tale of love and war on the English-Scottish border, his hearers, a duchess and her attendant ladies, ask him why he plods around Scotland to sing his songs; his harp would be much more appreciated in the south, in England, and the wealthy English would reward him more highly than the poor Scots are able to. The aged harper, although his harp is dear to him, rather resents the slight of putting his harp music above his poetry. He begins his next canto with what is probably the most famous expression of patriotism in poetry. He asks if there is a man who cannot say to himself that this is his own, his native land, whose heart has not been stimulated by a return home from foreign lands. If such an unenviable creature exists, take note of him, because he is a wretch who will die unwept, unhonored, and unsung. Scott's expression here is reminiscent of Achilles' characterization of the dead Hector (in Alexander Pope's translation of the *Iliad*); he said that the fallen warrior, lying on the plain, was "unwept, unhonor'd, uninterred."

Breathes there a man, with soul so dead,
Who never to himself hath said,
   This is my own, my native land?
Whose heart hath ne'er within him burned,
As home his footsteps he hath turned
   From wandering on a foreign strand?
If such there breathe, go, mark him well;
For him no minstrel raptures swell;
High though his titles, proud his name,
Boundless his wealth as wish can claim,—
Despite those titles, power, and pelf,
The wretch, concentred all in self,
Living, shall forfeit fair renown,
And, doubly dying, shall go down
To the vile dust from whence he sprung,
Unwept, unhonored, and unsung.

Up roos the sonne, and up roos Emelye

Source: THE CANTERBURY TALES ("The Knight's Tale," Line 2273)
Author: Geoffrey Chaucer (1343?–1400)
First transcribed: c. 1387–1392
Type of work: Collection of tales

Context: In "The Knight's Tale," a medieval romance and the first of *The Canterbury Tales,* Chaucer tells the story of the love of the knights Arcite and Palamon for the beautiful Emilia, sister-in-law to Theseus, ruler of Athens. Hopelessly in love with the maiden, the two young men are commanded by Theseus to meet in fifty weeks with one hundred followers to fight till death for the hand of their ideal. On the appointed day of the tournament, when Palamon prays to Venus, the goddess of love, and Arcite to Mars, the god of war, Emilia, a follower of Diana, the goddess of chastity, rises and makes her prayers to her own deity.

> The thridde houre inequal that Palamon
> Bigan to Venus temple for to gon,
> **Up roos the sonne, and up roos Emelye,**
> And to the temple of Dyane gan hye.
> Hir maydens, that she thider with hire ladde,
> Ful redily with hem the fyr they hadde,
> Th'encens, the clothes, and the remenant al
> That to the sacrifice longen shal;
> The hornes fulle of meeth, as was the gyse:
> Ther lakked noght to doon hir sacrifise.
> Smokynge the temple, ful of clothes faire,
> This Emelye, with herte debonaire,
> Hir body wessh with water of a welle.

Upper-crust

Source: THE WAYS OF THE HOUR (Chapter 6)
Author: James Fenimore Cooper (1789–1851)
First published: 1850
Type of work: Novel

Context: Thomas Chandler Halliburton (1796–1865) was a Canadian jurist who was also a humorist. His alter ego and pseudonym was Sam Slick. Sam first appeared in a series of letters that ran in *The Nova Scotian,* a weekly paper, in 1836. These were later issued in book form under the title, *The Clockmaker; or, the Sayings and Doings of Samuel Slick of Slickville.* Sam is a shrewd and ingenious Yankee peddler, dealing in clocks; he sells his wares among the Nova Scotians, who are usually not so quick-witted as he, and he never fails to take advantage of them. Like the later and somewhat similar creation of William Sidney Porter (O.

Henry), Jeff Peters, Sam is an unscrupulous but loveable rascal. His adventures were so popular that he appeared in a number of volumes, and at length Halliburton sent him abroad in 1843–1844 to provide a commentary on the British. In this book, *The Attaché; or, Sam Slick in England,* Sam makes the following comment (Chapter 24): "I want you to see Peel, Stanley, Graham, Shiel, Russell, Macauley, Old Joe, and so on. These men are all *upper-crust* here." However, credit for the more or less universal popularity of this term should, perhaps, go to James Fenimore Cooper, who used it six years later. Cooper was the first American novelist to reach widespread fame beyond the borders of this country. His historical novels of pioneer America were read avidly throughout the English-speaking world. He later wrote a number of works embodying social criticism and expressing his conservative point of view. *The Ways of the Hour* is one of these. In it he deals with the evils of the jury system, and of laws which restrict the individual but do not protect him. The story itself is a murder mystery. Mary Monson, a beautiful girl of unknown background, is accused of arson and murder; the old couple she has been staying with have apparently been killed and their house burned. Their money is missing. Jack Wilmeter, nephew of lawyer Tom Dunscomb, has fallen in love with Mary. In the following passage, Jack and the sheriff's wife speculate on the girl's background:

Although Mrs. Gott and John Wilmeter had very different ideas, at the bottom of the requisites to form a lady, and the pronunciation of the good woman was by no means faultless, she cordially assented to the truth of the young man's eulogy. Indeed, Mary Monson, for the hour, was her great theme; and, though still a young woman herself, and good-looking withal, she really seemed never to tire of uttering her praises.

"She has been educated, Mr. Wilmeter, far above any female hereabouts, unless it may be some of the ——s and ——s," the good woman continued. "Those families, you know, are our **upper crust**—not upper ten thousand, as the newspapers call it, but upper hundred, and their ladies may know as much as Mary; but, beyond *them,* no female hereabouts can hold a candle to her! Her books have been brought in, and I looked them over—there isn't more than one in three that I can read at all. What is more, they don't seem to be all in one tongue, the foreign books, but in three or four."

An upstart crow, beautified with our feathers

Source: A GROATSWORTH OF WIT BOUGHT WITH A MILLION OF REPENTANCE
Author: Robert Greene (c. 1560–1592)
First published: 1592
Type of work: Autobiography

Context: Robert Greene, a talented writer who lived a dissolute life in the slums of Elizabethan London, was much given to confessing his sins and follies in the form of penny pamphlets. In *A Groatsworth of Wit Bought with a Million of Repentance* he cautions several of his fellow University Wits to be warned by his deplorable example and mend their ways while yet there is time. The first one he addresses is Christopher Marlowe (1564–1593), the famous gracer of tragedies; he urges him not to defer his reformation until he, like Greene, is upon the point of death. He also tells Thomas Nashe (1567–1601), the prose satirist, not to make enemies with his biting words. To George Peele (1558?–1597?) he also urges the living of a better life. He then sneers at an unnamed writer, almost universally thought to be Shakespeare (1564–1616), who apparently bases his plays on the works of Greene's coterie, the University Wits. He calls him an upstart, because Greene and his fellows, all university educated, looked down upon those, like Shakespeare, who had not attended a university. The phrase "tiger's heart wrapped in a player's hide," with its glance at *King Henry the Sixth, Part Three* (Act I, sc. iv, l. 137), is generally held to be the first reference to Shakespeare as an actor and a reviser of old plays.

. . . There is **an upstart crow, beautified with our feathers,** that with his *tiger's heart wrapped in a player's hide,* supposes he is as well able to bombast out a blank verse as the best of you; and being an absolute *Johannes fac totum,* is in his own conceit the only Shake-scene in a country. Oh that I might entreat your rare wits to be employed in more profitable courses; and let those apes imitate your past excellence, and never more acquaint them with your admired inventions. . . .

The vain tribute of a smile

Source: THE LAY OF THE LAST MINSTREL (Canto IV, conclusion, l. 601)
Author: Sir Walter Scott (1771–1832)
First published: 1805
Type of work: Narrative poem

Context: The last of the border minstrels, feeble and old, is entertained by a duchess who, with her attendant ladies, listens to his story. He tells of the activities that center on Branksome Hall, a castle on the Scottish side of the English-Scottish border. An English force of three thousand men marches on Branksome Hall to demand the surrender of William Deloraine, who has foully ravaged English soil. In the English army is the young heir of Branksome Hall; he had been kidnaped from his own estate and carried to the south. The English say that if Deloraine is not surrendered to them, the boy will be sent to London to be employed as a page to the king. At this point, news of the approach of a large Scottish army is announced to the English, who agree to a fight at single combat between Deloraine and Musgrave, whom he had wronged. If Deloraine wins, the heir will be freed; if Musgrave has the victory, the lad goes to London. At this point the minstrel breaks off the story to rest. The listening ladies all applaud the old man's performance. He smiles at the reception given his tale, as poets are a simple race who waste their toil for the slight reward of a smile.

> The harper smiled, well pleased; for ne'er
> Was flattery lost on poet's ear.
> A simple race! they waste their toil
> For **the vain tribute of a smile;**
> E'en when in age their flame expires,
> Her dulcet breath can fan its fires:
> Their drooping fancy wakes at praise,
> And strives to trim the short-lived blaze.

Vanity, like murder, will out

Source: THE BELLE'S STRATAGEM (Act I, sc. iv)
Author: Hannah Parkhouse Cowley (1743–1809)
First published: 1780
Type of work: Dramatic comedy

Context: Mrs. Cowley's comedy, *The Belle's Stratagem,* appealed to the audiences of her day because it was humorous, without dragging in characters from low life, as did so many other plays. She did, however, extract fun from the broken French of some of the people. Most who appear are well bred, even if not elegant, yet they bring chuckles as well as sympathy. Audiences could identify with them. The basic incident is not very funny or credible. It is hard to accept the situation that a lady could play the part of a simpleton so convincingly. That episode is not the reason for one editor of the play speaking of its "forceful and pleasing occurrences." She refers to the subplot in which the newlywed Sir George and Lady Frances Touchwood figure. They are more than warmed-over type characters of the period in their love that never becomes mawkish. Yet her disguise at the masquerade, like Doricourt's sudden and violent passion for a masked woman in the main story, are hardly credible, though they do make for good theater. This, after all, is the reason for reading or attending a play. Though the powdered ladies in their silken gowns, and references to a masquerade party of the Queen of France, dated the play shortly after its first performance at Theatres Royal, Drury Lane, and Covent Garden in 1780, it long continued a favorite, with many revivals. Ellen Terry enjoyed playing Letitia. The opening scenes present the problem. Saville has left his friends who are shooting in the country, to come to Lincoln Inn, London, to meet his acquaintance, Doricourt, a mirror of fashions just back from Italy and about to marry the heiress Letitia Hardy, whom he has not seen since childhood. Having met her, he expresses pleasure in her beauty but laments her lack of spirit. In Scene iv we meet Letitia, bemoaning her cool treatment from Doricourt. But to Mrs. Rackett and Villers she announces her scheme. She will behave so badly that Doricourt will hate her. She is sure it is easier to change hatred into love than to modify indifference. That is her stratagem. In the rest of the play, Doricourt tries to break off their engagement after meeting a masked lady at a ball. To prevent this plot, Letitia's father pretends to be dying. Only the thought of his daughter safely married will permit him to depart in peace, so reluctantly Doricourt agrees to the wedding. Only then does he see the masked woman again. She turns out to be witty Letitia, for a happy ending. In Act I, before Letitia Hardy is introduced, Villers and Mrs. Rackett are discussing her.

VILLERS

So you brought Miss Hardy to town last night?

MRS. RACKETT

Yes, I should have brought her before, but I had a fall from my horse, that confined me a week.—I suppose in her heart she wished me hanged a dozen times an hour.

· · ·

MRS. RACKETT

Had she not an expecting lover in town all the time? She meets him this morning at the lawyer's.—I hope she'll charm him; she's the sweetest girl in the world.

VILLERS

Vanity, like murder, will out. You have convinced me you think yourself more charming.

MRS. RACKETT

How can that be?

VILLERS

No woman ever praises another, unless she thinks herself superior in the very perfections she allows.

Variety is the soul of pleasure

Source: THE ROVER; OR, THE BANISH'D CAVALIERS, PART TWO (Act I, sc. i)
Author: Aphra Behn (1640–1689)
First published: 1681
Type of work: Dramatic comedy

1176

Context: This quotation is apparently a variation of the proverb: "Variety is the spice of life." It appears in Aphra Behn's second play about the Rover, Willmore, a Cavalier banished by Parliamentary action. Her first play, apparently the rage of the London season in 1677, had made her famous; and this second play takes advantage of the theme which had proved so popular in her hands. The scene is Madrid, where are gathered a number of exiled Englishmen who have taken refuge from Parliamentarian persecution. Among them are Willmore, the Rover; Ned Blunt, an English country gentleman; Nicholas Fetherfool, a foolish country squire and Ned Blunt's friend; and Mr. Hunt, an ensign. These go in a group to the home of the English ambassador, where they meet Lieutenant Shift and Beaumond, friends of Willmore in earlier adventures. The conversation turns to women, in whom all the men, but especially Willmore, have a lively interest. Willmore, a widower who lost a wealthy wife he scarcely mourns, inquires about the pleasures of Madrid from Beaumond, turning the conversation away from his late wife:

WILLMORE
—But come, let's leave this mortifying Discourse, and tell me how the price of Pleasure goes.

BEAUMOND
At the old Rates still; he that gives most is happiest, some few there are for Love!

WILLMORE
Ah, one of the last, dear Beaumond; and if a Heart or Sword can purchase her, I'll bid as fair as the best. Damn it, I hate a Whore that asks me Mony.

BEAUMOND
Yet have I known thee venture all thy stock for a new Woman.

WILLMORE
Ay, such a Fool I was in my dull Days of Constancy, but I am now for Change, (and should I pay as often, 'twould undo me)—for Change, my Dear, of Place, Clothes, Wine, and Women. **Variety is the Soul of Pleasure,** a Good unkown; and we want faith to find it.

The vasty hall of death

Source: REQUIESCAT (Stanza 4)
Author: Matthew Arnold (1822–1888)
First published: 1853
Type of work: Lyric poem

Context: The title "Requiescat" means "may she rest." This poem expresses tenderly a person's reaction to the death of a lady he knew quite well. By saying "Strew on her roses, roses,/ And never a spray of yew!" in the first two lines, the speaker urges his listeners not to grieve because, as he goes on to point out, the lady is at peace. The next stanza tells of the deceased's former gaiety followed by weariness with life. The poem then advances, in the next stanza, the image of this weariness along with her desire for peaceful release from "the mazes of heat and sound." Finally the poem climaxes in contrasting how the lady's spirit, so confined during her life, is freed by entering "The vasty hall of death." Thus the spirit so bound in life finds liberty in the immense realm of death.

> Her life was turning, turning,
>   In mazes of heat and sound.
> But for peace her soul was yearning,
>   And now peace laps her round.
>
> Her cabin'd, ample spirit,
>   It flutter'd and fail'd for breath.
> To-night it doth inherit
>   **The vasty hall of death.**

Vengeance is mine

Source: ROMANS 12:19
Author: Paul
First transcribed: c. 50–60
Type of work: Religious epistle

Context: Romans is an epistle which Paul wrote to the Christian Church that was gradually building itself in Rome. He had not had a part in its founding and had not visited there; he was not acquainted with its members. Therefore, his letter is more a treatise on Christianity than an ordinary communication between good friends. Starting with a statement of his qualifications and an expression of his gospel, he declares the great mercies God has shown through Christ. Paul's principal concern is for the Jews; it has been his custom during his missionary activities to go to the synagogue whenever he enters a town, beginning his preaching and scriptural argumentation there. He has found the Jews difficult to convert, and has at times been treated roughly. Feeling that he can give converted Romans a better understanding of the Jews, he lists all the objections to Christianity that his experience has taught him a member of the Jewish faith would have. He supplies carefully reasoned answers to each of the objections; in this way he gives his readers a handbook for their missionary efforts. In Chapters 9 through 12 Paul's concern for the Jews is expressed in another way; here he admonishes his fellow Christians in regard to their possible attitude toward the Jews. He feels sorry for the latter and shows that he understands them; in Chapter 11 he points out that they must not be insulted, but treated with consideration and mercy. Chapter 12 is a little sermon on the proper attitude and conduct of a Christian. Paul reminds his readers that they must keep themselves pure as a sacrifice to God; that they should not conform themselves to this world; that they are unified through faith. He then lists a number of principles they should adhere to in their daily life, each using his special talents in the service of the Lord. He ends with a particular caution against the desire to be revenged:

Let love be without dissimulation. Abhor that which is evil; cleave to that which is good.

Be kindly affectioned one to another with brotherly love; in honour preferring one another;

Not slothful in business; fervent in spirit; serving the Lord;

Rejoicing in hope; patient in tribulation; continuing instant in prayer;

Distributing to the necessity of saints; given to hospitality.

Bless them which persecute you: bless, and curse not.

Rejoice with them that do rejoice, and weep with them that weep.

Be of the same mind one toward another. Mind not high things, but condescend to men of low estate. Be not wise in your own conceits.

Recompense to no man evil for evil. Provide things honest in the sight of all men.

If it be possible, as much as lieth in you, live peaceably with all men.

Dearly beloved, avenge not yourselves, but rather give place unto wrath: for it is written, **Vengeance is mine; I will repay,** saith the Lord.

Therefore if thine enemy hunger, feed him; if he thirst, give him drink: for in so doing thou shalt heap coals of fire on his head.

Be not overcome of evil, but overcome evil with good.

Vengeance of Jenny's case

Source: THE MERRY WIVES OF WINDSOR (Act IV, sc. i, l. 64)
Author: William Shakespeare (1564–1616)
First published: 1602
Type of work: Dramatic comedy

Context: During one of the minor interludes, Mistress Page asks the schoolmaster if her son is making progress in school. Sir Hugh Evans then asks several questions of young William Page in order to prove to his mother that the boy is learning. Mistress Quickly, who is a female messenger and informer and who has been discussing the Falstaff plot with Mistress Page, stands by to hear William's recital. As William answers the questions put to him by Evans, Mistress Quickly reflects her lack of learning in making rather vulgar humor out of his answers. For one of the questions, Evans asks William to recite the "genitive case plural" in Latin, and his answer is *"horum, harum, horum."* Mistress Quickly immediately pounces on this answer and proclaims that William has said that Jenny is a whore and calls for "Vengeance of Jenny's case!" Her misconstruction of the dialogue and her play on words is brought out in the quote below, which gave the title to Rossetti's famous poem "Jenny."

EVANS

What is your genitive case plural, William?

WILLIAM

Genitive case?

EVANS

Ay.

WILLIAM

Genitivo horum, harum, horum.

QUICKLY

Vengeance of Jenny's case! Fie on her!
Never name her, child, if she be a whore.

EVANS

For shame 'oman!

QUICKLY

You do ill to teach the child such words. He teaches him to hick and to hack; which they'll do fast enough of themselves, and to call horum; fie upon you!

A very ancient and fish-like smell

Source: THE TEMPEST (Act II, sc. ii, ll. 26–27)
Author: William Shakespeare (1564–1616)
First published: 1623
Type of work: Tragi-comedy

Context: Trinculo, a jester, one of several survivors of a shipwreck, comes upon Caliban, a deformed and beastlike creature who is a slave to Prospero, a magician and the rightful Duke of Milan, who has been living

1180

with his daughter Miranda on the island to which the survivors of the shipwreck have come. Believing Trinculo to be one of Prospero's captive spirits, Caliban attempts to hide, but Trinculo sees him and thinks that in England he could make his fortune exhibiting such a monster:

TRINCULO

· · ·

What have we here? A man, or a fish? Dead or alive? A fish: he smells like a fish. **A very ancient and fish-like smell.** A kind of, not of the newest, Poor-John. A strange fish. Were I in England now, as once I was, and had but this fish painted, not a holiday fool there but would give a piece of silver. There would this monster make a man. Any strange beast there makes a man. When they will not give a doit to relieve a lame beggar, they will lay out ten to see a dead Indian.

· · ·

The very ecstasy of love

Source: HAMLET (Act II, sc. i, l. 102)
Author: William Shakespeare (1564–1616)
First published: 1603
Type of work: Dramatic tragedy

Context: Polonius, Lord Chamberlain to King Claudius, has warned his daughter, Ophelia, not to waste her time in hearing the declared love of Hamlet, that she can only be hurt by what must be false attention. When the dutiful daughter rejects Hamlet, he bursts in on her as she is sewing in her closet. His action may be part of his pretended madness to entrap Claudius, but Polonius sees it only as madness for love of his daughter.

OPHELIA
He took me by the wrist, and held me hard;
Then goes he to the length of all his arm,
And with his other hand thus o'er his brow,
He falls to such perusal of my face
As 'a would draw it. . . .

· · ·

. . . he lets me go,
And with his head over his shoulder turned,
He seemed to find his way without his eyes,
For out a doors he went without their helps,
And to the last bended their light on me.

POLONIUS
Come, go with me, I will go seek the King.
This is **the very ecstasy of love,**
Whose violent property fordoes itself,

1181

And leads the will to desperate undertakings
As oft as any passion under heaven
That does afflict our natures. . . .

The very pink of courtesy

Source: ROMEO AND JULIET (Act II, sc. iv, l. 61)
Author: William Shakespeare (1564–1616)
First published: 1597
Type of work: Dramatic tragedy

Context: The morning after the masked ball at the home of the Capulets, Romeo's friend Mercutio learns from Benvolio that Romeo was not at home all night and that Juliet's fiery cousin Tybalt has sent a letter—apparently a challenge—to Romeo's home. Mercutio, unaware that Romeo has transferred his affection for haughty Rosaline to lovely Juliet Capulet, mocks both Romeo's love-stricken condition and Tybalt's exaggerated compliments and foppish ways, including his fencing style. When Romeo comes by, Mercutio engages in a play of verbal wit with him, each punning on the other's words. The word play begins with a pun on the name for a counterfeit coin—a slip.

MERCUTIO
· · ·
You gave us the counterfeit fairly last night.

ROMEO
Good morrow to you both. What counterfeit did I give you?

MERCUTIO
The slip sir, the slip, can you not conceive?

ROMEO
Pardon, good Mercutio, my business was great, and in such a case as mine a man may strain courtesy.

MERCUTIO
That's as much as to say, such a case as yours constrains a man to bow in the hams.

ROMEO
Meaning to curtsy.

MERCUTIO
Thou hast most kindly hit it.

1182

ROMEO
A most courteous exposition.

MERCUTIO
Nay I am **the very pink of courtesy.**

A very present help in trouble

Source: PSALMS 46:1
Author: Unknown
First transcribed: c. 400–200 B.C.
Type of work: Religious poetry

Context: This psalm is a statement of the confidence the Jews had in God to protect and help them: He was their refuge in time of tribulation and a source of strength; He was their help in times of trouble. God being what He is, the Jews had no fear, even though terrible convulsions might rend the earth and hurl the mountains into the sea. The waters might roar and the mountains tremble, but the Jews' faith in God would remain strong. The Lord of Hosts was with them, and the God of Jacob was their refuge. No one is exactly sure of the meaning of "Selah," that occurs frequently in the Psalms; perhaps it means "So be it," or "Notice."

God is our refuge and strength, **a very present help in trouble.**
Therefore will not we fear, though the earth be removed, and though the mountains be carried into the midst of the sea;
Though the waters thereof roar and be troubled, though the mountains shake with the swelling thereof. Selah.

A very riband in the cap of youth

Source: HAMLET (Act IV, sc. vii, l. 78)
Author: William Shakespeare (1564–1616)
First published: 1603
Type of work: Dramatic tragedy

Context: Together, Claudius and Laertes plot the death of Hamlet— Claudius because he fears the prince may know that he, Claudius, killed Hamlet's father; Laertes because Hamlet mistakenly killed Polonius, Laertes' father. They plan a friendly fencing-match in which Laertes' rapier will not be blunted, as a practice rapier should be, and will be touched with poison. Claudius is quite certain he can get Hamlet to agree to the match because Hamlet envies Laertes' reputation for swordsmanship

1183

and has desired to match himself against his rival. Swordplay, according to Claudius, is a mere ornament, like the ribbons courtiers sometimes wear in their caps, and yet it is as becoming to youth as furs and dignified attire are to the more aged, who must look after their health and dignity:

KING
A very riband in the cap of youth;
Yet needful too, for youth no less becomes
The light and careless livery that it wears
Than settled age his sables and his weeds
Importing health and graveness.

• • •

A very unclubable man

Source: THE LIFE OF SAMUEL JOHNSON, LL.D. (For 1764)
Author: James Boswell (1740–1795)
First published: 1791
Type of work: Biography

Context: Boswell relates how the famous club, which for a long time existed without a name, became known at the time of David Garrick's funeral as the Literary Club. This group, established by Sir Joshua Reynolds and Samuel Johnson, at the former's suggestion, began meeting once a week at seven in the evening, for dinner, at the Turk's Head Tavern, Gerrard Street, in London, later moving to other meeting places. The original membership, according to Boswell, consisted of Sir Joshua Reynolds, Dr. Johnson, Edmund Burke, Oliver Goldsmith, Dr. Nugent, Mr. Beauclerk, Mr. Langton, Mr. Chamier, and Sir John Hawkins. Over the years the number of members in the group increased, and some of the membership changed. Sir John Hawkins, although one of the original members, dropped from the group. He said his "domestick arrangements" were inconsistent with his belonging to the club, that its sessions lasted till too late in the evening. Boswell reports, however, that Hawkins was rude to Edmund Burke on one occasion, and that the next time the club met the members of the group all "testified their displeasure," so that Sir John never came again. It has also been reported, as noted in a footnote, that Sir John, because he usually ate no supper at home, refused to pay a portion of the club's reckoning for a meal; all this seems to have spurred Dr. Johnson to make his comment about the knight, with its famous nonce word:

"Sir John, Sir, is **a very unclubable man.**

1184

Vidth and visdom alvays grows together

Source: THE PICKWICK PAPERS (Chapter 54)
Author: Charles Dickens (1812–1870)
First published: 1836–1837
Type of work: Novel

Context: Sam Weller and his father discuss the will of Mrs. Weller, who has just died. Old Mr. Weller, having located the will in a teapot, after a good deal of searching, and, finding that he and Sam are the sole legatees, is ready to end the matter by tossing the document into the fire. Sam, however, insists upon taking the will to a lawyer to be probated and urges his father to hurry up in putting on his "veskit" and in getting ready to go to London. The old fellow replies in his Cockney accent:

> ". . . Vait a minit, Sammy; ven you grow as old as your father, you von't get into your veskit quite as easy as you do now, my boy."
> "If I couldn't get into it easier than that, I'm blessed if I'd vear vun at all," rejoined the son.
> "You think so now," said Mr. Weller, with the gravity of age, "but you'll find that as you get vider, you'll get viser. **Vidth and visdom,** Sammy, **alvays grows together.**

Vigil strange

Source: VIGIL STRANGE I KEPT ON THE FIELD ONE NIGHT (Line 1)
Author: Walt Whitman (1819–1892)
First published: 1865
Type of work: Elegy

Context: Whitman, who dedicated himself to caring for the wounded during the Civil War, writes of the death of one whom he calls comrade and son, who falls in battle, gives his friend an unforgettable look, and raises his arm to him before dying. The poet hurries on to care for other wounded men, but after the duties of the day have ended, he returns to his beloved dead friend, over whom he keeps a "vigil strange" all night. At dawn, the poet carefully wraps a blanket about the dead youth and buries him in a crude grave.

> **Vigil strange I kept on the field one night;**
> When you my son and my comrade dropt at my side
>   that day,
> One look I but gave which your dear eyes return'd
>   with a look that I shall never forget,
> One touch of your hand to mine O boy, reach'd up as

you lay on the ground,
Then onward I sped in the battle, the even-contested
    battle,
Till late in the night reliev'd to the place at last again
    I made my way,
Found you in death so cold dear comrade, found your
    body son of responding kisses, (never again on
    earth responding,)
Bared your face in the starlight, curious the scene. . . .

Virtue is the fount whence honor springs

Source: TAMBURLAINE THE GREAT (Part I, Act IV, sc. iv, l. 1769)
Author: Christopher Marlowe (1564–1593)
First published: 1590
Type of work: Dramatic tragedy

Context: Tamburlaine, a former scythian shepherd, defeats force after force to become ruler of the East, styling himself Emperor of Asia, and keeping kings and queens as slaves, laughing at their curses. Bajazeth, former ruler of the Turks, Tamburlaine keeps in a cage, letting him out to serve as a footstool upon which to mount the throne. Zenocrate, daughter of the Sultan of Egypt, held as a prisoner by Tamburlaine, comes to love her captor, as he deeply loves her. One day at a banquet Tamburlaine causes three crowns to be brought in for display. He looks to his three lieutenants—Theridamas, Techelles, and Usumcasane—bidding them finger the crowns, but they are hesitant, lest they seem too ambitious and arouse Tamburlaine's distrust. However, Tamburlaine makes Theridamas the King of Argier, Techelles the King of Fez, and Usumcasane the King of Morocco. Having crowned his loyal followers, Tamburlaine speaks in praise of them:

TAMBURLAINE
Kings of Argier, Morocco, and of Fez,
You that have marched with happy *Tamburlaine,*
As far from the frozen place of heaven,
Unto the watry morning's ruddy bower,
And thence by land unto the Torrid Zone,
Deserve these titles I endow you with
By valour and magnanimity.
Your births shall be no blemish to your fame,
For **virtue is the fount whence honor springs,**
And they are worthy she investeth kings.

1186

Visits, like those of angels, short, and far between

Source: THE GRAVE (Lines 588–589)
Author: Robert Blair (1699–1746)
First published: 1743
Type of work: Didactic poem

Context: The Grave is Blair's one important work; it is in the pattern of the so-called Graveyard School of poetry popular in the eighteenth century, akin to such poems as Gray's *Elegy in a Country Churchyard,* Young's *Night Thoughts,* and Henry's *Meditations and Contemplations among the Tombs,* and reprinted many times before 1800. Blair, a clergyman, has written a sermon in verse, dwelling upon man's passage from this life to death and, hopefully, to eternal life with God. Early in the poem Blair announces his theme: ". . . the task be mine/ To paint the gloomy horrors of the tomb,/ The appointed place of rendezvous, where all/ These travellers meet." In the verse paragraph in which the quotation about angels' visits occurs, Blair reminds the reader of the original happy state of man, as described in Genesis, telling in the poet's own terms of his bliss in the Garden of Eden before the Fall, and, then, because of his sin, his expulsion by "a mighty angel with a glaming sword":

> . . . Man has sinned!
> Sick of his bliss, and bent on new adventures,
> Evil he would needs try, nor tried in vain.
> Dreadful experiment! destructive measure!
> Where the worst thing could happen, is success!
> Alas, too well he sped; the good he scorned
> Retired reluctant, like an ill-used ghost,
> Not to return; or if it did, its **visits,**
> **Like those of angels, short, and far between;**
> Whilst the black demon, with his hell-'scaped train,
> Admitted once into its better room,
> Grew loud and mutinous, nor would be gone;
> Lording it o'er the man, who now too late
> Saw the rash error which he could not mend;
> An error fatal not to him alone,
> But to his future's sons, his fortune's heirs.

Voice of many waters

Source: REVELATION 14:2
Author: St. John the Divine
First transcribed: c. 90–96
Type of work: Apocalyptic epistle

1187

Context: The authorship of this tremendous and often bewildering vision is uncertain. The writer's name was John, and he has been variously identified as John the Apostle, John the Presbyter, and John of Patmos. The name may even be a pseudonym. It is likely that he was a Jew from Palestine who had been with the Christians at Ephesus and was exiled, as many Christians were, to labor in the penal settlement at Patmos. His literary style makes it most unlikely that he wrote either the first and second epistles of John or the fourth Gospel. *Revelation* elaborates a series of divinely inspired letters written to seven of the early churches in Asia. The time of its composition was one of great difficulty for Christianity; its principal purpose is to bolster the faith of Christians. Nero had confined his persecutions to Christians in Rome, but Domitian hated all Christians and rigidly enforced the practice of Caesar-worship throughout the empire. The result was a reign of terror lasting until his death in A.D. 96. John had a wide and searching knowledge of the Old Testament and makes frequent references to the apocalyptic visions therein. In likening the voice of God to the mighty surges of the sea, he harks back to Psalm 93, fourth verse: "The LORD on high is mightier than the noise of many waters, yea, than the mighty waves of the sea." John's own visions are transcendent in nature and often extremely difficult for him to describe, so that he frequently employs allegory and symbolism. His purpose is to show that spiritual forces triumph over material, and that God's cause on earth is not lost. A vision of heaven follows, in which the book of fate is opened, and John sees the glory of Christ's kingdom. Certain great woes, or catastrophes, will descend upon earth. An angel gives him a little book to eat and tells him to prophesy. He does so, saying that the third and greatest woe will usher in the coming of Christ. This calamity will be the temporary reign of Anti-Christ on earth. In Chapter 14 John gives his vision of the church triumphant.

And I looked, and, lo, a Lamb stood on the mount Sion, and with him an hundred forty and four thousand, having his Father's name written in their foreheads.

And I heard a voice from heaven, as the **voice of many waters,** and as the voice of a great thunder: and I heard the voice of harpers harping with their harps:

And they sung as it were a new song before the throne, and before the four beasts, and the elders: and no man could learn that song but the hundred and forty and four thousand, which were redeemed from the earth.

These are they which were not defiled with women, for they are virgins. These are they which follow the Lamb whithersoever he goeth. These were redeemed from among men, being the firstfruits unto God and to the Lamb.

And in their mouth was found no guile: for they are without fault before the throne of God.

And I saw another angel fly in the midst of heaven, having the

1188

everlasting gospel to preach unto them that dwell on the earth, and to every nation, and kindred, and tongue, and people,

Saying with a loud voice, Fear God, and give glory to him; for the hour of his judgment is come: . . .

The voice of the people has something divine

Source: THE ADVANCEMENT OF LEARNING (Book VI, Chapter 3, Antitheses, 9, as translated by Francis Headlam)
Author: Sir Francis Bacon (1561–1626)
First published: 1605
Type of work: Philosophy

Context: Sir Francis Bacon was, in several respects, a remarkable man. He served his country both politically and intellectually. Trained in the legal profession, he served many years in Parliament and associated himself with various royal favorites, including Essex (whom he helped to convict after the latter's rebellion) and George Villiers, Duke of Buckingham. The latter attachment at first resulted in a series of royal favors for Bacon; but when Buckingham's popularity vanished, Bacon was charged with accepting bribes from persons who had appeared in his court. He admitted the truth of this charge, but denied that he had perverted justice. Pardoned after a stiff fine and a brief imprisonment, he was forbidden to reenter politics and was allowed to retire. His last years were devoted to the literary and philosophical activities for which he is now remembered. A voluminous writer, Bacon concentrated largely upon the promotion and explanation of his intellectual ideals; and most of his principal writings were intended to be part of an enormous work entitled *The Great Instauration.* His plan was to reorganize all systems of knowledge on an experimental and inductive basis. *De Dignitate et Augmentis Scientiarium (Of the Dignity and Advancement of Learning,* usually shortened to *The Advancement of Learning*) was to form the first part; a full-length work in itself, it is a synopsis and summary of all knowledge and learning current in Bacon's time. In it he stresses his ideals of clear observation, objectivity, and critical awareness. Its influence upon the realists who followed him, and upon the much later utilitarian school of philosophy, was enormous. Book VI of *The Advancement of Learning* discusses rhetoric, discourse, and argument; here Bacon cites examples of fallacious reasoning (sophisms) and follows them with various "antitheses"—encapsulated commonplace arguments for and against certain things. An example follows:

IX. PRAISE, REPUTATION

FOR	AGAINST
Praise is the reflexion of	Fame is a worse judge than

virtue.

Praise is the honour that comes by free votes.

Honours are conferred by many forms of government; but praise comes everywhere of liberty.

The voice of the people has something divine; else how could so many agree in one thing?

Marvel not if the vulgar speak truer than the great, for they speak safer.   12

messenger.

What has a good man to do with the slaver of the common people?

Fame is like a river, it bears up the light and lets the solid sink.

The lowest virtues are praised by the common people, the middle are admired; but of the highest they have no sense or perception.

Praise is won by ostentation more than by merit, and follows the vain and windy more than the sound and real.   13

The voice of the sluggard

Source: MORAL SONGS ("The Sluggard," Line 1)
Author: Isaac Watts (1674–1748)
First published: 1720
Type of work: Didactic poem

Context: Watt's poem is a description of the lazy person and what happens to him, with a highly didactic ending; following his description of the sluggard, the poet expresses gratitude to God, knowing that he might well have become such a lazy person; he also expresses gratitude to his friends, who have seen to it that he has learned the joys of work and reading, thus avoiding the fate of the poem's subject. Watts describes the sluggard as one who lies abed late in the day, who trifles with his working hours, who fails to weed his garden, who fails to care for his clothing, who wastes his money, who seldom reads his Bible, who dislikes thinking, and who spends his time in reverie. In *Alice's Adventures in Wonderland,* Chapter 10, appears the famous parody of this poem—" 'Tis the voice of the lobster . . ." This is one of many instances of Carroll's parodies becoming more famous than the originals. Watts' description begins with the sluggard's hating to rise from his bed:

'Tis **the voice of the sluggard;** I hear him complain,
You have wak'd me too soon, I must slumber again.
As the door on its hinges, so he on his bed,
Turns his sides, and his shoulder, and his heavy head.
A little more sleep, and a little more slumber,
Thus he wastes half his days, and his hours without
          number:
And when he gets up, he sits folding his hands,
Or walks about sauntering, or trifling he stands.

The voice that breathed o'er Eden

Source: POEMS ("Holy Matrimony")
Author: John Keble (1792–1866)
First published: 1857
Type of work: Hymn

Context: John Keble was an Anglican clergyman and poet who initiated the Oxford Movement, a reform movement within the Church of England whose aim was a return of the Church to a purer and more fundamental religious outlook. A number of factors contributed to a need for reform: schisms within the Church; proliferation of other sects; political conditions; and the romantic influence on literature and popular thinking exerted by Sir Walter Scott, whose works glorified medieval life and religion. In 1833 Keble preached a sermon in which he accused the Whigs of attempting to do away with the sovereignty of God and the Church. The Oxford Movement, thus begun, gained impetus with a series of tracts written by its leaders. John Henry Newman became the movement's principal figure. The tracts crusaded for Church reform, advocating a return to ceremony, dignity, scholarship, and more basic theology. The movement also sought to revive much of the ritual and ornamentation that the Reformation had abolished. These efforts had a profound and lasting influence on the Reformed Churches. Keble's literary output, in addition to sermons and several of the tracts, consisted for the most part of poetry and hymns. His major work is *The Christian Year,* a series of poetical compositions and thoughts in verse pertaining to each of the sundays and annual Holy Days. It was intended to be a guide and companion to the Book of Common Prayer. Published in 1827, it expresses in poetry the outlook that led to the Oxford Movement. In it many of the more familiar and cherished passages of Scripture are expanded and illuminated. Characterized by simple piety and a love of nature, it contains a number of hymns which have since become favorites. The same religious sentiment is found in Keble's other poetry; in *Holy Matrimony* he expresses the deep sanctity of marriage and asks the blessing of God upon it:

The voice that breath'd o'er Eden,
  That earliest wedding-day,
The primal marriage blessing,
  It hath not pass'd away.

Still in the pure espousal
  Of Christian man and maid,
The holy Three are with us,
  The threefold grace is said.

        •   •   •

Be present, Holiest Spirit,
  To bless them as they kneel,

As thou for Christ, the Bridegroom,
    The heavenly Spouse dost seal.

Oh spread thy pure wing o'er them,
    Let no ill power find place,
When onward to thine altar
    The hallow'd path they trace,

To cast their crowns before thee
    In perfect sacrifice,
Till to the home of gladness
    With Christ's own Bride they rise. AMEN.

Voyaging through strange seas of thought

Source: THE PRELUDE (Book III, l. 63)
Author: William Wordsworth (1770–1850)
First published: 1850
Type of work: Autobiographical poem

Context: Composed as the first part of a massive philosophical poem, *The Prelude* is a long autobiographical history of "the growth of a poet's mind." Wordsworth first tells of his earliest childhood, a time when he was a creature of sensation that grew through beauty from his natural surroundings and fear usually resulting from his own selfish actions; childhood was a time of animal pleasures during which he lived in complete harmony with his environment. Next he passed into the experiences of youth, a time of unreflective ecstasy before the necessity of thought separated him from nature; however, the demands of adulthood were already pressing upon him. Very slowly he was being estranged from nature and cast into the world of men where he was later to become disillusioned. More than anything else his entrance into St. John's College, Cambridge, marked the separation between his life in harmony with nature and his unhappy and lonely period of faith in the rational philosophers. In this quotation, introducing his account of his college experience, he foreshadows the loneliness of the years that were to follow by describing the statue of Sir Isaac Newton, the great seventeenth century scientist whose discoveries helped to form the creed that man could, through the use of his reason, make an orderly society.

The Evangelist St. John my patron was:
Three Gothic courts are his, and in the first
Was my abiding-place, a nook obscure; . . .
And from my pillow, looking forth by light
Of moon or favouring stars, I could behold

1192

The antechapel where the statue stood
Of Newton with his prism and silent face,
The marble index of a mind forever
Voyaging through strange seas of thought, alone.

War is the trade of kings

Source: KING ARTHUR OR THE BRITISH WORTHY (Act II, sc. ii)
Author: John Dryden (1631–1700)
First published: 1691
Type of work: Dramatic opera

Context: The death of Charles II, friend of the theater, in 1685, ended the chances of the poet laureate, Dryden's, producing this opera intended as a sequel to *Albion and Albanius.* The Revolution of 1688 brought him further ruin. As a Catholic, he could not get a government position. But he worked on translations and wrote or revised a half dozen plays. Finally in 1691 *King Arthur* was performed with music by the famous Henry Purcell (1659–1695). It was published the same year. The story relates that after the Britons defeat the forces of the Saxon King Oswald of Kent, the magic of Oswald's wizard Osmond overcomes the magic of Arthur's Merlin. Meanwhile, blind Emmeline, promised to Arthur, is spirited away by the returning Oswald, who surprises her and her maid Matilda in a pavilion. Angered by the treachery of his vanquished foe, Arthur follows and overtakes them. He upbraids Oswald, not for persisting in the fight after his defeat, but for stealing Emmeline.

ARTHUR

For you have wronged me much.

OSWALD

Oh, you would tell me,
I called more Saxons in, to enlarge my bounds.
If those be wrongs, the war has well redress'd ye.

ARTHUR

Mistake me not; I count not war a wrong.
War is the trade of kings, that fight for empire;
And better be a lion, than a sheep.

OSWALD

In what, then, have I wronged ye?

ARTHUR

In my love.

1193

Even love's an empire, too; the noble soul,
Like kings, is covetous of single sway.

War its thousands slays: peace its ten thousands

Source: DEATH (Line 179)
Author: Beilby Porteus (1731–1808)
First published: 1759
Type of work: Philosophical poem

Context: Beilby Porteus must have been a melancholy youth. Or he was playing at being so when he wrote his long poem, *Death,* that won for him the Seatonian poetry, awarded at intervals for serious verse. This poem conforms. Perhaps he exhibited a happier side to King George III, who appointed him Court Chaplain in 1769, then named him Bishop of Chester in 1776. He served there for eleven years before being promoted to Bishop of London. Though no other poetry by Dr. Porteus seems to have survived, "Death" was much praised and admired. It was even published by Cornelius Davis of New York in 1797, in his *Poems of Religious and Moral Subjects, Extracted from the Most Celebrated Authors.* The long work begins with an apostrophe to Death: "Friend to the wretched whom every friend forsakes/ I woo thee, Death." The poet goes on to spurn Life and its joys, leaving them to those who prize them. Man always loses. Most of the time, there are wars somewhere to kill him off. Even if peace should come, Death follows along with it. Porteus pictures the frantic scene "Of midnight revel and tumultuous mirth/ Where in the intoxicating draught conceal'd/ Or crouched beneath the glance of lawless love/ He snares the simple youth, who naught suspecting/ Means to be blest—but finds himself undone." With Death waiting in peace as in war, what hope has a man? The poet complains, Job-like, to God: Ill-fated man, for whom such various forms/ Of Mis'ry vast—why, all-Righteous Father,/ Didst thou make this creature Man? Dr. Porteus sees only one hope. Live an upright life when you are young, so that when you are old, "Let cheerful memory lead forth a goodly train of virtues, cherished in thy youth." Then, having established something to remember, adopt the hedonistic philosophy of "Carpe diem." Take advantage of every moment, or, as he puts it, "Live then while Heav'n in pity lends thee life." Speaking of the dangers of peace, part way through his poem, Dr. Porteus writes:

Yet say, should Tryants learn at last to feel,
And the loud din of battle cease to bray:
Should dove-eyed peace o'er all the world extend
Her olive branch, and give the world repose,

1194

Would Death be foil'd? Would health and strength
Defy his power? Has he no arts in store, and youth
No other shafts save those of war? Alas!
Ev'n in the smile of Peace, that smile which sheds
A heav'nly sunshine o'er the soul, there basks
That serpent Luxury. **War its thousands slays:**
Peace its ten thousands.

Warm sea-scented beach

Source: MEETING AT NIGHT
Author: Robert Browning (1812–1889)
First published: 1845
Type of work: Dramatic monologue

Context: "Meeting at Night" was originally published with a companion piece, "Parting at Morning," as a single poem. In 1849 Browning divided the poem into two sections. Together they describe the fleeting nature of love. However, "Meeting at Night" shows the man en route to a rendezvous with his love, certain of the enduring nature of his feelings. He describes the landscape as he passes, and his sight is colored with the anticipated rapture of their meeting:

> . . . I gain the cove with pushing prow,
> And quench its speed i' the slushy sand.
>
> Then a mile of **warm sea-scented beach;**
> Three fields to cross till a farm appears;
> A tap at the pane, the quick sharp scratch
> And blue spurt of a lighted match.
> And a voice less loud, through its joys and fears
> Than the two hearts beating each to each!

The way to be a bore, for an author, is to say everything

Source: ON THE NATURE OF MAN (Lines 174–175, as translated by William F. Fleming)
Author: Voltaire (François Marie Arouet, 1694–1778)
First published: 1738
Type of work: Didactic poem

Context: Voltaire aroused controversy all his life and would doubtless have been pleased if he could have known that it would still rage for nearly two centuries after his death. The champion of freedom in thought and belief, he wrote voluminously in support of his ideas throughout a long

1195

and active life; as a result he was often in trouble with those in power. He wrote in many fields and was successful in all; beginning with the drama, he produced a tragedy which made him the fashionable poet of Paris. At the same time he was confined in the Bastille—first for writing satirical verses against the regent, and again a few years later for refusing to swallow an insult. He spent three years in England, returned to France, and became affluent through various investments. A few peaceful years were passed with the Marquise du Châtelet, but after her death his political insecurity returned. The genius of his wit and pen gained him royal favor and lost it for him; after a painful bout with the Prussian court he moved to Geneva and established an estate near that city, where he ruled almost as a monarch. Much of his later life was spent in exile; his most savage attacks were reserved for orthodox Christianity, priestcraft, and Catholicism, and he found it necessary to live outside France or upon its borders. Voltaire was not an atheist. He upheld theism with as much zeal as he employed in denouncing Christianity, and the atheists of his time considered him a reactionary. During all his long life he wrote steadily—poetry, drama, romance, history, philosophy, criticism, science, and the philosophical novels for which he is best known today. In addition, he carried on a vast correspondence. His utterances are keen and penetrating, often aphoristic or epigrammatic. His *On the Nature of Man* contains several examples, among them the lines *"The way to be a bore, for an author, is to say everything (Le secret d'ennuyer est . . . de tout dire)."* The following translation, by William F. Fleming, renders them in the style of Pope, whose *Essay on Man* (Voltaire's inspiration) had appeared in 1733–1734:

The night, perhaps, was lightsome as the day,
And winter bloomed with all the flowers of May;
Whilst man, the king of earth, in peace retired,
Wrapt up in self, himself alone admired.
But let us rest contented with our fate,
Our bliss is suited to our present state:
Against our Maker murmurs must prove vain,
Mortals should not the laws of God arraign:
Let us to serve him all our lives employ,
And gratefully the bliss he gives, enjoy.
If to two days the Almighty had confined
The time allotted to all humankind,
We should to God those two short days consign,
And consecrate the time to love divine.
He who assiduous every call attends,
Never complains that life too quickly ends.
A man in little time may sure live long,
This I could prove by reasons very strong;
But authors should not to instruct aspire,
Who speaks too much is ever sure to tire.

We are always doing something for posterity, but I would fain see posterity do something for us

Source: THE SPECTATOR (Number 583)
Author: Joseph Addison (1672–1719)
First published: August 20, 1714
Type of work: Essay

Context: As a forerunner of later newspapers and literary reviews, Joseph Addison, with Richard Steele (1672–1729), published a daily edition of *The Spectator,* of which Addison wrote 298 issues. For Number 583, dated Friday, August 20, 1714, he expressed his thoughts under the topic sentence: "Every station of life has duties which are proper to it." He complains that too many sons of Adam feel exempted from any labor which is either useful to themselves or beneficial to others. He expands the idea:

> Many country gentlemen, seek diversion in the chase or other hunting, unlike one man who spent his leisure emulating Cyrus the Great in beautifying his estate which at the same time increased its value for his successors.
>
> . . . I know when a man talks of posterity in matters of this nature, he is looked upon with an eye of ridicule by the cunning and selfish part of mankind. Most people are of the humor of an old fellow of a college who, when he was pressed by the society to come into something that might redound to the good of their successors, grew very peevish: **"We are always doing** (says he) **something for posterity, but I would fain see posterity do something for us."**

We are as near to Heaven by sea as by land

Source: A SHORT HISTORY OF THE ENGLISH PEOPLE, J. R. Green (Chapter 8, section IV, p. 506)
Author: Sir Humphrey Gilbert (1539–1583)
First published: 1874
Type of work: Attributed comment

Context: Sir Humphrey Gilbert, stepbrother of Sir Walter Raleigh, was one of the many Elizabethan navigators, explorers, and soldiers who added luster to that period of history. He was educated at Eton and Oxford and was intended for the law, but adopted a military career instead. He served with distinction in Ireland and in France, and was knighted in 1570. As early as 1566 he and Anthony Jenkinson had petitioned Queen Elizabeth for a voyage to discover the Northeast Passage, and again the same year for a similar effort to locate the Northwest Passage; the latter petition was in his own name. After a year as a member of Parliament in 1571 he campaigned in the Netherlands; following this episode, he wrote a book on the desirability of a search for the Northwest. The work was widely circulated and encouraged a number of other adventurers. His charter was granted in 1578, authorizing him to discover new lands and occupy them. His first expedition, undertaken that year, was unsuccessful. In 1583 he set out again with a small fleet, arriving at Newfoundland in August. Here, at St. John's harbor, he established the first British colony in North America. He lost the largest of his ships near Cape Breton, and his party set out for England in the two remaining vessels. Gilbert was in the smaller of the two, the *Squirrel*. A tempest was encountered off the Azores; the *Squirrel* nearly foundered but recovered herself; and Gilbert, a book in one hand, called across to the *Golden Hind* that they were as close to heaven by sea as by land. That night the *Squirrel's* lights were seen to go out suddenly, and the crew of the *Golden Hind* knew she had been swallowed by the sea. *In his Short History of the English People,* Green recounts the great struggle between Puritanism and the government of England, which resulted in the stern despotism of James I and the Puritan migration to New England. He then summarizes British activities in the New World prior to 1620:

> . . . England had reached the mainland even earlier than Spain, for before Columbus touched its shores Sebastian Cabot, a seaman of Genoese blood born and bred in England, sailed with an English crew from Bristol in 1497, and pushed along the coast of America to the south as far as Florida, and northward as high as Hudson's Bay. But no Englishman followed on the track of this bold adventurer; and while Spain built up her empire in the New World, the English seamen reaped a humbler harvest in the fisheries of Newfoundland. It was not till the reign of Elizabeth that the thoughts of Englishmen turned again to the New World. The dream of finding a passage to Asia by a voyage round the northern coast of the American continent drew a west-country seaman, Martin Frobisher, to the coast of Labrador, and the news which he brought back of the existence of gold mines there set adventurers cruising among the icebergs of Baffin's Bay. Luckily the quest for gold proved a vain one; and the nobler spirits among those who had engaged in it turned to plans of colonization. But the country, vexed by long winters and thinly peopled by warlike tribes of Indians, gave a rough welcome to the earlier colonists. After a fruitless attempt to form a settlement, Sir Humphry Gilbert, one of the noblest spirits of his time, turned homewards again, to find his fate in the stormy seas. **"We are as near to Heaven by sea as by land,"** were the famous words he was heard to utter, ere the light of his little bark was lost for ever in the darkness of the night. . . .

We are dust and a shadow

Source: ODES (Book IV, Ode 7, l. 16)
Author: Horace (65–8 B.C.)
First transcribed: 23–13 B.C.
Type of work: Ode

Context: As spring arrives, the poet reflects upon the changing seasons, but, with a melancholy tone, points out that man also passes through phases of life, but that he cannot repeat these phases, as the seasons of the year or the phases of the moon are repeated. Samuel Johnson translated the passage, with its line *Pulvis et umbra sumus:*

> The snow, dissolved, no more is seen;
> The fields and woods, behold, are green;
> The changing year renews the plain;
> The rivers know their banks again;
> The sprightly Nymph and naked Grace
> The mazy dance together trace;
> The changing year's successive plan
> Proclaims mortality to man.
> Rough Winter's blasts to Spring give way;
> Spring yields to Summer's sovereign ray;
> And Winter chills the world again.
> Her losses soon the moon supplies,
> But wretched man, when once he lies
> Where Priam and his sons are laid,
> Is naught but **ashes, and a shade.**

We are ruined by Chinese cheap labor

Source: PLAIN LANGUAGE FROM TRUTHFUL JAMES (Stanza 7)
Author: Bret Harte (1836–1902)
First published: 1870
Type of work: Humorous poem

Context: This humorous dialect poem, also known as "The Heathen Chinee," produced Bret Harte's great surge of popularity and resulted in his leaving the West, where he had won his original fame, for the East, where he accepted an offer to write for the *Atlantic Monthly*. The poem, subtitled "Table Mountain, 1870," describes how Truthful James and Bill Nye invite Ah Sin, a Chinese laborer, of whom there were many in the West, to join them in a game of euchre. Ah Sin, who smiles pensively and like a child, says he does not understand the game. Bill Nye and Truthful James intend to cheat the poor Chinese, for the cards are stacked, and Bill Nye's sleeve conceals a supply of extra aces and bowers. Despite their efforts to cheat him, Ah Sin gains many more points.

At last Ah Sin goes too far, putting down the same jack that Bill Nye had already dealt, dishonestly, to Truthful James. In the melee that follows, twenty-four jacks fall from Ah Sin's copious sleeve, and his fingernails are discovered to be coated with wax, for help in manipulating the cards. When the two white men discover they have been over-reached, Bill Nye makes his ironic comment:

> Then I looked up at Nye,
>   And he gazed upon me;
> And he rose with a sigh,
>   And said, "Can this be?
> **We are ruined by Chinese cheap labor,"—**
> And he went for that heathen Chinee.
>
> In the scene that ensued
>   I did not take a hand,
> But the floor it was strewed
>   Like the leaves on the strand
> With the cards Ah Sin had been hiding,
>   In the game "he did not understand."

We are symbols, and inhabit symbols

Source: THE POET
Author: Ralph Waldo Emerson (1803–1882)
First published: 1844
Type of work: Moral essay

Context: In his early essay entitled *Nature,* Emerson gives four uses which Nature subserves to mankind: commodity, beauty, language, and discipline. Nature, suggests Emerson, is the vehicle of thought in a threefold manner, speaking of course as the transcendentalist, the philosophical idealist, he is. In the first place, according to the Emersonian doctrine, words are symbols of facts in nature; secondly, each natural fact is in turn the symbol of a spiritual fact; and, finally, man and the universe he inhabits, what Emerson terms Nature, is a symbol of deity itself. Emerson even suggests that in its infancy language was all poetry. These ideas he takes up again in *The Poet,* which appeared in *Essays, Second Series,* in 1844, eight years after the publication of *Nature.* Emerson stresses the function of the poet and of poetry as expression; this he shows to be the understanding of the symbolic quality of the world about us and the language we use to communicate about it:

. . . For though life is great, and fascinates and absorbs; and though all men are intelligent of the symbols through which it is named; yet they cannot originally use them. **We are symbols**

1200

and inhabit symbols; workmen, work, and tools, words and things, birth and death, all are emblems; but we sympathize with the symbols, and, being infatuated with the economical uses of things, we do not know that they are thoughts. The poet, by an ulterior intellectual perception, gives them a power which makes their old use forgotten, and puts eyes and a tongue into every dumb and inanimate object. He perceives the independence of the thought on the symbol, the stability of the thought, the accidency and fugacity of the symbol. . . . He uses forms according to the life, and not according to the form. This is true science. The poet alone knows astronomy, chemistry, vegetation, and animation, for he does not stop at their facts, but employs them as signs. . . .

We are wiser than we know

Source: THE OVER-SOUL
Author: Ralph Waldo Emerson (1803–1882)
First published: 1841
Type of work: Moral essay

Context: As a philosophical idealist, Ralph Waldo Emerson believed that the soul of the individual human being is forever in existence as a part of the Deity, or Over-Soul. Thus it was that he could believe that every human being, insofar as he is a soul, is a part of God. The existence of the soul in the transcendental realm prior to this life is a key to understanding Emerson's transcendentalism, and a key to understanding the quotation. Emerson believed in absolutes, and he believed that every human being could know them because of the soul's continual existence. He believed we can know truth and the other absolutes if we will but trust the intuition of the soul:

The soul is the perceiver and revealer of truth. We know truth when we see it, let sceptic and scoffer say what they choose. Foolish people ask you, when you have spoken what they do not wish to hear, "How do you know it is truth, and not an error of your own?" We know the truth when we see it, from opinion, as we know when we are awake that we are awake. It was a grand sentence of Emanuel Swedenborg, which would alone indicate the greatness of that man's perception—"It is no proof of a man's understanding to be able to confirm whatever he pleases; but to be able to discern that what is true is true, and that what is false is false—this is the mark and character of intelligence." In the book I read, the good thought returns to me, as every truth will, the image of the whole soul. To the bad thought which I find in it, the same soul becomes a discerning, separating sword, and lops it away. **We are wiser than we know.** If we will not interfere with

our thought, but will act entirely, or see how the thing stands
in God, we know the particular thing, and every thing, and every
man. For the Maker of all things and all persons stands behind
us and casts his dread omniscience through us over things.

We can drink till all look blue

Source: THE LADY'S TRIAL (Act IV, sc. ii)
Author: John Ford (1586–1639?)
First published: 1639
Type of work: Dramatic comedy

Context: In this relatively little-known and short play, John Ford has written a comedy which, he says in his dedication, contrives to bring together "Language and matter, with a fit of mirth." One of the characters is a young girl named Amoretta, who is styled by her creator "a fantastic Maid." This girl is unfortunate in having a lisp which appears almost every time she speaks; the lisp is, naturally, part of the fun of the play. Amoretta is courted by Fulgoso, who brings a group of musicians to the house of Trelcatio, where Amoretta is staying, to serenade the young woman and thus prepare the way for him to appear in person to court her. Amoretta, hearing the music, comes to the room where Trelcatio, Piero, and Futelli are, to inquire about the music and its source. At her appearance a song is heard from the musicians, in part sung with a lisp:

SONG

What, ho! we come to be merry,
   Open the doors, a jovial crew,
Lusty boys and free, and very,
   Very, very lusty boys are we;
We can drink till all look blue,
   Dance, sing, and roar,
   Never give o'er,
As long as we have e'er an eye to see.
Pithee, pithee, leths come in,
   Oue thall all oua favous win,
Dently, dently, we thall passe;
   None kitheth like the lithping lasse.

PIERO

What call ye this, a song?

AMORETTA

Yeth, a delithious thing, and wondroth prety.

1202

We have heard the chimes at midnight

Source: KING HENRY THE FOURTH: PART TWO (Act III, sc. ii, l. 226)
Author: William Shakespeare (1564–1616)
First published: 1600
Type of work: Historical drama

Context: As a soldier with the forces of Henry IV, Falstaff, by cowardice which he chooses to call discretion, has managed to survive the first phase of the rebellion at Shrewsbury. So successfully has he carried off his false claim to have defeated Hotspur in single combat that he has been dispatched for further martial service at Gaultree Forest. Given a sum of money—which he has every intention of using for himself—for the impressment of foot soldiers, he travels through Gloucestershire where his old acquaintance Justice Shallow has summoned a group of men to be examined for possible service. Shallow, with his cousin Silence, is living out the senile dregs of his life in the memories of youth. Consequently, he is delighted at the opportunity of conversing with his old crony about activities—both fictional and actual—which recall his London days at the Inns of Court fifty-five years ago. With the dry rattle of old age he lecherously recounts the night when he and Sir John "lay all night in the windmill in St. George's field." And, with fond memory he recalls their old acquaintance in fun, Jane Nightwork, who has fallen victim to age if not the grave:

SHALLOW
Nay she must be old, she cannot choose but be old, certain she's old, and had Robin Nightwork by old Nightwork before I came to Clement's Inn.

SILENCE
That's fifty-five year ago.

SHALLOW
Ha cousin Silence, that thou hadst seen that that this knight and I have seen. Ha Sir John, said I well?

FALSTAFF
We have heard the chimes at midnight Master Shallow.

SHALLOW
That we have, that we have, that we have, in faith Sir John we have; our watchword was hem, boys! Come let's to dimmer, come let's to dinner. Jesu, the days that we have seen. Come, come.

We have scotched the snake, not killed it

Source: MACBETH (Act III, sc. ii, l. 13)
Author: William Shakespeare (1564–1616)
First published: 1623
Type of work: Dramatic tragedy

Context: Macbeth, promised by witches that he will be king, murders King Duncan of Scotland and usurps the throne. However, certain obstacles remain: (1) the witches advise that the heirs of Banquo shall be kings, (2) the sons of the slain king live in exile, and (3) in gaining power Macbeth has lost peace. Lady Macbeth encourages her lord to forget the past, but Macbeth says that their difficulties have not yet been overcome.

LADY MACBETH

. . .

How now my lord, why do you keep alone,
Of sorriest fancies your companions making,
Using those thoughts which should indeed have died
With them they think on? Things without all remedy
Should be without regard: what's done is done.

MACBETH

We have scotched the snake, not killed it.
She'll close, and be herself, whilst our poor malice
Remains in danger of her former tooth.
But let the frame of things disjoint, both the worlds
    suffer,
Ere we will eat our meal in fear, and sleep
In the affliction of these terrible dreams
That shake us nightly. Better be with the dead,
Whom we, to gain our peace, have sent to peace,
Than on the torture of the mind to lie
In restless ecstasy. . . .

We have seen the best of our time

Source: KING LEAR (Act I, sc. ii, ll. 122–123)
Author: William Shakespeare (1564–1616)
First published: 1608
Type of work: Dramatic tragedy

Context: Edmund, bastard son of the Earl of Gloucester, plots to have Edgar, Gloucester's legitimate and virtuous son, disinherited. He forges a letter from Edgar suggesting that they murder Gloucester and divide

1204

the inheritance; with a great show of unwillingness, Edmund reveals the letter to the earl, whose response is everything Edmund could desire. King Lear has just disinherited his virtuous and honest daughter, Cordelia, and banished the frank and loyal Earl of Kent, turning his kingdom over to the faithless and scheming daughters, Goneril and Regan. To Gloucester, his son's presumed treachery is further evidence that the world as he knew it is being destroyed:

GLOUCESTER

These late eclipses in the sun and moon portend no good to us; . . . Love cools, friendship falls off, brothers divide. In cities, mutinies; in countries, discord; in palaces, treason; and the bond cracked 'twixt son and father. This villain of mine comes under the prediction, there's son against father; the King falls from bias of nature, there's father against child. **We have seen the best of our time.** Machinations, hollowness, treachery, and all ruinous disorders, follow us disquietly to our graves. . . . And the noble and true-hearted Kent banished; his offence, honesty. 'Tis strange.

We love the precepts for the teacher's sake

Source: A RHYMED LESSON ("Urania," Line 189)
Author: Oliver Wendell Holmes (1809–1894)
First published: 1848
Type of work: Didactic poem

Context: On October 14, 1846, Holmes delivered this poem himself, to a mixed audience at the Boston Mercantile Library Association. Knowing his reputation among the persons—men and women, girls and boys—composing the audience, the poet tells them they will have the laughter they have learned to expect from his humorous, witty poetry, but that they will have to take some serious lessons in the poem first. He then speaks about religion and the purpose of religion in each person's life, and he notes that in our earliest days we accept religious teachings because we love the teacher and respect him, not because of our understanding as in later years:

Uncursed by doubt, our earliest creed we take;
We love the precepts for the teacher's sake;
The simple lessons which the nursery taught
Fell soft and stainless on the buds of thought,
And the full blossom owes its fairest hue
To those sweet tear-drops of affection's dew.
  Too oft the light that led our earlier hours
Fades with the perfume of our cradle flowers;
The clear, cold question chills to frozen doubt;

Tired of beliefs, we dread to live without;
O then, if Reason waver at thy side,
Let humbler Memory be thy gentle guide;
Go to thy birthplace, and, if faith was there,
Repeat thy father's creed, thy mother's prayer!

We must not make a scarecrow of the law

Source: MEASURE FOR MEASURE (Act II, sc. i, l. 1)
Author: William Shakespeare (1564–1616)
First published: 1623
Type of work: Tragi-comedy

Context: Vincentio, Duke of Vienna, has for many years ruled with a tolerant hand. As a result the laws of the land, "Dead to infliction, to themselves are dead,/ And liberty plucks justice by the nose; . . ." Convinced that he has permitted his people such a degree of freedom that the law commands no respect, he removes himself from office temporarily on the pretext that urgent political affairs have called him out of the country. In reality, he disguises himself as Friar Lodowick in order to observe the manner in which his appointed deputy, Angelo, will handle the situation.

Although the deputy is expressly granted full authority to exercise mercy or to enforce the letter of the law, he assumes that only a rigid enforcement of decree will impress the populace. His initial command is to arrest Claudio, a citizen who has violated the long-unenforced decree of capital punishment for one who gets a woman with child out of wedlock. Refusing to consider the plea for mercy, to "be keen, and rather cut a little,/ Than fall, and bruise to death," he is determined to make an example of the unfortunate young man:

ANGELO
We must not make a scarecrow of the law,
Setting it up to fear the birds of prey,
And let it keep one shape, till custom make it
Their perch and not their terror.
. . .
When I, that censure him, do so offend,
Let mine own judgment pattern out my death,
And nothing come in partial. Sir, he must die.

We never are but by ourselves betrayed

Source: THE OLD BACHELOR (Act III, sc. i)
Author: William Congreve (1670–1729)
First published: 1693
Type of work: Dramatic comedy

1206

Context: Heartwell is a surly bachelor who has fallen in love with Silvia,
Vainlove's cast-off mistress. It is
Heartwell who is the title character of
the comedy. Poor Silvia, however, is
still in love with Vainlove, even
though he has deserted her for Araminta, who also loves him. Lucy, Silvia's maid, is a down-to-earth creature who recommends that her
mistress, despite her passion for
Vainlove, hurry to marry Heartwell
while she can; as Lucy herself puts it
to Silvia, "Strike Heartwell home, before the bait's worn off the hook. Age
will come." What bothers Silvia most

is Vainlove's indifference, for he cannot even be bothered long enough to
read the letter she has sent him.
Overcome by jealousy, Silvia wishes
vengeance on Vainlove; her maid
suggests that to separate Vainlove
from Araminta all Silvia need do is
persuade Vainlove, a fickle man, that
Araminta really loves him. As they
talk about what course to take,
Heartwell comes in sight, apparently
to visit Silvia. Lucy advises her mistress to receive him amiably; the
couplet at the end of her speech indicates the end of the scene.

LUCY
. . . Hold, I'm mistaken or that's Heartwell who stands talking
at the corner—'tis he. Go, get you in, madam, receive him
pleasantly, dress up your face in innocence and smiles, and dissemble the very want of dissimulation.—You know what will
take him.

SILVIA
'Tis as hard to counterfeit love as it is to conceal it; but I'll
do my weak endeavour, though I fear I have no art.

LUCY
Hang art, madam! and trust to nature for dissembling.
    Man was by nature woman's cully made;
    We never are but by ourselves betrayed.

We never can be made happy by compulsion

Source: THE THREE GRAVES (Part IV, stanza 12)
Author: Samuel Taylor Coleridge (1772–1834)
First published: 1809 (Parts III and IV)
Type of work: Ballad

Context: Coleridge was one of the
uncompleted geniuses of English literature. Gifted, he wasted his talents,
and from his unmistakable poetic
genius left only a few important po-

ems. He spent the last part of his life
lamenting the loss of his poetic ability.
Perhaps his failure can be explained
by the quoted line. His trouble was
that he needed compulsion to get

things done. Two of his three greatest poems are incomplete. Of "Christabel," he published an excellent first part in 1797, a second passable part in 1800, and then dropped the idea. And "Kubla Khan" (1797) has only fifty lines. Only "The Rhyme of the Ancient Mariner" comes down completed to show Coleridge's real capabilities. It is a complex personality. As the thirteenth child of a country minister, he knew poverty from the beginning. Sent to a charity school in London, he began a lifelong friendship with Charles Lamb. He entered Cambridge, then, discouraged by poverty, this pacifist who hated horses left the university to enlist in the Light Dragoons. He suffered there until a brother got him released and he returned to Cambridge. Next, with Robert Southey, he concocted a scheme to establish a Utopian colony on the Susquehanna River in the United States, and since colonists were to be married, he found himself a wife. In 1796 he published one volume of poetry, followed by another in 1797. Then he met William Wordsworth (1770–1850), with whom he planned a volume of verse, to describe the loveliness and kindness of Nature and show that poetry could be written in simple language. Coleridge's part was to make the supernatural seem real. His "Ancient Mariner" was his chief contribution. The hard-working Wordsworth provided most of the rest of *Lyrical Ballads,* the volume that inaugurated the Romantic Movement in England. With Wordsworth's example to inspire him, Coleridge went on. One poem, started then, but not finished until 1809, was a tale in ballad form supposedly told by a sexton to a traveler whose curiosity had been roused by three graves side by side, but with only two gravestones. The first had a name and a date; the second had only a date and the words: "The Mercy of God is infinite." In a footnote, the poet declared the story "founded on fact." In the story, Edward, a young farmer, falls in love with Mary at the house of her friend Ellen. Mary's widowed mother gives Edward permission to court her daughter, but one day begs him to marry her instead. When he laughs at her, she curses him and her daughter. Mary, overhearing, faints. Quickly the young people marry. In church, the mother sits beside Ellen and curses her for her share in the marriage. The two girls vainly try to comfort each other. Edward is horrified to see the appearance of the mother in both of them. After that moment, there is no peace among them. Writing of the women's attempts to cheer each other, Coleridge declares:

And once when Mary was downcast
 She took her by the hand,
And gazed upon her, and at first
 She gently pressed her hand;

Then harder, till her grasp at length
 Did gripe like a convulsion!
"Alas!" said she, **we ne'er can be
Made happy by compulsion!"**

We owe God a death

Source: KING HENRY THE FOURTH: PART TWO (Act III, sc. ii, l. 252)
Author: William Shakespeare (1564–1616)
First published: 1600
Type of work: Historical drama

Context: Sir John Falstaff, rude and roguish knight, recruits men for the army of King Henry IV, who is beset by rebellion and by ill-health. In Gloucestershire at the house of Justice Shallow, Falstaff and his corporal Bardolph survey the available men. Some of the more likely candidates approach Bardolph with excuses and bribes to avoid service, but Feeble announces that he is willing to serve "his prince" since every man must die at his destined time anyway:

FEEBLE

By my troth I care not, a man can die but once, **we owe God a death.** I'll ne'er bear a base mind. An't be my destiny, so; an't be not, so; no man's too good to serve's prince. And let it go which way it will, he that dies this year is quit for the next.

BARDOLPH

Well said, thou'rt a good fellow.

FEEBLE

Faith I'll bear no base mind.

We rise with the lark and go to bed with the lamb

Source: THE COURT AND COUNTRY
Author: Nicholas Breton (1545?–1626?)
First published: 1618
Type of work: Dialogue

Context: Breton was a very popular writer in his time, and exhibited his versatility by his mastery of a variety of forms including satires, characters, letter-books, political pamphlets, philosophical treatises, religious poetry, and pastorals. He was a friend to Shakespeare and Ben Jonson and was patronized by the Countess of Pembroke. The present work is a pastoral dialogue between one who resides at the court and one who lives amid the rural beauties of the country, each describing the attractions and virtues of his way of life. The countryman has decidedly the best of the debate:

I haue heard moreouer that you haue among you certain Euesdroppers, that are tale carriers, that come among the rooles of Knaues. But for our howses in the Country they are so far one from another, that if we catch any of them about vs, wee should carry him before the Constable for a theefe.

But now leauing to speake more of these things: for pleasures, beleeue it, we will put you downe a world of steppes; for, first of all **we rise with the Larke and goe to bed with the Lambe,** so that we haue the breake of the day and the brightnes of the Sunne to cheere our Spirits in our going to our labours, which many of you barre your selues of, by making day of the night and night of the day, by sleeping after wearines vpon the labour of wantonnes, if not of wickedness, . . .

We shall die alone

Source: PENSÉES (Section III, number 211)
Author: Blaise Pascal (1623–1662)
First published: 1670
Type of work: Philosophic commentary

Context: French author and religious leader, Blaise Pascal was an ardent defender of the religious reform movement of Jansenism. Other than *Pensées,* his best known work is *Lettres Provinciales,* which began to appear anonymously in 1656 and later under the pseudonym of Montalte; in these letters he sharply attacked the Jesuit opponents of Jansenism. Before his conversion, he was acutely interested in science, devising a theory of probability which, in the opinion of some critics, anticipated the system of calculus. *Pensées,* a collection of reflections on religion and philosophy, was found among the effects of the author after his death, but publication in its entirety was delayed for more than two centuries (1884) for fear that the thoughts expressed were unorthodox. Actually these reflections represent the first notes for a projected defense of Christianity. Convinced of the inability of man's reason to solve the human dilemma or to satisfy its yearnings, Pascal exalts faith and mystic revelation, saying that the "heart has reasons of which reason itself knows nothing." Human history, indeed our own personal history, has taught us the bitter facts of man's indifference to his fellow man. God alone is immutable; human friends soon falter and fail:

We are fools to depend upon the society of our fellow-men. Wretched as we are, powerless as we are, they will not aid us; **we shall die alone.** We should therefore act as if we were alone, and in that case should we build fine houses? We should seek the truth without hesitation; and, if we refuse it, we show that we value the esteem of men more than the search for truth.

1210

We that are true lovers run into strange capers

Source: AS YOU LIKE IT (Act II, sc. iv, ll. 54–55)
Author: William Shakespeare (1564–1616)
First published: 1623
Type of work: Dramatic comedy

Context: Lovers gather in the Forest of Arden, a pleasant, Arcadian retreat. Among them is the banished Rosalind, daughter of the banished Duke Senior. Listening to the shepherd Silvius speak of his passion for the shepherdess Phebe, Rosalind is reminded of her own love "wound," given to her by the young Orlando. At this point the court fool, Touchstone, mocks the behavior of young men and women in love, remembering his own youth when he lunged at imaginary rivals, kissed everything his rustic mistress touched, including the small bat she used in washing clothes, and employed peapods as love tokens:

ROSALIND

Alas, poor shepherd! Searching of thy wound,
I have by hard adventure found mine own.

TOUCHSTONE

And I mine. I remember when I was in love I broke my sword upon a stone, and bid him take that for coming a-night to Jane Smile, and I remember the kissing of her batlet, and the cow's dugs that her pretty chopped hands had milked. And I remember the wooing of a peascod instead of her, from whom I took two cods, and giving her them again, said with weeping tears, wear these for my sake. **We that are true lovers run into strange capers;** but as all is mortal in nature, so is all nature in love mortal in folly.

The weak alone repent

Source: THE CORSAIR (Canto II, stanza 10)
Author: George Gordon, Lord Byron (1788–1824)
First published: 1814
Type of work: Narrative poem

Context: The Romantic Movement in its revolt against the cruel realities of life had two representative types. One was a sensitive figure driven to despair and retiring from the world to seek the solitude of Nature. He was first represented fictionally in Goethe's *The Sorrows of Young Wer-* *ther* (1774). The other was a powerful personality who refused to become a victim and rebelled against social injustice, best represented by *The Robbers* (1781) by Goethe's friend, Schiller. This Titan-like character can be easily symbolized by a pirate, at odds with authority and supreme when alone on the bridge of his craft, like the William Ernest Henley character who could proclaim: "I am the master of my fate;/ I am the captain of my soul." In another land, José de Espronceda (1818–1842) sometimes called the Spanish Byron, and an outstanding representative of Romanticism in his country, is remembered for his vigorous and melodic "Song of the Pirate." Both these representative types of Romanticism can be found in the poetry of Byron, the sensitive, nature-seeking man in *Childe Harold's Pilgrimage,* and the pirate in both *The Bride of Abydos* and *The Corsair.* Lord Conrad of *The Corsair* is described as a cynical daredevil with a glance that not only terrifies, but pierces into the heart of a man. Juan has prepared the ship under its red flag of piracy for a foray against an unnamed enemy, and he, Gonsalvo, and the crew await the return of their cruel, remorseless chief whose name strikes terror on every coast. However, as Byron declares, "None are all evil," and this cursing villain has one soft spot. He loves Medora. Yet, as he steals away to tell her farewell, he wonders whether his fate or his folly has provided a possibility that she may still redeem him. Nevertheless, he spurns her pleas to share with her the joys of peace, and departs for the raid. The second canto opens as Seyd the Pacha is assembling a Moslem fleet at Coron Bay to destroy the pirate lair. Before him is brought a "captive Dervise from the pirate's nest." The man reports how he was captured and then escaped; but when given food, he shuns the salt "which, once partaken, makes even contending tribes in peace unite." The suspicious Pacha orders him seized as a spy. Off comes Conrad's disguise to reveal a coat of mail underneath. But, though he fights bravely and wins the admiration of the Pacha's daughter, Gulnare, he is finally wounded and imprisoned. Still he will not plead for mercy; only a coward expresses regret. But Gulnare saves him by stabbing the Pacha and helping him aboard a ship. There, when she finds he does not love her, she uses the same dagger on herself. In the end, Lord Conrad reaches the Pirate Isle alive. Medora, alive, had not been able to persuade him, but the sight of her body on the bier touches his heart. He disappears, and at the conclusion the poet declares: "He left a Corsair's name to other times,/ Linked with one virtue and a thousand crimes." In the Pacha's prison, describing "proud Conrad, fetter'd and alone," the poet says:

'T were vain to paint to what his feelings grew—
It even were doubtful if their victim knew.
There is a war, a chaos of the mind,
When all its elements convulsed, combined,
Lie dark and jarring with perturbèd force,
And gnashing with impenitent Remorse;
That juggling fiend—who never spake before—
But cries "I warn'd thee!" when the deed is o'er.
Vain voice! the spirit burning but unbent,
May writhe, rebèl—**the weak alone repent!**

1212

The weaker sex, to piety more prone

Source: DOOMES-DAY (Hour V, stanza 55)
Author: Sir William Alexander, Earl of Stirling (1567?–1640)
First published: 1614 (Hours I–IV); 1637 (complete form)
Type of work: Epic poem

Context: Alexander is now considered a minor figure among the many writers of Eilzabethan times. A Scottish poet, he was a close friend of King James I and is better known today for the royal favors conferred upon him than for his writings. The largest of these favors was a grant of the entire eastern half of Canada, formerly known as Acadia; the king renamed it Nova Scotia for this occasion. Although Alexander lost this proprietorship through the French conquest of Canada, he was not without other profitable enterprises. The king made him sole printer of the King James version of the Psalms, the patent running for thirty-one years. Alexander achieved literary recognition through his *Monarchicke Tragedies,* a group of four Senecan dramas dealing with great political events of the ancient world. These employ the convention of a chorus and an alternately rhyming verse scheme; they are respectable works and exhibit considerable political wisdom, but do not observe the dramatic unities and lack interest for the modern reader.

He also wrote a number of sonnets and a religious epic. The latter, entitled *Doomes-day,* contains twelve books, or "Hours"; the first four were published in 1614. In its final form as printed in *Recreations with the Muses,* the poem was extended to twelve Hours and a total of some 11,000 lines. This was Alexander's most ambitious literary effort and greatly admired in his own day. The first Hour argues the reality of God and describes the Creation; the second discusses the prophecies of Doomsday as given in the Bible; and in the third Hour Christ descends in glory to judge mankind. In the fourth Hour the last trumpet is sounded and the dead arise. The fifth Hour describes the great assemblage of souls, their vast diversity, their sins and confusion. Judgment begins, its first wrath falling on hypocrites and atheists. The poet reviews Biblical and Classical literature at some length; mention of Coriolanus turns his attention to the place of women in history, and he cites the examples of Thoas' daughter and of Antigone:

> **The weaker sexe, to piety more prone,**
> By rare examples, oft have beene renown'd,
> When many murthers were bewail'd by none,
> An isles whole men in bloud by women drown'd,
> The aged *Thoas* (stolne out from his throne)
> His daughter sav'd, though next him to be crown'd,
>   Whose Lord (though milde) one cruell did acquire,
>   Who kill'd her children, where she sav'd her sire.

Where all were ill, that Lady only good,

1213

Who though she had (of worth what wonders rife?)
Incestuous parents, brothers stain'd with bloud,
Time, state, sexe, race, oppos'd, with all at strife,
Blinde father led, griev'd mothers comfort stood,
Her brothers funerals urg'd with ventred life:
    In *Thebes* she Altars more deserv'd to have,
    Then one to wine, to lust another slave.

Wearing his wisdom lightly

Source: A DEDICATION (Line 12)
Author: Alfred, Lord Tennyson (1809–1892)
First published: 1864
Type of work: Lyric poem

Context: Tennyson addressed this poem to his wife, Emily Sellwood. The poet first writes of his wife as being "Dear, near and true . . ." and adds that "Time" enhances these qualities. He goes on to say that because of her "faith" in him, he hopes to sustain levelheadedness with the wisdom he has gained through living. By maintaining his intellectual dignity in his "Autumn" years and later, he is "Wearing his wisdom lightly . . . ," thus avoiding the mental lethargy usually associated with old age. Therefore he may approach death sagaciously because he has attained the "wise indifference of the wise."

Dear, near and true—no truer Time himself
Can prove you, tho' he make you evermore
Dearer and nearer, as the rapid of life
Shoots to the fall—take this and pray that he
Who wrote it, honouring your sweet faith in him,
May trust himself; and after praise and scorn,
As one who feels the immeasurable world,
Attain the wise indifference of the wise;
And after Autumn past—if left to pass
His autumn into seeming-leafless days—
Draw toward the long frost and longest night,
Wearing his wisdom lightly, like the fruit
Which in our winter woodland looks a flower.

Weep the more because I weep in vain

Source: SONNET ON THE DEATH OF RICHARD WEST (Last line)
Author: Thomas Gray (1716–1771)
First published: 1775
Type of work: Sonnet

Yet Morning smiles the busy race to cheer,
  And new-born pleasure brings to happier men;
The fields to all their wonted tribute bear;
  To warm their little loves the birds complain;
I fruitless mourn to him that cannot hear,
  And **weep the more because I weep in vain.**

Well hast thou fought the better fight

Source: PARADISE LOST (Book VI, ll. 29–30)
Author: John Milton (1608–1674)
First published: 1667
Type of work: Epic poem

Context: Raphael, in his instruction of Adam, tells how Satan drew away from God a host of angels and proposed to them a revolt in heaven. Of all the millions who heeded his summons, only one, Abdiel, a seraph, refused to show such ingratitude to God as Satan and his cohorts were planning. Abdiel warned them all that God's golden scepter would turn into a rod of iron to bruise and break their disobedience. Milton here emphasizes the devil's disobedience so that he may contrast man's disobedience with it. Abdiel withdrew from the scornful host and made his way across the wide plain of heaven until morning came. There is a cave near the mount of God from which light and darkness issue to produce day and night in heaven, although the heavenly night corresponds to the earthly twilight.

Abdiel found on the plain the angelic squadrons drawn up for battle and found that the revolt, which he had thought only he knew about, was general knowledge. He was led to the sacred hill through general applause, and before the supreme seat a voice speaks:

> Servant of God, well done, **well hast thou fought**
> **The better fight,** who single hast maintained
> Against revolted multitudes the cause
> Of truth, in word mightier than they in arms;
> And for the testimony of truth hast borne
> Universal reproach, far worse to bear
> Than violence; for this was all thy care
> To stand approved in sight of God, though worlds
> Judged thee perverse; the easier conquest now
> Remains thee, aided by this host of friends,
> Back on thy foes more glorious to return
> Than scorned thou didst depart, and to subdue
> By force, who reason for their law refuse,
> Right reason for their law, and for their King
> Messiah, who by right of merit reigns.
> Go, Michael, of celestial armies prince,
> And thou in military prowess next,
> Gabriel, lead forth to battle these my sons
> Invincible, lead forth my armèd saints
> By thousands and by millions ranged for fight, . . .

Well paid that is well satisfied

Source: THE MERCHANT OF VENICE (Act IV, sc. i, l. 415)
Author: William Shakespeare (1564–1616)
First published: 1600
Type of work: Dramatic comedy

Context: Portia, fair bride of Bassanio, disguised as a youthful judge, pronounces sentence upon the vengeful Jew Shylock, who has insisted upon the forfeiture of the bond of the ill-fated "merchant of Venice," Antonio—the forfeiture being a pound of Antonio's flesh. Portia, wisely noting that the promise includes a pound of flesh, but no blood, directs Shylock to proceed with the forfeiture at his own risk. As Shylock retracts his demand, Portia adds that since he, an alien, has threatened the life of a Venetian, the law requires that his own possessions be forfeited, half to the wronged citizen and half to the state. Bassanio and Antonio seek to express their gratitude to the judge by paying a large fee, but Portia refuses to accept payment:

PORTIA

He is **well paid that is well satisfied,**
And I, delivering you, am satisfied,
And therein do account myself well paid.
My mind was never yet more mercenary.
I pray you know me when we meet again,
I wish you well, and so I take my leave.

BASSANIO

Dear Sir, of force I must attempt you further.
Take some remembrance of us as a tribute,
Not as a fee. Grant me two things I pray you,
Not to deny me, and to pardon me.

Well roared, Lion

Source: A MIDSUMMER NIGHT'S DREAM (Act V, sc. i, l. 270)
Author: William Shakespeare (1564–1616)
First published: 1600
Type of work: Dramatic comedy

Context: One of Shakespeare's favorite comic devices is the scene within a scene in which the spectators observe a group which in turn is observing another group. Such an occasion is the final act of *A Midsummer Night's Dream* in which Theseus, Hippolyta, and the royal wedding party are provided amateur dramatic entertainment by Quince and his fellow handicraftsmen. Their production is an utter fiasco; lines are transposed, punctuation is confused, words are mispronounced, tragic intent is destroyed by flamboyant histrionics. The sophisticated courtiers, though encouraged by Theseus to judge the performance with tolerant eyes, cannot avoid humorous remarks at moments of particular ineptness. The Lion, on entering, carefully explains his true identity as Snug the joiner in order that his performance will not frighten the ladies. In the climactic scene he is called upon to roar "in wildest rage" at the fair Thisby, who has come to Ninnus' tomb to meet Pyramus. The mispronunciation of *Ninnus'* and the feeble roar from the king of breasts trigger a volley of good-natured gibes from the royal spectators:

THISBY
This is old Ninny's tomb. Where is my love?

LION
[*The* LION *roars; exit* THISBY.]
O—!

DEMETRIUS
Well roared, Lion.

1217

THESEUS

Well run, Thisby.

HIPPOLYTA

Well shone, Moon. Truly the moon shines with a good grace.
[*The* LION *tears* THISBY'S *mantle, and exit.*]

THESEUS

Well moused, Lion.

Enter PYRAMUS
DEMETRIUS

And then came Pyramus.

LYSANDER

And so the lion vanished.

We'll pluck a crow together

Source: THE COMEDY OF ERRORS (Act III, sc. i, l. 83)
Author: William Shakespeare (1564–1616)
First published: 1623
Type of work: Dramatic comedy

Context: In the street in front of his house in Ephesus Antipholus loudly demands admittance for himself, his friends Angelo and Balthazar, and his servant Dromio. Antipholus does not know that his shipwrecked twin brother, Antipholus, reared in the enemy city of Syracuse, accompanied by his servant, Dromio of Syracuse (twin of Dromio of Ephesus), has come to Ephesus to search for his long-lost brother, and that Adriana, his wife, has discovered her husband's twin at an inn and has angrily brought him home to dinner, assuming him to be her husband. In a comical dialogue filled with double meanings Antipholus of Ephesus calls for a crowbar to gain admittance to his own home.

DROMIO OF EPHESUS
. . . I pray thee let me in.

DROMIO OF SYRACUSE [*within*]
Ay, when fowls have no feathers, and fish have no fin.

ANTIPHOLUS OF EPHESUS
Well, I'll break in. Go borrow me a crow.

DROMIO OF EPHESUS
A crow without feather, master, mean you so?
For a fish without a fin, there's a fowl without a feather.
If a crow help us in sirrah, **we'll pluck a crow together.**

ANTIPHOLUS OF EPHESUS
Go get thee gone; fetch me an iron crow.

A well-written Life is almost as rare as a well-spent one

Source: CRITICAL AND MISCELLANEOUS ESSAYS (Volume I, "J.P.F. Richter")
Author: Thomas Carlyle (1795–1881)
First published: 1827
Type of work: Book review

Context: Born in a small village of Scotland, the son of a stonemason, Carlyle was reared in poverty. After a grammar school education, he walked to Edinburgh, where he enrolled in the University at the age of fourteen. He was forced by his poverty to leave without a degree, and he returned to his old grammar school as a teacher of mathematics. Religious doubts dissuaded him from following his parents' wishes that he study for the ministry. Lack of interest ended his reading of law in an Edinburgh office. Dyspepsia weakened him, and in 1822 he had a breakdown and spiritual crisis that he recorded in *Sartor Resartus.* With the reading of some of the German philosophers, he began to establish a system of beliefs that helped him regain his stability, a condition also aided by his marriage in 1826 to Jane Welsh, possessor of a brilliant mind. To earn their living, he began reviewing books for several magazines, including the influential *Edinburgh Review.* One of his first assignments was a book in German by Heinrich Döring, *Jean Paul Richter's Life, with a Sketch of His Works* (Gotha, 1826). The review was an agreeable task, since Richter (1763–1825), along with Johann Fichte (1762–1814), had been the most influential philosophers in settling Carlyle's mind. It appeared in Issue 91 of the *Edinburgh Review.* In it, Carlyle praises the book highly, though with some reservations, such as the biographer's choppy style and labored transitions. He begins his review with a general observation on the writing of biographies.

Dr. Johnson, it is said, when he first heard of Boswell's intention to write a life of him, announced, with decision enough, that, if he thought Boswell really meant to *write his* life, he would prevent it by *taking Boswell's.* That great authors should actually employ this preventive against bad biographers is a thing we would by no means recommend: but the truth is, that, rich as we are in Biography, **a well-written Life is almost as rare as a well-spent one;** and there are certainly many more men whose

history deserves to be recorded, than persons willing and able
to record it. . . .

What a genius I had when I wrote that book!

Source: LIFE OF SWIFT (Volume II, p. 289)
Author: Jonathan Swift (1667–1745), as quoted in the biography by Sir Henry
   Craik (1846–1927)
First published: 1882
Type of work: Biography

Context: Jonathan Swift (1667–1745) was a master of clear, firm prose, a clergyman admired for his wit, and a satirist feared for his merciless tongue. His two earliest important works were published in 1704. One, *The Battle of the Books,* took the side of his employer Sir William Temple, in an argument about the comparative merits of the Ancients and the Moderns. Swift pictured books in the library taking part in the debate, and though in his prose mock-epic neither side is declared victor, it is evident that the author sides with the Ancients for their attempts to depict Nature. Entirely different was his other book, *The Tale of a Tub,* completed about five years earlier. In it appears the scorn of a vigorous man of thirty for effete pedantry. It satirizes divisions among Christians. A man has three sons, Peter (representing the Roman Catholics), Martin (representing the Protestants), and Jack (the dissenting churches). Upon his deathbed the man gives to each a coat that will last as long as its wearer lives, and will grow in proportion to the body, lengthening and widening so as always to fit. (The coat typifies the doctrines and faith of Christianity.) The father's will (that is, the New Testament) gives instructions about wearing and looking after the coats. In the tale, in spite of the father's injunctions not to make over the garments, each son begins to alter his according to his own wishes, while protesting the changes his brothers are making. The book was published anonymously, though a few friends knew the secret of its authorship. Many others tried to guess. During his lifetime Swift never publicly acknowledged it as his own, despite his pride in it. Nor did he make any money from it. (His only royalties from writing came from *Gulliver's Travels* (1726), and these only because a friend acted as his agent and insisted on payments in cash.) In the fifth edition, he provided a preface making fun of some of the attributions of authorship. With no income, to live on, Swift became dean of St. Patrick's Cathedral, Dublin. For knowledge of the author's opinion of *The Tale of a Tub,* the world is indebted to his cousin, Mrs. Martha Whiteway, daughter of Swift's Uncle Adam, who lived with Swift and looked after him in his later years, when he was declining in health. Her testimony has been quoted by two of Swift's biographers, Sir Walter Scott, who published a biography in 1814, and Sir Henry Craik, who devoted two volumes to Swift's life in 1882. In an appendix to the latter, the author presents evidence that many people knew Swift as the author of

A Tale of a Tub. Following is the Craik version of the testimony, first recorded by Scott in 1814:

> So generally accepted did the authorship at length become that Pulteney (Sir William Pulteney, 1684–1764, an English political leader), in a letter to Swift himself (June 3, 1740) actually names the book in some Latin verses, as one of the manifestations of his genius.
>
> Lastly, in the period of almost speechless apathy which preceded his death, Swift was heard by Mrs. Whiteway to mutter, as he turned over the leaves of the book, "Good God, **what a genius I had when I wrote that book!**"

What a goodly outside falsehood hath!

Source: THE MERCHANT OF VENICE (Act I, sc. iii, l. 103)
Author: William Shakespeare (1564–1616)
First published: 1600
Type of work: Dramatic comedy

Context: The young Venetian gentleman, Bassanio, asks the assistance of the merchant Antonio, in seeking a loan to aid in his quest for the hand of the lovely Portia. Antonio, however, cannot immediately supply the demand of Bassanio, since his wealth depends upon the return of his ships. Shylock, a Jew who has felt the hatred of Gentiles and who, in turn, has despised them, agrees, notwithstanding, to advance the loan. Antonio protests the Jewish custom of charging usury and condemns Shylock for backing his stand by quoting the scriptural story of Jacob's devious acquisition of the best of the flock of his father-in-law, Laban:

> ANTONIO
> Mark you this Bassanio,
> The devil can cite Scripture for his purpose.
> An evil soul producing holy witness
> Is like a villain with a smiling cheek,
> A goodly apple rotten at the heart.
> O, **what a goodly outside falsehood hath.**

What a man needs in gardening is a cast-iron back, with a hinge in it

Source: MY SUMMER IN A GARDEN (Third Week)
Author: Charles Dudley Warner (1829–1900)
First published: 1870
Type of work: Essay

1221

Context: Charles Dudley Warner, probably best known for his collaboration with Mark Twain in *The Gilded Age,* also did a great deal of predominantly journalistic writing on his own. It was while he was editor of the *Hartford Courant* that he wrote the series of articles entitled "My Summer in a Garden," which appeared in the newspaper between May 21 and October 22, 1870. Near the close of the same year the articles were published in book form, with the date 1871 on the title page. The nineteen articles, or chapters, are titled by weeks—"First Week," "Second Week," and so on. The quotation comes in the "Third Week." Here Warner describes his battle with grass, vines, and weeds in anything but a scientific vein. The grass symbolizes "total depravity"; the vine, "intelligence"; and the weeds, "hateful moral qualities." In destroying weeds, he feels that he is "destroying sin," and his "hoe becomes an instrument of retributive justice. . . . Hoeing becomes not a pastime, but a duty." The quotation follows:

Nevertheless, **what a man needs in gardening is a cast-iron back, with a hinge in it.** The hoe is an ingenious instrument, calculated to call out a great deal of strength at a great disadvantage.

What a piece of work is a man

Source: HAMLET (Act II, sc. ii, l. 315)
Author: William Shakespeare (1564–1616)
First published: 1603
Type of work: Dramatic tragedy

Context: Hamlet, shocked by his kingly father's death and his mother's hasty marriage to his uncle, who, so the Ghost of his father informs him, has murdered the noble king, broods about the court. Alarmed over Hamlet's suspicious behavior, his uncle Claudius sends Rosencrantz and Guildenstern, former friends of Hamlet, to seek out the reason for the prince's melancholy. Hamlet fends off their entreaties, delivers his estimate of the world and mankind, and comments on his own feelings.

HAMLET
. . . I have of late, but wherefore I know not, lost all my mirth, forgone all custom of exercises; and indeed it goes so heavily with my disposition, that this goodly frame the earth, seems to me a sterile promontory, this most excellent canopy the air, look you, this brave o'erhanging firmament, this majestical roof fretted with golden fire, why, it appeareth nothing to me but a foul and pestilent congregation of vapours. **What a piece of work is a man,** how noble in reason, how infinite in faculties, in form and moving, how express and admirable in action, how like an angel in apprehension, how like a god—the beauty of the world; the

paragon of animals; and yet to me, what is this quintessence of
dust? Man delights not me; . . .

What! all this for a song?

Source: SPENSER'S FAERIE QUEENE (Introduction VII–VIII)
Editor: John Upton (1707–1760)
First published: 1758
Type of work: Biographical introduction

Context: How much is a poem worth? One reason for the survival of much early poetry—besides the fact that its meter makes it easier to remember than prose—was the general impression that anyone could write prose, but it took special qualifications to compose poetry. This viewpoint and a bit of English history were tied up in an anecdote about the poet Edmund Spenser (c. 1552–1599). Dr. Thomas Birch (1705–1766) set down part of the story in his ten-folio volume *General Dictionary, Historical and Critical* (1734–1741) and in his six-volume *Biographia Britannica, or Lives of the Most Eminent Persons who have Flourished in Great Britain and Ireland* (1747–1766). He also alluded to it in his *Spenser the Poet* (1771). However, a more complete account of the affair appears in the Introduction to the edition of *The Faerie Queene* (London; Tonson, 1758), by John Upton. To understand its significance one must go back to English history. In 1553, Mary, daughter of Henry VIII of England, succeeded to the throne upon the death of her half brother, Edward VI. Her brother's Secretary of State had been William Cecil (1520–1598). When Mary reestablished the Roman Catholic religion in England, in 1555, Cecil conformed to it. In 1558, Mary was succeeded by another daughter of Henry VIII, Queen Elizabeth (1533–1603). Elizabeth recalled Cecil and made him Secretary of State. Not only did he maintain a spy system to keep her warned of plots against her throne, but he also originated and directed her policies so satisfactorily that she made him First Baron Burghley (or Burleigh). Among the poets writing in England at the time were Sir Philip Sidney and Edmund Spenser. The latter wrote the first work of Elizabethan literature, *The Shepheardes Calendar* in twelve eclogues, dedicated to Sidney, and started on a long work, *The Faerie Queene,* an imaginative allegory in vindication of Protestantism and Puritanism. Its first three books were published in 1590, dedicated to Elizabeth. But meantime Spenser had written a number of short poems, and the elegy *Astrophel* when Sidney was killed in battle in 1586. He presented the queen with some of his poetry. Queen Elizabeth, anxious to be a patron of arts, and delighted at a Protestant poet, to counteract the Catholic followers of the previous queen, directed Lord Burleigh to pay a hundred pounds to Spenser. The courtier did not admire Protestant Spenser; he was not fond of poetry; and he was laboring to balance the finances of England, because of the war with

1223

Spain. So he protested, in words that have frequently been paraphrased by later Philistines. As Upton tells the story:

> There passeth a story commonly told and believed, that Spenser presenting his poems to Queen Elizabeth, she highly affected herewith commanded the Lord Cecil her Treasurer to give him an hundred pounds; and when the Treasurer (a good steward of the Queen's money) cried, **"What! all this for a song?"** and alledged that the sum was too much, "Then give him" (quoth the Queen) "what is reason;" to which the Lord Treasurer consented; but was so busied belike about matters of higher concernment, that Spenser received no reward. Whereupon he presented this petition in a small piece of paper to the Queen in her progress,
>
>> I was promis'd on a time
>> To have reason for my rhyme;
>> From that time unto this season,
>> I receiv'd nor rhyme nor reason.
>
> Hereupon the Queen gave strict order (not without some check to her Treasurer) for the present payment of the hundred pounds she first intended unto him.

What avails the sceptered race

Source: ROSE AYLMER (Line 1)
Author: Walter Savage Landor (1775–1864)
First published: 1806
Type of work: Elegiac poem

Context: This short poem, in the twentieth century probably Landor's best-known work, was first published in his little volume entitled *Simonidea.* The real-life Rose Aylmer, whose death in 1800 prompted Landor to write the poem, was the daughter of Lord Aylmer. Landor had become a friend of the Aylmer family shortly after he left Oxford University in 1794, when he went to Wales. As a poet he was at least somewhat in debt to Rose Aylmer, as it was she who had introduced him to Clara Reeve's *Progress of Romance,* from which he admittedly received the suggestion for *Gebir* (1798), a long, blank-verse narrative poem. Rose Aylmer had been sent, after her mother's second marriage, to live with an aunt, in India, where the girl died. Landor wrote of her:

> Ah, **what avails the sceptered race,**
>> Ah, what the form divine!
> What every virtue, every grace!
>> Rose Aylmer, all were thine.
> Rose Aylmer, whom these wakeful eyes

May weep, but never see,
A night of memories and of sighs
I consecrate to thee.

What dire effects from civil discord flow

Source: CATO (Act V, sc. iv, l. 108)
Author: Joseph Addison (1672–1719)
First published: 1713
Type of work: Dramatic tragedy

Context: This tragedy of a banished leader of unimpeachable integrity held great attractions to both Whigs and Tories in the complex political situation of the early eighteenth century. Cato, the stern and austere champion of constitutional government, stands for Roman virtue against the popular military dictator, Caesar. But in the end truth and virtue fail against the forces of ambition and greed, and the efforts of Cato to save Rome from Caesar and from herself are doomed to failure. His cause lost, one son dead in battle, and his friends endangered, Cato, in true Stoic fashion, commits suicide. His corpse is discovered by his remaining son, Portius, and his friend, Lucius, who closes the play:

> There fled the greatest soul that ever warmed
> A Roman breast. O Cato! O my friend!
> Thy will shall be religiously observed.
> But let us bear this awful corpse to Caesar,
> And lay it in his sight, that it may stand
> A fence betwixt us and the victor's wrath;
> Cato, tho' dead, shall still protect his friends.
>   From hence, let fierce contending nations know
> **What dire effects from civil discord flow.**
> 'Tis this that shakes our country with alarms,
> And gives up Rome a prey to Roman arms,
> Produces fraud, and cruelty, and strife,
> And robs the guilty world of Cato's life.

What, frighted with false fire!

Source: HAMLET (Act III, sc. ii, l. 277)
Author: William Shakespeare (1564–1616)
First published: 1603
Type of work: Dramatic tragedy

Context: Hamlet has devised a stratagem to determine finally whether the Ghost who has appeared to him is really his father's spirit or a tempting demon. He has asked a group of traveling actors to perform a play, *The*

Murther of Gonzago, in which he will insert some lines, the performance closely parallelling the story of his father's murder as told him by the Ghost: "The play's the thing/ Wherein I'll catch the conscience of the King," Hamlet asserts at the close of Act II. During the performance itself, Hamlet speaks of the play as "The Mousetrap." When one of the actors pours poison into the ears of another who is asleep—the way, according to the Ghost, that Claudius killed Hamlet's father—Claudius reacts, rising and leaving the throneroom. His conscience has been caught, and Hamlet is now convinced. Hamlet's first, quite characteristic, comment is ironic: can the king be so overwrought by a mere play, by "false fire," the discharge of a gun loaded with powder only?

OPHELIA

The King rises.

HAMLET

What, frighted with false fire!

GERTRUDE

How fares my lord?

POLONIUS

Give o'er the play.

KING

Give me some light—Away!

What have kings, that privates have not too

Source: KING HENRY THE FIFTH (Act IV, sc. i, l. 255)
Author: William Shakespeare (1564–1616)
First published: 1600
Type of work: Historical drama

Context: The English forces are encamped at Agincourt in preparation for battle against the much stronger forces of France in a contest in which King Henry V of England will attain the crown of France, which he considers to be rightfully his. The king, in disguise, walks unrecognized among his troops, and, talking freely with them, learns the mind of his men. Alone again, Henry meditates upon his fate as king—he, though a man as all are men, must bear the weight of the responsibility for all his subjects, and his reward is but the emptiness of ceremony:

We must bear all. O hard condition,
Twin-born with greatness, subject to the breath
Of every fool, whose sense no more can feel
But his own wringing. What infinite heart's-ease
Must kings neglect, that private men enjoy.
And **what have kings, that privates have not too,**
Save ceremony, save general ceremony?
And what art thou, thou idol ceremony?
What kind of god art thou, that suffer'st more
Of mortal griefs, than do thy worshippers?
What are thy rents, what are thy comings-in?
O ceremony, show me but thy worth.

. . .

What her eyes enthralled her tongue unbound

Source: LESBIA (Last line)
Author: William Congreve (1670–1729)
First published: 1704
Type of work: Lyric poem

Context: The original Lesbia was a Greek poetess, Sappho, born in Lesbos, who lived and wrote during the seventh century B.C. Only a few fragments of her verse remain, quoted by admirers. The name was also given to Clodia, notorious sister of Clodius and wife of Quintus Metellus Celer, who was the subject of much verse by one of the greatest of Roman lyric poets, Gaius Valerius Catullus (84?–54 B.C.). When the Restoration poet, Congreve, sought a literary name under which to address one of the fine ladies of the late seventeenth century, he cloaked her identity under that "nom d'amour." Noted as the greatest writer of Restoration comedy who, in the words of his admirer Voltaire, raised the art "to a greater height than any other English writer before or since," Congreve showed a facility in verse as well. Samuel Johnson called his wit "a meteor." How-ever, while Johnson selected a dozen lines from his play *The Mourning Bride* as the most poetical passage in the whole mass of English poetry, he lamented that the poetic power of Congreve seemed to desert him when he left the stage. He had little favorable to say about Congreve's miscellaneous poetry except that he taught English writers that the odes of Pindar were regular, and that while Congreve lacked the fire for the higher species of lyric poetry, he could demonstrate that enthusiasm can still have rules, and that in mere confusion there is neither grace nor greatness. Perhaps Congreve himself did not esteem his brief poetry very highly because after he wrote "CURTAIN" at the end of his fourth comedy in 1700, he lived on government sinecures largely provided by his patron, Lord Halifax, and did practically no writing. But his poem to Les-

1227

bia has the dexterity and the felicity of expression that are so evident in his comedies. The idea of being "cured by the hair of the dog that bit you," or that "poison has its own antidote," is expressed engagingly. With Lesbia, eyes might enchain the lover, but her stupid speech quickly breaks the chain. The poem was first published in *Dryden's Fifth Poetical Miscellany* (1704), along with ten more by Congreve, but officially published in his own *Writings of Mr. William Congreve,* in 1710. Here is the whole poem.

When Lesbia first I saw so heavenly fair,
With eyes so bright, and with that awful air
I thought my heart, which durst so high aspire,
As bold as his who snatch'd celestial fire.

But soon as e'er the beautious idiot spoke,
Forth from her coral lips such folly broke,
Like balm the trickling nonsense heal'd my wound,
And **what her eyes enthrall'd her tongue unbound.**

What I tell you three times is true

Source: THE HUNTING OF THE SNARK (Fit I, The Landing, l. 8)
Author: Lewis Carroll (Charles Lutwidge Dodgson, 1832–1898)
First published: 1876
Type of work: Poem for children

Context: English literature has few writers of nonsense verse. Besides Edward Lear (1812–1888), known for his *Book of Nonsense* (1846) and others, the only writer who comes to mind is a minister and professor of mathematics of Oxford University, the Reverend Charles Dodgson, who alternated textbooks and such tomes as *Euclid and His Modern Rivals* (1879) with delightful books for children, like *Alice's Adventures in Wonderland* (1865), where he concealed his identity behind the pen name of Lewis Carroll. Another such book was *The Hunting of the Snark, An Agony in Eight Fits.* A crew under the command of a Bellman or town crier, sails with a crew consisting of a Barrister, a Bonnet maker, a Broker, a Banker, a Butcher, a Beaver, a Boots or shoeshine boy, and others. Their map shows only a shoreless ocean, without equator, zones, or meridians, which to the captain are "merely conventional signs." The Bellman furnishes characteristics to help identify a snark: its taste, its lack of humor, its ambition, and "Its habit of getting up late, you'll agree/ That it carries too far, when I say/ That it frequently breakfasts at five o'clock tea/ And dines on the following day." The author never describes the creature. Perhaps its name is one of his "portmanteau words" that pack two meanings, as "fuming" and "furious" became to him "frumious." Perhaps it is a snake (sea serpent) and a shark. Certainly the Bellman knows what he is looking for.

> "Just the place for a Snark!" the Bellman cried,
>   As he landed his crew with care;
> Supporting each man on the top of the tide
>   By a finger entwined in his hair.
> "Just the place for a Snark! I have said it twice;
>   That alone should encourage the crew.
> "Just the place for a Snark!—I have said it thrice;
>   **What I tell you three times is true."**

What I want is, Facts

Source: HARD TIMES (Book I, chapter 1)
Author: Charles Dickens (1812–1870)
First published: 1854
Type of work: Novel

Context: In *Hard Times* Charles Dickens attacks the materialism of the Victorian period. At the beginning of the book Thomas Gradgrind is explaining the system of his private school to the schoolmaster, Mr. M'Choakumchild; all that is required is facts. Later, Gradgrind explains that emotion, feelings, fancy are weaknesses that must be eradicated if the human being is to be adapted to his environment. The results of this system of schooling are shown in the development of four pupils: Gradgrind's son, Tom, a self-centered whelp who uses everyone around him for his own purposes and eventually turns out to be a thief; his daughter, Louisa, whose emotions have been so smothered that she allows herself to be forced into a loveless marriage that produces nothing but unhappiness; Bitzer, a creature who rises in the world by sneaking and spying to serve his own interests; and Sissy Jupe, upon whom the system has had no effect. She alone develops into a warm and delightful person. Through the character of Joseph Bounderby, Dickens shows the evils of the *laissez faire* system of enterprise, which grinds down powerless workers for the enrichment of the magnates. There is a close connection between the Gradgrind system of education and the prevailing economic theory, as both are practical and stripped of sentimentality.

> "Now, **what I want is, Facts.** Teach these boys and girls nothing but Facts. Facts alone are wanted in life. Plant nothing else, and root out everything else. You can only form the minds of reasoning animals upon Facts: nothing else will ever be of any service to them. This is the principle on which I bring up my own children, and this is the principle on which I bring up these children. Stick to Facts, sir!"

What ills from beauty spring

Source: THE VANITY OF HUMAN WISHES (Line 321)
Author: Samuel Johnson (1709–1784)
First published: 1749
Type of work: Didactic poem in imitation of the tenth satire of Juvenal

Context: Samuel Johnson, looking at the world and finding all the things that people most desire to be delusions and vanities, in turn assails wealth, which in its insecurity produces only fear and anxiety; high place in politics, which brings forth a host of sycophantic beggars while the holder of office is in the ascendant but which causes them to fall away when adversity sets in; wide and deep learning, which leads to poverty and woe and is never appreciated until the wise man is dead; military glory, which causes the general himself and, indeed, all the world to think him almost a god so long as he is winning his battles but which can depart forever with the losing of but one battle and leave him for all time an object of contempt; long life, which leads to dotage, ingratitude of dependents, miserliness, and general anxiety; a seemingly happy prime of life, which is attended by the sickness of near relatives, the death of kin, and gradual aging into senility; and beauty. Every mother desires her daughter to be beautiful, but the fairness of the daughters may lead them into becoming great men's mistresses, and as such they will lead lives of misery. But if this situation does not develop, the beautiful girl is worried by her rival beauties, her lover seeks to undermine her virtue, and she generally ends her career betrayed, despised, and distressed:

> The teeming mother, anxious for her race,
> Begs for each birth the fortune of a face;
> Yet Vane could tell **what ills from beauty spring;**
> And Sedley cursed the form that pleased a king.
> Ye nymphs of rosy lips and radiant eyes,
> Whom Pleasure keeps too busy to be wise,
> Whom Joys with soft varieties invite,
> By day the frolic, and the dance by night;
> Who frown with vanity, who smile with art,
> And ask the latest fashion of the heart;
> What care, what rules your heedless charms shall save,
> Each nymph your rival, and each youth your slave?
> Against your fame with Fondness Hate combines,
> The rival batters, and the lover mines.
> With distant voice neglected Virtue calls,
> Less heard, and less, the faint remonstrance falls;
> Tired with contempt, she quits the slippery reign
> And Pride and Prudence take her seat in vain.

What is past my help is past my care

Source: THE DOUBLE MARRIAGE (Act I, sc. i)
Authors: Francis Beaumont (1585?–1616) and John Fletcher (1579–1625)
First published: 1647
Type of work: Dramatic tragedy

Context: Virolet, a noble gentleman of Naples, discloses to his wife Juliana that there is a plot afoot to assassinate Ferrand, the tyrant of the city-state. Juliana encourages her husband to proceed with the plot, saying that she would be prouder to be the widow of a man who died liberating his country than one who tamely bore the ills of the time. Upon her exit, Brissonet, Camillo, and Ronvere enter; and Ronvere immediately begins a defense of himself, saying that he loves freedom as well as anyone living. He says that he has means to put into operation that which is merely at the moment being plotted. Virolet says that Ronvere, a faithful follower of Ferrand, will betray the whole plot and have all the plotters executed. Camillo and Brissonet, however, point out that Ronvere has lost favor with Ferrand, has been relieved of his military command, and has been disgraced. Virolet maintains that to make his peace with Ferrand, Ronvere will gladly betray his fellow plotters. He further says that if it were not for the laws of hospitality, if the creature were not at that moment in his own house, he would kill him on the spot. He adds, however, that what he can do nothing about he does not try to remedy.

RONVERE
        You are too suspicious,
And I have borne too much, beyond my temper.
Take your own ways. I'll leave you.

VIROLET
        You may stay now;
You have enough, and all indeed you fished for.
But one word, gentlemen: have you discovered
To him alone our plot?

BRISSONET
To him and others that are at his devotion.

VIROLET
Worse and worse:
For were he only conscious of our purposes,
Though with the breach of hospitable laws,
In my own house, I'd silence him for ever;
But **what is past my help is past my care.**

1231

What man has made of man

Source: LINES WRITTEN IN EARLY SPRING (Line 8)
Author: William Wordsworth (1770–1850)
First published: 1798
Type of work: Lyric poem

Context: Dismayed by the materialism of his contemporaries in England, and appalled by the horrors of the French Revolution, Wordsworth often brooded on the contrast between the world of external Nature which he loved so deeply, and the man-made world of moral and religious decay, political opportunism, laboring-class exploitation, and civil strife. Such a contrast is found in "Lines Written in Early Spring." Sitting in a grove, the poet listens pleasurably to the "blended notes" of Nature's world, and "sad thoughts" come to his mind. Since the beauties of Nature are linked to man's soul, he is grieved to recall what man has done to his fellows. The world about him seems so joyous that he is led to believe in a conscious joy in the life of natural objects. If he is right, he asks, has he not reason to lament what man has done? Stanzas two and six follow:

To her fair works did Nature link
The human soul that through me ran;
And much it grieved my heart to think
What man has made of man.

. . .

If this belief from heaven be sent,
If such be Nature's holy plan,
Have I not reason to lament
What man has made of man?

What millions died that Caesar might be great!

Source: PLEASURES OF HOPE (Part II, l. 174)
Author: Thomas Campbell (1777–1844)
First published: 1799
Type of work: Didactic poem

Context: One editor of a volume of Campbell's poetry expressed indignation at the present neglect of the works of a Scotsman, so celebrated during his lifetime. His rise to fame was meteoric. *Pleasures of Hope,* completed when he was barely twenty-one, immediately became popular, not only for its poetic beauty, but for its graphic lines about the downfall of Poland. Schoolboys orated about the massacre of the citizens of Warsaw, with that couplet: "Hope for a season bade the world farewell,/ And Freedom shrieked—as Kosciusko fell." Perhaps one reason for the loss of popularity of the last eighteenth century practitioner of the heroic couplet was that the era of Pope, Thomson, and Cowper was over. Yet Campbell's bold patriotic songs, such as "Ye Mariners of England," "Napoleon and the British Soldier," and "The Battle of the Baltic," should have kept his memory alive. A few of his quotable lines still live, but few people know either the source or the name of the author of, for example, "Distance lends enchantment," and "Like angel-visits, few and far between." For his first work, Campbell originally had a fifty-line introduction, full of personal references to his feelings during its composition. Wisely it was omitted in publication. He had also provided a prose analysis of both parts, which was not included until later. Another change was the expansion of Part II from 326 to 474 lines. He left the first part untouched. *Pleasures of Hope* opens with a comparison between imagination and reality. Anticipation is discussed in its influence on passions, with the story of man's guardian deities abandoning the world and leaving only Hope behind. "Hope inspires the mother, the prisoner, the wanderer." Then with a political twist, the poet hopes for improvement in society and in the humanizing arts among the uncivilized nations, despite the victory of the oppressors in Poland. In the section of Part II in which Campbell makes his contribution to the nature poetry, so popular in his time, he discusses a summer and a winter evening and the ideas they create in a person's mind. In the winter, he may think of furious storms at sea, or be moved by the reading of Schiller's tragedy, *The Robbers*. Other thoughts may intrude, happy thoughts or tragic ones about the two million estimated victims of Caesar's wars, or the more recent battle of Pultowa of 1709, under Charles XII of Sweden.

> Turn to the gentler melodies that suit
> Thalia's harp, or Pan's Arcadian lute;
> Or, down the stream of Truth's historic page
> From clime to clime descend, from age to age!
> Yet there, perhaps, may darker scenes obtrude
> Than Fancy fashions in her wildest mood;
> There shall he pause with horrent brow, to rate
> **What millions died—that Caesar might be great!**
> Or learn the fate that bleeding thousands bore,
> Marched by their Charles to Dneiper's swampy shore;
> Faint in his wounds, and shivering in the blast,
> The Swedish soldier sunk—and groaned his last!

What news on the Rialto?

Source: THE MERCHANT OF VENICE (Act I, sc. iii, l. 38 and others)
Author: William Shakespeare (1564–1616)
First published: 1600
Type of work: Dramatic comedy

Context: Bassanio, a young Venetian gentleman, in plying his quest for the hand of fair Portia, seeks an additional loan from Antonio, "the merchant of Venice." Antonio, however, whose funds are tied up with ships in many ports, must in turn seek a temporary creditor. Hence, Bassanio approaches the Jew, Shylock, who agrees to advance three thousand ducats with the stipulation that Antonio shall stand bond. Shylock, refusing Bassanio's invitation to discuss the deal while they dine, gives vent to his hatred for Gentiles and, on hearing Antonio approach, asks the latest report on the Venetian exchange, the Rialto:

SHYLOCK

Yes, to smell pork, to eat of the habitation which your prophet the Nazarite conjured the devil into. I will buy with you, sell with you, talk with you, walk with you, and so following. But I will not eat with you, drink with you, nor pray with you. **What news on the Rialto?**

Enter ANTONIO

Who is he come here?

What scourge for perjury?

Source: KING RICHARD THE THIRD (Act I, sc. iv, l. 50)
Author: William Shakespeare (1564–1616)
First published: 1597
Type of work: Historical drama

Context: Through the machinations of his brother, Richard, Duke of Gloucester (later King Richard the Third), George, Duke of Clarence, is imprisoned in the Tower of London. The Duke of Gloucester has persuaded King Edward the Fourth, brother to the two dukes, that a man whose name begins with "G" will murder the king's two sons. As Gloucester expected, the suspicion has landed upon George, Duke of Clarence. In prison the duke has a terrible dream, in which he sees himself thrown overboard from a ship by his brother Richard. As the night-mare continues, the duke dreams that he crosses the River Styx into Hell, where the first condemned soul he meets is that of his father-in-law, the Earl of Warwick, whom Clarence had deserted in the struggle for the kingdom in the Wars of the Roses, recently ended. After Warwick's ghost passes by, the ghost of Edward, Prince of Wales, son of Henry the Sixth, comes to add his curse, in return for the wounds given him at Tewkesbury by Clarence. The Duke of Clarence is relating his dream to his keeper at the Tower of London.

CLARENCE
. . . my dream was lengthen'd after life.

1234

O, then began the tempest to my soul.
I pass'd, methought, the melancholy flood,
With that sour ferryman which poets write of,
Unto the kingdom of perpetual night.
The first that there did greet my stranger soul,
Was my great father-in-law, renowned Warwick,
Who spake aloud, **what scourge for perjury**
Can this dark monarchy afford false Clarence?
And so he vanished.

What shelter to grow ripe is ours, what leisure to grow wise?

Source: STANZAS IN MEMORY OF THE AUTHOR OF "OBERMANN" (Lines 71–72)
Author: Matthew Arnold (1822–1888)
First published: 1852
Type of work: Elegy

Context: Obermann, a philosophical romance by Etienne Pivert de Senancour (1770–1846), is a melancholy book that alternates between florid descriptions of nature and lengthy discussions about the soul. Arnold, finding that life in the mid-nineteenth century was racked by contrary desires, "one drives him to the world without,/ And one to solitude," found in this romance an escape from pain into the calm of romantic melancholy. Modern life, however, does not sanction such escape, so Arnold with classical stoicism accepts his fate. There being no escape in dreams or in the cold melancholy of romance, man has no chance to find calm or peace. As he says in other poems, Fate has chosen the age into which a man is born, and the individual who does not accept his fate will find only misery while the one who reaches the maturity of dreamless adulthood will possibly discover the peace of suffering endured.

But we, brought forth and rear'd in hours
Of change, alarm, surprise—
What shelter to grow ripe is ours?
What leisure to grow wise?

Like children bathing on the shore,
Buried a wave beneath,
The second wave succeeds, before
We have had time to breathe.

Too fast we live, too much are tried,
Wordsworth's sweet calm, or Goethe's wide
And luminous view to gain.

What so wild as words are?

Source: A WOMAN'S LAST WORD (Line 5)
Author: Robert Browning (1812–1889)
First published: 1855
Type of work: Dramatic monologue

Context: This poem is one of Browning's most perfect short lyrical dramatic monologues. It portrays, with keen perception, the delicate adjustments which must be made in married life. The reader's sympathy is claimed by the wife who is the speaker in the poem. It is evening; she and her husband have just had a serious quarrel for which she seeks peace and reconciliation. She points out that facts can lie: "What so false as truth is,/ False to thee?" The lady wishes only to be held to her husband, either by charms or by his own arms. She declares that to hold his love tomorrow she will "Meet, if thou require it,/ Both demands,/ Laying flesh and spirit/ In thy hands." Tonight, however, she will foolishly weep a little, bury her sorrow, and fall asleep, secure in his love. She begins her plea for their love by saying to him:

> Let's contend no more, love,
> Strive nor weep;
> All be as before, Love,
> —Only sleep!
>
> **What so wild as words are?**
> I and thou
> In debate, as birds are,
> Hawk on bough!

What song the Sirens sang, or what name Achilles assumed

Source: HYDRIOTAPHIA: URN BURIAL (Chapter 5)
Author: Sir Thomas Browne (1605–1682)
First published: 1658
Type of work: Philosophy

Context: Sir Thomas Browne, a learned seventeenth century gentleman, an advocate of the sciences, and a philosopher who questioned accepted religious beliefs, wrote the five-chapter tract titled *Hydriotaphia: Urn Burial* upon the discovery of some ancient burial receptacles containing skeletal remains from the Roman era of British history. Noting that the bones remain while the identity, the features, and the deeds of their possessors are obliterated from the records of men and that time carelessly erases most of history, occasionally leaving the name of one man or the good deeds of another whose name is not recalled, Browne suggests that man's true hope for perpetuation lies in the Christian belief in immortality of the soul. It is more difficult, the philosopher states, to conjecture the history of those bones than to prove the song the Sirens sang to Odysseus or the name assumed by Achilles when he hid among the women to avoid serving in the Trojan War. The passage begins:

> **What song the Sirens sang, or what name Achilles assumed** when he hid himself among women, though puzzling questions, are not beyond all conjecture. What time the persons of these ossuaries entered the famous nations of the dead, and slept with princes and counselors, might admit a wide solution. . . .

What was he doing, the great god Pan

Source: A MUSICAL INSTRUMENT (Line 1)
Author: Elizabeth Barrett Browning (1806–1861)
First published: 1862
Type of work: Lyric poem

Context: During her confinement as a result of paralysis, the poet turned to classical literature in order to escape the monotony of her restricted life; this love of the classics led her to use Greek and Latin myths in a strangely personal manner. According to the ancients, Pan, the Greek god of flocks and pastures, created the *aulos* or shepherd's flute. In this poem, the god is described as he selects a reed and carefully cuts it to size, draws the pith out and drills holes, thus making the first *aulos*. The poet, however, has so associated the reed to a man that her description is also an account of the making of a poet: the god selects an individual, draws out his heart, and turns him into a musical instrument. Furthermore, the god is part man and part goat, yet he can still enchant nature with his music; in like manner, the handicapped poet cannot match her flawless contemporaries, yet she can entrance them with her poetry.

> **What was he doing, the great god Pan,**
>   Down in the reeds by the river?
> Spreading ruin, and scattering ban,
>   Splashing and paddling with hoofs of a goat,
> And breaking the golden lilies afloat
>   With the dragon-fly on the river.

What you desire is not mortal

Source: THE METAMORPHOSES (Book II, l. 55)
Author: Ovid (43 B.C.–A.D. 18)
First transcribed: Before A.D. 8
Type of work: Mythological tales in verse

Context: Ovid came of a wealthy family; although he was trained for an official career, he soon gave his time exclusively to poetry. He was a typical member of Roman society as it existed during the age of Augustus; he moved in a gay and sophisticated world that was preoccupied with sensual pleasures. Nearly all his early poetry deals with love. He was a gifted writer and was blessed with a winning personality; he was greatly admired by other poets of his time. His career in Rome ended in A.D. 8, when he was banished from the city and his books excluded from its libraries. His book *The Art of Love* served as the official reason for this action, and may have been partially responsible: it celebrates adultery, which was a capital crime. The real reason for Ovid's banishment, however, may have been that he was an unlucky witness to something he should not have seen. Just before he entered upon his exile he completed the *Metamorphoses,* a monumental work for which he is still best known. In it he retells from Greek mythology all the stories of persons who were transformed by the gods into other forms. The work involves some 250 of these accounts, all joined together with natural and careful transitions so that they are linked in an unbroken series. In Book II Ovid retells the legend of Phaeton, son of Clymene and of Phoebus the sun-god. In order to prove his supernatural origin to a friend, Phaeton goes to the Palace of the Sun and asks Phoebus to grant him a wish. Phoebus does so willingly; and upon obtaining this consent, Phaeton announces that he wants to drive the chariot of the sun across the heavens for one day. Phoebus tells his son that what he desires is not possible for mortal man, that the steeds are very difficult to manage, and that he should reconsider. But Phaeton insists, and goes to disaster. Phoebus' admonition, literally translated, is "What you desire is not mortal"; most translators phrase this more poetically. The metrical translation by Arthur Golding (c. 1536–c. 1589), with spelling modernized, is quoted below. Golding's translation was used by Shakespeare, and was long popular.

> Then did his father by and by forethink him of his oath,
> And shaking twenty times his head, as one that was full
>   wroth,
> Bespake him thus: "Thy words have made me rashly to
>   consent
> To that which shortly both of us, I fear me, shall repent.
> Oh, that I might retract my grant! My son, I do protest
> I would deny thee nothing else save this, thy fond request.
> I may dissuade; there lies herein more peril than thou ween,

The things the which thou dost desire of great importance
     been,
More than thy weakness well can wield, a charge (as well
     appears)
Of greater weight than may agree with these thy tender
     years.
Thy state is mortal, weak and frail, **the thing thou dost
     desire**
Is such whereto no mortal man is able to aspire.
Yea, foolish boy, thou dost desire (and all for want of wit)
A greater charge than any god could ever have as yet;
For were there any of them all so overseen and blind
To take upon him this my charge, full quickly should he
     find
That none but I could sit upon the fiery axletree.
No, not even he that rules this waste and endless space we
     see. . . ."

Whatever gods may be

Source: THE GARDEN OF PROSERPINE (Stanza 11)
Author: Algernon Charles Swinburne (1837–1909)
First published: 1866
Type of work: Lyric poem

Context: "The Garden of Proserpine" expresses the reaction of a person tired of striving and seeking for something in life. Indeed, he is weary of the very emotions of living. He longs for death where he will at least be "from hope and fear set free." At the time of death, the speaker will become part of mother earth for which Proserpine is a symbol. Proserpine "waits for all men born." The speaker goes on to give thanks that men are released from the trials of living by the gods, "Whatever gods may be," and return to the earth for eternal sleep, not to be disturbed again.

From too much love of living,
     From hope and fear set free,
We thank with brief thanksgiving
     Whatever gods may be
That no life lives for ever;
That dead men rise up never;
That even the weariest river
     Winds somewhere safe to sea.

Whatever happens at all happens as it should

Source: MEDITATIONS (Book IV, 8)
Author: Marcus Aurelius Antoninus (121–180)
First transcribed: c. 171–173
Type of work: Philosophical essay

Context: The Emperor Marcus Aurelius, a Stoic philosopher, expresses philosophical thoughts in proverb form in his *Meditations*. He reasons that everything in the world happens justly, not only as a result of inevitable consequences, but according to the just deserts of the individual. In the translation of Casaubon the passage reads

Whatsoever doth happen in the world, doth happen justly, and so if thou dost well take heed, thou shalt find it. I say not only in right order by a series of inevitable consequences, but according to justice and as it were by way of equal distribution, according to the true worth of everything. Continue then to take notice of it, as thou hast begun, and whatsoever thou dost, do it not without this proviso, that it be a thing of that nature that a good man (as the word good is properly taken) may do it. This observe carefully in every action.

Whatever is, is in its causes just

Source: OEDIPUS (Act III, 1)
Author: John Dryden (1631–1700) with Nathaniel Lee (1655–1692)
First published: 1679
Type of work: Dramatic tragedy

Context: Leaving the King's Company of actors, whose aging members, he thought, did injustice to his plays, Dryden collaborated with another playwright, Lee, and furnished manuscripts to the Duke's Company. They chose a theme magnificently treated by Sophocles, and, with less skill, by Seneca and Corneille. Dryden's addition of a subplot about the love of Adrastus and Eurydice contributed nothing to the merits or effect of the story of Oedipus and Jocasta. Unlike Sophocles, who kept Oedipus alive for a sequel, Dryden ended his tragedy with the death of the blinded king. Act III, entirely the work of Dryden, contains the magnificent incantation scene and the trial of Adrastus for the murder of Laius, late King of Thebes. Adrastus has falsely confessed, in order to take the blame from Eurydice, daughter of Laius and Jocasta. Into the setting of a sacred grove the blind prophet Tiresias enters, guided by his daughter Manto, and followed by black-clad priests. He replies to Eurydice's expressed hope that some god will protect her with the statement that everything that happens is fated. He says man is too blind to see the scales by which justice is measured and that his short measuring line and sinker cannot plumb the depths of heaven's abyss. He also uses the figure of the scales of justice with its balance bar so high above humans that they cannot see even the length of the chains hanging from either end to hold the balance pans.

TIRESIAS

The gods are just;
But how can finite measure infinite?
Reason! alas, it does not know itself!
Yet man, vain man, would with the short-lined plummet,
Fathom the vast abyss of heavenly justice.
Whatever is, is in its causes just;
Since all things are by fate. But purblind man
Sees but a part o' the chain; the nearest links;
His eyes not carrying to that equal beam,
That poises all above.

Whatever you have, spend less

Source: THE LIFE OF SAMUEL JOHNSON, LL.D. (For 1782)
Author: James Boswell (1740–1795)
First published: 1791
Type of work: Biography

Context: In 1782 Boswell was much of the time in Scotland, away from Dr. Johnson, but Johnson wrote him a series of letters during that time which Boswell uses in his biography of the great man. On December 7, 1782, Johnson wrote from London that he had been ill much of the year and had been busy seeking health, commenting, "I am afraid, however, that health begins, after seventy, and long before, to have a meaning different from that which it had at thirty." Johnson goes on in his letter to complain of not having letters from Boswell, in the querulous tone of an old man, as he is. He asks Boswell, who has inherited his father's estates, in Scotland, to let him know the "history" of Boswell's current life, including such specific items as the number of houses and cows Boswell now owns, the extent of his landholdings, and the agreements with his tenants. In the course of the letter Dr. Johnson offers some advice in management to his friend and biographer:

> Your economy, I suppose, begins now to be settled; your expences are adjusted to your revenue, and all your people in their proper places. Resolve not to be poor: **whatever you have, spend less.** Poverty is a great enemy to human happiness; it certainly destroys liberty, and it makes some virtues impracticable, and others extremely difficult.

1241

When a heroine goes mad, she always goes into white satin

Source: THE CRITIC (Act III, sc. 1)
Author: Richard Brinsley Sheridan (1751–1816)
First published: 1781
Type of work: Dramatic comedy

Context: Sheridan had a brief but at times brilliant career as a comic dramatist. In *The Critic* he is following the tradition of the play within a play technique as a means of satirizing both bombastic tragic drama and dramatic criticism. In the play, Dangle, a theatrical dilettante, and his friend, Sneer, go with their friend Puff, a hack playwrite, to see a rehearsal of a tragedy by the latter. As the rehearsal takes place the commentary of these three constitutes the satire of criticism while the play itself, as a ludicrous bombastic tragedy, satirizes the conventional tragedy of the day. Toward the end of the inner play the action suddenly accelerates as Puff explains it:

PUFF
True—Now enter Tilburnia!

SNEER
Egad, the business comes on quick here.

PUFF
Yes, Sir—now she comes in stark mad in white satin.

SNEER
Why in white satin?

PUFF
O Lord, Sir—**when a heroine goes mad, she always goes into white satin**—don't she Dangle.

DANGLE
Always—it's a rule.

PUFF
Yes—here it is—[*looking at the book.*] "Enter Tilburnia stark mad in white satin, and her confidante stark mad in white linen."
[*Enter* TILBURNIA *and* CONFIDANTE *mad, according to custom.*]

SNEER
But what the deuce, is the confidante to be mad too?

1242

To be sure she is, the confidante is always to do whatever her mistress does; weep when she weeps, smile when she smiles, go mad when she goes mad. . . .

When faith is lost, when honor dies, the man is dead!

Source: ICHABOD (Stanza 8)
Author: John Greenleaf Whittier (1807–1892)
First published: 1850
Type of work: Lyric poem

Context: Whittier wrote that this poem was occasioned by his reading of Daniel Webster's famous Seventh of March Speech in support of the Missouri Compromise on slavery in the United States and the Fugitive Slave Act. Although Whittier was ardent for the cause of the Negroes' freedom from slavery, he wrote that "No partisan or personal enmity" dictated his poem. The title of the poem is indicative of its tone, reminding the reader of Ichabod, in I Samuel, "And she named the child Ichabod, saying, The glory is departed from Israel." The reference is to let the reader know that Whittier felt that Webster had lost all the splendid influence he once had, the influence on men's minds that seemingly was destroyed by this new stand on the extension of Negro slavery. The poem is an excellent piece of the propagandist's art: what answer could be given by Webster to the charges when the poem proclaims his death? Whittier professes to mourn for Webster, rather than ridicule him: "Revile him not, the Tempter hath/ A snare for all;/ And pitying tears, not scorn and wrath,/ Befit his fall!" Whittier calls upon all America to make, in sadness, a long lament for the fallen hero, not to "brand with deeper shame his dim,/ Dishonored brow." Although written upon a specific occasion about a specific man, this poem has become a classic expression of aversion for any once-worshiped political leader whose acts and deeds have caused him to seem alien to his followers:

Of all we loved and honored, naught
    Save power remains;
A fallen angel's pride of thought,
    Still strong in chains.

All else is gone: from those great eyes
    The soul has fled:
When faith is lost, when honor dies,
    The man is dead!

Then pay the reverence of old days
    To his dead fame;

Walk backward, with averted gaze,
And hide the shame!

When Freedom from her mountain height

Source: THE AMERICAN FLAG (Line 1)
Author: Joseph Rodman Drake (1795–1820)
First published: 1836
Type of work: Lyric poem

Context: During his brief life which was ended by tuberculosis, Joseph Rodman Drake published anonymously (with Fitz-Greene Halleck, 1790–1867) *The Croaker Papers* (1819), a group of satirical topical verses which first appeared in the New York *Post*. Drake's other poetry was published posthumously in *The Culprit Fay and Other Poems* (1835). His best-known poems now are his romantically fanciful "Culprit Fay" with its background of Hudson River scenery, and "The American Flag," which is marked by the patriotic rhetoric of a young man proud of his new nation. Drake's friend Halleck wrote the last quatrain of "The American Flag." The first stanza of the poem follows:

> **When Freedom from her mountain height**
>   Unfurled her standard to the air,
> She tore the azure robe of night,
>   And set the stars of glory there.
> She mingled with its gorgeous dyes
> The milky baldric of the skies.
> And striped its pure celestial white
> With streakings of the morning light;
> Then from his mansion in the sun
> She called her eagle bearer down,
> And gave into his mighty hand
>   The symbol of her chosen land.

When he leaves our houses, let us count our spoons

Source: THE LIFE OF SAMUEL JOHNSON, LL.D. (For 1763)
Author: James Boswell (1740–1795)
First published: 1791
Type of work: Biography

Context: On the fourteenth of July, 1763, a Thursday, Boswell spent a quiet, rainy evening at the Miter, a tavern, with Dr. Johnson. By this time the friendship between the two had progressed to the point that Boswell could observe that he felt quite at ease with Johnson, though having

1244

"all possible reverence" for the great man. They talked of many things that evening: Boswell's father's wish that Boswell would become a lawyer, the excellence of rhyme over blank verse in English poetry, the greater ease of taking the negative side in an argument, Johnson's acceptance of a pension of three hundred pounds per annum from the crown, and the desirability of meeting people when traveling. Boswell tells how he mentioned to Johnson "an impudent fellow from Scotland [Boswell was himself a Scot], who affected to be a savage, and railed at all established systems." Johnson comments that such a person is seeking attention and will do anything to draw it to himself, even to tumbling about in a hog-sty. Johnson adds, "But let him alone, never mind him, and he'll soon give it over." Boswell proceeds to observe that this same man maintains that there is no difference or distinction between vice and virtue. This observation draws the following comment from Dr. Johnson:

. . . "Why, Sir, if the fellow does not think as he speaks, he is lying; and I see not what honour he can propose to himself from having the character of a lyar. But if he does really think that there is no distinction between virtue and vice, why, Sir, **when he leaves our houses let us count our spoons.**"

When I give, I give myself

Source: SONG OF MYSELF (Canto 40)
Author: Walt Whitman (1819–1892)
First published: 1855
Type of work: Lyric poem

Context: Walt Whitman first called attention to his new sort of poetry when he published at his own expense the first edition of *Leaves of Grass* in 1855. Just before his death, he arranged the tenth edition. The unrhymed lines of unequal length brought much criticism from readers accustomed to the classical form. But the poet's genius, shining through much of his writing, demanded recognition. An example of his democratic themes and of his descriptions of his outgoing nature is in Canto 40:

Earth, you seem to look for something at my hands,
Say, old top-knot, what do you want?

Man or woman, I might tell how I like you, but cannot,
And might tell what it is in me and what it is in you, but
    cannot,
And might tell that pining I have, that pulse of my nights
    and days.

1245

Behold, I do not give lectures or a little charity,
When I give I give myself.

When I was a child, I spake as a child

Source: I CORINTHIANS 13:11
Author: Paul
First transcribed: c. 54–57
Type of work: Religious epistle

Context: During Paul's second missionary journey he visited Corinth and spent eighteen months there. He began in his customary manner, preaching and arguing Scripture in the synagogue, but was rejected by the Jews; so he went among the Gentiles, to the house of a man named Justus, and preached there. He won many converts and by the time he left Corinth had established a growing church. After he had taken up residence in Ephesus, Paul was confronted by a severe crisis. Corinth was an important trading center with a cosmopolitan population; and among the religions already flourishing there, a number encouraged forms of license at odds with Christian ethics. The city was famous for the vice which permeated it. Though a few of the Christian converts were men of standing in the community, most came from the lower classes and brought pagan moral standards with them. Paul's first letter to the Corinthian congregation, now lost, warned them against loose sexual conduct. The Corinthians replied with a letter asking a number of questions; Paul now learned that their sexual ethics were worse than he had thought, that factions had sprung up in the church, and that his congregation was flouting his authority. At this point Paul wrote I Corinthians—a blistering rebuke censuring the congregation for its lapses from high standards. He begins by deploring their factiousness and calling for unity, implying that those doing the preaching are too superficially wise. Human wisdom, beside that of God, is nothing; and those who are swollen with their own wisdom are mere fools. Paul speaks of the holiness of the minister's calling: it is not for self-aggrandizement. He reproves them for fornication and incest, and for many other kinds of questionable behavior. He then describes spiritual gifts and love, and in Chapter 13 urges them to achieve spiritual maturity:

Though I speak with the tongues of men and of angels, and have not charity, I am become as sounding brass, or a tinkling cymbal.

And though I have the gift of prophecy, and understand all mysteries, and all knowledge; and though I have all faith, so that I could remove mountains, and have not charity, I am nothing.

And though I bestow all my goods to feed the poor, and though I give my body to be burned, and I have not charity, it profiteth

1246

me nothing.

Charity suffereth long, and is kind; charity envieth not; charity vaunteth not itself, is not puffed up,

Doth not behave itself unseemly, seeketh not her own, is not easily provoked, thinketh no evil;

Rejoiceth not in iniquity, but rejoiceth in the truth;

Beareth all things, believeth all things, hopeth all things, endureth all things.

Charity never faileth: but whether there be prophecies, they shall fail; whether there be tongues, they shall cease; whether there be knowledge, it shall vanish away.

For we know in part, and we prophesy in part.

But when that which is perfect is come, then that which is in part shall be done away.

When I was a child, I spake as a child, I understood as a child, I thought as a child: but when I became a man, I put away childish things.

When, in disgrace with Fortune and men's eyes

Source: SONNET 29 (Line 1)
Author: William Shakespeare (1564–1616)
First published: 1609
Type of work: Sonnet

Context: When, says the poet, he despairs, feeling sorry for himself and envying others, he recalls the love of his friend, and his spirit soars just as the lark breaks into song at the dawn of day. The entire sonnet follows:

> **When, in disgrace with Fortune and men's eyes,**
> I all alone beweep my outcast state,
> And trouble deaf heaven with my bootless cries,
> And look upon myself and curse my fate,
> Wishing me like to one more rich in hope,
> Featur'd like him, like him with friends possess'd,
> Desiring this man's art, and that man's scope,
> With what I most enjoy contented least;
> Yet in these thoughts myself almost despising,
> Haply I think on thee, and then my state,
> Like to the lark at break of day arising
> From sullen earth, sings hymns at heaven's gate;
>   For thy sweet love remember'd such wealth brings,
>   That then I scorn to change my state with kings.

When Music, heavenly maid, was young

Source: THE PASSIONS, AN ODE FOR MUSIC (Line 1)
Author: William Collins (1721–1759)
First published: 1746
Type of work: Ode

Context: Collins was a gifted minor poet whose output was quite small but of unusually high quality. His life was brief and much of it was desperately unhappy. Educated at Oxford, he settled in London and became a literary hack writer, but he was indolent and his health was bad; he failed to accomplish most of the projects he undertook. He was deeply in debt much of the time. When his odes, on which his poetical reputation rests, were first published, they attracted no attention and sold slowly. Collins was bitterly disappointed and burned the unsold copies. During his last years his health grew increasingly worse, and his mind was affected; he was confined for a time in an asylum. In his poetry he uses a number of conventional mannerisms characteristic of the eighteenth century—neoclassic effects and an abundance of personified abstractions. However, his verses are notable for subtle rhythms, imaginative phrases, and a delicate balance between classic restraint and poetic sentiment. They are now considered permanent masterpieces of lyric verse. In *The Passions*, Collins personifies the various passions and describes the effect which music (also personified) has on them. Music, very young and beautiful, has been playing on various instruments; and the Passions, much swayed by the sounds produced, decide to try out her instruments themselves. Each produces a result of supernatural power in keeping with his own characteristics: Fear, Anger, Despair, Hope, Revenge, Pity, Melancholy, and a number of others all portray themselves in sound. The ode ends with the poet's sorrow that music in his own day has lost the heavenly fire that it had when the world was young. The first portion of the poem describes Music and the Passions' reaction to her:

> **When Music, heavenly maid, was young,**
> While yet in early Greece she sung,
> The Passions oft, to hear her shell,
> Thronged around her magic cell,
> Exulting, trembling, raging, fainting,
> Possest beyond the Muse's painting:
> By turns they felt the glowing mind
> Disturbed, delighted, raised, refined;
> Till once, 'tis said, when all were fired,
> Filled with fury, rapt, inspired,
> From the supporting myrtles round
> They snatched her instruments of sound;
> And, as they oft had heard apart
> Sweet lessons of her forceful art,

Each (for Madness ruled the hour)
Would prove his own expressive power. . . .

When Rome falls—the World

Source: CHILDE HAROLD'S PILGRIMAGE (Canto IV, stanza 145)
Author: George Gordon, Lord Byron (1788–1824)
First published: 1818 (Canto IV)
Type of work: Narrative poem

Context: Changing his style of narrative, from the thoughts of its typical Byronic hero, Harold, to the personal reactions of the poet himself, Byron continued while living in Venice to work on the final canto of the travel poem that he had begun publishing in 1812. He writes of the great authors of old Italy, Petrarch, and Dante the "Bard of Hell," and of Ariosto, the "Bard of Chivalry." How many enemies have overrun the country, leaving many ruins never rebuilt! Byron shows his thorough familiarity with Italy, its history and its literature, by references that for the average reader require footnotes. Speaking of Ariosto, he is reminded how the iron laurels on the bust melted when struck by lightning while the poet's remains were being moved to the Ferrara Library. He calls the city of Florence ungrateful for not providing burial for some of her most distinguished citizens. Many of the poetic references are more interesting, however, to a historian than to a lover of poetry. Coming to a consideration of Rome, Byron calls it "My country! City of the soul," and in another stanza, "Niobe of Nations," after the Queen of Thebes whose scorn of a goddess with only two children, while Niobe had fourteen, caused the gods to kill all of them and leave her petrified, weeping for them. So Rome is bereft of her children. Its sepulchers have been plundered by barbarians, floods, and fire, and what has been called "The Eternal City," has suffered from the destructive hand of time. Byron comments on the destruction of one tyrant by another, and laments: "Can Freedom find no champion here such as Columbia saw arise in George Washington?" The efforts of France to achieve freedom have ended in a Saturnalia of blood. Everywhere he sees the sequence: Freedom, glory, and then corruption and barbarism. However, with Rome, each period of degradation has been followed by an upsurge of life. Rome *is* Eternal. Time's scythe and tyrants' rods have failed to bring it down. And the Coliseum is proof of that fact. In the phrase "While stands the Coliseum, Rome shall stand," Bryon is quoting a sentence from *The History of the Decline and Fall of the Roman Empire* (1776–1788) by Edward Gibbon (1737–1797), which the English historian found in reports by Anglo-Saxon pilgrims about the end of the seventh century. Gibbon used it to prove that at that time the edifice was still entire and not the ruins seen by tourists today.

1249

"While stands the Coliseum, Rome shall stand;
When falls the Coliseum, Rome shall fall;
And **when Rome falls—the World.**" From our own land
Thus spake the pilgrims o'er this mighty wall
In Saxon times, which we are wont to call
Ancient; and these three mortal things are still
On their foundations, and unalter'd all;
Rome and her Ruins past Redemption's skill,
The World the same wide den—of thieves, or what ye will.

When the fight begins within himself,
a man's worth something

Source: BISHOP BLOUGRAM'S APOLOGY (Lines 693–694)
Author: Robert Browning (1812–1889)
First published: 1855
Type of work: Dramatic monologue

Context: As Bishop Blougram and Gigadibs discuss the problem of faith and doubt, it becomes clear that what the bishop has to say is an apologia for his own life and attitudes. The bishop's life is one of faith diversified by doubt, which he feels is better than that of Gigadibs which is one of doubt diversified by faith. The bishop says he cannot help it if he seems out of step with his age; it is historical accident that has placed him where he is. As his argument develops, the bishop creates a deliberate ambiguity about his ideas. In his attack on Gigadibs' philosophy, the bishop believes "say, half he spoke." At the close of his argument he hints at a deeper faith that will not fail him: "if ground should break away/ I take my stand on, there's a firmer yet/ Beneath it." The bishop emphasizes to Gigadibs that doubt is a vital element in belief:

> With me, faith means perpetual unbelief
> Kept quiet like the snake 'neath Michael's foot
> Who stands calm just because he feels it writhe.
>   .   .   .
> "Leave it in peace!" advise the simple folk:
> Make it aware of peace by itching-fits,
> Say I—let doubt occasion still more faith!
>   .   .   .
> No, **when the fight begins within himself,
> A man's worth something.** God stoops o'er his head,
> Satan looks up between his feet—both tug—
> He's left, himself, i' the middle: the soul wakes
> And grows. . . .

1250

When the liquor's out, why clink the cannikin?

Source: THE FLIGHT OF THE DUCHESS (Line 788)
Author: Robert Browning (1812–1889)
First published: 1845
Type of work: Dramatic monologue

Context: Many of Browning's memorable characters live through the vitriolic intensity of their hate—characters to whom he gave life with astonishing passion such as the monk who detests Brother Lawrence in "Soliloquy of the Spanish Cloister" or the Duke of Ferrara in "My Last Duchess." Another such character is the duke in "The Flight of the Duchess," who—weaned on pride and ostentation and controlled by his mother —rules with the hauteur of a lord of the Middle Ages. " 'Twas not for the joy's self, but the joy of his showing it,/ Nor for the pride's self, but the pride of our seeing it." For the sake of custom he takes a wife, a frail and beautiful creature destined to be, not loved, but on display. The poetic narrative, related by an aged huntsman thirty years after the event, describes the mysterious manner in which the duchess escapes from her tyrannical husband. While the duke rides with a hunting party which she has refused to join, he sends to her a gipsy witch to terrify her by telling her fortune in ominous guise. The gipsy, instead, takes pity on the disconsolate lady and bewitches her attendants so that the two of them might escape from the castle. The duke and his mother are furious, of course, but, as the old huntsman says, once a deed is done, it cannot be recalled:

> **When the liquor's out why clink the cannikin?**
> I did think to describe you the panic in
> The redoubtable breast of our master the mannikin,
> And what was the pitch of his mother's yellowness,
> How she turned as a shark to snap the spare-rib
> Clean off, sailors say, from a pearl-diving Carib,
> When she heard, what she called the flight of the feloness
> —But it seems such child's play,
> What they said and did with the lady away!
> And to dance on, when we've lost the music,
> Always made me—and no doubt makes you—sick.

When we build, let us think we build forever

Source: THE SEVEN LAMPS OF ARCHITECTURE (Chapter 6, "The Lamp of Memory," section 10)
Author: John Ruskin (1819–1900)
First published: 1849
Type of work: Aesthetic criticism

Context: John Ruskin, the indefatigable prophet of Victorian England, devoted the early part of his life to describing the moral perception of beauty in both art and architecture. His *Modern Painters* is a manifesto proclaiming the indivisibility of sound character and artistic creativity. *The Stones of Venice* advocates the supremacy of the Gothic to Renaissance architecture because the Gothic age reflected a stronger Christian faith and because it allowed in its architecture a greater freedom for the craftsman's apprehension and expression of beauty. In *The Seven Lamps of Architecture* he describes as morally inseparable from the true architect the virtues of Sacrifice, Truth, Power, Beauty, Memory, and Obedience. While many of his judgments have long since been challenged, certainly he was a leading influence in awakening the people to the vital meaning of all forms of artistic expression as an ennobling faculty which raises the spirit and induces a longing for higher things. And his basic principle is firm: in architecture, as in the other fine arts, the final test of the excellence of the work is the spirit of which it is an expression and of which it gives evidence in its design and execution. That design must be firm, durable, and finely wrought:

> . . . Every human action gains in honour, in grace, in all true magnificence, by its regard to things that are to come . . . Therefore, **when we build, let us think we build forever.** Let it not be for present delight, nor for present use alone. . . . For, indeed, the greatest glory of a building is not in its stones or in its gold. Its glory is in its age, and in that deep sense of voicefulness, of stern watching, of mysterious sympathy, nay, even of approval or condemnation, which we feel in walls which have long been washed by the passing waves of humanity. It is in their lasting witness against men, in their quiet contrast with the transitional character of all things, . . . that we are to look for the real light, and colour, and preciousness of architecture; . . .

When we think we lead, we are most led

Source: THE TWO FOSCARI (Act II, sc. i, l. 361)
Author: George Gordon, Lord Byron (1788–1824)
First published: 1821
Type of work: Historical tragedy

Context: Lord Byron had lived a dramatic life; he had established a reputation as a poet; and so he decided to attempt some poetic drama, beginning with *Manfred*, in racy blank verse. However, it would be madness to attempt a presentation of his dramas on the stage. Only one such attempt is recorded. Like a number of other major poets of the nineteenth century, without any knowledge of stage technique or thought of their adaptability to the theater, he turned out several closet dramas, as they were called because they were meant to be read in seclusion. The year 1821 saw the publication of four such plays. He was living in Italy and had established a more or less permanent relationship with the Countess Teresa Guiccioli, with her husband's consent. She remained his acknowledged mistress for the rest of his life. He was dividing his time among Pisa, Genoa, and Venice. Naturally he was interested in Italian history, and saw in the story of the doges, or rulers of Venice, dramatic material for a historical tragedy. Francesco Foscari (1372?–1457) ruled Venice from 1423 until his death. His life was embittered by his only surviving son, Giacopo. Byron calls them Francis and Jacopo. The politically active son was tried and banished in 1445 for receiving bribes from candidates for state offices. Pardoned, he was next banished in 1450 for his share in the assassination of one of the ten ruling Councilmen. Six years later he became involved in treasonable correspondence with enemies of Venice. Partly because of the father's intercession for Jacopo, the aged doge was deposed (Oct. 24, 1457). He died a week later. These are the circumstances that Byron wove into his play, classical in its observation of the unity of time. The pathos of the elderly father, imploring the Council to permit his only son to

return, is good theater, as is the action of The Ten in granting the request, since the doge cannot properly attend to the affairs of state as long as he is distracted by worry about his son. Byron was being a dramatist, so he should not be criticized for dramatic license in bringing in the Bridge of Sighs, between the doge's palace and the dungeon, some years before it was actually constructed. One can also overlook his killing of Old Foscari the day he was deposed, instead of a week later, as history records. Act II, set in the Doge's Palace, shows the aged ruler too old to see to dip his pen and too shaky to sign a treaty. But the senator with him remembers the great man's contributions during thirty-four years to the security and glory of Venice. Then Marina, wife of Jacopo, enters, complaining that the Council will not permit her to visit her husband in the dungeon. She angrily denounces the doge for not doing something to save his son. At that moment, a messenger brings word that a meeting of the Council has decided on banishment instead of execution for the traitor. Instead of being satisfied, Marina breaks into a violent attack on Venice, its rulers, its courts, and the justice they hand out. In his lengthy reply, Francis Foscari declares that rulers are only mortal and subject to fate.

> So, we are slaves,
> The greatest as the meanest—nothing rests
> Upon our will; the will itself no less
> Depends upon a straw than on a storm;
> **And when we think we lead, we are most led,**
> And still towards death, a thing which comes as much
> Without our act or choice as birth, so that
> Methinks we must have sinn'd in some old world,
> And *this* is hell; the best is, that it is not
> Eternal.

1253

When you have nothing to say, say nothing

Source: LACON (Volume I, No. 183)
Author: Charles Caleb Colton (1780?–1832)
First published: 1820
Type of work: Aphoristic commentary

Context: The Spartans who lived in Laconia, Greece, were legendary for their simplicity. Their Council turned down the plea of Athens for help against a foreign invader because it came in the form of an hour-long oration. "Those people talk too much," was their decision. And the threat of Philip of Macedon (382–333 B.C.), "If I enter Laconia, I shall level Lacedaemon to the ground," was answered by the laconic magistrates in a single word: "If." Brevity, the soul of wit, has also been much admired in England. The editor of *Punch* uttered a famous admonition: "To those thinking about marriage—DON'T." Charles C. Colton, a student at Cambridge University and later canon of Salisbury, could be verbose, as in his *Plain and Authentic Narrative of the Sampford Ghost* (1810), and as he threatened to be when starting *Hypocrisy, a Satire in Three Books* (1812), but he caught himself in time and completed only one of the volumes. He was inspired by the publication of *Materials for Thinking* (1812) by William Burdon (1764–1818) to make use of his own reading of Bacon's *Essays* and his musings as a famous fisherman, to assemble a collection of edifying aphorisms to which he gave the title *Lacon* because of the conciseness of its contents. It was a small book that could be tucked into a pocket. Its subtitle, "Many things in few words addressed to those who think," increased its sale to would-be intellectuals so that six editions were sold out by the end of 1821. By 1824 it had enjoyed nineteen editions. A New York publisher, S. Marks, that year issued a reprint of the eighth edition. Colton assembled a second volume which, unfortunately, suffered from the weaknesses of sequels. However, both volumes have been reprinted, both together in 1866. Here is a sampling:

CLXXXII

Those missionaries who embark for India, like some other reformers, begin at the wrong end. They ought first to convert to *practical* christianity, those of their own countrymen who have crossed the Pacific, on a very different mission, to acquire money by every kind of rapine abroad, in order to squander it in every kind of revelry at home. But example is more powerful than precept, and the poor Hindoo is not slow in discovering how very unlike the Christians he sees, are to that christianity of which he hears.

CLXXXIII

When you have nothing to say, say nothing; a weak defence strengthens your opponent, and silence is less injurious than a bad reply.

We know the effects of many things, but the causes of few; experience, therefore, is a surer guide than imagination, and inquiry than conjecture. But those physical difficulties which you cannot account for, be very slow to arraign, for he that would be wiser than nature, would be wiser than God.

Where are the songs of Spring?

Source: TO AUTUMN (Line 23)
Author: John Keats (1795–1821)
First published: 1820
Type of work: Lyric poem

Context: Keats hails autumn as the season of fruitfulness, when the grapes that grow on the cottage wall are ripe and the apple trees are bent with their load; the gourds are swollen and the hazelnut shells are filled with sweet kernels; late-blooming flowers provide nectar for the bees, whose hives are overflowing with honey. Amidst all this plenty, Autumn himself is to be seen, perhaps on a granary floor or sound asleep on a half-reaped furrow; some-times he is by a brook and at other times by an oozing cider press. And at this time, where are the songs of Spring? Who thinks of spring when the land is overflowing with its products? The songs should be dismissed from the mind, as they are unseasonable; Autumn, too, has his melodies: the hum of gnats along the river, the bleating of full-grown lambs, the chirp of the hedge crickets, and the soft whistle of the robin.

> **Where are the songs of Spring?** Ay, where are they?
>   Think not of them, thou hast thy music too,—
> While barred clouds bloom the soft-dying day,
>   And touch the stubble-plains with rosy hue;
> Then in a wailful choir the small gnats mourn
>   Among the river sallows, borne aloft
>   Or sinking as the light wind lives or dies;
> And full-grown lambs loud bleat from hilly bourn;
>   Hedge-crickets sing; and now with treble soft
> The red-breast whistles from a garden-croft;
>   And gathering swallows twitter in the skies.

Where freedom broadens slowly down

Source: YOU ASK ME WHY, THO' ILL AT EASE (Stanza 3)
Author: Alfred, Lord Tennyson (1809–1892)
First published: 1842
Type of work: Lyric poem

Context: Tennyson was a patriot; he loved his country. He was nonetheless aware of the social ills of his day and often cried out against them. Doubtless there were times, since there was a melancholy side to his nature, when he saw enough of injustice to wish that he might abandon the nation of his birth. There are hints of this in *Locksley Hall* and in other poems. Part of it is of course a convention of the Romantic era. But his sympathy for others was undoubtedly sincere. Although he reacted to the spectacle of human suffering, Tennyson realized that he could not escape his feelings by running away from them; besides, he was part of an age of progress and was to some extent fascinated by it. He was not by nature a crusader; social protest did not really suit his temperament and artistry. However keenly he may have felt the inequities he saw and often protested, he was at heart reasonably content with his time. Present technical progress and, most of all, the noble and legendary history of the past: these were his real interests. He was essentially a maker of beauty, and to his critics his rage does not quite ring true. To them it seems as though he felt it his duty to lead popular thought when song was his natural preference. In the following poem, however, he speaks plainly and quietly on the subject, and there is no effect of mere rhetoric:

You ask me why, tho' ill at ease,
   Within this region I subsist,
   Whose spirits falter in the mist,
And languish for the purple seas.

It is the land that freemen till,
   That sober-suited Freedom chose,
   The land, where girt with friends or foes
A man may speak the thing he will;

A land of settled government,
   A land of just and old renown,
   Where Freedom broadens slowly down
From precedent to precedent;

Where faction seldom gathers head,
   But, by degrees to fullness wrought,
   The strength of some diffusive thought
Hath time and space to work and spread.

Should banded unions persecute
   Opinion, and induce a time
   When single thought is civil crime,
And individual freedom mute;

Tho' Power should make from land to land
   The name of Britain trebly great—
   Tho' every channel of the State
Should fill and choke with golden sand—

1256

Yet waft me from the harbour-mouth,
Wild wind! I seek a warmer sky,
And I will see before I die
The palms and temples of the South.

Where my heart lies, let my brain lie also

Source: ONE WORD MORE (XIV, l. 142)
Author: Robert Browning (1812–1889)
First published: 1855
Type of work: Dedicatory epilogue

Context: Browning wrote this poem as an epilogue to dedicate a volume of poetry to Elizabeth Browning, his wife. In it he discusses the importance of a private existence for the artist apart from his public personage: "God be thanked, the meanest of his creatures/ Boasts two soul-sides, one to face the world with,/ One to show a woman when he loves her!" The poet wishes he could turn to a new medium to express his love as did Dante, who painted to honor Beatrice, or as did Rafael, who wrote a century of sonnets for his love. These evidences of love are more precious to other lovers than are all the masterpieces that the artists created in their own fields. An artist wishes, at least once, to be only a man and to be judged for the joy of his love and not by the critical standards applicable to his public performance. Heaven-sent gifts bring with them commitments and responsibilities that the poet would this once eschew. But the poet concludes that he will never paint pictures, carve statues, or compose music for his love. Therefore, this once, he will make "a strange art of the familiar" by writing this poem in unrhymed trochaic pentameter in order to make his tribute distinctive for the occasion. Putting aside the dramatic monologue, he says:

Let me speak, this once in my true person,
Not as Lippo, Roland, or Andrea,
Though the fruit of speech be just this sentence:
Pray you, look on these my men and women,
Take and keep my fifty poems finished;
Where my heart lies, let my brain lie also!
Poor the speech; be how I speak, for all things!

Where mystery begins, religion ends

Source: A VINDICATION OF NATURAL SOCIETY
Author: Edmund Burke (1729–1797)
First published: 1756
Type of work: Essay

Context: Bolingbroke, an important political writer of the early eighteenth century, attacked revealed religion frequently and with vigor, proposing Deism in its place. When he died about the middle of the century, he left some posthumous writings in the same vein, which were published with great acclaim, especially for their inimitable style. Burke, who held great reverence for religious tradition, responded with this heavily ironic tract in which he imitated perfectly the style of Bolingbroke and showed that the same arguments that had been turned against revealed religion might just as easily be applied to civilized, or political, society:

> . . . In a state of nature, it is true that a man of superior force may beat or rob me; but then it is true, that I am at full liberty to defend myself, or make reprisal by surprise or by cunning, or by any other way in which I may be superior to him. But in political society, a rich man may rob me in another way. I cannot defend myself; for money is the only weapon with which we are allowed to fight. And if I attempt to avenge myself the whole force of that society is ready to complete my ruin.
>
> A good parson once said, that **where mystery begins, religion ends.** Cannot I say, as truly at least, of human laws, that where mystery begins, justice ends? It is hard to say, whether the doctors of law or divinity have made the greatest advances in the lucrative business of mystery.

Where wilt thou find their like again?

Source: MARMION (Introduction to Canto I, stanza 11)
Author: Sir Walter Scott (1771–1832)
First published: 1808
Type of work: Narrative poem

Context: In an Introduction to each canto, that had nothing to do with the mood of the main poem, Scott addresses various friends and discusses his thoughts and activities. The Introduction to the First Canto bears the name of William Stewart Rose, Esq. Perhaps Scott's description of the chill and drear November sky and the signs of dead Nature reminds him of some of England's great men who have died recently, especially William Pitt the Younger (1759–1806) and Charles James Fox (1749–1806). Even though rivals, they fought against Europe to preserve Britain and were joined in reputation, as now in death.

. . .

Genius and taste and talent gone,
Forever tombed beneath the stone
Where—taming thought to human pride!—
The mighty chiefs sleep side by side.

1258

Drop upon Fox's grave the tear,
'T will trickle to his rival's bier.
O'er Pitt's the mournful requiem sound,
And Fox's shall the notes rebound.
The solemn echo seems to cry,—
"Here let their discord with them die.
Speak not for those a separate doom
Whom Fate made brothers in the tomb;
But search the land, of living men,
Where wilt thou find their like again?"

A whiff of grapeshot

Source: THE FRENCH REVOLUTION (Part I, Book V, chapter 3)
Author: Thomas Carlyle (1795–1881)
First published: 1837
Type of work: History

Context: The French Revolution might have been avoided had those in power been alert to the needs of the country and moved toward policies of reform. However, they waited too long. France was wealthy, but its methods of taxation placed all the burden on those least able to pay— the lower and middle classes. This situation was enough to start a movement that would destroy an already shaky equilibrium. An example had just been set for the French people by the American colonists. By the spring of 1789 conflict seemed imminent. Louis XVI called a general assembly on May 5 because of the hopeless financial situation, but disputes arose among the three groups represented —the nobility, the clergy, and the third estate. This last, the free bourgeoisie, now claimed power equal to that of the other two. The meeting came to nothing, and on June 17 representatives of the third estate took the title of National Assembly and invited the other groups to meet with them; they were shortly to assume all power in France. The king reacted to this spirit of rebellion among the lower classes in ways calculated to infuriate them further and in June decided to bring foreign troops with cannon into Paris. The cannon would be loaded with either grapeshot or canister to disperse the mobs. Grapeshot is a cluster of small cannon-balls wired together, which scatter on firing; canister is another scattering charge which resembles a tin can full of ball bearings. Broglie, Minister of War, was confident of quelling the revolt; neither he nor the others among the ruling classes comprehended the extent of this spirit of open rebellion. Nor did they realize that the soldiers' sympathies lay with the common people. Carlyle's hectic, staccato prose vividly depicts the tension of those days:

. . . the hungry food-year, which runs from August to August, is getting older; becoming more and more a famine-year! With 'meal-husks and boiled grass,' Brigands may actually collect; and in crowds, at farm and mansion, howl angrily, *Food! Food!* It is in vain to send soldiers against them: at sight of soldiers they disperse, they vanish as under ground; then directly reassemble elsewhere for new tumult and plunder. . . . A universal hubbub there, as of dissolving worlds. . . . To the calmest man it is becoming too plain that battle is inevitable.

Inevitable, silently nod Messeigneurs and Broglie: Inevitable and brief! . . . those cannon of ours stand duly levelled; those troops are here. . . . The Parisians resist? scornfully cry Messeigneurs. As a meal-mob may! They have sat quiet, these five generations, submitting to all. Their Mercier declared, in these very years, that a Parisian revolt was henceforth 'impossible.' Stand by the royal Declaration of the Twenty-third of June. The Nobles of France, valorous, chivalrous as of old, will rally round us with one heart;—and as for this which you call Third Estate, and which we call *canaille* of unwashed Sansculottes, of Patelins, Scribblers, factious Spouters,—brave Broglie, 'with **a whiff of grapeshot** (*salve de canons*),' if need be, will give quick account of it. . . .

While listening senates hang upon thy tongue

Source: THE SEASONS: AUTUMN (Line 15)
Author: James Thomson (1700–1748)
First published: 1730
Type of work: Nature poem

Context: The completion of "Autumn" permitted publication of all four parts of *The Seasons* together, in an edition from which many passages were deleted in the second edition of 1744. One critic referred to its contents as "a volume on which reason bestows as many beauties as imagination." Part III of *The Seasons*, devoted to Autumn, is dedicated to Arthur Onslow, who was speaker of the British House of Commons from 1728 to 1761. After describing the fields and vineyards ready for harvest, Thomson comments on the barbarity of hunting. Then he further described the migrating birds, the fading leaves, and finally the joys of a philosophical life in the country. The Dorians of early Greece were supposed to have invented the choral lyric. Pan, one of their agricultural gods, invented the shepherd's pipe, made of reeds. "Front" is, of course, "forehead."

Crown'd with the sickle and the wheaten sheaf,
While Autumn, nodding o'er the yellow plain,
Comes jovial on, the Doric reed once more,
Well pleased, I tune. Whate'er the wintry Frost,
Nitrous, prepared; the various blossom'd Spring
Put in white promise forth; and summer-suns

1260

Concocted strong, rush boundless now to view,
Full, perfect all, and swell my glorious theme.
　　Onslow! the Muse, ambitious of thy name,
To grace, inspire, and dignify her song,
Would from the public voice thy gentle ear
A while engage. Thy noble cares she knows,
The patriotic virtues that distend thy thought,
Spread on thy front, and in thy bosom glow;
While listening senates hang upon thy tongue,
Devolving through the maze of eloquence
A roll of periods, sweeter than her song.

Whispering "I will never consent,"—consented

Source: DON JUAN (Canto I, stanza 117)
Author: George Gordon, Lord Byron (1788–1824)
First published: 1819 (Cantos I–II)
Type of work: Satiric poem

Context: Instead of following the usual custom of starting to tell a story "in medias res," that is, in the middle of exciting events, Byron decided to start with the childhood of his hero. He tells of young Juan's boyhood beside the waters of the Guadalquivir (which he rhymes with "river"). The Spanish original introduces its anti-hero in an inn of Seville after his year of roistering, love-making, and dueling in Italy. Chiefly, however, the first canto of Byron's poem pokes ridicule at the feminine cult of knowledge, since Juan's mother, Inez, seeks to know everything. Her perfection makes her insipid; so her husband, Don Jóse, goes "plucking various fruit without her leave," until he dies. Juan's mother takes over his education with books "expurgated by learned men," who leave out all the grosser parts but collect them into an appendix. Told in the first person by the narrator, the beginning informs the reader of Juan's training in fencing, riding, and shooting. But the boy does not need training when he finds himself alone one day with his mother's young friend, Donna Julia, married to an elderly husband. In a flippant style, the poet recounts Juan's growing realization of Julia's charms. The boy is described wandering in self-communion, like Wordsworth beside "glassy brooks," and turning like Coleridge into a metaphysician, staying away from home so long that he misses his dinner. Finally on the sixth of June ("I like to be particular in dates"), at about six-thirty, he and Julia are sitting in her bower. Perhaps she meant to "clasp his fingers in a pure Platonic squeeze," as she thinks about her husband Don Alfonso's fifty years, and resolves to remain true to him. The poet pauses to devote a stanza to the "confounded fantasies" of Plato, and his responsibility for more immoral conduct than all the poets and romancers. Julia protests, but perhaps, as in Act III of *Hamlet*, "The lady doth protest too much, methinks." And as Byron goes on:

1261

And Julia's voice was lost, except in sighs,
   Until too late for useful conversation;
The tears were gushing from her gentle eyes,
   I wish, indeed, they had not had occasion;
But who, alas! can love, and then be wise?
   Not that remorse did not oppose temptation;
A little still she strove, and much repented,
And **whispering, "I will ne'er consent"—consented.**

Whispering tongues can poison truth

Source: CHRISTABEL (Part II, l. 409)
Author: Samuel Taylor Coleridge (1772–1834)
First published: 1816
Type of work: Narrative poem

Context: The Lady Christabel, having resorted to a wood at midnight to pray for her absent love, discovers at the base of a tree the beautiful Geraldine, apparently totally exhausted from having been mysteriously abducted by five men who forced her to ride at great speed for a long time. As Christabel conducts Geraldine to her bedchamber they pass a sleeping dog that growls. In the chamber Geraldine mentions that she wishes Christabel's mother were present. A moment later Geraldine, apparently looking at empty air, commands the mother to leave, as this hour had been given to Geraldine. Christabel thinks that the ghastly ride has unsettled Geraldine's wits. When, however, Geraldine prepares for bed she uncovers her breast and side, which are such horrifying sights that no one could tell of them. She draws Christabel to her breast, which is icy cold, and while the girl is in her arms she lays a spell on her that will prevent her from telling any more about the whole episode than the discovery of Geraldine in the woods. The next day Christabel conducts Geraldine to her father, the Baron Sir Leoline; he listens to Geraldine's story and becomes pale when he hears that her father is Lord Roland de Vaux of Tryermaine. Sir Leoline and Lord Roland had been fast friends in youth, but someone had said something to make them quarrel so bitterly that they had long ago parted.

But when he heard the lady's tale,
And when she told her father's name,
Why waxed Sir Leoline so pale,
Murmuring o'er the name again,
Lord Roland de Vaux of Tryermaine?

Alas! they had been friends in youth;
But **whispering tongues can poison truth;**
And constancy lives in realms above;
And life is thorny; and youth is vain;

And to be wroth with one we love
Doth work like madness in the brain.
And thus it chanced, as I divine,
With Roland and Sir Leoline.

Whistle and she'll come to you

Source: WIT WITHOUT MONEY (Act IV, sc. i)
Authors: Francis Beaumont (1585?–1616) and John Fletcher (1579–1625)
First published: 1639
Type of work: Dramatic comedy

Context: Isabel, younger sister of the rich Widow, sees young Francisco and falls in love with him. Francisco's elder brother, Valentine, has spent all of his own money and has also squandered Francisco's annuity, leaving him penniless. Isabel has a man present Francisco with a bag of money, and for the time he is ignorant of the identity of the real donor. When the Widow discovers that Isabel has fallen in love with Francisco, she moves to block the romance by taking her household out of the city into the country. When preparations for the move are almost completed, the Widow meets Valentine, who has forced his way into the house. Instantly she falls in love with him and countermands the orders to vacate her residence. After Valentine leaves, Francisco appears, having learned that it was Isabel who sent him the money; he is accompanied by his friend Lance, a falconer who uses the language of falconry, to thank her for her gift. Because her sister, the Widow, is present during the interview, she denies having given him anything and treats him with contempt. She, however, presents him with a valuable ring which she says he has dropped. He is about to vow that he has done no such thing, but Isabel will not listen to him:

FRANCISCO

I vow—

ISABEL

Vow me no vows. He that dares do this has bred himself to boldness, to forswear, too. There, take your gewgaw. You are too much pampered, and I repeat my part; as you grow older, grow wiser, if you can. And so farewell, sir. [*Exeunt* ISABEL *and* LUCE.]

LANCE

Grow wiser, if you can? She has put it to you. 'Tis a rich ring. Did you drop it?

FRANCISCO

Never; ne'er saw it afore, Lance.

1263

Thereby hangs a tail, then. What slight she makes to catch herself!
Look up, sir; you cannot lose her if you would. How daintily she
flies upon the lure, and cunningly she makes her stoop. **Whistle
and she'll come to you.**

FRANCISCO
I would I were so happy.

A white bird—his own soul was like that

Source: MARIUS THE EPICUREAN (Part I, chapter 2)
Author: Walter Pater (1839–1894)
First published: 1885
Type of work: Novel

Context: Marius, a young Roman of the second century A.D.—who is finally to die as a Christian—lives with his widowed mother on his family estate, White-nights, in northern Italy. A meditative and devout boy, he takes pleasure in observing the rites of Roman belief, "the religion of Numa," with its many observances centered about the family funeral urn —"a tiny, delicately carved marble house, still white and fair, in the fam-ily-chapel, wreathed always with the richest flowers of the garden." Influ-enced by his mother's devotion to the memory of her dead husband, Marius develops a reverence for maternity and, in addition, "an urbane and fem-inine refinement" of temperament himself. He so loves the country life that in the harsh winters, when the flocks suffer as people do from the rigors of nature, he feels a sympathy for all creatures:

. . . It was a feeling which had in it something of religious veneration for life as such—for that mysterious essence which man is powerless to create in even the feeblest degree. One by one, at the desire of his mother, the lad broke down his cherished traps and springs for the hungry wild birds on the salt marsh. **A white bird,** she told him once, looking at him gravely, a bird which he must carry in his bosom across a crowded public place—**his own soul was like that!** Would it reach the hands of his good genius on the opposite side, unruffled and unsoiled? . . .

The white flower of a blameless life

Source: IDYLLS OF THE KING ("Dedication," Line 24)
Author: Alfred, Lord Tennyson (1809–1892)
First published: (with "Dedication") 1862
Type of work: Narrative poem

Context: Tennyson's version of the Arthurian legends is dedicated to the memory of Prince Albert, Consort of Queen Victoria. The *Idylls of the King,* a metrical romance, was published over a long period of time (from 1859 to 1885); the dedication was added in 1862, following Albert's death in December, 1861. That a cycle of poems dealing with the noble days of chivalry, in which knightly purity is emphasized, should be dedicated to Albert's memory is appropriate. Born in 1819, Albert was educated at Bonn; he studied the political and natural sciences, and also music and painting. He married Queen Victoria in 1840; they were an unusually devoted couple, and their marriage was a happy one. Albert took his duties as a public figure with great seriousness; he was always deeply and actively interested in the welfare of the English people. He also devoted himself to the cause of science and art, and his contribution in these areas was of considerable importance. The rebuilding of the Houses of Parliament and the great exhibition at the Crystal Palace in 1851 owed a large measure of their success to the time, knowledge, and judgment he had given to each project. Albert was a kindly man and a devoted husband and father in an age which considered such attributes of great importance; he was in addition a dedicated citizen of his adopted country. The people loved and admired him, and his untimely death from typhoid fever threw all England into deep and sincere mourning. When Tennyson dedicated his *Idylls of the King* to this good and public-spirited man, he did so with an elegiac tribute which enumerates those qualities for which Albert will be remembered:

> . . . indeed he seems to me
> Scarce other than my king's ideal knight,
> "Who reverenced his conscience as his king;
> Whose glory was, redressing human wrong;
> Who spake no slander, no, nor listen'd to it;
> Who loved one only and who clave to her—"
> Her—over all whose realms to their last isle,
> Commingled with the gloom of imminent war,
> The shadow of his loss drew like eclipse,
> Darkening the world. We have lost him: he is gone:
> We know him now: all narrow jealousies
> Are silent; and we see him as he moved,
> How modest, kindly, all-accomplish'd, wise,
> With what sublime repression of himself,
> And in what limits, and how tenderly;
> Not swaying to this faction or to that;
> Not making his high place the lawless perch
> Of wing'd ambitions, nor a vantage-ground
> For pleasure; but thro' all this tract of years
> Wearing **the white flower of a blameless life,**
> Before a thousand peering littlenesses,
> In that fierce light which beats upon a throne,
> And blackens every blot; . . .

Whither goest thou?

Source: JOHN 13:36
Author: Unknown (traditionally John the Apostle)
First transcribed: By 130
Type of work: Gospel

Context: In Chapters 13 through 16 of his Gospel John describes the events that took place in the Upper Room, immediately following the Last Supper. John's information, apparently, comes from an eyewitness who is probably the host. The account omits certain episodes, which probably occurred while he was absent checking on the movements of the authorities, or perhaps following Judas. For example, he does not mention the sacrament of the Last Supper. After the disciples have eaten their meal, Jesus washes their feet; this is an act of hospitality in a hot and dusty country and is customarily performed by a servant. Jesus thus humbles Himself as an example to His disciples; there have been signs of rivalry among them, and He wishes them to be reminded once more of the humility that must be theirs. Afterward He announces that one of those present will betray Him. Those present are reclining on couches about the table, and the eyewitness is close enough to Jesus that by leaning back he can speak to Him privately. At a sign from Peter he does so and asks Jesus who is the guilty man. It is customary to hand others morsels at table, and Jesus indicates that the next morsel He passes will go to the betrayer. The others present do not overhear the conversation between Jesus and the eyewitness: it is not recorded elsewhere in this circumstantial fashion. In any case, the culprit's identity will shortly be known to all. Jesus knows His disciples thoroughly, and what Judas has done is not something a weak character can successfully hide. He tells Judas to play out his part; Judas picks up the bag of money and leaves. It is probable that the witness follows him, to return only when the soldiers do; John does not describe the Agony in the Garden. The witness' account of what takes place immediately upon Jesus' announcement of betrayal is given below:

> Jesus answered, He it is, to whom I shall give a sop, when I have dipped it. And when he had dipped the sop, he gave it to Judas Iscariot, the son of Simon.
> And after the sop Satan entered into him. Then said Jesus unto him, That thou doest, do quickly.
> Now no man at the table knew for what intent he spake this unto him.
> For some of them thought, because Judas had the bag, that Jesus had said unto him, Buy those things that we have need of against the feast; or, that he should give something to the poor.
> He then having received the sop went immediately out: and it was night.

Therefore, when he was gone out, Jesus said, Now is the Son of man glorified, and God is glorified in him.

If God be glorified in him, God shall also glorify him in himself, and shall straightway glorify him.

Little children, yet a little while I am with you. Ye shall seek me: and as I said unto the Jews, Whither I go, ye cannot come; so now I say to you.

A new commandment I give unto you, That ye love one another; as I have loved you, that ye also love one another.

By this shall all men know that ye are my disciples, if ye have love one to another.

Simon Peter said unto him, Lord, **whither goest thou?** Jesus answered him, Whither I go, thou canst not follow me now; but thou shalt follow me afterwards.

Who, alas! can love, and then be wise?

Source: DON JUAN (Canto I, stanza 117)
Author: George Gordon, Lord Byron (1788–1824)
First published: 1819 (Cantos I and II)
Type of work: Satiric poem

Context: The lovely Donna Julia is twenty-three and married to a man of fifty. In a household dedicated to the young Don Juan's moral education, she is, besides his mother and the ancient household servants, the only female the youth has ever known. She has watched him grow, and " . . . as a pretty child,/ Caress'd him often— . . ." Now, no longer a "child," he is sixteen: she is tremulous and shy, while he broods in solitude, "Tormented with a wound he [can] not know." All these signs Donna Julia sees and recognizes for what they are. She vows to herself she never will disgrace the marriage ring she wears, while "Love, then, within its proper limits/ Was Julia's innocent determination." One day in June, toward evening, she finds herself and Juan alone in a sequestered bower. "One hand on Juan's carelessly was thrown,/ Quite by mistake —she thought it was her own; . . ./ Yet there's no doubt she only meant to clasp/ His fingers with a pure Platonic squeeze." And then the moon comes up and sheds the "loving languor" that spells the end of all her resolution.

> Oh Plato! Plato! you have paved the way,
>   With your confounded fantasies, to more
> Immoral conduct by the fancied sway
>   Your system feigns o'er the controlless core
> Of human hearts, than all the long array
>   Of poets and romancers:—You're a bore,
> A charlatan, a coxcomb—and have been,
> At best, no better than a go-between.

1267

And Julia's voice was lost, except in sighs,
   Until too late for useful conversation;
The tears were gushing from her gentle eyes,
   I wish, indeed, they had not had occasion;
But who, alas! can love, and then be wise?
   Not that remorse did not oppose temptation;
A little still she strove, and much repented,
And whispering "I will ne'er consent"—consented.

Who are a little wise, the best fools be

Source: THE TRIPLE FOOL (Line 22)
Author: John Donne (1572–1631)
First published: 1633
Type of work: Metaphysical poem

Context: The poet, a fool first for loving, makes himself a fool again by giving expression in verse to his love and consequent grief, as he attempts to assuage his pain. He is made a fool a third time when he hears his verse put to music, smarting once more with love. In the second and final stanza, the poet concludes (having accomplished the writing of the verse in question in the first stanza):

> But when I have done so,
>   Some man, his art and voice to show,
>   Doth set and sing my pain,
> And, by delighting many, frees again
>   Grief, which verse did restrain.
> To love and grief tribute of verse belongs,
> But not of such as pleases when 'tis read,
>   Both are increas'd by such songs,
> For both their triumphs so are publish'd,
> And I, which was two fools, do so grow three.
> **Who are a little wise, the best fools be.**

Who finds himself, loses his misery

Source: SELF-DEPENDENCE (Line 32)
Author: Matthew Arnold (1822–1888)
First published: 1852
Type of work: Lyric poem

Context: Reared by his liberal father and taught as a young man that his responsibility was to ask questions concerning the fundamentals of human life, Arnold developed a keenly analytical mind; however, his inability to find answers that were certain led increasingly to personal sorrow.

1268

In his late twenties he had found that his passionate search for certainty seemed to turn on itself so that he was unable to find intellectual or emotional rest. Living in an age of extreme intellectual probing in such areas as politics, religion, and science, Arnold represented the confusion and unhappiness of many of his thinking contemporaries; the diversity of opinion on even crucial questions was making men rely more on themselves than on others. In this poem he looks at the stars and asks them how he can regain the neutral calm of early childhood that they seem to possess; a voice comes from the night to answer him:

"Wouldst thou *be* as these are? *Live* as they.

"Unaffrighted by the silence round them,
Undistracted by the sights they see,
These demand not that the things without them
Yield them love, amusement, sympathy."

    . . .

O air-born voice! long since, severely clear,
A cry like thine in mine own heart I hear:
"Resolve to be thyself; and know that he,
Who finds himself, loses his misery!"

Who often reads, will sometimes wish to write

Source: TALES: EDWARD SHORE (Number XI, l. 109)
Author: George Crabbe (1754–1832)
First published: 1812
Type of work: Narrative poem

Context: Edward Shore, a very personable young man endowed with genius and learning, could not settle upon any course in life. In all ways he was a model young man, gracious, good-natured, sensible, spirited, conservative in his dress. He looked over all the professions and found them all wanting. He shrank from entering trade and could be a lawyer only if he approved of the cases he might have; physicians seemed dull and divines wrapped in dreams; war he could perhaps love, but, there again, he would have to approve the cause. He believed in absolute virtue, unconstrained by law; he would be good, but only because of his inner promptings: the coarse, common people were constrained to be good because the law compelled them to be, but not so with Edward Shore. While reason guided him, he would walk upright. He, however, had doubts, and applied to doubters for help in resolving them; but this action was like the blind leading the blind. Naturally, he read a great deal, and anyone who reads much finally desires to write; but he could not fix upon any form of literature in which to gain the fame he wished. Tragedies were tedious and gloomy; a serious story concerned ghosts, of which he became ashamed;

1269

his sermons were unread; a guide for the conduct of national affairs came to nothing because he could not fix upon a political party. In short, his dislike of labor and his vacillating mind kept him from doing anything.

> But though with shaken faith, and slave to fame,
> Vain and aspiring on the world he came;
> Yet was he studious, serious, moral, grave,
> No passion's victim, and no system's slave:
> Vice he opposed, indulgence he disdained,
> And o'er each sense in conscious triumph reigned.

> **Who often reads, will sometimes wish to write,**
> And Shore would yield instruction and delight;
> A serious drama he designed, but found
> 'Twas tedious traveling in that gloomy ground;
> A deep and solemn story he would try,
> But grew ashamed of ghosts, and laid it by;
> Sermons he wrote, but they who knew his creed,
> Or knew it not, were ill disposed to read;
> And he would lastly be the nation's guide,
> But, studying, failed to fix upon a side;
> Fame he desired, and talents he possessed,
> But loved not labor, though he could not rest,
> Nor firmly fix the vacillating mind,
> That, ever working, could no center find.

Who speaks the truth stabs Falsehood to the heart

Source: L'ENVOI (Line 160)
Author: James Russell Lowell (1819–1891)
First published: 1841
Type of work: Poetic epistle

Context: "L'Envoi" appeared at the end of Lowell's first volume of poetry, *A Year's Life*. The book was dedicated, though not formally, to Maria White, to whom the poet had become engaged in the fall of 1840. She is the "mine own betrothed" of the poem, to whom the poet dedicates these early works, which he terms "the firstlings of my muse,—/ Poor windfalls of unripe experience,/ Young buds plucked hastily by childish hands." In this poem he speaks of the themes appropriate to the work of American poets, who should ignore the tall peaks, great lakes, vast forests, and wide prairies, in order to write about "the freedom and divinity of man,/ The glorious claims of human brotherhood." The American poet, says Lowell, must not be willing, "though clad with angel-wings," to write about "dead men's dead thoughts." He issues a call for American poetry to bring forth new songs to equal the challenge and hope for freedom that America gives to men:

Never had poets such high call before,
Never can poets hope for higher one,
And if they be but faithful to their trust,
Earth will remember them with love and joy,
And, oh, far better, God will not forget.
For he who settles Freedom's principles
Writes the death-warrant of all tyranny;
Who speaks the truth stabs Falsehood to the heart,
And his mere word makes despots tremble more
Than ever Brutus with his dagger could.
Wait for no hints from waterfalls or woods,
Nor dream that tales of red men, brute and fierce,
Repay the finding of this Western World,
Or needed half the globe to give them birth . . .

Who think themselves most wise, are greatest fools

Source: THE TRAGEDY OF CROESUS (Act II, sc. i, l. 298)
Author: Sir William Alexander, Earl of Stirling (c. 1567–1640)
First published: 1607
Type of work: Dramatic tragedy

Context: Alexander, now considered a minor figure in the Elizabethan literary world, was a Scottish poet and a close friend of King James I. Educated in Glasgow and Germany, he achieved his first renown with four examples of Senecan drama composed between 1603 and 1607, and published during the latter year under the collective title *Monarchicke Tragedies.* He also wrote a number of sonnets and later composed an epic in twelve books entitled *Doomes-day.* He is best known today for the royal favors conferred upon him. One was a grant given him by James I: the entire eastern half of Canada, named Nova Scotia for the occasion; its older name was Acadia. Although the French conquest of Canada deprived Alexander of his proprietorship, he was not left destitute; the king made him sole printer of the King James version of the Psalms, and his patent ran for thirty-one years. His literary efforts, although respectable, are no longer greatly admired; and his *Monarchicke Tragedies* are now considered important more for the political wisdom they contain than for their dramatic interest. They deal with four important political events of the ancient world, and employ the conventions of chorus and alternately rhyming verse. *Croesus* was the second in the series, the other three being *Darius, The Alexandrian Tragedy,* and *Julius Caesar. Croesus* opens with a speech by Solon; this intellectual light of ancient Greece has been sent for by Croesus, King of Lydia. Croesus, famed for his wealth, does not wish to profit by Solon's wisdom; instead, he wants Solon to approve his great material happiness. In his speech Solon considers the nature of happiness and pities the man who loves only material things. A chorus follows which compares the passions with reason. The actual play then begins, with a conversation among Croesus, Aesop, and Solon. Croesus boasts of his good fortune and tells Solon he should be a courtier and share in it. Solon insists he prefers less worldly pleasures:

SOLON

Spare (courteous King) that undeserved praise,
I am but one who doe the world despise,
And would my thoughts to some perfection raise,
A wisedome-lover, willing to be wise:
Yet all that I have learn'd (huge toyles now past)
By long experience, and in famous Schooles,
Is but to know my ignorance at last;
Who think themselves most wise, are greatest fooles.

CROESUS

This is the nature of a noble minde,
It rather would be good, then be so thought,
As if it had no ayme, but fame to finde,
Such as the shadow, not the substance sought:
Yet forc'd to give that which thou wilt not take:
The world, what thou hold'st down, doth raise more high,
That which thy face thus shunnes, shines on thy back:
Praise followes them, who what they merit flye:
And now I thinke, on th'earth no creature lives,
Who better can instruct what I would learne,
Then thou to whom franke Nature largely gives
A minde to see, a judgement to discerne.

Who wooed in haste, and means to wed at leisure

Source: THE TAMING OF THE SHREW (Act III, sc. ii, l. 11)
Author: William Shakespeare (1564–1616)
First published: 1623
Type of work: Dramatic comedy

Context: The suitors of gentle Bianca, younger daughter of a rich gentleman of Padua, Baptista, cannot hope to win her until her waspish older sister, Katharine, has married. Petruchio, who comes from Verona to make a fortune, is convinced by his friend, Hortensio, a suitor of Bianca, that marrying the heiress, Katharine, is the solution to his problem. Petruchio's bid for Katharine's hand is accepted, and a hasty marriage planned, but at the appointed time Petruchio does not appear, thus beginning his course of action to subdue the shrewish bride. Shamed, Katharine says to the assembled wedding party:

KATHARINE
. . . I must forsooth be forced

1272

To give my hand, opposed against my heart,
Unto a mad-brain rudesby, full of spleen,
Who wooed in haste, and means to wed at leisure.
I told you, I, he was a frantic fool,
Hiding his bitter jests in blunt behaviour;
And to be noted for a merry man,
He'll woo as husband, 'point the day of marriage,
Make feast, invite friends, and proclaim the banns,
Yet never means to wed where he hath wooed.

. . .

Who would have thought the old man to have had so much blood in him

Source: MACBETH (Act V, sc. i, ll. 44–45)
Author: William Shakespeare (1564–1616)
First published: 1623
Type of work: Dramatic tragedy

Context: Lady Macbeth learns that three witches or "weird sisters" have prophesied that Macbeth will become king. When the opportunity arises to murder King Duncan as he rests, a guest in her home, the lady chides Macbeth if he should fail to murder the king and seize the throne. Yet when the deed is accomplished and the power is gained and numerous other murders have been committed, Lady Macbeth does not enjoy her royal estate; instead, she lapses into insanity. A lady in attendance and a doctor observe the deranged queen as she walks and talks in her sleep, reliving the murder of King Duncan.

LADY MACBETH
. . . Fie my lord, fie! A soldier, and afeard? What need we fear who knows it, when none can call our power to account? Yet **who would have thought the old man to have had so much blood in him?**

DOCTOR
Do you mark that?

LADY MACBETH
The Thane of Fife had a wife; where is she now? What, will these hands ne'er be clean? No more o'that my lord, no more o'that; you mar all with this starting.

DOCTOR
Go to, go to! You have known what you should not.

1273

The whole earth is the sepulchre of famous men

Source: HISTORY OF THE PELOPONNESIAN WAR (Book II, chapter 43, as trans-
lated by Benjamin Jowett)
Author: Thucydides (455?–400? B.C.)
First transcribed: 431–400 B.C.
Type of work: History

Context: The Peloponnesian War was a long and intermittent struggle (431–404 B.C.) between Sparta and Athens for the control of Greece. During the winter of 431–430 the Athenians, in accordance with ancestral custom, celebrated the funeral of those who had first fallen in the conflict. This was a public ceremony; three days beforehand the bones of the dead were laid out in tents, and everyone chose some offering and brought it to his own dead. "At the time of the funeral," says Thucydides, "the bones are placed in chests of cypress wood, which are conveyed on waggons; there is one chest for each tribe. They also carry a single empty litter decked with a pall for all whose bodies are missing, and cannot be recovered after the battle." Anyone who wishes to do so may accompany the procession, and most of the population does so. Female relatives lament the dead. The burial place is a beautiful spot outside the city walls, and all who fall in battle are buried there except those who, because of their great valor, were buried on the field at Marathon. After the cypress chests are solemnly interred, a person of great ability and reputation as a speaker is chosen to deliver the funeral oration; Pericles has been selected for the present occasion. The address he undertakes will still be famous over two thousand years after he is gone. In it he speaks first of the Athenians' ancestry and of their heritage; he praises their government and the high level of their society; he describes their greatness, destined to increase. He then speaks of the fallen, and of the bravery with which they met their end. It is because of such men that Athens is great; they valued their ideals and their way of life, and when it became necessary to do so gave their lives that these things might be preserved.

"Such was the end of these men; they were worthy of Athens, and the living need not desire to have a more heroic spirit, although they may pray for a less fatal issue. The value of such a spirit is not to be expressed in words. Any one can discourse to you for ever about the advantages of a brave defence which you know already. But instead of listening to him I would have you day by day fix your eyes upon the greatness of Athens, until you become filled with the love of her; and when you are impressed by the spectacle of her glory, reflect that this empire has been acquired by men who knew their duty and had the courage to do it, who in the hour of conflict had the fear of dishonour always present to them, and who, if ever they failed in an enterprize, would not allow their virtues to be lost to their country, but freely gave their lives to her as the fairest offering which they could present at her feast. The sacrifice which they collectively made was individually repaid to them; for they received again each one for himself a praise which grows not old, and the noblest of all sepulchres—I speak not of that in which their remains are laid, but of that in which their glory survives, and is proclaimed always and on every fitting occasion both in word and deed. **For the whole earth is the sepulchre of famous men;** not only are they commemorated by columns and inscriptions in their own country, but in foreign lands there dwells also an unwritten memorial of them, graven not on stone but in the hearts of men. . . ."

Whom they have injured they also hate

Source: EPISTULAE MORALES ("On Anger," 2, 33)
Author: Seneca (c. 4 B.C.–A.D. 65)
First transcribed: c. 63
Type of work: Moral essay

Context: Philosopher Seneca, one of a distinguished family of Córdoba, Spain, was educated in Rome, served as tutor to Nero, wrote both dramatic and philosophic works, and finally died as a result of political intrigue. Noted for the Stoic philosophy in his *Moral Essays*, Seneca contends in his "On Anger" that nothing is gained by anger, an unnatural passion, which aids neither the mind nor the strength of the body, and which is an indication of weakness. If one receives abuse at the hand of an important person, says Seneca, he should, for his own good, endure it with patience and good will:

> But those injuries that are done us by mighty men, are not onely to be suffered joyfully, but patiently. They will doe it againe, if they beleeve they have displeased thee. Those minds whom Fortune hath made insolent, have this detestable qualitie in them, that **they hate those whom they have harmed.** Famous and memorable is his speech who was become old in the service of Kings, when a certayne man asked him: *How he had attayned so rare a thing, as old age, in his service in Court? By suffering injuries* (saith he,) *and by giving thanks.* . . .

Whom universal nature did lament

Source: LYCIDAS (Line 60)
Author: John Milton (1608–1674)
First published: 1637
Type of work: Elegiac pastoral poem

1275

Context: In *Lycidas*, Milton laments the death of Edward King, a fellow student at Cambridge University, who was drowned in the Irish Sea. Although the poem purports to be an elegy for King, its essential subject is Milton and his desire for poetic fame. He pictures Lycidas, or King, and himself as feeding their flocks of sheep and melodiously piping. But a change comes about: Lycidas is dead, and all nature laments his passing. Milton asks where the Nymphs were when the sea closed over his head: they were not on the mountains of Wales where the ancient bards, the Druids, lie buried, nor where the River Dee flows into the sea. But, he asks, what could they have done for King, when even a great Muse was not able to preserve the life of the celebrated Orpheus, whose slaying by the maddened Thracian women was a universal calamity:

> Where were ye Nymphs when the remorseless deep
> Closed over the head of your loved Lycidas?
> For neither were ye playing on the steep,
> Where your old bards, the famous Druids, lie,
> Nor on the shaggy top of Mona high,
> Nor yet where Deva spreads her wizard stream:
> Ay me, I fondly dream!—
> Had ye been there—for what could that have done?
> What could the Muse herself that Orpheus bore,
> The Muse herself, for her enchanting son
> **Whom universal nature did lament,**
> When by the rout that made the hideous roar,
> His gory visage down the stream was sent,
> Down the swift Hebrus to the Lesbian shore?

Whose dice were human bones

Source: THE AGE OF BRONZE (Part III)
Author: George Gordon, Lord Byron (1788–1824)
First published: 1823
Type of work: Satiric poem

Context: Byron's hatred of tyrants was expressed by him on many occasions, but his attitude towards Napoleon was ambivalent. On the occasion of that emperor's defeat and abdication in 1814 to a brief retirement at Elba, Byron wrote an ode to Napoleon; in it he characterizes the latter as a monster who has ravaged Europe and is unfit to live. Napoleon is compared unfavorably to George Washington who, unlike the emperor, was content to ensure his country's greatness and step aside. When Napoleon returned to France in 1815 and raised another army, he was defeated at Waterloo; this time the defeat was final, and the great shadow that had lain across Europe was lifted. Napoleon was exiled to St. Helena, an island in a lonely spot west of Africa, and was guarded there by the British until his death in 1821. Much of Europe felt a vast relief at his passing. In 1823 Byron wrote a lengthy satire in verse entitled *The Age of Bronze*; in it he resurrects the emperor from a very different point-of-view. The poem's theme is that greatness does not endure, that mortality is a force to which all, even the most powerful, must succumb. He points to Alexander, who knew little of the world he tried to conquer and whose empire lies in ruins; then he turns to the present and to the spectacle of the once great Napoleon, now insignificant on St. Helena. The emperor, in his last years, is reduced to bickering over trifles:

> Yes! where is he, the champion and the child
> Of all that's great or little, wise or wild?
> Whose game was empires and whose stakes were thrones?
> Whose table earth—**whose dice were human bones?**
> Behold the grand result in yon lone isle,
> And, as thy nature urges, weep or smile.
> Sigh to behold the eagle's lofty rage
> Reduced to nibble at his narrow cage;
> Smile to survey the queller of the nations
> Now daily squabbling o'er disputed rations;
> Weep to perceive him mourning, as he dines,
> O'er curtail'd dishes and o'er stinted wines,
> O'er petty quarrels upon petty things,—
> Is this the man who scourged or feasted kings?
> Behold the scales in which his fortune hangs,
> A surgeon's statement and an earl's harangues!
> A bust delay'd, a book refused, can shake
> The sleep of him who kept the world awake.

Whose game was empires and whose stakes were thrones

Source: THE AGE OF BRONZE (Part III, l. 9)
Author: George Gordon, Lord Byron (1788–1824)
First published: 1823
Type of work: Satiric poem

Context: Byron hated Napoleon Bonaparte, as he hated all tyrants. When the emperor was defeated and forced to abdicate in April, 1814, retiring to the Island of Elba, Byron wrote an ode to him. In it Byron deplores the fact that this monster who had laid waste to all Europe is still alive; and he compares Napoleon to George Washington, who was content to ensure his country's greatness and then step aside. Napoleon returned unexpectedly to France in 1815 and raised still another army; this time he was administered a final and irrevocable defeat at Waterloo. He was then exiled to St. Helena, an island off the west coast of Africa, where he was guarded by the British against escape until his death in 1821. Only after Bonaparte was dead were many countries able to breathe freely again.

In 1823 Byron wrote a lengthy verse satire entitled *The Age of Bronze*, in which he once again examines the emperor. The underlying theme of the poem is that all greatness is fleeting and that the most powerful of men are mortal: "How peaceful and how powerful is the grave,/ Which hushes all!" He mentions Alexander, who in trying to conquer the world knew nothing of its extent and whose world now lies in ruins; then he turns to a much more modern example of the conqueror reduced to insignificant mortality: Napoleon on St. Helena. The man before whom all the world trembled now must squabble over petty things:

> But where is he, the modern, mightier far,
> Who, born no king, made monarchs draw his car;
> The new Sesostris, whose unharness'd kings,
> Freed from the bit, believe themselves with wings,
> And spurn the dust o'er which they crawled of late,
> Chain'd to the chariot of the chieftain's state?
> Yes! where is he, the champion and the child
> Of all that's great or little, wise or wild?
> **Whose game was empires and whose stakes were thrones?**
> Whose table earth—whose dice were human bones?
> Behold the grand result in yon lone isle,
> And, as thy nature urges, weep or smile.
> Sigh to behold the eagle's lofty rage
> Reduced to nibble at his narrow cage;
> Smile to survey the queller of the nations
> Now daily squabbling o'er disputed rations;
> Weep to perceive him mourning, as he dines,
> O'er curtail'd dishes and o'er stinted wines,
> O'er petty quarrels upon petty things,—
> Is this the man who scourged or feasted kings?
> Behold the scales in which his fortune hangs,
> A surgeon's statement and an earl's harangues!
> A bust delay'd, a book refused, can shake
> The sleep of him who kept the world awake.

Whose only fit companion is his horse

Source: CONVERSATION (Line 412)
Author: William Cowper (1731–1800)
First published: 1782
Type of work: Essay in verse

Context: In the catalog of poor conversationalists described by Cowper in his essay in rhymed couplets are the slow talkers, especially the pipe smokers who puff between each two sentences; the solemn fop whose words are as dreary and unrewarding as a parcel filled with stones; those who harp on their illnesses; and those too timid to express their ideas. Then

Cowper unburdens himself about one of the worst conversational bores, and one incapable of being cured, even by a farrier, or veterinarian: the sports lover who thinks he must recall every least detail of his last hunt. That sort of talker should confine his conversation to his horse, or, if that be too much cruelty to animals, to his groom.

> The reeking roaring hero of the chase,
> I give him over as a desperate case.
> Physicians write in hopes to work a cure,
> Never, if honest ones, when death is sure;
> And though the fox he follows may be tamed,
> A mere fox-follower never is reclaimed.
> Some farrier should prescribe his proper course,
> **Whose only fit companion is his horse,**
> Or if, deserving of a better doom,
> The noble beast judge otherwise, his groom.

Widows are the most perverse creatures in the world

Source: THE SPECTATOR (Number 335)
Author: Joseph Addison (1672–1719)
First published: March 25, 1712
Type of work: Essay

Context: In the five hundred and fifty-five regular issues of the *Spectator*, Joseph Addison and Richard Steele raised popular essay journalism to a level of perfection never before achieved and seldom matched since. One of the most interesting members of the "club" of fictitious characters who contributed to this periodical was Sir Roger de Coverley. Addison used the character of this lovable but crusty and eccentric old country squire as, among other things, a vehicle for subtle satire of the Tory party, of which Sir Roger was a member. In addition, Sir Roger was supposed for some considerable time to have wooed without success a fascinating widow. In this essay Sir Roger, in the company of Mr. Spectator and Captain Sentry, visits the playhouse to see a tragedy on a classical subject in which a widow steadfastly refuses her wooer's advances:

> When Sir Roger saw Andromache's obstinate refusal to her lover's importunities, he whispered me in the ear, that he was sure she would never have him; to which he added, with a more than ordinary vehemence, "You can't imagine, sir, what it is to have to do with a widow." Upon Pyrrhus his threatening afterwards to leave her, the knight shook his head, and muttered to himself, "Ay, do if you can." This part dwelt so much upon my friend's imagination, that at the close of the third act, as I was thinking of something else, he whispered me in my ear, "These **widows**, sir, **are the most perverse creatures in the world. . . .**"

A wilderness of sweets

Source: PARADISE LOST (Book V, l. 294)
Author: John Milton (1608–1674)
First published: 1667
Type of work: Epic poem

Context: After an unquiet night of dreaming by Eve, Adam and Eve hymn the glory of God and all that He has created. God summons Raphael to go down to earth to instruct Adam about his duty to God and about the great command not to eat of the tree of knowledge so that if he disobeys the command, he cannot plead ignorance. Raphael is to join Adam during his noontime rest from labor and converse with him as friend with friend. He is to emphasize the fact that Adam's will is free, and happiness is within his power. He is to tell him of his danger, as Satan has broken out of hell and is on earth with the intent to ruin Adam and Eve by guile, not force. Raphael, after receiving the divine orders, looks out upon the universe from the gate of heaven and then sails down between worlds to the earth. He descends like an eagle or a phoenix. As a seraph he has six wings: two on his shoulders, two at his waist, and two at his feet. Finally, like Maia's son Hermes, the messenger of Zeus, he stands on the earth.

> Straight knew him all the bands
> Of angels under watch; and to his state,
> And to his message high in honor rise;
> For on some message high they guessed him bound.
> Their glittering tents he passed, and now is come
> Into the blissful field, through groves of myrrh,
> And flow'ring odors, cassia, nard, and balm;
> **A wilderness of sweets;** for nature here
> Wantoned as in her prime, and played at will
> Her virgin fancies, pouring forth more sweet,
> Wild above rule or art, enormous bliss.
>   • • •

The wilderness of this world

Source: THE PILGRIM'S PROGRESS (Part I)
Author: John Bunyan (1628–1688)
First published: 1678
Type of work: Religious allegory

Context: Bunyan, one of the great dissenting preachers of Restoration England, wrote "the most influential religious book ever composed in the English language" while confined to jail, the "Den" of his opening sentence, to prevent his preaching. In this allegorical novel he symbolizes in vivid physical terms the many spiritual snares that beset the devout Christian in his efforts to reach the Heavenly City. Bunyan, in his own words, "could also have stepped into a style much higher than this," but he chose a homely, plain style, for his message was to the multitude of simple but pious faithful, appropriately represented by his protagonist named Christian. This hero, perceiving some impending doom, leaves his home, his neighbors, who deride him for his fears, his wife, who has no faith in him, and his children to seek his soul's salvation. The opening paragraph of the book explains its nature as a dream allegory:

> As I walked through **the wilderness of this world,** I lighted on a certain place where was a Den, and I laid me down in the place to sleep: and as I slept I dreamed a dream. I dreamed, and behold I saw a man clothed with rags, standing in a certain place, with his face from his own house, a book in his hand, and a great burden upon his back. I looked, and saw him open the book and read therein; and as he read, he wept and trembled; and not being able longer to contain, he brake out with a lamentable cry, saying, "What shall I do?"

Will she pass in a crowd?

Source: JOURNAL TO STELLA (Feb. 9, 1711)
Author: Jonathan Swift (1667–1745)
First published: 1766–1768
Type of work: Personal letters

Context: When Swift abandoned Dublin in 1710 for London, he left behind two dear friends, both unmarried but called, according to the customs of the times, Madame, or Mistress (or Mrs.). One was Esther Johnson, the other, Rebecca Dingley. Biographers are not sure of the relationship of "Mrs." Johnson and Swift, whether he ever married her or not. To the two women, Swift wrote regularly in the form of a journal recounting news from London. Though addressed to the two of them, the installments of the diary were preserved by Esther Johnson, whom Swift called Stella. After her death in 1728, they were returned to Swift and were finally published under the title of *Journal to Stella.* Letter XV covers the month of February 1710/1711. The double date is due to the fact that England at that time had not adopted the Gregorian calendar, and did not, until 1752. By the Julian or Old Style calendar, the new year did not begin till March 25th. By present terminology, this part covers February, 1711. In the entry for Feb. 9, Swift wrote:

. . . Poor Stella's eyes, God bless them, and send them better.

1281

Pray spare them, and write not above two lines a day in broad daylight. How does Stella look, Madame Dingley? Pretty well; a handsome woman still. **Will she pass in a crowd?** Will she make a figure in a country church?

"Will you walk into my parlor?" said the Spider to the Fly

Source: THE SPIDER AND THE FLY (Stanza 1)
Author: Mary Howitt (1799–1888)
First published: 1821
Type of work: Didactic poem

Context: Mary Howitt and her husband, William, were both devoted to literary activity; and both were prolific writers. She published over 100 works, and he produced about fifty. A number of other volumes were produced jointly. The husband began his career as a poet, but his abilities in this respect were inferior to those of his wife; his best work is found in descriptive books which deal with English history and life, in connection with the land's natural scenery. In 1840 the couple visited Germany and remained there for three years; during that time they wrote two books on their life in that country, which were translated into German. The books proved quite popular. During this period Mary Howitt translated the tales of Fredrika Bremer from Swedish into English, and also undertook the translation of several stories by Hans Christian Andersen. Andersen was enthusiastic over her work and encouraged her to translate all his writings, but she declined. In addition to her translations, Mary Howitt produced a number of other works for children, including poetry. The Howitts are virtually forgotten today in spite of the large amount of material they produced; it should be noted that while their books are not of the sort which become classics, they were nonetheless well written, carefully produced, and consisted of good popular fare. Mary Howitt's best work is in the poems she wrote for children, and among these is the universally-known and still delightful "The Spider and the Fly." This is a moral fable told with great good humor, depicting a common human weakness. The spider extends a cordial invitation to his potential victim, following it with all manner of inducements. The fly, well aware of the danger, fends him off until he appeals to her vanity. Preening herself, the fly enters his trap.

"Will you walk into my parlor?" said the Spider to the Fly.
" 'Tis the prettiest little parlor that ever you did spy;
The way into my parlor is up a winding stair,
And I have many curious things to show when you are there."
"Oh no, no," said the little Fly, "to ask me is in vain;
For who goes up your winding stair can ne'er come down again."
• • •

"Sweet creature," said the Spider, "you're witty and you're wise;
How handsome are your gauzy wings, how brilliant are your eyes!
I have a little looking-glass upon my parlor shelf;
If you'll step in one moment, dear, you shall behold yourself."
"I thank you, gentle sir," she said, "for what you're pleased to say,
And bidding you good morning now, I'll call another day."

. . .

Alas, alas! how very soon this silly little Fly,
Hearing his wily, flattering words, came slowly flitting by:
With buzzing wings she hung aloft, then near and nearer drew,—
Thinking only of her brilliant eyes, and green and purple hue;
Thinking only of her crested head—poor foolish thing! At last,
Up jumped the cunning Spider, and fiercely held her fast.
He dragged her up his winding stair, into his dismal den
Within his little parlor—but she ne'er came out again!

The wind bloweth where it listeth

Source: JOHN 3:8
Author: Unknown (traditionally John the Apostle)
First transcribed: By 130
Type of work: Gospel

Context: The fact that John's Gospel does not conform to the other three in many respects has led some scholars to reject its historical accuracy; such students have considered it almost purely doctrinal and devotional in nature. The opinion of others is that Christ's ministry may have lasted three years or more; that He may well have preached in Jerusalem on numerous occasions, especially at feast times when large crowds were gathered there; that in the first three Gospels much has necessarily been omitted; and that John's Gospel supplements them by supplying the missing material. They point out that if the events described by John are added to those of the other Gospels, the picture of Jesus as a real threat to the religious and political establishment of His time becomes far more significant. It is true that John, more than the other writers of Gospel, comments on the discourses of Jesus; clearly he was interpreting them for members of the early Church. In Chapter 3 John recounts the story of Nicodemus, a Jewish ruler and representative of the Pharisees, who approaches Jesus in a patronizing manner and questions Him. Jesus has been very much a thorn in the side of the Pharisees; He confounds their arguments, and whenever they try to accuse Him of breaking a law He turns their own accusations upon them. Not only does He have an answer for everything; He frequently leaves them with nothing whatever to say. They hate Him, but at the same time they fear Him. He is clearly a serious threat to their personal and institutional security. It may be that Nicodemus, as representative of the Pharisees, is trying to make some sort of deal with Jesus. Jesus' reply is patient but firm and uncompromising: He is obviously not to be bought if that is His questioner's intent. Nico- demus' incredulity earns him a more pointed rebuke: he calls himself a teacher but he is unwilling to learn.

There was a man of the Pharisees, named Nicodemus, a ruler of the Jews:

The same came to Jesus by night, and said unto him, Rabbi, we know that thou art a teacher come from God: for no man can do these miracles that thou doest, except God be with him.

Jesus answered and said unto him, Verily, verily, I say unto thee, Except a man be born again, he cannot see the kingdom of God.

Nicodemus saith unto him, How can a man be born when he is old? Can he enter the second time into his mother's womb, and be born?

Jesus answered, Verily, verily, I say unto thee, Except a man be born of water and of the Spirit, he cannot enter into the kingdom of God.

That which is born of the flesh is flesh; and that which is born of the Spirit is spirit.

Marvel not that I said unto thee, Ye must be born again.

The wind bloweth where it listeth, and thou hearest the sound thereof, but canst not tell whence it cometh, and whither it goeth: so is every one that is born of the Spirit.

Nicodemus answered and said unto him, How can these things be?

Jesus answered and said unto him, Art thou a master of Israel, and knowest not these things?

The wind-grieved Apennine

Source: DE GUSTIBUS (Line 16)
Author: Robert Browning (1812–1889)
First published: 1855
Type of work: Lyric poem

Context: The title of this poem is part of a quotation, *de gustibus non est disputandum,* or, "there is no arguing about taste." In Part I Browning says that if we love the same things after death that we love in life, the lover of trees will haunt the English countryside, where boys and girls make love in hazel groves. The poet says that he loves best a castle on the windy Apennine mountains of Italy. Or perhaps if he can get himself out of the grave and loosen his spirit's bands, he will inhabit far in the south a seaside house that looks out over a great unbroken expanse of blue sea. It will be a crumbling house with blistered walls sheltering scorpions. A barefoot peasant girl who brings in the melons will tell of someone's having shot at the Bourbon king and will hope that the assailant has not been caught. The poet concludes by saying that if you open up his body you will find "Italy" engraved on his heart.

> What I love best in all the world,
> Is, a castle, precipice-encurled,
> In a gash of **the wind-grieved Apennine.**
> Or look for me, old fellow of mine,
> (If I get my head from out the mouth
> O' the grave, and loose my spirit's bands,
> And come again to the land of lands)—
> In a sea-side house to the farther South,
> Where the baked cicala dies, of drouth,
> And one sharp tree—'tis a cypress—stands
> By the many hundred years red-rusted,
> Rough iron-spiked, ripe fruit-o'ercrusted,
> My sentinel to guard the sands
> To the water's edge. For, what expands
> Before the house, but the great opaque
> Blue breadth of sea without a break?

The wisdom of our ancestors

Source: THOUGHTS ON THE CAUSE OF THE PRESENT DISCONTENTS
Author: Edmund Burke (1729–1797)
First published: 1770
Type of work: Political treatise

Context: As an important Whig member of Parliament Burke was ever concerned with popular response to government action. In 1770 there was considerable discontent: royal policy was in public disfavor, riots were breaking out in London, the Colonies in America were restive, and there was extensive public doubt concerning foreign policy. Burke, who was usually a speaker rather than an essayist, produced this pamphlet in an attempt to explain the general unrest which was directed toward the government. At one point in the tract he discusses the enormous size to which the government has grown, the huge sums of money considered in national finances, and the resulting temptations and opportunities for corruption. The people are doubtful of such issues, he says, and history offers no precedent for them:

> . . . The power of discretionary disqualification by one law of Parliament, and the necessity of paying every debt of the civil list by another law of Parliament, if suffered to pass unnoticed, must establish such a fund of rewards and terrors as will make Parliament the best appendage and support of arbitrary power that ever

was invented by the wit of man. This is felt. The quarrel is begun between the representatives and the people. . . .

In such a strait the wisest may well be perplexed, and the boldest staggered. The circumstances are in a great measure new. We have hardly any landmarks from **the wisdom of our ancestors,** to guide us. At best we can only follow the spirit of their proceeding in other cases. I know the diligence with which my observations on our public disorders have been made; I am very sure of the integrity of the motives on which they are published: I cannot be equally confident in any plan for the absolute cure of those disorders, or for their certain future prevention.

With a body filled, and vacant mind

Source: KING HENRY THE FIFTH (Act IV, sc. i, l. 286)
Author: William Shakespeare (1564–1616)
First published: 1600
Type of work: Historical drama

Context: The English army is encamped at Agincourt in preparation for battle against the stronger army of France, in a contest which will grant to King Henry V of England the crown also of France. In the darkness before battle the king, disguised, walks among his troops and learns the feelings of his men. Alone again, Henry reflects upon his responsibilities as king that weigh upon his mind and drive away the sleep which is enjoyed by his lowliest subject. The monarch chides greatness for being unable to command health and repose with ceremony.

HENRY
. . .

Canst thou, when thou command'st the beggar's knee,
Command the health of it? No, thou proud dream,
That play'st so subtly with a king's repose.
I am a king that find thee; and I know,
'Tis not the balm, the sceptre, and the ball,
The sword, the mace, the crown imperial,
The intertissued robe of gold and pearl,
The farced title running 'fore the king,
The throne he sits on; nor the tide of pomp
That beats upon the high shore of this world—
No, not all these, thrice-gorgeous ceremony,
Not all these, laid in bed majestical,
Can sleep so soundly as the wretched slave,
Who **with a body filled, and vacant mind,**
Gets him to rest, crammed with distressful bread,
Never sees horrid night, the child of hell; . . .

1286

With a name like yours, you might be any shape

Source: THROUGH THE LOOKING-GLASS (Chapter 6)
Author: Lewis Carroll (Charles Lutwidge Dodgson, 1832–1898)
First published: 1871
Type of work: Imaginative tale for children

Context: Having won a literary name for himself with *Alice's Adventures in Wonderland*, the story that grew out of a rowboat trip on July 4, 1862, with the small daughters of his dean, Prof. Charles Dodgson finally got around to writing its sequel, *Through the Looking-glass and What Alice Found There*, seven years after the publication of the first book. By passing through the mirror into the Looking-Glass House, Alice finds herself in a situation where everything is reversed. The White Queen can remember things before they have happened. She screams, then sees blood on her finger, and only after seeing the blood is she pricked by the pin of her brooch. Then Alice visits a shop whose clerk is a sheep. For the sake of buying something, she asks the price of eggs. She is told that the price is five-pence farthing for one, but only two pence for two. However, if she buys two, she must eat both. Alice decides to buy one, but when the clerk sets it upright on a shelf, it begins to grow larger and more human; and when Alice gets near enough, she sees its eyes, nose, and mouth, and is sure it is Humpty Dumpty. He is proud to be called an egg, as he proclaims into space, never looking at her. Unable to get into a conversation with him, she repeats to herself the nursery rhyme about "Humpty Dumpty sat on a wall."

"Don't stand chattering to yourself like that," Humpty Dumpty said, looking at her for the first time, "but tell me your name and your business."

"My name is Alice, but—"

"It's a stupid name enough!" Humpty Dumpty interrupted impatiently. "What does it mean?"

"Must a name mean something?" Alice asked doubtfully.

"Of course it must," Humpty Dumpty said with a short laugh: "my name means the shape I am—and a good handsome shape it is, too. **With a name like yours, you might be any shape,** almost."

"Why do you sit out here all alone?" said Alice, not wishing to begin an argument.

"Why, because there's nobody with me!" cried Humpty Dumpty. "Don't you think I know the answer to that? Ask another?"

1287

With the dead there is no rivalry

Source: LORD BACON
Author: Thomas Babington Macaulay (1800–1859)
First published: July, 1837
Type of work: Biographical essay and book review

Context: Macaulay's essay on Bacon, the longest and most elaborate of his essays, is a two-part study, divided into a look at Bacon's personal and political life, and a criticism of him as a philosopher. In some respects, by not taking into consideration the circumstances of time, Macaulay has done an injustice to his subject. It was necessary, he thought, for one in government to comply and flatter. The essayist, however, does end with a recognizable character. It is in his discussion of Bacon's philosophy that Macaulay reveals the blind spots in his reading and thinking that are his greatest flaws, and have lessened his popularity in modern times. Ignoring previous and even contemporary philosophers, Macaulay presents Bacon as an unaccountable prodigy who opened up the way of truth to a public up to then interested only in theological disputes. Macaulay begins with a criticism of the leniency and tenderness with which Basil Montagu (1770–1851), author of the book under review, handles his subject. He gives examples of the way authors of the past have been kindly treated by later writers who learned from them. Since they no longer represent potential rivals, they can be studied without jealousy or resentment. Jacques Bossuet (1627–1704) a French prelate and orator, wrote a magnificent *Discourse on Universal History* (1681) of which an English translation appeared in 1821. Macaulay continues:

> **With the dead there is no rivalry.** In the dead there is no change. Plato is never sullen. Cervantes is never petulant. Demosthenes never comes unseasonably. Dante never stays too long. No difference of political opinion can alienate Cicero. No heresy can excite the horror of Bossuet.

With the persuasive language of a tear

Source: THE TIMES (Line 308)
Author: Charles Churchill (1731–1764)
First published: 1764
Type of work: Satiric poem

Context: When *The Times* was privately printed in pamphlet form in September, 1764, at two-and-six a copy, one critic stated that "Everyone must applaud the poet's indignation, but it would have had a stronger effect had it been less indiscriminate," and another commented, "It may soon be a libel not to be satirized by Mr. Churchill." The poet begins by

1288

describing the good old times, "when modesty was scarcely held a crime," and those who served Sin tried to conceal it; before "a great Nation, no less just than free,/ Was made a beggar by Economy." However, conditions have changed: "Our Times, more polish'd, wear a diff'rent face;/ Debts are an Honor; Payment a disgrace." The lords run up bills and ruin the tradesmen. Under the name "Faber," the poet attacks the callous attitude of Lord Halifax, "who feels no Conscience as he fears no Law." Then with a poetic shrug: "But why enlarge I on such petty crimes?" "We begin where our Sires ended and improve on Sin." Perhaps as a result, we shall "leave nothing new in vice and folly for our sons to do." Virtue has disappeared; immorality is rife. Seeking new examples of the demoralizing times, the poet then roams the world, with stanzas to discuss the low state of morality in Holland, France, Spain, Italy, and even the Orient. Having established that man is vile, Churchill next aims his shafts at those who cast aside women as out-of-date and useless, in favor of sodomy. He continues his theme with a long list of offenders, then apologizes for being so frank that he may have wounded the chaste ear. Yet it is man's duty to protect woman, and the poet intends to continue to do so till the modern Sodom is destroyed and until all sinners "pardon of Women with Repentance buy,/ And learn to honor them as much as I." In beginning his apostrophe to women, nearly halfway through his 702 line poem expressed in the rhymed couplets of Pope, Churchill writes:

> Woman, the pride and happiness of Man,
> Without whose soft endearments Nature's plan
> Had been a blank, and Life not worth a thought;
> Woman, by all the Loves and Graces taught,
> With softest arts, and sure, tho' hidden skill
> To humanize, and mould us to her will;
> Woman, with more than common grace form'd *here*,
> **With the persuasive language of a tear**
> To melt the rugged temper of our Isle,
> Or win us to her purpose with a smile; . . .

With this key Shakespeare unlocked his heart

Source: SCORN NOT THE SONNET; CRITIC, YOU HAVE FROWNED (Lines 2–3)
Author: William Wordsworth (1770–1850)
First published: 1827
Type of work: Sonnet

Context: Not since the glorious age of the lyric poem in the Renaissance had English poets indicated more than a passing interest in the sonnet. With the Romantic writers, however, came a new determination to breathe fresh life into verse. *Lyrical Ballads* was, as Wordsworth stated in the Preface to the second edition, an attempt to "choose incidents and situ-

1289

ations from common life" and to trace through them "the primary laws of our nature." The feeling of a poem, in short, is more important to the Romantic than the incident or the situation. Thus, it is not surprising to find in the Romantic era a revival of the sonnet as an aesthetically structured medium through which to express personal emotion, especially in the hands of Wordsworth, Coleridge, Keats, and Shelley. In "Scorn Not the Sonnet" Wordsworth defends the poetic form against those critics who would claim it too fragile and artificial. To the contrary, Wordsworth traces the history of its use—in Dante, Tasso, Petrarch, Spenser, Milton, and above all Shakespeare. Far from fragile, it has provided the format for the expression of powerful and profound emotional truths:

> Scorn not the sonnet; critic, you have frowned,
> Mindless of its just honours; **with this key**
> **Shakespeare unlocked his heart;** the melody
> Of this small lute gave ease to Petrarch's wound;
>   • • •
>   . . . a glow-worm lamp,
> It cheered mild Spenser, called from Faery-land
> To struggle through dark ways; and when a damp
> Fell round the path of Milton, in his hand
> The Thing became a trumpet; whence he blew
> Soul-animating strains—alas, too few!

With women the heart argues, not the mind

Source: MEROPE (Line 341)
Author: Matthew Arnold (1822–1888)
First published: 1858
Type of work: Tragedy

Context: Polyphontes, the present tyrant of Messenia, came to power by murdering Cresphontes and all but one of his sons and then forcing Merope, the widow, to marry him; however, twenty years later he is still not safe on his throne. Afraid of Aepytus, the only son of Merope and Cresphontes to escape, and worried because the widow has not forgiven him for murdering her first family, Polyphontes can sense the spirit of rebellion that Merope's continued mourning sparks. Unknown to him, Aepytus has already returned, and the plot to find vengeance is under way; he knows only that if Merope does not cease her actions, the people might rebel. Thus he argues that he saved the country by his coup and that the children's murders cannot be attributed to him; Merope is not convinced. She replies that the avenging gods, not her lamentations, are the cause of discord in the state.

1290

I ask thee not to approve thy husband's death,
No, nor expect thee to admit the grounds,
In reason good, which justified my deed.
With women the heart argues, not the mind.
But, for thy children's death, I stand assoil'd—
I saved them, meant them honour; but my friends
Rose, and with fire and sword assailed my house
By night; in that blind tumult they were slain.
To chance impute their deaths, then, not to me.

Wit's the noblest frailty of the mind

Source: A TRUE WIDOW (Act I, sc. i)
Author: Thomas Shadwell (1642?–1692)
First published: 1679
Type of work: Dramatic comedy

Context: Bellamour, a London gentleman, is visited in rapid succession by Stanmore, another London gentleman; Carlos, a gentleman recently returned from France; Selfish, a vain and clothes-mad coxcomb who boasts of his prowess with women; Young Maggot, a law student and poetaster who neglects his law studies in order to develop his feeble wit in writing songs; Prig, another coxcomb and poetaster whose talk runs to the many sports he relishes; and Old Maggot, a businessman who is as scornful of wit as his nephew is enamored of it. Warned that his uncle is coming, Young Maggot hides while Bellamour, Carlos, and Stanmore engage the old fellow in conversation. When Old Maggot complains that his nephew is neglecting law for literature, Stanmore answers, in a phrase that is a parody of a line from Dryden's *The Indian Emperor* (1667): "Love's the noblest frailty of the mind":

STANMORE
Poetry is an ornament to a man of any profession.

MAGGOT
'Tis a damn'd Weed, and will let nothing good or profitable grow by it, 'tis the Language of the Devil, and begun with Oracles. Where did you know a Wit thrive, or indeed keep his own?

CARLOS
They part with their Money for Pleasure, and Fools part with their Pleasure for Money; the one will make a better Last Will and Testament, but the other lead a happier Life.

Meanwhile the hidden nephew is so intent upon his versifying that he speaks aloud:

Profit begone, what art thou but a breath.
I'l live proud of my Infamy and shame,
Grac'd with the Triumphs of a Poets name:
Men can but say, Wit did my Reason blind,
And **Wit's the noblest frailty of the Mind.**

Woe to the vanquished

Source: HISTORY OF ROME (Book V, chapter 48)
Author: Livy (Titus Livius, 59 B.C.–A.D. 17)
First transcribed: c. 26 B.C.–A.D. 14
Type of work: History

Context: Titus Livius was a protégé of the Roman emperor Augustus and the greatest prose writer of his time; his *Annals of the Roman People*, now generally called his *History of Rome*, ran to 142 books. About one third of it remains today. According to Livy, the first significant step taken by Rome toward the conquest of all Italy was its capture of Veii; this was a powerful Etruscan city located some twelve miles north of Rome. The Roman leader Marcus Furius Camillus, it is said, managed to build a tunnel under the city walls and into the citadel. After Veii had fallen, however, his troubles were not over. The siege had lasted ten years, from 405–396 B.C. The Romans, occupying Veii, now found themselves also besieged—this time by the Gauls. When the Gauls invaded Italy, the Romans had panicked. At Rome they managed to hold the citadel, but much of the city was sacked and burned. Fortunately for the Romans, the Gauls were not prepared to undertake a siege. The defenders at Veii gathered strength; Camillus, now at Ardea, was declared dictator and asked to return. At Rome, famine began to take its toll on both sides, and the Gauls were suffering from an epidemic. When Camillus arrived with his forces, he routed the Gauls with his first charge; when they reorganized eight miles away, he fell upon them again and "annihilation of the enemy was so complete that not even a witness of the carnage survived." Camillus had barely been in time to save the honor of Rome. The city's defenders had concluded an armistice with the Gauls, who taunted them with their lack of food and urged them to surrender; and although they knew Camillus was gathering fresh troops and hastening to their defense, the Romans gave in to hints that the enemy could be bought off:

. . . the Roman soldiers were so exhausted from day and night sentry duty and weakened by hunger that as they marched to their posts they were hardly able to support the weight of their armor. After they had looked day after day in vain for help to arrive from the dictator, all hope disappeared along with their food supply. The senate was convened and the duty of bargaining for peace was assigned to the military tribunes. An agreement was reached between the tribune Quintus Sulpicius and Brennus the Gallic chieftain, and the ransom price of the nation destined soon to rule the world was fixed at a thousand pounds of gold. Insult was added to this penalty which in itself was so degrading: when the tribune objected that the Gauls had brought false weights a Gaul derisively added his sword to the scale, with the words so intolerable to Roman ears, **"Woe to the vanquished."**

A woman seldom asks advice before she has bought her wedding clothes

Source: THE SPECTATOR (Number 475)
Author: Joseph Addison (1672–1719)
First published: September 4, 1712
Type of work: Essay

Context: In the *Spectator*, Joseph Addison and Richard Steele raised popular essay journalism to a level of perfection never before achieved. For a large middle-class reading public they created an interest in public affairs, literary and dramatic criticism, public morality, and manners.

In this essay, Addison is discussing with subtle but gentle satire those people who ask for advice they do not intend to use simply because they cannot keep a secret. The request for advice is, says Addison, merely an excuse for revealing the secret:

It is an old observation, which has been made of politicians who would rather ingratiate themselves with their sovereign than promote his real service, that they accommodate their counsels to his inclinations, and advise him to such actions only as his heart is naturally set upon. The privy-councillor of one in love must observe the same conduct, unless he would forfeit the friendship of the person who desires his advice. I have known several odd cases of this nature. Hipparchus was going to marry a common woman, but being resolved to do nothing without the advice of his friend Philander, he consulted him upon the occasion. Philander told him his mind freely, and represented his mistress to him in such strong colors, that the next morning he received a challenge for his pains, and before twelve o'clock was run through the body by the man who had asked his advice. Celia was more prudent on the like occasion; she desired Leonilla to give her opinion freely upon a young fellow who made his addresses to her. Leonilla, to oblige her, told her with great frankness that she looked upon him as one of the most worthless—Celia, forseeing what a character she was to expect, begged her not to go on, for that she had been privately married to him above a fortnight. The truth of it is, **a woman seldom asks advice before she has bought her wedding clothes.**

When she has made her own choice, for form's sake she sends a
congé d'élire to her friends.

The woman that deliberates is lost

Source: CATO (Act IV, sc. i, l. 31)
Author: Joseph Addison (1672–1719)
First published: 1713
Type of work: Dramatic tragedy

Context: Addison's play relates the story of Marcus Porcius Cato (95–46 B.C.), who opposed Caesar on the question of the Catilinian conspiracy and, later, opposed the triumvirate. His daughter, the Marcia of Addison's play, was actually named Portia; she married Marcus Junius Brutus, one of Caesar's famed assassins. In Act IV, scene 1, of *Cato* Marcia talks with one of her friends, Lucia, the daughter of a Roman senator. As two young girls will, they discuss the men in their lives. Two men love Marcia: one is Sempronius, a senator; the other is Juba, Prince of Numidia. She characterizes Sempronius as a loud and boisterous man, whom she does not like at all, and Juba as a brave hero who is also loving and sweet. She adds, however, that though she would prefer to marry Juba she must wait to see which man her father chooses for her, commenting, "While Cato lives, his daughter has no right/ To love or hate, but as his choice directs." Lucia then asks Marcia what will happen if Cato gives Marcia to Sempronius in marriage. Marcia replies:

> I dare not think he will; but if he should—
> Why wilt thou add to all the griefs I suffer
> Imaginary ills, and fancied tortures?
> I hear the sound of feet! They march this way!
> Let us retire, and try if we can drown
> Each softer thought in sense of present danger.
> When love once pleads admission to our hearts
> (In spite of all the virtue we can boast)
> **The woman that deliberates is lost.**

Woman will be the last thing civilized by Man

Source: THE ORDEAL OF RICHARD FEVEREL (Chapter 1)
Author: George Meredith (1828–1909)
First published: 1859
Type of work: Novel

Context: Sir Austin Absworthy Bearne Feverel, Baronet, of Raynham Abbey, is a man who wants to rear his son according to his own Sys-

1294

tem, which virtually excludes women from the young lad's life till he is twenty-five. Sir Austin is a woman-hater because his wife, the daughter of a retired admiral, was unfaithful to him. Sir Austin's bailiff, Denzil Somers, was a college friend who ran through his own inheritance, a modest one, and then became Sir Austin's employee, as well as a poet. He wrote and published sentimental and satiric verse under the pseudonym of Diaper Sandow. Lady May, Sir Austin's wife, a "languishing, inexperienced" woman was at first jealous of her husband's friend and employee, but by degrees she comes to tolerate him. Toleration grows to affection, and the poet-bailiff becomes her lover, as she finds the fluent young man appeals more to her "little refinements of taste and sentiment" than does her husband. Therefore, she runs off with him, deserting her husband and five-year-old son. Among the results of her infidelity is a book her husband writes, entitled *The Pilgrim's Scrip*, a collection of aphorisms, many of them obviously from the pen of a misogynist. The book is published anonymously, except for Sir Austin's crest, which stands upon the title page. Through his little book the rejected husband gives "a bruised heart to the world":

> He made no pretensions to Novelty. "Our new thoughts have thrilled dead bosoms," he wrote; by which avowal may be seen that Youth had manifestly gone from him, since he had ceased to be jealous of the ancients, his forefathers. There was a half-sigh floating through his pages for those days of intellectual coxcombry, when Ideas come to us affecting the embraces of Virgins, and swear to us, they are ours alone, and no one else have they ever visited: and we believe them.
>
> .   .   .

Carrying forward his misogynistic theme he gravely declared, as one whose postulate was readily accepted universally:

"I expect that **Woman will be the last thing civilized by Man.**"

A woman's friendship ever ends in love

Source: DIONE (Act IV, sc. vi)
Author: John Gay (1685–1732)
First published: 1720
Type of work: Dramatic tragedy

Context: Gay was certainly one of the best minor poets of the early eighteenth century, although he was greatly overshadowed by his friend Alexander Pope. His verse was generally light, and his thought was seldom profound; his favorite mode was burlesque which frequently took the form of mock-epic. In drama the twentieth century knows him best for

1295

his *The Beggar's Opera* in both its original form and as the *Three-Penny Opera*. In *Dione*, however, Gay changed his humour and tried his hand at pastoral tragedy. In the play the heroine, Dione, must appear disguised as a youth, Alexis. In this garb she befriends Parthenia and thus rouses jealousy in Lycidas whom she loves and who loves Parthenia. Lycidas believes that Alexis (Dione in disguise) has seduced Parthenia, and in the fourth act charges Alexis with the supposed betrayal:

LYCIDAS
Boast then her favours; say, what happy hour
Next calls to meet her in th' appointed bower;
Say, when and where you met.

DIONE
———Be rage supprest.
In stabbing mine, you wound *Parthenia's* breast.
She said, she still defy'd Love's keenest dart;
Yet purer friendship might divide her heart,
Friendship's sincerer bands she wish'd to prove.

LYCIDAS
A woman's friendship ever ends in love.
Think not these foolish tales my faith command;
Did not I see thee press her snowy hand?
O may her passion like thy friendship last!
May she betray thee e'er a day be past!

A woman's preaching is like a dog's walking on his hind legs

Source: THE LIFE OF SAMUEL JOHNSON, LL.D. (For 1763)
Author: James Boswell (1740–1795)
First published: 1791
Type of work: Biography

Context: Boswell made every effort to be in Dr. Johnson's good graces and to spend as much time as possible in his subject's company. He wrote up their visits immediately afterward, before he could lose the material from his memory. Boswell was also extremely pleased to become Johnson's friend, as he almost worshiped the man about whom he was writing. In this passage, for example, Boswell expresses his pleasure, first over the fact that Johnson later visited Auchinleck, the Boswell family's home in Scotland, and described it in his *Journey to the Western Islands*; but Boswell also expresses his pleasure over Johnson's offer to go to Harwich with him, when Boswell leaves England to travel in Holland. Boswell tells also in this passage how on Sunday, July 31, 1763, he attended a Quaker meeting in the morning, visiting Dr. Johnson later on in the same day. Boswell, probably realizing that Johnson, a conservative and loyal Anglican, would disapprove of a Quaker meeting itself, much less a woman's preaching, tells Johnson about his religious adventure. Dr. Johnson's reply to the information is typically Johnsonian—colorful, dogmatic, and to the point:

. . . "Sir, **a woman's preaching is like a dog's walking on his hind legs.** It is not done well; but you are surprised to find it done at all."

A woman's whole life is a history of the affections

Source: THE SKETCH-BOOK OF GEOFFREY CRAYON, GENT. (The Broken Heart)
Author: Washington Irving (1783–1859)
First published: 1819–1820
Type of work: Miscellany

Context: Washington Irving has his persona, Geoffrey Crayon, say that he believes in the existence of broken hearts, that they are not unknown in men and occur with some frequency in women, that often a broken heart sends "a lovely woman into an early grave." In this matter, says Geoffrey Crayon, he recognizes that he will face disagreement, for it is commonplace that persons who have passed the age of youth and feeling, or who have been brought up in the heartlessness of a dissipated life, laugh at stories of romantic passion as the product of the imaginations of the poets and novelists. Crayon goes on, in the second paragraph of the essay, to compare the man and the woman:

Man is the creature of interest and ambition. His nature leads him forth into the struggle and bustle of the world. Love is but the embellishment of his early life, or a song piped in the intervals of the acts. He seeks for fame, for fortune, for space in the world's thought, and dominion over his fellow-men. But **a woman's whole life is a history of the affections.** The heart is her world; it is there her ambition strives for empire; it is there her avarice seeks for hidden treasures. She sends forth her sympathies on adventure; she embarks her whole soul in the traffic of affection; and if shipwrecked, her case is hopeless—for it is a bankruptcy of the heart.

Women and music should never be dated

Source: SHE STOOPS TO CONQUER (Act III)
Author: Oliver Goldsmith (1728–1774)
First published: 1773
Type of work: Dramatic comedy

1297

Context: Mr. Marlow, who, because he has always led the life of a student apart from refined society, is extremely bashful in the presence of a good woman but is full of boldness in the presence of one from the lower walks of life, comes down to the country to see Miss Hardcastle, with whom his father and Miss Hardcastle's are trying to arrange a marriage for him. Miss Hardcastle's loutish half-brother, Tony Lumpkin, a practical joker, meeting Mr. Marlow and his traveling companion, Mr. Hastings, at the local alehouse, sends them to the Hardcastle house, saying that it is an inn. Arriving at the house, the two young men act with the liberty permissible in an inn, their freedom of behavior much puzzling Mr. Hardcastle, who knows who they are, even if they do not know who he is. Mr. Marlow meets Miss Hardcastle while she is dressed in her best finery, but is so discomfited in her presence that, while carrying on a stilted and halting conversation, he never looks at her face. As a result of the conversation he decides that marriage with her would be insupportable and decides to return to London as soon as possible. He, however, catches a glimpse of her clad in a plain country dress and mistakes her for the barmaid of the establishment, a mistake that one of the maids confirms. Marlow meets Miss Hardcastle in her new guise and immediately is so struck by her appearance that he requests a kiss. He then tries to discover her age, but she tells him that people should never try to find out how old a woman or a piece of music is.

MARLOW

One may call in this house, I find, to very little purpose. Suppose I should call for a taste, just by the way of a trial, of the nectar of your lips; perhaps I might be disappointed in that too.

MISS HARDCASTLE

Nectar! nectar! That's a liquor there's no call for in these parts. French, I suppose. We sell no French wines here, sir.

MARLOW

Of true English growth, I assure you.

MISS HARDCASTLE

Then it's odd I should not know it. We brew all sorts of wines in this house, and I have lived here these eighteen years.

MARLOW

Eighteen years! Why, one would think, child, you kept the bar before you were born. How old are you?

MISS HARDCASTLE

O! sir, I must not tell my age. They say **women and music should never be dated.**

1298

Wonders are many, and none is more wonderful than man

Source: ANTIGONE (Line 332, as translated by R. C. Jebb)
Author: Sophocles (496–405 B.C.)
First transcribed: Fourth century B.C.
Type of work: Dramatic tragedy

Context: Antigone is third in the famous trilogy by Sophocles dealing with the legend of Oedipus, King of Thebes, who unwittingly slew his father and married his own mother. When the truth was revealed many years later, his mother Jocasta took her own life; Oedipus blinded himself and left Thebes, wandering about the earth in misery and repentance with only his faithful daughter Antigone to serve and care for him. After his death she returns to Thebes. Her brothers, Eteocles and Polynices, had agreed to reign alternate years after Oedipus' abdication; but Eteocles would not give up the throne to his younger brother. The latter engaged six other Argive chiefs to help him seize it by force; but he and five of the chiefs were killed, and in the battle he and Eteocles slew each other. The play opens immediately following Antigone's return. She learns that Creon, now King of Thebes, has forbidden anyone to bury the corpse of Polynices. Her loyalty to her brother takes first place in her mind: she is determined to see that he has a decent burial. She calls her sister Ismene to her and makes this determination known. Ismene reminds her of all the misery the family has passed through, and of the death they too must suffer if they brave the king's wrath. She refuses to assist Antigone, whose purpose is unshaken. The Chorus, representing a group of Theban elders, tells of the joys of peace and victory; then Creon enters and reaffirms his intention to hold a noble funeral for Eteocles, who defended the city, and to leave unburied Polynices, who tried to destroy it. The Chorus upholds him. A guard arrives to inform Creon that the body of Polynices has disappeared. Creon, convinced that this act is the work of persons who have been bribed, orders that the evil-doers be found. The Chorus now soliloquizes on the nature of man, whose greatness and baseness exist side by side:

Wonders are many, and none is more wonderful than man; the power that crosses the white sea, driven by the stormy south-wind, making a path under surges that threaten to engulf him; and Earth, the eldest of the gods, the immortal, the unwearied, doth he wear, turning the soil with the offspring of horses, as the ploughs go to and fro from year to year.

And the light-hearted race of birds, and the tribes of savage beasts, and the sea-brood of the deep, he snares in the meshes of his woven toils, he leads captive, man excellent in wit. And he masters by his arts the beast whose lair is in the wilds, who roams the hills; he tames the horse of shaggy mane, he puts the yoke upon its neck, he tames the tireless mountain bull.

And speech, and wind-swift thought, and all the moods that mould a state, hath he taught himself; and how to flee the arrows of the frost, when 'tis hard lodging under the clear sky, and the arrows of the rushing rain; yea, he hath resource for all; without resource he meets nothing that must come: only against Death shall he call for aid in vain; but from baffling maladies he hath devised escapes.

Cunning beyond fancy's dream is the fertile skill which brings him, now to evil, now to good. When he honours the laws of the land, and that justice which he hath sworn by the gods to uphold, proudly stands his city: no city hath he who, for his rashness, dwells with sin. . . .

Works done least rapidly, Art most cherishes

Source: OLD PICTURES IN FLORENCE (Line 132)
Author: Robert Browning (1812–1889)
First published: 1855
Type of work: Dramatic monologue

Context: By emphasizing that the development of art is a continuous progression to better, more perceptive pictures, Browning says that earlier, inferior periods of art should not be overlooked and laments the tendency to neglect the painters of the late Middle Ages who taught the great masters. Without these painters—the history of art is distorted, because while the masters perfected techniques that enabled them to portray the subtleties of the flesh, these painters—Giotto, Fra Angelico, or Ghirlandajo—stressed the qualities of the spirit. The art of the High Renaissance was technically perfect but, according to Browning, lacked soul; the work of these neglected artists did not have perfect techniques but was superior because it caused men to look toward heaven rather than at the painting itself. Inferior as works of art, the paintings of the late Middle Ages are superior as testimonies of the spiritual struggles of man. The quotation comes from the part of the poem in which Browning imagines how he would defend the old pictures from the scorn of a typical art critic.

The Artificer's hand is not arrested
  With us; we are rough-hewn, nowise polished:
They stand for our copy, and, once invested
  With all they can teach, we shall see them abolished.

'Tis a life-long toil till our lump be leaven—
  The better! What's come to perfection perishes.
Things learned on earth, we shall practise in heaven:
  Works done least rapidly, Art most cherishes.

The world forgetting, by the world forgot

Source: ELOISA TO ABELARD (Line 208)
Author: Alexander Pope (1688–1744)
First published: 1717
Type of work: Poetic monologue

Context: Pope is here giving verse form to John Hughes' translation of the letters of the famous medieval lovers. Abelard was the learned clergyman, philosopher, and theologian who fell in love with the daughter of a friend. The intensely passionate love affair was discovered by the authorities, who confined Abelard to a monastery and Eloisa to a convent. The present poem supposes that after many years separation Eloisa accidentally comes upon a letter written by Abelard to a friend in which he recounts his misfortune. This letter reawakens in Eloisa the old emotions, and she speaks to herself as if she were addressing her lost lover. At one point she laments the fact that she cannot forget her past offence, begging Abelard himself to assist her to overcome her own nature. She expresses her envy of the innocent virgin who has no sinful past to plague her with both desire and guilt:

> Oh come! oh teach me nature to subdue,
> Renounce my love, my life, my self—and you.
> Fill my fond heart with God alone, for He
> Alone can rival, can succeed to thee.
> How happy is the blameless Vestal's lot!
> **The world forgetting, by the world forgot.**
> Eternal sun-shine of the spotless mind!
> Each pray'r accepted, and each wish resign'd;
> Labour and rest, that equal periods keep;
> 'Obedient slumbers that can wake and weep';
> Desires compos'd, affections ever ev'n,
> Tears that delight, and sighs that waft to heav'n.
> Grace shines around her with serenest beams,
> And whisp'ring Angels prompt her golden dreams.

The world, I count it not an inn

Source: RELIGIO MEDICI (Part II, section 11)
Author: Sir Thomas Browne (1605–1682)
First published: 1642
Type of work: Philosophy

Context: Browne looks at the inner man, at the soul, and sees it as a great glory: ". . . I study to find how I am a Microcosm, or little World, I find myself something more than great." He says he knows there is a divinity in man, that Nature tells him, as does Scripture, that God made man in His image. This knowledge, says Browne, makes him content, and, he asks, ". . . what should Providence add more?" It is the soul that he sees as immortal, as the higher, more potent aspect of man; he suggests that even in sleep, when our souls dream, we are somewhat more than our waking selves, that "surely it is not a melancholy conceit to think we are all asleep in this World, and that the conceits of this life are as meer dreams to those of the next." Sir Thomas Browne is proud to be a man:

> Now for my life, it is a miracle of thirty years, which to relate, were not a History, but a piece of Poetry, and would sound to common ears like a Fable. For **the World, I count it not an Inn,** but an Hospital; and a place not to live, but to die in. The world that I regard is myself; it is the Microcosm of my own frame that I cast mine eye on; for the other, I use it but like my Globe, and turn it round sometimes for my recreation. Men that look upon my outside, perusing only my conditions and Fortunes, do err in my Altitude; for I am above Atlas his shoulders. The earth is a point not only in respect of the Heavens above us, but of that heavenly and celestial part within us. . . .

The world is mine

Source: THE TRAVELLER (Line 50)
Author: Oliver Goldsmith (1728–1774)
First published: 1764
Type of work: Descriptive and meditative poem

Context: The poet, "the traveller," sits upon a crag in the Alps, and, as he surveys the world spread before him, meditates first upon the friend he loves who is content to stay at his familiar hearth, and then, reflecting upon his own travels, concludes that in all realms exist both good and ill, but that each person holds his home land the dearest. As he gazes at the panorama before him, he is caught up in an exuberant spirit in which he feels that he is the possessor of all creation:

> Ye glitt'ring towns, with wealth and splendor crown'd;
> Ye fields, where summer spread profusion round,
> Ye lakes, whose vessels catch the busy gale,
> Ye bending swains, that dress the flow'ry vale,
> For me your tributary stores combine;
> Creation's heir, the world, **the world is mine!**

The world is weary of the past

Source: HELLAS (Line 1100)
Author: Percy Bysshe Shelley (1792–1822)
First published: 1822
Type of work: Poetic drama

Context: In *Hellas,* Shelley catalogues some of the early battles of the Greek war for independence from Turkey that began in 1821. Because the war was still in progress, Shelley could not conclude his poem with an account of victory for either Greeks or Turks. In the poem affairs seem to be going in favor of the Turks, but the chorus of captive Greek women looks into the future in the concluding choral passage. Although Shelley said that the concluding chorus is indistinct and obscure, it is perhaps the clearest and most distinct part of the whole poem. The chorus prophesies that a great age of the world is beginning and that the golden age will return. A brighter Greece will arise, with a new Argo to cut the waves with a cargo different from the golden fleece; a new Orpheus will sing once again; a new Ulysses will travel the seas on his way home. A new Athens will arise. Worshipers will strew tears and flowers on the altars of Saturn, the ruler of the world before the beginning of the reign of Jupiter and Love. The chorus pleads for no more war. Why must men kill and die? The world is weary of its long past of hate and death. May it die or be at rest and peace!

Another Athens shall arise,
    And to remoter time
Bequeath, like sunset to the skies,
    The splendour of its prime;
And leave, if nought so bright may live,
All earth can take or Heaven can give.

Saturn and Love their long repose
    Shall burst, more bright and good
Than all who fell, than One who rose,
    Than many unsubdued:
Not gold, not blood, their altar dowers,
But votive tears and symbol flowers.

Oh, cease! must hate and death return?
    Cease! must men kill and die?
Cease! drain not to its dregs the urn
    Of bitter prophecy.
The world is weary of the past,
Oh, might it die or rest at last!

The world is white with May

Source: IDYLLS OF THE KING ("The Coming of Arthur," Line 481)
Author: Alfred, Lord Tennyson (1809–1892)
First published: 1869
Type of work: Narrative poem

Context: The youthful King Arthur, successful in answering the call of King Leodgran to repel the Saxon invaders and the beast rampant in the wilderness of England under the rule of petty kings and weak Roman lead- ers, weds Guinevere, fair daughter of Leodgran. After the marriage Arthur and Guinevere, silently watched by Roman lords, march from the shrine as trumpets blow and the knights of Arthur sing:

> "Blow trumpet, for **the world is white with May!**
> Blow trumpet, the long night hath roll'd away!
> Blow thro' the living world—'Let the King reign!'
>
> "Shall Rome or Heathen rule in Arthur's realm?
> Flash brand and lance, fall battle-axe upon helm,
> Fall battle-axe, and flash brand! Let the King reign!
> • • •
> "Blow, for our Sun is mighty in his May!
> Blow, for our Sun is mightier day by day!
> Clang battle-axe, and clash brand! Let the King reign!
>
> "The King will follow Christ, and we the King,
> In whom high God hath breathed a secret thing.
> Fall battle-axe, and clash brand! Let the King reign!"

The world was all before them, where to choose

Source: PARADISE LOST (Book XII, l. 646)
Author: John Milton (1608–1674)
First published: 1667
Type of work: Epic poem

Context: Michael comes down from heaven to the garden to prepare Adam for his expulsion from paradise. He shows him the future; that is, most of the events of the Bible. He also gives him a lecture on how he is to behave and what qualities of mind he must have if he is to live a happy life. He tells him that for the paradise he is losing he will gain an internal paradise that will make him happier than the terrestrial paradise would have made him. Adam is to instruct Eve in what he has learned. Eve is awakened; she says that she has had comforting dreams. She says that Adam may lead on and she will gladly follow, as to be with him, no matter where he may be, is to be in paradise; but to be alone, is to be banished from it. Through her rashness in eating the forbidden fruit, she has lost everything, but from her will come the Promised Seed who will restore everything. Adam and Eve walk out through the eastern gate of the garden and down the cliff to the plain below:

> They looking back, all th'eastern side beheld
> Of paradise, so late their happy seat,
> Waved over by that flaming brand, the gate
> With dreadful faces thronged and fiery arms:
> Some natural tears they dropped, but wiped them soon;
> **The world was all before them, where to choose**
> Their place of rest, and providence their guide:
> They hand in hand with wand'ring steps and slow,
> Through Eden took their solitary way.

A world-without-end bargain

Source: LOVE'S LABOUR'S LOST (Act V, sc. ii, l. 799)
Author: William Shakespeare (1564–1616)
First published: 1598
Type of work: Dramatic comedy

Context: The "finale" of *Love's Labour's Lost* comes toward the end of Act V when the Princess of France receives word that her father has died suddenly and she must prepare to return home immediately. Ferdinand, King of Navarre, asks the princess to grant him her love, but she replies that the time is "too short" for either of them to commit themselves for the rest of their lives. The word *bargain* refers to an agreement of marriage —thus the time is too short to decide on a marriage. The princess, however, does promise she will consider Ferdinand's request after a year of mourning for her father and after the king has followed her prescribed penance (to give himself to the scholarly, ascetic life for a year and a day). The other nobles at court receive similar answers from their ladies.

KING
Now at the latest minute of the hour
Grant us your loves.

PRINCESS
A time methinks too short
To make **a world-without-end bargain** in.
No, no, my lord, Your Grace is perjured much,
Full of dear guiltiness; and therefore this:
If for my love, as there is no such cause,
You will do aught, this shall you do for me.
Your oath I will not trust, but go with speed

1305

To some forlorn and naked hermitage,
Remote from all the pleasures of the world;
There stay until the twelve celestial signs
Have brought about their annual reckoning.
If this austere insociable life
Change not your offer made in heat of blood,
If frosts and fasts, hard lodging and thin weeds
Nip not the gaudy blossoms of your love,
But that it bear this trial, and last love;
Then, at the expiration of the year,
Come challenge me, challenge me by these deserts,
And by this virgin palm now kissing thine,
I will be thine; . . .

        .   .   .

Worship is transcendent wonder

Source: HEROES AND HERO-WORSHIP ("The Hero as Divinity")
Author: Thomas Carlyle (1795–1881)
First published: 1841
Type of work: Moral essay

Context: In his introductory lecture, "The Hero as Divinity," Carlyle takes up the examination of heroes and the nature of that process of deification to which they are subject. He feels that if we can see the hero clearly we can understand a basic process of history; and as a means to that understanding, he inquires into the nature of religion. "It is well said, in every sense, that a man's religion is the chief fact with regard to him. A man's, or a nation of men's. By religion I do not mean here the church-creed which he professes, the articles of faith which he will sign and, in words or otherwise, assert; not this wholly, in many cases not this at all. We see men of all kinds of professed creeds attain to almost all degrees of worth or worthlessness under each or any of them. This is not what I call religion. But the thing a man does practically believe . . . and know for certain, concerning his vital re-lations to this mysterious Universe, and his duty and destiny there, that is in all cases the primary thing for him, and creatively determines all the rest. That is his *religion* . . . if you tell me what that is, you tell me to a very great extent what the man is, what the kind of things he will do is. Of a man or of a nation we inquire, therefore, first of all, What religion they had? . . . Answering of this question is giving us the soul of the history of the man or nation." First he takes up Paganism; we find it strange, says Carlyle, that men could have believed in such a chaos of divinity. Some feel that Paganism was merely quackery in which the people were duped by an unscrupulous priesthood, but Carlyle rejects this idea. "Quackery," he points out, "gives birth to nothing; gives death to all things." Men had found a basic truth in Paganism, and the quackery and dupery had come later. Having disregarded the quackery theory, he considers the allegory theory—that Paganism was a poetic kind of symbolism. This he also discards, feeling that men would not base a solid belief on what is merely a poetic sport. Carlyle's own belief is that to the primitive mind all things in nature have their air of divine mystery, and that the Pagan worship of natural objects and forces was based on man's sense of wonder.

> . . . What in such a time as ours it requires a Prophet or Poet to teach us, namely, the stripping-off of those poor undevout wrappages, nomenclatures and scientific hearsays,—this, the ancient earnest soul, as yet unencumbered with these things, did for itself. The world, which is now divine only to the gifted, was then divine to whosoever would turn his eye upon it. . . . Canopus shining-down over the desert, with its blue diamond brightness (that wild blue spirit-like brightness, far brighter than we ever witness here), would pierce into the heart of the wild Ishmaelitish man, whom it was guiding through the solitary waste there. To his wild heart, with all feelings in it, with no *speech* for any feeling, it might seem a little eye, that Canopus, glancing-out on him from the great deep Eternity; revealing the inner Splendour to him. Cannot we understand how these men *worshipped* Canopus; became what we call Sabeans, worshipping the stars? Such is to me the secret of all forms of Paganism. **Worship is transcendent wonder;** wonder for which there is now no limit or measure; that is worship. . . .

Wreathe iron pokers into true-love knots

Source: ON DONNE'S POETRY
Author: Samuel Taylor Coleridge (1772–1834)
First published: 1836
Type of work: Epigram

Context: Coleridge's writing of poetry, despite his great genius, continued for only a short time. His important works were completed within the space of a few years. In the presence of his friend Wordsworth he felt an inferiority complex, and some scholars maintain that Wordsworth discouraged his poetry writing after the publication of *Lyrical Ballads* (1798–1800). However, Coleridge was interested in German philosophy and literature, and when he could drag himself from his opium, and the even greater opiate of reading, he sometimes forced himself to write critical articles on that subject. Also driven to lecturing by the poverty he knew from birth to death, he discussed Shakespeare's plays and characters with great insight and the imagination of a poet. Despite advances in Shakespearean research in the century and a half since the publication of his *Essays and Lectures* and his *Biographia Literaria* (1817), his critical opinions are still worth consideration. He indulged in a number of

Epigrams which could be quickly completed. When they dealt critically with literary people, like the one on Donne's poetry, they were enlightening. They were not collected until 1850. John Donne (1573–1631) was the originator of the school of Metaphysical poetry, the members of which strove to find relationships in things apparently unlike and to exercise their intelligence in combining dissimilar images. Donne headed a revolt against the sweetness of Elizabethan poetry. Instead of its delicacy and charm, he worked for intellectual intensity. Taking his qualities into consideration, Coleridge summed Donne up in four lines. There was a camel-like irregularity in the swing of Donne's lines. His love-knot for a sweetheart's hair was more likely to be iron than ribbon, and the ideas were shaped with intensity as if in a blast furnace, or pushed into form as if by a press, tightened by screws.

With Donne, whose muse on dromedary trots,
Wreathe iron pokers into true-love knots;
Rhyme's sturdy cripple, fancy's maze and clue,
Wit's forge and fire-blast, meaning's press and screw.

The wretched have no friends

Source: ALL FOR LOVE (Act III, sc. i, l. 83)
Author: John Dryden (1631–1700)
First published: 1678
Type of work: Dramatic tragedy

Context: All for Love, or The World Well Lost, based on the last two acts of Shakespeare's *Antony and Cleopatra,* is generally considered to be Dryden's best tragedy. It was written as part of his contract to supply the King's Theatre of London with three plays a year. Dryden wrote a total of twenty-eight dramas, counting his reworkings of Shakespeare's *The Tempest* (1667), *Troilus and Cressida* (1679), and this one. In some of his earlier plays, he used rhymed couplets, but for *All for Love,* he returned to blank verse. The work shows French influence and dramatic theory. It maintains the unities by confining the action to the Temple of Isis, and the time to Antony's birthday. So the Shakespearean spectacle of the fate of a nation had to be changed to the tragedy of the fortunes of two people. There was little time for character development. Antony seems unmanly because of a lack of vices. Cleopatra, the idealized heroine, has become untrue to herself. Yet in the dialogue can be found lines comparable to those of Shakespeare, as, for instance, the descriptions of Cleopatra and her barge. In Act III, after the coronation of Antony, his general Ventidius appears to warn him of dangers ahead. Though he did defeat Caesar with great slaughter on one occasion, he cannot hope for a repetition. Caesar is now warned and ready, and he also has access to abundant supplies; Antony can draw only from Egypt. Besides, as one whose fortunes are fading, he has dis- covered that his fair-weather friends are abandoning him.

VENTIDIUS

Expect no more; Caesar is on his guard:
I know, sir, you have conquer'd against odds.
But still you draw supplies from one poor town,
And of Egyptians; he has all the world,
And at his back nations come pouring in,
To fill the gap you make. Pray, think again.

ANTONY

Why doest thou drive me from myself, to search
For foreign aid?—To hunt my memory,
And range all o'er a waste and barren place,
To find a friend? **The wretched have no friends.**

Years steal fire from the mind

Source: CHILDE HAROLD'S PILGRIMAGE (Canto III, stanza 8)
Author: George Gordon, Lord Byron (1788–1824)
First published: 1816 (Canto III)
Type of work: Narrative poem

Context: One reason for the importance of *Childe Harold's Pilgrimage* is that here for the first time is introduced the Byronic hero, who will reappear in half-a-dozen of his narrative poems, always with the same characteristics. He is a true romantic, satiated with life's pleasures, disgusted with civilized society, and though in love with some gentle woman, takes pride in suppressing all tender feelings. A deep regret over some youthful crime usually embitters his thoughts. This inherent melancholia was one reason for the poem's instant success. Elaborate descriptions of nature in exotic oriental countries added charm for its readers. Childe Harold ("Childe" meaning "Young Lord") is the chief character of a sort of travel book in verse, following the itinerary Byron himself took in the summer of 1809, in company with his friend John Cam Hobhouse (1786–1869). Instead of the usual postgraduate Grand Tour of France and Italy, Byron went through the Mediterranean as far as Greece and Turkey. After his return to England, the first two cantos were published, in 1812. The furor over them added to his charm and helped his courtship of Miss Anna Isabella Milbanke, a well-educated country girl, much given to moralizing. Immediately following the wedding, in January, 1815, Byron realized he had made a mistake and so did she. No reason was ever given for their separation, though some suspect it was her discovery of improper relations between Byron and his half-sister,

Augusta Leigh. In any case, a few weeks after the birth of his daughter, Ada, he left his wife and England. Following his departure came a storm of gossip that settled on him the reputation for dissoluteness. He traveled to Switzerland, where he spent the summer with Shelley and had an affair with Mary Shelley's sister, Jane Clairmont. Here he wrote the third canto of *Childe Harold's Pilgrimage,* that was published in 1816. Canto III is the most admired part of the poem. It opens with a message to his daughter Ada, whom he had not seen since she was five weeks old. Does she look like her mother? He declares himself "once more upon the waters" that are taking him away from England. Long ago, in his "youth's summer," he had first sung about Harold. How greatly things have changed since then! But he has retained one of his old traits, "the strength to bear what time cannot abate,/ and feed on bitter fruits without accusing Fate." So, too, has his hero Harold changed, and in stanza 8 the poet comments on the changes:

> Something too much of this; but now 'tis past,
> And the spell closes with its silent seal.
> Long absent Harold re-appears at last;
> He of the breast which fain no more would feel,
> Wrung with the wounds which kill not but ne'er heal;
> Yet Time, who changes all, had alter'd him
> In soul and aspect as in age; **years steal**
> **Fire from the mind** as vigor from the limb,
> And life's enchanted cup but sparkles near the brim.

Yet still we hug the dear deceit

Source: VISIONS, FOR THE ENTERTAINMENT AND INSTRUCTION OF YOUNG MINDS (Part IV, "Content")
Author: Nathaniel Cotton (1705–1788)
First published: 1751
Type of work: Didactic poem

Context: Although his works enjoyed considerable popularity in his own day, Dr. Nathaniel Cotton was a man who sedulously avoided publicity. All his writings were published anonymously, and his tombstone bears only the names of those who lie beneath it. His collected works were edited by his son after Cotton's death, but no biographical sketch of the poet was included; this lack was probably in accordance with his own wishes. Unusually humble, he seems also to have been a cultivated and kindly man. Dr. Cotton was a physician; he settled at St. Albans in 1740 and remained in practice there until his death. In conjunction with his medical practice, he operated a private asylum for the insane. The poet William Cowper (1731–1800) was confined there during his first severe mental breakdown, from December 1763 to June 1765; during this period he and Dr.

Cotton became close friends. The poet and playwright Edward Young (1683–1765) was another of Cotton's friends, and the doctor attended him during his last illness. Cotton is remembered today for his descriptions of these events and for his kindly influence on the participants, rather than for his poetry. The latter is quite typical of its period: it is didactic, pious, and the work of a cultivated mind. His best-known volume, *Visions, for the Entertainment and Instruction of Young Minds,* is based on the *Fables* of John Gay (1688–1732). Gay was an irrepressible spirit best known today for his libretto to *The Beggar's Opera.* His *Fables* was more popular in his own time; it ranges from cheerful burlesque through penetrating satire to bitter cynicism. In *Visions,* Cotton has attempted to transform his commentaries into verses that will provide a moral lesson for young readers. He deals first with slander, then with pleasure and health. Part IV is a little allegory wherein the poet finds himself in a magnificent palace. All is harmonious and beautiful. At length the host, splendid personage, appears and reveals that his name is Content. A sermon ensues in which the bases of true contentment are explored. The opening lines of Part IV are given below:

> Man is deceiv'd by outward show—
> 'Tis a plain, homespun truth, I know;
> The fraud prevails at ev'ry age,
> So says the school boy, and the sage;
> **Yet still we hug the dear deceit,**
> And still exclaim against the cheat.
> But whence this inconsistent part?
> Say, moralists, who know the heart;
> If you'll this labyrinth pursue,
> I'll go before and find the clue.
>
> I dream'd ('twas on a birth-day night)
> A sumptuous palace rose to sight;
> The builder had thro' ev'ry part
> Observ'd the chastest rules of art;
> Raphael and Titian had display'd
> All the full force of light and shade.
> Around the liv'ried servants wait;
> An aged porter kept the gate.
>
> As I was traversing the hall,
> Where Brussels looms adorn'd the wall,
>   •   •   •
> A graceful person came in view. . . .

You can make better use of iron than forging it into chains

Source: SPEECHES (First Series, "Harper's Ferry": Speech delivered at Brooklyn, November 1, 1859)
Author: Wendell Phillips (1811–1884)
First published: 1859
Type of work: Political speech

Context: A confirmed abolitionist, Wendell Phillips was also a widely known orator. He was a Harvard graduate and a lawyer by profession, who abandoned his original career and joined William Lloyd Garrison in the fight against slavery. Most of the great speakers of the day employed flowery and heroic oratory, but Phillips adopted a more natural and familiar style. He was dynamic and forceful, pleasant, and immensely popular. Among other leading abolitionist voices was that of Henry Ward Beecher. When John Brown carried out his raid on the arsenal at Harper's Ferry, Virginia, a famous weapon figured prominently in the episode: this was a breech-loading carbine invented by Christian Sharps. In fact, these arms became known as "Beecher's Bibles." Brown captured the arsenal at Harper's Ferry in 1859, hoping to set off a general uprising of slaves throughout the South. Abolitionists applauded this effort, though it was a failure; there was no uprising, and he and his men were taken after a brief siege. When Phillips, on the evening of November 1, spoke in Beecher's church his subject was "the lesson of the hour." This lesson, says Phillips, "is insurrection. . . . Insurrection of thought always precedes insurrection of arms. The last twenty years have been an insurrection of thought. We seem to be entering on a new phase of the great American struggle. . . ." He contrasts the Old World's distrust of "the average conscience" with the social awareness he sees in America. He describes the growing enlightenment of the nation and the extent of its intellectual and moral progress. Law, however, is nothing unless it is backed by public opinion; and Phillips does not advocate passive resistance if worst comes to worst. The public must see things as they are. Praising John Brown, Phillips likens him to the heroes of the American Revolution, and adds that he is no less heroic because the raid came to nothing. If slavery is to end, violence may be necessary:

I believe in moral suasion. The age of bullets is over. The age of ideas is come. I think that is the rule of our age. The old Hindoo dreamed, you know, that he saw the human race led out to its varied fortune. First, he saw men bitted and curbed, and the reins went back to an iron hand. But his dream changed on and on, until at last he saw men led by reins that came from the brain, and went back into an unseen hand. It was the type of governments; the first despotism, palpable, iron; and the last, our government, a government of brains, a government of ideas. I believe in it,—in public opinion.

Yet, let me say, in passing, I think **you can make a better use of iron than forging it into chains.** If you must have the metal, put it into Sharpe's rifles. It is a great deal better used that way than in fetters; types are better than bullets, but bullets a thousand times rather than a clumsy statue of a mock great man, for hypocrites to kneel down and worship in a State-House yard. . . . Some men seem to think that our institutions are necessarily safe, because we have free schools and cheap books, and a public opinion that controls. But that is no evidence of safety. . . . What India and France and Spain wanted was live men, and that is what we want to-day; men who are willing to look their own destiny, and their own responsibilities, in the face. . . .

You carry Caesar and his fortune

Source: PARALLEL LIVES ("Caesar," as translated by John Dryden)
Author: Plutarch (c. 45–c. 125)
First transcribed: c. 105–115
Type of work: Biography

Context: Plutarch was a Greek writer who spent considerable time in Rome, and one whose primary interest lay in biography. He wrote a number of essays, chiefly moral in nature, but his best-known work is *Parallel Lives of Illustrious Greeks and Romans.* His method was to write the biographical essays in pairs, one of a Greek and one of a Roman; each pair was then followed by a comparison of the two personages. In these works he quoted many sources, perhaps 250 authors in all; many of these writers survive only in Plutarch's use of them. In the biographies Plutarch's chief purpose is to delineate character, rather than to give a straightforward account; it is for this reason that the portraits are striking and filled with a life of their own. The reader is left with a strong impression that he knows, and perhaps understands, the men Plutarch has depicted. True to his purpose, the biographer uses anecdotes, comments, and incidents for the insight they will provide or for their value as illustration. Strict chronological order is sometimes ignored: to Plutarch, the understanding of character is of greater significance than mere tabulation. It is for this reason that Shakespeare found him so useful. In his essay on Julius Caesar, Plutarch described vividly that leader's burning ambition, determination, fearlessness, and untiring energy. One illustration occurs during Caesar's war with Pompey. Following a major victory, Caesar returns briefly to Rome; resigning his dictatorship, he declares himself consul and returns to the war. He marches so fast that most of his army cannot keep up; but the weary troops are shamed into a stronger effort by this leader, who has more endurance than they. Caesar arrives in Appolonia, but the army has not yet arrived from Brundusium and he cannot fight.

1313

. . . At last he resolved upon a most hazardous experiment, and embarked, without any one's knowledge, in a boat of twelve oars, to cross over to Brundusium, though the sea was at that time covered with a vast fleet of the enemy. He got on board in the night-time, in the dress of a slave, and throwing himself down like a person of no consequence, lay along at the bottom of the vessel. The river Anius was to carry them down to sea, and there used to blow a gentle gale every morning from the land, which made it calm at the mouth of the river, by driving the waves forward; but this night there had blown a strong wind from the sea, which overpowered that from the land, so that where the river met the influx of the sea-water and the opposition of the waves it was extremely rough and angry; and the current was beaten back with such a violent swell that the master of the boat could not make good his passage, but ordered his sailors to tack about and return.

Caesar, upon this, discovered himself, and taking the man by the hand, who was surprised to see him there said, "Go on, my friend, and fear nothing; **you carry Caesar and his fortune** in your boat." The mariners, when they heard that, forgot the storm, and laying all their strength to their oars, did what they could to force their way down the river. But when it was to no purpose, and the vessel now took in much water, Caesar finding himself in such danger at the very mouth of the river, much against his will permitted the master to turn back. When he was come to land, his soldiers ran to him in a multitude, reproaching him for what he had done. . . .

You come most carefully upon your hour

Source: HAMLET (Act I, sc. 1, l. 6)
Author: William Shakespeare (1564–1616)
First published: 1603
Type of work: Dramatic tragedy

Context: Twice the ghost of Hamlet's father has appeared an hour past midnight before the castle at Elsinore. He will, however, not speak to the guardsmen, who have invited Hamlet's friend, the scholar Horatio, "to watch the minutes of this night." Horatio, we learn shortly, is rather skeptical of the story, an attitude that contrasts sharply with his reaction to the arrival of the Ghost: "It harrows me with fear and wonder." Leading up to the appearance of the Ghost, Shakespeare carefully creates a mood of anticipation and suspense out of the changing of the guard. The sentinel Francisco is delighted to leave. His replacement, Bernardo, wishes that Horatio and the soldier Marcellus, who will be "rivals," partners, of his watch, would arrive:

BERNARDO

Who's there?

1314

FRANCISCO
Nay, answer me. Stand and unfold yourself.

BERNARDO
Long live the king.

FRANCISCO
Bernardo?

BERNARDO
He.

FRANCISCO
You come most carefully upon your hour.

BERNARDO
'Tis now struck twelve, get thee to bed Francisco.

FRANCISCO
For this relief much thanks, 'tis bitter cold,
And I am sick at heart.

. . .

BERNARDO
Well, good night,
If you do meet Horatio and Marcellus,
The rivals of my watch, bid them make haste.

You might prove anything by figures

Source: CHARTISM (Chapter 2)
Author: Thomas Carlyle (1795–1881)
First published: 1839
Type of work: Political essay

Context: Chartism was a labor movement which began in the 1830's and reached its high point during the following decade. Its basic ideal was to demand and establish a Charter which would guarantee certain rights to labor and laboring classes. It later became the two movements which followed it, co-operatives and trade-unionism; a number of badly-needed reforms were brought about through its efforts. Chartist agitation was re- sisted strongly at first by the British government, and by 1839 it was said that a Reform Ministry had abolished Chartism altogether. Carlyle knew that this assumption was false. He was aware that the motivation behind the movement had not been dealt with; as he points out in this essay, "Chartism means the bitter discontent grown fierce and mad, the wrong condition therefore or the wrong disposition, of the Working Classes of

England. It is a new name for a thing which has had many names, which will yet have many." If it be madness, he continues, then the nation must bring sanity to it, not try to crush it. In order to accomplish this end, the causes of the discontent must be found and measured. "We have heard it asked, Why Parliament throws no light on this question of the Working Classes, and the condition or disposition they are in? . . . A Reformed Parliament, one would think, should inquire into popular discontents be-*fore* they get the length of pikes and torches!" Parliament, he feels, has done nothing at all; the matter can no longer "be left to the Collective Folly of the Nation." Obviously, there is something these laboring classes are trying to say, and a clear interpretation of it must be made. "Certain researches and considerations of ours on the matter, since no one else will undertake it, are now to be made public." He admits that the researchers have yielded him little, and proceeds to explain why:

A witty statesman said, **you might prove anything by figures.** We have looked into various statistic works, Statistic-Society Reports, Poor-Law Reports, Reports and Pamphlets not a few, with a sedulous eye to this question of the Working Classes and their general condition in England; we grieve to say, with as good as no result whatever. . . . Tables are like cobwebs, like the sieve of the Danaides; beautifully reticulated, orderly to look upon, but which will hold no conclusion. Tables are abstractions, and the object a most concrete one. . . . Statistics is a science which ought to be honourable, the basis of many most important sciences; but it is not to be carried on by steam. . . . Vain to send the purblind and blind to the shore of a Pactolus never so golden: these find only gravel; the seer and finder alone picks up gold grains there. And now the purblind offering you, with asservation and protrusive importunity, his basket of gravel as gold, what steps are to be taken with him?—Statistics, one may hope, will improve gradually, and become good for something. Meanwhile, it is to be feared the crabbed satirist was partly right, as things go: "A judicious man," says he, "looks at Statistics, not to get knowledge, but to save himself from having ignorance foisted on him." With what serene conclusiveness a member of some Useful-Knowledge Society stops your mouth with a figure of arithmetic! To him it seems he has there extracted the elixir of the matter, on which now nothing more can be said. It is needful that you look into his said extracted elixir; and ascertain, alas, too probably, not without a sigh, that it is wash and vapidity, good only for the gutters.

You must not kiss and tell

Source: LOVE FOR LOVE (Act II, sc. ii)
Author: William Congreve (1670–1729)
First published: 1695
Type of work: Dramatic comedy

Context: Mrs. Foresight rebukes her sister, Mrs. Frail, a woman of the town, for injudiciously riding around London with gentlemen in hackney-coaches, strongly hinting that her behavior has been immoral. In the course of the conversation it comes to light that Mrs. Foresight is no more moral than is Mrs. Frail. Mrs. Frail then confesses that she must enter into a marriage that will provide her with security. She says that Ben, the wealthy Sir Sampson Legend's son, is expected back from sea. He is supposed to marry Miss Prue, Mrs. Foresight's awkward country stepdaughter, but it seems that Miss Prue is much attached to Tattle, a half-witted beau. Mrs. Frail tells Mrs. Foresight that she will encourage the affair, as a marriage between Miss Prue and Tattle would leave Ben on the matrimonial market. At this point Tattle and Miss Prue enter. Miss Prue displays a snuffbox filled with snuff that Tattle has given her and also shows a ring which he has given her for a kiss. Tattle objects that she should not kiss and tell, but she says that she will tell her mother, meaning her stepmother, Mrs. Foresight.

MISS PRUE

Look you here, madam, then, what Mr. Tattle has given me. —Look you here, cousin, here's a snuff-box; nay, there's snuff in't;—here, will you have any?—Oh good! how sweet it is. —Mr. Tattle is all over sweet, his peruke is sweet, and his gloves are sweet, and his handkerchief is sweet, pure sweet, sweeter than roses. —Smell him, mother, madam, I mean. —He gave me this ring for a kiss.

TATTLE

O fy, miss! **you must not kiss and tell.**

MISS PRUE

Yes; I may tell my mother. . . .

You never know what life means till you die

Source: THE RING AND THE BOOK ("Guido," Line 2375)
Author: Robert Browning (1812–1889)
First published: 1868–1869
Type of work: Dramatic monologue

Context: Of all Browning's works, this poem is the most long sustained; it is generally considered his masterpiece. He based it on an old book found in Florence which contained the transcript of a murder trial that occurred there in 1698. Browning's re-creation of the event takes its title from the ring, or circle, of evidence and from the book in which it was recorded. Browning presents the evidence as seen from twelve different viewpoints and weighs it carefully, bringing out the character of each actor as he does so. The central figure is Guido Franceschini; he is a Florentine nobleman spurred on by ambition and fierce pride, who has married a young heiress in an effort to save his decaying fortune. Guido is fifty years of age and incapable of love. He suspects his wife Pompilia of infidelity and is further enraged when he discovers she is not really the child of Pietro and Violante, but has been supplied by them in order that certain property might be kept out of Guido's hands. A trial is held to settle the property, and Guido's brutality asserts itself: Pompilia leaves him, traveling under the protection of a young priest named Caponsacchi. Guido pursues and captures them, and another trial is held after he charges them with adultery. It ends in a legal separation; Pompilia is placed in a convent and the priest is temporarily exiled. Since Pompilia is now expecting a child, she is soon allowed to go home to her parents. She sues for a divorce; the infuriated Guido retaliates by murdering Pompilia and her parents. She lives long enough to accuse him. When his trial for murder begins, Guido conveys the impression that he is an upright and honest man who has suffered an unbearable humiliation. His plea of justifiable homicide is not accepted, and as events go against him, Guido's evil nature becomes more and more apparent. The cardinal and the abate visit him in prison, offering him the consolation of the Church. Guido berates them and condemns the Church and its political activities. He attempts to make various deals with them, and through them with the authorities. He tries vainly to change the past, that his murders might be carried out more effectively. Gradually his bravado evaporates; Pompilia haunts him, and he tells of the abuses she suffered at his hands. He still wants her child, that he may bring it up brutally. Finally, with execution imminent, he begs for mercy. The breakdown is all the more shocking when contrasted with such bluster as the following:

What if I be o'ertaken, pushed to the front
By all you crowding smoother souls behind,
And reach, a minute sooner than was meant,
The boundary whereon I break to mist?
Go to! the smoothest safest of you all,
· · ·
Will rock vertiginously in turn, and reel,
And, emulative, rush to death like me.
Later or sooner by a minute then,
So much for the untimeliness of death!
And, as regards the manner that offends,
The rude and rough, I count the same for gain.
Be the act harsh and quick! Undoubtedly
The soul's condensed and, twice itself, expands
To burst through life, by alternation due,
Into the other state whate'er it prove.
You never know what life means till you die. . . .

You roll my log, and I will roll yours

Source: APOCOLOCYNTOSIS (Part IX)
Author: Seneca (c. 4 B.C.–A.D. 65)
First transcribed: Unknown
Type of work: Satire

Context: According to the ancient tradition, this piece, "The Pumpkinification of Claudius," is the work of Seneca; although scholars have long debated the truth of the tradition, they have proved it neither true nor false. They do agree, however, that it is clearly a member of the literary class named *Satura Menippea,* a satiric medley in prose and verse. The satire relates the fictional events which lead to the deification of the Emperor Claudius after his death.

Jove has Claudius led out of the chamber in which the question of his deification is being discussed. First to speak then is Janus, the two-faced god, who suggests that no mortals ought to be made gods. Next to speak is Diespiter, son of Vica Pota, who recommends that Claudius, as kin of Augustus, already deified, be made a member of the pantheon. While he is speaking, Hercules goes about the chamber seeking votes for his side in the matter.

. . . The meeting was divided, and it looked as though Claudius was to win the day. For Hercules saw his iron was in the fire, trotted here and trotted there, saying, "Don't deny me; I make a point of the matter. I'll do as much for you again, when you like; **you roll my log, and I'll roll yours** [*deinde tu si quid volueris, in vicam faciam*]: one hand washes another."

You shall comprehend all vagrom men

Source: MUCH ADO ABOUT NOTHING (Act III, sc. iii, l. 25)
Author: William Shakespeare (1564–1616)
First published: 1600
Type of work: Dramatic comedy

Context: Dogberry and Verges, Shakespear's clownish constables, are charged with enlisting and supervising the night watch in Messina. As a result of overhearing a conversation between Conrade and Borachio, Don John's henchmen, they gain possession of information which could refute the false charges later brought against Hero by her fiancé Claudio at the wedding ceremony. For the con-

stables learn that Borachio has wooed Margaret, Hero's maid, at Hero's window while Claudio observed from a distance assuming, as the villainous Don John charged, that his intended bride was entertaining a lover. The constables, though utterly naïve, at least have sense enough to realize this information should get to Leonato, Governor of Messina, immediately. But so laborious and repetitious is their report that the impatient Leonato, anxious to attend his daughter's wedding, leaves them to examine the prisoners themselves. If their ineptness very nearly permits tragic consequences, certainly in other ways it enhances the comic tone of the play. Like Hostess Quickly, they are linguistic bumblers whose malapropisms create comic confusion. Dogberry, having selected **Hugh Oatcake** and **George Seacoal** because they can read and write, issues his instructions to these night watchmen and, in so doing, illustrates the comedy of his verbal confusion:

DOGBERRY

Come hither neighbor Seacoal. God hath blessed you with a good name. To be a well-favoured man is the gift of fortune, but to write and read comes by nature.

SECOND WATCHMAN

Both which master constable—

DOGBERRY

You have. I knew it would be your answer. Well, for your favour sir, why give God thanks, and make no boast of it, and for your writing and reading, let that appear when there is no need of such vanity. You are thought here to be the most senseless [sensible] and fit man for the constable of the watch. Therefore bear you the lantern. This is your charge. **You shall comprehend all vagrom men,** you are to bid any man stand, in the Prince's name.

You would find a tale in everything

Source: SIMON LEE (Stanza 9)
Author: William Wordsworth (1770–1850)
First published: 1798
Type of work: Narrative

Context: Wordsworth, with the collaboration of Samuel Taylor Coleridge, set the stage for Romantic poetry through the publication of *Lyrical Ballads* in 1798. One of the cardinal purposes of this "new" literature was to depict the simple folk in the throes of credible human emotions. Included among Wordsworth's contributions is the narrative of Simon Lee, who in his youth was renowned in the community as a merry huntsman; "In those days [with his mind on blither tasks] he little cared/ For husbandry or tillage," preferring to outrun every one in the chase. Time has taken its inevitable toll, however, and now Simon is bent and broken. "His body, dwindled and awry,/ Rests upon ankles swoln and thick." With his aged wife Ruth, he feebly attempts to till a narrow strip of land which he had enclosed many years ago. The poet, having established his narrative, addresses the reader directly concerning the rather

1320

obvious possibilities of drawing a moral observation on life and the vagaries of time and fortune. But, after the exegesis, instead of constructing such a heavily didactic perspective, he describes how—after he has helped the feeble Simon cut a tree—the old man's gratitude touches him more profoundly than could any lamentation over his wretched plight:

. . .

My gentle Reader, I perceive
How patiently you've waited,
And now I fear that you expect
Some tale will be related.

O Reader! had you in your mind
Such stores as silent thought can bring,
O gentle Reader, **you would find
A tale in every thing.**
What more I have to say is short,
And you must kindly take it:
It is no tale; but, should you think,
Perhaps a tale you'll make it.

Young boys and girls are level now with men

Source: ANTONY AND CLEOPATRA (Act IV, sc. xv, ll. 65–66)
Author: William Shakespeare (1564–1616)
First published: 1623
Type of work: Dramatic tragedy

Context: With friction rather than harmony a triumvirate, Antony, Octavius Caesar, and Lepidus, rules the vast Roman Empire. Antony, whose charge is the Eastern portion of the kingdom, loses power to young Caesar when he falls foolishly in love with the voluptuous and beguiling Queen of Egypt, Cleopatra. Finally the forces of Antony and Caesar meet in battle. Antony, badly beaten, feels that Cleopatra has caused his downfall and vows to kill her. Cleopatra tries to bring her lover to repentance by sending him a message saying she is dead. Antony, receiving the false message and filled with grief, falls upon his sword. He is taken to die in the arms of Cleopatra, who says to her attendants:

CLEOPATRA
O see, my women,

[ANTONY *dies.*]

The crown o' th' earth doth melt. My lord!
O withered is the garland of the war,
The soldiers' pole is fall'n: **young boys and girls
Are level now with men;** the odds is gone,

1321

And there is nothing left remarkable
Beneath the visiting moon.
. . .

No more but e'en a woman, and commanded
By such poor passion as the maid that milks,
And does the meanest chores. It were for me
To throw my sceptre at the injurious gods,
To tell them that this world did equal theirs
Till they had stol'n our jewel. . . .

A young man married is a man that's marred

Source: ALL'S WELL THAT ENDS WELL (Act II, sc. iii, l. 315)
Author: William Shakespeare (1564–1616)
First published: 1623
Type of work: Dramatic comedy

Context: Bertram, the young Count of Rousillon, goes off to serve his ailing king, leaving behind his mother and Helena, daughter of a famous physician. Secretly in love with Bertram, Helena travels to the court, where she cures the king and asks as her fee one of the young lords of the court for a husband. When she chooses Bertram, he complains that her low rank can only defile his noble blood. Ordered by the king to marry Helena, the proud young man consents, but later tells his servant that he will send his new wife home and will "never bed her," but will instead be off to the war.

> BERTRAM
> Go with me to my chamber, and advise me.
> I'll send her straight away. To-morrow
> I'll to the wars, she to her single sorrow.

> PAROLLES
> Why these balls bound, there's noise in it. 'Tis hard.
> **A young man married is a man that's marred.**
> Therefore away, and leave her bravely; go.
> The King has done you wrong; but hush, 'tis so.

The younger generation will come knocking at my door

Source: THE MASTER BUILDER (Act I)
Author: Henrik Ibsen (1828–1906)
First published: 1892
Type of work: Realistic drama

Context: Halvard Solness, the master-builder of Ibsen's play, is, on one level of interpretation, an opportunist who builds his success upon the misfortunes and ruin of other persons. Although of little talent, except as an entrepreneur, he makes himself a reputation and a fortune as an architect and builder. Actually, the capital with which he starts is his wife's and comes in part from the destruction of her family home. The talent Solness uses is the talent of his former employer, Knut Brovik, and the latter's son, Ragnar. Realizing that his position at the head of his profession is a result of luck and, perhaps, his strange ability to force people and things to his own ends, Solness, mindful of the passage of time and the shortness of life, fears that his position is constantly in danger of being undermined. He has had such great good fortune that he fears that misfortune, when it comes, will be equally great. In a conversation with his friend and family physician, Dr. Herdal, he reveals his fear at having luck so much on his side and how he believes that the younger generation will be the instrument of his downfall:

SOLNESS

It terrifies me—terrifies me every hour of the day. For sooner or later the luck must turn, you see.

DR. HERDAL

Oh nonsense! What should make the luck turn?

SOLNESS

The younger generation.

DR. HERDAL

Pooh! The younger generation! You are not laid on the shelf yet, I should hope. Oh no—your position is probably firmer now than it has ever been.

SOLNESS

The luck will turn, I know it.—I feel the day approaching, Some one or other will take it into his head to say: Give me a chance! And then all the rest will come clamouring after him, and shake their fists at me and shout: Make room—make room— make room! Yes, just you see, doctor—presently **the younger generation will come knocking at my door——**

Your sin will find you out

Source: NUMBERS 32:23
Author: Unknown
First transcribed: c.1000–400 B.C.
Type of work: Religious history and law

1323

Context: After answering the call of the Lord and leading his people out of Egypt, Moses finds his task a thankless one. His followers are all too human. Shortsighted, impatient, turbulent, they incur the wrath of the Lord again and again. Moses never fails to intercede in their behalf; but they are an unruly group and shepherding them is a frustrating endeavor. Their first transgression occurs during the encampment at Sinai: while Moses is on the mountain receiving instructions from God concerning proper forms of worship, the Israelites fashion themselves an image of a golden calf, after the manner of the Egyptians, and hold an orgy around it. Moses returns and takes stern measures to stem the revolt, then begs the Lord's forgiveness. The Lord is not pleased but orders Moses to lead his people forth, following a guiding Angel, who will lead them to the land promised to their forebears long ago. Moses sends out scouts, or spies, to investigate the country they must cross; there are twelve of these, one for each tribe. They return with conflicting reports, and the people threaten to stone Moses. The Lord, His patience exhausted, condemns them to wander forty years in the wilderness; thus no one over twenty will live to enter the promised land. During the ensuing four decades the people of Israel wander about the deserts of the Near East; somehow Moses holds them together, but his trials are many. They are fed miraculously at times of extreme need, but the Lord does not shorten their sentence. At length they approach the Jordan; Moses climbs the mountain, Abarim or Nebo, that he may see the goal he will not live to reach. Then, in accordance with God's instructions, he names Joshua his successor. Representatives of the tribes of Reuben and Gad then ask Moses if they may settle on this side of the stream. Moses misunderstands them, thinking this request is waywardness, and replies angrily. But they reassure him:

And they came near unto him, and said, We will build sheepfolds here for our cattle, and cities for our little ones:

But we ourselves will go ready armed before the children of Israel, until we have brought them unto their place: and our little ones shall dwell in the fenced cities because of the inhabitants of the land.

We will not return unto our houses, until the children of Israel have inherited every man his inheritance.

For we will not inherit with them on yonder side Jordan, or forward; because our inheritance is fallen to us on this side Jordan eastward.

And Moses said unto them, If ye will do this thing, if ye will go armed before the Lord to war,

And will go all of you armed over Jordan before the Lord, until he hath driven out his enemies from before him,

And the land be subdued before the Lord: then afterward ye shall return, and be guiltless before the Lord, and before Israel; and this land shall be your possession before the Lord.

1324

But if ye will not do so, behold, ye have sinned against the LORD; and be sure **your sin will find you out.**

Build you cities for your little ones, and folds for your sheep; and do that which hath proceeded out of your mouth.

And the children of Gad and the children of Reuben spake unto Moses, saying, Thy servants will do as my lord commandeth.

Your true lover of literature is never fastidious

Source: THE DOCTOR (Chapter 17)
Author: Robert Southey (1774–1843)
First published: 1834–1847
Type of work: Literary miscellany

Context: Robert Southey was an important literary figure in his day. A leader and pioneer, he explored new paths in literature and opened up ways for others to follow. The only professional man of letters of his time who depended solely upon his literary efforts, Southey experimented widely and was active in many forms of writing. He attempted a number of new approaches and freedoms in the structure of verse and in the choice of subject matter. In his break with eighteenth century restrictions, he helped to reëstablish blank verse, contributed to popularization of the ballad, and introduced exotic settings which aroused interest in the Orient. He wrote a number of epics, which he hoped would insure his lasting fame. In addition to his poetry, Southey wrote a great deal of competent prose, including essays, criticism, and several historical works. He was named poet laureate in 1813. In spite of his historical importance, however, Southey's work does not seem to have stood the test of time. Critics of the present century are agreed that his talents were unequal to his ambitions, and that his work is largely mediocre. He was a conscientious workman, however, and an indefatigable scholar. His mind eventually gave way from overwork and he died insane. *The Doctor* is an interesting example of his prose writing, and a difficult one to classify. A lengthy and curious work with which Southey amused himself in his spare time, it is a compendium of anecdotes, fantasy, whimsy, facetiae, and all sorts of miscellaneous lore. These diverse materials are joined loosely and presented in humorous fashion; to a modern reader the facetiousness is labored, but the variety of subject matter has a fascination of its own. It is evident that Southey enjoyed writing these pages, in which he discourses at random. In Chapter 16 he discusses literary appetites in general, and in the following chapter he examines and appraises the reader whose tastes are fastidious:

A fastidious taste is like a squeamish appetite; the one has its origin in some disease of mind, as the other has in some ailment of the stomach. **Your true lover of literature is never fastidious.** I do not mean the *helluo librorum,* the swinish feeder, who thinks that every name which is to be found in a title-page, or on a tombstone, ought to be rescued from oblivion; nor those first cousins of the moth, who labour under a bulimy for black-letter, and believe every thing to be excellent which was written in the reign of Elizabeth. I mean the man of robust and healthy intellect, who gathers the harvest of literature into his barns, threshes the straw, winnows the grain, grinds it at his own mill, bakes it in his own oven, and then eats the true bread of knowledge. If he bake his loaf upon a cabbage leaf, and eat onions with his bread and cheese, let who will find fault with him for his taste,—not I!

Your wit's too hot, it speeds too fast, 'twill tire

Source: LOVE'S LABOUR'S LOST (Act II, sc. i, l. 120)
Author: William Shakespeare (1564–1616)
First published: 1598
Type of work: Dramatic comedy

Context: Ferdinand, King of Navarre, has taken an oath along with several other men to study for three years and to have no association with women. It follows that certainly no woman could enter his courtyard and residence. When the daughter of the King of France arrives on a diplomatic mission, Ferdinand meets the group in the field outside his court so that he breaks his oath only partially. This situation is the setting for the above dialogue. While Ferdinand and the Princess of France converse, Berowne, one of the men taking the study oath with the king, addresses Katharine, one of the ladies attending the princess. Berowne asks Katharine if he had once danced with her. Instead of answering, she only mockingly and pertly repeats his question. When he states he knows he danced with her, she sarcastically points out, "How needless was it then to ask the question." After one more heated exchange of words between the two, Berowne admonishes her that her wit is too quickly sarcastic and it will not be long-lasting. More bickering follows before they part company.

BEROWNE
Did not I dance with you in Brabant once?

KATHARINE
Did not I dance with you in Brabant once?

BEROWNE
I know you did.

KATHARINE
How needless was it then
To ask the question.

1326

BEROWNE
You must not be so quick.

KATHARINE
'Tis 'long of you that spur me with such questions.

BEROWNE
Your wit's too hot, it speeds too fast, 'twill tire.

KATHARINE
Not till it leave the rider in the mire.

BEROWNE
What time o' day?

KATHARINE
The hour that fools should ask.

Youth on the prow, and Pleasure at the helm

Source: THE BARD (Part II, stanza 2)
Author: Thomas Gray (1716–1771)
First published: 1757
Type of work: Pindaric ode

Context: The bards were the ancient poets of the Celtic tribes. In battle they raised the war cry and sang war songs; in time of peace they chronicled their nation's history through their songs of heroes and important events. As an institution, the bard symbolized patriotic fervor and the national heritage. He was held in high esteem, particularly in Wales; and like other ancient institutions and customs of the Britons, was preserved with stubborn determination against efforts by the English to eliminate him. It is said that Edward I considered the bards of Wales to be stirrers-up of sedition, and that when his conquest of the country was complete he gathered up all the bards and had them hanged. Gray's poem is inspired by this account. In it an old bard stands on a high crag and watches the banners and lances of Edward's men as they march through his homeland, leaving a trail of blood and wreckage in their wake. Striking his lyre, this aged survivor of his nation's heritage calls upon the spirits of his dead brethren to assist him in laying a curse upon the king and his posterity. The bard is granted a vision, and before his death he sees the future and the long succession of misfortunes that Edward's line must endure. Edward II, cursed with an adulterous wife, will be murdered; Edward III's son, the Black Prince, will die an untimely death; Richard II, the first part of his reign full of promise, will die of starvation; there will be wars between the Houses of Lancaster and York; heirs to the throne will be secretly

1327

murdered in the Tower of London; and so on until at last the line dies out, to be replaced by the Tudors. Like most prophecies, the bard's is none too clear; and Gray has supplied copious footnotes so that his meaning will not be lost. Following is that stanza which describes the Black Prince's death and the deceptive early magnificence of Richard II's reign:

> "Mighty Victor, mighty Lord,
> Low on his funeral couch he lies!
> No pitying heart, no eye, afford
> A tear to grace his obsequies.
> Is the sable Warrior fled?
> Thy son is gone. He rests among the dead.
> The swarm, that in thy noon-tide beam were born?
> Gone to salute the rising morn.
> Fair laughs the morn, and soft the zephyr blows,
> While proudly riding o'er the azure realm
> In gallant trim the gilded vessel goes;
> **Youth on the prow, and Pleasure at the helm;**
> Regardless of the sweeping whirlwind's sway,
> That, hushed in grim repose, expects his evening prey."

Youth will be served

Source: LAVENGRO (Chapter 92)
Author: George Borrow (1803–1881)
First published: 1851
Type of work: Novel

Context: In Chapter 92 of *Lavengro,* George Borrow's semi-autobiographical gipsy novel, the wandering hero-tinker, Lavengro, having earned a local reputation as a boxer by defeating a rival tinker, the Flaming Tinman, goes several times to a public house near where he is temporarily living. The landlord, a former boxer himself, enjoys chatting with the young fighter and reminiscing about the time when he "became the wonder and glory of this here neighbourhood" by beating a man named Tom of Hopton:

. . . The landlord appeared at all times glad to see me, and insisted that I should sit within the bar, where, leaving his other guests to be attended to by a niece of his who officiated as his housekeeper, he would sit beside me and talk of matters concerning "the ring," indulging himself with a cigar and a glass of sherry, which he told me was his favourite wine, whilst I drank my ale. "I loves the conversation of all you coves of the ring," said he once, "which is natural, seeing as how I have fought in a ring myself. Ah, there is nothing like the ring; I wish I was not rather too old

1328

to go again into it. I often think I should like to have another rally —one more rally, and then—but there's a time for all things— **youth will be served,** every dog has his day, and mine has been a fine one—let me be content. . . ."

You've a darned long row to hoe

Source: THE BIGLOW PAPERS (First Series, number I, l. 104)
Author: James Russell Lowell (1819–1891)
First published: 1848
Type of work: Satirical dialect poem

Context: The Biglow Papers is a series of poems in the New England rural dialect, supposedly written by a young, untutored genius, a farm lad named Hosea Biglow, son of Ezekiel Biglow, a farmer at Jaalam. This poem, the first, is the result of Hosea Biglow's meeting with an Army recruiting team in Boston and Hosea's subsequent thoughts about enlisting for service in the Mexican War. That war was an unpopular one, particularly in New England; as Hosea notes, many New Englanders believed the South had pressed for the war in order to bring new slaveholding territory into the United States. Hosea takes a hard look at soldiering and the cost of war. Noting the fancy uniforms and feathers, he reminds the reader that farmers pay the bills for the nation. As for war, any war, he says it is murder and calls upon the Bible to back him up, warning soldiers that God will place the guilt on the murderer, not on the government which hired him. He also notes that the newspaper editors who call for enlistments and bloodshed are not the men who go out to fight. As far as his enlistment is concerned, Hosea Biglow, the farm boy who loves Nancy, says:

> Jest go home an' ask our Nancy
>   Wether I'd be sech a goose
> Ez to jine ye,—guess you'd fancy
>   The etarnal bung wuz loose!
> She wants me fer home consumption,
>   Let alone the hay's to mow,—
> Ef you're arter folks o' gumption,
>   **You've a darned long row to hoe.**

AUTHOR INDEX

1331

AUTHOR INDEX

1335

AUTHOR INDEX

1337

AUTHOR INDEX

AUTHOR INDEX

AUTHOR INDEX

AUTHOR INDEX

1343

AUTHOR INDEX